MARKETING 7E

real
real

People

Choices

MARKETING 7E

real
People

real
Choices

Michael R. **SOLOMON**
SAINT JOSEPH'S UNIVERSITY

Greg W. **MARSHALL**
ROLLINS COLLEGE

Elnora W. **STUART**
THE UNIVERSITY OF SOUTH CAROLINA
UPSTATE

Prentice Hall
Boston   Columbus   Indianapolis   New York   San Francisco   Upper Saddle River
Amsterdam   Cape Town   Dubai   London   Madrid   Milan   Munich   Paris   Montreal   Toronto
Delhi   Mexico City   Sao Paulo   Sydney   Hong Kong   Seoul   Singapore   Taipei   Tokyo

Editorial Director: Sally Yagan
Editor in Chief: Eric Svendsen
Acquisitions Editor: Melissa Sabella
Director of Editorial Services: Ashley Santora
Editorial Project Manager: Kierra Bloom
Editorial Assistant: Elisabeth Scarpa
Director of Marketing: Patrice Lumumba Jones
Senior Marketing Manager: Anne Fahlgren
Marketing Assistant: Melinda Jensen
Senior Managing Editor: Judy Leale
Project Manager: Becca Richter
Senior Operations Supervisor: Arnold Vila

Creative Director: Jon Christiana
Senior Art Director: Blair Brown
Text and Cover Designer: Blair Brown
Media Project Manager, Production: Lisa Rinaldi
Media Project Manager, Editorial: Denise Vaughn
Full-Service Project Management: S4Carlisle Publishing
  Services
Composition: S4Carlisle Publishing Services
Printer/Bindery: Courier/Kendallville
Cover Printer: Courier/Kendallville
Text Font: Palatino

Library of Congress Cataloging-in-Publication Data

Solomon, Michael R.
  Marketing : real people, real choices / Michael R. Solomon, Greg W. Marshall, Elnora W. Stuart. – 7th ed.
    p. cm.
  ISBN-13: 978-0-13-217684-2
  ISBN-10: 0-13-217684-X
  1. Marketing--Vocational guidance. I. Marshall, Greg W. II. Stuart, Elnora W. III. Title.
  HF5415.35.S65 2011
  658.8--dc22

                              2010051148

10 9 8 7 6 5 4 3 2 1

Prentice Hall
is an imprint of

www.pearsonhighered.com

ISBN 10: 0-13-217684-X
ISBN 13: 978-0-13-217684-2

Corporations don't make decisions. **People do.**

Julie Cordua decision maker at (RED)

Meet the Real Marketer
Who makes big marketing decisions?
What makes them tick?
How did they get there?
How would **you** get there?
Get to know the people behind the decisions.

You Make the Call
What would you do?
Hear from a real marketer about
a business problem he or she
faced, get the options and
decide what you would do.

Chapter | **5**

Consumer Behavior:
How and Why We Buy

Real People **Profile**

Julie Cordua

Profile | Info

▼ **A Decision Maker at (RED)**

Julie Cordua is the vice president of marketing at (RED), a new brand created by U2 lead singer Bono and Bobby Shriver to engage business in the fight against AIDS in Africa. (RED) partners with the world's best brands to make uniquely branded products from which up to 50 percent of the profits are directed to the Global Fund to finance African HIV/AIDS programs with a focus on women and children. In her role at (RED), she is responsible for building the (RED) brand through innovative marketing programs including public relations, advertising, events, and co-branding.

Prior to joining (RED), Julie spent the bulk of her career in marketing in the wireless industry. Most recently, she was the senior director of buzz marketing and part of the start-up team at HELIO, a new mobile brand for young, connected consumers. Before HELIO, Julie spent five years at Motorola in the Mobile Devices division in Chicago. At Motorola, she led the global category marketing group and was part of the team that orchestrated the RAZR launch in 2002.

Julie started her career in public relations at Hill & Knowlton in Los Angeles. She holds a BA in communications with an emphasis in business administration from UCLA and an MBA from the Kellogg School at Northwestern University. She currently lives in Manhattan Beach, California, with her husband.

Julie's Info

What do I do when I'm not working?
A) Read, travel, and spend time with friends and family

First job out of school?
A) Account coordinator at Hill & Knowlton Public Relations.

Career high?
A) Two, introducing the MOTO RAZR and introducing (RED).

Business book I'm reading now?
A) *The End of Poverty* by Jeff Sachs.

My management style?
A) Give your team the tools it needs to do its best job and trust it.

Don't do this when interviewing with me?
A) Ask about the salary in the first part of the interview.

128

Find Out What Happened
Discover the choice the real marketer
made and see how it worked out.

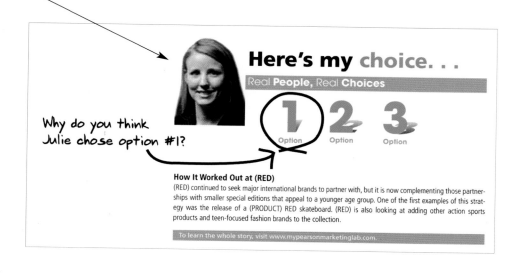

Here's my choice. . .

Real **People**, Real **Choices**

Why do you think Julie chose option #1?

① Option **2** Option **3** Option

How It Worked Out at (RED)
(RED) continued to seek major international brands to partner with, but it is now complementing those partnerships with smaller special editions that appeal to a younger age group. One of the first examples of this strategy was the release of a (PRODUCT) RED skateboard. (RED) is also looking at adding other action sports products and teen-focused fashion brands to the collection.

To learn the whole story, visit www.mypearsonmarketinglab.com.

▶Brief Contents

▶ Contents

▶Preface

WHAT'S **NEW** IN THE 7TH EDITION?

What's new in the 7th edition is what's new in marketing; more on metrics, a rethinking of advertising and promotions, and even stronger links to the real world of marketing by showing how concepts are linked with marketing planning.

Here's just a sample of what we changed.

Greater focus on marketing metrics:
- Specific exercises in every chapter and revised pedagogical material that includes focused in-class and homework activities and research that encourage improved critical thinking and decision-making skills.

Rethinking how companies are approaching advertising and promotion:
- Major revision and recasting of the entire promotion/marketing communication series of chapters (13, 14, 15) around messaging-to-many versus messaging-to-one models. Includes heightened attention to social networking as a marketing communication option of increasing importance. Covers emerging topics such as geospatial platforms, user-generated content (UCG), augmented reality, owned/earned/paid media, multichannel strategies.

Linking marketing planning with concepts:
- The addition of Part Openers that add value in two ways: (1) provide you with a brief overview of the key learning to come within the part chapters, and (2) link those learning elements to application in a threaded example marketing plan, with the suggestion "You can do it too"—leading readers to mymarketinglab and the opportunity to develop a semester marketing plan project assignment.

Marketing Executive Advisory Panel:
- We pride ourselves on our inclusion of cutting-edge, industry-relevant material in each new edition. In the 7th edition we've taken the extra step of reaching out to actual executives to be sure we're covering what you need to learn. Our *Marketing Executive Advisory Panel* is composed of industry leaders who have a handle on what the practice of marketing will probably look like when you graduate in a few years. We've asked these individuals to tell us what they believe students need to know— and to share with us what frustrates them about what current college graduates or new hires *don't* know. Our panel's feedback helped to shape the new content you will see in this edition.

And more!
- New boxed features on The Cutting Edge trends in technology in every chapter.
- Completely updated and integrated "figures" program for every chapter, with the figures tied to specific chapter objectives as a way to visually illustrate the main takeaways from each chapter. For your convenience, figures are labeled as either 📷 Snapshot or ⚡ Process, and the icons you see here appear in the text references to the figures.

Features of the 7th Edition of *Real People, Real Choices*

Meet Real Marketers

Many of the "Real People, Real Choices" vignettes are new to this edition, featuring a variety of decision makers, from CEOs to brand managers. Here is just a sample of the marketers we feature:

- Joe Kennedy, Pandora
- Jay Minkoff, First Flavor
- Ryan Garton, Discover
- Jim Multari, Sprout Networks
- David Clark, General Mills
- Mike Monello, Campfire
- Mark Brownstein, Brownstein Group
- Heather Mayo, Sam's Club
- Stan Clark, Eskimo Joe's

Ethics and Sustainability in Marketing

Because the role of ethics and sustainability in business and in marketing is so important, we focus on these topics not just in a single chapter but in EVERY CHAPTER of the book. These "Ripped from the Headlines" boxes feature real-life examples of ethical and sustainable decisions marketers are faced with on a day-to-day basis.

Cutting-Edge Technology

With technology evolving at a rapid-fire pace, it's now more important than ever for today's marketers to stay on the cutting edge of the latest technological developments. Viral marketing campaigns are just the tip of the iceberg! From Cargoshell's innovative sustainable shipping containers to virtual worlds accessed via a pair of Adidas sneakers, "The Cutting Edge" boxes feature the most current technological advances and explain how companies are using them to creatively get their messages out to consumers.

An Easy-to-Follow Marketing Plan Template

Marketing: Real People, Real Choices, 7th edition includes a tear-out template of a marketing plan you can use as you make your way through the book. The template provides a framework that will enable you to organize marketing concepts by chapter and create a solid marketing plan of your own. On the back of the template is a contemporary world map as a reminder that all marketing today is global. We encourage you to keep this tear-out as a handy reference after the class.

Learning How to Market Yourself: Brand You

Products aren't alone in benefiting from branding—people can benefit, too. Branding strategies help professionals get noticed and position them for exciting new career opportunities. Prepared by Kim Richmond of Saint Joseph's University, the *Brand You* handbook gives you concrete advice on how to thrive in a competitive marketplace and provides a hands-on approach to achieving career success. This separate *Brand You* supplement can be purchased at **www.mypearsonstore.com**.

End-of-chapter Study Map

Each chapter now has an integrative study map for students that includes an Objective Summary, Key Terms, and student assessment opportunities of several types: Concepts: Test Your Knowledge; Activities: Apply What You've Learned; Marketing Metrics Exercise; (more on this one below); Choices: What Do You Think?, and Miniproject: Learn By Doing. By completing these assessments students and instructors achieve maximum assurance of learning.

Measuring the Value of Marketing through Marketing Metrics

Just how do marketers add value to a company, and can that value be quantified? More and more, businesses demand accountability, and marketers respond as they develop a variety of "scorecards" that show how specific marketing activities directly affect their company's ROI—return on investment. And on the job, the decisions that marketers make increasingly come from data and calculations and less from instinct. Each end-of-chapter includes exercises that provide real-world examples of the measures marketers use to help them make good decisions.

All New and Updated End-of-Chapter Cases in This Edition

Each chapter concludes with an exciting "Marketing in Action" mini-case about a real firm facing real marketing challenges. Questions at the end let you make the call to get the company on the right track.

Student Resources

PEARSON
mymarketinglab

mymarketinglab gives you the opportunity to test yourself on key concepts and skills, track your own progress through the course, and use the personalized study plan activities—all to help you achieve success in the classroom.

Features include:

- Personalized study plans—Pre- and post-tests with remediation activities directed to help you understand and apply the concepts where you need the most help.

- Interactive elements—A wealth of hands-on activities and exercises let you experience and learn firsthand, whether it is with the online etext where you can search for specific keywords or page numbers, highlight specific sections, enter notes right on the etext page, and print reading assignments with notes for later review, or with other materials including *Real People, Real Choices* Video Cases, online end-of-chapter Study Map assessments, Active Flashcards, and much more.

- Mini-simulations—Move beyond the basics with interactive simulations that place you in a realistic marketing situation and let you make decisions based on marketing concepts.

www.mypearsonmarketinglab.com

Real People, Real Choices Videos

Featuring interviews with some of the real marketers from the text, these videos transport you from the abstract environment of the classroom to the exciting, dynamic world of real-life contemporary marketing practice. The marketers share their experiences as they discuss the challenges they face and decisions they make every day.

About the Authors

Michael R. Solomon, Elnora W. Stuart, Greg W. Marshall

Michael R. Solomon

MICHAEL R. SOLOMON, Ph.D., joined the Haub School of Business at Saint Joseph's University in Philadelphia as Professor of Marketing in 2006, where he also serves as Director of the Center for Consumer Research. From 1995 to 2006, he was the Human Sciences Professor of Consumer Behavior at Auburn University. Prior to joining Auburn in 1995, he was Chairman of the Department of Marketing in the School of Business at Rutgers University, New Brunswick, New Jersey. Professor Solomon's primary research interests include consumer behavior and lifestyle issues; branding strategy; the symbolic aspects of products; the psychology of fashion, decoration, and image; services marketing; and the development of visually oriented online research methodologies. He currently sits on the editorial boards of the *Journal of Consumer Behaviour, the European Business Review*, and the *Journal of Retailing*, and he recently completed a six-year term on the Board of Governors of the Academy of Marketing Science. In addition to other books, he is also the author of Prentice Hall's text *Consumer Behavior: Buying, Having, and Being*, which is widely used in universities throughout the world. Professor Solomon frequently appears on television and radio shows such as *The Today Show, Good Morning America*, Channel One, the *Wall Street Journal* Radio Network, and National Public Radio to comment on consumer behavior and marketing issues.

Greg W. Marshall

GREG W. MARSHALL, Ph.D., is the Charles Harwood Professor of Marketing and Strategy in the Crummer Graduate School of Business at Rollins College, Winter Park, Florida. For three years he also served as Vice President for Strategic Marketing for Rollins. Prior to joining Rollins, he served on the faculties of Oklahoma State University, the University of South Florida, and Texas Christian University. He earned a BSBA in Marketing and an MBA from the University of Tulsa, and a Ph.D. in Marketing from Oklahoma State University. Professor Marshall's research interests include sales force selection, performance, and evaluation; decision making by marketing managers; and intraorganizational relationships. He is editor of the *Journal of Marketing Theory and Practice* and former editor of the *Journal of Personal Selling & Sales Management*, and currently serves on the editorial boards of the *Journal of the Academy of Marketing Science, Journal of Business Research*, and *Industrial Marketing Management*. Professor Marshall is a Distinguished Fellow and President of the Academy of Marketing Science, Past-President of the American Marketing Association Academic Division, and a Fellow and Past-President of the Society for Marketing Advances. His industry experience prior to entering academe includes product management, field sales management, and retail management positions with firms such as Warner-Lambert, the Mennen Company, and Target Corporation.

Elnora W. Stuart

ELNORA W. STUART, Ph.D., is Professor of Marketing at the University of South Carolina Upstate. Prior to joining USC Upstate in 2008, she was Professor of Marketing and the BP Egypt Oil Professor of Management Studies at the American University in Cairo, Professor of Marketing at Winthrop University in Rock Hill, South Carolina, and on the faculty of the University of South Carolina. She is also a regular visiting professor at Instituto de Empresa in Madrid, Spain. She earned a BA in Theatre/Speech from the University of North Carolina at Greensboro and both a Master of Arts in Journalism and Mass Communication, and a Ph.D. in Marketing from the University of South Carolina. Professor Stuart's research has been published in major academic journals including the *Journal of Consumer Research, Journal of Advertising, Journal of Business Research*, and *Journal of Public Policy and Marketing*. For over 25 years she has served as a consultant for numerous businesses and not-for-profit organizations in the United States and in Egypt.

Acknowledgments

We feature many talented marketers and successful companies in this book. In developing it, we also were fortunate to work with a team of exceptionally talented and creative people at Prentice Hall. Melissa Sabella, Executive Editor, was instrumental in helping us solidify the vision for the 7th edition, and her assistance with decisions about content, organization, features, and supplements was invaluable. Anne Fahlgren also contributed great ideas from a marketing perspective. Kudos to Kierra Bloom for managing the project with great efficiency and patience. Becca Richter did yeoman work to smoothly integrate all the pieces of this project into one book.

A special note of appreciation goes to Tony Cooper of the Crummer Graduate School of Business at Rollins College for all his great work in helping assemble chapter materials to ensure this edition is as fresh and timely as possible.

Thank you to Leroy Robinson of the University of Houston who updated the Marketing in Action cases for this edition.

No book is complete without a solid supplements package. We extend our thanks to our dedicated supplement authors who devoted their time and shared their teaching ideas.

Finally, our utmost thanks and appreciation go to our families for their continued support and encouragement. Without them this project would not be possible.

Many people worked to make this 7th edition a reality. The guidance and recommendations of the following professors and focus group participants helped us update and improve the chapters and the supplements:

REVIEWERS

Camille Abbruscato, Stony Brook University
Lydia Anderson, Fresno City College
Gregory Spencer Black, Metropolitan State College of Denver
Koren Borges, University of North Florida
Charles R. Canedy, University of Hartford
Laura Dwyer, Rochester Institute of Technology
Mary Patricia Galitz, Southeast Community College
Debbie Gaspard, Southeast Community College
Michael Goldberg, Berkeley College
Karen Welte Gore, Ivy Tech Community College
John Hardjimarcou, University of Texas, El Paso
Debra Laverie, Texas Tech University
David Lehman, Kansas State University
Anne Weidemanis Magi, University of South Florida
Mohan K. Menon, University of South Alabama
Mark A. Neckes, Johnson & Wales University
John Edward Robbins, Winthrop University
Carlos M. Rodriguez, Delaware State University
Ann Renee Root, Florida Atlantic University
Charles Jay Schafer, Johnson & Wales University
Scott Thorne, Southeast Missouri State University
Casey Wilhelm, North Idaho University

EXECUTIVES

In addition to our reviewers and focus group participants, we want to extend our gratitude to the busy executives who gave generously of their time for the "Real People, Real Choices" features.

Executives Featured in "Real People, Real Choices" Vignettes

Chapter 1: Joe Kennedy, Pandora
Chapter 2: Jay Minkoff, First Flavor
Chapter 3: Robert Chatwani, eBay
Chapter 4: Ryan Garton, Discover Financial
Chapter 5: Julie Cordua, (RED)

Chapter 6: Brad Tracy, NCR Corporation
Chapter 7: Jim Multari, Sprout Network
Chapter 8: Palo Hawken, Bossa Nova Beverages
Chapter 9: David Clark, General Mills
Chapter 10: Lara Price, Philadelphia 76ers
Chapter 11: Danielle Blugrind, Taco Bell
Chapter 12: Mike Monello, Campfire
Chapter 13: Marc Brownstein, Brownstein Group
Chapter 14: Jeffery Brechman, Woodtronics
Chapter 15: Heather Mayo, Sam's Club
Chapter 16: Stan Clark, Eskimo Joe's

Executive Panel

Joe Barstys, Subaru of North America
Monique Brinson, Darden Restaurants
Michele R. Butler
Joe Chernov, BzzAgent
Rebecca Church, Massey Services
Peter Cornish
Laurie Demeritt, The Hartman Group
John Feehan, Virgin Mobile
Todd Fisher, Disney Corporation
Tisa Ford, General Mills
Marc Gobé, Desgrippes Gobé Group
Ric Hendee, Cotton, Inc.
Marlene M. Jones
Bharat Kapoor, Disney Corporation
Brian Kurtz, Boardroom Reports
Nat Martin, Darden Restaurants
Steve McCallion, Ziba Design
Jim Multari, Sprout Networks
Mary Lou Quinlan, Just Ask a Woman
Chad W. Russell
Jordan Stanley, Stanley Marketing
Jim Wilhelm, Baxter Healthcare
Mary Kay Williams, Medtronic
Jan Zlotnick, The Zlotnick Group

REVIEWERS OF PREVIOUS EDITIONS

The following individuals were of immense help in reviewing all or part of previous editions of this book and the supplement package:

Roy Adler, Pepperdine University
Gerald Athaide, Loyola College
Carole S. Arnone, Frostburg State University
Christopher Anicich, California State University–Fullerton
Nathan Austin, Morgan State University
Xenia Balabkins, Middlesex County College
Fred Beasley, Northern Kentucky University
Jas Bhangal, Chabot College
Silvia Borges, Miami Dade CC–Wolfson Campus
Deborah Boyce, State University of New York Institute of Technology, Utica, New York
Tom Boyd, California State University–Fullerton
Henry C. Boyd III, University of Maryland–College Park
Val Calvert, San Antonio College
Richard Celsi, California State University–Long Beach
Swee-Lim Chia, LaSalle University
Paul Cohen, Florida Atlantic University
Brian Connett, California State University–Northridge
Ruth Clottey, Barry University
Robert M. Cosenza, University of Mississippi
Brent Cunningham, Jacksonville State University
Patricia Doney, Florida Atlantic University
Rita Dynan, LaSalle University
Jill S. Dybus, Oakton Community College
Joyce Fairchild, Northern Virginia Community College
Elizabeth Ferrell, Southwestern Oklahoma State University
Joanne Frazier, Montgomery College
Jon Freiden, Florida State University
Mike Gates, South Hills School of Business and Technology
Kimberly D. Grantham, University of Georgia
David Hansen, Texas Southern University
Manoj Hastak, American University
John Heinemann, Keller Graduate School of Management
Dorothy Hetmer-Hinds, Trinity Valley Community College
Mark B. Houston, Texas Christian University
Gary Hunter, Case Western Reserve University
Annette Jajko, Triton College
Janice M. Karlen, LaGuardia Community College/ City University of New York
Jack E. Kant, San Juan College
Gail Kirby, Santa Clara University
David Knuff, Oregon State University–Cascades
Kathleen Krentler, San Diego State University
Sandra J. Lakin, Hesser College
Linda N. LaMarca, Tarleton State University
Debra A. Laverie, Texas Tech University
Freddy Lee, California State University–Sacramento
Ron Lennon, Barry University

Marilyn Liebrenz-Himes, George Washington University
Cesar Maloles, California State University–East Bay
Norton Marks, California State University–San Bernardino
Kelly Duggan Martin, Washington State University
Carolyn Massiah, University of Central Florida
Laura M. Milner, University of Alaska
Timothy R Mittan, Southeast Community College
Jakki Mohr, University of Montana
Linda Morable, Richland College
Michael Munro, Florida International University
Jeff B. Murray, University of Arkansas
Linda Newell, Saddleback College
Eric Newman, California State University-San Bernardino
David Oliver, Edison College
Beng Ong, California State University- Fresno
A.J. Otjen, Montana State University-Billings
Lucille Pointer, University of Houston- Downtown
Mohammed Rawwas, University of Northern Iowa
John E. Robbins, Winthrop University
Bruce Robertson, San Francisco State University
Leroy Robinson, University of Houston-Clear Lake
Barbara Rosenthal, Miami Dade Community College-Kendall Campus
Behrooz Saghafi, Chicago State University
Ritesh Saini, George Mason University
Marcianne Schusler, Prairie State College
Susan Silverstone, National University
Samuel A. Spralls III, Central Michigan University
Melissa St. James, California State University-Dominguez Hills
Frank Svestka, Loyola University of Chicago
James Swartz, California State Polytechnic University-Pomona
Kim Taylor, Florida International University-Park Campus
Steven Taylor, Illinois State University
Susan L. Taylor, Belmont University
John Thanopoulos, University of Piraeus, Greece
Jane Boyd Thomas, Winthrop University
Judee A. Timm, Monterey Peninsula College
Sue Umashankar, University of Arizona
Sal Veas, Santa Monica College
D. Roger Waller, San Joaquin Delta College
Leatha Ware, Waubonsee Community College
Steve Wedwick, Heartland Community College
Kathleen Williamson, University of Houston-Clear Lake
Mary Wolfinbarger, California State University-Long Beach
Kim Wong, Albuquerque TVI Community College
Steve Wong, Rock Valley College
Richard Wozniak, Northern Illinois University
Brent M. Wren, University of Alabama in Hunstville
Merv Yeagle, University of Maryland at College Park
Mark Young, Winona State University
Marybeth Zipperer, Montgomery College

MARKETING 7E

real
real

People

Choices

```
Make marketing value decisions
(Part One)                          ← You are here
         ↓
Understand consumers' value needs
(Part Two)
         ↓
Create the value proposition
(Part Three)
         ↓                    Process
Communicate the value proposition
(Part Four)
         ↓
Deliver the value proposition
(Part Five)
```

Make Marketing Value Decisions

Part One
Overview

Welcome to the first set of chapters in *Marketing: Real People, Real Choices*! The book is divided into five major sections called "Parts." Each of these Parts focuses on a key element of marketing as a value-adding element to any organization's success. Each Part Opener (like this one) provides you with a brief overview of the learning opportunities within that Part. Then, through a fictitious company called S&S Smoothie (which is published in its entirety in the book's Appendix), you will learn how the pieces of a marketing plan come together so that "You Can Do It Too!"

Whether or not you are assigned a marketing plan as a class project, you will find the Part Openers worth reading because linking each Part's content to the bigger picture of marketing planning will help you understand the "five W's and an H"—who, what,

when, where, why, and how—related to the way the particular material in that Part fits into the big picture of marketing. Don't be concerned right now if the notion of a marketing plan is brand-new to you. In Chapter 2 we'll focus on them and bring you up to speed on what marketing planning is all about. There we include a useful tear-out that serves as a roadmap for how each chapter's content fits into the process of developing a marketing plan.

Part One offers three chapters that kick off your study of marketing, with an overall focus on making marketing value decisions. In Chapter 1 you will learn what value is, as well as pick up a lot of great insights on the contemporary field of marketing to pique your interest in the course. You will notice right away that this book is about *people doing marketing*, as opposed to merely being a narrative about products, firms, and other inanimate objects. The *Real People, Real Choices* vignettes that begin each chapter help you connect marketing to actual people making decisions. As such, marketing truly comes alive! As mentioned, Chapter 2 takes you through the entire process of marketing planning. Finally, Chapter 3 addresses the fact that today *all marketing is global*. You'll get to see the various elements of the external environment that impact marketers' ability to do successful planning in both domestic and global markets.

Marketing Plan Connection:
Tricks of the Trade

As mentioned earlier, the Appendix at the end of the book provides you with an abbreviated marketing plan example for the fictitious S&S Smoothie Company. That plan is flagged to indicate what elements from the plan correspond to each of the Parts within the book. In addition, in Chapter 2 you will find a tear-out guide called "Build a Marketing Plan," which can be used as a template for marketing planning. It is also cross-referenced to chapters by section of the marketing plan.

In the chapters within Part One, there are major learning elements that guide you in developing four initial parts of a marketing plan: internal environmental analysis, external environmental analysis, SWOT analysis, and setting marketing objectives. Let's take a look at each of these elements.

Internal Environmental Analysis

Chapter 2 provides an overview of marketing planning from the perspective of a marketing firm. It might surprise you to learn that accomplishing a useful internal environmental analysis is often more challenging than is the analysis of the external environment. It's like the old saying, "We have found the enemy and it is us!" Some firms do not have a culture that supports honest self-reflection, and instead they tend to just sweep problems under the rug. This is, of course, very dangerous, since future marketing planning depends on a realistic assessment of the firm and its internal capabilities.

When you review the case of S&S Smoothie, take special note of their mission, how the firm is set up and who the key players are, the nature of their organizational culture, and how they are currently deploying the 4 Ps of the marketing mix. What is evidently working well for them already? What likely could be improved through marketing planning?

External Environmental Analysis

In Chapter 3 you will gain solid knowledge of the global environment in which marketers today do business. In contrast to the internal environment, the external environment consists of elements that are largely outside the direct control of a firm and its managers. The company operates within the context of its external environment, but in most instances it can do little directly to shape and form that environment. Because of this, it becomes incredibly important that firms accurately identify the external

factors that are likely to have the greatest impact on success and then work to develop approaches to proactively take these factors into account when developing plans and forecasts.

Key elements in the external environment include the following:

- *Competitive environment*—Who do you compete with and how?
- *Economic environment*—In what ways do economic forces impact the marketing success of the firm?
- *Technological environment*—What is the role of advancing technology on the business?
- *Political and legal environment*—How do these elements impact decisions the firm makes about products and markets?
- *Sociocultural environment*—What is the impact of changing societal tastes and values on the marketplace?

One of the most challenging aspects of doing external environmental analysis is that the information gathered is not static. It is constantly changing! This means that marketers need to continually scan the elements of the external environment for trends and (hopefully) make changes to their marketing plans before the trends get away from them. As you review S&S Smoothie's marketing plan, try to imagine which of the external environmental elements identified are most likely to change in the near future, and how the changes would impact their plan.

SWOT Analysis

A SWOT analysis (for <u>S</u>trengths, <u>W</u>eaknesses, <u>O</u>pportunities, and <u>T</u>hreats) is a convenient way of summarizing your situation analysis. You will note that the S&S Smoothie example has a very succinct set of 3–4 bulleted items under each of the SWOT subheadings. This is what you should strive for in a SWOT—a succinct prioritization of the main internal and external situational factors that you believe, based on your analysis, are most important to future planning for the firm.

Marketing Objectives

An objective is something that you set out to accomplish. You will learn in Chapter 2 that for objectives to be useful they must meet several important criteria in the way they are written. A well-stated objective is specific, measurable, and realistically attainable. Objectives are not very useful to marketers for planning purposes if they are vague, if you don't know what metrics tell you that you've succeeded, or if they are impossible to accomplish. S&S Smoothie has identified four important marketing objectives. See if you think they meet these criteria.

> **>>You Can Do It Too!**
> Now, if you are working on a marketing plan as part of your course, you can go to mymarketinglab to apply what you learn in Part One to your own marketing plan project.

Welcome to the World of Marketing
Create and Deliver Value

Real People Profiles

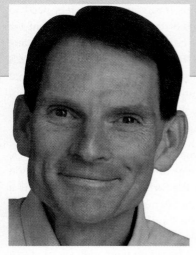

Joe Kennedy

Profile

▼ **A Decision Maker at Pandora**

Joe Kennedy is chief executive officer and president of Pandora, the Internet radio company that more than 65 million people use to create personalized radio stations that they can listen to from their computers, phones, TVs, and cars. Just type the name of one of your favorite songs or artists into Pandora and it will instantly generate a station with music pulled from its collection of more than 800,000 songs. Enter Rihanna and connect to similar artists like Loer Velocity and The Cab. Is Ludacris more your speed? Discover 112 or Sensational.

How does Pandora customize stations to each individual listener? It all has to do with the Music Genome Project; Pandora describes it as the most comprehensive analysis of music ever undertaken. Over the last decade the MGP's team of musician-analysts has classified each song based on up to 400 distinct musical characteristics. It takes an analyst 20–30 minutes to analyze a song and record the details that define it, such as melody, harmony, instrumentation, rhythm, vocals, and lyrics. Artists receive royalties from Pandora every time one of their songs is played on a station.

Joe Kennedy joined Pandora in 2004 following a five-year stint at E-LOAN, where he was president and chief operating officer. From 1995 to 1999, he was the vice president of sales, service and marketing for Saturn Corporation, which he grew to more than $4 billion in revenue and established as the top brand for customer satisfaction in the auto industry. Joe joined the initial startup team at Saturn, four months after it was founded, as a marketing manager and held positions of increasing marketing responsibility over the course of his 11-year tenure there.

Joe has an MBA from Harvard Business School and a BS degree in electrical engineering and computer science from Princeton University, where he dabbled in music theory and learned to compose his own Gregorian chants. According to his bio on the Pandora site, he is Pandora's resident pop music junkie. Joe has also been playing the piano for more than 30 years, spending a majority of that time attempting to master Gershwin's "Rhapsody in Blue."

Info

💬 **Joe's Info**

What do I do when I'm not working?
A) Working on my tennis game, trying to finally reach that elusive top 10 national ranking in my age group.

Business book I'm reading now?
A) *Checklist Manifesto* by Atul Gawande.

My hero?
A) Skip LeFauve, the president of Saturn from 1986 to 1995.

What drives me?
A) I love to bring about game-changing innovation in categories consumers are passionate about.

My management style?
A) Hire senior, experienced, self-motivated leaders who know more about their functional areas than I do and let them do their thing.

My pet peeve?
A) People who are always running late. It's a clear sign of self-centeredness when someone always keeps other people waiting.

Here's my problem...

The company was founded in January 2000 by Tim Westergren, a pianist who played in rock and jazz bands for 10 years before he became a film composer. As he analyzed music to decide what film directors would like, he got the idea of creating a technology that would reflect people's tastes and deliver music that fit those tastes. Tim raised $1.5 million and started Savage Beast Technologies, which sold music recommendations services to companies like Best Buy. But the company struggled as the dot-com boom of the late 1990s burst. Tim and his employees worked on an unpaid basis for several years before they got more financial backing in 2004 (after Tim made 347 unsuccessful pitches to investors!). Tim paid his employees, switched the company's name to Pandora, and changed its focus to consumers instead of businesses. To lead this strategic shift the newly christened Pandora hired Joe Kennedy, who had solid experience building consumer products. The company knew it was on to something when it first released Pandora in a beta version for family and friends. Within a week, 5,000 people had used the service to discover new music.

That was encouraging, but a 5,000-user base isn't nearly enough to entice advertisers to buy space on the site. Pandora needed to make money by attracting enough people to capture the interest of potential advertising clients; these companies in turn would pay to place ads that would reach Pandora's users. The challenge was to avoid the fate of many other Internet startups that offered cool features but never grew to the scale where they could turn a profit. Joe needed to build a solid customer base so he could develop a firm business model for Pandora. He knew that if he could just make music lovers aware of the value Pandora offered, he would be able to turn the fledgling service into a marketing success.

Things to remember

Pandora doesn't charge people to use its service. It makes its money by attracting advertisers who want to reach users. In order for the company to entice companies to advertise, it has to offer them access to large numbers of consumers who are likely to tune in on the ads they will encounter on the site.

Part of Pandora's unique product offering is the ability to customize music for each individual user. Everyone who registers can create their own "stations" that play songs with similar characteristics. This enables users to learn about artists they might not otherwise stumble upon, so potentially Pandora can create new audiences for independent musicians and for music labels.

Word of mouth is the least expensive way to attract large numbers of web surfers to Pandora's site. However, it's difficult to build buzz in an environment where many other products and services compete for the consumer's scarce attention.

Option 2. Build a buzz about Pandora through word of mouth. Put Tim Westergren, the company's founder, in front of groups of music lovers to tell the unique story of Pandora and how the Music Genome Project makes it work. Cultivate a dedicated fan base by reaching out to social networks on Twitter and Facebook, and then rely on these converts to spread the word to their friends. A buzz-building strategy is very inexpensive, and if done well, it can create a large group of devoted followers almost overnight. On the other hand, a startup has to compete with the thousands of others that are trying to recruit fans, and it might be difficult to reach a mass audience as opposed to hard-core music lovers without any catchy advertising.

Option 3. Sell the service to a large chain of record stores, a music magazine, or even a record label. Pandora could return to its roots as a music recommendation service for businesses. If a large company (like Virgin Records) could offer the service exclusively to its customers, almost instantly Pandora would have access to many thousands of music buyers. In the same way that *USA Today* is able to claim a huge circulation (and thus attract a lot of advertising dollars) because it is distributed free to hotel guests across the country, Pandora would inherit an impressive distribution network. However, this choice would entail giving up control of the unique Music Genome Project and its sophisticated database that the company had worked so hard to build. Hardcore music fans might accuse Pandora of "selling out," and they might question how objective its recommendations were.

Now, put yourself in Joe's shoes: Which option would you consider, and why?

Joe considered his Options 1·2·3

Option 1. Launch an advertising campaign on radio stations, in music magazines, and at record stores. Advertising is a great way to create awareness of a new product or service, but it takes a lot of money to cut through the clutter of competing messages. To afford advertising, Pandora would have had to convince financial backers that a substantial up-front investment would pay off as droves of users flocked to the site once they heard or read about it.

You Choose

Which **Option** would you choose, and **why**?

1. ☐YES ☐NO   2. ☐YES ☐NO   3. ☐YES ☐NO

See what **option** Joe chose on **page 33**

value
The benefits a customer receives from buying a good or service.

Check out chapter 1 **Study Map** on page 33

1

Welcome to Brand You

Alex wakes up with a groan as Vampire Weekend belts out a song from the next bedroom. Why does her roommate have to download these loud ringtones onto her cell phone and then leave it on so early in the morning? She throws back the Ralph Lauren sheets and rolls off her new Sleep Number mattress. As Alex stumbles across the room in her VS Signature pajamas from Victoria's Secret, her senses are further assaulted as she catches wafts of Amanda's trademark Juicy Couture perfume. She pours herself a steaming cup of Starbucks Verona Blend coffee from the Capresso CoffeeTeam Luxe coffeemaker and stirs in a heaping mound of Splenda. As she starts to grab a Yoplait from the SubZero, she checks her iPhone and suddenly remembers: Big job interview with Sprout Networks today! Yeah for LinkedIn! Good thing she gChatted her friends last night to get advice about what to wear so she won't have to think about it this morning. Alex does a quick scan of the *New York Times* on her Apple iPad, checks the forecast on Weather.com, and for one last time googles the executive who will be interviewing her. Hopefully *he* won't remember to check out her Facebook page; those photos she posted from her trip to Cancun don't exactly communicate a professional image! Well, he'll be more impressed by the volunteer work she's doing with Sweatshopwatch.org to build a buzz about horrific labor conditions in developing countries. Just in case, she glances down at her wrist to be sure she's wearing her turquoise advocacy bracelet (which new cause was that for, anyway?).

Alex slips into her sleek new BCBG suit, slides on her Prada shoes, grabs her Coach briefcase that was a graduation present from her parents, and climbs into her Jeep Grand Cherokee. As she listens to the Coke ad blaring over the loudspeakers while she gasses up at the Exxon station, Alex finds herself looking forward to tomorrow. The pressure will be off, and she can throw on her Madewell dress, Ray-Ban Aviators, and of course those new Frye wedges. Then, it'll be out to that hot new bar to look for Mr. Right—or maybe a few Mr. Wrongs. Oh yes, and perhaps a quick check on Craigslist for a new roommate.

Marketing is all around us. Indeed, some might say we live in a branded world. Like Alex, you have encounters with many marketers even before you leave for the day: ads, products, TV, the Web, charitable causes, podcasts.

What's more, like Alex, *you* are a product. That may sound weird, but companies like LinkedIn couldn't exist if you were not a product with value. We're going to use that word a LOT in this book, so let's define it now: **Value** refers to the benefits a customer receives from buying a good or service.

You have "market value" as a person—you have qualities that set you apart from others and abilities other people want and need. After you finish this course, you'll have even more value because you'll know about the field of marketing and how this field relates to you both as a future businessperson *and* as a consumer. In addition to learning about how marketing influences each of us, you'll have a better understanding of what it means to be "Brand You"—and hopefully some ideas about what you can do to increase your value to employers and maybe even to society.

Although it may seem strange to think about the marketing of people, in reality we often talk about ourselves and others in marketing terms. It is common for us to speak of "positioning" ourselves for job interviews or to tell our friends not to "sell themselves short." Some people who are cruising for potential mates even refer to themselves as "being on the market." In addition, many consumers hire personal image consultants to devise a "marketing strategy" for them, while others undergo plastic surgery or makeovers to improve their "product images." The desire to package and promote ourselves is the reason for personal goods and services markets ranging from cosmetics and exercise equipment to résumé specialists and dating agencies.[1]

So the principles of marketing apply to people, just as they apply to coffee, convertibles, and computer processors. Sure, there are differences in how we go about marketing each of these, but the general idea remains the same: Marketing is a fundamental part of our lives both as consumers and as players in the business world. We'll tell you why throughout this book. But first, we need to answer the basic questions of marketing: Who? Where? What? When? and Why? Let's start with Who and Where.

You are a product—hopefully a successful one!

The *Who* and *Where* of Marketing

Marketers come from many different backgrounds. Although many have earned marketing degrees, others have backgrounds in areas such as engineering or agriculture. Retailers and fashion marketers may have training in merchandising or design. Advertising copywriters often have degrees in English. E-marketers who do business over the Internet may have studied computer science.

Marketers work in a variety of locations. They work in consumer goods companies such as General Mills or at service companies like The Philadelphia 76ers basketball team. You'll see them in retail organizations like Sam's Club and at companies that manufacture products for other companies to use like NCR. You'll see them at philanthropic companies like Product (RED) and at cutting-edge advertising and social media agencies like Campfire and Pandora. We'll get to know these and other companies better as we make our way through this book.

And, although you may assume that the typical marketing job is in a large, consumer-oriented company like Disney, marketers work in other types of organizations too. There are many exciting marketing careers in companies that sell to other businesses. In small organizations, one person (perhaps the owner) may handle all the marketing responsibilities. In large organizations, marketers work on different aspects of the marketing strategy.

No matter where they work, all marketers are real people who make choices that affect themselves, their companies, and very often thousands or even millions of consumers. At the beginning of each chapter, we'll introduce you to marketing professionals like Joe Kennedy of Pandora in a feature we call "Real People, Real Choices." We'll tell you about a decision the marketer had to make and give you the possible options he or she considered. Think about these options as you read through the chapter so you can build an argument for selecting an option. At the end of each chapter, we'll tell you what option the marketer chose and why in a feature called "Real People, Real Choices: How It Worked Out."

Marketing's Role in the Firm: Cross-Functional Relationships

What role do marketers play in a firm? The importance organizations assign to marketing activities varies a lot. Top management in some firms is very marketing-oriented (especially when the chief executive officer comes from the marketing ranks), whereas in other companies marketing is an afterthought. However, analysts estimate that at least one-third of CEOs come from a marketing background—so stick with us!

Sometimes a company uses the term *marketing* when what it really means is sales or advertising. In some organizations, particularly small, not-for-profit ones, there may be no one in the company specifically designated as "the marketing person." In contrast, some firms realize that marketing applies to all aspects of the firm's activities. As a result, there has been a trend toward integrating marketing with other business functions (such as management and accounting) instead of making it a separate function.

No matter what size the firm, a marketer's decisions affect—and are affected by—the firm's other operations. Marketing managers must work with financial and accounting officers to figure out whether products are profitable, to set marketing budgets, and to determine prices. They must work with people in manufacturing to be sure that products are produced on time and in the right quantities. Marketers also must work with research-and-development specialists to create products that meet consumers' needs.

Where Do You Fit In? Careers in Marketing

Marketing is an incredibly exciting, diverse discipline that brims with opportunities. There are many paths to a marketing career; we've tried to summarize the most typical ones here. Check out Table 1.1 to start thinking about which path might be best for you. Okay, now that you've gotten a glimpse of who marketers are and where they work, it's time to dig into what marketing really is.

marketing
An organizational function and a set of processes for creating, communicating, and delivering value to customers and for managing customer relationships in ways that benefit the organization and its stakeholders.

2 Marketing Creates Value

OBJECTIVE

Explain what marketing is and how it provides value to everyone involved in the marketing process.
(pp. 8–12)

Marketing. Lots of people talk about it, but what is it? When you ask people to define **marketing**, you get many answers. Some people say, "That's what happens when a pushy salesman tries to sell me something I don't want." Other people say, "Oh, that's simple—TV commercials." Students might answer, "That's a course I have to take before I can get my business degree." Each of these responses has a grain of truth in it, but the official definition of marketing the American Marketing Association adopted in late 2007 is as follows:

"Marketing is the activity, set of institutions, and processes for creating, communicating, delivering, and exchanging offerings that have value for customers, clients, partners, and society at large."[2]

The basic idea of this somewhat complicated definition is that marketing is all about delivering value to everyone who is affected by a transaction. Let's take a closer look at some of the different ideas that relate to this definition.

Marketing Meets Needs

stakeholders
Buyers, sellers, or investors in a company, community residents, and even citizens of the nations where goods and services are made or sold—in other words, any person or organization that has a "stake" in the outcome.

One important part of our definition of marketing is that it meets the needs of diverse stakeholders. The term **stakeholders** here refers to buyers, sellers, or investors in a company, community residents, and even citizens of the nations where goods and services are made or sold—in other words, any person or organization that has a "stake" in the outcome. Thus, marketing is about satisfying everyone involved in the marketing process.

Table 1.1 | Careers in Marketing

Marketing Field	Where Can I Work?	What Entry-Level Position Can I Get?	What Course Work Do I Need?
Advertising	**Advertising agency:** Media, research, and creative departments; account work **Large corporation:** Advertising department: brand/product management **Media:** Magazine, newspaper, radio, and television selling; management consulting; marketing research	Account coordinator (traffic department); assistant account executive; assistant media buyer; research assistant; assistant brand manager	Undergraduate business degree
Brand Management	**Any size corporation:** Coordinate the activities of specialists in production, sales, advertising, promotion, R&D, marketing research, purchasing, distribution, package development, and finance	Associate brand manager	M.B.A. preferred, but a few companies recruit undergraduates. Expect a sales training program in the field from one to four months and in-house classes and seminars.
Business-to-Business Marketing	**Any size corporation:** Only a few companies recruit on campus, so be prepared to search out job opportunities on your own, as well as interview on campus.	Sales representative; market research administrator; product manager; pricing administrator; product administrator; assistant marketing manager; sales administrator; assistant sales manager; sales service administrator	Undergraduate business degree. A broad background of subjects is generally better than concentrating on just one area. A technical degree may be important or even required in high-technology areas. Courses in industrial marketing and marketing strategy are very helpful.
Direct–Response Marketing	**Any size corporation:** Marketing-oriented firms, including those offering consumer goods, industrial products, financial institutions, and other types of service establishments. Entrepreneurs seeking to enter business for themselves.	Direct-response marketing is expanding rapidly and includes direct mail; print and broadcast media, telephone marketing, catalogues, in-home presentations, and door-to-door marketing. Seek counsel from officers and directors of the Direct Marketing Association and the Direct Selling Association.	Undergraduate business degree. Supplemental work in communications, psychology, and/or computer systems recommended.
Supply-Channel Management	**Any size corporation, including transportation corporations:** The analysis, planning, and control of activities concerned with the procurement and distribution of goods. The activities include transportation, warehousing, forecasting, order processing, inventory control, production planning, site selection, and customer service.	Physical distribution manager; supply chain manager; inventory-control manager; traffic manager; distribution-center manager; distribution-planning analyst; customer service manager; transportation marketing and operations manager	Undergraduate business degree and M.B.A. Broad background in the core functional areas of business, with particular emphasis in distribution related topics such as logistics, transportation, purchasing, and negotiation.
International Marketing	**Large corporations:** Marketing Department at corporate headquarters	Domestic sales position with an international firm may be the best first step toward international opportunities.	M.B.A. A broad background in marketing is recommended, with some emphasis on sales management and market research.
Marketing Models and Systems Analysis	**Large corporations:** Consult with managers who are having difficulty with marketing problems.	Undergraduate: Few positions available unless you have prior work experience. Graduate: market analyst, market research specialist, and management scientist.	M.B.A. Preparation in statistics, mathematics, and the behavioral sciences.

(continued)

Table 1.1 | Careers in Marketing *(continued)*

Marketing Field	Where Can I Work?	What Entry-Level Position Can I Get?	What Course Work Do I Need?
Marketing Research	**Any size corporation:** Provide management with information about consumers, the marketing environment, and the competition	Assistant market analyst or assistant product analyst level.	M.B.A. or an M.S. in Marketing Research although prior experience and training may improve an undergraduate's chances.
New Product Planning	**Any size corporation:** Marketing of consumer products, consumer industries, advertising agencies, consulting firms, public agencies, medical agencies, retailing management	Assistant manager or director of product planning or new product development.	M.B.A.
Retail Management	**Retail corporations**	Assistant buyer positions; department manager positions	Undergraduate business degree
Sales and Sales Management	**Profit and nonprofit organizations:** Financial, insurance, consulting, and government	Trade sales representative who sells to a wholesaler or retailer; missionary sales representative in manufacturing who sells to retailers or decision makers (e.g., pharmaceutical representative); technical sales representative who sells to specified accounts within a designated geographic area.	Undergraduate business degree; M.B.A.; *Helpful courses:* consumer behavior, psychology, sociology, economics, anthropology, cost accounting, computer science, statistical analysis, communications, drama, creative writing. Language courses, if you're interested in international marketing; engineering or physical science courses if you're interested in technical selling.
Services Marketing	**Any size corporation:** Banking and financial service institutions, health care organizations, leisure-oriented businesses, and in various other service settings.	Assistant brand manager; assistant sales manager	Undergraduate business degree; M.B.A.; Additional course work in management policy, research, advertising and promotion, quantitative analysis, consumer behavior, and the behavioral sciences should prove useful.

Source: This information was based on an excellent compilation prepared by the marketing faculty of the Marshall School of Business, University of Southern California at **http://www.marshall.usc.edu/marketing/resources/resources-overview.htm** (accessed June 11, 2010). For average salaries broken down by job type and state consult the *Aquent/AMA Survey of Marketing Professionals* at **http://www.marketingsalaries.com/aquent/Home.form** or commercial websites such as **payscale.com** and **rileyguide.com**.

consumer
The ultimate user of a good or service.

marketing concept
A management orientation that focuses on identifying and satisfying consumer needs to ensure the organization's long-term profitability.

need
The recognition of any difference between a consumer's actual state and some ideal or desired state.

One important stakeholder is YOU. A **consumer** is the ultimate user of a good or service. Consumers can be individuals or organizations, whether a company, government, sorority, or charity. We like to say that the consumer is king (or queen), but it's important not to lose sight of the fact that the seller also has needs—to make a profit, to remain in business, and even to take pride in selling the highest-quality products possible. Products are sold to satisfy both consumers' and marketers' needs—it's a two-way street. When you strip away the big words, try this as a bumper sticker: *Marketers do it to satisfy needs*.

Needs, Wants, and Benefits

Most successful firms today practice the **marketing concept**—that is, marketers first identify consumer needs and then provide products that satisfy those needs, ensuring the firm's long-term profitability. A **need** is the difference between a consumer's actual state and some ideal or desired state. When the difference is big enough, the consumer is motivated to take action to satisfy the need. When you're hungry, you buy a snack. If you're not happy with your hair, you get a new hairstyle. When you need a job (or perhaps just get mad at your boss), you check out LinkedIn.

Needs relate to physical functions (such as eating) or to psychological ones (such as social acceptance). Levi Strauss & Company is one company that tries to meet the psychological needs of consumers to look good (as well as their basic need to be clothed). The company's research indicates that people wear Levi's jeans to say important things about themselves and their desired image. From time to time, the company even receives a beat-up, handed-down pair in the mail, with a letter from the owner requesting that the jeans be given a proper burial—that's a pretty "deep-seated" attachment to a pair of pants![3] The specific way a person satisfies a need depends on his or her unique history, learning experiences, and cultural environment. That explains why Nestlé's Kit Kat is the No. 1 candy brand in Japan—but the flavors you buy there include green tea, soy sauce, yubari melon, and sweet potato.[4]

A **want** is a desire for a particular product we use to satisfy a need in specific ways that are culturally and socially influenced. For example, two classmates' stomachs rumble during a lunchtime lecture, and both need food. However, each of the two may satisfy this need in quite a different way. The first student may be a health nut who fantasizes about gulping down a big handful of trail mix, while the second person may lust for a greasy cheeseburger and fries. The first student's want is trail mix, whereas the second student's want is fast food (and some antacid for dessert).

A product delivers a **benefit** when it satisfies a need or want. For marketers to be successful, they must develop products that provide one or more benefits that are important to consumers. The challenge is to identify what benefits people look for and then develop a product that delivers those benefits while also convincing consumers that their product is better than a competitor's product—making the choice of which product to buy obvious. As the late management guru Peter Drucker observed, "The aim of marketing is to make selling superfluous."[5]

Everyone can want your product, but that doesn't ensure sales unless consumers have the means to obtain it. When you couple desire with the buying power or resources to satisfy a want, the result is **demand**. So the potential customers looking for a snappy red BMW convertible are the people who want the car minus those who can't afford to buy or lease one (no, stealing the car doesn't count). A **market** consists of all the consumers who share a common need that can be satisfied by a specific product and who have the resources, willingness, and authority to make the purchase.

A *marketplace* used to be a location where buying and selling occurs face to face. In today's "wired" world, however, buyers and sellers might not even see each other. The modern **marketplace** may take the form of a glitzy shopping mall, a mail-order catalog, a television shopping network, an eBay auction, or an e-commerce Web site. In developing countries, the marketplace may be a street corner or an open-air market where people sell fruits and vegetables much as they did thousands of years ago. Indeed, a marketplace may not even exist in the physical world—as players of online games will tell you. Residents of cyberworlds like *Second Life* and *Habbo Hotel* buy and sell virtual real estate, home furnishings, and bling for their digital avatars; in 2010 alone they bought about $1.6 billion worth of **virtual goods** that exist only on a computer server.

Marketing Creates Utility

Marketing transactions create **utility**, which refers to the sum of the benefits we receive when we use a good or service. When it ensures that people have the type of product they want, where and when they want it, the marketing system makes our lives easier. Utility is what

Marketers create value for society when they help to promote worthy causes.

want
The desire to satisfy needs in specific ways that are culturally and socially influenced.

benefit
The outcome sought by a customer that motivates buying behavior—that satisfies a need or want.

demand
Customers' desires for products coupled with the resources needed to obtain them.

market
All the customers and potential customers who share a common need that can be satisfied by a specific product, who have the resources to exchange for it, who are willing to make the exchange, and who have the authority to make the exchange.

Joe Kennedy

APPLYING ▽ Demand

Joe needs to understand the potential demand for Pandora's services so he can develop a plan to maximize the number of these consumers who actually visit the site on a regular basis. ➡

marketplace
Any location or medium used to conduct an exchange.

virtual goods
Digital products consumers buy for use in online contexts.

utility
The usefulness or benefit consumers receive from a product.

exchange
The process by which some transfer of value occurs between a buyer and a seller.

product
A tangible good, service, idea, or some combination of these that satisfies consumer or business customer needs through the exchange process; a bundle of attributes including features, functions, benefits, and uses.

creates value. Marketing processes create several different kinds of utility to provide value to consumers:

- *Form utility* is the benefit marketing provides by transforming raw materials into finished products, as when a dress manufacturer combines silk, thread, and zippers to create a bridesmaid's gown.

- *Place utility* is the benefit marketing provides by making products available where customers want them. The most sophisticated evening gown sewn in New York's garment district is of little use to a bridesmaid in Kansas City if it isn't shipped to her in time.

- *Time utility* is the benefit marketing provides by storing products until they are needed. Some women rent their wedding gowns instead of buying them and wearing them only once (they hope!).

- *Possession utility* is the benefit marketing provides by allowing the consumer to own, use, and enjoy the product. The bridal store provides access to a range of styles and colors that would not be available to a woman outfitting a bridal party on her own.

As we've seen, marketers provide utility in many ways. Now, let's see how customers "take delivery" of this added value.

Rent the Runway is a new service started by two recent business school grads. It rents high-end dresses from designers like Diane Von Furstenberg, for about one-tenth of the cost of buying the same garment in a store. A woman can rent a dress for four nights; it's shipped directly to her doorstep much like a Netflix video. The customer returns the dress in a prepaid envelope and the rental price includes the cost of dry cleaning. Place utility at work![6]

Marketing and Exchange

At the heart of every marketing act—big or small—is something we refer to as an "exchange relationship." An **exchange** occurs when a person gives something and gets something else in return. The buyer receives an object, service, or idea that satisfies a need, and the seller receives something he or she feels is of equivalent value. A **product** is a good, a service, an idea, a place, a person—whatever is offered for sale in the exchange.

For an exchange to occur, at least two people or organizations must be willing to make a trade, and each must have something the other wants. Both parties must agree on the value of the exchange and how it will be carried out. Each party also must be free to accept or reject the other's terms for the exchange. Under these conditions, a gun-wielding robber's offer to "exchange" your money for your life does not constitute a valid exchange. In contrast, although someone may complain that a store's prices are "highway robbery," an exchange occurs if he still forks over the money to buy something there—even if he still grumbles about it weeks later.

To complicate things a bit more, everyone does not always agree on the terms of the exchange. Think, for example, about *music piracy*, which is a huge headache for music labels. On the one hand, they claim that they lose billions of dollars a year when consumers download songs without paying for them. On the other hand, a lot of people who engage in this practice don't feel that they participate in an unfair exchange that deprives manufacturers of the value of their products. They argue that music piracy is the fault of record companies that charge way too much for new songs. What do you think?

The debate over music downloading reminds us that an agreed upon transfer of value must occur for an exchange to take place. A politician can agree to work toward certain goals in exchange for your vote, or a minister can offer you salvation in return for your faith. Today, most exchanges occur as a monetary transaction in which currency (in the form of cash, check, or credit card) is surrendered in return for a good or a service.

3

OBJECTIVE

Explain the evolution of the marketing concept.

(pp. 13–18)

When Did Marketing Begin? The Evolution of a Concept

Now that we have an idea of how the marketing process works, let's take a step back and see how this process worked (or didn't work) in "the old days." Although it just sounds like common sense to us, believe it or not, the notion that businesses and other organizations succeed when they satisfy customers' needs actually is a pretty recent idea. Before the 1950s, marketing was basically a means of making production more efficient. Let's take a quick look at how the marketing discipline has developed. Table 1.2 tells us about some of the more recent events in this marketing history.

The Production Era

Many people say that Henry Ford's Model T changed America forever. Even from the start in 1908, when the "Tin Lizzie," or "flivver" as the T was known, sold for $825, Henry Ford continued to make improvements in production. By 1912, Ford got so efficient that the car sold for $575, a price even the Ford employees who made the car could afford.[7] As the price continued to drop, Ford sold even more flivvers. By 1921, the Model T Ford had 60 percent of the new-car market. In 1924, the ten millionth Model T rolled off the assembly line. The Model T story is perhaps the most well-known and most successful example of an organization that focuses on the most efficient production and distribution of products.

Ford's focus illustrates a **production orientation**, which works best in a seller's market when demand is greater than supply because it focuses on the most efficient ways to produce and distribute products. Essentially, consumers have to take whatever is available—there weren't a whole lot of other Tin Lizzies competing for drivers in the 1920s. Under these conditions, marketing plays a relatively insignificant role—the goods literally sell themselves because people have no other choices. In the former Soviet Union, the centralized government set production quotas, and weary shoppers lined up (often for hours) to purchase whatever happened to be on a store's shelves at the time.

Firms that focus on a production orientation tend to view the market as a homogeneous group that will be satisfied with the basic function of a product. Sometimes this view is too narrow. For example, Procter & Gamble's Ivory soap has been in decline for some time because the company viewed the brand as plain old soap, not as a cleansing product that could provide other benefits as well. Ivory soap lost business to newer deodorant and "beauty" soaps containing cold cream that "cleaned up" in this market.[8]

production orientation
A management philosophy that emphasizes the most efficient ways to produce and distribute products.

The Sales Era

When product availability exceeds demand in a buyer's market, businesses may engage in the "hard sell" in which salespeople aggressively push their wares. During the Great Depression in the 1930s, when money was scarce for most people, firms shifted their focus from a product orientation to moving their goods in any way they could.

This **selling orientation** means that management views marketing as a sales function, or a way to move products out of warehouses so that inventories don't pile up. The selling orientation gained in popularity after World War II. During the war, the United States dramatically increased its industrial capacity to manufacture tanks, combat boots, parachutes, and countless other wartime goods. After the war, this industrial capacity was converted to producing consumer goods.

Consumers eagerly bought all the things they couldn't get during the war years, but once they satisfied these initial needs and wants they got more selective. The race for consumers'

selling orientation
A managerial view of marketing as a sales function, or a way to move products out of warehouses to reduce inventory.

Table 1.2 | Marketing History

Year	Marketing Event
1955	Ray Kroc opens his first McDonald's.
1956	Lever Brothers launches Wisk, America's first liquid laundry detergent.
1957	Ford rolls out Edsel, loses more than $250 million in two years.
1959	Mattel introduces Barbie.
1960	The FDA approves Searle's Enovid as the first oral contraceptive.
1961	Procter & Gamble launches Pampers.
1962	Walmart, Kmart, Target, and Woolco open their doors.
1963	The Pepsi Generation kicks off the cola wars.
1964	Blue Ribbon Sports (now known as Nike) ships its first shoes.
1965	Donald Fisher opens The Gap, a jeans-only store in San Francisco.
1971	Cigarette advertising is banned on radio and television.
1973	Federal Express begins overnight delivery services.
1976	Sol Price opens the first warehouse club store in San Diego.
1980	Ted Turner creates CNN.
1981	MTV begins.
1982	Gannett launches *USA Today.*
1983	Chrysler introduces minivans.
1984	Apple Computer introduces the Macintosh.
1985	New Coke is launched; Old Coke is brought back 79 days later.
1990	Saturn, GM's first new car division since 1919, rolls out its first car.
1993	Phillip Morris reduces price of Marlboros by 40 cents a pack and loses $13.4 billion in stock market value in one day.
1994	In the largest switch in ad history, IBM yanks its business from scores of agencies worldwide and hands its entire account to Ogilvy & Mather.
1995	eBay goes online as an experimental auction service.
1997	McDonald's gives away Teenie Beanie Babies with Happy Meals. Consumer response is so overwhelming that McDonald's is forced to take out ads apologizing for its inability to meet demand. Nearly 100 million Happy Meals are sold during the promotion.[a]
1998	Germany's Daimler-Benz acquires America's Chrysler Corporation for more than $38 billion in stock to create a new global automaking giant called Daimler-Chrysler.[b]
2003	Amazon debuts its "Search Inside the Book" feature that allows you to search the full text of more than 33 million pages from over 120,000 printed books.
2004	Online sales in the United States top $100 billion.[c]
2007	About 30 open source companies were purchased for more than $1 billion.[d]
2008	MySpace boasts over 225 million members worldwide.[d]
2010	Apple launches the iPad; sells 300,000 of the tablets on the first day and one million iPads in 28 days —less than half of the 74 days it took to sell one million iPhones. Consumers watch more than 30 billion videos online per month.[e]

Sources: Patricia Sellers, "To Avoid Trampling, Get Ahead of the Mass," *Fortune,* 1994, 201–2 except as noted. [a] Tod Taylor, "The Beanie Factor," *Brandweek,* June 16, 1997, 22–27. [b] Jennifer Laabs, "Daimler-Benz and Chrysler: A Merger of Global HR Proportions," *Workforce,* July 1998, 13. [c] Keith Regan, "Report: Online Sales Top $100 Billion," *E-Commerce Times,* June 1, 2004, **www.ecommercetimes.com/story/34148.html**. [d] Frank Rose, "Wired Business Trends 2008," *Wired* **http://www.wired.com/techbiz/it/ magazine/16-04/bz_opensource**, December 2007. [e] Eliot Van Buskirk, "Apple iPad Reaches '1 Million Sold' Twice as Fast as iPhone" (May 3, 2010), *Wired,* **http://www .wired.com/epicenter/2010/05/apple-ipad-reaches-one-million-sold-twice-as-fast-as-iphone/#ixzz0qBrfv3tj**, accessed June 7, 2010; Mashable.com (April 5, 2010), **http://mashable.com/2010/04/05/ipad-stats-300000-sold/**, accessed June 7, 2010; "30 Billion Videos Watched Online in April" (June 11, 2010), Center for Media Research, **http://www.mediapost.com/publications/?fa=Articles.showArticle&art_aid=129561**, accessed June 11, 2010.

hearts and pocketbooks was on. The selling orientation prevailed well into the 1950s. But consumers as a rule don't like to be pushed, and the hard sell gave marketing a bad image.

Companies that still follow a selling orientation tend to be more successful at making one-time sales rather than at building repeat business. We are most likely to find this focus among companies that sell *unsought goods*—products that people don't tend to buy without some prodding. For example, most of us aren't exactly "dying" to shop for cemetery plots, so some encouragement may be necessary to splurge on a final resting place.

The Relationship Era

At Direct Tire Sales in Watertown, Massachusetts, customers discover an unusual sight: The customer lounge is clean, there is free coffee with fresh cream and croissants, employees wear ties, and the company will even pay your cab fare home if your car isn't ready on time. People don't mind paying 10 to 15 percent more for these extra services.[9] Direct Tire Sales has found that it pays to have a **consumer orientation** that satisfies customers' needs and wants.

As the world's most successful firms began to adopt a consumer orientation, marketers had a way to outdo the competition—and marketing's importance was also elevated in the firm. Marketers did research to understand the needs of different consumers, assisted in tailoring products to the needs of these various groups, and did an even better job of designing marketing messages than in the days of the selling orientation.

The marketing world was humming along nicely, but then inflation in the 1970s and recession in the 1980s took their toll on company profits. The marketing concept needed a boost. Firms had to do more than meet consumers' needs—they had to do this better than the competition and do it repeatedly. They increasingly concentrated on improving the quality of their products. By the early 1990s, many in the marketing community followed an approach termed **Total Quality Management (TQM)**. The TQM perspective takes many forms, but essentially it's a management philosophy that involves all employees from the assembly line onward in continuous product quality improvement.

Indeed, rapid improvements in manufacturing processes give forward-thinking firms—even small ones—a huge edge in the marketplace because they are more nimble and thus able to create products consumers want when they want them and at the price they want. One way they do is to manufacture *on demand*—this means that they don't actually produce a product until a customer orders it. The Japanese pioneered this idea with their *just-in-time model* that we'll learn more about in Chapter 15.

Today, however, even small mom and pop companies can compete in this space. Technology is creating a new class of business person that we call an **instapreneur**. All you need is a design; even amateurs can produce jewelry, T-shirts, furniture, and indeed almost anything we can imagine. They don't have to pay to store their inventory in huge warehouses and they don't need any money down. For example, the German firm Spreadshirt hosts 500,000 individual T-shirt shops. You see a design you like, place an order, and bam—it gets produced and sent to your door.[10] Spreadshirt even partnered with Stardoll, a Swedish virtual world that lets girls create fashion designs and see what they look like on virtual celebrities. Now, they can actually transfer their own designs to the real world.

The Triple Bottom Line Orientation

Over time, many forward-thinking organizations began to see their commitment to quality even more intensely than "just" satisfying consumers' needs during a single transaction. A few realized that making monetary profit is

consumer orientation
A business approach that prioritizes the satisfaction of customers' needs and wants.

Total Quality Management (TQM)
A management philosophy that focuses on satisfying customers through empowering employees to be an active part of continuous quality improvement.

instapreneur
A businessperson who only produces a product when it is ordered.

RUBBISH CAN BE RECYCLED. NATURE CANNOT.

Marketing messages like this Romanian one for the World Wildlife Fund focus on the environmental bottom line.

triple bottom line orientation
A business orientation that looks at financial profits, the community in which the organization operates, and creating sustainable business practices.

customer relationship management (CRM)
A systematic tracking of consumers' preferences and behaviors over time in order to tailor the value proposition as closely as possible to each individual's unique wants and needs. CRM allows firms to talk to individual customers and to adjust elements of their marketing programs in light of how each customer reacts.

attention economy
A company's success is measured by its share of mind rather than share of market, where companies make money when they attract eyeballs rather than just dollars.

social marketing concept
A management philosophy that marketers must satisfy customers' needs in ways that also benefit society and also deliver profit to the firm.

important—but there's more to think about than just the financial bottom line. Instead, they began to focus on a **triple bottom line orientation** that meant building long-term bonds with customers rather than merely selling them stuff today.[11] This new way of looking at business emphasizes the need to maximize three components:

1. *The financial bottom line:* Financial profits to stakeholders

2. *The social bottom line:* Contributing to the communities in which the company operates

3. *The environmental bottom line:* Creating sustainable business practices that minimize damage to the environment or that even improve it

Is it possible to contribute in a positive way to society and the earth and still contribute to your paycheck? Walmart, the nation's largest retailer, seems to think so. The huge company announced in 2010 its goal to cut 20 million metric tons of greenhouse gas emissions from its supply chain by the end of 2015—the equivalent of removing more than 3.8 million cars from the road for a year. It's asking suppliers to take a hard look at the carbon their products emit. Walmart will work with its vendors to make their manufacturing processes more efficient—and hopefully pass cost savings on to customers. The chain has introduced more modest initiatives already; for example, it's working to change the labels on clothing it sells to indicate the products can be washed in cold water (therefore lowering customers' electricity bills) and in partnership with 20th Century Fox Home Entertainment it eliminated the plastic knob in the center of CD cases to cut greenhouse gas emissions.[12]

One outgrowth of this new way of thinking was the concept of **customer relationship management (CRM)**, which involves systematically tracking consumers' preferences and behaviors over time in order to tailor the value proposition as closely as possible to each individual's unique wants and needs. With the advent of the Internet, a CRM approach got a lot easier to implement as more and more firms started to rely heavily on the Web to connect with consumers. The Internet provides the ultimate opportunity for implementation of the marketing concept because it allows a firm to personalize its messages and products to better meet the needs of each individual consumer. More on this in Chapter 12.

Although dot-com companies took a beating in the marketplace during the first "bubble" in the early 1990s, many analysts believe that this was just a preliminary shakeout—the heyday of the Internet is yet to come. More recent success stories like Google, Twitter, Facebook, and Flickr seem to be proving analysts right. Indeed, some marketing analysts suggest that the Internet creates a *paradigm shift* for business. This means that companies must adhere to a new model to profit in a wired world. They argue that we live in an **attention economy**, one in which a company's success will be measured by its share of mind rather than share of market, where companies make money when they attract eyeballs rather than just dollars. For example, Google sells advertising to many other companies, so the more consumers it can persuade to "google" rather than "bing" or "yahoo," the more it can charge to place ads on search pages.

This means that companies must find new and innovative ways to stand out from the crowd and become an integral part of consumers' lives rather than just being a dry company that makes and sells products. For example, major consumer packaged foods companies are drawing many more customers to their Web sites than in the past. More important, the sites are "sticky," meaning that they tend to keep visitors long enough to make a lasting impression on them and motivate people to come back for more.

Another result of this new way of long-term thinking is the **social marketing concept**, which maintains that marketers must satisfy customers' needs in ways that also benefit society while still delivering a profit to the firm. This perspective is even more important since the terrorist attacks of

"I REALIZED good coffee can be good for the world."

GREEN MOUNTAIN COFFEE®

A REVELATION IN EVERY CUP™

Green Mountain Coffee uses sustainable business practices.

2001, which led many people and firms to reexamine their values and redouble their commitments to community and country.

Many big and small firms alike practice this philosophy. Their efforts include satisfying society's environmental and social needs for a cleaner, safer environment by developing recyclable packaging, adding extra safety features such as car air bags, voluntarily modifying a manufacturing process to reduce pollution, and sponsoring campaigns to address social problems. Servus Credit Union, a Canadian bank, even handed out $200,000 in $10 increments to finance small good deeds.[13]

A very important trend now is for companies to think of ways to design and manufacture products with a focus on **sustainability**, which we define as "meeting present needs without compromising the ability of future generations to meet their needs."[14] Some refer to this philosophy as *"cradle to cradle"*; this term describes the ideal condition where a product is made from natural materials and is fully reusable, recyclable, or biodegradable so the net depletion of resources a company needs to make it is zero. When players in the 2010 World Cup ran onto the field, many wore Nike jerseys made from plastic bottles the company retrieved from landfills in Japan and Taiwan. Walmart is a leader in sustainability practices. The giant retail chain makes and sells photo frames from plastic waste products it creates and recycles materials left over from manufacturing its private label diapers into building materials when it constructs new stores. Sustainability is good business because it reduces costs while conserving resources; Walmart estimates savings of $100 million in one year when it switched to a recyclable variety of cardboard it uses to ship goods to its stores. Consumers love it too: In the United States alone we spend more than $500 billion per year on sustainable products.[15]

Sustainability applies to many aspects of doing business, including social and economic practices (e.g., humane working conditions and diplomacy to prevent wars that deplete food supplies, atmospheric quality, and of course lives). One other crucial pillar of sustainability is the environmental impact of the product. **Green marketing**, the development of marketing strategies that support environmental stewardship by creating an environmentally founded differential benefit in the minds of consumers, is being practiced by most forward-thinking firms today. Green marketing is one aspect of a firm's overall commitment to sustainability. A recent study on the impact of green marketing uncovered some interesting results:

- About half the companies reported that they are consciously taking steps to become more green.

- More than 80 percent of respondents indicated they expect to spend more on green marketing in the future.

- Companies with smaller marketing budgets tend to spend more on green marketing and also think green marketing is more effective than larger companies do.

- By far the most popular medium for green marketing was the Internet, with 74.2 percent of respondents having spent money online.

- Marketers that track marketing spending and its relation to sales believe people will pay more for green products.

- Marketers tend to lead green initiatives; 50 percent of firm managers surveyed agree that control of the green (sustainability) program is in the hands of marketers.[16]

In addition to building long-term relationships and focusing on social responsibility, triple bottom line firms place a much greater focus on *accountability*—measuring just how

Game sites like Candystand are "sticky" (this one is built around candy, after all) so many advertisers find these media outlets an attractive place to advertise.

sustainability
A product design focus that seeks to create products that meet present consumer needs without compromising the ability of future generations to meet their needs.

green marketing
A marketing strategy that supports environmental stewardship, thus creating a differential benefit in the minds of consumers.

Green marketing in action.

©Solo Cup Company

return on investment (ROI)
The direct financial impact of a firm's expenditure of a resource such as time or money.

OBJECTIVE
Understand the range of services and goods that organizations market.
(pp. 18–21)

much value marketing activities create. This means that marketers at these organizations ask hard questions about the true value of their efforts and their impact on the bottom line. These questions all boil down to the simple acronym of **ROI (return on investment)**. Marketers now realize that if they want to assess just how much value they create for the firm, they need to know exactly what they are spending and what the concrete results of their actions are.

However, it's not always so easy to assess the value of marketing activities. Many times managers state their marketing objectives using vague phrases like "increase awareness of our product" or "encourage people to eat healthier snacks." These goals are important, but their lack of specificity makes it pretty much impossible for senior management to determine marketing's true impact. Because management may view these efforts as costs rather than investments, marketing activities often are among the first to be cut out of a firm's budget. To win continued support for what they do (and sometimes to keep their jobs), marketers in triple bottom line firms do their best to prove to management that they are generating measurable value by aligning marketing activities with the firm's overall business objectives.[17]

What Can We Market?

Marketers' creations surround us. It seems that everywhere we turn we get bombarded by advertisements, stores, and products that compete fiercely and loudly for our attention and our dollars. Marketers filter much of what we learn about the world, such as when we see images of rich or beautiful people on television commercials or magazines. Ads show us how we should act and what we should own. Marketing's influence extends from "serious" goods and services such as health care to "fun" things such as extreme skateboarding equipment and hip-hop music (though many people take these products as seriously as their health).

Lasers to Lady Gaga

popular culture
The music, movies, sports, books, celebrities, and other forms of entertainment consumed by the mass market.

Popular culture consists of the music, movies, sports, books, celebrities, and other forms of entertainment that the mass market consumes. The relationship between marketing and popular culture is a two-way street. The goods and services that are popular at any time often mirror changes in the larger society. Consider, for example, some U.S. products that reflected underlying cultural changes at the time they were introduced:

- The TV dinner signaled changes in family structure, such as a movement away from the traditional family dinner hour filled with conversation about the day's events.

- Cosmetics made of natural materials and not tested on animals reflected social concerns about pollution and animal rights.

- Condoms marketed in pastel carrying cases intended for female buyers signaled changing attitudes toward sexual responsibility.

myths
Stories containing symbolic elements that express the shared emotions and ideals of a culture.

Marketing messages often communicate **myths**, stories containing symbolic elements that express the shared emotions and ideals of a culture. Consider, for example, how McDonald's takes on mythical qualities. To some, the golden arches are virtually synonymous with American culture.[18] These familiar structures offer sanctuary to Americans in foreign lands who are grateful to know exactly what to expect once they enter. Basic struggles of good versus evil play out in the fantasy world of McDonald's advertising, as when Ronald McDonald confounds the Hamburglar. McDonald's even runs Hamburger University, where fast-food majors learn how to make the perfect burger.

Is there any limit to what marketers can market? Marketing applies to more than just canned peas or cola drinks. Some of the best marketers come from the ranks of services companies such as American Express or not-for-profit organizations such as Greenpeace. Politicians, athletes, and performers use marketing to their advantage (just think about that $30 T-shirt you may have bought at a baseball game or rock concert). Ideas such as political systems (democracy, totalitarianism), religion (Christianity, Islam), and art (realism, abstract) also compete for acceptance in a "marketplace." In this book, we'll refer to any good, service, or idea that can be marketed as a product, even though what you're buying may not take a physical form.

Marketing messages sometimes refer to familiar cultural stories, like this ad from Chile that borrows imagery from Little Red Riding Hood.

Consumer Goods and Services

Consumer goods are the tangible products that individual consumers purchase for personal or family use. **Services** are intangible products that we pay for and use but never own. Service transactions contribute on average more than 60 percent to the gross national product of all industrialized nations. Marketers need to understand the special challenges that arise when marketing an intangible service rather than a tangible good.[19]

In both cases, though, keep in mind that the consumer looks to obtain some underlying value, such as convenience, security, or status, from a marketing exchange. That value can come from a variety of competing goods and services, even those that don't resemble one another on the surface. For example, a new CD and a ticket to a local concert may cost about the same, and each may provide the benefit of musical enjoyment, so consumers often have to choose among competing alternatives if they can't afford (or don't want) to buy them all.

Business-to-Business Goods and Services

Business-to-business marketing is the marketing of goods and services from one organization to another. Although we usually relate marketing to the thousands of consumer goods begging for our dollars every day, the reality is that businesses and other organizations buy a lot more goods than consumers do. They purchase these **industrial goods** for further processing or to use in their own business operations. For example, automakers buy tons of steel to use in the manufacturing process, and they buy computer systems to track manufacturing costs and other information essential to operations.

Similarly, there is a lot of buzz about **e-commerce** and the buying and selling of products—books, CDs, cars, and so forth—on the Internet. However, just like in the off-line world, much of the real online action is in the area of business-to-business marketing.

Marketing an intangible service like the assistance this British realtor offers poses unique challenges.

consumer goods
The goods individual consumers purchase for personal or family use.

services
Intangible products that are exchanged directly between the producer and the customer.

business-to-business marketing
The marketing of goods and services from one organization to another.

Ripped from the Headlines!

Ethical/Sustainable Decisions in the Real World

Back in the day, the "typical" marijuana smoker (or at least the stereotype) was a bearded, bell-bottomed hippie who zoned out in front of the TV watching reruns on *Nick at Night* and eating Oreos by the bagful. Today, there's a good chance a user is a senior citizen or a suburban housewife who smokes joints to fight the negative effects of glaucoma or chemotherapy. Pot is going mainstream. The drug is legal with a prescription in 14 states including California, Colorado, and New Jersey, and some feel it's only a matter of time before American voters decide in favor of full-scale legalization.

Some businesspeople smell opportunity through the smoke. One consulting firm called CannBe (advocates prefer the term *cannabis* to marijuana) offers seminars to budding marketers

ETHICS CHECK:
Find out what other students taking this course **would do** and **why** on www.mypearsonmarketinglab.com

(pun intended) who want to learn about the best techniques to merchandise the drug and related paraphernalia in a cleaned-up context. The firm's president observes, "If we can't demonstrate professionalism and legitimacy, we're never going to gain the trust of our citizens." Taking a page from marketers like General Motors and General Mills, the firm is diversifying its product line as it offers a weaker version of weed to attract first-time potheads. California dispensaries (there are more in the state than there are Starbucks outlets) offer regular promotions including coupons and even free parking to lure customers.[20] At the Harborside Health Center in Oakland, customers can check out different strains on display under a glass counter with brand names like Blue Dreams, Super Diesel, and Original Purple. Shoppers who enjoy reading detailed wine reviews will feel at home with write-ups of recommended varieties like this one: ". . . lush and spicy . . . reminiscent of Cali mist yet fatter and more body. The high is up and giggly and long lived as well. I was baked for four hours after smoking some."[21]

> Should marijuana be marketed like makeup or milk? Would you open a cannabis dispensary in your community?
>
> ☐YES ☐NO

industrial goods
Goods individuals or organizations buy for further processing or for their own use when they do business.

e-commerce
The buying or selling of goods and services electronically, usually over the Internet.

shrinkage
Losses experienced by retailers due to shoplifting, employee theft, and damage to merchandise.

anticonsumption
The deliberate defacement of products.

not-for-profit organizations
Organizations with charitable, educational, community, and other public service goals that buy goods and services to support their functions and to attract and serve their members.

Shrinkage

Someone steals from a store every five seconds. **Shrinkage** is the industry term for inventory and cash losses from shoplifting and employee theft. As we'll see in Chapter 16, this is a massive problem for businesses that they in turn pass on to consumers in the form of higher prices. Analysts attribute about 40 percent of the losses to employees rather than shoppers.

Anticonsumption

Some types of destructive consumer behavior are **anticonsumption**, when people deliberately deface products. This practice ranges from relatively mild acts like spray-painting graffiti on buildings and subways, to serious incidences of product tampering or even the release of computer viruses that can bring large corporations to their knees.

Not-for-Profit Marketing

As we noted earlier, you don't have to be a businessperson to use marketing principles. Many **not-for-profit organizations**, including museums, zoos, and even churches, practice the marketing concept. Local governments are adopting marketing techniques to create more effective taxpayer services and to attract new businesses and industries to their counties and cities. Even states are getting into the act: We've known for a long time that I ♥ NY, but recently Kentucky and Oregon hired advertising agencies to develop statewide branding campaigns (the official state motto of Oregon is now "Oregon. We love dreamers.").[22] The intense competition for support of civic and charitable activities means that only the not-for-profits that meet the needs of their constituents and donors will survive.

Idea, Place, and People Marketing

Marketing principles also encourage people to endorse ideas or to change their behaviors in positive ways. Many organizations work hard to convince consumers to use seat belts, not to litter our highways, to engage in safe sex, or to believe that one political system is preferable to another. In addition to ideas, places and people also are marketable. We are all familiar with tourism marketing that promotes exotic resorts like Club Med ("the antidote for civilization"). For many developing countries like Thailand, tourism provides an important opportunity for economic growth.

You may have heard the expression, "Stars are made, not born." There's a lot of truth to that. Lady Gaga may have a killer voice and Ryan Howard may have a red-hot baseball bat, but talent alone doesn't make thousands or even millions of people buy CDs or stadium seats. Entertainment events do not just happen. People plan them. Whether for a concert or a baseball game, the application of sound marketing principles helps ensure that patrons will continue to support the activity and buy tickets. Today, sports and the arts are hotbeds of marketing activity. Many of the famous people you pay to see became famous with the help of shrewd marketing: They and their managers developed a "product" that they hoped would appeal to some segment of the population. To appreciate how far these efforts can go (maybe too far!), recently reports circulated that the Russian government plans to rebrand the infamous dictator Josef Stalin as part of an effort to improve its global image. Since Stalin "purged" (i.e., executed) about 20 million people, this campaign may be a bit ambitious.[23]

Some of the same principles that go into "creating" a celebrity apply to you. An entertainer—whether Adam Lambert or Tony Bennett—must "package" his talents, identify a market that is likely to be interested, and work hard to gain exposure to these potential customers by appearing in the right musical venues.

In the same way, everyday people like Alex "package" themselves when they sum up their accomplishments on LinkedIn and join professional groups to link with as many "buyers" as they can. And this person marketing perspective is more valid than ever—now that almost everyone can find "15 minutes of fame" on a Web site, a blog, or a YouTube video. We even have a new word—*microcelebrity*—to describe those who are famous, not necessarily to millions of people, but certainly to hundreds or even thousands who follow their comings and goings on Facebook, Flickr, or Twitter. Some of these stories reveal heartbreak and despair—including the chronicle of a woman named Jennifer who described her husband's betrayal in intimate detail to the 55,000 readers of her blog, NakedJen.com.[24] Others focus on more crucial issues like how to handle a bad hair day—Blogger.com lists more than 4,000 postings that ask readers: "Should I cut my hair?" In a way, when you post some text about how you spent your day on your blog or Facebook wall, you're basically sending out a press release about yourself (we'll find out more about those in Chapter 13). So, be careful what you broadcast—you might make the news sooner than you think![25]

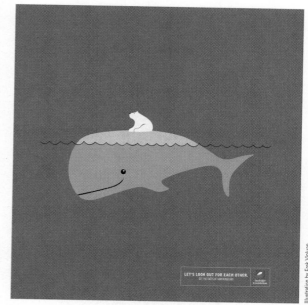

Not-for-profit organizations also use marketing tools.

Illustration by Erek Vinluan

5 The Value of Marketing and the Marketing of Value

OBJECTIVE
Understand value from the perspectives of customers, producers, and society.
(pp. 21–29)

So far, we've talked a lot about marketing practices that deliver value to customers. As we noted at the beginning of this chapter, value refers to the benefits a customer receives from buying a good or service. Marketers communicate these benefits to the customer in the form of a **value proposition**, a marketplace offering that fairly and accurately sums up the value that the customer will realize if he or she purchases the product. The challenge to the marketer is to create an attractive value proposition. A big part of this challenge is to convince customers that this value proposition is superior to others they might choose from competitors.

How do customers (such as your potential employers) decide how much value they will get from a purchase? One way to look at value is to think of it simply as a ratio of benefits to costs—that is, customers "invest" their precious time and money to do business with a firm, and they expect a certain bundle of benefits in return.

value proposition
A marketplace offering that fairly and accurately sums up the value that will be realized if the good or service is purchased.

Marketing strategies exert an important influence on major social problems such as finding a cure for cancer.

But here's the tricky part: Value is in the eye of the beholder; this means that something (or someone) may be worth a lot to one person but not to another. Your mother may believe that you are the greatest person on the planet, but a prospective employer may form a different opinion. A big role marketers play in an organization is to ensure that consumers appreciate the value of a product, service, or idea. Let's look at value from the different perspectives of the parties that are involved in an exchange: the customers, the sellers, and society.

Value from the Customer's Perspective

Think about something you would like to buy, say, a new pair of shoes. You have narrowed the choice down to several options. Your purchase decision no doubt will be affected by the ratio of costs versus benefits for each type of shoe. When you buy a pair of shoes, you consider the price (and other costs) along with all the other benefits (utilities) that each competing pair of shoes provides you.

As we noted previously, the value proposition includes the whole bundle of benefits the firm promises to deliver, not just the benefits of the product itself. For example, although most people probably couldn't run faster or jump higher if they were wearing Nikes versus Reeboks, many die-hard loyalists swear by their favorite brand. These archrival brands are largely marketed in terms of their images—meanings their respective advertising agencies have carefully crafted with the help of legions of athletes, slickly produced commercials, and millions of dollars. When you buy a Nike "swoosh," you're doing more than choosing shoes to wear to the mall—you may also be making a statement about the type of person you are or wish you were. In addition to providing comfort or letting you run faster, that statement also is part of the value the product delivers to you.

You can probably think of possessions you own with which you've "bonded" in some way—that is, their value to you goes beyond their function. Marketers who understand this know that in the long run, their value proposition will be successful if they manage to build a relationship between their product and the people who buy it.

Value from the Seller's Perspective

We've seen that marketing transactions produce value for buyers, but how do sellers experience value, and how do they decide whether a transaction is valuable? One answer is obvious: They determine whether the exchange is profitable to them. Has it made money for the company's management, its workers, and its shareholders?

That's a very important factor, but not the only one. Just as we can't measure value from the consumer's perspective only in functional terms, value from the seller's perspective can take many forms. For example, in addition to making a buck or two, many firms measure value along other dimensions, such as prestige among rivals or pride in doing what they do well. Some firms by definition don't even care about making money, or they may not even be allowed to make money; nonprofits like Greenpeace, the Smithsonian Institution, or National Public Radio regard value in terms of their ability to motivate, educate, or delight the public.

Because value is such a complicated but important concept, now more than ever marketers search for new and better ways to accurately measure just what kind of value they deliver. They also try to learn how this stacks up to the competition, and—as we'll see next—in some cases even whether the relationship they have with a customer possesses enough value for them to continue it.

Build Value: Market with Customers, Not to Them

Smart companies today understand that making money from a single transaction doesn't provide the kind of value they desire. Instead, their goal is to satisfy the customer over and over again so that they can build a long-term relationship rather than just having a "one-night stand."

In recent years many firms have transformed the way they do business. They now regard consumers as *partners* in the transaction rather than as passive "victims." That explains why it's becoming more common for companies to host events (sometimes called **brandfests**) to thank customers for their loyalty. Harley-Davidson builds strong bonds with riders when it sponsors activities every year (including test drives of its new bikes) at the massive motorcycle rally in Sturgis, S.D.[26] This is one venue where thousands of members of Harley chapters called HOGs (Harley Owners Groups) come to hang out and commune with fellow brand loyalists.

brandfests
Events companies host to thank customers for their loyalty.

Customers Have Value (Some More Than Others)

Harley's cultivation of its HOGs reflects an important lesson the company understands very well: *It is more expensive to attract new customers than it is to retain current ones.* Although this notion has transformed the way many companies do business, it doesn't always hold true. In recent years, companies have been working harder to calculate the true value of their relationships with customers by asking, "How much is this customer *really* worth to us?" Firms recognize that it can be very costly in terms of both money and human effort to do whatever it takes to keep some customers loyal to the company. Very often these actions pay off, but there are cases in which keeping a customer is a losing proposition.

This way of thinking is similar to how we may decide which friends are "worth keeping." You may do a lot of favors for two friends, only to discover that when you need something, one of them is always there for you, while the other is nowhere to be found. Over time, you may decide that maintaining a friendship with that second person just doesn't make sense. Similarly, a company may use a lot of resources to appeal to two customers and find that one returns the favor by buying a lot of its products, while the other buys hardly anything. In the long run, the firm may decide to "fire" that second customer. Perhaps you once ordered something in a catalog, and you get that catalog in your mailbox every month. If you don't order anything for a certain period of time, the company will stop sending you the catalog. In the words of Donald Trump, "You're fired!" In a promotion, Burger King went a step farther: The chain created a Facebook app that awarded a coupon for a free hamburger. The catch: All you had to do was delete ten people from your friends list. Just how much is a Facebook "friend" worth to you?[27]

Joe Kennedy

APPLYING ▽ Customer Value

Joe understands that it's more expensive to attract new customers than it is to retain current ones. He needs to find ways to motivate Pandora's users to visit the site more often and to recommend it to their friends to build a loyal customer base. ➤

Companies that calculate the **lifetime value of a customer** look at how much profit they expect to make from a particular customer, including each and every purchase he or she will make from them now and in the future. To calculate lifetime value, companies estimate the amount the person will spend and then subtract what it will cost to maintain this relationship.

lifetime value of a customer
The potential profit a single customer's purchase of a firm's products generates over the customer's lifetime.

Provide Value Through Competitive Advantage

How does a firm go about creating a competitive advantage? The first step is to identify what it does really well. A **distinctive competency** is a firm's capability that is superior to that of its competition. For example, Coca-Cola's success in global markets—Coke commands 50 percent of the world's soft-drink business—is related to its distinctive competencies in distribution and marketing communications. Coke's distribution system got a jump on the competition during World War II. To enable U.S. soldiers fighting overseas to enjoy a five-cent Coke, the U.S. government assisted Coca-Cola in building 64 overseas bottling plants. Coke's skillful marketing communications program, a second distinctive competency, has contributed to its global success. In addition to its television commercials, Coke blankets less-developed countries such as Tanzania with signs posted on roads and on storefronts so that even people without televisions will think of Coke when they get thirsty.

distinctive competency
A superior capability of a firm in comparison to its direct competitors.

The second step in developing a competitive advantage is to turn a distinctive competency into a **differential benefit**—value that competitors don't offer. Differential benefits set products apart from competitors' products by providing something unique that customers want. Differential benefits provide reasons for customers to pay a premium for a firm's products and exhibit a strong brand preference. For many years, loyal Apple computer users benefited from superior

differential benefit
Properties of products that set them apart from competitors' products by providing unique customer benefits.

Joe Kennedy

Pandora's distinctive competency is the site's ability to build customized "radio stations" that offer the listener the specific types of music he or she likes to hear based on a similar song or artist. ➡

value chain

A series of activities involved in designing, producing, marketing, delivering, and supporting any product. Each link in the chain has the potential to either add or remove value from the product the customer eventually buys.

marketing scorecards

Feedback vehicles that report (often in quantified terms) how the company or brand is actually doing in achieving various goals.

metrics

Measurements or "scorecards" marketers use to identify the effectiveness of different strategies or tactics.

graphics capability compared to their PC-using counterparts. Later, when PC manufacturers caught up with this competitive advantage, Apple relied on its inventive product designers to create another differential benefit—futuristic-looking computers in a multitude of colors. This competitive advantage even tempted many loyal PC users to take a bite of the Apple.

Note that a differential benefit does not necessarily mean simply offering something different. For example, Mennen marketed a deodorant with a distinctive feature: It contained vitamin D. Unfortunately, consumers did not see any reason to pay for the privilege of spraying a vitamin under their arms. Despite advertising claims, consumers saw no benefit, and the product failed. The moral: *Effective product benefits must be both different from the competition and things customers want.* A firm that delivers these desired benefits provides value to its customers and other stakeholders.

Add Value Through the Value Chain

Many different players—both within and outside a firm—need to work together to create and deliver value to customers. The **value chain** is a useful way to appreciate all the players that work together to create value. This term refers to a series of activities involved in designing, producing, marketing, delivering, and supporting any product. In addition to marketing activities, the value chain includes business functions such as human resource management and technology development.[28]

The value chain concept reminds us that every product starts with raw materials that are of relatively limited value to the end customer. Each link in the chain has the potential to either add or remove value from the product the customer eventually buys. The successful firm is the one that can perform one or more of these activities better than other firms—this is its competitive advantage. The main activities of value-chain members include the following:

- *Inbound logistics:* Bringing in materials to make the product
- *Operations:* Converting the materials into the final product
- *Outbound logistics:* Shipping out the final product
- *Marketing:* Promoting and selling the final product
- *Service:* Meeting the customer's needs by providing any additional support required

For example, when you buy a new iPad at your local Apple store, do you think about all the people and steps involved in designing, manufacturing, and delivering that product to the store? Not to mention other people who create brand advertising, conduct consumer research to figure out what people like or dislike about their mobile music players, or even make the box it comes in or those little plastic peanuts that keep the unit from being damaged in shipment?

As 📷 Figure 1.1 shows, all these companies (and more) belong to Apple's value chain. This means that Apple must make a lot of decisions. What electronic components will go into its music players? What accessories will it include in the package? What trucking companies, wholesalers, and retailers will deliver the iPods to stores? What service will it provide to customers after the sale? And what marketing strategies will it use? In some cases, members of a value chain will work together to coordinate their activities to be more efficient and thus create a competitive advantage.

We've organized this book around the sequence of steps necessary to ensure that the appropriate value exchange occurs and that both parties to the transaction are satisfied—making it more likely they'll continue to do business in the future. 🏃 Figure 1.2 shows these steps. Basically, we're going to learn about what marketers do as a product makes its way through the value chain from manufacturers into your hands. We'll start with a focus on how companies decide what to make, how and where to sell it, and to whom to sell it. Then we'll take a look at how they decide to "position" the product in the marketplace, including choices about what it should look like, how its value should be communicated to customers, and how much to charge for it. As we reach the end of our marketing journey, we'll talk about how the product actually gets delivered to consumers.

Figure 1.1 📷 *Snapshot* | Apple's Value Chain

Apple's value chain includes inbound logistics, operations, outbound logistics, marketing and sales, and service.

Inbound Logistics	Operations	Outbound Logistics	Marketing and Sales	Service
• Planar lithium battery (Sony) • Hard drive (Toshiba) • MP3 decoder and controller chip (PortalPlayer) • Flash memory chip (Sharp Electronics Corp.) • Stereo digital-to-analog converter (Wolfson Microelectronics Ltd.) • Firewire interface controller (Texas Instruments)	• Consumer research • New product development team • Engineering and production	• Trucking companies • Wholesalers • Retailers	• Advertising • Sales force	• Computer technicians

Source: Based on information from Erik Sherman, "Inside the Apple iPod Design Triumph," Electronics Design Chain (May 27, 2006), accessed at <http://www.designchain.com/coverstory.asp?issue=summer02>http://www.designchain.com/coverstory.asp?issue=summer02"

How Do We Know What's Valuable?

How do marketers measure value? Increasingly, they develop **marketing scorecards** that report (often in quantified terms) how the company or brand is actually doing in achieving various goals. We can think of a scorecard as a marketing department's report card. Scorecards tend to be short and to the point, and they often use charts and graphs to summarize information in an easy-to-read format. They might report "grades" on factors such as actual cost per sale, a comparison of Web hits (the number of people who visit an e-commerce site) versus Web transactions (the number who actually buy something at the site), a measure of customers' satisfaction with a company's repair facilities, or perhaps even a percentage of consumers who respond to a mail piece that asks them to make a donation to a charity that the firm sponsors. You can see an example of a simple scorecard in Table 1.3. Throughout this book, we'll give you the opportunity to "get your hands dirty" as you calculate ROI using various kinds of scores, or **metrics**.

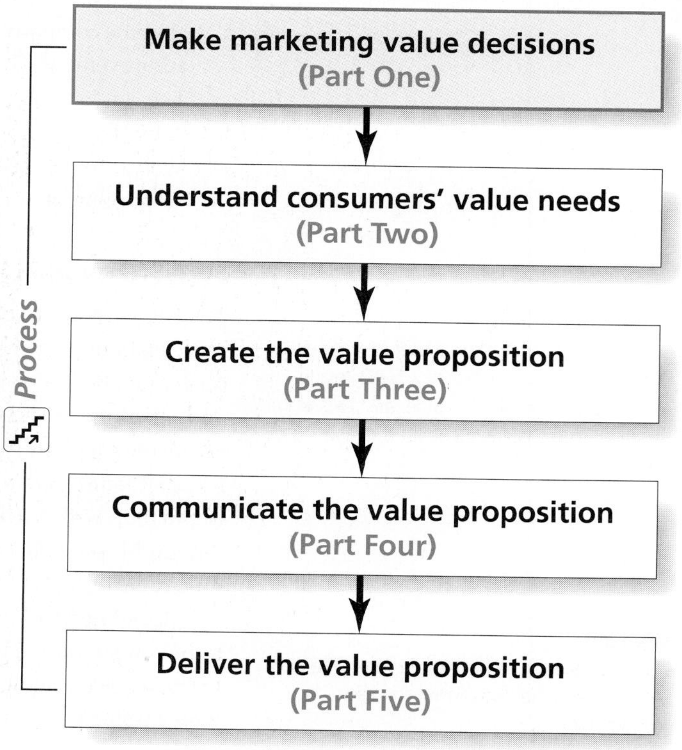

Consumer-Generated Value: From Audience to Community

One of the most exciting developments in the marketing world is the evolution of how consumers interact with marketers. In particular, we're seeing everyday people actually *generating* value instead of just buying it—consumers are turning into advertising directors, retailers, and new-product-development consultants. They create their own ads (some flattering, some not) for products and post them on sites like YouTube. They buy and sell merchandise ranging from Beatles memorabilia to washing machines (to body parts, but that's another story) on eBay. They share ideas for new styles with fashion designers and customize their own unique versions of products on Web sites. Some even proudly announce the latest stuff they've bought at websites like Blippy or in "haul videos" they shoot and post on YouTube. These changes mean that marketers need to adjust their thinking about customers: They need to stop thinking of buyers as a passive audience and start thinking of

Figure 1.2 〽️ *Process* | Create and Deliver Value

This book is organized around the sequence of steps necessary to ensure that the appropriate value exchange occurs and that both parties to the transaction are satisfied. Each step corresponds to one of the books five parts.

Make marketing value decisions
(Part One)

↓

Understand consumers' value needs
(Part Two)

↓

Create the value proposition
(Part Three)

↓

Communicate the value proposition
(Part Four)

↓

Deliver the value proposition
(Part Five)

| Table 1.3 | An Example of a Customer Service Scorecard |

| | Quarterly Scores | | |
Item Text	1st Qtr.	2nd Qtr.	3rd Qtr.
Satisfaction with			
C1 Employee responsiveness	60%	65%	68%
C2 Product selection	60%	62%	63%
C3 Service quality	60%	62%	55%
C4 Cleanliness of facility	75%	80%	85%
C5 Knowledge of employees	62%	62%	58%
C6 Appearance of employees	60%	62%	63%
C7 Convenience of location	60%	65%	68%

Source: Adapted From C. F. Lunbdy and C. Rasinowich, "The Missing Link," *Marketing Research,* Winter 2003, 14–19 p. 18. Copyright © 2003 American Marketing Association.

amafessionals
Consumers who contribute ideas to online forums for the fun and challenge rather than to receive a paycheck, so their motivation is to gain *psychic income* rather than financial income.

consumer-generated content
Everyday people functioning in marketing roles, such as participating in creating advertisements, providing input to new product development, or serving as wholesalers or retailers.

them as a community that is motivated to participate in both the production and the consumption of what companies sell. Some of these consumers are **amafessionals**: They contribute ideas for the fun and challenge rather than to receive a paycheck, so their motivation is to gain *psychic income* rather than financial income. We'll talk more about this phenomenon later, but for now think about these recent examples of **consumer-generated content**:

- Ghirardelli Chocolate broadcast consumer-generated comments in New York's Times Square about when and where they most enjoyed eating its chocolate squares.[29]

- On MySpace more than five million amafessional artists and bands place their songs right next to those of professionals—about 15 percent of the total active music participants.[30]

- Rite-Solutions, a software company that builds advanced command-and-control systems for the Navy, set up an internal "prediction market" in which any employee can propose that the company acquire a new technology, enter a new business, or make an efficiency improvement. These proposals become stocks, complete with ticker symbols, discussion lists, and e-mail alerts. Employees buy or sell the stocks, and prices change to reflect the sentiments of the company's engineers, computer scientists, and project managers—as well as its marketers, accountants, and even the receptionist. One "stock" resulted in the development of a new product that now accounts for 30 percent of the company's sales.[31]

Social Networking

social networking
Online platforms that allow a user to represent him- or herself via a profile on a Web site and provide and receive links to other members of the network to share input about common interests.

The tremendous acceleration of **social networking** fuels this fire. In a social network a user represents him- or herself via a profile on a Web site and provides and receives links to other members of the network to share input about common interests. The odds are you and most of your classmates checked your Facebook page before (or during?) class today. Social media platforms like this are very hot today; more and more advertisers realize that these sites are a great way to reach an audience that tunes in regularly and enthusiastically to catch up with friends, check out photos of what they did at that outrageous party Saturday night, proclaim opinions about political or social issues, or share discoveries of new musical artists.

Web 2.0
The new generation of the World Wide Web that incorporates social networking and user interactivity.

Social networking is an integral part of what many call **Web 2.0**, which is like the Internet on steroids. The key difference between Web 1.0 and the new version is the interactivity we see among producers and users, but these are some other characteristics of a Web 2.0 site:[32]

The Cutting Edge

Social Media

What isn't an app these days? StickyBits software turns a Coke can, iPhone, or box of detergent into an app that lets users link video, photos, text, or audio to any object that has a barcode. Some call these apps **physical URLs**; they enable user-generated clouds of content to form around products you encounter in the store or on the street. When you scan the barcode you can upload your own content or see what others have already uploaded. Brands such as Ben & Jerry's, Campbell Soup, and Doritos already have content forming around their products. A similar app lets users link for good causes; when they participate in CauseWorld, they earn money for charity as they scan products from P&G and Kraft.[35] Before long, will we all be remembering to scan our cans?

- It improves as the number of users increases. For example, Amazon's ability to recommend books to you based on what other people with similar interests have bought gets better as it tracks more and more people who are entering search queries.

- Its currency is eyeballs. Google makes its money by charging advertisers according to the number of people who see their ads after they type in a search term.

- It's version-free and in perpetual beta. Unlike static Web sites or books, content is always a work in progress. Wikipedia, the online encyclopedia, gets updated constantly by users who "correct" others' errors.

- It categorizes entries according to **folksonomy** rather than "taxonomy." In other words, sites rely on users rather than preestablished systems to sort contents. Listeners at Pandora.com create their own "radio stations" that play songs by artists they choose as well as other similar artists.[33]

This last point highlights a key change in the way some new media companies approach their businesses: Think of it as marketing strategy by committee. The **wisdom of crowds** perspective (from a book by that name) argues that under the right circumstances, groups are smarter than the smartest people in them. If this is true, it implies that large numbers of (non-expert) consumers can predict successful products.[34]

physical URLs
New apps that enable user-generated clouds of content to form around products; barcode scans allow the user to upload content or see what others have already uploaded.

folksonomy
A classification system that relies on users rather than preestablished systems to sort contents.

wisdom of crowds
Under the right circumstances, groups are smarter than the smartest people in them, meaning that large numbers of consumers can predict successful products.

Open Source Business Models

Another related change is the rise of the **open source model** that turns some of our conventional assumptions about the value of products and services on its head. This model started in the software industry where the Linux system grows by leaps and bounds—even IBM uses it now. Unlike the closely guarded code that companies like Microsoft use, open source developers post their programs on a public site, and a community of volunteers is free to tinker with it, develop other applications using the code, then give their changes away for free. For example, the company that gives out (for free) the Mozilla Firefox Internet browser that competes with Microsoft commands over 20 percent market share among users.[36] We'll talk more about this—and answer the question of how in the world you can make money from something when you give it away—in Chapter 11.

open source model
A practice used in the software industry in which companies share their software codes with one another to assist in the development of a better product.

Value from Society's Perspective

Every company's activities influence the world around it in ways both good and bad. Therefore, we must also consider how marketing transactions add or subtract value from society. In many ways, we are at the mercy of marketers because we trust them to sell us products that are safe and perform as promised. We also trust them to price and distribute these products fairly. Conflicts often arise in business when the pressure to succeed in the marketplace provokes dishonest business practices—the huge failure of major financial services organizations like AIG and Goldman Sachs is a painful case in point.

Companies usually find that stressing ethics and social responsibility also is good business, at least in the long run. Some find out the hard way: Toyota squandered massive amounts of consumer loyalty when the company allegedly hid evidence of safety defects from customers and regulators before it was forced to recall cars due to acceleration problems. BP's handling of the massive Gulf oil spill and the subsequent cleanup attempts similarly eroded its image in the marketplace as consumers boycotted the company's gas stations to protest the tragic incident and its consequences for the environment.[37] In contrast, Procter & Gamble voluntarily withdrew its Rely tampons from the market following reports of women who had suffered toxic shock syndrome (TSS). Although scientists did not claim a causal link between Rely and TSS, the company agreed with the Food and Drug Administration that they would undertake extensive advertising notifying women of the symptoms of TSS and asking them to return their boxes of Rely for a refund. The company took a $75 million loss and sacrificed an unusually successful new product that had already captured about one-quarter of the billion-dollar sanitary product market.[38]

Is Marketing Evil?

For some—hopefully not many and hopefully not *you* after you read this book—marketing is a four-letter word. The field sometimes gets attacked for a number of reasons.[39] Here are some primary ones:

Criticism: Marketing corrupts society. The marketing system comes under fire from both ends of the political spectrum. On the one hand, some members of the Religious Right believe that marketers contribute to the moral breakdown of society because they present images of hedonistic pleasure and encourage the pursuit of secular humanism at the expense of spirituality and the environment. On the other hand, some leftists argue that the same deceitful promises of material pleasure function to buy off people who would otherwise be revolutionaries working to change the system.[40]

A Response: A need *is a basic biological motive; a* want *represents one way that society has taught us to satisfy the need.* For example, thirst is biologically based; we are taught to want Coca-Cola to satisfy that thirst rather than, say, goat's milk. Thus, the need is already there; marketers simply recommend ways to satisfy it. A basic objective of marketing is to create awareness that needs exist, not to create needs.

Criticism: Advertising and marketing are unnecessary. Marketers arbitrarily link products to desirable social attributes, fostering a materialistic society in which people measure us by what we own.

A Response: Products are designed to meet existing needs, and advertising only helps to communicate their availability.[41] Advertising is a service for which consumers are willing to pay, because the information it provides reduces search time.

Criticism: Marketers promise miracles and manipulate consumers. Through advertising, consumers are led to believe that products have magical properties; products will do special and mysterious things for consumers in a way that will transform their lives. Consumers will be beautiful, have power over others' feelings, be successful, and be relieved of all ills.

A Response: Advertisers simply do not know enough about people to manipulate them. Consider that the failure rate for new products ranges from 40 to 80 percent. Although people think that advertisers have an endless source of magical tricks and scientific techniques to manipulate them, in reality the industry is successful when it tries to sell good products and unsuccessful when selling poor ones.[42]

The Dark Side of Marketing

Whether intentionally or not, some marketers *do* violate their bond of trust with consumers, and unfortunately the "dark side" of marketing often is the subject of harsh criticism.[43] In some cases, these violations are illegal, such as when a retailer adopts a "bait-and-switch" selling strategy, luring consumers into the store with promises of inexpensive products with the sole intent of getting them to switch to higher-priced goods.

In other cases, marketing practices have detrimental effects on society even though they are not actually illegal. Some alcohol and tobacco companies advertise in low-income neighborhoods where abuse of these products is a big problem. Others sponsor commercials depicting groups of people in an unfavorable light or sell products that encourage antisocial behavior. An online game based on the Columbine High School massacre drew criticism from some who say it trivializes the actions of the two teen killers.

Despite the best efforts of researchers, government regulators, and concerned industry people, sometimes consumers' worst enemies are themselves. We tend to think of ourselves as rational decision makers, calmly doing our best to obtain products and services that will maximize our health and well-being and that of our families and society. In reality, however, our desires, choices, and actions often result in negative consequences to ourselves and the society in which we live. Some of these actions are relatively harmless, but others have more onerous consequences. Some harmful consumer behaviors such as excessive drinking or cigarette smoking stem from social pressures, and the cultural value people place on money encourages activities such as shoplifting or insurance fraud. Exposure to unattainable ideals of beauty and success can create dissatisfaction with the self. Let's briefly review some dimensions of "the dark side" of consumer behavior:

Terrorism: The terrorist attacks of 2001 revealed the vulnerability of nonmilitary targets and reminded us that disruptions of our financial, electronic, and supply networks can potentially be more damaging to our way of life than the fallout from a conventional battlefield. The hours many of us spend as we wait to pass through security lines in airports is but one consequence of these attacks.

Addictive consumption: Consumer addiction is a physiological or psychological dependency on goods or services. These problems, of course, include alcoholism, drug addiction, and cigarettes—and many companies profit from addictive products or by selling solutions. Although most people equate addiction with drugs, consumers can use virtually anything to relieve (at least temporarily) some problem or satisfy some need to the point that reliance on it becomes extreme. "Shopaholics" turn to shopping much the way addicted people turn to drugs or alcohol.[44] Numerous treatment centers in China, South Korea, and Taiwan (and now a few in the United States also) deal with cases of Internet addiction—some hard-core gamers have become so hooked they literally forget to eat or drink and die of dehydration. There is even a Chap Stick Addicts support group with approximately 250 active members![45]

Exploited people: Sometimes people are used or exploited, willingly or not, for commercial gain in the marketplace; these situations range from traveling road shows that feature dwarfs and little people to the selling of body parts and babies on eBay. *Consumed consumers* are people who themselves become commodities.

Illegal activities: The cost of crimes consumers commit against businesses has been estimated at more than $40 billion per year. A survey the McCann-Erickson advertising agency conducted revealed the following tidbits:[46]

- Ninety-one percent of people say they lie regularly. One in three fibs about their weight, one in four about their income, and 21 percent lie about their age. Nine percent even lie about their natural hair color.

- Four out of ten Americans have tried to pad an insurance bill to cover the deductible.

- Nineteen percent say they've snuck into a theater to avoid paying admission.

- More than three out of five people say they've taken credit for making something from scratch when they have done no such thing. According to Pillsbury's CEO, this "behavior is so prevalent that we've named a category after it—speed scratch."

OBJECTIVE

Explain the basics of marketing planning and the marketing mix tools we use in the marketing process.

(pp. 30–32)

Marketing as a Process

Our definition of marketing also refers to *processes*. This means that marketing is not a one-shot operation. When it's done right, marketing is a decision process in which marketing managers determine the strategies that will help the firm meet its long-term objectives and then execute those strategies using the tools they have at their disposal. In this section, we'll look at how marketers make business decisions and plan actions and the tools they use to execute their plans. We'll build on this brief overview in the next chapter, where we'll also provide you with a "road map" in the form of a pullout planning template you can use to understand the planning process as you work your way through the book.

Marketing Planning

A big part of the marketing process is *marketing planning,* where we think carefully and strategically about the "big picture" and where our firm and its products fit within it. The first phase of marketing planning is to analyze the marketing environment. This means understanding the firm's current strengths and weaknesses by assessing factors that might help or hinder the development and marketing of products. The analysis must also take into account the opportunities and threats the firm will encounter in the marketplace, such as the actions of competitors, cultural and technological changes, and the economy.

Firms (or individuals) that engage in marketing planning ask questions like these:

- What product benefits will our customers look for in three to five years?

- What capabilities does our firm have that set it apart from the competition?

- What additional customer groups might provide important market segments for us in the future?

- How will changes in technology affect our production process, our communication strategy, and our distribution strategy?

- What changes in social and cultural values are occurring now that will impact our market in the next few years?

- How will customers' awareness of environmental issues affect their attitudes toward our manufacturing facilities?

- What legal and regulatory issues may affect our business in both domestic and global markets?

Answers to these and other questions provide the foundation for developing an organization's **marketing plan**. This is a document that describes the marketing environment, outlines the marketing objectives and strategy, and identifies who will be responsible for carrying out each part of the marketing strategy. As we noted earlier, in Chapter 2 we'll give you a template you can use to construct your own marketing plan that will help bring this important process to life. If you want, you can even use it to develop a plan to market "Brand You!"

A major marketing decision for most organizations is which products to market to which consumers without simultaneously turning off other consumers. Some firms choose to reach as many customers as possible, so they offer their goods or services to a **mass market** that consists of all possible customers in a market regardless of the differences in their specific needs and wants. Marketing planning then becomes a matter of developing a basic product and a single strategy to reach everyone.

marketing plan
A document that describes the marketing environment, outlines the marketing objectives and strategy, and identifies who will be responsible for carrying out each part of the marketing strategy.

mass market
All possible customers in a market, regardless of the differences in their specific needs and wants.

Although this approach can be cost-effective, the firm risks losing potential customers to competitors whose marketing plans instead try to meet the needs of specific groups within the market. A **market segment** is a distinct group of customers within a larger market who are similar to one another in some way and whose needs differ from other customers in the larger market. For example, automakers such as Ford, General Motors, and BMW offer different automobiles for different market segments. Depending on its goals and resources, a firm may choose to focus on one segment. A **target market** is the segment(s) on which an organization focuses its marketing plan and toward which it directs its marketing efforts. A product's **market position** is how the target market perceives the product in comparison to competitors' brands. We'll learn more about these ideas in Chapter 7.

Marketing's Tools: The Marketing Mix

When they decide upon the best way to present a good or service for consumers' consideration, marketers have to make many decisions, so they need many tools. The marketer's strategic toolbox is the **marketing mix**, which consists of the tools the organization uses to create a desired response among a set of predefined consumers. These tools include the product itself, the price of the product, the promotional activities that introduce it to consumers, and the places where it is available. We commonly refer to the elements of the marketing mix as the **Four Ps**: *product*, *price*, *promotion*, and *place*. As 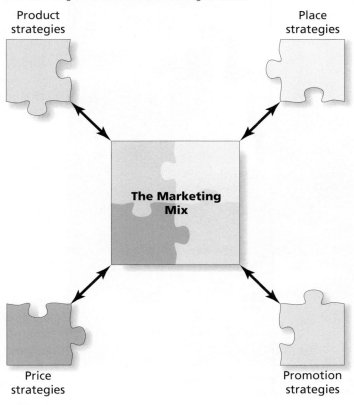 Figure 1.3 shows, each P is a piece of the puzzle that the marketer must combine with other pieces. Just as a radio DJ puts together a collection of separate songs (a musical mix) to create a certain mood, the idea of a mix in this context reminds us that no single marketing activity is sufficient to accomplish the organization's objectives.

Although we talk about the Four Ps as separate parts of a firm's marketing strategy, in reality, product, price, promotion, and place decisions are totally interdependent. Decisions about any single one of the four are affected by and affect every other marketing-mix decision. For example, assume that a firm is introducing a superior quality product, one that is more expensive to produce than its existing line of products. The price the firm charges for this new product must cover these higher costs, but in addition the firm must create advertising and other promotional strategies to convey a top-quality image. At the same time, the price of the product must cover not only the costs of production but also the cost of advertising. Furthermore, the firm must include high-end retailers in its distribution strategy. The elements of the marketing mix therefore work hand-in-hand.

We'll examine these components of the marketing mix in detail later in this book. For now, let's briefly look at each P to gain some insight into its meaning and role in the marketing mix.

Product

We've already seen that the product is a good, a service, an idea, a place, a person—whatever is offered for sale in the exchange. This aspect of the marketing mix includes the design and packaging of a good, as well as its physical features and any associated services, such as free delivery. So we can see that the product is a combination of many different elements, all of which are important to the product's success. For example,

Figure 1.3 📷 *Snapshot* | The Marketing Mix
The marketing mix is the marketer's strategic toolbox.

market segment
A distinct group of customers within a larger market who are similar to one another in some way and whose needs differ from other customers in the larger market.

target market
The market segments on which an organization focuses its marketing plan and toward which it directs its marketing efforts.

market position
The way in which the target market perceives the product in comparison to competitors' brands.

marketing mix
A combination of the product itself, the price of the product, the place where it is made available, and the activities that introduce it to consumers that creates a desired response among a set of predefined consumers.

Four Ps
Product, price, promotion, and place.

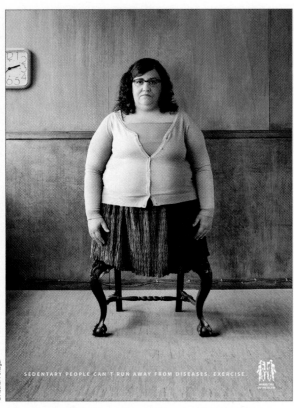

©Fischer Portugal

SEDENTARY PEOPLE CAN'T RUN AWAY FROM DISEASES. EXERCISE

A "product" can be an idea. In this Portuguese ad that idea is to encourage people to exercise.

price
The assignment of value, or the amount the consumer must exchange to receive the offering.

promotion
The coordination of a marketer's communication efforts to influence attitudes or behavior.

place
The availability of the product to the customer at the desired time and location.

Joe Kennedy

APPLYING ▽ Promotion

Joe has to decide on a communications strategy for Pandora. Part of this decision is to choose which promotional elements he should use to attract more users. His options include paid advertising, publicity releases and "buzz building."

when the British firm Virgin introduced Virgin Cola in the United States, the company attempted to make the product stand out from the competition through its distinctive packaging. Advertising that introduced the brand told customers about the curved squeezable bottles: "If all you got is Va Va, You got to get some Voom; It's in the curvy bottle, Yeah, Virgin Drinks got Voom. . . . Virgin puts the Voom in your Va Va."[47] We're not quite sure what that means, but it does get your attention. Whether the focus is on the bottle or some other element, the product is an important part of the marketing mix.

Price

Price is the assignment of value, or the amount the consumer must exchange to receive the offering. Marketers often turn to price to increase consumers' interest in a product. This happens when they put an item on sale, but in other cases marketers actually try to sell a product with a *higher* price than people are used to if they want to communicate that it's high quality or cutting edge. For example, the Adidas 1 computerized running shoe got a lot of attention in the media. Some of the fuss was that the shoe was billed as the first "smart shoe" because it contains a computer chip that adapts its cushioning level to a runner's size and stride. But a lot of the press coverage also revolved around the hefty price tag of $250 per pair, which makes buying the shoe a status statement for the hard-core runner.[48]

Promotion

Promotion includes all the activities marketers undertake to inform consumers about their products and to encourage potential customers to buy these products. Promotions can take many forms, including personal selling, television advertising, store coupons, billboards, magazine ads, and publicity releases.

Place

Place refers to the availability of the product to the customer at the desired time and location. This *P* relates to a *supply chain*—the set of firms that work together to get a product from a producer to a consumer. For clothing or electronics, this channel includes local retailers as well as other outlets, such as retail sites on the Web that strive to offer the right quantity of products in the right styles at the right time.

To achieve a competitive advantage over rivals in the minds of consumers, the marketer carefully blends the four Ps of the marketing mix—that is, the organization develops product, price, place, and promotion strategies to meet the needs of its target market. These strategies may vary from one country to another, and marketers may inject them with fresh ideas over time to maintain or change the product's position.

Now that you've learned the basics of marketing, read "Here's My Choice . . ." to see which strategy Joe selected for Pandora.

Here's my choice. . .

Real **People**, Real **Choices**

1 Option 2 Option 3 Option

Why do you think
Joe chose option 2?

How It Worked Out at Pandora

Pandora relied exclusively on personal communication to build awareness, via town halls led by the company's founder, e-mail, blog posts, Twitter, and eventually a Facebook fan page. Pandora solved its distribution problem by making the service available on as many Internet-enabled devices as possible. As of mid-2010 the company boasted more than 50 million listeners.

To learn the whole story, visit www.mypearsonmarketinglab.com.

Brand **YOU**!

Do you want to stand out among all the new grads seeking their first job out of college?

Learn how in *Brand You,* a supplemental text to *Marketing: Real People, Real Choices.* Discover how to realize professional success, whether it's landing a great internship or job, getting paid what you're worth, or launching your own startup. Start the process of creating your own personal brand by reading Chapter 1 in *Brand You.*

Objective Summary ➡ Key Terms ➡ Apply

CHAPTER 1
Study Map

1. Objective Summary (pp. 6–8)

Understand who marketers are, where they work, and marketing's role in a firm.

Marketers come from many different backgrounds and work in a variety of locations, from consumer goods companies to non-profit organizations to financial institutions to advertising and public relations agencies. Marketing's role in a firm depends on the organization. Some firms are very marketing-oriented, whereas others do not focus on marketing. However, marketing is increasingly being integrated with other business functions. Therefore, no matter what firm marketers work in, their decisions affect and are affected by the firm's other operations. Marketers must work together with other executives.

Key Term

value, p. 6

2. Objective Summary (pp. 8–12)

Explain what marketing is and how it provides value to everyone involved in the marketing process.

Marketing is the activity, set of institutions, and processes for creating, communicating, delivering, and exchanging offerings that have value for customers, clients, partners, and society at large. Therefore, marketing is all about delivering value to stakeholders, that is, to everyone who is affected by a transaction. Organizations that seek to ensure their long-term profitability by identifying and satisfying customers' needs and wants have adopted the marketing concept. Marketing is also about exchanges or the transfer of value between a buyer and a seller.

Key Terms

marketing, p. 8

stakeholders, p. 8

consumer, p. 10

marketing concept, p. 10

need, p. 10

want, p. 11

benefit, p. 11

demand, p. 11

market, p. 11

marketplace, p. 11

virtual goods, p. 11

utility, p. 11

exchange, p. 12

product, p. 12

3. Objective Summary (pp. 13–18)

Explain the evolution of the marketing concept.

Early in the twentieth century, firms followed a production orientation in which they focused on the most efficient ways to produce and distribute products. Beginning in the 1930s, some firms adopted a selling orientation that encouraged salespeople to aggressively sell products to customers. In the 1950s, organizations adopted a consumer orientation that focused on customer satisfaction. This led to the development of the marketing concept. Today, many firms are moving toward a triple bottom line orientation that includes not only a commitment to quality and value, but also a concern for both economic and social profit.

Key Terms

production orientation, p. 13

selling orientation, p. 13

consumer orientation, p. 15

Total Quality Management (TQM), p. 15

instapreneur, p. 15

triple bottom line orientation, p. 16

customer relationship management (CRM), p. 16

attention economy, p. 16

social marketing concept, p. 16

sustainability, p. 17

green marketing, p. 17

return on investment (ROI), p. 18

4. Objective Summary (pp. 18–21)

Understand the range of services and goods that organizations market.

Any good, service, or idea that can be marketed is a product, even though what is being sold may not take a physical form. Consumer goods are the tangible products that consumers purchase for personal or family use. Services are intangible products that we pay for and use but never own. Business-to-business goods and services are sold to businesses and other organizations for further processing or for use in their business operations. Not-for-profit organizations, ideas, places, and people can also be marketed.

Key Terms

popular culture, p. 18

myths, p. 19

consumer goods, p. 19

services, p. 19

business-to-business marketing, p. 19

industrial goods, p. 19

e-commerce, p. 19

shrinkage, p. 20

anticonsumption, p. 20

not-for-profit organizations, p. 20

5. Objective Summary (pp. 21–29)

Understand value from the perspectives of customers, producers, and society.

Value is the benefits a customer receives from buying a good or service. Marketing communicates these benefits as the value proposition to the customer. For customers, the value proposition includes the whole bundle of benefits the product promises to deliver, not just the benefits of the product itself. Sellers determine value by assessing whether their transactions are profitable, whether they are providing value to stakeholders by creating a competitive advantage, and whether they are providing value through the value chain. Customers generate value when they turn into advertising directors, retailers, and new product development consultants, often through social networking. Society receives value from marketing activities when producers and consumers engage in ethical, profitable, and environmentally friendly exchange relationships.

Key Terms

value proposition, p. 21

brandfests, p. 23

lifetime value of a customer, p. 23

distinctive competency, p. 23

differential benefit, p. 23

value chain, p. 24

marketing scorecards, p. 25

metrics, p. 25

amafessionals, p. 26

consumer-generated content, p. 26

social networking, p. 26

web 2.0, p. 26

physical URLs, p. 27

folksonomy, p. 27

wisdom of crowds, p. 27

open source model, p. 27

6. Objective Summary (pp. 30–32)

Explain the basics of marketing planning and the marketing mix tools managers use in the marketing process.

The strategic process of marketing planning begins with an assessment of factors within the organization and in the external environment that could help or hinder the development and marketing of products. On the basis of this analysis, marketers set objectives and develop strategies. Many firms use a target marketing strategy in which they divide the overall market into segments and then target the most attractive one. Then they design the marketing mix to gain a competitive position in the target market. The marketing mix includes product, price, place, and promotion. The product is what satisfies customer needs. The price is the assigned value or amount to be exchanged for the product. The place or channel of distribution gets the product to the customer. Promotion is the organization's efforts to persuade customers to buy the product.

Key Terms

marketing plan, p. 30

mass market, p. 30

market segment, p. 31

target market, p. 31

market position, p. 31

marketing mix, p. 31

four Ps, p. 31

price, p. 32

promotion, p. 32

place, p. 32

Chapter **Questions** and **Activities**

Questions: Test Your Knowledge

1. Where do marketers work, and what role does marketing play in the firm?
2. Briefly explain what marketing is.
3. Explain needs, wants, and demands. What is the role of marketing in each of these?
4. What is utility? How does marketing create different forms of utility?
5. Trace the evolution of the marketing concept.
6. Define the terms *consumer goods, services,* and *industrial goods.*
7. To what does the *lifetime value of the customer* refer, and how is it calculated?
8. What does it mean for a firm to have a competitive advantage? What gives a firm a competitive advantage?
9. What is involved in marketing planning?
10. List and describe the elements of the marketing mix.

Activities: Apply What You've Learned

1. ***Creative Homework/Short Project*** An old friend of yours has been making and selling vitamin-fortified smoothies to acquaintances and friends of friends for some time. He is now thinking about opening a shop in a small college town, but he is worried about whether he'll have enough customers who want these smoothies to keep a business going. Knowing that you are a marketing student, he's asked you for some advice. What can you tell him about product, price, promotion, and place (distribution) strategies that will help him get his business off the ground?

2. ***In Class 10–25 Min. for Teams*** Assume that you are employed by your city's Chamber of Commerce. One major focus of the chamber is to get industries to move to your city. As a former marketing student, you know that there are issues involving product, price, promotion, and place (distribution) that can attract business. Next week you and your consulting firm have an opportunity to speak to the members of the chamber, and your topic will be "Marketing a City." Develop an outline for that presentation.

3. ***In Class 10–25 Min. for Teams*** Successful firms have a competitive advantage because they are able to identify distinctive competencies and use these to create differential benefits for their customers. Consider your business school or your university. What distinctive competencies does it have? What differential benefits does it provide for students? What is its competitive advantage? What are your ideas as to how your university could improve its competitive position? Write an outline of your ideas.

4. *Creative Homework/Short Project* As a marketing professional, you have been asked to write a short piece for a local business newsletter about the state of marketing today. You think the best way to address this topic is to review how the marketing concept has evolved and to discuss the triple bottom line orientation. Write the short article you will submit to the editor of the newsletter.

5. *In Class 10–25 Min. for Teams* As college students, you and your friends sometimes discuss the various courses you are taking. One of your friends says to you, "Marketing's not important. It's just dumb advertising." Another friend says, "Marketing doesn't really affect people's lives in any way." As a role-playing exercise, present your arguments against these statements to your class.

6. *For further research (individual):* The chapter discusses the recent development of physical URLs; where packages come with codes that unlock online content. This new technology is also known as "the internet of things." What is the current status of physical URLs? Can you identify marketers that use this approach to help them gain consumer awareness of their products?

7. *For further research (groups):* Consumer-generated value is one of the big marketing stories today. In addition to sharing in the creation of advertising and submitting ideas for new products, some consumers also participate in the marketing value chain. For example, at the T-shirt design site Threadless.com, visitors vote on their favorite styles and the company only manufactures the most popular choices. Other sites like Groupon pool potential customers so that all participants get a sizeable discount on a product or service because they offer a volume purchase to the merchant. As a group, devise a new approach to this kind of group-oriented purchasing. Create a simple marketing strategy that integrates the 4Ps: Describe how you would promote the site, where you would sell it, how you would price it, and what you would sell. Prepare a short presentation that summarizes the current status of group purchasing and illustrates how your idea fits within this framework.

Marketing Metrics Exercise

The chapter discusses the growing importance of sustainability, and it notes that companies and consumers increasingly consider other costs in addition to financial kinds when they decide what to sell or buy. One of these cost categories is damage to the environment. How can marketers make it easier for shoppers to compute these costs? The answer is more apparent in some product categories than in others. For example, American consumers often are able to compare the power consumption and annual costs of appliances by looking at their EnergyStar™ rating. In other situations we can assess the *carbon footprint* implications of a product or service; this tells us how much CO_2 our purchase will emit into the atmosphere (e.g., if a person flies from New York to London). The average American is responsible for 9.44 tons of CO_2 per year![49] A carbon footprint comes from the sum of two parts, the direct, or primary, footprint and the indirect, or secondary, footprint:

1. The *primary footprint* is a measure of our direct emissions of CO_2 from the burning of fossil fuels, including domestic energy consumption and transportation (e.g., cars and planes).

2. The *secondary footprint* is a measure of the indirect CO_2 emissions from the whole lifecycle of products we use, from their manufacture to their eventual breakdown.[50]

Although many of us are more aware today that our consumption choices carry unseen costs, there is still a lot of confusion about the best way to communicate the environmental costs of our actions—and in many cases consumers aren't motivated to take these issues into account unless the costs impact them directly and in the short term. What other metrics would you suggest that might address this important measurement problem?

Choices: What Do You Think?

1. *Ethics* Have you ever pirated software? How about music? Is it ethical to give or receive software instead of paying for it? Does the answer depend on the person's motivation and/or if the person could otherwise afford to buy the product?

2. *Critical thinking* The marketing concept focuses on the ability of marketing to satisfy customer needs. As a typical college student, how does marketing satisfy your needs? What areas of your life are affected by marketing? What areas of your life (if any) are not affected by marketing?

3. *Critical thinking* In both developed and developing countries, not all firms have implemented programs that follow the marketing concept. Can you think of firms that still operate with a production orientation? A selling orientation? What changes would you recommend for these firms?

4. *Critical thinking* Ideally, each member of a value chain adds value to a product before someone buys it. Thinking about a music CD you might buy in a store, what kind of value does the music retailer add? How about the label that signs the artist? The public relations firm that arranges a tour by the artist to promote the new CD? The production company that shoots a music video to go along with the cut?

5. *Critical thinking* User-generated commercials seem to be part of a broader trend toward user-generated content of all sorts. Examples include MySpace, Flickr (where users post photos and comment on others' pictures), blogging, and video-sharing sites like YouTube. Do you think this is a passing fad or an important trend? How (if at all) should marketers be dealing with these activities?

6. *Ethics* Some marketing or consumption activities involve the (literal) consumption of people—voluntarily or not. In one recent controversial incident, a man in Germany advertised on the Internet to find someone who wanted to be killed and eaten (we are not making this up). He actually found a willing volunteer and did just what he promised—he's now on trial for murder. If a person consents to be "consumed" in some way, is this still an ethical problem?

7. *Ethics* The American Psychological Association does not yet recognize Internet addiction as a problem. Should it?

Miniproject: Learn by Doing

The purpose of this miniproject is to develop an understanding of the importance of marketing to different organizations.

1. Working as a team with two or three other students, select an organization in your community that practices marketing. It may be a manufacturer, a service provider, a retailer,

a not-for-profit organization—almost any organization will do. Then schedule a visit with someone within the organization who is involved in the marketing activities. Arrange for a short visit during which the person can give your group a tour of the facilities and explain the organization's marketing activities.

2. Divide the following list of topics among your team and ask each person to be responsible for developing a set of questions to ask during the interview to learn about the company's program:

- What customer segments the company targets
- How it determines needs and wants
- What products it offers, including features, benefits, and goals for customer satisfaction
- What its pricing strategies are, including any discounting policies it has

- What promotional strategies it uses and what these emphasize to position the product(s)
- How it distributes products and whether it has encountered any problems
- How marketing planning is done and who does it
- Whether social responsibility is part of the marketing program and, if so, in what ways

3. Develop a team report of your findings. In each section of the report, share what you learned that is new or surprising to you compared to what you expected.
4. Develop a team presentation for your class that summarizes your findings. Conclude your presentation with comments on what your team believes the company was doing that was particularly good and what was not quite so good.

Marketing in **Action** Case

Real Choices at Colgate-Palmolive

What do you do when you want fresh breath and a clean mouth, and do not have your toothbrush or water? This can be a challenge to the person on the go with little time and limited access to the necessary things and places. The Colgate-Palmolive Company has introduced an option that claims to provide "a clean, fresh mouth anywhere, anytime—no water or rinsing required." The new Colgate Wisp is a new oral care aide made to remove food and particles from between the teeth and release a liquid-filled bead of freshness in the mouth.

Based in New York City, the Colgate-Palmolive Company "is an American diversified multinational corporation focused on the production, distribution, and provision of household, health care, and personal products, such as soaps, detergents, and oral hygiene products (including toothpaste and toothbrushes)." The oral hygiene market encompasses products offering cleansing, disinfecting, breath freshening, and whitening. This market in the United States represents over $7.5 billion at retail prices. In this spirited market, innovation is necessary for companies to attain and hold market share. Competitors in this marketplace include some of the largest multinational firms, such as, GlaxoSmithKline, Pfizer Inc, Procter & Gamble, Gillette Co, Oral-B Laboratories, and Unilever NV.

The Wisp is a disposable mini-toothbrush with a "breath-freshening bead" in the bristles. The bead dissolves during brushing, eliminating the need for toothpaste, and there is no need to rinse, making it easy to brush at work or on the go. Packaging with an "innovative slim shell design with individually foil-sealed brushes," allows for easy disposal of the used brush. To prevent abrasion, the brush head of the Wisp contains tiny, soft, and flexible plastic bristles similar to those of a toothbrush. Three flavors are available: a blue bead for peppermint flavor, a green bead for spearmint flavor, and a red bead for "cinnamint" flavor.

Innovation must be accompanied with value in the minds of consumers. The price for a pack of four Wisps is $2.39 and the price for a 16-pack is $7.99. This pricing strategy is formulated to reflect the convenient and disposable nature of the product. Colgate-Palmolive's goal is that this pricing strategy

will result in gross sales of over $62 million annually during the early years of the product's introduction.

The Wisp will be distributed through the traditional outlets for oral hygiene products. This includes, but is not limited to, drug stores, supermarkets, and mass merchandisers. In addition, the Wisp will be available for purchase online at major retailers such as, Amazon.com, Walgreens.com, and Drugstore.com.

Colgate-Palmolive has developed a web site dedicated to the Wisp (**www.colgatewisp.com**). The web site covers aspects of the product including frequently asked questions, customer reviews, and Internet coupons. The Wisp's promotion campaign includes traditional promotions like print and television advertisements to attract customers that are more traditional. For the young, urban target audience of 18 to 25-year olds, Colgate-Palmolive promotions include social networking, online video, and mobile applications.

The success of the Colgate Wisp is not guaranteed. There is a great deal of competition in the marketing for oral hygiene products and the major players have a good track record for defending their respective market shares. The original marketing strategy for the Wisp's four Ps—product, price, place, and promotion—has been designed to attract as many customers as possible. However, plans do not always achieve the desired goals. There must always be consideration for what may right as well as what may go wrong.

You Make the Call

1. What is the decision facing Colgate-Palmolive?
2. What factors are important in understanding this decision situation?
3. What are the alternatives?
4. What decision(s) do you recommend?
5. What are some ways to implement your recommendation?

Based on: Matthew Boyle, "Colgate's World-Beating Performance," *Bloomberg BusinessWeek*, March 26, 2009, (Website: **http://www .businessweek.com/magazine/content/09_14/b4125048865641.htm**); Shawn Watson, "What is the Colgate Wisp?" *About.com*, April 24, 2009, (Website: **http://www.businessweek.com/magazine/content/09_14/b4125048865641.htm**); Colgate-Palmolive, *Wikipedia*, http://en.wikipedia.org/wiki/Colgate-Palmolive (accessed July 13, 2010).

Chapter 2

Strategic Market Planning:
Take the Big Picture

Real People Profiles

Jay Minkoff

| Profile | Info |

▼ A **Decision Maker** at First Flavor, Inc.

Jay Minkoff is a serial entrepreneur who specializes in creating innovative marketing solutions. Currently, Jay is the co-founder and president of First Flavor, which provides the patent-pending Peel 'n Taste® flavor sampling platform for marketing food, beverage, and flavored product industries using edible film technology. Prior to this, he co-founded HomeBuilder.com, an online marketing and listing site for the home building industry, which was sold to Homestore, Inc. (now Move.com) in 1999 and which he continued to manage until 2003. His prior business, Tri-State Publishing & Communications, publisher of the *Apartment Shoppers Guide* and *New Homes Guide* consumer real estate magazines, was sold to Primedia in 1996. This company was recognized in 1990 as the 91st fasting growing company in the country on *Inc. Magazine*'s Inc. 500 List. Prior to this, Jay was a successful commercial real estate broker, having sold or financed over a quarter billion dollars of institutional properties.

A graduate of Tufts University majoring in civil engineering, he holds an MBA in entrepreneurial management and real estate finance from The Wharton School at the University of Pennsylvania. Jay lives in Wynnewood, PA with his wife and two daughters.

Jay's Info

What do I do when I'm not working?
  A) Staying fit by cycling, playing golf, scuba diving, and skiing.

First job out of school?
  A) Real estate investment banking.

Career high?
  A) Getting offered a cash-out on selling my first company at 50 percent more than I felt the company was worth!

A job-related mistake I wish I hadn't made?
  A) Raising my voice to *any* employee when it was not appropriate.

Business book I'm reading now?
  A) *Buy-ology* by Martin Lindstrom.

My hero?
  A) William Jefferson Clinton, a brilliant man who has dedicated his life to making a difference in the world for hundreds of millions of people. A true global citizen.

My motto to live by?
  A) Make a difference and enjoy what you do!

What drives me?
  A) Doing what hasn't been done before. My version of Star Trek's "exploring strange new worlds and civilizations."

My management style?
  A) Micro management meets delegation with accountability.

Don't do this when interviewing with me?
  A) Playing with a pen, tapping your fingers, any nervous habit.

My pet peeve?
  A) Not keeping your word. If you can't do what you told me you're going to do, renegotiate your promise vs. dropping the ball.

Here's my problem. . .

First Flavor had just completed product development of its marketing services product, the Peel 'n Taste® marketing system. This product provides marketers, for the first time, with the ability to use the sense of taste to market a consumer product. The company's technology allows it to infuse virtually any taste onto an edible flavor strip (à la popular breath strips). The consumer can "sample" the product—whether it's fruit juice, toothpaste, frozen desserts, or any beverage—simply by plucking a strip from a dispenser in a grocery aisle or peeling one off a magazine ad. The strip completely dissolves on the tongue and provides a realistic approximation of what the item will taste like. This new taste sampling vehicle had the potential to be for the food and beverage industry what Scratch 'n Sniff® was for the fragrance industry; it's a way to sample a sensory attribute without actually purchasing the product! Better yet, it could be included in any printed marketing media.

As First Flavor started to see its first sales of Peel 'n Taste® from consumer product manufacturers (Arm & Hammer toothpaste, Old Orchard fruit juice, Welch's grape juice, Sunny Delight Elations®, etc.), the startup became aware of other uses for its capability to produce great-tasting edible film strips. Several different applications presented themselves. Here are a few examples:

- When people saw samples of edible films that tasted like Krispy Kreme® glazed donuts, buttered popcorn, and butter pecan ice cream, some of them asked, "How many calories do they have?" and "Can I use these when I'm on a diet?" Jay realized that providing dieters with no-calorie edible film strips in indulgent flavors could be a new market for First Flavor given the size of the $30 billion diet industry.

- Several people during those early years also contacted the company as a result of online searches to provide convalescing relatives with flavor strips. The intended recipients of the flavor strips had a medical condition that prevented them from swallowing (dysphagia) and thus they could not taste food. Quite literally, one of their five senses was not being activated. First Flavor's strips could improve the quality of life for many people and possibly generate a new revenue stream.

- One of First Flavor's clients had a line of herbal-flavored waters it wanted to sell on QVC. Because the water weighed so much compared to the cost, it was as expensive to ship the flavored water as it was to buy it. The owner of the water company asked Jay if First Flavor could create "flavor strips" that contained the flavoring used in these herbal flavored waters. The consumer could simply drop a flavoring strip in a bottle of water to create the herbal flavor at home.

Things to remember

First Flavor's new technology allows it to duplicate virtually any taste in a plastic strip that dissolves on a person's tongue. This provided several potential benefits, including novelty/entertainment, risk reduction (people could taste a product before they bought it), and a new way to promote a product in-store or even in print media (by attaching a flavor strip to a mailing or a magazine ad). Jay has to understand which application(s) hold the most promise and also to decide on a strategic focus so that First Flavor can identify marketing objectives based on what the company hopes to accomplish in the short term and then farther into the future.

As entrepreneurs, Jay and his partners wanted to jump on all of these new opportunities. But they were concerned with losing focus while in the middle of launching First Flavor's first product, Peel 'n Taste®. Also, they didn't think they would be able to secure intellectual property protection (such as patents) for any of these three new product ideas. In addition, as an under-capitalized company that Jay was primarily funding, First Flavor was also concerned with the cost of launching these other products. The decision regarding whether to diversify into new product categories was a major strategic crossroads for the young company.

Jay considered his options 1·2·3

1 **Option**

Investigate all three new business ideas and start product development even as Peel 'n Taste® was still a fledgling product trying to gain market acceptance. This strategy could create new revenue opportunities and give the company other options to fall back upon if Peel 'n Taste® took off slower than First Flavor hoped. And, since the new applications couldn't be patented, the extra lead time would give First Flavor a first-to-market advantage. On the other hand, these other initiatives would drain the company's limited financial resources. And management needed to stay focused on maximizing the market's acceptance of Peel 'n Taste® at this crucial point in its young life-cycle.

2 **Option**

Continue to focus on introducing Peel 'n Taste® into the market until it gained market acceptance. This product would provide the company with the cash flow to invest in new product launches at a later point. A single approach will keep management and staff focused on the company's initial mission. It will reduce costs and thus the initial investment required to bring the company to profitability. Still, it's not clear how long this process will take. There may be missed market opportunities if another company picks up on one or more of these ideas and brings them to market first.

3 **Option**

Pick just one or two of these new products and investigate the opportunity of launching it with limited resources and management attention while Peel 'n Taste® remained the company's primary focus. This more selective approach would minimize the cost of launching a new product. Management's time and attention would be diverted, but not on such a significant basis. And this strategy would force First Flavor to look at each of the opportunities more critically because it would have to pick only one to push forward. Still, there was the problem of the "road not taken." Two of the ideas would not get implemented in the near future, and First Flavor faced a possible loss of first-mover advantage in the marketplace for these new products. Now, put yourself in Jay's shoes: Which option would you pick, and why?

You Choose

Which **Option** would you choose, and **why**?

1. ☐ Yes ☐ No   2. ☐ Yes ☐ No   3. ☐ Yes ☐ No

See what **option** Jay chose on **page 61**

The great success Jay Minkoff and First Flavor have had with its innovative product line didn't just happen by luck. A great deal of planning went into creating value with the innovative First Flavor Peel 'n Taste® Marketing System. The company's ongoing business planning at all levels of the firm—strategic, marketing, and operational—drives the market success of its patent-pending technology; this process replicates the flavor of a product in quick-dissolving edible film strips that prospective customers can sample by tasting individually packaged pouches. Implementation of these plans led to First Flavor's ability to pitch easy integration of Peel 'n Taste® into a variety of clients' promotional marketing programs in order to drive consumer trial—a powerful service. In this chapter, you will experience the power of effective business planning and lay the groundwork for your own capability to do the kind of planning that has led to Jay's success at First Flavor. We even include a handy foldout guide later in this chapter that shows you step-by-step how to build a plan and where to find the information throughout the book to be able to do it.

For Jay Minkoff at First Flavor, or any marketer engaged in planning for the future of the business, the knowledge you gain from going through a formal planning process is worth its weight in gold! You see, without market planning as an ongoing activity in a business, there's no real way to know where you want the firm to go, how it will get there, or even if it is on the right or wrong track right now. There's nothing like a clear map when you're lost in the wilderness.

As part of the planning process, firms like First Flavor must come to grips with their own resources and capabilities—or *internal environment*—as one part of the *Situation Analysis* section of their Marketing Plan. Jay has to have a clear understanding of First Flavor's mission and marketing objectives before he can develop plans to invest in future products and markets for company growth.

1 Business Planning: Compose the Big Picture

Jay Minkoff at First Flavor understands that planning is everything—well, almost. Part of Jay's role as a planner is to define his offering's distinctive identity and purpose. Careful planning enables a firm to speak in a clear voice in the marketplace so that customers understand what the firm is and what it has to offer that competitors don't—especially as it decides how to create value for customers, clients, partners, and society at large.

We think this process is so important that we're launching into our exploration of marketing by starting with a discussion about what planners do and the questions they (both First Flavor and marketers in general) need to ask to be sure they keep their companies and products on course. The foldout marketing planning "road map" we mentioned earlier is useful to help you make your way through the book, keeping the big picture in mind no matter which chapter you're reading. In many ways, developing great business planning is like taking a great digital photo. The metaphor works because success in photography is built around capturing the right information in the lens of your camera, positioning the image correctly, and snapping the picture you'll need to set things in motion. A business plan is a lot like that.

Whether a firm is a well-established company like General Mills (which we'll feature in a later chapter) or a relatively new firm like First Flavor, planning for the future is a key to prosperity. Sure, it's true that a firm can succeed even if it makes some mistakes in planning, and there are times when even the best planning cannot anticipate the future accurately. It's also true that some seat-of-the-pants businesses are successful. But without good planning for the future, firms will be less successful than they could be. In the worst-case scenario, a lack of planning can be fatal for both large and small businesses. So, like a Boy Scout, it's always better to be prepared.

Business planning is an ongoing process of decision making that guides the firm both in the short term and the long term. Planning identifies and builds on a firm's strengths, and it helps managers at all levels make informed decisions in a changing business environment. *Planning* means that an organization develops objectives before it takes action. In large firms like Microsoft and Honda, which operate in many markets, planning is a complex process involving many people from different areas of the company's operations. At a very small business like Mac's Diner in your home town, however, planning is quite different. Mac himself is chief cook, occasional dishwasher, and the sole company planner. With more entrepreneurial firms the planning process falls somewhere in between, depending on the size of the firm and the complexity of its operations.

In this chapter, we'll look at the different steps in an organization's planning. First, we'll see how managers develop a **business plan** that includes the decisions that guide the entire organization or its business units. Then we'll examine the entire strategic planning process and the stages in that process that lead to the development and implementation of a **marketing plan**—a document that describes the marketing environment, outlines the marketing objectives and strategies, and identifies how the company will implement and control the strategies embedded in the plan. But first, let's consider one of the most important overarching issues in planning—ethics.

Ethics Is Up Front in Marketing Planning

It's hard to overemphasize the importance of ethical marketing decisions. Businesses touch many stakeholders, and they need to do what's best for all of them where possible. On a more selfish level, unethical decisions usually come back to bite you later. The consequences of low ethical standards become very visible when you consider a slew of highly publicized corporate scandals that have made news headlines since the turn of the century. These include the fall of Enron and WorldCom due to unsavory financial and management practices, Martha Stewart's stint as a jailbird for using insider information in stock trading, the subprime mortgage meltdown that contributed to the woes of AIG and other financial giants, and Bernie Madoff's infamous Ponzi scheme that robbed thousands of their retirement nest eggs. And these are only a few especially high-profile examples!

The fallout from these and other cases raises the issue of how damaging unethical practices can be to society at large. The business press is filled with articles about accountability, corporate accounting practices, and government regulation as the public and corporate worlds rethink what we define as ethical behavior. When major companies defraud the public, everyone suffers. Thousands of people lose their jobs, and in many cases the pensions they counted on to support them in retirement vanish overnight.

Other stakeholders are punished as well, including stockholders who lose their investments, and consumers who end up paying for worthless merchandise or services. Even confidence in our political system suffers, as was the case with the 2007–2008 government bailouts of major financial institutions while some of these same firms continued to pay

business planning
An ongoing process of making decisions that guides the firm both in the short term and for the long term.

business plan
A plan that includes the decisions that guide the entire organization.

marketing plan
A document that describes the marketing environment, outlines the marketing objectives and strategy, and identifies who will be responsible for carrying out each part of the marketing strategy.

Ripped from the Headlines

Ethical/Sustainable Decisions in the Real World

In late 2009 Anheuser-Busch rolled out a new marketing campaign that features Bud Light beer cans emblazoned with local college and university team colors. Not surprisingly, many college administrators contend that the promotions near college campuses will contribute to underage and binge drinking and give the impression—because of the color connection—that the colleges are endorsing the brew and associated behaviors. The "Fan Cans" renewed the debate over the role of beer makers in encouraging college drinking.

ETHICS CHECK: ↖
Find out what other students taking this course **would do** and **why** on **www .mypearsonmarketinglab .com**

Bud Light's school-colors campaign, also called "Team Pride" in the marketing materials, aims to use "color schemes to connect with fans of legal drinking age in fun ways in select markets across a variety of sports," says Carol Clark, Anheuser-Busch's vice president of corporate social responsibility. She also says that the program is voluntary and that roughly half the brand's wholesalers have chosen to participate. A number of schools asked Anheuser-Busch to drop the campaign near their campuses.

"Show your true colors with Bud Light," the company says, according to copies of internal marketing materials obtained by colleges. "This year, only Bud Light is delivering superior drinkability in 12-ounce cans that were made for game day." Ms. Clark says Anheuser-Busch values its relationships with college administrators and has "a longstanding commitment to promoting responsible drinking." Since 1982, the company and its U.S. wholesalers have spent more than $750 million to fight alcohol abuse, including underage drinking and drunk driving, she says.

The National Institute on Alcohol Abuse and Alcoholism says 45 percent of college students report engaging in binge drinking, which is defined as five or more alcoholic drinks in one sitting. Nearly 600,000 students between the ages of 18 and 24 are injured annually because of alcohol, it says, and 97,000 are the victims of alcohol-related sexual assault. What would you do?

As a college administrator, would you ask Budweiser to pull its Bud Light Fan Can promotion if it involved your institution?

☐ **Yes** ☐ **No**

business ethics
Rules of conduct for an organization.

code of ethics
Written standards of behavior to which everyone in the organization must subscribe.

managers healthy performance bonuses. All taxpayers will wind up paying for some of these ethical transgressions for decades to come.[1]

Codes of Business Ethics

Ethics are rules of conduct—how most people in a culture judge what is right and what is wrong. **Business ethics** are basic values that guide a firm's behavior. These values govern all sorts of marketing planning decisions that managers make, including what goes into their products, where they source raw materials, how they advertise, and what type of pricing they establish. Developing sound business ethics is a major step toward creating a strong relationship with customers and others in the marketplace.

With many rules about doing business—written and unwritten—floating around, how do marketers know what upper management, investors, and customers expect of them? In order to answer this question definitively, many firms develop their own **code of ethics**—written standards of behavior to which everyone in the organization must subscribe—as part of the planning process. These documents eliminate confusion about what the firm considers to be ethically acceptable behavior by its people, and also set standards for how the organization interacts with its stakeholders. For example, the Dow Chemical Company's Code of Business Conduct, available in 20 different languages through its Web site at **www.dow.com**, is based on Dow's stated corporate values of integrity and respect for people. The code deals with the following issues: diversity; the environment; financial integrity; accurate company records; conflicts of interest; obligations to customers, competitors, and regulators; computer systems and telecommunications security; safeguarding important information; interactions with the public; and corporate social responsibility.[2]

To help marketers adhere to ethical behavior in their endeavors, the American Marketing Association (AMA) developed the code of ethics that we reproduce in Table 2.1. Note that this code spells out norms and expectations relating to all aspects of the marketing process, from pricing to marketing research.

The Three Levels of Business Planning

We all know what planning is—we plan a vacation or a great Saturday night party. Some of us even plan how we're going to study and get our assignments completed without stressing out at the last minute. When businesses plan, the process is more complex. As

Table 2.1 | Statement of Ethics

Ethical Norms and Values for Marketers

PREAMBLE

The American Marketing Association commits itself to promoting the highest standard of professional ethical norms and values for its members (practitioners, academics, and students). Norms are established standards of conduct that are expected and maintained by society and/or professional organizations. Values represent the collective conception of what communities find desirable, important and morally proper. Values also serve as the criteria for evaluating our own personal actions and the actions of others. As marketers, we recognize that we not only serve our organizations but also act as stewards of society in creating, facilitating, and executing the transactions that are part of the greater economy. In this role, marketers are expected to embrace the highest professional ethical norms and the ethical values implied by our responsibility toward multiple stakeholders (e.g., customers, employees, investors, peers, channel members, regulators, and the host community).

ETHICAL NORMS

As Marketers, we must:

1. **Do no harm.** This means consciously avoiding harmful actions or omissions by embodying high ethical standards and adhering to all applicable laws and regulations in the choices we make.

2. **Foster trust in the marketing system.** This means striving for good faith and fair dealing so as to contribute toward the efficacy of the exchange process as well as avoiding deception in product design, pricing, communication, and delivery of distribution.

3. **Embrace ethical values.** This means building relationships and enhancing consumer confidence in the integrity of marketing by affirming these core values: honesty, responsibility, fairness, respect, transparency, and citizenship.

ETHICAL VALUES

Honesty—to be forthright in dealings with customers and stakeholders. To this end, we will:

- Strive to be truthful in all situations and at all times.
- Offer products of value that do what we claim in our communications.
- Stand behind our products if they fail to deliver their claimed benefits.
- Honor our explicit and implicit commitments and promises.

Responsibility—to accept the consequences of our marketing decisions and strategies. To this end, we will:

- Strive to serve the needs of customers.
- Avoid using coercion with all stakeholders.
- Acknowledge the social obligations to stakeholders that come with increased marketing and economic power.
- Recognize our special commitments to vulnerable market segments such as children, seniors, the economically impoverished, market illiterates, and others who may be substantially disadvantaged.
- Consider environmental stewardship in our decision making.

Fairness—to balance justly the needs of the buyer with the interests of the seller. To this end, we will:

- Represent products in a clear way in selling, advertising, and other forms of communication; this includes the avoidance of false, misleading, and deceptive promotion.
- Reject manipulations and sales tactics that harm customer trust.
- Refuse to engage in price fixing, predatory pricing, price gouging, or "bait-and-switch" tactics.
- Avoid knowing participation in conflicts of interest.
- Seek to protect the private information of customers, employees, and partners.

(continued)

Table 2.1 | Statement of Ethics *(continued)*

Ethical Norms and Values for Marketers

Respect—to acknowledge the basic human dignity of all stakeholders. To this end, we will:
- Value individual differences and avoid stereotyping customers or depicting demographic groups (e.g., gender, race, sexual orientation) in a negative or dehumanizing way.
- Listen to the needs of customers and make all reasonable efforts to monitor and improve their satisfaction on an ongoing basis.
- Make every effort to understand and respectfully treat buyers, suppliers, intermediaries, and distributors from all cultures.
- Acknowledge the contributions of others, such as consultants, employees, and coworkers, to marketing endeavors.
- Treat everyone, including our competitors, as we would wish to be treated.

Transparency—to create a spirit of openness in marketing operations. To this end, we will:
- Strive to communicate clearly with all constituencies.
- Accept constructive criticism from customers and other stakeholders.
- Explain and take appropriate action regarding significant product or service risks, component substitutions or other foreseeable eventualities that could affect customers or their perception of the purchase decision.
- Disclose list prices and terms of financing as well as available price deals and adjustments.

Citizenship—to fulfill the economic, legal, philanthropic, and societal responsibilities that serve stakeholders. To this end, we will:
- Strive to protect the ecological environment in the execution of marketing campaigns.
- Give back to the community through volunteerism and charitable donations.
- Contribute to the overall betterment of marketing and its reputation.
- Urge supply chain members to ensure that trade is fair for all participants, including producers in developing countries.

IMPLEMENTATION

We expect AMA members to be courageous and proactive in leading and/or aiding their organizations in the fulfillment of the explicit and implicit promises made to those stakeholders. We recognize that every industry sector and marketing sub-discipline (e.g., marketing research, e-commerce, Internet selling, direct marketing, and advertising) has its own specific ethical issues that require policies and commentary. An array of such codes can be accessed through links on the AMA Web site. Consistent with the principle of subsidiarity (solving issues at the level where the expertise resides), we encourage all such groups to develop and/or refine their industry and discipline-specific codes of ethics to supplement these guiding ethical norms and values.

The American Marketing Association helps its members adhere to ethical standards of business through its Code of Ethics.

Source: Copyright © American Marketing Association.

Figure 2.1 shows, planning occurs at three levels: strategic, functional, and operational. The top level is "big picture" stuff, while the bottom level specifies the "nuts-and-bolts" actions the firm will need to take to achieve these lofty goals.

strategic planning
A managerial decision process that matches an organization's resources and capabilities to its market opportunities for long-term growth and survival.

- **Strategic planning** is the managerial decision process that matches the firm's resources (such as its financial assets and workforce) and capabilities (the things it is able to do well because of its expertise and experience) to its market opportunities for long-term growth. In a strategic plan, top management—usually the chief executive officer (CEO), president, and other top executives—define the firm's purpose and specify what the firm hopes to achieve over the next five years or so. For example, a firm's strategic plan may set an objective to increase total revenues by 20 percent in the next five years.

Figure 2.1 📷 *Snapshot* | Levels of Planning

During planning, an organization determines its objectives and then develops courses of action to accomplish them. In larger firms, planning takes place at the strategic, functional, and operational levels.

Strategic Planning	**Functional** Planning (In Marketing Department, called Marketing Planning)	**Operational** Planning
Planning done by top-level corporate management	Planning done by top functional-level management such as the firm's chief marketing officer (CMO)	Planning done by supervisory managers
1. Define the mission 2. Evaluate the internal and external environment 3. Set organizational or SBU objectives 4. Establish the business portfolio (if applicable) 5. Develop growth strategies	1. Perform a situation analysis 2. Set marketing objectives 3. Develop marketing strategies 4. Implement marketing strategies 5. Monitor and control marketing strategies	1. Develop action plans to implement the marketing plan 2. Use marketing metrics to monitor how the plan is working

Source: Copyright © American Marketing Association

Large firms, such as the Walt Disney Company, have a number of self-contained divisions we call **strategic business units (SBUs)**—individual units that represent different areas of business within a firm that are unique enough to each have their own mission, business objectives, resources, managers, and competitors. Disney's SBUs include its theme park, television network, and cruise line divisions, and strategic planning occurs both at the overall corporate level (Disney headquarters planning for the whole corporation) and at the individual business unit level (at the theme park, television network, and cruise line level). We'll discuss these two levels later in the chapter.

- The next level of planning is **functional planning**. This level gets its name because the various functional areas of the firm, such as marketing, finance, and human resources, are involved. Vice presidents or functional directors usually do this. We refer to what the functional planning marketers do as *marketing planning*. The person in charge of such planning may have the title of Director of Marketing, Vice President of Marketing, or Chief Marketing Officer. Marketers like Jay Minkoff at First Flavor might set an objective to gain 40 percent of a particular market by successfully introducing three new products during the coming year. This objective would be part of a marketing plan. Marketing planning typically includes both a broad 3–5-year plan to support the firm's strategic plan and a detailed annual plan for the coming year.

- Still farther down the planning ladder are the managers who are responsible for planning at a third level we call **operational planning**. In marketing, these include people such as sales managers, marketing communications managers, brand managers, and marketing research managers. This level of planning focuses on the day-to-day execution of the functional plans and includes detailed annual, semiannual, or quarterly plans. Operational plans might show exactly how many units of a product a salesperson needs to sell per month, or how many television commercials the firm will place on certain networks during a season. At the operational planning level, First Flavor, for example, may develop plans for a marketing campaign to promote the product by creating buzz via social networking outlets.

Of course, marketing managers don't just sit in their offices dreaming up plans without any concern for the rest of the organization. Even though we've described each layer separately,

strategic business units (SBUs)
Individual units within the firm that operate like separate businesses, with each having its own mission, business objectives, resources, managers, and competitors.

functional planning
A decision process that concentrates on developing detailed plans for strategies and tactics for the short term, supporting an organization's long-term strategic plan.

operational planning
A decision process that focuses on developing detailed plans for day-to-day activities that carry out an organization's functional plans.

all business planning is an integrated activity. This means that the organization's strategic, functional, and operational plans must work together for the benefit of the whole, always within the context of the organization's mission and objectives. So planners at all levels must consider good principles of accounting, the value of the company to its stockholders, and the requirements for staffing and human resource management—that is, they must keep the "big picture" in mind even as they plan for their corner of the organization's world.

In the next sections, we'll further explore planning at each of the three levels that we've just introduced.

JAY MINKOFF

APPLYING ▽ The Mission Statement

First Flavor's mission statement is "to facilitate the success of its clients through the innovative technology of its Peel 'n Taste® Marketing System, creating opportunities for firms to build brands by effectively sampling and promoting their products to consumers." ➡

2 Strategic Planning: Frame the Picture

OBJECTIVE

Describe the steps in strategic planning.
(pp. 46–53)

Many large firms realize it's risky to put all their eggs in one basket and rely on only one product, so they have become multiproduct companies with self-contained divisions organized around products or brands. You know that firms such as Disney operate several distinctly different businesses (Disney's theme parks, television networks, and cruise line, for example).

In firms with multiple SBUs, the first step in strategic planning is for top management to establish a mission for the entire corporation. Top managers then evaluate the internal and external environments of the business and set corporate-level objectives that guide decision making within each individual SBU. In small firms that are not large enough to have separate SBUs, strategic planning simply takes place at the overall firm level. Whether or not a firm has SBUs, the process of strategic planning is basically the same. Let's look at the planning steps in a bit more detail, guided by 📈 Figure 2.2.

Step 1: Define the Mission

Theoretically, top management's first step in the strategic planning stage is to answer questions such as:

- What business are we in?
- What customers should we serve?
- How should we develop the firm's capabilities and focus its efforts?

Figure 2.2 📈 *Process* | Steps in Strategic Planning

The strategic planning process includes a series of steps that result in the development of growth strategies.

Step 1: Define the Mission

↓

Step 2: Evaluate the Internal & External Environment

↓

Step 3: Set Organizational or SBU Objectives

↓

Step 4: Establish the Business Portfolio

↓

Step 5: Develop Growth Strategies

In many firms, the answers to questions such as these become the lead items in the organization's strategic plan. The answers become part of a **mission statement**—a formal document that describes the organization's overall purpose and what it hopes to achieve in terms of its customers, products, and resources. For example, the mission of Mothers Against Drunk Driving (MADD) is "to stop drunk driving, support the victims of this violent crime, and prevent underage drinking."[3] The ideal mission statement is not too broad, too narrow, or too shortsighted. A mission that is too broad will not provide adequate focus for the organization. It doesn't do much good to claim, "We are in the business of making high-quality products" or "Our business is keeping customers happy" as it is hard to find a firm that doesn't make these claims. It's also important to remember that the need for a clear mission statement applies to virtually any type of organization, even those like Mothers Against Drunk Driving, whose objective is to serve society rather than to sell goods or services.

Step 2: Evaluate the Internal and External Environment

The second step in strategic planning is to assess the firm's internal and external environments. We refer to this process as a **situation analysis**, *environmental analysis*, or sometimes a *business review*. The analysis includes a discussion of the firm's internal environment, which can identify a firm's strengths and weaknesses, as well as the external environment in which the firm does business so the firm can identify opportunities and threats.

By **internal environment** we mean all the controllable elements inside a firm that influence how well the firm operates. Internal strengths may lie in the firm's technologies. What is the firm able to do well that other firms would find difficult to duplicate? What patents does it hold? A firm's physical facilities can be an important strength or weakness, as can its level of financial stability, its relationships with suppliers, its corporate reputation, its ability to produce consistently high-quality products, and its ownership of strong brands in the marketplace.

Internal strengths and weaknesses often reside in the firm's employees— the firm's *human and intellectual capital*. What skills do the employees have? What kind of training have they had? Are they loyal to the firm? Do they feel a sense of ownership? Has the firm been able to attract top researchers and good decision makers?

The **external environment** consists of elements outside the firm that may affect it either positively or negatively. The external environment for today's businesses is global, so managers/marketers must consider elements such as the economy, competition, technology, law, ethics, and sociocultural trends. Unlike elements of the internal environment that management can controls to a large degree, the firm can't directly control these external factors, so management must respond to them through its planning process.

Chapter 3 develops in depth the various elements of the external environment in which marketing takes place, within the context of today's global enterprise. For now, it is important for you to be aware that opportunities and threats can come from any part of the external environment. On the one hand, trends or currently unserved customer needs may provide opportunities for growth. On the other hand, if changing customer needs or buying patterns mean customers are turning away from a firm's products, it's a signal of possible danger or threats down the road. Even very successful firms have to change to keep up with

Rainy days really are brighter when you save.

With a little help from Xerox, you can reduce your company's document-related expenses by up to 30%. For 40 years, we've helped businesses manage documents and information more cost-efficiently. Whether it's with software and services designed to reduce expensive paper-driven processes, or a full line of MFP's and printers starting at $179, there are lots of ways your office can save enough to weather the occasional storm.

1-800-ASK-XEROX
xerox.com

Ready For Real Business **xerox**

A mission statement that is *too narrow* may inhibit managers' ability to visualize possible growth opportunities. If, for example, a firm sees itself in terms of its product only, consumer trends or technology can make that product obsolete—and the firm is left with no future. Years ago, Xerox was the undisputed king of the photocopier—to the point where many people used the verb "xeroxing" to refer to many forms of print duplication (just as today in online search we all "google"). But in the digital age, if Xerox had continued to define its mission in terms of just producing copy machines instead of providing a broad array of "document solutions," the shift to electronic documents would have left them in the dust the way the Model T Ford replaced the horse and buggy. Take a look at how today's Xerox defines itself:

> Xerox is the world's leading document management technology and services enterprise. A nearly $18 billion company, with steadily increasing revenue and strong profits even throughout the recent recession, Xerox provides the document industry's broadest portfolio of offerings. Digital systems include color and black-and-white printing and publishing systems, digital presses and "book factories," multifunction devices, laser and solid ink network printers, copiers and fax machines. Xerox's services expertise is unmatched and includes helping businesses develop online document archives, analyzing how employees can most efficiently share documents and knowledge in the office, operating in-house print shops or mailrooms, and building Web-based processes for personalizing direct mail, invoices, brochures, and more. Xerox also offers associated software, support, and supplies such as toner, paper, and ink.[4]

mission statement
A formal statement in an organization's strategic plan that describes the overall purpose of the organization and what it intends to achieve in terms of its customers, products, and resources.

situation analysis
An assessment of a firm's internal and external environments.

JAY MINKOFF

Jay needs to have a realistic sense of the goals his employees can achieve. This will help to determine First Flavor's strategic direction as it takes its flavor strips to market. ➡

internal environment
The controllable elements inside an organization, including its people, its facilities, and how it does things that influence the operations of the organization.

external environment
The uncontrollable elements outside an organization that may affect its performance either positively or negatively.

SWOT analysis
An analysis of an organization's strengths and weaknesses and the opportunities and threats in its external environment.

external environmental pressures. First Flavor's business, like that of most marketing-related suppliers, is greatly impacted by the marketing budgets of its clients, which in turn are driven by economic conditions and ultimately consumer demand.

What is the outcome of an analysis of a firm's internal and external environments? Managers often synthesize their findings from a situation analysis into a format we call a **SWOT analysis**. This document summarizes the ideas from the situation analysis. It allows managers to focus clearly on the meaningful strengths (S) and weaknesses (W) in the firm's internal environment and opportunities (O) and threats (T) coming from outside the firm (the external environment). A SWOT analysis enables a firm to develop strategies that make use of what the firm does best in seizing opportunities for growth, while at the same time avoiding external threats that might hurt the firm's sales and profits. Table 2.2 shows an example of a partial SWOT analysis for McDonald's.

Step 3: Set Organizational or SBU Objectives

After they construct a mission statement, top management translates it into *organizational* or *SBU objectives*. These goals are a direct outgrowth of the mission statement and broadly identify what the firm hopes to accomplish within the general time frame of the firm's long-range business plan. If the firm is big enough to have separate SBUs, each unit will have its own objectives relevant to its operations.

To be effective, objectives need to be *specific, measurable* (so firms can tell whether they've met them or not), *attainable*, and *sustainable*. Attainability is especially important—firms that establish "pie in the sky" objectives they can't realistically obtain can create frustration for their employees (who work hard but get no satisfaction of accomplishment) and other stakeholders in the firm, such as vendors and shareholders who are affected when the firm doesn't meet its objectives. That a firm's objectives are sustainable is also critical—what's the point of investing in attaining an objective for only a very short term? This often happens when a firm underestimates the likelihood a competitor will come to market with a better offering. Without some assurance that an objective is sustainable, the financial return on an investment likely will not be positive.

Objectives may relate to revenue and sales, profitability, the firm's standing in the market, return on investment, productivity, product development, customer satisfaction, social responsibility, and many other attributes. To ensure measurability, marketers increasingly try to state objectives in numerical terms. For example, a firm might have as an objective a 10 percent increase in profitability. It could reach this objective by increasing productivity, by reducing costs, or by selling off an unprofitable division. Or it might meet this 10 percent objective by developing new products, investing in new technologies, or entering a new market.

For many years, one of Procter & Gamble (P&G)'s objectives was to have a number-one brand in every product category in which it competed. This objective was specific and clearly it was attainable, since P&G could boast of market leaders such as Crest in the toothpaste category, Folgers in coffee, Pampers in diapers, and Head & Shoulders in shampoo. It also was measurable in terms of the share of market of P&G's products versus those competitors sold. However, in the long run this objective is very difficult to sustain because of competitive activity and ever-changing consumer tastes. Sure enough, over time some P&G brands continued to hold a respectable market share,

Southwest Airlines has always been very focused on hiring and developing employees who reflect the "Southwest Spirit" to customers. Anyone who has flown on Southwest can attest to the fact that the atmosphere is lively and fun, and flight attendants are likely to do most any crazy stunt—bowling in the aisle, or serenading the captain and first officer (and passengers) with a favorite tune. One of our favorites is a guy who does galloping horse hooves and neighing sounds during takeoff and landing to promote a fun atmosphere. For Southwest, a real strength—one that's hard for the competition to crack—lies in this employee spirit.

QUESTIONS the Plan Addresses	**CHAPTERS** Where You'll Find These Questions
• How does marketing support my company's mission, objectives, and growth strategies? • What is the corporate culture and how does it influence marketing activities? • What has my company done in the past with its: Target markets? Products? Pricing? Promotion? Supply chain? • What resources including management expertise does my company have that make us unique? How has the company added value through its offerings in the past?	**Chapter 1:** Welcome to the World of Marketing: Create and Deliver Value **Chapter 2:** Strategic Market Planning: Take the Big Picture **Chapter 3:** Thrive in the Marketing Environment: The World Is Flat **Chapter 4:** Marketing Research: Gather, Analyze, and Use Information
• What is the nature of the overall domestic and global market for our product? How big is the market? Who buys our product? • Who are our competitors? What are their marketing strategies? • What are the key trends in the economic environment? The technological environment? The regulatory environment? The social and cultural environment?	
• Based on this analysis of the internal and external environments, what are the key Strengths, Weaknesses, Opportunities, and Threats (SWOT)?	
• What does marketing need to accomplish to support the objectives of my firm?	**Chapter 2:** Strategic Market Planning: Take the Big Picture **Chapter 3:** Thrive in the Marketing Environment: The World Is Flat
• How do consumers and organizations go about buying, using, and disposing of our products? • Which segments should we select to target? If a consumer market: What are the relevant demographic, psychographic, and behavioral segmentation approaches and the media habits of the targeted segments? If a business market: What are the relevant organizational demographics? • How will we position our product for our market(s)?	**Chapter 4:** Marketing Research: Gather, Analyze, and Use Information **Chapter 5:** Consumer Behavior: How and Why People Buy **Chapter 6:** Business-to-Business Markets: How and Why Organizations Buy **Chapter 7:** Sharpen the Focus: Target Marketing Strategies and Customer Relationship Management
• What is our core product? Actual product? Augmented product? • What product line/product mix strategies should we use? • How should we package, brand, and label our product? • How can attention to service quality enhance our success?	**Chapter 8:** Create the Product **Chapter 9:** Manage the Product **Chapter 10:** Services and Other Intangibles: Marketing the Product That Isn't There
• How will we price our product to the consumer and through the channel? How much must we sell to break even at this price? What pricing tactics should we use?	**Chapter 11:** Price the Product
• How do we develop a consistent message about our product? How do we best generate buzz? • What approaches to advertising, public relations, sales promotion, and newer forms of communication (such as social networking) should we use? • What role should a sales force play in the marketing communications plan? How should direct marketing be used?	**Chapter 12:** One-to-Many to Many-to-Many: Traditional and New Media **Chapter 13:** One-to-Many: Advertising, Public Relations, and Consumer Sales Promotion **Chapter 14:** One-to-One: Trade Promotion, Direct Marketing, and Personal Selling
• How do we get our product to consumers in the best and most efficient manner? • What types of retailers, if any, should we work with to sell our product? • How do we integrate supply chain elements to maximize the value we offer to our customers and other stakeholders?	**Chapter 15:** Deliver Value through Supply Chain Management, Channels of Distribution, and Logistics **Chapter 16:** Retailing: Bricks and Clicks
• How do we make our marketing plan happen? • Who is responsible for accomplishing each aspect of implementing the marketing plan? • What is the timing for the elements of our marketing plan? • What budget do we need to accomplish our marketing objectives? • How do we measure the actual performance of our marketing plan and compare it to our planned performance and progress toward reaching our marketing objectives?	**Chapter 2:** Strategic Market Planning: Take the Big Picture **Chapter 4:** Marketing Research: Gather, Analyze, and Use Information **Appendix:** Marketing Plan: The S&S Smoothie Companyy

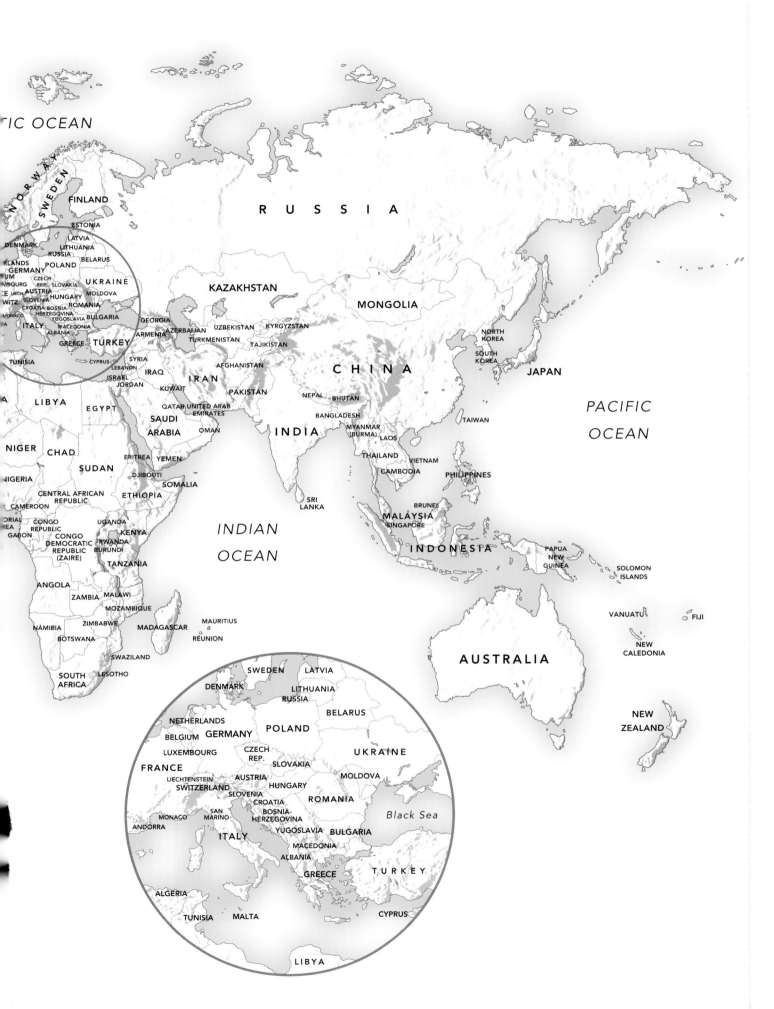

build a
Marketing
Plan

HOW TO USE This Tear-out Template

Here's a handy tear-out template that serves as a road map both to develop a marketing plan and to guide you through the course.

1. The first column provides the basic marketing plan **OUTLINE**.

2. The second column gives you **QUESTIONS** you must answer in each of the sections of the marketing plan.

3. The third column shows you where to go to find the answers as you work your way through the **CHAPTERS** of the book.

By the time you're done, all these pieces will come together and you'll understand how real marketers make real choices. And by the way, there's a **world map** on the other side of this tear-out that you can use to locate the many countries we discuss in the chapters.

Table 2.2	Example of a Partial SWOT Analysis for McDonald's
Strengths	World-class research and product development. Global franchise system that is second to none. Strong cash position. Consistency of product and service quality across the globe. Growing presence in the coffee/bistro market.
Weaknesses	Until recently, slow to react to changing consumer trends and preferences (organics, low-fat options).
Opportunities	Changing consumer tastes and dining preferences signals opportunity to continue to remake locations into more upscale bistro formats to compete directly with Starbucks in coffee. Reconnecting with Baby Boomers and Gen X while cultivating Gen Y and Millennials provides opportunity for product innovation and more flexibility by market area. High cost of gasoline means more people are seeking dining experiences closer to home. Greatly increased sales and profits during the recession due to high perceived value—opportunity to keep those customers postrecession.
Threats	The image of McDonald's is inextricably linked to the image of America globally. Strongly negative media coverage surrounding obesity and unhealthy eating, especially among children and teens, has tarnished the brand. Burger King has emerged as an innovator, and they are currently aggressively reimaging their stores. The rival chain has been hugely successful with offbeat advertising strategies both off-line and online that appeal to younger consumers.

but they dropped from the number-one position. Should P&G withdraw from a product category simply because its brand is not number one? Management realized the answer to this question was clearly "no," and the objective morphed from category leadership into one focused on profitability for each brand.[5]

Step 4: Establish the Business Portfolio

For companies with several different SBUs, strategic planning includes making decisions about how to best allocate resources across these businesses to ensure growth for the total organization. Each SBU has its own focus within the firm's overall strategic plan, and each has its own target market and strategies for reaching its objectives. Just like an independent business, each SBU is a separate *profit center* within the larger corporation—that is, each SBU within the firm is responsible for its own costs, revenues, and profits. These items can be accounted for separately for each SBU.

Just as we call the collection of different stocks an investor owns a portfolio, the range of different businesses that a large firm operates is its **business portfolio**. These different businesses usually represent very different product lines, each of which operates with its own budget and management. Having a diversified business portfolio reduces the firm's dependence on one product line or one group of customers. For example, if consumers don't travel as much and Disney has a bad year in theme park attendance and cruises, its managers hope that the sales will be made up by stay-at-homers who watch Disney's television networks and DVDs.

Portfolio analysis is a tool management uses to assess the potential of a firm's business portfolio. It helps management decide which of its current SBUs should receive more—or less—of the firm's resources, and which of its SBUs are most consistent with the firm's

business portfolio
The group of different products or brands owned by an organization and characterized by different income-generating and growth capabilities.

portfolio analysis
A management tool for evaluating a firm's business mix and assessing the potential of an organization's strategic business units.

Jeep's product development strategy offers vehicles for different needs.

Courtesy of Chrysler LLC

JAY MINKOFF

APPLYING ▽ Portfolio Analysis

First Flavor needs to evaluate the potential of new markets in addition to its initial focus on selling flavor strips to manufacturers for use in in-store product sampling to determine whether it should expand its portfolio to other applications. ➡

BCG growth–market share matrix
A portfolio analysis model developed by the Boston Consulting Group that assesses the potential of successful products to generate cash that a firm can then use to invest in new products.

stars
SBUs with products that have a dominant market share in high-growth markets.

cash cows
SBUs with a dominant market share in a low-growth-potential market.

overall mission. There are a host of portfolio models available for use. To illustrate how one works, let's examine the especially popular model the Boston Consulting Group (BCG) developed: the **BCG growth–market share matrix**.

The BCG model focuses on determining the potential of a firm's existing successful SBUs to generate cash that the firm can then use to invest in other businesses. The BCG matrix in 📷 Figure 2.3 shows that the vertical axis represents the attractiveness of the market: the *market growth rate*. Even though the figure shows "high" and "low" as measurements, marketers might ask whether the total market for the SBU's products is growing at a rate of 10, 50, 100, or 200 percent annually.

The horizontal axis in 📷 Figure 2.3 shows the SBU's current strength in the market through its relative market share. Here, marketers might ask whether the SBU's share is 5, 25, or perhaps 75 percent of the current market. Combining the two axes creates four quadrants representing four different types of SBUs. Each quadrant of the BCG grid uses a symbol to designate business units that fall within a certain range for market growth rate and market share. Let's take a closer look at each cell in the grid:

- **Stars** are SBUs with products that have a dominant market share in high-growth markets. Because the SBU has a dominant share of the market, stars generate large revenues, but they also require large amounts of funding to keep up with production and promotion demands. Because the market has a large growth potential, managers design strategies to maximize market share in the face of increasing competition. The firm aims at getting the largest share of loyal customers so that the SBU will generate profits that it can reallocate to other parts of the company. For example, in recent years, Disney has viewed its television operations as a star, so it invested heavily in such franchise players as *Hannah Montana* and *Narnia*. Likewise, at Disney/Pixar *Toy Story 3* and the re-release of *Toy Story 1* and *2* in 3D continued the sensational success of that business unit as a contributor to overall Disney profits.

- **Cash cows** have a dominant market share in a low-growth- potential market. Because there's not much opportunity for new companies, competitors don't often enter the market. At the same time, the SBU is well established and enjoys a high market share that the firm can sustain with minimal funding. Firms usually milk cash cows of their profits to fund the growth of other SBUs. Of course, if the firm's objective is to increase

Figure 2.3 📷 *Snapshot* | BCG Matrix

The Boston Consulting Group's (BCG) growth–market share matrix is one way a firm can examine its portfolio of different products or SBUs. By categorizing SBUs as stars, cash cows, question marks, or dogs, the matrix helps managers make good decisions about how the firm should grow.

Source: Product Portfolio Matrix, © 1970, The Boston Consulting Group

revenues, having too many cash cows with little or no growth potential can become a liability. For Disney, its theme parks unit fits into the cash cow category in that sales have been basically steady or only slightly increasing/decreasing for an extended period of time.

- **Question marks**—sometimes called "problem children"— are SBUs with low market shares in fast-growth markets. When a business unit is a question mark, it suggests that the firm has failed to compete successfully. Perhaps the SBU's products offer fewer benefits than competing products. Or maybe its prices are too high, its distributors are ineffective, or its advertising is too weak. The firm could pump more money into marketing the product and hope that market share will improve. But the firm may find itself "throwing good money after bad" if it gains nothing but a negative cash flow and disappointment. For Disney, its brick and mortar Disney Stores are in the question-mark category, as their performance compared to the overall specialty retail market has lagged in recent years. The online version of the Disney Store, in contrast, performs much better.

- **Dogs** have a small share of a slow-growth market. They are businesses that offer specialized products in limited markets that are not likely to grow quickly. When possible, large firms may sell off their dogs to smaller firms that may be able to nurture them—or they may take the SBU's products off the market. Disney, being a savvy strategic planner, apparently identified its Miramax film studio as a long-term dog (to Pluto and Goofy: no pun intended), as they announced in 2009 that they plan to shut it down.

Like Disney, Jay Minkoff at First Flavor could use the BCG matrix to evaluate his product lines in order to make important decisions about where to invest for future growth. He would look across First Flavor's various offerings to assess the market growth rate and relative market share, determine the degree to which each is a cash generator or a cash user, and decide whether to invest further in these or other business opportunities.

Step 5: Develop Growth Strategies

Although the BCG matrix can help managers decide which SBUs they should invest in for growth, it doesn't tell them much about *how* to make that growth happen. Should the growth of an SBU come from finding new customers, from developing new variations of the product, or from some other growth strategy? Part of the strategic planning at the SBU level entails evaluating growth strategies.

Marketers use the product-market growth matrix that 📷 Figure 2.4 shows to analyze different growth strategies. The vertical axis in 📷 Figure 2.4 represents opportunities for growth, either in existing markets or in new markets. The horizontal axis considers whether the firm would be better off putting its resources into existing products or if it should acquire new products. The matrix provides four fundamental marketing strategies: market penetration, market development, product development, and diversification:

- **Market penetration strategies** seek to increase sales of existing products to existing markets such as current users, nonusers, and users of competing brands within a market. For example, both Quaker Oatmeal and General Mills' Cheerios (also an oats product) have been aggressively advertising a new use for their products as products that can help lower total cholesterol and LDL ("bad") cholesterol, and that can help keep

COLUMBIA PICTURES/MARVEL ENTERTAINMENT/Newscom

The recent acquisition of Marvel Comics by Disney most likely will add to the entertainment company's stable of stars.

question marks
SBUs with low market shares in fast-growth markets.

dogs
SBUs with a small share of a slow-growth market. They are businesses that offer specialized products in limited markets that are not likely to grow quickly.

market penetration strategies
Growth strategies designed to increase sales of existing products to current customers, nonusers, and users of competitive brands in served markets.

Figure 2.4 📷 *Snapshot* | Product-Market Growth Matrix

Marketers use the product-market growth matrix to analyze different growth strategies.

Product Emphasis

	Existing **Products**	New **Products**
Existing Markets	**Market penetration strategy** • Seek to increase sales of existing products to existing markets	**Product development strategy** • Create growth by selling new products in existing markets
New Markets	**Market development strategy** • Introduce existing products to new markets	**Diversification strategy** • Emphasize both new products and new markets to achieve growth

(Market Emphasis)

market development strategies
Growth strategies that introduce existing products to new markets.

product development strategies
Growth strategies that focus on selling new products in existing markets.

diversification strategies
Growth strategies that emphasize both new products and new markets.

arteries clean and healthy. General Mills advertises that a clinical study showed that eating two half-cup servings daily of Cheerios cereal for six weeks reduced bad cholesterol about 4 percent (when eaten as part of a diet low in saturated fat and cholesterol). Quaker's Web site reads as much like a health provider's as it does a food manufacturer's—main tabs include "Oats Do More," which provides an impressive bank of information extolling the virtues of the product on health, fitness, and even environmental issues, and "For Healthcare Professionals," which offers that industry a portal into the "science of oats." Both Cheerios' and Quaker Oats' approaches aim to increase usage based on important new product claims.[6]

- **Market development strategies** introduce existing products to new markets. This strategy can mean expanding into a new geographic area, or it may mean reaching new customer segments within an existing geographic market. For example, the wildly popular Wii home gaming system by Nintendo has also become popular with older consumers because its active functionality during the game provides an opportunity for a light and fun physical workout. Wii exercise sessions have become especially popular in retirement homes where the activity takes on a strong social and community-building flavor. And because the technology part of Wii is so straightforward and user-friendly, even the most technophobic of seniors are not reluctant to join in the Wii events.[7]

- **Product development strategies** create growth by selling new products in existing markets. *Product development* may mean extending the firm's product line by developing new variations of the item, or it may mean altering or improving the product to provide enhanced performance.

- **Diversification strategies** emphasize both new products and new markets to achieve growth. After a long period of sluggish performance in the fast-food market, McDonald's has reenergized itself over the past several years through successful strategic planning. For example, planners at McDonald's in the late 1990s decided that the company was starting to max out in the hamburger business. The company tried to attract different customers when it offered new lines of business to diversify its portfolio of food offerings. Among those are Donatos Pizza, Boston Market, and a controlling interest in Chipotle Mexican Grills. Interestingly, now that their core hamburger and fries business has been back on track for several years, McDonald's has divested these other brands and is shifting from a diversification strategy back to more of a product development strategy around the core McDonald's brand.[8]

For Jay Minkoff at First Flavor, the product-market growth matrix can be a very important way to analyze where his future opportunities lie. Consider these options for future growth: Is he primarily focused on growing totally new customers for the First Flavor Peel 'n Taste® Marketing System (market development)? Or will he eventually also be moving current users into new product lines as the company creates them (product development)? And to what degree does the First Flavor Peel 'n Taste® Marketing System afford him the chance to grow current customers in usage of existing product lines (market penetration)? Jay has

Without DIRECTV High Definition your LCD TV is in the past

DIRECTV
▷HD

DIRECTV® hopes to penetrate new markets. This ad is from Ecuador.

© La Faculttad

to weigh these options for future product-market investment against the potential returns of each over both the short and long term.

To review what we've learned so far, strategic planning includes developing the mission statement, assessing the internal and external environment (resulting in a SWOT analysis), setting objectives, establishing the business portfolio, and developing growth strategies. In the next section, we'll look at marketers' functional plans as we examine the process of marketing planning.

3
OBJECTIVE
Describe the steps in marketing planning.
(pp. 53–61)

Marketing Planning:
Select the Camera Setting

Until now, we have focused on fairly broad strategic plans. This big-picture perspective, however, does not provide details about how to reach the objectives we set. Strategic plans "talk the talk" but put the pressure on lower-level functional-area managers, such as the marketing manager, production manager, and finance manager, to "walk the walk" by developing the functional plans—the nuts and bolts—to achieve organizational and SBU objectives. Since this is a marketing course and marketing book, our focus at the functional planning level is naturally on developing marketing plans, which is the next step in planning as we showed back in  Figure 2.1.

Lee jeans diversifies its product portfolio.

The Four Ps of the marketing mix we discussed in Chapter 1 remind us that successful firms must have viable *products* at *prices* consumers are willing to pay, a way to *promote* the products to the right consumers, and the means to get the products to the *place* where consumers want to buy them.

Making this happen requires a tremendous amount of planning by the marketer. The steps in this marketing planning process are quite similar to the steps at the strategic planning level. An important distinction between strategic planning and marketing planning, however, is that marketing professionals focus much of their planning efforts on issues related to the *marketing mix*—the firm's product, its price, promotional approach, and distribution (place) methods. In the end, as you learned in Chapter 1, marketing focuses on creating, communicating, delivering, and exchanging offerings that have value, and marketing planning plays a central role in making these critical components of marketing successful. Let's use Figure 2.5 as a guide to look at the steps involved in the marketing planning process in a bit more detail.

Step 1: Perform a Situation Analysis

The first step to develop a marketing plan is to conduct an analysis of the *marketing environment*. To do this, managers build on the company's SWOT analysis; they search out information about the environment that specifically affects the marketing plan. For example, for Jay Minkoff at First Flavor to develop an effective marketing communication program, it's not enough for him to have a general understanding of the target market. He needs to know *specifically* what media potential customers like to connect with, what messages about the product are most likely to make them buy, and how they prefer to communicate with his firm about new services and customer care issues. Jay also must know how his competitors are marketing to customers so that he can plan effectively.

Figure 2.5 *Process* | **Steps in Marketing Planning**

The steps in marketing planning are quite similar to those in strategic planning, with the important distinction that marketing professionals focus much of their planning efforts on issues related to the marketing mix—the firm's product, price, promotional approach, and distribution (place) methods. Marketing planning facilitates creating, communicating, delivering, and exchanging offerings that have value.

Step 1: Perform a Situation Analysis

↓

Step 2: Set Marketing Objectives

↓

Step 3: Develop Marketing Strategies

↓

Step 4: Implement and Control the Marketing Plan

Step 2: Set Marketing Objectives

Once marketing managers have a thorough understanding of the marketing environment, the next step is to develop specific marketing objectives. How do marketing objectives differ from corporate objectives? Generally, marketing objectives are more specific to the firm's brands, sizes, product features, and other marketing mix–related elements. Think of the connection between business objectives and marketing objectives this way: Business objectives guide the entire firm's operations, while marketing objectives state what the marketing function must accomplish if the firm is ultimately to achieve these overall business objectives. So for Jay Minkoff at First Flavor, setting marketing objectives means deciding what he wants to accomplish in terms of First Flavor's marketing mix–related elements: product development, pricing strategies, or specific marketing communication approaches.

Step 3: Develop Marketing Strategies

In the next stage of the marketing planning process, marketing managers develop their actual marketing strategies—that is, they make decisions about what activities they must accomplish to achieve the marketing objectives. Usually this means they decide which markets to target and actually develop the marketing mix strategies (product, price, promotion, and place [supply chain]) to support how they want to position the product in the market. At this stage, marketers must figure out how they want consumers to think of their product compared to competing products.

Select a Target Market

As we mentioned in Chapter 1, the target market is the market segment(s) a firm selects because it believes its offerings are most likely to win those customers. The firm assesses the potential demand—the number of consumers it believes are willing and able to pay for its products—and decides if it is able to create a sustainable competitive advantage in the marketplace among target consumers.

Develop Marketing Mix Strategies

Marketing mix decisions identify how marketing will accomplish its objectives in the firm's target markets by using product, price, promotion, and place. To make the point, we'll compare several different airlines' approaches.

- Because the product is the most fundamental part of the marketing mix—firms simply can't make a profit without something to sell—carefully developed *product strategies* are essential to achieving marketing objectives. Product strategies include decisions such as product design, packaging, branding, support services (e.g., maintenance), if there will be variations of the product, and what product features will provide the unique benefits targeted customers want. For example, product planners for JetBlue Airways decided to include in-seat video games and television as a key product feature during the flight. Their planes get you from point A to point B just as fast (or slow) as the other airlines—that is, the basic product is the same—but the flight seems shorter because there is more to do while you're in the air.

- The *pricing strategy* determines how much a firm charges for a product. Of course, that price has to be one that customers are willing to pay. If not, all the other marketing efforts are futile. In addition to setting prices for the final consumer, pricing strategies usually establish prices the company will charge to wholesalers and retailers. A firm may base its pricing strategies on costs, demand, or the prices of competing prod-

California's almond growers have a marketing strategy to increase consumption by promoting the nut's health benefits.

ucts. Southwest Airlines uses a pricing strategy to successfully target customers who could not previously afford air travel. Southwest does not compete solely on price; however, consumers do perceive Southwest as a low-priced airline compared with others, and the airline reinforces this theme regularly in its ads targeting travelers on a tight budget.

- A *promotional strategy* is how marketers communicate a product's value proposition to the target market. Marketers use promotion strategies to develop the product's message and the mix of advertising, sales promotion, public relations and publicity, direct marketing, and personal selling that will deliver the message. Many firms use all these elements to communicate their message to consumers. American Airlines strives to portray an image of quality and luxury for the serious business traveler. To do so, it combines television ads focused on that target with sales promotion in the form of the AAdvantage™ loyalty program, personal selling to companies and conventions to promote usage of American as the "official carrier" for the group events, direct marketing via mail and e-mail providing information to loyal users, and (its managers hope) positive publicity through word-of-mouth about the airline's good service and dependability. A panel of wine judges *Global Traveler Magazine* created recently named American as the airline with the "Best Wine Selections." An official wine consultant, a "sommieler" who is a classically trained winemaker and viticulturist, personally selects the wines American offers. Cheers![9]

Nature Valley's target market includes people who look for other benefits in addition to taste when they choose a snack.

- *Distribution strategies* outline how, when, and where the firm will make the product available to targeted customers (the *place* component). When they develop a distribution strategy, marketers must decide whether to sell the product directly to the final customer or to sell through retailers and wholesalers. And the choice of which retailers should be involved depends on the product, pricing, and promotion decisions. For example, if the firm produces a luxury good, it may wish to avoid being seen on the shelves of discount stores for fear that it will cheapen the brand image. Recently the airline industry has made major changes in its distribution strategy. For many years, most customers bought their airline tickets through travel agencies or at the ticket counters of the major airlines. Today, most airlines actually penalize customers who don't opt for online purchase of "ticketless" flight reservations by charging them a "ticketing fee" of $5 or $10. This strategy has molded the behavior of many consumers to go online 24/7 to save money as well as experience the convenience of personally scheduling the flight they want.

Step 4: Implement and Control the Marketing Plan

Once the plan is developed, it's time to get to work and make it succeed. In practice, marketers spend much of their time managing the various elements involved in implementing the marketing plan. Once Jay Minkoff and his team at First Flavor understand the marketing environment, determine the most appropriate objectives and strategies, and get their ideas organized and on paper in the formal plan, the rubber really hits the road. Like all firms, how First Flavor implements its plan is what will make or break it in the marketplace.

During the implementation phase, marketers must have some means to determine to what degree they actually meet their stated marketing objectives. Often called **control**, this formal process of monitoring progress entails three steps:

1. Measure actual performance.

2. Compare this performance to the established marketing objectives or strategies.

3. Make adjustments to the objectives or strategies on the basis of this analysis. This issue of making adjustments brings up one of the most important aspects of successful marketing planning: Marketing plans aren't written in stone, and marketers must be flexible enough to make such changes when changes are warranted.

control
A process that entails measuring actual performance, comparing this performance to the established marketing objectives, and then making adjustments to the strategies or objectives on the basis of this analysis.

For effective control, Jay Minkoff at First Flavor has to establish appropriate *metrics* related to his marketing objectives and then track those metrics to know how successful his marketing strategy is, as well as whether he needs to make changes in the strategy along the way. For example, what happens if First Flavor sets an objective for the first quarter of a year to increase the number of manufacturers that use its Peel 'n Taste® flavor sampling platform to promote their products by 20 percent, but after the first quarter sales are only even with those of last year? The *control process* means that Jay would have to look carefully at why the company isn't meeting its objectives. Is it due to internal factors, external factors, or a combination of both? Depending on the cause, Jay would then have to either adjust the marketing plan's strategies (such as to implement product alterations, modify the price, or increase or change advertising). Alternatively, he could decide to adjust the marketing objective so that it is more realistic and attainable. This scenario illustrates the important point we made earlier in our discussion of strategic planning: Objectives must be specific and measurable, but also *attainable* (and *sustainable*) in the sense that if an objective is not realistic, it can become very demotivating for everyone involved in the marketing plan.

For First Flavor and all firms, effective control requires appropriate *marketing metrics*, which, as we discussed in Chapter 1, are concrete measures of various aspects of marketing performance. You will note throughout the book a strong emphasis on metrics. But marketing control and the measurement of marketing performance must be tempered with an eye toward sustainability. Recall from Chapter 1 that sustainability has to do with firms doing well by doing good—that is, paying attention to important issues such as ethics, the environment, and social responsibility as well as the bottom line. In marketing planning, we certainly don't want to drive firms toward strategies that compromise sustainability by focusing only on controlling relatively short-term aspects of performance.

Today's CEOs are keen to quantify just how an investment in marketing has an impact on the firm's success, financially and otherwise, over the long haul. You've heard of the term *return on investment (ROI)*—think of this overall notion as **return on marketing investment (ROMI)**. *In fact it's critical to consider marketing as an investment rather than an expense*—this distinction drives firms to use marketing more strategically to enhance the business. For many firms nowadays, ROMI is the metric *du jour* to analyze how the marketing function contributes to the bottom line.

So, what exactly is ROMI? It is the revenue or profit margin (both are widely used) generated by investment in a specific marketing campaign or program divided by the cost of that program (expenditure) at a given risk level (the risk level is determined by management's analysis of the particular program). Again, the key word is *investment*—that is, in the planning process, thinking of marketing as an investment rather than an expense keeps managers focused on using marketing dollars to achieve specific goals.[10]

But is ROMI always appropriate or sufficient to judge marketing's effectiveness and efficiency? Here are six common objections to relying exclusively on ROMI for measuring marketing success:

1. In a company's accounting statements, marketing expenditures tend to appear as a cost, not an investment. This perpetuates the "marketing is an expense" mentality in the firm.

2. ROMI requires the profit to be divided by expenditure, yet all other bottom-line performance measures (like the ones you learned in your finance course) consider profit or cash flow after deducting expenditures.

3. Calculating ROMI requires knowing what would have happened if the marketing expenditure in question had never taken place. Few marketers have those figures.

4. ROMI has become a fashionable term for marketing productivity in general, yet much evidence exists that firms interpret how to calculate ROMI quite differently. When executives discuss ROMI with different calculations of it in mind, only confusion can result.

---

return on marketing investment (ROMI)
Quantifying just how an investment in marketing has an impact on the firm's success, financially and otherwise.

5. ROMI, by nature, ignores the effect of marketing assets of the firm (for example, its brands) and tends to lead managers toward a more short-term decision perspective. That is, it typically considers only short-term incremental profits and expenditures without looking at longer-term effects or any change in brand equity.

6. And speaking of short-term versus long-term decisions, ROMI (like a number of other metrics focused on snapshot information—in this case, a particular marketing campaign) often can lead to actions by management to shore up short-term performance to the detriment of a firm's sustainability commitment. Ethics in marketing should not be an oxymoron—but often unethical behavior is driven by the demand for quick, short-term marketing results.

For an organization to use ROMI properly it must: (a) identify the most appropriate and consistent measure to apply; (b) combine review of ROMI with other critical marketing metrics (one example is marketing payback—how quickly marketing costs are recovered); and (c) fully consider the potential long-term impact of the actions ROMI drives (that is, their sustainability).[11]

Fortunately for the marketer, there are many other potential marketing metrics beyond ROMI that measure specific aspects of marketing performance. Just to give you a sense of a few of them, Table 2.3 provides some examples of metrics that managers apply across an array of marketing planning situations, including all the marketing mix variables.

Table 2.3 | Examples of Marketing Metrics

- Cost of a prospect
- Value of a prospect
- ROI of a campaign
- Value of telesales
- Conversion rates of users of competitor products
- Long-term value of a customer
- Customer commitment to relationship/partnership
- Referral rate
- Response rates to direct marketing
- Perceived product quality
- Perceived service quality
- Customer loyalty/retention
- Customer turnover
- Customer/segment profitability
- Customer mind set/customer orientation
- Customer satisfaction
- Company/product reputation
- Customer word-of-mouth (buzz) activity
- Salesperson's self-ratings of effectiveness
- Timeliness and accuracy of competitive intelligence
- Usage rates of technology in customer initiatives
- Reach and frequency of advertising
- Recognition and recall of message
- Sales calls per day/week/month
- Order fulfillment efficiency/stock-outs
- Timeliness of sales promotion support

Action Plans

action plans

Individual support plans included in a marketing plan that provide the guidance for implementation and control of the various marketing strategies within the plan. Action plans are sometimes referred to as "marketing programs."

How does the implementation and control step actually manifest itself within a marketing plan? One very convenient way is through the inclusion of a series of **action plans** that support the various marketing objectives and strategies within the plan. We sometimes refer to action plans as "marketing programs." The best way to use action plans is to include a separate action plan for each important element involved in implementing the marketing plan. Table 2.4 provides a template for an action plan.

For example, let's consider the use of action plans in the context of supporting Jay's objective at First Flavor to increase the number of manufacturers that use its Peel 'n Taste® flavor sampling platform to promote their products by 20 percent in the first quarter of the year. To accomplish this, the marketing plan would likely include a variety of strategies related to how he will use the marketing mix elements to reach this objective. Important questions will include:

- What are the important needs and wants of this target market?
- How will the product be positioned in relation to this market?
- What will be his product and branding strategies?
- What will be his pricing strategy for this group?
- How will the product be promoted to them?
- What is the best distribution strategy to access the market?

Any one of these important strategic issues may require several action plans to implement.

Action plans also help managers when they need to assign responsibilities, time lines, budgets, and measurement and control processes for marketing planning. Notice in Table 2.4 that these four elements are the final items an action plan documents. Sometimes when we view a marketing plan in total, it can seem daunting and nearly impossible to actually implement. Like most big projects, implementation of a marketing plan is best done one step at a time, paying attention to maximizing the quality of executing that step. In practice, what happens is that marketers combine the input from these last four elements of each action plan to form the overall implementation and control portion of the marketing plan. Let's examine each element a bit further.

Table 2.4 | Template for an Action Plan

Title of Action Plan	Give the action plan a relevant name.
Purpose of Action Plan	What do you hope to accomplish by the action plan—that is, what specific marketing objective and strategy within the marketing plan does it support?
Description of Action Plan	Be succinct, but still thorough, in explaining the action plan. What are the steps involved? This is the core of the action plan. It describes what must be done in order to accomplish the intended purpose of the action plan.
Responsibility for the Action Plan	What person(s) or organizational unit(s) are responsible for carrying out the action plan? What external parties are needed to make it happen? Most importantly, who specifically has final "ownership" of the action plan—that is, who is accountable for it?
Time Line for the Action Plan	Provide a specific timetable of events leading to the completion of the plan. If different people are responsible for different elements of the time line, provide that information.
Budget for the Action Plan	How much will implementation of the action plan cost? This may be direct costs only, or may also include indirect costs, depending on the situation. The sum of all the individual action plan budget items will ultimately be aggregated by category to create the overall budget for the marketing plan.
Measurement and Control of the Action Plan	Indicate the appropriate metrics, how and when they will be measured, and who will measure them.

The Cutting Edge

Social Networks and Marketing Planning

Many companies have begun to incorporate social networks into their larger marketing plans and strategies—typically either to promote brands or to be on the lookout for complaints about services and products. But there are other ways marketers can mine the wealth of data that are available on social media platforms like Facebook or Yelp! Let's say, for example, that a marketing manager of a hotel wants to send a targeted e-mail to people looking for "hotels in Dublin." A search pulls up all the people on Twitter talking about and looking for hotels in Dublin. Twitter very nicely gives you an RSS feed of these results in the top right-hand corner. Copy the URL of this link. Then you can add a subscription button in Google Reader (you can easily sign up if you don't have an account). Paste in the URL of the Twitter RSS feed, then click "Show Details" in the top right corner, where you will see a blank graph. After a few days this will show some fantastic data on what day of the week, month, and time people were talking about "hotels in Dublin." From this information you can determine when will be the very best time to send the e-mail.[12] Faith and Begorrah! That's how you lure visitors to your little piece of Ireland.

Assign Responsibility

A marketing plan can't be implemented without people. And not everybody who will be involved in implementing a marketing plan is a marketer. The truth is, marketing plans touch most areas of an organization. Upper management and the human resources department will need to deploy the necessary employees to accomplish the plan's objectives. You learned in Chapter 1 that marketing isn't the responsibility only of a marketing department. Nowhere is that idea more apparent than in marketing plan implementation. Sales, production, quality control, shipping, customer service, finance, information technology—the list goes on—all will likely have a part in making the plan successful.

Create a Time Line

Notice that each action plan requires a time line to accomplish the various tasks it requires. This is essential to include in the overall marketing plan. Most marketing plans portray the timing of tasks in flowchart form so that it is easy to visualize when the pieces of the plan will come together. Marketers often use *Gantt charts* or *PERT charts*, popular in operations management, to portray a plan's time line. These are the same types of tools that a general contractor might use to map out the different elements of building a house from the ground up. Ultimately, managers develop budgets and the financial management of the marketing plan around the time line so they know when cash outlays are required.

Set a Budget

Each action plan carries a *budget item*, assuming there are costs involved in carrying out the plan. Forecasting the needed expenditures related to a marketing plan is difficult, but one way to improve accuracy in the budgeting process overall is to ensure estimates for expenditures for the individual action plans that are as accurate as possible. At the overall marketing plan level, managers create a master budget and track it throughout the market planning process. They report variances from the budget to the parties responsible for each budget item. For example, a firm's vice president of sales might receive a weekly or monthly report that shows each sales area's performance against its budget allocation. The VP would note patterns of budget overage and contact affected sales managers to determine what, if any, action they need to take to get the budget back on track. The same approach would be repeated across all the different functional areas of the firm on which the budget has an impact. In such a manner, the budget itself becomes a critical element of control.

Decide on Measurements and Controls

Earlier we described the concept of control as a formal process of monitoring progress to measure actual performance, compare the performance to the established marketing objectives or strategies, and make adjustments to the objectives or strategies on the basis of this analysis. The metric(s) a marketer uses to monitor and control individual action plans ultimately forms the overall control process for the marketing plan. It is an unfortunate fact that many marketers do not consistently do a good job of measurement and control, which, of course, compromises their marketing planning. And remember that selection of good metrics needs to take into account short-term objectives balanced against the firm's focus on long-term sustainability.

Make Your Life Easier! Use the Marketing Planning Template

Ultimately, the planning process we've described in this section is documented in a formal, written marketing plan. You'll find a tear-out template for a marketing plan in the foldout located in this chapter. The template will come in handy as you make your way through the book, as each chapter will give you information you can use to "fill in the blanks" of a marketing plan. You will note that the template is cross-referenced with the questions you must answer in each section of the plan and that it also provides you with a general road map of the topics covered in each chapter that need to flow into building the marketing plan. By the time you're done, we hope that all these pieces will come together and you'll understand how real marketers make real choices.

As we noted earlier, a marketing plan should provide the best possible guide for the firm to successfully market its products. In large firms, top management often requires such a written plan because putting the ideas on paper encourages marketing managers to formulate concrete objectives and strategies. In small entrepreneurial firms, a well-thought-out marketing plan is often the key to attracting investors who will help turn the firm's dreams into reality.

Operational Planning: Day-to-Day Execution of Marketing Plans

Recall that planning happens at three levels: strategic, functional (such as marketing planning), and operational. In the previous section, we discussed marketing planning—the process by which marketers perform a situation analysis; set marketing objectives; and develop, implement, and control marketing strategies. But talk is cheap: The best plan ever written is useless if it's not properly carried out. That's what **operational plans** are for. They put the pedal to the metal by focusing on the day-to-day execution of the marketing plan.

The task of operational planning falls to the first-line managers we discussed earlier, such as sales managers, marketing communications managers, brand managers, and marketing research managers. Operational plans generally cover a shorter period of time than either strategic plans or marketing plans—perhaps only one or two months—and they include detailed directions for the specific activities to be carried out, who will be responsible for them, and time lines for accomplishing the tasks. In reality, the action plan template we provide in Table 2.4 is most likely applied at the operational level.

Significantly, many of the important marketing metrics managers use to gauge the success of plans actually get used at the operational planning level. For example, sales managers in many firms are charged with the responsibility of tracking a wide range of metrics related to the firm–customer relationship, such as number of new customers, sales calls per month, customer turnover, and customer loyalty. The data are collected at the operational level and then sent to upper management for use in planning at the functional level and above.

To summarize what we've discussed in this chapter, business planning—a key element of a firm's success—occurs in several different stages. Strategic planning takes place at both the corporate and the SBU level in large firms and in a single stage in smaller businesses. Marketing planning, one of the functional planning areas, comes next. Operational planning ensures proper implementation and control of the marketing plan. It is critical that firms approach the marketing planning process in a highly ethical manner, mindful of the importance of establishing an organizational code of ethics to eliminate ambiguity about which

operational plans
Plans that focus on the day-to-day execution of the marketing plan. Operational plans include detailed directions for the specific activities to be carried out, who will be responsible for them, and time lines for accomplishing the tasks.

behaviors by organization members are acceptable and which are not. And it is also important that the application of metrics to provide effective control of marketing performance take into account not just short-term results but also impact on long-term sustainability issues. In the next chapter, we'll continue the dialogue by focusing on how marketing can best help firms thrive in today's global business environment.

Now that you've learned the basics of strategic market planning, go to **www.mypearsonmarketinglab.com** to see which strategy Jay selected to develop a market for First Flavor.

Here's my choice. . .
Real **People**, Real **Choices**

1 Option 2 Option **3** Option

Why do you think Jay chose option 3?

How It Worked Out at First Flavor
Jay and his partners decided to defer the flavoring strip concept, as they felt that it required a more capital-intensive consumer product launch rather than working through a corporate partner with an existing supply chain. Focusing on their core marketing services product, Peel 'n Taste®, First Flavor was able to achieve profitability for the first time in Q1 2010 as a result of new orders.

To learn the whole story, visit www.mypearsonmarketinglab.com.

Brand **YOU**!

Do you cringe when someone asks you, "What do you want to do when you graduate?"

Learn about yourself and what professions might be best for you in Chapter 2 of *Brand You.* You'll create a mission statement, complete a skills inventory, and identify your career objectives. In today's competitive world, it's never too early to plan your career.

1. Objective Summary (pp. 40–46)

Explain business planning and its three levels.

Strategic planning is the managerial decision process in which top management defines the firm's purpose and specifies what the firm hopes to achieve over the next five or so years. For large firms that have a number of self-contained business units, the first step in strategic planning is for top management to establish a mission for the entire corporation. Top managers then evaluate the internal and external environment of the business and set corporate-level objectives that guide decision making within each individual SBU. In small firms that are not large enough to have separate SBUs, strategic planning simply takes place at the overall firm level. For companies with several different SBUs, strategic planning also includes (1) making decisions about how to best allocate resources across these businesses to ensure growth for the total organization, and (2) developing growth strategies.

Planning takes place at three key levels. Strategic planning is the managerial decision process that matches the firm's resources and capabilities to its market opportunities for long-term growth. Functional planning gets its name because the various functional areas of the firm such as marketing, finance, and human resources get involved. And operational planning focuses on the day-to-day execution of the functional plans and includes detailed annual, semiannual, or quarterly plans.

Key Terms

business planning, p. 41

business plan, p. 41

marketing plan, p. 41

business ethics, p. 42

code of ethics, p. 42

strategic planning, p. 44

strategic business units (SBUs), p. 45

functional planning, p. 45

operational planning, p. 45

2. Objective Summary (pp. 46–53)

Describe the steps in strategic planning.

Marketing planning is one type of functional planning. Marketing planning begins with an evaluation of the internal and external environments. Marketing managers then set marketing objectives usually related to the firm's brands, sizes, product features, and other marketing mix–related elements. Next, marketing managers select the target market(s) for the organization and decide what marketing mix strategies they will use.

Product strategies include decisions about products and product characteristics that will appeal to the target market. Pricing strategies state the specific prices to be charged to channel members and final consumers. Promotion strategies include plans for advertising, sales promotion, public relations, publicity, personal selling, and direct marketing used to reach the target market. Distribution (place) strategies outline how the product will be made available to targeted customers when and where they want it. Once the marketing strategies are developed, they must be implemented. Control is the measurement of actual performance and comparison with planned performance. Maintaining control implies the need for concrete measures of marketing performance called "marketing metrics."

Key Terms

mission statement, p. 47

situation analysis, p. 47

internal environment, p. 47

external environment, p. 47

SWOT analysis, p. 48

business portfolio, p. 49

portfolio analysis, p. 49

BCG growth–market share matrix, p. 50

stars, p. 50

cash cows, p. 50

question marks, p. 51

dogs, p. 51

market penetration strategies, p. 51

market development strategies, p. 52

product development strategies, p. 52

diversification strategies, p. 52

3. Objective Summary (pp. 53–61)

Describe the steps in marketing planning.

Operational planning is done by first-line supervisors such as sales managers, marketing communication managers, and marketing research managers, and focuses on the day-to-day execution of the marketing plan. Operational plans generally cover a shorter period of time and include detailed directions for the specific activities to be carried out, who will be responsible for them, and time lines for accomplishing the tasks. To ensure effective implementation, a marketing plan must include individual action plans, or programs, that support the plan at the operational level. Each action plan necessitates providing a budget estimate, schedule, or time line for its implementation, and appropriate metrics so that the marketer can monitor progress and control for discrepancies or variation from the plan. Sometimes variance from a plan requires shifting or increasing resources to make the plan work; other times, it requires changing the objectives of the plan to recognize changing conditions.

Key Terms

control, p. 55

return on marketing investment (ROMI), p. 56

action plans, p. 58

operational plans, p. 60

Chapter **Questions** and **Activities**

Concepts: Test Your Knowledge

1. What is strategic, functional, and operational planning? How does strategic planning differ at the corporate and the SBU levels?
2. What is a mission statement? What is a SWOT analysis? What role do these play in the planning process?
3. What is a strategic business unit (SBU)? How do firms use the Boston Consulting Group model for portfolio analysis in planning for their SBUs?
4. Describe the four business growth strategies: market penetration, product development, market development, and diversification.
5. Explain the steps in the marketing planning process.
6. How does operational planning support the marketing plan?
7. What are the elements of a formal marketing plan?
8. What is an action plan? Why are action plans such an important part of marketing planning? Why is it so important for marketers to break the implementation of a marketing plan down into individual elements through action plans?
9. What is return on marketing investment (ROMI)? How does considering marketing as an investment instead of an expense affect a firm?
10. Give several examples of marketing metrics. How might a marketer use each metric to track progress of some important element of a marketing plan?
11. What is corporate culture? What are some ways that the corporate culture of one organization might differ from that of another? How does corporate culture affect marketing decision making?
12. Why is it essential, even in firms with a strong corporate culture, to have a written Code of Ethics? What are some important potential negative consequences of not formalizing a Code of Ethics in written form?

Activities: Practice What You've Learned

1. Assume that you are the marketing director for a small firm that manufactures educational toys for children. Your boss, the company president, has decided to develop a mission statement. He's admitted that he doesn't know much about developing a mission statement and has asked you to help guide him in this process. Write a memo

outlining exactly what a mission statement is, why firms develop such statements, how firms use mission statements, and your thoughts on what the firm's mission statement might be.

2. As a marketing student, you know that large firms often organize their operations into a number of strategic business units (SBUs). A university might develop a similar structure in which different academic schools or departments are seen as separate businesses. Consider how your university might divide its total academic units into separate SBUs. What would be the problems with implementing such a plan? What would be the advantages and disadvantages for students and for faculty? Be prepared to share your analysis of university SBUs to your class.

3. An important part of planning is a SWOT analysis, understanding an organization's strengths, weaknesses, opportunities, and threats. Choose a business in your community with which you are familiar. Develop a brief SWOT analysis for that business.

4. As an employee of a business consulting firm that specializes in helping people who want to start small businesses, you have been assigned a client who is interested in introducing a new concept in health clubs—one that offers its customers both the usual exercise and weight-training opportunities and certain related types of medical assistance such as physical therapy, a weight-loss physician, and diagnostic testing. As you begin thinking about the potential for success for this client, you realize that developing a marketing plan is going to be essential. Take a role-playing approach to present your argument to the client as to why she needs to invest in formal marketing planning.

5. Review the Code of Ethics for any three business organizations of your choosing. What elements do you find in common across the three examples? Which Code of Ethics do you think is the most effective overall, and why?

Marketing Metrics Exercise

Most marketers today feel pressure to measure (quantify) their level of success in marketing planning. In your opinion, is it easy to measure marketing's success (compared to, say, measuring the success of a firm's financial management or production quality)? Explain your viewpoint.

Choices: What Do You Think?

1. The Boston Consulting Group matrix identifies products as stars, cash cows, question marks, and dogs. Do you think this is a useful way for organizations to examine their businesses? What are some examples of product lines that fit in each category?

2. In this chapter we talked about how firms do strategic, functional, and operational planning. Yet some firms are successful without formal planning. Do you think planning is essential to a firm's success? Can planning ever hurt an organization?

3. Most planning involves strategies for growth. But is growth always the right direction to pursue? Can you think of some organizations that should have contraction rather than expansion as their objective? Do you know of any organizations that have planned to get smaller rather than larger in order to be successful?

4. When most people think of successful marketing, internal firm culture doesn't immediately come to mind as a contributing factor. What is a corporate culture? What are some reasons a firm's corporate culture is important to the capability of doing good marketing? Give some examples of what you consider to be a good corporate culture for marketing.

5. Review the *AMA Code of Ethical Norms and Values for Marketers*, provided in the chapter. Which of the areas represented within the document do you anticipate are the most challenging for marketers to consistently follow? What makes these issues particularly troublesome? Do you think marketing in general does a good job adhering to the AMA Code? Provide specific evidence from your knowledge and experience to support your position.

Miniproject: Learn by Doing

The purpose of this miniproject is to gain an understanding of marketing planning through actual experience.

1. Select one of the following for your marketing planning project:
   - Yourself (in your search for a career)
   - Your university
   - A specific department in your university

2. Next, develop the following elements of the marketing planning process:
   - A mission statement
   - A SWOT analysis
   - Objectives
   - A description of the target market(s)
   - A positioning strategy
   - A brief outline of the marketing mix strategies—the product, pricing, distribution, and promotion strategies—that satisfy the objectives and address the target market

3. Prepare a brief outline of a marketing plan using the basic template provided in this chapter as a guide.

Marketing in **Action** Case — Real Choices for the Apple iPhone

Time magazine named it the Invention of the Year. Experts and consumers alike called it "revolutionary." Introduced in June 2007, the iPhone is Apple's Internet-enabled multimedia mobile phone. In the first six months after Steve Jobs announced the planned launch of the iPhone at the Macworld Expo in January 2007, the invention was the subject of 11,000 print articles and 69 million hits on Google.

So why is the iPhone revolutionary? For starters, the iPhone is a quad-band mobile phone that uses GSM standard, thus having international calling capability. It is a portable media player or iPod and an Internet browser, thus accessing owners' e-mail. It does text messaging, visual voice-mail, and has local Wi-Fi connectivity. It's sleek, slim, and is outfitted with a multitouch screen with virtual keyboard. The multitouch screen technique means the owner can expand or shrink the screen image by sliding her finger and thumb apart or together. The iPhone offers owners three types of radio: cellular, Wi-Fi, and Bluetooth. As an added benefit, one iPhone battery charge provides 8 hours of calls, 7 hours of video, or 24 hours of music.

Indeed, the iPhone was the year's most desired gadget. Customers stood in line to be the first to own one. In fact, some more entrepreneurially-minded customers bought more than one, convinced they could sell one at a profit and make enough to pay for the second!

Apple made the iPhone available to U.S. consumers through an alliance that made AT&T the exclusive carrier and under which AT&T subsidized the cost of the iPhone. To use an iPhone, customers had to sign a two-year contract with AT&T for cellular and Internet service. The price of the phone itself was $499 for the four-gigabyte model or $599 for the eight-gig version.

But consumers' love affair with the iPhone soon faced trouble. Just two months after the iPhone introduction, Apple dropped the price from $600 to $399, angering customers who had paid top dollar only two months before. And those customers immediately let Apple know of their dissatisfaction by phone, by e-mail, and on blogs. In response, Steve Jobs admitted that the company had abused its core customers and offered a $100 store credit to early iPhone buyers.

Furthermore, consumers were not happy that they were restricted to AT&T with their iPhones. Soon after the phone's introduction, hackers posted directions on the Internet for consumers to unlock the cellular service feature of their phone, allowing them to use the iPhone with any cellular service provider. Even though Apple was quick to warn consumers that unlocking the phone might damage the iPhone software, eventually making downloading with upgraded software impossible, unlocked phones continued to be available.

To make matters worse, various European countries have laws to protect consumers from being forced to buy something as a condition of buying a product, thus creating barriers for the global iPhone business. The courts in both France and Germany have refused to allow Apple to sell the iPhone locked to a long-term contract with a single cellular service supplier.

For Apple, the iPhone is the product of the future with plans for introducing software upgrades and newer versions to stimulate increased world sales. Steve Jobs is betting that the iPhone will enjoy the same success he has had with the iPod and with Apple computers. But for that success to materialize, Apple must carefully consider what long-term strategies are necessary to make the iPhone both popular and profitable.

You Make the Call

1. What is the decision facing Apple?
2. What factors are important in understanding this decision situation?
3. What are the alternatives?
4. What decision(s) do you recommend?
5. What are some ways to implement your recommendation?

Based on: Katie Hafner and Brad Stone, "iPhone Owners Crying Foul over Price Cut," *New York Times*, September 7, 2007, **http://www .nytimes.com/2007/09/07/technology/07apple.html**; Times Topics, iPhone, **http://topics.nytimes.com/top/reference/timestopics/ subjects/i/iphone/index.html?8qa&scp=1-spot&sq=iphone&st=nyt**; The Associated Press, "Altered iPhones at Risk of Failure," *New York Times*, September 25, 2007, **http://www.nytimes.com/2007/09/25/technology/25iphone.html?sq=iphone%20unlocked&st= nyt&scp=6&pagewanted=print**; Victoria Shannon, "Iphone Must Be Offered Without Contract Restrictions, German Court Rules," *New York Times*, November 21, 2007, **http://www.nytimes.com/2007/11/21/technology/21iphone.html?scp=3&sq=iphone+unlocked&st= nyt**; David Pogue, "The iPhone Matches Most of Its Hype," *New York Times*, June 27, 2007, **http://www.nytimes.com/2007/06/27/ technology/circuits/27pogue.html.**

Thrive in the Marketing Environment:
The World *Is* Flat

Robert Chatwani

Profile | Info

▼ A **Decision Maker** at eBay

Robert Chatwani oversees the marketing, strategic planning, operations, and business development for eBay's marketplace for socially responsible shopping. Formerly a senior manager on eBay's Internet marketing team, Robert helped to manage the company's relationships with Google, Yahoo!, and Microsoft. Robert joined eBay in 2003 as manager of platform strategy, and he helped transform eBay into the world's largest Web services platform.

Prior to joining eBay, Robert was the co-founder and COO of MonkeyBin, the leading software company to the global barter and corporate trading industry. Before starting MonkeyBin, Robert worked with McKinsey & Company where he served *Fortune* 500 clients and also helped to start McKinsey's Globalization Practice.

Robert has a bachelor of science degree from DePaul University, has completed graduate work in computer science at the University of Chicago, and holds an MBA from UC Berkeley's Haas School of Business.

💬 Robert's Info ✎

What do I do when I'm not working?
A) Practice my digital photography, play the sitar, and spend as much time as possible reading to my daughter.

First job out of school?
A) In management consulting at McKinsey & Company.

Career high?
A) Pitching a new marketplace business concept to eBay's founder and chairman, Pierre Omidyar.

A job-related mistake I wish I hadn't made?
A) Brought in an outside CEO to run a software company that I co-founded—he had relevant experience, but he was the absolute wrong cultural fit for the organization.

Business book I'm reading now?
A) *The Mystery of Capital: Why Capitalism Triumphs in the West and Fails Everywhere Else* by Hernando De Soto.

My hero?
A) My father, who always taught me the importance of integrity.

My motto to live by?
A) True success is best achieved through humility, fierce resolve, and a focus on doing what's right for others.

What drives me?
A) Creating new technology businesses, particularly when it involves ideas that are untested, but hold tremendous potential for creating economic value and social impact.

Here's my problem...

A small, entrepreneurial group of eBay employees was developing a new online marketplace to help small producers and artisans throughout the world gain improved access to global consumers.

The group was particularly interested in creating a marketplace for products that were ethically sourced, ensuring that the people and organizations that created them could directly benefit from the income generated from sale of the products. The team's research showed that there was an abundant supply of products such as handcrafted artisan goods and consumables such as coffee, tea, and chocolate. The group referred to these products as "People Positive" goods, meaning that the sale of the products positively impacts the producers and their community.

The group faced a key business question: Should it create a new, separately branded online marketplace or should it integrate the concept directly into eBay's existing online marketplace?

Robert's role as general manager of the business was to ensure that the team made a decision that could maximize both long-term revenue and social impact. And because eBay Inc. typically added new marketplace businesses to its portfolio through acquisition rather than by developing them internally, there was not much of a precedent for the decision he needed to make.

Things to remember

It's difficult enough to start a new business; having an unknown brand doesn't help matters. One consideration is whether the well-known eBay name will help the new enterprise get on its feet quickly.

Just because a country is poor doesn't mean there aren't many business opportunities that can benefit foreign companies as well as its inhabitants. As consumers are increasingly exposed to other cultures via the media and travel, their interest in locally made products grows as well.

Robert considered his **Options** 1·2·3

1

Option

Customize the existing eBay shopping experience on eBay.com by adding additional categories to accommodate the supply of artisans' products, and do not create a separate brand. The listings could be highlighted or marked in some way to indicate that the products were ethically sourced and a benefit to the producer. This would ensure that all listings would be visible to millions of eBay users who currently shop on **eBay.com**. In addition, existing eBay users would not have to register on a new site. Custom page designs could be created to highlight inventory, and merchandising and marketing could be easily featured on the eBay home page that millions of unique users visit each day. And the availability of socially responsible products on **eBay.com**, such as fair trade and ethically sourced artisan goods, could help shed positive light on the eBay brand and lead to increased intangible brand value for eBay Inc. The financial risk of this approach was also low due to the quick development and rapid time-to-market for the solution.

On the other hand, this option would position the business primarily as an incremental extension of eBay rather than a whole new business with an independent identity and its own customers. Plus, historically, artisan goods and fair trade products have sold on eBay with only moderate success; simple customization to eBay's current shopping experience might not significantly improve sales volume.

2

Option

Create a completely separate, custom-branded marketplace. It would exist as a separate new brand and offer a unique and highly tailored online shopping experience for consumers. There was some precedent for this among eBay's competitors. For example, **Amazon.com** had recently launched a newly branded marketplace for designer shoes and handbags called **Endless.com**. By developing a new brand identity, the business might attract new users who currently did not shop on eBay Inc. properties. This option also would allow for the creation of new, stand-alone marketing and merchandising campaigns, as opposed to marketing efforts that were simply "tacked on" to current eBay marketing programs. The unit would have the ability to fully customize a shopping experience that would be specifically designed around the needs of consumers who shop for "People Positive" goods such as home décor, furniture, artwork, paintings, and other handcrafted and fair trade goods and consumables. It would also provide the opportunity to create a custom online community specifically targeted toward socially conscious consumers who purchase fair trade and ethically sourced handcrafted artisan goods.

But this option would be very expensive. Developing a new brand and independent marketplace from scratch requires a large investment. It would also be time-consuming, because the team would have to recreate many existing eBay functions and features for the marketplace such as a billing infrastructure, a search and browse experience, and checkout flows. And it was risky because there was little precedent for creating entirely new marketplaces within the company, and it would be hard to predict how this new business would work.

3

Option

Create a hybrid model to take advantage of everything that the core eBay.com platform and brand offered with the flexibility and customization of an independent marketplace with a different brand. License a brand name that socially responsible consumers were already familiar with, and that was reinforced by eBay as the ingredient brand (e.g., **XYZ.com** by eBay). Sellers' listings would appear in both the newly branded marketplace as well as the core **eBay.com** marketplace. The new marketplace and its listings would have an entirely distinct visual experience, while the exact same listings on **eBay.com** would look just like all other eBay listings. This option might attract a new market of socially conscious consumers who buy ethically sourced goods, but who are not currently active on eBay. The marketplace experience could be customized, but the business unit would avoid the heavy investment that an entirely new platform would need. And nearly 300 million registered eBay users would automatically be users of the new marketplace because they would retain the same username and password information. On the other hand, the brand licensing option would require the unit to establish a brand alliance with another company to co-brand the marketplace. This would present complexities in terms of a licensing agreement and a need to adhere to certain trademark and brand quality standards of another organization.

Now, put yourself in Robert's shoes: Which option would you choose, and why?

You Choose

Which **Option** would you choose, and **why**?
1. ☐ YES ☐NO **2.** ☐YES ☐NO **3.** ☐YES ☐NO

See what **option** Robert chose on **page 93**

67

Check out chapter 3 **Study Map** on page 93

Decisions, Decisions

As we discussed in Chapter 2, in order to plan for the future, marketers need a clear picture of where they are now. When marketers understand what's going on NOW in both their internal and external environments, they can make good decisions about where they should go in the future. In this chapter we'll better understand the worldwide marketing playing field and look at the decisions firms face when they think about global opportunities.

Whether they're at home or moving into the global marketplace, marketers know that it's critical to clearly understand what's going on around them in order to make good decisions. Otherwise they'd be "flying blind" as weather conditions change constantly and other planes (i.e., the competition) maneuver around them. That's why they include information about their external environment in the *Situation Analysis* section of their Marketing Plan. For example, when the planners at Walmart think about their future efforts at home or in a foreign country, they need to understand the economic picture, their competition, the legal and political climate, and a host of other factors that can make or break their future marketing efforts. In the Appendix at the end of this book, we can see how the Marketing Plan our (fictional) friends at S&S Smoothie wrote describes the firm's external environment. We'll also see how they use the analysis of both their internal and external environments to develop a SWOT analysis.

1

OBJECTIVE

Understand the big picture of international marketing and the decisions firms must make when they consider globalization. (pp. 68–71)

Take a Bow: Marketing on the Global Stage

Whether you think of yourself as a member of a global community or only a resident of Smalltown, USA, you are a citizen of the world and a participant in a global marketplace. You may eat strawberries from Peru and sip wine from Australia. When you come home, you may take off your shoes that were made in Thailand, put your feet up on the cocktail table imported from Indonesia, and watch the World Cup football (soccer) match on your HDTV made in China. You may even have been one of the millions of people around the world who donated money to help the people of Haiti hit by an earthquake in 2010. And you may be looking for an exciting career with a firm that does business around the globe.

Of course, not everyone thinks of a single global marketplace as an advantage. Some argue that the development of free trade will benefit us all, because it allows people in developing and least developed countries to enjoy the same economic benefits as citizens of more developed countries. Others warn of problems such as global warming and stress the need for international agreements that would force industries and governments to develop and adhere to environmental standards to protect the future of the planet. However, critics argue for limits on trade to protect domestic industries or because some imported products, produced in countries with inadequate industry regulations and controls, are dangerous.

In his bestselling book, *The World Is Flat: A Brief History of the Twenty-first Century*, Thomas Friedman argues that technology creates a level playing field for all countries and that marketers must recognize that national borders are not as important as they once were. Today, businesses like eBay must seek new and improved ways to attract customers down the street and around the globe in order to stay relevant.

The global marketing game is exciting, the stakes are high—and it's easy to lose your shirt. Competition comes from both local and foreign firms, and differences in national laws, customs, and consumer preferences can make your head spin. Like many American companies that feel they are running out of growth opportunities in the American marketplace, the retail giant Walmart aggressively expands its international presence. But you can be sure that when its planners plot future growth, they're keenly aware of competitors in their external environment who have other ideas. While the giant U.S. retailer ranks number one in *Fortune* magazine's 2010 list of the top 500 global firms, other retailers hope to steal some of the chain's thunder. French company Auchan, now the world's 14th biggest retailer with over 1,200 stores in 13 countries, is rapidly expanding into China, Russia, and Eastern Europe.[1] In China, Auchan outperforms Walmart, as the firm opens an average of two new stores per month. The success attests to Auchan's understanding of the Chinese market, where middle-class consumers often assume that cheaper products are unsafe or counterfeit. Auchan has created an image of a retailer with higher quality products; it makes store aisles wider and provides better lighting than its competitors.

Expanding into foreign markets is not the right decision for all firms. For some, globalization may mean simply being a customer of large and small companies around the world as they import products they need to run their business. Still, even very small firms may want to consider global opportunities—as we saw at the beginning of this chapter, eBay's experience with indigenous crafts is a powerful demonstration of the potential to find buyers for locally made products in many other markets. In this section we will first discuss the status of world trade today and then look at the decisions firms must make as they consider their global opportunities.

World Trade

World trade refers to the flow of goods and services among different countries—the total value of all the exports and imports of the world's nations. In 2009, as the world suffered in a global economic crisis after years of double-digit increases, worldwide exports of merchandise decreased from $15.7 trillion to just a little over $12 trillion.[2]

Of course, not all countries participate equally in the trade flows among nations. Understanding the "big picture" of who does business with whom is important to marketers when they devise global trade strategies. 📷 Figure 3.1 shows the amount of merchandise North American countries traded with major partners around the world in 2008.

It's often a good thing to have customers in remote markets, but to serve their needs well requires flexibility because you have to run your business differently to adapt to local social and economic conditions. For example, you often have to accommodate the needs of trading partners when those foreign firms can't pay cash for the products they want to purchase. Believe it or not, the currency of as many as 70 percent of all countries (including China) is not *convertible*; it cannot be spent or exchanged outside the country's borders. In other countries, because sufficient cash or credit is simply not available, trading firms work out elaborate deals in which they trade (or *barter*) their products with each other or even supply goods in return for tax breaks from the local government. This **countertrade** accounts for between 20 and 25 percent of all world trade. For instance, for many years, because Russian currency was no good outside the Russian borders, buyers paid for Coca-Cola in vodka while Poland paid Coke in beer.

world trade
The flow of goods and services among different countries—the value of all the exports and imports of the world's nations.

countertrade
A type of trade in which goods are paid for with other items instead of with cash.

Like many American companies that feel they are running out of growth opportunities in the American marketplace, the retail giant Walmart aggressively expands its international presence.

Stevens Frederic/Sipa/Newscom

Figure 3.1 📷 *Snapshot* | North American Merchandise Trade Flows (in $ Billions)

Knowing who does business with whom is essential to develop an overseas marketing strategy. As this figure shows, North America trades most heavily with Asia, Europe, and Latin America.

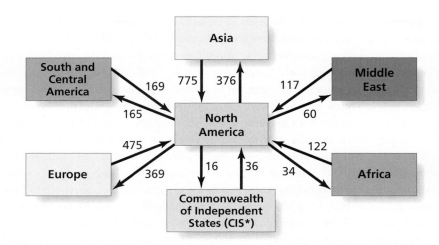

* Armenia, Azerbaijan, Belarus, Kazakhstan, Kyrgyzstan, Republic of Moldova, Russian Federation, and Ukraine

Our ever-increasing access to products from around the world does have a dark side: The growth in world trade in recent years has been accompanied by a glut of unsafe products, many of which have come from China. In 2006 alone, Chinese imports of toys, tires, toothpaste, cat and dog food, and farm-raised fish were found to be unsafe. More recently, an investigative report by the Associated Press reported on high levels of cadmium, a cancer-causing substance, in children's jewelry, causing Walmart and other retailers to pull suspected products from their shelves.[3] Although most of the thousands of Chinese manufacturers produce quality products, some unscrupulous producers have damaged the reputation of Chinese manufacturers and prompted U.S. and European officials to increase their inspections of Chinese imports.

Should We Go Global?

📈 Figure 3.2 shows that when firms consider going global they must think about this in four steps:

- Step 1. "Go" or "no go"—is it in our best interest to focus exclusively on our home market or should we cast our net elsewhere as well?

- Step 2. If the decision is "go," which global markets are most attractive? Which country or countries offer the greatest opportunity for us?

- Step 3. What market-entry strategy and thus what level of commitment is best? As we'll see, it's pretty low risk to simply export products to overseas markets, while the commitment and the risk is substantial if the firm decides to build and run manufacturing facilities in other countries (though the payoff may be worth it).

- Step 4. How do we develop marketing mix strategies in the foreign markets—should we standardize what we do in other countries, or develop a unique localized marketing strategy for each country?

We'll look at the first of these decisions now—whether or not to go global.

Although the prospect of millions—or even billions—of consumers salivating for your goods in other countries is very tempting, not all firms can or should go global, and certainly not all global markets are alike. When they make these decisions, marketers need to consider a number of factors that may enhance or detract from their success abroad. Let's review some big ones now.

Figure 3.2 📈 *Process* | Steps in the Decision Process for Entering Global Markets

Entering global markets involves a sequence of decisions.

Look at Domestic and Global Market Conditions

Many times, a firm decides to go global because domestic demand is declining while demand in foreign markets grows. For example, the market for personal computers has leveled off in the United States; more Americans replace old or obsolete machines than buy a personal computer for the first time. In contrast, the demand is much greater in some parts of the world where consumers and businesses are only now beginning to tune into the power of the Web. So it's no coincidence that a few years ago IBM sold its entire personal computing business to Lenovo, a Chinese company.

Identify Your Competitive Advantage

In Chapter 1, we saw how firms hope to create competitive advantage over rivals. When firms compete in a global marketplace, this challenge is even greater. There are more players involved, and typically local firms have a "home-court advantage." It's like soccer—increasing numbers of Americans play the game, but they are up against an ingrained tradition of soccer fanaticism in Europe and South America where kids start dribbling a soccer ball when they start to walk.

If it wants to go global, a firm needs to examine the competitive advantage that makes it successful in its home country. Will this leg-up "travel" well to other countries? For example, the many competitive advantages enjoyed by Silicon Valley companies such as Microsoft and HP have allowed the companies to be successful first in exporting their products to markets around the globe. That success has led to direct investment in research facilities and service centers around the globe. In contrast, developing countries typically do not have engineering expertise, highly trained workers, or high-tech facilities, but they do have a large labor force and low wages. Thus, firms in these countries can compete better in the global marketplace with products that rely on low-cost manufacturing or even handmade crafts.

Some of the most significant U.S. exports are foods, industrial supplies, and services, including tourism and entertainment—industries in which consumers around the world value American products. As we'll see next, barriers to trade and memberships in economic communities also affect a firm's success in global markets.

Of course, it isn't only Western countries that are going global. For years China was a huge export market for Western firms as consumers there began to prosper and crave foreign goods. Now the Chinese are turning the tables as they carve out a larger role in the global marketplace. Dozens of Chinese companies have global ambitions, including government-owned Chery Automobile. Chery, founded in 1997, realizes that growth in its home Chinese market has slowed while competition has increased, and it sees opportunities around the globe. In July 2007, Chery signed an agreement with Chrysler to develop international markets in North America and Europe.[4] A second agreement with Fiat includes a 50:50 joint venture to produce Chery, Fiat, and Alfa Romeo cars. Chery has overseas plants in Iran, Russia, Ukraine, Indonesia, Egypt, and Uruguay; it plans to expand overseas assembly plants to include Argentina and India. Other Chinese carmakers such as Great Wall and Geely are also hungrily looking to the United States.[5] Watch for a flood of new, low-priced cars from Asia—including one that features a karaoke player in the dashboard!

2

OBJECTIVE

Explain how both international organizations such as the World Trade Organization (WTO) and economic communities and individual country regulations both facilitate and limit a firm's opportunities for globalization.

(pp. 71–73)

Understand International, Regional, and Country Regulations

Alas, even the most formidable competitive advantage does not guarantee success in foreign markets because the local government may "stack the deck" in favor of domestic competitors. Although many governments say they support the idea that the world should be one big open marketplace where companies from every country are free to compete for business, their actions frequently say the reverse. Often they erect roadblocks (or at least those pesky speed bumps) designed to favor local businesses over outsiders that hinder a company's efforts to expand into foreign markets.

Initiatives in International Cooperation and Regulation

In recent years a number of international initiatives have diminished barriers to unfettered world trade. Most notably, after World War II the United Nations established the **General Agreement on Tariffs and Trade (GATT)**, which did a lot to establish free trade among nations. During a meeting in 1984 known as the Uruguay Round, GATT created the **World Trade Organization (WTO)**. With 153 members (and around 30 more negotiating membership now), the WTO member nations account for over 97 percent of world trade. The World Trade Organization has made giant strides in creating a single, open world market and is the only international organization that deals with the global rules of trade between nations. Its main function is "to ensure that trade flows as smoothly, predictably and freely as possible." With over three-fourths of its membership drawn from the world's poorer countries, negotiations in recent years have largely focused on issues concerning economic development.[6]

If you spend any time in Asia, you immediately notice the huge numbers of luxury watches, leather bags, and current music CDs that sell for ridiculously low prices. Who can resist a Rolex watch for $20? Of course, there is a catch: They're fake or pirated illegally. Protection of copyright and patent rights is a huge headache for many companies, and it's a priority the WTO tries to tackle. *Pirating* is a serious problem for U.S. companies because illegal sales significantly erode their profits. All too often, we see news headlines from New York or Rome or Dubai about police confiscating millions of dollars worth of goods—from counterfeit luxury handbags to fake Viagra. And, while things have improved in recent years, Microsoft recently found that 25 percent of Russian software outlets still sell bootleg copies of Microsoft software.[7]

Protected Trade: Quotas, Embargoes, and Tariffs

In some cases, a government adopts a policy of **protectionism**; it enforces rules on foreign firms to give home companies an advantage. Many governments set **import quotas** on foreign goods to reduce competition for their domestic industries. Quotas can make goods more expensive to a country's citizens, because the absence of cheaper foreign goods reduces pressure on domestic firms to lower their prices.

We can look at Russia as an example. As the economy of the country has improved, the demand for meat has increased much faster than the production capacity of Russian meat producers. To protect the local industry and to encourage its growth, Russia has instituted import quotas. In 2010 Russia's import quotas on U.S. meat products allowed a maximum of 600,000 tons of poultry, 21,700 tons of beef, and 57,500 tons of pork to make their way to Russian dinner tables.[8]

An **embargo** is an extreme quota that prohibits commerce and trade with a specified country altogether. Much to the distress of hard-core cigar smokers in the United States, the U.S. government prohibits the import of Cuban cigars as well as rum and other products because of political differences with its island neighbor.

Governments also use **tariffs**, or taxes on imported goods, to give domestic competitors an advantage in the marketplace by making foreign competitors' goods more expensive than their own products. For example, in September 2009, President Barack Obama imposed a three-year tariff on Chinese-made tires in order to protect American jobs in that industry. The Chinese-made products sell for about half the price of tires made in the United States.[9]

Economic Communities

Groups of countries may also band together to promote trade among themselves and make it easier for member nations to compete elsewhere. These **economic communities** coordinate trade policies and ease restrictions on the flow of products and capital across their borders. Economic communities are important to marketers because they set policies in areas such as product content, package labeling, and advertising regulations. The United States, for example, is a member of the North American Free Trade Agreement (NAFTA) that includes

---

General Agreement on Tariffs and Trade (GATT)
International treaty to reduce import tax levels and trade restrictions.

World Trade Organization (WTO)
An organization that replaced GATT; the WTO sets trade rules for its member nations and mediates disputes between nations.

protectionism
A policy adopted by a government to give domestic companies an advantage.

import quotas
Limitations set by a government on the amount of a product allowed to enter or leave a country.

embargo
A quota completely prohibiting specified goods from entering or leaving a country.

tariffs
Taxes on imported goods.

economic communities
Groups of countries that band together to promote trade among themselves and to make it easier for member nations to compete elsewhere.

Table 3.1 | Major Economic Communities around the World

Community	Member Countries
The Andean Community **www.comunidadandina.org**	Bolivia, Colombia, Ecuador, Peru
APEC Asia-Pacific Economy Cooperation **www.apecsec.org**	Australia, Brunei Darussalam, Canada, Chile, China, Hong Kong (China), Indonesia, Japan, Malaysia, Mexico, New Zealand, Papua New Guinea, Peru, Philippines, Republic of Korea, Russian Federation, Singapore, Chinese Taipei, Thailand, United States, Vietnam
ASEAN Association of Southeast Asian Nations **www.aseansec.org**	Brunei, Cambodia, Indonesia, Lao PDR, Malaysia, Myanmar, Philippines, Singapore, Thailand, Vietnam
CAFTA Central American Free Trade Agreement	Costa Rica, Dominican Republic, El Salvador, Guatemala, Honduras, Nicaragua, United States
CEFTA Central European Free Trade Agreement	Albania, Bosnia and Herzegovina, Bulgaria, Croatia, Czech Republic, Hungary, Kosovo, Moldova, Montenegro, Poland, Republic of Macedonia, Romania, Serbia, Slovak Republic, Slovenia
COMESA Common Market for Eastern and Southern Africa **www.comesa.int**	Angola, Burundi, Comoros, Democratic Republic of Congo, Djibouti, Egypt, Eritrea, Ethiopia, Kenya, Libya, Madagascar, Malawi, Mauritius, Namibia, Rwanda, Seychelles, Sudan, Swaziland, Uganda, Zambia, Zimbabwe
EU European Union **www.Europa.eu.int**	Austria, Belgium, Bulgaria, Cyprus, Czech Republic, Denmark, Estonia, Finland, France, Germany, Greece, Hungary, Ireland, Italy, Latvia, Lithuania, Luxembourg, Malta, Netherlands, Poland, Portugal, Slovakia, Slovenia, Spain, Sweden, United Kingdom
MERCOSUR **www.mercosur.org**	Brazil, Paraguay, Uruguay, Argentina
NAFTA North American Free Trade Agreement **www.nafta-sec-alena.org**	Canada, Mexico, United States
SAARC South Asian Association for Regional Cooperation **www.south-asia.com**	Afghanistan, Bangladesh, Bhutan, India, Maldives, Nepal, Pakistan, Sri Lanka

the United States, Canada, and Mexico. The European Union (EU) represents 490 million consumers, over 300 million of whom use the euro as their currency. Table 3.1 lists major economic communities.

3

OBJECTIVE

Understand how factors in a firm's external business environment influence marketing strategies and outcomes in both domestic and global markets.

(pp. 73–87)

Analyze the Marketing Environment

Whether or not you've decided to venture into a foreign market, it's essential to understand your external environment. For firms that choose to limit themselves to their domestic market, having a sharp picture of the marketing environment allows them to make good decisions about marketing strategies. If you've decided to go global, understanding local conditions in potential new country or regional markets helps you to figure out just where to go. 📷 Figure 3.3 provides a snapshot of these different external environments. In this section, we'll look at the economic, competitive, technological, political/legal, and sociocultural factors in the external environment that we need to think about.

Figure 3.3 📷 *Snapshot* | Elements of the External Environment

It's essential to understand elements of the firm's external environment to succeed in both domestic and global markets.

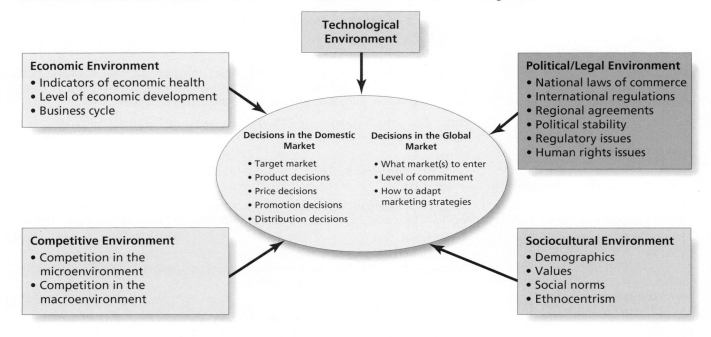

Technological Environment

Economic Environment
- Indicators of economic health
- Level of economic development
- Business cycle

Political/Legal Environment
- National laws of commerce
- International regulations
- Regional agreements
- Political stability
- Regulatory issues
- Human rights issues

Decisions in the Domestic Market
- Target market
- Product decisions
- Price decisions
- Promotion decisions
- Distribution decisions

Decisions in the Global Market
- What market(s) to enter
- Level of commitment
- How to adapt marketing strategies

Competitive Environment
- Competition in the microenvironment
- Competition in the macroenvironment

Sociocultural Environment
- Demographics
- Values
- Social norms
- Ethnocentrism

The Economic Environment

Marketers need to understand the state of the economy from two different perspectives: (1) the overall economic health and level of development of a country, and (2) the current stage of its business cycle. Let's take a look at each now.

Indicators of Economic Health

gross domestic product (GDP)
The total dollar value of goods and services produced by a nation within its borders in a year.

gross national product (GNP)
The value of all goods and services produced by a country's citizens or organizations, whether located within the country's borders or not.

Just as a doctor takes your temperature during a medical checkup, companies need to know about the overall "health" of a country's *economic environment* before they conduct a more detailed exam. You can easily find information about most countries in the *World Factbook* of the Central Intelligence Agency (CIA) (no, you don't need high-level security clearance to access this information online).

The most commonly used measure of economic health is a country's **gross domestic product (GDP)**: the total dollar value of goods and services it produces within its borders in a year. A similar but less frequently used measure of economic health is the **gross national product (GNP)**, which measures the value of all goods and services a country's individuals or organizations produce, whether located within the country's borders or not. Table 3.2 shows the GDP and other economic and demographic characteristics of a sampling of countries. In addition to total GDP, marketers may also compare countries on the basis of *per capita GDP*: the total GDP divided by the number of people in a country. The per capita GDP is often the better indicator of economic health since it is adjusted for the population size of each country.

Still, these comparisons may not tell the whole story. Per capita GDP can be deceiving, because the wealth of a country may be concentrated in the hands of a few while

Courtesy of Leo Burnett Cairo

BIG BORGAR

HELPING EGYPTIAN FAST-FOOD RESTAURANTS STAY IN BUSINESS SINCE 1992

Large packaged goods companies like Heinz continually scan the global environment to identify opportunities to sell their products in new markets. This ad is from Egypt.

Table 3.2 | Selected Comparisons of Economic and Demographic Characteristics

	United States	China	Japan	Spain	Hungary	Ecuador
Total GDP	$14.14 trillion	$8.748 trillion	$4.15 trillion	$1.362 trillion	$186 billion	$108.8 billion
Per capita GDP	$46,000	$6,600	$32,700	$33,600	$18,800	$7,500
Population below poverty level	12%	2.8%	NA	19.8%	12%	35.1%
Inflation rate	−0.3%	−0.7%	−1.4%	−0.8%	4.2%	4.3%
Unemployment rate	9.3%	4.3%	5.1%	18%	10.8%	8.5%
Population	307.2 million	1.3 trillion	127.1 million	40.525 million	9.9 million	14.6 million
Birth rate per 1,000 population	13.83	14.00	7.64	9.72	9.51	20.77
Population growth rate	0.977%	0.655%	−0.191%	0.072%	−0.257%	1.497%
Population aged 0–14	20.2%	19.8%	13.5%	14.5%	15.0%	31.1%
Population aged 15–64	67.0%	72.1%	64.3%	67.4%	69.3%	62.7%
Population aged 65 and over	12.8%	8.1%	22.2%	18.1%	15.8%	6.2%

Source: Adapted from Central Intelligence Agency, *The World Factbook*, **https://www.cia.gov/library/publications/the-world-factbook/index.html** (accessed August 26, 2010).
Note: *The World Factbook* is updated bi-weekly.

most of its citizens don't have the means to obtain basic necessities. Furthermore, the costs of the same goods and services are much lower in some global markets. *The Economist* magazine has developed its Big Mac Index based on the theory that with purchasing power parity, the exchange rate would equalize prices for goods and services. The Big Mac Index shows that a Big Mac that costs an average of $3.58 in the United States would cost over $7.00 in Norway, $2.50 in Mexico, and less than $2.00 in China.[10]

Of course, GDP alone does not provide the information marketers need to decide if a country's economic environment makes for an attractive market. They also need to consider whether they can conduct "business as usual" in another country. The **economic infrastructure** refers to the quality of a country's distribution, financial, and communications systems. For example, countries with less-developed financial institutions may still operate on a cash economy in which consumers and business customers must pay for goods and services with cash rather than with credit cards or checks. In poorer countries without good road systems, sellers may use donkey carts, hand trucks, or bicycles to deliver goods to the many small retailers who are their customers.

economic infrastructure
The quality of a country's distribution, financial, and communications systems.

Level of Economic Development

These are just some of the issues marketers must think about when they determine whether a country will be a good prospect. However, there are other economic conditions we must understand as well, including the broader economic picture of a country that we call its **level of economic development**.

When marketers scout the world for opportunities, it helps if they consider a country's level of economic development to understand the needs of people who live there and the infrastructure conditions with which they must contend. Economists look past simple facts such as growth in GDP to decide this; they also look at what steps the country is taking to reduce poverty, inequality, and unemployment. Analysts also take into account a country's **standard of living**, an indicator of the average quality and quantity of goods and services a country consumes. They describe the following three basic levels of development:

1. A country at the lowest stage of economic development is a **least developed country (LDC)**. In most cases, its economic base is agricultural. Analysts consider many nations

level of economic development
The broader economic picture of a country.

standard of living
An indicator of the average quality and quantity of goods and services consumed in a country.

least developed country (LDC)
A country at the lowest stage of economic development.

The low wages they can pay to local workers often entice U.S. firms to expand their operations overseas. Although they provide needed jobs, some companies have been criticized for exploiting workers when they pay wages that fall below local poverty levels, for damaging the environment, or for selling poorly made or unsafe items to consumers. Gap responded to criticism by establishing programs that help workers and their families in developing countries.

developing countries
Countries in which the economy is shifting its emphasis from agriculture to industry.

BRIC countries
Refers to Brazil, Russia, India, and China, the largest and fastest growing of the developing countries with over 40 percent of the world's population.

developed country
A country that boasts sophisticated marketing systems, strong private enterprise, and bountiful market potential for many goods and services.

Group of 8 (G8)
An informal forum of the eight most economically developed countries that meets annually to discuss major economic and political issues facing the international community.

business cycle
The overall patterns of change in the economy—including periods of prosperity, recession, depression, and recovery—that affect consumer and business purchasing power.

in Africa and South Asia to be LDCs. In least developed countries, the standard of living is low, as are literacy levels. Opportunities to sell many products, especially luxury items such as diamonds and caviar, are minimal because most people don't have enough spending money. They grow what they need and barter for the rest. These countries are attractive markets for staples such as rice and inexpensive goods like shoes and fabrics from which clothes can be made. They may export important raw materials, such as minerals or rubber, to industrialized nations. For example, most of us know that raw diamonds are exported from LDCs including Sierra Leone and Congo. LDCs in central Africa export copper. Haiti, one of the poorest of the LDCs (even before the 2010 earthquake devastated its economy), exports vetiver essence. Vetiver is a fragrant plant, similar to lemon grass. The oil from the plant is one of the major ingredients in perfumes.[11]

2. When an economy shifts its emphasis from agriculture to industry, standards of living, education, and the use of technology rise. These countries are **developing countries**. In such locales, there may be a viable middle class, often largely composed of entrepreneurs working hard to run successful small businesses. Because over 8 out of 10 consumers now live in developing countries, the number of potential customers and the presence of a skilled labor force attract many firms to these areas. Marketers see these developing countries as the future market for consumer goods like skin care products and mobile phones. Procter & Gamble, Unilever, and other companies meet these needs when they offer cleaning products, fabric softeners, and shampoo in one-use sachet packaging. Some mobile phone companies offer phones with limited functions but with a built-in flashlight for use in countries where there are frequent power outages.[12]

The largest of the developing countries, Brazil, Russia, India, and China, are referred to as the **BRIC countries** or simply as the BRICs. These four countries are the fastest growing of the developing countries, and they represent over 40 percent of the world's population. Marketers are attracted to these countries because of the masses of consumers who are not wealthy but who are beginning their move toward economic prosperity.

A **developed country** boasts sophisticated marketing systems, strong private enterprise, and bountiful market potential for many goods and services. Such countries are economically advanced, and they offer a wide range of opportunities for international marketers.

The United States, the United Kingdom, Australia, Canada, France, Italy, Germany, and Japan are the most economically developed countries in the world. In 1975 they established the **Group of Eight (G8)** to serve as an informal forum for these nations. The G8 meets annually to deal with the major economic and political issues that the countries and the international community face. In addition to topics of the world economy and international trade, G8 summits have more recently included discussions of other issues such as energy, terrorism, unemployment, the information highway, crime and drugs, arms control, and the environment.[13]

The Business Cycle

The **business cycle** describes the overall pattern of changes or fluctuations of an economy. All economies go through cycles of *prosperity* (high levels of demand, employment, and income), *recession* (falling demand, employment, and income), and *recovery* (gradual improvement in production, lowering unemployment, and increasing income). A severe recession is a *depression*, a period during which prices fall but there is little demand because few people have money to spend and many are out of work.

Inflation occurs when prices and the cost of living rise while money loses its purchasing power because the cost of goods escalates. For example, between 1960 and 2004, prices increased over 5 percent per year so that an item worth $1.00 in 1960 would cost over $6.00 in 2004. During inflationary periods, dollar incomes may increase, but real income—what the dollar will buy—decreases because goods and services cost more.

The business cycle is especially important to marketers because of its effect on customer purchase behavior. During times of prosperity, consumers buy more goods and services. Marketers try to grow the business and maintain inventory levels and even to develop new products to meet customers' willingness to spend. During periods of recession, such as that experienced by countries all over the globe beginning in 2008, consumers simply buy less.

We clearly see that pattern in recent years as many people have scaled back on buying houses, expensive cars and vacations, and even restaurant dinners. The challenge to most marketers is to maintain their firm's level of sales by convincing the customers who *do* buy to select the firm's product over the competition. Of course, even recessions aren't bad for all businesses. Although it may be harder to sell luxury items, firms that make basic necessities are not likely to suffer significant losses. The Great Recession of 2009 actually was pretty great for businesses including dollar stores and frozen foods manufacturers (as more people chose to skip eating out and to cook at home to save money).

It is important to note that when firms assess the economic environment, they evaluate all factors that influence consumer and business buying patterns, including the amount of confidence people have in the health of the economy. This "crystal ball" must be a global one because events in one country can have an impact on the economic health of other countries. For instance, the economic impact of the terrorist attacks on the United States in September 2001 affected the fortunes of businesses around the world, as did the meltdown in the American subprime mortgage industry in 2007.

The Competitive Environment

A second important element of a firm's external environment is the *competitive environment*. For products ranging from toothpaste to sport utility vehicles, firms must keep abreast of what the competition is doing so they can develop new product features, new pricing schedules, or new advertising to maintain or gain market share.

Analyze the Market and the Competition

Before we can create a competitive advantage in the marketplace, we need to know who our competitors are and what they're doing. Like players in a global chess game, marketing managers size up their competitors according to their strengths and weaknesses, monitor their marketing strategies, and try to predict their moves.

An increasing number of firms around the globe engage in **competitive intelligence (CI)** activities where they gather and analyze publicly available information about rivals. In fact, many firms have budgets in the millions for CI activities. Banks continually track home loan, auto loan, and certificate of deposit (CD) interest rates of their competitors. Major airlines change hundreds of fares daily as they respond to competitors' price cuts or increases. Car manufacturers keep abreast of cuts and increases in their rivals' production numbers, sales, and sales incentives (e.g., rebates and low or no interest loan rates) and use the information in their own marketing strategies. When Toyota suddenly confronted a crisis due to massive recalls of many of its best-selling models in 2010, American carmakers pounced on this "gift" as an opportunity to steal sales from the company.

Most of the information that companies need to know about their competitors is available from rather mundane sources, including the Internet, the news media, and publicly available government documents such as building permits and patent grants (or even for some hardball

competitive intelligence (CI)
The process of gathering and analyzing publicly available information about rivals.

players a rival's garbage, if they're into "dumpster diving!"). Successful CI means that a firm learns about a competitor's new products, its manufacturing, or the management styles of its executives. Then the firm uses this information to develop superior marketing strategies (we'll learn more about collecting marketing intelligence in Chapter 4, so stay tuned).

Competition in the Microenvironment

Competition in the *microenvironment* means the product alternatives from which members of a target market may choose. We think of these choices at three different levels.

discretionary income
The portion of income people have left over after paying for necessities such as housing, utilities, food, and clothing.

1. At a broad level, marketers compete for consumers' **discretionary income**: the amount of money people have left after paying for necessities such as housing, utilities, food, and clothing. Few consumers are wealthy enough to buy anything and everything, so each of us is constantly faced with choices: Do we plow "leftover" money into a new MP3 player, donate it to charity, or turn over a new leaf and lose those extra pounds by investing in a healthy lifestyle? Thus, the first part of understanding who the competition is means understanding *all* the alternatives consumers consider for their discretionary income—not just the brands against which the firm directly competes within a product category.

product competition
When firms offering different products compete to satisfy the same consumer needs and wants.

2. A second type of choice is **product competition**, in which competitors offering different products attempt to satisfy the same consumers' needs and wants. So, for example, if a couch potato decides to use some of his discretionary income to get buff, he may join a health club or buy a Soloflex machine and pump iron at home.

brand competition
When firms offering similar goods or services compete on the basis of their brand's reputation or perceived benefits.

3. The third type of choice is **brand competition**, in which competitors offering similar goods or services vie for consumer dollars. So, if our flabby friend decides to join a gym, he still must choose among competitors within this industry, such as between Gold's Gym and the YMCA. Or he may forgo the exercise thing altogether and count on the South Beach diet to work its magic by itself—or just buy bigger pants.

Competition in the Macroenvironment

When we talk about examining competition in the *macroenvironment*, we mean that marketers need to understand the big picture—the overall structure of their industry. This structure can range from one firm having total control to numerous firms that compete on an even playing field.

Four structures describe differing amounts of competition. Let's review each structure, beginning with total control by one organization and ending with tons of competitors.

monopoly
A market situation in which one firm, the only supplier of a particular product, is able to control the price, quality, and supply of that product.

1. No, it's not just a board game: A **monopoly** exists when one seller controls a market. Because the seller is "the only game in town," it feels little pressure to keep prices low or to produce quality goods or services. In the old days, the U.S. Postal Service had a monopoly on the delivery of written documents. Now, the days of a snail-mail monopoly are over because the U.S. Postal Service must battle fax machines, e-mail, scanners, and couriers such as FedEx for market share.

   In most U.S. industries today, the government attempts to ensure consumers' welfare by limiting monopolies through the prosecution of firms that engage in activities that would limit competition and thus violate antitrust regulations. Of course, these laws may generate controversy as powerful firms argue that they dominate a market simply because they provide a product most people want. This is at the heart of the ongoing controversy about Walmart's domination of the retail business. The world's largest retailer (and getting bigger all the time) produces some amazing statistics. In 2008, Walmart generated $401 billion in sales through its more than 4,200 facilities in the United States and more than 3,600 in 16 markets worldwide. Over 200 million shoppers visit Walmart stores each year.[14]

2. In an **oligopoly**, there are a relatively small number of sellers, each holding substantial market share, in a market with many buyers. Because there are few sellers, the actions of each directly affect the others. Oligopolies most often exist in industries that require substantial investments in equipment or technology to produce a product—this means only a few competitors have the resources to enter the game. The airline industry is an oligopoly. It is pretty hard for an entrepreneur with little start-up cash to enter—that's left to billionaires like Richard Branson, who can afford to launch a start-up like Virgin Airlines. Relatively smaller firms like JetBlue and Frontier succeed by offering something special, such as onboard entertainment, direct routes to smaller cities, or more leg room. Others that just can't compete either on price or amenities (like Mesa, Frontier, or Aloha Airlines) simply fly to that Great Hangar in the Sky.

3. In a state of **monopolistic competition**, there are many sellers who compete for buyers in a market. Each firm, however, offers a slightly different product, and each has only a small share of the market. For example, many athletic shoe manufacturers, including Nike, New Balance, and more recently Under Armour, vigorously compete with one another to offer consumers some unique benefit—even though only Adidas (at least for now) offers you a $250 computerized running shoe that senses how hard the ground is where you are running and adapts to it.

4. Finally, **perfect competition** exists when there are many small sellers, each offering basically the same good or service. In such industries, no single firm has a significant impact on quality, price, or supply. Although true conditions of perfect competition are rare, agricultural markets (in which there are many individual farmers who each produce the same corn or jalapeño peppers) come the closest. Even in the case of food commodities, though, there are opportunities for marketers to distinguish their offerings. Egg-Land's Best Inc., for example, says it feeds its hens a high-quality, all-vegetarian diet, so the eggs they lay contain less cholesterol and six times more vitamin E than regular eggs.[15] It brands each egg with a red "EB" seal. The company scrambled the competition when it created an "egg-straordinary" difference where none existed before.

The Technological Environment

Firms today see technology as an investment they can't afford not to make, as technology provides firms with important competitive advantages. The *technological environment* profoundly affects marketing activities. Of course, the Internet and continuing innovations in Internet applications is the biggest technological change in marketing. The Internet allows consumers to buy virtually anything they want (and even some things they don't want) without ever leaving home. Increasingly, marketers are using social media such as Facebook and Twitter to have two-way conversations with customers and prospective customers. Easy computer access to customer databases facilitates one-to-one marketing. And distribution has improved because of automated inventory control afforded by advancements such as bar codes, RFID (radio frequency identification) chips, and computer light pens.

Changes in technology can dramatically transform an industry, as when transistors revolutionized the field of consumer electronics. Successful marketers continuously scan the external business environment in search of ideas and trends to spark their own research efforts. They also monitor ongoing research projects in government and private organizations. When inventors feel they have come across something exciting, they usually want to protect their exclusive right to produce and sell the invention by applying for a **patent**. This is a legal document that grants inventors exclusive rights to produce and sell a particular invention in that country.

The Political and Legal Environment

The *political and legal environment* refers to the local, state, national, and global laws and regulations that affect businesses. Legal and regulatory controls can be prime motivators for

oligopoly
A market structure in which a relatively small number of sellers, each holding a substantial share of the market, compete in a market with many buyers.

monopolistic competition
A market structure in which many firms, each having slightly different products, offer unique consumer benefits.

perfect competition
A market structure in which many small sellers, all of whom offer similar products, are unable to have an impact on the quality, price, or supply of a product.

Robert Chatwani
APPLYING ▽ Technology

Robert knows that as increasing numbers of consumers around the world gain access to the World Wide Web, the global marketplace will continue to expand. This growth works in favor of an online enterprise like eBay. ➡

patent
A legal mechanism to prevent competitors from producing or selling an invention, aimed at reducing or eliminating competition in a market for a period of time.

The Cutting Edge

Sustainable Global Packaging

What invention, other than the Internet, has had the greatest impact on globalization? Believe it or not, it just may be the lowly shipping container. Introduced in the 1950s, standardized containers allow manufacturers to easily move massive quantities of cargo on ships, trucks, and planes. Containers have dramatically decreased the cost of global shipping because they can be loaded and unloaded with only a high crane and a few workers.

Now a new container named the Cargoshell, the invention of Dutch businessman and entrepreneur René Giesbers, promises to provide even more benefits. Although for now it costs three times more than a traditional container, the Cargoshell offers a number of advantages over traditional containers:

- It collapses in 30 seconds to one-fourth its original size.
- Because many containers are shipped back to their originating country empty after goods have been unloaded, the Cargoshell will reduce the number of trips a ship, truck, or plane must make.

- The Cargoshell has a roll-up door rather than one that has to be opened outward, so containers can be placed closer together and thus more can be loaded on a ship.
- Because the Cargoshell is made of composite material rather than steel, manufacture of the Cargoshell produces only one-third the amount of CO_2, so it will reduce global warming.
- The Cargoshell weighs less, reducing the carbon footprint ships create when they transport cargo.
- The composite material provides insulation and better protects contents from fungi and insects.
- A large percentage of traditional containers end up in the sea each year. Because it is fitted with float bags, the Cargoshell can be retrieved if it falls off a ship, so it reduces ocean pollution and financial losses.

---

many business decisions. Although firms that choose to remain at home only have to worry about local regulations, global marketers must understand more complex political issues that can affect how they are allowed to do business around the world.

American Laws

Laws in the United States governing business have two purposes. Some, such as the Sherman Antitrust Act and the Wheeler–Lea Act, make sure that businesses compete fairly with each other. Others, such as the Food and Drug Act and the Consumer Products Safety Commission Act, make sure that businesses don't take advantage of consumers. Although some businesspeople argue that excessive legislation only limits competition, others say that laws ultimately help firms because they maintain a level playing field for businesses and support troubled industries.

As world trade increases and problems with defective imports continue, it is likely that new regulations will be created to address the problems. So far, the United States has signed safety agreements with China that require that Chinese producers must register with the Chinese government, that China will inspect food and feed exports to the United States, and that the two countries will notify each other of public health risks they discover.[16] Still, China continues to find problems in its domestic food production, many revolving around the addition of melamine, a chemical that causes kidney stones and kidney failure, to dairy products. In response, China has tightened regulations and is cooperating with U.S. officials to increase inspections of producers and exporters. In 2009 China executed a farmer and a milk salesman for producing and distributing milk tainted with melamine.[17]

Table 3.3 lists some of the major federal laws that protect and preserve the rights of U.S. consumers and businesses. Federal and state governments have created a host of regulatory agencies—government bodies that monitor business activities and enforce laws. Table 3.4 lists some of the agencies whose actions affect marketing activities.

Sometimes firms learn the hard way that government watchdog activities can put a stop to their Marketing Plans. The Federal Trade Commission (FTC), for example, recently cried foul over KFC ads claiming that

Verizon hopes to expand its market by launching communications services that span geographic regions.

Table 3.3 | Significant American Legislation Relevant to Marketers

Law	Purpose
Sherman Antitrust Act (1890)	Developed to eliminate monopolies and to guarantee free competition. Prohibits exclusive territories (if they restrict competition), price fixing, and predatory pricing.
Food and Drug Act (1906)	Prohibits harmful practices in the production of food and drugs.
Clayton Act (1914)	Prohibits tying contracts that require a dealer to take other products in the seller's line. Prohibits exclusive dealing if it restricts competition.
Federal Trade Commission Act (FTC) (1914)	Created the Federal Trade Commission to monitor unfair practices.
Robinson–Patman Act (1936)	Prohibits price discrimination (offering different prices to competing wholesalers or retailers) unless cost-justified.
Wheeler–Lea Amendment to FTC Act (1938)	Revised the FTC Act. Makes deceptive and misleading advertising illegal.
Lanham Trademark Act (1946)	Protects and regulates brand names and trademarks.
Fair Packaging and Labeling Act (1966)	Ensures that product packages are labeled honestly.
National Traffic and Motor Vehicle Safety Act (1966)	Sets automobile and tire safety standards.
Cigarette Labeling Act (1966)	Requires health warnings on cigarettes.
Child Protection Act (1966)	Bans dangerous products children use.
Child Protection and Toy Safety Act (1969)	Sets standards for child-resistant packaging.
Consumer Credit Protection Act (1968)	Protects consumers by requiring full disclosure of credit and loan terms and rates.
Fair Credit Reporting Act (1970)	Regulates the use of consumer credit reporting.
Consumer Products Safety Commission Act (1972)	Created the Consumer Product Safety Commission to monitor and recall unsafe products. Sets product safety standards.
Magnuson–Moss Consumer Product Warranty Act (1975)	Regulates warranties.
Children's Television Act (1990)	Limits the amount of television commercials aired on children's programs.
Nutrition Labeling and Education Act (1990)	Requires that new food labeling requirements be set by the Food and Drug Administration.
National Do Not Call Registry (2003)	Established by the Federal Trade Commission to allow consumers to limit number of telemarketing calls they receive.
Controlling the *Assault* of *Non-Solicited Pornography And Marketing* Act of 2003 (CAN–SPAM)	While it makes spam legal, the CAN–SPAM Act regulates commercial e-mail and makes misleading e-mail illegal.
Family Smoking and Prevention and Tobacco Control Act of 2009	Bans candy and fruit-flavored cigarettes.
Credit CARD Accountability, Responsibility, and Disclosure Act of 2009	Bans unfair rate increases, prevents unfair fee traps, requires disclosures be in plain language, and protects students and young people.

"Two KFC breasts have less fat than a BK Whopper." The FTC said that although two fried chicken breasts have slightly less total fat and saturated fat than a Whopper, they also have more than three times the trans fat and cholesterol, more than twice the sodium, and more calories. The FTC also said the company made false claims that its fried chicken is compatible with certain popular weight-loss programs, and it ordered KFC not to run these ads or others making similar claims about the nutritional value, weight-loss benefits, or other health benefits of its chicken products and meals.

Table 3.4 | U.S. Regulatory Agencies and Responsibilities

Regulatory Agency	Responsibilities
Consumer Product Safety Commission (CPSC)	Protects the public from potentially hazardous products. Through regulation and testing programs, the CPSC helps firms make sure their products won't harm customers.
Environmental Protection Agency (EPA)	Develops and enforces regulations aimed at protecting the environment. Such regulations have a major impact on the materials and processes that manufacturers use in their products and thus on the ability of companies to develop products.
Federal Communications Commission (FCC)	Regulates telephone, radio, and television. FCC regulations directly affect the marketing activities of companies in the communications industries, and they have an indirect effect on all firms that use broadcast media for marketing communications.
Federal Trade Commission (FTC)	Enforces laws against deceptive advertising and product labeling regulations. Marketers must constantly keep abreast of changes in FTC regulations to avoid costly fines.
Food and Drug Administration (FDA)	Enforces laws and regulations on foods, drugs, cosmetics, and veterinary products. Marketers of pharmaceuticals, over-the-counter medicines, and a variety of other products must get FDA approval before they can introduce products to the market.
Interstate Commerce Commission (ICC)	Regulates interstate bus, truck, rail, and water operations. The ability of a firm to efficiently move products to its customers depends on ICC policies and regulations.

Political Constraints on Trade

Global firms know that the political actions a government takes can drastically affect their business operations. At the extreme, of course, when two countries go to war the business environment changes dramatically. Sometimes it's consumers and not governments that disrupt trade in global markets. This was the case when the United States invaded Afghanistan in 2001 and sent troops to Iraq a few years later, and more recently when a Danish newspaper printed cartoons that highly offended Muslims around the globe. In such times, it's common for symbols of a country's culture, like McDonald's Golden Arches, to be the first target of boycotts, demonstrations, vandalism, and in some cases destruction.

Short of war, a country may impose *economic sanctions* that prohibit trade with another country (as the United States has done with several countries, including Cuba and North Korea), so access to some markets may be cut off. For example, trying to stop Iran's alleged efforts to build nuclear weapons, the U.S. government imposed financial and economic sanctions against that country, some as recently as October 2007. These rules prevented any American from engaging in financial transactions with the Revolutionary Guards or any of their many associated businesses and with three state-owned banks.[18] The revelation in late 2009 that Iran was producing uranium and a later announcement by President Ahmadinejad in 2010 that Iran had the capacity to produce weapons-grade nuclear fuel brought a call for the United Nations to impose even greater sanctions against Iran.[19]

nationalization
When a domestic government reimburses a foreign company (often not for the full value) for its assets after taking it over.

expropriation
When a domestic government seizes a foreign company's assets without any reimbursement.

In some situations, internal pressures may prompt the government to take over the operations of foreign companies that do business within its borders. **Nationalization** occurs when the domestic government reimburses a foreign company (often not for the full value) for its assets after taking it over. **Expropriation** is when a domestic government seizes a foreign company's assets without any reimbursement (and that firm is just out of luck). To keep track of the level of political stability or instability in foreign countries, firms often engage in formal or informal analyses of the potential political risk in various countries, or hire specialized consulting firms to do this for them.

Regulatory Constraints on Trade

Governments and economic communities regulate what products are allowed in the country, what products should be made of, and what claims marketers can make about them. For example, when the blockbuster hit movie *Avatar* drew long lines in China, government officials replaced the movie in many theaters with a locally produced film on Confucius. Although the reasons for the switch were not clear, many suspected it was because of the plot's similarity to the actions of local property developers who evict ordinary Chinese from their homes to make way for new buildings.[20]

Other regulations ensure that the host country gets a piece of the action. **Local content rules** are a form of protectionism that stipulates a certain proportion of a product must consist of components supplied by industries in the host country or economic community. For example, under NAFTA rules, cars must have 62.5 percent of their components made in North America to be able to enter Mexico and Canada duty-free. That explains why Asian automakers such as Toyota, Hyundai, and Kia have already beefed up their local presence by opening manufacturing plants in the United States and hiring local workers to run them.

local content rules
A form of protectionism stipulating that a certain proportion of a product must consist of components supplied by industries in the host country or economic community.

Human Rights Issues

Some governments and companies are vigilant about denying business opportunities to countries that mistreat their citizens. They are concerned about conducting trade with local firms that exploit their workers or that keep costs down by employing children or prisoners for slave wages. The **U.S. Generalized System of Preferences (GSP)** is a program Congress established to promote economic growth in the developing world. GSP regulations allow developing countries to export goods duty-free to the United States. The catch is that each country must constantly demonstrate that it is making progress toward improving the rights of its workers.[21]

U.S. Generalized System of Preferences (GSP)
A program to promote economic growth in developing countries by allowing duty-free entry of goods into the U.S.

On the other side of the coin, the low wages they can pay to local workers often entice U.S. firms to expand their operations overseas. Although they provide needed jobs, some companies have been criticized for exploiting workers when they pay wages that fall below local poverty levels, for damaging the environment, or for selling poorly made or unsafe items to consumers. For example, in 2004 Gap Inc. conceded that working conditions were far from perfect at many of the 3,000 overseas factories that make its clothing. The company also observed that the situation is even worse in many of the overseas factories that *don't* earn its business—about 90 percent of foreign manufacturers who apply for a Gap contract fail the retailer's initial evaluation.[22] In 2007, Gap again faced disturbing publicity when news reports surfaced that an Indian company forced children as young as 10 years old to work 16 hours a day for no pay to hand-embroider decorations on blouses for GapKids. Gap, embarrassed by the reports, established a grant of $200,000 to improve working conditions, pay back wages, and provide an education for the children.[23] Today, Gap takes social responsibility seriously. For example, the company helps homeless people in Madagascar through its partnership with Merci, a furniture and fashion boutique in Paris that offers designer items from around the world.[24]

The Sociocultural Environment

The *sociocultural environment* refers to the characteristics of the society, the people who live in that society, and the culture that reflects the values and beliefs of the society. Whether at home or in global markets, marketers need to understand and adapt to the customs, characteristics, and practices of its citizens. Basic beliefs about cultural priorities, such as the role of family or proper relations between the sexes, affect people's responses to products and promotional messages in any market.

Demographics

The first step toward understanding the characteristics of a society is to look at its **demographics**. These are statistics that measure observable aspects of a population, such as population size, age, gender, ethnic group, income, education, occupation, and family structure. The information demographic studies reveal is of great value to marketers when they

demographics
Statistics that measure observable aspects of a population, including size, age, gender, ethnic group, income, education, occupation, and family structure.

want to predict the size of markets for many products, from home mortgages to brooms and can openers. We'll talk more about how demographic factors impact marketing strategies in Chapter 7.

Values

More than 8.2 million women read *Cosmopolitan* in 28 different languages—even though, because of local norms about modesty, some of them have to hide the magazine from their husbands. Adapting the *Cosmo* credo of "Fun, Fearless, Female" in all these places gets a bit tricky. Different cultures emphasize varying belief systems that define what it means to be female, feminine, or appealing—and what is considered appropriate to see in print on these matters. For example, in China *Cosmo* can't even mention sex at all, so local editors replace spicy articles with stories about youthful dedication. Ironically, there isn't much down-and-dirty material in the Swedish edition either—but for the opposite reason. The culture is so open about this topic that it doesn't grab readers' attention the way it would in the United States.[25]

cultural values
A society's deeply held beliefs about right and wrong ways to live.

As this example shows, every society has a set of **cultural values**, or deeply held beliefs about right and wrong ways to live, that it imparts to its members.[26] Those beliefs influence virtually every aspect of our lives, even the way we mark the time we live them. For example, for most Americans *punctuality* is a core value; indeed, business leaders often proclaim that "Time is money." For countries in Latin America and other parts of the world, this is not at all true. If you schedule a business meeting at 10:00, you can be assured most people will not arrive until around 10:30—or later.

These differences in values often explain why marketing efforts that are a big hit in one country can flop in another. Italian housewives spend about five times as many hours per week as do their American counterparts on household chores. On average they wash their kitchen and bathroom floors at least four times a week, and they typically iron everything they wash, including socks! This dedication (obsession?) should make them perfect customers for cleaning products—but when Unilever launched an all-purpose spray cleaner there, the product flopped. And when Procter & Gamble tested its top-selling Swiffer Wet mop, which eliminates the need for a clunky bucket of water, the product bombed so badly in Italy that P&G took it off the market. These successful consumer-products companies failed to realize that the benefit of labor-saving convenience is a huge turnoff to Italian women who want products that are tough cleaners, not timesavers. Unilever had to make big adjustments in order to clean up in the Italian market—including making the bottles 50 percent bigger because Italians clean so frequently.[27]

collectivist cultures
Cultures in which people subordinate their personal goals to those of a stable community.

individualist cultures
Cultures in which people tend to attach more importance to personal goals than to those of the larger community.

One important dimension on which cultures differ is their emphasis on collectivism versus individualism. In **collectivist cultures**, such as those we find in Venezuela, Pakistan, Taiwan, Thailand, Turkey, Greece, and Portugal, people tend to subordinate their personal goals to those of a stable community. In contrast, consumers in **individualist cultures**, such as the United States, Australia, Great Britain, Canada, and the Netherlands, tend to attach more importance to personal goals, and people are more likely to change memberships when the demands of the group become too costly.[28] This difference can be a big deal to marketers who appeal to one extreme or the other—try selling a garment that is "sure to make you stand out" to consumers who would much prefer to "fit in."

Social Norms

social norms
Specific rules dictating what is right or wrong, acceptable or unacceptable.

Values are general ideas about good and bad behaviors. From these values flow **social norms**, or specific rules that dictate what is right or wrong, acceptable or unacceptable within a society. Social norms indicate what ways to dress, how to speak, what to eat (and how to eat), and how to behave.

A meal of dog may be taboo in the United States, whereas Hindus would shun a steak, and Muslims avoid pork products. A custom dictates the appropriate hour at which the meal should be served—many Europeans, Middle Easterners, and Latin Americans do not begin dinner until around 9:00 or later, and they are amused by American visitors whose stomachs growl by 7:00. Customs tell us how to eat the meal, including such details as the utensils, table etiquette, and even the appropriate apparel for dinnertime (no thongs at the dinner table!).

Conflicting customs can be a problem when U.S. marketers try to conduct business in other countries where executives have different ideas about what is proper or expected. These difficulties even include body language; people in Latin countries tend to stand much closer to each other than do Americans, and they will be insulted if their counterpart tries to stand farther away. In many countries, even casual friends greet each other with a kiss (or two) on the cheek. In the United States, one should only kiss a person of the opposite sex, and one kiss only, please. In Spain and other parts of Europe, kissing includes a kiss on each cheek for both people of the same and the opposite sex, while in the Middle East, unless a very special friend, it is unacceptable for a man to kiss a woman or a woman to kiss a man. Instead it is the norm to see two men or two women holding hands or walking down the street with their arms entwined.

Language

The language barrier is one obvious problem that confronts marketers who wish to break into foreign markets. Travelers abroad commonly encounter signs in tortured English such as a note to guests at a Tokyo hotel that said, "You are invited to take advantage of the chambermaid," a notice at a hotel in Acapulco that proclaimed "The manager has personally passed all the water served here," or a dry cleaner in Majorca that urged passing customers to "drop your pants here for best results."

These translation snafus are not just embarrassing. They can affect product labeling and usage instructions, advertising, and personal selling. It's vital for marketers to work with local people who understand the subtleties of language to avoid confusion. For example, the meaning of a brand name—one of the most important signals a marketer can send about the character and quality of a product—can get mangled as it travels around the world. Local product names often raise eyebrows to visiting Americans who may be surprised to stumble on a Japanese coffee creamer called Creap, a Mexican bread named Bimbo, or a Scandinavian product that unfreezes car locks called Super Piss.[29]

AMERICANO, MAS COM UM TOQUE DE MÉXICO.

Marketers often "borrow" imagery from other cultures to communicate with local customers. This ad is for a Mexican restaurant in Brazil.

Ethnocentrism

Ethnocentrism refers to the belief that one's own norms and the products made in one's country are superior. This bias occurs because we tend to use our own cultural frame of reference to judge other people.

Sometimes a willingness to try products made elsewhere comes slowly. For example, the French tend to be a bit finicky about their cuisine, and they evaluate food products from other countries critically. However, the upscale British department store Marks & Spencer is making inroads in France by selling English-style sandwiches like egg and watercress on whole wheat bread and ethnic dishes such as chicken tikka masala. Young office workers view these as convenience foods, and they are less expensive than the traditional French loaf split down the middle and lathered with butter and ham or Camembert cheese.

ethnocentrism
The tendency to prefer products or people of one's own culture.

When Is a Bribe Not a Bribe? Ethical Issues for Global Business

Whether the organization operates in one's own home market or in a global environment, marketers face ethical dilemmas on an almost daily basis. Thus, understanding the environment where you do business means you need to stay on top of the ethical values and norms of the business culture in the marketplace—often not an easy task. Indeed, there are vast differences in what people consider ethical business behavior around the world.

Business leaders who have experienced a sheltered life in American companies are often shocked to find that they cannot expect the same ethical standards of others in the global community. Westerners, for example, are often painfully honest. If an American business contact cannot meet a deadline or attend a meeting or provide the needed services, he will normally say so. In other cultures the answer, even if untrue, will always be "yes." Westerners see such dishonest answers as unethical, but in some areas of the world, people just believe saying "no" to any request is extremely rude—even if there's no way they intend to honor the request.

In many least developed and developing countries, salaries for mid-level people are sadly very low; the economy runs on a system we would call blatant bribery. Some of these "payments" are only petty corruption and the "favors" are inconsequential, while others may involve high-level government or business officials and can have devastating consequences. If you need to park your car or your delivery truck illegally where there is no parking space, you give a little money to the policeman. If the shopkeeper wants the policeman to watch out for his store, he gives the policeman a shirt from his stock once in a while. If an importer wants to get his merchandise out of customs before it spoils, he pays off the government worker who can hold up his shipment for weeks. And if someone wants the contract to build a new building or wants an unsafe building to pass inspection—well, you get the idea.

Bribery occurs when someone voluntarily offers payment to get an illegal advantage. **Extortion** occurs when someone in authority extracts payment under duress. Some businesspeople give bribes to speed up required work, secure a contract, or avoid having a contract cancelled. Such payments are a way of life in many countries because many people consider them as natural as giving a waiter a tip for good service. The Foreign Corrupt Practices Act of 1977 (FCPA), however, puts U.S. businesses at a disadvantage because it bars them from paying bribes to sell overseas. The FCPA does, however, allow payments for "routine governmental action . . . such as obtaining permits, licenses, or other official documents; processing governmental papers, such as visas and work orders; [and] providing police protection." But FCPA does not permit payment to influence "any decision by a foreign official to award new business or to continue business with a particular party."[30] So under U.S. rules bribes are out.

Transparency International, an anticorruption organization, publishes an annual survey, the *Bribe Payers Index,* that measures the propensity of firms from 30 various countries to pay bribes. Table 3.5 provides the results of a recent survey and shows that even among developed countries, there is great variation in the frequency of this practice.

bribery
When someone voluntarily offers payment to get an illegal advantage.

extortion
When someone in authority extracts payment under duress.

Table 3.5 | The Transparency International 2008 *Bribe Payers Index*: Some Winners and Some Losers

2008 Country Rank	Country	2008 BPI Score*
1	Belgium	8.8
1	Canada	8.8
3	Netherlands	8.7
3	Switzerland	8.7
5	Germany	8.6
5	United Kingdom	8.6
5	Japan	8.6
9	United States	8.1
19	India	6.8
20	Mexico	6.6
21	China	6.5

*A lower score such as those for Mexico and China indicates a higher propensity to pay bribes.

Source: Adapted from Transparency International, "Bribe Payers Index 2008,"
http://www.transparency.org/news_room/latest_news/press_releases/2008/bpi_2008 (Accessed January 18, 2010).

Ripped from the Headlines

Ethical/Sustainable Decisions in the Real World

Retailers are constantly faced with the problem of returned merchandise. When a consumer returns a shirt or a pair of shoes or even a designer gown, the garment is often damaged and cannot be resold. The store then has to figure out what to do with the merchandise. These decisions are especially difficult for global firms that must comply with the varying ethical values of many different countries. Executives of a large Swedish fashion retail chain with stores in 35 countries were faced with this problem. After considering the alternatives, they decided that they should destroy the returned and damaged clothing. Employees at the firm's retail outlets around the globe were instructed to slash the garments, thus making them unwearable, and place them in the garbage. When the practice was made known, some consumer advocates complained that the clothing should be given to the poor. They argued that it was callous of the firm to destroy clothing when many people around the globe could use it. If you were a marketer with this firm, what would you do?

> **ETHICS CHECK:** ↘
> Find out what other students taking this course **would do** and **why** on www**.mypearsonmarketinglab.com**

> Would you destroy clothing and other products that had been worn and then returned?
>
> ☐YES ☐NO

4

OBJECTIVE

Explain some of the strategies and tactics that a firm can use to enter global markets.
(pp. 87–92)

Is the World Flat or Not? How "Global" Should a Global Marketing Strategy Be?

Going global is not a simple task. Even a popular television show may have to make "adjustments" as it travels across borders. Consider, for example, the incredibly popular show *American Idol*, which isn't really American at all—the concept originated in the United Kingdom. More than 100 million people around the globe tune into over 20 local versions of the *Idol* show, but sometimes the format has to be fine-tuned:[31]

- When a South African contestant was bluntly told to work on her clothes and her appearance, she broke down and told the judges she was too poor to afford nicer things. The station was swamped with calls from angry viewers who offered to donate clothing.

- Because the word "idol" has Hitler-like connotations for Germans, producers there had to change the show's title to *Germany Seeks the Superstar*. Similarly, "idol" is sacrilegious in Arabic countries and can't be used in those markets.

- A riot broke out in Beirut when a Lebanese contestant was voted out in favor of a Jordanian woman—viewers accused the producers of fixing the show for political reasons.

Of course it isn't only U.S. companies that seek to "go global." Gold medal–winning gymnast Li Ning is a hero in China. Li Ning, the company, is also the largest Chinese manufacturer of athletic shoes and sports apparel with 6,300 stores in the home market. Now Li Ning wants to take on Nike and Adidas and become a global brand.[32] But if a firm decides to expand beyond its home country, it must make important decisions about how to structure its business and whether to adapt its product marketing strategy to accommodate local needs. First, the company must decide on the level of its commitment, which dictates the type of entry strategy it will use. Is the firm better off to simply export to another country, to partner with another firm, or to go it alone in the foreign market? It also has to make specific decisions about the marketing mix for a particular product. In this final section, we'll consider issues related to these two crucial aspects of global strategy: decisions at the company level and the product level.

Company-Level Decisions: The Market Entry Strategy

Just like a romantic relationship, a firm must determine the level of commitment it is willing to make to operate in another country. This commitment ranges from casual involvement to a full-scale "marriage." At one extreme, the firm simply exports its products, while at the other extreme it directly invests in another country by buying a foreign subsidiary or opening its own stores or manufacturing facility. This decision about the extent of commitment entails a trade-off between *control* and *risk*. Direct involvement gives the firm more control over what happens in the country, but its risk also increases if the operation is not successful.

Let's review four globalization strategies representing increased levels of involvement: exporting, contractual arrangements, strategic alliances, and direct investment. Table 3.6 summarizes these options.

Exporting

If a firm chooses to export, it must decide whether it will attempt to sell its products on its own or rely on intermediaries to represent it in the target country. These specialists, or **export merchants**, understand the local market and can find buyers and negotiate terms. An exporting strategy allows a firm to sell its products in global markets and cushions it against downturns in its domestic market. Because the firm actually makes the products at home, it is able to maintain control over design and production decisions.

Robert Chatwani

APPLYING ▼ Exporting

Robert sees huge potential for locally-made goods to find markets around the world. He wants the new eBay service to be an intermediary in this process. ➡

Table 3.6 | Market Entry Strategies

Strategy	Exporting Strategy	Contractual Agreements		Strategic Alliances	Direct Investment
Level of Risk	Low	Medium		Medium	High
Level of Control	Low	Medium		Medium	High
Options	Sell on its own	Licensing	Franchising	Joint venture where firm and local partner pool their resources	Complete ownership often through buying a local company
	Rely on export merchants	License a local firm to produce the product	A local firm adopts your entire business model		
Advantages	Low investment so lowest risk of financial loss	Avoid barriers to entry	Local franchisee avoids barriers to entry	Easy access to new markets	Maximum freedom and control
	Can control quality of product	Limit financial investment and thus risk	Limit financial investment and risk	Preferential treatment by governments and other entities	Avoid import restrictions
	Avoid difficulties of producing some products in other countries				
Disadvantages	May limit growth opportunities	Lose control over how product is produced and marketed, which could tarnish company and brand image	Franchisee may not use the same quality ingredients or procedures, thus damaging brand image	High level of financial risk	Highest level of commitment and financial risk
	Perceived as a "foreign" product	Potential unauthorized use of formulas, designs or other intellectual property			Potential for nationalization or expropriation if government is unstable

Choosing a market-entry strategy is a critical decision for companies that want to go global. Decisions vary in terms of risk and control.

Contractual Agreements

The next level of commitment a firm can make to a foreign market is a contractual agreement with a company in that country to conduct some or all of its business there. These agreements take several forms. Two of the most common are licensing and franchising:

1. In a **licensing agreement**, a firm (the *licensor*) gives another firm (the *licensee*) the right to produce and market its product in a specific country or region in return for royalties on goods sold. Because the licensee produces the product in its home market, it can avoid many of the barriers to entry that the licensor would have encountered. However, the licensor also loses control over how the product is produced and marketed, so if the licensee does a poor job this may tarnish the company's reputation. Often licensors must provide the licensee with its formulas, designs or other intellectual property, thus risking unauthorized use for production of copied products. Licensors also have to accept the possibility that local licensees will alter its product to suit local tastes. That's what's happened with America's loveable *Sesame Street* characters. The show now is licensed in many countries, including India, France, Japan, and South Africa with some editorial changes that include new characters with names like Nac, Khokha, and Kami.

2. **Franchising** is a form of licensing that gives the franchisee the right to adopt an entire way of doing business in the host country. Again, there is a risk to the parent company if the *franchisee* does not use the same-quality ingredients or procedures, so firms monitor these operations carefully. McDonald's, perhaps the best known of all franchises, has over 30,000 restaurants that serve 52 million people in 119 countries.[33] In India, where Hindus do not eat beef, all McDonald's have vegetarian and nonvegetarian burger-cooking lines and offer customers vegetarian specialties such as Pizza McPuff and McAloo Tikki (a spiced-potato burger).[34] However, don't make the mistake of thinking that the only kind of franchise is a fast-food restaurant! The International Franchise Association estimates that there are more than 3,000 franchise systems in the United States that offer business opportunities from pet care to tutoring services.[35] These U.S. franchising companies, including 7-Eleven, Century 21, Fuddruckers, and Chili's, operate thousands of outlets internationally.

Strategic Alliances

Firms that choose to develop an even deeper commitment to a foreign market enter a **strategic alliance** with one or more domestic firms in the target country. These relationships often take the form of a **joint venture**: Two or more firms create a new entity to allow the partners to pool their resources for common goals. Strategic alliances also allow companies easy access to new markets, especially because these partnerships often bring with them preferential treatment in the partner's home country. For example, General Motors has an alliance with the Chinese firm SAIC. In 2009, GM sold 1.83 million cars in China and projects sales of over 2 million vehicles annually.[36]

Of course, joint ventures are not always successful. In India, where import taxes can be as high as 40 percent and retail shop rental rates are high, international marketers find their activities simply cannot be profitable. Thus, over a dozen global brands, including GAS, Replay, and the Etam women's apparel chain have ended their joint venture or franchisee relationships in that country.[37]

Direct Investment

An even deeper level of commitment occurs when a firm expands internationally through ownership, often when it buys a business in the host country outright. Instead of starting from scratch in its quest to become multinational, buying part or all of a domestic firm allows

---

export merchants
Intermediaries a firm uses to represent it in other countries.

licensing agreement
An agreement in which one firm gives another firm the right to produce and market its product in a specific country or region in return for royalties.

franchising
A form of licensing involving the right to adapt an entire system of doing business.

strategic alliance
Relationship developed between a firm seeking a deeper commitment to a foreign market and a domestic firm in the target country.

joint venture
A strategic alliance in which a new entity owned by two or more firms allows the partners to pool their resources for common goals.

a foreign firm to take advantage of a domestic company's political savvy and market position in the host country.

Sometimes firms have no option other than to invest directly in a local business. In most countries, McDonald's purchases its lettuce and pickles from local farms. When the company entered Russia in 1990, there were no private businesses to supply the raw ingredients for its burgers. McDonald's had to build its own facility, the McComplex, outside Moscow. As the country's economy booms, however, domestic businesses develop to take up the slack. Today, McDonald's purchases 80 percent of its ingredients from local farmers, some of whom have become millionaires as a result.[38]

Product-Level Decisions: The Marketing Mix Strategy

In addition to "big picture" decisions about how a company will operate in other countries, managers must decide how to market their product in each country. They may need to modify the famous Four Ps—product, price, promotion, and place—to suit local conditions. To what extent will the company need to adapt its marketing communications to the specific styles and tastes of each local market? Will the same product appeal to people there? Will it have to be priced differently? And, of course, how does the company get the product into people's hands? Let's consider each of these questions in turn.

Standardization Versus Localization

The executive in charge of giant VF Corporation's overseas operations recently observed that when most American brands decide to branch out to other countries, they "tend to take every strategy used in their home market—products, pricing, marketing—and apply it in the same way." VF, which owns several fashion brands including Tommy Hilfiger and Nautica, discovered that this doesn't necessarily work very well because local tastes can differ so dramatically. On the other hand, Spanish fashion retailer Zara, which prides itself on being able to design, manufacture, and deliver new clothing designs to its stores within just two weeks, provides trendy consumers the same designs worldwide.

So which strategy is right? Advocates of standardization argue that the world has become so small that basic needs and wants are the same everywhere. A focus on the similarities among cultures certainly is appealing. After all, if a firm didn't have to make any changes to its marketing strategy to compete in foreign countries, it would realize large economies of scale because it could spread the costs of product development and promotional materials over many markets. Widespread, consistent exposure also helps create a global brand because it forges a strong, unified image all over the world—Coca-Cola signs are visible on billboards in London and on metal roofs deep in the forests of Thailand.

In contrast, those in favor of localization feel that the world is not *that* small; you need to tailor products and promotional messages to local environments. These marketers feel that each culture is unique, with a distinctive set of behavioral and personality characteristics. For example, Egyptians like their beverages very sweet, but alcoholic beverages are prohibited for Muslims. When the Al Ahram Beverage Company introduced its Farouz brand beer alternative—a super-sweet nonalcoholic malt beverage—the local firm enjoyed surprising success. In less than five years, Farouz captured a 12 percent market share from giants Coke and Pepsi.

To P or Not to P: Tweak the Marketing Mix

Once a firm decides whether it will adopt standardization or a localization strategy, it is time to plan for the Four Ps.

Product Decisions

MTV is betting its hit show *Jersey Shore*, that chronicles the (uniquely American?) drunken antics of a group of tanned "guidos" during a summer in New Jersey, will become a hit among young people the world over who have never had the experience of "going down the shore." The network exported the show to 30 countries after it became a runaway hit in the U.S. One overseas promotion boasts, "In the show that's got America talking . . . prepare to meet a whole new kind of crazy." Another advertising poster pretty much sums up why MTV believes it can export the show to many different cultures: "Muscles + gel + tanning bed = sex."[39]

A firm has three choices when it decides on a product strategy:

1. Sell the same product in the new market.

2. Modify it for that market.

3. Develop a brand-new product to sell there.

A **straight extension strategy** retains the same product for domestic and foreign markets. For generations, proper etiquette in Japan was for girls to bow and never raise their eyes to a man.[40] However, the new generation of Japanese women wants to look straight at you, showing their eyes and eyelashes. Japanese eyelashes are very short, so they have to be curled to show. To meet this need, L'Oréal introduced its Maybelline brand Wonder Curl that dramatically thickens and curls lashes as a woman applies it. The launch was such a success in Japan that local television news showed Japanese customers standing in line to buy the product.

A **product adaptation strategy** recognizes that in many cases people in different cultures do have strong and different product preferences. Sometimes these differences can be subtle yet important. In India, Pizza Hut offer pizzas with traditional toppings such as paneer and tikka.[41] Many people in Argentina pronounce "Pepsi" as "Pesci" so the company adapted to the local dialect by formally changing its name there.[42] Kraft had a tough time for years persuading Chinese consumers to eat its Oreo cookies. People thought they were too sweet and they were too expensive. The package was too big for small Chinese families. Kraft International embraced a product adaptation strategy as it reformulated the snack to be less sugary and cheaper. As a result Oreos now account for about 7% of the $1.6 billion Chinese cookie market.[43]

A **product invention strategy** means a company develops a new product as it expands to foreign markets. For example, in India Coca-Cola and Pepsi now offer their versions of a traditional lemonade, Nimbu Panni.[44] In some cases, a product invention strategy takes the form of **backward invention**. For example, there are still nearly one and a half billion people on the earth without electricity, primarily in Africa, Asia, and the Middle East. This provides a challenge for firms to develop products such as refrigerators and air conditioning systems that can operate without electric power.[45]

Promotion Decisions

Marketers must also decide whether it's necessary to modify how they speak to consumers in a foreign market. Some firms endorse the idea that the same message will appeal to everyone around the world, while others feel the need to customize it. The 2006 World Cup was broadcast in 189 countries to one of the biggest global television audiences ever. This mega-event illustrates how different marketers make different decisions—even when they create ads that run during the same game. MasterCard ran ads that appeared in 39 countries, so its ad agency came up with a spot called "Fever," in which 100-odd cheering fans from 30 countries appear. There's no dialogue, so it works in any language. At the end, the words, "Football fever. Priceless" appeared under the MasterCard logo.[46] In 2009, Coke launched its first global ad campaign with the tagline "Open Happiness." More recently, Sprite followed with

Local customs provide opportunities for product invention strategies. Most American consumers would not be familiar with this Indian product, cooling hair oil.

straight extension strategy
Product strategy in which a firm offers the same product in both domestic and foreign markets.

product adaptation strategy
Product strategy in which a firm offers a similar but modified product in foreign markets.

product invention strategy
Product strategy in which a firm develops a new product for foreign markets.

backward invention strategy
Product strategy in which a firm develops a less advanced product to serve the needs of people living in countries without electricity or other elements of a developed infrastructure.

its global "The Spark" ad campaign (along with a new global package) in Europe, North America, Africa, and Asia.[47]

Price Decisions

It's often more expensive to manufacture a product in a foreign market than at home. This is because there are higher costs stemming from transportation, tariffs, differences in currency exchange rates, and the need to source local materials. To ease the financial burden of tariffs on companies that import goods, some countries have established **free trade zones**. These are designated areas where foreign companies can warehouse goods without paying taxes or customs duties until they move the goods into the marketplace.

One danger of pricing too high is that competitors will find ways to offer their product at a lower price, even if they do so illegally. **Gray market goods** are items that are imported without the consent of the trademark holder. While gray market goods are not counterfeit, they may be different from authorized products in warranty coverage and compliance with local regulatory requirements. The Internet offers exceptional opportunities for marketers of gray market goods from toothpaste to textbooks. But, as the saying goes, "If it seems too good to be true, it probably is." Consumers may be disappointed when they find gray market goods may not be of the same quality, so the deal they got may not look as good after they take delivery.

Another unethical and often illegal practice is **dumping**, in which a company prices its products lower than it offers them at home. This removes excess supply from home markets and keeps prices up there. In 2009, even with the economic downturn, China speeded up its manufacture of steel products. With government subsidies of between 40 and 90 percent, companies dumped a lot of very low-priced steel on the U.S. market. In response, U.S. steelmakers filed complaints against China because they claimed that the dumping threatened the livelihoods of American workers.[48] Later in the year, China in retaliation conducted its own subsidy and dumping investigations and imposed import duties on U.S. steel products based on allegations of dumping by the U.S. firms.[49]

Distribution Decisions

Getting your product to consumers in a remote location can be quite a challenge. It's essential for a firm to establish a reliable distribution system if it's going to succeed in a foreign market. Marketers used to dealing with a handful of large wholesalers or retailers in their domestic market may have to rely instead on thousands of small "mom-and-pop" stores or distributors, some of whom transport goods to remote rural areas on oxcarts, wheelbarrows, or bicycles. In least developed countries, marketers may run into problems when they want to package, refrigerate, or store goods for long periods.

Even the retailing giant Walmart occasionally stumbles when it expands to new markets. The company joined the ranks of multinationals like Nokia, Nestlé, and Google that have failed to adjust to the tastes of South Korean consumers. Walmart (as well as European rival Carrefour) stuck to Western marketing strategies that concentrated on dry goods from electronics to clothing. It failed to figure out in time that local rivals like E-Mart and Lotte emphasize food and beverages that are more likely to attract South Koreans to large stores. Local customers also didn't take to a relatively sterile environment where products sell by the box; their competitors enticed shoppers with eye-catching displays and clerks who hawked their goods with megaphones and hand-clapping. Walmart bailed out of South Korea entirely in 2006.[50]

Now that you've learned about global marketing, read "Real People, Real Choices: How It Worked Out" to see which strategy Robert Chatwani of eBay selected.

---

free trade zones
Designated areas where foreign companies can warehouse goods without paying taxes or customs duties until they move the goods into the marketplace.

gray market goods
Items manufactured outside a country and then imported without the consent of the trademark holder.

dumping
A company tries to get a toehold in a foreign market by pricing its products lower than it offers them at home.

Here's my choice. . .

Real **People**, Real **Choices**

1 Option **2** Option **3** Option

*Why do you think
Robert chose option #3?*

How It Worked Out at eBay
The unit decided that the name of the new marketplace would be **WorldofGood.com**, an eBay Marketplace. They decided to launch the new business in two phases. Phase 1 was the launch of the **WorldofGood.com** Community (**http://community.worldofgood.com**), and Phase 2 was the launch of the e-commerce marketplace. Phase 1, the community, was designed to attract consumers interested in commerce as a force for social change. Phase 2 integrated both the community and commerce platforms into a single online shopping experience.

To learn the whole story, visit www.mypearsonmarketinglab.com.

Brand **YOU**!

Do what you love and love what you do.

It's a mantra for life. Explore what you love to do (and don't love to do) and how that can translate into your career in Chapter 3 of the Brand You supplement. You'll be surprised at the choices you have and how easily you'll be able to narrow down the direction that is best for you.

Objective Summary ➡ Key Terms ➡ Apply

CHAPTER 3
Study Map

1. Objective Summary (pp. 68–71)

Understand the big picture of international marketing and the decisions firms must make when they consider globalization.

The increasing amount of world trade—the flow of goods and services among countries—may take place through cash, credit payments, or countertrade. A decision to go global often comes when domestic market opportunities dwindle and the firm perceives a likelihood for success in foreign markets due to a competitive advantage. After a firm has decided to go global, they must consider which markets are most attractive, what market-entry strategy is best and how to best develop the marketing mix.

Key Terms

world trade, p. 69

countertrade, p. 69

2. Objective Summary (pp. 71–73)

Explain how both international organizations such as the World Trade Organization (WTO) and economic communities and individual country regulations facilitate and limit a firm's opportunities for globalization.

Established by the General Agreement on Tariffs and Trade (GATT) in 1984, the World Trade Organization with its 153 members seeks to create a single open world market where trade flows "freely, fairly, and predictably." Some governments, however, adopt policies of protectionism with rules designed to give home companies an advantage. Such policies may include trade quotas, embargoes, or tariffs that increase the costs of foreign goods. Many countries have banded together to form economic communities to promote free trade.

Key Terms

general Agreement on Tariffs and Trade (GATT), p. 72

world Trade Organization (WTO), p. 72

protectionism, p. 72

import quotas, p. 72

embargo, p. 72

tariffs, p. 72

economic communities, p. 72

3. Objective Summary (pp. 73–87)

Understand how factors in a firm's external business environment influence marketing strategies and outcomes in both domestic and global markets.

The economic environment refers to the economic health of a country that may be gauged by its gross domestic product and its economic infrastructure, its level of economic development, and its stage in the business cycle. Marketers use competitive intelligence to examine brand, product, and discretionary income competition in the microenvironment. They also consider the structure of the industry, that is competition in the macroenvironment. A country's political and legal environment includes laws and regulations that affect business. Marketers must understand any local political constraints, that is, the prospects for nationalization or expropriation of foreign holdings, regulations such as local content rules, and labor and human rights regulations. Because technology can affect every aspect of marketing, marketers must be knowledgeable about technological changes, often monitoring government and private research findings. Marketers also examine a country's sociocultural environment including demographics, values, social norms and customs, language, and ethnocentricity. The ethical environment in some countries can cause problems for

marketers if they do not understand the differences in the ethical perspective of such things such as honesty. In many least developed and developing countries, corruption is a major stumbling block for Western businesses. Bribery and extortion present ethical dilemmas for U.S. companies who must abide by the Foreign Corrupt Practices Act of 1977 (FCPA).

Key Terms

gross domestic product (GDP), p. 74

gross national product (GNP), p. 74

economic infrastructure, p. 75

level of economic development, p. 75

standard of living, p. 75

least developed country (LDC), p. 75

developing countries, p. 76

BRIC countries, p. 76

developed countries, p. 76

group of 8 (G8), p. 76

business cycle, p. 76

competitive intelligence (CI), p. 77

discretionary income, p. 78

product competition, p. 78

brand competition, p. 78

monopoly, p. 78

oligopoly, p. 79

monopolistic competition, p. 79

perfect competition, p. 79

patent, p. 79

nationalization, p. 82

expropriation, p. 82

local content rules, p. 83

U.S. Generalized System of Preferences (GSP), p. 83

demographics, p. 83

cultural values, p. 84

collectivist cultures, p. 84

individualist cultures, p. 84

social norms, p. 84

ethnocentrism, p. 85

bribery, p. 86

extortion, p. 86

4. Objective Summary (pp. 87–92)

Explain some of the strategies and tactics that a firm can use to enter global markets.

Different foreign-market-entry strategies represent varying levels of commitment for a firm. Exporting of goods entails little commitment but allows little control over how products are sold. Contractual agreements such as licensing or franchising allow greater control. With strategic alliances through joint ventures, commitment increases. Finally, the firm can choose to invest directly by buying an existing company or starting a foreign subsidiary in the host country. Firms that operate in two or more countries can choose to standardize their marketing strategies by using the same approach in all countries or choose to localize by adopting different strategies for each market. The firm needs to decide whether to sell an existing product, change an existing product, or develop a new product. In many cases, the promotional strategy, the pricing strategy, the distribution strategy and the product itself must be tailored to fit the needs of consumers in another country.

Key Terms

export merchants, p. 88
licensing agreement, p. 89

franchising, p. 89
strategic alliances, p. 89
joint venture, p. 89
straight extension strategy, p. 91
product adaptation strategy, p. 91
product invention strategy, p. 91
backward inventions, p. 91
free trade zones, p. 92
gray market goods, p. 92
dumping, p. 92

Chapter **Questions** and **Activities**

Questions: Test Your Knowledge

1. Describe the market conditions that influence a firm's decision to enter foreign markets.
2. Explain what world trade means. What is the role of the WTO and economic communities in encouraging free trade? What is protectionism? Explain import quotas, embargoes, and tariffs.
3. Explain how GDP, the categories of economic development, and the business cycle influence marketers' decisions in entering global markets. What are the BRIC countries? What is the Group of Eight (G8)?
4. Explain the types of competition marketers face: discretionary income competition, product competition, and brand competition.
5. What are a monopoly, an oligopoly, monopolistic competition, and pure competition?
6. What aspects of the political and legal environment influence a firm's decision to enter a foreign market? Why are human rights issues important to firms in their decisions to enter global markets?
7. What do marketers mean when they refer to technological and sociocultural environments? Why do they need to understand these environments in a global marketplace?
8. What is ethnocentrism? How does it affect a firm that seeks to enter a foreign market?
9. How is a firm's level of commitment related to its level of control in a foreign market? Describe the four levels of involvement that are options for a firm: exporting, contractual agreements, strategic alliances, and direct investment.
10. What are the arguments for standardization of marketing strategies in the global marketplace? What are the arguments for localization? What are some ways a firm can standardize or localize its marketing mix?

Activities: Apply What You've Learned

1. Tide laundry detergent, McDonald's food, and Dell computers are very different U.S. products that are marketed

globally. Develop ideas about why the marketers for each of these products
   a. Standardize product strategies.
   b. Localize product strategies.
   c. Standardize promotion strategies.
   d. Localize promotion strategies.
2. Select one of the following product categories. Think about how a firm's offering in the product category would need to differ for least developed countries, developing countries, and developed countries. Develop recommendations for the product, pricing, promotion, and distribution in these different markets.
   a. Shampoo
   b. Automobiles
   c. Diapers
   d. Washing machines
   e. Athletic shoes
3. Consider the pros and cons of localization and standardization of marketing strategies. Are the advantages and disadvantages different for different products? In different countries? Organize a debate in your class to argue the merits of the standardization perspective versus the localization perspective.
4. Assume you are the director of marketing for a firm that produces refrigerators and other home appliances. Your firm is considering going global and is faced with the decision of the best entry strategy. Should they simply export their products or would a strategic alliance, licensing, or a joint venture be a better choice? Select one of the countries listed below. Then develop your ideas for a best entry strategy. Be specific in your recommendations for a strategy, how to implement the strategy, and your reasons for your recommendations.
   a. Germany
   b. Mexico
   c. China
   d. Sudan
   e. New Zealand
5. Ethnocentrism is the tendency for individuals to prefer products or people of one's own culture. Sometimes people think products made at home are better than imported goods. Develop a small study to find out what students at

your university think about products made at home and abroad. Develop a survey that asks other students to evaluate 10 or more products (not brands) that are imported versus made at home. You might wish to ask if they feel the domestic or imported products are superior in quality and which they would purchase. Prepare a report on your study for your class.

6. Assume that you are a marketing director for a firm that is interested in the global market potential for a chain of coffee shops in Italy, Brazil, and India. You recognize that an understanding of the external environments in each of these potential markets is essential. First, decide which environmental factors are most important to your business. Then, use your library to gather information about the environments of each of these countries. If possible, talk with someone who is from that country or who has visited that country. Finally, tell how the differences among the environments might affect marketing strategies for coffee shops. Develop a report for your class.

7. In this chapter we learned that many countries practice protectionism in order to protect their domestic industries. But do you know what protectionist policies and regulations are practiced by your own government? Go to the library or the Internet to find out as much as you can about your government's protectionism policies. Prepare a report for your class that presents your findings and your ideas about the pros and cons of these government policies.

Marketing Metrics Exercise

Many Western firms see their futures in the growing populations of developing countries, where eight out of 10 consumers now live. Consumers from countries such as Brazil, India, China, and Russia offer new opportunities for firms because growing numbers of them are accumulating small but significant amounts of disposable income. Firms like worldwide cosmetics giant Beirsdorf, producer of Nivea products, are adapting their products and their marketing activities to meet the needs of these populations. Often this means selling miniature or even single-use packages of shampoo, dishwashing detergent, or fabric softener for only a few cents. The huge Swiss company Nestlé sells shrimp-flavored instant soup cubes for two cents each in Ghana while the financial company Allianz, in a joint program with CARE, sells microinsurance for five cents a month to the very poor in India.

But how do these firms measure their success in these new markets? Firms normally use such marketing metrics as customer awareness or satisfaction, increases in market share or profits, or return on marketing investment (ROMI). These metrics may not be right for the new markets in the developing world where many millions of people buy streamlined versions of a firm's products at a fraction of their usual price.

What do you think? Develop a list of possible metrics that firms might use to measure their success in these new developing markets.

Choices: What Do You Think?

1. Do you think U.S. firms should be allowed to use bribes to compete in countries where bribery is an accepted and legal form of doing business? Why or why not?

2. In 2006, the National Institutes of Health released results of a study showing that young people tend to drink more in areas with more alcohol advertising compared to areas with less advertising.[51] Do alcohol companies have an ethical obligation to curtail their advertising in order to decrease drinking rates among young people?

3. Some countries have been critical of the exporting of American culture by U.S. businesses. What about American culture might be objectionable? Can you think of some products that U.S. marketers export that can be objectionable to some foreign markets?

4. The World Trade Organization seeks to eventually remove all barriers to world trade. Do you think this will ever be a reality? What do you think are the positive and negative aspects of a totally free marketplace? Which countries will win and which will lose in such a world?

5. Some companies have been criticized for moving their manufacturing to other countries where laws protecting the environment are more lenient and goods can be produced more cheaply because the firms do not have to invest in ways to protect the environment. What do you think of this practice? What can governments and/or consumers do to prevent such actions?

6. Many people feel that governments should protect local industries and local jobs with protectionist laws. Do you feel that your country's government should do more to protect local industries? What are your reasons?

7. In recent years, terrorism and other types of violent activities around the globe have made the global marketplace seem very unsafe. How concerned should firms with international operations be about such activities? Should these firms consider abandoning some global markets? How should firms weigh their concerns about terrorism against the need to help the economies of developing countries? Would avoiding countries such as those in the Middle East make good sense in terms of economic profit? What about in terms of social profit?

8. We noted in this chapter that consumers often use country-of-origin as a heuristic to judge a product. Sometimes this tendency can backfire: While one study found that around the world, "the Golden Arches are now more widely recognized than the Christian cross," the strong link between McDonald's and the United States has been a liability for the food chain in recent years. As antiwar protests in many countries give vent to raw anti-American sentiment, the familiarity of McDonald's has made it a widespread target. In Quito, Ecuador, protesters burned a Ronald McDonald statue. In Paris, demonstrators smashed a McDonald's restaurant window. South Korean activists calling for an end to the war sought attention by scaling a McDonald's sign. Other McDonald's outlets in Karachi and in Buenos Aires have been ringed with police officers to stave off trouble. Should a company that takes credit for its association with its country-of-origin in good times have to take its lumps in bad times? What steps can marketers take to avoid these problems?[52]

Miniproject: Learn by Doing

The purpose of this miniproject is to begin to develop an understanding of a culture other than your own and of how customer differences lead to changes in the ways marketing strategies and socially responsible decision making can be implemented in that culture.

1. Select a country you would like to know more about and a product you think could be successful in that market. As a first step, gather information about the country. Many campuses have students from different countries. If possible, find a fellow student from the country and talk with him or her about the country. You will probably also wish to investigate other sources of information, such as books and magazines found in your library, or to access information from the Web.

2. Prepare a summary of your findings that includes the following:

   a. An overall description of the country, including facts such as its history, economy, religions, and so on,

that might affect marketing of the product you have selected

   b. A description of the cultural values and business ethics dominant in the country
   c. The current status of this product in the country
   d. Your recommendations for a product strategy (product design, packaging, brand name, and so on)
   e. Your recommendations for a pricing strategy
   f. Your recommendations for promotional strategies
   g. A discussion of the ethical and social responsibility issues in the recommendations you have made

3. Present your findings and recommendations to the class.

Marketing in Action Case   Real Choices at Mattel

In 1945 Mattel's founders, Ruth and Elliott Handler, were manufacturing picture frames out of a garage workshop. The couple also ran a side business making dollhouse furniture from the frame scraps; this became so successful that they turned to making toys. In 1955, Mattel began advertising its toys through the *Mickey Mouse Club* TV show and thus revolutionized the way toys are sold. In 1959, Ruth Handler, noting her own daughter Barbara's love for cut-out paper dolls, created the idea of a three-dimensional paper doll. Barbie was born and very quickly propelled Mattel to the forefront of the toy industry. The 1960s saw Mattel grow with such new products as Barbie's boyfriend Ken, See-and-Say toys, and Hot Wheels toy cars. In the 1980s Mattel became a global company with the purchase of Hong Kong–based ARCO industries, Corelle, SA, a maker of collector-quality dolls based in France, a British company, Corgi Toys Ltd., and a joint venture with Japan's largest toy company, Bandai.

Mattel stresses social responsibility. Its Sustainability Mission states "We regard the thoughtful management of the environment and the health and safety of our employees, customers, and neighbors as among our highest priorities and as key elements of our responsibility to be a sustainable company." In 2006, Mattel's Children's Foundation donated approximately $4.8 million in cash grants and approximately $10 million in toys to organizations serving children around the world. Over 2,500 Mattel employees volunteered for charitable activities and Special Olympics programs in 13 countries.

In 2007 trouble arrived in Toyland. Like many other toy makers, in recent years Mattel commissioned Chinese companies to produce its products. In August, Mattel was forced to recall 1.5 million of its Fisher-Price toys, including such favorites as Elmo and Big Bird, because they were suspected of containing hazardous levels of lead paint. Later in August, Mattel recalled over 19 million more Chinese-made toys because they contained magnets that could be swallowed by children or because they were made with dangerous lead paint. Following the second recall the company purchased full-page ads in the *New York Times* and the *Wall Street Journal* to assure parents that it understands how they feel. CEO Robert Eckert, a father of four, appeared on an online video to state, "I can't change what has happened in the past, but I can change how we work

in the future." Mattel pledged to test the paint in every batch of paint delivered to all of its toy producers and to take other safety measures. Consumers, however, were not all convinced. Video clips appeared on YouTube mocking the company's efforts. One video referred to the recall of "Tickle Me Lead-Mo."

The recall dramatically cut into Mattel's revenues. Sales of Dora the Explorer toys fell 34 percent in the United States and 21 percent internationally. Barbie sales fell 19 percent in the United States, and Brazil banned imports of all Mattel products while it evaluated whether or not the company was complying with its safety regulations.

Again in 2010, Mattel recalled over 10 million of its Fisher-Price products including about seven million Fisher-Price Trikes and Tough Trikes. The tricycles have a plastic ignition key near the seat that kids can sit on or fall, potentially leading to injuries. Fisher-Price offered customers free repair or replacements.

Mattel must continue to work hard to recover from these disasters. Are apologies and claims for new safety regulations enough? Because some but not all of the recalls were because of production in other countries, should the company stop producing its toys in China and other developing countries where costs are low? Or should Mattel return to its roots and produce the millions of Polly Pockets, "Sarge" toy cars, and Barbie playsets in the United States, where costs are substantially higher but standards are tougher?

You Make the Call

1. What is the decision facing Mattel?
2. What factors are important in understanding this decision situation?
3. What are the alternatives?
4. What decision(s) do you recommend?
5. What are some ways to implement your recommendation?

Based on: http://www.mattel.com/about_us/history/default.asp; Nicholas Casey and Nicholas Zamiska, "Mattel Does Damage Control after Recall," *The Wall Street Journal* (August 17, 2007; accessed January 16, 2008 at http://on-line.wsj.com/article/SB118709567221897168 .html); "Key Dates in China Export Scares," *The Wall Street Journal* (October 21, 2007; accessed January 16, 2008, at http://on-line.wsj.com/article/SB118606827156686195.html); Roger Parloff, "Not Exactly Counterfeit," *Fortune* (May 1, 2006): 108–116; "Mattel, Battered by Recalls, Posts Quarterly Profit Drop," *The International Herald Tribune* (October 16, 2007): 19; Associated Press, "Fisher-Price Recalls 10 Million Items," *New York Times*, September 6, 2010, B6.

Part Two

```
┌─────────────────────────────────┐
│  Make marketing value decisions │
│           (Part One)            │
└─────────────────────────────────┘
                 ↓
┌─────────────────────────────────┐
│  Understand consumers' value needs │  ← You are here
│           (Part Two)            │
└─────────────────────────────────┘
                 ↓
┌─────────────────────────────────┐
│   Create the value proposition  │
│          (Part Three)           │
└─────────────────────────────────┘
                 ↓
┌─────────────────────────────────┐
│ Communicate the value proposition │
│          (Part Four)            │
└─────────────────────────────────┘
                 ↓
┌─────────────────────────────────┐
│  Deliver the value proposition  │
│          (Part Five)            │
└─────────────────────────────────┘
```

Process

Understand Consumers' Value Needs

Part Two Overview Part Two continues the focus on making marketing decisions by providing insights in Chapter 4 on how marketers conduct research to gather the information they need to make excellent decisions. Information is the fuel that drives the engine of marketing decision making, and bad input information generally leads to bad output in the form of poor decisions by marketers. In Chapter 4 you learn about the steps in the marketing research process and gain insights on effective approaches to collecting data.

In marketing, a useful and convenient way to consider markets and customers is by splitting them up as end-user consumer markets, which are composed of folks that purchase products for their own personal consumption/use, and business markets, which are composed of a variety of organizational customers that are purchasing products and services for use within their enterprise. Chapter 5 provides insights on consumer behavior including the fascinating topics of how and why individuals make their purchase decisions. Chapter 6 outlines the process of business-to-business (B2B) purchasing, which has numerous important differences from end-user consumer buying. Although you're probably more familiar with marketing from a consumer's perspective, the truth is that B2B accounts for a huge volume of transactions around the world—most students go to work for a B2B firm at some point during their professional careers.

Finally, in Chapter 7 you have the opportunity to explore target marketing, a fascinating process that includes market segmentation, selection of target markets, and positioning. Because consumer markets are more diverse than ever on many dimensions, doing market segmentation has become increasingly complex. Fortunately, today's more sophisticated research methodologies allow marketers to derive very precise profiles of their markets so that they can laser target the ones that offer the best return on investment. Marketers use positioning strategies to influence how a particular market segment perceives a good or service in comparison to the competition.

Marketing Plan Connection:
Tricks of the Trade

Recall that the Appendix at the end of the book provides you with an abbreviated marketing plan example for the fictitious S&S Smoothie Company. That plan is flagged to indicate what elements from the plan correspond to each of the Parts within the book. In addition, in Chapter 2 you found a tear-out guide called "Build a Marketing Plan," which can be used as a template for marketing planning. It is also cross-referenced to chapters by section of the marketing plan.

In the chapters within Part Two, there are major learning elements that guide you in developing three critical elements of your marketing plan: marketing objectives, target market strategies, and positioning the offering. But before you deal with those elements, a good bit of information is required. This information is attained via marketing research designed to find out all you can about the consumer marketplace and the business marketplace so you can make better decisions as a marketer.

Marketing Research

As you will read in Chapter 4, "Information is the fuel that runs the marketing engine." Nowhere is the value of working with good information for decision making more apparent than in marketing planning.

In the S&S Smoothie Marketing Plan, you will notice that research has been used to gather information about such things as customer awareness and loyalty, the sociocultural environment, and customer demographics. The results of marketing research—assuming the research is conducted properly—are invaluable in allowing you to decide on the best marketing objectives, the right target markets, and the most attractive positioning of your offering for those markets.

Marketing Objectives

The information from the situation analysis and from research on consumer and B2B markets leads an organization to formulate appropriate marketing objectives. You learned in Chapter 2 that good objectives must be specific, measurable, attainable, and sustainable over time.

The following are the marketing objectives set by S&S Smoothie:

- To increase the awareness of S&S Smoothie products by at least 10 percent among the target market
- To increase gross sales by 50 percent over the next two years
- To introduce two new product lines over the next three years: a line of low-carb smoothies and a line of gourmet flavored smoothies
- To increase distribution of S&S Smoothie products to include new retail outlets both in the United States and globally

Consumer and Business-to-Business Target Markets

Consumer markets consist of end-users of products and services—people like you who buy things for your own use at the nearby Target or online. Chapter 5 gives you the lowdown on consumer behavior. In S&S Smoothie's case, most (but not all) of their marketing planning is for the consumer market. To develop successful target marketing strategies, they (and you) need to be able to actually describe the market segments in each category that have the most potential. Perusal of the S&S Smoothie marketing plan in the Appendix will reveal that they do a great job of specifying which consumer segments they want to target.

In Chapter 6 you will learn that B2B markets differ from consumer markets in that the purchaser of the product or service is buying it for resale or for use in their own business. In the past, S&S Smoothie has targeted two categories of reseller markets: (1) health clubs and gyms, and (2) small upscale specialty food markets. To increase distribution and sales of its products, they aim to target several different B2B customers in the future: hotels and resorts in the United States and in selected international markets; golf and tennis clubs; and college and university campuses.

The final element in targeting in Chapter 7 is positioning, influencing how a particular market segment perceives a good or service in comparison to the competition. To develop a positioning strategy, marketers must clearly understand the criteria target customers use to evaluate the different brands in a product category and then convince those customers that their brand will better meet their needs. One way to think of positioning is that it is the application of the marketing mix (4Ps) elements in a unique way to appeal to a particular target market.

S&S Smoothie seeks to position its products as the first-choice smoothie beverage for the serious health-conscious consumer, including those who are seeking to lower their carbohydrate intake. The justification for this positioning is as follows: Many smoothie beverages are available. The S&S Smoothie formula provides superior flavor and nutrition in a shelf-stable form. S&S Smoothie has developed its product, packaging, pricing, and promotion to communicate a superior, prestige image. This positioning is thus supported by all its marketing strategies.

>> You Can **Do It Too!**
Now, if you are working on a marketing plan as part of your course, go to **www.mypearsonmarketinglab.com** to apply what you learn in Part Two to your own marketing plan project.

Chapter 4

Marketing Research:
Gather, Analyze, and Use Information

Ryan Garton

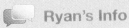

Profile

Info

▼ A Decision Maker at Discover Financial Services

Ryan Garton is director, Consumer Insights at Discover Financial Services. Promoted to his current position in January 2008, Ryan and the Consumer Insights team are responsible for all Market Research activities for the firm including brand and advertising tracking/effectiveness, new product development/innovation screeners, financial attitudes and usage studies, overall voice of the customer, and other ad hoc quantitative and qualitative studies as requested by business lines. Prior to this assignment, Ryan joined Discover Financial Services as the director, Corporate Brand Strategy, where he and his team of brand specialists were responsible for overall corporate brand strategy for all Discover Card products and programs including Discover More Card, Miles by Discover, Discover Open Road Card, Discover Motiva Card, and Stored Value card products. Additionally, the team was responsible for brand and marketing strategy for Discover Banking products such as student loans, deposits, and personal loans. The brand team is also responsible for integrating product development, innovation cycles, marketing strategy, and ensuring communication efforts are fully leveraged across all business activities.

Prior to joining Discover Financial Services, Ryan had an 11-year career at United Airlines, which spanned several marketing leadership roles in international marketing—STAR Alliance, market research, product development, and brand marketing strategy. He and his team were responsible for all United branding, the new United aircraft livery, development of airport lounge products, EasyCheck-in, sub-brand development (TED), and overall partnership strategy (Starbucks, Pepsi, and AOL). His assignment prior to joining the Marketing Division was as the marketing and sales manager for the Midwest Region–Chicago, where he was responsible for revenue and profitability within United's largest North American Region.

💬 Ryan's Info

What do I do when I'm not working?
A) Activities with my three kids—soccer, dance, swimming, and music lessons. Restoring our 1910 home (I am a bit of a carpenter! Think of *This Old House*)

First job out of school?
A) Marketing research for The Gallup Organization

Business book I'm reading now?
A) *Buyology* by Martin Lindstrom

My motto to live by?
A) "Make no small plans, for they have not the power to stir the hearts and minds of men." Daniel Burnham

My management style?
A) Competitive—strategic—achiever—individualization—relator

Don't do this when interviewing with me?
A) Make excuses

My pet peeve?
A) Others not taking ownership of their actions

Before his airline career, Ryan worked for The Gallup Organization in survey research and political tracking. He worked with several key accounts including Volkswagen, NationsBank, CNN News, and numerous political polls. He has an MBA from the University of Nebraska with an emphasis on international marketing and strategy, and an undergraduate degree from St. Olaf College in economics and political science.

Here's my problem. . .

Ryan's problem at Discover Card was simple: Too much of a good thing. The company had a lot of very good new product and services ideas: new card products, new technologies to help people manage their finances/bills, enhancements to its Web site, new insurance products, and new banking products. However, Ryan lacked an integrated approach to determine which of the ideas would be most likely to fit cardholders' desires, fit with the Discover brand image as the card that is all about cashback and other rewards to cardholders, and fit with company resources (financial and technical).

In fact, Ryan had such a good thing that he didn't have the internal resources to evaluate each product idea. In particular, he was missing a crucial piece of the puzzle: customer input. Typically Discover would prioritize new product ideas using metrics such as revenue projections, resource consumption estimates, and internal assessments of strategic fit. But these estimates largely occur in a vacuum because they don't include the "reality check" that actual users could provide.

Ryan knew he had to seriously consider whether it was worthwhile to invest crucial resources to develop a system that could screen a large number of new product ideas with input from current or potential users of these products. He convened a cross-functional team of colleges from Consumer Insights, Brand Strategy, and New Product Strategy to outline what this new screening process might look like. The "old" process was one where Ryan would gather these business partners together to look at the financial information available and the technology resources available. They would then determine the best course of action, typically without necessarily considering consumers' needs.

Things to remember

Like many companies, Discover Financial collected a lot of data from different sources to stay on top of changes in the financial services industry and to monitor the types of credit card options competitors offered to customers. But (also like many companies), the recognition that consumers' preferences should play a role when decisions are made regarding which products to take to market is a fairly new one for Discover. The marketing research process also gets more complicated when more input is included, so Ryan has to decide if his internal organization has the resources to make the best use of all the information. He also recognizes that internal decision-making often has a "political" side to it, as executives often have a vested interest in which paths the company will choose to follow.

learn a new process. But decisions about new features would continue to rely on internal projections and the intuition of managers without benefiting from input by actual consumers.

2 Option **Modify the current process to include existing consumer input Discover can easily access.** The team could look more carefully at feedback the company received in blogs, letters, and telephone calls to help it gauge the likelihood of success. Again, this extra layer of information wouldn't significantly hold up the progress of product ideas in the pipeline. And, if the information contradicted management's priorities, at least this would be a red flag to force decision makers to take a second look. However, some of the new ideas broke new ground so there was no primary or syndicated research to indicate if they would fly. Consumers can't spontaneously provide feedback about products that don't yet exist.

3 Option **Engage an outside firm to assist Discover in developing a new process.** Ideally Ryan wanted to test consumers' reactions to several key measures: market potential, consumer likeability, brand fit, and comparisons with launches by other financial services companies. This new process would involve hiring an outside firm to apply a standardized set of measures to assess all potential offerings so Discover could use an "apples to apples" comparison. Decision makers could access one score for each concept that encompasses all relevant research results. They could more easily identify how a concept might be improved so that cardholders would think more highly of it. And the score would include an assessment of how well each concept fits with the Discover brand.

But this radical new approach would be politically challenging within the organization because it would challenge some internal stakeholders' existing beliefs and priorities regarding which offerings they would like to develop. And a new approach would involve a big financial investment, most likely in the neighborhood of $100,000. There would also be a potential cost in that it would add weeks to the decision-making process so a competitor might get to market with the idea first.

Now, put yourself in Ryan Garton's shoes.

Ryan considered his Options 1·2·3

1 Option **Don't muddy the waters.** Continue to use the same project prioritization process that Discover had been using for many years. A passive approach would not put additional roadblocks in front of project time lines; new card features and other offerings could get to market faster because they wouldn't have to undergo another evaluation. Decision makers wouldn't have to

You Choose

Which option would you choose, and why?

1. ☐YES ☐NO **2.** ☐YES ☐NO **3.** ☐YES ☐NO

See what **option** Ryan chose on **page 123**

marketing research ethics
Taking an ethical and above-board approach to conducting marketing research that does no harm to the participant in the process of conducting the research.

marketing information system (MIS)
A process that first determines what information marketing managers need and then gathers, sorts, analyzes, stores, and distributes relevant and timely marketing information to system users.

1

Knowledge Is Power

By now we know that successful planning means that managers make informed decisions to guide the organization. But how do marketers actually make these choices? Specifically, how do they find out what they need to know to develop marketing objectives, select a target market, position (or reposition) their product, and develop product, price, promotion, and place strategies?

The answer is (drumroll . . .): Information. Information is the fuel that runs the marketing engine. To make good decisions, marketers must have information that is accurate, up-to-date, and relevant. To understand these needs, marketers first need to conduct *marketing research* to identify them. In this chapter, we will discuss some of the tools that marketers use to get that information. In the chapters that follow, we will look at consumer behavior, how and why organizations buy, and then how marketers sharpen their focus via target marketing strategies.

A marketer who conducts research to learn more about her customers shouldn't encounter any ethical challenges, right? Well, maybe. In reality, several aspects of marketing research are fraught with the *potential* for ethics breaches. **Marketing research ethics** refers to taking an ethical and above-board approach to conducting marketing research that does no harm to the participant in the process of conducting the research.

When the organization collects data, important issues of privacy and confidentiality come into play. Marketers must be very clear when they work with research respondents about how they will use the data and give respondents full disclosure on their options for confidentiality and anonymity. For example, it is unethical to collect data under the guise of marketing research when your real intent is to develop a database of potential customers for direct marketing. Firms who abuse the trust of respondents run a serious risk of damaging their reputation when word gets out that they are engaged in unethical research practices. This makes it difficult to attract participants in future research projects—and it "poisons the well" for other companies when consumers believe that they can't trust them.

The Marketing Information System

Many firms use a **marketing information system (MIS)** to collect information. The MIS is a process that first determines what information marketing managers need. Then it gathers, sorts, analyzes, stores, and distributes relevant and timely marketing information to users. As you can see in Figure 4.1, the MIS system includes three important components:

- Four types of data (internal company data, marketing intelligence, marketing research, and acquired databases)

- Computer hardware and software to analyze the data and to create reports

- Output for marketing decision makers

Various sources "feed" the MIS with data, and then the system's software "digests" it. MIS analysts use the output to generate a series of regular reports for various decision makers. For example, Frito-Lay's MIS generates daily sales data by product line and by region. Its managers then use this informa-

Ripped from the Headlines

Ethical/Sustainable Decisions in the Real World

Did you catch Burger King's "Whopper Freakout" online and TV ads that showed what happened at two Burger King outlets in Nevada when real customers were told the Whopper had been taken off the menu? The videotaped hoax was actually a twist on a real market research technique called "deprivation research," in which marketers measure how loyal consumers are to a brand or product by taking it away from them. The insight gained helps marketers design new marketing and ad ploys that will resonate better with consumers. The difference is, this time the "research" made its way into commercials—a rare translation of research into promotion.

Burger King has been conducting deprivation studies for several years; it gets loyal customers to voluntarily forgo eating Whoppers. As part of the experiment, the people typically keep food diaries so Burger King can analyze what they ate instead. Russ Klein, the chain's chief marketing officer, says he conducts such research because fast-food customers are "promiscuous" when it comes to food choices. "While our core customers frequent Burger King five times a month,

they frequent other fast-food restaurants 11 times a month," he says. Burger King hopes the research will help it improve customer loyalty.

Staged at two Las Vegas outlets over two full days, the ads featured actors who played the role of cashiers. Eight hidden cameras recorded the results. In another twist, some customers who asked for a Whopper were given burgers from rivals such as McDonald's and Wendy's. The result: Irate customers ended up returning the burgers, sometimes disparaging the competing brand. "I hate McDonald's," said a young male consumer. All this was captured on film and viewed millions of times on a special Burger King Web site and on YouTube.

Staging the colossal prank wasn't without problems. For one, Los Angeles was abandoned as the filming site because of the difficulty of navigating California laws governing when people can be secretly videotaped. Another challenge: All the consumers who walked into the stores during the experiment had to be chased down afterward to sign release forms so they could be shown in the video and ads. Not everyone could be caught in time. One irate consumer who demanded Burger King's "corporate number" to call in his complaint was so upset he jumped in his pickup truck and drove off. That footage will never see the light of day.

ETHICS CHECK:

Find out what other students taking this course **would do** and **why** on www.mypearsonmarketinglab.com.

If you were a participant in Burger King's deprivation research, would you allow yourself to be featured in a Whopper commercial that used your video footage?

☐**YES** ☐**NO**

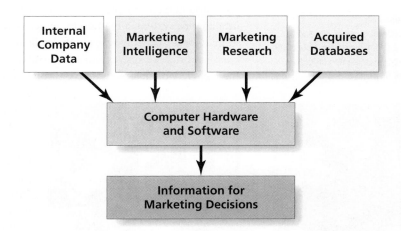

Figure 4.1 *Process* | The Marketing Information System

A firm's marketing information system (MIS) stores and analyzes data from a variety of sources and turns the data into information for useful marketing decision making.

tion to evaluate the market share of different Frito-Lay products compared to one another and to competing snack foods in each region where the company does business.[1]

Let's take a closer look at each of the four different data sources for the MIS.

1. Internal Company Data

The *internal company data system* uses information from within the organization to produce reports on the results of sales and marketing activities. Internal company data include a firm's sales records—information such as which customers buy which products in what quantities and at what intervals, which items are in stock and which are back-ordered because they are out of stock, when items were shipped to the customer, and which items have been returned because they are defective.

Often, an MIS allows salespeople and sales managers in the field to access internal records through a company **intranet**. This is an internal corporate communications network that uses Internet technology to link company departments, employees, and databases. Intranets are secured so that only authorized employees have access. When salespeople and sales managers in the field can use an intranet to access their company's MIS, they can better serve their customers because they have immediate access to information on pricing, inventory levels, production schedules, shipping dates, and the customer's sales history. But equally important, because salespeople and sales managers are the ones in daily direct contact with customers, the company intranet enters *their* reports directly into the system. This means the reports can provide an important source of information to upper management on changes in sales patterns or new sales opportunities.

Marketing managers at HQ also can see daily or weekly sales data by brand or product line from the internal company data system. They can view monthly sales reports to measure progress toward sales goals and market share objectives. For example, managers and buyers at Target's headquarters in Minneapolis use up-to-the-minute sales information they obtain from store cash registers around the country so they can quickly detect problems with products, promotions, and even the firm's distribution system.

2. Marketing Intelligence

As we saw in Chapter 2, to make good decisions marketers need to have information about the marketing environment. Thus, a second important element of the MIS is the **marketing intelligence system**, a method by which marketers get information about what's going on in the world that is relevant to their business. Although the name *intelligence* may suggest cloak-and-dagger spy activities, in reality nearly all the information companies need about their environment—including the competitive environment—is available by monitoring everyday sources: Web sites, industry trade publications, or simple observations of the marketplace. And because salespeople are the ones "in the trenches" every day, talking with customers, distributors, and prospective customers, they too can provide valuable information. Retailers often hire "mystery shoppers" to visit their stores and those of their competitors posing as customers to see how people are treated. (Imagine being paid to shop!) Other information may come from speaking with organizational buyers about competing products, attending trade shows, or simply purchasing competitors' products.

3. Marketing Research

Marketing research refers to the process of collecting, analyzing, and interpreting data about customers, competitors, and the business environment to improve marketing effectiveness. Although companies collect marketing intelligence data continuously to keep managers abreast of happenings in the marketplace, marketing research also is called for when managers need unique information to help them make specific decisions. Whether their business is selling cool stuff to teens or coolant to factories, firms succeed when they know what cus-

intranet
An internal corporate communication network that uses Internet technology to link company departments, employees, and databases.

marketing intelligence system
A method by which marketers get information about everyday happenings in the marketing environment.

marketing research
The process of collecting, analyzing, and interpreting data about customers, competitors, and the business environment in order to improve marketing effectiveness.

Marketing managers may use marketing intelligence data to predict fluctuations in sales due to economic conditions, political issues, and events that heighten consumer awareness, or to forecast the future so that they will be on top of developing trends. For example, knowledge of trends in consumer preferences, driven by the younger teen generation, prompted plucky cellular provider Sprint to best AT&T and Verizon Wireless with an in-your-face plan that for $69.99 provided unlimited messaging, data, GPS, and calls to any mobile phone in the United States. Sprint's CEO personally plugged the "More Perks, Same Price" deal and hawked the promotion in ads; the net effect is that Sprint's competitors come across by comparison as nickel-and-diming consumers—especially on text messaging, which for all practical purposes costs cellular providers nothing. Nothing speaks to young consumers like an easier or cheaper way to text their friends![2]

tomers want, when they want it, where they want it—and what competing firms are doing about it. In other words, the better a firm is at obtaining valid marketing information, the more successful it will be. Therefore, virtually all companies rely on some form of marketing research, though the amount and type of research they conduct vary dramatically. In general, marketing research data available in an MIS include syndicated research reports and custom research reports.

Syndicated research is general information specialized firms collect on a regular basis and then sell to other firms. INC/The QScores Company, for instance, reports on consumers' perceptions of over 1,700 celebrity performers for companies that want to feature a well-known person in their advertising. The company also rates consumer appeal of cartoon characters, sports stars, and even deceased celebrities.[3] Other examples of syndicated research reports

115 years of research and we're just getting warmed up.

PURINA
A DIFFERENCE YOU CAN SEE

Companies conduct marketing research to improve their products and to understand their customers' needs.

include Nielsen's television ratings and Arbitron's radio ratings. Experian Simmons Market Research Bureau and Mediamark Research Inc. are two syndicated research firms that combine information about consumers' buying behavior and their media usage with geographic and demographic characteristics.

As valuable as it may be, syndicated research doesn't provide all the answers to marketing questions because the information it collects typically is broad but shallow; it gives good insights about general trends such as who is watching what television shows or what brand of perfume is hot this year. In contrast, **custom research** is research a single firm conducts to provide answers to specific questions. This kind of research is especially helpful for firms when they need to know more about *why* certain trends have surfaced.

Some firms maintain an in-house research department that conducts studies on its behalf. Many firms, however, hire outside research companies that specialize in designing and conducting projects based on the needs of the client. These custom research reports are another kind of information an MIS includes. Marketers may use marketing research to identify opportunities for new products, to promote existing ones, or to provide data about the quality of their products, who uses them, and how.

syndicated research
Research by firms that collect data on a regular basis and sell the reports to multiple firms.

custom research
Research conducted for a single firm to provide specific information its managers need.

4. Acquired Databases

A large amount of information that can be useful in marketing decision making is available in the form of external databases. Firms may acquire these databases from any number of sources. For example, some companies are willing to sell their customer database to noncompeting firms. Government databases, including the massive amounts of economic and demographic information the U.S. Census Bureau just collected in 2010, are available at little or no cost. State and local governments may make information such as automobile license data available for a fee.

In recent years, the use of such databases for marketing purposes has come under increased government scrutiny as some consumer advocates protest against the potential invasion of privacy these may cause. Using the data to analyze consumer trends is one thing—using it for outbound mailings and unsolicited phone calls and e-mails has evoked a backlash resulting in a plethora of "do-not-call" lists and antispam laws. Maybe you have noticed that when you sign up for most anything on the Web that requires your contact information, you receive an invitation to "opt out" of receiving promotional mailings from the company or from others who may acquire your contact information from the organization later. By law, if you decide to opt out, companies cannot use your information for marketing purposes.

Figure 4.2 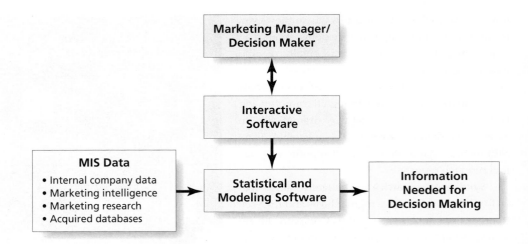 *Process* | The MDSS

Although an MIS provides many reports managers need for decision making, it doesn't answer all their information needs. The marketing decision support system (MDSS) is an enhancement to the MIS that makes it easy for marketing managers to access the MIS system and find answers to their questions.

marketing decision support system (MDSS)
The data, analysis software, and interactive software that allow managers to conduct analyses and find the information they need.

data mining
Sophisticated analysis techniques to take advantage of the massive amount of transaction information now available.

Ryan Garton

APPLYING ▼
Marketing Decision Support Systems

Ryan has to decide on the best system to integrate data from different sources so that Discover can make intelligent choices as it competes in the credit card marketplace. ➡

The Marketing Decision Support System

As we have seen, a firm's marketing information system generates regular reports for decision makers on what is going on in the internal and external environment. But sometimes these reports are inadequate. Different managers may want different information, and in some cases, the problem they must address is too vague or unusual for the MIS process to easily answer. As a result, many firms beef up their MIS with a **marketing decision support system (MDSS)**. An MDSS includes analysis and interactive software that allows marketing managers, even those who are not computer experts, to access MIS data and conduct their own analyses, often over the company intranet. Figure 4.2 shows the elements of an MDSS.

Typically an MDSS includes sophisticated statistical and modeling software tools. Statistical software allows managers to examine complex relationships among factors in the marketplace. For example, a marketing manager who wants to know how consumers perceive her company's brand in relation to the competition's brand might use a sophisticated statistical technique called "multidimensional scaling" to create a "perceptual map," or a graphic presentation of the various brands in relationship to each other. You'll see an example of a perceptual map in Chapter 7.

Modeling software allows decision makers to examine possible or preconceived ideas about relationships in the data—to ask "what-if" questions. For example, media modeling software allows marketers to see what would happen if they made certain decisions about where to place their advertising. A manager may be able to use sales data and a model to find out how many consumers stay with her brand and how many switch, thus developing projections of market share over time. Table 4.1 gives some examples of the different marketing questions an MIS and an MDSS might answer.

Table 4.1 | Examples of Questions an MIS and an MDSS Might Answer

Questions an MIS Answers	Questions an MDSS Answers
What were our company sales of each product during the past month and the past year?	Has our decline in sales simply reflected changes in overall industry sales, or is there some portion of the decline that industry changes cannot explain?
What changes are happening in sales in our industry, and what are the demographic characteristics of consumers whose purchase patterns are changing the most?	Do we see the same trends in our different product categories? Are the changes in consumer trends very similar among all our products? What are the demographic characteristics of consumers who seem to be the most and the least loyal?
What are the best media for reaching a large proportion of heavy, medium, or light users of our product?	If we change our media schedule by adding or deleting certain media buys, will we reach fewer users of our product?

2

Searching for Gold:
Data Mining

As we have explained, most MIS systems include internal customer transaction databases and many include acquired databases. Often these databases are extremely large. To take advantage of the massive amount of data now available, a sophisticated analysis technique called **data mining** is now a priority for many firms. This refers to a process in which analysts sift through data (often measured in terabytes—much larger than kilobytes or even gigabytes) to identify unique patterns of behavior among different customer groups.

Data mining uses computers that run sophisticated programs so that analysts can combine different databases to understand relationships among buying decisions, exposure to marketing messages, and in-store promotions. These operations are so complex that often companies need to build a *data warehouse* (which can cost more than $10 million) simply to store and process the data.[4] Marketers at powerful consumer data generators Google, Yahoo!, Facebook, and Twitter are onto data mining big time. For example, Yahoo! collects between 12 and 15 terabytes of data each day, and Facebook has access to valuable information that its over 50 million users post. Both firms want to use the data to facilitate targeted advertising by clients who are willing to pay big bucks to get their online ads in front of people who are likely to buy.[5]

Even cellular providers are getting into the data mining act. Signals among phones and base stations can be detected by commercial sensing devices. But the detailed records of who is calling whom belong entirely to the phone companies. Right now, they make little use of that data, in part because they fear alienating subscribers who worry about privacy infringement. But cellular operators have begun signing deals with business partners who are eager to market products based on specific phone users' location and calling habits. If *reality mining* catches on, phone companies' calling records will become precious assets. And these will only grow in value as customers use their phones to browse the Web, purchase products, and update their Facebook pages—and as marketers apply reality mining's toolkit to these activities.[6]

As illustrated in 🎿 Figure 4.3, Data mining has four important applications for marketers:[7]

1. *Customer acquisition:* Many firms include demographic and other information about customers in their database. For example, a number of

What do all these Las Vegas casino brands have in common: Caesar's Palace, Paris Las Vegas, Flamingo, Bally's, Rio, Imperial Palace, Planet Hollywood Resort and Casino, and Harrah's Las Vegas? Answer: They are all part of Harrah's Entertainment. So how in the world does Harrah's possibly create customized offerings for patrons of these very different properties? The answer is sophisticated data mining. By mining the data, Harrah's identifies customer segments whose preferences indicate that they may respond to different types of promotional offers. If the data show that some of the company's clientele favor one property over another, one form of gaming over another, or even one type of show over another, those customers will receive promotional materials tailored to their specific preferences. Slot players are notified of slot tournaments, while fans of magic shows get a heads up when Lance Burton is scheduled to appear. And the database tracks what casino visitors actually do (including how much they wager at the tables) so that that the hotels can "comp" active gamblers (winners or losers) and encourage them to drop even more.

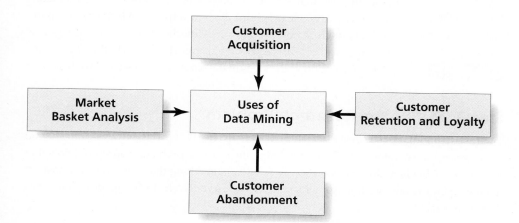

Figure 4.3 🎿 *Process* | Uses of Data Mining

Data mining has four primary applications for marketers.

Market basket analysis helps companies to understand when customers are most likely to consume their products so they can promote them more heavily during these occasions.

supermarkets offer weekly special price discounts for store "members." These stores' membership application forms require that customers indicate their age, family size, address, and so on. With this information, the supermarket determines which of its current customers respond best to specific offers and then sends the same offers to noncustomers who share the same demographic characteristics.

2. *Customer retention and loyalty:* The firm identifies big-spending customers and then targets them for special offers and inducements other customers won't receive. Keeping the most profitable customers coming back is a great way to build business success because keeping good customers is less expensive than constantly finding new ones.[8]

3. *Customer abandonment:* Strange as it may sound, sometimes a firm wants customers to take their business elsewhere because servicing them actually costs the firm too much. Today, this is popularly called "firing a customer." For example, a department store may use data mining to identify unprofitable customers—those who are not spending enough or who return most of what they buy. In recent years, data mining has allowed Sprint to famously identify customers as "the good, the bad, and the ugly."[9]

4. *Market basket analysis* develops focused promotional strategies based on the records of which customers have bought certain products. Hewlett-Packard, for example, carefully analyzes which of its customers recently bought new printers and targets them to receive e-mails about specials on ink cartridges and tips to get the most out of their machines.

So far, we have looked at the MIS and the MDSS, the overall systems that provide the information marketers need to make good decisions. We've seen how MIS and MDSS data include internal company data, marketing intelligence data gathered by monitoring everyday sources, acquired databases, and information gathered to address specific marketing decisions through the marketing research process. In the rest of the chapter, we'll look at the steps that marketers take when they conduct marketing research.

3 Steps in the Marketing Research Process

OBJECTIVE

List and explain the steps and key elements of the marketing research process.
(pp. 108–122)

The collection and interpretation of strategic information is hardly a one-shot deal that managers engage in "just out of curiosity." Ideally, marketing research is an ongoing process, a series of steps marketers take repeatedly to learn about the marketplace. Whether a company conducts the research itself or hires another firm to do it, the goal is the same: to help managers make informed marketing decisions. Figure 4.4 shows the steps in the research process, and we'll go over each of these now.

Step 1: Define the Research Problem

The first step in the marketing research process is to clearly understand what information managers need. We refer to this step as defining the research problem. You should note that the word *problem* here does not necessarily refer to "something that is wrong," but instead it refers to the overall questions for which the firm needs answers. Defining the problem has three components:

1. *Specify the research objectives:* What questions will the research attempt to answer?

2. *Identify the consumer population of interest:* What are the characteristics of the consumer group(s) of interest?

3. *Place the problem in an environmental context:* What factors in the firm's internal and external business environment might influence the situation?

It's not as simple as it may seem to provide the right kind of information for each of these pieces of the problem. Suppose a luxury car manufacturer wants to find out why its sales have fallen off dramatically over the past year. The research objective could revolve around any number of possible questions: Is the firm's advertising failing to reach the right consumers? Is the right message being sent? Do the firm's cars have a particular feature (or lack of one) that's turning customers away? Is there a problem with the firm's reputation for providing quality service? Do consumers believe the price is right for the value they get? The particular objective researchers choose depends on a variety of factors, such as the feedback the firm gets from its customers, the information it receives from the marketplace, and sometimes even the intuition of the people who design the research.

Often the focus of a research question comes from marketplace feedback that identifies a possible problem. Mercedes-Benz is a great example of a firm that for years has continually monitored drivers' perceptions of its cars. When the company started to get reports from its dealers in the 1990s that more and more people viewed Mercedes products as "arrogant" and "unapproachable," even to the point at which they were reluctant to sit in showroom models, the company undertook a research project to better understand the reasons for this perception.

The *research objective* determines the consumer population the company will study. In the case of Mercedes, the research could have focused on current owners to find out what they especially like about the car. Or it could have been directed at nonowners to understand their lifestyles, what they look for in a luxury automobile, or their beliefs about the company itself that keep them from choosing its cars. So what did Mercedes find out? Research showed that although people rated its cars very highly on engineering quality and status, many were too intimidated by the elitist Mercedes image to consider actually buying one. Mercedes dealers reported that a common question from visitors to showrooms was, "May I actually sit in the car?" Based on these findings, Mercedes in recent years has worked hard to adjust perceptions by projecting a slightly more down-to-earth image in its advertising, and it ultimately created new downsized classes of vehicles to appeal to consumers who want something a little less ostentatious.[10]

Step 2: Determine the Research Design

Once we isolate specific problems, the second step of the research process is to decide on a "plan of attack." This plan is the **research design**, which specifies exactly what information marketers will collect and what type of study they will do. ⚡ Figure 4.5 summarizes many of the types of research designs in the researcher's arsenal. As you can see, research designs fall into two broad categories: *secondary research* and *primary research.* All marketing problems do not call for the same research techniques, and marketers solve many problems most effectively with a combination of techniques.

Define the Research Problem
- Specify the research objectives
- Identify the consumer population of interest
- Place the problem in an environmental context

Determine the Research Design
- Determine whether secondary data are available
- Determine whether primary data are required
  —Exploratory research
  —Descriptive research
  —Causal research

Choose the Method to Collect Primary Data
- Determine which survey methods are most appropriate
  —Mail questionnaires
  —Telephone interviews
  —Face-to-face interviews
  —Online questionnaires
- Determine which observational methods are most appropriate
  —Personal observation
  —Unobtrusive measures
  —Mechanical observation

Design the Sample
- Choose between probability sampling and nonprobability sampling

Collect the Data
- Translate questionnaires and responses if necessary
- Combine data from multiple sources (if available)

Analyze and Interpret the Data
- Tabulate and cross-tabulate the data
- Interpret or draw conclusions from the results

Prepare the Research Report
- In general, the research report includes the following:
  —An executive summary
  —A description of the research methods
  —A discussion of the results of the study
  —Limitations of the study
  —Conclusions and recommendations

Figure 4.4 ⚡ *Process* | Steps in the Marketing Research Process

The marketing research process includes a series of steps that begins with defining the problem or the information needed and ends with the finished research report for managers.

Figure 4.5 🏃 *Process* | Marketing Research Designs

For some research problems, the secondary research may provide the information needed. At other times, one of the primary research methods may be needed.

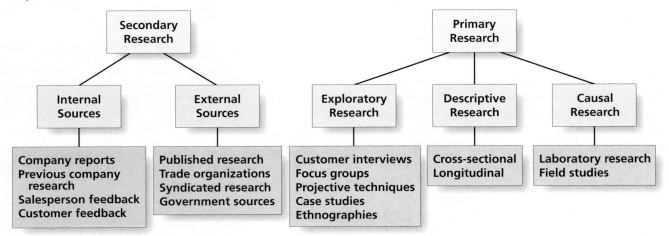

research design
A plan that specifies what information marketers will collect and what type of study they will do.

secondary data
Data that have been collected for some purpose other than the problem at hand.

primary data
Data from research conducted to help make a specific decision.

Secondary Research

The first question marketers must ask when they determine their research design is whether the information they require to make a decision already exists. For example, a coffee producer who needs to know the differences in coffee consumption among different demographic and geographic segments of the market may find that the information it needs is already available from one or more studies already conducted by the National Coffee Association, the leading trade association of U.S. coffee companies and a major generator of industry research. We call data that have been collected for some purpose other than the problem at hand **secondary data**.

Many marketers thrive on going out and collecting new, "fresh" data from consumers. However, if secondary data are available, it saves the firm time and money because the expense to design and implement a study has already been incurred. Sometimes the data that marketers need may be "hiding" right under the organization's nose in the form of company reports; previous company research studies; feedback received from customers, salespeople, or stores; or even in the memories of longtime employees. More typically, though, researchers need to look elsewhere for secondary data. They may obtain reports published in the popular and business press, studies that private research organizations or government agencies conduct, and published research on the state of the industry from trade organizations.

For example, many companies subscribe to reports such as the *National Consumer Study*, a national survey conducted by syndicated research firm Experian Simmons. Simmons publishes results that it then sells to marketers, advertising agencies, and publishers. Access to their data is even available in some college libraries. This database contains over 60,000 data variables with usage behavior on all major media, over 450 product categories, and over 8,000 brands. Data from Experian Simmons can give a brand manager a profile of who uses a product, identify heavy users, or even provide data on what magazines a target market reads.[11] Of course, marketers can readily turn to the Internet for numerous external information sources. Table 4.2 lists several Web sites helpful to marketers when they look for secondary research topics.

Primary Research

Of course, secondary research is not always the answer. When a company needs to make a specific decision, it often needs to collect **primary data**: information it gathers directly from respondents to specifically address the question at hand. Primary data include demographic and psychological information about customers and prospective customers, customers' attitudes

Table 4.2 | Helpful Internet Sites for Marketing Research

URL	Description
www.opinionresearch.com	Opinion Research Corporation offers numerous industry and trend reports that are useful as secondary data sources.
www.census.gov	The U.S. Census Bureau publishes separate reports on specific industries (such as agriculture, construction, and mining) as well as on housing, population growth and distribution, and retail trade. Some 2010 Census data will be available in 2011, but most won't be out until 2012.
www.marketingpower.com	The American Marketing Association provides many resources to its members on a variety of industry topics.
www.dialog.com	Dialog sorts companies by location, size, and industry. The user can request telemarketing reports, preaddressed mailing labels, and company profiles.
www.lexisnexis.com	LexisNexis is a large database featuring information from sources such as Dun & Bradstreet, the *New York Times*, CNN, and National Public Radio transcripts.

and opinions about products and competing products, as well as their awareness or knowledge about a product and their beliefs about the people who use those products. In the next few sections, we'll talk briefly about the various designs options to conduct primary research.

Exploratory (Qualitative) Research

Marketers use **exploratory research** to come up with ideas for new strategies and opportunities or perhaps just to get a better handle on a problem they are currently experiencing with a product. Because the studies are usually small scale and less costly than other techniques, marketers may use exploratory research to test their hunches about what's going on without too much risk.

Exploratory studies often involve in-depth probing of a few consumers who fit the profile of the "typical" customer. Researchers may interview consumers, salespeople, or other employees about products, services, ads, or stores. They may simply "hang out" and watch what people do when they choose among competing brands in a store aisle. Or they may locate places where the consumers of interest tend to be and ask questions in these settings. For example, some researchers find that younger people often are too suspicious or skeptical in traditional research settings, so they may interview them while they wait in line to buy concert tickets or in clubs.[12]

We refer to most exploratory research as *qualitative*: that is, the results of the research project tend to be nonnumeric and instead might be detailed verbal or visual information about consumers' attitudes, feelings, and buying behaviors in the form of words rather than in numbers. For example, when DuPont wanted to know how women felt about panty hose, marketers asked research participants to collect magazine clippings that expressed their emotions about the product.

Intuit, the software company that produces the personal finance software packages Turbo-Tax and Quicken, used personal interviews to better understand consumers' frustrations when they try to install and use its products. When customers told researchers that the software itself should "tell me how to do it," they took this advice literally and developed software that used computer audio to give verbal instructions. Intuit's probing went one step beyond interviews. Its researchers left respondents microcassette recorders so that whenever they were having problems, they could simply push a button and tell the company of their frustration.

The **focus group** is the technique that marketing researchers use most often for collecting exploratory data. Focus groups typically consist of five to nine consumers who have been recruited because they share certain characteristics (they all play golf at least twice a month, are women in their twenties, and so on). These people sit together to discuss a product, ad,

exploratory research
A technique that marketers use to generate insights for future, more rigorous studies.

focus group
A product-oriented discussion among a small group of consumers led by a trained moderator.

or some other marketing topic a discussion leader introduces. Typically, the leader records (by videotape or audiotape) these group discussions, which may be held at special interviewing facilities that allow for observation by the client who watches from behind a one-way mirror.

Today it's common to find focus groups in cyberspace as well. Firms such as DelMonte, Coca-Cola, and Disney use online focus group sites that often bear some resemblance to other social-networking sites, where members create profile pages and post to discussion boards. Companies use them to administer polls, chat in real time with consumers, and even ask members to go to the store to try out specific products. DelMonte handpicked 400 members for its private network, which the company uses to help create products, test marketing campaigns, and stir up buzz. The rapid back-and-forth between the company and the online community allows for real-time data collection that can help substantially shorten the product development cycle.[13]

case study
A comprehensive examination of a particular firm or organization.

The **case study** is a comprehensive examination of a particular firm or organization. In business-to-business marketing research in which the customers are other firms, for example, researchers may try to learn how one particular company makes its purchases. The goal is to identify the key decision makers, to learn what criteria they emphasize when choosing among suppliers, and perhaps to learn something about any conflicts and rivalries among these decision makers that may influence their choices.

ethnography
An approach to research based on observations of people in their own homes or communities.

An **ethnography** is a different kind of in-depth report. It uses a technique marketers borrow from anthropologists who go to "live with the natives" for months or even years. Some marketing researchers visit people's homes or participate in real-life consumer activities to get a handle on how they really use products. Imagine having a researcher follow you around while you shop and then while you use the products you bought to see what kind of consumer you are. This is basically marketers' version of a reality show—though hopefully the people they study are a bit more "realistic"!

Descriptive (Quantitative) Research

We've seen that marketers have many tools in their arsenal, including focus groups and observational techniques, to help them better define a problem or opportunity. These are usually modest studies of a small number of people, enough to get some indication of what is going on but not enough for the marketer to feel confident about generalizing what she observes to the rest of the population.

descriptive research
A tool that probes more systematically into the problem and bases its conclusions on large numbers of observations.

The next step in marketing research, then, often is to conduct **descriptive research**. This kind of research probes systematically into the marketing problem and bases its conclusions on a large sample of participants. Results typically are expressed in quantitative terms—averages, percentages, or other statistics that result from a large set of measurements. In such quantitative approaches to research, the project can be as simple as counting the number of Listerine bottles sold in a month in different regions of the country or as complex as statistical analyses of responses to a survey mailed to thousands of consumers. In each case, marketers conduct the descriptive research to answer a specific question, in contrast to the "fishing expedition" that may occur in exploratory research.

cross-sectional design
A type of descriptive technique that involves the systematic collection of quantitative information.

Marketing researchers who employ descriptive techniques most often use a **cross-sectional design**. This approach usually involves the systematic collection of responses to a consumer survey instrument, such as a *questionnaire*, from one or more samples of respondents at one point in time. The data may be collected on more than one occasion but generally not from the same pool of respondents.

longitudinal design
A technique that tracks the responses of the same sample of respondents over time.

In contrast to these one-shot studies, a **longitudinal design** tracks the responses of the same sample of respondents over time. Market researchers sometimes create consumer panels to get information; in this case a sample of respondents that are representative of a larger market agrees to provide information about purchases on a weekly or monthly basis. Major consumer packaged goods firms like P&G, Unilever, Colgate Palmolive, and Johnson &

Johnson, for instance, recruit consumer advisory panels on a market-by-market basis to keep their fingers on the pulse of local shoppers.

Causal Research

It's a fact that purchases of both diapers and beer peak between 5:00 PM and 7:00 PM. Can we say that purchasing one of these products caused shoppers to purchase the other as well—and, if so, which caused which? Does taking care of a baby drive a parent to drink? Or is the answer simply that this happens to be the time when young fathers stop at the store on their way home from work to pick up some brew and Pampers?[14]

The descriptive techniques we've examined do a good job of providing valuable information about what is happening in the marketplace, but by its very nature descriptive research can only *describe* a marketplace phenomenon—it cannot tell us *why* it occurs. Sometimes marketers need to know if something they've done has brought about some change in behavior. For example, does placing one product next to another in a store mean that people will buy more of each? We can't answer this question through simple observation or description.

GlowImages/Masterfile

To rule out alternative explanations, researchers carefully design **experiments** that test predicted relationships among variables in a controlled environment. Because this approach tries to eliminate competing explanations for the outcome, researchers may bring respondents to a laboratory so they can control precisely what the participants experience. For example, a study to test whether the placement of diapers in a grocery store influences the likelihood that male shoppers will buy them might bring a group of men into a testing facility and show them a "virtual store" on a computer screen. Researchers would ask the men to fill a grocery cart as they click through the "aisles." The experiment might vary the placement of the diapers—next to shelves of beer in one scenario, near paper goods in a different scenario. The objective is to see which placement gets the guys to put diapers into their carts.

Causal research attempts to identify cause-and-effect relationships. Marketers use causal research techniques when they want to know if a change in something (for example, placing cases of beer next to a diaper display) is responsible for a change in something else (for example, a big increase in diaper sales). They call the factors that might cause such a change *independent variables* and the outcomes *dependent variables*. The independent variable(s) cause some change in the dependent variable(s). In our example, then, the beer display is an independent variable, and sales data for the diapers are a dependent variable—that is, the study would investigate whether an increase in diaper sales "depends" on the proximity of beer. Researchers can gather data and test the causal relationship statistically.

causal research
A technique that attempts to understand cause-and-effect relationships.

experiments
A technique that tests predicted relationships among variables in a controlled environment.

Step 3: Choose the Method to Collect Primary Data

When the researcher decides to work with primary data, the next step in the marketing research process is to figure out just how to collect it. We broadly describe primary data collection methods as either *survey* or *observation*. There are many ways to collect data, and marketers try new ones all the time. Today, a few marketing researchers even turn to sophisticated brain scans to directly measure our brains' reactions to various advertisements or products. These "neuromarketers" hope to be able to tell companies how people will react to their brands by scanning consumers' brains rather than collecting data the old-fashioned way—by asking them.[15] These techniques are still in their infancy, so for now we still rely on other methods to collect primary data.

Survey Methods

Survey methods involve some kind of interview or other direct contact with respondents who answer questions. Questionnaires can be administered on the phone, in person, through the mail, or over the Internet. Table 4.3 summarizes the advantages and disadvantages of different methods to collect data.

Table 4.3 | Advantages and Disadvantages of Data Collection Methods

Data Collection Method	Advantages	Disadvantages
Mail questionnaires	<ul><li>Respondents feel anonymous</li><li>Low cost</li><li>Good for ongoing research</li></ul>	<ul><li>May take a long time for questionnaires to be returned</li><li>Low rate of response; many may not return questionnaires</li><li>Inflexible questionnaire</li><li>Length of questionnaire limited by respondent interest in the topic</li><li>Unclear whether respondents understand the questions</li><li>Unclear who is responding</li><li>No assurance that respondents are being honest</li></ul>
Telephone interviews	<ul><li>Fast</li><li>High flexibility in questioning</li><li>Low cost</li><li>Limited interviewer follow-up</li></ul>	<ul><li>Decreasing levels of respondent cooperation</li><li>Limited questionnaire length</li><li>High likelihood of respondent misunderstanding</li><li>Respondents cannot view materials</li><li>Cannot survey households without phones</li><li>Consumers screen calls with answering machines and caller ID</li><li>Do-not-call lists allow many research subjects to opt out of participation</li></ul>
Face-to-face interviews	<ul><li>Flexibility of questioning</li><li>Can use long questionnaires</li><li>Can determine whether respondents have trouble understanding questions</li><li>Take a lot of time</li><li>Can use visuals or other materials</li></ul>	<ul><li>High cost</li><li>Interviewer bias a problem</li></ul>
Online questionnaires	<ul><li>Instantaneous data collection and analysis</li><li>Questioning very flexible</li><li>Low cost</li><li>No interviewer bias</li><li>No geographic restrictions</li><li>Can use visuals or other materials</li></ul>	<ul><li>Unclear who is responding</li><li>No assurance that respondents are being honest</li><li>Limited questionnaire length</li><li>Unable to determine whether respondent understands the question</li><li>Self-selected samples</li></ul>

Questionnaires

Questionnaires differ in their degree of structure. With a totally *unstructured questionnaire*, the researcher loosely determines the items in advance. Questions may evolve from the respondent's answers to previous questions. At the other extreme, the researcher uses a *completely structured questionnaire*. She asks every respondent the exact same questions and each participant responds to the same set of fixed choices. You have probably experienced this kind of questionnaire, where you might have had to respond to a statement by saying if you "strongly agree," "somewhat agree," and so on. *Moderately structured questionnaires* ask each respondent the same questions, but the respondent is allowed to answer the questions in her own words.

Mail questionnaires are easy to administer and offer a high degree of anonymity to respondents. On the downside, because the questionnaire is printed and mailed, researchers have little flexibility in the types of questions they can ask and little control over the circumstances under which the respondent answers them. Mail questionnaires also take a long time to get back to the company and are likely to have a much lower response rate than other types of data collection methods because people tend to ignore them.

Telephone interviews usually consist of a brief phone conversation in which an interviewer reads a short list of questions to the respondent. There are several problems with using telephone interviews as a data collection method. The respondent also may not feel comfortable speaking directly to an interviewer, especially if the survey is about a sensitive subject.

Another problem with this method is that the growth of **telemarketing**, in which businesses sell directly to consumers over the phone, has eroded consumers' willingness to participate in phone surveys. In addition to aggravating people by barraging them with telephone sales messages (usually during dinnertime!), some unscrupulous telemarketers disguise their pitches as research. They contact consumers under the pretense of doing a study when, in fact, their real intent is to sell the respondent something or to solicit funds for some cause. This in turn prompts increasing numbers of people to use voice mail and caller ID to screen calls, which further reduces the response rate. And, as we noted earlier, state and federal *do-not-call lists* allow many would-be research subjects to opt out of participation both in legitimate marketing research and unscrupulous telemarketing.[16]

Using *face-to-face interviews*, a live interviewer asks questions of one respondent at a time. Although in "the old days" researchers often went door-to-door to ask questions, that's much less common today because of fears about security and because the large numbers of two-income families make it less likely to find people at home during the day. Typically, today's face-to-face interviews occur in a **mall-intercept** study in which researchers recruit shoppers in malls or other public areas. You've probably seen this going on in your local mall, where a smiling person holding a clipboard stops shoppers to see if they are willing to answer a few questions.

Mall-intercepts offer good opportunities to get feedback about new package designs, styles, or even reactions to new foods or fragrances. However, because only certain groups of the population frequently shop at malls, a mall-intercept study does not provide the researcher with a representative sample of the population (unless the population of interest is mall shoppers). In addition to being more expensive than mail or phone surveys, respondents may be reluctant to answer questions of a personal nature in a face-to-face context.

Online questionnaires are growing in popularity, but the use of such questionnaires is not without concerns. Many researchers question the quality of responses they will receive—particularly because (as with mail and phone interviews) no one can be really sure who is typing in the responses on the computer. In addition, it's uncertain whether savvy online consumers are truly representative of the general population.[17] However, these concerns are rapidly evaporating as research firms devise new ways to verify identities; present surveys in novel formats, including the use of images, sound, and animation; and recruit more diverse respondents.[18]

Observational Methods

As we said earlier, the second major primary data collection method is *observation*. This term refers to situations where the researcher simply records the consumer's behaviors.

When researchers use *personal observation*, they simply watch consumers in action to understand how they react to marketing activities. Although a laboratory allows researchers to exert control over what test subjects see and do, marketers don't always have the luxury of conducting this kind of "pure" research. But it is possible to conduct field studies in the real world, as long as the researchers still can control the independent variables. For example, a diaper company might choose two grocery stores that have similar customer bases in terms of age, income, and so on. With the cooperation of the grocery store's management, the company might place its diaper display next to the beer in one store and next to the paper goods in the other and then record diaper purchases men make over a two-week period. If a lot

telemarketing
The use of the telephone to sell directly to consumers and business customers.

mall-intercept
A study in which researchers recruit shoppers in malls or other public areas.

more guys buy diapers in the first store than in the second (and the company was sure that nothing else was different between the two stores, such as a dollar-off coupon for diapers being distributed in one store and not the other), the diaper manufacturer might conclude that the presence of beer in the background does indeed result in increased diaper sales.

unobtrusive measures
Measuring traces of physical evidence that remain after some action has been taken.

When they suspect that subjects will probably alter their behavior if they know someone is watching them, researchers may use **unobtrusive measures** to record traces of physical evidence that remain after people have consumed something. For example, instead of asking a person to report on the alcohol products currently in her home, the researcher might go to the house and perform a "pantry check" by actually counting the bottles in her liquor cabinet. Another option is to sift through garbage to search for clues about each family's consumption habits. The "garbologists" can tell, for example, which soft drink accompanied what kind of food. Since people in these studies don't know that researchers are looking through products they've discarded, the information is totally objective—although a bit smelly!

Mechanical observation is a primary data–collection method that relies on nonhuman devices to record behavior. For example, one of the classic applications of mechanical observation is the Nielsen Company's famous use of "people meters"—boxes the company attaches to the television sets of selected viewers to record patterns of television watching. The data Nielsen obtains from these devices indicate who is watching which shows. These "television ratings" help network clients determine how much to charge advertisers for commercials and which shows to cancel or renew. The service is so popular that Nielsen tripled the size of its reporting panel between 2007 and 2011—currently about 37,000 homes and 100,000 people are involved in the data collection.[19]

Similarly, Arbitron deploys thousands of "portable people meters," or PPMs. PPMs resemble pagers and automatically record the wearer's exposure to any media that has inserted an inaudible code into its promotion (TV ad, shelf display, and so forth). Thus, when the consumer is exposed to a broadcast commercial, cinema ad, Internet banner ad, or other form of commercial the PPM registers, records, and time-stamps the signal. At day's end, a home docking station downloads the media history. Portability ensures that all exposures register; this eliminates obtrusive people meters and written diaries that participants often forget to fill out.[20]

Online Research

The Internet rewrote some of the rules of the marketing research process. Many companies find that the Web is a superior way to collect data—it's fast, it's relatively cheap, and it lends itself well to forms of research from simple questionnaires to online focus groups. In fact, some large companies like P&G now collect a large portion of their consumer intelligence

The Cutting Edge

Measuring Multimedia Activity

Who watches old-fashioned TV anymore? As more and more people tune in Hulu or YouTube instead of catching their favorite shows on network television, TV ratings alone grossly underestimate actual viewership of program content. NBC Universal, broadcaster of the most recent Summer and Winter Olympics in Beijing and Vancouver, respectively, used the occasions to do some groundbreaking market research. The company measured how viewers actually watched the games across the full array of diverse media platforms today, including mobile devices and the Web. "To some extent, these Olympics are starting to influence how people use new technology," said Alan Wurtzel, president of research and media development, NBC Universal. "About half of people who used mobile [to watch NBC Olympics content] are using it for the first time."

As more people start to get information and entertainment from venues other than the living room TV, measuring the overall activity will play a large role in whether big networks such as NBC can get advertisers to pay significant dollars for it. To capture the full scope, the network unveiled a metric dubbed "TAMi," or *total audience measurement index*. The data capture in basic fashion the numbers of people watching Olympics content on TV, online, via mobile, and through video-on-demand. Results are far from perfect and some of the numbers may represent duplication of viewership. Even so, NBC is rolling out TAMi across all its program offerings as a means of helping advertisers track cross-media promotions. "It gives you an insight that you normally wouldn't have about TV viewership across platforms," Wurtzel said.[21]

online. Developments in online research are happening quickly, so let's take some time now to see where things are headed.

There are two major types of online research. One type is information we gather by tracking consumers while they surf the Web. The second type is information we gather through questionnaires on Web sites, through e-mail, or from focus groups virtual moderators conduct in chat rooms.

The Internet offers an unprecedented ability to track consumers as they search for information. Marketers can better understand where people look when they want to learn about products—and which advertisements they stop to browse along the way. How can marketers do this? Beware the Cookie Monster! **Cookies** are text files a Web site sponsor inserts into a user's hard drive when the user connects with the site. Cookies remember details of a visit to a Web site and they track which pages the user visits. Some sites request or require that visitors "register" on the site by answering questions about themselves and their likes and dislikes. In such cases, cookies also allow the site to access these details about the customer.

This technology allows Web sites to customize services, such as when **Amazon.com** recommends new books to users on the basis of what books they have ordered in the past. Consider this one. A shopper at the retail site **FigLeaves.com** takes a close look at a frilly pair of women's slippers. Next, a recommendation pops up for a man's bathrobe. Is this a mistake—or is the site showing the shopper just what she wanted to see? These surprising connections will happen more often as e-marketers adopt newer generation of **predictive technology** that use shopping patterns of large numbers of people to determine which products are likely to be purchased if others are. So, why the bathrobe? ATG, a Cambridge (Mass.) e-commerce software company that crunches data for FigLeaves, has found that certain types of female shoppers at certain times of the week are likely to be shopping for men. Like all Web recommendations, this one will be wrong a good portion of the time. But as marketers scrutinize online shoppers in greater detail, they're edging closer to their ultimate goal: teaching computers to blend data smarts with something close to the savvy of a flesh-and-blood sales clerk.[22]

Most consumers have no idea that technologies such as cookies allow Web sites to gather and store all this information. You can block cookies or curb them, although this can make life difficult if you are trying to log on to many sites, such as online newspapers or travel agencies that require this information to admit you. The information generated from tracking consumers' online journeys has become a product as well—companies sell records to other companies that want to target prospects. But consumers increasingly are concerned about the sharing of these data. In a study of 10,000 Web users, 84 percent objected to the reselling of their information to other companies. Although Internet users can delete cookie files manually or install anticookie software on their computers, many people feel there is a need for privacy regulation and for cookies to limit potential abuses.

To date, the Federal Trade Commission has relied on the Internet industry to develop and maintain its own standards instead of developing its own extensive privacy regulations, but many would like to see that situation changed. Privacy rights proponents advocate the following guiding principles:

- Information about a consumer belongs to the consumer.

- Consumers should be made aware of information collection.

- Consumers should know how information about them will be used.

- Consumers should be able to refuse to allow information collection.

- Information about a consumer should never be sold or given to another party without the permission of the consumer.

No data collection method is perfect, and online research is no exception—though many of the criticisms of online techniques also apply to offline techniques. One potential problem

cookies
Text files inserted by a Web site sponsor into a Web surfer's hard drive that allows the site to track the surfer's moves.

predictive technology
Analysis techniques that use shopping patterns of large numbers of people to determine which products are likely to be purchased if others are.

is the representativeness of the respondents. Although the number of Internet users continues to grow, many segments of the consumer population, mainly the poor and elderly, do not have equal access to the Internet. In addition, in many studies (just as with mail surveys or mall intercepts) there is a self-selection bias in the sample. That is, because respondents have agreed to receive invitations to take part in online studies, by definition they tend to be the kind of people who like to participate in surveys. As with other kinds of research such as live focus groups, it's not unusual to encounter "professional respondents"—people who just enjoy taking part in studies (and getting paid for it). Online research specialists such as Harris Interactive, SSI—Survey Sampling International, and Toluna address this problem by monitoring their participants and regulating how often they are allowed to participate in different studies over a period of time.

There are other disadvantages of online research. Hackers can actually try to influence research results. Competitors can learn about a firm's marketing plans, products, advertising, and so forth when they intercept information from these studies (though this can occur in offline studies just as easily). Because cheating has become so rampant, some companies today use fraud-busting software that creates a digital fingerprint of each computer involved in a survey to identify respondents who fake responses or professionals who game the industry by doing as many surveys as possible.[23]

Data Quality: Garbage In, Garbage Out

We've seen that a firm can collect data in many ways, including focus groups, ethnographic approaches, observational studies, and controlled experiments. But how much faith should marketers place in what they find out from the research?

All too often, marketers who commission a study assume that because the researchers give them a massive report full of impressive-looking numbers and tables, they must be looking at the "truth." Unfortunately, there are times when this "truth" is really just one person's interpretation of the facts. At other times, the data researchers use to generate recommendations are flawed. As the expression goes, "Garbage in, garbage out!"[24] That is, your conclusions can only be as good as the information you use to make them. Typically, three factors influence the quality of research results—validity, reliability, and representativeness.

validity
The extent to which research actually measures what it was intended to measure.

Validity is the extent to which the research actually measures what it was intended to measure. This was part of the problem underlying the famous New Coke fiasco in the 1980s, in which Coca-Cola underestimated people's loyalty to its flagship soft drink after it replaced "Old Coke" with a new, sweeter formula. In a blind taste test, the company assumed testers' preferences for one anonymous cola over another was a valid measure of consumers' preferences for a cola brand. Coca-Cola found out the hard way that measuring taste only is not the same as measuring people's deep allegiances to their favorite soft drinks. After all, Coke is a brand that elicits strong consumer loyalty and is nothing short of a cultural icon. Tampering with the flavors was like assaulting Mom and apple pie. Sales eventually recovered after the company brought back the old version as "Coca-Cola Classic."[25]

reliability
The extent to which research measurement techniques are free of errors.

Reliability is the extent to which the research measurement techniques are free of errors. Sometimes, for example, the way a researcher asks a question creates error by biasing people's responses. Imagine that an attractive female interviewer working for Trojans condoms stopped male college students on campus and asked them if they used contraceptive products. Do you think their answers might change if they were asked the same questions on an anonymous survey they received in the mail? Most likely, their answers would be different because people are reluctant to disclose what they actually do when their responses are not anonymous. Researchers try to maximize reliability by thinking of several different ways to ask the same questions, by asking these questions on several occasions, or by using several analysts to interpret the responses. Thus, they can compare responses and look for consistency and stability.

Reliability is a problem when the researchers can't be sure the consumer population they're studying even understands the questions. For example, kids are difficult subjects for market researchers because they tend to be undependable reporters of their own behavior, they have poor recall, and they often do not understand abstract questions. In many cases, the children cannot explain why they prefer one item over another (or they're not willing to share these secrets with grown-ups).[26] For these reasons, researchers have to be especially creative when they design studies involving younger consumers. ▢ Figure 4.6 shows part of a completion test a set of researchers used to measure children's preferences for television programming in Japan.

Representativeness is the extent to which consumers in the study are similar to a larger group in which the organization has an interest. This criterion underscores the importance of **sampling**: the process of selecting respondents for a study. The issue then becomes how large the sample should be and how to choose these people. We'll talk more about sampling in the next section.

Step 4: Design the Sample

Once the researcher defines the problem, decides on a research design, and determines how to collect the data, the next step is to decide from whom to obtain the needed information. Of course, he or she *could* collect data from every single customer or prospective customer, but this would be extremely expensive and time consuming if possible at all (this is what the U.S. Census spends millions of dollars to do every 10 years). Not everyone has the resources of the U.S. government (or what's left of them) to poll everyone in their market. So, they typically collect most of their data from a small proportion or sample of the population of interest. Based on the answers from this sample, researchers generalize to the larger population. Whether such inferences are accurate or inaccurate depends on the type and quality of the study sample. There are two main types of samples: probability and nonprobability samples.

Probability Sampling

In a **probability sample**, each member of the population has some known chance of being included. Using a probability sample ensures that the sample represents the population and that inferences we make about the population from what members of the sample say or do are justified. For example, if a larger percentage of males than females in a probability sample say they prefer action movies to "chick flicks," one can infer with confidence that a larger percentage of males than females in the general population also would rather see a character get sliced and diced (okay, we wouldn't really use these descriptions in a study, but you get the idea).

The most basic type of probability sample is a *simple random sample* in which every member of a population has a known and equal chance of being included in the study. For example, if we simply take the names of all 40 students in your class and put them in a hat and draw one out, each member of your class has a one in 40 chance of being included in the sample. In most studies, the population from which the sample will be drawn is too large for a hat, so marketers use a computer program to generate a random sample from a list of members.

Sometimes researchers use a *systematic sampling procedure* to select members of a population; they select the *n*th member of a population after a random start. For example, if we want a sample of 10 members of your class, we might begin with the second person on the roll and select every fourth name after that—the 2nd, the 6th, the 10th, the 14th, and so on. Researchers know that studies that use systematic samples are just as accurate as those that use simple random samples. But unless a list of members of the population of interest is already in a computer data file, it's a lot simpler just to create a simple random sample.

Yet another type of probability sample is a *stratified sample*, in which a researcher divides the population into segments that relate to the study's topic. For example, imagine you want to study what movies most theatergoers like. You have learned from previous studies that men and women in the population differ in their attitudes toward different types of

Figure 4.6 ▢ *Snapshot* | Completion Test

It can be especially difficult to get accurate information from children. Researchers often use visuals such as this Japanese completion test to encourage children to express their feelings. The test asked boys to write in the empty balloon what they think the boy in the drawing will answer when the girl asks, "What program do you want to watch next?"

representativeness
The extent to which consumers in a study are similar to a larger group in which the organization has an interest.

sampling
The process of selecting respondents for a study.

probability sample
A sample in which each member of the population has some known chance of being included.

movies—men like action flicks and women like romances. To create a stratified sample, you would first divide the population into male and female segments. Then you would randomly select respondents from each of the two segments in proportion to their percentage of the population. In this way, you have created a sample that is proportionate to the population on a characteristic that you know will make a difference in the study results.

Nonprobability Sampling

nonprobability sample
A sample in which personal judgment is used to select respondents.

Sometimes researchers do not believe the time and effort required to develop a probability sample is justified, perhaps because they need an answer quickly or they just want to get a general sense of how people feel about a topic. They may choose a **nonprobability sample**, which entails the use of personal judgment to select respondents—in some cases they just ask whomever they can find. With a nonprobability sample, some members of the population have no chance at all of being included. Thus, there is no way to ensure that the sample is representative of the population. Results from nonprobability studies can be generally suggestive of what is going on in the real world but are not necessarily definitive.

convenience sample
A nonprobability sample composed of individuals who just happen to be available when and where the data are being collected.

A **convenience sample** is a nonprobability sample composed of individuals who just happen to be available when and where the data are being collected. For example, if you simply stand in front of the student union and ask students who walk by to complete your questionnaire, the "guinea pigs" you get to agree to do it would be a convenience sample.

Finally, researchers may also use a *quota sample* that includes the same proportion of individuals with certain characteristics as in the population. For example, if you are studying attitudes of students in your university, you might just go on campus and find freshmen, sophomores, juniors, and seniors in proportion to the number of members of each class in the university. The quota sample is much like the stratified sample except that with a quota sample, the researcher uses his or her individual judgment to select respondents.

Step 5: Collect the Data

At this point, the researcher has determined the nature of the problem she needs to address. She has decided on a research design that will specify how to investigate the problem and what kinds of information (data) she will need. The researcher has also selected the data collection and sampling methods. Once she has made these decisions, the next task is to actually collect the data.

Garbage In, Garbage Out

We noted earlier that the quality of your conclusions is only as good as the data you use. The same logic applies to the people who collect the data: The quality of research results is only as good as the poorest interviewer in the study. Careless interviewers may not read questions exactly as written, or they may not record respondent answers correctly. So marketers must train and supervise interviewers to make sure they follow the research procedures exactly as outlined. In the next section, we'll talk about some of the problems in gathering data and some solutions.

Challenges to Gathering Data in Foreign Countries

Conducting market research around the world is big business for U.S. firms. In 2009, among the top 50 U.S. research firms nearly 50 percent of revenues came from projects outside the United States.[27] However, market conditions and consumer preferences vary worldwide, and there are major differences in the sophistication of market research operations and the amount of data available to global marketers. In Mexico, for instance, because there are still large areas where native tribes speak languages other than Spanish, researchers may end up bypassing these groups in surveys. In Egypt, where the government must sign off on any survey, the approval process can take months or years. And in many developing countries, infrastructure is an impediment to executing phone or mail surveys and lack of online connectivity blocks Web-based research.

For these and other reasons, choosing an appropriate data collection method is difficult. In some countries, many people may not have phones, or low literacy rates may interfere with mail surveys. Understanding *local customs* can be a challenge, and *cultural differences* also affect responses to survey items. Both Danish and British consumers, for example, agree that it is important to eat breakfast. However, the Danish sample may be thinking of fruit and yogurt while the British sample has toast and tea in mind. Sometimes marketers can overcome these problems by involving local researchers in decisions about the research design.

Another problem with conducting marketing research in global markets is *language*. Sometimes translations just don't come out right. In some cases entire subcultures within a country might be excluded from the research sample. In fact, this issue is becoming more and more prevalent inside the United States as non-English speakers increase as a percentage of the population.

To overcome language difficulties, researchers use a process of **back-translation**, which requires two steps. First, a native speaker translates the questionnaire into the language of the targeted respondents. Then they translate this new version back into the original language to ensure that the correct meanings survive the process. Even with precautions such as these, researchers must interpret data they obtain from other cultures with care.

View Stock/Alamy

Estimated expenditures for research by marketing research companies rank China number two in Asia Pacific markets with nearly $500 million, topped only by Japan. In fact, the amount firms spend on marketing research in China is growing faster than in any other country in the world, with growth rates of over 25 percent per year. The reason for such expenditures is obvious: China is an emerging market of more than 1.3 billion potential consumers. Interestingly, however, there's an erroneous impression among foreign marketers that most of the population lives in large cities. Coupled with real infrastructure and transportation challenges, this demographic misconception has left large portions of the vast Chinese countryside virtually untouched by modern marketing—at least so far.

Step 6: Analyze and Interpret the Data

Once marketing researchers collect the data, what's next? It's like a spin on the old "if a tree falls in the woods" question: "If results exist but there's no one to interpret them, do they have a meaning?" Well, let's leave the philosophers out of it and just say that marketers would answer "no." Data need interpretation if the results are going to be useful.

To understand the important role of data analysis, let's take a look at a hypothetical research example. Say a company that markets frozen foods wishes to better understand consumers' preferences for varying levels of fat content in their diets. They conducted a descriptive research study where they collected primary data via telephone interviews. Because they know that dietary preferences relate to gender, they used a stratified sample that includes 175 males and 175 females.

Typically, marketers first tabulate the data as Table 4.4 shows—that is, they arrange the data in a table or other summary form so they can get a broad picture of the overall responses. The data in Table 4.4 show that 43 percent of the sample prefers a low-fat meal. In addition, there may be a desire to cross-classify or cross-tabulate the answers to questions by other variables. *Cross-tabulation* means that we examine the data we break down into *subgroups*, in this case males and females separately, to see how results vary between categories. The cross-tabulation in Table 4.4 shows that 59 percent of females versus only 27 percent of males prefer a meal with low-fat content. In addition, researchers may wish to apply additional statistical tests, which you'll probably learn about in subsequent courses (something to look forward to).

Based on the tabulation and cross-tabulations, the researcher interprets the results and makes recommendations. For example, the study results in Table 4.4 may lead to the conclusion that females are more likely than males to be concerned about a low-fat diet. Based on these data, the researcher might then recommend that the firm should target females when it introduces a new line of low-fat foods.

back-translation
The process of translating material to a foreign language and then back to the original language.

Ryan Garton

APPLYING ▼ Data Analysis

Ryan's decision relates to the process by which Discover will incorporate consumer data with other sources and how much weight each data component will carry when researchers process information from both internal and external sources. ➡

Table 4.4 | Examples of Data Tabulation and Cross-Tabulation Tables

Fat Content Preference (number and percentages of responses)		
Questionnaire Response	Number of Responses	Percentage of Responses
Do you prefer a meal with high fat content, medium fat content, or low fat content?		
High fat	21	6
Medium fat	179	51
Low fat	150	43
Total	350	100

Fat Content Preference by Gender (number and percentages of responses)						
Questionnaire Response	Number of Females	Percentage of Females	Number of Males	Percentage of Males	Total Number	Total Percentage
Do you prefer a meal with high fat content, medium fat content, or low fat content?						
High fat	4	2	17	10	21	6
Medium fat	68	39	111	64	179	51
Low fat	103	59	47	27	150	43
Total	175	100	175	100	350	100

Step 7: Prepare the Research Report

The final step in the marketing research process is to prepare a report of the research results. In general, a research report must clearly and concisely tell the readers—top management, clients, creative departments, and many others—what they need to know in a way that they can easily understand and that won't put them to sleep (kind of like a good textbook). A typical research report includes the following sections:

- An Executive Summary of the report that covers the high points of the total report

- An understandable description of the research methods

- A complete discussion of the results of the study, including the tabulations, cross-tabulations, and additional statistical analyses

- Limitations of the study (no study is perfect)

- Conclusions drawn from the results and the recommendations for managerial action based on the results

Here's my choice. . .

Real **People**, Real **Choices**

Why do you think
Ryan chose option #3?

1 Option   **2** Option   **3** Option

How It Worked Out at Discover Card

Ryan's team undertook the first Innovation Screening in Discover's history. A large consumer panel evaluated a total of 16 concepts.: The consumer research showed that, in fact, some of management's initial estimates about the likely appeal of new products was significantly off the mark. Some products were less appealing than sponsors assumed, and some showed evidence of greater demand than Discover's internal finance teams predicted.

To learn the whole story, visit www.mypearsonmarketinglab.com.

Brand **YOU**!

Or, "Don't skate to where the puck is; skate to where the puck will be."

Learn how to apply this futuristic philosophy to your job search. Find out how to identify the fastest growing companies, the best places to work, the best small businesses, top companies, and trends in your target industry in Chapter 4 of *Brand You*. Don't put it off . . . the future is now!

Objective Summary ➠ **Key Terms** ➠ **Apply**

1. Objective Summary (pp. 102–106)

Explain the role of a marketing information system and a marketing decision support system in marketing decision making.

A marketing information system (MIS) is composed of internal data, marketing intelligence, marketing research data, acquired databases, and computer hardware and software. Firms use an MIS to gather, sort, analyze, store, and distribute information needed by managers for marketing decision making. The marketing decision support system (MDSS) allows managers to use analysis software and interactive software to access MIS data and to conduct analyses and find the information they need.

Key Terms

marketing research ethics, p. 102

marketing information system (MIS), p. 102

intranet, p. 104

marketing intelligence system, p. 104

marketing research, p. 104

syndicated research, p. 105

custom research, p. 105

marketing decision support system (MDSS), p. 106

2. Objective Summary (pp. 107–108)

Understand data mining and how marketers can put it to good use.

When marketers data mine they methodically sift through large datasets using computers that run sophisticated programs to understand relationships among things like consumer buying decisions, exposure to marketing messages, and in-store promotions. Data mining leads to the ability to make important decisions about which customers to invest in further and which to abandon.

Key Term

data mining, p. 107

3. Objective Summary (pp. 108–122)

List and explain the steps and key elements of the marketing research process.

The research process begins by defining the problem and determining the research design or type of study. Next, researchers choose the data-collection method—that is, whether there are secondary data available or if primary research with a communication study or through observation is necessary. Then researchers determine what type of sample is to be used for the study and then collect the data. The final steps in the research are to analyze and interpret the data and prepare a research report.

Exploratory research typically uses qualitative data collected by individual interviews, focus groups, or observational methods such as ethnography. Descriptive research includes cross-sectional and longitudinal studies. Causal research goes a step further by designing controlled experiments to understand cause-and-effect relationships between independent marketing variables, such as price changes, and dependent variables, such as sales.

Researchers may choose to collect data via survey methods and observation approaches. Survey approaches include mail questionnaires, telephone interviews, face-to-face interviews, and online questionnaires. A study may use a probability sample such as a simple random or stratified sample, in which inferences can be made to a population on the basis of sample results. Nonprobability sampling methods include a convenience sample and a quota sample. The researcher tries to ensure that the data are valid, reliable, and representative.

Online research accounts for a rapidly growing proportion of all marketing research. Online tracking uses cookies to record where consumers go on a Web site. Consumers have become increasingly concerned about privacy and how this information is used and made available to other Internet companies. The Internet also provides an attractive alternative to traditional communication data-collection methods because of its speed and low cost. Many firms use the Internet to conduct online focus groups.

Key Terms

research design, p. 109

secondary data, p. 110

primary data, p. 110

exploratory research, p. 111

focus group, p. 111

Chapter **Questions** and **Activities**

Concepts: Test Your Knowledge

1. What is a marketing information system (MIS)? What types of information are included in a marketing information system? How does a marketing decision support system (MDSS) allow marketers to easily get the information they need?
2. What is data mining? How is it used by marketers?
3. What are the steps in the marketing research process? Why is defining the problem to be researched so important to ultimate success with the research project?
4. What techniques are used to gather data in exploratory research? How can exploratory research be useful to marketers?
5. What are some advantages and disadvantages of telephone interviews, mail questionnaires, face-to-face interviews, and online interviews?
6. When considering data quality, what are the differences among validity, reliability, and representativeness? How do you know the data have high levels of these characteristics?
7. How do probability and nonprobability samples differ? What are some types of probability samples? What are some types of nonprobability samples?
8. What is a cross-tabulation? How are cross-tabulations useful in analyzing and interpreting data?
9. What is a cookie? What ethical and privacy issues are related to cookies?
10. What important issues must researchers consider when planning to collect their data online?

Activities: Apply What You've Learned

1. Your firm is planning to begin marketing a consumer product in several global markets. You have been given the responsibility of developing plans for marketing research to be conducted in South Africa, in Spain, and in China. In a role-playing situation, present the difficulties you expect to encounter, if any, in conducting research in each of these areas.
2. As an account executive with a marketing research firm, you are responsible for deciding on the type of research to be used in various studies conducted for your clients. For each of the following client questions, list your choices of research approaches.
   a. Will television or magazine advertising be more effective for a local bank to use in its marketing communication plan?
   b. Could a new package design for dry cereal do a better job of satisfying the needs of customers and, thus, increase sales?
   c. Are consumers more likely to buy brands that are labeled as environmentally friendly?
   d. How do female consumers determine if a particular perfume is right for them?
   e. What types of people read the local newspaper?
   f. How frequently do consumers switch brands of soft drinks?
   g. How will an increase in the price of a brand of laundry detergent affect sales?
   h. What are the effects of advertising and sales promotion in combination on sales of a brand of shampoo?
3. Your marketing research firm is planning to conduct surveys to gather information for a number of clients. Your boss has asked you and a few other new employees to do some preliminary work. She has asked each of you to choose three of the topics (from among those listed next) that will be included in the project and to prepare an analysis of the advantages and disadvantages of these communication methods of collecting data: mail questionnaires, telephone interviews, face-to-face interviews, and online questionnaires.
   a. The amount of sports nutrition drinks consumed in a city
   b. Why a local bank has been losing customers

    c. How heavily the company should invest in manufacturing and marketing home fax machines

    d. The amount of money being spent "over the state line" for lottery tickets

    e. What local doctors would like to see changed in the city's hospitals

    f. Consumers' attitudes toward several sports celebrities

4. For each of the topics you selected in item 3, how might a more passive (observation) approach be used to support the communication methods employed?

Marketing Metrics Exercise

It's a fact that many marketers tend to overrely on click-through rates—basically the mere number of pages a visitor to a Web site lands on—to provide a metric of the success of a firm's online/interactive marketing initiatives. According to Forrester senior analyst Emily Riley, "Brand marketers gravitate toward metrics that measure quantity, not quality. Clicks and impressions—metrics that are easy to track—measure little more than campaign volume."

Consider what you learned in this chapter about approaches to marketing research. What other two or three data collection approaches to measuring the success of a Web site might be fruitful in providing more meaningful data than just clicks? Hint: Just because the metric relates to the Web doesn't mean non-Web-based research approaches are inappropriate.

Choices: What Do You Think?

1. Some marketers attempt to disguise themselves as marketing researchers when their real intent is to sell something to the consumer. What is the impact of this practice on legitimate researchers? What do you think might be done about this practice?

2. Do you think marketers should be allowed to conduct market research with young children? Why or why not?

3. Are you willing to divulge personal information to marketing researchers? How much are you willing to tell, or where would you draw the line?

4. What is your overall attitude toward marketing research? Do you think it is a beneficial activity from a consumer's perspective? Or do you think it merely gives marketers new insights on how to convince consumers to buy something they really don't want or need?

5. Sometimes firms use data mining to identify and abandon customers who are not profitable because they don't spend enough to justify the service needed or because they return a large proportion of the items they buy. What do you think of such practices? Is it ethical for firms to prune out these customers?

6. Many consumers are concerned about online tracking studies and their privacy. Do consumers have the right to "own" data about themselves? Should governments limit the use of the Internet for data collection?

7. One unobtrusive measure mentioned in this chapter involved going through consumers' or competitors' garbage. Do you think marketers should have the right to do this? Is it ethical?

8. Consider the approach to tracking consumers' exposure to promotions via portable people meters, or PPMs. How would you feel about participating in a study that required you to use a PPM? What would be the advantage of a PPM approach versus keeping a written diary of television shows you watched and ads you saw?

Miniprojects: Learn by Doing

Miniproject 1

The purpose of this miniproject is to familiarize you with marketing research techniques and to help you apply these techniques to managerial decision making.

1. With a group of three other students in your class, select a small retail business or fast-food restaurant to use as a "client" for your project. (Be sure to get the manager's permission before conducting your research.) Then choose a topic from among the following possibilities to develop a study problem:
   - Employee–customer interactions
   - The busiest periods of customer activity
   - Customer perceptions of service
   - Customer likes and dislikes about offerings
   - Customer likes and dislikes about the environment in the place of business
   - The benefits customers perceive to be important
   - The age groups that frequent the place of business
   - The buying habits of a particular age group
   - How customer complaints are handled

2. Develop a plan for the research.
   a. Define the problem as you will study it.
   b. Choose the type of research you will use.
   c. Select the techniques you will use to gather data.
   d. Develop the mode and format for data collection.

3. Conduct the research.

4. Write a report (or develop a class presentation) that includes four parts:
   a. Introduction: a brief overview of the business and the problem studied
   b. Methods: the type of research used, the techniques used to gather data (and why they were chosen), the instruments and procedures used, the number of respondents, duration of the study, and other details that would allow someone to replicate your study
   c. Results: a compilation of the results (perhaps in table form) and the conclusions drawn
   d. Recommendations: a list of recommendations for actions management might take based on the conclusions drawn from the study

Miniproject 2

As we discussed in this chapter, monitoring changes in demographics and other consumer trends is an important part of the marketing intelligence included in an MIS. Today, much of this information is gathered by government research and is available on the Internet.

The U.S. Census Bureau provides tabled data for cities and counties across the nations at its site, **www.census.gov.** On the home page, click on Statistical Abstract. In addition, most states produce their own statistical abstract publications that are available on the Web. You should be able to locate the statistical abstract for your state by using a search engine such as Google and entering something like "Florida Statistical Abstract." Using both state data and U.S. Census data, develop a report on a city or county of your choice that answers these questions:

1. What is the total population of the city or county?
2. Describe the population of the area in terms of age, income, education, ethnic background, marital status, occupation, and housing.

3. How does the city or county compare to the demographic characteristics of the entire U.S. population?
4. What is your opinion of the different Web sites you used? How useful are they to marketers? How easy were they to navigate? Was there information that you wanted that was not available? Was there more or less information from the sites than you anticipated? Explain.

Marketing in **Action** Case   Real Choices at IMMI

Marketing executives claim, "Half the money I spend on advertising is wasted; I just don't know which half." With more than half of all ad dollars spent on broadcast media like television and radio, advertisers need to have a way to determine the exposure and effectiveness of these media. The people meters and diaries that firms have used to track television and radio audiences for decades provide some estimates, but they do not track the other media (like the Internet) that are also key today.

Integrated Media Measurement Inc., also known as IMMI, uses existing technologies to measure broadcast audiences in a new way. IMMI recruits adults and teens, aged 13 to 54, to carry a special cell phone at all times for two years. The phone captures 10 seconds of audio from its surroundings every 30 seconds, 24 hours a day, seven days a week. The samples are then compressed into small digital files and uploaded to the company's servers where they are compared to samples of the media being measured using a technology called *acoustic matching*. This allows IMMI to measure the number of people who have been exposed to an advertisement not only on television or radio but also on digital video recorders, game players, cellphones, DVDs, and CDs. Based on the data, IMMI produces real-time reports that get to individual behavior, not just group averages, thus connecting advertising to consumer behavior more accurately than possible with older methodologies. IMMI can answer questions such as the following: How many people are actually watching my network including outside the home and with time-shifting devices? How many people actually see my commercial? What songs cause radio listeners to change stations? What programs cause TV viewers to change channels?

Of course, IMMI's research methodology is not without potential problems. For example, IMMI only tracks audible media—not print or Internet advertising. Furthermore, many people are unwilling to participate in the study because they feel the technology is an invasion of their privacy. IMMI has been able to recruit an initial 3,000 panelists, but it will have to work hard to replenish that group when its two-year participation ends. While the cell phones only tracks broadcast media, many people are concerned that the company will also record their personal phone conversations.

For IMMI and for advertisers, the future is unclear. IMMI founders agree that this is not the last step in the attempt to more accurately understand media usage and advertising effectiveness. Surely better methodologies will follow. IMMI must consider its future and plan now in order to remain on top.

You Make the Call

1. What is the decision facing IMMI?
2. What factors are important in understanding this decision situation?
3. What are the alternatives?
4. What decision(s) do you recommend?
5. What are some ways to implement your recommendation?

Based on: "How It Works," **http://immi.com/howItWorks.html**; Jason Pontin, "Are Those Commercials Working? Just Listen," New York Times, September 9, 2007; **http://immi.com;09stream.html** (accessed February 28, 2008).

Consumer Behavior:
How and Why We Buy

Real People **Profile**

Julie Cordua

Profile   **Info**

▼ A **Decision Maker** at (RED)

Julie Cordua is the vice president of marketing at (RED), a new brand created by U2 lead singer Bono and Bobby Shriver to engage business in the fight against AIDS in Africa. (RED) partners with the world's best brands to make uniquely branded products from which up to 50 percent of the profits are directed to the Global Fund to finance African HIV/AIDS programs with a focus on women and children. In her role at (RED), she is responsible for building the (RED) brand through innovative marketing programs including public relations, advertising, events, and co-branding.

Prior to joining (RED), Julie spent the bulk of her career in marketing in the wireless industry. Most recently, she was the senior director of buzz marketing and part of the start-up team at HELIO, a new mobile brand for young, connected consumers. Before HELIO, Julie spent five years at Motorola in the Mobile Devices division in Chicago. At Motorola, she led the global category marketing group and was part of the team that orchestrated the RAZR launch in 2002.

Julie started her career in public relations at Hill & Knowlton in Los Angeles. She holds a BA in communications with an emphasis in business administration from UCLA and an MBA from the Kellogg School at Northwestern University. She currently lives in Manhattan Beach, California, with her husband.

💬 Julie's Info

What do I do when I'm not working?
A) Read, travel, and spend time with friends and family.

First job out of school?
A) Account coordinator at Hill & Knowlton Public Relations.

Career high?
A) Two: introducing the MOTO RAZR and introducing (RED).

Business book I'm reading now?
A) *The End of Poverty* by Jeff Sachs.

My management style?
A) Give your team the tools it needs to do its best job and trust it.

Don't do this when interviewing with me?
A) Ask about the salary in the first part of the interview.

Here's my problem. . .

(RED) works with the world's best brands to make unique (PRODUCT) RED-branded products and directs up to 50 percent of its gross profits to the Global Fund to invest in African AIDS programs with a focus on the health of women and children. (RED) is not a charity or "campaign." It is an economic initiative that aims to deliver a sustainable flow of private sector money to the Global Fund.

> **Things to remember**
>
> A sizeable portion of consumers have strong negative attitudes toward big corporations. They don't necessarily want to deal with companies now aligned with (RED) as part of their charitable activities.

Launch product partners included Converse, Gap, Motorola, Emporio Armani, Apple, and American Express (U.K. only). In its first year, (RED) added Hallmark, Dell, and Microsoft as partners. These companies were chosen because they were strong international consumer brands that could drive significant awareness and sell large volumes of products. And, more importantly, they were the few brave companies that were willing to take a risk on the idea of (RED) before it was a proven concept.

By fall 2007, with a successful first year behind it, (RED) was evaluating how to ensure sustained success for the brand. One of the main inputs Julie needed was more consumer insights about how shoppers related to the (RED) concept and to cause marketing where purchases are linked to donations to a non-profit organization in general. The company had not done this research before launch, so Julie decided it was time to do an extensive consumer research study in the United States.

Specifically, Julie wanted to know what consumers thought about the following (and how their beliefs affected their purchasing/participation actions):

- A corporation's role in solving social issues
- Churches/community organizations' roles in solving social issues
- An individual's role in solving social issues (via donation or volunteering)
- Government's role in solving social issues
- Celebrity involvement in solving social issues
- The idea of combining charity with capitalism (buying and contributing at the same time)

The research project included three stages: (1) interviews with a variety of consumers to qualitatively understand major issues on people's minds, how consumers relate to shopping and charity, and what people know about (RED); (2) a nationwide quantitative survey to identify major attitudinal and behavioral trends across the population; and (3) ethnographies where researchers actually spent time with people as they went about their daily lives and that helped bring some of the key insights from the survey to life.

The research showed that teens were most open to the idea of cause marketing. This finding made sense to Julie; this is a group that has grown up with the idea of "creative capitalism" and doesn't understand why doing good and having what you want should be separated. Also, this group looked up to celebrities more than any other age segment; they cited famous people across music, film, TV, and sports as major influences on their opinions and behaviors. However, when describing how they relate to (RED), they often commented that the brands that were current partners were not relevant to them.

A surprisingly large portion of the population rejected the idea of combining charity and capitalism. These "traditionalists" believed that social issues were best taken care of by the government or churches and community organizations. They were highly skeptical of corporations that promoted an ability to do good by buying a product. These consumers wanted a more traditional way to get involved—through donations, volunteering, or simply through paying taxes and allowing their government to address the issues.

With these insights in hand, Julie and her colleagues, including the head of business development, several outside advisors, and the CEO, had to decide if the (RED) model—partnering with mass market international brands for long-term deals—was the optimal way to generate the most money for the Global Fund.

Julie considered her **Options** 1·2·3

1 Option **Expand the (RED) model based on what the research revealed about the teen market.** Complement the bigger deals involving mainstream brands with the introduction of smaller "special edition" deals with younger, more relevant brands. Engage celebrities that specifically appeal to the younger demographic. If young people buy into the concept now, this would build loyalty and they would remain long-term fans of the brand. On the down side, this additional investment in smaller brands would require additional resources and divert (RED)'s small staff from its primary task of working with larger companies.

2 Option **Stick with the existing (RED) model.** Continue to partner only with large, international brands that make significant marketing and contribution commitments. Use celebrity engagement to draw attention to the brand. This option would let (RED) tap into the growing sentiment toward combining charity and capitalism. It would provide opportunities for significant exposure for (RED) through large-scale marketing programs.

On the other hand, this approach might alienate those who prefer more traditional avenues of giving to charity; these people might not give to the Global Fund under these circumstances. And, with such a mass-market approach, (RED) might not maximize engagement with the high-potential teen segment, which might be valuable long-term.

3 Option **Expand the (RED) model to include more traditional non-profit aspects, such as donation and volunteering, in order to appeal to all consumer groups and increase engagement.** This would allow (RED) to expand its reach to a much broader audience and potentially drive more revenue for the Global Fund through donations. But such an expansion might create brand confusion since (RED) is all about shopping and doing good at the same time. Julie feared that the company might not be able to be "all things to all people" by appealing to those who endorse the idea of "creative capitalism" and to those who want to contribute via more traditional avenues.

Now, put yourself in Julie's shoes: Which option would you choose, and why?

You Choose

Which **Option** would you choose, and **why**?

1. ☐Yes ☐No   2. ☐Yes ☐No   3. ☐Yes ☐No

See what **option** Julie chose on **page 150**

consumer behavior
The process involved when individuals or groups select, purchase, use, and dispose of goods, services, ideas, or experiences to satisfy their needs and desires.

Decisions, Decisions

Nothing is more important than understanding consumers and how they make decisions when you need to plan marketing strategy. In this chapter we'll look at the consumer decision-making process and the multitude of factors that influence those choices. And we'll show how understanding consumers boosts ROI as these insights help marketers to figure out the best way to win customers by meeting their needs.

We include consumer insights in many parts of the marketing plan—from what type of product to offer to where to advertise. This knowledge is key when we select a target market. For example, Julie's understanding of (RED)'s consumer base showed her that teens were the most receptive to social marketing and thus an ideal target for the organization's message.

1

OBJECTIVE

Define *consumer behavior* and explain the purchase decision-making process. (pp. 130–138)

The Consumer Decision-Making Process

Compelling new products, clever packaging, and creative advertising surround us, clamoring for our attention—and our money. But consumers don't all respond in the same way. Each of us is unique, with our own reasons to choose one product over another. Remember: The focus of the marketing concept is to satisfy consumers' wants and needs. To accomplish that crucial goal, first we need to appreciate what those wants and needs are. What causes one consumer to step into Denny's for a huge cholesterol-laden breakfast, while another opts for a quick Starbucks latte and Danish, and a third will only eat a healthy serving of "natural" Kashi cereal and fruit? And what, other than income, will cause one consumer to buy that box of Kashi cereal only when it's "on deal" while her neighbor never even looks at the price?

Consumer behavior is the process individuals or groups go through to select, purchase, use, and dispose of goods, services, ideas, or experiences to satisfy their needs and desires. Marketers recognize that consumer decision making is an ongoing process—it's much more than what happens at the moment a consumer forks over the cash and in turn receives a good or service.

Let's go back to the shoppers who want to buy a box of dry cereal. Although this may seem like a simple purchase, in reality there are quite a few steps in the process that cereal marketers need to understand. The first decision in the process is where to buy your cereal. If you eat a lot of it, you may choose to make a special trip to a warehouse-type retailer that sells super-duper-sized boxes rather than just picking up a box while you're at the local supermarket. Of course, if you get a craving for cereal in the middle of the night, you may dash to the local convenience store. Then there is the decision of the type of cereal. Do you eat only low-fat, high-fiber bran cereals, or do you go for the sugar-coated varieties with marshmallows? Of course, you may also like to have a variety of cereals available so you can "mix and match."

Marketers also need to know how and when you consume their products. Do you eat cereal only for breakfast, or do you snack on it while you sit

Check out chapter 5 **Study Map** on page 151

in front of the TV at night? Do you eat certain kinds of cereal only at certain times (like sugary "kids' cereals" that serve as comfort food when you're pulling an all-nighter)? What about storing the product (if it lasts that long)? Do you have a kitchen pantry where you can store the supersized box, or is space an issue?

And there's more. Marketers also need to understand the many factors that influence each of these steps in the consumer behavior process—internal factors unique to each of us, situational factors at the time of purchase, and the social influences of people around us. In this chapter, we'll talk about how all these factors influence how and why consumers do what they do. But first we'll look at the types of decisions consumers make and the steps in the decision-making process.

Not All Decisions Are the Same

Traditionally, researchers assumed that we carefully collect information about competing products, determine which products possess the characteristics or product attributes important to our needs, weigh the pluses and minuses of each alternative, and arrive at a satisfactory decision. But how accurate is this picture of the decision-making process? Is this the way *you* buy cereal?

Although it does seem that people take these steps when they make an important purchase such as a new car, is it realistic to assume that they do this for everything they buy, like that box of cereal? Today we realize that decision makers actually employ a set of approaches that range from painstaking analysis to pure whim, depending on the importance of what they are buying and how much effort they choose to put into the decision.[1] Researchers find it convenient to think in terms of an "effort" continuum that is anchored on one end by *habitual decision making*, such as deciding to purchase a box of cereal, and at the other end by *extended problem solving*, such as deciding to purchase a new car.

When consumers engage in extended problem solving, indeed we do carefully go through the steps Figure 5.1 outlines: problem recognition, information search, evaluation of alternatives, product choice, and postpurchase evaluation.

When we make habitual decisions, however, we make little or no conscious effort. We may not search much if at all for more information, and we may not bother to compare alternatives. Rather, we make purchases automatically. You may, for example, simply throw the same brand of cereal in your shopping cart week after week without thinking about it. Figure 5.2 provides a summary of the differences between extended problem solving and habitual decision making.

Many decisions fall somewhere in the middle and are characterized by *limited problem solving*, which means that we do *some* work to make a decision but not a great deal. This is probably how you decide on a new pair of running shoes or a new calculator for math class. We often rely on simple "rules of thumb" instead of painstakingly learning all the ins-and-outs of every product alternative. So, rather than devoting a week of your life to learning all there is to know about calculators, you may use a simple rule like: "Buy a well-known electronics brand."

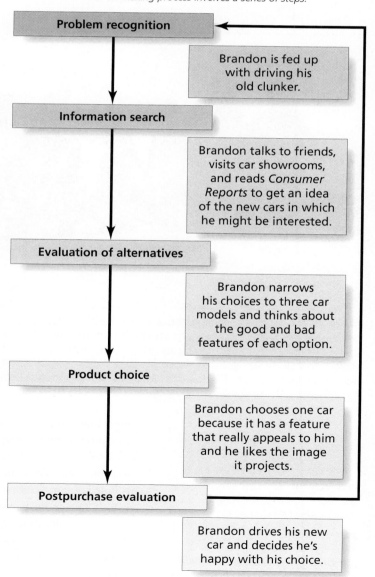

Figure 5.1 *Process* | The Consumer Decision-Making Process

The consumer decision-making process involves a series of steps.

Problem recognition

Brandon is fed up with driving his old clunker.

Information search

Brandon talks to friends, visits car showrooms, and reads *Consumer Reports* to get an idea of the new cars in which he might be interested.

Evaluation of alternatives

Brandon narrows his choices to three car models and thinks about the good and bad features of each option.

Product choice

Brandon chooses one car because it has a feature that really appeals to him and he likes the image it projects.

Postpurchase evaluation

Brandon drives his new car and decides he's happy with his choice.

Figure 5.2 ⚡ *Process* | Extended Problem Solving versus Habitual Decision Making

Decisions characterized as extended problem solving versus habitual decision making differ in a number of ways.

	Extended Problem Solving	*Habitual Decision Making*
Product	New car	Box of cereal
Level of involvement	High (important decision)	Low (unimportant decision)
Perceived risk	High (expensive, complex product)	Low (simple, low-cost product)
Information processing	Careful processing of information (search advertising, magazines, car dealers, Web sites)	Respond to environmental cues (store signage or displays)
Learning model	Cognitive learning (use insight and creativity to use information found in environment)	Behavioral learning (ad shows product in beautiful setting, creating positive attitude)
Needed marketing actions	Provide information via advertising, salespeople, brochures, Web sites. Educate consumers to product benefits, risks of wrong decisions, etc.	Provide environmental cues at point-of-purchase, such as product display

Marketers at the beginning of the walking shoe craze assumed that all recreational walkers were just burned-out joggers. Subsequent psychographic research that examined the AIOs of these walkers showed that there were actually several psychographic segments within the larger group who engaged in the activity for very different reasons. These different motivations included walking for fun, walking to save money, and walking for exercise. This research resulted in walking shoes for different segments, from Footjoy Walkers to Nike Healthwalkers.

Just how much effort do we put into our buying decisions? The answer depends on our level of **involvement**—how important we perceive the consequences of the purchase to be. As a rule, we are more involved in the decision-making process for products that we think are risky in some way. **Perceived risk** may be present if the product is expensive or complex and hard to understand, such as a new computer or a sports car. Perceived risk also can play a role when we think that making a bad choice will result in embarrassment or social rejection. For example, a person who wears a pair of Skechers on a job interview may jeopardize the job if the interviewer doesn't approve of his footwear.

When perceived risk is low—such as when we buy a box of cereal—we experience a small amount of involvement in the decision-making process. In these cases we're not overly concerned about which option we choose because it is not especially important or risky. The worst-case scenario is that you don't like the taste and pawn off the box on your unsuspecting roommate! In *low-involvement* situations, the consumer's decision is often a response to environmental cues, such as when you decide to try a new type of cereal because the grocery store prominently displays it at the end of the aisle. Under these circumstances, managers must concentrate on how a store displays products at the time of purchase to influence the decision maker. For example, a cereal marketer may decide to spend extra money to be sure its brand stands out in a store display or feature a cool athlete like Olympic speed skater Apolo Ohno on the box so consumers notice it.

For *high-involvement* purchases, such as when we buy a house or a car, we are more likely to carefully process all the available information and to have thought about the decision well before we buy the item. The consequences of the purchase are important and risky, especially because a bad decision may result in significant financial losses, aggravation, or

involvement
The relative importance of perceived consequences of the purchase to a consumer.

perceived risk
The belief that choice of a product has potentially negative consequences, whether financial, physical, and/or social.

embarrassment. Most of us would not just saunter into a real estate agent's office at lunchtime and casually plunk down a deposit on a new house. For high-involvement products, managers must start to reduce perceived risk by educating the consumer about why their product is the best choice well in advance of the time that the person is ready to make a decision.

To understand each of the steps in the decision-making process, we'll follow the fortunes of a consumer named Brandon, who, as 📊 Figure 5.1 shows, is in the market for a new ride—a highly involving purchase decision, to say the least.

Step 1: Problem Recognition

Problem recognition occurs whenever a consumer sees a significant difference between his or her current state of affairs and some desired or ideal state. A woman whose 10-year-old Hyundai lives at the mechanic's shop has a problem, as does the man who thinks he'd have better luck getting dates if he traded his Hyundai for a new sports car. Brandon falls into the latter category—his old clunker runs okay, but he wants to sport some wheels that will get him admiring stares instead of laughs.

Do marketing decisions have a role in consumers' problem recognition? Although most problem recognition occurs spontaneously or when a true need arises, marketers often develop creative advertising messages that stimulate consumers to recognize that their current state (that old car) just doesn't equal their desired state (a shiny, new convertible). 📊 Figure 5.3 provides examples of marketers' responses to consumers' problem recognition and the other steps in the consumer decision-making process.

problem recognition
The process that occurs whenever the consumer sees a significant difference between his current state of affairs and some desired or ideal state; this recognition initiates the decision-making process.

Campbell's asks, "What shape are your kids in?" This question kick-starts problem recognition for parents who may need to reconsider what they feed their children.

Figure 5.3 *Process* | Responses to Decision Process Stages

Understanding the consumer decision process means marketers can develop strategies to help move the consumer from recognizing a need to being a satisfied customer.

Stage in the Decision Process	Marketing Strategy	Example
Problem recognition	Encourage consumers to see that existing state does not equal desired state	• Create TV commercials showing the excitement of owning a new car
Information search	Provide information when and where consumers are likely to search	• Target advertising on TV programs with high target-market viewership • Provide sales training that ensures knowledgeable salespeople • Make new-car brochures available in dealer showrooms • Design exciting, easy-to-navigate, and informative Web sites • Provide information on blogs and social networks to encourage word-of-mouth strategies • Use search marketing to ensure that your Web site has preferential search engine positioning • Participate in consumer review/advisory Web sites such as tripadvisor.com
Evaluation of alternatives	Understand the criteria consumers use in comparing brands and communicate own brand superiority	• Conduct research to identify most important evaluative criteria • Create advertising that includes reliable data on superiority of a brand (e.g., miles per gallon, safety, comfort)
Product choice	Understand choice heuristics used by consumers and provide communication that encourages brand decision	• Advertise "Made in America" (country of origin) • Stress long history of the brand (brand loyalty)
Postpurchase evaluation	Encourage accurate consumer expectations	• Provide honest advertising and sales presentations

Step 2: Information Search

information search
The process whereby a consumer searches for appropriate information to make a reasonable decision.

Once Brandon recognizes his problem—he wants a newer car!—he needs adequate information to resolve it. **Information search** is the step of the decision-making process in which the consumer checks his memory and surveys the environment to identify what options are out there that might solve his problem. Advertisements in newspapers, on TV or the radio, information we "Google" on the Internet, or a video on YouTube often provide valuable guidance during this step. Brandon might rely on recommendations from his friends, Facebook drivers' clubs, information he finds at **www.caranddriver.com**, in brochures from car dealerships, or on the manufacturers' Web sites.

The Internet as a Search Tool

Increasingly, consumers use the Internet to search for information about products. Search engines, sites such as Google (**www.google.com**) and Bing (**www.Bing.com**), help us locate useful information as they search millions of Web pages for key words and return a list of sites that contain those key words.

Of course, the problem for marketers is that consumers seldom follow up on more than a page or two of results they get from these searches—we're all bombarded by way too much information these days to ever look at all of it. This has led marketers to develop sophisticated **search marketing** techniques. With **search engine optimization (SEO)** marketers first find what key words consumers use most in their searches. Then they edit their site's content or HTML to increase its relevance to those keywords so they can try to place their site high up in the millions of sites the search might generate. With **search engine marketing (SEM)** the search engine company charges marketers to display **sponsored search ads** that appear at the top or beside the search results.

Comparison shopping agents (or **shopbots**) such as **Shopzilla.com** and **NexTag.com** are Web applications that can help online shoppers to find what they are looking for at the lowest price. In addition to listing where a product is available and the price, these sites often provide customer reviews and ratings of the product and the sellers. They enable consumers to view both positive and negative feedback about the product and the online retailer from other consumers. Increasingly consumers also search out other consumers' opinions and experience through networking Web sites such as YouTube and Facebook. We'll talk more about these sites and others similar to them later in the chapter.

When a consumer recognizes a problem such as the need to shed a few pounds, he or she will be more receptive to products that offer to help.

Behavioral Targeting

During information search, the marketer's goal is to make the information consumers want and need about their product easily accessible. The challenge today is how to get the right message to the right consumer. One answer to this challenge is **behavioral targeting**, a strategy that presents individuals with advertisements based on their Internet use. In other words, with today's technology it has become fairly easy for marketers to tailor the ads you see to Web sites you've visited.

Cable TV stations offer the newest behavioral targeting strategy.[2] Using existing systems in digital set-top boxes, cable companies can deliver ads to specific households based on such demographic data as income, ethnicity, gender, and household size. For example, an ad for diapers would only go to households with infants, while one for the Lexus SC convertible (beginning price of over $68,000) would target high-income households. In addition, a viewer will be able to press a button on her remote to get more information about a product, see a movie trailer, view a demonstration video of a new product, or order a sample or a coupon.

Some critics feel this is a mixed blessing because of privacy issues. While most agree using demographic information is acceptable, many fear that viewing habits will be tracked and also used in behavioral targeting. What do you think?

Step 3: Evaluation of Alternatives

Once Brandon has identified his options, it's time to decide on a few true contenders. There are two components to this stage of the decision-making process. First, a consumer armed with information identifies a small number of products in which he is interested. Then he

search marketing
Marketing strategies that involve the use of Internet search engines.

search engine optimization (SEO)
A systematic process of ensuring that your firm comes up at or near the top of lists of typical search phrases related to your business.

search engine marketing (SEM)
Search marketing strategy in which marketers pay for ads or better positioning.

sponsored search ads
Paid ads that appear at the top or beside the Internet search engine results.

comparison shopping agents
or shopbots
Web applications that help online shoppers find what they are looking for at the lowest price and provide customer reviews and ratings of products and sellers.

behavioral targeting
The marketing practice by which marketers deliver advertisements for products a consumer is looking for by watching what the consumer does online.

Ripped from the Headlines

Ethical/Sustainable Decisions in the Real World

Considering a new TV? What brand is best? Will you be happy with the new state-of-the-art 50-inch Samsung 3D or should you go with the lower-priced Sylvania? Many consumers turn to Internet review sites to help them make important purchase decisions. Internet sites such as Epinions, Google, ZDNet, and Yelp that provide customer reviews of products and retailers are sprouting up all over. The reason: Research has shown that review sites do influence consumers' purchases. Retailers such as BestBuy and Walmart even advertise the availability of customer reviews on their Web sites. But buyer beware: Review sites are not without their critics.

Consumers who use the review Web sites assume the reviews are written by ordinary consumers who are "just like me." In reality, some reviews may be written by the companies that produce the products. And there are other issues as well. At least one review site has been accused of allowing businesses that advertise on their site to give better placement to positive reviews, placing negative reviews at the bottom where consumers are less likely to see them. Other companies say they have been pressured to buy advertising on the site, and some have claimed that their ratings actually fell when they refused to be a paid advertiser. As a marketer, what would you do?

ETHICS CHECK: ✎
Find out what other students taking this course **would do** and **why** on www.mypearsonmarketinglab.com

What policies should review sites have toward companies that do and that do not advertise on their sites?

If your business was reviewed on a Web site, would you buy advertising in order to get preferential treatment?

☐YES ☐NO

evaluative criteria
The dimensions consumers use to compare competing product alternatives.

heuristics
A mental rule of thumb that leads to a speedy decision by simplifying the process.

narrows down his choices as he decides which of the possibilities are feasible and by comparing the pros and cons of each remaining option.

Brandon has always wanted a red Ferrari. But, after he allows himself to daydream for a few minutes, he returns to reality and reluctantly admits that an Italian sports car is probably not in the cards for him right now. He decides that the cars he likes—and can actually afford—are the Scion, the Ford Focus, and the Honda Element. He has narrowed down his options by considering only affordable cars that come to mind or that his buddies suggest.

Now it's decision time! Brandon has to look more systematically at each of the three possibilities and identify the important characteristics, or **evaluative criteria**, that he will use to decide among them. The criteria may be power, comfort, price, the style of the car, and even safety. Keep in mind that marketers often play a role in educating consumers about which product characteristics they should use as evaluative criteria—usually they will "conveniently" emphasize the dimensions in which their product excels. To make sure customers like Brandon come to the "right" conclusions in their evaluation of the alternatives, marketers must understand which criteria consumers use, and which are more or less important. With this information, sales and advertising professionals can point out a brand's superiority on the most important criteria as *they* have defined them.

Step 4: Product Choice

When Brandon examines his alternatives and takes a few test drives, it's time to "put the pedal to the metal." Deciding on one product and acting on this choice is the next step in the decision-making process. After agonizing over his choice for a few weeks, Brandon decides that even though the Element and the Scion have attractive qualities, the Focus has the affordability he needs and its carefree image is the way he wants others to think about him. All this thinking about cars is "driving" him crazy, and he's relieved to make a decision to buy the Focus and get on with his life.

So, just how do consumers like Brandon choose among the alternatives they consider? These decisions often are complicated because it's hard to juggle all the product characteristics in your head. One car may offer better gas mileage, another is $2,000 cheaper, while another boasts a better safety record. How do we make sense of all these qualities and arrive at a decision?

We saw earlier that consumers often rely on decision guidelines when they weigh the merits of competing brands claims that companies make. These **heuristics**, or mental rules-of-thumb, provide consumers with shortcuts that simplify the decision-making process. One such heuristic is "price = quality;" many people willingly buy the more expensive brand because they assume that if it costs more, it must be better (even though this isn't always true).

Perhaps the most common heuristic is **brand loyalty**; this occurs when we buy the same brand over and over, and as you can guess it's the Holy Grail for marketers. Consumers who have strong brand loyalty feel that it's not worth the effort to consider competing options. People form preferences for a favorite brand and then may never change their minds in the course of a lifetime. Needless to say, this makes it extremely difficult for rivals to persuade them to switch.

Still another heuristic is based on *country-of-origin*. We assume that a product has certain characteristics if it comes from a certain country. In the car category, many people associate German cars with fine engineering and Swedish cars with safety. Brandon assumed that the Japanese-made Honda would be a bit more reliable than the Ford or Saturn, so he factored that into his decision.

Sometimes a marketer wants to encourage a country association even when none exists. For example, U.S. firm General Mills offers consumers Swiss-sounding Yoplait yogurt while Stonyfield Farms has introduced its Greek-sounding Oikos Organic Greek Yogurt. Häagen-Dazs ice cream comes from that exotic Scandinavian area we call . . . New Jersey.

When you're dieting and you'll only consider low-calorie options, taste becomes an evaluative criterion.

Step 5: Postpurchase Evaluation

In the last step of the decision-making process, the consumer evaluates just how good a choice he made. Everyone has experienced regret after making a purchase ("What was I *thinking*?"), and (hopefully) we have all been pleased with something we've bought. The evaluation of the product results in a level of **consumer satisfaction/dissatisfaction**. This refers to the overall feelings, or attitude, a person has about a product after she purchases it.

Just how do we decide if we're satisfied with what we bought? The obvious answer would be, "That's easy. The product is either wonderful or it isn't." However, it's a little more complicated than that. When we buy a product, we have some *expectations* of product quality. How well a product or service meets or exceeds these expectations determines customer satisfaction. In other words, we tend to assess product quality by comparing what we have bought to a preexisting performance standard. We form this standard via a mixture of information from marketing communications, informal information sources such as friends and family, and our own prior experience with the product category. That's why it's very important that marketers create accurate expectations of their product in advertising and other communications.

Even when a product performs to expectations, consumers may suffer anxiety or regret, or **cognitive dissonance**, after making a purchase. When we reject product alternatives with attractive features, we may second-guess our decision. Brandon, for example, might begin to think, "Maybe I should have chosen the Honda Element—everyone says Hondas are great cars." To generate satisfied customers and remove dissonance, marketers often seek to reinforce purchases through direct mail or other personalized contacts after the sale.

So, even though Brandon's new Focus is not exactly as powerful as a Ferrari, he's still happy with the car, because he never really expected a fun little car to eat up the highway like a high-performance sports car that costs ten times as much. Brandon has "survived" the consumer decision-making process: He recognized a problem, conducted an informational search to resolve it, identified the (feasible) alternatives available, made a product choice, and then evaluated the quality of his decision.

Apart from understanding the mechanics of the consumer decision-making process, marketers also try to ascertain what influences in consumers' lives affect this process. There are three main categories: internal, situational, and social influences. In Brandon's case, for

brand loyalty
A pattern of repeat product purchases, accompanied by an underlying positive attitude toward the brand, based on the belief that the brand makes products superior to those of its competition.

consumer satisfaction/dissatisfaction
The overall feelings or attitude a person has about a product after purchasing it.

cognitive dissonance
The anxiety or regret a consumer may feel after choosing from among several similar attractive choices.

Figure 5.4 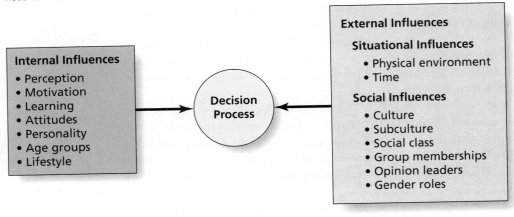 *Process* | Influences on Consumer Decision-Making

A number of different factors in consumers' lives influence the consumer decision-making process. Marketers need to understand these influences and which ones are important in the purchase process.

example, the evaluative criteria he used to compare cars and his feelings about each were influenced by:

1. Internal factors such as the connection he learned to make between a name like Ford Focus and an image of "slightly hip, yet safe and solid"

2. Situational factors such as the way the Ford salesperson treated him

3. Social influences such as his prediction that his friends would be impressed when they saw him cruising down the road in his new wheels.

Figure 5.4 shows the influences in the decision-making process and emphasizes that all these factors work together to affect the ultimate choice each person makes. Now, let's consider how each of these three types of influences work, starting with internal factors.

2 Internal Influences on Consumers' Decisions

OBJECTIVE

Explain how internal factors influence consumers' decision-making processes.
(pp. 138–145)

Like Brandon, your dream ride may be a sporty Ferrari. However, your roommate dreams of a pimped-out Escalade and your dad is set on owning a big Mercedes. As the saying goes, "That's why they make chocolate and vanilla." We can attribute much of these differences to internal influences on consumer behavior—those things that cause each of us to interpret information about the outside world, including which car is the best, differently from one another. Let's see how internal factors relating to the way people absorb and interpret information influence the decision-making process.

Perception

Perception is the process by which people select, organize, and interpret information from the outside world. We receive information in the form of sensations, the immediate response of our sensory receptors—eyes, ears, nose, mouth, and skin—to basic stimuli such as light, color, odors, touch, and sound. We try to make sense of the sensations we receive as we interpret them in light of our past experiences. For example, when we encounter a new product, we look at and perhaps touch the product or its package. Then we interpret that product based on our past experiences—or lack of experiences—with similar products.

perception
The process by which people select, organize, and interpret information from the outside world.

Take the computer keyboard, for example. When typewriters were introduced in the 1870s the keys got stuck if you typed too fast. Then in 1874 an inventor named Christopher Latham Sholes developed the QWERTY keyboard (named for the first six letters on the top row); this layout arranged the letters of the alphabet so that it decreased how fast a person could type. We don't have physical keys in computers and cell phones, so why do we still use QWERTY keyboards? Because we're used to them and it would be a hassle to learn a different configuration.

We are bombarded with information about products—thousands of ads, in-store displays, special offers, our friends' opinions, and on and on. The perception process has important implications for marketers: As we absorb and make sense of the vast quantities of information that compete for our attention, the odds are that any single message will get lost in the clutter. And, if we do notice the message, there's no guarantee that the meaning we give it will be the same one the marketer intended. The issues that marketers need to understand during this process include *exposure, attention*, and *interpretation*.

Exposure

The stimulus must be within range of people's sensory receptors to be noticed; in other words, people must be physically able to see, hear, taste, smell, or feel the stimulus. For example, the lettering on a highway billboard must be big enough for a passing motorist to read easily, or the message will be lost. **Exposure** is the extent to which a person's sensory receptors are capable of registering a stimulus.

exposure
The extent to which a stimulus is capable of being registered by a person's sensory receptors.

Marketers work hard to achieve exposure for their products, but sometimes it's just a matter of making sure that cool people use your product—and that others observe them doing this. After finding out that a close friend was flying to Los Angeles to audition for the film *Any Given Sunday*, the president of the high-performance sportswear company Under Armour sent along with him a bunch of free samples of its athletic wear to give to the film's casting director as a gift. The director liked the quality of the clothes so much he gave them to the wardrobe company the filmmakers hired and they also really liked the clothes. The next thing you know, the movie (starring Al Pacino and Jamie Foxx) featured both the actors wearing Under Armour clothes on screen—and there was even a scene in the film when Jamie Foxx undressed in the locker room with a clear shot of the Under Armour logo on his jock strap. After the movie's release, hits on Under Armour's Web site spiked, and, as they say, the rest is history.[3]

Many people believe that even messages they can't see will persuade them to buy advertised products. Claims about **subliminal advertising** of messages hidden in ice cubes (among other places) have been surfacing since the 1950s. A survey of American consumers found that almost two-thirds believe in the existence of subliminal advertising, and over one-half are convinced that this technique can get them to buy things they don't really want.[4]

subliminal advertising
Supposedly hidden messages in marketers' communications.

There is very little evidence to support the argument that this technique actually has any effect at all on our perceptions of products. But still, concerns persist. In 2006 ABC rejected a commercial for KFC that invites viewers to slowly replay the ad to find a secret message, citing the network's long-standing policy against subliminal advertising. The ad (which other networks aired) is a seemingly ordinary pitch for KFC's $.99 Buffalo Snacker chicken sandwich. But if you replay it slowly on a digital video recorder or VCR, it tells you that viewers can visit KFC's Web site to receive a coupon for a free sandwich. Ironically, this technique is really the *opposite* of subliminal advertising because instead of secretly placing words or images in the ad, KFC blatantly publicized its campaign by informing viewers that it contains a message and how to find it.[5] The short story: Hidden messages are intriguing and fun to think about (if a little scary), but they don't work. Sorry for the letdown.

Attention

As you drive down the highway, you pass hundreds of other cars. But to how many do you pay attention? Probably only one or two—the bright pink and purple VW Bug and the Honda with the broken taillight that cut you off at the exit ramp. **Attention** is the extent to

attention
The extent to which a person devotes mental processing to a particular stimulus.

which we devote mental-processing activity to a particular stimulus. Consumers are more likely to pay attention to messages that speak to their current needs. For example, you're far more likely to notice an ad for a fast-food restaurant when you're hungry, while smokers are more likely than nonsmokers to block out messages about the health hazards of smoking.

Grabbing consumers' attention is becoming harder than ever, because people's attention spans are shorter than ever. Now that we are accustomed to *multitasking*, flitting back and forth between our e-mails, TV, IMs, and so on, advertisers have to be more creative by mixing up the types of messages they send. That's why we see both long (60-second) commercials that almost feel like miniature movies and short (some as brief as five seconds) messages that are meant to have surprise value: They are usually over before commercial-haters can zap or zip past them. Indeed, brief blurbs that are long enough to tantalize viewers but short enough not to bore them are becoming commonplace. In contrast to the old days when most commercials on television networks were 30-second spots, today more than one-third run for only 15 seconds.[6]

Interpretation

interpretation
The process of assigning meaning to a stimulus based on prior associations a person has with it and assumptions he or she makes about it.

Interpretation is the process of assigning meaning to a stimulus based on prior associations we have with it and assumptions we make about it. Extra Strength Maalox Whip Antacid flopped, even though a spray can is a pretty effective way to deliver this kind of tummy ache relief. But to consumers, aerosol whips mean dessert toppings, not medication.[7] If we don't interpret the product the way it was intended because of our prior experiences, the best marketing ideas will be "waisted."

Motivation

motivation
An internal state that drives us to satisfy needs by activating goal-oriented behavior.

Motivation is an internal state that drives us to satisfy needs. Once we activate a need, a state of tension exists that drives the consumer toward some goal that will reduce this tension by eliminating the need.

Think again about Brandon and his old car. He began to experience a gap between his present state (he owns an old car) and a desired state (he craves a car that gets him noticed and is fun to drive). This activated the need for a new car, which in turn motivated Brandon to test different models, to talk with friends about different makes, and finally to buy a new car.

hierarchy of needs
An approach that categorizes motives according to five levels of importance, the more basic needs being on the bottom of the hierarchy and the higher needs at the top.

Psychologist Abraham Maslow developed an influential approach to motivation.[8] He formulated a **hierarchy of needs** that categorizes motives according to five levels of importance, the more basic needs being on the bottom of the hierarchy and the higher needs at the top. The hierarchy suggests that before a person can meet needs at a given level, he must first meet the lower level's needs—somehow those hot new Seven jeans don't seem as enticing when you don't have enough money to buy food.

As you can see from 📷 Figure 5.5, people start at the lowest level with basic physiological needs for food and sleep. Then they progress to higher levels to satisfy more complex needs, such as the need to be accepted by others or to feel a sense of accomplishment. Ultimately, they can reach the highest-level needs, where they will be motivated to attain such goals as self-fulfillment. As the figure shows, if marketers understand the level of needs relevant to consumers in their target market, they can tailor their products and messages to them.

Learning

learning
A relatively permanent change in behavior caused by acquired information or experience.

Learning is a change in behavior caused by information or experience. Learning about products can occur deliberately, as when we set out to gather information about different MP3 players before we buy one brand. We also learn even when we don't try. Consumers recognize many brand names and can hum many product jingles, for example, even for products they themselves do not use. Psychologists who study learning have advanced several theories to explain the learning process, and these perspectives are important because a major goal for marketers is to "teach" consumers to prefer their products. Let's briefly review the most important perspectives on how people learn.

Figure 5.5 📷 Snapshot | Maslow's Hierarchy of Needs and Related Products

Abraham Maslow proposed a hierarchy of needs that categorizes motives. Savvy marketers know they need to understand the level of needs that motivates a consumer to buy a particular product or brand.

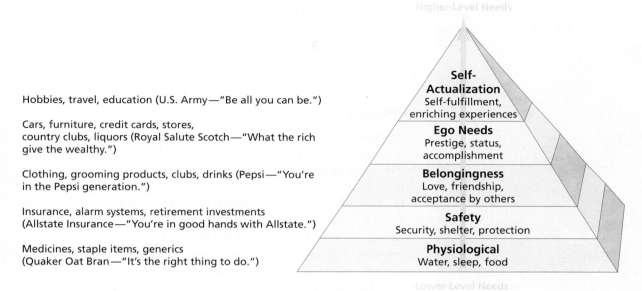

Hobbies, travel, education (U.S. Army—"Be all you can be.")

Cars, furniture, credit cards, stores, country clubs, liquors (Royal Salute Scotch—"What the rich give the wealthy.")

Clothing, grooming products, clubs, drinks (Pepsi—"You're in the Pepsi generation.")

Insurance, alarm systems, retirement investments (Allstate Insurance—"You're in good hands with Allstate.")

Medicines, staple items, generics (Quaker Oat Bran—"It's the right thing to do.")

Higher-Level Needs

Self-Actualization
Self-fulfillment, enriching experiences

Ego Needs
Prestige, status, accomplishment

Belongingness
Love, friendship, acceptance by others

Safety
Security, shelter, protection

Physiological
Water, sleep, food

Lower-Level Needs

Source: Maslow's Hierarchy of Needs and Related Products—Maslow's *Hierarchy of Needs: Motivation and Personality,* 3rd ed., by A.H. Maslow, 1987. Reprinted by permission of Prentice Hall, Inc., Upper Saddle River, NJ.

Behavioral Learning

Behavioral learning theories assume that learning takes place as the result of connections we form between events. In one type of behavioral learning, **classical conditioning**, a person perceives two stimuli at about the same time. After a while, the person transfers his response from one stimulus to the other. For example, an ad shows a product and a breathtakingly beautiful scene so that (the marketer hopes) you will transfer the positive feelings you get when you look at the scene to the advertised product. Hint: Did you ever notice that car ads often show a new auto on a beautiful beach at sunset or speeding down a mountain road with brightly colored leaves blowing across the pavement?

Another common form of behavioral learning is **operant conditioning**, which occurs when people learn that their actions result in rewards or punishments. This feedback influences how they will respond in similar situations in the future. Just as a rat in a maze learns the route to a piece of cheese, consumers who receive a reward such as a prize in the bottom of a box of cereal will be more likely to buy that brand again. We don't like to think that marketers can train us like lab mice, but that kind of feedback does reward us for the behavior. Will that be American or Swiss for you?

Cognitive Learning

In contrast to behavioral theories of learning, **cognitive learning theory** views people as problem-solvers who do more than passively react to associations between stimuli. Supporters of this viewpoint stress the role of creativity and insight during the learning process. *Cognitive learning* occurs when consumers make a connection between ideas or by observing things in their environment.

Observational learning occurs when people watch the actions of others and note what happens to them as a result. They store these observations in memory and at some later point use the information to guide their own behavior. Marketers often use this process to create advertising and other messages that allow consumers to observe the benefits of using

behavioral learning theories
Theories of learning that focus on how consumer behavior is changed by external events or stimuli.

classical conditioning
The learning that occurs when a stimulus eliciting a response is paired with another stimulus that initially does not elicit a response on its own but will cause a similar response over time because of its association with the first stimulus.

operant conditioning
Learning that occurs as the result of rewards or punishments.

cognitive learning theory
Theory of learning that stresses the importance of internal mental processes and that views people as problem solvers who actively use information from the world around them to master their environment.

observational learning
Learning that occurs when people watch the actions of others and note what happens to them as a result.

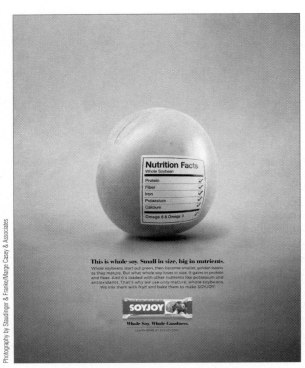

Cognitive learning theory views people as problem-solvers. Marketing messages facilitate this process when they provide factual information to help consumers make decisions.

attitude
A learned predisposition to respond favorably or unfavorably to stimuli on the basis of relatively enduring evaluations of people, objects, and issues.

affect
The feeling component of attitudes; refers to the overall emotional response a person has to a product.

Marketers often try to influence our attitudes via the affective component when they use images that arouse either negative or positive feelings. This ad for a gym in Bogotá, Colombia, focuses on consumers' emotional reactions to unattractive faces and attractive bodies.

their products. Health clubs and manufacturers of exercise equipment feature well-muscled men and women pounding away on treadmills, while mouthwash makers show that fresh breath is the key to romance.

Now we've discussed how the three internal processes of perception, motivation, and learning influence how consumers absorb and interpret information. But the results of these processes—the interpretation the consumer gives to a marketing message—differ depending on unique consumer characteristics. Let's talk next about some of these characteristics: existing consumer attitudes, the personality of the consumer, and consumer age groups.

Attitudes

An **attitude** is a lasting evaluation of a person, object, or issue.[9] Consumers have attitudes toward brands, such as whether McDonald's or Wendy's has the best hamburgers. They also evaluate more general consumption-related behaviors such as whether high-fat foods, including hamburgers, are a no-no in a healthy diet. A person's attitude has three components: affect, cognition, and behavior.

Affect is the *feeling* component of attitudes. This term refers to the overall emotional response a person has to a product. Affect is usually dominant for expressive products, such as perfume, where we choose a fragrance if it makes us feel happy.

Some marketing researchers are trying to understand how consumers' emotional reactions influence how they feel about products. A company called Sensory Logic, for example, studies videotapes of people's facial reactions—to products and commercials—in increments as fleeting as 1/30 of a second. Staffers look for the difference between, say, a true smile (which includes a relaxation of the upper eyelid) and a social smile (which occurs only around the mouth). Whirlpool hired the company to test consumers' emotional reactions to its Duet washers and dryers. Its (perhaps ambitious) goal was to design appliances that would actually make people happy. The research led Whirlpool to change some design options on the Duet products, including geometric patterns and certain color combinations. Smile, it's Laundry Day! More recently, Disney has built a lab where it will measure heart rate and skin conductivity and track the eye gaze of consumers while they view ads over the Internet, mobile devices, and their TVs.[10]

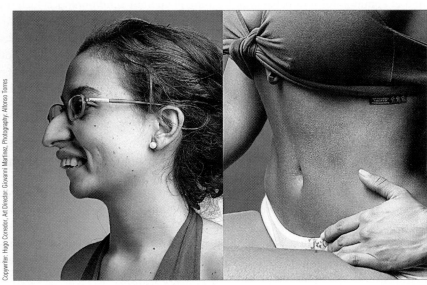

Cognition, the *knowing* component, refers to the beliefs or knowledge a person has about a product and its important characteristics. You may believe that a Mercedes is built better than most cars, or (like Brandon) that a Ford Focus is slightly hip, yet solid. Cognition is important for complex products, such as computers, for which we may develop beliefs on the basis of technical information.

Behavior, the *doing* component, involves a consumer's intention to do something, such as the intention to purchase or use a certain product. For products such as cereal, consumers act (purchase and try the product) on the basis of limited information and then form an evaluation of the product simply on the basis of how the product tastes or performs.

Personality and the Self: Are You What You Buy?

Personality is the set of unique psychological characteristics that consistently influences the way a person responds to situations in the environment. One adventure-seeking consumer may always be on the lookout for new experiences and cutting-edge products, while another is happiest in familiar surroundings using the same brands over and over. Today, popular online matchmaking services like **match.com**, **Matchmaker.com**, and **Tickle.com** offer to create your "personality profile" and then hook you up with other members whose profiles are similar.

It makes sense to assume that consumers buy products that are extensions of their personalities. That's why marketers try to create brand personalities that will appeal to different types of people. For example, consider the different "personalities" fragrance marketers invent: A brand with a "wholesome, girl-next-door" image such as Clinique's Happy would be hard to confuse with the sophisticated image of Christian Dior's Dolce Vita. We'll talk more about this in Chapter 9.

A person's **self-concept** is his attitude toward himself. The self-concept is composed of a mixture of beliefs about one's abilities and observations of one's own behavior and feelings (both positive and negative) about one's personal attributes, such as body type or facial features. The extent to which a person's self-concept is positive or negative can influence the products he buys and even the extent to which he fantasizes about changing his life.

Self-esteem refers to how positive a person's self-concept is. Alberto Culver uses a self-esteem pitch to promote its Soft & Beautiful, Just for Me hair relaxer for children. The company's Web site "Mom's Blog" encourages mothers to provide affirmation of their daughters' beauty to encourage their self-esteem. The site also provides "conversation starters" to help parents talk to their daughters about self-image.[11]

Age

A person's age is another internal influence on purchasing behavior. Many of us feel we have more in common with those of our own age because we share a common set of experiences and memories about cultural events, whether these involve Woodstock, Woodstock II, or even Woodstock III.

Goods and services often appeal to a specific age group. Although there are exceptions, it is safe to assume that most buyers of Lil' Kim's CDs are younger than those who buy Barbra Streisand disks. Thus, many marketing strategies appeal to the needs of different age groups such as children, teenagers, the middle-aged, and the elderly. These various needs result in different types of consumer behavior both offline

cognition
The knowing component of attitudes; refers to the beliefs or knowledge a person has about a product and its important characteristics.

behavior
The doing component of attitudes; involves a consumer's intention to do something, such as the intention to purchase or use a certain product.

personality
The set of unique psychological characteristics that consistently influences the way a person responds to situations in the environment.

self-concept
An individual's self-image that is composed of a mixture of beliefs, observations, and feelings about personal attributes.

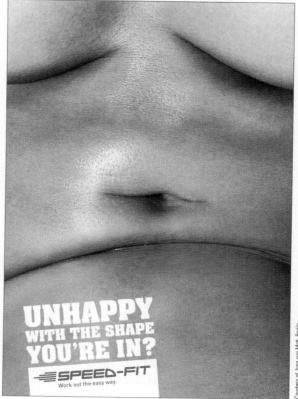

This German ad appeals directly to the self-concepts of potential customers who want to shed a few pounds.

Jordan Strauss/WireImage/Getty Images

Marketers recognize that it's often helpful to group people into market segments based on similarities in lifestyle preferences. For example, skateboarding has morphed from an activity we associate with the law-breaking daredevils from the movie *Dogtown and Z-Boys* depicted to become a full-fledged lifestyle, complete with a full complement of merchandise that boarders need to live the life. Shows on MTV feature professional skateboarders, and sales of a skateboarding video game, Tony Hawk by Activision, are over $1 billion. Many kids happily fork over $20 for T-shirts and more than $60 for skate shoes in addition to the hundreds they may spend on the latest boards.[12]

family life cycle
A means of characterizing consumers within a family structure on the basis of different stages through which people pass as they grow older.

and now online as many people incorporate the Web into their shopping patterns.

Age is important, but actually regardless of how old we are, what we buy often depends more on our current position in the **family life cycle**—the stages through which family members pass as they grow older. Singles (of any age) are more likely to spend money on expensive cars, entertainment, and recreation. Couples with small children purchase baby furniture, insurance, and a larger house, while older couples whose children have "left the nest" are more likely to buy a retirement home in Florida.

Lifestyle

A **lifestyle** is a pattern of living that determines how people choose to spend their time, money, and energy and that reflects their values, tastes, and preferences. We express our lifestyles in our preferences for activities such as sports, interests such as music, and opinions on politics and religion. Consumers often choose goods, services, and activities that they associate with a certain lifestyle. Brandon may drive a Ford Focus, hang out in Internet cafes, and go extreme skiing during Spring Break because he views these choices as part of a cool college student lifestyle.

If lifestyles are so important, how do marketers identify them so that they can reach consumers who share preferences for products that they associate with a lifestyle that appeals to them? *Demographic* characteristics, such as age and income, tell marketers *what* products people buy, but they don't reveal *why*. Two consumers can share the same demographic characteristics, yet be totally different people—all 20-year-old male college students are hardly identical to one another. That's why it is often important to further profile consumers in terms of their passions and how they spend their leisure time.

To breathe life into demographic analyses, marketers turn to **psychographics**, which groups consumers according to psychological and behavioral similarities. One way to do this is to describe people in terms of their activities, interests, and opinions (**AIOs**). These dimensions are based on preferences for vacation destinations, club memberships, hobbies, political and social attitudes, tastes in food and fashion, and so on. Using data from large samples, marketers create profiles of customers who resemble one another in terms of their activities and patterns of product use.[14]

The Cutting Edge

Social Networks

Has social media gone to the dogs? Mattel hopes so. The toy company is targeting pet owners, especially those who think their pets are totally—or at least pretty close to—human, with its first foray into the pet products market. Puppy Tweets is a high-tech toy that attaches to a dog's collar—and sends Tweets to the pet's Twitter page. No, Puppy Tweets doesn't know what a pet is thinking.

Instead, the toy responds to the dog's movement or barking to randomly send one of 500 Tweets. With tweets such as "I bark because I miss you. There, I said it. Now hurry home" and "I finally caught that tail I've been chasing, and . . . OOUUUCHH!" Mattel's toy may be only the beginning of new products that use social media to allow people to interact with their pets.[13]

3

OBJECTIVE

Show how situational factors and consumers' relationships with other people influence consumer behavior.
(pp. 145–150)

Situational and Social Influences on Consumers' Decisions

We've seen that internal factors such as how people perceive marketing messages, their motivation to acquire products, and their unique personalities, age groups, family life cycle, and lifestyle influence the decisions they make. In addition, situational and social influences—factors external to the consumer—have a big impact on the choices consumers make and how they make them.

Situational Influences

When, where, and how consumers shop—what we call *situational influences*—shape their purchase choices. Some important situational cues are our physical surroundings and time pressures.

Marketers know that dimensions of the physical environment, including factors such as decor, smells, lighting, music, and even temperature, can significantly influence consumption. If you don't believe this, consider that one study found that pumping certain odors into a Las Vegas casino actually increased the amount of money patrons fed into slot machines.[15] **Sensory marketing** is becoming big business. Westin Hotels spray a blend of green tea, geranium, and black cedar into hotel lobbies while Sheraton uses a combination of jasmine, clove, and fig. Sony scents its stores with orange, vanilla, and cedar, and Cadillac puts that "new car" smell into its autos artificially, all to influence the consumer's decision process.[16]

Let's see how some other situational factors influence the consumer decision-making process.

The Physical Environment

It's no secret that physical surroundings strongly influence people's moods and behaviors. Despite all their efforts to presell consumers through advertising, marketers know that the store environment influences many purchases. For example, one classic study showed that consumers decide on about two out of every three of their supermarket product purchases in the aisles (so always eat before you go to the supermarket).[17] A more recent study in Germany showed that almost 70 percent of shoppers decide what to buy at the point of sale.[18] The messages consumers receive at the time and their feelings about being in the store strongly influence these decisions.

Two dimensions, *arousal* and *pleasure*, determine whether a shopper will react positively or negatively to a store environment. In other words, the person's surroundings can be either dull or exciting (arousing) and either pleasant or unpleasant. Just because the environment is arousing doesn't necessarily mean it will be pleasant—we've all been in crowded, loud, hot stores that are anything but. Maintaining an upbeat feeling in a pleasant context is one factor behind the success of theme parks such as Disney World, which tries to provide consistent doses of carefully calculated stimulation to visitors.[19]

The importance of these surroundings explains why many retailers focus on packing as much entertainment as possible into their stores. For example, Bass Pro Shops, a chain of outdoor sports equipment stores, features giant aquariums, waterfalls, trout ponds, archery

lifestyle
The pattern of living that determines how people choose to spend their time, money, and energy and that reflects their values, tastes, and preferences.

psychographics
The use of psychological, sociological, and anthropological factors to construct market segments.

AIOs
Measures of consumer activities, interests and opinions used to place consumers into dimensions.

sensory marketing
Marketing techniques that link distinct sensory experiences such as a unique fragrance with a product or service.

and rifle ranges, putting greens, and free classes in everything from ice fishing to conservation. A company called Privy Promotions and others like it even sell ad space on restroom walls in stadiums. According to the company's president, "It's a decided opportunity for an advertiser to reach a captive audience."[20] Guess so.

Time

Time is one of consumers' most limited resources. We talk about "making time" or "spending time," and we remind one another that "time is money." Marketers know that the time of day, the season of the year, and how much time a person has to make a purchase affects decision making.

time poverty
Consumers' belief that they are more pressed for time than ever before.

Indeed, many consumers believe that they are more pressed for time than ever before. This sense of **time poverty** makes consumers responsive to marketing innovations that allow them to save time, including services such as one-hour photo processing, drive-through lanes at fast-food restaurants, and ordering products on the Web. A number of Web sites, including Apple's iTunes and even Walmart, now offer consumers the speed and convenience of downloading music or movies. These sites allow consumers to browse through thousands of titles, preview selections, and order and pay for them—all without setting foot inside a store. This saves the customer time, plus the "store" is always open.

Social Influences on Consumers' Decisions

Although we are all individuals, we are also members of many groups that influence our buying decisions. Families, friends, and classmates often sway us, as do larger groups with which we identify, such as ethnic groups and political parties. Now let's consider how social influences such as culture, social class, influential friends and acquaintances, and trends within the larger society affect the consumer decision-making process.

culture
The values, beliefs, customs, and tastes a group of people values.

Culture

As we saw in Chapter 3, we think of **culture** as a society's personality. It is the values, beliefs, customs, and tastes a group of people produce or practice. Although we often assume that what people in one culture (especially our own) think is desirable or appropriate will be appreciated in other cultures as well, that's far from the truth. Middle Eastern youth may not agree with U.S. politics, but they love Western music and find Arab TV music channels boring. Enter MTV Arabia, a 24-hour free satellite channel. Sure, many U.S. and European videos have to be cleaned up for the Arab audience and many are simply too edgy to air. To meet the values of the Middle Eastern audience, bad language and shots of kissing, revealing outfits, or people in bed are blurred or removed and sometimes replaced by more acceptable copy.[21] Culture matters.

Rituals

Every culture associates specific activities and products with its *rituals*, such as weddings and funerals. Some companies are more than happy to help us link products to cultural events. Consider the popularity of the elaborate weddings Disney stages for couples who want to reenact their own version of a popular fairy tale. At Disney World, the princess bride wears a tiara and rides to the park's lakeside wedding pavilion in a horse-drawn coach, complete with two footmen in gray wigs and gold lamé pants. At the exchange of vows, trumpets blare as Major Domo (he helped the Duke in his quest for Cinderella) walks up the aisle with two wedding bands in a glass slipper on a velvet pillow. Disney stages about 2,000 of these extravaganzas each year.[22]

In most countries, rituals are involved in the celebration of holidays. Americans purchase and/or cook turkeys, cranberry sauce, and pumpkin

THE SKINNY COW TRUFFLE BAR
A.K.A. 100 CALORIES OF PURE BLISS.

NEW!

Introducing The Skinny Cow® Truffle Bar, in Chocolate or French Vanilla flavors. Did we mention it's only 100 calories? Indulgence at its skinniest...

GET THE SKINNY.™

Dreyer's Grand Ice Cream

Our culture rewards skinny people.

pies to have the perfect Thanksgiving dinner. In Christian cultures, the Christmas ritual is so strongly tied to gifts, Christmas trees, lights, and decorations that it becomes the make-or-break sales season of the year for retailers. In many Muslim countries, the Ramadan season means fasting during the day but consuming gigantic amounts of food after sunset each day. And New Year's Eve parties all around the globe must include fancy party dresses and champagne. Is it any wonder that marketers of so many companies study consumer rituals?

Values (Again)

As we also saw in Chapter 3, cultural values are deeply held beliefs about right and wrong ways to live.[23] Marketers who understand a culture's values can tailor their product offerings accordingly. Consider, for example, that the values for collectivist countries differ greatly from those of individualistic cultures where immediate gratification of one's own needs come before all other loyalties. In collectivist cultures, loyalty to a family or a tribe overrides personal goals. Collectivist cultures put value on self-discipline, accepting one's position in life, and honoring parents and elders. Individualist cultures, on the other hand, stress equality, freedom, and personal pleasure. Today, we see the economic growth of some collectivist countries such as India, Japan, and China, making many consumers more affluent—and individualistic. For marketers, this means growth opportunities for products such as travel, luxury goods, sports activities like tennis and golf, and entertainment.

Subcultures

A **subculture** is a group that coexists with other groups in a larger culture but whose members share a distinctive set of beliefs or characteristics, such as members of a religious organization or an ethnic group. **Microcultures** are groups of consumers who identify with a specific activity or art form. These form around music groups such as the Dave Matthews Band, media creations such as *World of Warcraft*, or leisure activities such as extreme sports. Social media has been a real boon to subcultures and microcultures; it provides an opportunity for like-minded consumers to share their thoughts, photographs, videos, and so on. More on these important new sharing platforms later in the book.

For marketers, some of the most important subcultures are racial and ethnic groups because many consumers identify strongly with their heritage, and products that appeal to this aspect of their identities appeal to them. To grow its business, cereal maker General Mills targets Hispanic consumers. The company hopes to reach mothers who want better ways to nurture their children through its *Que Vida Rica* marketing program that tells mothers about the benefits of its products and offers nutrition tips and recipe suggestions. Advertising for General Mills' Nature Valley brand shows Hispanic couples "savoring nature instead of conquering it."[24]

Emerging Lifestyle Trends: Consumerism and Environmentalism

Powerful new social movements within a society also contribute to how we decide what we want and what we don't. One such influence is **consumerism**, the social movement directed toward protecting consumers from harmful business practices. Many consumers are becoming very aware of the social and environmental consequences of their purchases—and making their decisions accordingly.

Organized activities that bring about social and political change are not new to the American scene. Women's right to vote, child labor laws, the minimum wage, equal employment opportunity, and the ban on nuclear weapons testing all have resulted from social movements in which citizens, public and private organizations, and businesses worked to change society. In today's connected world, criticisms from consumerists can be especially damaging. A company's best way to combat such attacks and maintain a good image is to be proactive by practicing good business.

Related to the consumerism movement is **environmentalism**; this is a social movement that grows out of the worldwide growing concern for the many ways in which our

subculture
A group within a society whose members share a distinctive set of beliefs, characteristics, or common experiences.

microcultures
Groups of consumers who identify with a specific activity or art form.

consumerism
A social movement that attempts to protect consumers from harmful business practices.

environmentalism
A broad philosophy and social movement that seeks conservation and improvement of the natural environment.

Kyoto Protocol
A global agreement among countries that aims at reducing greenhouse gases that create climate change.

environmental stewardship
A position taken by an organization to protect or enhance the natural environment as it conducts its business activities.

green marketing
A marketing strategy that supports environmental stewardship, thus creating a differential benefit in the minds of consumers.

social class
The overall rank or social standing of groups of people within a society according to the value assigned to factors such as family background, education, occupation, and income.

status symbols
Visible markers that provide a way for people to flaunt their membership in higher social classes (or at least to make others believe they are members).

mass-class
The hundreds of millions of global consumers who now enjoy a level of purchasing power that's sufficient to let them afford high-quality products—except for big-ticket items like college educations, housing, or luxury cars.

consumption behaviors impact the physical world in which we live. Environmentalists seek solutions that enable companies to manage resources responsibly.

The **Kyoto Protocol** is an agreement the United Nations Framework Convention on Climate Change (UNFCCC) crafted in 1997. The Kyoto Protocol covers 170 countries worldwide. It aims to reduce greenhouse gases that create climate change. The protocol has been ratified by 175 countries. The United States has not ratified the agreement because of objections that China, as a developing country, is exempt from the emissions requirements of the agreement even though it is the world's second largest emitter of carbon dioxide. It's unlikely that the United States will ratify the Kyoto Protocol before it expires in 2012. In November 2009, the United Nations Climate Change Conference (referred to as the Copenhagen Summit) was unable to reach consensus on a post-2012 agreement.

Still, global concerns are mounting and a lot of businesses are acting even in the absence of government regulations because they understand that consumers will reward companies who do. Many firms now assume a position of **environmental stewardship** when they make socially responsible business decisions that also protect the environment. A **green marketing** strategy describes efforts to choose packages, product designs, and other aspects of the marketing mix that are earth-friendly but still profitable.

Green marketing practices can indeed result in black ink for a firm's bottom line. As mainstream marketers recognize this change, they are starting to alter their practices to satisfy Americans' desires for healthy and earth-friendly products. Coca-Cola, for example, demonstrated its commitment to the environment during the 2010 Vancouver Olympics. The company sponsored a 100 percent environmentally sustainable, carbon-neutral café. It featured bottles, furniture, and other products made from recycled material. Going even further, Coke made every aspect of its involvement with the Olympics green—from staff uniforms to delivery trucks to compostable coffee cups.[25]

Social Class

Social class is the overall rank of people in a society. People who are within the same class tend to exhibit similarities in occupation, education, and income level, and they often have similar tastes in clothing, decorating styles, and leisure activities. Class members also share many political and religious beliefs as well as preferences for AIOs.

Many marketers design their products and stores to appeal to people in a specific social class. Working-class consumers tend to evaluate products in more utilitarian terms like sturdiness or comfort instead of trendiness or aesthetics. They are less likely to experiment with new products or styles, such as modern furniture or colored appliances, because they tend to prefer predictability to novelty.[26] Marketers need to understand these differences and develop product and communication strategies that appeal to different social classes.

Luxury goods often serve as **status symbols**; visible markers that provide a way for people to flaunt their membership in higher social classes (or at least to make others believe they are members). The bumper sticker, "He who dies with the most toys wins," illustrates the desire to accumulate these badges of achievement. However, it's important to note that over time, the importance of different status symbols rises and falls. For example, when James Dean starred in the movie *Giant*, the Cadillac convertible was the ultimate status symbol car in America. Today, wealthy consumers who want to let the world know of their success are far more likely to choose a Mercedes, a BMW, or an Escalade. The "in" car five years from now is anyone's guess—perhaps with today's emphasis on the environment the Prius and other hybrids will emerge as the new status symbols?

In addition, traditional status symbols today are available to a much wider range of consumers around the world with rising incomes. This change fuels demand for mass-consumed products that still offer some degree of panache or style. Think about the success of companies like Nokia, H&M, Zara, ING, Dell Computers, Gap, Nike, EasyJet, or L'Oréal. They cater to a consumer segment that analysts have labeled **mass-class.** This term refers to the hundreds of millions of global consumers who now enjoy a level of purchasing power that's sufficient to let them afford high-quality products offered by well-known multinational companies.

Group Membership

Anyone who's ever "gone along with the crowd" knows that people act differently in groups than they do on their own. When there are more people in a group, it becomes less likely that any one member will be singled out for attention, and normal restraints on behavior may evaporate (think about the last wild party you attended). In many cases, group members show a greater willingness to consider riskier alternatives than they would if each member made the decision alone.[27]

A **reference group** is a set of people a consumer wants to please or imitate. Consumers "refer to" these groups when they decide what to wear, where they hang out, and what brands they buy. This influence can take the form of family and friends, respected statesmen like Martin Luther King Jr., celebrities like Angelina Jolie, or even (dare we say it!) your professors.

Opinion Leaders

If, like Brandon, you are in the market for a new car, is there a certain person to whom you'd turn for advice? An **opinion leader** is a person who influences others' attitudes or behaviors because they believe that he possesses expertise about the product.[29] Opinion leaders usually exhibit high levels of interest in the product category. They continuously update their knowledge as they read blogs, talk to salespeople, or subscribe to podcasts about the topic. Because of this involvement, opinion leaders are valuable information sources.

Unlike commercial endorsers, who are paid to represent the interests of just one company, opinion leaders have no ax to grind and can impart both positive and negative information about the product (unless they're being compensated to blog on behalf of a brand, which is not unheard of these days!). In addition, these knowledgeable consumers often are among the first to buy new products, so they absorb much of the risk and reduce uncertainty for others who are not as courageous.

Gender Roles

Some of the strongest pressures to conform come from our **gender roles**, society's expectations regarding the appropriate attitudes, behaviors, and appearance for men and women.[30] Of course, marketers play a part in teaching us how society expects us to act as men and women. Marketing communications and products often portray women and men differently. These influences teach us what the "proper" gender roles of women or men should be and which products are appropriate for each gender. Some of these "sex-typed" products have come under fire from social groups. For example, feminists claim the Barbie doll reinforces unrealistic ideas about what women's bodies should look like—even though a newer version of the doll isn't quite as skinny and buxom.

Sex roles constantly evolve—in a complex society like ours we often encounter contradictory messages about "appropriate" behavior. We can clearly see this in the messages girls have been getting from the media for the last several years: It's cool to be overly provocative. Role models like Paris Hilton, Lindsay Lohan, Britney Spears, and even Bratz dolls convey standards about how far preteens and teens should go to broadcast their sexuality. Now we see signs of a backlash. At the Pure Fashion Web site, girls get style tips including skirts and dresses that fall no more than four fingers above the knee and no tank tops without a sweater or jacket over them. Several other sites such as **ModestApparelU.S.A.com** advocate a return to styles that leave almost everything to the imagination.[31] Is our culture moving from a celebration of "girls gone wild" to "girls gone mild"?

Scott Broehm/Getty Images

Since we consume many of the things we buy in the presence of others, group behaviors are very important to marketers. Sometimes group activities create new business opportunities. Consider, for example, the increasing popularity of tailgating during football games, long a tradition at some college campuses. Now many companies have figured out that there's as much, if not more, money to be made in the stadium parking lot as on the field. Coleman sells grills designed just for tailgating as part of its RoadTrip line. The *American Tailgater* catalog features tailgate flags, tailgate tents, and even a gas-powered margarita blender. Ragu offers tailgating training camps that John Madden hosts, and Jack Daniels sponsors parking-lot contests. The National Football League sells over $100 million per year of tailgating merchandise, including keg-shaped grills.[28]

reference group
An actual or imaginary individual or group that has a significant effect on an individual's evaluations, aspirations, or behavior.

opinion leader
A person who is frequently able to influence others' attitudes or behaviors by virtue of his or her active interest and expertise in one or more product categories.

gender roles
Society's expectations regarding the appropriate attitudes, behaviors, and appearance for men and women.

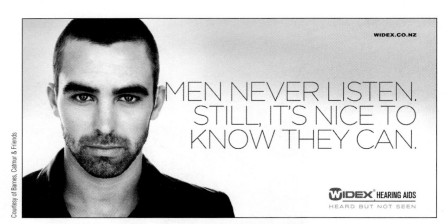

This ad from New Zealand reinforces a widely-held assumption about the male gender role.

metrosexual

A straight, urban male who is keenly interested in fashion, home design, gourmet cooking, and personal care.

Men's sex roles are changing too. For one, men are concerned as never before with their appearance. Guys spend $7.7 billion on grooming products globally each year. In Europe, 24 percent of men younger than age 30 use skincare products—and 80 percent of young Korean men do.[32] In fact, no doubt one of the biggest marketing buzzwords over the past few years is the **metrosexual**—a straight, urban male who is keenly interested in fashion, home design, gourmet cooking, and personal care. But just how widespread is the metrosexual phenomenon? Clearly, our cultural definition of masculinity is evolving as men try to redefine sex roles while they stay in a "safety zone" of acceptable behaviors bounded by danger zones of sloppiness at one extreme and effeminate behavior at the other. For example, a man may decide that it's okay to use a moisturizer but draw the line at an eye cream that he considers too feminine.[33] And, much like the "girls gone milder" trend we just discussed, some cultural observers report the emergence of "retrosexuals"—men who want to emphasize their old-school masculinity as they get plastic surgery to create a more rugged look that includes hairier chests and beards, squarer chins, and more angular jaw lines.[34]

Miller Genuine Draft conducted a survey of American men aged 21 to 34 to try to get a handle on these new definitions so that it could position its brand to appeal to them. The company found that, indeed, many "average Joes" are moving on from the days of drinking whatever beer is available and wearing baseball hats backward, but they also don't want to sacrifice their identities as regular guys. They care more about preparing a good meal, meeting friends for a beer, and owning a home than they do about amassing shoes, savoring fine wine, or dining at expensive restaurants. This new man is discerning when it comes to some important everyday and lifestyle decisions but isn't overly concerned about fitting into cultural molds or trends.[35]

Now that you've learned about consumer behavior, read "Real People, Real Choices: How It Worked Out" to see which strategy Julie selected to promote the (RED) brand.

Why do you think Julie chose option #1?

How It Worked Out at (RED)

(RED) continued to seek major international brands to partner with, but it is now complementing those partnerships with smaller special editions that appeal to a younger age group. One of the first examples of this strategy was the release of a (PRODUCT) RED skateboard. (RED) is also looking at adding other action sports products and teen-focused fashion brands to the collection.

To learn the whole story, visit www.mypearsonmarketinglab.com.

Brand **YOU**!

Why are you in college? To get a good job, of course. But how do you know what job is best for you? And how can you increase your chances of getting that perfect job? Think of yourself as the product and prospective employers as customers who might eventually "buy" you. Then you see that you need to understand each customer, how he makes the decision to hire someone, and what criteria he uses to evaluate future employees. So you have to ask yourself, which customer needs can you satisfy best—where will you find the best fit? Take a look into Chapter 5 of the *Brand You* supplement to learn how to identify what employers want and how to decide which is your top choice.

Objective Summary ➡ Key Terms ➡ Apply

CHAPTER 5
Study Map

1. Objective Summary (pp. 130–138)

Define *consumer behavior* and explain the purchase decision-making process.

Consumer behavior is the process individuals or groups go through to select, purchase, use, and dispose of goods, services, ideas, or experiences to satisfy their needs and desires. Consumer decisions differ greatly, ranging from habitual, repeat (low-involvement) purchases to complex, extended problem-solving activities for important, risky (high-involvement) purchases. When consumers make important purchases, they go through a series of five steps. First, they recognize there is a problem to be solved. Then they search for information to make the best decision. Next they evaluate a set of alternatives and judge them on the basis of various evaluative criteria. At this point, they are ready to make their purchasing decision. Following the purchase, consumers decide whether the product matched their expectations.

Key Terms

consumer behavior, p. 130

involvement, p. 132

perceived risk, p. 132

problem recognition, p. 133

information search, p. 134

search marketing, p. 135

search engine optimization (SEO), p. 135

search engine marketing (SEM), p. 135

sponsored search ads, p. 135

comparison shopping agents or shopbots, p. 135

behavioral targeting, p. 135

evaluative criteria, p. 136

heuristics, p. 136

brand loyalty, p. 137

consumer satisfaction/dissatisfaction, p. 137

cognitive dissonance, p. 137

2. Objective Summary (pp. 138–145)

Explain how internal factors influence consumers' decision-making processes.

Several internal factors influence consumer decisions. Perception is how consumers select, organize, and interpret stimuli. Motivation is an internal state that drives consumers to satisfy needs. Learning is a change in behavior that results from information or experience. Behavioral learning results from external events, while cognitive learning refers to internal mental activity. An attitude is a lasting evaluation of a person, object, or issue and includes three components: affect, cognition, and behavior. Personality traits such as innovativeness, materialism, self-confidence, sociability, and the need for cognition may be used to develop market segments. Marketers seek to understand a consumer's self-concept in order to develop product attributes that match some aspect of the consumer's self-concept.

The age of consumers, family life cycle, and their lifestyle also are strongly related to consumption preferences. Marketers may use psychographics to group people according to activities, interests, and opinions that may explain reasons for purchasing products.

Key Terms

perception, p. 138

exposure, p. 139

subliminal advertising, p. 139

attention, p. 139

interpretation, p. 140

motivation, p. 140

hierarchy of needs, p. 140

learning, p. 140

behavioral learning theories, p. 141

classical conditioning, p. 141

operant conditioning, p. 141

cognitive learning theory, p. 141

observational learning, p. 141

attitude, p. 142

affect, p. 142

cognition, p. 143

behavior, p. 143

personality, p. 143

self-concept, p. 143

family life cycle, p. 144

lifestyle, p. 144

psychographcs, p. 144

AIOs, p. 144

3. Objective Summary (pp. 145–150)

Show how situational factors and consumers' relationships with other people influence consumer behavior.

Situational influences include our physical surroundings and time pressures. Dimensions of the physical environment including decor, smells, lighting, music, and even temperature can influence consumption. The time of day, the season of the year, and how much time one has to make a purchase also affect decision making.

Consumers' overall preferences for products are determined by the culture in which they live and their membership in different subcultures. Consumerism is a social movment directed toward protecting consumers from harmful business practices. Environmentalism, another social movement, seeks ways to protect the natural environment. Firms practice environmental stewardship when they make decisions that protect the environment. Green marketing strategies include earth-friendly packaging and product designs. Social class, group memberships, and opinion leaders are other types of social influences that affect consumer choices. A reference group is a set of people a consumer wants to please or imitate, and this affects the consumer's purchasing decisions. Purchases also often result from conformity to real or imagined group pressures. Another way social influence is felt is in the expectations of society regarding the proper roles for men and women. Such expectations have led to many gender-typed products.

Key Terms

sensory marketing, p. 145

time poverty, p. 146

culture, p. 146

subculture, p. 147

microcultures, p. 147

consumerism, p. 147

environmentalism, p. 147

Kyoto Protocol, p. 148

environmental stewardship, p. 148

green marketing, p. 148

social class, p. 148

status symbols, p. 148

mass-class, p. 148

reference group, p. 149

opinion leader, p. 149

gender roles, p. 149

metrosexual, p. 150

Chapter **Questions** and **Activities**

Questions: Test Your Knowledge

1. What is consumer behavior? Why is it important for marketers to understand consumer behavior?
2. Explain habitual decision making, limited problem solving, and extended problem solving. What is the role of perceived risk in the decision process?
3. What are the steps in the consumer decision-making process?
4. What is search engine marketing and how is it related to the consumer decision process?
5. What is perception? Explain the three parts of the perception process: exposure, attention, and interpretation. For marketers, what are the implications of each of these components?
6. What is motivation? What is the role of motivation in consumer behavior?

7. What is behavioral learning? What is cognitive learning? How is an understanding of behavioral and cognitive learning useful to marketers?

8. What are the three components of attitudes? What is personality?

9. Explain what lifestyle means. What is the significance of family life cycle and lifestyle in understanding consumer behavior and purchasing decisions?

10. What are cultures, subcultures, and microcultures? How do cultures, subcultures, and microcultures influence consumer behavior? What is the significance of social class to marketers?

11. What are reference groups, and how do they influence consumers? What are opinion leaders?

12. What are gender roles? How do metrosexuals differ from other male consumers?

13. What is consumerism? What is environmentalism? How do firms respond to these social movements?

Activities: Apply What You've Learned

1. Assume that you are in the marketing department of a manufacturer of one of the products listed below. You know that internal factors including (1) perception, (2) motivation, (3) learning, (4) attitudes, and (5) personality influence consumers' decision making. With your classmates, develop your ideas about why each of these internal factors is important in the purchase of the product and how you might use these factors in developing marketing strategies for your firm. Report your ideas to your class.
   a. Automobiles
   b. Designer jeans
   c. An iPad or other tablet book
   d. Fragrances (for men or for women)
   e. Furniture

2. Sometimes advertising or other marketing activities cause problem recognition by showing consumers how much better off they would be with a new product or by pointing out problems with products they already own. Discuss problem recognition for the following product categories. Make a list of some ways marketers might try to stimulate problem recognition for each product. Present your ideas to your class.
   a. Life insurance
   b. Mouthwash
   c. A new automobile
   d. A health club membership

3. Assume that you are a marketing manager for a major hotel chain with outlets in major tourism sites around the world. You are concerned about the effects of current consumer trends, including changing ethnic populations, changing roles of men and women, increased concern for time and for the environment, and decreased emphasis on status goods. Others in your firm do not understand or care about these changes. They believe that the firm should continue to do business just as it always has. Develop a role-playing exercise to discuss these two different points of view for your class. Be sure to include the importance of each of these trends to your firm and offer suggestions for marketing strategies to address these trends.

4. This chapter indicated that consumers go through a series of steps (from problem recognition to postpurchase evaluation) as they make purchases. Write a detailed report describing what you would do in each of these steps when deciding to purchase one of the following products:
   a. An iPhone or similar device
   b. A university
   c. A fast-food lunch
   Then make suggestions for what marketers might do to make sure that consumers like you who are going through each step in the consumer decision process move toward the purchase of their brand. (*Hint:* Think about product, place, price, and promotion strategies.)

5. In 1991, a survey of American consumers found that almost two-thirds believe in the existence of subliminal advertising, and over one-half are convinced that this technique can get them to buy things they don't really want. Conduct your own survey on perceptions of subliminal advertising with students in your school. You may wish to ask them what they know about subliminal advertising, how much subliminal advertising they believe exists today, and whether they feel subliminal advertising works, that is, whether it causes people to buy things they don't really want. Report the results of your research to your class.

6. In this chapter we learned that some products are status symbols and serve as visible markers that provide a way for people to flaunt their membership in higher social classes. Using the Internet and magazines (your library probably has a collection of magazines), find ads and Web sites for status symbol products. Examine how the Web sites and the ads communicate that the product is a status symbol. How do they relate to a higher social class? Make a list of the products and the visuals and words that are used to promote the status symbol products.

7. In different cultures, perceptions about the proper roles for men and women, that is, gender roles, can vary greatly. Select one of the countries listed below or some other country of your choice. Conduct research to learn about the beliefs about gender roles held by people in that country. You should be able to find some information about the country on the Internet. If possible, find someone who is a native of the country or has visited the country. Prepare a report on the results of your research and the implications for global marketers.
   a. France
   b. China
   c. Japan
   d. Mexico
   e. Egypt

Marketing Metrics Exercise

Marketers use some or all of a variety of metrics to better understand how consumers make decisions involving a marketer's brand. Below are a list of some of these metrics. Which of these metrics would be useful to better understand each item listed below. Explain how the metrics suggested could be used.
   a. A firm's existing customers
   b. Potential new customers for a firm
   c. The market potential market for a new product

- *Awareness* is the percentage of all customers who recognize or know the name of a brand. Unaided brand recognition for toothpaste may be measured by asking consumers to name all the brands of toothpaste that come to mind. Aided recognition is measured by asking consumers questions such as, "Have you heard of Tom's of Maine toothpaste?"

- *Top of Mind Awareness (TOMA)* is the first brand that comes to mind when a consumer thinks of a product category. Marketers measure TOMA with questions such as, "What brand comes to mind when you think of toothpaste?"

- *Brand Knowledge* is measured by asking consumers if they have specific knowledge about a brand. To measure brand knowledge, marketers may ask consumers if they believe the brand possesses certain attributes or characteristics.

- *Measures of Attitudes* toward a brand may include survey questions about (1) beliefs that the brand possesses certain characteristics, (2) the relative importance of those characteristics to the product category, and (3) the overall measure of how much the consumer likes the brand.

- *Intentions* are consumers' stated willingness to buy or their likelihood of certain behavior. A consumer survey may ask, "If you are in the market for a new pair of shoes, what is the likelihood that you would purchase a pair of Nike shoes?"

- *Purchase Habits* measure consumers' self-reported behavior. Marketers ask consumers questions such as, "On average, how many times a month do you eat out? Which restaurant did you go to the last time you ate out? How much do you normally spend on a dinner out with your family?"

- *Loyalty* is a measure of consumers' commitment to a specific brand. Marketers measure loyalty by asking such questions as, "If on your next trip to the store you plan to purchase hand soap and your favorite brand of hand soap is not available, would you buy another brand or wait until you find your favorite brand to make the purchase?"

- *Customer satisfaction* is generally based on a survey in which consumers are asked if they are (1) very satisfied, (2) somewhat satisfied, (3) neither satisfied nor dissatisfied, (4) somewhat dissatisfied, or (5) very dissatisfied with a brand.

Choices: What Do You Think?

1. Demographic or cultural trends are important to marketers. What are some current trends that may affect the marketing of the following products?
   a. Housing
   b. Food
   c. Education
   d. Clothing
   e. Travel and tourism
   f. Automobiles

2. What are the core values of your culture? How do these core values affect your behavior as a consumer? Are they collectivist or individualistic? What are the implications for marketers?

3. Consumers often buy products because they feel pressure from reference groups to conform. Does conformity exert a positive or a negative influence on consumers? With what types of products is conformity more likely to occur?

4. Retailers often place impulse purchase items such as magazines and candy bars near the entrance to the store or near the checkout area. How would you describe the decision process for these products? Why are these locations effective? What are the problems with these decisions?

5. Behavioral targeting on the Internet involves tracking where people go online and then feeding them advertising information that's related to what they're looking for. Now, cable TV providers are also considering their own version of behavioral targeting. While proponents of this approach argue that it's a very efficient and convenient way for people to conduct information-search, others who are concerned about a potential invasion of privacy aren't so enthusiastic. What are some other arguments for and against behavioral targeting? What's your opinion? Do you mind having marketers know what sites you visit or what TV shows and movies you watch in return for receiving more relevant information on products?

6. Today, consumers are increasingly demanding "green" products. And marketers are responding with more and more products to meet that demand. Some companies, however, are "greenwashing" their products, that is, they are claiming they are more environmentally friendly than they really are. What are some examples of products that you suspect are being greenwashed? What should be done about this problem? Should there be laws about greenwashing or should marketers do more to patrol their own actions?

Miniproject: Learn by Doing

The purpose of this miniproject is to increase your understanding of the roles of personal, social, and situational factors in consumer behavior.

1. Select one of the following product categories (or some other product of your choice):
   - Hairstyling
   - Large appliances, such as refrigerators or washing machines
   - A restaurant
   - Banking
   - Fine jewelry

2. Visit three stores or locations where the product may be purchased. (Try to select three that are very different from each other.) Observe and make notes on all the elements of each retail environment.

3. At each of the three locations, observe people purchasing the product. Make notes about their characteristics (e.g., age, race, gender, and so on), their social class, and their actions in the store in relation to the product.

4. Prepare a report for your class describing the situational variables and individual consumer differences among the three stores and how they relate to the purchase of the product. Present your findings to your class.

Source: Adapted from Paul W. Farris, Neil T. Bendle, Phillip E. Pfeifer, and David J. Reibstein, *Marketing Metrics: 50+ Metrics Every Executive Should Master*, Pearson Education, 2006.

Marketing in **Action** Case   Real Choices at Lexus

In 1983 at a top-secret meeting, Toyota chairman Eiji Toyoda suggested that the time was right for Toyota to introduce a true luxury automobile that would challenge the best luxury vehicles in the world. A six-year development process followed that involved 60 designers and 450 prototypes at a cost of over $1 billion. In 1989 the Lexus was launched. In 1999, Lexus sold its millionth car in the United States and within a little over a decade, Lexus became America's best selling line of luxury vehicles. Following its success in the United States, Toyota introduced the Lexus in markets outside America, and today the luxury cars are available in over 40 different countries. Since its introduction, the Lexus has repeatedly won top awards and accolades for customer satisfaction, dependability, appeal, design, and engineering from the Motoring Press Association, J.D. Power and Associates studies, *The Robb Report, Popular Science, Car and Driver, Popular Mechanics, Automobile Magazine*, and *Motor Trend*.

Why has Lexus been such a success? According to North America President and CEO Atsushi Niimi, "Lexus is a success story because there is no compromise in its manufacture, as it always reflects the voice of the customer." Toyota President Ray Tanguay noted, "Manufacturing Lexus demands a deep understanding of what customers want, expect, and deserve in a luxury vehicle. We call it the relentless pursuit of perfection."

How did Toyota listen to the voices of its consumers? As early as 1985 while the Lexus was only a concept, Toyota sent a study team to the United States to conduct focus groups with potential customers. More recently, Lexus Great Britain introduced a unique program that helps Lexus consultants better understand customers by giving them a taste of luxury. Staff from Lexus centers are pampered at top-class hotels in order to experience for themselves the kind of quality and service their customers expect. In another program, Lexus GB gets feedback from actual customers. Thousands of U.K. Lexus owners are invited to spend the day at luxury spa hotels to share their opinions on where Lexus is succeeding and where it could be better, all while enjoying the spa facilities.

Such attention to providing the best for luxury car owners has led to Lexus's latest innovation: the Advanced Parking Guidance System. Most consumers find parallel parking a real pain, or worse, they simply avoid parallel parking spaces altogether. Enter the 2007 Lexus LS 460 sedan. The car actually parks itself—or almost. In theory, a driver only need pull up ahead of the empty parking space, make a few minor adjustments on a computer screen, and lift his or her foot off the brake. As the car backs up, the steering wheel turns as needed, and, "voila," the car is in the space, just where you want it to be. Of course, the LS isn't perfect. It must have a parking space considerably (about six feet) longer than the car, so it isn't useful in those tight city spots. And the system won't work on downward inclines—only on level ground where it can move at a "creeping" speed. As you might expect, the price of the Lexus with the Advanced Parking Guidance System is over $70,000— not a price tag to be taken lightly.

The question many observers ask is whether the parking capability of the Lexus is truly a benefit luxury car owners want and will use—or is it just a gimmick? And were customers really asking for this feature? Some argue that the Lexus automatic parking capability isn't really useful and that Lexus should have waited to introduce the feature until the company had worked out all the kinks in the system. Has Lexus stepped away from its focus on customer needs, and if so, what should the company do now?

You Make the Call

1. What is the decision facing Lexus?
2. What factors are important in understanding this decision situation?
3. What are the alternatives?
4. What decision(s) do you recommend?
5. What are some ways to implement your recommendation?

Based on: "Lexus History," Conceptcarz.com, **http://www.conceptcarz.com/view/makehistory/94,0/Lexus_History.aspx** (accessed March 15, 2008); "Lexus Luxury Lifestyle Training," Carpages, **http://www.carpages.co.uk/lexus/lexus-lifestyle-12-11-05.asp** (accessed March 10, 2008); Trevor Hoffman, "First Luxury Lexus Built outside Japan Rolls off the Line in Cambridge, Ontario," (October 1, 2003), Automobile.com, **http://car-reviews.automobile.com/news/worlds-first-lexus-built-outside-of-japan-rolls-off-canadian-line/456/** (accessed March 15, 2008); "Lexus," Wikipedia, **http://wikipedia.org/wiki/Lexus**.

Chapter 6

Business-to-Business Markets:
How and Why Organizations Buy

Brad Tracy

Profile

Info

▼ **A Decision Maker at NCR Corporation**

Brad Tracy is VP of Americas Marketing Deployment for NCR Corporation, head-quartered in Dayton, Ohio. In this role, Brad has the responsibility for developing and deploying NCR marketing programs for NCR's full portfolio of products throughout the Americas region (that is, North and South America). This includes solutions and best practices for the retail, financial, hospitality, health care, and travel industries. He joined NCR in 1988 as a retail sales representative in Portland, Oregon. His experience includes positions in sales, product management, product marketing, and industry marketing. Prior to his current assignment, he led the Global Marketing team for NCR's retail solutions division, responsible for all aspects of marketing for NCR retail products. Brad holds a bachelor of science degree in business administration from the University of Oregon.

💬 **Brad's Info**

What do I do when I'm not working?
 A) I enjoy golf, coaching soccer, and traveling.

First job out of school?
 A) NCR sales rep right after college.

My motto to live by?
 A) Passion, integrity, and effort.

What drives me?
 A) A sense of accomplishment and the belief in what I do and the impact it can have on our customers.

My management style?
 A) I am very transparent and direct.

Don't do this when interviewing with me?
 A) Come unprepared.

My pet peeve?
 A) People who don't assume accountability for their results.

Here's my problem...

NCR had just released a new generation point-of-sale (POS) workstation that was ahead of the competition by almost a year. The POS workstation is the computer that drives the retail checkout process. It is responsible for accepting input from the scanners and other peripherals, pricing the merchandise, offering discounts, calculating tax, and finalizing the transaction via cash, credit, debit, or other financial instrument. The official launch occurred in January at a major trade show. This launch was to be followed up by other industry shows and events, webinars, and advertising. As Brad and his colleagues planned these events, they questioned NCR's participation in a particular trade show because this would entail a significant amount of resources. The company had sent representatives to the event for many years, and many of its customers regularly participated in the show. While it had traditionally been a great venue for meeting with key clients and marketing NCR's newest solutions, in recent years attendance had been waning and other competing shows had grown in popularity. Suffering from this downturn in attendance and increased competition, the event had decided to combine with another event to boost the number of attendees. This combination involved moving the venue from its traditional location and renaming the combined show.

Things to remember

Especially in B2B contexts, trade shows are a major element in a firm's marketing mix. Show attendees gather a lot of information about competing products as they contemplate purchases, but they also use these venues as an opportunity to connect personally with company representatives.

With a superior solution to promote and a legacy of attending the show, the retail division's sales managers made an impassioned case for NCR's continued participation. They felt that this venue would be their last chance to demonstrate the new workstation before the competition responded with its own next-generation product. NCR would miss a golden opportunity to capitalize on its market leadership. In the end, the discussions became quite political as these managers argued their case. The discussion was extremely difficult as a number of key sales leaders were pushing to attend while Brad felt it would be best to skip the show.

Complicating this situation, NCR's retail division (the organization responsible for developing and selling solutions to retailers) had "shared" a booth with another division in prior years. Despite being told of the retail division's concerns, the other division proceeded on the assumption that retail would again participate and fund a significant portion of the event. As the event drew closer, this group pushed hard to force the retail division to continue to fund the event.

Brad considered his Options 1·2·3

1 Option

Attend the show as in past years. This would allow Brad's division to reinforce the product launch and further solidify its market leadership while the competition again showed an outdated product. But attending the show would consume limited sales and marketing resources. The *cost per touch* (that is, the number of potential clients the team could talk to at the show divided by the total cost of exhibiting at the show) would increase as the number of people attending the show declined.

2 Option

Skip the show this year and reallocate sales and marketing resources to one or more of the other alternatives for marketing the new workstation. The freed-up budget would allow NCR to attend two smaller but more targeted events in which the company had not previously participated. Because these events are highly targeted and have more of a conference format, they tend to be more intimate, and NCR's representatives could spend more quality time with retail clients. However, while costs for these smaller shows would be lower, since NCR hadn't been to these shows before Brad didn't know what kinds of opportunities to interact with customers would actually occur, so it was hard to predict the cost per touch.

3 Option

Forgo the show this year and find out whether the changes in venue and sponsorship would really diminish the value of the event. If it turned out that the newly combined show continued to draw enough attendees, NCR could participate the following year. Sitting it out would let the retail division conserve its limited marketing resources. On the other hand, NCR would miss the window to further exploit its market leadership by showcasing its new POS product. And, if Brad decided not to attend, the division would lose its position in the booth selection process. This loss of "seniority" could mean a poor position on the show floor in subsequent years, which would result in decreased foot traffic if NCR's booth was in an out-of-the-way location.

Now, put yourself in Brad's shoes: Which option would you choose, and why?

You Choose

Which **Option** would you choose, and **why**?
1. ☐YES ☐NO   2. ☐YES ☐NO   3. ☐YES ☐NO

See what **option** Brad chose on **page 177** ➡

business-to-business (B2B) markets
The group of customers that include manufacturers, wholesalers, retailers, and other organizations.

organizational markets
Another name for business-to-business markets.

Business Markets: Buying and Selling When the Customer Is Another Firm

You might think most marketers spend their days dreaming up the best way to promote cutting-edge products for consumers like new apps for your iPhone, a new power drink to keep you fit, or some funky shoes to add to your closet collection. But this is not the whole picture. Many marketers know that the "real action" also lies in products that companies sell to businesses and organizations rather than to end-user consumers like you—software applications to make a business more efficient, group medical insurance, safety shoes for industrial plants, or the First Flavor Peel 'n Taste Marketing System used by brands from Bacardi rum to Campbell's soup. In fact, some of the most interesting and lucrative jobs for young marketers are in businesses you've never heard of because these companies don't deal directly with consumers.

Like an end consumer, a business buyer makes decisions—but with an important difference: The purchase may be worth millions of dollars, and both the buyer and the seller have a lot at stake (maybe even their jobs). A consumer may decide to buy two or three T-shirts at one time, each emblazoned with a different design. *Fortune* 500 companies such as ExxonMobil, PepsiCo Inc., and FedEx buy hundreds, even thousands, of employee uniforms embroidered with their corporate logos in a single order.

Consider these transactions: Dell makes computer network servers to sell to its business customers. Procter & Gamble contracts with several advertising agencies to promote its brands at home and around the globe. The Metropolitan Opera buys costumes, sets, and programs. Mac's Diner buys a case of canned peas from BJ's Wholesale Club. The U.S. government places an order for 3,000 new HP laser printers. Perhaps at the extreme, the country of Qatar purchases five new Boeing 787 Dreamliners to add to their fleet—at a price that can exceed $200 million each![1]

All the above exchanges have one thing in common: they're part of *business-to-business (B2B) marketing*. As we first saw in Chapter 1, this is the marketing of goods and services that businesses and other organizations buy for purposes other than personal consumption. Some firms resell these goods and services, so they are part of a *channel of distribution*, a concept we'll revisit in Chapters 15 and 16. Other firms use the goods and services they buy to produce still other goods and services that meet the needs of their customers or to support their own operations. These **business-to-business (B2B) markets**, also called **organizational markets**, include manufacturers, wholesalers, retailers, and a variety of other organizations, such as hospitals, universities, and governmental agencies.

To put the size and complexity of business markets into perspective, let's consider a single product—a pair of jeans. A consumer may browse through several racks of jeans and ultimately purchase a single pair, but the buyer who works for the store at which the consumer shops had to purchase many pairs of jeans in different sizes, styles, and brands from different manufacturers. Each of these manufacturers purchases fabrics, zippers, buttons, and thread

Check out chapter 6 **Study Map** on page 178

from other manufacturers, which in turn purchase the raw materials to make these components. In addition, all the firms in this chain need to purchase equipment, electricity, labor, computer systems, legal and accounting services, insurance, office supplies, packing materials, and countless other goods and services. So, even a single purchase of a pair of Seven For All Mankind jeans is the culmination of a series of buying and selling activities among many organizations—many people have been keeping busy while you're out shopping!

In this chapter, we'll look at the big picture of the business marketplace, a world in which the fortunes of business buyers and sellers can hang in the balance of a single transaction, along with characteristics of B2B demand. Then we'll learn about different types of B2B customers. And finally, we'll examine different business buying situations and the elements of the business buying decision process.

Factors That Make a Difference in Business Markets

In theory, the same basic marketing principles should hold true in both consumer and business markets—firms identify customer needs and develop a marketing mix to satisfy those needs. For example, take the company that made the desks and chairs in your classroom. Just like a firm that markets consumer goods, the classroom furniture company first must create an important competitive advantage for its target market of universities. Next the firm develops a marketing mix strategy beginning with a product—classroom furniture that will withstand years of use by thousands of students while it provides a level of comfort that a good learning environment requires (and you thought those hardback chairs were intended just to keep you awake during class). The firm must offer the furniture at prices that universities will pay and that will allow the firm to make a reasonable profit. Then the firm must develop a sales force or other marketing communication strategy to make sure your university (and hundreds of others) considers—and hopefully chooses—its products when it furnishes classrooms.

Although marketing to business customers does have a lot in common with consumer marketing, there are differences that make this basic process more complex.[2] 📷 Figure 6.1 summarizes the key areas of difference and Table 6.1 provides a more extensive set of comparisons between the two types of markets.

Multiple Buyers

In business markets, products often have to do more than satisfy an individual's needs. They must meet the requirements of everyone involved in the company's purchase decision. If you decide to buy a new chair for your room or apartment, you're the only one who has to be satisfied. For your classroom, the furniture must satisfy not only students but also faculty, administrators, campus planners,

Although marketing to business customers does have a lot in common with consumer marketing, there are differences that make this basic process more complex.

Frank Uyttenhove

Figure 6.1 📷 *Snapshot* | Key Differences in Business versus Consumer Markets

There are a number of differences between business and consumer markets. To be successful, marketers must understand these differences and develop strategies specific to organizational customers.

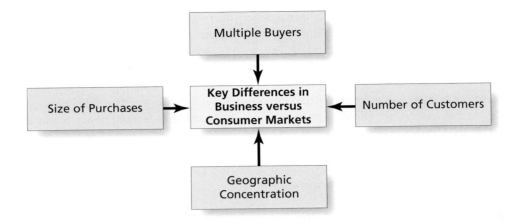

Table 6.1 | Differences between Organizational and Consumer Markets

Organizational Markets	Consumer Markets
• Purchases made for some purpose other than personal consumption	• Purchases for individual or household consumption
• Purchases made by someone other than the user of the product	• Purchases usually made by ultimate user of the product
• Decisions frequently made by several people	• Decisions usually made by individuals
• Purchases made according to precise technical specifications based on product expertise	• Purchases often based on brand reputation or personal recommendations with little or no product expertise
• Purchases made after careful weighing of alternatives	• Purchases frequently made on impulse
• Purchases based on rational criteria	• Purchases based on emotional responses to products or promotions
• Purchasers often engage in lengthy decision processes	• Individual purchasers often make quick decisions
• Interdependencies between buyers and sellers; long-term relationships	• Buyers engage in limited-term or one-time-only relationships with many different sellers
• Purchases may involve competitive bidding, price negotiations, and complex financial arrangements	• Most purchases made at "list price" with cash or credit cards
• Products frequently purchased directly from producer	• Products usually purchased from someone other than producer of the product
• Purchases frequently involve high risk and high cost	• Most purchases are relatively low risk and low cost
• Limited number of large buyers	• Many individual or household customers
• Buyers often geographically concentrated in certain areas	• Buyers generally dispersed throughout total population
• Products often complex; classified based on how organizational customers use them	• Products: consumer goods and services for individual use
• Demand derived from demand for other goods and services, generally inelastic in the short run, subject to fluctuations, and may be joined to their demand for other goods and services	• Demand based on consumer needs and preferences, is generally price-elastic, steady over time and independent of demand for other products
• Promotion emphasizes personal selling	• Promotion emphasizes advertising

and the people at your school who actually do the purchasing. If your school is a state or other governmental institution, the furniture may also have to meet certain government-mandated engineering standards. If you have a formal green initiative, the purchase must satisfy environmental-friendly criteria.

Number of Customers

Organizational customers are few and far between compared to end-user consumers. In the United States, there are about 100 million consumer households but less than half a million businesses and other organizations.

Size of Purchases

B2B products dwarf consumer purchases both in the quantity of items ordered and how much they cost. A company that rents uniforms to other businesses, for example, buys hundreds of large drums of laundry detergent each year to launder its uniforms. In contrast, even a hard-core soccer mom who deals with piles of dirty socks and shorts only goes through a box of detergent every few weeks.

Organizations purchase many products, such as a highly sophisticated piece of manufacturing equipment or computer-based marketing information systems, that can cost a million dollars or more. Recognizing such differences in the size of purchases allows marketers to develop effective marketing strategies. Although it makes perfect sense to use mass-media advertising to promote laundry detergent to consumers who buy it at their nearby Target, selling thousands of dollars' worth of laundry detergent to Marriott Hotels or a million-dollar machine tool to Northrop Grumman is best handled by a strong personal sales force. More on the differences in promotion approaches to businesses versus consumers later in the book.

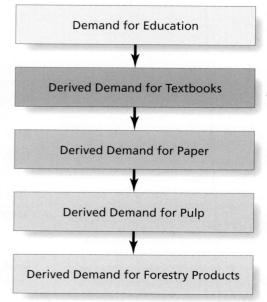

Our color prints run on just pennies a page. Our of color. Our total satisfaction guarantee* protects

tracking software increases the mileage you get out your investment. Xerox Color. It makes business sense.

xerox.com/frugalcolor 1-800-ASK-XEROX

xerox

Courtesy of Xerox, Inc.

Xerox employs a colorful pitch to sell office products to other companies.

derived demand
Demand for business or organizational products caused by demand for consumer goods or services.

Geographic Concentration

Another difference between business markets and consumer markets is *geographic concentration*, meaning that many business customers are located in a small geographic area rather than being spread out across the country. Whether they live in the heart of New York City or in a small fishing village in Oregon, consumers buy and use toothpaste and televisions. This is not necessarily so for B2B customers, who may be almost exclusively located in a single region of the country. For years Silicon Valley, a 50-mile-long corridor close to the California coast, has been home to thousands of electronics and software companies because of its high concentration of skilled engineers and scientists. And the U.S. commercial jet aircraft industry is centered in the Seattle area (Boeing and dozens of subcontractors). For B2B marketers who wish to sell to these markets, this means that they can concentrate their sales efforts and perhaps even locate distribution centers in a single geographic area.

B2B Demand

Demand in business markets differs from consumer demand. Most demand for B2B products is derived, inelastic, fluctuating, and joint. Understanding how these factors influence B2B demand is important for marketers when they forecast sales and plan effective marketing strategies. Let's look at each of these concepts in a bit more detail.

Derived Demand

Consumer demand is based on a direct connection between a need and the satisfaction of that need. But business customers don't purchase goods and services to satisfy their own needs. Businesses instead operate on **derived demand**, because a business's demand for goods and services comes either directly or indirectly from consumers' demand for what it produces.

To better understand derived demand, take a look at Figure 6.2. Demand for forestry products comes from the demand for pulp that paper publishers buy to make the textbooks you use in your classes. The demand for textbooks comes from the

Figure 6.2 *Process* | Derived Demand

B2B demand is derived demand. That is, the demand is derived directly or indirectly from consumer demand for another good or service. Some of the demand for forestry products is derived indirectly from the demand for education. At least until the day when all textbooks are only available online, publishers will need to buy paper.

Demand for Education

↓

Derived Demand for Textbooks

↓

Derived Demand for Paper

↓

Derived Demand for Pulp

↓

Derived Demand for Forestry Products

demand for education (yes, education is the "product" you're buying—with the occasional party or football game thrown in as a bonus). As a result of derived demand, the success of one company may depend on another company in a different industry. The derived nature of business demand means that marketers must constantly be alert to changes in consumer trends that ultimately will have an effect on B2B sales. So if fewer students attend college and fewer books are sold, the forestry industry has to find other sources of demand for its products.

Inelastic Demand

inelastic demand

Demand in which changes in price have little or no effect on the amount demanded.

Inelastic demand means that it usually doesn't matter if the price of a B2B product goes up or down—business customers still buy the same quantity. Demand in B2B markets is mostly inelastic because what a firm sells often is just one of the many parts or materials that go into producing the consumer product. It is not unusual for a large increase in a business product's price to have little effect on the final consumer product's price.

For example, you can buy a Limited Edition Porsche Boxster S "loaded" with options for about $60,000.[3] To produce the car, Porsche purchases thousands of different parts. If the price of tires, batteries, or stereos goes up or down, Porsche will still buy enough to meet consumer demand for its cars. As you might imagine, increasing the price by $30 or $40 or even $100 won't change consumer demand for Boxsters—so demand for parts remains the same. (If you have to ask how much it costs, you can't afford it!)

But B2B demand isn't always inelastic. Sometimes a consumer good or service requires only one or a few materials or component parts to produce. If the price of the part increases, demand may become elastic if the manufacturer of the consumer good passes the increase on to the consumer. Currently, for example, the price of corn is skyrocketing, largely due to the demand for ethanol-based fuel and high-fructose corn syrup sweetener (which is a cheaper substitute for sugar in many products). As a result, other food products overall that use corn or corn by-products are much more expensive.

Fluctuating Demand

Business demand also is subject to greater fluctuations than is consumer demand. There are two reasons for this. First, even modest changes in consumer demand can create large increases or decreases in business demand. Take, for example, air travel. A rise in jet fuel prices, causing higher ticket prices and a shift by some consumers from flying to driving vacations, can cause airlines to postpone or cancel orders for new equipment. This change in turn creates a dramatic decrease in demand for planes from manufacturers such as Boeing and Airbus.

A product's life expectancy is another reason for fluctuating demand. Business customers tend to purchase certain products infrequently. They may only need to replace some types of large machinery every 10 or 20 years. Thus, demand for such products fluctuates—it may be very high one year when a lot of customers' machinery wears out but low the following year because everyone's old machinery works fine. One solution to keep production more constant is to use price reductions to encourage companies to order products *before* they actually need them.

joint demand

Demand for two or more goods that are used together to create a product.

producers

The individuals or organizations that purchase products for use in the production of other goods and services.

resellers

The individuals or organizations that buy finished goods for the purpose of reselling, renting, or leasing to others to make a profit and to maintain their business operations.

Joint Demand

Joint demand occurs when two or more goods are necessary to create a product. For example, Porsche needs tires, batteries, and spark plugs to make that Limited Edition Boxster S that piqued your interest earlier. If the supply of one of these parts decreases, Porsche will be unable to manufacture as many automobiles, and so it will not buy as many of the other items either.

Types of Business-to-Business Customers

As we noted before, many firms buy products in business markets so they can produce other goods. Other B2B customers resell, rent, or lease goods and services. Still other customers, including governments and not-for-profit institutions such as the Red Cross or a local church, serve the public in some way. In this section, we'll look at the three major classes of B2B customers that  Figure 6.3 shows (producers, resellers, and organizations). Then we'll look at how marketers classify specific industries.

Producers

Producers purchase products for the production of other goods and services that they, in turn, sell to make a profit. For this reason, they are customers for a vast number of products from raw materials to goods that still other producers manufacture. For example, Dell buys microprocessor chips from Intel and AMD that go into its line of computers, and Marriott hotels buys linens, furniture, and food to produce the accommodations and meals their guests expect.

Resellers

Resellers buy finished goods for the purpose of reselling, renting, or leasing to consumers and other businesses. Although resellers do not actually produce goods, they do provide their customers with the time, place, and possession utility we talked about in Chapter 1 because they make the goods available to consumers when and where they want them. For example, Walmart buys toothpaste and peanuts and kids' shoes and about a gazillion other products to sell in its over 4,000 stores worldwide.

Trade associations often try to stimulate joint demand by suggesting new uses for their products. In this case Mexican avocado growers advocate more consumption of guacamole, which, in turn, may stimulate demand for taco chips or even tequila.

Figure 6.3 📷 *Snapshot* | The Business Marketplace

The business marketplace consists of three major categories of customers: producers, resellers, and organizations. B2B marketers must understand the different needs of these customers if they want to build successful relationships with them.

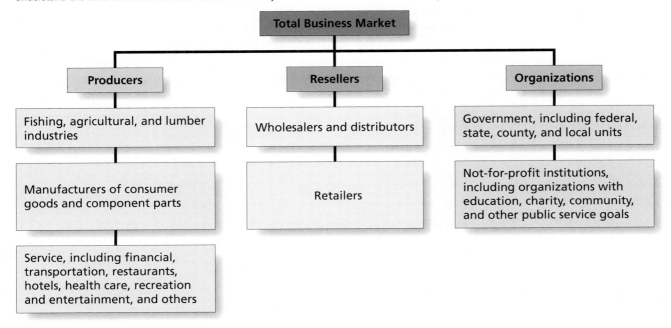

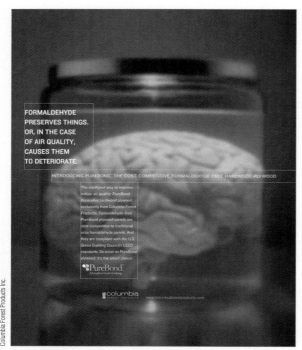

Companies like Columbia Forest Products that sell building supplies differentiate themselves.

Government and Not-for-Profit Organizations

Governments and not-for-profit institutions are two other types of organizations in the business marketplace. **Government markets** make up the largest single business and organizational market in the United States. The U.S. government market includes more than 3,000 county governments, 35,000 municipalities and townships, 28,000 special district governments, 50 states and the District of Columbia, plus the federal government. State and local government markets alone account for 15 percent of the U.S. gross national product.[4]

And, of course, there are thousands more government customers around the globe, and many of those governments are just about the only customers for certain products—for example, jet bombers and nuclear power plants. But many government expenditures are for more familiar items. Pens, pencils, and paper for offices; cots, bedding, and toiletries for jails and prisons; and cleaning supplies for routine facilities maintenance are just a few examples of items consumers buy one at a time but that governments purchase in bulk.

Not-for-profit institutions are organizations with educational, community, and other public service goals, such as hospitals, churches, universities, museums, and charitable and cause-related organizations like the Salvation Army and the Red Cross. These institutions tend to operate on low budgets. Because nonprofessional part-time buyers who have other duties often make purchases, these customers may rely on marketers to provide more advice and assistance before and after the sale.

The North American Industry Classification System

In addition to looking at B2B markets within these three general categories, marketers rely upon the **North American Industry Classification System (NAICS)** to identify their customers. This is a numerical coding of industries the United States, Canada, and Mexico developed. Table 6.2 shows the NAICS coding system. NAICS replaced the U.S. Standard Industrial Classification (SIC) system in 1997 so that the North American Free Trade Agreement (NAFTA) countries could compare economic and financial statistics.[5] The NAICS reports the number of firms, the total dollar amount of sales, the number of employees, and the growth rate for industries, all broken down by geographic region. Many firms use the NAICS to assess potential markets and to determine how well they are doing compared to others in their industry group.

Firms may also use the NAICS to find new customers. A marketer might first determine the NAICS industry classifications of her current customers and then evaluate the sales potential of other firms occupying these categories. For example, Brad may find that several of NCR's large customers are in the grocery industry. To find new customers, he could contact other firms in the same industrial group.

government markets
The federal, state, county, and local governments that buy goods and services to carry out public objectives and to support their operations.

not-for-profit institutions
The organizations with charitable, educational, community, and other public service goals that buy goods and services to support their functions and to attract and serve their members.

North American Industry Classification System (NAICS)
The numerical coding system that the United States, Canada, and Mexico use to classify firms into detailed categories according to their business activities.

Table 6.2 | North American Industry Classification System

	Frozen Fruit Example		Cellular Telecommunications Example	
• Sector (two digits)	31–33	Manufacturing	51	Information
• Subsector (three digits)	311	Food manufacturing	513	Broadcasting and Telecommunications
• Industry group (four digits)	3114	Fruit and vegetable preserving and speciality food manufacturing	5133	Telecommunications
• Industry (five digits)	31141	Frozen food manufacturing	51332	Wireless Telecommunications Carriers (except satellite)
• U.S. Industry (six digits)	311311	Frozen fruit, juice, and vegetable manufacturing	513322	Cellular and Other Wireless Telecommunications

2

OBJECTIVE

Appreciate opportunities for using e-commerce and social media in business-to-business settings. (pp. 165–168)

Business-to-Business E-Commerce and Social Media

We know that the Internet transformed marketing—from the creation of new products to providing more effective and efficient marketing communications to the actual distribution of some products. This is certainly true in business markets as well. **Business-to-business (B2B) e-commerce** refers to Internet exchanges between two or more businesses or organizations. This includes exchanges of information, goods, services, and payments. It's not as glitzy as consumer e-commerce, but it sure has changed the way businesses operate. Using the Internet for e-commerce allows business marketers to link directly to suppliers, factories, distributors, and their customers, radically reducing the time necessary for order and delivery of goods, tracking sales, and getting feedback from customers.

In the simplest form of B2B e-commerce, the Internet provides an online catalog of goods and services that businesses need. Companies find that their Internet site is important to deliver online technical support, product information, order status information, and customer service to corporate customers. Many companies, for example, save millions of dollars a year when they replace hard-copy manuals with electronic downloads. And, of course, B2B e-commerce creates some exciting opportunities for a variety of B2B service industries.

business-to-business (B2B) e-commerce
Internet exchanges between two or more businesses or organizations.

Intranets, Extranets, and Private Exchanges

Although the Internet is the primary means of B2B e-commerce, many companies maintain an *intranet*, which provides a more secure means of conducting business. As we said in Chapter 4, this term refers to an internal corporate computer network that uses Internet technology to link a company's departments, employees, and databases. Intranets give access only to authorized employees. They allow companies to process internal transactions with greater control and consistency because of stricter security measures than those they can use on the entire Web. Businesses also use intranets to videoconference, distribute internal documents, communicate with geographically dispersed branches, and train employees.

In contrast to an intranet, an **extranet** allows certain suppliers, customers, and others outside the organization to access a company's internal system. A business customer that a company authorizes to use its extranet can place orders online. Extranets can be especially useful for companies that need to have secure communications between the company and its dealers, distributors, and/or franchisees.

extranet
A private, corporate computer network that links company departments, employees, and databases to suppliers, customers, and others outside the organization.

As you can imagine, intranets and extranets are very cost-efficient. Prudential Health Care's extranet allows its corporate customers to enroll new employees and check eligibility and claim status themselves. This saves Prudential money because it can hire fewer customer service personnel, there are no packages of insurance forms to mail back and forth, and Prudential doesn't even have to input policyholder data into the company database.

In addition to saving companies money, extranets allow business partners to collaborate on projects (such as product design) and build relationships. Companies like HP and Procter & Gamble swap marketing plans and review ad campaigns with their advertising agencies through extranets. They can exchange ideas quickly without having to spend money on travel and meetings. GE's extranet, the Trading Process Network, began as a set of online purchasing procedures and has morphed into an extensive online extranet community that connects GE with large buyers such as Con Edison.

Some of the most interesting online activity in the B2B world takes place on **private exchanges**. No, these aren't "adult sites"; they are systems that link a specially invited group of suppliers and partners over the Web. A private exchange allows companies to collaborate with suppliers they trust—without sharing sensitive information with others.

private exchanges
Systems that link an invited group of suppliers and partners over the Web.

Walmart, IBM, and HP are among the giant firms that operate private exchanges. Many other companies are getting on board as well. For example, the director of inventory control for Ace Hardware can click a mouse and instantly receive an up-to-the minute listing of the screwdrivers, hammers, and other products her suppliers have in stock. In addition, suppliers Ace invites to participate in its private exchange (and *only* those suppliers) can submit bids when Ace stores start to run low on hammers. In the "old days" before Ace implemented this process it would take 7 to 10 days to purchase more hammers, and Ace's suppliers could only guess how many they should have on hand to supply the store chain at any given time. The system benefits everyone because Ace keeps tighter controls on its inventories, and its suppliers have a more accurate picture of the store's needs so they can get rid of unneeded inventory and streamline their costs.

The Dark Side of B2B E-Commerce

Doing business the Web-enabled way sounds great—perhaps too great. There are also security risks because so much information gets passed around in cyberspace. You've no doubt heard all the recent stories about hackers obtaining vast lists of consumers' credit card numbers from retailers and other sources. But companies have even greater worries. When hackers break into company sites, they can destroy company records and steal trade secrets. Both B2C and B2B e-commerce companies worry about *authentication* and ensuring that transactions are secure. This means making sure that only authorized individuals are allowed to access a site and place an order. Maintaining security also requires firms to keep the information transferred as part of a transaction, such as a credit card number, from criminals' hard drives.

Well-meaning employees also can create security problems. They can give out unauthorized access to company computer systems by being careless about keeping their passwords into the system a secret. For example, hackers can guess at obvious passwords—nicknames, birthdates, hobbies, or a spouse's name. To increase security of their Internet sites and transactions, most companies now have safeguards in place—firewalls and encryption devices, to name the two most common methods.

A *firewall* is a combination of hardware and software that ensures that only authorized individuals gain entry into a computer system. The firewall monitors and controls all traffic between the Internet and the intranet to restrict access. Companies may even place additional firewalls within their intranet when they wish only designated employees to have access to certain parts of the system. Although firewalls can be fairly effective (even though none is totally foolproof), they require costly, constant monitoring.

Encryption means scrambling a message so that only another individual (or computer) with the right "key" can unscramble it. Otherwise, it looks like gobbledygook. The message is inaccessible without the appropriate encryption software—kind of like a decoder ring you might find in a cereal box. Without encryption, it would be easy for unethical people to get a credit card number by creating a "sniffer" program that intercepts and reads messages. A sniffer finds messages with four blocks of four numbers, copies the data, and voila!— someone else has your credit card number.

Despite firewalls, encryption, and other security measures, Web security for B2B marketers remains a serious problem. The threat to intranet and extranet usage goes beyond competitive espionage. The increasing sophistication of hackers and Internet criminals who create viruses and worms and other approaches to disrupting individual computers and entire company systems mean that all organizations—and consumers—are vulnerable to attacks and must remain vigilant.

B2B and Social Media

Another way B2B marketers drive brand awareness and generate buzz is by playing games—yes, *games*. Check out Office Depot's "Strange Little Office Beings" as an example of a viral game that appeals to business customers' playful sides. As we'll see in Chapter 12, a viral technique refers to a message that people spread to others (just like catching a cold, but more fun).[6] And speaking of viral, there's hardly a B2B firm of any size today that doesn't promote itself through social networking sites such as LinkedIn, Twitter, and Facebook.

When it comes to developing an effective B2B social media marketing strategy, one size definitely does not fit all. A recent study of more than 2,300 people and the social media resources they turn to for business-relevant information found the following were the five most popular resources people turn to at work to get the information they need for their day-to-day jobs:

1. Webinars and podcasts

2. Online ratings and reviews of business products or services

3. Company pages on social networking sites such as Facebook or LinkedIn

4. Company blogs

5. Searches of business-related information on social media sites

However, use of these formats varied considerably across company size, job role, and industry. Social media channels were most effective to reach and engage prospects at mid-to-large-size companies. Respondents who work at small companies with fewer than 100 employees were less likely to use almost all social media resources for business, with one exception: online ratings and reviews. Also, while the use of Twitter for business was 60 percent lower than for webinars or podcasts overall, Twitter is indeed a viable channel to reach senior managers at mid-to-large-size companies. Among those using any type of social media for business, 41 percent use Twitter. Certain industries (advertising and marketing, computers and software, and the Internet) and job roles (marketing and consulting) are also heavier users of social media for business than other industries (health care, legal and retail) and job responsibilities (accounting, finance, customer support and sales).[7]

Among the social media sites, the one that has become most associated with B2B networking is LinkedIn. Here are key reasons why it is the site *du jour* for so many businesspeople.

LinkedIn reduces the separation gap. Like other social networking sites, LinkedIn allows you to connect with people you know. However, it has one distinct benefit—it also allows you to see the degree of separation between you and others with whom you are not yet connected. This allows you to discover who your connections are connected with, and many times they're just the people you need to know.

LinkedIn is primarily for corporate professionals. Sites like Facebook mainly cater to people looking to have fun, post pictures, take quizzes, and so on. After all, the site was created by college kids to reach out to other kids. Most people do not use Facebook as a business tool, and most members aren't on it to network or build their brand. However, LinkedIn was created for business professionals. Almost everyone on LinkedIn is a member of the white-collar business world, which not only helps you to reach a large audience, it helps you to reach your target audience.

LinkedIn can lead to quality introductions. When you are trying to land a big account or grow your business, sometimes all it takes is an introduction to the right person. LinkedIn addresses this very need. It has a unique tool that allows you to ask people you are connected with to connect you with people they know in a professional way. A quality introduction like this is a great way to get your foot in the door and gives you more credibility than a cold call would.

LinkedIn can help you reconnect with alumni and colleagues. LinkedIn has an extensive and comprehensive search engine that will allow you to locate and reconnect with past colleagues and peers. Who knows what company your old roommate from college works for, or what quality connections your long-lost coworker can offer you? LinkedIn can help you to revive these old relationships to network and build your brand.

The Cutting Edge

Trade Shows Gone Virtual

Trade shows are a staple in the B2B world. Traditionally, firms ship samples of their latest and greatest wares to a convention center and company reps man a booth for several days of prospecting and networking. But tight travel budgets and busier-than-ever clients have caused many firms to shift to virtual trade shows, where exhibitors and attendees participate through their Web browsers. The events resemble virtual worlds such as Second Life and may last only a few hours or span several days. There are presentations from speakers, exhibit halls, and even lounges—sans virtual cocktails—where attendees can "mingle" with other participants.

Setting up a virtual booth is quick and easy. Exhibitors choose from pre-designed displays, add their company logos, and upload promotional materials. When a visitor clicks on a company's booth, employees (who are logged into their own computers but may be multitasking) receive an alert. They can talk to the visitor through a chat window or, if both parties have Web cameras, by video.

Procuring a booth at a virtual trade show isn't always cheap, but it tends to be less than its brick-and-mortar counterpart, which can exceed $15,000 before travel costs. A virtual booth costs $3,000 to $8,000 on average. Importantly, virtual shows often provide more detailed data about attendees than a physical event can—a rich source of information for future follow-up by sales and marketing.

Still, the virtual expos don't get nearly as many visitors as in-person events—maybe a couple thousand versus 8,000 or so. And because of the lower costs—admission is usually free—attendees at virtual expos tend to be smaller companies rather than large corporations. But the intimacy of virtual trade shows sometimes allows smaller firms to get more attention than they would receive at a big expo, a benefit for both parties. Although the absence of real face-to-face interaction is a downside, given that companies are tightening their budgets for many B2B buyers and sellers, virtual shows have become the primary channel for initial contact, and the medium is projected to continue growing for the foreseeable future.[9]

LinkedIn is a professional site. Because it was designed specifically for business professionals, LinkedIn users follow good business manners. Unlike on the other social networking sites, you won't have to weed your way through party pictures and drunken status updates in order to reach your target audience.[8]

3
OBJECTIVE

Identify and describe the different business buying situations and the business buying decision process.
(pp. 168–176)

Business Buying Situations and the Business Buying Decision Process

So far we've talked about how B2B markets are different from consumer markets and about the different types of customers that make up business markets. In this section, we'll discuss some of the important characteristics of business buying situations. This is important because just like companies that sell to end consumers, a successful B2B marketer needs to understand how her customers make decisions. Armed with this knowledge, the company is able to participate in the buyer's decision process from the start.

The Buyclass Framework

Like end-user consumers, business buyers spend more time and effort on some purchases than on others. This usually depends on the complexity of the product and how often they need to make the decision. A **buyclass** framework, illustrated in 📷 Figure 6.4, identifies the degree of effort required of the firm's personnel to collect information and make a purchase decision. These classes, which apply to three different buying situations, are straight rebuys, modified rebuys, and new-task buys.

Straight Rebuy

A **straight rebuy** refers to the routine purchase of items that a B2B customer regularly needs. The buyer has purchased the same items many times before and routinely reorders them when supplies are low, often from the same suppliers. Reordering the items takes little time. Buyers typically maintain a list of approved vendors that have demonstrated their ability to meet the firm's criteria for pricing, quality, service, and delivery. GE Healthcare's customers

buyclass
One of three classifications of business buying situations that characterizes the degree of time and effort required to make a decision.

straight rebuy
A buying situation in which business buyers make routine purchases that require minimal decision making.

routinely purchase its line of basic surgical scrubs (the clothing and caps doctors and nurses wear in the operating room) without much evaluation on each occasion.

Because straight rebuys often contribute the "bread and butter" revenue a firm needs to maintain a steady stream of income, many business marketers go to great lengths to cultivate and maintain relationships with customers who submit reorders on a regular basis. Salespeople may regularly call on these customers to personally handle orders and to see if there are additional products the customer needs. The goal is to be sure that the customer doesn't even think twice about just buying the same product every time she is running low. Rebuys keep a supplier's sales volume up and help cover selling costs.

Modified Rebuy

Life is sweet for companies whose customers automatically do straight rebuys. Unfortunately, these situations do not last forever. A **modified rebuy** occurs when a firm decides to shop around for suppliers with better prices, quality, or delivery times. This situation also can occur when the organization confronts new needs for products it already buys. A buyer who purchased many BlackBerry smart phones, for example, may have to reevaluate several other options if the firm upgrades its cellular telecommunications system.

Modified rebuys require more time and effort than straight rebuys. The buyer generally knows the purchase requirements and she has a few potential suppliers in mind. Marketers know that modified rebuys can mean that some vendors get added to a buyer's approved supplier list while others may be dropped. So even if in the past a company purchased its smart phones from BlackBerry's manufacturer Research in Motion (RIM), this doesn't necessarily mean it will do so in the future. Now, other platforms like Apple, Palm, and Google's Android may gain approved supplier status going forward and the race is on. Astute marketers routinely call on buyers to detect and define problems that can lead to winning or losing in such situations.

New-Task Buy

A first-time purchase is a **new-task buy**. Uncertainty and risk characterize buying decisions in this classification, and they require the most effort because the buyer has no previous experience on which to base a decision.

Your university, for example, may decide (if it hasn't done so already) to go into the "distance learning" business—delivering courses to off-site students. Buying the equipment to set up classrooms with two-way video transmission is an expensive and complex new-task buy for a school. The buyer has to start from scratch to gather information on purchase specifications that may be highly technical and complex and require detailed input from others. In new-task buying situations, not only do buyers lack experience with the product, but they also are often unfamiliar with firms that supply the product. Supplier choice is critical, and buyers gather much information about quality, pricing, delivery, and service from several potential suppliers.

A prospective customer's new-task buying situation represents both a challenge and an opportunity. Although a new-task buy can be significant in and of itself, many times the chosen supplier gains the added advantage of becoming an "in" supplier for more routine purchases that will follow. A growing business that needs an advertising agency for the first time, for example, may seek exhaustive information from several firms before it selects one, but then it may continue to use the chosen agency's services for future projects without bothering to explore other alternatives.

Marketers know that to get the order in a new-buy situation, they must develop a close working relationship with the business buyer. There are many situations in which marketers focus on selling their product by wooing people who recommend their products—over and

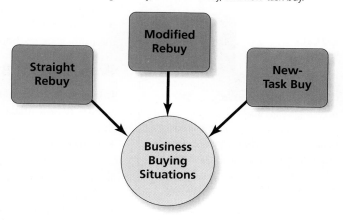

Figure 6.4 📷 *Snapshot* | Elements of the Buyclass Framework

The classes of the buyclass framework relate to three different organizational buying situations: straight rebuy, modified rebuy, and new-task buy.

modified rebuy
A buying situation classification used by business buyers to categorize a previously made purchase that involves some change and that requires limited decision making.

new-task buy
A new business-to-business purchase that is complex or risky and that requires extensive decision making.

Brad Tracy

buying center
The group of people in an organization who participate in a purchasing decision.

above the end consumers who actually buy them. To use an example close to home, think about all of the goods and services that make up the higher-education industry. For instance, even though you are the one who shelled out the money for this extremely awesome textbook, your professor was the one who made the exceptionally wise decision to assign it. She made this choice (did we mention it was a really wise choice?) only after carefully considering numerous textbooks and talking to several publishers' sales representatives.

Professional Buyers and Buying Centers

Just as it is important for marketers of consumer goods and services to understand their customers, it's essential that B2B marketers understand who handles the buying for business customers. Trained professional buyers typically carry out buying in B2B markets. These people have titles such as *purchasing agents, procurement officers,* or *directors of materials management*.

While some consumers like to shop 'til they drop almost every day, most of us spend far less time roaming the aisles. However, professional purchasers do it all day, every day—it's their job and their business to buy! These individuals focus on economic factors beyond the initial price of the product, including transportation and delivery charges, accessory products or supplies, maintenance, and other ongoing costs. They are responsible for selecting quality products and ensuring their timely delivery. They shop as if their jobs depend on it—because they do.

Many times in business buying situations, several people work together to reach a decision. Depending on what they need to purchase, these participants may be production workers, supervisors, engineers, administrative assistants, shipping clerks, or financial officers. In a small organization, everyone may have a voice in the decision. The **buying center** is the group of people in the organization who participate in the decision-making process. Although this term may conjure up an image of "command central" buzzing with purchasing activity, a buying center is not a place at all. Instead, it is a cross-functional team of decision makers. Generally, the members of a buying center have some expertise or interest in the particular decision, and as a group they are able to make the best decision.

Hospitals, for example, frequently make purchase decisions through a large buying center. When they need to purchase disposable protective masks, one or more physicians, the director of nursing, and purchasing agents may work together to determine quantities and select the best products and suppliers. A separate decision regarding the types of pharmaceutical supplies to stock might call for a different cast of characters to advise the purchasing agent, likely including pharmacists and pharmacy technicians. Marketers must continually identify which employees in a firm take part in every purchase decision and develop relationships with them all.

Depending on the complexity of the purchase and the size of the buying center, a participant may assume one, several, or all of the six roles that Table 6.3 shows. Let's review them now.

Table 6.3 | Roles in the Buying Center

Role	Potential Player	Responsibility
• Initiator	• Production employees, sales manager, almost anyone	• Recognizes that a purchase needs to be made
• User	• Production employees, secretaries, almost anyone	• Individual(s) who will ultimately use the product
• Gatekeeper	• Buyer/purchasing agent	• Controls flow of information to others in the organization
• Influencer	• Engineers, quality control experts, technical specialists, outside consultants	• Affects decision by giving advice and sharing expertise
• Decider	• Purchasing agent, managers, CEO	• Makes the final purchase decision
• Buyer	• Purchasing agent	• Executes the purchase decision

- The *user* is the member of the buying center who actually needs the product. The user's role in the buying center varies. For example, an administrative assistant may give her input on the features a new copier should have because she will be chained to it for several hours a day. Marketers need to inform users of their products' benefits, especially if the benefits outweigh those that competitors offer.

- The *initiator* begins the buying process by first recognizing that the firm needs to make a purchase. A production employee, for example, may notice that a piece of equipment is not working properly and notify a supervisor that it is slowing up the production line. At other times, the initiator may suggest purchasing a new product because it will improve the firm's operations. Depending on the initiator's position in the organization and the type of purchase, the initiator may or may not influence the actual purchase decision. For marketers, it's important to make sure that individuals who might initiate a purchase are aware of improved products they offer.

- The *gatekeeper* is the person who controls the flow of information to other members. Typically the gatekeeper is the purchasing agent, who gathers information and materials from salespeople, schedules sales presentations, and controls suppliers' access to other participants in the buying process. For salespeople, developing and maintaining strong personal relationships with gatekeepers is critical to being able to offer their products to the buying center.

Airlines like the German carrier Lufthansa appeal strongly to business travelers, even though the person who flies on business may not be the one deciding which airline he or she will use.

- An *influencer* affects the buying decision when she dispenses advice or shares expertise. Highly trained employees like engineers, quality-control specialists, and other technical experts in the firm generally have a great deal of influence in purchasing equipment, materials, and component parts the company uses in production. The influencers may or may not wind up using the product. Marketers need to identify key influencers in the buying center and persuade them of their product's superiority.

- The *decider* is the member of the buying center who makes the final decision. This person usually has the greatest power within the buying center; she often has power within the organization to authorize spending the company's money. For a routine purchase, the decider may be the purchasing agent. If the purchase is complex, a manager or even the chief executive officer (CEO) may be the decider. Quite obviously, the decider is critical to a marketer's success and deserves a lot of attention in the selling process.

- The *buyer* is the person who has responsibility to execute the purchase. Although the buyer often has a role in identifying and evaluating alternative suppliers, this person's primary function is to handle the details of the transaction. The buyer obtains competing bids, negotiates contracts, and arranges delivery dates and payment plans. Once a firm makes the purchase decision, marketers turn their attention to negotiating the details of the purchase with the buyer. Successful marketers are well aware that providing exemplary service in this stage of the purchase can be a critical factor in achieving future sales from this client.

The Business Buying Decision Process

We've seen that there are a number of players in the business buying process, beginning with an initiator and ending with a buyer. To make matters even more challenging to marketers, members of the buying team go through several stages in the decision-making process before the marketer gets an order. The *business buying decision process*, as 📈 Figure 6.5 shows, is a

Figure 6.5  *Process* | Steps in the Business Buying Process

The steps in the business buying decision process are the same as those in the consumer decision process. But for business purchases, each step may be far more complex and require more attention from marketers.

Step 1: Recognize the problem
- Make purchase requisition or request
- Form buying center, if needed

↓

Step 2: Search for Information
- Develop product specifications
- Identify potential suppliers
- Obtain proposals and quotations

↓

Step 3: Evaluate the Alternatives
- Evaluate proposals
- Obtain and evaluate samples

↓

Step 4: Select the Product and Supplier
- Issue purchase order

↓

Step 5: Evaluate Postpurchase
- Survey users
- Document performance

Brad Tracy

APPLYING ▽
The Search for Information

Brad knows that prospective customers need a lot of information about a complex purchase like a POS workstation. He needs to decide upon the best places to make this information available, including which trade shows NCR should attend.

series of steps similar to those in the consumer decision process we discussed in Chapter 5. To help understand these steps, let's say you've just started working at the Way Radical Skateboard Company and your boss just assigned you to the buying center for the purchase of new software for Web-page design—a new-task buy for your firm.

Step 1: Recognize the Problem

As in consumer buying, the first step in the business buying decision process occurs when someone sees that a purchase can solve a problem. For straight rebuy purchases, this may occur because the firm has run out of paper, pens, or garbage bags. In these cases, the buyer places the order, and the decision-making process ends. Recognition of the need for modified rebuy purchases often comes when the organization wants to replace outdated existing equipment, from changes in technology, or from an ad, brochure, or some other marketing communication that offers the customer a better product or one at a lower price. Two events may occur in the problem-recognition step. First, a firm makes a request or requisition, usually in writing. Then, depending on the complexity of the purchase, the firm may form a buying center.

The need for new-task purchases often occurs because the firm wants to enhance its operations in some way or when a smart salesperson tells the business customer about a new product that will increase the efficiency of the firm's operations or improve the firm's end products. In the case of Way Radical's new software purchase, your marketing department has previously hired an outside agency to design and maintain its Web page. The company has become dissatisfied with the outside supplier and has decided to move the design function in-house. Now the company needs to select new software to create a truly Way Radical Web site.

Step 2: Search for Information

In the second step of the decision process (for purchases other than straight rebuys) the buying center searches for information about products and suppliers. Members of the buying center may individually or collectively refer to reports in trade magazines and journals, seek advice from outside consultants, and pay close attention to marketing communications from different manufacturers and suppliers. As in consumer marketing, it's the job of marketers to make sure that information is available when and where business customers want it—by placing ads in trade magazines, by mailing brochures and other printed material to prospects, and by having a well-trained sales force regularly calling on customers to build long-term relationships. For Way Radical's purchase, you may try to find out what software your outside supplier uses (if the supplier will tell you), talk to the information technology experts in your firm, or review ads and articles in trade magazines.

There are thousands of specialized publications out there that cater to just about any industry you can think of. Usually sponsored by leading industry trade associations, each is bursting with information from competing companies that cater to a specific niche. Who needs that fluffy romance novel at the beach? Try leafing through the latest issue of *Chemical Processing* or *Meat and Poultry Magazine* instead.

Of course, sometimes B2B marketers try to get the information about their product into the hands of buyers via less-specialized media. For example, in recent years AFLAC, American Family Life Assurance Company of Columbus—the firm behind the famous duck—has heavily advertised on television even though most of its customers are in the B2B space. In fact, many end-user consumers don't have the foggiest notion what AFLAC sells—but they sure love to "quack up" over the duck's antics. The truth is, AFLAC's primary business is working with businesses (over 400,000 of them, in fact) to enhance their employee benefits packages with various types of insurance and other benefits in order to improve recruiting and retention of the firms' people. But their strategy of advertising directly on mass media was brilliant; now when an organizational buyer or HR manager searches for these services, AFLAC's name will surely be at the top of the list (aided by great search engine optimization). Now there's a duck that's not out of water![10]

Business buyers often develop **product specifications**, that is, a written description of the quality, size, weight, color, features, quantity, training, warranty, service terms, and delivery requirements for the purchase. When the product needs are complex or technical, engineers and other experts are the key players who identify specific product characteristics they require and determine whether the organizations can get by with standardized/off-the-shelf items or if they need to acquire customized/made-to-order goods and services. Although excellent Web-design software is available off the shelf, for some computer applications like the ones Way Radical needs, custom-designed software may be necessary.

Once the product specifications are in hand, the next step is to identify potential suppliers and obtain written or verbal proposals, or *bids*, from one or more of them. For standardized or branded products in which there are few if any differences in the products of different suppliers, this may be as simple as an informal request for pricing information, including discounts, shipping charges, and confirmation of delivery dates. At other times, the potential suppliers receive a formal written *request for proposal* or *request for quotation* that requires detailed information from vendors. For the Way Radical software, which is likely to be a standardized software package, you will probably just ask for general pricing information.

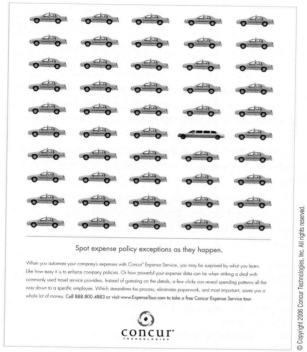

Many companies sell services—like expense monitoring—to other companies (rather than to end consumers) that allow their business customers to operate at peak efficiency.

Step 3: Evaluate the Alternatives

In this stage of the business buying decision process, the buying center assesses the proposals it receives. Total spending for goods and services can have a major impact on the firm's profitability so, all other things being equal, price can be a primary consideration. Pricing evaluations must take into account discount policies for certain quantities, returned-goods policies, the cost of repair and maintenance services, terms of payment, and the cost of financing large purchases. For capital equipment, cost criteria also include the life expectancy of the purchase, the expected resale value, and disposal costs for the old equipment. In some cases, the buying center may negotiate with the preferred supplier to match the lowest bidder.

Although a firm often selects a bidder because it offers the lowest price, there are times when it bases the buying decision on other factors. For example, in its lucrative B2B market, American Express wins bids for its travel agency business because it offers extra services other agencies don't or can't such as a corporate credit card, monthly reports that detail the company's total travel expenses, and perks tied to AMEX's customer loyalty program.

The more complex and costly the purchase, the more time buyers spend searching for the best supplier—and the more marketers must do to win the order. In some cases, a company may even ask one or more of its current customers to participate in a **customer reference program**. In these situations customers formally share success stories and actively recommend products to other potential clients, often as part of an online community composed of people with similar needs.

Marketers often make formal presentations and product demonstrations to the buying center group. In the case of installations and large equipment, they may arrange for buyers to speak with or even visit other customers to examine how the product performs. For less complex products, the buying firm may ask potential suppliers for samples of the products so its people can evaluate them personally. The buying center may ask salespeople from various companies to demonstrate their software for your Way Radical group so that you can all compare the capabilities of different products.

product specifications
A written description of the quality, size, weight, and other details required of a product purchase.

customer reference program
A formalized process by which customers formally share success stories and actively recommend products to other potential clients, usually facilitated through an on-line community.

Ripped from the Headlines

Ethical/Sustainable Decisions in the Real World

Drug maker Merck's political action committee donated more than $572,000 to federal candidates in the 2008 presidential election and racked up $4.6 million in expenses to lobby Congress and the executive branch that same year, federal records show. What federal records don't show is that Merck also spent millions on payments to the Pharmaceutical Research and Manufacturers of America (PRMA) and several other trade groups that lobbied intensely on the massive bill to revamp the nation's health care system. PRMA pumped nearly $19.9 million into lobbying during the first nine months of 2009, up from $14.1 million during the same period the previous year.

Sweeping ethics rules passed by Congress in 2007 require corporate interests that lobby Washington to reveal more information than ever, such as how much they donate to politicians' favorite charities. Yet companies don't have to detail how much money they give to powerful trade associations, nor does federal law require trade groups to disclose the amount they receive from each member for political activity.

> **ETHICS CHECK:** ✎
> Find out what other students taking this course **would do** and **why** on **www .mypearsonmarketinglab .com**

"This is a stealth loophole," said Lisa Gilbert of U.S. Public Interest Research Group, a nonpartisan watchdog group. "These corporations have a big stake in how legislation plays out, but it's pretty egregious that the public doesn't know exactly how their money is being spent." Current law allows "companies to hide behind trade associations and engage in lobbying and political activity they don't want to be associated with," said Bruce Freed, president of the Center for Political Accountability. "The public needs to know how money is being spent politically," he said, "because of the tremendous influence it has on policymaking, the political process and their daily lives."

Merck started disclosing association dues in 2008. It is one of a handful of companies shedding more light on their political activity under pacts with the nonprofit Center for Political Accountability. Others include Microsoft, Time Warner, Campbell Soup, and Wisconsin Energy—each of which has agreed to detail their trade-association donations, along with other political spending. Dan Bross, Microsoft's senior director of corporate citizenship, said the company wanted "to lead by example." Microsoft has posted its political-related dues online for the first time. The largest payment: $2.1 million in fiscal year 2009 to the Computing Technology Industry Association, a high-tech trade group. To date, 50 companies have voluntarily agreed to disclose payments to trade groups, and 24 have started doing so on the Internet, said Maureen O'Brien, research director for the Center for Political Accountability.

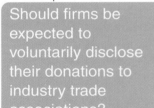

Should firms be expected to voluntarily disclose their donations to industry trade associations?

☐ **YES** ☐ **NO**

Why or why not?

single sourcing
The business practice of buying a particular product from only one supplier.

multiple sourcing
The business practice of buying a particular product from several different suppliers.

Step 4: Select the Product and Supplier

Once buyers have assessed all proposals, it's time for the rubber to hit the road. The next step in the buying process is the purchase decision when the group selects the best product and supplier to meet the firm's needs. Reliability and durability rank especially high for equipment and systems that keep the firm's operations running smoothly without interruption. For some purchases, warranties, repair service, and regular maintenance after the sale are important. For Way Radical, the final decision may be based not only on the capabilities of the software itself but also on the technical support the software company provides. What kind of support is available and at what cost to the customer?

One of the most important decisions a buyer makes is how many suppliers can best serve the firm's needs. Sometimes having one supplier is more beneficial to the organization than having multiple suppliers. **Single sourcing**, in which a buyer and seller work quite closely, is particularly important when a firm needs frequent deliveries or specialized products. Single sourcing also helps assure consistency of quality of materials input into the production process. But reliance on a single source means that the firm is at the mercy of the chosen supplier to deliver the needed goods or services without interruption. If the single source doesn't come through, the firm's relationship with its own end users will very likely be affected.

However, using one or a few suppliers rather than many has its advantages. A firm that buys from a single supplier becomes a large customer with a lot of clout when it comes to negotiating prices and contract terms. Having one or a few suppliers also lowers the firm's administrative costs because it has fewer invoices to pay, fewer contracts to negotiate, and fewer salespeople to see than if it uses many sources.

In contrast, **multiple sourcing** means buying a product from several different suppliers. Under this system, suppliers are more likely to remain price-competitive. And if one supplier has problems with delivery, the firm has others to fall back upon. The automotive industry practices this philosophy: A vehicle manufacturer often won't buy a new product from a supplier unless the vendor's rivals also are capable of making the same item! This policy tends to stifle innovation, but it does ensure a steady supply of parts to feed to the assembly line.

Sometimes supplier selection is based on **reciprocity**, which means that a buyer and seller agree to be each other's customers by saying essentially, "I'll buy from you, and you buy from me." For example, a firm that supplies parts to a company that manufactures trucks would agree to buy trucks from only that firm.

The U.S. government frowns on reciprocal agreements and often determines that such agreements between large firms are illegal because they limit free competition—new suppliers simply don't have a chance against the preferred suppliers. Reciprocity between smaller firms, that is, firms that are not so large as to control a significant proportion of the business in their industry, is legal in the United States if both parties voluntarily agree to it. In other countries, reciprocity is a practice that is common and even expected in B2B marketing.

Outsourcing occurs when firms obtain outside vendors to provide goods or services that might otherwise be supplied in-house. For example, Sodexo is the world's largest outsourcer for food and facilities management services with over 6,000 U.S. client sites. Colleges and universities are a major category of clientele for Sodexo (are they your school's vendor?), as these educational institutions want to focus on educating students rather than preparing and serving food. (Fortunately, your professors don't have to cook as well as teach!)

Outsourcing is an increasingly popular strategy, but in some cases it can be controversial. Many critics object when American companies contract with companies or individuals in remote places like China or India to perform work they used to do at home. These tasks range from complicated jobs like writing computer code to fairly simple ones like manning reservations desks, staffing call centers for telephone sales, and even taking drive-through orders at American fast-food restaurants. (Yes, in some cases it's actually more efficient for an operator in India to relay an order from a customer for a #3 Burger Combo to the restaurant's cooks than for an on-site person to take the order!)

Controversy aside, many companies find that it's both cost-efficient and productive to call on outsiders from around the world to solve problems their own scientists can't handle. We call this process **crowdsourcing**: put simply, a way to harness "crowds" to "source" solutions to business problems. Among the more interesting areas for crowdsourcing by marketers: brainstorming and feedback (www.kluster.com), brand names (www.namethis.com), product redesign (www.redesignme.com), and logo design (www.99designs.com), which hawks itself as follows: "Need a logo? No problem. Simply turn your logo/design project needs into a contest on 99designs. Submit a brief and determine a fee for the contest winner (minimum is around $150), then sit back and watch the crowd go to work. More than 40,000 designers use 99designs. After all the submissions are in you can choose a design. What could be simpler?"[11]

Yet another type of buyer–seller partnership is **reverse marketing**. Instead of sellers trying to identify potential customers and then "pitching" their products, buyers try to find suppliers that can produce specifically needed products and then attempt to "sell" the idea to the suppliers. The seller aims to satisfy the buying firm's needs. Often large poultry producers practice reverse marketing. Perdue supplies baby chickens, chicken food, financing for chicken houses, medications, and everything else necessary for farmers to lay "golden eggs" for the company. This assures the farmer that she will have a buyer, while at the same time guaranteeing Perdue's chicken supply.

Step 5: Evaluate Postpurchase

Just as consumers evaluate purchases, an organizational buyer assesses whether the performance of the product and the supplier lives up to expectations. The buyer surveys the users to determine their satisfaction with the product as well as with the installation, delivery, and service the supplier provides. For producers of goods, this may relate to the level of satisfaction

reciprocity
A trading partnership in which two firms agree to buy from one another.

outsourcing
The business buying process of obtaining outside vendors to provide goods or services that otherwise might be supplied in-house.

crowdsourcing
A practice in which firms outsource marketing activities (such as selecting an ad) to a community of users.

reverse marketing
A business practice in which a buyer firm attempts to identify suppliers who will produce products according to the buyer firm's specifications.

of the final consumer of the buying firm's product. Has demand for the producer's product increased, decreased, or stayed the same? By documenting and reviewing supplier performance, a firm decides whether to keep or drop the supplier. Many suppliers recognize the importance of conducting their own performance reviews on a regular basis. Measuring up to a customer's expectations can mean winning or losing a big account. Many a supplier has lost business because of a history of late deliveries or poor equipment repairs and maintenance.

An important element in postpurchase evaluation is measurement. When you think about measuring elements of a customer's experience with a company and its products and brands, we'll bet you automatically think about end-user consumers—like travelers' views of their Marriott hotel stay or the taste of that new Starbucks coffee flavor. Similarly, in the B2B world managers pay a lot of attention to the feedback they get about the purchases they've made. Here are some metrics organizational buyers use to measure how well a product or service performs:

- *Satisfaction:* Yes, customer satisfaction is still very relevant in B2B and in the buying center; ultimately it is the user of the product that should provide this feedback. You can bet that if users are dissatisfied, they will quickly relay this information to the rest of the buying center.

- *Quality:* Is the product meeting, exceeding, or falling short of expectations, and (for the latter) what can be done to correct the deficiency?

- *Customer Engagement:* It is important to find ways to get and keep customers involved in your business after the sales have been made through customer reference programs or other means.

- *Purchase Intentions:* A common metric is to determine the general budgetary plan a client has for the year ahead, leading to the ability to determine what appropriate sales goals might be going forward.

- *Promptness and Effectiveness of Problem Resolution:* The complexities of the B2B market ensure that problems will occur between vendor and client. The true test is how well and how quickly problems are resolved when they do come up.

A final tip: Remember that B2B customers are busy professionals. They have even less time to fill out lengthy questionnaires than do end-user consumers. Make sure you collect feedback efficiently in a manner most comfortable to the client.[12]

Here's my choice. . .

Real **People**, Real **Choices**

Why do you think Brad chose option 3?

1
Option

2
Option

3
Option

How It Worked Out at NCR Corporation

NCR's retail division passed on the show and reallocated its sales and marketing resources to the two smaller events. One show, sponsored by a national trade association, drew a solid number of customers and prospects while the second event, sponsored by a trade publication, did not. The division will continue to focus its resources in two areas: (1) large industry-leading shows that have sustainable momentum with its targeted customers, and (2) small focused conference events that offer the opportunity to have high-quality interactions with attendees.

To learn the whole story, visit www.mypearsonmarketinglab.com.

Brand **YOU**!

It's hard to start your job search without knowing how the hiring process works inside companies.

What can you expect in the interview process? Whom will you meet during interviews? Who makes the hiring decision? How do you know what comes next? Learn the ins and outs of how employers select candidates and how to create a competitive advantage for your brand. Check out Chapter 6 of *Brand You* and get the inside track.

| Kim Richmond Fourth Edition |

Brand YOU

MARKETING 7E real People, real Choices

Solomon | Marshall | Stuart

Objective Summary ➡ Key Terms ➡ Apply

1. Objective Summary (pp. 158–164)

Understand the characteristics of business-to-business markets, business-to-business market demand, and how marketers classify business-to-business customers.

B2B markets include business or organizational customers that buy goods and services for purposes other than personal consumption. There are a number of major and minor differences between organizational and consumer markets. To be successful, marketers must understand these differences and develop strategies that can be effective with organizational customers. For example, business customers are usually few in number, they may be geographically concentrated, and they often purchase higher-priced products in larger quantities. Business demand derives from the demand for another good or service, is generally not affected by price increases or decreases, is subject to great fluctuations, and may be tied to the demand and availability of some other good.

Business customers include producers, resellers, governments, and not-for-profit organizations. Producers purchase materials, parts, and various goods and services needed to produce other goods and services to be sold at a profit. Resellers purchase finished goods to resell at a profit as well as other goods and services to maintain their operations. Governments and other not-for-profit organizations purchase the goods and services necessary to fulfill their objectives. The North American Industry Classification System (NAICS), a numerical coding system developed by NAFTA countries, is a widely used classification system for business and organizational markets.

Key Terms

business-to-business (B2B) markets, p. 158

organizational markets, p. 158

derived demand, p. 161

inelastic demand, p. 162

joint demand, p. 162

producers, p. 163

resellers, p. 163

government markets, p. 164

not-for-profit institutions, p. 164

North American Industry Classification System (NAICS), p. 164

2. Objective Summary (pp. 165–168)

Appreciate opportunities for using e-commerce and social media in business-to-business settings.

Business-to-business (B2B) e-commerce refers to Internet exchanges between two or more businesses or organizations. This includes exchanges of information, goods, services, and payments. Using the Internet for e-commerce allows business marketers to link directly to suppliers, factories, distributors, and their customers, radically reducing the time necessary for order and delivery of goods, tracking sales, and getting feedback from customers.

Besides the Internet itself, intranets, extranets, and private exchanges also provide useful means for firms and their employees, customers, and suppliers to conduct business. As with the consumer side, B2B e-commerce has a potential "dark side" fraught with problems such as security breaches, fraud, password theft, sophisticated hackers, and nasty viruses. Despite firewalls, encryption, and other security measures, overall Web security for B2B marketers remains a serious issue with high potential for financial loss.

Social media usage has made its way into B2B, especially through the use of LinkedIn. LinkedIn was developed specifically for professional business users. However, don't ignore opportunities to connect your business via Facebook, Twitter, and other more consumer-focused social network sites.

Key Terms

business-to-business (B2B) e-commerce, p. 165

extranet, p. 165

private exchanges, p. 165

3. Objective Summary (pp. 168–176)

Identify and describe the different business buying situations and the business buying decision process.

The buyclass framework identifies the degree and effort required to make a business buying decision. Purchase situations can be straight rebuy, modified rebuy, and new-task buying. A buying center is a group of people who work together to make a buying decision. The roles in the buying center are (1) the initiator, who recognizes the need for a purchase; (2) the user, who will ultimately use the product; (3) the gatekeeper, who controls the flow of information to others; (4) the influencer, who shares advice and expertise; (5) the decider, who makes the final decision; and (6) the buyer, who executes the purchase.

Key Terms

buyclass, p. 168

straight rebuy, p. 168

modified rebuy, p. 169

new-task buy, p. 169

buying center, p. 170

product specifications, p. 173

customer reference program, p. 173

single sourcing, p. 174

multiple sourcing, p. 174

reciprocity, p. 175

outsourcing, p. 175

crowdsourcing, p. 175

reverse marketing, p. 175

Chapter Questions and Activities

Concepts: Test Your Knowledge

1. How do B2B markets differ from consumer markets? How do these differences affect marketing strategies?
2. Explain what we mean by derived demand, inelastic demand, fluctuating demand, and joint demand.
3. How do we generally classify B2B markets? What is the NAICS?
4. Describe new-task buys, modified rebuys, and straight rebuys. What are some different marketing strategies each calls for?
5. What are the characteristics of business buyers?
6. What is a buying center? What are the roles of the various people in a buying center?
7. What are the steps in the business buying decision process? What happens in each step?
8. How are the steps in the business buying decision process similar to the steps in the consumer buying process? How are they different?
9. What is single sourcing? Multiple sourcing? Outsourcing?
10. Explain how reciprocity and reverse marketing operate in B2B markets.
11. Explain the role of intranets, extranets, and private exchanges in B2B e-commerce.
12. Describe the security issues firms face in B2B e-commerce. What are some safeguards firms use to reduce their security risks?

Activities: Apply What You've Learned

1. As a director of purchasing for a firm that manufactures motorcycles, you have been notified that the price of an important part used in the manufacture of the bikes has nearly doubled. You see your company having three choices: (1) buying the part and passing the cost on to the customer by increasing your price; (2) buying the part and absorbing the increase in cost, keeping the price of your bikes the same; and (3) buying a lower-priced part that will be of lower quality. Prepare a list of pros and cons for each alternative. Then explain your recommendation and justification for it.
2. Assume that you are the marketing manager for a small securities firm (a firm that sells stocks and bonds) whose customers are primarily businesses and other organizations.

Your company has so far not made use of the Internet to provide information and service to its customers. You are considering whether this move is in the best interests of your firm. Write a memo outlining the pros and cons of e-commerce for your firm, the risks your firm would face, and your recommendations.

3. Assume you are a sales manager for a firm that is a distributor of hospital equipment and supplies. Your company offers its customers a wide range of products—everything from disposable rubber gloves to high-tech patient monitors. Thus, purchases made by your customers include straight rebuys, modified rebuys, and new-task purchases. Your job is to explain to your new salesperson the differences among these types of purchases and how to effectively "get the business" for all three types of purchases. In a role-playing exercise with another classmate, provide the needed information and advice.
4. As chief marketing officer (CMO) for a four-year-old software firm specializing in applications for use in billing and scheduling systems in medical offices, you are interested in providing a forum for your clients to share their success stories and best practices. You believe that building a community of this type can lead to numerous leads and referrals for new business. What characteristics might a customer reference program have that would best serve you, your firm, and its customers? Be as specific as you can about what this program would be like and how it would work to gain the desired references.

Marketing Metrics Exercise

B2B customers are very busy professionals and notoriously reluctant to take time to provide data to marketers. In order to measure important issues described in the chapter such as client satisfaction, quality, customer engagement, repurchase intentions, and problem resolution turnaround and effectiveness, marketers must employ the most user-friendly and efficient data collection methods available—else the customer will be highly unlikely to provide the needed data.

Review what you learned in Chapter 4 about approaches to collecting data and propose an approach to collecting the above information from a busy B2B customer in a way that is most likely to result in his or her cooperation. Be as specific as you can in describing your chosen approach and explain why you selected it.

Choices: What Do You Think?

1. E-commerce is dramatically changing the way B2B transactions take place. What are the advantages of B2B e-commerce to companies? To society? Are there any disadvantages of B2B e-commerce?
2. The practice of buying business products based on sealed competitive bids is popular among all types of business buyers. What are the advantages and disadvantages of this practice to buyers? What are the advantages and disadvantages to sellers? Should companies always give the business to the lowest bidder? Why or why not?
3. When firms implement a single sourcing policy in their buying, other possible suppliers do not have an opportunity. Is this ethical? What are the advantages to the company? What are the disadvantages?
4. Many critics say that strict engineering and other manufacturing requirements for products purchased by governments increase prices unreasonably and that taxpayers end up paying too much because of such policies. What are the advantages and disadvantages of such purchase restrictions? Should governments loosen restrictions on their purchases?
5. In the buying center, the gatekeeper controls information flow to others in the center. Thus, the gatekeeper determines which possible sellers are heard and which are not. Does the gatekeeper have too much power? What policies might be implemented to make sure that all possible sellers are treated fairly?
6. Some critics complain that outsourcing sends much-needed jobs to competitors overseas (like Airbus) while depriving American workers of these opportunities. Should a company consider this factor when deciding where to obtain raw materials or brainpower in order to compete efficiently?

Miniproject: Learn by Doing

The purpose of this miniproject is to gain knowledge about one B2B market using the NAICS codes and other government information.

1. Select an industry of interest to you and use the NAICS information you find on the Internet (**http://www.census .gov**, then find the NAICS page) or in your library.
   a. What are the codes for each of the following classifications?

   NAICS Sector (two digits)
   NAICS Subsector (three digits)
   NAICS Industry Group (four digits)
   NAICS Industry (five digits)
   U.S. Industry (six digits)

   b. What types of products are or are not included in this industry?
2. Locate the *U.S. Industrial Outlook* or *Standard & Poor's Industry Surveys* in your library to find the answers to the following:
   a. What was the value of industry shipments (sales) for the United States in the latest year reported?
   b. What were worldwide sales for the industry in the most recent year reported?
3. The U.S. Census Bureau publishes a number of economic censuses every five years covering years ending in the digits 2 and 7. These include the following publications: *Census of Retail Trade, Census of Wholesale Trade, Census of Service Industries, Census of Transportation, Census of Manufacturers, Census of Mineral Industries,* and *Census of Construction Industries.* Use the appropriate publication to determine the value of shipments in your industry for the most recent year reported.
4. *Ward's Business Directory* provides useful industry-specific information. Use it to find the names and addresses of the top four public companies in the industry and their sales revenues.
5. *Compact Disclosure* provides information from company annual reports on CD-ROM (usually available in your school library). Use it or some other similar source to provide the following for the four companies listed in question 4:
   a. Income statements
   b. Net sales, gross profits, and income before tax
6. *The Statistical Abstract of the United States* provides information on the economic, demographic, social, and political structures of the United States. It provides data on the sales of products in consumer markets. Use it to complete the following:
   a. Find a product in the consumer market that is produced by your industry (or is down the value chain from your industry, for example, automobiles from the steel industry).
   b. Determine the sales of the consumer product category for the most recent year reported.

Marketing in **Action** Case Real Choices at The Filter

How often do Web site recommendations work for the average customer? **Yahoo.com** offers advice as customers browse its music and video catalog and suggests selections based on what other shoppers chose. In many cases, however, the connections it proposes aren't very helpful. Many businesses develop proprietary algorithms to make suggestions for their customers. However, others choose not to take on this task and outsource this activity to firms that specialize in recommendation engine technology. Recommendation engines apply the information collected from user activity to suggest other items for consump-

tion. The type of items can range from music to television content, videos, books, news, Web pages, and so on.

Operating in a business-to-business environment, the companies that develop recommendation engines have to carefully consider the specific needs of their diverse clients in order to be successful. The Filter is a company that thinks it can do a better job for those companies that need this type of functionality, like **Yahoo.com**. Doug Merrill, current director and a former chief information officer at Google, says, "Recommendations—from friends, from newspapers, from colleagues—are the most common way to find new content. However, there is more information available than there are people to recommend. The Filter analyzes data to provide measurably better, more relevant recommendations, automatically."

Based in Bath, England, The Filter is a privately held company that provides recommendation technology for various companies on the Web. Its founder is Martin Hopkins, a physicist who is also a passionate music fan. In 2004, he started The Filter due to his own frustration as he tried to keep track of his digital music collection of over 10,000 tracks. Hopkins developed an algorithm using artificial intelligence that learned his likes and dislikes and then suggested playlists. This software would later become the foundation for the decision-making procedure that controls The Filter's recommendation engine.

The Filter's client list includes firms such as Sony Music, Nokia, and Comcast. In 2010, The Filter entered into a deal with Dailymotion, a Web site of over 66 million monthly users, to make video-to-video recommendations. During the trial and optimization period, the company's software captured over 5 billion video views and delivered over 1 billion recommendations.

Just as Netflix uses its extensive database of customers' posted opinions to help locate movies they might not have thought of on their own, The Filter guides customers toward music and video choices that are not obvious. One of the program's advantages over other recommendation engines is that it only deals with digital media that can be tracked after a customer actually purchases a song online. This advantage allows The Filter to monitor postpurchase consumption behavior. For instance, some customers only listen to or watch parts of the media they download, so this behavior may signal that the customer may

not be truly interested in all the material he or she purchased. This type of knowledge could make a significant difference in what the software recommends the next time the user accesses the system.

Initially The Filter aimed its services at individual consumers; however, it did not win enough business to be profitable. As a result, the company shifted direction to a business-to-business environment and began to promote its recommendation engine to media firms, who utilized the service to make recommendations for visitors at their Web sites. The pressure is on to prove that its recommendation algorithms do provide the kind of improvements it claims. The ultimate goal for The Filter is to market its service to companies in industries other than media, entertainment, and technology. The firm has to define its long-term strategy and find ways to ensure profitability well into the future.

You Make the Call

1. What is the decision facing The Filter?
2. What factors are important in understanding this decision situation?
3. What are the alternatives?
4. What decision(s) do you recommend?
5. What are some ways to implement your recommendation?

Based on: Devin Leonard, "Tech Entrepreneur Peter Gabriel Knows What You Want," *Bloomberg Businessweek*, April 8, 2010 (http://www.businessweek.com/magazine/content/10_16/b4174046688330.htm); The Filter, *Wikipedia*, http://en.wikipedia.org/wiki/The_Filter (accessed June 22, 2010); Rachel Carr and Arielle Himy, "The Filter Recommendation Engine Launched on Dailymotion to Further Boost User Engagement," Marketwire, March 2, 2010 (http://www.marketwire.com/press-release/Filter-Recommendation-Engine-Launched-on-Dailymotion-Further-Boost-User-Engagement-1124739.htm); Erick Schonfeld, "The Filter Reboots as Recommendation Engine for Hire, Ex-Googler Doug Merrill Joins Board," *TechCrunch*, February 8, 2010 (http://techcrunch.com/2010/02/08/the-filter-reboots-doug-merrill/).

Chapter 7

Sharpen the Focus:
Target Marketing Strategies and Customer Relationship Management

Real People **Profiles**

Jim Multari

Profile

▼ A Decision Maker at PBS Kids Sprout

Jim Multari is the director of research for PBS Kids Sprout, the first 24-hour preschool destination available on TV, on demand, and online for kids ages 2–5 and their parents and caregivers. Sprout's programming features trusted favorites like *The Wiggles* and *Sesame Street*, plus innovative originals such as *The Sunny Side Up Show* and *The Good Night Show*.

Jim manages marketing, programming, and ad sales research for Sprout. He collaborates with all internal business units and has been a contributor to numerous initiatives related to custom studies and new methodologies. Sprout's recent research on kids' usage of video on demand (VOD), alternative media viewership metrics, and creative concept testing has been a key driver of network strategy and has won multiple industry awards, including a silver David Ogilvy Award (the Advertising Research Foundation's award for excellence in advertising research) and the Cable & Telecommunications Association for Marketing (CTAM) Research Case Study Award. He received a BA in communications and psychology from Marymount University in Arlington, VA, and an MBA from Saint Joseph's University.

Info

💬 Jim's Info

What do I do when I'm not working?
A) Running.

First job out of school?
A) Research analyst for a customer satisfaction research company. In those days, surveys were still paper and pencil!

Career high?
A) Winning a David Ogilvy Award.

Business book I'm reading now?
A) *7 Habits of Highly Effective People* by Stephen Covey.

My motto to live by?
A) Your answer to the question "What are you reading?" should never be "Nothing."

What drives me?
A) My family.

My management style?
A) Collaborate, communicate, and think strategically.

Don't do this when interviewing with me?
A) Not ask questions.

Here's my problem...

The Sprout marketing team faced three significant challenges when they launched the channel in 2005. First, Sprout was (and still is today) considered an "emerging network," relatively small compared to the more established kids' networks (Disney Channel, Nickelodeon, etc.). As a result, the marketing team had to develop creative ways to reach viewers of the network, nonviewers of the network, as well as cable and satellite TV operators, to communicate Sprout's unique content and format. Sprout's programming is designed to foster parent-preschooler interaction through gold-standard, curriculum-based shows and short-form original programs. It inspires conversation, activities (i.e., making crafts), exploration/discovery, play, learning, exercise, healthy eating, and so on. Sprout is different from other networks because it really is an active viewing experience and truly a network "made for you, by you." Whether it's sharing homemade birthday cards and crafts with Chica on *The Sunny Side Up Show*, watching viewer-submitted videos on *The Sprout Sharing Show*, or making a craft and reading bedtime stories on *The Good Night Show*, Sprout is the only network that actually shares with its audience, while also encouraging parent-child interaction at home.

The second marketing challenge was that Sprout is essentially a "library channel"; its programming mainly consists of previously aired kids' shows, repackaged and represented around short original content and brand identity links. Although the presentation makes the entire package feel new and fresh, there was a risk that parents wouldn't see a reason to tune in, and cable and satellite providers wouldn't see a reason to launch the channel. Sprout needed to find a way to break through and be heard by both audiences in order to support its unique claim that it fosters parent-child interaction.

The third and most significant challenge was that Sprout is not a brand that is fully distributed (available in all U.S. television households). Early on, Sprout was available in just 30 million households. Thus, the channel's target audiences consisted of both preschool families that were aware of watching Sprout and families that were unaware of Sprout and/or had never interacted with the brand.

In early 2007, Sprout began work on its first-ever consumer-targeted brand awareness advertising campaign. The critical marketing decision was to decide which audience to target: Should the upstart channel target viewers of Sprout, nonviewers of Sprout, or should it somehow find a way of reaching both audiences with the same campaign?

Current viewers understand and enjoy the Sprout brand, are seamlessly navigating across all of Sprout's platforms, and are likely submitting content. Reaching them with the campaign would likely mean television spots on Sprout, print ads in parenting and other relevant magazines, as well as a highly targeted digital media approach (banner ads, promotions via social media outlets, etc.).

Nonviewers have little understanding at all of Sprout, though they may have immediate positive associations due to Sprout's relationship with PBS

Kids (Sprout is a partnership in which PBS has an interest) Because moms are the key media decision makers in preschool households, the campaign would need to resonate with them (both functionally and emotionally) while also indirectly being of some interest to preschoolers. Reaching this audience would require a broader mix of media and markets to maximize the campaign's reach.

As director of research, Jim's role was to ensure that all strategic decisions were supported by actionable consumer insights.

Jim and the Sprout marketing team considered their **Options** 1·2·3

1 Option
Target Sprout viewers with the marketing campaign. This option would enable the channel to develop a tightly focused campaign that its core audience could rally behind. Hopefully this identification would be a catalyst to motivate them to tell their friends and family about Sprout, invite them to further participate in the Sprout experience, and so on. But Sprout's viewer base at the time was relatively small. Also, there was no guarantee that busy Sprout families would be motivated to help "spread the word" about the programming.

2 Option
Produce a campaign that was specifically designed for nonviewers of Sprout. This approach would require a more functionally descriptive campaign that introduced consumers to the network, its unique programming format, the different usage platforms, and so forth. A campaign that targeted nonviewers would attract a much larger audience. If it was executed properly, families in general (regardless of whether they already viewed Sprout) would be interested in the message. Of course, the marketing team would need to do a lot of heavy lifting to educate unaware audiences about Sprout, how the brand works, and how they could participate. This approach would not engage Sprout enthusiasts, so there would not be an opportunity to reinforce them for their loyalty.

3 Option
Target both Sprout viewers/awares as well as nonviewers, all within the same creative campaign. An all-inclusive campaign would maximize Sprout's exposure and attract families in general. However, speaking to two audience segments with the same campaign would be complicated. The campaign would need to communicate both the functional benefits of the brand to attract nonviewers and also reinforce the emotional rewards that Sprout viewers receive when they watch the channel's programs with their preschoolers.

Things to remember

Sprout is a relatively small presence in the children's TV programming market. Jim needs to weigh the value of providing more value to the current viewership versus attracting new viewers.

There are really two segments of viewers—young kids and their parents. Both groups play different roles in deciding what shows the kids will watch.

Sprout's position in the market is a bit ambiguous. It is affiliated with PBS (Public Broadcasting) but it also offers other programming.

You Choose

Which **Option** would you choose, and **why**?

1. ☐YES ☐NO   2. ☐YES ☐NO   3. ☐YES ☐NO

See what **option** Jim chose on **page 209** ➡

market fragmentation
The creation of many consumer groups due to a diversity of distinct needs and wants in modern society.

target marketing strategy
Dividing the total market into different segments on the basis of customer characteristics, selecting one or more segments, and developing products to meet the needs of those specific segments.

1

OBJECTIVE

Identify the steps in the target marketing process.
(pp. 184–185)

Target Marketing Strategy: Select and Enter a Market

By now, you've read over and over that the goal of the marketer is to create value, build customer relationships, and satisfy needs. But in our modern, complex society, it's naive to assume that everyone's needs are the same. Understanding people's needs is an even more complex task today because technological and cultural advances in modern society create a condition of **market fragmentation**. This means that people's diverse interests and backgrounds divide them into numerous groups with distinct needs and wants. Because of this diversity, the same good or service will not appeal to everyone.

Consider, for example, the effects of fragmentation in the health-and-fitness industry—one that has gained increasing attention due to recent data about skyrocketing rates of obesity among adults and children. Back in the 1960s, dieting was simple. Pritikin was a best-selling weight loss system that emphasized very low fat and high fiber, and health-conscious consumers thought that this combination would surely yield a lean body and good health. Today's consumers, however, have a cornucopia of diets from which to choose including such brands as NutriSystem, Weight Watchers, Jenny Craig, Optifast, FitAmerica, the Atkins diet, and many more. Calories, fat, carbs, or all of the above—which to cut?

Marketers must balance the efficiency of mass marketing where they serve the same items to everyone, with effectiveness that comes when they offer each individual exactly what he or she wants. Mass marketing certainly costs much less; when we offer one product to everyone we eliminate the need for separate advertising campaigns and distinctive packages for each item. However, consumers see things differently; from their perspective the best strategy would be to offer the perfect product just for them. Unfortunately, that's often not realistic. To this day, Burger King touts its longtime motto "Have It Your Way," but BK can only deliver this promise to a point: "Your way" is fine as long as you stay within the confines of familiar condiments such as mustard or ketchup. Don't dream of topping your burger with blue cheese, mango sauce, or some other "exotic" ingredient.

Instead of trying to sell something to everyone, marketers select a **target marketing strategy** in which they divide the total market into different segments based on customer characteristics, select one or more segments, and develop products to meet the needs of those specific segments. Figure 7.1 illustrates the three-step process of segmentation, targeting, and positioning, and it's what we're going to check out in this chapter. Let's start with the first step—segmentation.

Check out chapter 7 Study Map on page 210

Figure 7.1 ⚡ *Process* | Steps in the Target Marketing Process

Target marketing strategy consists of three separate steps. Marketers first divide the market into segments based on customer characteristics, then select one or more segments, and finally develop products to meet the needs of those specific segments.

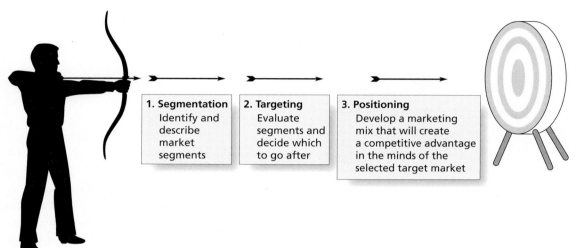

1. Segmentation
Identify and describe market segments

2. Targeting
Evaluate segments and decide which to go after

3. Positioning
Develop a marketing mix that will create a competitive advantage in the minds of the selected target market

2

Step 1: Segmentation

Segmentation is the process of dividing a larger market into smaller pieces based on one or more meaningfully shared characteristics. This process is a way of life for almost all marketers in both consumer and business-to-business markets. The truth is that you can't please all the people all the time, so you need to take your best shot. Just how do marketers segment a population? How do they divide the whole pie into smaller slices they can "digest"? The marketer must decide on one or more useful **segmentation variables**—that is, dimensions that divide the total market into fairly homogeneous groups, each with different needs and preferences. In this section, we'll take a look at this process, beginning with the types of segmentation variables that marketers use to divide up end-user consumers. Then we'll move on to business-to-business segmentation.

segmentation
The process of dividing a larger market into smaller pieces based on one or more meaningfully shared characteristics.

segmentation variables
Dimensions that divide the total market into fairly homogeneous groups, each with different needs and preferences.

Segment Consumer Markets

At one time, it was sufficient to divide the sports shoe market into athletes and nonathletes. But take a walk through any sporting goods store today: You'll quickly see that the athlete market has fragmented in many directions. Shoes designed for jogging, basketball, tennis, cycling, cross training, and even skateboarding beckon us from the aisles.

During the late 1990s Converse began falling well behind its competitors such as Reebok and Nike, which successfully targeted the younger demographic as they tied their shoes (pun intended!) to popular athletes who acted as marketing machines for the brands. Converse needed to find a way to appeal to the younger generation as well. More specifically, the marketers at Converse (which Nike acquired in 2003) wanted to target **Generation Y**—people born between 1979 and 1994.[1] They found their stride when they reminded these consumers that cultural icons they admired like Kurt Cobain and Jackson Pollock once wore Converse shoes. These messages appealed to Gen Y "optimistic rebels" who were looking for a "blank canvas for self-expression."[2]

Generation Y
The group of consumers born between 1979 and 1994.

We need several segmentation variables if we want to slice up the market for all the shoe variations available today. First, not everyone is willing or able to drop $150 on the latest sneakers, so marketers consider income. Second, men may be more interested in

Figure 7.2 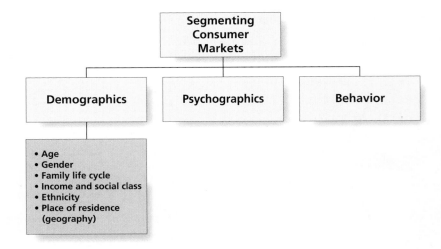 *Snapshot* |
Segmenting Consumer Markets

Consumer markets can be segmented by demographic, psychographic, or behavioral criteria.

demographics
Statistics that measure observable aspects of a population, including size, age, gender, ethnic group, income, education, occupation, and family structure.

generational marketing
Marketing to members of a generation, who tend to share the same outlook and priorities.

Apple is a masterful marketer to teens, yet its product line appeals to other age groups as well. The iPod in its various forms enables teens to be content creators and empowers them to be masters of their own music world. This satisfies a strong need among this age group for individuality. The iPhone is coveted by youth as the smartphone *du jour*—any other brand is viewed as subpar. Teens don't particularly like to be marketed to, which is a great fit for Apple's approach of letting fans and the media do their marketing for them. The iPod and iPhone are iconic symbols of modern youth— stylish, nonconforming, and an expression of a clear difference from the past.

basketball shoes while women snap up the latest Pilates styles, so marketers also consider gender. Because not all age groups are equally interested in buying specialized athletic shoes, we can slice the larger consumer "pie" into smaller pieces in a number of ways, including demographic, psychographic, and behavioral differences. In the case of demographic segmentation there are several key subcategories of demographics: age (including generational differences), gender, family life cycle, income and social class, ethnicity, and place of residence, sometimes referred to separately as geographic segmentation. 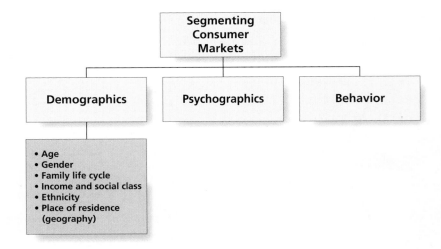 Figure 7.2 summarizes the various approaches to segmenting consumer markets.

In the sections that follow we'll consider each of these segmentation approaches in turn, but first a note of caution. When it comes to marketing to some groups—in particular, lower income individuals, the poorly educated, non-native language speakers, and children—it is incumbent on marketers to exercise the utmost care not to take undue advantage of their circumstances. Ethical marketers are sensitive to the different conditions in which people find themselves and proactively work to uphold a high level of honesty and trust with all segments of the public. Doing so is nothing short of marketing's social responsibility.

Segment by Demographics: Age

As we stated in Chapter 3, **demographics** are statistics that measure observable aspects of a population, including size, age, gender, ethnic group, income, education, occupation, and family structure. These descriptors are vital to identify the best potential customers for a good or service. Because they represent objective characteristics, they usually are easy to identify, and then it's just a matter of tailoring messages and products to relevant groups. Let's take a quick look at how marketers use each of these dimensions to slice up the consumer pie.

Consumers of different age groups have different needs and wants. Members of a generation tend to share the same outlook and priorities. We call such a focus **generational marketing**.

As Jim Multari's experience with Sprout TV programming shows, *children* are an attractive age segment for many marketers. Although kids obviously have a lot to say about purchases of toys and games, they influence other family purchases as well (just watch them at work in the grocery store!). By one estimate, American children aged 4 to 12 have a say in family-related purchases of more than $130 billion a year.[3] The ongoing popularity of shows such as Disney's *Hannah Montana* propelled Miley Cyrus into a wildly successful singing career and has also successfully translated into a booming toy business including blond wigs, replicas of Hannah's tour van, and even toy musical instruments. The music on the show has spawned several new musical acts—including the Jonas Brothers—and sold millions of CDs and tens of millions of downloads. The younger girl market segment loves the idea of being a pop star, and the girls live their dream vicariously through Hannah as well as *American Idol* and the *High School Musical* movie series, which lives on, immortal even though its stars are now all twenty-somethings.[4]

Teens are also an attractive market segment. The 12- to 17-year-old age group is growing nearly twice as fast as the general population—and teens and *tweens* (kids between the ages of 8 and 14) spend an average of $3,000 per year.[5] Much of this money goes toward "feel-good" products: cosmetics, posters, and fast food—with the occasional tattoo thrown in as well. Because they are so interested in many different products and have the resources to obtain them, many marketers avidly court the teen market.[6]

As we said, Generation Y consists of people born between the years 1979 and 1994. Sometimes labeled the "baby boomlet," Generation Y is made up of the 71 million children of the baby boomers.[7] They are the first generation to grow up online and are more ethnically diverse than earlier generations. Generation Y is an attractive market for a host of consumer products because of its size (approximately 26 percent of the population) and free-spending nature—as a group they spend about $200 billion annually.

But Generation Y consumers are also hard to reach because they resist reading and increasingly turn off the TV. When they do watch TV, they tend toward alternative fare such as the late-night lineup on Adult Swim, which is consistently the number-one show on basic cable for this age group—outperforming even the *Late Show with David Letterman* with young men.[8] As a result, many marketers have had to develop other ways to reach this generation "where they live," including through social networking, online chat rooms, e-mail promotions, and a variety of other new-age marketing communications techniques we'll talk about later in this book.

As a snapshot on Gen Y values, a recent Pew Research Center study asked Gen Y respondents whether a variety of elements are one of the most important things in their lives. Results revealed "Being a good parent" (52 percent), "Having a successful marriage" (30 percent), "Helping others in need" (21 percent), "Owning a home" (20 percent), "Living a very religious life" (15 percent), "Having a high-paying career "(15 percent), "Having lots of free time (9 percent), and "Becoming famous" (1 percent). Among other Gen Y tidbits: 38 percent have a tattoo, and half of those have two to five, but 72 percent say their tats are hidden by clothing; 41 percent use only a cell phone and have no landline; and 66 percent voted for Barack Obama for president in 2008, compared with 50 percent of those 30 and older—the largest disparity between younger and older voters in four decades of exit polling. They also vote at a rate higher than did other generations at their age.[9]

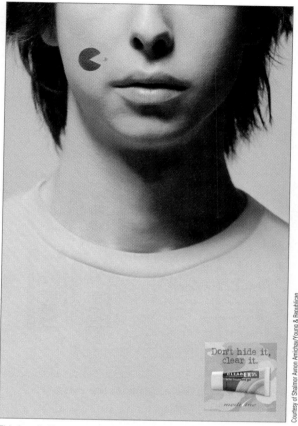

This Israeli skincare product targets adolescents.

Don't hide it, clear it.

The Cutting Edge

Ford Fiesta Looks for Gen Y "Where They Live"

Ford's Fiesta launched in the United States in 2010, but a year earlier the company gave away 100 of the cars to influential Gen Y's in the hope of building some buzz from the ground up. The "recruitment call" went out for 100 "agents" to receive the car in April 2009, complete Ford-assigned "missions," and chronicle their experiences through their social networks such as Facebook, Flickr, and YouTube. The company has dubbed this effort its "Fiesta Movement," and it's the anchor of a plan to build excitement and spread the word about the arrival of the new Ford Fiesta to the next generation of customers—clearly strong targets for this economy-priced vehicle. Sam De La Garza, small car marketing manager for Ford, says, "Socially vibrant campaigns are so important be-

cause of their power in delivering authentic and genuine messages across a broad spectrum of media, which will only help us deliver a more positive consumer experience when the car launches in the U.S. next year."

The company set up a Web site where people could upload a two- to-five-minute video to explain why they want to become one of the agents. By 2010, Gen Y will account for 28 percent of the country's driving population (a total of 70 million new drivers). The movement gives the company an opportunity to connect with the group before they have established brand loyalty, while Ford also appeals to their affinity for social networking and technology. Using social networking as a way to reach Gen Y is a sound strategy, provided that the company is upfront about its relationship with the agents and is willing to let them craft the message as they see fit.[10]

no
gray™

Just add **no gray™** to your favorite hair color for **Longer Lasting Color**

no gray™ penetrates your hair to ensure **100% Gray Coverage**

Also available for MEN!

Prove it to yourself!

• Use **no gray™** with your favorite hair color.
• Covers stubborn gray hair completely.
• For in-home or salon use.

For more information go to developlus.com/nogray

Boomers are willing to invest a ton of money, time, and energy to maintain their youthful image

Generation X
The group of consumers born between 1965 and 1978.

baby boomers
The segment of people born between 1946 and 1964.

metrosexual
A straight, urban male who is keenly interested in fashion, home design, gourmet cooking, and personal care.

The group of consumers born between 1965 and 1978 consists of 46 million Americans known as **Generation X**, who unfortunately and undeservedly came to be called slackers, or busters (for the "baby bust" that followed the "baby boom"). Many of these people have a cynical attitude toward marketing—a chapter in a famous book called *Generation X* is entitled "I am not a target market!"[11] As one 20-year-old Japanese Xer commented, "I don't like to be told what's trendy. I can make up my own mind."[12]

Despite this tough reputation, members of Generation X, the oldest of whom are now in their late 40s, have mellowed with age. In retrospect, they also have developed an identity for being an entrepreneurial group. One study revealed that Xers are already responsible for 70 percent of new start-up businesses in the United States—they led much of the modern technology revolution and are now highly sought after by firms for their entrepreneurial talents. An industry expert observed, "Today's Gen Xer is both values-oriented and value-oriented. This generation is really about settling down."[13] Many people in this segment seem to be determined to have stable families after being latchkey children themselves. Seven out of ten regularly save some portion of their income, a rate comparable to that of their parents. Xers tend to view the home as an expression of individuality rather than material success. More than half are involved in home improvement and repair projects.[14] So much for Gen Xers as slackers!

Baby boomers, consumers born between 1946 and 1964 and who are now in their 40s, 50s, and 60s, are an important segment to many marketers—if for no other reason than that there are so many of them who make a lot of money. The baby boom occurred when soldiers came flooding home after World War II and there was a rush to get married and start families. Back in the 1950s and 1960s, couples started having children younger and had more of them than the previous generation. The resulting glut of kids really changed the infrastructure of the country: more single-family houses, more schools, migration to the suburbs, and so on.

One aspect of boomers marketers should always remember—they never age. At least, that's the way they look at it. Boomers are willing to invest a ton of money, time, and energy to maintain their youthful image. For the past several years the show *Nip/Tuck* on FX has chronicled the experiences of two cosmetic surgeons in Los Angeles, baby boomers themselves, who crassly market their surgical fountain of youth to a seemingly endless stream of 50-somethings with whom they begin the patient consult by asking, "Tell us what you don't like about yourself." Other boomer-appealing TV fare includes *Cougar Town,* in which Courtney Cox, who has aged a bit since her starring role on *Friends,* now trolls for younger men, and *Lost's* cosmic-philosophical commentary on life, age, and other ultimate questions of the universe, which ended in 2010 with a five-hour reveal-all finale that proved to be a ratings blockbuster with Boomers. Time Warner even formed a separate unit to publish magazines, including *Health, Parenting,* and *Cooking Light,* that specifically address baby boomers' interests in staying young, healthy, and (relatively) sane.

Currently, there are nearly 40 million Americans aged 65 or older—a 22 percent increase in this age segment since 1990.[15] Many *mature consumers* enjoy leisure time and continued good health. Indeed, a key question today is: Just what is a senior citizen when people live longer and "80 is the new 60"? As we will see later in the chapter, perhaps it isn't age but rather lifestyle factors, including mobility, that best define this group. More and more marketers offer products that have strong appeal to active-lifestyle seniors. And they often combine the product appeal with a nostalgia theme that includes music popular during the seniors' era of youth. People tend to prefer music that was released when they were teenagers or young adults, with interest peaking between ages 24–25. Sandals Resorts uses the song "(I've Had) The Time of My Life" in commercials for its romantic vacation destinations in the Caribbean. The song, recorded by Bill Medley and Jennifer Warnes, was made famous in the 1987 movie *Dirty Dancing*. As nostalgia, it does double duty because the movie itself was set in 1963, so it conjures up memories of both the 1980s and the 1960s. People who were in their 20s in 1963 are now in their 60s and 70s. Those in their 20s in 1987 are now in their 40s and 50s. Both age groups are key demographics for Sandals.[16]

Segment by Demographics: Gender

Many products, from fragrances to footwear, specifically appeal to men or women. Segmenting by gender starts at a very early age—even diapers come in pink for girls and blue for boys. As proof that consumers take these differences seriously, market researchers report that most parents refuse to put male infants in pink diapers.[17]

In some cases, manufacturers develop parallel products to appeal to each sex. For example, male grooming products have traditionally been Gillette's priority since the company's founder King Gillette (yes, his first name was actually King) introduced the safety razor in 1903.

Metrosexual is a marketing buzzword that gained popularity in recent years. The term describes a straight, urban man who is keenly interested in fashion, home design, gourmet cooking, and personal care. Metrosexuals are usually well-educated urban dwellers who are in touch with their feminine side.[18] While many men are reluctant to overtly identify with the metrosexual, there's no denying that a renewed interest in personal care products, fashion accessories, and other "formerly feminine" product categories creates many marketing opportunities. Mainstream newspapers such as the *New York Times* offer regular segments dedicated to male fashion and grooming. This Web posting from *The Urban Dictionary* sums up the metrosexual stereotype.[19]

You might be "metrosexual" if:

1. You just can't walk past a Banana Republic store without making a purchase.

2. You own 20 pairs of shoes, half a dozen pairs of sunglasses, just as many watches, and you carry a man-purse.

3. You see a stylist instead of a barber, because barbers don't do highlights.

4. You can make her lamb shanks and risotto for dinner and eggs Benedict for breakfast . . . all from scratch.

5. You only wear Calvin Klein boxer-briefs.

6. You shave more than just your face. You also exfoliate and moisturize.

7. You would never, ever own a pickup truck.

8. You can't imagine a day without hair styling products.

9. You'd rather drink wine than beer . . . but you'll find out what estate and vintage first.

10. Despite being flattered (even proud) that gay guys hit on you, you still find the thought of actually getting intimate with another man truly repulsive.

An interesting trend related to gender segmentation has been fueled by the recent recession. Men now are increasingly likely to marry wives with more education and income than they have, and the reverse is true for women. In recent decades, with the rise of well-paid working wives, the economic gains of marriage have been a greater benefit for men. The education

A phone with a feature adapted specifically to the needs of mature callers.

Personal care products typically appeal to one gender exclusively.

and income gap has grown even more in the latest recession, when men held about three in four of the jobs that were lost. In 1970, 28 percent of wives had husbands who were better educated, and 20 percent were married to men with less education. By 2007, the comparable figures were 19 percent and 28 percent. In 1970, 4 percent of husbands had wives who made more money; in 2007, 22 percent did.[20]

Segment by Demographics: Family Life Cycle

Because family needs and expenditures change over time, one way to segment consumers is to consider the stage of the family life cycle they occupy. (You learned about the family life cycle in Chapter 5.) Not surprisingly, consumers in different life-cycle segments are unlikely to need the same products, or at least they may not need these things in the same quantities. Folger's Classic Roast Coffee Singles are designed for people who live alone and don't need to brew a full pot of coffee at a time, while Marriott and other hoteliers actively market vacation ownership (timeshare) opportunities to young couples—because these consumers can easily tailor these getaways to their changing lifestyles and preferences since they tend to not want to do the same trip year after year as many of their parents did.

But not all attempts at marketing to the family life cycle succeed. Gerber once tried to market single-serving food jars to singles; a quick meal for one person who lives alone. The manufacturer called these containers "Singles." However, Gerber's strong identification with baby food worked against it: The product flopped because people misperceived that Gerber was trying to sell baby food to adults.[21]

As families age and move into new life stages, different product categories ascend and descend in importance. Young bachelors and newlyweds are the most likely to exercise, go to bars and movies, and consume alcohol (in other words, party while you can). Older couples and bachelors are more likely to use maintenance services. Seniors are a prime market for resort condominiums and golf products. Marketers need to identify the family life-cycle segment of their target consumers by examining purchase data by family life-cycle group.

Cultural changes continually create new opportunities as people's roles change. For example, Boomer women in their 50s are a hot new market for what the auto industry calls "reward cars": sexy and extravagant vehicles. These buyers say that for years they had let the roles of wife and mother restrict them to minivans or stodgy family sedans. As their kids grow up and leave home, it's reward time. As one woman who bought a snazzy Mercedes convertible for herself stated, "I don't have the disease to please anymore . . . I'm pleasing me." She's not alone. Vehicle registration records show that the number of women over age 45 who purchased cars in the niche known as "mid-sized sporty," which includes two-door models like the Mazda RX-8 and the Chrysler Crossfire, is up 277 percent since 2000. Among women 45 and over earning at least $100,000, smaller luxury cars like the BMW 3 Series and the Audi A4 are up 93 percent.[22]

Segment by Demographics: Income and Social Class

The distribution of wealth is of great interest to marketers because it determines which groups have the greatest *buying power*. It should come as no surprise that many marketers yearn to capture the hearts and wallets of high-income consumers. Perhaps that explains a recent proliferation of ultra-high-end bottled waters such as Voss—which bills itself as extracted from a real Norwegian glacier. To taste this delicacy in gourmet restaurants and mini-bars of top hotels, expect to pay well over $10 a bottle. Tap water, anybody?[23] At the same time, other marketers target lower-income consumers (defined as households with annual incomes of $25,000 or less), who make up about

A South African ad for a TV show speaks to kids.

Courtesy of FOXP2

40 percent of the U.S. market. Stores such as Sam's Club and Costco sell generic bottled water in flats of 24 bottles for less than 50 cents per bottle! Baby Boomers in particular lost a big chunk of their retirement savings in just a few months during the financial "meltdown" of 2008–2009. Although the stock market came back to a degree, Boomers are increasingly cautious about spending their present income at prerecession levels. Much evidence exists that they are down-shopping—that is, Walmart can look much more palatable to upscale Boomers when 40 percent of their retirement nest egg has gone up in smoke.

After a 50-year run during which the truly wealthy just kept getting richer, the Great Recession has taken some of the wind out of their sails due to heavy investment losses. Just how much poorer the rich will ultimately end up is unclear. Any major shift in the financial status of the rich could have big implications for some marketers. For example, a drop in their income and wealth would complicate life for elite universities, museums, and other institutions that received lavish donations in recent decades. Governments—federal and state—could struggle, too, because they rely heavily on the taxes paid by the affluent.[24] Households making $100,000 or more certainly do not in most cases come close to being part of that "truly wealthy" crowd, but if a recovery is to come, particularly in consumer spending, it will have to come from households making $100,000 or more. They represent only 20 percent of U.S. households, but they control more than half of all income and are far less likely than everyone else to be restrained by tight credit markets. On average, the affluent are 2.6 times more likely to buy everything, and when they do, they spend 3.7 times more.[25]

In the past, it was popular for marketers to consider *social class segments*, such as upper class, middle class, and lower class. However, many consumers do not buy according to where they actually fall in that framework, but rather according to the image they wish to portray. For example, over the years readily available credit has facilitated many a sale of a BMW to a consumer whose income doesn't easily support the steep price tag. The recent financial crisis also nipped a good portion of this free-flowing credit in the bud. It remains to be seen over the long run how much the new austere era of credit permanently changes consumer buying behavior.

Segment by Demographics: Ethnicity

A consumer's national origin is often a strong indicator of his or her preferences for specific magazines or TV shows, foods, apparel, and leisure activities. Marketers need to be aware of these differences and sensitivities—especially when they invoke outmoded stereotypes to appeal to consumers of diverse races and ethnic groups.

African Americans, Asian Americans, and Hispanic Americans are the largest ethnic groups in the United States. The Census Bureau projects that by the year 2050, non-Hispanic whites will make up just less than 50 percent of the population (compared to 74 percent in 1995) as these other groups grow. Let's take a closer look at each of these important ethnic segments.

African Americans account for about 12 percent of the U.S. population. This percentage has held steady for 20 years. Reflecting the growing consumer power fueled by the hip-hop and urban scene, magazines such as *The Source* and *Vibe* target this market.[26] Television shows that feature African American heroes and heroines, unheard of until the late 1960s, are commonplace today, and BET is an advertising force to be reckoned with. In many cities, urban-sound radio stations are among the elite few in audience ratings.

These media examples demonstrate the opportunities that await those who develop specialized products to connect with segments of consumers who share an ethnic or racial identity. And what had been the original rap culture has migrated from the inner-city streets to mainstream hip-hop clubs, creating substantial opportunities for marketers to parlay what started out as an urban street trend among the African American community to a broader cultural phenomenon that appeals to young people of many ethnicities.

Products targeted to African Americans often appear in specialized media like *Ebony* magazine.

Though their numbers are still relatively small, *Asian Americans* are the fastest-growing minority group in the United States. The Asian American population is projected to grow from 11.3 million in 2000 to 19.6 million in 2020.[27] The American advertising industry spends between $200 million and $300 million to court these consumers.[28] Ford set up a toll-free consumer hotline that it staffs with operators fluent in three Asian languages, and JCPenney holds one-day sales in stores in Asian communities during certain holidays such as the Chinese Moon Festival.[29] Wonder Bra even launched a special line it sized for the slimmer Asian body.[30]

The *Hispanic American* population is the real sleeping giant, a segment that mainstream marketers today actively cultivate. Hispanics have overtaken African Americans as the nation's largest minority group. In the United States, Hispanics command well over $400 billion in purchasing power. In addition to its rapid growth, five other factors make the Hispanic segment attractive to marketers:[31]

- Hispanics tend to be brand loyal, especially to products made in their country of origin.

- They tend to be highly concentrated by national origin, which makes it easy to fine-tune the marketing mix to appeal to those who come from the same country.

- This segment is young (the median age of Hispanic Americans is 23.6, compared with the U.S. average of 32), which is attractive to marketers because it is a great potential market for youth-oriented products such as cosmetics and music.

- The average Hispanic household contains 3.5 people, compared to only 2.7 people for the rest of the United States. For this reason, Hispanic households spend 15 to 20 percent more of their disposable income than the national average on groceries and other household products.

- In general, Hispanic consumers are very receptive to relationship-building approaches to marketing and selling. For this reason there are many opportunities to build loyalty to brands and companies by emphasizing relationship aspects of the customer encounter.[32]

As with any ethnic group, appeals to Hispanic consumers need to take into account cultural differences. For example, Hispanics didn't appreciate the successful "Got Milk?" campaign because biting, sarcastic humor is not part of their culture. In addition, the notion of milk deprivation is not funny to a Hispanic mother—if she runs out of milk, this means she has failed her family. To make matters worse, "Got Milk?" translates as "Are You Lactating?" in Spanish. Thus, new Spanish-language versions were changed to "And you, have you given them enough milk today?" with tender scenes centered on cooking *flan* (a popular pudding) in the family kitchen.

Latino youth are changing mainstream culture. Many of these consumers are "young biculturals" who bounce back and forth between hip-hop and rock en Español, blend Mexican rice with spaghetti sauce, and spread peanut butter and jelly on tortillas. By the year 2020, the Census Bureau estimates, the number of Hispanic teens will grow by 62 percent, compared with 10 percent growth in teens overall. They seek spirituality, stronger family ties, and more color in their lives—three hallmarks of Latino culture. Music crossovers from the Latin charts to mainstream lead the trend, including pop idols Shakira and Enrique Iglesias, and Reggaeton sensation Daddy Yankee.

One caution about the Hispanic market is that the term *Hispanic* itself is a misnomer. For example, Cuban Americans, Mexican Americans, and Puerto Ricans may share a common language, but their history, politics, and culture have many differences. Marketing to them as though they are a homogeneous segment can be a big mistake. However, the term is still widely used as a demographic descriptive.

An important outcome of the increase in multiethnicity in the United States is the opportunity for increased cultural diversity in the workplace and elsewhere. **Cultural diversity**, a management practice that actively seeks to include people of different sexes, races, ethnic groups, and religions in an organization's employees, customers, suppliers, and distribu-

cultural diversity
A management practice that actively seeks to include people of different sexes, races, ethnic groups, and religions in an organization's employees, customers, suppliers, and distribution channel partners.

tion channel partners, is today business as usual rather than an exception. Marketing organizations benefit from employing people of all kinds because they bring different backgrounds, experiences, and points of view that help the firm develop strategies for its brands that will appeal to diverse customer groups.

Segment by Demographics: Place of Residence

Recognizing that people's preferences often vary depending on where they live, many marketers tailor their offerings to geographic regions. Pabst Brewing Company pushes different brands of beer in different parts of the country, so drinkers in Texas buy the company's Lone Star and Pearl brands, while those in other states buy Old Milwaukee, Olympia, and Stroh's.

When marketers want to segment regional markets even more precisely, they sometimes combine geography with demographics using the technique of **geodemography**. A basic assumption of geodemography is that "birds of a feather flock together"—people who live near one another share similar characteristics. Sophisticated statistical techniques identify geographic areas that share the same preferences for household items, magazines, and other products. This lets marketers construct segments of households with a common pattern of preferences. This way they can hone in on those customers most likely to be interested in its specific offerings, in some cases so precisely that families living on one block will belong to a segment while those on the next block will not.

geodemography
A segmentation technique that combines geography with demographics.

Companies can even customize Web advertising by **geocoding** so that people who log on in different places will see ad banners for local businesses. For example, the Weather Channel links localized ads to 1,300 U.S. weather-reporting stations. A surfer can get both the local weather forecast and information about businesses in an area by simply typing a city and state, or an airport code, into the forecast request box.

geocoding
Customizing Web advertising so that people who log on in different places will see ad banners for local businesses.

One widely used geodemographic system is PRIZM, which is a large database developed by Nielsen Claritas. This system classifies the U.S. population into 66 segments based on various socioeconomic data, such as income, age, race, occupation, education and household composition, as well as lifestyle attributes that are critical to marketing strategies, shopping patterns such as where they vacation, what they drive and their favorite brands, and media preferences.

The 66 segments range from the highly affluent "Upper Crust" and "Blue Blood Estates" to the lower income "Big City Blues or "Low-Rise Living" neighborhoods. To learn about how the system classifies your ZIP code, visit **www.mybestsegments.com**.

Here are a few thumbnail sketches of different segments of relatively younger consumers a marketer might want to reach depending on the specific product or service he or she sells:

- Young Digerati are tech-savvy and live in fashionable neighborhoods on the urban fringe. Affluent, highly educated, and ethnically mixed, Young Digerati communities are typically filled with trendy apartments and condos, fitness clubs and clothing boutiques, casual restaurants and all types of bars—from juice to coffee to microbrew. The Young Digerati are much more likely than the average American consumer to shop at Banana Republic, order from J. Crew, read *Elle Decor* magazine, watch the Independent Film Channel, and drive a Range Rover SUV.

- Kids & Cul-de-Sacs are upper-middle class, suburban, married couples with children. With a high rate of Hispanic and Asian Americans, this segment is a refuge for college-educated, white-collar professionals with administrative jobs and upper-middle-class incomes. Their nexus of education, affluence, and children translates into large outlays for child-centered products and services. They are much more likely than the average American consumer to shop at The Disney Store, eat at Chuck E. Cheese, read parenting magazines, watch Nickelodeon, and drive a Nissan Armada SUV.

- Shotguns & Pickups scores near the top of all lifestyles for owning hunting rifles and pickup trucks. These Americans tend to be young, working-class couples with large

Digital enhancement portrait of mature bike couple

Over the years, Harley-Davidson has done a great job of understanding buyers on the basis of psychographics. A Harley user's profile includes both thrill-seeking and affinity for a countercultural image (at least on weekends). In fact, your doctor, banker, lawyer, or even marketing professor may be a member of HOG (the Harley Owners Group). However, demographics also come into play. Over the past decade, the age of the typical Harley buyer has risen to about 46, older than the motorcycle industry average of 38. But because the company knows the psychographics of its target buyers, it isn't lulled into age stereotypes of safety and conservatism. Harley-Davidson knows that in spite of the older age demographic, its buyers are still a thrill-seeking bunch (they may just need a little more time and some aspirin to recover after a long ride).

families—more than half have two or more kids—living in small homes and manufactured housing. Nearly a third of residents live in mobile homes, more than anywhere else in the nation. They are much more likely than the average American consumer to own a tent, go to auto races, read *North American Hunter* magazine, watch Country Music TV, and drive a Dodge Ram.

Other examples of PRIZM clusters are fully described in the Segment Lookup feature at **www.mybestsegments.com**.

Segment by Psychographics

Demographic information is useful, but it does not always provide enough information to divide consumers into meaningful segments. Although we can use demographic variables to discover, for example, that the female college student segment uses perfume, we won't be able to tell whether certain college women prefer perfumes that express an image of, say, sexiness rather than athleticism.

As we said in Chapter 5, **psychographics** segments consumers in terms of psychological and behavioral similarities such as shared activities, interests, and opinions, or AIOs.[33] Marketers often develop profiles of the typical customers they desire to paint a more vivid picture of them. For example, in 2010 Buick's marketers named their target consumers Greg and Laurie Robbins. They say they're in their early 40s with two kids and together, they make $130,000 a year and live in a $363,000 house. They are Facebook fans of Target, Starbucks, Apple, J. Crew, Whole Foods, and the Westin. This (fictional) couple is younger than Buick's current user and their interests extend beyond the golf course, which is where many older Buick drivers spend their time. To woo them, the company is cutting back on ads in golf magazines and instead promoting Buick in culinary- and travel-related venues and on *The Wall Street Journal*'s iPad application. The goal of this psychographic exercise: Put a Buick in the Robbins's garage where a Lexus is probably parked now.[34]

Although some advertising agencies and manufacturers develop their own psychographic techniques to classify consumers, other agencies subscribe to services that divide the entire U.S. population into segments and then sell pieces of this information to clients for specific strategic applications. The best known of these systems is **VALS™ (Values and Lifestyles)**. The original VALS™ system was based on social values and lifestyles. Today, VALS™ is based on psychological traits that correlate with consumer behavior. If you go to **www.strategicbusinessinsights.com** and click on "VALS™ Survey" you can complete a brief, free questionnaire to find out your own VALS™ type (you might be surprised). VALS™ divides U.S. adults into eight groups according to what drives them psychologically as well as by their economic resources.

As 📷 Figure 7.3 shows, three primary consumer motivations are key to the system: ideals, achievement, and self-expression. Consumers who are motivated primarily by ideals are guided by knowledge and principles. Consumers who are motivated primarily by achievement look for goods and services that

Courtesy of Chiquisa Mares, Advertising and Planning

Toyota targets consumers who prioritize environmental issues (as well as gas savings) with the Prius hybrid vehicle.

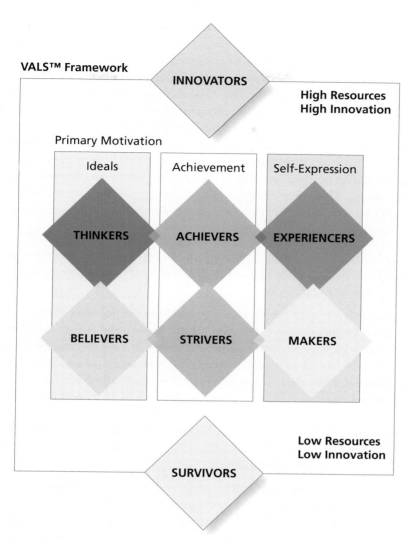

VALS™ Framework

INNOVATORS

High Resources
High Innovation

Primary Motivation

Ideals   Achievement   Self-Expression

THINKERS   ACHIEVERS   EXPERIENCERS

BELIEVERS   STRIVERS   MAKERS

Low Resources
Low Innovation

SURVIVORS

Figure 7.3 📷 *Snapshot* | VALS™ Framework

VALS™ uses psychological characteristics to segment the U.S. market into eight unique consumer groups.

Source: Strategic Business Insights (SBI); www.strategicbusiness insights.com/VALS

demonstrate success to their peers. And consumers who are motivated primarily by self-expression desire social or physical activity, variety, and risk.

VALS™ helps match products to particular types of people. For example, VALS™ survey data show that 12 percent of American adults (many of whom are on the younger side) are Experiencers who tend to be thrill seekers. VALS™ helped Isuzu market its Rodeo sport-utility vehicle by targeting Experiencers who believe it's fun to break rules. The company and its advertising agency promoted the car as a vehicle that lets a driver break the rules by going off-road. One ad showed a kid jumping in mud puddles after his mother went to great lengths to keep him clean. Another ad showed a schoolchild scribbling outside the lines after the teacher made a big deal about coloring carefully within the lines. Isuzu sales increased significantly after this campaign, and the company recently introduced a worthy next-generation SUV called the Ascender.[35]

As another example of a psychographic segmentation system developed for the luxury car market, German research firm Sigma categorized consumers in a way that inspired BMW's highly publicized product line reinvention and expansion. This system included "upper liberals" (socially conscious, open-minded professionals who prefer the roominess and flexibility of SUVs), "postmoderns" (high-earning innovators like architects, entrepreneurs, and artists who like the individualistic statements made by driving convertibles and roadsters), "upper conservatives" (made up of wealthy, traditional thinkers who like upper-crust, traditional sedans), and "modern mainstream" (family-oriented up-and-comers who want a luxury brand but likely can't afford more than the lowest-end model). Using this segmentation scheme as an anchor, BMW created vehicles for each category and added

psychographics
The use of psychological, sociological, and anthropological factors to construct market segments.

VALS™ (Values and Lifestyles)
A psychographic system that divides the entire U.S. population into eight segments.

to its success with multiple segments by acquiring Rolls-Royce and the Mini to serve the extreme ends.[36]

Finally, the recent economic recession sparked the identification of four distinct consumer psychographic segments as consumers emerge from the bad economy. Marketing strategy and research firm Decitica labels these segments as follows: (1) Steadfast Frugalists, (2) Involuntary Penny-Pinchers, (3) Pragmatic Spenders, and (4) Apathetic Materialists. These categories were derived by analyzing the frequency, satisfaction, and self-efficacy associated with a variety of spending, purchase, and consumption behaviors. Steadfast Frugalists are committed to self-restraint, engaging in prudence with unequivocal enthusiasm. They make up about one-fifth of the American consumers, representing all income and age groups. This group could be quite challenging, as they are the least brand loyal and most likely to discount marketing messages. Consider how these psychographic segments differ:

- Eighty percent of Steadfast Frugalists say the new behaviors they have adopted will likely stay with them for a long time. This is in contrast to 24 percent of Apathetic Materialists who feel this way.

- Involuntary Penny-Pinchers, about 29 percent of the population, have been severely affected by the recession. They are mainly made up of households with less than $50,000 in income, with more women than men. This segment has been forced to embrace thrift like never before. Presently, their actual behaviors do not differ widely from those of Steadfast Frugalists. Where they drastically diverge is in their aversion to expending effort in money-saving strategies. Only 17 percent find buying store or generic labels to be satisfying, compared to 59 percent of Steadfast Frugalists. Also, the recession has had a heavy emotional impact on Involuntary Penny-Pinchers; they admit to being more scared (77 percent), stressed (81 percent), and worried (87 percent) about the future than other groups.

- Pragmatic Spenders are the most attractive group for marketers because of their higher spending power. Although it is true that they have also curbed their spending, they are the most capable, both psychologically and financially, to willfully resurrect their past spending patterns. This group comprises 29 percent of consumers. Income has blunted the effects of the recession on this segment. Only 28 percent of Pragmatic Spenders feel the recession has changed what and how they will buy in the future, compared to 55 percent of Steadfast Frugalists.

- Apathetic Materialists seem least changed by the recession. They have not embraced the new frugality to the same extent as others and get minimal satisfaction from such behaviors. Only about 6 percent in this group find price comparison to be satisfying, in contrast to 85 percent in the Steadfast Frugalists camp. The Apathetic Materialists segment has more men (55 percent) and younger consumers (72 percent are below the age of 40). They are the least driven by price: Only 8 percent admit to being very focused on value compared to 30 percent of Pragmatic Spenders and 52 percent of Involuntary Penny-Pinchers.[37]

Segment by Behavior

People may use the same product for different reasons, on different occasions, and in different amounts. So, in addition to demographics and psychographics, it is useful to study what consumers actually do with a product. **Behavioral segmentation** slices consumer segments on the basis of how they act toward, feel about, or use a product. One way to segment based on behavior is to divide the market into users and nonusers of a product. Then marketers may attempt to reward current users or try to win over new ones. In addition to distinguishing between users and nonusers, marketers can describe current customers as heavy, mod-

behavioral segmentation
A technique that divides consumers into segments on the basis of how they act toward, feel about, or use a good or service.

erate, and light users. They often do this according to a rule of thumb we call the **80/20 rule**: 20 percent of purchasers account for 80 percent of the product's sales (the ratio is an approximation, not gospel). This rule means that it often makes more sense to focus on the smaller number of people who are really into a product rather than on the larger number who are just casual users. Kraft Foods began a $30 million campaign to remind its core users not to "skip the zip" after its research showed that indeed 20 percent of U.S. households account for 80 percent of the usage of Miracle Whip. Are you surprised to learn that in this product category "heavy" users consume 17 pounds of Miracle Whip a year?[38]

While the 80/20 rule still holds in the majority of situations, the Internet's ability to offer an unlimited choice of goods to billions of people has changed how marketers think about segmentation. An approach called the **long tail** turns traditional thinking about the virtues of selling in high volume on its head. The basic idea is that we need no longer rely solely on big hits (like blockbuster movies or best-selling books) to find profits. Companies can also make money when they sell small amounts of items that only a few people want—if they sell enough different items. For example, Amazon.com maintains an inventory of 3.7 million books compared to the 100,000 or so you'll find in a Barnes & Noble retail store. Most of these will sell only a few thousand copies (if that), but the 3.6 million books that Barnes & Noble doesn't carry make up a quarter of Amazon's revenues! Similarly, about a fifth of the videos Netflix delivers to its customers are older or obscure titles rather than the blockbusters you'd find at, well, Blockbuster (if there's still a store in your neighborhood!). Blizzard's World of Warcraft's massively multiplayer online game is another long tail. Instead of having to constantly release new sequels, Blizzard only has to release a few updates here and there. The sheer volume of users and the game's open world/do anything environment allows its users to constantly keep it interesting at no additional development costs to Blizzard. Other examples of the long tail include successful microbreweries and TV networks that make money on reruns of old shows on channels like Nick at Night.[39]

Another way to segment a market based on behavior is to look at **usage occasions**, or when consumers use the product most. We associate many products with specific occasions, whether time of day, holidays, business functions, or casual get-togethers. Businesses often divide up their markets according to when and how their offerings are in demand.

In a similar vein, Google enables its advertising clients to target certain ads to certain segments of search engine users based on data such as Google domain, query entered, IP address, and language preference. This way, companies can have Google automatically sort and send the intended ad to certain market segments. Thus, it is possible for advertisers on Google to tailor their automatically targeted ads based on seasonality—you will see more TurboTax ads on Google pages during tax season, even if people aren't querying tax software.[40]

Segment Business-to-Business Markets

We've reviewed the segmentation variables marketers use to divide up the consumer pie, but how about all those business-to-business marketers out there? Adding to what we learned about business markets in Chapter 6, it's important to know that

80/20 rule
A marketing rule of thumb that 20 percent of purchasers account for 80 percent of a product's sales.

long tail
A new approach to segmentation based on the idea that companies can make money by selling small amounts of items that only a few people want, provided they sell enough different items.

usage occasions
An indicator used in behavioral market segmentation based on when consumers use a product most.

The Biltmore Estate in Asheville, North Carolina, increased attendance during its annual Christmas celebration as part of a strategy to segment by usage occasion. Set on 8,000 acres and featuring four acres of lavishly decorated floor space under one roof, the Biltmore is the largest private home in America. Although more than 750,000 people typically visit the house annually, several years ago attendance was starting to stagnate. Then the estate's marketers mixed things up; they developed four separate strategies to target different types of visitors—heavy users such as those who have made a Christmas pilgrimage an annual family tradition versus light users who have visited only once. Each segment received a different invitation that included a customized package calculated to appeal to that segment. As a result, visits increased by 300 percent in one season, resulting in a merry Christmas for the Biltmore.

B. Anthony Stewart/National Geographic/Getty Images

segmentation also helps them better understand their customers. Though the specific variables may differ, the underlying logic of classifying the larger market into manageable pieces that share relevant characteristics is the same whether the product you sell is pesto or pesticides.

Organizational demographics also help a business-to-business marketer to understand the needs and characteristics of its potential customers. These classification dimensions include the size of the firms, either in total sales or number of employees; the number of facilities, whether they are a domestic or a multinational company, purchasing policies, and the type of business they are in. Business-to-business markets may also be segmented on the basis of the production technology they use and whether the customer is a user or a nonuser of the product.

Many industries use the North American Industry Classification System (NAICS) we discussed in Chapter 6 to obtain information about the size and number of companies operating in a particular industry. Business-to-business marketers often consult information sources on the Web. For example, Hoovers Online (**www.hoovers.com**) provides subscribers with up-to-date information on private and public companies worldwide.

3

OBJECTIVE

Explain how marketers evaluate segments and choose a targeting strategy.
(pp. 198–201)

targeting
A strategy in which marketers evaluate the attractiveness of each potential segment and decide in which of these groups they will invest resources to try to turn them into customers.

target market
The market segments on which an organization focuses its marketing plan and toward which it directs its marketing efforts.

Step 2: Targeting

We've seen that the first step in a target marketing strategy is segmentation, in which the firm divides the market into smaller groups that share certain characteristics. The next step is **targeting**, in which marketers evaluate the attractiveness of each potential segment and decide in which of these groups they will invest resources to try to turn them into customers. The customer group or groups they select are the firm's **target market**.

Targeting in Three Steps

In this section, we'll review the three phases of targeting: evaluate market segments, develop segment profiles, and choose a targeting strategy. Figure 7.4 illustrates these three phases.

Evaluate Market Segments

Just because a marketer identifies a segment does not necessarily mean that it's a useful target. A viable target segment should satisfy the following requirements:

- *Are members of the segment similar to each other in their product needs and wants and, at the same time, different from consumers in other segments?* Without real differences in consumer needs, firms might as well use a mass-marketing strategy. For example, it's a waste of time to develop two separate lines of skin care products for working women and nonworking women if both segments have the same complaints about dry skin.

  - *Can marketers measure the segment?* Marketers must know something about the size and purchasing power of a potential segment before they decide if it's worth their efforts.

  - *Is the segment large enough to be profitable now and in the future?* For example, a graphic designer who hopes to design Web pages for Barbie-doll collectors must decide whether there are enough hard-core aficionados to make this business worthwhile and whether the trend will continue.

  - *Can marketing communications reach the segment?* It is easy to select television programs or magazines that will efficiently reach older consumers, consumers with certain levels of education, or residents of major cities because

Figure 7.4 Process | Phases of Targeting
Targeting involves three distinct phases of activities.

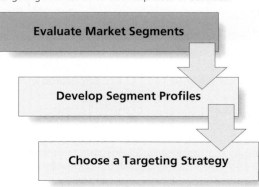

the media they prefer are easy to identify. It is unlikely, however, that marketing communications can reach only left-handed blondes with tattoos who listen to Lady Gaga overdubbed in Mandarin Chinese.

- *Can the marketer adequately serve the needs of the segment?* Does the firm have the expertise and resources to satisfy the segment better than the competition? Some years ago, consumer-products manufacturer Warner-Lambert (now a part of Pfizer) made the mistake of trying to enter the pastry business by purchasing Entenmann's Bakery. Entenmann's sells high-end boxed cakes, cookies, pastries, and pies in supermarkets. Unfortunately, Warner-Lambert's expertise at selling Listerine mouthwash and Trident gum did not transfer to baked goods and it soon lost a lot of dough on the deal.

Develop Segment Profiles

Once a marketer identifies a set of usable segments, it is helpful to generate a profile of each to really understand segment members' needs and to look for business opportunities. This segment profile is a description of the "typical" customer in that segment. A **segment profile** might, for example, include customer demographics, location, lifestyle information, and a description of how frequently the customer buys the product.

Years ago, when the R.J. Reynolds Company made plans to introduce a new brand of cigarettes called Dakota that it would target to women, it created a segment profile of a possible customer group: the "Virile Female." The profile included these characteristics: Her favorite pastimes are cruising, partying, going to hot-rod shows and tractor pulls with her boyfriend, and watching evening soap operas. Her chief aspiration is to get married in her early 20s.[41] Anyone you know?

segment profile
A description of the "typical" customer in a segment.

Choose a Targeting Strategy

A basic targeting decision revolves around how finely tuned the target should be: Should the company go after one large segment or focus on meeting the needs of one or more smaller segments? Let's look at four targeting strategies, which Figure 7.5 summarizes.

A company like Walmart that selects an **undifferentiated targeting strategy** appeals to a broad spectrum of people. If successful, this type of operation can be very efficient because production, research, and promotion costs benefit from economies of scale—it's cheaper to develop one product or one advertising campaign than to choose several targets and create separate products or messages for each. But the company must be willing to bet that people have similar needs so the same product and message will appeal to many customers.

A company that chooses a **differentiated targeting strategy** develops one or more products for each of several customer groups with different product needs. A differentiated strategy is called for when consumers choose among well-known brands that have distinctive images, and the company can identify one or more segments that have distinct needs for different types of products.

Despite its highly publicized product safety issues in 2010, Toyota historically has been a leader in differentiated strategy with distinct product lines that cater to multiple customer groups. Its Lexus product line caters to consumers who want luxury, performance, and the newest technology. The Prius hybrid provides value to drivers who want to save gas money and the environment. And finally, the Scion product line caters to younger drivers who look for a relatively inexpensive car that is highly customizable and stylish.[42]

Differentiated marketing can also involve connecting one product with different segments by communicating differently to appeal to those segments. Again using the "Got Milk?" campaign as an example, one of their most classic ads featured Aerosmith's Steven Tyler to appeal to both aging boomers who got into the band in the 1970s and Gen Yers who discovered the band in the 1990s due to Run-DMC's remake of "Walk This Way."

When a firm offers one or more products to a single segment, it uses a **concentrated targeting strategy**. Smaller firms that do not have the resources or the desire to be all things to

undifferentiated targeting strategy
Appealing to a broad spectrum of people.

differentiated targeting strategy
Developing one or more products for each of several distinct customer groups and making sure these offerings are kept separate in the marketplace.

concentrated targeting strategy
Focusing a firm's efforts on offering one or more products to a single segment.

Figure 7.5 📷 *Snapshot* | Choose a Targeting Strategy

Marketers must decide on a targeting strategy. Should the company go after one total market, one or several market segments, or even target customers individually?

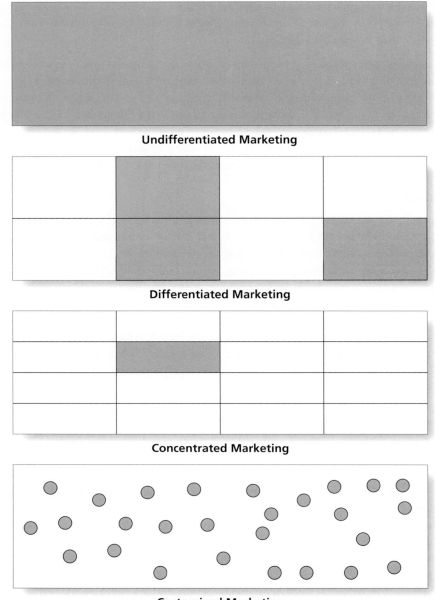

Undifferentiated Marketing

Differentiated Marketing

Concentrated Marketing

Customized Marketing

custom marketing strategy
An approach that tailors specific products and the messages about them to individual customers.

mass customization
An approach that modifies a basic good or service to meet the needs of an individual.

positioning
Develop a marketing strategy to influence how a particular market segment perceives a good or service in comparison to the competition.

all people often do this. Blacksocks.com is a mail-order sock company that only makes black dress socks; it targets businessmen who are too busy to go to the store and buy new socks when their old ones wear out. Blacksocks ship 3-packs of black socks once a month to its "sockscribers." The company argues that every guy who wears a business suit wears socks, and most wear black socks. For these busy men, going to the store just to buy socks is boring, time-consuming, and simply unnecessary. Periodically the company wrestles with the dilemma of whether or not to also sell white socks because this expansion will dilute the brand (and force the company to change its name!).[43]

Ideally, marketers should be able to define segments so precisely that they can offer products that exactly meet the unique needs of each individual or firm. This level of concentration does occur (we hope) in the case of personal or professional services we get from doctors, lawyers, and hairstylists. A **custom marketing strategy** also is common in industrial contexts where a manufacturer often works with one or a few large clients and develops products that only these clients will use.

Ripped from the Headlines

Ethical/Sustainable Decisions in the Real World

Most major brands are gearing up to more deeply target consumers in emerging markets. China has 1.3 billion people. India has 1.1 billion. Other nations such as Brazil and Russia offer the dazzling prospect of massive revenue for savvy brands. Coca-Cola is particularly known for successful targeting for many reasons, including the firm's ability to identify untapped target markets and win over consumers not only by aggressively pursuing them, but also by wanting to know them.

Currently 30 million people, one in three of India's population, constitute the BOP "bottom-of-pyramid" marketplace. The BOP refers to the masses in developing countries that account for over 65 percent of the world's population. Buyers at the BOP not only behave differently from their counterparts in developed countries but also from the upper and middle income consumers in their own societies.

Now, Coke is reaching out to this group in India with Vitingo, a new drink aimed at low-income consumers. Coke isn't alone as it pursues this target market, and for good reason. Statistics show that 40 million Indian families are moving from outright poverty to the BOP demographic every year. Remember, that's not 40 million people, that is 40 million *families*. Each *year*. Like Coke, Glaxo Smith Kline, the pharmaceutical firm, knows there is no greater brand advocate than a family member. In fact, GSK is launching its own milk-based drink, Asha, in India that is designed to appeal to the BOP demographic. Also like Coke, GSK is doing more than offering a product. It is selling the product to a specific group of consumers that the brand values and actively targets. Says Zubair Ahmed, managing director at GSK India: "We are building a robust go-to-market model to ensure the products reach the right consumers because it's not enough just to have the right products."

Other familiar brands investing in India's BOP market are Nestlé, Pepsi, and Hindustan Unilever with the idea that the successful brands of tomorrow are already courting these up-and-coming BOP consumers and demographics that will provide important revenue streams in the years to come.

ETHICS CHECK: ➤
Find out what other students taking this course **would do** and **why** on **www .mypearsonmarketinglab .com**

Is it appropriate for firms such as Coke and GSK to target the BOP market in countries like India?

☐ **Yes** ☐ **No**

Of course, in most cases this level of segmentation is neither practical nor possible when mass-produced products such as computers or cars enter the picture. However, advances in computer technology, coupled with the new emphasis on building solid relationships with customers, have focused managers' attention on devising new ways to tailor specific products and the messages about them to individual customers. Thus, some forward-looking, consumer-oriented companies are moving toward **mass customization** in which they modify a basic good or service to meet the needs of an individual.[44] Dell does this when it offers customized computer products over the Internet at Dell.com where users configure their own computers—everything from personal computers to networking systems. We'll return to the issue of customization later in this chapter when we introduce the idea of customer relationship management.

4

OBJECTIVE

Understand how marketers develop and implement a positioning strategy.
(pp. 201–204)

Step 3: Positioning

The final stage of developing a target marketing strategy is to provide consumers who belong to a targeted market segment with a good or service that meets their unique needs and expectations. **Positioning** means developing a marketing strategy to influence how a particular market segment perceives a good or service in comparison to the competition. To position a brand, marketers have to clearly understand the criteria target consumers use to evaluate competing products and then convince them that their product, service, or organization will meet those needs. In addition, the organization has to come up with way to communicate this "position" to its target market.

Positioning happens in many ways. Sometimes it's just a matter of making sure that cool people use your product—and that others observe them doing this. After finding out that a close friend was flying to Los Angeles to audition for the film *Any Given Sunday*, the president of the high-performance sportswear company Under Armour sent along with him a bunch of free samples of its athletic wear to give to the film's casting director as a gift. The

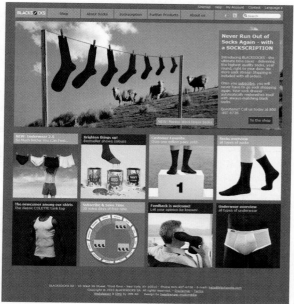

Blacksocks practices a highly concentrated targeting strategy.

Courtesy of Blacksocks US

Figure 7.6 *Process* | Stages in a Positioning Decision

Four key elements comprise the decision-making process in positioning.

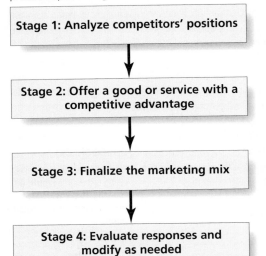

```
┌─────────────────────────────────────────┐
│ Stage 1: Analyze competitors' positions  │
└─────────────────────────────────────────┘
                    │
                    ▼
┌─────────────────────────────────────────┐
│ Stage 2: Offer a good or service with a  │
│           competitive advantage          │
└─────────────────────────────────────────┘
                    │
                    ▼
┌─────────────────────────────────────────┐
│    Stage 3: Finalize the marketing mix   │
└─────────────────────────────────────────┘
                    │
                    ▼
┌─────────────────────────────────────────┐
│     Stage 4: Evaluate responses and      │
│              modify as needed            │
└─────────────────────────────────────────┘
```

Jim Multari

Sprout offers a different viewing experience than its larger competitions as it tries to encourage a lot of parent/child interaction. It is also essentially a "library channel"; its programming mainly consists of previously aired kids' shows, repackaged and represented around short original content and brand identity links. ➡

director liked the quality of the clothes so much he gave them to the wardrobe company the filmmakers hired and they also really liked the clothes. The next thing you know, the movie (starring Al Pacino and Jamie Foxx) featured both the actors wearing Under Armour clothes on screen—and there was even a scene in the film when Jamie Foxx undressed in the locker room with a clear shot of the Under Armour logo on his jock strap. After the movie's release, hits on Under Armour's Web site spiked, and, as they say, the rest is history.[45]

Steps in Positioning

 Figure 7.6 shows the stages marketers use to decide just how to position their product or service: analyze competitors' positions, offer a good or service with a competitive advantage, finalize the marketing mix, and evaluate responses and modify as needed. Let's take a closer look at each of the positioning stages.

Analyze Competitors' Positions

The first stage is to analyze competitors' positions in the marketplace. To develop an effective positioning strategy, marketers must understand the current lay of the land. What competitors are out there, and how does the target market perceive them? Aside from direct competitors in the product category, are there other goods or services that provide similar benefits?

Sometimes the indirect competition can be more important than the direct, especially if it represents an emerging consumer trend. For years, McDonald's developed positioning strategies based only on its direct competition, which it defined as other large fast-food hamburger chains (translation: Burger King and Wendy's). McDonald's failed to realize that in fact many indirect competitors fulfilled consumers' needs for a quick, tasty, convenient meal—from supermarket delis to frozen microwavable single-serving meals to call-ahead takeout from full-service restaurants like T.G.I. Friday's, Outback, and Chili's. Only recently, McDonald's has begun to understand that it must react to this indirect competition by serving up a wider variety of adult-friendly food and shoring up lagging service. Their latest home run is the McCafe concept, with coffee products aimed squarely at taking business away from morning mainstays Starbucks and Dunkin Donuts.

Define Your Competitive Advantage

The second stage is to offer a good or service with a competitive advantage to provide a reason why consumers will perceive the product as better than the competition. If the company offers only a "me-too product," it can induce people to buy for a lower price. Other forms of competitive advantage include offering a superior image (Giorgio Armani), a unique product feature (Levi's 501 button-fly jeans), better service (Cadillac's roadside assistance program), or even better-qualified people (the legendary salespeople at Nordstrom's department stores).

Finalize the Marketing Mix

Once they settle on a positioning strategy, the third stage for marketers is to finalize the marketing mix by putting all the pieces into place. The elements of the marketing mix must match the selected segment. This means that the good or service must deliver benefits that the segment values, such as convenience or status. Put another way, it must add value and satisfy consumer needs. Furthermore, marketers must price this offering at a level these consumers will pay, make the offering available at places consumers are likely to go, and correctly communicate the offering's benefits in locations where consumers are likely to take notice.

Evaluate Responses and Modify as Needed

In the fourth and final stage, marketers evaluate the target market's responses so they can modify strategies as needed. Over time, the firm may find that it needs to change which segments it targets or even alter a product's position to respond to marketplace changes. Consider this classic example: Macho Marlboro cigarettes originally were a smoke for women—complete with a red tip to hide lipstick stains!

A change strategy is **repositioning**, and it's fairly common to see a company try to modify its brand image to keep up with changing times. Take as an example Charles Schwab, which used to be pegged primarily as a self-service stock brokerage. Competition in the budget broker business, especially from online brokers, prompted Schwab's repositioning to a full-line, full-service financial services firm that still pays attention to frugal prices for its services. Think of it this way: There's not much value Schwab can add as one of a dozen or more online providers of stock trades. In that environment, customers simply will view the firm as a commodity (i.e., just a way to buy stocks) with no real differentiation. Schwab still has its no-frills products, but the real growth in sales and profits comes from its expanded product lines and provision of more information—both online and through personal selling—that warrant higher fees and build deeper customer relationships. Repositioning also occurs when a marketer revises a brand thought to be dead or at least near death. Sometimes these products arise from their deathbeds to ride a wave of nostalgia and return to the marketplace as **retro brands**—venerable brands like Oxydol laundry detergent, Breck Shampoo, Ovaltine cereal, and Tab cola have gotten a new lease on life in recent years.[46]

repositioning
Redoing a product's position to respond to marketplace changes.

retro brand
A once-popular brand that has been revived to experience a popularity comeback, often by riding a wave of nostalgia.

Bring a Product to Life: The Brand Personality

In a way, brands are like people: We often describe them in terms of personality traits. We may use adjectives such as *cheap, elegant, sexy,* or *cool* when we talk about a store, a perfume, or a car. That's why a positioning strategy often tries to create a **brand personality** for a good or service—a distinctive image that captures its character and benefits. An advertisement for *Elle,* which bills itself as the number-one fashion magazine for women, proclaimed, "She is not a reply card. She is not a category. She is not shrink-wrapped. *Elle* is not a magazine. She is a woman."

Products as people? It seems funny to say, yet marketing researchers find that most consumers have no trouble describing what a product would be like "if it came to life." People often give clear, detailed descriptions, including what color hair the product would have, the type of house it would live in, and even whether it would be thin, overweight, or somewhere in between.[47] If you don't believe us, try doing this yourself.

Part of creating a brand personality is developing an identity for the product that the target market will prefer over competing brands. How do marketers determine where their product actually stands in the minds of consumers? One solution is to ask consumers what characteristics are important and how competing alternatives would rate on these attributes, too. Marketers use this information to construct a **perceptual map**, a vivid way to construct a picture of where products or brands are "located" in consumers' minds.

For example, suppose you wanted to construct a perceptual map of how American women in their 20s perceive magazines to help you develop an idea for a new publication that these readers would like. After you interview a sample of female readers, you might identify two key questions women ask when they select a magazine: (1) Is it "traditional," that is, oriented toward family, home, or personal issues, or is it "fashion-forward," oriented toward personal appearance and fashion? (2) Is it for "upscale" women who are older and established in their careers or for relatively "downscale" women who are younger and just starting out in their careers?

To summarize the steps we take to position a product, look at the strategy the SoBe Beverage Company developed. SoBe is a small drink manufacturer based in Connecticut that offers a line of teas, elixirs, and power drinks. The company first segmented the market in terms of age and psychographics. Then it targeted a segment of 18- to 35-year-olds whose profiles indicated they were into "New Age" beverages that would give them a feeling of energy without unhealthy additives. SoBe created XTC, a drink inspired by "herbal ecstasy" cocktails of extracts and amino acids first made popular at 1990s' "raves" featuring all-night gyrations to techno music. As an industry executive noted, this strategy provides a unique position for the elixir: "People are taking something that provides a four-times-removed high without having to get arrested or wrecking their bodies. It carries the image of being a little further out there without carrying the risk." Today, XTC has given way to an amazing line of products in various flavors under such thematic purposes as Purify, C-boost, N-Dure, Electrify, Lean Machine, and D-Fence for the ever-moving and multitasking Gen Y as well as a line of teas and elixirs with broader generational appeal.

Figure 7.7 📷 *Snapshot* | Perceptual Map

Perceptual mapping allows marketers to identify consumers' perceptions of their brand in relation to the competition.

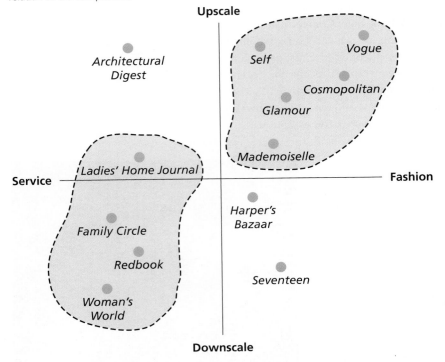

The perceptual map in 📷 Figure 7.7 illustrates how these ratings might look for a set of major women's magazines. The map provides some guidance as to where you might position your new magazine. You might decide to compete directly with either the cluster of "service magazines" in the lower left or the traditional fashion magazines in the upper right. In this case, you would have to determine what benefits your new magazine might offer that these existing magazines do not. Condé Nast, for example, positioned *Allure* to compete against fashion magazines by going into more depth than they do on beauty issues, such as the mental, physical, and emotional dangers of cosmetic surgery.

You might try to locate an unserved area in this perceptual map. There may be room for a magazine that targets "cutting-edge" fashion for college-age women. An unserved segment is the "Holy Grail" for marketers: With luck, they can move quickly to capture a segment and define the standards of comparison for the category. This tactic paid off for Chrysler, which first identified the minivan market for soccer moms; JetBlue, which found a spot for low fares and high tech without the poor-boy service attitude and cattle-call boarding procedure of other budget airlines; and Liz Claiborne, which pioneered the concept of comfortable, "user-friendly" clothing for working women. In the magazine category, perhaps *Marie Claire* comes closest to this position.

brand personality

A distinctive image that captures a good's or service's character and benefits.

perceptual map

A technique to visually describe where brands are "located" in consumers' minds relative to competing brands.

customer relationship management (CRM)

A systematic tracking of consumers' preferences and behaviors over time in order to tailor the value proposition as closely as possible to each individual's unique wants and needs. CRM allows firms to talk to individual customers and to adjust elements of their marketing programs in light of how each customer reacts.

5 Customer Relationship Management (CRM): Toward a Segment of One

OBJECTIVE

Explain how marketers increase long-term success and profits by practicing customer relationship management.

(pp. 204–208)

We've talked about how marketers identify a unique group of consumers and then develop products specifically to meet their needs. And we talked about how marketers today build products to meet the needs of individual consumers by using mass customization techniques. As we discussed in Chapter 1, currently many highly successful marketing firms embrace **customer relationship management (CRM)** programs that involve systematically tracking consumers' preferences and behaviors over time in order to tailor the value proposition as closely as possible to each individual's unique wants and needs. CRM allows firms to talk to individual customers and to adjust elements of their marketing programs in light of how each customer reacts.[48] The CRM trend facilitates *one-to-one marketing*, which includes several steps.[49]

1. Identify customers and get to know them in as much detail as possible.

2. Differentiate among these customers in terms of both their needs and their value to the company.

3. Interact with customers and find ways to improve cost efficiency and the effectiveness of the interaction.

4. Customize some aspect of the goods or services that you offer to each customer. This means treating each customer differently based on what has been learned through customer interactions.[50]

Table 7.1 suggests some specific activities to implement these four steps of one-to-one marketing. Remember, successful one-to-one marketing depends on CRM, which allows a company to identify its best customers, stay on top of their needs, and increase their satisfaction.[51]

CRM: A New Perspective on an Old Problem

CRM is about communicating with customers, and about customers being able to communicate with a company "up close and personal." CRM systems are applications that use computers, specialized computer software, databases, and often the Internet to capture information at each **touchpoint**, which is any point of direct interface between customers and a company (online, by phone, or in person).

These systems include everything from Web sites that let you check on the status of a bill or package to call centers that solicit your business. When you log on to the FedEx Web site to track a lost package, that's part of a CRM system. When you get a phone message from the dentist reminding you about your appointment tomorrow to get a root canal, that's CRM (sorry about that). And

Marketers know that one way to more finely segment consumers is to allow them to personalize products. That's the message behind this Danish ad for McDonald's.

Table 7.1	The Four Steps of One-to-One Marketing

Step	Suggested Activities
Identify	Collect and enter names and additional information about your customers.
	Verify and update, deleting outdated information.
Differentiate	Identify top customers.
	Determine which customers cost the company money.
	Find higher-value customers who have complained about your product more than once.
	Find customers who buy only one or two products from your company but a lot from other companies.
	Rank customers into A, B, and C categories based on their value to your company.
Interact	Call the top three people in the top 5 percent of dealers, distributors, and retailers that carry your product and make sure they're happy.
	Call your own company and ask questions; see how hard it is to get through and get answers.
	Call your competitors and compare their customer service with yours.
	Use incoming calls as selling opportunities.
	Initiate more dialogue with valuable customers.
	Improve complaint handling.
Customize	Find out what your customers want.
	Personalize your direct mail.
	Ask customers how and how often they want to hear from you.
	Ask your top 10 customers what you can do differently to improve your product.
	Involve top management in customer relations.

Source: Adapted by permission of *Harvard Business Review* from Don Peppers, Martha Rogers, and Bob Dorf, "Is Your Company Ready for One-to-One Marketing?" *Harvard Business Review* (January–February 1999), 151–60. Copyright © 1999 by the Harvard Business School Publishing Corporation. All rights reserved.

touchpoint
Any point of direct interface between customers and a company (online, by phone, or in person).

when you get a call from the car dealer asking how you like your new vehicle, that's also CRM. Remember how in Chapter 4 we said information is the fuel that runs the marketing engine? It is through CRM that companies act upon and manage the information they gather from their customers.

To fully appreciate the value of a CRM strategy, consider the experience of USAA, which began as an insurance company catering to the military market and today is a leading global financial services powerhouse. In 1922, when 25 army officers met in San Antonio and decided to insure each other's vehicles, they could not have imagined that their tiny organization would one day serve 6 million members and become the only fully integrated financial services company in America. Unlike State Farm, Allstate, and other traditional insurance providers, USAA does not provide field agents with an office you can go to, sit down, and shoot the breeze. In fact, USAA's employees conduct business almost entirely over the phone. But just ask any USAA member how they feel about the service, and you'll get a glowing report.

The secret to USAA's success is largely due to its state-of-the-art CRM system. No matter where on the globe you are, no matter what time of day or night, a USAA representative will pull up your profile and you'll feel that he knows you. Of course, it takes a good dose of employee training to enable those folks to use the system to its potential. But USAA does a great job of building and maintaining long-term customer relationships, and (more importantly) getting customers to move many or all of their business over to USAA including banking, credit cards, money management, investments, and financial planning. To further build loyalty, USAA even runs an online company store that sells all sorts of popular product lines and brands for which members get purchase discounts.[52]

USAA's success helps explain why CRM has become a driving philosophy in many successful firms. A study by the Services & Support Professionals Association (SSPA) estimates that in 2008, organizations with more than $1 billion in revenue spent approximately $565 million on e-service, CRM, contact center, and field service technology. Small and midsized businesses spent about $884 million. And Forrester Research estimates the CRM market reached about $11 billion in 2010.[53] Here are some current examples of CRM at work:

- Amazon.com is the world champion master of the happy customer approach to CRM. For loyal users, Amazon tracks visits so it can customize advertisements, product promotions, and discounts for each shopper. And, if you happen to have a passion for, say, grunge bands of the 1990s, the Web site is quick to recommend that new retrospective on Pearl Jam the next time you visit.[54]

- Coca-Cola launched its My Coke Rewards online program, the multiyear customer-loyalty marketing blitz into which it poured millions of dollars.

- JCPenney uses the power of its CRM system to develop lasting consumer relationships. Its JCP Rewards program lets customers earn points to snag members-only benefits. Rival Macy's West, one of the retailer's biggest divisions, also has been investing in CRM to decipher a more effective media mix and gauge reaction to digital efforts.[55]

Characteristics of CRM

In addition to having a different mind-set, companies that successfully practice CRM have different goals, use different measures of success, and look at customers in some different ways. Followers of CRM look at four critical elements, as portrayed in 📷 Figure 7.8: share of customer, lifetime value of a customer, customer equity, and customer prioritization. Let's have a look at each of these ideas now.

Share of Customer

Historically, marketers measured success in a product category by their *market share*. For example, if people buy 100 million pairs of athletic shoes each year, a firm that sells 10 million of them claims a 10 percent market share. If the shoemaker's marketing objective is to in-

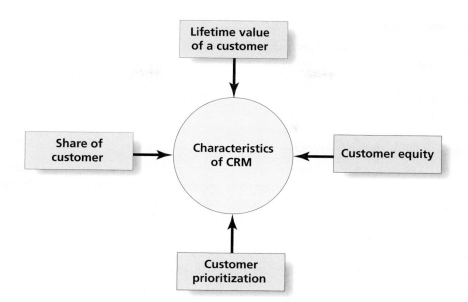

Figure 7.8 📷 *Snapshot* |
Characteristics of CRM

Followers of CRM look at share of customer, lifetime value of a customer, customer equity, and customer prioritization.

crease market share, it may lower the price of its shoes, increase its advertising, or offer customers a free basketball with every pair of shoes they purchase. These tactics may increase sales in the short run. Unfortunately, they may not do much for the long-term success of the shoemaker. In fact, they may actually decrease the value of the brand because they cheapen its image with giveaways.

Because it is always easier and less expensive to keep an existing customer than to get a new customer (yes, we've said that already), CRM firms try to increase their **share of customer**, not share of market. Let's say that a consumer buys six pairs of shoes a year—two pairs from each of three different manufacturers. Assume one shoemaker has a CRM system that allows it to send letters to its current customers inviting them to receive a special price discount or a gift if they buy more of the firm's shoes during the year. If the firm can get the consumer to buy three or four or perhaps all six pairs from it, it has increased its share of customer. And that may not be too difficult, because the customer already likes the firm's shoes. Without the CRM system, the shoe company would probably use traditional advertising to increase sales, which would be far more costly than the customer-only direct-mail campaign. So the company can increase sales and profits at a much lower cost than it would spend to get one, two, or three new customers.

share of customer
The percentage of an individual customer's purchase of a product that is a single brand.

Lifetime Value of a Customer

As you'll recall from Chapter 1, the **lifetime value of a customer** is the potential profit a single customer's purchase of a firm's products generates over the customer's lifetime. It just makes sense that a firm's profitability and long-term success are going to be far greater if it develops long-term relationships with its customers so that those customers buy from it again and again. Costs will be far higher and profits lower if each customer's purchase is a first-time sale.

How do marketers calculate the lifetime value of a customer? They first estimate a customer's future purchases across all products from the firm over the next 20 or 30 years. The goal is to try to figure out what profit the company could make from the customer in the future (obviously, this will just be an estimate). For example, an auto dealer might calculate the lifetime value of a single customer by first calculating the total revenue the customer will generate for the company during his or her life. This figure includes the number of automobiles he will probably buy times their average price, plus the service the dealership would provide over the years, and even possibly the income from auto loan financing. The lifetime value of the customer would be the total profit the revenue stream generates.

lifetime value of a customer
The potential profit a single customer's purchase of a firm's products generates over the customer's lifetime.

Customer Equity

Today an increasing number of companies consider their relationships with customers as financial assets. These firms measure success by calculating the value of their **customer equity**—the financial value of a customer throughout the lifetime of the relationship.[56] To do this, they compare the investments they make to acquire customers and then to retain them to the financial return they'll get on those investments.

customer equity
The financial value of a customer relationship throughout the lifetime of the relationship.

Focus on High-Value Customers

Using a CRM approach, the organization prioritizes its customers and customizes its communications to them accordingly. For example, any banker will tell you that not all customers are equal when it comes to profitability. Some generate a lot of revenue because they bank interest on loans or credit cards, while others basically just use the bank as a convenient place to store a small amount of money and take out a little bit each week to buy beer. Banks use CRM systems to generate a profile of each customer based on factors such as value, risk, attrition, and interest in buying new financial products. This automated system helps the bank decide which current or potential customers it will target with certain communications or how much effort it will expend to retain an account—all the while cutting its costs by as much as a third. It just makes sense to use different types of communication contacts based on the value of each individual customer. For example, personal selling (the most expensive form of marketing communication per contact) may constitute 75 percent of all contacts with high-volume customers, while direct mail or telemarketing is more often the best way to talk to low-volume customers.

Here's my choice. . .

Real **People**, Real **Choices**

1 2 (3)
Option   Option   Option

Why do you think Jim chose option 3?

How It Worked Out at PBS Kids Sprout

Sprout implemented a dual target audience strategy with a campaign it called "We share." The campaign featured the fresh and playful spirit of Sprout's brand, while reinforcing the network's core vision of bringing parents and kids together into a child's world. Using the theme of "together time" for parents and preschoolers, print, outdoor, and TV ads linked users to SproutOnline.com, which includes crafts, activities, games, videos, and more for parents to share with their preschoolers.

To learn the whole story, visit www.mypearsonmarketinglab.com.

Brand **YOU**!

Great brands are NOT all things to all people.

The best brands target their customers and understand what is important to them. Learn how to target your brand and work smarter, not harder, to land your perfect job. Chapter 7 in *Brand You* helps your job search come into focus.

Objective Summary ➡ Key Terms ➡ Apply CHAPTER 7
Study Map

1. Objective Summary (pp. 184–185)

Identify the steps in the target marketing process.

Marketers must balance the efficiency of mass marketing, serving the same items to everyone, with the effectiveness of offering each individual exactly what she wants. To accomplish this, instead of trying to sell something to everyone, marketers follow these steps: (1) select a target marketing strategy, in which they divide the total market into different segments based on customer characteristics; (2) select one or more segments; and (3) develop products to meet the needs of those specific segments.

Key Terms

market fragmentation, p. 184
target marketing strategy, p. 184

2. Objective Summary (pp. 185–198)

Understand the need for market segmentation and the approaches available to do it.

Market segmentation is often necessary in today's marketplace because of market fragmentation—that is, the splintering of a mass society into diverse groups due to technological and cultural differences. Most marketers can't realistically do a good job of meeting the needs of everyone, so it is more efficient to divide the larger pie into slices in which members of a segment share some important characteristics and tend to exhibit the same needs and preferences. Marketers frequently find it useful to segment consumer markets on the basis of demographic characteristics, including age, gender, family life cycle, social class, race or ethnic identity, and place of residence. A second dimension, psychographics, uses measures of psychological and social characteristics to identify people with shared preferences or traits. Consumer markets may also be segmented on the basis of how consumers behave toward the product, for example, their brand loyalty, usage rates (heavy, moderate, or light), and usage occasions. Business-to-business markets are often segmented on the basis of industrial demographics, type of business based on the North American Industry Classification (NAICS) codes, and geographic location.

Key Terms

segmentation, p. 185
segmentation variables, p. 185
Generation Y, p. 185

demographics, p. 186
generational marketing, p. 186
Generation X, p. 188
baby boomers, p. 188
metrosexual, p. 189
cultural diversity, p. 192
geodemography, p. 193
geocoding, p. 193
psychographics, p. 194
VALS™ (Values and Lifestyles), p. 194
behavioral segmentation, p. 196
80/20 rule, p. 197
long tail, p. 197
usage occasions, p. 197

3. Objective Summary (pp. 198–201)

Explain how marketers evaluate segments and choose a targeting strategy.

To choose one or more segments to target, marketers examine each segment and evaluate its potential for success as a target market. Meaningful segments have wants that are different from those in other segments, can be identified, can be reached with a unique marketing mix, will respond to unique marketing communications, are large enough to be profitable, have future growth potential, and possess needs that the organization can satisfy better than the competition.

After marketers identify the different segments, they estimate the market potential of each. The relative attractiveness of segments also influences the firm's selection of an overall marketing strategy. The firm may choose an undifferentiated, differentiated, concentrated, or custom strategy based on the company's characteristics and the nature of the market.

Key Terms

targeting, p. 198
target market, p. 198
segment profile, p. 199
undifferentiated targeting strategy, p. 199
differentiated targeting strategy, p. 199
concentrated targeting strategy, p. 199
custom marketing strategy, p. 200
mass customization, p. 201

4. Objective Summary (pp. 201–204)

Understand how marketers develop and implement a positioning strategy.

After marketers select the target market(s) and the overall strategy, they must determine how they wish customers to perceive the brand relative to the competition—that is, should the brand be positioned like, against, or away from the competition? Through positioning, a brand personality is developed. Marketers can compare brand positions by using such research techniques as perceptual mapping. In developing and implementing the positioning strategy, firms analyze the competitors' positions, determine the competitive advantage offered by their product, tailor the marketing mix in accordance with the positioning strategy, and evaluate responses to the marketing mix selected. Marketers must continually monitor changes in the market that might indicate a need to reposition the product.

Key Terms

positioning, p. 201

repositioning, p. 203

retro brands, p. 203

brand personality, p. 203

perceptual map, p. 203

5. Objective Summary (pp. 204–208)

Explain how marketers increase long-term success and profits by practicing customer relationship management.

Companies using customer relationship management (CRM) programs establish relationships and differentiate their behavior toward individual customers on a one-to-one basis through dialogue and feedback. Success is often measured one customer at a time using the concepts of share of customer, lifetime value of the customer, and customer equity. In CRM strategies, customers are prioritized according to their value to the firm, and communication is customized accordingly.

Key Terms

customer relationship management (CRM), p. 204

touchpoint, p. 205

share of customer, p. 207

lifetime value of a customer, p. 207

customer equity, p. 208

Chapter Questions and Activities

Concepts: Test Your Knowledge

1. What is market segmentation, and why is it an important strategy in today's marketplace?
2. List and explain the major demographic characteristics frequently used in segmenting consumer markets.
3. Explain consumer psychographic segmentation.
4. What is behavioral segmentation?
5. What are some of the ways marketers segment industrial markets?
6. List the criteria marketers use to determine whether a segment may be a good candidate for targeting.
7. Explain undifferentiated, differentiated, concentrated, and customized marketing strategies. What is mass customization?
8. What is product positioning? What do marketers mean by creating a brand personality? How do marketers use perceptual maps to help them develop effective positioning strategies?
9. What is CRM? How do firms practice CRM?
10. Explain the concepts of share of customer, lifetime value of a customer, customer equity, and customer prioritization.

Activities: Apply What You've Learned

1. Assume that a small regional beer brewery has hired you to help them with their target marketing. They are pretty unsophisticated about marketing—you will need to explain some things to them and provide ideas for their future. In the past, the brewery has simply produced and sold a single beer brand to the entire market—a mass-marketing strategy. As you begin work, you come to believe that the firm could be more successful if it developed a target marketing strategy. Write a memo to the owner outlining the following:
   a. The basic reasons for doing target marketing in the first place
   b. The specific advantages of a target marketing strategy for the brewery
   c. An initial "short list" of possible target segment profiles
2. As the marketing director for a company that is planning to enter the business-to-business market for photocopy machines, you are attempting to develop an overall marketing strategy. You have considered the possibility of using mass marketing, concentrated marketing, differentiated marketing, and custom marketing strategies.
   a. Prepare a summary explaining what each type of strategy would mean for your marketing plan in terms of product, price, promotion, and distribution channel.
   b. Evaluate the desirability of each type of strategy.
   c. What are your final recommendations for the best type of strategy?
3. As an account executive for a marketing consulting firm, your newest client is a university—your university. You have been asked to develop a positioning strategy for the university. Develop an outline of your ideas, including the following:
   a. Who are your competitors?
   b. What are the competitors' positions?

c. What target markets are most attractive to the university?

d. How will you position the university for those segments relative to the competition?

4. Assume that a firm hires you as marketing manager for a chain of retail bookstores. You believe that the firm should develop a CRM strategy. Outline the steps you would take in developing that strategy.

Marketing Metrics Exercise

In the chapter discussion about CRM, you read about four key characteristics of CRM: share of customer, lifetime value of a customer, customer equity, and customer prioritization. Each of these elements is discussed in the context of monitoring and assessing the effectiveness of a CRM initiative.

Consider JCPenney's relatively new loyalty program, JCP Rewards. Go to their Web site (**www.jcprewards.com**) and click on "How it works." In what ways could JCPenney expect to measure the four elements of CRM above within the context of a reward program such as this? How would data be collected for each element, and how might management at JCPenney utilize that data to provide loyal customers with a very strong relationship with the firm?

Choices: What Do You Think?

1. Some critics of marketing have suggested that market segmentation and target marketing lead to an unnecessary proliferation of product choices that wastes valuable resources. These critics suggest that if marketers didn't create so many different product choices, there would be more resources to feed the hungry and house the homeless and provide for the needs of people around the globe. Are the results of segmentation and target marketing harmful or beneficial to society as a whole? Should firms be concerned about these criticisms? Why or why not?

2. One of the criteria for a usable market segment is its size. This chapter suggested that to be usable, a segment must be large enough to be profitable now and in the future and that some very small segments get ignored because they can never be profitable. So how large should a segment be? How do you think a firm should go about determining if a segment is profitable? Have technological advances made it possible for smaller segments to be profitable? Do firms ever have a moral or ethical obligation to develop products for small, unprofitable segments? When?

3. A few years ago, Anheuser-Busch Inc. created a new division dedicated to marketing to Hispanics and announced it would boost its ad spending in Hispanic media by two-thirds to more than $60 million, while Miller Brewing Co. signed a $100 million, three-year ad package with Spanish-language broadcaster Univision Communications Inc. But Hispanic activists immediately raised public-health concerns about the beer ad blitz on the grounds that it targets a population that skews young and is disproportionately likely to abuse alcohol. Surveys of Hispanic youth show that they are much more likely to drink alcohol, get drunk, and to engage in binge drinking, than their white or black peers. A senior executive at Anheuser-Busch responded, "We would disagree with anyone who suggests beer billboards increase abuse among Latino or other minority communities. It would be poor business for us in today's world to ignore what is the fastest-growing segment of our population."[56]

Manufacturers of alcohol and tobacco products have been criticized for targeting unwholesome products to certain segments of the market—the aged, ethnic minorities, the disabled, and others. Do you view this as a problem? Should a firm use different criteria in targeting such groups? Should the government oversee and control such marketing activities?

4. Customer relationship management (CRM) relies on data collected from customers to create customized or one-to-one experiences for those customers. Data are collected at various touchpoints—places in which the customer interfaces with the firm to provide information, such as at a checkout lane, on the phone, on the Web site, and so on. Do firms have an obligation to explain to customers that they are collecting information from them to populate and drive their CRM initiative, or is it inherently obvious in today's world that such practices are routine? In general, what is your personal viewpoint of database-driven positioning strategies? What are the potential pros and cons to the company and to the customer?

Miniproject: Learn by Doing

This miniproject will help you to develop a better understanding of how firms make target marketing decisions. The project focuses on the market for women's beauty-care products.

1. Gather ideas about different dimensions useful for segmenting the women's beauty products market. You may use your own ideas, but you probably will also want to examine advertising and other marketing communications developed by different beauty care brands.

2. Based on the dimensions for market segmentation that you have identified, develop a questionnaire and conduct a survey of consumers. You will have to decide which questions should be asked and which consumers should be surveyed.

3. Analyze the data from your research and identify the different potential segments.

4. Develop segment profiles that describe each potential segment.

5. Generate several ideas for how the marketing strategy might be different for each segment based on the profiles. Develop a presentation (or write a report) outlining your ideas, your research, your findings, and your marketing strategy recommendations.

Marketing in **Action** Case   Real Choices at Subaru

How do companies "share the love" with their customers? Subaru of America, the automobile manufacturing division and brand name of Japanese transportation conglomerate Fuji Heavy Industries, attempts to "share the love" through its marketing efforts. Alexander Edwards, president of market researcher Strategic Vision, says, "In their marketing they've been focusing on what creates love between the owner and the automobile." The focus of Subaru's promotional campaign is to build the connection of fun and adventure with the Subaru brand.

In 1968, Subaru of America began in Philadelphia and subsequently moved its headquarters to Cherry Hill, New Jersey. In 1986, the company was acquired by Fuji Heavy Industries. Internationally, the Subaru brand is identified by its use of boxer engines and the all-wheel drive train layout. In 2008, Subaru was the nineteenth seller of automobiles in the United States. The next year Subaru moved up to the number 11 slot. Subaru was the fastest growing mass-market automobile brand in the United States, outselling BMW.

As it grew, Subaru decided to move away from its traditional customers who were concentrated in regions like the North American Rocky Mountains, New England, and the Pacific Northwest. The challenge is to appeal to drivers who don't necessarily live in such a rough terrain, but not lose ground with its core customers.

Edwards states that the average household income of a Subaru owner is $88,000, the same as Honda Motor and $10,000 more than Toyota. The average owner is younger than the industry average and more likely to be college educated. Subaru customers are penny-wise and do not make automobile purchases that stretch their budgets. This market wants to acquire exciting driving experiences, but not with a big price tag.

Kevin Mayer, Subaru's U.S.A.'s director of marketing communications, says, "We wanted to develop the next stage of that partnership. The idea was to emotionally connect with the customers." The company's research showed that its' target market is particularly eco-friendly. One of the brand-building strategies was to build a manufacturing plant located in an official wildlife preserve with no landfill waste. Another is that at an annual sales event, customers can donate $250 of their Subaru purchase to one of five charities. The end result of these activities is that the company's acquisition costs per customer are lower than those of its competition.

Subaru takes a holistic approach to marketing its brand with the goal to demonstrate to customers that it "cares about their passion points." Subaru managers believe that the market for the upscale buyer who values freedom and frugality exceeds 60 million. There are currently 2.4 million Subarus in use, which makes for a huge opportunity in the U.S.A. In order to maintain or grow market share, the firm will have to attract more customers. Its past tactics may or may not work in other regions of the country. If Subaru has to adjust its marketing tactics, will it harm its relationships with current customers who value the company's outdoors, eco-friendly brand personality?

You Make the Call

1. What is the decision facing Subaru?
2. What factors are important in understanding this decision situation?
3. What are the alternatives?
4. What decision(s) do you recommend?
5. What are some ways to implement your recommendation?

Based on: Jeff Green and Alan Ohnsman, "At Subaru, Sharing the Love Is a Market Strategy," *Bloomberg Businessweek*, May 20, 2010 (http://www.businessweek.com/magazine/content/10_22/b4180018655478.htm); Subaru, *Wikipedia*, http://en.wikipedia.org/wiki/Subaru (accessed June 21, 2010); Andrew Hampp, "Subaru Puts Dogs in the Driver Seat for New Campaign," *Advertising Age*, February 4, 2010 (http://adage.com/article?article_id5141915).

Make marketing value decisions
(Part One)

Understand consumers' value needs
(Part Two)

Create the value proposition
(Part Three)

Process

You are here

Communicate the value proposition
(Part Four)

Deliver the value proposition
(Part Five)

Create the Value Proposition

Part Three
Overview

Part Three focuses on the value offering a firm brings to the market. This offering—which often is generically referred to as simply the "product"—can be in the form of an actual physical good, service, or other intangible. It has often been said that among the four elements of the marketing mix—product, price, promotion, and distribution—if the product itself isn't right, the other three elements of the mix probably won't overcome that deficiency in the mind of the consumer. Making decisions about developing new products and how individual consumers and organizations decide to adopt those products is critical to any marketer, and that is the topic of Chapter 8. Chapter 9 then addresses important issues marketers face in managing products, that is, the product life cycle, branding, packaging, and long-term product management.

You've no doubt heard the phrase "service economy" to describe today's marketplace. Services and other intangible offerings comprise a very large percentage of the purchase transactions nowadays throughout the world. In Chapter 10 you have the opportunity to learn about the unique characteristics of services and understand what it takes to deliver value to customers through service quality. Finally, a big part of creating the value proposition is making decisions about how to price the offering. Remember that value is like a give/get ratio—the customer gives something up (money, for instance) in the belief that a good or service will have benefits that equal or exceed the price paid. Chapter 11 provides you with great ideas on how to go about pricing your offering.

Marketing Plan Connection:
Tricks of the Trade

Recall that the Appendix at the end of the book provides you with an abbreviated marketing plan example for the fictitious S&S Smoothie Company. That plan is flagged to indicate what elements from the plan correspond to each of the Parts within the book. In addition, in Chapter 2 you found a tear-out guide called "Build a Marketing Plan," which can be used as a template for marketing planning. It is also cross-referenced to chapters by section of the marketing plan.

In the chapters within Part Three, there are major learning elements that guide you in developing two critical elements of your marketing plan: your product strategies in which you outline how you will develop and manage the offering (both physical product and service components) and your pricing strategies.

Recall that S&S Smoothie seeks to position its products as the first-choice smoothie beverage for the serious health-conscious consumer, including those who are seeking to lower their carbohydrate intake. The justification for this positioning is as follows: Many smoothie beverages are available. The S&S Smoothie formula provides superior flavor and nutrition in a shelf-stable form. S&S Smoothie has developed its product (including packaging) and pricing in support of this positioning strategy. Let's review what they're doing with these two marketing mix elements to support that positioning.

Product Strategies

To increase its leverage in the market and to meet its sales objectives, S&S Smoothie needs additional products. Two new product lines are planned:

1. *S&S Smoothie Gold:* This product will be similar to the original S&S Smoothie beverage but will come in six unique flavors:
   a. Piña Colada
   b. Chocolate Banana
   c. Apricot Nectarine Madness
   d. Pineapple Berry Crush
   e. Tropical Tofu Cherry
   f. Peaches and Dreams

   The nutritional content, critical to the success of new products in this category, will be similar to that of the original S&S Smoothie beverages. The packaging for S&S Smoothie Gold will also be similar to that used for the original product, utilizing the unique easy-to-hold, hourglass-shaped, frosted glass bottle and providing the new beverage with the same upscale image. But to set the product apart from the original-flavor Smoothie beverages in store refrigerator cases, labels will include the name of the beverage and the logo in gold lettering. The bottle cap will be black.

2. *Low-Carb S&S Smoothie:* The Low-Carb S&S Smoothie beverage will have approximately 50 percent fewer grams of carbohydrates than the original Smoothie beverage or the S&S Smoothie Gold. Low-Carb S&S Smoothie will come in the following four flavors:
   a. Strawberry
   b. Blueberry
   c. Banana
   d. Peach

   Packaging for the Low-Carb S&S Smoothie will be similar to other S&S Smoothie beverages but will include the term "Low-Carb" in large type. The label will state that the beverage has 50 percent fewer carbs than regular smoothies.

Pricing Strategies

The current pricing strategy will be maintained for existing and new products. This pricing is appropriate for communicating a high-quality product image for all S&S Smoothie products. The company believes that creating different pricing for the new beverages would be confusing and create negative attitudes among consumers. Thus, there is no justification for increasing the price of the new products.

>> You Can Do It Too!
Now, if you are working on a marketing plan as part of your course, go to **www.mypearsonmarketinglab.com** to apply what you learn in Part Three to your own marketing plan project.

Create the Product

Palo Hawken

Profile   **Info**

▼ A **Decision Maker** at **Bossa Nova Superfruit Company**

Palo Hawken is co-founder and vice president of research and innovation at Bossa Nova. His dream from an early age was to become an inventor, which led him to pursue both a degree in physics from UC Santa Cruz and a degree in industrial design from the Rhode Island School of Design. When he completed his degree at RISD in 1996, he was invited to join his mentor and former professor Stephan Copeland to help develop his consulting business. After three years of working at the Copeland studio, primarily in the contract furniture industry for companies like Steelcase, Knoll, and Innovant, Palo moved to New York to start a furniture company. It was not a very successful venture, but it eventually led him to Los Angeles, where he met Alton Johnson and joined forces to launch Bossa Nova. Palo's specialty is harnessing the underappreciated power of design from formulation, to functionality, to packaging, to maximize any given market opportunity.

💬 Palo's Info ✏

What do I do when I'm not working?
   A) Tracking wild cats in Topanga Canyon.

My hero?
   A) My father, Paul Hawken.

My motto to live by?
   A) Don't complain, don't explain.

What drives me?
   A) Knowing that there is more to do in this lifetime than I could possibly achieve.

My management style?
   A) MBA (Management By Absence).

My pet peeve?
   A) Not doing what you say you are going to do.

Here's my problem . . .

Bossa Nova was born out of the founder Alton Johnson's fascination with the fruits of Brazil. While visiting there on business, he was constantly served platters of local fruits with unrecognizable flavors and names that invariably were accompanied by intriguing stories of health and healing. Because many of these legends seemed too good to be true, he initiated one of the first university studies to analyze them in greater depth. The results were compelling enough to launch a multiyear R&D effort to find the best way to commercialize the two most promising items: the açai and guarana fruits.

In the summer of 2004, Bossa Nova was completing a regional southern California test market of its launch product: a line of premium, guarana-flavored carbonated energy drinks. This line had four SKUs: a rainforest refresher and an energy drink in both regular and diet versions. At the same time Bossa Nova was also putting the finishing touches on the crowning achievement of its R&D department—the world's first juice from an unknown Brazilian palm berry called açai. Açai had been overlooked by those outside Brazil for decades as it was notoriously hard to work with—spoiling within hours of picking and containing naturally occurring fats that looked and smelled awful. But it was also rumored to be the world's highest antioxidant fruit (the company's university research partners confirmed this finding). In the fall of 2004, after years of work, Bossa Nova had finally commercialized a method for extracting the bright purple, antioxidant-rich juice from the brownish pulp.

Palo and his partner had succeeded in creating a compelling (and expensive) new ingredient, but he wasn't sure how it fit into the product line Bossa Nova was currently selling. If indeed the company had just created the highest antioxidant juice ingredient in the world, what was the product that best took advantage of this opportunity? Palo's role as head of product development was to make sure the new company could capitalize on this opportunity with the right new product strategy.

> ## Things to remember
>
> Bossa Nova makes specialty products; people who are looking for healthy beverages aren't likely to be turned off by relatively expensive alternatives because quality is more important to them than price.
>
> A new product needs to have a crisp, clear message that shows consumers how it's different and worth switching to. Most people have never heard of açai juice so Bossa Nova will need to educate them about just what that is and why they should care.

Palo considered his Options 1·2·3

1 **Option** **Add the new açai juice ingredient to one of the three products Bossa Nova was already making to create a carbonated "antioxidant superfruit refresher."** This would create a unique health proposition in the carbonated beverage category, not known for substantive health or functional claims. This option lent itself to an easy and rapid product development cycle because Bossa Nova would be leveraging its current product platform rather than having to create a new manufacturing process. It would be fairly easy to stimulate sales because the company would be working with the same buyers, making it unnecessary to forge relationships with new retail customers. On the other hand, the powerful health story of açai could get lost in an essentially unhealthy product platform (basically, sugar water). And the new ingredient would only be included in one of the company's four SKUs, so it wouldn't create the splash Palo hoped for. In addition, the dark açai juice looked murky and intimidating in the cobalt blue bottle that gave Bossa Nova's energy drinks so much life. The company's technical people weren't sure how to change that property of the juice.

2 **Option** **Go all out: Create a new line of pure açai juices in a new package that would showcase its world-class nutritional features and benefits.** Açai would not be an ingredient in an energy drink (as in Option 1); it would be the core ingredient of a whole new product line. At that time the market leader in premium antioxidant juices, POM Wonderful, was pulling in about $20–$30 million annually in sales by promoting its antioxidant message, and Palo saw Bossa Nova as a fast follower that could grab a piece of that market. Adding a new product line could diversify the firm's product portfolio, which would also build brand awareness in two places in the store instead of one (on the carbonated, 4-pack dry shelf, and in the fresh juice case in the produce department). Bossa Nova could help define the emerging beverage category of premium/functional antioxidant juices.

- On the other hand, another product line could overextend Bossa Nova; it would force the company to spread already scarce capital and human resources across two product lines rather than focusing on one. This option would also be risky because the current product line wasn't yet firmly established in the market. Finally, the brand wasn't originally designed to embody the health message of the new açai juice line. It was too playful and needed more science/credibility, which Palo was unclear on how to achieve.

3 **Option** **Rewrite, reraise, rebuild.** Rewrite the business plan to focus on developing a single product line that could stake the claim to the title of highest antioxidant juice in the world. This option was the riskiest, because it entailed raising a significant amount of capital, selling off the existing carbonated inventory, rebranding the company, and generally moving back to square one. If this option were successful, it would result in a strong seductive product concept with a radical value proposition (both a "world's first . . ." and a "world's highest . . ."). The company would also be able to ride the coattails of $5 million of advertising by POM Wonderful designed to educate consumers about the benefits of antioxidants. Of course, this choice would entail huge risk; it would mean a decision to jettison a small but successful product line and remake/rebrand a new company that had already burned through $500,000 in seed capital. And, although the new açai juice ingredient was the world's highest antioxidant juice, it was very expensive to produce and the margins were dangerously low.

Now, put yourself in Palo's shoes: Which option would you pick, and why?

You Choose

Which **Option** would you choose, and **why**?

1. ☐YES ☐NO   **2.** ☐YES ☐NO   **3.** ☐YES ☐NO

See what **option** Palo chose on **page 239** ➡

good
A tangible product that we can see, touch, smell, hear, or taste.

attributes
Include features, functions, benefits, and uses of a product. Marketers view products as a bundle of attributes that includes the packaging, brand name, benefits, and supporting features in addition to a physical good.

Check out chapter 8 **Study Map** on page 240

1

OBJECTIVE

Explain how value is derived through different product layers.
(pp. 218–220)

Build a Better Mousetrap—And Add Value

"Build a better mousetrap and the world will beat a path to your door." Although we've all heard that adage, the truth is that just because a product is better there is no guarantee it will succeed. For decades, the Woodstream Company built Victor brand wooden mouse-traps. Then the company decided to build a better one. Woodstream's product-development people researched the eating, crawling, and nesting habits of mice (hey, it's a living). They built prototypes of different mousetraps to come up with the best possible design and tested them in homes. Then the company unveiled the sleek-looking "Little Champ," a black plastic miniature inverted bathtub with a hole. When the mouse went in and ate the bait a spring snapped upward—and the mouse was history.

Sounds like a great new product (unless you're a mouse), but the Little Champ failed. Woodstream studied mouse habits, *not* consumer preferences. The company later discovered that husbands set the trap at night, but in the morning it was the wives who disposed of the trap holding the dead mouse. Unfortunately, many of them thought the Little Champ looked too expensive to throw away, so they felt they should empty the trap for reuse. This was a task most women weren't willing to do—they wanted a trap they could happily toss into the garbage.[1]

Woodstream's failure in the "rat race" underscores the importance of creating products that provide the benefits people want rather than just new gizmos that sound like a good idea. It also tells us that any number of products, from low-tech cheese to high-tech traps, potentially deliver these benefits. Despite Victor's claim to be the "World's Leader in Rodent Control Solutions," in this case cheese and a shoe box could snuff out a mouse as well as a high-tech trap.

We need to take a close look at how products successfully trap consumers' dollars by providing value. Chapter 1 showed us that the *value proposition* is the consumer's perception of the benefits she will receive if she buys a good or service. So, the marketer's task is twofold: first, to create a better value than what's out there already and second, to convince customers that this is true.

As we defined it in Chapter 1, a *product* is a tangible good, service, idea, or some combination of these that satisfies consumer or business customer needs through the exchange process; it is a bundle of attributes including features, functions, benefits, and uses. Products can be physical goods, services, ideas, people, or places. A **good** is a *tangible* product, something that we can see, touch, smell, hear, taste, or possess. It may take the form of a pack of cookies, a digital camera, a house, a fancy new smartphone, or a chic but pricey Coach handbag. In contrast, *intangible* products—services, ideas, people, places—are products that we can't always see, touch, taste, smell, or possess. We'll talk more about intangible products in Chapter 10.

Marketers think of the product as more than just a thing that comes in a package. They view it as a bundle of **attributes** that includes the packaging, brand name, benefits, and supporting features in addition to a physical good.

We are now in Part 3 of this book, "Create the Value Proposition." The key word here is *create*, and a large part of the marketer's role in creating the value proposition is to develop and market products appropriately. In this chapter, we'll first examine what a product is and see how marketers classify consumer and business-to-business products. Then we'll go on to look at new products, how marketers develop new products, and how markets accept them (or not). In the chapters that follow, we'll look at how marketers manage and assign a price to goods and services.

Layers of the Product Concept

No doubt you've heard someone say, "It's the thought, not the gift that counts." This means that the gift is a sign or symbol that the gift giver has remembered you (or possibly it means that you hate the gift but are being polite!). When we evaluate a gift, we may consider the following: Was it presented with a flourish? Was it wrapped in special paper? Was it obviously a "re-gift"—something the gift giver had received as a gift for herself but wanted to pass on to you? These dimensions are a part of the total gift you receive in addition to the actual goodie in the box.

Like a gift, a product is everything that a customer receives in an exchange. As 📷 Figure 8.1 shows, we distinguish among three distinct layers of the product—the core product, the actual product, and the augmented product. When they develop product strategies, marketers need to consider how to satisfy customers' wants and needs at each of these three layers—that is, how they can create value. Let's consider each layer in turn.

Figure 8.1 📷 *Snapshot* | Layers of the Product

A product is everything a customer receives—the basic benefits, the physical product and its packaging, and the "extras" that come with the product.

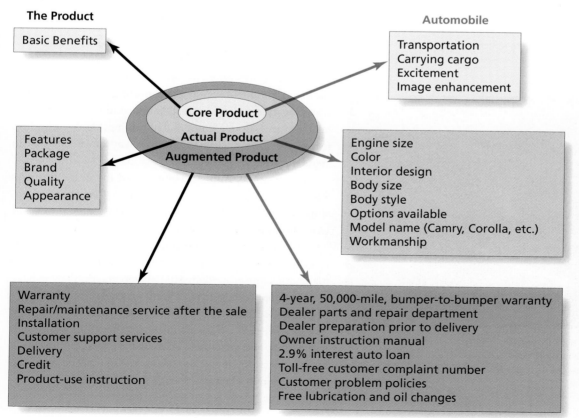

The Core Product

core product
All the benefits the product will provide for consumers or business customers.

The **core product** consists of all the benefits the product will provide for consumers or business customers. As we noted in Chapter 1, a *benefit* is an outcome that the customer receives from owning or using a product. Wise old marketers (and some young ones, too) will tell you, "A marketer may make and sell a half-inch drill bit, but a customer buys a half-inch hole." This tried-and-true saying tells us that people buy the core product, in this case, the ability to make a hole. If a new product, such as a laser, comes along that provides that outcome in a better way or more cheaply, the drill-bit maker has a problem. The moral of this story? *Marketing is about supplying benefits,* not *attributes.*

Many products actually provide multiple benefits. For example, the primary benefit of a car is transportation—all cars (in good repair) provide the ability to travel from point A to point B. But products also provide customized benefits—benefits customers receive because manufacturers add "bells and whistles" to win customers. Different drivers seek different customized benefits in a car. Some simply want economical transportation; others appreciate an environmentally friendly hybrid car; and still others want a top-of-the-line, all-terrain vehicle, or perhaps a hot sports car that will be the envy of their friends.

The Actual Product

actual product
The physical good or the delivered service that supplies the desired benefit.

The second layer—the **actual product**—is the physical good or the delivered service that supplies the desired benefit. For example, when you buy a washing machine, the core product is the ability to get clothes clean, but the actual product is a large, square, metal apparatus. When you get a medical exam, the core service is maintaining your health, but the actual one is a lot of annoying poking and prodding. The actual product also includes the unique features of the product, such as its appearance or styling, the package, and the brand name. Sony makes a wide range of televisions from tiny, battery-powered TVs for camping trips, to massive plasma televisions that can display a resolution rivaling reality—but all offer the same core benefit of enabling you to catch Stewie Griffin's antics on the latest episode of *Family Guy.*

augmented product
The actual product plus other supporting features such as a warranty, credit, delivery, installation, and repair service after the sale.

The Augmented Product

Finally, marketers offer customers an **augmented product**—the actual product plus other supporting features such as a warranty, credit, delivery, installation, and repair service after the sale. Marketers know that adding these supporting features to a product is an effective way for a company to stand out from the crowd.

For example, Apple revolutionized the music business when it created its iTunes Music Store that enables consumers to download titles directly to their digital music and video libraries. It also conveniently saves you the trouble of correctly inserting, labeling, and sorting new music on your iPod because it does that automatically. Plus, because so many of us tote around an MP3 player, you don't even have to worry about where to store all those stacks of CDs. Apple's augmented product (convenience, extensive selection, and ease of use) pays off handsomely for the company in sales and profits, and customers adore the fact that you can do it all on your laptop if you want. You crave a track or video clip and two minutes later you've got it.

© Woody Stock/Alamy

Are record albums doomed to the fate of the dinosaur? Maybe, but old-style phonograph records from the '80s and earlier are something of a cult product on sites like eBay, and connoisseurs of real "albums" swear that the analog sound is "richer" (static and all) than the crisp digital recordings of today.

2 How Marketers Classify Products

OBJECTIVE

Describe how marketers classify products.
(pp. 221–225)

So far we've learned that a product may be a tangible good or an intangible service or idea and that there are different layers to the product through which a consumer can derive value. Now we'll build on these ideas as we look at how products differ from one another. Marketers classify products into categories because they represent differences in how consumers and business customers feel about products and how they purchase different products. Such an understanding helps marketers develop new products and a marketing mix that satisfies customer needs.

Generally, products are either consumer products or business-to-business products, although sometimes consumers and businesses buy the same products, such as toilet paper, vacuum cleaners, and light bulbs. In these cases, though, businesses tend to buy a lot more of them at once. Of course, as we saw, customers differ in how they decide on a purchase, depending on whether the decision maker is a consumer or a business purchaser. Let's first consider differences in consumer products based on how long the product will last and on how the consumer shops for the product. Then we will discuss the general types of business-to-business products.

How Long Do Products Last?

Marketers classify consumer goods as durable or nondurable depending on how long the product lasts. You expect a refrigerator to last many years, but a gallon of milk will last only a week or so until it turns into a science project. **Durable goods** are consumer products that provide benefits over a period of months, years, or even decades, such as cars, furniture, and appliances. In contrast, we consume **nondurable goods**, such as newspapers and food, in the short term.

We are more likely to purchase durable goods under conditions of *high involvement* (as we saw in Chapter 5), while nondurable goods are more likely to be *low-involvement* decisions. When consumers buy a computer or a house, they will spend a lot of time and energy on the decision process. When they offer these products, marketers need to understand consumers' desires for different product benefits and the importance of warranties, service, and customer support. So they must be sure that consumers can find the information they need. One way is to provide a "Frequently Asked Questions" (FAQs) section on a company Web site. Another is to host a Facebook page, Twitter feed, message board, or blog to build a community around the product. When a company itself sponsors such forums, odds are the content will be much more favorable and the firm can keep track of what people say about its products. For example, the section of the Microsoft Web site called "Microsoft Technical Communities" allows users to interact with Microsoft employees, experts, and peers in order to share knowledge and news about Microsoft products and related technologies.[2]

In contrast, consumers usually don't "sweat the details" so much when they choose among nondurable goods. There is little if any search for information or deliberation. Sometimes this means that consumers buy whatever brand is available and reasonably priced. In other instances, they base their decisions largely on past experience. Because a certain brand has performed satisfactorily before, customers see no reason to consider other brands, and they choose the same one out of habit. For example, even though there are other brands available most consumers buy that familiar yellow bottle of French's Mustard again and again. In such cases, marketers can probably be less concerned with developing new product features to attract customers; they should focus more on creating new

durable goods
Consumer products that provide benefits over a long period of time, such as cars, furniture, and appliances.

nondurable goods
Consumer products that provide benefits for a short time because they are consumed (such as food) or are no longer useful (such as newspapers).

Figure 8.2 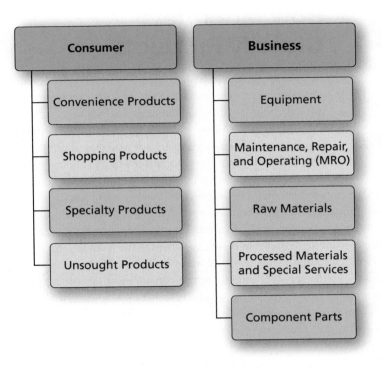 *Snapshot* |
Classification of Products

Products are classified differently depending on whether they are in the consumer or business market.

uses of the existing product, as well as pricing and distribution strategies. In fact, mustard has had something of a "condiment field day" in recent years as it is extremely low in calories and fat compared to its mayonnaise and ketchup competitors!

How Do Consumers Buy Products?

Marketers also classify products based on where and how consumers buy the product. 📷 Figure 8.2 portrays product classifications in the consumer and business marketplaces. We'll consider the consumer market first. In these contexts we think of both goods and services as convenience products, shopping products, specialty products, or unsought products. Recall that we talked about how consumer decisions differ in terms of effort they put into habitual decision making to limited problem solving to extended problem solving. We can use this idea when we want to understand why it's important to classify products. For example, it's a good guess that shoppers don't put a lot of thought into buying convenience products, so a company that sells products like white bread might focus its strategy on promoting awareness of a brand name as opposed to providing a detailed "spec sheet" we might expect to find for a smartphone.

A **convenience product** typically is a nondurable good or service that consumers purchase frequently with a minimum of comparison and effort. As the name implies, consumers expect these products to be handy and they will buy whatever brands are easy to obtain. In general, convenience products are low-priced and widely available. You can buy a gallon of milk or a loaf of bread at most any grocery store, drug store, or convenience store. Consumers generally already know all they need or want to know about a convenience product, devote little effort to purchases, and willingly accept alternative brands if their preferred brand is not available in a convenient location. Most convenience product purchases are the results of habitual consumer decision making. What's the most important thing for marketers of convenience products? You guessed it—make sure the product is easily obtainable in all the places where consumers are likely to look for it.

There are several types of convenience products:

- **Staple products** such as milk, bread, and gasoline are basic or necessary items that are available almost everywhere. Most consumers don't perceive big differences among

convenience product
A consumer good or service that is usually low-priced, widely available, and purchased frequently with a minimum of comparison and effort.

staple products
Basic or necessary items that are available almost everywhere.

brands. When selling staples, marketers must offer customers a product that consistently meets their expectations for quality and make sure it is available at a price comparable to the competition's prices. While a staple is something we usually decide to buy in advance (or at least before the fuel needle sits on "E" for too long), we buy **impulse products** on the spur of the moment. When you throw a copy of *People* magazine into your shopping cart because it has a cool photo of Lady Gaga on the cover, you're acting on impulse. When they want to promote impulse products, marketers have two challenges: to create a product or package design that is enticing and that "reaches out and grabs the customer," and to make sure their product is highly visible, for example, by securing prime end-aisle or checkout-lane space.

- As the name suggests, we purchase **emergency products** when we're in dire need; examples include bandages, umbrellas, and something to unclog the bathroom sink. Because we need the product badly and immediately, price and sometimes product quality may be irrelevant to our decision to purchase. If you ever go to Disney World in Florida during the summer months, chances are at some point you will get caught in a sudden downpour. When that happens, Disney knows that any umbrella at any price may do and the company stocks its concessions with the product. The company also rolls out the Mickey Mouse ponchos because once the sky opens up everybody's gotta have one.

- In contrast to convenience products, **shopping products** are goods or services for which consumers will spend time and effort to gather information on price, product attributes, and product quality. They are likely to compare alternatives before they buy. The purchase of shopping products is typically a limited problem-solving decision. Often consumers have little prior knowledge about these products. Because they gather new information for each purchase occasion, consumers are only moderately brand loyal; they will typically switch whenever a different brand offers new or better benefits. They may visit several stores and devote considerable effort to comparing products. Laptop computers are a good example of a shopping product because they offer an ever-expanding array of new features and functions. There are trade-offs and decisions to make about a variety of features that can be bundled including speed, screen size, weight, and battery life.

In business-to-consumer e-commerce, consumers sometimes can shop more efficiently when they use **intelligent agents** or *shopbots*—computer programs that find sites selling a particular product. Some of these programs also provide information on competitors' prices, and they may even ask customers to rate the various e-businesses that they have listed on their site so consumers can learn from other shoppers which sellers are good and which are less than desirable. We should note, however, that some sites do not wish to compete on price and don't give shopbots access to their listings.

Specialty products have unique characteristics that are important to buyers at almost any price. You can buy a mop at Target for well under $10, right? Yet the iRobot Corporation has models of its Scooba Floor Washing Robot that sell for upwards of $500! They also make equally pricey robot vacuums, pool cleaners, and gutter cleaners.[3] Other examples of specialty products include Rolex watches and Big Bertha golf clubs.

Consumers usually know a good deal about specialty products, and they tend to be loyal to specific brands. Generally, a specialty product is an extended problem-solving purchase that requires a lot of effort to choose. That means firms that sell these kinds of products need to create marketing strategies that make their product stand apart from the rest.

Unsought products are goods or services (other than convenience products) for which a consumer has little awareness or interest until a need arises. For college graduates with their first "real" jobs, retirement plans and disability insurance are unsought products. It requires a good deal of advertising or personal selling to interest people in these kinds of

impulse products
A product people often buy on the spur of the moment.

emergency products
Products we purchase when we're in dire need.

shopping products
Goods or services for which consumers spend considerable time and effort gathering information and comparing alternatives before making a purchase.

intelligent agents
Computer programs that find sites selling a particular product.

specialty products
Goods or services that has unique characteristics and is important to the buyer and for which she will devote significant effort to acquire.

unsought products
Goods or services for which a consumer has little awareness or interest until the product or a need for the product is brought to her attention.

products—just ask any life insurance salesperson. It's a real challenge to find convincing ways to interest consumers in unsought products. One solution may be to make pricing more attractive; for example, reluctant consumers may be more willing to buy an unsought product for "only pennies a day" than if they have to think about their yearly or lifetime cash outlay.

How Do Businesses Buy Products?

Although consumers purchase products for their own use, as we saw in Chapter 6 organizational customers purchase items to use in the production of other goods and services or to facilitate the organization's operation. Marketers classify business-to-business products based on how organizational customers use them. As with consumer products, when marketers know how their business customers use a product, they are better able to design products and craft the entire marketing mix. Let's briefly review the five different types of business-to-business products 📷 Figure 8.2 depicts.

equipment
Expensive goods that an organization uses in its daily operations that last for a long time.

- **Equipment** refers to the products an organization uses in its daily operations. *Heavy equipment*, sometimes called *installations* or *capital equipment*, includes items such as buildings and robotics Ford uses to assemble automobiles. Installations are big-ticket items and last for a number of years. Computers, photocopy machines, and water fountains are examples of *light* or *accessory equipment*; they are portable, cost less, and have a shorter life span than capital equipment. Marketing strategies for equipment usually emphasize personal selling and may mean custom-designing products to meet an industrial customer's specific needs.

maintenance, repair, and operating (MRO) products
Goods that a business customer consumes in a relatively short time.

- **Maintenance, repair, and operating (MRO) products** are goods that a business customer consumes in a relatively short time. *Maintenance products* include light bulbs, mops, cleaning supplies, and the like. Repair products are items such as nuts, bolts, washers, and small tools. *Operating supplies* include computer paper and oil to keep machinery running smoothly. Although some firms use a sales force to promote MRO products, others rely on catalog sales, the Internet, and telemarketing in order to keep prices as low as possible.

raw materials
Products of the fishing, lumber, agricultural, and mining industries that organizational customers purchase to use in their finished products.

- **Raw materials** are products of the fishing, lumber, agricultural, and mining industries that organizational customers purchase to use in their finished products. For example, a food company may transform soybeans into tofu, and a steel manufacturer changes iron ore into large sheets of steel used by other firms to build automobiles, washing machines, and lawn mowers. And turning one industry's waste materials into another's raw material is a great business model. Did you know that producers use cotton seeds left over from making textiles to make mayonnaise (check the ingredients on the back for cottonseed oil)?[4]

processed materials
Products created when firms transform raw materials from their original state.

- Firms produce **processed materials** when they transform raw materials from their original state. Organizations purchase processed materials that become a part of the products they make. A builder uses treated lumber to add a deck onto a house, and a company that creates aluminum cans for Red Bull buys aluminum ingots for this purpose.

- In addition to tangible materials, some business customers purchase *specialized services* from outside suppliers. Specialized services may be equipment-based, such as repairing a copy machine or fixing an assembly line malfunction, or non-equipment-based, such as market research and legal services. These services are essential to the operation of an organization but are not part of the production of a product.

component parts
Manufactured goods or subassemblies of finished items that organizations need to complete their own products.

- **Component parts** are manufactured goods or subassemblies of finished items that organizations need to complete their own products. For example, a computer manufacturer needs silicon chips to make a computer, and an automobile manufacturer needs batteries, tires, and fuel injectors. As with processed materials, marketing strategies for component parts usually involve nurturing relationships with customer firms and on-time delivery of a product that meets the buyer's specifications.

To review, we now understand what a product is. We also know how marketers classify consumer products based on how long they last and how they are purchased, and we've seen how they classify business-to-business products according to how they use them. In the next section we'll learn about the marketing of new products, or *innovations*.

From a marketing standpoint an innovation is *anything* that customers perceive as new and different.

3 "New and Improved!" The Process of Innovation

OBJECTIVE

Understand the importance and types of product innovations.
(pp. 225–227)

"New and improved!" What exactly do we mean when we use the term *new product*? The Federal Trade Commission says that (1) a product must be entirely new or changed significantly to be called new, and (2) a product may be called new for only six months.

That definition is fine from a legal perspective. From a marketing standpoint, though, a new product or an **innovation** is *anything* that customers perceive as new and different. An innovation may be a game-changing product with cutting-edge style like the Apple iPhone that is a phone *and* an iPod, or the Gillette Fusion MVP razor that looks like a device from Star Trek. It can also be an innovative communications approach such as Skype VoIP telephony over the Internet, or a new way to power a vehicle such as hydrogen fuel cell cars like the BMW Hydrogen 7, the Ford Focus FCV, or the Honda FCX Clarity. An innovation may be a completely new product that provides benefits never available before, such as personal computers when they were first introduced, or it may simply be an existing product with a new style, in a different color, or with some new feature, like Chocolate Cheerios.

innovation
A product that consumers perceive to be new and different from existing products.

Types of Innovations

Innovations differ in their degree of newness, and this helps to determine how quickly the target market will adopt them. Because innovations that are more novel require us to exert greater effort to figure out how to use them, they are slower to spread throughout a population than new products that are similar to what is already available.

As 📷 Figure 8.3 shows, marketers classify innovations into three categories based on their degree of newness: continuous innovations, dynamically continuous innovations, and discontinuous innovations. However, it is better to think of these three types as ranges along a continuum that goes from a very small change in an existing product to a totally new product. We can then describe the three types of innovations in terms of the amount of change they bring to people's lives. For example, the first automobiles caused tremendous changes in the lives of people who were used to getting places by "horse power." While a more recent innovation like GPS systems that feed us driving directions by satellite is undoubtedly cool, in a relative sense, we have to make fewer changes in our lives to adapt to them (other than not having to ask a stranger for directions when we're lost). And how about the Lexus LS 460 that can actually parallel park itself?[5]

A sweet alternative to sugar or chemicals is an innovation.

Figure 8.3 📷 *Snapshot* | Types of Innovations

Three types of innovations are continuous, dynamically continuous, and discontinuous, based on their degree of newness.

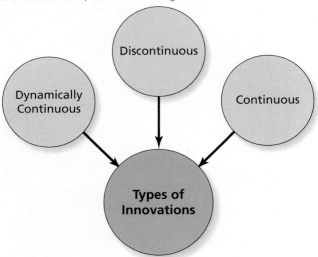

continuous innovation
A modification of an existing product that sets one brand apart from its competitors.

knockoff
A new product that copies, with slight modification, the design of an original product.

dynamically continuous innovation
A change in an existing product that requires a moderate amount of learning or behavior change.

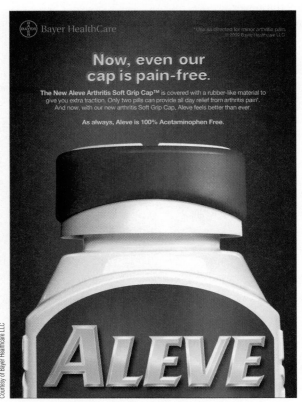

A continuous innovation makes the package easier to open.

Continuous Innovations

A **continuous innovation** is a modification to an existing product, such as when Crocs reinvigorated the market for clogs by offering a version of the comfy shoe with big holes punched in it. This type of modification can set one brand apart from its competitors. For example, people associate Volvo cars with safety, and Volvo comes out with a steady stream of safety-related innovations. Volvo was the first car to offer full front and side air bags, and beginning with some of its 2009 models you can get "Low Speed Collision Avoidance" and "Volvo City Safety." The cars have a radar system that monitors the distance of the car to the car in front of you, and if you get too close, the car's computer automatically applies the brakes.[6]

The consumer doesn't have to learn anything new to use a continuous innovation. From a marketing perspective, this means that it's usually pretty easy to convince consumers to adopt this kind of new product. For example, the current generation of high-definition plasma flat-screen monitors didn't require computer users to change their behaviors. We all know what a computer monitor is and how it works. The system's continuous innovation simply gives users the added benefits of taking up less space and being easier on the eyes than old-style monitors.

A **knockoff** is a new product that copies, with slight modification, the design of an original product. Firms deliberately create knockoffs of clothing and jewelry, often with the intent to sell to a larger or different market. For example, companies may copy the *haute couture* clothing styles of top designers and sell them at lower prices to the mass market. It's likely that a cheaper version of the gown Jennifer Aniston wears to the Academy Awards ceremony will be available at numerous Web sites within a few days after the event. It is difficult to legally protect a design (as opposed to a technological invention), because an imitator can argue that even a very slight change—different buttons or a slightly wider collar on a dress or shirt—means the knockoff is not an exact copy.

Dynamically Continuous Innovations

A **dynamically continuous innovation** is a pronounced modification to an existing product that requires a modest amount of learning or change in behavior to use it. The history of audio equipment is a series of dynamically continuous innovations. For many years, consumers enjoyed listening to their favorite Frank Sinatra songs on record players. In the 1960s they swooned as they listened to the Beatles on a continuous-play eight-track tape (requiring the purchase of an eight-track tape player, of course). Then came cassette tapes to listen to the Eagles (oops, now a cassette player is needed). In the 1980s, consumers could hear Metallica songs digitally mastered on compact discs (that, of course, required the purchase of a new CD player).

In the 1990s, recording technology moved one more step forward with MP3 technology; it allowed Madonna fans to download music from the Internet or to exchange electronic copies of the music with others, and when Mobile MP3 players hit the scene in 1998, fans could download the tunes directly into a portable player. Then, in November 2001, Apple Computer introduced its first iPod. With the original iPod, music fans could take 1,000 songs with them wherever they went. By 2006, iPods could hold 15,000 songs, 25,000 photos, and 150 hours of video. (In 2010, iPods could hold 40,000 songs, 25,000 photos, and 200 hours of video.)[7] Music fans go to the Apple iTunes music store or elsewhere to download songs and to get suggestions for new music they might enjoy. Of course, today you can do all this on your smartphone—you don't even need an iPod to have a portable music player. From radio to smartphone—an amazing journey in dynamically continuous innovation!

Discontinuous Innovations

To qualify as a **discontinuous innovation**, the product must create *major changes* in the way we live. Consumers must learn a great deal to use a discontinuous innovation because no similar product has ever been on the market. Major inventions such as the airplane, the car, and the television radically changed modern lifestyles. Another discontinuous innovation, the personal computer—facilitated by the advent of the Internet—changed the way we shop and allowed more people to work from home or anywhere else. What's the next discontinuous innovation? Is there a product out there already that will gain that distinction? Usually, marketers only know for sure through 20–20 hindsight; in other words, it's tough to plan for the next big one (what the computer industry calls "the killer app").

Convergence is one of the most talked-about forms of dynamically continuous innovations in the digital world. This term means the coming together of two or more technologies to create new systems that provide greater benefit than the original technologies alone. Originally, the phone, organizer, and camera all came together in the Palm Treo and then the Motorola Q. Cable companies now provide cellular service, land phone lines, and high-speed Internet. Today devices like Apple's iPad integrate numerous functions on one platform.

© David Levenson/Alamy

How Do We Measure Innovation?

Innovation is a complicated item to try to measure. This is because it involves not only marketing, but the firm's overall culture, leadership, and processes in place that foster innovation. Here's a short list of measures that when taken as a whole can provide a firm's "innovation report card":

Firm Strategy

- How aware are organization members of a firm's goals for innovation?

- How committed is the firm and its leadership to those goals?

- How actively does the firm support innovation among its organization members? Are there rewards and other incentives in place to innovate? Is innovation part of the performance evaluation process?

- To what degree do organization members perceive that resources are available for innovation (money and otherwise)?

Firm Culture

- Does the organization have an appetite for learning and trying new things?

- Do organization members have the freedom and security to try things, fail, and then go forward to try different things?

Outcomes of Innovation

- Does the organization have an appetite for learning and trying new things?

- Do organization members have the freedom and security to try things, fail, and then go forward to try different things?

- Number of innovations launched in the past three years

- Percentage of revenue attributable to launches of innovations during the past three years[8]

discontinuous innovation
A totally new product that creates major changes in the way we live.

convergence
The coming together of two or more technologies to create a new system with greater benefits than its separate parts.

new product development (NPD)
The phases by which firms develop new products including idea generation, product concept development and screening, marketing strategy development, business analysis, technical development, test marketing, and commercialization.

idea generation
The first step of product development in which marketers brainstorm for products that provide customer benefits and are compatible with the company mission.

product concept development and screening
The second step of product development in which marketers test product ideas for technical and commercial success.

OBJECTIVE
Show how firms develop new products.
(pp. 228–233)

4 New Product Development

Building on our knowledge of different types of innovations, we'll now turn our attention to how firms actually develop new products. There are seven phases in the process of **new product development (NPD)**, as shown in Figure 8.4: idea generation, product concept development and screening, marketing strategy development, business analysis, technical development, test marketing, and commercialization. Let's take a look at what goes on during each of these phases.

Phase 1: Idea Generation

In the initial **idea generation** phase of product development, marketers use a variety of sources to come up with great new product ideas that provide customer benefits and that are compatible with the company mission. Sometimes ideas come from customers. Ideas also come from salespeople, service providers, and others who have direct customer contact.

Often firms use marketing research activities such as the *focus groups* we discussed in Chapter 4 in their search for new product ideas. For example, a company such as ESPN that is interested in developing new channels or changing the focus of its existing channels might hold focus-group discussions across different groups of sports-minded viewers to get ideas for new types of programs.

Phase 2: Product Concept Development and Screening

The second phase in developing new products is **product concept development and screening**. Although ideas for products initially come from a variety of sources, it is up to marketers to expand these ideas into more complete product concepts. Product concepts describe what features the product should have and the benefits those features will provide for consumers.

Continuing with our Golden Arches theme (hungry yet?), everyone knows that McDonald's makes the world's best french fries—a fact that has annoyed archrival Burger King for decades. Unfortunately for BK, the chain achieved technical success but not commercial success when the chain invested heavily to out-fry Mickey D's. BK's food engineers came up with a potato stick coated with a layer of starch that makes the fry crunchier and keeps the heat in to stay fresh longer. Burger King created 19 pages of specifications for its new contender, including a requirement that there must be an audible crunch present for seven or more chews. The $70 million rollout of the new product included a "Free Fryday" when BK gave away 15 million orders of fries to customers, placed lavish advertising on the Super Bowl, and engineered official proclamations by the governors of three states. Unfortunately, the new fry was a "whopper" of a product failure. Burger King blamed the product failure on inconsistent cooking by franchisees and a poor potato crop, but a more likely explanation is that consumers simply did not like the fry as well as those they might find at certain (golden) archrivals. Just because it's new doesn't always make it better.

On the other hand, did you know that Sony was originally working *with* archrival Nintendo to create a new video game system? Executives from both sides were happy because Nintendo had the market, the intellectual property, and the know-how to do it and Sony had the financial means. However, Nintendo eventually decided not to move forward with the deal and essentially ditched Sony. The man at Sony who would have been the head guy for the joint project approached the company's president and told him that Sony could enter the market anyway without the big N's help because of the headway it had already made. Sony's CEO reportedly felt dishonored by Nintendo's behavior and approved the project. This rebuff resulted in Sony's highly regarded Playstation, which went on to seriously challenge Nintendo for gaming supremacy.[9]

Figure 8.4 *Process* | Phases in New Product Development

New product development generally occurs in seven phases.

In new product development, failures often come as frequently (or more so) than successes. BK's french fry failure illustrates the importance of screening ideas for *both* their technical and their commercial value. When screening, marketers and researchers examine the chances that a new product concept might be successful, while they weed out concepts that have little chance to make it in the market. They estimate *technical success* when they decide whether the new product is technologically feasible—is it possible to actually build this product? Then they estimate *commercial success* when they decide whether anyone is likely to buy the product. And speaking of technology-driven product innovation, take a look at Table 8.1 for some examples of "pushing out the envelope"—new products that have their roots in some pretty old-fashioned ones. But caution: Any new product today can easily be obsolete tomorrow!

Phase 3: Marketing Strategy Development

The third phase in new product development is to develop a marketing strategy to introduce the product to the marketplace, a process we began to talk about back in Chapter 2. This means that marketers must identify the target market, estimate its size, and determine how they can effectively position the product to address the target market's needs. And, of course, marketing strategy development includes planning for pricing, distribution, and promotion expenditures both for the introduction of the new product and for the long run.

Some companies encourage their designers to "think outside the box" by exposing them to new ideas, people, and places. The director of culinary innovation at McDonald's is a chef who trained at the Culinary Institute of America. He runs the chain's test kitchen and he's challenged with the tricky assignment of finding new menu concepts that work within the context of a McDonald's store. Recently, he came up with a simple idea: He took the breaded chicken the chain uses in its Chicken Selects strips, topped it with shredded cheddar jack cheese and lettuce, added a few squirts of ranch sauce, and wrapped it in a flour tortilla. McDonald's dubbed it the "Snack Wrap" and put it on the menu at a starter price of $1.29. A hit was born—the Snack Wrap is one of the most successful new product launches in company history with sales exceeding projections by 20 percent.

Phase 4: Business Analysis

Once a product concept passes the screening stage, the next phase is a **business analysis**. Even though marketers have evidence that there is a market for the product, they still must find out if the product can make a profitable contribution to the organization's product mix.

business analysis
The step in the product development process in which marketers assess a product's commercial viability.

The Cutting Edge

Facebook for NPD

During Phase Two of the new product development process—product concept development and screening—marketers frequently engage in qualitative research approaches such as focus groups to enhance the development process. In the past these have largely been in-person rather than via social networking. Today, however, Facebook looms as an effective way to get feedback. Some firms offer free product samples on their Facebook pages, but Splenda (the artificial sweetener folks) took a different approach. The company planned to introduce a pocket-size spray form of the product it called Splenda Mist. It turned to Facebook to gather valuable input from its target, women 25 and older, as well as those outside its target. Splenda used the data to plan the next stages of the product rollout.

"It's another tool in which to expose a product idea, concept, or actual product to a particular target in a very efficient way," said Ivy Brown, group product director at Splenda. Tom Arrix, VP-U.S. sales at Facebook, said other consumer-products companies are taking note of the ever-expanding possibilities the social network has to offer. "There are conversations on an ongoing basis about brands out there," Arrix said. "Innovative brand teams can come into a platform like Facebook, glean insights, and make real-time decisions." Facebook offers marketers the following guidelines for conducting market research on their site:

- The Facebook experience won't replace a formal focus group, but it can provide plenty of information that you wouldn't necessarily gather in street sampling.
- As people interact with you in such an engagement, reach of your product can be extended. Just as in the offline world, if you are giving participants samples, you want to make sure you don't run out.
- Once you've invited people in, don't abandon them. Give them regular product updates to encourage a sense of ownership.[10]

Table 8.1 | Products Yesterday, Today, and Tomorrow

YESTERDAY	TODAY	TOMORROW
Typewriter	Personal Computer	**Dragon Naturally Speaking 10** This software for computers, MP3 players, and cell phones allows you to send e-mails and instant messages, and surf the Web with voice commands. *$100,* **www.shop.nuance.com**.
Drinking Fountain	Bottled Water	**AquaSafeStraw** This portable, reusable straw removes 99.9 percent of waterborne bacteria from any water. $45, **www.aquasafestraw.com**.
Wine Cork	Synthetic Cork and Screwcap	**Skybar Wine Preservation and Optimization System** A wine bar that stores, refrigerates, pours, and preserves three bottles of wine for up to 10 days after opening. *$1,000,* **www.skybarhome.com**.
Blackboard	Dry-Erase Board	**Interactive Smart Board** This whiteboard lets you write in multiple colors, erase, zoom, and move objects around with your fingers or with one of its ink-free pens. *From $700 to $4,450,* **www.smarttech.com**.
Payphone	Cell Phone	**Google's Nexus One** This smartphone with a 3.7-inch touchscreen, a 5-megapixel camera, and Wi-Fi connectivity will help you forget the scary parts of the movie *Phone Booth*. *$529,* **www.google.com/phone**.
Mechanical Bell	Electronic Bell (Alarm Clock)	**Soleil Sun Alarm Ultima SA-2008** The 10-watt bulb grows brighter as wake-up time approaches, just like the sunrise. *$90,* **www.soleilsunalarm.com**.
Boombox	Sony Walkman	**Sony Ericsson Portable Bluetooth Speaker MBS-100** Set the speakers around the room, keep your MP3 player or smartphone in your pocket, and DJ from the dance floor. *$64,* **www.amazon.com**.
Hotel Key	Electronic Keycard	**Openways** This system sends a series of tones to a cell phone that will unlock doors. The manufacturer planned to install it in three major U.S. hotel chains and two Las Vegas casinos in 2010. **www.openways.com**.
Road Map	GPS Navigation Device	**Garmin nüvi 1690** This GPS provides real-time fuel prices, movie times, and Google Local search, along with hands-free calling. *$500,* **www.target.com**.
Checkbook	Debit Card	**RedLaser App** This iPhone application lets you scan a barcode for an item, comparison-shop online, and purchase with your phone. *$2,* **www.iTunes.com**.
Lick-and-Stick Stamp	Peel-and-Press Stamp	**Stamps.com** Pay a monthly service charge on this site, and you can print official USPS postage directly onto your envelopes. No licking, no peeling, no nothing. *$16 per month,* **www.stamps.com**.
Photo Film	Digital Camera	**Sony Cyber-shot DSC-HX5V/B** This still camera was the first of its kind to include GPS, a compass, and full advanced video codec high-definition video capability. *$350,* **www.sonystyle.com**.

Source: Lauren Parajon, "Last Tech," *Southwest Airlines Spirit Magazine*, March 2010, pp. 82–92. Prices are as of this writing.

How much potential demand is there for the product? Does the firm have the resources it will need to successfully develop and introduce the product?

The business analysis for a new product begins with assessing how the new product will fit into the firm's total product mix. Will the new product increase sales, or will it simply cannibalize sales of existing products? Are there possible synergies between the new product and the company's existing offerings that may improve visibility and the image of both? And what are the marketing costs likely to be?

Phase 5: Technical Development

technical development
The step in the product development process in which company engineers refine and perfect a new product.

If it survives the scrutiny of a business analysis, a new product concept then undergoes **technical development**, in which a firm's engineers work with marketers to refine the design and production process. For example, when Sharp Electronics began to look into the next big product innovation in home television, it soon settled on the potential of adding a fourth color pixel (yellow) to the standard palette of red, green, and blue. The company labeled the innovation "Quattron technology" and introduced it in 2010 via an innovative promotional campaign that featured actor George Takei (Sulu in the original *Star Trek* series) dressed in an engineer's lab coat talking in very scientific terms about the distinct advantages of Quattron over competitors' mere four-pixel sets. The translation of technical developments into terms that consumers can easily understand and respond to is a critical marketing function, and Sharp did this brilliantly without ever attempting to show the new screen in its ads (after all, how could you view the fourth color if you don't already have a Quattron set?). But the reaction on Takei's face when he sees the picture and says "Oh man, you have to see it" was enough to drive consumers into Best Buy and other electronics retailers in droves to see if they could tell the difference between Quattron and all the other sets lined up on the wall.[11]

The better a firm understands how customers will react to a new product, the better its chances of commercial success. For this reason, typically, a company's research-and-development (R&D) department usually develops one or more physical versions or **prototypes** of the product. Prospective customers may evaluate these mockups in focus groups or in field trials at home.

Prototypes also are useful for people within the firm. Those involved in the technical development process must determine which parts of a finished good the company will make and which ones it will buy from other suppliers. If it will be manufacturing goods, the company may have to buy new production equipment or modify existing machinery. Someone has to develop work instructions for employees and train them to make the product. When it's a matter of a new service process, technical development includes decisions such as which activities will occur within sight of customers versus in the "backroom," and whether the company can automate parts of the service to make delivery more efficient.

Technical development sometimes requires the company to apply for a **patent**. Because patents legally prevent competitors from producing or selling the invention, this legal mechanism may reduce or eliminate competition in a market for many years so that a firm gains some "breathing room" to recoup its investments in technical development.

New flavors need to undergo rigorous technical development so companies can be sure they will satisfy consumers' expectations.

prototypes
Test versions of a proposed product.

patent
A legal mechanism to prevent competitors from producing or selling an invention, aimed at reducing or eliminating competition in a market for a period of time.

Phase 6: Test Marketing

The next phase of new product development is **test marketing**. This means the firm tries out the complete marketing plan—the distribution, advertising, and sales promotion—in a small geographic area that is similar to the larger market it hopes to enter.

There are both pluses and minuses to test marketing. On the negative side, test marketing is extremely expensive. It can cost over a million dollars to conduct a test market even in a single city. A test market also gives the competition a free look at the new product, its introductory price, and the intended promotional strategy—and an opportunity to get to the market first with a competing product. On the positive side, when they offer a new product in a limited area marketers can evaluate and improve the marketing program. Sometimes test marketing uncovers a need to improve the product itself. At other times, test marketing indicates product failure; this advanced warning allows the firm to save millions of dollars by "pulling the plug."

For years, Listerine manufacturer Warner-Lambert (now owned by McNeil-PPC) wanted to introduce a mint-flavored version of the product to compete with Procter & Gamble's Scope (it originally introduced this alternative under the brand Listermint). Unfortunately, every time Warner-Lambert tried to run a test market, P&G found out and poured

test marketing
Testing the complete marketing plan in a small geographic area that is similar to the larger market the firm hopes to enter.

substantial extra advertising and coupons for Scope into the test market cities. This counterattack reduced the usefulness of the test market results for Warner-Lambert when its market planners tried to decide whether to introduce Listermint nationwide. Because P&G's aggressive response to Listermint's test marketing actually *increased* Scope's market share in the test cities, there was no way to determine how well Listermint would actually do under normal competitive conditions. Warner-Lambert eventually introduced Listermint nationally, but achieved only marginal success, so the company ultimately pulled it from the market. Today, Listerine itself is available in mint flavor as well as several other choices.[12]

As we saw in Chapter 4, because of the potential problems and expense of test marketing, marketers instead may use special computer software to conduct simulated tests that imitate the introduction of a product into the marketplace. These simulations allow the company to see the likely impact of price cuts and new packaging—or even to determine where in the store it should try to place the product. The process entails gathering basic research data on consumers' perceptions of the product concept, the physical product, the advertising, and other promotional activity. The test market simulation model uses that information to predict the product's success much less expensively (and more discreetly) than a traditional test market. As this simulated test market technology improves, traditional test markets may become a thing of the past.

Phase 7: Commercialization

commercialization
The final step in the product development process in which a new product is launched into the market.

The last phase in new product development is **commercialization**. This means the launching of a new product, and it requires full-scale production, distribution, advertising, sales promotion—the works. For this reason, commercialization of a new product cannot happen overnight. A launch requires planning and careful preparation. Marketers must implement trade promotion plans that offer special incentives to encourage dealers, retailers, or other members of the channel to stock the new product so that customers will find it on store shelves the very first time they look. They must also develop consumer sales promotions such as coupons. Marketers may arrange to have point-of-purchase displays designed, built, and delivered to retail outlets. If the new product is especially complex, customer service employees must receive extensive training and preparation.

As launch time nears, preparations gain a sense of urgency—like countdown to blastoff at NASA. Sales managers explain special incentive programs to salespeople. Soon the media announce to prospective customers why they should buy and where they can find the new product. All elements of the marketing program—ideally—come into play like a carefully planned lift-off of a Delta rocket.

Innovation genius and Apple CEO Steve Jobs has never been one to squelch precommercialization hype about his new product introductions. It has been estimated that Apple achieved prelaunch publicity worth over $500 million on the iPhone before it spent a penny on any advertising. The introduction of the iPad in 2010 was no exception to the Apple hype-creation machine. Jobs claimed that the iPad would offer an experience superior to that of netbooks, and that the 75+ million people who already owned iPhones and iPod Touches already knew how to use the iPad, which uses the same operating system and touch-screen interface. But some analysts thought the iPad would be a tougher sell than its prior product brethren in part because it is a more complex innovation than those before. Critical questions driving the long-term success of the iPad include: What apps ultimately will be made for it and how quickly will they come out? Over time, how much will the iPad cannibalize, or take sales away from, other Apple products and in particular the MacBook laptop or (more likely) the iPod Touch? How long will the iPad be available only from Apple's own stores and Best Buy? And how aggressively will Apple ultimately lower the price or introduce new models with additional features like a built-in camera?[13] The questions raised about the iPad's introduction here provide a perfect segue to the next section on adoption and diffusion of innovation.

Ripped from the Headlines

Ethical/Sustainable Decisions in the Real World

When P&G's breakthrough new Pampers Dry Max diaper was introduced in 2009, it was hailed by company executives as "the iPod of baby care." It was supposed to be a breakthrough innovation: a diaper that could legitimately claim to be 20 percent thinner and way more absorbent than its Pampers predecessors or the competition based on credible consumer tests. Dry Max uses revamped, more permeable material, which allowed P&G to eliminate the traditional mesh liner and a considerable amount of wood-based fiber that was in the old Pampers, resulting in considerably less environmental impact.

But after the introduction, a group of mostly Internet-centered critics have been increasingly vocal—review boards like **www.diapers.com** quickly lit up with highly negative comments by users (one source says the online reviews are 5 to 1 negative). Anti–Dry Max Facebook pages quickly cropped up; the main page for critics boasts more than 7,000 members, The noise is undercutting what P&G had expected to be positive buzz about the most significant innovation in 24 years for Pampers, P&G's largest global brand that has sales approaching $9 billion.

So what is the "big rub," so to speak? Basically, according to information released from a $5 million class-action lawsuit on the matter filed against P&G in mid-2010, the key issue is increased cases of diaper rash, sometimes severe, among babies who wear Dry Max. P&G is "shifting blame to parents" for the rashes, according to the complaint, "implying that [the parents] fail to change their children's diapers with sufficient frequency." In general, P&G has taken a tough stance; it denies that Dry Max contributes to increased cases of diaper rash and cites data that the malady affects more than 2.5 million babies, or one in four, at any given moment, and of those, 250,000 cases typically are severe. The company claims that a small number of vocal critics dominate the online activity and cites evidence that one person has posted complaints on at least 75 sites, with more than 50 posts on P&G's own PampersVillage.

The marketers at P&G for Dry Max need to get on top of this situation quickly in order to avoid broad and long-term damage to the Pampers brand new product introduction.

ETHICS CHECK: ↖
Find out what other students taking this course **would do** and **why** on www **.mypearsonmarketinglab .com**

5
Adoption and Diffusion of New Products

OBJECTIVE

Explain the process of product adoption and the diffusion of innovations.

(pp. 233–239)

If you were in charge of marketing for Dry Max at P&G, would you recall all the new Pampers Dry Max diapers?

☐ **YES** ☐ **NO**

In the previous section, we talked about the steps marketers take to develop new products from generating ideas to launch. Now we'll look at what happens *after* that new product hits the market—how an innovation spreads throughout a population.

A painting is not a work of art until someone views it. A song is not music until someone sings it. In the same way, new products do not satisfy customer wants and needs until the customer uses them. **Product adoption** is the process by which a consumer or business customer begins to buy and use a new good, service, or idea.

The term **diffusion** describes how the use of a product spreads throughout a population. One way to understand how this process works is to think about a new product as if it were a computer virus that spreads from a few computers to infect many machines. A brand like Hush Puppies, for example, might just slog around—sometimes for years and years. At first only a small number of people buy it, but change happens in a hurry when the process reaches the moment of critical mass. This moment of truth is called the **tipping point**.[14] For example, Sharp created the low-price, home/small-office fax market in 1984 and sold about 80,000 in that year. There was a slow climb in the number of users for the next three years. Then, suddenly, in 1987 enough people had faxes that it made sense for everyone to have one—Sharp sold a million units that year as it reached its tipping point. Along with such diffusion almost always come steep price declines—today you can buy a Sharp fax machine at Amazon for about $35.[15] The question, of course, is how long a market for traditional fax machines can be sustained, given all the other document transmission possibilities today including scan and send via e-mail attachment. That's a question we'll take up in the next chapter.

After they spend months or even years to develop a new product, the real challenge to firms is to get consumers to buy and use the product and to do so quickly so they can recover the costs of product development and launch. To accomplish this, marketers must

product adoption
The process by which a consumer or business customer begins to buy and use a new good, service, or idea.

diffusion
The process by which the use of a product spreads throughout a population.

tipping point
In the context of product diffusion, the point when a product's sales spike from a slow climb to an unprecedented new level, often accompanied by a steep price decline.

understand the product adoption process. In the next section, we'll discuss the stages in this process. We'll also see how consumers and businesses differ in their eagerness to adopt new products and how the characteristics of a product affect its adoption (or "infection") rate.

Stages in Consumers' Adoption of a New Product

Whether the innovation is better film technology or a better mousetrap, individuals and organizations pass through six stages in the adoption process. 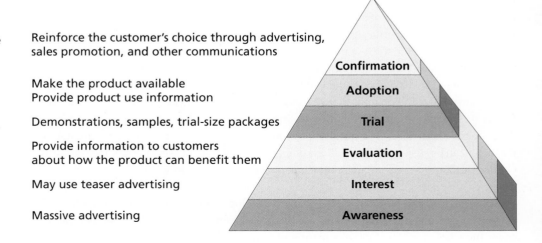 Figure 8.5 shows how a person goes from being unaware of an innovation through the stages of awareness, interest, evaluation, trial, adoption, and confirmation. At every stage, people drop out of the process, so the proportion of consumers who wind up using the innovation on a consistent basis is a fraction of those who are exposed to it.

Awareness

media blitz
A massive advertising campaign that occurs over a relatively short time frame.

Awareness that the innovation exists at all is the first step in the adoption process. To educate consumers about a new product, marketers may conduct a massive advertising campaign: a **media blitz**. For example, let's revisit our discussion of Sharp's new Quattron technology: To raise awareness that it was going to incorporate this new attribute in its AQUOS TV line the company fed bits and pieces about the product into a variety of outlets, including previews of George Takei's "Oh, my!" commercial on Twitter, Facebook, and YouTube. Within three days the ad had been viewed more than 100,000 times via Sharp's dedicated YouTube channel—remember, that's FREE promotion for Sharp![16]

At this point, some consumers will say, "So there's a new television set out there. So what?" Many of these consumers, of course, will fall by the wayside and thus drop out of the adoption process. But this strategy works for new products when at least some consumers see a new product as something they want and need and just can't live without.

Interest

For some of the people who become aware of a new product, a second stage in the adoption process is *interest*. In this stage, a prospective adopter begins to see how a new product might satisfy an existing or newly realized need. Interest also means that consumers look for and are open to information about the innovation. Volkswagen's Jetta, for instance, developed panache with the young 20s crowd around 2000 or so. But, as today's 20- and 30-something car buyers started having families and needed bigger cars with more carrying space, they began to lose interest in the Jetta. To get the lucrative young-parent group interested in the product again, Volkswagen reverted to a stronger emphasis on safety and also touted the quality and reliability virtues of German engineering. Today the

Figure 8.5 📊 *Process* | Adoption Pyramid

Consumers pass through six stages in the adoption of a new product—from being unaware of an innovation to becoming loyal adopters. The right marketing strategies at each stage help ensure a successful adoption.

Reinforce the customer's choice through advertising, sales promotion, and other communications — **Confirmation**

Make the product available
Provide product use information — **Adoption**

Demonstrations, samples, trial-size packages — **Trial**

Provide information to customers about how the product can benefit them — **Evaluation**

May use teaser advertising — **Interest**

Massive advertising — **Awareness**

brand has become successful in its positioning, which takes advantage of German mechanical prowess but at a lower price point than the other cars from Deutschland.[17] Marketers often design teaser advertisements that give prospective customers just enough information about the new product to make them curious and to stimulate their interest. Despite marketers' best efforts, however, some more consumers drop out of the process at this point.

Evaluation

In the *evaluation* stage, we weigh the costs and benefits of the new product. On the one hand, for complex, risky, or expensive products, people think about the innovation a great deal before they will try it. For example, a firm will carefully evaluate spending hundreds of thousands of dollars on manufacturing robotics prior to purchase. Marketers for such products help prospective customers see how such products can benefit them.

But as we've seen in the case of impulse products, sometimes little evaluation may occur before someone decides to buy a good or service. A person may do very little thinking before she makes an **impulse purchase**, like the virtual *Tamagotchi* (Japanese for "cute little egg") pets. For these goods, marketers design the product to be eye-catching and appealing to get consumers to notice the product quickly. Tamagotchis certainly did grab the attention of consumers—40 million of them bought the first generation of them. Toymaker Bandai Co. has since come out with a new generation of Tamagotchis—the current version allows the pet owner to control aspects of the Tamagotchi's life such as career choices and who they eventually become. Bandai's newest tagline for the product is "Start livin' the Tamagotchi life!"—a not-too-veiled reference to virtual worlds such as Second Life.[18] Some potential adopters will evaluate an innovation positively enough to move on to the next stage. Those who do not think the new product will provide adequate benefits drop out at this point.

Trial

Trial is the stage in the adoption process when potential buyers will actually experience or use the product for the first time. Often marketers stimulate trial when they provide opportunities for consumers to sample the product. Even if the trial is satisfactory, however, some prospective buyers still won't actually adopt the new product because it costs too much. Initially, this was the case with GPS systems in cars. Consumers could try out the system in rental cars from Hertz and Avis, but the price (over $2,000) understandably put off most prospective customers. Today, as prices dip below $100 at Walmart and elsewhere, many more consumers buy the units for their own cars and order them with new vehicles.[19]

Travel through some U.S. airports and you'll see Dell demonstration kiosks—a big departure from the company's usual focus on online direct marketing. That's because there is a drawback to online direct marketing: Some consumers just can't stand to buy without first touching, holding, and using a product—in short, conducting a "trial." Interestingly, people also buy Dells right at the kiosks. In retrospect, this is not too surprising, given that the passenger demographics tend toward 24 to 49 years of age, most with annual household incomes above $70,000—just the type of people who want the latest computer. Dell also showcases the PC gaming power of its higher-end computers kiosks at Gamestop locations around the country, in part because of its acquisition of Alienware—a long-time champion of high-powered PC gaming. For gamers, it's really important to touch, feel, and experience the product first-hand before they buy.[20]

It's like eating a mango.

Except it doesn't take a machete to open.

INTRODUCING FRUIT2DAY®
Real fruit bits in a blend of rich juice

All natural
No sugar added
110–120 calories
2 servings of fruit*

Find it in the produce section
A NEW WAY TO EAT FRUIT

fruit2day.com

Fruit2day
real fruit bits
in 100% juice blend

Mango Peach

Courtesy of Hero Whitewater and its agency, Kirchenbaum Bond Senecal and Partners

In the interest stage, a prospective adopter begins to see how a new product might satisfy an existing or newly realized need. This juice drinks bills itself as "a new way to eat fruit."

impulse purchase
A purchase made without any planning or search effort.

Adoption

In the *adoption* stage, a prospect actually buys the product (Hallelujah!). If the product is a consumer or business-to-business good, this means buying the product and learning how to use and maintain it. If the product is an idea, this means that the individual agrees with the concept.

Does this mean that all individuals or organizations that first choose an innovation are permanent customers? That's a mistake many firms make. Marketers need to provide follow-up contacts and communications with adopters to ensure they are satisfied and remain loyal to the new product over time.

Confirmation

After she adopts an innovation, a customer weighs expected versus actual benefits and costs. Favorable experiences make it more likely that she will become a loyal adopter as her initially positive opinions result in *confirmation*. Of course, nothing lasts forever—even a loyal customer may decide that a new product no longer meets her expectations and reject it (sort of like dropping a boyfriend). Some marketers feel that reselling the customer in the confirmation stage is important. They provide advertisements, sales presentations, and other communications to reinforce a customer's choice.

Innovator Categories

As we saw earlier, *diffusion* describes how the use of a product spreads throughout a population. Of course, marketers prefer their entire target market to immediately adopt a new product, but this is not the case. Consumers and business customers differ in how eager or willing they are to try something new, lengthening the diffusion process by months or even years. Based on adopters' roles in the diffusion process, experts classify them into five categories.

Some people like to try new products. Others are so reluctant you'd think they're afraid of anything new (do you know anyone like that?). As 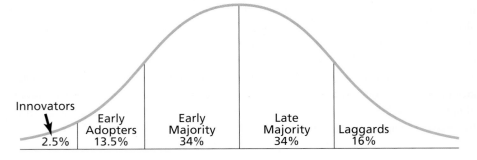 Figure 8.6 shows, there are five categories of adopters: innovators, early adopters, early majority, late majority, and laggards.[21] To understand how the adopter categories differ, we'll focus on an example of the adoption of one specific technology from the past that has had a big impact on all of us today—Wi-Fi (wireless fidelity).

Innovators

innovators
The first segment (roughly 2.5 percent) of a population to adopt a new product.

Innovators make up roughly the first 2.5 percent of adopters. This segment is extremely adventurous and willing to take risks with new products. Innovators are typically well educated, younger, better off financially than others in the population, and worldly. Innovators who

Figure 8.6 📷 *Snapshot* | Categories of Adopters

Because consumers differ in how willing they are to buy and try a new product, it often takes months or years for most of the population to adopt an innovation.

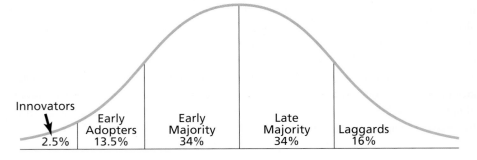

were into new technology knew all about Wi-Fi before other people had heard of it. Because innovators pride themselves on trying new products, they purchased laptops with Wi-Fi cards way back in 1999 when Apple Computer first introduced them in its laptops.

Early Adopters

Early adopters, approximately 13.5 percent of adopters, buy product innovations early in the diffusion process but not as early as innovators. Unlike innovators, early adopters are very concerned about social acceptance, so they tend to gravitate toward products they believe will make others think they are cutting-edge or fashionable. Typically, they are heavy media users and often are heavy users of the product category. Others in the population often look to early adopters for their opinions on various topics, making early adopters key to a new product's success. For this reason, marketers often target them in their advertising and other communications efforts.

Columnists who write about personal technology for popular magazines like *Time* were testing Wi-Fi in mid-2000. They experienced some problems (like PCs crashing when they set up a wireless network at home), but still they touted the benefits of wireless connectivity. Road warriors adopted the technology as Wi-Fi access spread into airports, hotels, city parks, and other public spaces. Intel, maker of the Centrino mobile platform, launched a major campaign with Condé Nast's *Traveler* magazine and offered a location guide to T-Mobile hotspots nationwide.

Early adopters like to try new products soon after a company introduces them into the market.

Early Majority

The **early majority**, roughly 34 percent of adopters, avoid being either first or last to try an innovation. They are typically middle-class consumers and are deliberate and cautious. Early majority consumers have slightly above-average education and income levels. When the early majority adopts a product, we no longer consider it new or different—it is, in essence, already established. By 2002, Wi-Fi access was available in over 500 Starbucks cafés, and monthly subscription prices were dropping rapidly (from $30 to $9.95 per month).

early adopters
Those who adopt an innovation early in the diffusion process, but after the innovators.

early majority
Those whose adoption of a new product signals a general acceptance of the innovation.

Late Majority

Late majority adopters, about 34 percent of the population, are older, even more conservative, and typically have lower-than-average levels of education and income. The late majority adopters avoid trying a new product until it is no longer risky. By that time, the product has become an economic necessity or there is pressure from peer groups to adopt. By 2004, Wi-Fi capability was being bundled into almost all laptops and you could connect in mainstream venues like McDonald's restaurants and sports stadiums. Cities across the country began considering blanket Wi-Fi coverage throughout the entire town through WiMax technology.

late majority
The adopters who are willing to try new products when there is little or no risk associated with the purchase, when the purchase becomes an economic necessity, or when there is social pressure to purchase.

Laggards

Laggards, about 16 percent of adopters, are the last in a population to adopt a new product. Laggards are typically lower in social class than other adopter categories and are bound by tradition. By the time laggards adopt a product, it may already be superseded by other innovations. By 2006, it would have seemed strange if Wi-Fi or a similar capability was not part of the standard package in even the lowest-priced laptop computer, and people began to become annoyed if Wi-Fi access wasn't available just about everywhere they might go.[22]

Understanding these adopter categories allows marketers to develop strategies that will speed the diffusion or widespread use of their products. For example, early in the diffusion

laggards
The last consumers to adopt an innovation.

A timeless classic.

JOHNSON'S® Baby Lotion. For over fifty years, women have trusted its clinically proven gentle formula to give them that unmistakable fresh scent and 24 hours of baby soft skin.

Johnson's

"Classic" brands appeal to consumers who value consistency and predictability.

relative advantage
The degree to which a consumer perceives that a new product provides superior benefits.

compatibility
The extent to which a new product is consistent with existing cultural values, customs, and practices.

Palo Hawken

APPLYING ▽ Complexity

Palo and his colleagues realized they were better off with a simple, focused message to make it more likely that consumers would adopt their new Bossa Nova beverage product. ➡

process, marketers may put greater emphasis on advertising in special-interest magazines to attract innovators and early adopters. Later they may lower the product's price or come out with lower-priced models with fewer "bells and whistles" to attract the late majority. We will talk more about strategies for new and existing products in the next chapter.

Product Factors That Affect the Rate of Adoption

Not all products are successful, to say the least. Let's see if you've ever heard of these classic boo-boos in new product introduction:

- Crystal Pepsi—Same Pepsi taste but clear in color. Consumers didn't equate the look with the flavor.

- Clairol Look of Buttermilk shampoo—Consumers pondered what exactly *was* the "Look of Buttermilk" and why would they want it?

- Betamax video player—Sony refused to allow anyone else to make the players and the rest of the industry went to VHS format.

- Snif-T-Panties—Yes, women's underwear that smelled like bananas, popcorn, whiskey, or pizza. What were they thinking![23]

The reason for most product failures is really pretty simple—consumers did not perceive that the products satisfied a need better than competitive products already on the market. If you *could* predict which new products will succeed and which will fail, you'd quickly be in high demand as a marketing consultant by companies worldwide. That's because companies make large investments in new products, but failures are all too frequent. Experts suggest that between one-third and one-half of all new products fail. As you might expect, a lot of people try to develop research techniques that enable them to predict whether a new product will be hot or not.

Researchers identify five characteristics of innovations that affect the rate of adoption: relative advantage, compatibility, complexity, trialability, and observability.[24] The degree to which a new product has each of these characteristics affects the speed of diffusion. It may take years for a market to widely adopt a new product. Let's take a closer look at the humble microwave oven—a product that was highly innovative in its early days but now is generally a low-priced staple of every kitchen (and every college apartment and dorm)—as an example to better understand why each of these five factors is important.

- **Relative advantage** describes the degree to which a consumer perceives that a new product provides superior benefits. In the case of the microwave oven, consumers in the 1960s did not feel that the product provided important benefits that would improve their lives. But by the late 1970s, that perception had changed because more women had entered the workforce. The 1960s woman had all day to prepare the evening meal, so she didn't need the microwave. In the 1970s, however, when many women left home for work at 8:00 A.M. and returned home at 6:00 P.M., an appliance that would "magically" defrost a frozen chicken and cook it in 30 minutes provided a genuine advantage.

- **Compatibility** is the extent to which a new product is consistent with existing cultural values, customs, and practices. Did consumers see the microwave oven as being compatible with existing ways of doing things? Hardly. Cooking on paper plates? If you put a paper plate in a conventional oven, you'll likely get a visit from the fire department. By anticipating compatibility issues early in the new-product development stage, marketing strategies can address such problems in planning communications programs, or there may be opportunities to alter product designs to overcome some consumer objections.

- **Complexity** is the degree to which consumers find a new product or its use difficult to understand. Many microwave users today haven't a clue about how a microwave oven cooks food. When appliance manufacturers introduced the first microwaves, they explained that this new technology causes molecules to move and rub together, which creates friction that produces heat. Voilà! Cooked pot roast. But that explanation was too complex and confusing for the homemaker of the Ozzie and Harriet days back in the 1950s.

- **Trialability** is the ease of sampling a new product and its benefits. Marketers took a very important step in the 1970s to speed up adoption of the microwave oven—product trial. Just about every store that sold microwaves invited shoppers to visit the store and sample an entire meal a microwave cooked.

- **Observability** refers to how visible a new product and its benefits are to others who might adopt it. The ideal innovation is easy to see. For example, for a generation of kids, scooters like the Razor became the hippest way to get around as soon as one preteen saw her friends flying by. That same generation observed its friends trading Pokémon cards and wanted to join in. In the case of the microwave, it wasn't quite so readily observable for its potential adopters—only close friends and acquaintances who visited someone's home would likely see an early adopter using it. But the fruits of the microwave's labors—tasty food dishes—created lots of buzz at office water coolers and social events and its use spread quickly.

Now that you've learned the basics of creating a product, read "Real People, Real Choices: How It Worked Out" to see which strategy Palo Hawken selected for Bossa Nova.

complexity
The degree to which consumers find a new product or its use difficult to understand.

trialability
The ease of sampling a new product and its benefits.

observability
How visible a new product and its benefits are to others who might adopt it.

Here's my choice. . .

Real **People**, Real **Choices**

Why do you think Palo chose option 3?

1 Option   **2** Option   **3** Option

How It Worked Out at Bossa Nova
Bossa Nova clung to Options 1 and 2 for many months. Then Palo and his colleagues took the leap and chose Option 3. They created Bossa Nova Açai juice in three flavors. Bossa Nova took its first order from Whole Foods Market and went on to be picked up by most other major grocery retailers in the United States.

To learn the whole story, visit www.mypearsonmarketinglab.com.

Brand **You**!

Companies don't just hire people—they hire people who produce results.

Show prospective employers how you can deliver results by identifying your features, benefits, and extras in Chapter 8 of *Brand You*.

Kim Richmond Fourth Edition

Brand YOU

MARKETING 7E **real** People, **real** Choices

Solomon | Marshall | Stuart

Objective Summary ➡ Key Terms ➡ Apply

CHAPTER 8
Study Map

---

1. Objective Summary (pp. 218–220)

Explain how value is derived through different product layers.

Products can be physical goods, services, ideas, people, or places. A good is a *tangible* product, something that we can see, touch, smell, hear, taste, or possess. In contrast, *intangible* products—services, ideas, people, places—are products that we can't always see, touch, taste, smell, or possess. Marketers think of the product as more than just a thing that comes in a package. They view it as a bundle of attributes that includes the packaging, brand name, benefits, and supporting features in addition to a physical good. The key issue is the marketer's role in creating the value proposition in order to develop and market products appropriately.

A product may be anything tangible or intangible that satisfies consumer or business-to-business customer needs. Products include goods, services, ideas, people, and places. The core product is the basic product category benefits and customized benefit(s) the product provides. The actual product is the physical good or delivered service, including the packaging and brand name. The augmented product includes both the actual product and any supplementary services, such as warranty, credit, delivery, installation, and so on.

Key Terms

good, p. 218

attributes p. 218

core product, p. 220

actual product, p. 220

augmented product, p. 220

2. Objective Summary (pp. 221–225)

Describe how marketers classify products.

Marketers generally classify goods and services as either consumer or business-to-business products. They further classify consumer products according to how long they last and by how they are purchased. Durable goods provide benefits for months or years, whereas nondurable goods are used up quickly or are useful for only a short time. Consumers purchase convenience products frequently with little effort. Customers carefully gather information and compare different brands on their attributes and prices before buying shopping products. Specialty products have unique characteristics that are important to the buyer. Customers have little interest in unsought products until a need arises. Business products are for commercial uses by organizations. Marketers classify business products according to how they are used, for example, equipment; maintenance, repair, and operating (MRO) products; raw and processed materials; component parts; and business services.

Key Terms

durable goods, p. 221

nondurable goods, p. 221

convenience product, p. 222

staple products, p. 222

impulse products, p. 223

emergency products, p. 223

shopping products, p. 223

intelligent agents, p. 223

specialty product, p. 223

unsought products, p. 223

equipment, p. 224

maintenance, repair, and operating (MRO) products, p. 224

raw materials, p. 224

processed materials, p. 224

component parts, p. 224

3. Objective Summary (pp. 225–227)

Understand the importance and types of product innovations.

Innovations are anything consumers perceive to be new. Understanding new products is important to companies because of the fast pace of technological advancement, the high cost to companies for developing new products, and the contributions to society that new products can make. Marketers classify innovations by their degree of newness. A continuous innovation is a modification of an existing product, a dynamically continuous innovation provides a greater change in a product, and a discontinuous innovation is a new product that creates major changes in people's lives.

Key Terms

innovation, p. 225

continuous innovation, p. 226

knockoff, p. 226

dynamically continuous innovation, p. 226

discontinuous innovation, p. 227

convergence, p. 227

4. Objective Summary (pp. 228–233)

Show how firms develop new products.

In new product development, marketers generate product ideas from which product concepts are first developed and then screened. Next they develop a marketing strategy and conduct a business analysis to estimate the profitability of the new product. Technical development includes planning how the product will be manufactured and may mean obtaining a patent. Next, the effectiveness of the new product may be assessed in an actual or a simulated test market. Finally, the product is launched, and the entire marketing plan is implemented.

Key Terms

new product development (NPD) p. 228

idea generation, p. 228

product concept development and screening, p. 228

business analysis, p. 229

technical development, p. 230

prototypes, p. 231

patent p. 231

test marketing, p. 231

commercialization, p. 232

5. Objective Summary (pp. 233–239)

Explain the process of product adoption and the diffusion of innovations.

Product adoption is the process by which an individual begins to buy and use a new product, whereas the diffusion of innovations is how a new product spreads throughout a population. The stages in the adoption process are awareness, interest, trial, adoption, and confirmation. To better understand the diffusion process, marketers classify consumers—according to their readiness to adopt new products—as innovators, early adopters, early majority, late majority, and laggards.

Five product characteristics that have an important effect on how quickly (or if) a new product will be adopted by consumers are relative advantage, compatibility, product complexity, trialability, and observability. Similar to individual consumers, organizations differ in their readiness to adopt new products based on characteristics of the organization, its management, and characteristics of the innovation.

Key Terms

product adoption, p. 233

diffusion, p. 233

tipping point, p. 233

media blitz, p. 234

impulse purchase, p. 235

innovators, p. 236

early adopters, p. 237

early majority, p. 237

late majority, p. 237

laggards, p. 237

relative advantage, p. 238

compatibility, p. 238

complexity, p. 239

trialability, p. 239

observability, p. 239

Chapter **Questions** and **Activities**

Concepts: Test Your Knowledge

1. What is the difference between the core product, the actual product, and the augmented product?
2. What is the difference between a durable good and a nondurable good? What are the main differences among convenience, shopping, and specialty products?
3. What is an unsought product? How do marketers make such products attractive to consumers?
4. What types of products are bought and sold in business-to-business markets?
5. What is a new product? Why is understanding new products so important to marketers? What are the types of innovations?
6. List and explain the steps marketers undergo to develop new products.
7. What is a test market? What are some pros and cons of test markets?
8. Explain the stages a consumer goes through in the adoption of a new product.
9. List and explain the categories of adopters.
10. What product factors affect the rate of adoption of innovations?
11. Explain how organizations may differ in their willingness to buy and use new industrial products.

Activities: Apply What You've Learned

1. Assume that you are the director of marketing for the company that has developed a smartphone to outdo the iPhone. How would you go about convincing the late majority to go ahead and adopt it—especially since they still haven't quite caught onto the iPhone yet?
2. Assume that you are employed in the marketing department of a firm that is producing a hybrid automobile. In developing this product, you realize that it is important to provide a core product, an actual product, and an augmented product that meets the needs of customers. Develop an outline of how your firm might provide these three product layers in the hybrid car.
3. Firms go to great lengths to develop new product ideas. Sometimes new ideas come from brainstorming, in which groups of individuals get together and try to think of as many different, novel, creative—and hopefully profitable—ideas for a new product as possible. With a group of other students, participate in brainstorming for new product ideas for one of the following (or some other product of your choice):
   • An exercise machine with some desirable new features
   • A combination shampoo and body wash
   • A new type of university
   Then, with your class, screen one or more of the ideas for possible further product development.
4. As a member of a new product team with your company, you are working to develop an electric car jack that would make changing tires for a car easier. You are considering conducting a test market for this new product. Outline the

pros and cons for test marketing this product. What are your recommendations?

Marketing Metrics Exercise

The chapter provides a discussion on measuring innovation and outlines some important metrics related to firm strategy, firm culture, and outcomes of innovation—an "Innovation Report Card." Apple is often cited as an example of a highly innovative firm that is highly engaged in new product development and continuous product innovation. Their success, both with consumers and in the financial markets, has been incredible in recent years. Between the unveiling of the iPad in late January 2010 and its first sale in early April, Apple's stock rose more than 10 percent by riding on the hype around the new product. Most firms would like to come even close to the success Apple achieves through innovation.

Review the questions in the chapter section "Measuring Innovation." Your job is to go to the Apple Web site and also to review some articles and news stories online about Apple's new product introductions. Look for evidence to be able to answer these metrics questions related to innovation as applied to Apple. How does Apple score on the "Innovation Report Card"?

Choices: What Do You Think?

1. Technology is moving at an ever-increasing speed, and this means that new products enter and leave the market faster than ever. What are some products you think technology might be able to develop in the future that you would like? Do you think these products could add to a company's profits?
2. In this chapter, we talked about the core product, the actual product, and the augmented product. Does this mean that marketers are simply trying to make products that are really the same seem different? When marketers understand these three layers of the product and develop products with this concept in mind, what are the benefits to consumers? What are the hazards of this type of thinking?
3. Discontinuous innovations are totally new products—something seldom seen in the marketplace. What are some examples of discontinuous innovations introduced in the past 50 years? Why are there so few discontinuous innovations? What products have companies recently introduced that you believe will end up being regarded as discontinuous innovations?
4. Consider the differences in marketing to consumer markets versus business markets. Which aspects of the processes of product adoption and diffusion apply to both markets? Which aspects are unique to one or the other? Provide evidence of your findings.
5. In this chapter, we explained that knockoffs are slightly modified copies of original product designs. Should knockoffs be illegal? Who is hurt by knockoffs? Is the marketing of knockoffs good or bad for consumers in the short run? In the long run?

6. It is not necessarily true that all new products benefit consumers or society. What are some new products that have made our lives better? What are some new products that have actually been harmful to consumers or to society? Should there be a way to monitor or "police" new products that are introduced to the marketplace?

Miniproject: Learn by Doing

What product characteristics do consumers think are important in a new product? What types of service components do they demand? Most important, how do marketers know how to develop successful new products? This miniproject is designed to let you make some of these decisions.

1. Create (in your mind) a new product item that might be of interest to college students such as yourself. Develop a written description and possibly a drawing of this new product.

2. Show this new product description to a number of your fellow students who might be users of the product. Ask them to tell you what they think of the product. Some of the questions you might ask them are the following:
   - What is your overall opinion of the new product?
   - What basic benefits would you expect to receive from the product?
   - What about the physical characteristics of the product? What do you like? Dislike? What would you add? Delete? Change?
   - What do you like (or would you like) in the way of product packaging?
   - What sort of services would you expect to receive with the product?
   - Do you think you would try the product? How could marketers influence you to buy the product?

Develop a summary based on what you found. Include your recommendations for changes in the product and your beliefs about the potential success of the new product.

Marketing in **Action** Case   Real Choices at KFC

If there is no bread, is it really a sandwich? That's the question that many customers have been asking the Kentucky Fried Chicken (KFC) fast-food retail chain. In 2010, KFC released its latest addition to its menu, the "Double Down." KFC promotes the new item in its advertisements, stating that it is "so much 100-per-cent premium chicken, we didn't have room for a bun." The sandwich is an attempt to grow revenue in a very competitive business. The United States has the largest fast-food market in the world. Many competitors offer products that are considered the same, and the rivalry compels prices that constrain profit margins.

KFC began in a gas station in North Corbin, Kentucky, during the Great Depression. The success of the eating establishment called Sanders Court & Café led to expansion. The first Kentucky Fried Chicken retail store opened in 1952 in South Salt Lake, Utah. Eventually expanding to Canada, by the early 1960s, Kentucky Fried Chicken was sold in over 600 franchised outlets. Since that time, the fast-food restaurant has changed ownership multiple times. Today the brand is owned by Yum! Brands and is based in Louisville, Kentucky. There are more than 14,000 KFC outlets in more than 80 countries and territories around the world, serving some 12 million customers each day.

According to **KFC.com**, the Double Down "features two thick and juicy boneless white meat chicken filets (Original Recipe® or Grilled), two pieces of bacon, two melted slices of Monterey Jack and pepper jack cheese and Colonel's Sauce." Although it was initially offered on a limited-time basis, KFC decided to add the item to its menu permanently. The company's change of course was related to strong sales driven in part by people eating the sandwich on YouTube and popular television personality Stephen Colbert consuming one on *The Colbert Report* television show. KFC reports that the launch is one of their most successful ever.

From a nutritional standpoint, the Double Down is 540 calories, 32 grams of fat, and 1,380 milligrams of sodium. The grilled version is 460 calories, 23 grams of fat and 1,430 milligrams of sodium. The level of sodium in the sandwich is drawing a great deal of concern from customers and health advocacy organizations. Many critics are questioning why KFC introduced this option in the midst of building its brand image as a fast-food restaurant offering healthier menu choices. Lona Sandon, a registered dietitian and spokesperson for the American Dietetic Association, says, "You are getting large amounts of total fat and saturated fat by eating a sandwich like this, and this is very detrimental to your overall heart health."

The fast-food retail market is in a constant state of competitive fervor. Are sandwiches like the Double Down the future of fast-food chains? The dilemma for companies like KFC is, how do you appeal to both the healthy market and the indulgent market? Many customers prefer healthy choices when considering fast food. However, there are also numerous diners to whom the appeal of fat, salt, and processed carbs is irresistible. But the general issue of obesity as an epidemic leading to major health problems has become front page news. The choice of menu items must lead to long-term profitability and competitive market advantage, but KFC will have to find a way to balance potential public relations concerns and still maintain its bottom line.

You Make the Call

1. What is the decision facing KFC?
2. What factors are important in understanding this decision situation?
3. What are the alternatives?
4. What decision(s) do you recommend?
5. What are some ways to implement your recommendation?

Based on: Sam Sifton, "On Ingesting KFC's New Product, the 'Double Down,'" *The New York Times*, April 12, 2010 (http://dinersjournal .blogs.nytimes.com/2010/04/12/on-ingesting-kfcs-new-product-the-double-down/ ?scp51&sq5new%20product&st5cse); KFC, *Wikipedia*, http://en.wikipedia.org/wiki/Kfc (accessed June 25, 2010); Double Down (sandwich), *Wikipedia*, http://en.wikipedia .org/wiki/Double_Down_(sandwich) (accessed June 25, 2010); Rosemary Black, "KFC's New 'Double Down' Sandwich Swaps Bun for Two Deep-Fried Chicken Breasts, Extra Calories," *New York Daily News*, August 26, 2009; Gerrick D. Kennedy, "KFC's Double Down: A Cheesy, Sodium-Filled Sandwich—Will You Be Buying?" *Los Angeles Times*, April 12, 2010 (http://dinersjournal.blogs.nytimes.com/2010/04/12/ on-ingesting-kfcs-new-product-the-double-down/ ?scp51&sq5new%20product&st5cse).

Manage the Product

David Clark

Profile | **Info**

▼ A Decision Maker at General Mills

David Clark is vice president, Big G Adult Cereals at General Mills. Since July 2007, he has been responsible for leading the development and execution of growth strategies for several iconic brands including Wheaties, Total, Chex, and Fiber One. In November 2008, he was recognized as being among the Marketing Top 50 by *Advertising Age*.

Prior to his responsibilities in the Big G division, David was the marketing director for General Mills Foodservice from November 2003 to July 2007. In this assignment, David led the Brand Marketing, Channel Marketing, and Promotions Marketing teams in driving growth across 13 product platforms within the Foodservice Distributor channel.

From June 1997 to November 2003, David held various marketing roles including marketing manager for Progresso Soup, marketing manager for Green Giant Frozen Vegetables, and associate marketing manager for Old El Paso Mexican Food.

Although David has spent the majority of his career in marketing and general management leadership positions, his early career experience in marketing research, category management, and sales were instrumental in building a foundational understanding of consumer behavior and the consumer packaged goods industry.

David holds a bachelor's degree from the University of Tennessee, Knoxville, and an MBA from the University of Minnesota Carlson School. He currently resides in Minneapolis, Minnesota, with his wife, Molly, and three children.

💬 David's Info

What do I do when I'm not working?
A) Tennis, running, and all things digital.

Career high?
A) Leading the Wheaties brand and working with five top athletes (Peyton Manning, Albert Pujols, Kevin Garnett, Bryan Clay, and Hunter Kemper) to co-create a new Breakfast of Champions, Wheaties Fuel.

A job-related mistake I wish I hadn't made?
A) Thinking that it's easier to gain new consumers than keep current ones. A lesson no one wants to learn twice.

My hero?
A) My mom, who taught me that honest, hard work and treating others with respect are the real secrets to success.

My motto to live by?
A) See what everyone sees; think what no one has thought.

What drives me?
A) The possibilities that can come from a great idea.

Here's my problem...

Fiber One cereal was launched in 1985. One of the first high-fiber cereals on the market, the product delivered 57 percent of one's daily value of fiber per bowl. It gained a small but intensely loyal following of older consumers who often learned about the brand from a doctor or pharmacist.

Fiber One sat quietly on the shelf as an average performer until 2002. Then the Atkins Diet generated a lot of interest in fiber as a tool to offset carbohydrate levels in foods. Fiber One sales started to grow. In the years following, increased coverage in the media and medical community about the benefits of fiber increased consumer awareness and interest in the nutrient.

Due to the boom in consumer interest in fiber, Fiber One was uniquely positioned for growth from increased marketing investment that would build awareness about the brand. General Mills launched new brand extensions including Fiber One Honey Clusters Cereal and Fiber One Oats and Chocolate Snack Bars. The brand took on a fresh, more contemporary look with a packaging redesign. Now, the big question was how the core Fiber One brand should be positioned and grow as it matured through its life cycle.

Things to remember

David needed to define a strategy that would reinforce a consistent and desirable brand meaning for Fiber One as it "aged" through its product life-cycle.

Consumers already had strong feelings about fiber—basically it's good for you but it tastes bad.

Fiber's positive relationship to digestive health is attractive to older consumers, but this link is a turnoff to younger ones.

to add fiber to their diets. A superiority message would appeal to their greatest need. However, products in the fiber supplement category (Benefiber, Metamucil) already advertised their superiority over other high-fiber foods. And younger consumers who were just beginning to seek more fiber in their diets were less willing to trade off taste; they often described the taste of fiber products as "cardboard." They thought high-fiber products were "old people food," and this was a turnoff.

David considered his **Options** 1·2·3

Option 1

Own the position of "Fiber Superiority." Fiber One is very high in fiber. For example, it takes 3.5 cups of broccoli to get the same fiber as one bowl of Fiber One Original Cereal. Bringing this comparison to life could make a powerful marketing visual on which to build a campaign. The cereal's heaviest users tend to be older consumers (age 55+) who have the greatest desire

Option 2

Own the position of "Great Tasting High Fiber." Consumers pointed to the poor taste of fiber as the number-one barrier to getting more fiber in their diets. They rated the taste of recent new product launches like Fiber One Honey Clusters Cereal and Oats and Chocolate Snack Bars as surprisingly good given their high fiber content. On the other hand, fiber delivers many important health benefits to consumers (weight management, heart health, digestive health). Failure to position against the health benefits of fiber could be an opportunity lost to competition. In addition, consumers might have such a negative association with fiber products that they might not believe a message that stressed its good taste.

Option 3

Own the position of "Digestive Health." Consumers primarily think about fiber in terms of its digestive benefits. This is particularly appealing to the growing baby boomer demographic. They were already snapping up products in other categories (especially yogurt) because of their digestive health benefits. However, other cereal brands already were talking about digestive health benefits. And this topic tended to polarize shoppers. While older consumers valued digestive efficiency, younger consumers found this a turnoff or even comical.

Now, put yourself in David's shoes: Which option would you choose, and why?

You Choose

Which **Option** would you choose, and **why**?
1. ☐YES ☐NO   2. ☐YES ☐NO   3. ☐YES ☐NO

See what **option** David chose on **page 267** ➡

Chapter 9

Objective Outline

1. Explain the different product objectives and strategies a firm may choose. (pp. 246–251)

   PRODUCT PLANNING: USE PRODUCT OBJECTIVES TO DECIDE ON A PRODUCT STRATEGY (p. 246)

2. Understand how firms manage products throughout the product life cycle. (pp. 252–255)

   MARKETING THROUGHOUT THE PRODUCT LIFE CYCLE (p. 252)

3. Discuss how branding strategies create product identity. (pp. 255–262)

   CREATE PRODUCT IDENTITY: BRANDING DECISIONS (p. 255)

4. Explain how packaging and labeling contribute to product identity. (pp. 262–265)

   CREATE PRODUCT IDENTITY: THE PACKAGE AND LABEL (p. 262)

5. Describe how marketers structure organizations for new and existing product management. (pp. 266–267)

   ORGANIZE FOR EFFECTIVE PRODUCT MANAGEMENT (p. 266)

product management
The systematic and usually team-based approach to coordinating all aspects of a product's marketing initiative including all elements of the marketing mix.

1

OBJECTIVE

Explain the different product objectives and strategies a firm may choose.
(pp. 246–251)

Product Planning: Use Product Objectives to Decide on a Product Strategy

What makes one product fail and another succeed? It's worth re-emphasizing what you learned in Chapter 2: *Firms that plan well succeed.* Product planning plays a big role in the firm's *marketing planning.* Strategies the product plan outlines spell out how the firm expects to develop a value proposition that will meet marketing objectives. Product planning is guided by the continual process of **product management**, which is the systematic and usually team-based approach to coordinating all aspects of a product's marketing initiative including all elements of the marketing mix. In some companies, product management is sometimes also called *brand management*, and the terms refer to essentially the same thing. The organization members that coordinate these processes are called *product managers* or *brand managers.* We'll discuss the role of these individuals in more detail later in the chapter.

As more and more competitors enter the global marketplace and as technology moves forward at an ever-increasing pace, firms create products that grow, mature and then decline at faster and faster speeds. This means that smart product management strategies are more critical than ever. Marketers just don't have the luxury of trying one thing, finding out it doesn't work, and then trying something else.

In Chapter 8, we talked about how marketers think about products—both core and augmented—and about how companies develop and introduce new products. In this chapter, we'll finish the product part of the story as we see how companies manage products, and then we'll examine the steps in product planning as Figure 9.1 outlines. These steps include developing product objectives and the strategies required to successfully market products as they evolve from "new kids on the block" to tried-and-true favorites—and in some cases finding new markets for these favorites. Next, we'll discuss branding and packaging, two of the more important tactical decisions product planners make. Finally, we'll examine how firms organize for effective product management. Let's start with how firms develop product-related objectives.

When marketers develop product strategies, they make decisions about product benefits, features, styling, branding, labeling, and packaging. But what do they want to accomplish? Clearly stated product objectives provide focus and direction. They should support the broader marketing objectives of the business unit in addition to being consistent with the firm's overall mission. For example, the objectives of the firm may focus on return on investment (ROI). Marketing objectives then may concentrate on building market share and/or the unit or dollar sales volume necessary to attain that return on investment. Product objectives need to specify how product decisions will contribute to reaching a desired market share or level of sales.

To be effective, product-related objectives must be measurable, clear, and unambiguous—and feasible. Also, they must indicate a specific time frame.

Check out chapter 9 Study Map on page 268

Consider, for example, how Amy's, a popular organic and health-conscious frozen ethnic entrée manufacturer, might state its product objectives:

- "In the upcoming fiscal year, reduce the fat and calorie content of our products to satisfy consumers' health concerns."

- "Introduce three new items this quarter to the product line to take advantage of increased consumer interest in Mexican foods."

- "During the coming fiscal year, improve the chicken entrées to the extent that consumers will rate them better-tasting than the competition."

Planners must keep in touch with their customers so that their objectives accurately respond to their needs. An up-to-date knowledge of competitive product innovations also is important to develop product objectives. Above all, these objectives should consider the *long-term implications* of product decisions. Planners who sacrifice the long-term health of the firm to reach short-term sales or financial goals choose a risky course. Product planners may focus on one or more individual products at a time, or they may look at a group of product offerings as a whole. In this section, we'll briefly examine both of these approaches. We'll also look at one important product objective: product quality.

Figure 9.1  *Process* | Steps to Manage Products

Effective product strategies come from a series of orderly steps.

Objectives and Strategies for Individual Products

Everybody loves the MINI Cooper. But it wasn't just luck or happenstance that turned this product into a global sensation. Just how do you launch a new car that's only 142 inches long and makes people laugh when they see it? BMW deliberately called attention to the small size and poked fun at the car. The original launch of the MINI Cooper a few years back included bolting the MINI onto the top of a Ford Excursion with a sign, "What are you doing for fun this weekend?" BMW also mocked up full-size MINIs to look like coin-operated kiddie rides you find outside grocery stores with a sign proclaiming: "Rides $16,850. Quarters only." The advertising generated buzz in the 20- to 34-year-old target market and today the MINI is no joke.

As a smaller brand, the MINI didn't have a huge advertising budget—in fact it was the first launch of a new car in modern times that didn't include TV advertising. Instead, the MINI launched with print, outdoor billboards, and Web ads. The aim wasn't a heavy car launch but more of a "discovery process." Ads promoted "motoring" instead of driving, and magazine inserts included MINI-shaped air fresheners and pullout games. *Wired* magazine ran a cardboard foldout of the MINI suggesting readers assemble and drive it around their desks making "putt-putt" noises. *Playboy* came up with the idea of a six-page MINI "centerfold" complete with the car's vital statistics and hobbies. By the end of its first year on the market, the MINI was the second most memorable new product of the year!

Some product strategies focus on a single new product. (As an interesting sidebar, enough customers have complained about the cramped quarters in the MINI's back seat— it is, after all, a "mini"—that BMW has since introduced a larger MINI. Now that's an oxymoron—something like a "jumbo shrimp"!)[1] Strategies for individual products may be quite different for new products, for regional products, or for mature products. For new products, not surprisingly, the objectives relate to successful introduction. After a firm experiences success with a product in a local or regional market, it may decide to introduce it nationally. Coors, for example, started out in 1873 as a regional beer you could buy only in Colorado. It didn't move east of the Mississippi until 1981 and took another decade to move into all 50 states.

For mature products like cheddar Goldfish snack crackers that Campbell's Soup Company manufactures under its Pepperidge Farm label, product objectives may focus on bringing

David Clark

APPLYING ▽ Product Strategy

A major part of defining a brand's strategy is to decide on how to position it relative to competing brands. David needs to decide how to emphasize the healthy aspects of fiber while still attracting young consumers who don't identify with this benefit. ➥

product line
A firm's total product offering designed to satisfy a single need or desire of target customers.

product line length
Determined by the number of separate items within the same category.

new life to a product while holding on to the traditional brand personality. For Goldfish, "The snack that smiles back," this means introducing a host of spin-offs—peanut butter–flavored, giant-sized, multicolored, and color-changing, to name a few. The Goldfish brand has been around since 1962 but it continues to stay fresh with 25 varieties it sells in more than 40 countries. In fact, people eat over 75 billion Goldfish per year—if strung together, enough to wrap around the earth 30 times![2]

Objectives and Strategies for Multiple Products

Although a small firm might get away with a focus on one product, a larger firm often sells a set of related products. This means that strategic decisions affect two or more products simultaneously. The firm must think in terms of its entire portfolio of products. As Figure 9.2 shows, product planning means developing *product line* and *product mix* strategies to encompass multiple offerings.

A **product line** is a firm's total product offering to satisfy a group of target customers. For example, Procter & Gamble's (P&G's) line of cleaning products includes three different liquid dish detergent brands: Dawn stresses grease-cutting power, Ivory emphasizes mildness, and Joy is for people who want shiny dishes. To do an even better job of meeting varying consumer needs, each of the three brands comes in more than one formulation. In addition to regular Dawn, you can also buy Dawn with Bleach Alternative, Dawn Simple Pleasures (smells nice with botanicals), Dawn Direct Foam (detergent comes out already foaming so "One pump and my dishes are done"), and Dawn Plus with Power Scrubbers ("Finally, an answer to tough, stuck-on food").[3] The **product line length** is determined by the number of separate items within the same category.

We describe a large number of variations in a product line as a *full line* that targets many customer segments to boost sales potential. A *limited-line strategy*, with fewer product variations, can improve the firm's image if consumers perceive it as a specialist with a clear, spe-

Figure 9.2 *Process* | Objectives for Single and Multiple Products

Product objectives provide focus and direction for product strategies. Objectives can focus on a single product or a group of products.

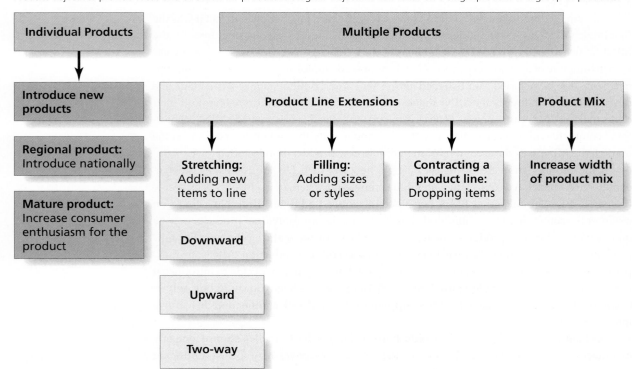

cific position in the market. A great example is Rolls-Royce Motor Cars, which BMW now owns. Rolls-Royce makes expensive, handcrafted cars built to each customer's exact specifications, and for decades maintained a unique position in the automobile industry. Every Rolls Phantom that rolls out the factory door is truly a unique work of art.[4]

Organizations may decide to extend their product line by adding more brands or models when they develop product strategies. For example, Patagonia, Gap, and Lands' End extended their reach when they added children's clothing. When a firm stretches its product line, it must decide on the best direction to go. If a firm's current product line includes middle and lower-end items, an *upward line stretch* adds new items—higher priced entrants that claim better quality or that offer more bells and whistles. Hyundai decided it could tap the market for bigger, more luxurious cars and SUVs, and stretched its line upward in the form of models such as the Azera sedan, Tucson and Santa Fe SUVs, and the Entourage minivan. It positions each of these against top-end products by Toyota and Honda but prices its cars thousands of dollars less. Hyundai does the same thing in the sedan category; it offers its popular Sonata alternative to the pricier Accord and Camry. These product line changes positioned Hyundai for considerable success with value-conscious consumers during the recent recession, and Hyundai (and its sister firm Kia) took away considerable market share from Toyota and other brands—even before Toyota ran into problems with its faulty accelerators.[5]

Conversely, a *downward line stretch* augments a line when it adds items at the lower end. Here the firm must take care not to blur the images of its higher-priced, upper-end offerings. Rolex, for example, may not want to run the risk of cheapening its image with a new watch line to compete with Timex or Swatch.

In some cases, a firm may decide that its target is too small a market. In this case, the product strategy may call for a *two-way stretch* that adds products at both the upper and lower ends. Marriott Hotels, for example, added Fairfield Inns and Courtyard at the lower end and J.W. Marriott and Ritz-Carlton at the upper end to round out its product line.

A *filling-out strategy* adds sizes or styles not previously available in a product category. Nabisco did this when it introduced "bite-size" versions of its popular Oreo and Nutter Butter cookies. In other cases, the best strategy may be to *contract* a product line, particularly when some of the items are not profitable. For example, Heinz scrapped its "Bite Me" brand of frozen pizza snacks because of poor sales. The product, targeted to teens, failed to meet company expectations.[6]

We've seen that there are many ways a firm can modify its product line to meet the competition or take advantage of new opportunities. To further explore these strategic decisions, let's return to the "glamorous" world of dish detergents. What does P&G do if the objective is to increase market share? One possibility would be to expand its line of liquid dish detergents—as the company did with its Dawn brand when it introduced Dawn Direct Foam and other extensions. If the line extension meets a perceived consumer need the company doesn't currently address, this would be a good strategic objective.

But whenever a manufacturer extends a product line or a product family, there is risk of **cannibalization**. This occurs when the new item eats up sales of an existing brand as the firm's current customers simply switch to the new product. That may explain why P&G met consumer demands for an antibacterial dish liquid by creating new versions of the existing brands Joy and Dawn.

Product Mix Strategies

A firm's **product mix** describes its entire range of products. For example, in addition to a deep line of shaving products, P&G's acquisition of Gillette a few years back gave P&G Oral B toothbrushes, Braun oral care products, and Duracell batteries.

When they develop a product mix strategy, planners usually consider the **product mix width**: the number of different product lines the firm produces. If it develops several different

cannibalization
The loss of sales of an existing brand when a new item in a product line or product family is introduced.

product mix
The total set of all products a firm offers for sale.

product mix width
The number of different product lines the firm produces.

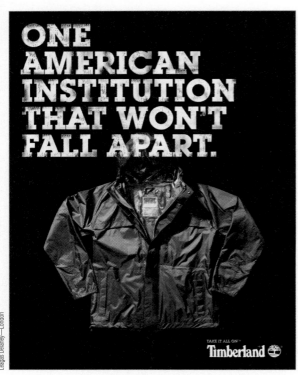

Timberland uses a patriotic message to underscore an emphasis on quality.

product quality
The overall ability of the product to satisfy customers' expectations.

total quality management (TQM)
A management philosophy that focuses on satisfying customers through empowering employees to be an active part of continuous quality improvement.

ISO 9000
Criteria developed by the International Organization for Standardization to regulate product quality in Europe.

ISO 14000
Standards of the International Organization for Standardization concerned with "environmental management" aimed at minimizing harmful effects on the environment.

product lines, a firm reduces the risk of putting all its eggs in one basket. Normally, firms develop a mix of product lines that have some things in common.

Wine and spirits distributor Constellation Brands' entry into the mainstream supermarket wine space through its acquisition of Robert Mondavi is an example of a successful product mix expansion strategy. Americans drink more wine (and hard liquor) of late (perhaps to help them forget the recession), and the Mondavi brand gives Constellation the crown jewel in the $4+ billion *supermarket wine channel* (i.e., mass market wines that people buy in large volume where they shop for groceries rather than at specialty wine shops).[7]

Quality as a Product Objective: The Science of TQM

Product objectives often focus on **product quality**, which is the overall ability of the product to satisfy customers' expectations. Quality is tied to how customers *think* a product will perform, and not necessarily to some technological level of perfection. Product quality objectives coincide with marketing objectives for higher sales and market share and to the firm's objectives for increased profits.

In 1980, just when the economies of Germany and Japan were finally rebuilt from World War II and were threatening American markets, an NBC documentary on quality titled *If Japan Can Do It, Why Can't We?* demonstrated to the American public—and to American CEOs—the poor quality of American products.[8] So began the **total quality management (TQM)** revolution in American industry.

TQM is a business philosophy that calls for company-wide dedication to the development, maintenance, and continuous improvement of all aspects of the company's operations. Indeed, some of the world's most admired, successful companies—top-of-industry firms such as Nordstrom, 3M, Boeing, and Coca-Cola—endorse a total quality focus.

Product quality is one way that marketing adds value to customers. However, TQM as an approach to doing business is far more sophisticated and effective than simply paying attention to product quality. TQM firms promote the attitude among employees that *everybody* working there serves its customers—even employees who never interact with people outside the firm. In such cases, employees' customers are *internal customers*—other employees with whom they interact. In this way, TQM maximizes customer satisfaction by involving all employees, regardless of their function, in efforts to continually improve quality. For example, TQM firms encourage all employees, even the lowest-paid factory workers, to suggest ways to improve products—and then reward them when they come up with good ideas.

Quality Guidelines

Around the world, many companies look to the uniform standards of the International Organization for Standardization (ISO) for quality guidelines. This Geneva-based organization developed a set of criteria in 1987 to improve and standardize product quality in Europe. The **ISO 9000** is a broad set of guidelines that establishes voluntary standards for quality management. These guidelines ensure that an organization's products conform to the customer's requirements. In 1996, the ISO developed **ISO 14000** standards, which concentrate on "environmental management." This means the organization works to minimize any harmful effects it may have on the environment. Because members of the European Union and other European countries prefer suppliers with ISO 9000 and ISO 14000 certification, U.S. companies must comply with these standards to be competitive there.[9]

One way that companies can improve quality is to use the **Six Sigma** method. The term *Six Sigma* comes from the statistical term *sigma*, which is a standard deviation from the mean. Six Sigma refers to six standard deviations from a normal distribution curve. In practical terms, that translates to no more than 3.4 defects per million—getting it right 99.9997 percent of the time. As you can imagine, achieving that level of quality requires a very rigorous approach (try it on your term papers—even when you use spell-check!), and that's what Six Sigma offers. The method involves a five-step process called "DMAIC" (*define, measure, analyze, improve,* and *control*). The company trains its employees in the method, and as in karate they progress toward "black belt" status when they successfully complete all the levels of training. Employees can use Six Sigma processes to remove defects from services, not just products. In these cases a "defect" means failing to meet customer expectations. For example, hospitals use Six Sigma processes to reduce medical errors, and airlines use the system to improve flight scheduling.

It's fine to talk about product quality, but exactly what is it? 📷 Figure 9.3 summarizes the many meanings of product quality. In some cases, product quality means durability. For example, athletic shoes shouldn't develop holes after their owner shoots hoops for a few weeks. Reliability also is an important aspect of product quality—just ask Maytag and the "lonely repairman" it featured in its commercials for years. For many customers, a product's versatility and its ability to satisfy their needs are central to product quality.

For other products, quality means a high degree of precision. For example, purists compare HDTVs in terms of the number of pixels and their refresh rate. Quality, especially in business-to-business products, also relates to ease of use, maintenance, and repair. Yet another crucial dimension of quality is product safety. Finally, the quality of products such as a painting, a movie, or even a wedding gown relates to the degree of aesthetic pleasure they provide. Of course, evaluations of aesthetic quality differ dramatically among people: To one person, the quality of a mobile device may mean simplicity, ease of use, and a focus on reliability in voice signal (think a basic Samsung or LG flip phone), while to another it's the cornucopia of applications and multiple communication modes available (think Apple iPhone).

Six Sigma
A process whereby firms work to limit product defects to 3.4 per million or fewer.

Christopher Smith, The New York Times/Redux Pictures

In 2009, the five most memorable new products were KFC's Grilled Chicken, McDonald's McCafe, the Beatles Rock Band video game, the Blackberry Storm from Research in Motion—and the "Snuggie" blanket. Each of these products owes its success largely to exceptionally well-executed product planning and management.[11]

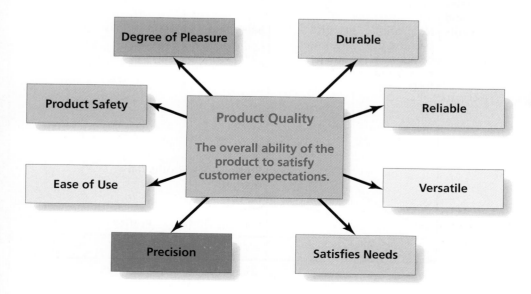

Figure 9.3 📷 *Snapshot* | Product Quality

Some product objectives focus on quality, which is the ability of a product to satisfy customer expectations—no matter what those expectations are.

product life cycle (PLC)
A concept that explains how products go through four distinct stages from birth to death: introduction, growth, maturity, and decline.

introduction stage
The first stage of the product life cycle in which slow growth follows the introduction of a new product in the marketplace.

2

OBJECTIVE

Understand how firms manage products throughout the product life cycle.
(pp. 252–255)

Marketing throughout the Product Life Cycle

Many products have very long lives, while others are "here today, gone tomorrow." The **product life cycle (PLC)** is a useful way to explain how the market's response to a product and marketing activities change over the life of a product. In Chapter 8, we talked about how marketers go about introducing new products, but the launch is only the beginning. Product marketing strategies must evolve and change as they continue through the product life cycle.

Alas, some brands don't have long to live. Who remembers the Nash car or Evening in Paris perfume? In contrast, other brands seem almost immortal. For example, Coca-Cola has been the number-one cola brand for more than 120 years, General Electric has been the number-one light bulb brand for over a century, and Kleenex has been the number-one tissue brand for over 80 years.[10] Let's take a look at the stages of the PLC.

The Introduction Stage

Like people, products are born, they "grow up" (well, most people grow up, anyway), and eventually they die. We divide the life of a product into four separate stages. The first stage we see in 📷 Figure 9.4 is the **introduction stage**. Here customers get the first chance to purchase the good or service. During this early stage, a single company usually produces the product. If it clicks and is profitable, competitors usually follow with their own versions.

During the introduction stage, the goal is to get first-time buyers to try the product. Sales (hopefully) increase at a steady but slow pace. As is also evident in 📷 Figure 9.4, the company usually does not make a profit during this stage. Why? Research and development (R&D) costs and heavy spending for advertising and promotional efforts cut into revenue.

Celebrities (like singer Amy Winehouse), need to manage their image just as other brands do throughout their product life cycle. This Israeli ad reminds us of that.

Figure 9.4 📷 *Snapshot* | The Product Life Cycle (PLC)

The PLC helps marketers understand how a product changes over its lifetime and suggests how to modify their strategies accordingly.

$ Sales and Profits	Introduction Stage	Growth Stage	Maturity Stage	Decline Stage
	No profits because the company is recovering R&D costs	Profits increase and peak	Sales peak	Market shrinks: Sales fall
			Profit margins narrow	Profits fall

Sales

Profits

0

Time

As 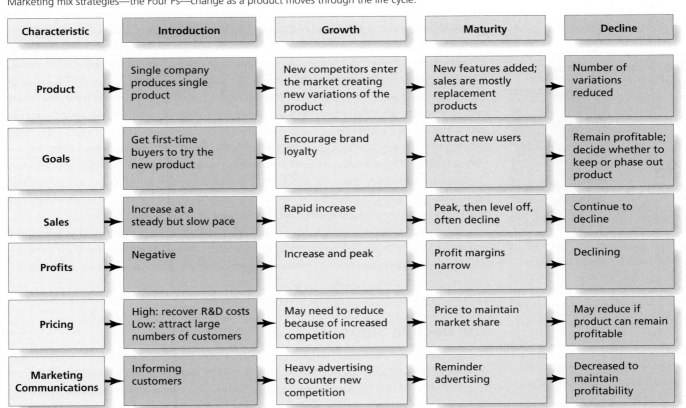 Figure 9.5 illustrates, during the introduction stage pricing may be high to recover the R&D costs (demand permitting) or low to attract a large numbers of consumers. For example, the introductory base price of the Lexus GS450h was $54,900, nearly the same as the BMW 550i's base price of $57,400 at the time. Lexus intended the price to appeal to consumers who are willing to pay for the GS450h's unique combination of comfort, great gas mileage, and superb performance. The high price is also necessary so that Lexus can recover its R&D costs for this revolutionary new engineering design, and ultimately develop more hybrid products like the LS 600h L, which hit the market at $104,000.

How long does the introduction stage last? As we saw in Chapter 8's microwave oven example, it can be quite long. A number of factors come into play, including marketplace acceptance and the producer's willingness to support its product during start-up. Sales for hybrid cars started out pretty slowly except for the Prius, but now with gas prices at astronomical levels and sales reaching new heights, hybrids are well past the introduction stage. Now, electric cars like the Chevy Volt and the Tesla have replaced them.

It is important to note that many products never make it past the introduction stage. For a new product to succeed, consumers must first know about it. Then they must believe that it is something they want or need. Marketing during this stage often focuses on informing consumers about the product, how to use it, and its promised benefits. However, this isn't nearly as easy as it sounds: Would you believe that the most recent data indicate that as many as 95 percent of new products introduced each year fail? Shocking as that number is, it's true. Ever heard of Parfum Bic, Pierre Cardin frying pans, or Jack Daniels mustard? These product blunders—which must have seemed good to some product manager at the time but sound crazy now—certainly didn't last on shelves very long. Ever heard of the Microsoft "Kin" mobile phone, positioned as a product for teens and tweens? It was both introduced

Figure 9.5 📷 *Snapshot* | Marketing Mix Strategies through the Product Life Cycle

Marketing mix strategies—the Four Ps—change as a product moves through the life cycle.

Characteristic	Introduction	Growth	Maturity	Decline
Product	Single company produces single product	New competitors enter the market creating new variations of the product	New features added; sales are mostly replacement products	Number of variations reduced
Goals	Get first-time buyers to try the new product	Encourage brand loyalty	Attract new users	Remain profitable; decide whether to keep or phase out product
Sales	Increase at a steady but slow pace	Rapid increase	Peak, then level off, often decline	Continue to decline
Profits	Negative	Increase and peak	Profit margins narrow	Declining
Pricing	High: recover R&D costs Low: attract large numbers of customers	May need to reduce because of increased competition	Price to maintain market share	May reduce if product can remain profitable
Marketing Communications	Informing customers	Heavy advertising to counter new competition	Reminder advertising	Decreased to maintain profitability

Scary smart.

The big, fluffy chocolate you've always loved and *45% less fat* than the average of the leading chocolate brands. Simply brilliant.
www.3musketeers.com

3Musketeers
A Lighter Way to Enjoy Chocolate®
ALSO AVAILABLE IN **Mint**

New products often have an advantage at the starting gate if they are offshoots of a well-known brand.

and subsequently withdrawn from the market in 2010—sales were abysmal (if you have one, keep it—it could be worth a fortune as a collector's item). It's noteworthy that these (as are many) product failures were backed by big companies and attached to already well-known brands. Just think of the product introduction risks for startups and unknown brands![12]

The Growth Stage

In the **growth stage**, sales increase rapidly while profits increase and peak. Marketing's goal here is to encourage brand loyalty by convincing the market that this brand is superior to others. In this stage, marketing strategies may include the introduction of product variations to attract market segments and increase market share. The smartphone is an example of a product that is still in its growth stage, as worldwide sales continue to increase. Continual new product introductions (Droid, iPhone, and others) fuel what seems for now to be an endless growth opportunity due to relentless product innovation as manufacturers continue to build in more and more communication features and developers create more useful apps.

When competitors appear on the scene, marketers must heavily rely on advertising and other forms of promotion. Price competition may develop, which drives profits down. Some firms may seek to capture a particular segment of the market by positioning their product to appeal to a certain group. And, if it initially set the price high, the firm may now reduce it to meet increasing competition.

The Maturity Stage

growth stage
The second stage in the product life cycle, during which consumers accept the product and sales rapidly increase.

maturity stage
The third and longest stage in the product life cycle, during which sales peak and profit margins narrow.

David Clark

APPLYING ▼ The Maturity Stage of the Product Life Cycle

As Fiber One starts to enter the maturity stage, David needs to consider how to use the marketing mix to tweak its position in the market for the long-term. ➡

decline stage
The final stage in the product life cycle, during which sales decrease as customer needs change.

The **maturity stage** of the product life cycle is usually the longest. Sales peak and then begin to level off and even decline while profit margins narrow. Competition gets intense when remaining competitors fight for their share of a shrinking pie. Firms may resort to price reductions and reminder advertising ("Did you brush your teeth today?") to maintain market share. Because most customers have already accepted the product, they tend to buy to replace a "worn-out" item or to take advantage of product improvements. For example, almost everyone in the United States owns a TV (there are still more homes without indoor toilets than without a TV set), which means most people who buy a new set replace an older one—especially when television stations nationwide stopped using analog signals and began to broadcast exclusively in a digital format in February 2009. TV manufacturers hope that a lot of the replacements will be sets with the latest and greatest new technology—Samsung would love to sell you a 3D television to replace that worn-out basic model. During the maturity stage, firms try to sell their product through as many outlets as possible because availability is crucial in a competitive market. Consumers will not go far to find one particular brand if satisfactory alternatives are close at hand.

To remain competitive and maintain market share during the maturity stage, firms may tinker with the marketing mix in order to extend this profitable phase for their product. Food manufacturers constantly monitor consumer trends, which of late have been heavily skewed toward more healthy eating. This has resulted in all sorts of products that trumpet their low-carb, organic, or no trans-fat credentials.

The Decline Stage

We characterize the **decline stage** of the product life cycle by a decrease in product category sales. The reason may be obsolescence forced by new technology—where (other than in a museum) do you see a typewriter today? Although a single firm may still be profitable, the market as a whole begins to shrink, profits decline, there are fewer variations of the product, and suppliers pull out. In this stage there are usually many competitors but none has a distinct advantage.

A firm's major product decision in the decline stage is whether to keep the product at all. An unprofitable product drains resources that it could use to develop newer products. If the firm decides to keep the product, it may decrease advertising and other marketing communications to cut costs, and reduce prices if the product can still remain profitable. If the firm decides to drop the product, it can eliminate it in two ways: (1) phase it out by cutting production in stages and letting existing stocks run out, or (2) simply dump the product immediately. If the established market leader anticipates that there will be some residual demand for the product for a long time, it may make sense to keep the product on the market. The idea is to sell a limited quantity of the product with little or no support from sales, merchandising, advertising, and distribution and just let it "wither on the vine."

Now that e-commerce is a significant factor for marketing, some products that would have died a natural death in brick-and-mortar stores continue to sell online to a cadre of fans, backed by zero marketing support (translation: high profits for the manufacturer). Online purveyors such as **candydirect.com** sell Beeman's gum direct to consumers. In the "old days" (that is, B.I.—Before the Internet), a brand like Beeman's would have been doomed by aggressive marketing budgets for all the crazy and continuous new product introductions in the category by behemoth gum competitors Wrigley and American Chicle. eBay has certainly helped proliferate the life cycle of many products—yes, you can buy Beeman's there too (as well as occasionally its sister products Clove and Blackjack gum), hopefully with current expiration dates for freshness!

FRESH BLADE. MORE COMFORTABLE SHAVE.

Even the best blades get dull after a while. So, when the Gillette Fusion Power Indicator strip fades to white...

It may be time to change your blade for a more comfortable shave.

Gillette
Fusion
POWER

Gillette
The Best a Man Can Get

Courtesy of Procter & Gamble

Disposable razor blades are a mature product, so companies like Gillette need to keep introducing new variations to maintain consumers' interest.

3 Create Product Identity: Branding Decisions

OBJECTIVE

Discuss how branding strategies create product identity.

(pp. 255–262)

Successful marketers keep close tabs on their products' life cycle status, and they plan accordingly. Equally important, though, is to give that product an *identity* and a *personality*. For example, the word "Disney" evokes positive emotions around fun, playfulness, family, and casting day-to-day cares out the window. Folks pay a whole lot of money at Disney's theme parks in Florida and California to act on those emotions. Disney achieved its strong identity through decades of great branding. Branding is an extremely important (and expensive) element of product strategies. In this section, we'll examine what a brand is and how certain laws protect brands. Then we'll discuss the importance of branding and how firms make branding decisions.

What's in a Name (or a Symbol)?

How do you identify your favorite brand? By its name? By the logo (how the name appears)? By the package? By some graphic image or symbol, such as Nike's swoosh? A **brand** is a name, a term, a symbol, or any other unique element of a product that identifies one firm's product(s) and sets it apart from the competition. Consumers easily recognize the Coca-Cola logo, the Jolly Green Giant (a *trade character*), and the triangular red Nabisco logo (a *brand mark*) in the corner of the box. Branding provides the recognition factor products need to succeed in regional, national, and international markets.

A brand name is probably the most used and most recognized form of branding. Smart marketers use brand names to maintain relationships with consumers "from the cradle to

brand
A name, a term, a symbol, or any other unique element of a product that identifies one firm's product(s) and sets it apart from the competition.

the grave." McDonald's would like nothing better than to bring in kids for their Happy Meal and then convert them over time to its more adult Southwest Salad (hopefully followed by a Mocha Frappé). A good brand name may position a product because it conveys a certain image (Ford Mustang) or describes how it works (Drano). Brand names such as Caress and Shield help position these different brands of bath soap by saying different things about the benefits they promise. Irish Spring soap provides an unerring image of freshness (can't you just smell it now?). The Nissan Xterra combines the word *terrain* with the letter *X*, which many young people associate with extreme sports, to give the brand name a cutting-edge, off-road feel. Apple's use of "i-everything" is a brilliant branding strategy, as it conveys individuality and personalization—characteristics that Gen Y buyers prize.

How does a firm select a good brand name? Good brand designers say there are four "easy" tests: *easy to say, easy to spell, easy to read, and easy to remember*—like P&G's Tide, Cheer, Dash, Bold, Gain, Downy, and Ivory Snow (P&G is probably the undisputed branding king of all time). And the name should also "fit" four ways:

1. *Fit the target market*

2. *Fit the product's benefits*

3. *Fit the customer's culture*, and

4. *Fit legal requirements.*

When it comes to graphics for a brand symbol, name, or logo, the rule is that it must be recognizable and memorable. No matter how small or large, the triangular Nabisco logo in the corner of the box is a familiar sight. And it should have visual impact. That means that from across a store or when you quickly flip the pages in a magazine, the brand will catch your attention.

A **trademark** is the legal term for a brand name, brand mark, or trade character. The symbol for legal registration in the United States is a capital "R" in a circle ®. Marketers register trademarks to make their use by competitors illegal. Because trademark protection ap-

trademark
The legal term for a brand name, brand mark, or trade character; trademarks legally registered by a government obtain protection for exclusive use in that country.

The Cutting Edge

iPad's Branding Strategy Had Some "Bugs"

In its inimitable way, Apple generated an amazing amount of buzz in 2010 with its new iPad tablet. But this time, some of it might not have been quite the conversation it wanted. Many women immediately tweeted, posted, and blogged that the name evokes awkward associations with feminine hygiene products. In the hours after the iPad launch announcement, "iTampon" became one of the most popular trending topics on Twitter. Apple's communication team fielded a wave of queries on the subject but characteristically declined to comment.

Various marketing experts and pundits quickly weighed in that a lot of women, when they hear the word "pad," are automatically going to associate it with feminine hygiene products. Michael Cronan, a naming consultant in Berkeley, Calif., whose company has helped come up with brands like TiVo and Kindle, said many naming experiments show that women tend to reflexively relate words like "pad" and "flow" to bodily concerns. He's not sure Apple could have found an alternative that ties in as perfectly to its famous brands. "I think we're going to get over this fairly quickly and we'll get on with enjoying the experience."

If this wasn't enough drama for Apple in its iPad's first few days out of the chute, it turns out folks of both sexes from Boston to Ireland complained that the verbalization of "iPad," in their regional brogue sounds almost indistinguishable from "iPod," Apple's music player. In addition, there were more se-

rious conflicts. It turns out two other high-tech companies already market products—albeit relatively obscure ones—called iPad and laid claim to the trademark. Fujitsu, the Japanese technology firm, applied for the iPad trademark in the United States and already was selling a $2,000 hand-held device that shop clerks use to check inventory. Swiss semiconductor company STMicroelectronics owned the iPad trademark in Europe, where it uses the name as an acronym for integrated passive and active devices—which sounds less fun than playing games on a tablet.

Naming conflicts have not stopped Apple before. In 2007, on the eve of the introduction of the iPhone, technology giant Cisco Systems pointed out that it already sold an Internet handset called the iPhone. Legend has it that Apple CEO Steve Jobs personally strong-armed Cisco into submission by peppering Cisco executives with calls at all hours and telling them he was prepared to claim that Cisco was underutilizing the trademark (he's a persuasive guy—Cisco surrendered the trademark with a vague promise to market their products jointly—a partnership that never materialized). "Jobs is a very tough businessman and tough negotiator," said Charles Giancarlo, a former Cisco executive who dealt directly with him on the issue. "I feel sorry for the poor guy at Fujitsu who is going to be negotiating with Steve directly." As for the "iTampon" crowd—likely by now the technological wonders of the tablet have long since erased any confusion about what product category the brand represents.[13]

plies only in individual countries where the owner registers the brand, unauthorized use of marks on counterfeit products is a huge headache for many companies.

A firm can claim protection for a brand even if it has not legally registered it. In the United States, *common-law protection* exists if the firm has used the name and established it over a period of time (sort of like a common-law marriage). Although a registered trademark prevents others from using it on a similar product, it may not bar its use for a product in a completely different type of business. Consider the range of "Quaker" brands: Quaker Oats (cereals), Quaker Funds (mutual funds), Quaker State (motor oil), Quaker Bonnet (gift food baskets), and Quaker Safety Products Corporation (firemen's clothing). A court applied this principle when Apple Corp., the Beatles' music company, sued Apple Computers in 2006 over its use of the Apple logo. The plaintiff wanted to win an injunction to prevent Apple Computer from using the Apple logo in connection with its iPod and iTunes products; it argued that the application to music-related products came too close to the Beatles' musical products. The judge didn't agree; he ruled that Apple Computer clearly used the logo to refer to the download service, not to the music itself.[14] Of course, now that Apple Corp. and Apple Computer have agreed to make Beatles songs available on iTunes, all bets are off.

Why Brands Matter

A brand is *a lot* more than just the product it represents—the best brands build an emotional connection with their customers. Think about the most popular diapers—they're branded Pampers and Luvs, not some functionally descriptive name like Absorbency Master or Dry Bottom. The point is that Pampers and Luvs evoke the joys of parenting, not the utility of the diaper.

Marketers spend huge amounts of money on new-product development, advertising, and promotion to develop strong brands. When they succeed, this investment creates **brand equity**. This term describes a brand's value over and above the value of the generic version of the product. For example, how much extra will you pay for a golf shirt with a Ralph Lauren or Lacoste logo on it than for the same shirt with no logo? The difference reflects the polo player or gator's brand equity in your mind.

brand equity
The value of a brand to an organization.

Brand equity means that a brand enjoys customer loyalty because people believe it is superior to the competition. For a firm, brand equity provides a competitive advantage because it gives the brand the power to capture and hold on to a larger share of the market and to sell at prices with higher profit margins. For example, among pianos the Steinway name has such powerful brand equity that its market share among concert pianists is 95 percent.[15]

Marketers identify different levels of loyalty, or lack thereof, by observing how customers feel about the product. At the lowest level, customers really have no loyalty to a brand and they will change brands for any reason—often they will jump ship if they find something else at a lower price. At the other extreme, some brands command fierce devotion, and loyal users will go without rather than buy a competing brand.

Escalating levels of attachment to a brand begin when consumers become aware of a brand's existence. Then, they might look at the brand in terms of what it literally does for them or how it performs relative to competitors. Next, they may think more deeply about the product and form beliefs and emotional reactions to it. The truly successful brands, however, are those that truly "bond" with their customers so that people feel they have a real relationship with the product. Here are some of the types of relationships a person might have with a product:

- *Self-concept attachment:* The product helps establish the user's identity. (For example, do you feel better in Ralph Lauren or Sean John clothing?)

- *Nostalgic attachment:* The product serves as a link with a past self. (Does eating the inside of an Oreo cookie remind you of childhood? How about a vintage T-shirt with a picture of Strawberry Shortcake or Mayor McCheese—both recent fashion hits?)[16]

- *Interdependence:* The product is a part of the user's daily routine. (Could you get through the day without a Starbucks coffee?

- *Love:* The product elicits emotional bonds of warmth, passion, or other strong emotion. (Hershey's Kiss, anyone?)[17]

brand meaning
The beliefs and associations that a consumer has about the brand.

Ultimately, the way to build strong brands is to forge strong bonds with customers—bonds based on **brand meaning.** This concept encompasses the beliefs and associations that a consumer has about the brand. In many ways, the practice of brand management revolves around the management of meanings. Brand managers, advertising agencies, package designers, name consultants, logo developers, and public relations firms are just some of the collaborators in a global industry devoted to the task of *meaning management.* Table 9.1 summarizes some important dimensions of brand meaning.

Nowadays, for many consumers brand meaning builds virally as people spread its story online. "Tell to sell," once a mantra of top Madison Avenue ad agencies, is making a comeback as marketers seek to engage consumers with compelling stories rather than peddle products in hit-and-run fashion with interruptive advertising like 30-second commercials—which Gen Y and younger largely block out anyway. The method of **brand storytelling** captures the notion that powerful ideas do self-propagate when the audience is connected by digital technology. It conveys the constant reinvention inherent in interactivity in that whether it's blogging, content creation through YouTube or other means, or social media, there will always be new and evolving perceptions and dialogues about a brand real-time. A cadre of start-up firms have emerged over the last few years to aid companies in storytelling about their brand (we'll meet one of them, Campfire, in a later chapter).[18]

brand storytelling
Marketers seek to engage consumers with compelling stories about brands.

If we could name the key elements that make a brand successful, what would they be? Here is a list of 10 characteristics of the world's top brands:[19]

1. The brand excels at delivering the benefits customers truly desire.

2. The brand stays relevant.

3. The pricing strategy is based on consumers' perceptions of value.

Table 9.1 | Dimensions of Brand Meaning

Dimension	Example
Brand identification markers	Coca-Cola's red and white colors, the Nike swoosh logo, Harley-Davidson's characteristic sound
Product attribute and benefit	Starbucks as good coffee; BMW as "The Ultimate Driving Machine"
Gender	NASCAR, Harley-Davidson, Marlboro and masculinity; Laura Ashley and femininity
Social class	Mercedes and the old-guard elite; Jell-O and the lower-middle class
Age	Facebook, MySpace, Skechers, iPod, Adult Swim
Reference group	Dockers and the casual workforce; Williams-Sonoma and the serious cook
Life stage	Dewar's and the coming of age; Parent's Soup and new mothers
Lifestyles and taste subcultures	BMW and the yuppie; Red Bull and the club culture
Place	Coke and America; Ben & Jerry's and rural Vermont
Time and decade	Betty Crocker and the 1950s; VW and the 1960s countercultural revolution
Trends	Pottery Barn and cocooning; Starbucks and small indulgences
Traditions and rituals	Häagen-Dazs ice cream and the pampering of self

Source: Parts of the table are adapted from Fournier, Susan G., Michael R. Solomon, and Basil G. Englis, "Brand Resonance," in ed. Bernd Schmitt, *Handbook on Brand and Experience Management*, Elgar Publishing, 2009.

4. The brand is properly positioned.

5. The brand is consistent.

6. The brand portfolio and hierarchy make sense.

7. The brand makes use of and coordinates a full repertoire of marketing activities to build equity.

8. The brand's managers understand what the brand means to consumers.

9. The brand is given proper support, and that support is sustained over the long run.

10. The company monitors sources of brand equity.

Products with strong brand equity provide exciting opportunities for marketers. A firm may leverage a brand's equity via **brand extensions**—new products it sells with the same brand name. Because of the existing brand equity, a firm is able to sell its brand extension at a higher price than if it had given it a new brand, and the brand extension will attract new customers immediately. Of course, if the brand extension does not live up to the quality or attractiveness of its namesake, brand equity will suffer, as will brand loyalty and sales.

One other related approach is **sub-branding**, or creating a secondary brand within a main brand that can help differentiate a product line to a desired target group. Dodge, like many U.S. automobile brands, has had its problems recently. Although the brand features a line of sedans, Dodge is by far best known for the Ram truck. To help clarify things for consumers, in 2009 Dodge made Ram a sub-brand (minus the Dodge name) that is marketed separately from all other Dodge products. Now the Dodge name is all about cars, which sport a new Dodge logo to clearly differentiate them from Ram, which has the same Ram symbol as before but now displayed more prominently than ever on the trucks. In terms of future positioning, the trucks will focused on hard-core commercial and recreational users and the cars on young attitudes and lifestyles rather than age groups or price classes.[20]

Sometimes a brand's meaning simply becomes so entrenched with a particular consumer group that it can be tough to find ways to branch out and achieve new users through extensions. Take, for example, Quiksilver, whose original line of wetsuits and swimwear was aimed squarely at teenage boys who identified with the surf and skate cultures. But now, Quiksilver hopes to appeal to women who may have never hit the waves with items from sweaters to jeans. The new line is in Quiksilver's 650+ stores as well as Nordstrom and other high-end retail outlets. The competition will be fierce, though—Urban Outfitters' Anthropologie and Liz Claiborne's Lucky Brand Jeans are formidable in the 20-something female market and are aimed at the same genre of retailer as Quiksilver uses for its new line.[21]

Branding Strategies

Because brands contribute to a marketing program's success, a major part of product planning is to develop and execute branding strategies. Marketers have to determine which branding strategy approach(es) to use. 📷 Figure 9.6 illustrates the options: individual or family brands, national or store brands, generic brands, licensing, and cobranding. This decision is critical but it is not always an easy or obvious choice.

brand extensions
A new product sold with the same brand name as a strong existing brand.

sub-branding
Creating a secondary brand within a main brand that can help differentiate a product line to a desired target group.

Figure 9.6 📷 *Snapshot* | Branding Strategies

Marketing managers have several options for which branding strategy or strategies to employ.

Campbell's uses a family branding strategy to identify its Chunky line of soups.

family brand
A brand that a group of individual products or individual brands share.

national or manufacturer brands
Brands that the product manufacturer owns.

private-label brands
Brands that a certain retailer or distributor owns and sells.

Individual Brands versus Family Brands

Part of developing a branding strategy is to decide whether to use a separate, unique brand for each product item—an *individual brand strategy*—or to market multiple items under the same brand name—a **family brand** or *umbrella brand* strategy. Individual brands may do a better job of communicating clearly and concisely what the consumer can expect from the product, while a well-known company like Apple may find that its high brand equity in other categories (like computers) can sometimes "rub off" on a new brand (like the iPod and iPhone). The decision often depends on characteristics of the product and whether the company's overall product strategy calls for introduction of a single, unique product or for the development of a group of similar products. For example, Microsoft serves as a strong umbrella brand for a host of diverse, individually branded products like Windows 7, Office, Xbox 360, and Bing, while P&G prefers to brand each of its household products separately.

But there's a potential dark side to having too many brands, particularly when they become undifferentiated in the eyes of the consumer due to poor positioning. Over the last decade, venerable General Motors continually suffered from muddy differentiation among the eight brands in its portfolio—namely, Chevrolet, GMC, Pontiac, Saturn, Cadillac, Buick, Hummer, and Saab. The brands often competed with each other—both for customers and a slice of GM's marketing budget. For example, at one time GM had four mainstream midsize sedans. It backed its top-selling Chevy Malibu with an aggressive ad campaign, while the Buick LaCrosse, Pontiac G6, and Saturn Aura struggled to build the awareness and recognition these lines need to compete. Fast forward to today: When GM got into financial difficulty and was "bailed out" by the government, one of the first moves for the leaner, meaner GM was to cut out all the fat in its product lines. Of the models listed above, only the Malibu is still around![22]

National and Store Brands

Retailers today often are in the driver's seat when it comes to deciding what brands to stock and push. In addition to choosing from producers' brands, called **national or manufacturer brands**, retailers decide whether to offer their own versions. **Private-label brands**, also called *store brands*, are the retail store's or chain's exclusive trade name. Walmart, for example, sells store brand Sam's Cola and Sam's cookies along with national brands such as Coke and Oreos. During the recent recession store brands gained substantially in popularity for many value-conscious shoppers, and the projection is that many consumers will not switch back to the parallel national brands as the economy rebounds because they are satisfied with the private labels.

In addition, if you stock a unique brand that consumers can't find in other stores, it's much harder for shoppers to compare "apples to apples" across stores and simply buy the brand where they find it sold for the lowest price. Loblaws, Canada's largest supermarket chain, sells over 4,000 food items under the "premium quality" President's Choice label, from cookies to beef, olive oil, curtains, and kitchen utensils. Sales of President Choice items run from 30 to 40 percent of total store volumes. Under the private label, Loblaws can introduce new products at high quality but for lower prices than brand names. It can also keep entire categories profitable by its mix of pricing options. Competitors that sell only national brands can cut prices on those brands, but that hurts their overall profitability. Loblaws can bring prices down on national brands but still make money on its private-label products.[23]

Generic Brands

An alternative to either national or store branding is **generic branding**, which is basically no branding at all. Generic branded products are typically packaged in white with black lettering that names only the product itself (for example, "Green Beans"). Generic branding is one strategy to meet customers' demand for the lowest prices on standard products such as dog food or paper towels. Generic brands first became popular during the inflationary period of the 1980s when consumers became especially price conscious because of rising prices. Lately, they have experienced a resurgence with the soft economy. Walmart has set the pharmacy business on end by offering some types of generic prescriptions, such as basic antibiotics, for $4.00.[24]

Licensing

Some firms choose to use a **licensing** strategy to brand their products. This means that one firm sells another firm the right to use a legally protected brand name for a specific purpose and for a specific period of time. Why should an organization sell its name? Licensing can provide instant recognition and consumer interest in a new product, and this strategy can quickly position a product for a certain target market as it trades on the high recognition of the licensed brand among consumers in that segment. For example, distiller Brown-Forman licensed its famous Jack Daniel's bourbon name to T.G.I. Friday's to use on all sorts of menu items from shrimp to steak to chicken. In addition to this "Jack Daniel's Grill," Friday's features menu items inspired by the popular Food Network reality show *Ultimate Recipe Showdown*.[25]

A familiar form of licensing occurs when movie producers license their properties to manufacturers of a seemingly infinite number of products. Each time a blockbuster Harry Potter movie hits the screens, a plethora of Potter products packs the stores. In addition to toys and games, you can buy Harry Potter candy, clothing, all manner of back-to-school items, home items, and even wands and cauldrons. And in 2010, Harry and the gang showed up in the form of an attraction at Universal Orlando called "The Wizarding World of Harry Potter."[26]

Cobranding

Frito-Lay sells K.C. Masterpiece–flavored potato chips, and Post sells Oreo O's cereal. Strange marriages? Not at all! Actually, these are examples of a great strategy called **cobranding**, as are the Jack Daniel's and Food Network combinations with T.G.I. Friday's that we already mentioned. Cobranding benefits both partners when combining the two brands provides more recognition power than either enjoys alone. For example, Panasonic markets a line of digital cameras that use Leica lenses, which are legendary for their superb image quality. Panasonic is known for its consumer electronics. Combining the best in traditional camera optics with a household name in consumer electronics helps both brands.

A new and fast-growing variation on cobranding is *ingredient branding*, in which branded materials become "component parts" of other branded products.[27] This was the strategy behind the classic "Intel inside" campaign that convinced millions of consumers to ask by name for a highly technical computer part (a processor) that they wouldn't otherwise recognize if they fell over it.[28] Today, consumers can buy Breyer's Ice Cream with Reese's Peanut Butter Cups or M&M's candies, Twix cookies or Snickers bars. Van De Camp's Fish & Dips come with Heinz ketchup dipping cups.

Jelly Belly cobrands with several soft drink brands to offer new flavor options.

The practice of ingredient branding has two main benefits. First, it attracts customers to the host brand because the ingredient brand is familiar and has a strong brand reputation for quality. Second, the ingredient brand's firm can sell more of its product, not to mention the additional revenues it gets from the licensing arrangement.[29]

Brand Metrics

Recall from our earlier discussion that brand equity represents the value of a product with a particular brand name compared to what the value of the product would be without that brand name (think Coca-Cola versus generic supermarket soda). Companies, marketing research firms, and creative agencies create metrics of brand equity because this is an important way to assess whether a branding strategy has been successful. For example, Harris Interactive conducts its EquiTrend® study twice a year to measure the brand equity of over 1,000 brands. The company interviews over 25,000 consumers to determine how they feel about competing brands.[30] Each year, *BusinessWeek* applies its brand equity formulas to come up with a list of its top 100 global brands. In 2009, the top 10 in order of brand value were Coca-Cola, Microsoft, IBM, GE, Nokia, McDonald's, Google, Toyota, Intel, and Disney. Of these, McDonald's and Google moved up in the rankings versus 2008 while Toyota, Intel, and Disney moved down. The estimated brand value for Coca-Cola was $68.7 billion (with a "b") in 2009.[31]

If consumers have strong, positive feelings about a brand and are willing to pay extra to choose it over others, you are in marketing heaven. Each of the following approaches to measuring brand equity has some good points and some bad points:

1. *Customer mind-set metrics* focus on consumer awareness, attitudes, and loyalty toward a brand. However, these metrics are based on consumer surveys and don't usually provide a single objective measure that a marketer can use to assign a financial value to the brand.

2. *Product-market outcomes metrics* focus on the ability of a brand to charge a higher price than the one an unbranded equivalent charges. This usually involves asking consumers how much more they would be willing to pay for a certain brand compared to others. These measures often rely on hypothetical judgments and can be complicated to use.

3. *Financial market metrics* consider the purchase price of a brand if it is sold or acquired. They may also include subjective judgments about the future stock price of the brand.

4. A team of marketing professors proposed a simpler measure that they claim reliably tracks the value of a brand over time. Their *revenue premium metric* compares the revenue a brand generates with the revenue generated by a similar private-label product (that doesn't have any brand identification). In this case, brand equity is just the difference in revenue (net price times volume) between a branded good and a corresponding private label.[32]

package
The covering or container for a product that provides product protection, facilitates product use and storage, and supplies important marketing communication.

Universal Product Code (UPC)
The set of black bars or lines printed on the side or bottom of most items sold in grocery stores and other mass-merchandising outlets. The UPC, readable by scanners, creates a national system of product identification.

4 Create Product Identity: The Package and Label

OBJECTIVE
Explain how packaging and labeling contribute to product identity.
(pp. 262–265)

How do you know if the soda you are drinking is "regular" or "caffeine-free"? How do you keep your low-fat grated cheese fresh after you have used some of it? Why do you always leave your bottle of new "fresh, sexy, enticing" blue Glow by JLO perfume out on your dresser so everyone can see it? The answer to all these questions is effective packaging and labeling. So far, we've talked about how marketers create product identity with branding. In this section, we'll learn that packaging and labeling decisions also help to create product identity. We'll also talk about the strategic functions of packaging and some of the legal issues that relate to package labeling.

What Packages Do

A **package** is the covering or container for a product, but it's also a way to create a competitive advantage. So, the important functional value of a package is that it protects the product. For example, packaging for computers, TV sets, and stereos protects the units from damage during shipping and warehousing. Cereal, potato chips, or packs of grated cheese wouldn't be edible for long if packaging didn't provide protection from moisture, dust, odors, and insects. The multilayered, soft box you see in 📷 Figure 9.7 prevents the chicken broth inside from spoiling. In addition to protecting the product, effective packaging makes it easy for consumers to handle and store the product. 📷 Figure 9.7 shows how packaging serves a number of different functions.

Over and above these utilitarian functions, however, the package communicates brand personality. Effective product packaging uses colors, words, shapes, designs, and pictures to provide brand and name identification for the product. In addition, packaging provides product facts including flavor, fragrance, directions for use, suggestions for alternative uses (for example, recipes), safety warnings, and ingredients. Packaging may also include warranty information and a toll-free telephone number for customer service.

A final communication element is the **Universal Product Code (UPC)**, which is the set of black bars or lines printed on the side or bottom of most

A range of package sizes allows a company to expand its product line.

Figure 9.7 📷 *Snapshot* | Functions of Packaging

Great packaging provides a covering for a product, and it also creates a competitive advantage for the brand.

A waterproof camera is a packaging innovation—and a differential advantage—for Fuji.

A next-generation bar code called an *Aztec code* is starting to pop up on everything from cereal boxes to airline boarding passes. It holds much more data and can be read by cellphones that have the necessary software.

items sold in grocery stores and other mass-merchandising outlets. The UPC is a national system of product identification. It assigns each product a unique 10-digit number. These numbers supply specific information about the type of item (grocery item, meat, produce, drugs, or a discount coupon), the manufacturer (a five-digit code), and the specific product (another five-digit code). At checkout counters, electronic scanners read the UPC bars and automatically transmit data to a computer in the cash register so that retailers can easily track sales and control inventory.

Design Effective Packaging

Should the package have a zip-lock, feature an easy-to-pour spout, be compact for easy storage, be short and fat so it won't fall over, or be tall and skinny so it won't take up much shelf space? Effective package design involves a multitude of decisions.

Planners must consider the packaging of other brands in the same product category. For example, when P&G introduced Pringles potato chips, it packaged them in a cylindrical can instead of in bags like Lay's and others. This was largely out of necessity, since P&G doesn't have all the local trucks to deliver to stores that Frito-Lay does, and the cans keep the chips fresher much longer. However, P&G discovered that not all customers will accept a radical change in packaging, and retailers may be reluctant to adjust their shelf space to accommodate such packages. To partly answer the concern, Pringles now comes in an amazing array of products and package types and sizes including Stix, Snack Stacks, Grab & Go, and 100 Calorie (apportioned for those who want a snack while they also watch their weight).[33]

Who says people don't judge a book by its cover? NXT, a new brand of shaving gel targeted at younger men, makes a glitzy statement on the shelf. It's sold in an arresting triangular container that lights up from the bottom to illuminate air bubbles suspended in the clear gel. The plastic is tinted blue, and when its base lights up (yes, this package requires batteries!), the whole thing looks like a miniature lava lamp or tiny fishless aquarium. How does NXT afford such a fancy container? It doesn't spend a dime on traditional advertising—the brand counts on its innovative package to sell the gel in the grocery aisle. What's NXT? NXT body wash and NXT deodorant, of course.[34]

Firms that wish to act in a socially responsible manner must also consider the environmental impact of packaging. Shiny gold or silver packaging transmits an image of quality and opulence, but certain metallic inks are not biodegradable. Some firms are developing innovative *green packaging* that is less harmful to the environment than other materials. Of course, there is no guarantee that consumers will accept such packaging. They didn't take to plastic pouch refills for certain spray bottle products even though the pouches may take up less space in landfills than the bottles do. They didn't like pouring the refill into their old spray bottles. Still, customers have accepted smaller packages of concentrated products such as laundry detergent, dishwashing liquid, and fabric softener.

What about the shape: Square? Round? Triangular? Hourglass? How about an old-fashioned apothecary jar that consumers can reuse as an attractive storage container? What color should it be? White to communicate purity? Yellow because it reminds people of lemon freshness? Brown because the flavor is chocolate? Sometimes we can trace these decisions back to personal preferences. The familiar Campbell's Soup label—

Ripped from the Headlines

Ethical/Sustainable Decisions in the Real World

Because of the power of branding, marketers constantly are on the lookout for new trends and ways they can connect to those trends through their packaging and labeling. One of the hottest consumer trends now is organic "food, as in organically grown agricultural products. A lot of products use the word "organic" on their product labels. Unfortunately for consumers, there is no precise definition of organic, so a lot of food products that carry this label may really be stretching it. Recently, the U.S. Department of Agriculture (USDA) has addressed this controversial topic as it tries to categorize ingredients as organic or not organic.

Also, unfortunately for consumers, the big food companies are pressuring the USDA to add a whole bunch of ingredients to the organic list; these include numerous nonorganic ingredients they want to use in products that qualify to bear the "USDA Organic" seal. Remarkably, some of these are artificial food colorings that will ensure your organic food has pleasing eye appeal.

Assume you are a retailer like Whole Foods whose business (and reputation) is built around giving consumers true healthy choices. You have to decide whether to feature the "USDA Organic" designation as part of your product strategy. Under the circumstances, what would you do?

ETHICS CHECK:
Find out what other students taking this course **would do** and **why** on **www.mypearsonmarketinglab.com**

Would you describe products labeled USDA Organic as organic to your customers even if they may contain nonorganic ingredients?

☐ **YES** ☐ **NO**

immortalized as art by Andy Warhol—is red and white because a company executive many years ago liked the football uniforms at Cornell University!

Finally, there are many specific decisions brand managers must make to ensure a product's packaging reflects well on its brand and appeals to the intended target market. What graphic information should the package show? Should there be a picture of the product on the package? Should cans of green beans always show a picture of green beans? Should there be a picture that demonstrates the results of using the product, such as beautiful hair? Should there be a picture of the product in use, perhaps a box of crackers that shows them with delicious-looking toppings arranged on a silver tray? Should there be a recipe or coupon on the back? Of course, all these decisions rest on a marketer's understanding of consumers, ingenuity, and perhaps a little creative luck.

Labeling Regulations

The Federal Fair Packaging and Labeling Act of 1966 controls package communications and labeling in the United States. This law aims to make labels more helpful to consumers by providing useful information. More recently, the requirements of the *Nutrition Labeling and Education Act of 1990* forced food marketers to make sweeping changes in how they label products. Since August 18, 1994, the U.S. Food and Drug Administration (FDA) requires most foods sold in the United States to have labels telling, among other things, how much fat, saturated fat, cholesterol, calories, carbohydrates, protein, and vitamins are in each serving of the product. These regulations force marketers to be more accurate when they describe the contents of their products. Juice makers, for example, must state how much of their product is real juice rather than sugar and water.

As of January 1, 2006, the FDA also requires that all food labels list the amount of trans fats in the food, directly under the line for saturated fat content. The new labeling reflects scientific evidence showing that consumption of trans fat, saturated fat, and dietary cholesterol raises "bad" cholesterol levels, which increase the risk of coronary heart disease. The new information is the first significant change on the Nutrition Facts panel since it was established.[36]

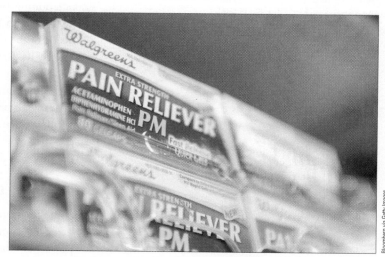

Some store brands opt for copycat packaging, mimicking the look of the national branded product they want to knock off. Walgreen's is a master of such copycat packaging—look on any shelf in its medicinal categories and you will see a Walgreen's brand proudly merchandised on the shelf right next to the leading national brand in that category, with the package design and colors so similar that you have to look carefully to discern what you are actually buying.[35]

brand manager
An individual who is responsible for developing and implementing the marketing plan for a single brand.

product category managers
Individuals who are responsible for developing and implementing the marketing plan for all the brands and products within a product category.

David Clark

APPLYING ▽ Brand Manager

David is responsible for coordinating all the marketing activities for Fiber One to ensure that it continues to attract customers and even expand its market share. ➡

Figure 9.8 📷 *Snapshot* | Types of Product Management

Product management can take several forms: brand managers, product category managers, and market managers, depending on the firm's needs and the market situation.

Three Types of Product Management

5

OBJECTIVE

Describe how marketers structure organizations for new and existing product management.
(pp. 266–267)

Organize for Effective Product Management

Of course, firms don't create great packaging, brands, or products—people do. Like all elements of the marketing mix, product strategies are only as effective as their managers make them and carry them out. In this section, we'll talk about how firms organize to manage existing products and to develop new products.

Manage Existing Products

In small firms, a single marketing manager usually handles the marketing function. She is responsible for new-product planning, advertising, working with the company's few sales representatives, marketing research, and just about everything else. But in larger firms, there are a number of managers who are responsible for different brands, product categories, or markets. As illustrated in 📷 Figure 9.8, depending on the organization's needs and the market situation, product management may include brand managers, product category managers, and market managers. Let's take a look at how each operates.

Brand Managers

Sometimes a firm sells several or even many different brands within a single product category. Take the detergent aisle in the supermarket, for example. P&G manufactures and markets all these brands: Bounce, Cheer, Downy, Dreft, Era, Febreze, Gain, Ivory, and Tide. In such cases, each brand may have its own **brand manager** who coordinates all marketing activities for a brand; these duties include positioning, identifying target markets, research, distribution, sales promotion, packaging, and evaluating the success of these decisions.

While this job title and assignment is still common throughout industry, some big firms are changing the way they allocate responsibilities. For example, today P&G's brand managers function more like internal consultants to cross-functional teams located in the field that have responsibility for managing the complete business of key retail clients across all product lines. Brand managers still are responsible for positioning of brands and developing brand equity, but they also work heavily with folks from sales, finance, logistics, and others to serve the needs of the major retailers that comprise the majority of P&G's business.

By its very nature, the brand management system is not without potential problems. Acting independently and sometimes competitively against each other, brand managers may fight for increases in short-term sales for their own brand. They may push too hard with coupons, cents-off packages, or other price incentives to a point at which customers will refuse to buy the product when it's not "on deal." Such behavior can hurt long-term profitability and damage brand equity.

Product Category Managers

Some larger firms have such diverse product offerings that they need more extensive coordination. Take IBM, for example. Originally known as a computer manufacturer, IBM now generates much of its revenue from a wide range of consulting and related client services across the spectrum of IT applications (and the company doesn't even sell personal computers anymore!). In cases such as IBM, organizing for product management may include **product category managers**, who coordinate the mix of product lines within the more general product category and who consider the addition of new-product lines based on client needs.

Market Managers

Some firms have developed a **market manager** structure in which different people focus on specific customer groups rather than on the products the company makes. This type of organization can be useful when firms offer a variety of products that serve the needs of a wide range of customers. For example, Raytheon, a company that specializes in consumer electronics products, special-mission aircraft, and business aviation, sells some products directly to consumer markets, others to manufacturers, and still others to the government. It serves its customers best when it focuses separately on each of these very different markets.

market manager
An individual who is responsible for developing and implementing the marketing plans for products sold to a particular customer group.

Organize for New-Product Development

You read in Chapter 8 about the steps in new-product development, and learned earlier in this chapter about the importance of the Introductory Phase of the Product Life Cycle. Because launching new products is so important, the management of this process is a serious matter. In some instances, one person handles new-product development, but within larger organizations new-product development almost always requires many people. Often especially creative people with entrepreneurial skills get this assignment.

The challenge in large companies is to enlist specialists in different areas to work together in **venture teams**. These teams focus exclusively on the new-product development effort. Sometimes the venture team is located away from traditional company offices in a remote location called a "skunk works." This colorful term originated with the Skunk Works, an illicit distillery in the comic strip *Li'l Abner*. Because illicit distilleries were bootleg operations, typically located in an isolated area with minimal formal oversight, organizations adopted the colorful description "skunk works" to refer to a small and often isolated department or facility that functions with minimal supervision (not because of its odor).[37]

venture teams
Groups of people within an organization who work together to focus exclusively on the development of a new product.

Why do you think David chose option #2?

How It Worked Out at General Mills

David chose to position Fiber One as a great-tasting, high-fiber product. By emphasizing Fiber One's great taste, General Mills would offer a solution to the biggest obstacle people associated with eating fiber.

Under the "Surprisingly Great-Tasting High-Fiber" campaign, Fiber One has expanded to over eight product categories, and sales have increased tenfold over four years. The brand now exceeds $500 million in retail sales annually.

To learn the whole story, visit www.mypearsonmarketinglab.com.

Brand **YOU**!

What makes you special? What makes your brand unique? For example, do you describe yourself as "good with people" or do you make the description into a compelling advantage by saying you are a "collaborative problem solver"? Turn your features into benefits that a company wants by creating your personal brand value proposition. Chapter 9 in the Brand You supplement takes you through this important process, which creates the framework for your resume.

Kim Richmond Fourth Edition

MARKETING 7E **real** People, **real** Choices
Solomon | Marshall | Stuart

Objective Summary ➡ Key Terms ➡ Apply

CHAPTER 9
Study Map

1. Objective Summary (pp. 246–251)

Explain the different product objectives and strategies a firm may choose.

Objectives for individual products may be related to introducing a new product, expanding the market of a regional product, or rejuvenating a mature product. For multiple products, firms may decide on a full- or a limited-line strategy. Often companies decide to extend their product line with an upward, downward, two-way stretch or with a filling-out strategy, or they may decide to contract a product line. Firms that have multiple product lines may choose a wide product mix with many different lines or a narrow one with few. Product quality objectives refer to the durability, reliability, degree of precision, ease of use and repair, or degree of aesthetic pleasure.

Key Terms

product management, p. 246

product line, p. 248

product line length, p. 248

cannibalization, p. 249

product mix, p. 249

product mix width, p. 249

product quality, p. 250

total quality management (TQM), p. 250

ISO 9000, p. 250

ISO 14000, p. 250

Six Sigma, p. 251

2. Objective Summary (pp. 252–255)

Understand how firms manage products throughout the product life cycle.

The product life cycle explains how products go through four stages from birth to death. During the introduction stage, marketers seek to get buyers to try the product and may use high prices to recover research and development costs. During the growth stage, characterized by rapidly increasing sales, marketers may introduce new-product variations. In the maturity stage, sales peak and level off. Marketers respond by adding desirable new-product features or market-development strategies. During the decline stage, firms must decide whether to phase a product out slowly, to drop it immediately, or, if there is residual demand, to keep the product.

Key Terms

product life cycle (PLC), p. 252

introduction stage, p. 252

growth stage, p. 254

maturity stage, p. 254

decline stage, p. 254

3. Objective Summary (pp. 255–262)

Discuss how branding strategies create product identity.

A brand is a name, term, symbol, or other unique element of a product used to identify a firm's product. A brand should be selected that has a positive connotation and is recognizable and memorable. Brand names need to be easy to say, spell, read, and remember, and should fit the target market, the product's benefits, the customer's culture, and legal requirements. To protect a brand legally, marketers obtain trademark protection. Brands are important because they help maintain customer loyalty and because brand equity or value means a firm is able to attract new customers. Firms may develop individual brand strategies or market multiple items with a family or umbrella brand strategy. National or manufacturer brands are owned and sold by producers, whereas private-label or store brands carry the retail or chain store's trade name. Licensing means a firm sells another firm the right to use its brand name. In a cobranding strategy, two brands form a partnership to market a new product.

Key Terms

brand, p. 255

trademark, p. 256

brand equity, p. 257

brand meaning, p. 258

brand storytelling, p. 258

brand extensions, p. 259

sub-branding, p. 259

family brand, p. 260

national or manufacturer brands, p. 260

private-label brands, p. 260

generic branding, p. 261

licensing, p. 261

cobranding, p. 261

4. Objective Summary (pp. 262–265)

Explain how packaging and labeling contribute to product identity.

Packaging is the covering or container for a product and serves to protect a product and to allow for easy use and storage of the product. The colors, words, shapes, designs, pictures, and materials used in package design communicate a product's identity, benefits, and other important product information. Package designers must consider cost, product protection, and communication in creating a package that is functional, aesthetically pleasing, and not harmful to the environment. Product labeling in the United States is controlled by a number of federal laws aimed at making package labels more helpful to consumers.

Key Terms

package, p. 263

Universal Product Code (UPC), p. 263

5. Objective Summary (pp. 266–267)

Describe how marketers structure organizations for new and existing product management.

To successfully manage existing products, the marketing organization may include brand managers, product category managers, and market managers. Large firms, however, often give new-product responsibilities to new-product managers or to venture teams, groups of specialists from different areas who work together for a single new product.

Key Terms

brand manager, p. 266

product category managers, p. 266

market manager, p. 267

venture teams, p. 267

Chapter **Questions** and **Activities**

Concepts: Test Your Knowledge

1. What are some reasons a firm might determine it should expand a product line? What are some reasons for contracting a product line? Why do many firms have a product mix strategy?
2. Why is quality such an important product strategy objective? What are the dimensions of product quality? How has e-commerce affected the need for quality product objectives?
3. Explain the product life cycle concept. What are the stages of the product life cycle?
4. How are products managed during the different stages of the product life cycle?
5. What is a brand? What are the characteristics of a good brand name? How do firms protect their brands?
6. What is a national brand? A store brand? Individual and family brands?
7. What does it mean to license a brand? What is cobranding?
8. What are the functions of packaging? What are some important elements of effective package design?
9. What should marketers know about package labeling?
10. Describe some of the ways firms organize the marketing function to manage existing products. What are the ways firms organize for the development of new products?

Activities: Apply What You've Learned

1. The Internet allows consumers to interact directly through blogs and other means with other people so they can praise products they like and slam those they don't. With several of your classmates, conduct a brief survey of students and of older consumers. Find out if consumers complain to each other about poor product quality. Have they ever used a Web site to express their displeasure over product quality? Make a report to your class.

2. You may think of your college or university as an organization that offers a line of different educational products. Assume that you have been hired as a marketing consultant by your university to examine and make recommendations for extending its product line. Develop alternatives that the university might consider:
   a. Upward line stretch
   b. Downward line stretch
   c. Two-way stretch
   d. Filling-out strategy

   Describe how each might be accomplished. Evaluate each alternative.

3. Assume that you are the vice president of marketing for a firm that markets a large number of specialty food items (gourmet sauces, marinades, relishes, and so on). Your firm is interested in improving its marketing management structure. You are considering several alternatives: using a brand manager structure, having product category managers, or focusing on market managers. Outline the advantages and disadvantages of each type of organization. What is your recommendation?

4. Assume that you are working in the marketing department of a major manufacturer of athletic shoes. Your firm is introducing a new product, a line of disposable sports clothing. That's right—wear it once and toss it! You wonder if it would be better to market the line of clothing with a new brand name or use the family brand name that has already gained popularity with your existing products. Make a list of the advantages and disadvantages of each strategy. Develop your recommendation.

5. Assume that you have been recently hired by Kellogg, the cereal manufacturer. You have been asked to work on a plan for redesigning the packaging for Kellogg's cereals. In a role-playing situation, present the following report to your marketing superior:
   a. Discussion of the problems or complaints customers have with current packaging
   b. Several different package alternatives
   c. Your recommendations for changing packaging or for keeping the packaging the same

Marketing Metrics Exercise

The chapter introduces you to the concept of brand equity, an important measurement of the value vested in a product's brand in and of itself. Different formulas for calculating brand equity exist. One well-publicized approach is that of Interbrand, which annually publishes its Best 100 Global Brands list. Go to the location on the Interbrand Web site where they provide these rankings for the present and past years **(http://www .interbrand.com/best_global_brands.aspx)**. Peruse the list of brands and select any five in which you have interest. For each, observe whether brand equity has been trending up or down over the past few years. How does Interbrand explain the changes (or stability) in each? Do you agree with Interbrand's assessment or do you have another opinion about why your brand's equity is what it is?

Choices: What Do You Think?

1. Brand equity means that a brand enjoys customer loyalty, perceived quality, and brand name awareness. To what brands are you personally loyal? What is it about the product that creates brand loyalty and, thus, brand equity?

2. Quality is an important product objective, but quality can mean different things for different products, such as durability, precision, aesthetic appeal, and so on. What does quality mean for the following products?
   a. Automobile
   b. Pizza
   c. Running shoes
   d. Hair dryer
   e. Deodorant
   f. College education

3. Many times firms take advantage of their popular, well-known brands by developing brand extensions because they know that the brand equity of the original or parent brand will be transferred to the new product. If a new product is of poor quality, it can damage the reputation of the parent brand, while a new product that is of superior quality can enhance the parent brand's reputation. What are some examples of brand extensions that have damaged and that have enhanced the parent brand equity?

4. Sometimes marketers seem to stick with the same packaging ideas year after year regardless of whether they are the best possible design. Following is a list of products. For each one, discuss what, if any, problems you have with the package of the brand you use. Then think of ways the package could be improved. Why do you think marketers don't change the old packaging? What would be the results if they adopted your package ideas?
   a. Dry cereal
   b. Laundry detergent
   c. Frozen orange juice
   d. Gallon of milk
   e. Potato chips
   f. Loaf of bread

5. You learned in this chapter that it's hard to *legally* protect brand names across product categories—Quaker and Apple, for example, and also Delta—which is an airline and a faucet. But what about the *ethics* of borrowing a name and applying it to some unrelated products? Think of some new business you might like to start up. Now consider some possible names for the business that are already in use as brands in other unrelated categories. Do you think it would be ethical to borrow one of those names? Why or why not?

Miniproject: Learn by Doing

In any supermarket in any town, you will surely find examples of all the different types of brands discussed in this chapter: individual brands, family brands, national brands, store brands, and cobranded and licensed products. This miniproject is designed to give you a better understanding of branding as it exists in the marketplace.

1. Go to a typical supermarket in your community.
2. Select two product categories of interest to you: ice cream, cereal, laundry detergent, soup, paper products, and so on.
3. Make a list of the brands available in each product category. Identify what type of brand each is. Count the number of shelf facings (the number of product items at the front of each shelf) for each brand.
4. Arrange to talk with the store manager at a time that is convenient with him or her. Ask the manager to discuss the following:
   a. How the store decides which brands to carry
   b. Whether the store is more likely to carry a new brand that is an individual brand versus a family brand
   c. What causes a store to drop a brand
   d. The profitability of store brands versus national brands
   e. Other aspects of branding that the store manager sees as important from a retail perspective
5. Present a summary to your class on what you learned about the brands in your two product categories.

Marketing in **Action** Case   Real Choices at Starbucks

Starbucks began as a local coffee bean roaster and retailer of whole bean and ground coffee, tea, and spices. From 1971, a lone store in Seattle's Pike Place Market has grown into the largest coffeehouse company in the world. The Seattle-based Starbucks Corporation is an international coffee and coffeehouse chain with 16,635 stores in 49 countries, including 11,068 in the United States, nearly 1,000 in Canada and more than 800 in Japan. The Starbucks product selection includes drip brewed coffee, espresso-based hot drinks, other hot and cold drinks, coffee beans, salads, hot and cold sandwiches and paninis, pastry, snacks, and items such as mugs and tumblers.

One of Starbuck's prominent brands that suffered in the recession at the beginning of the 21st century is the Frappuccino™". At its height, annual sales of this specialty drink exceeded $2 billion annually. However, sales have declined over the past few years. In 2010 the Frappuccino™ brand was estimated to represent between 15 percent and 20 percent of annual sales at Starbucks retail outlets. Dunkin' Donuts and McDonald's, along with many other smoothie chains are gearing up to snatch market share away from Starbucks with their own coffee drinks. Since the Frappuccino™ plays such an important role in Starbucks' product mix, the company takes these challenges very seriously.

Frappuccino™ is a registered trademark of the Starbucks Corporation and it has been a brand for over 15 years. The blended ice beverage is a mixture of frappé and cappuccino, an Italian-style coffee with a topping of frothed milk. Starbucks sells it at the counter and also in bottles. Like the terms "Kleenex" and "Band-Aid," the word "Frappuccino" has become almost generic and many customers think the product is also available at other coffee purveyors.

Starbucks has tried various strategies to extend the brand name. Two new Frappuccino-flavored ice creams are available on supermarket shelves. Vanilla Frappuccino Light, a bottled beverage, was created in a joint venture with PepsiCo. In addition, Starbucks globally introduced new blends, such as Black Sesame Frappuccino in China, and Red Bean Frappuccino in other Asian markets. Still other plans are in the works including new bottled versions, new "wacky" ingredients, and other products under the same brand banner.

The chain also is looking closely at a "however-you-want-it-Frappuccino" customization program at a premium price. Customization empowers the consumer to co-create value by beginning with an empty slate and personalizing the beverage with his or her own choice of milk, coffee intensity, syrup, and any optional toppings. Annie Young-Scrivner, global chief marketing officer for Starbucks, observes that one of the target markets for the Frappuccino™ is an 18- to 24-year-old woman. The customization option allows calorie-counting customers to create nonfat milk, light syrup, and no whipped cream version with only 160 calories. According to Young-Scrivner, this market is ideal for the custom-made Frappuccino™. She told the *Wall Street Journal,* "Millennials (otherwise known as Gen Y) are the iPod age group . . . accustomed to selecting exactly what they want. Now, they can choose an extra shot of espresso, no whipped cream, or a dab more caramel, for instance."

With any product extension strategy, there are inevitable challenges. The Frappuccino has an involved preparation process and takes longer to produce than other Starbucks beverages. This may present a problem if the new program is successful. The extra time needed for *baristas* to customize each drink may lead to long lines, customer irritation, more complicated employee training, and slower-than-expected sales growth. Starbucks has questions to answer concerning, among other things, pricing, training, and competition.

You Make the Call

1. What is the decision facing Starbucks?
2. What factors are important in understanding this decision situation?
3. What are the alternatives?
4. What decision(s) do you recommend?
5. What are some ways to implement your recommendation?

Based on: Bruce Horovitz, "Starbucks' Strategy: Whip It Good," *USA Today,* April 27, 2010, p. 3B; Starbucks Corporation Official Web site, "Company Profile" (http://www.starbucks.com/about-us/company-information); Starbucks, *Wikipedia,* http://en.wikipedia.org/wiki/Starbucks (accessed April 28, 2010); Kevin Helliker, "At Long Last, Customized Frappuccino," *Wall Street Journal* (Eastern Edition), New York, March 17, 2010 p. D.3.

Chapter 10

Services and Other Intangibles:
Marketing the Product That Isn't There

Lara L. Price

Profile | Info

▼ A **Decision Maker** at the Philadelphia 76ers

Lara Price is senior vice president of business operations for the Philadelphia 76ers professional basketball team. When Lara was elevated to vice president of marketing in August 1998, she became one of only 18 female vice presidents in the NBA (National Basketball Association). After being named the team's senior vice president in August 2001, Price was promoted to her current position in June 2003 and continues to oversee the day-to-day activities of the 76ers business operation. She is responsible for the team's sales and marketing along with the communications department, which includes public relations, community relations, and new media, as well as game entertainment. She also oversees the Sixers' television and radio broadcasts.

The recipient of several awards for excellence in advertising and public relations, Price joined the 76ers in 1996 as director of marketing after serving as manager of team services for the NBA. She also served as director of team services for the Continental Basketball Association. A native of Boulder, Colorado, Price is a graduate of Colorado State University, where she was also a member of the women's basketball team.

💬 Lara's Info

What do I do when I'm not working?
A) Running or walking my Rottweiler, Deuce.

First job out of school?
A) Continental Basketball Association.

Career high?
A) Going to the NBA Finals in 2001 and helping to organize the NBA All-Star Weekend Celebration that honored the 50 greatest players. Having the opportunity to stand with all of them and organize them before they went out on the court.

A job-related mistake I wish I hadn't made?
A) Letting a vendor talk me into using more fireworks than we should have used for opening night. The haze/smoke didn't lift for at least 5 minutes. This delayed the game and the team was fined.

Business book I'm reading now?
A) *Competing on Analytics* by Thomas H. Davenport and Jeanne G. Harris.

My hero?
A) My parents.

My motto to live by?
A) Never quit and the Golden Rule.

What drives me?
A) Passion.

My management style?
A) Hands on!

My pet peeve?
A) People who blame others and don't try to resolve the issue or problem at hand. Figure out why it happened, correct it, and move on.

Here's my ~~problem~~. . .

To better serve its fans (customers), the 76ers needed to compile more detailed information about its customer base. The team's management had access to several data sources; these included some surveys, notes from customer service representatives that recorded highlights of conversations with fans, and a ticketing system (which showed past purchases)—but this system only recorded a ticket buyer's name, address, length of being a season ticket holder, and any miscellaneous notes that customer service representatives added to the account. Lara knew that she needed a better system to compile buying habit information to predict what Sixers fans wanted, as opposed to the poorly organized "spray and pray" strategy the team was currently using.

Sports have been a little bit slower than other industries to jump on board with CRM techniques (customer relationship management; see Chapter 7). Many professional teams don't have the resources or type of internal culture that encourages a lot of rigorous analysis of what fans want and do, but Lara recognized the value of systematically tracking this information to fine-tune her marketing strategies. Still, she acknowledged that you can't run before you can walk: The company (not just the 76ers but the team's parent company, Comcast Spectacor, which owns the Flyers, 76ers, Phantoms, the Wachovia Center/Spectrum, and Comcast SportsNet) needed to find a workable CRM solution. This solution had to grow with Comcast's business needs; it wouldn't work to put an overly sophisticated system in place that was too complicated to use and would be rejected before it had a chance to show why it was superior to the way the team tracked customers' buying habits now.

Things to remember

The Philadelphia 76ers didn't have a rigorous system in place to measure their fans' experiences. The team needed to do a better job of tracking the specific aspects of its service that either attracted or turned off potential ticket buyers.

Lara considered her **Options** 1·2·3

1

Option

Phase in a CRM database approach. This would allow Lara to obtain a full view of her customers and segment her base according to relevant drivers, such as purchasing behaviors, Web site viewing habits (even which specific pages customers were going to on the site), which e-mails people are opening, who responds to direct mail/letters, text messages, and so on. This system is more efficient in the long run because it tracks behaviors (purchasing) and requires minimal human input. However, to adopt such a system would require buy-in from the company at all levels (including senior management), and it wasn't clear that her colleagues would be receptive to this more analytical approach to monitoring fans' behavior as opposed to a more traditional "hands-on" perspective. And, depending upon the CRM system the company adopted, this could be a pricey option, ranging from six figures to more than $2 million.

2

Option

Send out several surveys to season ticket holders each year. These would request feedback about many topics including game operations, payment options, broadcast preferences, and the general direction of the team. Although this is a proven (and relatively inexpensive) method to get feedback from customers, mail surveys might not capture rapid changes in preferences. In addition, it's risky to base business decisions on customers' opinions rather than taking into account their actual behaviors.

3

Option

Analyze the lifetime value of customers by projecting how their spending habits over time will provide revenue to the organization. This technique would allow Lara to identify her most profitable customers to be sure she was allocating her marketing dollars toward satisfying their needs. The Sixers' full season ticket holders are the lifeblood of the team's business, but other segments such as partial plan holders, individual game purchasers, and broadcast viewers are very important as well. This approach would let Lara's staff identify which types of customers provide the largest revenue to the company over time and tailor its promotions accordingly. A lifetime value analysis is useful because it's based on actual behavior rather than on what fans say they will do in the future. On the other hand, these behaviors don't tell the whole story: It's still important to know about customers' demographics and psychographics (see Chapter 5) to enable the team to market one-to-one. For example, a lifetime value analysis doesn't indicate if a customer wants her Sixers information delivered via the Web, phone, or mail.

Now, put yourself in Lara's shoes: Which option would you choose, and why?

You Choose

Which **Option** would you choose, and **why**?
1. ☐YES ☐NO 2. ☐YES ☐NO 3. ☐YES ☐NO

See what **option** Lara chose and its success on **page 291**

intangibles
Experience-based products.

services
Intangible products that are exchanged directly from the producer to the customer.

1

OBJECTIVE

Describe the characteristics of services and the ways marketers classify services.
(pp. 274–280)

Marketing What Isn't There

What do a Lady Gaga concert, a college education, a Cubs baseball game, and a visit to Walt Disney World have in common? Easy answer—each is a product that combines experiences with physical goods to create an event that the buyer consumes. You can't have a concert without musical instruments (or bizarre masks, in Lady Gaga's case), a college education without textbooks (Thursday night parties don't count), a Cubbies game without a hot dog, or a Disney experience without the mouse ears. But these tangibles are secondary to the primary product, which is some act that, in these cases, produces enjoyment, knowledge, or excitement.

In this chapter we'll consider some of the challenges and opportunities that face marketers whose primary offerings are **intangibles**: services and other experience-based products that we can't touch. The marketer whose job is to build and sell a better football, automobile, or smartphone—all tangibles—deals with issues that are somewhat different from the job of the marketer who wants to sell tickets to a basketball game, limousine service to the airport, or allegiance to a hot new rock band. In the first part of this chapter, we'll discuss services, a type of intangible that also happens to be the fastest-growing sector in our economy. As we'll see, all services are intangible, but not all intangibles are services. Then we'll look at a few other types of intangibles as well.

What Is a Service?

Services are acts, efforts, or performances exchanged from producer to user without ownership rights. Like other intangibles, a service satisfies needs when it provides pleasure, information, or convenience. In 2010, service industry jobs accounted for over 75 percent of all employment in the United States and over two-thirds of the gross domestic product (GDP).[1] If you pursue a marketing career, it's highly likely that you will work somewhere in the services sector of the economy. Got your interest?

Of course, the service industry includes many consumer-oriented services, ranging from dry cleaning to body piercing. But it also encompasses a vast number of services directed toward organizations. Some of the more common *business services* include vehicle leasing, information technology services, insurance, security, Internet transaction services (**Amazon.com**, Google, online banking, etc.), legal advice, food services, consulting, cleaning, and maintenance. In addition, businesses also purchase some of the same services as consumers, such as electricity, telephone service, and gas (although as we saw in Chapter 6 these purchases tend to be in much higher quantities).

The market for business services has grown rapidly because it is often more cost effective for organizations to hire outside firms that specialize in these services than to hire a workforce and handle the tasks themselves.

Characteristics of Services

Services come in many forms, from those done *to* you, such as a massage or a teeth cleaning, to those done to *something you own*, such as having your computer tuned up by the Geek Squad or getting a new paint job on your classic 1965 Mustang. Regardless of whether they affect our bodies or our posses-

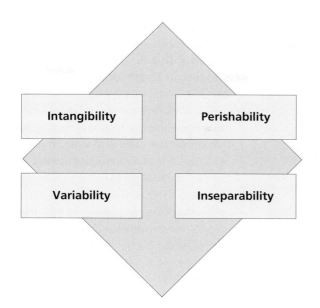

Figure 10.1 📷 *Snapshot* |
Characteristics of Services
Services have four unique characteristics versus products.

sions, all services share four characteristics, which are summarized in 📷 Figure 10.1: intangibility, perishability, inseparability, and variability. The discussion that follows shows how marketers can address the unique issues related to these characteristics of services that don't pop up when they deal with tangible goods.

Intangibility

Part of the title of this chapter is "Marketing the Product That Isn't There." The essence is that unlike a bottle of Izzo soda or a flat screen TV—both of which have physical, tangible properties—services do assume a tangible form. **Intangibility** means customers can't see, touch, or smell good service. Unlike the purchase of a tangible good, we can't inspect or handle services before we buy them. This makes it much more difficult for consumers to evaluate many services. Although it may be easy to evaluate your new haircut, it is far less easy to determine whether the dental hygienist did a great job when she cleaned your teeth.

Because they're buying something that isn't there, customers look for reassuring signs before they purchase—so marketers must ensure that these signs are readily available. That's why they try to overcome the problem of intangibility by providing *physical cues* to reassure the buyer. These cues might be the "look" of the facility, its furnishings, logo, stationery, business cards, appearance of its employees, or well-designed advertising and Web sites.

Perishability

Perishability refers to the characteristic of a service that makes it impossible to store for later sale or consumption—it's a case of use it or lose it. When rooms go unoccupied at a ski resort, there is no way to make up for the lost opportunity to rent them for the weekend. Marketers try to avoid these problems when they use the marketing mix to encourage demand for the service during slack times. One popular option is to reduce prices to increase demand for otherwise unsold services. Airlines do this when they offer more lower-priced seats in the final days before a flight by direct e-mail to customers who sign up for last-minute deals or online through outlets like **Priceline.com**. In a last-ditch effort to fill their ships to the highest possible capacity, Disney Cruise Lines offers Walt Disney World Resort employees discounts in excess of 50 percent off about a week before the ship sets sail. We'll talk more about these and other pricing tactics in Chapter 11.

intangibility
The characteristic of a service that means customers can't see, touch, or smell good service.

perishability
The characteristic of a service that makes it impossible to store for later sale or consumption.

Because services are intangible, marketers often find it useful to link them to very vivid images—like talking money.

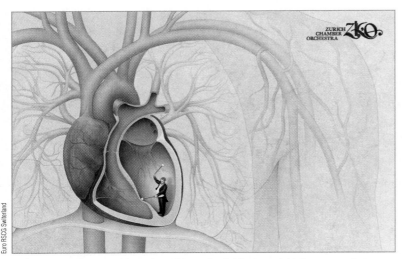

A symphony orchestra provides an intangible service that is also variable from one performance to another.

capacity management
The process by which organizations adjust their offerings in an attempt to match demand.

variability
The characteristic of a service that means that even the same service performed by the same individual for the same customer can vary.

inseparability
The characteristic of a service that means that it is impossible to separate the production of a service from the consumption of that service.

Capacity management is the process by which organizations adjust their services in an attempt to match supply with demand. This strategy may mean adjusting the product, or it may mean adjusting the price. In the summer, for example, the Winter Park Ski Resort in Colorado combats its perishability problem when it opens its lifts to mountain bikers who tear down the sunny slopes. Rental car companies offer discounts on days of the week when business travel is light, and many hotels offer special weekend packages to increase weekend occupancy rates. Las Vegas might add free meals, room discounts, show passes, or other incentives to lure travelers during slow weeks, yet during a big convention or major boxing match prices go sky high and amenities disappear.

Variability

An NFL quarterback may be hot one Sunday and ice cold the next, and the same is true for most services. **Variability** means that over time even the same service the same individual performs for the same customer changes—even only in minor ways. It's rare when you get exactly the same cut from a hairstylist each time you visit him. Even your physician might let a rough day get in the way of her usual charming bedside manner with patients.

It's difficult to standardize services because service providers and customers vary. Think about your experiences in your college classes. A school can standardize its offerings to some degree—course catalogs, course content, and classrooms are fairly controllable. Professors, however, vary in their training, life experiences, and personalities, so there is little hope of being able to make teaching uniform (not that we'd want to do this anyway). And because students with different backgrounds and interests vary in their needs, the lecture that you find fascinating might put your friend to sleep (trust us on this). The same is true for customers of organizational services. Differences in the quality of individual security guards or cleaning personnel mean variability in how organizations deliver these services.

The truth is, if you really stop and think about it, we don't necessarily *want* standardization when we purchase a service. Most of us desire a hairstyle that fits our face and personality, and a personal trainer who will address our unique physical training needs. Businesses like McDonald's, Wendy's, and Burger King want unique advertising campaigns to set them apart from each other, not cookie-cutter messages. Because of the nature of the tasks service providers perform, customers often appreciate the one that customizes its service for each individual.

Inseparability

In services, **inseparability** means that it is impossible to divide the production of a service from the consumption of that service. Think of the concept of inseparability this way: A firm can manufacture goods at one point in time, distribute them, and then sell them later (likely at a different location than the original manufacturing facility). In contrast, by its nature a service can take place only at the time the actual service provider performs an act on either the customer or the customer's possession. Nobody wants to eat a meal at a restaurant that was prepared yesterday at another location—that's inseparability. And you can't bulk up haircuts or empty seats on airplanes as inventory for future use!

Still, it's difficult if not impossible to detach the expertise, skill, and personality of a provider or the quality of a firm's employees, facilities, and equipment from the offering itself. The central role that employees play in making or breaking a service underscores the importance of the **service encounter**, or the interaction between the customer and the service provider.[2] The most expertly cooked meal is just plain mush if a surly or incompetent waiter brings it to the table.

To minimize the potentially negative effects of bad service encounters and to save on labor costs, some service businesses turn to **disintermediation**, which means removing the "middleman" and thus eliminating the need for customers to interact with people at all. Examples include self-checkouts at the supermarket or home improvement store, self-service gas pumps, and bank ATMs. Even salad and dessert bars reduce reliance on a restaurant server. Although some consumers resist dealing with machines, pumping their own gas, or fixing their own salad, most prefer or at least don't mind the speed and efficiency disintermediation provides. The remaining consumers who want a Caesar salad prepared table-side by your server with old fashioned flare or a fill-up that includes an oil check and a clean windshield provide marketing opportunities for full-service restaurants and the few gas stations that still provide these higher levels of service—usually at a higher price.

The Internet provides many opportunities for disintermediation, especially in the financial services area. Banking customers can access their accounts, transfer funds from one account to another, and pay their bills with the click of a mouse. Many busy consumers can check out mortgage interest rates and even apply for a loan at their convenience—a much better option than taking an afternoon off from work to sit in a mortgage company office. Online brokerage services are popular, as many consumers seek to handle their investments themselves so they can avoid the commission a full-service brokerage firm charges. Insurance companies like GEICO and Progressive aggressively lead consumers to the Web instead of to an agent's office to get rate quotes and visit about the weather and fishing.

The Service Encounter

Earlier we said that a service encounter occurs when the customer comes into contact with the organization—which usually means she interacts with one or more employees who represent that organization. The *service encounter* has several dimensions that are important to marketers.[3] First, there is the social contact dimension—one person interacting with another person. The physical dimension is also important—customers often pay close attention to the environment where they receive the service.

Despite all the attention (and money) firms pay to create an attractive facility and deliver a quality product, this contact is "the moment of truth"—the employee often determines whether the customer will come away with a positive or a negative impression of the service. Our interactions with service providers can range from the most superficial, such as when we buy a movie ticket, to telling a psychiatrist (or bartender) our most intimate secrets. In each case, though, the quality of the service encounter exerts a big impact on how we feel about the service we receive.

Because services are intimately tied to company employees who deliver the service, *the quality of a service is only as good as its worst employee.* The employee represents the organization; her actions, words, physical appearance, courtesy, and professionalism reflect its values. Customers entrust themselves and/or their possessions to the care of the employee, so it is important that employees look at the encounter from the customer's perspective.

However, the customer also plays a part in the type of experience that results from a service encounter. When you visit a doctor, the quality of the health care you receive depends not only on the physician's competence. It's also influenced by your ability to accurately and clearly communicate the symptoms you experience and how well you follow the regimen she prescribes to treat you. The business customer must provide accurate information to her accounting firm. And even the best personal trainer is not going to make the desired improvements in a client's physique if the client refuses to do the workout designed for her.

service encounter
The actual interaction between the customer and the service provider.

disintermediation
A service that requires the customer to obtain an outcome without the intervention of a human provider.

How We Classify Services?

When they understand the characteristics of different types of services, marketers can develop strategies to ramp up customer satisfaction. As Table 10.1 shows, we classify services in terms of whether the service is performed directly on the customer or on something the customer owns, and whether the service consists of tangible or intangible actions. Customers themselves receive tangible services to their bodies—a haircut or a heart transplant. The education (we hope!) you are receiving in this course is an intangible service directed at the consumer. A customer's possessions are the recipient of tangible services such as the repair of a favorite carpet. Intangible services directed at a consumer's possessions include insurance and home security.

In reality, most products are a combination of goods and services. The purchase of a "pure good" like a Cadillac Escalade still has service components, such as bringing it to the dealer for maintenance work or using its OnStar service to figure out how to find the dealer in the first place. The purchase of a "pure service" like a makeover at a department store has product components, for example, lotions, powders, and lipsticks the cosmetologist uses to create the "new you." Either tangible or intangible elements dominate some products, such as salt versus teaching, whereas others such as a commercial airline flight tend to include more of a mixture of goods and services. To make sense of this, it's useful to consider a firm's offerings within the context of three categories: goods-dominated products, equipment- or facility-based services, and people-based services.

Goods-Dominated Products

Even if this means only that the company maintains a toll-free telephone line for questions or provides a 30-day warranty against defects, companies that primarily sell tangible products still must provide support services. Automobile, major appliance, and electronics firms can realize a competitive advantage when they provide customers with this support better than the competition. Services may be even more important for marketers of B2B tangibles. Business customers often will not even consider buying from manufacturers who don't provide services after the sale like employee training and equipment maintenance. For example, hospitals that buy lifesaving patient care and monitoring equipment costing hundreds of thousands of dollars demand not only in-service training for their nursing and technician

Table 10.1 | Marketing Strategies for Different Service Characteristics

Characteristic	Marketing Response
Intangibility	Provide tangibility through physical appearance of the facility
	Furnishings
	Employee uniforms
	Logo
	Web sites
	Advertising
Perishability	Adjust pricing to influence demand
	Adjust services to match demand (*capacity management*)
Variability	Institute total quality management programs
	Offer service guarantees
	Conduct gap analysis to identify gaps in quality
Inseparability	Train employees about successful service encounters
	Explore means for disintermediation

personnel, but also quick response to breakdowns and regular maintenance of the equipment.

Equipment- or Facility-Based Services

Some products include a mixture of tangible and intangible elements. Although a restaurant is a balanced product because it includes the preparation and delivery of the food to your table plus the food itself, for many other offerings the tangible elements of the service are less evident. For example, in the case of hospitals and hotels, customers do not take away a tangible good from the service encounter, but clearly these organizations do rely on expensive equipment or facilities to deliver a their offerings. Equipment- or facility-based services such as automatic car washes, amusement parks, museums, movie theaters, health clubs, tanning salons, and zoos all must be concerned with important operational, locational, or environmental factors of the service encounter.

An amusement park is an equipment-based service.

- *Operational factors:* Clear signs and other guidelines must show customers how to use the service (think about the infamous roped waiting spaces at airport ticket counters, banks, and hotel check-in lobbies. In particular, firms need to minimize waiting times (or at least give that illusion). Marketers employ a number of tricks to give impatient customers the illusion that they aren't waiting too long. One hotel chain, responding to complaints about the long wait for elevators, installed mirrors in the lobby: People tended to check themselves out until the elevators arrived, and lo and behold, protests decreased.[4]

- *Locational factors:* These are especially important for frequently purchased services, such as dry cleaning or retail banking, that we obtain at a fixed spot. When you select a bank, a restaurant, or a health club, its location often factors into your decision. Marketers of these services make sure their service sites are convenient and in neighborhoods that are attractive to prospective customers.

- *Environmental factors:* Service managers who operate a storefront service that requires people to come to their location realize they must create an attractive environment to lure customers. One trend is for such services to adopt a more retail-like philosophy, borrowing techniques from clothing stores or restaurants to create a pleasant environment as part of their marketing strategy. Banks, for example, increasingly create signature looks for their branches through the careful use of lighting, color, and art.[5]

People-Based Services

We've already pointed out that the unique service characteristics of inseparability and variability are largely due to the fact that individual service providers—even for the same firm—are inherently unique and different. When dad takes his six-year-old son to get male-bonding haircuts at Big League Barbers, one can only hope that the cut will be basically consistent time and again! Because people have less and less time to get things done today, the importance of people-based services is increasing. Self-improvement services such as those wardrobe consultants and personal trainers offer are increasingly popular, and in some locales even professional dog walkers and mobile pet washing trucks do a brisk business. Many of us hire someone to do our legal work, repair our cars and appliances, or do our tax returns.

Core and Augmented Services

When we buy a service, we may actually purchase a *set* of services. The **core service** is a benefit that a customer gets from the service. For example, when your car breaks down, repairing the problem is a core service you seek from an auto dealer or a garage. In most

core service
The basic benefit of having a service performed.

Ripped from the Headlines

Ethical/Sustainable Decisions in the Real World

The fast food industry certainly is a great example of a product that is about equal in tangible and intangible elements. And employees and customers interact to create a sale. McDonald's is the 800-pound gorilla in fast food. The chain is by far number one 1 in revenue, and it also ranks as the sixth biggest brand in the world in terms of brand value ($32.3 billion in 2009). With such size comes a certain, shall we say, visibility, and McDonald's comes under the scrutiny of many consumer and governmental groups. Recently much of that focus has been related to the epidemic of childhood obesity and how McDonald's, through its sheer market power, could contribute to solutions.

ETHICS CHECK: ↖
Find out what other students taking this course **would do** and **why** on **www .mypearsonmarketinglab .com**

A recent study focused on an aspect of Mc-Donald's service, specifically the likelihood that a counter or drive-through employee will mention healthier choices to consumers when they purchase a kid's Happy Meal. Nutrition researchers working for the Center for Science in the Public Interest visited 44 McDonald's restaurants around the United States and ordered 75 Happy Meals without specifying the side dish or beverage. The side dish options are French fries or apple slices with a low-fat caramel dipping sauce (apple slices alone apparently don't cut it). The beverage options are 1 percent low-fat milk, 100 percent juice, or standard sodas. The result: 93 percent of the time McDonald's employees served fries automatically without offering the apple choice, and 84 percent of the time sugar-loaded sodas were the first option mentioned for the accompanying drink (think: Would you like a Coke with that?). More than 75 percent of stores had toy displays for the Happy Meals, essentially implying a reward for ordering and consuming a high-fat, high-calorie, high-sugar meal.

Of all 24 possible Happy Meal product combinations McDonald's describes on its Web site, calories range from 380 to 650 per meal. At the high end, 650 is half of the 1,300-calorie recommended daily intake for kids 4 to 8 years old. McDonald's, along with Coca-Cola and other providers of food products heavily consumed by children, is becoming increasingly sensitive about its role in childhood obesity.

What should McDonald's do to ensure that healthier options are offered to customers by its service personnel? Would you make menu changes to the Happy Meal to make it healthier?

☐ YES ☐ NO

augmented services
The core service plus additional services provided to enhance value.

servicescape
The actual physical facility where the service is performed, delivered, and consumed.

cases though, the core service alone just isn't enough. To attract customers, a service firm often tries to offer **augmented services**—additional service offerings that differentiate the firm from the competition. When the auto dealership provides pickup and delivery of your car, a free car wash, or a customer lounge with donuts and coffee, it gains your loyalty as a customer.

And what about your own college education? Over the last decade, increased competition for students prompted many colleges and universities to emphasize a whole variety of augmented products such as full-service gyms and fitness centers, comprehensive on-site health services, upgraded dining options, writing and editing centers for term paper development, expanded hours for campus support departments, more variety of housing options including boutique and upscale dorms, user-friendly grant and scholarship counseling, and convenient bill payment plans. With so many augmented services, hopefully in their spare moments students even squeeze in a few classes along the way!

2

OBJECTIVE
Appreciate the importance of service quality to marketers.
(pp. 280–286)

Physical Elements of the Service Encounter: Servicescapes and Other Tangibles

As we noted earlier in the chapter, because services are intangible, marketers have to be mindful of the *physical evidence* that goes along with them. An important part of this physical evidence is the **servicescape**: the environment in which the service is delivered and where the firm and the customer interact. Servicescapes include facility exteriors—elements such as a building's architecture, the signage, parking, and even the landscaping. They also include interior elements, such as the design of the office or store, equipment, colors, air quality, temperature, and smells. For hotels, restaurants, banks, airlines, and even schools, the servicescape is quite elaborate. For other services, such as an express mail drop-off, a dry cleaner, or an ATM, the servicescape can be very simple.

Marketers know that carefully designed servicescapes can have a positive influence on customers' purchase decisions, their evaluations of service quality, and their ultimate satisfaction with the service. Thus, for a service such as a pro basketball game that Lara Price sells, much planning goes into designing not only the actual court, but also the exterior design and entrances of the stadium, landscaping, seating, restrooms, concession stands, and ticketing area. Similarly, marketers pay close attention to the design of other tangibles that facilitate the performance of the service or provide communications. For the basketball fan, these include the signs that direct people to the stadium, the game tickets, the programs, the team's uniforms, and the hundreds of employees who help to deliver the service.

Nowadays, for many consumers the first tangible evidence of a business (service or otherwise) is its Web site. Web sites send a strong cue to customers about you, and sites that are unattractive or frustratingly dysfunctional provide a horrible first impression of the company and its service. Searchability is important, as is paying attention to **search engine optimization (SEO)**: a systematic process of ensuring that your firm comes up at or near the top of lists of typical search phrases related to your business. SEO is critical, because if your organization's name doesn't come up when someone Googles, she'll just click on one of the competitors that does appear on the list (try Googling our book's title *Real People, Real Choices*, and see what happens).

search engine optimization (SEO)
A systematic process of ensuring that your firm comes up at or near the top of lists of typical search phrases related to your business.

How We Provide Quality Service

If a service experience isn't positive, it can quickly turn into a *disservice* with nasty consequences. Quality service ensures that customers are satisfied with what they have paid for. However, satisfaction is relative because the service recipient compares the current experience to some prior set of expectations. That's what makes delivering quality service tricky. What may seem like excellent service to one customer may be mediocre to another person who has been "spoiled" by earlier encounters with an exceptional service provider. So, marketers must identify customer expectations and then work hard to exceed them.

In air travel, lots of "little things" that used to be considered a normal part of the service are now treated by most airlines as extras. Many fliers believe the airlines are "nickel and diming" them for extra bag weight, blankets and pillows, small snacks and drinks, and prime seat locations. Southwest, though, has continued to offer all these perks as part of the basic service. Thus, by essentially doing nothing different from what they've always done, Southwest now stands out from the crowd and exceeds customer expectations. No surprise that for over five straight years Southwest has been ranked among the top three in customer satisfaction among low-priced carriers by J.D. Power and Associates.[6]

The Cutting Edge

Airlines Introduce Handheld Devices to Improve Service

The beleaguered airline industry is looking for any ways it can use handheld technology to improve performance with customers (and save time and money in the process!). Airline agents are increasingly going mobile at airports, with tools in hand to help passengers check in and print boarding passes, and eventually help sell augmented services (which is where they get a lot of their profit).

American Airlines recently equipped its agents at several U.S. airports with mobile devices. The plan is to eventually assign them at every gate. Delta introduced agents with mobile devices last year too, and the airline has since increased the number of devices to 900 units used at all domestic airports.

Services in place or planned via the devices include printing boarding passes, providing flight and gate information, displaying maps of other airports, printing bag tags, making upgrade purchases and other bundled offerings, adding passengers to standby lists, rebooking canceled flights and issuing meal vouchers, and paying for oversized bags that shouldn't have cleared security.

Despite the industry's generally bad service reputation, one thing they have done well over time is integrating technology into the service encounter. As travelers, we've all been trained to use the Internet to buy tickets and self-serve kiosks to check in and print boarding passes. Our expectations are very low for having an actual human encounter throughout the process. With the handhelds, the airlines can reintroduce a human touchpoint and maximize opportunities for up-sale to travelers while at the same time speeding along the airport process.[7]

Insurance companies like this one in Germany need to reassure customers about what they will receive if and when they actually need the service they sell.

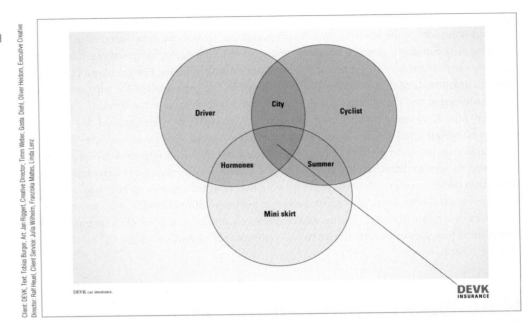

Client: DEVK, Text: Tobias Burger, Art: Jan Riggert, Creative Director: Timm Weber, Gosta Diehl, Oliver Heidon, Executive Creative Director: Ralf Heuel, Client Service: Julia Wilhelm, Franziska Mattes, Linda Lenz

Of course, it's not always so easy to meet or exceed customer expectations. The stories we hear from friends and acquaintances may influence our standards, and these may not always be realistic in the first place.[8] In some cases, there is little marketers can do to soothe ruffled feathers. Exaggerated customer expectations, such as providing a level of personal service impossible for a large company to accomplish, account for about 75 percent of the complaints service businesses report. However, providing customers with logical explanations for service failures and compensating them in some way can substantially reduce dissatisfaction.

Service Quality Attributes

Because services are inseparable in that an organization doesn't produce one until the time a customer consumes it, it is difficult to estimate how good a service will be until you buy it. Most service businesses cannot offer a free trial. Because services are variable, it is hard to predict consistency of quality and there is little or no opportunity for comparison shopping. The selection process for services is somewhat different than for goods, especially for services that are highly intangible. Service marketers have to come up with creative ways to illustrate the benefits their service will provide. A useful way to begin to develop approaches to marketing services effectively is to consider three types of service quality attributes—search qualities, experience qualities, and credence qualities.

search qualities
Product characteristics that the consumer can examine prior to purchase.

- **Search qualities** are product attributes that the consumer can examine prior to purchase. These include color, style, price, fit, smell, and texture. Tangible goods, of course, are more likely to have these characteristics, so services need to build them in by paying attention to details such as the style of flight attendants' uniforms or the decor of a hotel room.

experience qualities
Product characteristics that customers can determine during or after consumption.

- **Experience qualities** are product attributes that customers identify during or after consumption. For example, we can't really predict how good a vacation will be until we have it, so marketers need to reassure customers *before* the fact that they are in for a positive experience. A travel agency may invest in a slick presentation complete with alluring images of a tropical resort and perhaps even supply enthusiastic recommendations from other clients who had a positive experience at the same location. On the other hand, the last thing a marketer wants to do is overpromise and then fall short in the actual delivery—so conveniently cropping out that construction site that's located right next to the resort may not be a great idea.

- **Credence qualities** are product attributes we find difficult to evaluate even *after* we've experienced them. For example, most of us don't have the expertise to know if our doctor's diagnosis is correct.[9] To a great extent the client must trust the service provider. That is why tangible clues of professionalism, such as diplomas, an organized office, or even the professional's attire (for example, a physician in a lab coat instead of blue jeans) count toward purchase satisfaction.

credence qualities
Product characteristics that are difficult to evaluate even after they have been experienced.

How We Measure Service Quality

Because the customer's experience of a service determines if she will return to the provider in the future, service marketers feel that measuring positive and negative service experiences is the "Holy Grail" for the services industry. Marketers gather consumer responses in a variety of ways. For example, some companies hire "mystery shoppers" to check on hotels and airlines and report back. These shoppers usually work for a research firm, although some airlines reportedly recruit "spies" from the ranks of their most frequent flyers. Some firms also locate "lost customers" (former patrons) so they can find out what turned them off and correct the problem.

SERVQUAL

The **SERVQUAL** scale is one popular instrument to measure consumers' perceptions of service quality. SERVQUAL identifies five dimensions, or components, of service quality:

- *Tangibles:* the physical facilities and equipment and the professional appearance of personnel

- *Reliability:* the ability to provide dependably and accurately what was promised

- *Responsiveness:* the willingness to help customers and provide prompt service

- *Assurance:* the knowledge and courtesy of employees, and the ability to convey trust and confidence

- *Empathy:* the degree of caring and individual attention customers receive[10]

SERVQUAL
A multiple-item scale used to measure service quality across dimensions of tangibles, reliability, responsiveness, assurance, and empathy.

Thousands of service businesses apply the SERVQUAL scale. They usually administer it in a survey format through a written, online, or phone questionnaire. Firms often track SERVQUAL scores over time to understand how their service quality is (hopefully) improving. They also can use this measure to apply the gap analysis approach we describe next.

Gap Analysis

Gap analysis (no, nothing to do with a Gap clothing store) is a measurement approach that gauges the difference between a customer's expectation of service quality and what actually occurs. By identifying specific places in the service system where there is a wide gap between what customers expect and what they receive, services marketers can get a handle on what needs improvement. 🎵 Figure 10.2 illustrates where the gaps can occur in service, both on the consumer's side (often referred to as "in front of the curtain") and on the marketer's side ("behind the curtain"). Some major gaps include the following:[11]

gap analysis
A marketing research method that measures the difference between a customer's expectation of a service quality and what actually occurred.

- *Gap between consumers' expectations and management's perceptions:* A major quality gap occurs when the firm's managers don't understand what its customers' expectations are in the first place. Many service organizations have an *operations orientation* rather than a *customer orientation.* For example, banks often used to close branches at midday to balance transactions because that's more efficient for them, even though it's not convenient for customers who want to do their banking during their lunch hour. Today more and more banks are open late and on weekends.

- *Gap between management's perception and quality standards the firm sets:* Quality suffers when a firm fails to establish a quality-control program. Successful service firms, such

Figure 10.2 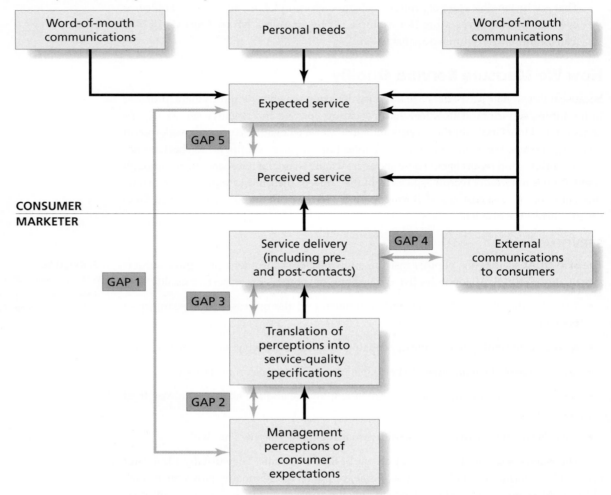 *Process* | The Gap Model of Service Delivery

A gap analysis identifies specific places in the service system where there is a wide gap between what customers expect and what they receive, allowing marketers to get a handle on what needs improvement.

A. Parasuraman, Valarie A. Zeithaml, and Leonard L. Berry, "A Conceptual Model of Service Quality and its Implications for Future Research," *Journal of Marketing* (Fall 1985), pp. 41–50.

as American Express, Ritz-Carlton, and JetBlue, develop written quality goals. American Express found that customers complained most about its responsiveness, accuracy, and timeliness. The company established 180 specific goals to correct these problems, and it now monitors how fast employees answer phones in an effort to be more responsive.

- *Gap between established quality standards and service delivery:* One of the biggest threats to service quality is poor employee performance. When employees do not deliver the service at the level the company specifies, quality suffers. Teamwork is crucial to service success. Unfortunately, many companies don't clearly specify what they expect of employees. Merrill Lynch addressed this problem when the brokerage firm assembled its operations personnel into quality groups of 8 to 15 employees each to clarify its expectations for how its personnel should interact with clients.

- *Gap between service quality standards and consumers' expectations:* Sometimes a firm makes exaggerated promises or does not accurately describe its service to customers. When the Holiday Inn hotel chain developed an advertising campaign based on the promise that guests would receive "No Surprises," many operations personnel opposed the idea. They pointed out that no service organization, no matter how good, can anticipate every single thing that can go wrong. Sure enough, the campaign was unsuccessful. A services firm is better off when it communicates exactly what the customer can expect and how the company will make it right if it doesn't deliver on its promises.

- *Gap between expected service and actual service:* Sometimes consumers misperceive the quality of the service. Thus, even when communications accurately describe what service quality the firm provides and what customers can expect, buyers are less than satisfied. Some diners at fine restaurants are so demanding that even their own mothers couldn't anticipate their every desire (that's probably why they're eating out in the first place).

The Critical Incident Technique

The **critical incident technique** is another way to measure service quality.[12] Using this approach, the company collects and closely analyzes very specific customer complaints. It can then identify *critical incidents*—specific contacts between consumers and service providers that are most likely to result in dissatisfaction.

Some critical incidents happen when the service organization simply can't meet a customer's expectations. For example, it is impossible to satisfy a passenger who says to a flight attendant, "Come sit with me. I don't like to fly alone." In other cases, though, the firm is capable of meeting these expectations but fails to do so. For example, the customer might complain to a flight attendant, "My seat won't recline."[13] A service provider can turn a potentially dissatisfied customer into a happy one if it addresses the problem or perhaps even tells the customer why the problem can't be solved at this time. Customers tend to be fairly forgiving if the organization gives them a reasonable explanation for the problem.

Disney Parks and Resorts is a real champion of consistency between standards and delivery. Disney makes all employees, or "Cast Members" (whether they sell ice cream on Main Street USA or they come in from another company to fill an executive role), go through "Traditions" training, as well as many other training programs, to help ensure that all Disney cast members know how they should interact with guests. They follow up frequently with refresher seminars and meetings to remind everyone of the company's history and traditions.

critical incident technique
A method for measuring service quality in which marketers use customer complaints to identify critical incidents—specific face-to-face contacts between consumer and service providers that cause problems and lead to dissatisfaction.

Strategic Issues When We Deliver Service Quality

We've seen that delivering quality is the goal of every successful service organization. What can the firm do to maximize the likelihood that a customer will choose its service and become a loyal customer? Because services differ from goods in so many ways, decision makers struggle to market something that isn't there. But, just as in goods marketing, the first step is to develop effective marketing strategies. Table 10.2 illustrates how three different types of service organizations might devise effective marketing strategies.

Of course, no one (not even your marketing professor) is perfect, and mistakes happen. Some failures, such as when your dry cleaner places glaring red spots on your new white sweater, are easy to see at the time the firm performs the service. Others, such as when the dry cleaner shrinks your sweater, are less obvious and you recognize them only at a later time when you're running late and get a "surprise." But no matter when or how you discover the failure, the important thing is that the firm takes fast action to resolve the problem. A timely and appropriate response means that the problem won't occur again (hopefully) and that the customer's complaint will be satisfactorily resolved. The key is speed; research shows that customers whose complaints are resolved quickly are far more likely to buy from the same company again than from those that take longer to resolve complaints.[14]

To make sure that they keep service failures to a minimum and that when they do blow it they can recover quickly, managers should first understand the service and the potential points at which failures are most likely to occur so they can plan how to recover ahead of time. That's why it's so important to identify critical incidents. In addition, employees

Table 10.2 | Marketing Strategies for Service Organizations

	Dry Cleaner	City Opera Company	A State University
Marketing objective	Increase total revenues by 20 percent within one year by increasing business of existing customers and obtaining new customers	Increase to 1,000 the number of season memberships to opera productions within two years	Increase applications to undergraduate and graduate programs by 10 percent for the coming academic year
Target markets	Young and middle-aged professionals living within a five-mile radius of the business	Clients who attend single performances but do not purchase season memberships Other local residents who enjoy opera but do not normally attend local opera performances	Primary market: prospective undergraduate and graduate students who are residents of the state Secondary market: prospective undergraduate and graduate students living in other states and in foreign countries
Benefits offered	Excellent and safe cleaning of clothes in 24 hours or fewer	Experiencing professional-quality opera performances while helping ensure the future of the local opera company	High-quality education in a student-centered campus environment
Strategy	Provide an incentive offer to existing customers such as one suit cleaned for free after 10 suits cleaned at regular price Use newspaper and direct mail advertising to communicate a limited-time discount offer to all customers	Correspond with former membership holders and patrons of single performances encouraging them to purchase new season memberships Arrange for opera company personnel and performers to be guests for local television and radio talk shows	Increase number of recruiting visits to local high schools; arrange a special day of events for high-school counselors to visit campus Communicate with alumni encouraging them to recommend the university to prospective students they know

should be trained to listen for complaints and be empowered to take appropriate actions immediately. Many hoteliers allow front desk employees the discretion to spend up to a certain amount per service failure to compensate guests for certain inconveniences.

Marketing People, Places, and Ideas

OBJECTIVE

Explain the marketing of people, places, and ideas.
(pp. 286–290)

By now, you understand that services are intangibles that marketers work hard to sell. But as we said earlier, services are not the only intangibles that organizations need to market. Intangibles such as people, places, and ideas often need to be "sold" by someone and "bought" by someone else. Let's consider how marketing is relevant to each of these.

Marketing People

As we saw in Chapter 1, people are products, too. If you don't believe that, you've never been on a job interview or spent a Saturday night in a singles bar! Many of us find it distasteful to equate people with products. In reality, though, a sizable number of people hire personal image consultants to devise a marketing strategy for them, and others undergo plastic surgery, physical conditioning, or cosmetic makeovers to improve their "market position" or "sell" themselves to potential employers, friends, or lovers.[15] Let's briefly touch on a few prominent categories of people marketing.

Sophisticated consultants create and market politicians when they "package"" candidates (clients) who then compete for "market share" as measured by votes. We trace this perspective all the way back to the 1952 and 1956 presidential campaigns of Dwight Eisenhower. Advertising executive Rosser Reeves (one of the original "Mad Men" who shaped the industry) repackaged the bland but amiable army general as he invented jingles and slogans such as "I like Ike" and contrived man-on-the-street interviews to improve the candidate's market position.[16] For better or worse, Reeves's strategies revolutionized the political landscape as people realized they could harness the tactics they use to sell soap to sell candidates for public office. Today, the basic idea remains the same, even though the techniques are more sophisticated.

In the age of electronic everything, marketing politics gets a little wackier. For example, comedian Stephen Colbert announced on his show that he was running for president in the 2008 election as "both a Democrat and a Republican." After his announcement, an online group was set up, and through links with social networking sites such as Facebook, he managed to acquire one million supporters! In fact, his fans' responses inspired the creation of the "1,000,000 Strong for Stephen T. Colbert" Facebook group, which modeled itself after a similarly named group set up for Democratic candidate Barack Obama's campaign. It took more than eight months for Obama to gain 380,000 supporters, while it took less than two weeks for Colbert's group to become one of the largest political groups on Facebook.[17]

From actors and musicians to athletes and supermodels, the famous and near-famous jockey for market position in popular culture. Agents carefully package celebrities as they connive to get their clients exposure on TV, starring roles in movies, recording contracts, or product endorsements.[18] Like other products, celebrities even rename themselves to craft a "brand identity." They use the same strategies marketers use to ensure that their products make an impression on consumers, including memorability (Evel Knievel), suitability (fashion designer Oscar Renta reverted to his old family name of de la Renta because it sounded more elegant), and distinctiveness (Steveland Morris Hardaway became Stevie Wonder).

It's hard to imagine anyone topping Stefani Joanne Angelina Germanotta for pure marketing chutzpah. Oh, by the way, that's Lady Gaga's real name. Her stage name was inspired by the Queen song "Radio Ga Ga" and in 2010 she laid claim to the most Facebook friends of any living person with over 11 million. A lot of corporate marketing gurus could take a lesson or two from Lady Gaga's marketing playbook!

Celebrities and the services they sell (i.e., concerts) get packaged and promoted in many ways, including these innovative messages from a ticket agency in Israel.

Table 10.3 | Strategies to Sell a Celebrity

Marketing Approach	Implementation
Pure Selling Approach	Agent presents a client
	– to record companies
	– to movie studios
	– to TV production companies
	– to talk show hosts
	– to advertising agencies
	– to talent scouts
Product Improvement Approach	*Client is modified*
	– New name
	– New image
	– Voice lessons
	– Dancing lessons
	– Plastic surgery
	– New back-up band
	– New music genre
Market Fulfillment Approach	*Agent looks for market opening*
	– Identify unmet need
	– Develop a new product (band, singer) to the specifications of consumer wants

In addition to these branding efforts, there are other strategies marketers use to "sell" a celebrity as Table 10.3 shows. These include the following:

1. The *pure selling approach*: An agent presents a client's qualifications to potential "buyers" until she finds one who is willing to act as an intermediary.

2. The *product improvement approach*: An agent works with the client to modify certain characteristics that will increase her market value.

3. The *market fulfillment approach*: An agent scans the market to identify unmet needs. After identifying a need, the agent then finds a person or a group that meets a set of minimum qualifications and develops a new "product."

Marketing Places

place marketing
Marketing activities that seek to attract new businesses, residents, or visitors to a town, state, country, or some other site.

Place marketing strategies regard a city, state, country, or other locale as a brand. Marketers use the marketing mix to create a suitable identity so that consumers choose this brand over competing destinations when they plan their travel. Because of the huge amount of money tourism generates, the competition to attract visitors is fierce. There are about 1,600 visitors' bureaus in the United States alone that try to brand their locations. In addition, almost every town or city has an economic development office charged with luring new businesses or residents. For example, after the 2001 attack on the World Trade Center, New York City unveiled a new tourism advertising campaign that November with the slogan "The New York Miracle: Be a Part of It." The campaign included six 30-second TV commercials and some of New York's biggest celebrities such as Woody Allen and Robert DeNiro.[19] Since then, NYC & Company, the city's official tourism marketer, reports that both the domestic and overseas visitor counts are returning to pre-9/11 levels.[20]

Marketing Ideas

You can see people. You can stand in a city. So how do you market something you can't see, smell, or feel? **Idea marketing** refers to strategies that seek to gain market share for a concept, philosophy, belief, or issue. Even religious organizations market ideas about faith and desirable behavior when they adopt secular marketing techniques to attract young people. Some evangelists use the power of television to convey their messages. So-called *megachurches* are huge steel and glass structures, with acres of parking and slickly produced services complete with live bands and professional dancers that draw huge audiences. Some offer aerobics, bowling alleys, and multimedia Bible classes inspired by MTV to attract "customers" turned off by traditional approaches to religion.[21]

But make no mistake about it, the marketing of ideas can be even more difficult than marketing goods and services. Consumers often do not perceive that the *value* they receive when they wear seat belts or recycle garbage or designate a driver or even when they conserve to reduce global warming is worth the *cost*—the extra effort necessary to realize these goals. Governments and other organizations use marketing strategies, often with only limited success, to sell ideas that will save the lives of millions of unwilling consumers or that will save our planet.

The marketers whose job is to promote Las Vegas as a tourist destination have changed course several times. First they tried to clean up the city's original image as a den of corruption and vice to encourage family visits. Then they switched direction and plugged the city's bawdy roots with the slogan "What happens in Vegas stays in Vegas." Oops, then the recession hit and companies clamped down on business and convention travel to "Sin City." Now, Vegas no longer promotes its famous tagline as it opens its arms to families once again with all sorts of kid-friendly activities and incentives.
Pascal Le Segretain/Getty Images

idea marketing
Marketing activities that seek to gain market share for a concept, philosophy, belief, or issue by using elements of the marketing mix to create or change a target market's attitude or behavior.

The Future of Services

As we look into the future, we recognize that service industries will continue to play a key role in the growth of both the United States and the global economy. In fact, in recent years the accelerating impact of service as an integral part of any firm's value proposition has led some analysts to argue that there is now a **new dominant logic for marketing**. This means that we need to rethink our traditional distinction between services and goods. Instead, we need to recognize that a service is the central (core) deliverable in *every* exchange; any physical products involved are relatively minor in terms of their contribution to the value proposition.[22] Figure 10.3 provides several trends for us to consider that will provide both opportunities and challenges for the marketers of services down the road (that means you). In the future, we can expect services we can't even imagine yet. Of course, they will

new dominant logic for marketing
A reconceptualization of traditional marketing to redefine service as the central (core) deliverable and the actual physical products purveyed as comparatively incidental to the value proposition.

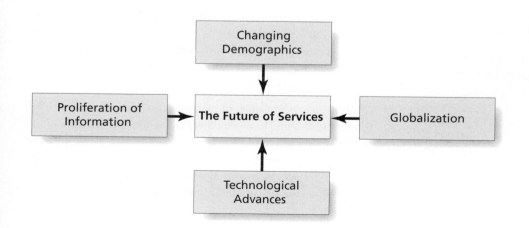

Figure 10.3 *Snapshot* | Factors That Shape the Future of Services

Changing demographics, globalization, technological advances, and proliferation of information all impact services.

This Australian ad promotes the idea of safe driving.

Non-profit organizations often use vivid imagery to communicate the seriousness of their causes.

also provide many new and exciting job opportunities for future marketers.

- *Changing demographics:* As the population ages, service industries that meet the needs of older consumers will see dramatic growth. Companies that offer recreational opportunities, health care, and living assistance for seniors will be in demand.

- *Globalization:* The globalization of business will increase the need for logistics and distribution services to move goods around the world (we'll talk more about these in Chapter 15) and for accounting and legal services that facilitate these global exchanges. In addition, global deregulation will affect the delivery of services by banks, brokerages, insurance, and other financial service industries because globalization means greater competition. For example, many "medical tourists" now journey to countries like Thailand and India to obtain common surgical procedures that may cost less than half what they would in the United States. Meanwhile, hospitals back home often look more like luxury spas as they offer amenities such as adjoining quarters for family members, choice of different ethnic cuisines, and in-room Internet access. In the hotel industry, demand for luxury properties is growing around the world. Hyatt International is expanding aggressively in China with 14 luxury properties either open or scheduled to open. Hyatt expects to have as many as 24 properties there within a decade.[23]

- *Technological advances:* Changing technology provides opportunities for growth and innovation in global service industries such as telecommunications, health care, banking, and Internet services. And we can also expect technological advances to provide opportunities for services that we haven't even thought of yet but that will dramatically change and improve the lives of consumers. Best Buy's Geek Squad makes the company a ton of money by showing people how to set up and use their home computers—with new advances there will always be "clueless" customers who need help to keep up with progress! Meanwhile, social media Web sites, smartphones, blogs, and the Internet in general all are central to successfully marketing all kinds of intangibles. In the political realm, the U.S. presidential campaign of 2008 was a breakthrough in the use of digital platforms as handlers for both parties' candidates invested heavily to support these "real-time" methods of communicating with tech-savvy voters about their candidate's ideas and position on the issues *du jour.*

- *Proliferation of information:* In many ways, we have become an information society. The availability of, flow of, and access to information are critical to the success of organizations. These changes will provide greater opportunities for database services, artificial intelligence systems, communications systems, and other services that facilitate the storage and transfer of knowledge.

Here's my choice...

Real **People**, Real **Choices**

1 Option   **2** Option   **3** Option

Why do you think Lara chose option 1?

How It Worked Out at the Philadelphia 76ers

The Sixers hired a Web-based company that provided a data warehouse, and the vendor also developed software to help the Sixers track their customer base. The team realized a 150-to-1 return on its investment due to the money it saved in advertising spending (TV, print, and radio). The CRM approach has proven to be so successful that the company is in the process of developing more sophisticated systems.

To learn the whole story, visit www.mypearsonmarketinglab.com.

Brand **YOU**!

Corporate life is not for everyone. You can blaze a trail to success in many different ways. Learn about the myths and realities of the job market and how you can explore different options for your career, including being a contract employee with flexible hours, a free agent with many clients and projects, or even pursuing your personal passion while you are working. Consider your options in Chapter 10 of the Brand You supplement.

| Kim Richmond Fourth Edition |

Brand YOU

MARKETING 7E **real** People, **real** Choices

Solomon | Marshall | Stuart

1. Objective Summary (pp. 274–280)

Describe the characteristics of services and the ways marketers classify services.

Services are products that are intangible and that are exchanged directly from producer to customer without ownership rights. Generally, services are acts that accomplish some goal and may be directed either toward people or toward an object. Both consumer services and business-to-business services are important parts of the economy. Important service characteristics include the following: (1) intangibility (they cannot be seen, touched, or smelled), (2) perishability (they cannot be stored), (3) variability (they are never exactly the same from one time to the next), and (4) inseparability from the producer (most services are produced, sold, and consumed at the same time).

In reality, most products are a combination of goods and services. Some services are goods-dominant (i.e., tangible products are marketed with supporting services). Some are equipment- or facility-based (i.e., the creation of the service requires elaborate equipment or facilities). Other services are people-based (i.e., people are actually a part of the service marketed).

Like goods, services include both a core service, or the basic benefit received, and augmented services, including innovative features and convenience of service delivery. Banking and brokerages, computer software, music, travel, dating services, career services, distance learning, and medical care are among some of the services available on the Internet. Marketers know that both the social elements of the service encounter (i.e., the employee and the customer) and the physical evidence including the servicescape are important to a positive service experience.

Key Terms

intangibles, p. 274

services, p. 274

intangibility, p. 275

perishability, p. 275

capacity management, p. 276

variability, p. 276

inseparability, p. 276

service encounter, p. 277

disintermediation, p. 277

core service, p. 279

augmented services, p. 280

servicescape, p. 280

2. Objective Summary (pp. 280–286)

Appreciate the importance of service quality to marketers.

The customer's perception of service quality is related to prior expectations. Because services are intangible, evaluation of service quality is more difficult, and customers often look for cues to help them decide whether they have received satisfactory service. Marketers improve customers' perceptions of services by designing important search qualities, experience qualities, and credence qualities.

SERVQUAL is a multiple-item scale used to measure consumer perceptions of service quality across dimensions of tangibles, reliability, responsiveness, assurance, and empathy. Gap analysis measures the difference between customer expectations of service quality and what actually occurred. Using the critical incident technique, service firms can identify the specific contacts between customers and service providers that create dissatisfaction. When service quality does fail, marketers must understand the points at which failures occur and take fast action.

Key Terms

search engine optimization (SEO), p. 281

search qualities, p. 282

experience qualities, p. 282

credence qualities, p. 283

SERVQUAL, p. 283

gap analysis, p. 283

critical incident technique, p. 285

3. Objective Summary (pp. 286–290)

Explain the marketing of people, places, and ideas.

Managers follow the steps for marketing planning when marketing other intangibles as well. People, especially politicians and celebrities, are often packaged and promoted. Place marketing aims to create or change the market position of a particular locale, whether a city, state, country, resort, or institution. Idea marketing (gaining market share for a concept, philosophy, belief, or issue) seeks to create or change a target market's attitude or behavior. Marketing is used by religious organizations and to promote important causes. Marketing of ideas may be especially difficult, as consumers may not consider the value to be worth the cost.

Key Terms

place marketing, p. 288

idea marketing, p. 289

new dominant logic for marketing, p. 289

Chapter **Questions** and **Activities**

Concepts: Test Your Knowledge

1. What are intangibles? How do basic marketing concepts apply to the marketing of intangibles?
2. What is a service? What are the important characteristics of services that make them different from goods?
3. What is the service continuum? What are goods-dominated services, equipment- or facility-based services, and people-based services?
4. What are core and augmented services? How do marketers increase market share with augmented services?
5. What are the social and physical elements of the service encounter?
6. What are search qualities, experience qualities, and credence qualities?
7. What dimensions do consumers and business customers use to evaluate service quality? How do marketers measure service quality?
8. How should marketers respond to failures in service quality?
9. What is the so-called "new dominant logic for marketing"? Why is it especially relevant to someone just starting a career in business (either in marketing or otherwise)?
10. What do we mean by marketing people? Marketing places? Marketing ideas?

Activities: Apply What You've Learned

1. Because of increased competition in its community, you have been hired as a marketing consultant by a local bank. You know that the characteristics of services (intangibility, perishability, variability, and inseparability) create unique marketing challenges. You also know that these challenges can be met with creative marketing strategies. Outline the challenges for marketing the bank created by each of the four characteristics of services. List your ideas for what might be done to meet each of these challenges.
2. Assume that you are a physician. You are opening a new family practice clinic in your community. You feel that you have the best chance of being successful if you can create a product that is superior to that offered by competing businesses. Put together a list of ways in which you can augment the basic service offering to develop a better product. List the advantages and disadvantages of each.

3. You are currently a customer for a college education, a very expensive service product. You know that a service organization can create a competitive advantage by focusing on how the service is delivered after it has been purchased—making sure the service is efficiently and comfortably delivered to the customer. Develop a list of recommendations for your school for improving the delivery of its service. Consider both classroom and nonclassroom aspects of the educational product.
4. Assume that you work for a marketing firm that has been asked to develop a marketing plan for an up-and-coming rock band called Stalagmite and its new CD, *Slow Drip*. Prepare an outline for your marketing plan. First, list the special problems and challenges associated with marketing people rather than a physical product. Then outline your ideas for product, price, and promotion strategies.
5. Address the same issues in question #4 for a marketing plan for your hometown.
6. Assume that you have been recently hired by your city government to head up a program to create 100 percent compliance with recycling regulations. Develop a presentation for the city council in which you will outline the problems in "selling" recycling. Develop an outline for the presentation. Be sure to focus on each of the *Four Ps*.

Choices: What Do You Think?

1. Why are first impressions we form about a service through the Internet so important? What can a service firm do to ensure a favorable first impression online? (*Hint:* Consider issues beyond the Web site itself.)
2. Sometimes service quality may not meet customers' expectations. What problems have you experienced with quality in the delivery of the following services?
   a. A restaurant meal
   b. An airline flight
   c. Automobile repairs
   d. Your college education
   What do you think is the reason for the poor quality?
3. Internet dating services, while becoming very popular, may present some dangers for those who use their services. Who do you think uses Internet dating services? What, if anything, should dating services do to protect their clients?

4. What "service" do providers such as MySpace convey? What core and augmented services do they offer? How should we evaluate MySpace's service quality?

5. There has been a lot of criticism about the way politicians have been marketed in recent years. What are some of the ways marketing has helped our political process? What are some ways the marketing of politicians might have an adverse effect on our government?

6. Many not-for-profit and religious organizations have found that they can be more successful by marketing their ideas. What are some ways that these organizations market themselves that are similar to and different from the marketing by for-profit businesses? Is it *ethical* for churches and religious organizations to spend money on marketing? Why or why not?

7. In the chapter we mentioned that most of the airlines have transformed elements of their core service (extra bags, pillows and blankets, etc.) into "extras." They claim that this is better for customers because they can now pay for only what they want instead of paying for a bundle of services they do not even use. How do you react to their premise? Do you agree or disagree?

8. Many developed countries, including the United States, have in recent decades become primarily service economies; that is, there is relatively little manufacturing of goods, and most people in the economy are employed by service industries. Why do you think this has occurred? In what ways is this trend a good and/or a bad thing for a country? Do you think this trend will continue?

Marketing Metrics Exercise

The consulting firm Market Metrix employs a metric it calls the Marketing Metrix Hospitality Index (MMHI) to measure customer satisfaction with hotel, airline, and car rental companies. The metric is based on 35,000 in-depth consumer interviews. The MMHI includes most major brand hotels, airlines, travel industry Web sites, and car rental companies—each rated on over 50 different dimensions. Subscribers to the quarterly report can measure their company's stand-alone performance and also benchmark its ratings against those of competitors and highly ranked companies within and across the other hospitality industries. Go to the MMHI Web site (**www.marketmetrix.com**), then click on "Hospitality Index."

Review the information on MMHI Winners, Brand History, and MMHI Brand List. Based on recent results, how are your favorite brands faring on their index? Do you agree with the results provided about your favorites?

Miniprojects: Learn by Doing

Miniproject 1

1. Select a service that you, as a consumer, will purchase in the next week or so.
2. As you experience the service, record the details of every aspect, including the following:
   a. People
   b. Physical facilities
   c. Location
   d. Waiting time
   e. Hours
   f. Transaction
   g. Other customers
   h. Tangible aspects
   i. Search qualities
   j. Credence qualities
3. Recommend improvements for this service encounter.

Miniproject 2

Theme and entertainment parks like Universal Studios fall in the middle of the goods/services continuum—half goods and half services. To be successful in this highly competitive market, these parks must carefully develop targeting and positioning strategies. Visit the Web sites of the four top theme park organizations: Walt Disney World (**www.disneyworld.com**), Six Flags parks (**www.sixflags.com**), Universal's Orlando® Theme Park (**www.universalstudios.com**), and Busch Gardens (**www.buschgardens.com**). Thoroughly investigate each site.

1. How is the Web site designed to appeal to each theme park organization's target markets?
2. How does each park position its product? How is this positioning communicated through the Web site?
3. What changes or improvements would you recommend for each Web site?

Marketing in **Action** Case   Real Choices at Clear & SIMPLE™

Want to know how to fit your very complicated life into your very small apartment? How to organize your clothes so you can find that great pink sweater on Friday night? What to do with those very valuable high school football trophies? Like many people, you may be faced with a seemingly insurmountable problem of clutter.

As evidenced by the increasing popularity of TV programs like *Clean Sweep* (TLC), *Clean House* (Style Network), and *Mission: Organization* (HGTV), many consumers recognize that they suffer from home chaos. For some of us, the clutter comes from excessive buying or an attachment to things, while for others the problem is simply a lack of organizational skills. A disorganized home or office not only lowers our efficiency but also create stress and interrupts the harmony of the space. Fortunately, there is help.

Clear & SIMPLE™, founded in 1999, is one of a number of professional organizing companies that meets the growing need for home and office organization skills. Because many of us seem to be missing a gene for good organizational skills, professional organizers like Clear & SIMPLE™ help clients to build a harmonized life and restore order to their homes and workplaces.

Clear & SIMPLE™ owners Marla Dee and Lisa Parsons try to convince homeowners and businesses that "Getting Organized can be Fun, Simple, and Freeing!" The company offers clutter-afflicted consumers a variety of services. Their two major systems, SEE IT • MAP IT • DO IT and S.T.A.C.K.S.™, aim to train clients how to identify their problems with clutter and chaos and then show them how to better organize their space.

Most of the objects we accumulate relate to our memories; we're afraid to throw away and/or give away these things because it means losing part of our past. Thus, a major part of the training is learning how to separate meaningful things that are also useful from those that no longer are very meaningful. In addition to its training programs, Clear & SIMPLE™ products include workshops, individual consultation and needs assessment, plus a variety of organizational skills books, kits, and self-study courses. Clear & SIMPLE™ also introduced a certificate program to train more professional organizers to meet the growing demand in the market.

Despite its current success, Clear & SIMPLE™ faces a number of challenges. The increasing number of competitors in the industry and the growing number of Internet Web sites on delivering organizing skills can have a direct impact on Clear & SIMPLE's™ future success. While we wouldn't classify Clear & SIMPLE™ as a luxury product, consumers may question if help in organizing their space is a necessary expense in times of economic recession. How can Clear & SIMPLE™ build on its current success for a sustainable future that will endure economic ups and downs? Even more important, what should Marla and her colleagues do to make their brand stand out among their other "neat" competitors?

You Make the Call

1. What is the decision facing Clear & SIMPLE™?
2. What factors are important in understanding this decision situation?
3. What are the alternatives?
4. What decision(s) do you recommend?
5. What are some ways to implement your recommendation?

Based on: Russell W. Belk, Joon Yong Seo, and Eric Li, "Dirty Little Secret: Home Chaos and Professional Organizers," *Consumption, Markets and Culture*, Volume 10, Number 2, June 2007, pp. 133–40; Clear & SIMPLE™ Official Web site, "About Us," Clear & SIMPLE™ Official Web site (http://www.clearsimple.com/aboutus.html).

Chapter 11

Price the Product

Real People **Profiles**

Danielle Blugrind

Profile   Info

▼ **A Former Decision Maker at Taco Bell**

Danielle Blugrind was Director of Consumer and Brand Insights for Taco Bell Corporation. After she received her BA from the University of California, Irvine, in 1989, she earned an MBA in marketing at Claremont Graduate School. Her first job out of the MBA program was as an analyst in the Consumer Research department of Mattel Toys. At first, she worked on research for sports toys, activity toys, and action figures. Then she was promoted to senior analyst working on the Barbie brand, and she spent the next six years on Barbie for girls and Barbie Collectibles before working her way up to senior manager. At Taco Bell, Danielle oversaw all research related to overall brand and advertising strategy, value products, late night, beverages, promotions, and combos. She left the company in 2008 to open her own consulting practice.

💬 **Danielle's Info**   ✎

What do I do when I'm not working?
   A) I'm a mom to a wonderful daughter! And I can't get enough of reading.

Career high?
   A) Every day is a new one! There is always something to look forward to.

Business book I'm reading now?
   A) *The Sweet Spot* by Lisa Fortini Campbell.

Don't do this when interviewing with me?
   A) Never act nervous! Don't try to sell me on what a big Taco Bell fan you are. And don't try to tell me you don't have a single question about the job or the company.

My management style?
   A) Too hands-on, at times! Let's say it is evolving into a better demonstration of my belief in people and their abilities.

My motto to live by?
   A) There is always a bright side.

Here's my problem...

Back in the 1990s, Taco Bell realized that a major barrier to broadening its reach and sales was the fact that many consumers found its food too expensive. To combat this problem, the company developed a 59–79–99¢ Value Menu. Taco Bell's sales shot through the roof as consumers responded positively to the price-based approach. However, after several years, the competition began to offer similar alternatives (such as the McDonald's Value Meals), so Taco Bell no longer "owned" a value position in the industry as it had in the mid-1990s. In response, the company tried to refocus its strategy and move away from a value emphasis—a decision that wound up hurting the company.

Fast-forward to the year 2000. Taco Bell knew that value was here to stay in the fast-food industry, but it had abandoned its 59–79–99¢ menu and needed a new direction. The firm test-marketed several value menus and ideas, but nothing really generated a much-needed boost in sales. Danielle and her colleagues were forced to step back and think hard about what value means to their customers and how the chain could deliver the food people wanted at the price they wanted. Danielle knew that as competitors began to claim they were providing greater value, Taco Bell needed to break through the cluttered value landscape that is fast food and "think outside the bun."

The company looked at numerous alternatives, including new products, new ways to price its menu, and new product combinations. A pricing strategy began to take shape. Many of Taco Bell's competitors continued to focus on the $.99 price point, which is virtually synonymous with value in the fast-food world. Although it was tempting for Taco Bell to follow suit by adding items to the menu for $.99, most of the company's products could not feasibly be offered at such a low price. And Taco Bell wanted to show that it was different from other fast-food restaurants—this wouldn't happen if it used the same pricing strategy as everyone else.

Danielle and her team began to test other pricing options, including the idea of pricing all menu items the same. She knew from other research that the "value threshold" for Taco Bell's menu items was $1.29; this represents the highest possible price that consumers might still consider to be a value for some items. In total, the company tested eight different price configurations that it determined would make financial sense; these included four options in which each menu item was priced the same and would cost $.99, $1.09, $1.19, or $1.29 as well as four other mixed price options. These are the eight combinations they tested:

Things to remember

Danelle knew that Taco Bell couldn't afford to get into a price war with its fast food competitors. The major chains had already responded to the company's value prices by offering their own versions so she needed to do something else to grab the attention of hungry, but price-conscious, customers.

	$.99 Menu	$1.09 Menu	$1.19 Menu	$1.29 Menu	Mixed Price #1	Mixed Price #2	Mixed Price #3	Mixed Price #4
Burrito #1	$.99	$1.09	$1.19	$1.29	$1.29	$1.29	$.99	$1.29
Burrito #2	$.99	$1.09	$1.19	$1.29	$1.19	$1.19	$1.29	$1.29
Burrito #3	$.99	$1.09	$1.19	$1.29	$1.29	$1.29	$1.29	$1.29
Taco #1	$.99	$1.09	$1.19	$1.29	$.99	$1.09	$.99	$.99
Taco #2	$.99	$1.09	$1.19	$1.29	$.99	$.99	$.99	$.99
Nachos	$.99	$1.09	$1.19	$1.29	$.99	$.99	$1.19	$.99
Specialty item	$.99	$1.09	$1.19	$1.29	$1.19	$1.19	$1.29	$1.29

Danielle considered her **Options** 1·2·3

Based on the results from the concept testing of the eight different menus, Danielle identified three possible ways to proceed:

Option 1

Price the entire menu at $1.29. This would make things simple for the company, and it would be easy for consumers to understand. This option would also offer the most potential profit per item. But the challenge would be to convince people that these $1.29 items were *all* truly a "value" in a world where competitors offered many items for $.99. This problem surfaced in Taco Bell's research; consumers rated the $1.29 menu the lowest of the eight menus it tested.

Option 2

Price items at $.99 and $1.29 (Mixed Price Menu #4). Purchase intent and overall liking were much stronger than for the $1.29 menu. The pricing structure was still pretty simple since any item would cost either $.99 or $1.29. Not surprisingly, though, consumers didn't rate a menu that included some $1.29 items as high as one that included only $.99 items.

Option 3

Price items at $.99, $1.19, and $1.29 (Mixed Price Menu #1). Danielle's research showed that purchase intent, overall liking, and ratings of uniqueness were all strong for this menu. On the downside, the pricing structure was more complex. If customers were to accept it, they would have to be made to understand why there are three price points on a value menu and why certain items cost more than others.

Now, put yourself in Danielle's shoes: Which option would you choose, and why?

You Choose

Which **Option** would you choose, and **why**?
1. ☐YES ☐NO 2. ☐YES ☐NO 3. ☐YES ☐NO

See what **option** Danielle chose and its success on **page 330** ➡

price
The assignment of value, or the amount the consumer must exchange to receive the offering.

Check out chapter 11 Study Map on page 331

1

OBJECTIVE

Explain the importance of pricing and how marketers set objectives for their pricing strategies. (pp. 298–302)

"Yes, But What Does It Cost?"

"If you have to ask how much it is, you can't afford it!" We've all heard that, but how often do you buy something without asking the price? If price weren't an issue, we'd all drive dream cars, take trips to exotic places, and live like royalty. In the real world, though, most of us need to at least consider a product's price before we buy it.

In the past three chapters, we've talked about creating and managing tangible and intangible products. But to create value for customers, marketers must do more. Of course, a successful marketing plan must include a fantastic new (or existing) widget with all the bells and whistles consumers want. But equally (if not more) important is pricing the new offering so that consumers are willing to fork over their hard-earned cash to own the product. The question of what to charge for a product is a central part of the marketing plan.

In this chapter, we'll tackle the basic question—what is price? We'll also see how marketers develop pricing objectives, and we'll look at the roles demand, costs, revenues, and the environment play in the pricing decision process. Then we'll explore how the pricing decision process leads to specific pricing strategies and tactics. Finally, we'll look at the dynamic world of pricing on the Internet and at some psychological, legal, and ethical aspects of pricing.

What Is Price?

As we said in Chapter 1, **price** is the assignment of value, or the amount the consumer must exchange to receive the offering or product. Payment may be in the form of money, goods, services, favors, votes, or anything else that has *value* to the other party. As we also explained in Chapter 1, marketing is the process that creates exchanges of things of value. We usually think of this exchange as people trading money for a good or a service. But in some marketplace practices, price can mean exchanges of nonmonetary value as well. Long before societies minted coins, people exchanged one good or service for another. This practice still occurs today. For example, someone who owns a home at a mountain ski resort may exchange a weekend stay for car repair or dental work. No money changes hands, but there still is an exchange of value (just ask the IRS).

Other nonmonetary costs often are important to marketers. What is the cost of wearing seat belts? What is it worth to people to camp out in a clean national park? It is also important to consider an *opportunity cost*, or the value of something we give up to obtain something else. For example, the cost of going to college includes more than tuition—it also includes the income that the student could have earned by working instead of going to classes (no, we're not trying to make you feel guilty). And what about a public service campaign designed to reduce alcohol-related accidents? The cost to the individual is either agreeing to abstain and be a designated driver or shelling out for taxi fare. The value is reducing the risk of having a serious or possibly fatal accident. Unfortunately, too many people feel the chance of having an accident is so slim that the cost of abstaining from drinking is too high.

As  Figure 11.1 shows, the elements of price planning include six steps: developing pricing objectives, estimating demand, determining costs, evaluating the pricing environment, choosing a pricing strategy and developing pricing tactics: In this chapter we will talk about how marketers go through these steps for successful price planning.

Step 1: Set Pricing Objectives
- Profit
- Sales
- Market share
- Competitive effect
- Customer satisfaction
- Image enhancement

Step 2: Estimate Demand
- Shifts in demand
- Price elasticity of demand

Step 3: Determine Costs
- Variable costs
- Fixed costs
- Break-even analysis
- Marginal analysis
- Markups and margins

Step 4: Examine the Pricing Environment
- The economy
- The competition
- Government regulation
- Consumer trends
- The international environment

Step 5: Choose a Pricing Strategy
- Based on cost
- Based on demand
- Based on the competition
- Based on customers' needs
- New-product pricing

Step 6: Develop Pricing Tactics
- For individual products
- For multiple products
- Distribution-based tactics
- Discounting for channel members

Figure 11.1 *Process* | Elements of Price Planning

Successful price planning includes a series of orderly steps beginning with setting pricing objectives.

Figure 11.2 *Process* | Pricing Objectives

The first step in price planning is to develop pricing objectives that support the broader objectives of the firm.

Sales or Market Share
Develop bundle pricing offers in order to increase market share

Profit
Set prices to allow for an 8 percent profit margin on all goods sold.

Image Enhancement
Alter pricing policies to reflect the increased emphasis on the product's quality image.

Pricing Objectives

Competitive Effect
Alter pricing strategy during first quarter of the year to increase sales during competitor's introduction of a new product.

Customer Satisfaction
Alter price levels to match customer expectations.

Step 1: Develop Pricing Objectives

The first crucial step in price planning is to develop pricing objectives. These must support the broader objectives of the firm, such as maximizing shareholder value, as well as its overall marketing objectives, such as increasing market share. Figure 11.2 provides examples of different types of pricing objectives. Let's take a closer look at these.

Profit Objectives

As we discussed in Chapter 2, often a firm's overall objectives relate to a certain level of profit it hopes to realize. This is usually the case in B2B marketing. When pricing strategies are determined by profit objectives, the focus is on a target level of profit growth or a desired net profit margin. A profit objective is important to firms that believe profit is what motivates shareholders and bankers to invest in a company.

Because firms usually produce an entire product line and/or a product mix, profit objectives may focus on pricing for the firm's entire portfolio of products. In such cases, marketers develop pricing strategies that maximize the profits of the entire portfolio rather than focusing on the costs or profitability of each individual product. For example, it may be better to price one product especially high and lose sales on it if that decision causes customers to instead purchase a product that has a higher profit margin.

Cannibalization, a subject we discussed in Chapter 9, is also something to worry about. For example, what happens when a firm that markets several brands of hair care products offers a special price promotion of 15 percent off on one of its shampoos? If customers who normally buy

How important are good pricing decisions? Even during the best of economic times, most consumers consider a reasonable price, one that makes the product affordable and seems fair, as an important part of their purchase decisions. During recessionary times, price is even more important. The plight of U.S. airlines is a good example of how bad pricing decisions can hurt an entire industry. In 1978 the U.S. Congress passed the Airline Deregulation Act that allowed airlines to set their own fares and fly whatever domestic routes they wished while allowing new airlines to enter the industry. From about 1982 to 1992, the airline industry engaged in a fierce price war, lowering the per-mile fare nearly 25 percent (accounting for inflation of the dollar) while costs such as labor and fuel more than doubled. As a result, during that time period the airlines lost over $10 billion—more than they had earned since the start of commercial air travel. Of course, things haven't gotten much better for airlines today. In 2009 alone the international airline industry lost over $9 billion.

another of the firm's offerings are attracted to the price-off promotion and buy the discounted brand, the promotion can mean a loss to the firm instead of the desired increase in sales and profits.[1]

Although profits are an important consideration in the pricing of all goods and services, they are critical when the product is a *fad*. Fad products, from pet rocks to Beanie Babies, have a short market life; this makes a profit objective essential to allow the firm to recover its investment in a short time. In such cases, the firm must harvest profits before customers lose interest and move on to the next fad. Think about the Teen Buzz fad (aka Mosquito Ringtone), for example. This high-pitched, annoying tone that only younger people can detect (before their hearing deteriorates as they reach middle age) was originally intended to keep them from loitering near convenience stores in the United Kingdom. Kids adapted this weapon to their own advantage; they use the Teen Buzz in classrooms to alert them to incoming text messages on their mobile phones without their (old and decrepit) teachers' knowledge.[2] A company that hawks a tone like this has to move quickly to unload its "inventory" before the next cool idea replaces it.

Sales or Marketing Share Objectives

Often the objective of a pricing strategy is to maximize sales (either in dollars or in units) or to increase market share. Does setting a price intended to increase unit sales or market share simply mean pricing the product lower than the competition? Sometimes, yes. Providers of cable and satellite TV services such as Time Warner, Dish Network, DIRECTV, and Comcast relentlessly offer consumers better deals that include more TV, wireless Internet, and telephone service. Similarly, mobile phone providers compete with deals that include a set number of minutes for a standard fee, free nighttime and weekend minutes, rollover minutes, and low or no-cost phones to keep them ahead in the "mobile wars." But lowering prices is not always necessary to increase market share. If a company's product has a competitive advantage, keeping the price at the same level as other firms may satisfy sales objectives. And such "price wars" can have a negative effect when consumers switch from one producer to another simply because the price changes.

Competitive Effect Objectives

Sometimes strategists design the pricing plan to dilute the competition's marketing efforts. In these cases a firm may deliberately try to preempt or reduce the impact of a rival's pricing changes. That's what happened when new low-fare airline JetBlue entered Delta's hub Atlanta market with flights from Atlanta to Los Angeles. Delta slashed its fares in response, forcing JetBlue to abandon the Atlanta market.[3] Similarly, when Aloha Airlines filed for bankruptcy in 2008, it accused Mesa Air Group Inc.'s go! airline of *predatory pricing*; we'll return to this concept later in the chapter.[4]

Customer Satisfaction Objectives

Many quality-focused firms believe that profits result from making customer satisfaction the primary objective. These firms believe that if they focus solely on short-term profits, they will lose sight of their objective to retain customers for the long term. Recognizing that many people hate to buy new cars because they feel the dealers are untrustworthy hucksters, in 1985 General Motors introduced a totally new car, the Saturn. With its value pricing strategy, in which customers get one price and one price only—no haggling, no negotiation, and no "deals," Saturn experienced initial success and created a loyal core of Saturn owners. Unfortunately, when GM faced bankruptcy in 2009, Saturn was one of four divisions it put on the auction block. Unable to find a buyer for Saturn, GM's only alternative was to shut Saturn down.[5]

Image Enhancement Objectives

Consumers often use price to make inferences about the quality of a product. In fact, marketers know that price is often an important means of communicating not only quality but also image to prospective customers. The image enhancement function of pricing is particularly important with **prestige products** (or luxury products) that have a high price and appeal to status-conscious consumers. Most of us would agree that the high price tag on a Rolex watch, a Louis Vuitton handbag, or a Rolls-Royce car, although representing the higher costs of producing the product, is vital to shaping an image of an extraordinary product that only the wealthy can afford (not counting the "real" Rolex you buy for $10 from that guy on the street).

Figure 11.3 *Process* | Factors in Price Setting

To set the right price, marketers must understand a variety of quantitative and qualitative factors.

Costs	Demand
Revenue	Pricing Environment

2 Costs, Demand, Revenue, and the Pricing Environment

OBJECTIVE

Describe how marketers use costs, demands, revenue, and the pricing environment to make pricing decisions. (pp. 302–316)

Once a marketer decides on its pricing objectives, it is time to begin the actual process of price setting. In order to set the right price, marketers must understand a variety of quantitative and qualitative factors that can mean success or failure for the pricing strategy. As shown in Figure 11.3, these include an estimate of demand, knowledge of costs and revenue, and an understanding of the pricing environment.

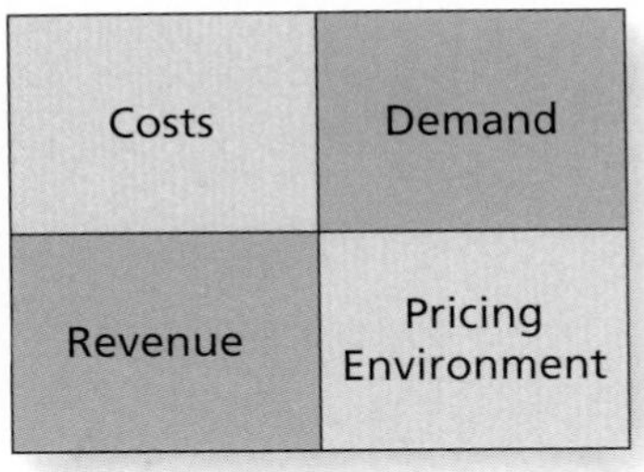

Step 2: Estimate Demand

The second step in price planning is to estimate demand. *Demand* refers to customers' desire for a product: How much of a product are they willing to buy as the price of the product goes up or down? Obviously, marketers should know the answer to this question before they set prices. Therefore, one of the earliest steps marketers take in price planning is to estimate demand for their products.

Demand Curves

Economists use a graph of a *demand curve* to illustrate the effect of price on the quantity demanded of a product. The demand curve, which can be a curved or straight line, shows the quantity of a product that customers will buy in a market during a period of time at various prices if all other factors remain the same.

Figure 11.4 shows demand curves for normal and prestige products. The vertical axis for the demand curve represents the different prices that a firm might charge for a product (P). The horizontal axis shows the number of units or quantity (Q) of the product demanded. The demand curve for most goods (that we show on the left side of Figure 11.4) slopes downward and to the right. As the price of the product goes up (P_1 to P_2), the number of units that customers are willing to buy goes down (Q_1 to Q_2). If prices decrease, customers will buy more. This is the *law of demand*. For example, if the price of bananas goes up, customers will probably buy fewer of them. And if the price gets really high, customers will eat their cereal without bananas.

There are, however, exceptions to this typical price–quantity relationship. In fact, there are situations in which (otherwise sane) people desire a product more as it *increases* in price. For prestige products such as luxury cars or jewelry, a price hike may actually result in an *increase* in the quantity consumers demand because they see the product as more valuable. In such cases, the demand curve slopes upward. The right-hand side of Figure 11.4 shows the "backward-bending" demand curve we associate with prestige products. If the price decreases, consumers perceive the product to be less desirable, and demand may decrease. You can see that if the price decreases from P_2 to P_3, the quantity demanded decreases from Q_2 to Q_1. On the other hand, if the price increases, consumers think the product is more desirable. This is what happens if the price begins at P_3 and then goes up to P_2; quantity increases from Q_1 to Q_2. Still, the higher-price/higher-demand relationship has its limits. If the

Figure 11.4 📷 *Snapshot* | Demand Curves for Normal and Prestige Products

There is an inverse relationship between price and demand for normal products. For prestige products, demand will increase—to a point—as price increases or will decrease as price decreases.

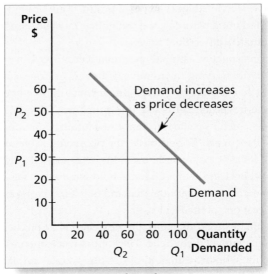

Normal Products

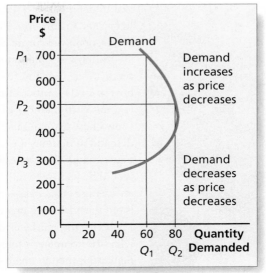

Prestige Products

firm increases the price too much (say from P_2 to P_1), making the product unaffordable for all but a few buyers, demand will begin to decrease. The direction the backward-bending curve takes shows this.

Shifts in Demand

The demand curves we've shown assume that all factors other than price stay the same. But what if they don't? What if the company improves the product? What happens when there is a glitzy new advertising campaign that turns a product into a "must-have" for a lot of people? What if stealthy *paparazzi* catch Brad Pitt using the product at home? Any of these things could cause an *upward shift* of the demand curve. An upward shift in the demand curve means that at any given price, demand is greater than before the shift occurs. And the demand shift would no doubt be even more precipitous if toddler Shiloh Nouvel Jolie-Pitt were also to make an appearance in the pic!

　📷 Figure 11.5 shows the upward shift of the demand curve as it moves from D_1 to D_2. At D_1, before the shift occurs, customers will be willing to purchase the quantity Q_1 (or 80 units in 📷 Figure 11.5) at the given price, P (or $60 in 📷 Figure 11.5). For example, customers at a particular store may buy 80 barbecue grills at $60 a grill. But then the store runs a huge advertising campaign featuring Queen Latifah on her patio using the barbecue grill. The demand curve shifts from D_1 to D_2. (The store keeps the price at $60.) Take a look at how the quantity demanded has changed to Q_2. In our example, the store is now selling 200 barbecue grills at $60 per grill. From a marketing standpoint, this shift is the best of all worlds. Without lowering prices, the company can sell more of its product. As a result, total revenues go up and so do profits, unless, of course, the new promotion costs as much as those potential additional profits.

　Demand curves may also shift downward. That's what happens, for example, when there is a beef recall. Sales of beef decline at any given price as risk-averse consumers seek alternative meats. Then, even with the price remaining at $60, the curve would shift downward and the quantity demanded would drop so that the store could sell only 30 or 40 grills.

Figure 11.5 📷 *Snapshot* | Shift in Demand Curve

Changes in the environment or in company efforts can cause a shift in the demand curve. A great advertising campaign, for example, can shift the demand curve upward.

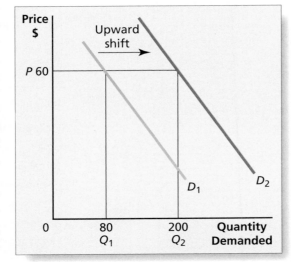

In the real world, factors other than the price and marketing activities influence demand. If it rains, the demand for umbrellas increases and the demand for tee times on a golf course is a wash. The development of new products may influence demand for old ones. Even though a few firms may still produce phonographs, the introduction of cassette tapes and then CDs and iPods has all but eliminated the demand for new vinyl records and turntables on which to play them.

price elasticity of demand

The percentage change in unit sales that results from a percentage change in price.

Estimate Demand

It's extremely important for marketers to understand and accurately estimate demand. A firm's production scheduling is based on anticipated demand that must be estimated well in advance of when products are brought to market. In addition, all marketing planning and budgeting must be based on reasonably accurate estimates of potential sales.

So how do marketers reasonably estimate potential sales? Marketers predict total demand first by identifying the number of buyers or potential buyers for their product and then multiplying that estimate times the average amount each member of the target market is likely to purchase. Table 11.1 shows how a small business, such as a start-up pizza restaurant, estimates demand in markets it expects to reach. For example, the pizza entrepreneur may estimate that there are 180,000 consumer households in his market who would be willing to buy his pizza and that each household would purchase an average of six pizzas a year. The total annual demand is 1,080,000 pizzas (hold the anchovies on at least one of those, please).

Once the marketer estimates total demand, the next step is to predict what the company's market share is likely to be. The company's estimated demand is then its share of the whole (estimated) pie. In our pizza example, the entrepreneur may feel that he can gain 3 percent of this market, or about 2,700 pizzas per month—not bad for a new start-up business. Of course, such projections need to take into consideration other factors that might affect demand, such as new competitors entering the market, the state of the economy, and changing consumer tastes like a sudden demand for low-carb take-out food.

Price Elasticity of Demand

Marketers also need to know how their customers are likely to react to a price change. In particular, it is critical to understand whether a change in price will have a large or a small impact on demand. How much can a firm increase or decrease its price if it sees a marked change in sales? If the price of a pizza goes up one dollar, will people switch to subs and burgers? What would happen if the pizza went up two dollars? Or even five dollars?

Price elasticity of demand is a measure of the sensitivity of customers to changes in price: If the price changes by 10 percent, what will be the percentage change in demand for the product? The word *elasticity* indicates that changes in price usually cause demand to stretch or retract like a rubber band. We calculate price elasticity of demand as follows:

$$\text{Price elasticity of demand} = \frac{\text{percentage change in quantity demanded}}{\text{percentage change in price}}$$

Table 11.1	Estimating Demand for Pizza	
Number of families in market		180,000
Average number of pizzas per family per year		6
Total annual market demand		1,080,000
Company's predicted share of the total market		3%
Estimated annual company demand		32,400 pizzas
Estimated monthly company demand		2,700
Estimated weekly company demand		675

Sometimes customers are very sensitive to changes in prices, and a change in price results in a substantial change in the quantity they demand. In such instances, we have a case of **elastic demand**. In other situations, a change in price has little or no effect on the quantity consumers are willing to buy. We describe this as **inelastic demand**.

Let's use the formula in this example: Suppose the pizza maker finds (from experience or from marketing research) that lowering the price of his pizza 10 percent (from $10 per pizza to $9) will cause a 15 percent increase in demand. He would calculate the price elasticity of demand as 15 divided by 10. The price elasticity of demand would be 1.5. If the price elasticity of demand is greater than one, demand is elastic; that is, consumers respond to the price decrease by demanding more. Or, if the price increases, consumers will demand less. 📷 Figure 11.6 shows these calculations.

As 📷 Figure 11.7 illustrates, when demand is elastic, changes in price and in total revenues (total sales) work in opposite directions. If the price is increased, revenues decrease. If the price is decreased, total revenues increase. With elastic demand, the demand curve shown in 📷 Figure 11.7 is more horizontal. With an elasticity of demand of 1.5, a decrease in price will increase the pizza maker's total sales.

We saw earlier that in some instances demand is *inelastic* so that a change in price results in little or no change in demand. For example, if the 10 percent decrease in the price of pizza resulted in only a 5 percent increase in pizza sales, then the price elasticity of demand calculated would be 5 divided by 10, which is 0.5 (less than one), and our pizza maker faces inelastic demand. When demand is inelastic, price and revenue changes are in the same direction; that is, increases in price result in increases in total revenue, while decreases in price result in decreases in total revenue. With inelastic demand, the demand curve in 📷 Figure 11.7

elastic demand
Demand in which changes in price have large effects on the amount demanded.

inelastic demand
Demand in which changes in price have little or no effect on the amount demanded.

Elastic demand

Price changes from $10 to $9.

$10 − 9 = $1

1/10 = 10% change in price

Demand changes from 2,700 per month to 3,100 per month

$$\begin{array}{r} 3,100 \\ -2,700 \\ \hline \end{array}$$

Increase $\qquad$ 400 pizzas

Percentage increase $\qquad$ 400/2,700 = .148 ~ 15% change in demand

$$\text{Price elasticity of demand} = \frac{\text{percentage change in quantity demanded}}{\text{percentage change in price}}$$

$$\text{Price elasticity of demand} = \frac{15\%}{10\%} = 1.5$$

Inelastic demand

Price changes from $10 to $9.

$10 − 9 = $1

1/10 = 10% change in price

Demand changes from 2,700 per month to 2,835 per month

$$\begin{array}{r} 2,835 \\ -2,700 \\ \hline \end{array}$$

Increase $\qquad$ 135 pizzas

Percentage increase $\qquad$ 135/2,700 = 0.05 ~ 5% change in demand

$$\text{Price elasticity of demand} = \frac{\text{percentage change in quantity demanded}}{\text{percentage change in price}}$$

$$\text{Price elasticity of demand} = \frac{5\%}{10\%} = 0.5$$

Figure 11.6 📷 *Snapshot* | Price Elasticity of Demand

Marketers know that elasticity of demand is an important pricing metric.

Figure 11.7 📷 *Snapshot* | Price Elastic and Inelastic Demand Curves

Price elasticity of demand represents how demand responds to changes in prices. If there is little change in demand, then demand is said to be price inelastic. If there is a large change in demand, demand is price elastic.

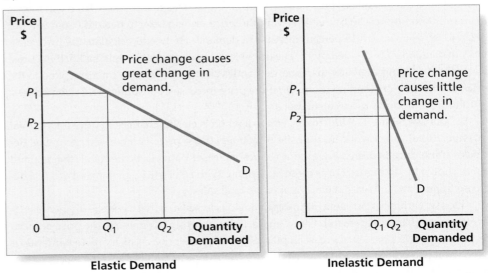

Elastic Demand   Inelastic Demand

becomes more vertical. Generally, the demand for necessities, such as food and electricity, is inelastic. Even large price increases do not cause us to buy less food or to give up our lights and hot water (though we may take fewer bubble baths).

If demand is price inelastic, can marketers keep raising prices so that revenues and profits will grow larger and larger? And what if demand is elastic? Does it mean that marketers can never raise prices? The answer to these questions is no (surprise!). Elasticity of demand for a product often differs for different price levels and with different percentages of change.

As a general rule, pizza makers and other companies can determine the *actual* price elasticity only after they have tested a pricing decision and calculated the resulting demand (as Taco Bell did with its value menu). Only then will they know whether a specific price change will increase or decrease revenues.

To estimate what demand is likely to be at different prices for new or existing products, marketers often do research. One approach is to conduct a study in which consumers tell marketers how much of a product they would be willing to buy at different prices. For example, researchers might ask participants if they would download fewer iTunes songs if the price per track goes from $.89 to $1.50 or how many bags of their favorite chocolate chip cookies they would buy at $3, $4, or $5. At other times, researchers conduct *field studies* in which they vary the price of a product in different stores and measure how much is actually purchased at the different price levels.

Other factors can affect price elasticity and sales. Consider the availability of *substitute* goods or services. If a product has a close substitute, its demand will be elastic; that is, a change in price will result in a change in demand, as consumers move to buy the substitute product. For example, all but the most die-hard cola fans might consider Coke and Pepsi close substitutes. If the price of Pepsi goes up, many people will buy Coke instead. Marketers of products with close substitutes are less likely to compete on price because they recognize that doing so could result in less profit as consumers switch from one brand to another. And many consumers find that the cost of mobile phone service is so reasonable that they give up their land lines to have totally cellular households.

Changes in prices of other products also affect the demand for an item, a phenomenon we label **cross-elasticity of demand**. When products are substitutes for each other, an increase in the price of one will increase the demand for the other. For example, if the price of

cross-elasticity of demand
When changes in the price of one product affect the demand for another item.

bananas goes up, consumers may instead buy more strawberries, blueberries, or apples. However, when products are *complements*—that is, when one product is essential to the use of a second—an increase in the price of one decreases the demand for the second. So if the price of gasoline goes up, consumers may drive less, carpool, or take public transportation, and thus demand for tires (as well as gasoline) will decrease.

As a final note on demand, consumer insights are critical to understanding demands. The current recessionary economic environment is driving changes in consumers' budgets and in their spending habits. How is this affecting demand and how will it affect demand in the future? While we talk about demand in terms of the relationship of price to quantity demanded, such relationships cannot be fully understood or used in pricing without a full understanding of exactly how consumers respond not only to the offering and its price but also to the offerings of competitors, the marketing communications, and the influence of other consumers.

Step 3: Determine Costs

Estimating demand helps marketers determine possible prices to charge for a product. It tells them how much of the product they think they'll be able to sell at different prices. Knowing this brings them to the third step in determining a product's price: making sure the price will cover costs. Before marketers can determine price, they must understand the relationship of cost, demand, and revenue for their product. In this next section, we'll talk about different types of costs that marketers must consider in pricing. Then we'll show two types of analyses that marketers use to make pricing decisions.

Variable and Fixed Costs

It's obvious that the cost of producing a product plays a big role when firms decide what to charge for it. If an item's selling price is lower than the cost to produce it, it doesn't take a rocket scientist to figure out that the firm will lose money. Before looking at how costs influence pricing decisions, we need to understand the different types of costs that firms incur.

First, a firm incurs **variable costs**—the per-unit costs of production that will fluctuate depending on how many units or individual products a firm produces. For example, if it takes 25¢ worth of nails—a variable cost—to build one bookcase, it will take 50¢ worth for two, 75¢ worth for three, and so on. Make cents? For the production of bookcases, variable costs would also include the cost of lumber and paint as well as the wages the firm would pay factory workers.

📷 Figure 11.8 shows some examples of the variable cost per unit or average variable cost and the total variable costs at different levels of production (for producing 100, 200, and

variable costs
The costs of production (raw and processed materials, parts, and labor) that are tied to and vary depending on the number of units produced.

Figure 11.8 📷 *Snapshot* | Variable Costs at Different Levels of Production

Variable Costs to Produce 100 Bookcases		Variable Costs to Produce 200 Bookcases		Variable Costs to Produce 500 Bookcases	
Wood	$13.25	Wood	$13.25	Wood	$9.40
Nails	0.25	Nails	0.25	Nails	0.20
Paint	0.50	Paint	0.50	Paint	0.40
Labor (3 hours × $12.00 per hr)	$36.00	Labor (3 hours × $12.00 per hr)	$36.00	Labor (2½ hours × $12.00 per hr)	$30.00
Cost per unit	$50.00	Cost per unit	$50.00	Cost per unit	$40.00
Multiply by number of units	100	Multiply by number of units	200	Multiply by number of units	500
Cost for 100 units	$5,000	Cost for 200 units	$10,000	Cost for 500 units	$20,000

One bookcase = one unit.

500 bookcases). If the firm produces 100 bookcases, the average variable cost per unit is $50, and the total variable cost is $5,000 ($50 × 100). If it doubles production to 200 units, the total variable cost now is $10,000 ($50 × 200).

In reality, calculating variable costs is usually more complex than what we've shown here. As the number of bookcases the factory produces increases or decreases, average variable costs may change. For example, if the company buys just enough lumber for one bookcase, the lumberyard will charge top dollar. If it buys enough for 100 bookcases, the guys at the lumberyard will probably offer a better deal. And if it buys enough for thousands of bookcases, the company may cut variable costs even more. Even the cost of labor goes down with increased production as manufacturers are likely to invest in laborsaving equipment that allows workers to produce bookcases faster. [camera] Figure 11.8 shows this is the case. By purchasing wood, nails, and paint at a lower price (because of a volume discount) and by providing a means for workers to build bookcases more quickly, the company reduces the cost per unit of producing 500 bookcases to $40 each.

Variable costs don't always go down with higher levels of production. Using the bookcase example, at some point the demand for the labor, lumber, or nails required to produce the bookcases may exceed the supply: The bookcase manufacturer may have to pay employees higher overtime wages to keep up with production. The manufacturer may have to buy additional lumber from a distant supplier that will charge more to cover the costs of shipping. The cost per bookcase rises. You get the picture.

fixed costs
Costs of production that do not change with the number of units produced.

Fixed costs are costs that *do not* vary with the number of units produced—the costs that remain the same whether the firm produces 1,000 bookcases this month or only 10. Fixed costs include rent or the cost of owning and maintaining the factory, utilities to heat or cool the factory, and the costs of equipment such as hammers, saws, and paint sprayers used in the production of the product. While the cost of factory workers to build the bookcases is part of a firm's variable costs, the salaries of a firm's executives, accountants, human resources specialists, marketing managers, and other personnel not involved in the production of the product are fixed costs. So too are other costs such as advertising and other marketing activities, at least in the short term. All these costs are constant no matter how many items the factory manufactures.

average fixed cost
The fixed cost per unit produced.

Average fixed cost is the fixed cost per unit, the total fixed costs divided by the number of units (bookcases) produced. Although total fixed costs remain the same no matter how many units are produced, the average fixed cost will decrease as the number of units produced increases. Say, for example, that a firm's total fixed costs of production are $300,000. If the firm produces one unit, it applies the total of $300,000 to the one unit. If it produces two units, it applies $150,000, or half of the fixed costs, to each unit. If it produces 10,000 units, the average fixed cost per unit is $30.00 and so on. As we produce more and more units, average fixed costs go down, and so does the price we must charge to cover fixed costs.

Of course, like variable costs, in the long term, total fixed costs may change. The firm may find that it can sell more of a product than it has manufacturing capacity to produce, so it builds a new factory, its executives' salaries go up, and more money goes into purchasing manufacturing equipment.

total costs
The total of the fixed costs and the variable costs for a set number of units produced.

Combining variable costs and fixed costs yields **total costs** for a given level of production. As a company produces more and more of a product, both average fixed costs and average variable costs may decrease. Average total costs may decrease, too, up to a point. As we said, as output continues to increase, average variable costs may start to increase. These variable costs ultimately rise faster than average fixed costs decline, resulting in an increase to average total costs. As total costs fluctuate with differing levels of production, the price that producers have to charge to cover those costs changes accordingly. Therefore, marketers need to calculate the minimum price necessary to cover all costs—the *break-even price*.

The Cutting Edge

Virtual Wallets

History shows a series of innovations in how consumers buy shoes, toothpaste, and candy bars. Coins replaced bartering and were the first currency. Paper money followed coins, and in the 1950s the credit card was introduced. Today Americans use plastic more than money, and some airlines and restaurants won't even take cash. So what's next? Most likely the transition to digital cash. In the future, money as we know it may cease to exist. Instead, consumers will carry virtual wallets, with their credit card and bank information stored on remote computers. And since everyone, it seems, has a cell phone, that's the ob-

vious access vehicle. ShopSavvy is one new cell phone app that uses the phone camera to scan an item's bar code, checks to see if it's available for a lower price online, and then buys it with a credit card number and shipping information stored on a Web site. MasterCard with its partner Obopay now makes it possible for consumers to send money to anyone via cell phone text messages. In Malaysia, Visa has begun installing chips into cell phones so that consumers can swipe their cell phone instead of their credit card. And Starbucks has an iPhone app that allows its customers to upload money and then swipe their phone at the cash register to pay for their double macchiato.[6]

Break-Even Analysis

Break-even analysis is a technique marketers use to examine the relationship between costs and price. This method lets them determine what sales volume the company must reach at a given price before it will completely cover its total costs and past which it will begin to turn a profit. Simply put, the **break-even point** is the point at which the company doesn't lose any money and doesn't make any profit. All costs are covered, but there isn't a penny extra. A break-even analysis allows marketers to identify how many units of a product they will have to sell at a given price to exceed the break-even point and be profitable.

Figure 11.9 uses our bookcase example to demonstrate break-even analysis assuming the manufacturer charges $100 per unit. The vertical axis represents the amount of costs and revenue in dollars and the horizontal axis shows the quantity of goods the manufacturer produces and sells. In this break-even model, we assume that there is a given total fixed cost and that variable costs do not change with the quantity produced.

In this example, let's say that the total fixed costs (the costs for the factory, the equipment, and electricity) are $200,000 and that the average variable costs (for materials and labor) are constant. The figure shows the total costs (variable costs plus fixed costs) and total revenues if varying quantities are produced and sold. The point at which the total revenue and total costs lines intersect is the break-even point. If sales are above the break-even point, the company makes a profit. Below that point, the firm will suffer losses.

To determine the break-even point, the firm first needs to calculate the **contribution per unit**, or the difference between the price the firm charges for a product (the revenue per unit)

break-even analysis
A method for determining the number of units that a firm must produce and sell at a given price to cover all its costs.

break-even point
The point at which the total revenue and total costs are equal and beyond which the company makes a profit; below that point, the firm will suffer a loss.

contribution per unit
The difference between the price the firm charges for a product and the variable costs.

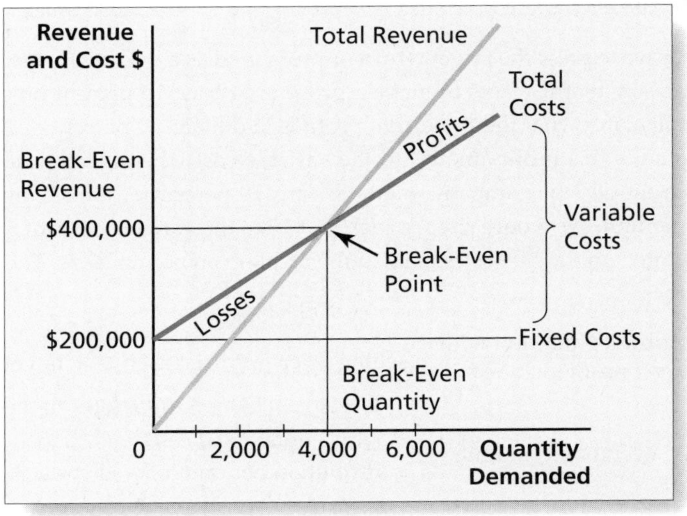

Figure 11.9 *Snapshot* | Break-Even Analysis Assuming a Price of $100

Using break-even analysis, marketers can determine what sales volume must be reached before the company makes a profit. This company needs to sell 4,000 bookcases at $100 each to break even.

and the variable costs. This figure is the amount the firm has after it pays for the wood, nails, paint, and labor to contribute to meeting the fixed costs of production. For our example, we will assume that the firm sells its bookcases for $100 each. Using the variable costs of $50 per unit that we had before, contribution per unit is $100 − $50 = $50. Using the fixed cost for the bookcase manufacturing of $200,000, we can now calculate the firm's break-even point in units of the product:

$$\text{Break-even point (in units)} = \frac{\text{total fixed costs}}{\text{contribution per unit to fixed costs}}$$

$$\text{Break-even point (in units)} = \frac{\$200,000}{\$50} = 4,000 \text{ units}$$

We see that the firm must sell 4,000 bookcases at $100 each to meet its fixed costs and to break even. We can also calculate the break-even point in dollars. This shows us that to break even the company must sell $400,000 worth of bookcases:

$$\text{Break-even point (in dollars)} = \frac{\text{total fixed costs}}{1 - \dfrac{\text{variable cost per unit}}{\text{price}}}$$

$$\text{Break-even point (in dollars)} = \frac{\$200,000}{1 - \dfrac{\$50}{\$100}} = \frac{\$200,000}{1 - 0.5} = \frac{\$200,000}{0.5} = \$400,000$$

After the firm's sales have met and passed the break-even point, it begins to make a profit. How much profit? If the firm sells 4,001 bookcases, it will make a profit of $50. If it sells 5,000 bookcases, we calculate the profit as follows:

$$\begin{aligned}\text{Profit} &= \text{quantity above break-even point} \times \text{contribution margin}\\ &= \$1,000 \times 50\\ &= \$50,000\end{aligned}$$

Often a firm will set a *profit goal*, the dollar profit figure it wants to earn. Its managers may calculate the break-even point with a certain dollar profit goal in mind. In this case, it is not really a "break-even" point we are calculating, because we're seeking profits. It's more of a "target amount." If our bookcase manufacturer thinks it is necessary to realize a profit of $50,000, his calculations look like this:

$$\begin{array}{l}\text{Break-even point (in units)}\\ \text{with target profit included}\end{array} = \frac{\text{total fixed costs} + \text{target profit}}{\text{contribution per unit to fixed costs}}$$

$$\text{Break-even point (in units)} = \frac{\$200,000 + 50,000}{\$50} = 5,000 \text{ units}$$

Sometimes we express the target return or profit goal as a *percentage of sales*. For example, a firm may say that it wants to make a profit of at least 10 percent on sales. In such cases, it first calculates what the 10 percent profit is in dollars: 10 percent of $100 is $10.00. Then the firm adds this profit amount to the variable cost when it calculates break-even point. In our example, the company wants to earn 10 percent of the selling price of the bookcase, or per unit. We would simply add this $10 to the variable costs of $50 and calculate the new target amount as we calculated the break-even point before. The contribution per unit becomes:

$$\begin{array}{l}\text{Contribution per unit with}\\ \text{target profit included}\end{array} = \text{selling price} - (\text{variable costs} + \text{target profit})$$

$$= \$100 - (\$50 + \$10) = \$40$$

$$\text{Break-even point (in units)} = \frac{\text{total fixed costs}}{\text{contribution per unit to fixed costs}}$$

$$\text{Break-even point (in units)} = \frac{\$200,000}{\$40} = 5,000 \text{ units}$$

Break-even analysis does not provide an easy answer for pricing decisions. Yes, it provides answers about how many units the firm must sell to break even and to make a profit—but without knowing whether demand will equal that quantity at that price, companies can make big mistakes. It is, therefore, useful for marketers to estimate the demand for their product and then perform a marginal analysis. Now let's see how to do that.

Marginal Analysis

Marginal analysis provides a way for marketers to look at cost and demand at the same time and to identify the output and the price that will generate the maximum profit. 📷 Figure 11.10 shows the various cost and revenue elements we consider in marginal analysis. Like 📷 Figure 11.9, the vertical axis in 📷 Figure 11.10 represents the cost and revenues in dollars, and the horizontal axis shows the quantity produced and sold. 📷 Figure 11.10 shows the average revenue, average cost, marginal revenue, and marginal cost curves.

When they do a marginal analysis, marketers examine the relationship of **marginal cost** (the increase in total costs from producing one additional unit of a product) to **marginal revenue** (the increase in total income or revenue that results from selling one additional unit of a product). Average revenue is also the demand curve and thus represents the amount customers will buy at different prices—people buy more only if price, and thus revenue, decrease. Thus, both average revenue and marginal revenue decrease with each additional unit sold.

If the manufacturer produces only one bookcase, the average total cost per unit is the same as the marginal cost per unit. After the first unit, the cost of *producing each additional unit* (marginal cost) and the average cost at first decrease. Eventually, however, both marginal costs and average costs begin to increase since, as we discussed earlier, both average fixed costs and average variable costs may increase in the long term.

Profit is maximized at the point at which marginal cost is *exactly* equal to marginal revenue. At that point, the cost of producing one unit is exactly equal to the revenue to be realized from selling that one unit. If, however, the company produces one additional unit, the cost of producing that unit is *greater than* the revenue from the sale of the unit, and total profit actually begins to decrease. So it's a no-brainer that firms should maintain production and sales at the point of maximum profit.

One word of caution when you use marginal analysis: Although in theory the procedure is straightforward, in the real world things seldom are. Production costs may vary unexpectedly

marginal analysis
A method that uses cost and demand to identify the price that will maximize profits.

marginal cost
The increase in total cost that results from producing one additional unit of a product.

marginal revenue
The increase in total income or revenue that results from selling one additional unit of a product.

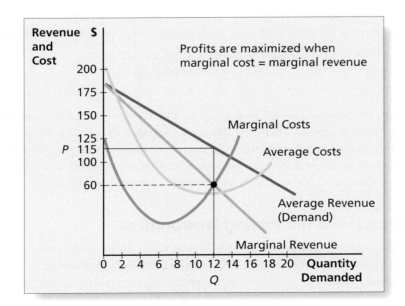

Figure 11.10 📷 *Snapshot* | Marginal Analysis

Marginal analysis allows marketers to consider both costs and demand in calculating a price that maximizes profits.

because of shortages, inclement weather, unexpected equipment repairs, and so on. Revenues may also unexpectedly move up and down because of the economy, what the competition is doing, or a host of other reasons. Predicting demand, an important factor in marginal analysis, is never an exact science. This makes marginal analysis a less-than-perfect way to determine the best price for a product. Indeed, it is theoretically sounder than break-even analysis, but most firms find the break-even approach more useful on a day-to-day basis.

Markups and Margins: Pricing through the Channel

markup
An amount added to the cost of a product to create the price at which a channel member will sell the product.

gross margin
The markup amount added to the cost of a product to cover the fixed costs of the retailer or wholesaler and leave an amount for a profit.

retailer margin
The margin added to the cost of a product by a retailer.

wholesaler margin
The amount added to the cost of a product by a wholesaler.

list price or manufacturer's suggested retail price (MSRP)
The price the end customer is expected to pay as determined by the manufacturer; also referred to as the suggested retail price. The appropriate price for the end customer to pay as determined by the manufacturer.

So far we have talked about costs simply from the perspective of a manufacturer selling directly to a consumer. But in reality, most products are not sold directly to the consumers or business buyers of the product. Instead a manufacturer may sell a consumer good to a wholesaler, distributor, or jobber who in turn sells to a retailer who finally sells the product to the ultimate consumer. In organizational markets, the manufacturer may sell his product to a distributor who will then sell to the business customer. Each of these members of the channel of distribution buys a product for a certain amount and adds a **markup** amount to create the price at which they will sell a product. This markup amount is the **gross margin**, also referred to as the **retailer margin** or the **wholesaler margin.** The margin must be great enough to cover the fixed costs of the retailer or wholesaler and leave an amount for a profit. When a manufacturer sets his price, he must consider these margins. To understand pricing through the channel better, we'll look at a simple example of channel pricing.

Many times, a manufacturer builds its pricing structure around list prices. A **list price,** that we also refer to as a **manufacturer's suggested retail price (MSRP)**, is the price that the manufacturer sets as the appropriate price for the end consumer to pay. Let's say we have a consumer good with an MSRP of $10. This means the retailer will sell the product to the consumer for $10. But, as we said, retailers need money to cover their fixed costs and their profits. Thus, the retailer may determine that he must have a certain percentage gross or retailer margin, say 30%.

This means that the retailer must be able to buy the product for no more than

$$\text{Price to the retailer} = \$10.00 \times (1.00 - .30)$$
$$= \$10.00 \times .70$$
$$= \$7.00$$

If the channel of distribution also includes a wholesaler, the wholesaler must be able to mark up the product in order to pay for his fixed costs and profits. This means that the wholesaler must also have a certain percentage gross or wholesaler margin, say 20%.

This means that the wholesaler must be able to buy the product for no more than

$$\text{Price to the wholesaler} = \$7.00 \times (1.00 - .20)$$
$$= \$7.00 \times .80$$
$$= \$5.40$$

Thus, the manufacturer will sell the product not for $10.00 but for $5.40. Of course, the manufacturer may sell the product to the wholesaler for less than that, but he cannot sell it for more and meet the margin requirements of the retailer and the wholesaler. If the manufacturer's variable costs for producing the product are $3.00, then his contribution to fixed costs is $2.40. It is this amount that is used to calculate the break-even point.

Step 4: Examine the Pricing Environment

In addition to demand and costs, marketers look at factors in the firm's external environment when they set prices. This is especially important in today's recessionary economic environment. Thus, the fourth step in developing pricing strategies is to examine and evaluate the pricing environment. Only then can marketers set a price that not only covers costs but also provides a *competitive advantage*—a price that meets the needs of customers better than the competition. This section will discuss some important external influences on pricing strategies—the economic environment, competition, and consumer trends. Before we begin this discussion, it is especially important to note that price decisions are interdependent and must take into account demand and costs and the pricing environment together as a whole.

The Economy

Broad economic trends, like those we discussed in Chapter 3, tend to direct pricing strategies. The business cycle, inflation, economic growth, and consumer confidence all help to determine whether one pricing strategy or another will succeed. Should a firm keep prices stable, reduce them, or even raise them in today's recessionary economy? Of course, the upswings and downturns in a national economy do not affect all product categories or all regions equally. Marketers need to understand how economic trends will affect their particular business.

In general, during *recessions*, consumers grow more price-sensitive. They switch brands to get a better price and patronize discount stores and warehouse outlets. They are less likely to take luxury vacations and instead are happy with a "staycation" where they entertain the family at home. Many consumers lose their jobs and others are fearful of losing theirs. Even wealthy households, relatively unaffected by the recession, tend to cut back on their consumption. As a result, to keep factories in operation during periods of recession, some firms find it necessary to cut prices to levels at which they cover their costs but don't make a profit.

Consumers are very price-sensitive when economic conditions are bleak.

During the recession that started in 2008, many consumers were affected by the subprime mortgage crisis and discovered that they could no longer spend as freely as they had become accustomed to doing. Some companies actually found ways to profit from the credit crunch. For example, Sekurus Inc. created a product that used car dealers install in vehicles they sell to poor credit risks: It's a box underneath the dashboard that flashes a light when a payment is due. If the buyer doesn't make the payment and punch in a code when the dealer receives it, the car won't start and the repo man pays a visit.[7] Walmart removed many national brands from its shelves to make more space for its own brands when it found that shoppers were increasingly opting for the lower-priced versions. This proved a mistake for Walmart as it aggravated customers. Walmart quickly responded by returning hundreds of national brands to its stores.[8]

There are also some economic trends that allow firms to increase prices, altering what consumers see as an acceptable or unacceptable price range for a product. *Inflation* may give marketers causes to either increase or decrease prices. First, inflation gets customers accustomed to price increases. Customers may remain insensitive to price increases, even when inflation goes away, allowing marketers to make real price increases, not just those that adjust

Procter & Gamble is the world's biggest consumer-product maker, producing many premium-priced brands, some at prices twice the category average. But during the 2008 recession, P&G found sales, market share, and profits declining as consumers switched to store brands and other cheaper options. P&G responded with a number of price-cutting and product enhancement strategies. For example, P&G began offering larger packs of Duracell batteries and more absorbent Pamper's diapers without increasing prices. The company has also repositioned both Era and Cheer detergent as bargain brands. But will customers return to premium brands after the recession? Many believe that the recession of 2008, the worst since the Great Depression, will probably have a permanent effect on the American consumer. Consumers, even those whose income has not declined, are spending less and saving more.[9]

Not everyone cuts prices in a recession. Starbucks' strategy to cope with the downturn was to keep a premium image while the chain retained price-sensitive customers who threatened to defect to lower-priced competitors such as McDonald's. To do this, Starbucks raised the prices of its sugary coffees with several ingredients, like Frappuccinos and caramel macchiatos, by 10, 15, or even 30 cents. At the same time, the company reduced prices of more popular beverages such as lattes and brewed coffee from 5 to 15 cents.[10]

for the inflation. Of course, during periods of inflation, consumers may grow fearful of the future and worry about whether they will have enough money to meet basic needs. In such a case, they may cut back on purchases. Then, as in periods of recession, inflation may cause marketers to lower prices and temporarily sacrifice profits to maintain sales levels.

The Competition

Marketers try to anticipate how the competition will respond to their pricing actions. They know that consumers' expectations of what constitutes a fair price largely depend on what the competition charges. However, it's not always a good idea to fight the competition with lower and lower prices. Pricing wars such as those in the fast-food industry can change consumers' perceptions of what is a "fair" price, leaving them unwilling to buy at previous price levels.

Most industries, such as the airline, restaurant, and wheat farm industries, consist of a number of firms. As we discussed in Chapter 3, these industries can belong to one of three industry structures—an oligopoly, monopolistic competition, or pure competition. The industry structure a firm belongs to will influence price decisions. In general, firms like Delta Airlines that do business in an oligopoly, in which the market has few sellers and many buyers, are more likely to adopt *status quo* pricing objectives in which the pricing of all competitors is similar. Such objectives are attractive to oligopolistic firms because avoiding price competition allows all players in the industry to remain profitable. In a business like the restaurant industry, which is characterized by monopolistic competition in which there are a lot of sellers each offering a slightly different product, it is more possible for firms to differentiate products and to focus on nonprice competition. Then each firm prices its product on the basis of its cost without much concern for matching the exact price of competitors' products. People don't tend to "comparison shop" between the prices of a burger at Applebee's versus one at Chili's before deciding which chain to patronize. Of course, this doesn't mean that firms in an oligopoly can just ignore pricing by the competition. When one fast-food chain offers a "value meal," others often respond with their own versions.

Organizations like wheat farmers that function in a purely competitive market have little opportunity to raise or lower prices. Rather, supply and demand directly influence the price of wheat, soybeans, corn, or fresh peaches. When bad weather decreases the supply of crops, prices go up. And prices for almost any kind of fish have increased dramatically since health-conscious consumers began to turn away from red meat.

Of course, as we said, the elements of the pricing environment are interdependent. When the economy turns down and firms are faced with declining sales from a recession such as began in 2008, many will simply lower their prices and sacrifice profits to drive sales. Other firms in the industry have to decide whether to maintain their current prices or follow suit and lower prices. The trick is to balance the two—to maintain customer loyalty and the corresponding sales while ensuring an adequate level of profits.

Government Regulation

Another important factor in the environment that influences how marketers develop pricing strategies is government regulations. Governments in the United States and other countries develop two different types of regulations that have an effect on pricing. First, a large number of regulations increase the costs of production. Regulations for health care, environmental protection, occupational safety, and highway safety, just to mention a few, cause the costs of producing many products to increase. Other regulations of specific industries such as those imposed by the Food and Drug Administration (FDA) on the production of food and pharmaceuticals increase the costs of developing and producing those products.

In addition, some regulations directly address prices. In 1971, in order to fight what was thought to be an unacceptable level of inflation, President Nixon announced an unprecedented 90-day price freeze on most products that in reality actually lasted nearly three years. More recently, Congress enacted the Credit Card Responsibility and Disclosure Act, which limits credit card rates and other fees.[11] In March of 2010, a massive health care overhaul bill was enacted which, when it takes effect in 2013, will have a dramatic effect on health insurance premiums and will likely affect pricing for a vast number of firms in the health care industry.[12]

Consumer Trends

Consumer trends also can strongly influence prices. Culture and demographics determine how consumers think and behave, and so these factors have a large impact on all marketing decisions. Take, for example, the buying habits of the women who opted for a career in their twenties but who are hearing the ticking of their biological clocks as they enter their late thirties and forties. Couples who have babies later in their lives are often better off financially than younger parents, and on average they will have fewer children to spoil, so they are more willing to spend whatever it costs to give their babies the best.

Another important trend is that even well-off people no longer consider it shameful to hunt for bargains—in fact, it's becoming fashionable to boast that you found one. As a marketing executive for a chain of shopping malls observed, "Everybody loves to save money. It's a badge of honor today." Luxury consumers are looking for prestigious brands at low prices, though they're still willing to splurge for some high-ticket items. Industry analysts have called this new interest in hunting for sales "strategic shopping."[13]

The International Environment

As we discussed in Chapter 3, the marketing environment often varies widely from country to country. This can have important consequences in developing pricing strategies. Can prices be standardized for all global markets or must there be localization in pricing?

For some product such as jet airplanes, companies such as Boeing and Airbus standardize their prices. This is possible, first, because about the only customers for the wide-bodies and other popular jets are major airlines and governments of countries who buy for their military or for use by government officials, two groups that are able to pay. Second, companies building planes have little or no leeway in cutting their costs without sacrificing safety.

For other products including most consumer goods, unique environmental factors in different countries mean marketers must adapt their pricing strategies. As we noted in Chapter 3, the economic conditions in developing countries often means that consumers simply cannot afford $3 or $4 or more for a bottle of shampoo or laundry detergent. As a result, marketers offer their brands at lower prices, often by providing them in one-use packages called **sachets** that sell for just a few cents. In other cases, companies must save on costs by using less expensive ingredients in their brands in order to provide toothpaste or soap that is affordable.

sachets
Single use packages of products such as shampoo often sold in developing countries.

The competitive environment in different countries also contributes to different pricing strategies. In countries such as China, long-established manufacturers of packaged foods and toiletries have been successful for decades by providing products at affordable prices. New entrants into these markets must price their products more or less in line with the local firms.

Another factor that can have an effect on a firm's pricing in the international environment is government regulation. In some countries, the government dictates what the prices of products such as pharmaceuticals will be. With this kind of government control, a firm's only options are to use cheaper ingredients to produce the product or not make their products available.

Finally, channels of distribution often vary both in the types and sizes of available intermediaries and in the availability of an infrastructure to facilitate product distribution. Often these differences can mean that trade margins will be higher, as will the cost of getting the products to consumers.

3 Pricing the Product: Establishing Strategies and Tactics

OBJECTIVE

Understand key pricing strategies and tactics.
(pp. 316–322)

An old Russian proverb says, "There are two kinds of fools in any market. One doesn't charge enough. The other charges too much."[14] In modern business, there seldom is any one-and-only, now-and-forever, best pricing strategy. Like playing a chess game, making pricing moves and countermoves requires thinking two and three moves ahead. Figure 11.11 provides a summary of the different pricing strategies and tactics.

Step 5: Choose a Pricing Strategy

The next step in price planning is to choose a pricing strategy. Some strategies work for certain products, with certain customer groups, in certain competitive markets. When is it best for the firm to undercut the competition and when to just meet the competition's prices? When is the best pricing strategy one that covers costs only and when is it best to use one based on demand?

Pricing Strategies Based on Cost

Marketing planners often choose cost-based strategies because they are simple to calculate and are relatively risk free. They promise that the price will at least cover the costs the company incurs in producing and marketing the product.

Cost-based pricing methods have drawbacks, however. They do not consider factors such as the nature of the target market, demand, competition, the product life cycle, and the product's image. Moreover, although the calculations for setting the price may be simple and straightforward, accurate cost estimating may prove difficult.

Think about firms such as 3M, General Electric, and Nabisco, all of which produce many products. How does a cost analysis allocate the costs for the plant, research and development, equipment, design engineers, maintenance, and marketing personnel among the different products so that the pricing plan accurately reflects the cost of producing any

Figure 11.11 📷 *Snapshot* |
Pricing Strategies and Tactics

Marketers develop successful pricing programs by choosing from a variety of pricing strategies and tactics.

Pricing strategies	Pricing tactics

• Based on cost
   Cost plus
• Based on demand
   Target costing
   Yield management
• Based on the competition
   Price leadership
• Based on customers' needs
   Value (EDLP) pricing
• New product pricing
   Skimming pricing
   Penetration pricing
   Trial pricing
	• Pricing for individual products
	   Two-part pricing
	   Payment pricing
	• Pricing for multiple products
	   Price bundling
	   Captive pricing
	• Distribution-based pricing
	• Discounting for channel members

one product? For example, how do you allocate the salary of a marketing executive who oversees many different products? Should the cost be divided equally among all products? Should costs be based on the actual number of hours spent working on each product? Or should costs be assigned based on the revenues generated by each product? There is no one right answer. Even with these limitations, though, cost-based pricing strategies often are a marketer's best choice.

The most common cost-based approach to pricing a product is **cost-plus pricing**, in which the marketer totals all the costs for the product and then adds an amount (or marks up the cost of the item) to arrive at the selling price. Many marketers, especially retailers and wholesalers, use cost-plus pricing because of its simplicity—users need only know or estimate the unit cost and add the markup. To calculate cost-plus pricing, marketers usually calculate either a markup on cost or a markup on selling price. With both methods, you calculate the price by adding a predetermined percentage to the cost, but as the names of the methods imply, for one the calculation uses a percentage of the costs and for the other a percentage of the selling price. Which of the two methods is used seems often to be little more than a matter of the "the way our company has always done it." You'll find more information about cost-plus pricing and how to calculate markup on cost and markup on selling price in the Chapter 11 Supplement at the end of this chapter.

cost-plus pricing
A method of setting prices in which the seller totals all the costs for the product and then adds an amount to arrive at the selling price.

Pricing Strategies Based on Demand

Demand-based pricing means that the firm bases the selling price on an estimate of volume or quantity that it can sell in different markets at different prices. To use any of the pricing strategies based on demand, firms must determine how much product they can sell in each market and at what price. As we noted earlier, marketers often use customer surveys, in which consumers indicate whether they would buy a certain product and how much of it they would buy at various prices. They may obtain more accurate estimates by conducting an experiment *like* the ones we described in Chapter 4. For example, a firm might actually offer the product at different price levels in different test markets and gauge the reaction. Two specific demand-based pricing strategies are target costing and yield management pricing. Let's take a quick look at each approach.

demand-based pricing
A price-setting method based on estimates of demand at different prices.

Today, firms find that they can be more successful if they match price with demand using a **target costing** process.[15] They first determine the price at which customers would be willing to buy the product and then work backwards to design the product in such a way that it can produce and sell the product at a profit.

With target costing, firms first use marketing research to identify the quality and functionality needed to satisfy attractive market segments and what price they are willing to pay *before the product is designed*. As 📷 Figure 11.12 shows, the next step is to determine what margins retailers and dealers require as well as the profit margin the company requires. On the basis of this information, managers can calculate the target cost—the maximum it can cost the firm to manufacture the product. If the firm can meet customer quality and functionality requirements and control costs to meet the required price, it will manufacture the product. If not, it abandons the product.

target costing
A process in which firms identify the quality and functionality needed to satisfy customers and what price they are willing to pay before the product is designed; the product is manufactured only if the firm can control costs to meet the required price.

Yield management pricing is another type of demand-based pricing strategy that hospitality companies like airlines, hotels, and cruise lines use. These businesses charge different prices to different customers in order to manage capacity while maximizing revenues. Many service firms practice yield management pricing because they recognize that different customers have different sensitivities to price—some customers will pay top dollar for an airline ticket, while others will travel only if there is a discount fare. The goal of yield management pricing is to accurately predict the proportion of customers who fall into each category and allocate the percentages of the airline's or hotel's capacity accordingly so that no product goes unsold.

yield management pricing
A practice of charging different prices to different customers in order to manage capacity while maximizing revenues.

For example, an airline may charge two prices for the same seat: the full fare ($899) and the discount fare ($299). The airline must predict how many seats it can fill at full fare and

Figure 11.12 📷 *Snapshot* | Target Costing Using a Jeans Example

With target costing, a firm first determines the price at which customers would be willing to buy the product and then works backward to design the product in such a way that it can produce and sell the product at a profit.

Step 1: Determine the price customers are willing to pay for the jeans
$79.99

Step 2: Determine the markup required by the retailer
40% (.40)

Step 3: Calculate the maximum price the retailer will pay, the price customers are willing to pay minus the markup amount

Formula: Price to the retailer = Selling price × (1.00 − markup percentage)
Price to the retailer = $79.99 × (1.00 − .40)
= $79.99 × 0.60 = **$47.99**

Step 4: Determine the profit required by the firm
15% (.15)

Step 5: Calculate the target cost, the maximum cost of producing the jeans
Formula: Target cost = Price to the retailer × (1.00 − profit percentage)
Target cost = $47.99 × 0.85 = **$40.79**

how many it can sell only at the discounted fare. The airline begins months ahead of the date of the flight with a basic allocation of seats—perhaps it will place 25 percent in the full-fare "bucket" and 75 percent in the discount-fare "bucket." While it can't sell the seats in the full-fare bucket at the discounted price, the airline may sell the seats it allocated at the discounted price for the full fare if it's lucky (and the passenger isn't).

As flight time gets closer, the airline might make a series of adjustments to the allocation of seats in the hope of selling every seat on the plane at the highest price possible. If the New York Mets need to book the flight, chances are the airline will be able to sell some of the discount seats at full fare, which in turn decreases the number available at the discounted price. If, as the flight date nears, the number of full-fare ticket sales falls below the forecast, the airline will move some of those seats over to the discount bucket. Then, the suspense builds! The pricing game continues until the day of the flight as the airline attempts to fill every seat by the time the plane takes off. This is why you may be able to get a fantastic price on an airline ticket through an Internet auction site such as **Priceline.com** if you wait until the last minute to buy your ticket. It also tells you why you often see the ticket agents frantically looking for "volunteers" who are willing to give up their seats because the airline sold more seats than actually fit in the plane.

Pricing Strategies Based on the Competition

Sometimes a firm's pricing strategy involves pricing its wares near, at, above, or below the competition's prices. In the "good old days," when U.S. automakers had the American market to themselves, pricing decisions were straightforward: Industry giant General Motors would announce its new car prices, and Ford, Chrysler, Packard, Studebaker, Hudson, and the others got in line or dropped out. A **price leadership** strategy, which usually is the rule in an oligopolistic industry that a few firms dominate, may be in the best interest of all players because it minimizes price competition. Price leadership strategies are popular because they provide an acceptable and legal way for firms to agree on prices without ever coordinating these rates with each other. There's a good reason to avoid explicitly working together to set rates: That's called *collusion* and it's illegal in most cases.

price leadership

A pricing strategy in which one firm first sets its price and other firms in the industry follow with the same or very similar prices.

Pricing Strategies Based on Customers' Needs

When firms develop pricing strategies that cater to customers, they are less concerned with short-term results than with keeping customers for the long term. U.S. Cellular refines its pricing strategies by talking to customers to determine the best blend of minutes, plan features, and price.[16] The firm even designed its FarmFlex Plan to offer farmers one rate during the planting season and a lower rate in the off-season.

Firms that practice **value pricing**, or **everyday low pricing (EDLP)**, develop a pricing strategy that promises ultimate value to consumers. What this really means is that in the customers' eyes the price is justified by what they receive. At Walmart EDLP is a fundamental part of the company's success. The world's largest retailer demands tens of billions of dollars in cost efficiencies from its supply chain and passes these savings on to its customers. To compete, other retailers must reduce their prices.

When firms base price strategies solely or mainly on cost, they operate under the old production orientation we discussed in Chapter 1 rather than under a customer orientation. Value-based pricing begins with customers, then considers the competition, and then determines the best pricing strategy.

In order to compete more effectively with Walmart, warehouse clubs, and other low-price retailers, some retail chains have adopted a "hybrid EDLP" strategy that combines lower prices on hundreds or thousands of items with programs designed to offer consumers additional value in the form of a more fun shopping experience. For supermarket chains, the hybrid EDLP strategies mean abandoning short-term price promotions such as coupon wars and "buy-one-get-one-free" offers in favor of long-term price reductions combined other incentives to keep the shopper coming back. One supermarket provides customers with a customized ad flier each week based on products that are of interest to them. Another replaced its weekly sale advertising with newsletter-type fliers that offer recipes and "fun facts," while still another competitor allows frequent shoppers to receive 20 personalized offers each week when they use a biometric finger-scan identification system.[17]

> **value pricing** or **everyday low pricing (EDLP)**
> A pricing strategy in which a firm sets prices that provide ultimate value to customers.

New Product Pricing

New products are vital to the growth and profits of a firm—but they also present unique pricing challenges. When a product is new to the market or when there is no established industry price norm, marketers may use a skimming price strategy, a penetration pricing strategy, or trial pricing when they first introduce the item to the market. Let's take a closer look at each approach.

Setting a **skimming price** means that the firm charges a high, premium price for its new product with the intention of reducing it in the future in response to market pressures. When Apple introduced the iPhone in 2007 the company charged $599.00, clearly a skimming price. However, when the firm dropped the price $200 a few months later early adopters were so angered that Apple agreed to give them a $100 Apple store credit. Some questioned whether the same would happen when Apple introduced its iPad in 2010 with prices from $499 to $829.[18]

> **skimming price**
> A very high, premium price that a firm charges for its new, highly desirable product.

If a product is highly desirable and it offers unique benefits, demand is price inelastic during the introductory stage of the product life cycle, allowing a company to recover research and development and promotion costs. When rival products enter the market, the firm lowers the price to remain competitive. Firms that focus on profit objectives when they develop their pricing strategies often set skimming prices for new products.

A skimming price is more likely to succeed if the product provides some important benefits to the target market that make customers feel they must have it no matter what the cost. Handheld calculators were such a product when they entered the market in the late 1960s. To the total astonishment of consumers at that time, these magic little devices could add, subtract, multiply, and divide

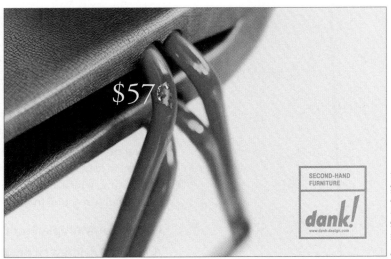

Secondhand products often meet the price needs of frugal consumers. This ad for a used furniture store ran in Turkey.

with just the push of a button. It's equally hard for consumers today to believe that back then these gizmos sold for as much as $200—a fortune 40 years ago. Today Hewlett-Packard's HP 17bII+ financial calculator features over 250 functions and allows owners to calculate loan payments, interest rates, standard deviations, and net present value—all for under $100.[19]

Second, for skimming pricing to be successful, there should be little chance that competitors can get into the market quickly. With highly complex, technical products, it may be quite a while before competitors can put a rival product into production. Finally, a skimming pricing strategy is most successful when the market consists of several customer segments with different levels of price sensitivity. There must be a substantial number of initial product customers who have very low price sensitivity. After a period of time, the price can go down, and a second segment of the market with a slightly higher level of price sensitivity will purchase, and so on.

penetration pricing
A pricing strategy in which a firm introduces a new product at a very low price to encourage more customers to purchase it.

Penetration pricing is the opposite of skimming pricing. In this situation, the company prices a new product very low to sell more in a short time and gain market share early. One reason marketers use penetration pricing is to discourage competitors from entering the market. The firm first out with a new product has an important advantage. Experience shows that a pioneering brand often is able to maintain dominant market share for long periods. Penetration pricing may act as a *barrier-to-entry* for competitors if the prices the market will bear are so low that the company will not be able to recover development and manufacturing costs. Bayer aspirin and Hoover vacuum cleaners are examples of brands that were first-to-market decades ago and still dominate their industries today.

trial pricing
Pricing a new product low for a limited period of time in order to lower the risk for a customer.

Trial pricing means that a new product carries a low price for a limited time to generate a high level of customer interest. Unlike penetration pricing, in which the company maintains the low price, in this case it increases the trial price after the introductory period. The idea is to win customer acceptance first and make profits later, as when a new health club offers an introductory membership to start pulling people in. When Microsoft first introduced the Access database program, it hit the market at the short-term promotional price of $99 (the suggested retail price was a whopping $495). Microsoft hoped to lure people to try the product at the lower price; it was banking on the idea that they would be so impressed with the program that they would persuade others to buy it at the full price.

Step 6: Develop Pricing Tactics

Once marketers have developed pricing strategies, the last step in price planning is to implement them. The methods companies use to set their strategies in motion are their *pricing tactics*.

Pricing for Individual Products

Once marketers have settled on a product's price, the way they present it to the market can make a big difference:

- *Two-part pricing* requires two separate types of payments to purchase the product. For example, golf and tennis clubs charge yearly or monthly fees plus fees for each round of golf or tennis. Likewise, many cellular phone service providers offer customers a set number of minutes for a monthly fee plus a per-minute rate for extra usage.

- *Payment pricing* makes the consumer think the price is "do-able" by breaking up the total price into smaller amounts payable over time. For example, many customers now opt to lease rather than buy a car. The monthly lease amount is an example of payment pricing, which tends to make people less sensitive to the total price of the car (we call a negative reaction to the total retail price *sticker shock*).

Pricing for Multiple Products

A firm may sell several products that consumers typically buy at one time. As fast-food restaurants like Burger King know, a customer who buys a burger for lunch usually goes for a soft drink and fries as well. The sale of a paper-cup dispenser usually means a package of cups is not far behind. The two most common tactics for pricing multiple products are price bundling and captive pricing.

Price bundling means selling two or more goods or services as a single package for one price—a price that is often less than the total price of the items if bought individually. A music buff can buy tickets to an entire concert series for a single price. A PC typically comes bundled with a monitor, a keyboard, and software. Even an all-you-can-eat special at the local diner is an example of price bundling. Traditional cable television providers like Cox, Comcast, and Time Warner have gotten into the price bundling act as they entice their customers to sign on for a package of cable television, high-speed Internet and local phone service or (in some cases) wireless phone service.

From a marketing standpoint, price bundling makes sense. If we price products separately, it's more likely that customers will buy some but not all the items. They might choose to put off some purchases until later, or they might buy from a competitor. Whatever revenue a seller loses from the reduced prices for the total package it often makes up in increased total purchases.

Captive pricing is a pricing tactic a firm uses when it has two products that work only when used together. The firm sells one item at a very low price and then makes its profit on the second high-margin item. This tactic is commonly used to sell shaving products where the razor is relatively cheap but the blades are not. Similarly, companies such as HP and Canon offer consumers a desktop printer that also serves as a fax, copier, and scanner for under $100 in order to keep selling ink cartridges.

Distribution-Based Pricing

Distribution-based pricing is a pricing tactic that establishes how firms handle the cost of shipping products to customers near, far, and wide. Characteristics of the product, the customers, and the competition figure in the decision to charge all customers the same price or to vary according to shipping cost.

F.O.B. pricing is a tactic used in business-to-business marketing. Often a company states a price as *F.O.B. factory* or *F.O.B. delivered*. F.O.B. stands for "free on board," which means the supplier pays to have the product loaded onto a truck or some other carrier. Also—and this is important—*title passes to the buyer* at the F.O.B. location. F.O.B. factory or **F.O.B. origin pricing** means that the cost of transporting the product from the factory to the customer's location is the responsibility of the customer. **F.O.B. delivered pricing** means that the seller pays both the cost of loading and the cost of transporting to the customer, amounts it includes in the selling price.

Delivery terms for pricing of products sold in international markets are especially important. Some of the more common terms are the following—get ready for a bunch of initials![20]

- *CIF* (cost, insurance, freight) is the term used for ocean shipments and means the seller quotes a price for the goods (including insurance), all transportation, and miscellaneous charges to the point of debarkation from the vessel.

- *CFR* (cost and freight) means the quoted price covers the goods and the cost of transportation to the named point of debarkation, but the buyer must pay the cost of insurance. The CFR term is also used for ocean shipments.

- *CIP* (carriage and insurance paid to) and *CPT* (carriage paid to) include the same provisions as CIF and CFR but are used for shipment by modes other than water.

Another distribution-based pricing tactic used primarily in B2B marketing, **basing-point pricing**, means marketers choose one or more locations to serve as intermediate delivery locations. Customers pay shipping charges from these *basing points* to their final destinations, whether the goods are actually shipped from these points or not. For example, a customer in Los Angeles may order a product from a company in San Diego. The product

---

price bundling
Selling two or more goods or services as a single package for one price.

captive pricing
A pricing tactic for two items that must be used together; one item is priced very low, and the firm makes its profit on another, high-margin item essential to the operation of the first item.

F.O.B. origin pricing
A pricing tactic in which the cost of transporting the product from the factory to the customer's location is the responsibility of the customer.

F.O.B. delivered pricing
A pricing tactic in which the cost of loading and transporting the product to the customer is included in the selling price and is paid by the manufacturer.

basing-point pricing
A pricing tactic in which customers pay shipping charges from set basing-point locations, whether the goods are actually shipped from these points or not.

ships to Los Angeles from the San Diego warehouse. However, if the designated basing point is Dallas, the customer pays shipping charges from Dallas to Los Angeles, charges that the seller never incurred.

When a firm uses **uniform delivered pricing**, it adds an average shipping cost to the price, no matter what the distance from the manufacturer's plant—within reason. For example, when you order a CD from a music supplier, you may pay the cost of the CD plus $2.99 shipping and handling, no matter what the actual cost of the shipping to your particular location. Internet sales, catalog sales, home television shopping, and other types of nonstore retail sales usually use uniform delivered pricing.

Freight absorption pricing means the seller takes on part or all of the cost of shipping. This policy works well for high-ticket items, for which the cost of shipping is a negligible part of the sales price and the profit margin. Marketers are most likely to use freight absorption pricing in highly competitive markets or when such pricing allows them to enter new markets. More recently, online marketers such as **Amazon.com** have found that offering free shipping makes a big difference to consumers and to their sales volume.

Discounting for Channel Members

So far we've talked about pricing tactics used to sell to end customers. Now we'll talk about tactics firms use to price to members of their *distribution channels*.

- *Trade or functional discounts:* We discussed earlier how manufacturers often set a list or suggested retail price for their product and then sell the product to members of the channel, for less, allowing the channel members to cover their costs and make a profit. Thus, the manufacturer's pricing structure will normally include **trade discounts** to channel intermediaries. These discounts are usually set percentage discounts off the suggested retail or list price for each channel level. In today's marketing environment dominated by large retail chains such as Walmart, Costco, and Target, the amount of the trade discount is dictated by the retailers who, because of their size, have the most power in the channel. We'll talk more about channel power in Chapter 15.

- *Quantity discounts:* To encourage larger purchases from distribution channel partners or from large organizational customers, marketers may offer **quantity discounts**, or reduced prices for purchases of larger quantities. *Cumulative quantity discounts* are based on a total quantity bought within a specified time period, often a year, and encourage a buyer to stick with a single seller instead of moving from one supplier to another. Cumulative quantity discounts often take the form of *rebates*, in which case the firm sends the buyer a rebate check at the end of the discount period or, alternatively, gives the buyer credit against future orders. *Noncumulative quantity discounts* are based only on the quantity purchased with each individual order and encourage larger single orders but do little to tie the buyer and the seller together.

- *Cash discounts:* Many firms try to entice their customers to pay their bills quickly by offering **cash discounts**. For example, a firm selling to a retailer may state that the terms of the sale are "2 percent 10 days, net 30 days," meaning that if the retailer pays the producer for the goods within 10 days, the amount due is cut by 2 percent. The total amount is due within 30 days, and after 30 days the payment is late.

- *Seasonal discounts:* **Seasonal discounts** are price reductions offered only during certain times of the year. For seasonal products such as snow blowers, lawn mowers, and water-skiing equipment, marketers use seasonal discounts to entice retailers and wholesalers to buy off-season and either store the product at their locations until the right time of the year or pass the discount along to consumers with off-season sales programs. Alternatively, they may offer discounts when products are in-season to create a competitive advantage during periods of high demand.

uniform delivered pricing
A pricing tactic in which a firm adds a standard shipping charge to the price for all customers regardless of location.

freight absorption pricing
A pricing tactic in which the seller absorbs the total cost of transportation.

trade discounts
Discounts off list price of products to members of the channel of distribution who perform various marketing functions.

quantity discounts
A pricing tactic of charging reduced prices for purchases of larger quantities of a product.

cash discounts
A discount offered to a customer to entice them to pay their bill quickly.

seasonal discounts
Price reductions offered only during certain times of the year.

4 Pricing and Electronic Commerce

OBJECTIVE

Understand the opportunities for Internet pricing strategies.
(pp. 323–324)

As we have seen, price planning is a complex process in any firm. But if you are operating in the "wired world," get ready for even more pricing options!

Because sellers are connected to buyers around the globe as never before through the Internet, corporate networks, and wireless setups, marketers can offer deals they tailor to a single person at a single moment. On the other hand, they're also a lot more vulnerable to smart consumers, who can easily check out competing prices with the click of a mouse.

Many experts suggest that technology is creating a consumer revolution that might change pricing forever—and perhaps create the most efficient market ever. The music industry provides the most obvious example: Music lovers from around the globe purchase and download billions of songs from numerous Internet sites including the iTunes Music Store.[21] And mobile music is just beginning—43 percent of mobile users across the globe access music through their phones. In the United States, consumers spent $1.1 billion on recorded music for their phones in 2007. This figure is about 12 percent of the $9 billion people spent globally on mobile music; analysts expect the total to jump to $17.5 billion by 2012.[22] And many of the sellers find that it is easy to compete on price.

The Internet also enables firms that sell to other businesses (B2B firms) to change their prices rapidly as they adapt to changing costs. For consumers who have lots of stuff in the attic they need to put in someone else's attic the Internet means an opportunity for consumers to find ready buyers. And for B2C firms, firms that sell to consumers, the Internet offers other opportunities. In this section, we will discuss some of the more popular Internet pricing strategies shown in 📷 Figure 11.13.

Figure 11.13 📷 *Snapshot* |
Internet Pricing Strategies
The Internet provides an opportunity to use some unique pricing strategies.

| Dynamic Pricing |
| Online Auctions |
| Freenomics |

Dynamic Pricing Strategies

One of the most important opportunities the Internet offers is **dynamic pricing**, in which the seller can easily adjust the price to meet changes in the marketplace. If a bricks-and-mortar retail store wants to change prices, employees/workers must place new price tags on items, create and display new store signage and media advertising, and input new prices into the store's computer system. For business-to-business marketers, employees/workers must print catalogs and price lists and distribute to salespeople and customers. These activities can be very costly to a firm, so they simply don't change their prices very often.

dynamic pricing
A pricing strategy in which the price can easily be adjusted to meet changes in the marketplace.

Online Auctions

Most consumers are familiar with eBay. But what about eCrater, Bonanzle, eBid, and CQout? These too are some of the many **online auctions** that allow shoppers to bid on everything from bobbleheads to health-and-fitness equipment to a Sammy Sosa home-run ball. Auctions provide a second Internet pricing strategy. Perhaps the most popular auctions are the C2C auctions such as those on eBay. The eBay auction is an *open auction*, meaning that all the buyers know the highest price bid at any point in time. On many Internet auction sites, the seller can set a *reserve price*, a price below which the item will not be sold.

A *reverse auction* is a tool used by firms to manage their costs in business-to-business buying. While in a typical auction buyers compete to purchase a product, in reverse auctions, sellers compete for the right to provide a product at, hopefully, a low price.

on-line auctions
E-commerce that allows shoppers to purchase products through online bidding.

Freenomics: What If We Just Give It Away?

It turns out that one of the most exciting revolutions in e-commerce is happening in the area of pricing. Yes folks, once again the Internet is changing the way we look at doing business.[23] In this case this is because the Net makes it possible to give products away FOR FREE.

No, you're not hallucinating—we said for free. You're probably thinking this is the dumbest idea you've ever heard of—but it turns out that a new business model based on pricing goods at zero or close to zero actually makes dollars and sense. For example, music groups like Radiohead, Trent Reznor of Nine Inch Nails, and R.E.M. understand that when they make their music freely available online they build a fan base that flocks to their concerts and buys their merchandise. Many online video games are free to players because they are ad-supported, and almost everything Google "sells" such as unlimited search, Gmail, and Picasa is actually free to consumers.

This new business model of **freenomics** is based on the idea that economists call *externalities*; this means that the more people you get to participate in a market, the more profitable it is. So, for example, the more people Google convinces to use its Gmail e-mail service, the more eyeballs it attracts, which in turn boosts the rates advertisers are willing to pay to talk to those people. Here are a few examples of how freenomics is changing the way at least some savvy marketers think about pricing:

- The hugely successful European discount airline Ryanair currently flies passengers from London to Barcelona for about $20. The company's CEO says he hopes eventually to turn all of his flights into a free ride. Don't lose any sleep over the airline's profitability— it makes money when it sells ancillary services *a la carte* such as food, beverages, extra fees for preloading, checked baggage, and flying with an infant. Ryanair charges extra for credit card transactions, sells in-flight advertising, and the plan is to introduce gambling so that passengers who are riding for free will drop a bundle while en route to their destinations.

- The singer Prince launched his new *Planet Earth* album by putting a free copy of the CD—normally worth about $19—into 2.8 million copies of London's *Daily Mail* newspaper. The Purple One lost a bundle doing that—and then more than made it up by posting record ticket sales to the 21 shows he proceeded to sell out at London's O$_2$ Arena.

- Cable giant Comcast has given about nine million subscribers free set-top digital video recorders. How do you make money by giving away DVRs? Try adding installation fees to put the boxes in and charge customers a monthly fee to use the box. Comcast also hopes to lure new customers with the offer, and then sell them other services like high-speed Internet. All told, Comcast earns back the cost of its free DVR in 18 months, and then the company goes into the black. The next time someone tells you there's no such thing as a free lunch, point them to the Web for a mouse sandwich.

Pricing Advantages for Online Shoppers

The Internet also creates unique pricing challenges for marketers because consumers and business customers are gaining more control over the buying process. Access to sophisticated "shopbots" and search engines mean that consumers are no longer at the mercy of firms that dictate a price they must accept. The result is that customers have become more price-sensitive. Many computer-savvy computer shoppers find that shopbots provide them with the best price on both hardware and software. As one illustration, a comparison study found that the price of Panasonic Viera TC-P50X1 HD TV ranges from a high of $999.99 at **Amazon.com** to a low of $795 at Abe's of Maine. Similarly, the price of a red Canon Power-Shot A480 digital camera is $94.99 at **Amazon.com** and $129.99 online from Sears.

Detailed information about what products actually cost manufacturers, available from sites such as Consumerreports.org, can give consumers more negotiating power when shopping for new cars and other big-ticket items. Finally, e-commerce potentially can lower consumers' costs because of the gasoline, time, and aggravation they save when they avoid a trip to the mall.

freenomics
A business model that encourages giving products away for free because of the increase in profits that can be achieved by getting more people to participate in a market.

5 Psychological, Legal, and Ethical Aspects of Pricing

OBJECTIVE

Describe the psychological, legal, and ethical aspects of pricing.
(pp. 325–330)

So far, we've discussed how marketers use demand, costs, and an understanding of the pricing environment to plan effective pricing strategies and tactics. There are, however, other aspects of pricing that marketers must understand and deal with in order to maximize the effectiveness of their pricing plans. In this section we discuss a number of psychological, legal, and ethical factors related to pricing that are important for marketers. Figure 11.14 provides a quick look at these aspects of pricing.

Psychological Issues in Setting Prices

Much of what we've said about pricing depends on economists' notion of a customer who evaluates price in a logical, rational manner. For example, we express the concept of demand by a smooth curve, which assumes that if a firm lowers a product's price from $10.00 to $9.50 and then from $9.50 to $9.00 and so on, then customers will simply buy more and more. In the real world, though, it doesn't always work that way—consumers aren't nearly as rational as that! Let's look at some psychological factors that keep economists up at night.

Buyers' Pricing Expectations

Often consumers base their perceptions of price on what they perceive to be the customary or *fair price*. For example, for many years a candy bar or a pack of gum was priced at five cents (yes, five). Consumers would have perceived any other price as too high or low. It was a nickel candy bar—period. So when costs went up or inflation kicked in, some candy makers tried to shrink the size of the bar instead of changing the price. Eventually, inflation prevailed, consumers' salaries rose, and that candy bar goes for 10 to 12 times one nickel today—a price that consumers would have found unacceptable a few decades ago.

When the price of a product is above or even sometimes when it's below what consumers expect, they are less willing to purchase the product. If the price is above their expectations, they may think it is a rip-off. If it is below expectations, consumers may think quality is below par. By understanding the pricing expectations of their customers, marketers are better able to develop viable pricing strategies. These expectations can differ across cultures and countries. For example, in one study researchers did in southern California, they found that Chinese supermarkets charge significantly lower prices (only half as much for meat and seafood) than mainstream American supermarkets in the same areas.[24]

Psychological Issues in Pricing	Psychological Pricing Strategies
• Buyer' Expectations • Internal Reference Prices • Price-Quality inferences	• Odd-Even Pricing • Price Lining • Prestige Pricing
Legal and Ethical Issues in B2C Pricing	Legal and Ethical Issues in B2B Pricing
• Bait-and-Switch • Loss-Leader pricing	• Price Discrimination • Price-Fixing • Predatory Pricing

Figure 11.14 *Snapshot*
Psychological, Legal, and Ethical Aspects of Pricing

Price planning is influenced by psychological issues and strategies and by legal and ethical issues.

Internal Reference Prices

internal reference price

A set price or a price range in consumers' minds that they refer to in evaluating a product's price.

Sometimes consumers' perceptions of the customary price of a product depend on their **internal reference price**. That is, based on past experience, consumers have a set price or a price range in mind that they refer to in evaluating a product's cost. The reference price may be the last price paid, or it may be the average of all the prices they know of for similar products. No matter what the brand, the normal price for a loaf of sandwich bread is about $2.99. In some stores it may be $2.79, and in others it is $3.19, but the average is $2.99. If consumers find a comparable loaf of bread priced much higher than this—say, $4.99—they will feel it is overpriced and grab a competing brand. If they find bread priced significantly lower—say, at $.99 or $1.29 a loaf—they may shy away from the purchase, wondering "what's wrong" with the bread.

In some cases, marketers try to influence consumers' expectations of what a product should cost when they use reference pricing strategies. For example, manufacturers may compare their price to competitors' prices when they advertise. Similarly, a retailer may display a product next to a higher-priced version of the same or a different brand. The consumer must choose between the two products with different prices.

Two results are likely: On the one hand, if the prices (and other characteristics) of the two products are fairly close, the consumer will probably feel the product quality is similar. This is an *assimilation effect*. The customer might think, "The price is about the same, they must be alike. I'll be smart and save a few dollars." And so the customer chooses the lower-price item because the low price makes it look attractive next to the higher-priced alternative. This is why store brands of deodorant, vitamins, pain relievers, and shampoo sit beside national brands, often accompanied by a shelf talker pointing out how much shoppers can save if they purchase the store brands. On the other hand, if the prices of the two products are too far apart, a *contrast effect* may result, in which the customer equates the gap with a big difference in quality: "Gee, this lower-priced one is probably not as good as the higher-priced one. I'll splurge on the more expensive one." Using this strategy, an appliance store may place an advertised $300 refrigerator next to a $699 model to convince a customer that the bottom-of-the-line model just won't do.

Price–Quality Inferences

Imagine that you go to a shoe store to check out running shoes. You notice one pair that costs $89.99. On another table you see a second pair that looks almost identical to the first pair— but its price is only $24.95. Which pair do you want? Which pair do you think is the better quality? Many of us will pay the higher price because we believe the bargain-basement shoes aren't worth the risk at any price.

Consumers make *price–quality inferences* about a product when they use price as a cue or an indicator of quality. (An inference means we believe something to be true without any direct evidence.) If consumers are unable to judge the quality of a product through examination or prior experience, they usually assume that the higher-priced product is the higher-quality product.

In fact, new research on how the brain works even suggests that the price we pay can subtly influence how much pleasure we get from the product. Brain scans show that— contrary to conventional wisdom—consumers who buy something at a discount experience less satisfaction than people who pay full price for the very same thing. For example, in one recent study volunteers who drank wine that they were told cost $90 a bottle actually registered more brain activity in pleasure centers than did those who drank the very same wine but who were told it only cost $10 a bottle. Researchers call this the *price-placebo effect*. This is similar to the placebo effect in medicine where people who think they are getting the real thing but who are actually taking sugar pills still experience the effects of the real drug.[25]

Psychological Pricing Strategies

Setting a price is part science, part art. Marketers must understand psychological aspects of pricing when they decide what to charge for their products or services.

Odd–Even Pricing

In the U.S. market, we usually see prices in dollars and cents—$1.99, $5.98, $23.67, or even $599.95. We see prices in even dollar amounts—$2.00, $10.00, or $600.00—far less often. The reason? Marketers assume that there is a psychological response to odd prices that differs from the response to even prices. Habit might also play a role here. Whatever the reason, research on the difference in perceptions of odd versus even prices indeed supports the argument that prices ending in 99 rather than 00 lead to increased sales.[26]

But there are some instances in which even prices are the norm or perhaps a necessity. Theater and concert tickets, admission to sporting events, and lottery tickets tend to be priced in even amounts. Professionals normally quote their fees in even dollars. If a doctor or dentist charged $39.99 for a visit, the patient might think the quality of medical care was less than satisfactory. Many luxury items such as jewelry, golf course fees, and resort accommodations use even dollar prices to set them apart.

Restaurants (and the menu engineers who work with them) have discovered that how prices for menu items are presented has a major influence on what customers order—and how much they pay. When prices are given with dollar signs or even the word dollar, customers spend less. Thus, a simple 9 is better on a menu than $9. For high-end restaurants, the formats that end in 9 such as $9.99 indicate value but not quality.[27]

Price Lining

Marketers often apply their understanding of the psychological aspects of pricing in a practice they call **price lining**, whereby items in a product line sell at different prices, or *price points*. If you want to buy a new digital camera, you will find that most of the leading manufacturers have one "stripped-down" model for $100 or less. A better-quality but still moderately priced model likely will be around $200, while a professional quality camera with multiple lenses might set you back $1,000 or more. Price lining provides the different ranges necessary to satisfy each segment of the market.

Why is price lining a smart idea? From the marketer's standpoint, it's a way to maximize profits. In theory, a firm would charge each individual customer the highest price that customer was willing to pay. If the maximum one particular person would be willing to pay for a digital camera is $150, then that would be the price. If another person would be willing to pay $300, that would be his price. But charging each consumer a different price is really not possible. Having a limited number of prices that generally fall at the top of the different price ranges customers find acceptable is a more workable alternative.

price lining
The practice of setting a limited number of different specific prices, called price points, for items in a product line.

Prestige Pricing

Finally, although a "rational" consumer should be more likely to buy a product or service as the price goes down, in the real world sometimes this assumption gets turned on its head. Remember that earlier in the chapter we talked about situations where we want to meet an image enhancement objective to appeal to status-conscious consumers. For this reason, sometimes luxury goods marketers use a *prestige pricing strategy* that turns the typical assumption about price-demand relationships on its head: Contrary to the "rational" assumption that we value a product or service more as the price goes down, in these cases, believe it or not, people tend to buy more as the price goes up!

Legal and Ethical Considerations in B2C Pricing

The free enterprise system is founded on the idea that the marketplace will regulate itself. Prices will rise or fall according to demand. Firms and individuals will supply goods and services at fair prices if there is an adequate profit incentive. Unfortunately, the business world includes the greedy and the unscrupulous. Federal, state, and local governments find it necessary to enact legislation to protect consumers and to protect businesses from predatory rivals. In this section, we'll talk about deceptive prices, unfair prices, discriminatory prices, and price-fixing, and some regulations to combat them.

Deceptive Pricing Practices: Bait-and-Switch

bait-and-switch
An illegal marketing practice in which an advertised price special is used as bait to get customers into the store with the intention of switching them to a higher-priced item.

Unscrupulous businesses may advertise or promote prices in a deceptive way. The Federal Trade Commission (FTC), state lawmakers, and private bodies such as the Better Business Bureau have developed pricing rules and guidelines to meet the challenge. They say retailers (or other suppliers) must not claim that their prices are lower than a competitor's unless that claim is true. A going-out-of-business sale should be the last sale before going out of business. A fire sale should be held only when there really was a fire.

Another deceptive pricing practice is the **bait-and-switch** tactic, whereby a retailer will advertise an item at a very low price—the *bait*—to lure customers into the store. An example might be a budget model appliance, such as a washing machine or television that has been stripped of all but the most basic features. But it is almost impossible to buy the advertised item—salespeople like to say (privately) that the item is "nailed to the floor." The salespeople do everything possible to get the unsuspecting customers to buy a different, more expensive, item—the *switch*. They might tell the customer "confidentially" that "the advertised item is really poor quality, lacking important features, and full of problems." It's complicated to enforce laws against bait-and-switch tactics because these practices are similar to the legal sales technique of "trading up." Simply encouraging consumers to purchase a higher-priced item is acceptable, but it is illegal to advertise a lower-priced item when it's not a legitimate, *bona fide* offer that is available if the customer demands it. The FTC may determine if an ad is a bait-and-switch scheme or a legitimate offer by checking to see if a firm refuses to show, demonstrate, or sell the advertised product; disparages it; or penalizes salespeople who do sell it.

Loss-Leader Pricing and Unfair Sales Acts

loss-leader pricing
The pricing policy of setting prices very low or even below cost to attract customers into a store.

Not every advertised bargain is a bait-and-switch. Some retailers advertise items at very low prices or even below cost and are glad to sell them at that price because they know that once in the store, customers may buy other items at regular prices. Marketers call this **loss-leader pricing**; they do it to build store traffic and sales volume. For example, some office-supply stores and mass merchandisers recognize that "back-to-school" shopping means more than pencils and erasers and protractors.[28] These retailers use loss-leader pricing—eight pencils for a penny, 24 Crayola crayons for a quarter, or a watercolor set for fifty cents—in order to entice mothers to fork out $60 for a new back-to-school outfit.

unfair sales acts
State laws that prohibit suppliers from selling products below cost to protect small businesses from larger competitors.

Some states frown on loss leader practices, so they have passed legislation called **unfair sales acts** (also called *unfair trade practices acts*). These laws or regulations prohibit wholesalers and retailers from selling products below cost. These laws aim to protect small wholesalers and retailers from larger competitors because the "big fish" have the financial resources that allow them to offer loss leaders or products at very low prices—they know that the smaller firms can't match these bargain prices.

Legal Issues in B2B Pricing

Of course, illegal pricing practices are not limited to business-to-consumer pricing situations. Some of the more significant illegal B2B pricing activities include price discrimination, price fixing, and predatory pricing.

Illegal Business-to-Business Price Discrimination

The *Robinson–Patman Act* includes regulations against price discrimination in interstate commerce. Price discrimination regulations prevent firms from selling the same product to different retailers and wholesalers at different prices if such practices lessen competition. In addition to regulating the price companies charge, the Robinson–Patman Act specifically

Ripped from the Headlines

Ethical/Sustainable Decisions in the Real World

Mexico City has five million automobiles; it's frequently cited as the most polluted city on earth. But in an attempt to improve its brand image and attract tourism, the city is following the lead of Paris, Milan, and Rio de Janeiro as it launches a public bike-sharing program. The program will initially have 85 stations and over 1,000 bikes. Riders will pay 300 pesos ($23) a year for the privilege of taking a bike for a 30-minute ride. They will pay additional fees for longer rides. But the program is not without hazards. When a similar program was launched in New York City, all of the bikes were stolen in a few days! Even in Paris, where crime rates are much lower, many of the bikes have been stolen or destroyed—some have been found in eastern Europe, in North Africa, floating in the Seine river, and hanging from lampposts. In fact, 80 percent of the bikes in Paris have been damaged or stolen. With so much crime in the city, does it make sense for Mexico City to launch the bike-sharing program? What would you do?

ETHICS CHECK: ☜
Find out what other students taking this course **would do** and **why** on www **.mypearsonmarketinglab .com**

↓

If you were advising the Mexico City government, would you approve the launch of the bike-sharing program?

☐YES ☐ NO

prohibits offering such "extras" as discounts, rebates, premiums, coupons, guarantees, and free delivery to some but not all customers.

There are exceptions, however:

- The Robinson–Patman Act does not apply to consumers—only resellers.

- A discount to a large channel customer is legal if it is based on the quantity of the order and the resulting efficiencies, such as transportation savings.

- The act allows price differences if there are physical differences in the product, such as different features. A name-brand appliance may be available through a large national retail chain at a lower price than an almost identical item a higher-priced retailer sells because only the chain sells that specific model.

Price-Fixing

Price-fixing occurs when two or more companies conspire to keep prices at a certain level. For example, General Electric Co. and De Beers Centenary AG were charged with fixing the prices in the $600-million-per-year world market for industrial diamonds used in cutting tools. This type of illicit agreement can take two forms: horizontal and vertical.

In 2008, the U.S. Justice Department found three makers of flat screens guilty of price-fixing of their liquid crystal display panels used in televisions, personal computers, and cell-phones.[29] In a similar ruling, the European Commission fined Dutch brewers Heineken and Grolsch for sharing pricing policy and levels.[30] Because such practices mean higher prices for customers, such practices are against the regulations of the Sherman Antitrust Act we discussed in Chapter 3. *Horizontal price-fixing* occurs when competitors making the same product jointly determine what price they each will charge. In industries in which there are few sellers, there may be no specific price-fixing agreement, but sellers will still charge the same price to "meet the competition." Such parallel pricing is not in and of itself considered price-fixing. There must be an exchange of pricing information between sellers to indicate illegal price-fixing actions.

Sometimes manufacturers or wholesalers attempt to force retailers to charge a certain price for their product. When *vertical price-fixing* occurs, the retailer that wants to carry the product has to charge the "suggested" retail price. The *Consumer Goods Pricing Act* of 1976 limited this practice, leaving retail stores free to set whatever price they choose without interference by the manufacturer or wholesaler. Today, retailers don't need to adhere to "suggested" prices.

price-fixing
The collaboration of two or more firms in setting prices, usually to keep prices high.

Predatory Pricing

Predatory pricing means that a company sets a very low price for the purpose of driving competitors out of business. Later, when they have a monopoly, they turn around and increase prices. The Sherman Act and the Robinson–Patman Act prohibit predatory pricing.

predatory pricing
Illegal pricing strategy in which a company sets a very low price for the purpose of driving competitors out of business.

For example, in 1999 the Justice Department accused American Airlines of predatory pricing at its Dallas–Ft. Worth hub.[31] In the mid-1990s, three small rivals started flying into the airport. American responded by lowering the prices of its flights on four routes. The Justice Department claimed that the airline planned to scare the three carriers away and monopolize the routes. While American was exonerated in court, the case did send a message to airlines that they must be careful when they set prices.

Now that you've learned about product pricing, read "Real People, Real Choices: How It Worked Out" to see which strategy Danielle Blugrind of Taco Bell selected for the chain's value menu.

Here's my choice. . .

Real **People**, Real **Choices**

1 Option   2 Option   **3** Option

Why do you think Danielle chose option 3?

How It Worked Out at Taco Bell

Danielle went with the Mixed Price Menu, #3. Consumers responded very well to the Big Bell Value Menu. They told Taco Bell that they liked the $1.19 price point because it helped make the menu feel less disjointed and more like a collection of products rather than two separate sets of higher-priced and lower-priced items. The middle price point also allows for some premium pricing where necessary (for example, on chicken) without resorting to the highest price point of $1.29.

To learn the whole story, visit www.mypearsonmarketinglab.com.

Brand **YOU**!

Do you know how much you are worth?

The first step in getting the salary you want is knowing how much you are worth. Find out the latest in salary trends, how and when to negotiate your offer and what else you can ask for as part of your compensation in Chapter 11 in Brand You.

| Kim Richmond Fourth Edition |

Brand YOU

MARKETING 7E **real** People, **real** Choices

Solomon | Marshall | Stuart

Objective Summary ➡ Key Terms ➡ Apply

1. Objective Summary (pp. 298–302)

Explain the importance of pricing and how marketers set objectives for their pricing strategies.

Pricing is important to firms because it creates profits and influences customers to purchase or not. Prices may be monetary or nonmonetary, as when consumers or businesses exchange one product for another. Effective pricing objectives are designed to support corporate and marketing objectives and are flexible. Pricing objectives often focus on a desired level of profit growth or profit margin, on sales (to maximize sales or to increase market share), on competing effectively, on increasing customer satisfaction, or on communicating a certain image.

Key Terms

price, p. 298

prestige products, p. 302

2. Objective Summary (pp. 302–316)

Describe how marketers use costs, demands, revenue, and the pricing environment to make pricing decisions.

In developing prices, marketers must estimate demand and determine costs. Marketers often use break-even analysis and marginal analysis to help in deciding on the price for a product. Break-even analysis uses fixed and variable costs to identify how many units must be sold at a certain price in order to begin making a profit. Marginal analysis uses both costs and estimates of product demand to identify the price that will maximize profits. Marketers must also consider the requirements for adequate trade margins for retailers, wholesalers and other members of the channel of distribution. Like other elements of the marketing mix, pricing is influenced by a variety of external environmental factors. This includes economic trends such as inflation and recession and the firm's competitive environment—that is, whether the firm does business in an oligopoly, a monopoly, or a more competitive environment. Government regulations can also affect prices by increasing the cost of production or through actual regulations of a firm's pricing strategies. Consumer trends that influence how consumers think and behave may also influence pricing. While marketers of some products may develop standardized pricing strategies for global markets, unique environmental factors in different countries mean marketers must localize pricing strategies.

Key Terms

price elasticity of demand, p. 304

elastic demand, p. 305

inelastic demand, p. 305

cross-elasticity of demand, p. 306

variable costs, p. 307

fixed costs, p. 308

average fixed cost, p. 308

total costs, p. 308

break-even analysis, p. 309

break-even point, p. 309

contribution per unit, p. 309

marginal analysis, p. 311

marginal cost, p. 311

marginal revenue, p. 311

markup, p. 312

gross margin, p. 312

retailer margin, p. 312

wholesaler margin, p. 312

list price or manufacturer's suggested retail price (MSRP), p. 312

sachets, p. 315

3. Objective Summary (pp. 316–322)

Understand key pricing strategies and tactics.

Though easy to calculate and "safe," frequently used cost-based strategies do not consider demand, the competition, the stage in the product life cycle, plant capacity, or product image. The most common cost-based strategy is cost-plus pricing.

Pricing strategies based on demand, such as target costing and yield management pricing, can require that marketers estimate demand at different prices in order to be certain they can sell what they produce. Strategies based on the competition may represent industry wisdom but can be tricky to apply. A price leadership strategy is often used in an oligopoly.

Firms that focus on customer needs may consider everyday low price or value pricing strategies. New products may be priced using a high skimming price to recover research, development, and promotional costs, or a penetration price to encourage more customers and discourage competitors from entering the market. Trial pricing means setting a low price for a limited time.

To implement pricing strategies with individual products, marketers may use two-part pricing or payment pricing tactics. For multiple products, marketers may use price bundling, wherein two or more products are sold and priced as a single package. Captive pricing is often chosen when two items must be used together; one item is sold at a very low price and the other at a high, profitable price.

Distribution-based pricing tactics, including F.O.B., basing-point, and uniform delivered pricing, address differences in how far products must be shipped. Similar pricing tactics are used for products sold internationally.

Pricing for members of the channel may include trade or functional discounts, cumulative or noncumulative quantity discounts to encourage larger purchases, cash discounts to encourage fast payment, and seasonal discounts to spread purchases throughout the year or to increase off-season or in-season sales.

cost-plus pricing, p. 317

demand-based pricing, p. 317

target costing, p. 317

yield management pricing, p. 317

price leadership, p. 318

value pricing, p. 319

everyday low pricing (EDLP), p. 319

skimming price, p. 319

penetration pricing, p. 320

trial pricing, p. 320

price bundling, p. 321

captive pricing, p. 321

F.O.B. origin pricing, p. 321

F.O.B. delivered pricing, p. 321

basing-point pricing, p. 321

uniform delivered pricing, p. 322

freight absorption pricing, p. 322

trade discounts, p. 322

quantity discounts, p. 322

cash discounts, p. 322

seasonal discounts, p. 322

4. Objective Summary (pp. 323–324)

Understand the opportunities for Internet pricing strategies.

E-commerce may offer firms an opportunity to initiate dynamic pricing—meaning prices can be changed frequently with little or no cost. Auctions offer opportunities for customers to bid on items in C2C, B2C, and B2B e-commerce. The Internet allows buyers to compare products and prices, gives consumers more control over the price they pay for items, and has made customers more price sensitive.

Key Terms

dynamic pricing, p. 323

online auctions, p. 323

freenomics, p. 324

5. Objective Summary (pp. 325–330)

Describe the psychological, legal, and ethical aspects of pricing.

Consumers may express emotional or psychological responses to prices. Customers may use an idea of a customary or fair price as an internal reference price in evaluating products. Sometimes marketers use reference pricing strategies by displaying products with different prices next to each other. A price–quality inference means that consumers use price as a cue for quality. Customers respond to odd prices differently than to even-dollar prices. Marketers may practice price lining strategies in which they set a limited number of different price ranges for a product line. With luxury products, marketers may use a prestige pricing strategy, assuming that people will buy more if the price is higher.

Most marketers try to avoid unethical or illegal pricing practices. One deceptive pricing practice is the illegal bait-and-switch tactic. Many states have unfair sales acts, which are laws against loss leader pricing that make it illegal to sell products below cost. Federal regulations prohibit predatory pricing, price discrimination, and horizontal or vertical price-fixing.

Key Terms

internal reference price, p. 326

price lining, p. 327

bait-and-switch, p. 328

loss-leader pricing, p. 328

unfair sales acts, p. 328

price fixing, p. 329

predatory pricing, p. 329

Chapter **Questions** and **Activities**

Questions: Test Your Knowledge

1. What is price, and why is it important to a firm? What are some examples of monetary and nonmonetary prices?
2. Describe and give examples of some of the following types of pricing objectives: profit, market share, competitive effect, customer satisfaction, and image enhancement.
3. Explain how the demand curves for normal products and for prestige products differ. What are demand shifts and why are they important to marketers? How do firms go about estimating demand? How can marketers estimate the elasticity of demand?
4. Explain variable costs, fixed costs, average variable costs, average fixed costs, and average total costs.
5. What is break-even analysis? What is marginal analysis? What are the comparative advantages of break-even analysis and marginal analysis for marketers?
6. What are trade margins? How do they relate to the pricing for a producer of goods?
7. How does recession affect consumers' perceptions of prices? How does inflation influence perceptions of prices? What are some ways that the competitive environment, government regulations, consumer trends, and the global environment influence a firm's pricing strategies?
8. Explain cost-plus pricing, target costing, and yield management pricing. Explain how a price leadership strategy works.
9. For new products, when is skimming pricing more appropriate, and when is penetration pricing the best strategy? When would trial pricing be an effective pricing strategy?
10. Explain two-part pricing, payment pricing, price bundling, captive pricing, and distribution-based pricing tactics. Give an example of when each would be a good pricing tactic for marketers to use.
11. Why do marketers use trade or functional discounts, quantity discounts, cash discounts, and seasonal discounts in pricing to members of the channel?
12. What is dynamic pricing? Why does the Internet encourage the use of dynamic pricing?
13. Explain these psychological aspects of pricing: price–quality inferences, odd–even pricing, internal reference price, price lining, and prestige pricing.
14. Explain how unethical marketers might use bait-and-switch tactics, price-fixing, and predatory pricing. What is loss-leader pricing? What are unfair sales acts?

Activities: Apply What You've Learned

1. Assume that you are the director of marketing for a firm that manufactures candy bars. Your boss has suggested that the current economic conditions merit an increase in the price of your candy bars. You are concerned that increasing the price might not be profitable because you are unsure of the price elasticity of demand for your product. Develop a plan for the measurement of price elasticity of demand for your candy bars. What findings would lead you to increase the price? What findings would cause you to rethink the decision to increase prices? Develop a presentation for your class outlining (1) the concept of elasticity of demand, (2) why raising prices without understanding the elasticity would be a bad move, (3) your recommendations for measurement, and (4) the potential impact on profits for elastic and inelastic demand.

2. As the vice president for marketing for a firm that markets computer software, you must regularly develop pricing strategies for new software products. Your latest product is a software package that automatically translates any foreign language e-mail messages to the user's preferred language. You are trying to decide on the pricing for this new product. Should you use a skimming price, a penetration price, or something in between? Argue in front of your class the pros and cons for each alternative.

3. Assume that you have been hired as the assistant manager of a local store that sells fresh fruits and vegetables. As you look over the store, you notice that there are two different displays of tomatoes. In one display the tomatoes are priced at $1.39 per pound, and in the other the tomatoes are priced at $.89 per pound. The tomatoes look very much alike. You notice that many people are buying the $1.39 tomatoes. Write a report explaining what is happening and give your recommendations for the store's pricing strategy.

4. We know that marketers must consider not only the monetary costs of products but also the nonmonetary costs. Take, for example, the cost of your college education. While you pay tuition and other fees, there are also nonmonetary costs that students must bear. Talk with five to 10 of your fellow university students. Ask them what nonmonetary costs they feel are important and would like reduced. Develop a report with your recommendations for how your university might change policies or practices that would reduce nonmonetary costs.

5. Select one of the product categories below. Identify two different firms that offer consumers a line of product offerings in the category. For example, Dell, HP, and Toshiba each market a line of laptop computers while Hoover, Eureka, and Bissell offer lines of vacuum cleaners. Using the Internet or by visiting a retailer who sells your selected product, research the product lines and pricing of the two firms. Based on your research, develop a report on the price lining strategies of the two firms. Your report should discuss (1) the specific price points of the product offerings of each firm and how the price lining strategy maximizes revenue, (2) your ideas for why the specific price points were selected, (3) how the price lining strategies of the two firms are alike and how they are different, and (4) possible reasons for differences in the strategies.
   a. Laptop computers
   b. Vacuum cleaners
   c. Refrigerators
   d. HD televisions

6. Assume that you are the V.P. of marketing for a firm that produces refrigerated prepared pasta dishes for sale to consumers through various retail channels. You are considering producing a new line of all-natural one-serving pasta

dishes. Your research suggests that consumers would only be willing to buy the pasta if the price is less than $6.00 per package. You will be selling the pasta through specialty food brokers who will distribute to natural food stores that will sell to consumers. The natural food stores require a 30 percent retailer margin and the brokers require a 20 percent wholesaler margin.

   a. Assuming the natural food stores will sell the product for $5.99 per package, what price will the specialty food brokers charge the food stores for the product?
   b. What price will the manufacturer charge the specialty food brokers?
   c. If the manufacturer costs are $0.95 per package, what will the manufacturer's contribution per unit be?

Marketing Metrics Exercise

Contribution analysis and break-even analysis are surely the most important and most frequently used marketing metrics. These analyses are essential to determine if a firm's marketing opportunity will mean a financial loss or be profitable. As explained in the chapter, *contribution* is the difference between the selling price per unit and the variable cost per unit. Break-even analysis that includes contribution tells marketers how much must be sold to break even or to earn a desired amount of profit.

Happy Days Dairy is a producer of high-quality organic yogurt, sour cream, and crème fraiche. They are considering marketing a new line of drinkable yogurt for children. The new yogurt will be offered in packages of six 6-ounce individual containers and it will be available in four flavors.

The company plans to use TV and newspaper advertising to promote the new product. Distribution will be through major supermarket chains, which currently have over 90 percent of the U.S. yogurt market. The suggested retail price for each 6-ounce individual container will be $0.60. Because the retailer requires a 30 percent markup, Happy Days' price to the supermarkets will be $0.42 per six-ounce container. The unit variable costs for the product including packaging will be $0.15.

The company estimates its advertising and promotion expenses for the first year will be $1,500,000.

1. What is the contribution per unit for the new children's yogurt product?
2. What is the break-even unit volume for the first year that will cover the planned advertising and promotion? The break-even in dollars?
3. How many units of the yogurt must Happy Days sell to earn a profit of $800,000?

Choices: What Do You Think?

1. Governments sometimes provide price subsidies to specific industries; that is, they reduce a domestic firm's costs so that it can sell products on the international market at a lower price. What reasons do governments (and politicians) use for these government subsidies? What are the benefits and disadvantages to domestic industries in the long run? To international customers? Who would benefit and who would lose if all price subsidies were eliminated?
2. In many oligopolistic industries, firms follow a price leadership strategy, in which an accepted industry leader sets, raises, or lowers prices and the other firms follow. Why is this good policy for the industry? In what ways is this good or bad for consumers? What is the difference between price leadership and price fixing? Should governments allow industries to use price leadership strategies?
3. Many very successful retailers use a loss leader pricing strategy, in which they advertise an item at a price below their cost and sell the item at that price to get customers into their store. They feel that these customers will continue to shop with their company and that they will make a profit in the long run. Do you consider this an unethical practice? Who benefits and who is hurt by such practices? Do you think the practice should be made illegal, as some states have done? How is this different from "bait-and-switch" pricing?
4. Consumers often make price–quality inferences about products. What does this mean? What are some products for which you are likely to make price–quality inferences? Do such inferences make sense?
5. In pricing new products, marketers may choose a skimming or a penetration pricing strategy. While it's easy to see the benefits of these practices for the firm, what are the advantages and/or disadvantages of the practice for consumers? For an industry as a whole?

Miniprojects: Learn by Doing

The purpose of this miniproject is to help you become familiar with how consumers respond to different prices by conducting a series of pricing experiments.

For this project, you should first select a product category that students such as yourself normally purchase. It should be a moderately expensive purchase such as athletic shoes, a bookcase, or a piece of luggage. You should next obtain two photographs of items in this product category or, if possible, two actual items. The two items should not appear to be substantially different in quality or in price.

Note: You will need to recruit separate research participants for each of the activities listed in the next section.

- *Experiment 1: Reference Pricing*
   a. Place the two products together. Place a sign on one with a low price. Place a sign on the other with a high price (about 50 percent higher will do). Ask your research participants to evaluate the quality of each of the items and to tell which one they would probably purchase.
   b. Reverse the signs and ask other research participants to evaluate the quality of each of the items and to tell which one they would probably purchase.
   c. Place the two products together again. This time place a sign on one with a moderate price. Place a sign on the other that is only a little higher (less than 10 percent higher). Again, ask research participants to evaluate the quality of each of the items and to tell which one they would probably purchase.
   d. Reverse the signs and ask other research participants to evaluate the quality of each of the items and to tell which one they would probably purchase.
- *Experiment 2: Odd–Even Pricing.* For this experiment, you will only need one of the items from experiment 1.

a. Place a sign on the item that ends in $.99 (for example, $62.99). Ask research participants to tell you if they think the price for the item is very low, slightly low, moderate, slightly high, or very high. Also ask them to evaluate the quality of the item and to tell you how likely they would be to purchase the item.

b. This time place a sign on the item that is slightly lower but that ends in $.00 (for example, $60.00). Ask different research participants to tell you if they think the price for the item is very low, slightly low, moderate, slightly high, or very high. Also ask them to evaluate the quality of the item and to tell you how likely they would be to purchase the item.

Develop a presentation for your class in which you discuss the results of your experiments and what they tell you about how consumers view prices.

Marketing in **Action** Case — Real Choices at Amazon

What's your favorite way to read books? Do you prefer hard or soft covers? Do you prefer reading physical books or reading books on the Internet? Recently one more option has been added to the decision process: the e-book reader. As the print industry declines, the e-book reader may exert a dramatic impact on book, magazine, and newspaper pricing. **Amazon.com** jumped into this market with the the Kindle, which consists of a hardware and software device that displays content from various e-books and other digital media. It can access content through downloads using the Sprint EVDO network. Free access to the Internet via cellular networks is available at no cost to the consumer. The goal of Amazon is to change the way people enjoy media content.

Amazon offers over 540,000 titles for the Kindle, containing the largest selection of the books available for reading devices, including U.S. and international newspapers, magazines, and blogs. *New York Times* best sellers and new releases sell for $9.99, most daily newspapers are available for $5 to $10 per month, and magazines are approximately $1.50 per month. The Kindle store offers thousands of free popular classics including titles such as *The Adventures of Sherlock Holmes, Pride and Prejudice*, and *Treasure Island*. In addition, customers can download over 1.8 million free, pre-1923, out-of-copyright titles from other Web sites.

In 2010, Macmillan, a group of publishing companies in the United States, requested that Amazon increase the price of its book selections from $9.99 to around $15. Amazon, in response to the request for new pricing, temporarily removed Macmillan books from the Kindle store. Macmillan proposed using an agency model in which the publisher sets the retail price and collects 70 percent of the sale. Amazon would receive the remaining 30 percent of the proceeds. If Amazon did not agree to the proposal, Macmillan would offer Amazon the opportunity to purchase e-books using the current wholesale model and pay 50 percent of the hardcover list price. Amazon would be free to set the retail price at any level; however, Macmillan would only allow access to the e-book version seven months after the hardcover release.

Another key player in the e-book pricing environment is Apple. Apple offers publishers the chance to sell their content through its new iBooks store. All publishers who choose the iBooks store to distribute their content have the ability to set the retail price. Apple would also collect 30 percent of the retail price using the agency model. This agency model used by Apple gives publishers more control in pricing. Typically, the prices for newly released e-book editions are $12.99 to $14.99. At the time, many other publishers nervously watched from the sidelines as Amazon and Apple offered competing pricing strategies.

At the turn of the early 21st century the print industry was well into a steep decline. Consumers were moving their consumption from print materials to electronic materials. This environmental change could have a dramatic impact on print pricing. Amazon's introduction of the Kindle is a response to the new market dynamics. Amazon's insistence of a $9.99 price point was an attempt to offer a flat, easy-to-understand rate to help build a new market. However, the correct retail price, along with its impact on publisher pricing, has yet to be determined for the long run. How much power do publishers have over the retailers? What pricing strategy should Amazon adopt for the long-term success of the Kindle and e-books?

You Make the Call

1. What is the decision facing Amazon?
2. What factors are important in understanding this decision situation?
3. What are the alternatives?
4. What decision(s) do you recommend?
5. What are some ways to implement your recommendation?

Based on: Brad Stone, "Amazon Pulls Macmillan Books over E-Book Price Disagreement," *The New York Times* (January 29, 2010, **http://bits.blogs.nytimes.com**); Motoko Rich and Brad Stone, "Publisher Wins Fight with Amazon over E-Books," *The New York Times* (January 31, 2010, http://bits.blogs.nytimes.com); Matt Buchanan, "Why (and How) Apple Killed the $9.99 Ebook," *Gizmodo* (February 5, 2010, **http://gizmodo.com/5465323/why-and-how-apple-killed-the-999-ebook**); Amazon Kindle, *Wikipedia*, **http://en.wikipedia.org/wiki/Amazon_Kindle** (accessed June 2, 2010); **Amazon.com**, "Kindle Wireless Reading Device," (**http://www.amazon.com/Kindle-Wireless-Reading-Display-Generation/dp/B0015T963C**); Macmillan Corporation, "About Macmillan" (**http://us.macmillan.com/splash/about/index.html**).

Marketing Math

To develop marketing strategies to meet the goals of an organization effectively and efficiently, it is essential that marketers understand and use a variety of financial analyses. This supplement provides some of these basic financial analyses, including a review of the income statement and balance sheet, as well as some basic performance ratios. In addition, this supplement includes an explanation of some of the specific calculations that marketers use routinely to set prices for their goods and services.

Income Statement and Balance Sheet

The two most important documents used to analyze the financial situation of a company are the income statement and the balance sheet. The *income statement* (which is sometimes referred to as the *profit and loss statement* or the *P&L*) provides a summary of the revenues and expenses of a firm—that is, the amount of income a company received from sales or other sources, the amount of money it spent, and the resulting income or loss that the company experienced.

The major elements of the income statement are as follows:

- **Gross sales** are the total of all income the firm receives from the sales of goods and services.

- **Net sales revenue** is the gross sales minus the amount for returns and promotional or other allowances given to customers.

- **Cost of goods sold** (sometimes called the *cost of sales*) is the cost of inventory or goods that the firm has sold.

- **Gross margin** (also called *gross profit*) is the amount of sales revenue that is in excess of the cost of goods sold.

- **Operating expenses** are expenses other than the cost of goods sold that are necessary for conducting business. These may include salaries, rent, depreciation on buildings and equipment, insurance, utilities, supplies, and property taxes.

- **Operating income** (sometimes called *income from operations*) is the gross margin minus the operating expenses. Sometimes accountants prepare an *operating statement*, which is similar to the income statement except that the final calculation is the operating income—that is, other revenues or expenses and taxes are not included.

- **Other revenue and expenses** are income and/or expenses other than those required for conducting the business. These may include items such as interest income/expenses and any gain or loss experienced from the sale of property or plant assets.

- **Taxes** are the amount of income tax the firm owes calculated as a percentage of income.

- **Net income** (sometimes called *net earnings* or *net profit*) is the excess of total revenue over total expenses.

Table 11S.1 shows the income statement for an imaginary company, DLL Incorporated. DLL is a typical merchandising firm. Note that the income statement is for a specific year and includes income and expenses inclusively from January 1 through December 31. The following comments explain the meaning of some of the important entries included in this statement.

- DLL Inc. has total or gross sales during the year of $253,950. This figure was adjusted, however, by deducting the $3,000 worth of goods returned and special allowances given to customers and by $2,100 in special discounts. Thus, the actual or net sales generated by sales is $248,850.

- The cost of goods sold is calculated by adding the inventory of goods on January 1 to the amount purchased during the year and then subtracting the inventory of goods on December 31. In this case, DLL had $60,750 worth of inventory on hand on January 1. During the year the firm made purchases in the amount of $135,550. This amount, however,

Table 11S.1 | **DLL Income Statement for the Year Ended December 31, 2008**

Gross Sales		$253,950	
Less: Sales Returns and Allowances	$ 3,000		
Sales Discounts	2,100	5,100	
Net Sales Revenue			$248,850
Cost of Goods Sold			
Inventory, January 1, 2008		60,750	
Purchases	135,550		
Less: Purchase Returns and Allowances	1,500		
Purchase Discounts	750		
Net Purchases	133,300		
Plus: Freight-In	2,450	135,750	
Goods Available for Sale		196,500	
Less: Inventory, December 31, 2008		60,300	
Cost of Goods Sold			136,200
Gross Margin			112,650
Operating Expenses			
Salaries and Commissions		15,300	
Rent		12,600	
Insurance		1,500	
Depreciation		900	
Supplies		825	
Total Operating Expenses			31,125
Operating Income			81,525
Other Revenue and (Expenses)			
Interest Revenue		1,500	
Interest Expense		(2,250)	(750)
Income Before Tax			80,775
Taxes (40%)			32,310
Net Income			$ 48,465

was reduced by purchase returns and allowances of $1,500 and by purchase discounts of $750, so the net purchases are only $133,300.

There is also an amount on the statement labeled "Freight-In." This is the amount spent by the firm in shipping charges to get goods to its facility from suppliers. Any expenses for freight from DLL to its customers (Freight-Out) would be an operating expense. In this case, the Freight-In expense of $2,450 is added to net purchase costs. Then these costs of current purchases are added to the beginning inventory to show that during the year the firm had a total of $196,500 in goods available for sale. Finally, the inventory of goods held on December 31 is subtracted from the goods available for sale, to reveal the total cost of goods sold of $136,200.

We mentioned that DLL Inc. is a merchandising firm—a retailer of some type. If DLL were instead a manufacturer, calculation of the cost of goods sold would be a bit more complicated and would probably include separate figures for items such as inventory of finished goods, the "work-in-process" inventory, the raw materials inventory, and the cost of goods delivered to customers during the year. Continuing down the previous income statement we have the following:

- The cost of goods sold is subtracted from the net sales revenue to get a gross margin of $112,650.

- Operating expenses for DLL include the salaries and commissions paid to its employees, rent on facilities and/or equipment, insurance, depreciation of capital items, and the cost of operating supplies. DLL has a total of $31,125 in operating expenses, which is deducted from the gross margin. Thus, DLL has an operating income of $81,525.

- DLL had both other income and expenses in the form of interest revenues of $1,500 and interest expenses of $2,250, making a total other expense of $750, which was subtracted from the operating income, leaving an income before taxes of $80,775.

- Finally, the income before taxes is reduced by 40 percent ($32,310) for taxes, leaving a net income of $48,465. The 40 percent is an average amount for federal and state corporate income taxes incurred by most firms.

The *balance sheet* lists the assets, liabilities, and stockholders' equity of the firm. Whereas the income statement represents what happened during an entire year, the balance sheet is like a snapshot; it shows the firm's financial situation at one point in time. For this reason, the balance sheet is sometimes called the *statement of financial position*.

Table 11S.2 shows DLL Inc.'s balance sheet for December 31. Assets include any economic resource that is expected to benefit the firm in the short or long term. *Current assets* are items that are normally expected to be turned into cash or used up during the next 12 months or during the firm's normal operating cycle. Current assets for DLL include cash, securities, accounts receivable (money owed to the firm and not yet paid), inventory on hand, prepaid insurance, and supplies: a total of $84,525. *Long-term assets* include all assets that are not current assets. For DLL, these are furniture and fixtures (less an amount for depreciation) and land, or $45,300. The *total assets* for DLL are $129,825.

A firm's *liabilities* are its economic obligations, or debts that are payable to individuals or organizations outside the firm. *Current liabilities* are debts due to be paid in the coming year or during the firm's normal operating cycle. For DLL, the current liabilities—the accounts payable, unearned sales revenue, wages payable, and interest payable—total $72,450. *Long-term liabilities* (in the case of DLL, a note in the amount of $18,900) are all liabilities that are not due to be paid during the coming cycle. *Stockholders' equity* is the value of the stock and the corporation's capital or retained earnings. DLL has $15,000 in common stock and $23,475 in retained earnings for a total stockholders' equity of $38,475. Total liabilities always equal total assets—in this case $129,825.

Table 11S.2 | DLL Inc. Balance Sheet: December 31, 2008

Assets

Current assets		
Cash		$ 4,275
Marketable securities		12,000
Accounts receivable		6,900
Inventory		60,300
Prepaid insurance		300
Supplies		150
Total current assets		84,525
Long-term assets—property, plant and equipment		
Furniture and fixtures	$42,300	
Less: accumulated depreciation	4,500	37,800
Land		7,500
Total long-term assets		45,300
Total assets		$129,825

Liabilities

Current liabilities		
Accounts payable	$70,500	
Unearned sales revenue	1,050	
Wages payable	600	
Interest payable	300	
Total current liabilities		72,450
Long-term liabilities		
Note payable		18,900
Total liabilities		91,350
Stockholders' equity		
Common stock		15,000
Retained earnings		23,475
Total stockholders' equity		38,475
Total liabilities and stockholders' equity		$129,825

Important Financial Performance Ratios

How do managers and financial analysts compare the performance of a firm from one year to the next? How do investors compare the performance of one firm with that of another? As the book notes, managers often rely upon various metrics to measure performance.

Often a number of different financial ratios provide important information for such comparisons. Such *ratios* are percentage figures comparing various income statement items to net sales. Ratios provide a better way to compare performance than simple dollar sales or cost figures for two reasons. They enable analysts to compare the performance of large and small firms, and they provide a fair way to compare performance over time without having to take inflation and other changes into account. In this section, we will explain the basic operating ratios. Other measures of performance that marketers frequently use and that are also explained here are the inventory turnover rate and return on investment (ROI).

Operating Ratios

Measures of performance calculated directly from the information in a firm's income statement (sometimes called an operating statement) are called the *operating ratios*. Each ratio compares some income statement item to net sales. The most useful of these are the *gross margin ratio*, the *net income ratio*, the *operating expense ratio*, and the *returns and allowances ratio*. These ratios vary widely by industry but tend to be important indicators of how a firm is doing within its industry. The ratios for DLL Inc. are shown in Table 11S.3.

- **Gross margin ratio** shows what percentage of sales revenues is available for operating and other expenses and for profit. With DLL, this means that 45 percent, or nearly half, of every sales dollar is available for operating costs and for profits.

- **Net income ratio** (sometimes called the *net profit ratio*) shows what percentage of sales revenues is income or profit. For DLL, the net income ratio is 19.5 percent. This means that the firm's profit before taxes is about 20 cents of every dollar.

- **Operating expense ratio** is the percentage of sales needed for operating expenses. DLL has an operating expense ratio of 12.5 percent. Tracking operating expense ratios from one year to the next or comparing them with an industry average gives a firm important information about the efficiency of its operations.

- **Returns and allowances ratio** shows what percentage of all sales is being returned, probably by unhappy customers. DLL's returns and allowances ratio shows that only a little over 1 percent of sales is being returned.

Table 11S.3 | Hypothetical Operating Ratios for DLL Inc.

Gross margin ratio	$= \dfrac{\text{gross margin}}{\text{net sales}}$	$= \dfrac{\$112,650}{248,850}$	$= 45.3\%$
Net Income ratio	$= \dfrac{\text{net income}}{\text{net sales}}$	$= \dfrac{\$48,465}{248,850}$	$= 19.5\%$
Operating expense ratio	$= \dfrac{\text{total operating expenses}}{\text{net sales}}$	$= \dfrac{\$31,125}{248,850}$	$= 12.5\%$
Returns and allowances ratio	$= \dfrac{\text{return and allowances}}{\text{net sales}}$	$= \dfrac{\$3,000}{248,850}$	$= 1.2\%$

Inventory Turnover Rate

The *inventory turnover rate*, also referred to as the stockturn rate, is the number of times inventory or stock is turned over (sold and replaced) during a specified time period, usually a year. Inventory turnover rates are usually calculated on the basis of inventory costs, sometimes on the basis of inventory selling prices, and sometimes by number of units.

In our example, for DLL Inc. we know that for the year the cost of goods sold was $136,200. Information on the balance sheet enables us to find the average inventory. By adding the value of the beginning inventory to the ending inventory and dividing by 2, we can compute an average inventory. In the case of DLL, this would be as follows:

$$\frac{\$60,750 + \$60,300}{2} = \$60,525$$

Thus,

$$\frac{\text{inventory turnover rate}}{\text{(in cost of goods sold)}} = \frac{\text{costs of goods sold}}{\text{average inventory at cost}} = \frac{\$136,200}{\$60,525} = 2.25 \text{ times}$$

Return on Investment

Firms often develop business objectives in terms of *return on investment (ROI)*, and ROI is often used to determine how effective (and efficient) the firm's management has been. First, however, we need to define exactly what a firm means by investment. In most cases, firms define investment as the total assets of the firm. To calculate the ROI, we need the net income found in the income statement and the total assets (or investment) found in the firm's balance sheet.

Return on investment is calculated as follows:

$$\text{ROI} = \frac{\text{net income}}{\text{total investment}}$$

For DLL Inc., if the total assets are $129,825 then the ROI is as follows:

$$\frac{\$48,465}{\$129,825} = 37.3\%$$

Sometimes return on investment is calculated by using an expanded formula:

$$\text{ROI} = \frac{\text{net profit}}{\text{sales}} \times \frac{\text{sales}}{\text{investment}}$$

$$= \frac{\$48,465}{\$248,850} \times \frac{\$248,850}{\$129,825} = 37.3\%$$

This formula makes it easy to show how ROI can be increased and what might reduce ROI. For example, there are different ways to increase ROI. First, if the management focuses on cutting costs and increasing efficiency, profits may be increased while sales remain the same:

$$\text{ROI} = \frac{\text{net profit}}{\text{sales}} \times \frac{\text{sales}}{\text{investment}}$$

$$= \frac{\$53,277}{\$248,850} \times \frac{\$248,850}{\$129,825} = 41.0\%$$

But ROI can be increased just as much without improving performance simply by reducing the investment—by maintaining less inventory:

$$\text{ROI} = \frac{\text{net profit}}{\text{sales}} \times \frac{\text{sales}}{\text{investment}}$$

$$= \frac{\$48,465}{\$248,850} \times \frac{\$248,850}{\$114,825} = 42.2\%$$

Sometimes, however, differences among the total assets of firms may be related to the age of the firm or the type of industry, which makes ROI a poor indicator of performance. For this reason, some firms have replaced the traditional ROI measures with *return on assets managed* (ROAM), *return on net assets* (RONA), or *return on stockholders' equity* (ROE).

Price Elasticity

Price elasticity, discussed in Chapter 11, is a measure of the sensitivity of customers to changes in price. Price elasticity is calculated by comparing the percentage change in quantity to the percentage change in price:

$$\text{Price elasticity of demand} = \frac{\text{percentage change in quantity}}{\text{percentage change in price}}$$

$$E = \frac{(Q_2 - Q_1)Q_1}{(P_2 - P_1)P_1}$$

where Q = quantity and *P* = price

For example, suppose a manufacturer of jeans increased its price for a pair of jeans from $30.00 to $35.00. But instead of 40,000 pairs being sold, sales declined to only 38,000 pairs. The price elasticity would be calculated as follows:

$$E = \frac{(38,000 - 40,000)/40,000}{(\$35.00 - 30.00)/\$30.00} = \frac{-0.05}{0.167} = 0.30$$

Note that elasticity is usually expressed as a positive number even though the calculations create a negative value.

In this case, a relatively small change in demand (5 percent) resulted from a fairly large change in price (16.7 percent), indicating that demand is inelastic. At 0.30, the elasticity is less than 1.

On the other hand, what if the same change in price resulted in a reduction in demand to 30,000 pairs of jeans? Then the elasticity would be as follows:

$$E = \frac{(30,000 - 40,000)/40,000}{(\$35.00 - 30.00)/\$30.00} = \frac{-0.25}{0.167} = 1.50$$

In this case, because the 16.7 percent change in price resulted in an even larger change in demand (25 percent), demand is elastic. The elasticity of 1.50 is greater than 1.

Note: Elasticity may also be calculated by dividing the change in quantity by the average of Q_1 and Q_2 and dividing the change in price by the average of the two prices. However, we have chosen to include the formula that uses the initial quantity and price rather than the average.

Cost-Plus Pricing

As noted in Chapter 11, the most common cost-based approach to pricing a product is *cost-plus pricing*, in which a marketer figures all costs for the product and then adds an amount to cover profit and, in some cases, any costs of doing business that are not assigned to specific products. The most frequently used type of cost-plus pricing is *straight markup pricing*. The price is calculated by adding a predetermined percentage to the cost. Most retailers and wholesalers use markup pricing exclusively because of its simplicity—users need only estimate the unit cost and add the markup.

The first step requires that the unit cost be easy to estimate accurately and that production rates are fairly consistent. As Table 11S.4 shows, we will assume that a jeans manufacturer has fixed costs (the cost of the factory, advertising, managers' salaries, etc.) of $2,000,000. The variable cost, per pair of jeans (the cost of fabric, zipper, thread, and labor) is $20.00. With the current plant, the firm can produce a total of 400,000 pairs of jeans, so the fixed cost per pair is $5.00. Combining the fixed and variable costs per pair means that the jeans are produced at a total cost of $25.00 per pair and the total cost of producing 400,000 pairs of jeans is $10,000,000.

The second step is to calculate the markup. There are two methods for calculating the markup percentage: markup on cost and markup on selling price. For *markup on cost pricing*, just as the name implies, a percentage of the cost is added to the cost to determine the firm's selling price. As you can see, we have included both methods in our example shown in Table 11S.4.

Markup on Cost

For markup on cost, the calculation is as follows:

$$\text{Price} = \text{total cost} + (\text{total cost} \times \text{markup percentage})$$

But how does the manufacturer or reseller know which markup percentage to use? One way is to base the markup on the total income needed for profits, for shareholder dividends, and for investment in the business. In our jeans example, the total cost of producing the 400,000 pairs of jeans is $10,000,000. If the manufacturer wants a profit of $2,000,000, what markup percentage would it use? The $2,000,000 is 20 percent of the $10 million total cost, so 20 percent. To find the price, the calculations would be as follows:

$$\text{Price} = \$25.00 + (\$25.00 \times 0.20) = \$25.0 + \$5.00 = \$30.00$$

Note that in the calculations, the markup percentage is expressed as a decimal; that is, 20% = 0.20, 25% = 0.25, 30% = 0.30, and so on.

Markup on Selling Price

Some resellers, that is, retailers and wholesalers, set their prices using a markup on selling price. The markup percentage here is the seller's gross margin, the difference between the cost to the wholesaler or retailer and the price needed to cover overhead items such as salaries, rent, utility bills, advertising, and profit. For example, if the wholesaler or retailer

Table 11S.4 | Markup Pricing Using Jeans as an Example

Step 1: Determine Costs

1.a: Determine total fixed costs

Management and other nonproduction-related salaries	$ 750,000
Rental of factory	600,000
Insurance	50,000
Depreciation on equipment	100,000
Advertising	500,000
Total fixed costs	**$2,000,000**

1.b: Determine fixed costs per unit

Number of units produced = 400,000
Fixed cost per unit ($2,000,000/400,000)   **$ 5.00**

1.c: Determine variable costs per unit

Cost of materials (fabric, zipper, thread, etc.)	$ 7.00
Cost of production labor	10.00
Cost of utilities and supplies used in production process	3.00
Variable cost per unit	**$20.00**

1.d: Determine total cost per unit

$20.00 + $5.00 = $25.00
Total cost per unit   **$25.00**

Total cost for producing 400,000 units = $10,000,000

Step 2: Determine markup and price

***Manufacturer's markup on cost* (assuming 20% markup)**

Formula: Price = total cost + (total cost × markup percentage)
Manufacturer's Price to the Retailer   **$30.00**
   = $25.00 + ($25.00 × .20) = $25.00 + 5.00 =

***Retailer's markup on selling price* (assuming 40% markup)**

Formula: Price = $\dfrac{\text{total cost}}{(1.00 - \text{markup percentage})}$

Retailer's Price to the Consumer = $\dfrac{\$30.00}{(1.00 - .40)} = \dfrac{\$30.00}{.60} =$ **$50.00**

***Retailer's alternative markup on cost* (assuming 40% markup)**

Formula: Price = total cost + (total cost × markup percentage)

Retailer's Price to the Consumer   **$42.00**
   = $30.00 + ($30.00 × .40) = $30.00 + $12.00 =

knows that it needs a margin of 40 percent to cover its overhead and reach its target profits, that margin becomes the markup on the manufacturer's selling price. Markup on selling price is particularly useful when firms negotiate prices with different buyers because it allows them to set prices with their required margins in mind.

Now let's say a retailer buys the jeans from the supplier (wholesaler or manufacturer) for $30.00 per pair. If the retailer requires a margin of 40 percent, it would calculate the price as a 40 percent markup on selling price. The calculation would be as follows:

$$\text{Price} = \frac{\text{total cost}}{1.00 - \text{markup percentage}}$$

$$\text{Price} = \frac{\$30.00}{(1.00 - 0.40)} = \frac{\$30.00}{.60} = \$50.00$$

Therefore, the price of the jeans with the markup on selling price is $50.00.

Just to compare the difference in the final prices of the two markup methods, Table 11S.4 also shows what would happen if the retailer uses a markup on cost method. Using the same product cost and price with a 40 percent markup on cost would yield $42.00, a much lower price. The markup on selling price gives you the percentage of the selling price that the markup is. The markup on cost gives you the percentage of the cost that the markup is. In the markup on selling price the markup amount is $20.00, which is 40 percent of the selling price of $50.00. In the markup on cost, the markup is $12.00, which is 40 percent of the cost of $30.00.

| Make marketing value decisions (Part One) |
| Understand consumers' value needs (Part Two) |
| Create the value proposition (Part Three) |
| Communicate the value proposition (Part Four) |
| Deliver the value proposition (Part Five) |

Process

You are here

Communicate the Value Proposition

Part Four
Overview

Now that you have your offering developed and priced—all with a great value proposition that you think will be a home run with your target market—it's time to make important decisions about how you'll communicate that value proposition to your potential purchasers. The chapters in Part Four take you on a fascinating journey through the various marketing communication approaches you can employ to get your message out there. Should you advertise on TV, send free samples of your product in the mail, use Facebook to sponsor a consumer do-it-yourself advertising contest, or something else? Making the right choice of approach is critical, largely because most of the available promotion tools come at a very high cost to the marketer!

Chapter 12 introduces you to these options for communicating the marketing message—called the promotion mix. You'll enjoy learning about building buzz in the marketplace and using various forms of new media to do the trick. Then in Chapter 13, you'll get some great guidelines on doing "mass" communication through advertising, public relations, and consumer sales promotion—communicating "one to many." Finally, Chapter 14 is devoted to "one to one" promotion through trade sales promotion, direct marketing, and personal selling. The overarching theme of the chapters in Part Four is how to go about making a decision on which elements of the promotion mix will be most effective for communicating the value proposition of your offering to your target markets.

Marketing Plan Connection:
Tricks of the Trade

Recall that the Appendix at the end of the book provides you with an abbreviated marketing plan example for the fictitious S&S Smoothie Company. That plan is flagged to indicate what elements from the plan correspond to each of the Parts within the book. In addition, in Chapter 2 you found a tear-out guide called "Build a Marketing Plan," which can be used as a template for marketing planning. It is also cross-referenced to chapters by section of the marketing plan.

In the chapters within Part Four, there are major learning elements that guide you in developing an integrated approach to marketing communication within your marketing plan. In doing so, not all possible promotion elements are appropriate for a given offering at a given time. Marketers must apply the different promotion elements based on the positioning strategy. That is, along with the other marketing mix elements, promotion helps communicate the positioning to the consumer. Recall that S&S Smoothie seeks to position its products as the first-choice smoothie beverage for the serious health-conscious consumer, including those who are seeking to lower their carbohydrate intake. The justification for this positioning is as follows: Many smoothie beverages are available. The S&S Smoothie formula provides superior flavor and nutrition in a shelf-stable form. S&S Smoothie has developed its product (including packaging) and pricing in support of this positioning strategy. Let's review how S&S Smoothie has chosen to support this positioning through promotional strategies.

Promotional Strategies

In the past, S&S Smoothie has used mainly personal selling to promote its products to the trade channel. To support this effort, signage has been provided for the resellers to promote the product at the point of purchase. Posters and stand-alone table cards show appealing photographs of the product in the different flavors and communicate the brand name and the healthy benefits of the product. Similar signage will be developed for use by resellers who choose to stock the S&S Smoothie Gold and the Low-Carb Smoothies.

Selling has previously been handled by a team of over 75 manufacturers' agents who sell to resellers. In addition, in some geographic areas, an independent distributor does the selling. To support this personal selling approach, S&S Smoothie plans for additional promotional activities to introduce its new products and meet its other marketing objectives. These include the following:

1. *Television advertising:* S&S Smoothie will purchase a limited amount of relatively inexpensive and targeted cable channel advertising. A small number of commercials will be shown during prime-time programs with high viewer ratings by the target market. Television advertising can be an important means of not only creating awareness of the product, but also enhancing the image of the product.

2. *Magazine advertising:* Because consumers in the target market are not avid magazine readers, magazine advertising will be limited and will supplement other promotion activities. During the next year, S&S Smoothie will experiment with limited magazine advertising in such titles as *Sports Illustrated*. The company will also investigate the potential of advertising in university newspapers.

3. *Sponsorships:* S&S Smoothie will attempt to sponsor several marathons in major cities. The advantage of sponsorships is that they provide visibility for the product while at the same time showing that the company supports activities of interest to the target market.

4. *Digital Marketing:* S&S Smoothie will continue its use of social media to communicate with consumers and to monitor customers' postings about S&S products. In addition, S&S TV commercials will be available on the company Web site and on YouTube. In the latter part of the year, the company will sponsor a do-it-yourself ad competition through its Web site. The winning ads will be aired on cable TV.

5. *Sampling:* Sampling of S&S Smoothie beverages at select venues will provide an opportunity for prospective customers to become aware of the product and to taste the great flavors. Sampling will include only the two new products being introduced. Venues for sampling will include the following:
   a. Marathons
   b. Weight-lifting competitions
   c. Gymnastics meets
   d. Student unions located on selected college campuses

One-to-Many to Many-to-Many:
Traditional and New Media

 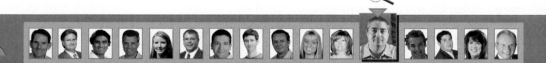

Michael Monello

Profile | Info

▼ A **Decision Maker** at Campfire

Mike Monello is partner/executive creative director at Campfire, a communication agency based in New York. Mike started out as a DIY filmmaker, and in 1998 he created *The Blair Witch Project* with four other film school friends. This integrated, interactive experience forged a community around the film's mythology. It resulted in a pop-culture phenomenon with over $240 million in worldwide box-office and changed the way marketers approach the Internet.

Excited by this marketing/entertainment hybrid, Mike co-founded Campfire, where he has been intimately involved in the creative development of every project that has come through Campfire's doors. From "Beta-7" for Sega and "Art of the Heist" for Audi to "Frenzied Waters" for Discovery Channel's Shark Week, he's led work that has been awarded top honors at the One Show, Clio, Mixx, ad:Tech, and Addy awards. A vocal force in the world of transmedia storytelling, Mike has spoken at many prestigious events, including Futures of Entertainment at M.I.T. and SXSW Interactive.

💬 Mike's Info

What do I do when I'm not working?
A) Creative projects with my kids, travel with my family, collecting tiki mugs and other Polynesian pop, playing amateur mixologist.

First job out of school?
A) Commissioned salesman at Circuit City. I still use what I learned on that job.

Career high?
A) Standing shell-shocked in Barnes & Noble looking at *The Blair Witch Project* on the covers of both *Time* and *Newsweek.*

A job-related mistake I wish I hadn't made?
A) Put off making a tough decision too long until it turned into a crisis.

Business book I'm reading now?
A) I don't read too many traditional business books. For inspiration, I'm currently reading *Signal and Noise: Media, Infrastructure, and Urban Culture in Nigeria* by Brian Larkin, and *Experience Design 1* by Nathan Shedroff.

My hero?
A) Too many to list, but some of my professional heroes are George C. Tilyou, Frederic Thompson, Elmer Dundy, and the entrepreneurs of Coney Island for figuring it all out.

What drives me?
A) Passion. It's the one constant across every successful thing I've done.

My management style?
A) Could be better.

Here's my problem...

Campfire's growth has been completely organic. It started as a small group of associates and collaborators who would come together to work on a project and evolved to a "real" agency with offices in New York City. Campfire is a project-based agency that is not reliant on specific media platforms to generate revenue (30-second TV spots, or banner ads and Flash-based Web sites, for example). Most advertising agencies seek **AOR (Agency of Record)** relationships, where the client pays a monthly retainer fee to the agency for creative services. The AOR relationship, however, can create a structure that supports only the most common and "safe" work to be presented to the client, since entire teams of people depend on that retainer for their jobs.

Campfire's work centers around storytelling and experience, and the marketing programs it develops for clients aren't easily put into the usual traditional/digital silos. For example, Campfire's work for Verizon FiOS encompasses a 30-minute technology home makeover show, large block-party events, a robust online experience, local PR outreach, direct mail, casting events, and more. Most clients, including Verizon, usually build a roster of specialized agencies and put them in silos to develop their own particular pieces, so the traditional ad agency develops for TV and print while the event agency does all the public events and sponsorships, the direct mail agency works on their pieces, branded content companies may be in the mix for product placement, digital agencies for online work, and so on. The result is almost never integrated beyond simple things like an overall look and feel and perhaps a tagline. Campfire's expertise is not in any one particular silo but in developing all these elements as part of the total integrated project. Campfire sits at the intersection of entertainment and marketing, and this is one reason why the company's position in the agency landscape is a bit of a mystery to some. Since its campaigns cross all media channels, Campfire has been called, at one time or another, a digital agency, a branded content agency, a transmedia agency, a social media agency, and simply a creative shop. That mystery has served Mike and his partners well, as it tends to attract clients who want to take bold chances; they often are willing to take risks with Campfire and approve projects that they would never accept from their traditional agencies.

In 2007, *Advertising Age* listed Campfire as one of "The Hottest Digital Agencies Around."[1] The company had only really been a full-time agency for about a year at that point, and it had never identified itself as a "digital agency." This was fantastic recognition that opened many new doors for the agency. As a result, Mike and his partners found themselves at a crossroads soon after when a potential client approached them to become their digital agency of record (AOR). Campfire had only seven employees at the time, and this was both a big opportunity as well as a significant change in the young agency's business model. While it had built Web sites, banner ads, and other more traditional media, these efforts were always in the service of a larger project. Campfire's leaders had to decide if they were to take the leap to become a full-service digital agency.

Things to *remember*

Campfire is largely a "new media" agency; this means that Mike and his colleagues employ a number of nontraditional channels to tell stories about their clients' brands. Mike has to choose between retaining that independence from "business as usual" and gaining access to resources (including employees and clients) that work in more established areas like television advertising.

Mike considered his **Options** 1·2·3

1 *Option*

Become the client's digital AOR. To do this Campfire would have to hire new creative, account, and production people and develop a more traditional digital offering. As a small agency built up organically, it would gain some breathing room in the race for new business, as well as a longer window into its financial future. On the other hand, the culture and structure required to develop the kinds of projects Campfire is known for is quite different from that of a traditional digital shop. While most agencies have strong hierarchies with creative directors, account planning, account management, art directors and copywriter teams, studio creatives and more, Campfire develops projects with smaller teams of higher level people whose skills and knowledge cross the boundaries of their titles. The agency would have to make adjustments to accommodate the new work as well as consider what building out that offering would mean for its own brand and differentiation in the marketplace.

2 *Option*

Partner with a smaller, more traditional agency and split the work according to capabilities in order to handle all the client's needs. Each agency could do what it does best with the added benefit of bridging strategy, research, and creative across both agencies, something that's often difficult for clients to manage on their own. While Campfire had worked successfully with partners in the past, the process would be complicated, and it would have to be managed very closely in order to keep it simple for the client. Dividing account services in particular could be tricky: Who owns the overall creative strategy when there are disagreements between agencies?

3 *Option*

Walk away. Campfire could turn the client away gracefully, explain that the agency isn't structured to service the kind of work they require on an ongoing basis, and hope to keep the door open for a future project that more closely aligns with Campfire's services. Turning away any work for a growing agency is not easy, especially when you need the income. While Campfire would stay true to its brand, would it also toss away a great opportunity to expand the scope of its business? After all, there are a lot more potential clients who want traditional digital work rather than the kind of fully integrated projects Campfire had done up to that time.

Now, put yourself in Mike's shoes: Which option would you choose, and why?

You Choose

Which **Option** would you choose, and **why**?
1. ☐YES ☐NO   **2.** ☐YES ☐NO   **3.** ☐YES ☐ NO

See what **option** Michael chose on **page 373**

AOR (Agency of Record) relationship
A relationship where the client pays a monthly retainer fee to an agency for creative services.

promotion
The coordination of a marketer's communication efforts to influence attitudes or behavior.

Check out chapter 12 **Study Map** on page 374

1

OBJECTIVE
Understand the communication process and the traditional promotion mix. (pp. 350–357)

One-to-Many:
The Traditional Communication Model

Test your advertising memory:*

1. What energy drink "gives you wiiings?"

2. What product advertises that "Even a caveman can do it?"

3. What character do Energizer battery ads feature?

4. At Burger King, you can have it "_____," whereas at Hardees the burgers are "_____" broiled.

5. Which paper towel brand is "The Quicker Picker-Upper?"[1]

Did you get them all right? You owe your knowledge about these and a thousand other trivia questions to the efforts of people who specialize in marketing communication. Of course today, these slogans are "old school" as marketers have followed consumers onto Facebook and Twitter and into virtual worlds to talk with their customers.

As we said in Chapter 1, **promotion** is the coordination of marketing communication efforts to influence attitudes or behavior. This function is one of the famous *Four Ps* of the marketing mix and it plays a vital role—whether the goal is to sell hamburgers, insurance, ringtones, or healthy diets. Of course, virtually *everything* an organization says and does is a form of marketing communication. The ads it creates, the packages it designs, the uniforms its employees wear, and what other consumers say about their experiences with the firm contribute to the thoughts and feelings people have of the company and its products. In fact, savvy marketers should consider that *every element of the marketing mix is actually a form of communication*. After all, the price of a product, where it is sold, and of course the quality of the product itself contribute to our impression of it.

In the previous four chapters we talked about creating, managing, and pricing tangible and intangible products. But it's not enough just to produce great products—successful marketing plans must also provide effective marketing communication strategies. Just what do we mean by communication? Today messages assume many forms: quirky television commercials, innovative Web sites, viral videos, sophisticated magazine ads, funky T-shirts, blimps blinking messages over football stadiums—even do-it-yourself, customer-made advertising. Some marketing communications push specific products (like the Apple iPad) or actions (like donating blood), whereas others try to create or reinforce an image that represents the entire organization (like General Electric or the Catholic Church).

Marketing communication in general performs one or more of four roles:

1. It *informs* consumers about new goods and services.

2. It *reminds* consumers to continue using certain brands.

---

*Answers: (1) Red Bull energy drink, (2) GEICO Insurance, (3) the Energizer Bunny, (4) "your way," "char," (5) Bounty paper towels

3. It persuades consumers to choose one brand over others.

4. It *builds* relationships with customers.

Many marketing experts now believe a successful promotional strategy should blend several diverse forms of marketing communication. **Integrated marketing communication (IMC)** is the process that marketers use "to plan, develop, execute, and evaluate coordinated, measurable, persuasive brand communication programs over time"[2] to plan, develop, execute, and evaluate coordinated, measurable, persuasive brand communication programs over time to targeted audiences. The IMC approach argues that consumers come in contact with a company or a brand in many different ways before, after, and during a purchase. Consumers see these points of contact or *touchpoints* as we described in Chapter 7—a TV commercial, a company Web site, a coupon, an opportunity to win

Promotion takes many forms, including humorous print ads like this one for a German company that makes pens.

a sweepstakes, or a display in a store—as a whole, as a single company that speaks to them in different places and different ways. IMC marketers understand that to achieve their marketing communication goals, they must selectively use some or all of these touchpoints to deliver a consistent message to their customers in a **multichannel promotional strategy** where they combine traditional advertising, sales promotion, and public relations activities with online buzz-building activities. That's a lot different from most traditional marketing communication programs of the past that made little effort to coordinate the varying messages consumers received. When an advertising campaign runs independently of a sweepstakes, which in turn has no relation to a NASCAR racing sponsorship, consumers often get conflicting messages that leave them confused and unsure of the brand's identity. With IMC, marketers seek to understand what information consumers want as well as how, when, and where they want it—and then to deliver information about the product using the best combination of communication methods available to them.

It's great to talk about a multichannel strategy, but that still leaves a lot of questions about how we get our customers to understand what we're trying to say. And, in today's high-tech world these questions get even more complicated because the communication options available to marketers change literally almost every day—there will probably be new formats that appear on the scene between the time you start and finish this course!

It helps to understand these options when we look at how we as consumers get our information. 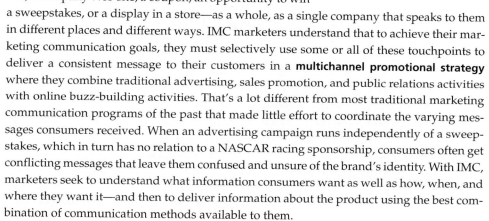 Figure 12.1 shows three communication models. The first, traditional communication model is a "One-to-Many" view in which a single marketer develops and sends messages to many, perhaps even millions of consumers at once. The one-to-many approach involves traditional forms of marketing communication such as *advertising* including traditional mass media (TV, radio, magazines, and newspapers), *out-of-home* (like billboards), and Internet advertising. This model also benefits from *consumer sales promotions* such as coupons, samples, rebates, or contests; and press releases and special events that *public relations* professionals organize.

Today, these traditional methods still work in some circumstances—but there are a lot of other options available that often mesh better with our "wired" 24/7 culture. When you take a break from posting to your friends on Facebook, you'll recognize that you also learn about products and services from your own social network in addition to ads, billboards, or coupons. For this reason we need to consider an *updated communication model* where marketing messages are what we think of as many-to-many. This newer perspective recognizes the huge impact of **word-of-mouth communication** where consumers look to each other for information and recommendations. Many of us are more likely to choose a new restaurant

integrated marketing communication (IMC)
A strategic business process that marketers use to plan, develop, execute, and evaluate coordinated, measurable, persuasive brand communication programs over time to targeted audiences.

multichannel promotional strategy
A marketing communication strategy where they combine traditional advertising, sales promotion, and public relations activities with online buzz-building activities.

word-of-mouth communication
When consumers provide information about products to other consumers.

Figure 12.1 📷 *Snapshot* | Three Models of Marketing Communication

Marketers today make use of the traditional one-to-many communication model and the updated many-to-many communication model as well as talking one-to-one with consumers and business customers.

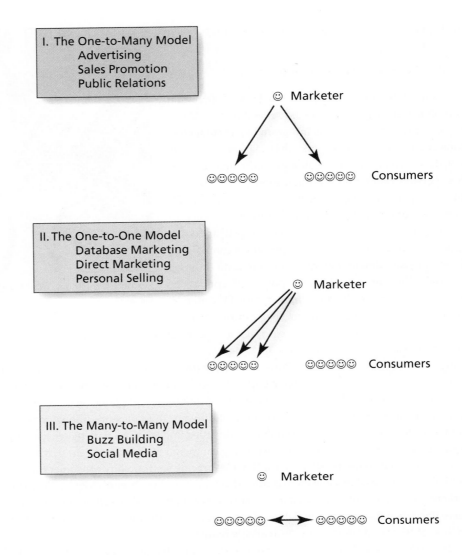

I. The One-to-Many Model
  Advertising
  Sales Promotion
  Public Relations

☺ Marketer

☺☺☺☺ ☺☺☺☺ Consumers

II. The One-to-One Model
  Database Marketing
  Direct Marketing
  Personal Selling

☺ Marketer

☺☺☺☺ ☺☺☺☺ Consumers

III. The Many-to-Many Model
  Buzz Building
  Social Media

☺ Marketer

☺☺☺☺ ⟷ ☺☺☺☺ Consumers

based on users' reviews we read on Yelp than because we saw a cool commercial for the place on TV. Ditto for nail salons, bike stores, and maybe even cars.

In the updated model, marketers add new tools to their communications toolbox including *buzz-building* activities that use *viral* and *evangelical marketing techniques* as well as new social media platforms such as *brand communities*, *product review sites*, and *social networking sites*. The odds are you're using many of these platforms already, though you may not call them by these names. By the end of this section, you will.

We also need to expand our traditional communication model to include *one-to-one marketing*, where marketers speak to consumers and business customers individually. The one-to-one forms of marketing communication include *personal selling*, *trade sales promotion activities* used to support personal selling, and a variety of *database marketing* activities that include direct marketing. In this chapter and the following two we'll examine each of these different ways to communicate with our customers.

The Communication Model

Wired or not, the **communication model** in 📊 Figure 12.2 is a good way to understand the basics of how any kind of message works. In this perspective, a *source* transmits a *message* through some *medium* to a *receiver* who (we hope) listens and understands the message. The

communication model
The process whereby meaning is transferred from a source to a receiver.

encoding
The process of translating an idea into a form of communication that will convey meaning.

source
An organization or individual that sends a message.

Figure 12.2 _Process_ | Communication Model

The communication model explains how organizations create and transmit messages from the marketer (the source) to the consumer (the receiver) who (we hope) understands what the marketer intends to say.

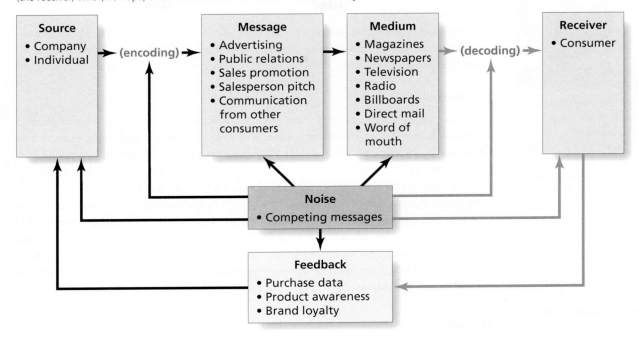

Source		**Message**		**Medium**		**Receiver**
• Company • Individual	→ (encoding) →	• Advertising • Public relations • Sales promotion • Salesperson pitch • Communication from other consumers	→	• Magazines • Newspapers • Television • Radio • Billboards • Direct mail • Word of mouth	→ (decoding) →	• Consumer

Noise
• Competing messages

Feedback
• Purchase data
• Product awareness
• Brand loyalty

basic idea is that _any_ way a marketer reaches out to consumers—a hat with a Caterpillar tractor logo on it, a personal sales pitch from a Mary Kay representative, or a televised fashion show with supermodels strutting their stuff for Victoria's Secret—this is part of the basic communication process.

The communication model specifies the elements necessary for effective communication to occur: a source, a message, a medium, and a receiver. Regardless of how a marketer sends messages, her objective is to capture receivers' attention and relate to their needs.

The Source Encodes

Let's start to explore this basic model from a good place: the beginning. **Encoding** is the process by which a source translates an idea into a form of communication that conveys the desired meaning. The **source** is the organization or individual that sends the message. It's one thing for marketers to form an idea about a product in their own minds, but it's not quite as simple to express the idea to their customers. To make their messages more believable or more attractive to consumers, marketers sometimes choose a real person (like the computer users that appeared in Microsoft's "Windows 7 Was My Idea" advertising), hire an actor or a model (William Shatner of _Star Trek_ fame for Priceline.com or Queen Latifah for Cover Girl Cosmetics) or create a character (the GEICO gecko with the Cockney accent) to represent the source.[3]

In other cases the message features actual customers. In advertising to counter negative consumers' responses to Toyota's massive recall, the company used ads in which Toyota customers told why they were going to continue to buy the cars.

Many marketing messages rely on an expert or highly credible source to encourage recipients to take them seriously.

Courtesy of Colgate Palmolive

Mike Monello

APPLYING ▽ The Medium

Campfire's current work typically relies on nontraditional media like online videos. Traditional media have advantages (such as the ability to reach a big audience at one time) and disadvantages (such as higher costs). The mix of media to send a campaign's messages is a crucial strategic decision. ➡

message
The communication in physical form that goes from a sender to a receiver.

medium
A communication vehicle through which a message is transmitted to a target audience.

receiver
The organization or individual that intercepts and interprets the message.

An Italian candy ad communicates the product's caffeine content quite vividly.

The Message

The **message** is the actual content that goes from the source to a receiver. It includes information necessary to persuade, inform, remind, or build a relationship. Advertising messages may include both verbal and nonverbal elements, such as beautiful background scenery or funky music. The marketer must select the ad elements carefully so that the message connects with end consumers or business customers in its target market. Otherwise effective communication simply does not occur and the organization just wastes its money.

The Medium

No matter how the source encodes the message, it must then transmit it via a **medium**, a communication vehicle that reaches members of a target audience. This vehicle can be television, radio, social media sites such as Facebook or Twitter, a magazine, a company Web site, an Internet blog, a personal contact, a billboard, or even a coffee mug that displays a product logo. Marketers face two major challenges when they select a medium. First, they must make sure the target market will be exposed to the medium—that the intended receivers actually read the magazine or watch the TV show where the message appears. Second, the attributes of the advertised product should match those of the medium. For example, magazines with high prestige are more effective to communicate messages about overall product image and quality, whereas specialized magazines do a better job when they convey factual information.[4]

The Receiver Decodes

If a tree falls in the forest and no one hears it, did it make a sound? Zen mysteries aside, communication cannot occur unless a **receiver** is there to get the message. The receiver is any individual or organization that intercepts and interprets the message. Assuming that the customer is even paying attention (a big assumption in our overloaded, media-saturated society), she interprets the message in light of her unique experiences. **Decoding** is the process whereby a receiver assigns meaning to a message; that is, she translates the message she sees or hears back into an idea that makes sense to her.

Marketers hope that the target consumer will decode the message the way they intended, but effective communication occurs only when the source and the receiver share a mutual frame of reference. Too often sources and receivers aren't on the same page, and the results can range from mildly embarrassing to downright disastrous. As we saw way back in Chapter 3, this mismatch is especially likely to happen when the source and the receiver don't share the same cultural background or language.

Noise

The communication model also acknowledges that **noise**—anything that interferes with effective communication—can block messages. As the many arrows between noise and the other elements of the communication model in 🎵 Figure 12.2 indicate, noise can occur at any stage of communication. It can pop up at the encoding stage if the source uses words or symbols that the receiver will not understand. Or a nearby conversation may distract the receiver. There may be a problem with transmission of the message through the medium— especially if it's drowned out by the chorus of other marketers clamoring for us to look at *their* messages instead. Marketers try to minimize noise when they place their messages where there is less likely to be distractions or competition for consumers' attention. Calvin Klein, for example, will often buy a block of advertising pages in a magazine so that the reader sees only pictures of its clothing as she leafs through that section.

Feedback

To complete the communication loop, the source gets **feedback** from receivers. Feedback is a reaction to the message that helps marketers gauge the effectiveness of the message so they can fine-tune it. Sometimes consumers eagerly provide this feedback—especially if they are unhappy. They may call a toll-free number or post an e-mail to the manufacturer to resolve a problem. More often, though, marketers must actively seek their customers' feedback. The need for this "reality check" reminds us of the importance of conducting marketing research (as we discussed in Chapter 4) to verify that a firm's strategies are working. And, keep in mind that even though nobody likes to be yelled at, we actually *want* customers to complain so that we have an opportunity to address their concerns before they say negative things to others.

Gillette employs a creative medium to get its message to customers.

decoding
The process by which a receiver assigns meaning to the message.

noise
Anything that interferes with effective communication.

feedback
Receivers' reactions to the message.

The Traditional Promotion Mix

As we said earlier, promotion, or marketing communication, is one of the Famous Four Ps. Marketers use the term **promotion mix** to refer to the communication elements that the marketer controls. These elements of the traditional promotion mix include:

- Advertising

- Sales promotion

- Public relations

- Personal selling

- Direct marketing

Just as a DJ combines different songs or phrases to create an entertainment experience, the term *mix* implies that a company's promotion strategy focuses on more than one element. And as we said, promotion works best when the marketer/DJ skillfully combines all of the elements of the promotion mix to deliver a single consistent message about a brand.

Another challenge is to be sure that the promotion mix works in harmony with the overall *marketing mix* to combine elements of promotion with place, price, and product to position the firm's offering in people's minds. For example, marketers must design ads for luxury products such as Rolex watches or Jaguar automobiles to communicate that same luxury character of the product, and the ads should appear in places that reinforce that upscale image. A chic commercial that appears before a showing of the latest *Jackass* movie just won't cut it.

Marketers have a lot more control over some kinds of marketing communication messages than they do others. As 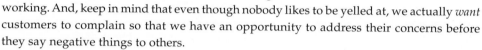 Figure 12.3 shows, *mass-media advertising* and *sales promotion* are at one end of the continuum, where the marketer has total control over the message she delivers. At the other end

Surrender, tough messes. Conquer them with our thick wipes.

For effective decoding to occur, the source and the receiver must share a mutual frame of reference. In this ad the receiver needs to understand the meaning of a "white flag" in order for the message to make sense.

Figure 12.3 📷 *Snapshot* | Control Continuum

The messages that consumers receive about companies and products differ in terms of how much the marketer can control the content.

High	Extent of marketer's control over communication	Low

Advertising	Sales promotion	Personal selling	Direct marketing	Public relations	Word of mouth

---

Table 12.1 | A Comparison of Elements of the Traditional Promotion Mix

Promotional Element	Pros	Cons
Advertising	• The marketer has control over what the message will say, when it will appear, and who is likely to see it.	• Because of the high cost to produce and distribute, it may not be an efficient means of communicating with some target audiences. • Some ads may have low credibility and/or be ignored by audience.
Sales promotion	• Provides incentives to retailers to support one's products. • Builds excitement for retailers and consumers. • Encourages immediate purchase and trial of new products. • Price-oriented promotions cater to price-sensitive consumers.	• Short-term emphasis on immediate sales rather than a focus on building brand loyalty. • The number of competing promotions may make it hard to break through the promotional clutter. • If marketers use too many price-related sales promotion activities, consumers' perception of a fair price for the brand may be lowered.
Public relations	• Relatively low cost • High credibility	• Lack of control over the message that is eventually transmitted and no guarantee that the message will ever reach the target. • It is difficult to measure the effectiveness of PR efforts.
Personal selling	• Direct contact with the customer gives the salesperson the opportunity to be flexible and modify the sales message to coincide with the customer's needs. • The salesperson can get immediate feedback from the customer.	• High cost per contact with customer. • Difficult to ensure consistency of message when it is delivered by many different company representatives. • The credibility of salespeople often depends on the quality of their company's image, which has been created by other promotional strategies.
Direct marketing	• Targets specific groups of potential customers with different offers. • Marketers can easily measure the results. • Provides extensive product information and multiple offers within a single appeal. • Provides a way for a company to collect feedback about the effectiveness of its messages in an internal database.	• Consumers may have a negative opinion of some types of direct marketing. • Costs more per contact than mass appeals.

promotion mix

The major elements of marketer-controlled communication, including advertising, sales promotion, public relations, personal selling, and direct marketing.

is *word-of-mouth (WOM) communication,* where everyday people rather than the company run the show. WOM is a vitally important component of the brand attitudes consumers form—and of their decisions about what and what not to buy. Sandwiched between the ends we find *personal selling* and *direct marketing,* where marketers have some but not total control over the message they deliver, and *public relations,* where marketers have even less control. Table 12.1 presents some of the pros and cons of each element of the promotion mix.

Mass Communication

Some elements of the promotion mix include messages intended to reach many prospective customers at the same time. Whether a company offers customers a coupon for 50 cents off or airs a television commercial to millions, it promotes itself to a mass audience. These are the elements of the promotion mix that use **mass communication,** i.e., TV radio, magazines, and newspapers:

NO ONE GROWS KETCHUP LIKE HEINZ.

That's because every red, ripe tomato in every bottle is grown only from Heinz seeds. It's what helps us deliver the uniquely thick, rich flavor that America loves.

HEINZ. GROWN, NOT MADE.™

Advertising can convey rich and dynamic images that establish and reinforce a distinctive brand identity.

- *Advertising:* **Advertising** is, for many, the most familiar and visible element of the promotion mix. It is nonpersonal communication from an identified sponsor using the mass media. The most important advantage of advertising is that it reaches large numbers of consumers at one time. In addition, advertising can convey rich and dynamic images that establish and reinforce a distinctive brand identity. This helps marketers bond with customers and boost sales. Advertising also is useful to communicate factual information about the product or to remind consumers to buy their favorite brand. However, it sometimes suffers from a credibility problem: Cynical consumers tune out messages they think are biased or are intended to sell them something they don't need. Advertising can also be very expensive, so firms must ensure that their messages deliver the best bang for the buck.

- *Sales promotion: Consumer sales promotion* includes programs such as contests, coupons, or other incentives that marketers design to build interest in or encourage purchase of a product during a specified period. Unlike other forms of promotion, sales promotion intends to stimulate immediate action (often in the form of a purchase) rather than build long-term loyalty.

- *Public relations: Public relations* describes a variety of communication activities that seek to create and maintain a positive image of an organization and its products among various *publics*, including customers, government officials, and shareholders. Public relations programs also include efforts to present negative company news in the most positive way so that this information will have less damaging consequences. In contrast to sales promotion, public relations components of the promotion mix usually do not seek a short-term increase in sales. Instead, they try to influence feelings, opinions, or beliefs for the long term.

mass communication
Relates to television, radio, magazines, and newspapers.

advertising
Nonpersonal communication from an identified sponsor using the mass media.

Personal Communication

Sometimes marketers want to communicate with consumers on a personal, one-on-one level. The most immediate way for a marketer to make contact with customers is simply to tell them how wonderful the product is. This is part of the *personal selling* element of the promotion mix we mentioned previously. It is the direct interaction between a company representative and a customer that can occur in person, by phone, or even over an interactive computer link.

Salespeople are a valuable source of communication because customers can ask questions and the salesperson can immediately address objections and describe product benefits. Personal selling can be tremendously effective, especially for big-ticket consumer items and for industrial products for which the "human touch" is essential.

Marketers also use direct mail, telemarketing, and other *direct marketing* activities to create personal appeals. Like personal selling, direct marketing provides direct communication with a consumer or business customer. Because direct marketing activities seek to gain a direct response from individual consumers, the source can target a communication to market segments of a few or—with today's technology—even segments of one.

2

OBJECTIVE
Understand how
marketers
communicate using
an updated
communication
model that
incorporates buzz
marketing activities
and new social
media.
(pp. 358–366)

Many-to-Many: The New Media Communication Model

groundswell
A social trend in which people use technology to get the things they need from each other, rather than from traditional institutions like corporations.

It seems as if most of us are "on" 24/7 these days, whether we're checking our e-mail while on vacation or Tweeting about the fabulous new restaurant we just discovered. Authors Charlene Li and Josh Bernoff refer to the changing communication landscape as the **groundswell**: "a social trend in which people use technology to get the things they need from each other, rather than from traditional institutions like corporations."[5] In other words, today's consumers are increasingly getting their information on running shoes, nightclubs, cars, new bands, or even last week's economics class lecture from one another rather than from the original source.

The Web Revolution is here! What has led to this new communication model and how is it changing marketing? Much of the answer lies in changing technology. Everyone is online now. Millions of people around the globe surf the Web, talk with their friends, watch TV, and purchase products from traditional marketers, from Internet-only marketers, and from each other on their computers or their mobile phones with broadband Internet connections. For example, at last report, Facebook had over 400 million users, more than the population of any country except India and China. These users all have the potential to connect with each other and to share feedback—whether it's about how hard that statistics test was this morning or where they bought a great new swimsuit for summer and how much they paid for it. Marketers are no longer the only ones who talk about their products—millions of consumers have the ability and the desire to spread the good (or bad) news about the goods and services they buy. That's why we're moving from a one-to-many communication model to the new world of many-to-many.

At the same time, traditional advertising has diminished as a way to talk to customers. As consumers, especially younger ones, spend more and more time online, they don't lounge in front of the TV as much and they don't tend to read printed magazines. For those who do watch TV, there are literally hundreds of channels to choose from. This abundance of choice fragments the TV audience and makes the job of reaching a mass market both complex and costly.

As one telling example of this realignment, in 2010 Pepsi decided to forego advertising on the Super Bowl for the first time in 23 years in order to put money into online formats, especially Facebook. The Pepsi Refresh Project combined online activities and a charitable campaign that Pepsi hoped would let young consumers know it was serious about doing good for the world—and increase its market share. Pepsi accepted one thousand ideas a month online from consumers on ways to improve their communities. The best ideas were chosen by online consumer voting. In all, Pepsi offered a total of $20 million in grants of between $5,000 and $250,000 to implement the best ideas.[6] After the tremendous success of the Pepsi Refresh project (over 45 million votes were cast by more than 1 million Facebook users in the first nine months), Pepsi decided to expand the project in 2011 to Europe, Latin America and Asia, as well as to continue to fund the project in the U.S. and Canada.[7]

Like Pepsi, many other marketers are moving money away from traditional communication vehicles such as TV advertising and investing heavily in new media. In 2010, global advertisers spent over $60 billion on online advertising! Retailers also find that their online business is growing but the Internet customer is harder to please and less loyal since she has easy access to competing prices and to the reviews of products and sellers from other online shoppers. The growth of Internet C2C shopping sites such as eBay and Craigslist means more and more consumers buy from each other than (gulp) pay retail prices. In order to better understand this new communication model and its consequences, we need to first look at how marketers encourage and enable consumers to talk about their products in "buzz" building activities. Then we'll look at some of the specific new media that pop up in the marketing communication landscape.

Buzz Building

Why do the heavy lifting when you can put your customers to work for you? The many-to-many communication model relies on consumers like you to talk to one another about goods, services, and organizations. Marketers think of **buzz** as everyday people helping their marketing efforts when they share their opinions with their friends and neighbors.[8] The idea is nothing new. It's basically the so-called "office water-cooler effect" where coworkers dish about the latest TV sitcom on Monday morning.

buzz
Word-of-mouth communication that customers view as authentic.

The trick is to create buzz that works for you, not against you. How does this happen? Or more specifically, how do marketers make sure it happens? Let's look at Volvo's recent online-only campaign called "The Naughty Volvo" to see buzz in action. The carmaker's goal was to get driving enthusiasts to talk about the new S60 model's innovative design and technology. The campaign was called "naughty" because instead of focusing on Volvo's traditional image of safety, it included online demonstrations of the S60's performance and handling. Online viewers could use a virtual dial to go from a "tame" test of the auto to one where the car swerved around a goldfish bowl or, in an even "naughtier" one, to drive the car in reverse (okay, maybe that's not so naughty). Fans could also submit their ideas for more "naughty" films.[9]

Companies today spend millions to create consumer positive buzz. Firms like Dell have named word-of-mouth (WOM) marketing managers, and the WOMMA (Word-of-Mouth Marketing Association) membership roster includes most of the top consumer brand companies.[10] According to advertising agency JWT Worldwide, over 85 percent of the top 1,000 marketing firms now use word-of-mouth tactics.[11] Techniques to encourage consumers to spread information about companies and their products come under a variety of names such as *word-of-mouth marketing*, *viral marketing*, *buzz marketing*, and *evangelist marketing*.

As we've noted, buzz isn't *really* new. In fact, we can point to the fame of none other than the *Mona Lisa* portrait as one of the first examples of buzz marketing. In 1911 the painting was stolen from the Louvre museum in Paris. The theft created buzz around the globe while it catapulted da Vinci's masterpiece into the limelight (note: we're not advocating that you arrange to get your product stolen to build buzz).

What *is* new is the magnifying effect that technology exerts on the spread of buzz: When you think of the effect of consumers talking one-on-one a century ago, imagine the exponential increase in influence of the individual consumer "connectors" or "e-fluentials" who use Facebook, blogs, and other social media to increase their reach.[12] How many online "friends" do you have? Compared to traditional advertising and public relations activities, these endorsements are far more credible and thus more valuable to the brand.

People like to share their experiences, good or bad, with others. Truly happy customers will share their excitement about a brand. Unfortunately, the unhappy ones will be even more eager to tell their friends about their unpleasant experiences. When Honda's PR staff set up a Facebook fan page for the 2010 Honda Accord Crosstour, customers disliked the car's visual appearance and responded with such comments as "Oh god, it looks like the mutant redheaded offspring of a Chrysler Crossfire and a Pontiac Aztec."[13] By the way, that unpredictability is a good reason to think twice before you post those photos from last Saturday night on your Facebook page.

Of course, marketers don't necessarily create the buzz around their product anyway—sometimes they just catch a wave that's building and simply ride it home. WOMMA refers to buzz that comes from deliberate buzz marketing campaigns as "amplified WOM" while it calls buzz that occurs naturally "organic WOM." Organic buzz allowed Procter & Gamble to discover that its Home Café coffee maker had a tendency to start fires after 3,000 people complained.[14] Naturally occurring buzz also can create negative publicity as Southwest Airlines learned firsthand after a director and actor named Kevin Smith was removed from a Southwest plane because he was too fat to fit in his seat. He used Twitter to express his displeasure. Southwest responded to Smith's tweets, apologized, and offered him a seat.[15]

Ripped from the Headlines

Ethical/Sustainable Decisions in the Real World

Social media sites like Facebook and Twitter are great places for users to get together with their friends, to talk about what they are doing right now ("dropping off my dry cleaning!"), and to share news. But sometimes the news isn't exactly true—and unfortunately the fun goes too far.

ETHICS CHECK: ↖

Find out what other students taking this course would do and why on **www.mypearsonmarketinglab.com**

When Ed McMahon, Farrah Fawcett, and Michael Jackson died over the span of a few days, the Web was full of made-up death reports about various celebrities. Within a week, rumors that Harrison Ford had died at sea in his capsized yacht, George Clooney's private plane had nosedived, and Jeff Goldblum had fallen to his death on a movie set quickly spread on Twitter and Facebook. Most of the rumors started on a prank Web site called **Fakeawish.com**, where a user can enter a celebrity's name and then gets a list of fake stories to circulate about him or her.

But is this ethical? Does it damage the credibility of Web sites? Does it seriously harm any celebrities or their families? Should such prankster Web sites be allowed to exist? Should consumers participate in a prankster Web site such as Fakeawish?

What would you do?

> **Would you spread rumors about celebrities on the Web as an online prank?**
>
> ☐ YES ☐ NO

viral marketing
Marketing activities that aim to increase brand awareness or sales by consumers passing a message along to other consumers.

Mike Monello

APPLYING ▽ Viral Marketing

A lot of Mike's work has involved viral marketing, where his team creates an engaging message and relies on viewers to disseminate it broadly. This was the key to the success of the groundbreaking "Blair Witch Project." ➡

Ethical Problems in Buzz Marketing

Just as firms are discovering there are a myriad of opportunities for buzz marketing, there are equally large opportunities for unethical or at least questionable marketing behavior. Some of these are the following:

- *Activities designed to deceive consumers.* Buzz works best when companies put unpaid consumers in charge of creating their own messages. As Table 12.2 shows, WOMMA considers hiring actors to create buzz deceptive and unethical. This is just what Sony Ericsson Mobile Communications did when the company hired 60 actors to go to tourist attractions. Their role was to act like tourists and get unsuspecting passersby to take their photos using the new Sony Ericsson camera phone, and then hype the phone. WOMMA now has rules that state that anyone talking up products should identify the client for whom they work.[16]

- *Directing buzz marketing at children or teens.* Some critics say buzz marketing should never do this, as these consumers are more impressionable and easier to deceive than adults.[17]

- *Buzz marketing activities that damage property.* Puma encouraged consumers to stencil its cat logo all over Paris. Such activities lead to damage or vandalism, which the company will ultimately have to pay for. In addition, individual consumers could find themselves in trouble with the law, a problem that could ultimately backfire and damage the company image.

- *Stealth marketing activities that deliberately deceive or lie on behalf of clients.* WOMMA considers such activities—whether authoring a positive product review on a shopbot, pretending to read a new novel on the subway, or calling a supermarket to ask the manager why she is not stocking a certain product—to be unethical.

Viral Marketing

One form of buzz building is **viral marketing**. This term refers to marketing activities that aim to increase brand awareness or sales by consumers passing a message along to other consumers, hopefully in an exponential fashion—much like your roommate passes a cold on to you and you pass it along to all your other friends. Some of the earliest examples of viral marketing were messages at the bottom of e-mails by Yahoo! and Hotmail that advertised the free e-mail services, much like the tag today at the bottom of e-mails, "Sent from my BlackBerry." Consumers could not choose whether they wanted to participate in these viral marketing programs. Today, most viral marketing tactics are more subtle and consist of marketers' use of video clips, interactive games, or other activities that consumers will find so interesting or unique that they want to share them with their friends using digital technology. To see a classic viral spot in action, visit **www.subservientchicken.com**.

Table 12.2 | Positive and Unethical Word-of-Mouth Marketing Strategies

Positive Word-of-Mouth Marketing Strategies	Unethical Word-of-Mouth Marketing Strategies
1. Encourage communication. Develop tools to make telling a friend easier. Create forums and feedback tools. Work with social networks.	**1. Stealth Marketing** Any practice designed to deceive people about the involvement of marketers in a communication.
2. Give people something to talk about. Transmit information they can share or forward. Create advertising, stunts, and other publicity that encourage conversation. Work with product development to build WOM elements into products.	**2. Shilling** Pay people to talk about (or promote) a product without disclosing that they are working for the company; impersonate a customer.
3. Create communities and connect people. Create user groups and fan clubs. Support independent groups that form around your product. Host discussions and message boards about your products. Support grassroots organizations such as local meetings and other real-world participation.	**3. Infiltration** Use fake identities in an online discussion to promote a product; take over a Web site, conversation, or live event against the wishes or rules set by the proprietor.
4. Work with influential communities. Find people who are likely to respond to your message. Identify people who are able to influence your target customers. Inform these individuals about what you do and encourage them to spread the word. Promote good-faith efforts to support issues and causes that are important to these individuals.	**4. Comment Spam** Use automated software ("bots") to post unrelated or inappropriate comments to blogs or other online communities. **5. Defacement** Vandalize or damage property to promote a product.
5. Create evangelist or advocate programs. Provide recognition and tools to active advocates. Recruit new advocates, teach them about the benefits of your products, and encourage them to talk about them.	**6. Spam** Send bulk or unsolicited e-mail or other messages without clear, voluntary permission.
6. Research and listen to customer feedback. Track online and off-line conversations by supporters, detractors, and neutrals. Listen and respond to both positive and negative conversations.	**7. Falsification** Knowingly disseminate false or misleading information.
7. Engage in transparent conversation. Encourage two-way conversations with interested parties. Create blogs and other tools to share information. Participate openly on online blogs and discussions.	
8. Co-creation and information sharing. Involve consumers in marketing and creative executions (solicit feedback on ads, allow enthusiasts to create their own commercials, etc.). Let customers go "behind the curtain" to obtain first access to information and content.	

Source: Adapted from "Word-of-Mouth 101: An Introduction to Word-of-Mouth Marketing," WOMMA, **www.womma.org/wom101.htm** (accessed March 12, 2008).

brand ambassadors or brand evangelists
Loyal customers of a brand recruited to communicate and be salespeople with other consumers for a brand they care a great deal about.

Brand Ambassadors and Evangelists

Many marketers realize that they can't create buzz by themselves; they recruit loyal customers as **brand ambassadors** or **brand evangelists** to help them. These zealous consumers can be the best salespeople a company can ever find—and they often work for free. They are heavy users, take a product seriously, care a great deal about it, and want it to succeed.[18] In addition, they know the target audience better than anyone because they are a part of it. A new twist in evangelist marketing is the brand party in the intimate settings provided by consumers' homes. For example, to introduce Windows 7, Microsoft enlisted nearly 60,000 hosts who held parties attended by an estimated 7 million consumers worldwide. Each Windows 7 host received an autographed edition of the operating system, a tote bag, a deck of cards, and other party favors.[19]

So how do marketers identify and motivate these loyal customers to be brand ambassadors? Sometimes they seek out customers who already blog about the product and share what they love about the brand. One way to motivate brand ambassadors is to give them special access or privileges to the company and its marketing strategies. Some might be recruited and featured through a brand contest. Months before its Ford Fiesta launch in the United States, Ford initiated its "Fiesta Movement" program to build buzz among the 70 million Millennials, also known as Generation Y consumers, for its car. The campaign sought to recruit 100 "agents" to complete Ford-assigned "missions" and write about their experiences on social networks Facebook, Flickr, and YouTube. To be considered for the "agent" job, consumers were asked to upload a two- to five-minute video to the company Web site explaining why they wanted to become an agent.[20]

New Social Media

social media
Internet-based platforms that allow users to create their own content and share it with others who access these sites.

In addition to buzz building, **social media** are an important part of the Updated Communication Model. This term refers to Internet-based platforms that allow users to create their own content and share it with others who access these sites. It's hard to grasp just how much these new formats will transform the way we interact with marketers; they "democratize" messages because they give individual consumers a seat at the table when organizations shape brand meanings and promote themselves in the marketplace. This makes it much easier for companies to tap into their brand evangelists to help them spread the word. The flip side is that the bad stuff also gets out much quicker and reaches people a lot faster: In one survey 20 percent of respondents said they had used social media to share a negative experience with a brand or service.[21]

There's no doubt that social media is the place to be in marketing communication now, even if many organizations haven't quite figured out just what to do with these platforms. Traditional brands such as McDonald's, Pizza Hut, and Church's Chicken are scrambling to move hefty portions of their promotion budgets out of advertising and into social media. Pizza Hut has over a million fans on its Facebook page, and the franchise launched a campaign on Twitter looking for summer "twiterns" who would blog to their fans about all things pizza. Church's Chicken sponsored a "pay it forward" promotion on Twitter, promising to donate $1 to the company pledge fund for each person who joined their Twitter feed during a 30-day period.[22]

Social media include blogs, forums, picture- and video-sharing sites, wikis, and podcasts, to name a few. While

AFP PHOTO/JOHNNY BIVERA/Newscom

A brand community is a group of people who are organized around a lifestyle or idea that is representative of a brand. The brand community members are admirers of the brand and share in the rituals and traditions they associate with it. They feel connected to the brand and as a result they bond with each other. After near bankruptcy in 1983, Harley focused on building a brand community. The Harley Owners Group®, fondly referred to as H.O.G., is credited with helping to turn the company around. Harley supports riders' passions for their bikes by sponsoring huge rallies around the country where members can meet up. In 2009, Harley enjoyed revenues of over $4 billion.

marketers can and do use all these types of sites, we are going to focus on just a few platforms: social networking sites, virtual worlds, product review sites, and geospatial mobile apps.

Social Networks

Social networks are sites used to connect people with other similar people. Successful networking sites ask users to develop profiles of themselves so that those with similar backgrounds, interests, hobbies, religious beliefs, racial identities, or political views can "meet" online. Social networks such as Facebook and LinkedIn are some of the most popular sites on the Internet with millions of users from around the globe. Once a user has created a profile, it's easy to connect with old and new friends.

So what's in all this social networking for marketers? First, social networks make it easy for marketers to reach influential people such as journalists and consumers who are opinion leaders. But even more important is the opportunity social networks provide to create a brand community. We'll talk later about brand communities but first, let's examine a couple of the most popular social media sites.

Facebook

Facebook is the most popular of all social networking sites with over 500 million users as we write this book—and no doubt tons more as you're reading it. Users of Facebook first develop a profile that remains private unless they choose to connect with a "friend." While this social media site was originally created to allow college students to keep in touch with their friends (in those days you had to have ".edu" in your e-mail address to join), it is no longer just for students. Today there are many significant user segments including baby-boomer women and even grandparents who use the platform to locate long-lost friends (and keep tabs on their grandchildren).[23] Despite this "invasion," at least for now Facebook is the social media site of choice for college students. In one recent survey of American students, an overwhelming 82 percent of males and 90 percent of females gave it the ultimate compliment: They rated it "cool" and the Go To place over all other networking platforms, and even over Web sites in general, including Google.[24] A major advantage for marketers is that you can establish Facebook groups around topics and you can recruit fans for your product. Many firms are rolling out promotions that tap into this fan base. A typical one is the Burgerville restaurant chain. It invites its network of over 10,000 Facebook fans to participate in "Tasting Tuesdays," where they can sample new menu items and provide feedback. The chain also alerts fans to upcoming visits to their areas by the Burgerville "Nomad," a 24-foot-long mobile restaurant.[25]

Twitter

Twitter is a free microblogging service that lets users post short text messages with a maximum of 140 characters. People who subscribe to an individual's Twitter feed are called "followers." Users can follow anyone they like, unlike Facebook where you have to be recognized and accepted as a "friend." Attesting to its popularity, Twitter now has 106 million registered users who "tweet" 55 million posts a day.[26]

The good news for marketers is that one in five (20 percent) tweets posted on Twitter is either a question or a comment about a brand-related product or service.[27] Thus it is especially important that marketers monitor Twitter to understand what consumers say about their products. Unlike other social media, Twitter is a broadcast medium, which means that marketers can send messages to hundreds of thousands of people at a time. They can use this platform to alert customers to deals and to generate sales. Dell, for example, used Twitter to tell followers about exclusive deals; these tweets generated over $3 million in revenue in 24 months.[28]

Virtual Worlds

What if a sophisticated video game like *Madden Football* married a chatroom that enables multiple participants to talk to each other in real time? Suppose they had a baby: This would probably be a **virtual world**. This term refers to an online, highly engaging digital environment

social networks
Sites used to connect people with other similar people.

twitter
A free microblogging service that lets users post short text messages with a maximum of 140 characters.

virtual worlds
Online, highly engaging digital environments where avatars live and interact with other avatars in real time.

The Cutting Edge

Where Is Twitter Going?

During its few years of existence, Twitter has seen exponential growth. Nevertheless, at least two problems have the potential to make the social media site's future less rosy than its brief past. First, Twitter has to deal with the same basic issue that has confounded many Web 2.0 media platforms—how to "monetize" the site (a fancy way to say make money from it). Second, the site's future popularity is not guaranteed—it could be overshadowed by the next social media darling idea, just as MySpace lost a lot of its luster when many users defected to Facebook.

Twitter is hoping to address the monetization problem as it embarks on a program to sell advertising, or what it calls Promoted Tweets.[29] In much the same way that Google makes money when people use its site to search for information, ads will be activated when users search for keywords that advertisers have bought to link to their ads. If a Twitter user searches for information

on vacations in Bali, she may see a Promoted Tweet from an airline that offers—guess what?—special fares on flights to Bali. The messages will appear at the top of the posts no matter when they were added. Later, even when users don't search for those keywords, the ads that are relevant to a particular user based on his previous searches will be posted in a stream of Twitter posts. The program will also allow Twitter advertisers to respond to negative tweets. When a tweet about a brand is negative (Twitter already has the software to measure the sentiments of tweets), an ad can be inserted. For example, if a Twitter user says something negative about a movie, the studio can use its ads to link the user to a positive review.

Time will tell if Twitter's strategy is successful. One potential pitfall: Will users get turned off by the Promoted Tweets and defect to another site that (at least for now) offers an environment with no advertising? If so, cue up problem #2 . . .

---

avatars
Graphic representations of users of virtual worlds.

where **avatars**—graphic representations of users—live and interact with other avatars in real time. The blockbuster movie *Avatar* exposed many people to this basic idea as it told the story of a wounded soldier who takes on a new (10 ft. tall and blue) identity in the world of Pandora.

In virtual worlds, residents can hang out at virtual clubs, shop for clothing and bling for their avatars, buy furniture to deck out virtual homes, and yes, even go to college in virtual universities. Some people find it hard to believe, but it's common for people to spend real money to buy digital products that don't exist in the real world. Indeed, the **virtual goods** market is booming: In the United States alone, consumers spend well over $1 billion each year to buy items they use only in virtual worlds!

virtual goods
Digital products bought and sold in virtual worlds that don't exist in the real world.

Second Life is one of the largest and best-known virtual worlds, although in reality there are several hundred of these environments up and running. This platform is one of many virtual worlds that has become a booming marketplace for budding fashion designers, musicians, and businesspeople who sell their products and services. A few have even become real-world millionaires by selling virtual goods to users who want to buy bling for their avatars. A sampling of other virtual worlds includes:

- Coke Studios, a promotional virtual world for Coca-Cola that targets teens and young adults. Avatars called "V-egos" create their own customized music mixes in a virtual music studio, games, and contests for Coca-Cola and its partners.

- Disney's Toontown offers kids a brightly colored cartoon environment where they can outfit their toon avatars and play games. Like offline Disney World, Toontown is designed to be a place where kids feel they are in charge.

- Habbo Hotel is a virtual world where teens and young adults inhabit a room (a "habbo") and decorate it with furniture they purchase with Habbo credits.

- FooPets, especially popular with 12- to 14-year-old girls, allows users to "adopt" digitally animated pets, then care for them and feed them. If the pets are not properly cared for, they will be taken to a virtual shelter.[30]

Most virtual goods, whether sold in virtual worlds or through other social media sites, have micro-prices—from less than $1 to $3. So what's in it for real-world marketers? Some firms enter the market for virtual goods to keep in touch with consumers, improve the brand's image and develop loyal customers. MTV Networks gave away virtual replicas of celebrity accessories such as Beyoncé's diamond ring in its campaign to increase viewership for the Video Music Awards. H&M showed viewers its collection of denim and blue garments and encouraged consumers to visit H&M retail stores on Mytown. And Volvo Cars of North America offered virtual goods on the iPhone app MyTown in a program to improve its image.[32]

Product Review Sites

Product review sites are social media sites that enable people to post stories about their experiences with products and services. Marketers hope that product review sites create a connection between the consumer and the brand. Product review sites give users both positive and negative information about companies:

- TripAdvisor provides unbiased hotel reviews complete with photos and advice. The site gives consumers an opportunity to rate and comment on a hotel that they recently stayed in or to use other consumers' comments to select a hotel for an upcoming trip.

- Yelp is a product review site that provides reviews of local businesses such as places to eat, shop, drink, or play. Consumers can access Yelp either through the Internet or a mobile phone. Businesses can create pages to enable them to track reviews.

- The *Zagat Survey* began in 1979 in offline form. Today the online version provides consumer survey-based information on restaurants, hotels, nightspots and leisure activities in over 100 countries based on surveys of more than 375,000 consumers. Zagat reviews are available to consumers online, through mobile phones and in-car personal navigation devices.

In anticipation of its 2011 launch of the "Cars 2" movie, a sequel to the original 2006 hit, "Cars," Disney launched an online community it calls "World of Cars." Subscribers to the community interact with characters from the movie, design their own car and race it on an online track.[31]

product review sites
Social media sites that enable people to post stories about their experiences with products and services.

Mobile Apps and Geospatial Platforms

It's obvious to almost anyone who's conscious today that the future of marketing communication lies in that magic little device you practically sleep with—whether it's a smartphone or perhaps a computer/phone hybrid like Apple's iPad. Combine Web browsing capability with built-in cameras and the race is on to bring to the world to your belt or purse. Apple lit up this market when it introduced the iPhone and now everyone is scrambling to "monetize" the mobile market through sales of ringtones, on-demand video, online coupons, and "apps" that entertain or educate. A few to watch include.[33]

- ShopSavvy finds the lowest prices online and at nearby brick-and-mortar retailers, as well as coupons, and lets users make transactions.

- RetrevoQ uses texts and tweets to provide information about electronics products. Shoppers can text 41411 or tweet @retrevoq, including the make and model of the electronics product they're considering, and RetrevoQ will respond with advice on whether it's a good buy, a fair price, the price range available online for that product, and a link to reviews at **Retrevo.com**, a consumer-electronics shopping and review site.

- Fastmall provides interactive maps of malls, highlights the quickest route to stores, and even helps shoppers remember where they parked their cars. Even better: Shake your phone and it shows you the nearest restroom location.

Geospatial platforms integrate sophisticated GPS technology (like the navigation system you may have in your car) that enables users to alert friends of their exact whereabouts via their mobile phones. Foursquare is one of the most popular of these new sites with nearly 3 million users; one of its addicting features is that users compete to become "mayor" of a location by checking in from there more than anyone else. Other hot location-based sites

geospatial platforms
Digital applications that integrate sophisticated GPS technology to enable users to alert friends of their exact whereabouts via their mobile phones.

include Loopt, Gowalla, Booyah, Shopkick, Google's Latitude and Facebook's location based service. Many top retailers including Starbucks, Sephora, Gap, Macy's, Best Buy and American Eagle are finding that the use of check-in sites such as Foursquare, Gowalla, and Shopkick that reach customers on the go increases sales.[34] Businesses can ride this wave by offering discounts or free services to people who check in to their locations, or in Foursquare to those who reach the rank of "Mayor," which obviously encourages consumers to visit the place frequently. Foursquare also provides a "dashboard" to businesses that tells them who checks into their locations and at what times so they can get a handle on how specific marketing communications such as a time-limited sales promotion are working (or not) to drive traffic.[35]

3 Promotional Planning in a Web 2.0 World

OBJECTIVE

Describe the steps in traditional and multichannel promotional planning.
(pp. 366–373)

Now that we've talked about communication and the traditional and new tools marketers can use to deliver messages to their customers, we need to see how to make it all happen. How do we go about the complex task of developing a promotional plan—one that delivers just the right message to a number of different target audiences when and where they want it in the most effective and cost-efficient way?

Just as with any other strategic decision-making process, the development of this plan includes several steps, as Figure 12.4 shows. First, we'll go over the steps in promotional planning. Then we'll take a look at how marketers today are developing multichannel promotional strategies.

Step 1. Identify the Target Audience(s)

An important part of overall marketing planning is to identify the target audience(s). IMC marketers recognize that we must communicate with a variety of stakeholders who influence the target market. Of course, the intended customer is the most important target audience and the one that marketers focus on the most.

Figure 12.4 *Process* | Steps to Develop the Promotional Plan

Development of successful promotional plans involves organizing the complex process into a series of several orderly steps.

Step 1: Identify the Target Audiences

Step 2: Establish the Communication Objectives

Step 3: Determine and Allocate the Marketing Communication Budget
- Determine the Total Promotion Budget
- Decide on a Push or a Pull Strategy
- Allocate the Budget to a Specific Promotion Mix

Step 4: Design the Promotion Mix

Step 5: Evaluate the Effectiveness of the Communication Program

Step 2. Establish the Communication Objectives

The whole point of communicating with customers and prospective customers is to let them know in a timely and affordable way that the organization has a product to meet their needs. It's bad enough when a product comes along that people don't want or need. An even bigger marketing sin is to have a product that they *do* want—but you fail to let them know about it. Of course, seldom can we deliver a single message to a consumer that magically transforms her into a loyal customer. In most cases, it takes a series of messages that moves the consumer through several stages.

We view this process as an uphill climb, such as the one 📷 Figure 12.5 depicts. The marketer "pushes" the consumer through a series of steps, or a **hierarchy of effects**, from initial awareness of a product to brand loyalty. The task of moving the consumer up the hierarchy becomes more difficult at each step. Many potential buyers may drop out along the way, leaving fewer of the target group inclined to go the distance and become loyal customers. Each part of this path entails different communication objectives to "push" people to the next level.

To understand how this process works, imagine how a firm would have to adjust its communication objectives as it tries to establish a presence in the market for Hunk, a new men's cologne. Let's say that the primary target market for the cologne is single men age 18 to 24 who care about their appearance and who are into health, fitness, working out, and looking ripped. The company would want to focus more on some promotion methods (such as advertising) and less on others (such as personal selling). Here are some communication objectives the company might develop for its Hunk promotion.

Create Awareness

The first step is to make members of the target market aware that there's a new brand of cologne on the market. The fragrance's marketers might place simple, repetitive advertising in magazines, on television, and on the radio that push the brand name. The company could develop a "teaser" ad campaign, in which messages heighten interest because they don't initially reveal the exact nature of the product (for example, newspaper ads that simply proclaim,

hierarchy of effects
A series of steps prospective customers move through, from initial awareness of a product to brand loyalty.

Figure 12.5 📷 *Snapshot* | The Hierarchy of Effects
Communication objectives move consumers through the hierarchy of effects.

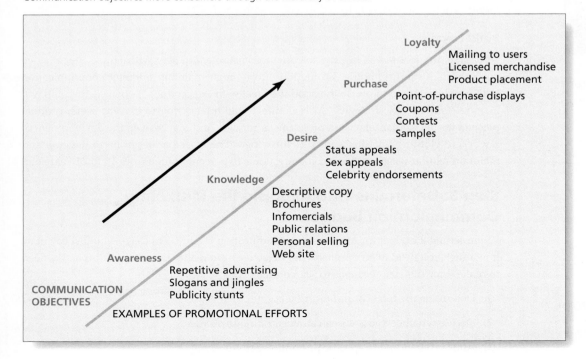

Attention-getting messages ("fat is sexy") capture consumers' attention and inform them about new products.

"Hunk is coming!"). The promotion objective might be to create an 80 percent awareness of Hunk cologne among 18- to 24-year-old men in the first two months. Note how this objective is worded. Objectives are best when they are quantitative (80 percent), when they specify the target consumer or business group (18- to 24-year-old men), and when they specify the time frame during which the plan is expected to reach the objective (in the first two months).

Inform the Market

The next step is to provide prospective users with knowledge about the benefits the new product has to offer—to *position* it relative to other colognes (see Chapter 7). Perhaps the cologne has a light, slightly mentholated scent with a hint of a liniment smell to remind wearers of how they feel after a good workout. Promotion would focus on communications that emphasize this position. The objective at this point might be to communicate the connection between Hunk and muscle building so that 70 percent of the target market develops some interest in the product in the first six months of the communication program.

Create Desire

The next task is to create favorable feelings toward the product and to convince at least some members of this group that they would rather splash on some Hunk instead of other colognes. Communication at this stage might consist of splashy advertising spreads in magazines, perhaps with an endorsement by a well-known celebrity "hunk" such as The Rock. The specific objective might be to create positive attitudes toward Hunk cologne among 50 percent of the target market and brand preference among 30 percent of the target market in the first six months.

Encourage Purchase and Trial

As the expression goes, "How do ya know 'til ya try it?" The company now needs to get some of the men who have become interested in the cologne to try it. A promotion plan might encourage trial by mailing samples of Hunk to members of the target market, inserting "scratch-and-sniff" samples in bodybuilding magazines, placing elaborate displays in stores that dispense money-saving coupons, or even sponsoring a contest in which the winner gets to have The Rock as his personal trainer for a day. The specific objective now might be to encourage trial of Hunk among 25 percent of 18- to 24-year-old men in the first two months (note: we have *not* cleared this plan with The Rock).

Build Loyalty

Of course, the real test is loyalty: to convince customers to stay with Hunk after they've gone through the first bottle. Promotion efforts must maintain ongoing communication with current users to reinforce the bond they feel with the product. As before, this step will include some mix of strategies, such as direct-mail advertising to current users, product placements in popular television programs or movies, and maybe even the development of a workout clothing line that sports a Hunk logo. The objective might be to develop and maintain regular usage of Hunk cologne among 10 percent of men from 18 to 24 years old.

Step 3: Determine and Allocate the Marketing Communication Budget

While setting a budget for marketing communication might seem easy—you just calculate how much you need to accomplish your objectives—in reality it's not that simple. We need to make three distinct decisions to set a budget:

1. Determine the total communication budget.

2. Decide whether to use a push strategy or a pull strategy.

3. Allocate spending to specific promotion activities.

top-down budgeting
Allocation of the promotion budget based on management's determiniation of the total amount to be devoted to marketing communication.

Determine the Total Promotion Budget

In the real world, firms often view communication costs as an expense rather than as an investment leading to greater profits (shame on them!). When sales are declining or the company is operating in a difficult economic environment, it is often tempting to cut costs by reducing spending on advertising, promotion, and other "soft" activities whose contributions to the bottom line are hard to quantify. When this is the case, marketers must work harder to justify these expenses.

Economic approaches to budgeting rely on *marginal analysis* (we discussed these in Chapter 11), in which the organization spends money on promotion as long as the revenues it realizes through these efforts continue to exceed the costs of the promotions themselves. This perspective assumes that a company always intends promotions solely to increase sales, when in fact these activities may have other objectives such as enhancing a firm's image.

Also, the effects of marketing communication often lag over time. For example, a firm may have to spend a lot on advertising and other forms of marketing communication when it first launches a product without seeing any immediate return. Because of these limitations, most firms rely on two budgeting techniques: top-down and bottom-up. **Top-down budgeting techniques** require top management to establish the overall amount that the organization allocates for promotion activities

The most common top-down technique is the **percentage-of-sales method** in which the promotion budget is based on last year's sales or on estimates for the present year's sales. The percentage may be an industry average provided by trade associations that collect objective information on behalf of member companies. The advantage of this method is that it ties spending on promotion to sales and profits. Unfortunately, this method can imply that sales cause promotional spending rather than viewing sales as the *outcome* of promotional efforts.

The **competitive-parity method** is a fancy way of saying "keep up with the Joneses." In other words, match whatever competitors spend. Some marketers think this approach simply mirrors the best thinking of others in the business. However, this method often results in each player simply maintaining the same market share year after year. This method also assumes that the same dollars spent on promotion by two different firms will yield the same results, but spending a lot of money doesn't guarantee a successful promotion. Firms certainly need to monitor their competitors' promotion activities, but they must combine this information with their own objectives and capacities.

The problem with top-down techniques is that budget decisions are based more on established practices than on promotion objectives. Another approach is to begin at the beginning: Identify promotion goals and allocate enough money to accomplish them. That is what **bottom-up budgeting techniques** attempt.

This bottom-up logic is at the heart of the **objective-task method**, which is gaining in popularity. Using this approach, the firm first defines the specific communication goals it hopes to achieve, such as increasing by 20 percent the number of consumers who are aware of the brand. It then tries to figure out what kind of promotional efforts—how much advertising, sales promotion, buzz marketing, and so on—it will take to meet that goal. Although this is the most rational approach, it is hard to implement because it obliges managers to specify their objectives and attach dollar amounts to them. This method requires careful analysis—and a bit of lucky "guesstimating."

Decide on a Push or a Pull Strategy

The second important decision in promotion budgeting is whether the company will primarily push or pull. A **push strategy** means that the company wants to move its products by convincing channel members to offer them and entice their customers to select these

Many brands have discovered that a great way to build loyalty is to give back to worthy causes.

percentage-of-sales budgeting method
A method for promotion budgeting that is based on a certain percentage of either last year's sales or on estimates of the present year's sales.

competitive-parity budgeting method
A promotion budgeting method in which an organization matches whatever competitors are spending.

bottom-up budgeting techniques
Allocation of the promotion budget based on identifying promotion goals and allocating enough money to accomplish them.

objective-task method
A promotion budgeting method in which an organization first defines the specific communication goals it hopes to achieve and then tries to calculate what kind of promotion efforts it will take to meet these goals.

push strategy
The company tries to move its products through the channel by convincing channel members to offer them.

Courtesy of Giovanni + DRAFTFCB

Small businesses need to budget carefully to be sure they get the bang for their scarce bucks. This food delivery company in Brazil decided to invest in an eye-catching print ad.

pull strategy
The company tries to move its products through the channel by building desire for the products among consumers, thus convincing retailers to respond to this demand by stocking these items.

items—it pushes them through the channel. This approach assumes that if consumers see the product on store shelves, they will be motivated to make a trial purchase. In this case, promotion efforts will "push" the products from producer to consumers by focusing on personal selling, trade advertising, and trade sales promotion activities such as exhibits at trade shows.

In contrast, a company that relies on a **pull strategy** is counting on consumers to demand its products. This popularity will then convince retailers to respond by stocking these items. In this case, efforts focus on media advertising and consumer sales promotion to stimulate interest among end consumers who will "pull" the product onto store shelves and then into their shopping carts.

Whether we use a push or a pull strategy and the promotion mix that we use for a product varies over time because some promotion strategies work better than others at different points in the product life cycle (which we reviewed back in Chapter 9).

As an example, we might think about the state of electronics in today's market and the relative positions in the product life cycle. In the *introduction phase*, the objective is to build awareness of and encourage trial of the product among consumers, often by relying on a pull strategy. That's the situation today with 3G (third generation) mobile telephone technology that allows voice and data transmission at incredible speeds. This enables you to watch television, have video conversations with your friends, log into your bank account to pay your bills, view video clips of local tourist attractions, and manage your inventory of items that need restocking from your home's "smart" refrigerator—all from your 3G mobile phone. Advertising is the primary promotion tool to create awareness, and a publicity campaign to generate news reports about the new product may help as well. A company may use sales promotion to encourage trial. Business-to-business marketing that emphasizes personal selling—the marketing that a manufacturer does to retailers and other business customers—is important in this phase in order to get channel members to carry the product. For consumer goods that retailers sell, trade sales promotion may be necessary to encourage retailers to stock the product.

In the *growth phase*, promotions stress product benefits. For products such as MP3 players, advertising increases, while consumer sales promotions that encourage trial usually decline because people are more willing to try the product without being offered an incentive.

The opposite pattern often occurs with products now in their *maturity phase* such as DVD players. In these situations many people have already tried the product. The strategy now shifts to encouraging people to switch from competitors' brands as sales stabilize. This can be tough if consumers don't see enough differences among the options to bother. Usually, sales promotion activities, particularly coupons and special price deals, have greater chances of success than advertising. In some cases an industry revamps a widely used technology when it introduces one or more new versions or formats that force consumers to convert (sometimes kicking and screaming), thus transforming a mature category back to a new one. That's what's happening now in the "DVD format wars," a high-stakes showdown between the HD DVD and Blu-ray disk formats that Blu-ray won after it gained the backing of a large number of consumer electronics and entertainment companies.[36]

All bets are off for VCR players, now well into their *decline phase*. As sales plummet, the company dramatically reduces spending on all elements of the promotion mix. Sales will be driven by the continued loyalty of a small group of users who keep the product alive until it is sold to another company or discontinued.

Allocate the Budget to a Specific Promotion Mix

Once the organization decides how much to spend on promotion and whether to use a push or a pull strategy, it must divide its budget among the elements in the promotion mix. Although advertising used to get the lion's share of the promotion budget, today sales promotion and digital marketing such as buzz building and the use of social media we talked about earlier in this chapter are playing a bigger role in marketing strategies. Overall advertising spending, for example, declined 12.3 percent in 2009 compared to spending in 2008 while at the same time companies were investing more in Internet display ads (up 7.3 percent) and coupon inserts (up 3 percent).[37] In one study, up to 60 percent of marketers said they were shifting funds from traditional media to interactive marketing, including social media, and mobile marketing. While only 12 percent of those surveyed said they were cutting TV ad budgets, 40 percent were cutting direct mail, and more than 25 percent were cutting newspapers and magazines.[38]

In today's dynamic media environment, there are few clear guidelines for how to divide up the promotional pie. In some cases managers may simply have a preference for advertising versus sales promotion or other elements of the promotion mix. Also, consumers vary widely in the likelihood that they will respond to various communication elements. Some thrifty consumers like to clip coupons or stock up with two-for-one offers while others throw away those Sunday newspaper coupons without a glance. College students are especially likely to spend most of their time on the Internet (but you knew that).The size and makeup of a geographic market also influence promotion decisions. In larger markets, the cost of buying media, such as local TV, can be quite high. If only a small percentage of the total market includes potential customers, then mass media advertising can be a very inefficient use of a promotion budget.

Consumers can't wait to read their novels and newspapers on a table instead of toting around all those hard copies but it's unclear which format will prevail. Will it be Amazon's Kindle, the Apple iPad, the Barnes & Noble Nook, the Sony Reader—or maybe some upstart we haven't seen quite yet?

Chris Ratcliffe/Bloomberg/Getty Images

Step 4: Design the Promotion Mix

Designing the promotion mix is the most complicated step in marketing communication planning. It includes determining the specific communication tools to use, what message to communicate, and the communication channel(s) that will be used to send the message.

Planners must ask how they can use advertising, sales promotion, personal selling, and public relations most effectively to communicate with different target audiences. Each element of the promotion mix has benefits and shortcomings, so—as we've seen—often a combination of a few techniques works the best.

The message ideally should accomplish four objectives (though a single message can rarely do all of these): It should get attention, hold interest, create desire, and produce action. We call these communication goals the **AIDA model**. Here we'll review some different forms the message can take as well as how we might structure the message.

There are many ways to say the same thing, and marketers must take care when they choose how they will encode their message. To illustrate, consider two strategies rival car companies used to promote similar automobiles: Toyota's advertising for its Lexus model used a rational appeal that focused on the technical advancements in the car's design. This approach is often effective for promoting products that are technically complex and require a substantial investment. Nissan, in contrast, focused on the spiritual fulfillment a driver might feel tooling down the road in a fine machine.

AIDA model
The communication goals of attention, interest, desire, and action.

This Turkish ad for bird seed gets attention and holds interest!

Step 5: Evaluate the Effectiveness of the Communication Program

The final step to manage marketing communication is to decide whether the plan is working. It would be nice if a marketing manager could simply report, "The $3 million campaign for our revolutionary glow-in-the-dark surfboards brought in $15 million in new sales!" It's not so easy. There are many random factors in the marketing environment: a rival's manufacturing problem, a coincidental photograph of a movie star toting one of the boards, or perhaps a surge of renewed interest in surfing sparked by a cult movie hit like *Blue Crush*.

Still, there are ways to monitor and evaluate the company's communication efforts. The catch is that it's easier to determine the effectiveness of some forms of communication than others. As a rule, various types of sales promotion are the easiest to evaluate because they occur over a fixed, usually short period, making it easier to link to sales volume. Advertising researchers measure brand awareness, recall of product benefits communicated through advertising, and even the image of the brand before and after an advertising campaign. The firm can analyze and compare the performance of salespeople in different territories, although again it is difficult to rule out other factors that make one salesperson more effective than another. Public relations activities are more difficult to assess because their objectives relate more often to image building than sales volume.

Multichannel Promotional Strategies

As we said early in this chapter, marketers today recognize that the traditional one-to-many communication model in which they spent millions of dollars broadcasting ads to a mass audience is less and less effective. At the same time, it isn't yet clear how effective the new many-to-many model is—or what marketing metrics we should use to measure how well new media campaigns are working. Thus, many marketers opt for multichannel promotional strategies where they combine traditional advertising, sales promotion, and public relations activities with online buzz-building activities. For marketers who choose multi-

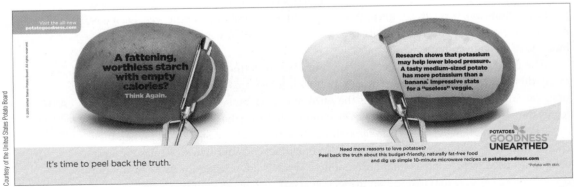

A communication objective may focus on educating consumers about a product like potatoes. The sponsor can measure the effectiveness of a campaign by assessing people's knowledge before and after the messages have run to determine if they had any impact.

channel marketing there are important benefits. First, multichannel strategies boost the effectiveness of either online or offline strategies used alone. And multichannel strategies allow marketers to repeat their messages across various channels; this lets them strengthen brand awareness, and it provides more opportunities to convert customers.

Perhaps the best way to really understand how marketers develop multichannel strategies is to look at how some actually do it:

- As part of its recent communication program to encourage consumers to buy its Athenos brand of hummus, Kraft combined traditional radio media with online messages. The campaign featured a three-city restaurant sampling program in Atlanta, Denver, and Chicago. The multichannel campaign also included a "true or false" quiz on the Internet and radio stations promotions in which listeners participated in live quiz events conducted by stations' morning show hosts. The campaign was also promoted on the Athenos Facebook page.[39]

- The Mexican restaurant chain Del Taco created a Facebook-based entertainment webisode, "The Del Taco Super Special Show." Traditional TV and radio ads promoted the webisode and offered consumers a coupon for a free Classic Taco.[40]

- Ghiradelli Chocolate combined an online sweepstakes, a 10-city sampling tour, promotional packaging, in-store displays, an online banner campaign, and a month-long Times Square billboard in its "Million Moments of Timeless Pleasure" campaign. Consumers were asked to visit a Web site and create a 75-character message about the "sweet little moments" when they enjoyed Ghiradelli. The comments were then streamed live. Selected posts were also shown in lights on a billboard in New York City's Times Square. To sweeten the campaign even more, Ghiradelli distributed one million Ghiradelli squares in a sampling program. Hungry consumers were able to find out where the sampling was taking place by following the campaign on Twitter.[41]

Why do you think Mike chose option #3?

Here's my choice. . .

Real **People**, Real **Choices**

1 2 ③

Option   Option   Option

How It Worked Out at Campfire

Mike and his partners declined the account. They felt that moving in that direction would reduce the agency's differentiation in the marketplace. Today the agency has grown to 25 employees and works on innovative forms of marketing and storytelling, such as recent work for Discovery Channel's Shark Week, a transmedia experience that used influencer outreach, Facebook Connect, and a chilling Web site to bring the visceral terror of a shark attack directly to its audience.

To learn the whole story, visit www.mypearsonmarketinglab.com.

Brand **YOU!**

Get the word out about your brand ... to all the right people.

Create an integrated marketing communication plan for your personal brand. It's easy to increase your chances of getting interviews when you use all the available "media" to get your cover letter and résumé to your target audiences. Plan your personal brand marketing communication plan in Chapter 12 of the *Brand You* supplement.

CHAPTER 12

Objective Summary ➡ Key Terms ➡ Apply **Study Map**

1. Objective Summary (pp. 350–357)

Understand the communication process and the traditional promotion mix.

Firms use promotion and other forms of marketing communication to inform consumers about new products, remind them of familiar products, persuade them to choose one alternative over another, and build strong customer relationships. Recognizing that consumers come in contact with a brand at many different touch points, firms today often practice integrated marketing communication to reach consumers through a multichannel promotional strategy. Because marketers understand the impact of word-of-mouth communication, they are likely to supplement the traditional one-to-many communication model with a newer many-to-many model and also talk one-to-one with consumers.

The traditional communication model includes a message source that creates an idea, encodes the idea into a message, and transmits the message through some medium. The message is delivered to the receiver, who decodes the message and may provide feedback to the source. Anything that interferes with the communication is called "noise."

The promotion mix refers to the marketing communication elements that the marketer controls. Advertising, sales promotion, and public relations use the mass media to reach many consumers at a single time while personal selling and direct marketing allow marketers to communicate with consumers one-on-one.

Key Terms

AOR (Agency of Record) relationship, p. 349

promotion, p. 350

integrated marketing communication (IMC), p. 351

multichannel promotional strategy, p. 351

word-of-mouth communication, p. 351

communication model, p. 352

encoding, p. 353

source, p. 353

message, p. 354

medium, p. 354

receiver, p. 354

decoding, p. 354

noise, p. 354

feedback, p. 355

promotion mix, p. 355

mass communication, p. 357

2. Objective Summary (pp. 358–366)

Understand how marketers communicate using an updated communication model that incorporates buzz marketing activities and social media.

Because consumers spend more time online and less time watching TV or reaching magazines, traditional advertising has diminished as a way to talk to consumers. Consumers today are increasingly getting their information on products from one another rather than from firms as technology magnifies the spread of consumer buzz. Marketers use buzz-building activities to encourage consumers to share their opinions about products with friends and neighbors. While organic word-of-mouth (WOM) occurs naturally, buzz marketing campaigns create amplified WOM.

Viral marketing refers to activities that aim to increase brand awareness or sales by consumers passing a message along to other consumers. Marketers may recruit loyal customers who care a great deal about a product and want it to succeed as brand ambassadors or brand evangelists to help create buzz.

Social media are Internet-based platforms that allow users to create their own content and share it with others. Social networking sites or social networks such as Facebook, Twitter, virtual worlds, product review sites, mobile apps, and geospatial platforms connect people with other similar people.

Key Terms

advertising, p. 357

groundswell, p. 358

buzz, p. 359

viral marketing, p. 360

brand ambassadors or brand evangelists, p. 362

social media, p. 362

social networks, p. 363

twitter, p. 363

virtual worlds, p. 363

avatars, p. 364

virtual goods, p. 364

product review sites, p. 365

geospatial platforms, p. 365

3. Objective Summary (pp. 366–373)

Describe the steps in traditional and multichannel promotional planning.

Recognizing the importance of communicating with a variety of stakeholders who influence the target market, marketers begin the promotional planning process by identifying the target audience(s). Next they establish communication objectives. Objectives often are to create awareness, inform the market, create desire, encourage purchase and trial, and/or build loyalty.

Marketers develop promotion budgets from rules of thumb such as the percentage-of-sales method, the competitive-parity method, and the objective-task method. They then decide on a push or a pull strategy and allocate monies from the total budget to various elements of the promotion mix.

Next marketers design the promotion mix by deciding how they can use advertising, sales promotion, personal selling, and public relations most effectively to communicate with different target audiences. The final step is to evaluate the effectiveness of the communication program in order to determine whether the plan is working.

Marketers today often opt for multichannel promotional strategies where they combine traditional advertising, sales promotion, and public relations activities with online buzz-building activities. Multichannel strategies boost the effectiveness of either online or offline strategies used alone and allow marketers to repeat their messages across various channels, thus strengthening brand awareness and providing more opportunities to convert customers.

Key Terms

hierarchy of effects, p. 367

top-down budgeting techniques, p. 369

percentage-of-sales method, p. 369

competitive-parity method, p. 369

bottom-up budgeting techniques, p. 369

objective-task method, p. 369

push strategy, p. 369

pull strategy, p. 370

AIDA model, p. 371

Chapter **Questions** and **Activities**

Questions: Test Your Knowledge

1. What is integrated marketing communication? What are multichannel promotional strategies? Why is word-of-mouth communication so important?
2. Describe the traditional communication model.
3. List the elements of the promotion mix and describe how they are used to deliver personal and mass appeals.
4. Explain the many-to-many communication model and why it is important for marketers today.
5. What is buzz? How do marketers practice buzz building?
6. What are some ethical problems in buzz marketing?
7. What is viral marketing? How do marketers use brand ambassador or brand evangelists?
8. What is social media? What are social networks? Describe Facebook, Twitter, virtual worlds, product review sites, mobile apps, and geospatial platforms.
9. List and explain the steps in promotion planning.
10. Explain the hierarchy of effects and how it is used in communication objectives.
11. Describe the major ways in which firms develop marketing communication budgets.
12. Describe push versus pull strategies. How are push and pull strategies useful in different stages of the product life cycle?

Activities: Apply What You've Learned

1. Assume you are the director of marketing for a firm that markets one of the following products.
   i. Environmentally friendly household cleaning supplies
   ii. Hand-made wooden toys for 2- to 5-year-old children
   iii. A line of designer book bags for students

You are developing a promotional plan. Develop suggestions for each of the following items.

a. Marketing communication objectives
b. A method for determining the communication budget
c. The use of a push strategy or a pull strategy
d. Elements of the traditional promotion mix you will use
e. Use of buzz-building and social media activities

Then, in a role-playing situation, present your recommendations to your boss.

2. Many firms today are using a variety of buzz-building activities to encourage word-of-mouth communication about their products. Select a product that you and your classmates might purchase. You might, for example, think about (1) a specialty coffee shop, (2) a night spot where you and your friends might hang out on the weekends, or (3) a local theme or amusement park.

For your selected product, develop ideas for at least three different buzz-building activities. Outline the details as to exactly how these activities would be implemented. Next, rank order the activities as to which you feel are the top three, and tell why you feel that way. Develop a report for your class on your ideas.

3. As a marketing consultant, you are frequently asked by clients to develop recommendations for marketing communication strategies. The traditional elements used include advertising, sales promotion, public relations, and personal selling. Which of these do you feel would be most effective for each of the following clients?

a. A company that provides cellular phone service
b. A hotel
c. A university
d. A new soft drink
e. A sports equipment company

4. Assume that you are a marketing consultant for one of the clients in question 3 above. You believe that the client would benefit from non-traditional marketing. Develop several ideas for buzz building and social-media tactics that you feel would be successful for the client.

5. First, schedule an appointment with your university's marketing communication or university relations department to discuss their communication program. You will probably want to ask them about

a. The target audiences for their communication program
b. The objectives of their communication program
c. The different types of traditional and nontraditional communication methods they use
d. Their use of social media
e. How they evaluate the effectiveness of their communication program(s)

Based on your discussions, develop a report that (1) provides a critique of the university's communication program and (2) makes recommendations for improvement.

6. More and more firms are engaged in multichannel promotional programs. You can learn about many of these by searching library or Internet sources. Some Internet sources that may be useful are

Brandchannel.com
Adweek.com (*Adweek* magazine)
NYTimes.com (*New York Times*)
Adage.com (*Advertising Age* magazine)

Gather information on one or more multichannel promotional programs. Develop a report that describes the program(s) and makes suggestions for how it/they might be improved.

Marketing Metrics Exercise

One of the important benefits of social media such as Facebook and Twitter is that they allow marketers to learn what consumers are saying about their brand—and about the competition. To better understand that process, you can research what consumers are saying about a brand on Twitter.

1. Select a brand or a product category to study. If you are doing a marketing plan project for your marketing course, you may use that product. If not, choose a brand or product that you use—or one that you dislike.
2. Go to **Twitter.com**. Search for the product. Keep a record of the results. You might want to categorize the results in some way such as the categories listed below. Of course, you may be able to develop even better categories based on your product and the specific characteristics of the product.

a. Number of tweets that are positive (and negative) about the benefits of the product
b. Number of tweets that are positive (and negative) about the style or looks of the product
c. Number of tweets that are positive (and negative) about the quality of the product
d. Number of tweets that are positive (and negative) about using the product
e. Number of tweets that ask questions

Choices: What Do You Think?

1. Some buzz marketing activities engage buzz "agents" to tell their friends about a product, ask store managers to stock the product, and in other ways purposefully create word-of-mouth. Are these activities ethical?
2. There is increasing concern about consumer privacy on social networking sites such as Facebook. How do you feel about privacy on social networks? Is allowing personal information to be available to others without a user's specific permission unethical? Should the network owners do more to protect users' privacy? Should there be greater government regulation or should the sites be free to develop as they want to meet the needs of users? How much responsibility should users accept in protecting their own private information?
3. Marketing seems to be moving at breakneck speed toward greater use of the Internet. Where do you think this is headed? Will social media become even more important in the future? Will some types of social media grow in popularity and usefulness to marketers while others decline? What are the major factors in the growth or decline of an individual social media site?
4. Many companies are using brand ambassadors or brand evangelists to spread the word about their product. For what types of products do you think brand ambassadors are likely to be most useful? When would they be less useful? Would you be willing to be a brand ambassador for a product? If so, which product(s)? If not, why not?
5. Recently Twitter has joined other Internet sites in selling preferred positions on the site to generate revenue. Do you feel that such revenue-generating activities make sites such as Twitter less attractive? If you know that the top

comments on a site have their positions because firms paid for them, are you likely to change your use of the sites? Are there other ways that an Internet site such as Twitter can generate revenue?

6. While marketers are spending less in mass media advertising today than in previous times, TV, radio, magazine, and newspaper advertising remains an important means of communicating with customers for many products. What products do you think most benefit from mass media advertising? Why is this so? Do you feel traditional advertising will continue to decline in importance as a means for marketing communication or will it rebound in the future?

Miniproject: Learn by Doing

This miniproject is designed to help you understand how important word-of-mouth marketing is to consumers like yourself.

1. Ask several of your classmates to participate in a focus-group discussion about how they communicate with others about products. Some questions you might ask are the following:

   a. What products that you buy do you discuss with others at least from time to time?
   b. What experiences have you had discussing products face-to-face with others?
   c. What experiences have you had discussing products or reading comments of others about products on blogs, social networks, or other Internet sites?
   d. What are your experiences with product-related Web sites? Do you participate in games and entertainment opportunities on product-related Web sites?
   e. How do you think firms could improve their Web sites to provide more information for you?

2. Make a presentation of your findings and to your class.

Marketing in **Action** Case

Real Choices at American Express

What do Robert DeNiro, Ellen DeGeneres, Tiger Woods, Kate Winslet, and Laird Hamilton have in common? Let's see, Robert DeNiro is one of the greatest living actors; Ellen DeGeneres is a famous comedienne; Tiger Woods is arguably the best golfer ever; Kate Winslet is a multiple Academy Award nominee; and Laird Hamilton is perhaps the greatest surfer who ever lived. However, being famous and best in their fields are not the only things these folks have in common. They also all carry the American Express credit card and have appeared in television or print commercials to promote the card in the company's "My Life, My Card" campaign.

The fast pace of today's busy lifestyles and the rapid changes in information technology mean that, more than ever, companies like American Express have to rely on the familiar faces of celebrities to get its messages across. In late 2004, American Express started to feature famous and recognizable people as attractive spokespersons in the "My Life, My Card" advertising campaign in an attempt to capture the attention of current and potential consumers. Each of the AMEX ads included brief biographical information on the celebrity such as where they live, profession, greatest triumphs or greatest disappointments, and basic philosophy on life. The final point of each ad showed how the American Express card helps enable individuals to pursue what is important to them. American Express sought to communicate to its current and potential customers that they are just like these celebrities—simply trying to live life at its best. So, the slogan of "My Life, My Card" was perfect for the ad campaign. Consumers loved the ads.

Unfortunately for American Express, its "My Life, My Card" advertising campaign had some serious competition. Visa had been running ads for some time with the slogan of "Life takes Visa," which is a clever variation on Amex's campaign theme. American Express's other main competitor, MasterCard, was using its "Priceless" theme commercials that are aimed at encouraging customers to use the card to create priceless moments.

In the end, however, the "My Life, My Card" campaign, while well-liked, really wasn't working. Measures of customer loyalty showed that American Express was first in its product category in 1997, but by 2007, the American Express card was fifth, trailing Discover, Capital One, Visa, and MasterCard.

So in 2007, American Express replaced its "My Life, My Card" ads with a campaign that that presented a productoriented approach rather than the general image-oriented approach. New ads asked consumers the question, "Are you a cardmember?"

Historically, American Express has not switched campaigns quickly. The "Do you know me?" campaign ran from 1974 to 1987 and is still a well-known advertising saying. "Membership has its privileges" was used from 1987 to 1996, and the "Do More" campaign ran from 1996 to 2004. With only three campaigns in thirty years, how could consumers respond to this quick change of focus? Was American Express risking confusing consumers about American Express's positioning? And what if the new "Are you a cardmember?" campaign didn't improve loyalty ratings. Should American Express move quickly to develop still another new campaign or stick with this one?

You Make the Call

1. What is the decision facing American Express?
2. What factors are important in understanding this decision situation?
3. What are the alternatives?
4. What decision(s) do you recommend?
5. What are some ways to implement your recommendation?

Based on: Brian Steinberg, "Now Showing: Clustered Ad Spots on Television," *Wall Street Journal*, February 15, 2006, B3; Business Wire Inc., "American Express Launches the Restaurant Partnership Program with Savings, Access and Information," *Business Wire*, June 8, 2006; Centaur Communications Ltd., "Amex Expands Tourist Podcast After Turin Olympics Success," *New Media Age*, March 2, 2006, 2; Dan Sewell, "Companies Use Online Magazines to Woo Customers," *Associated Press Financial Wire*, January 2, 2006; Sentido Comun, "American Express Launches New Promotion Campaign in Mexico," *Latin American News Digest*, February 14, 2006; Stuart Elliott, "American Express Gets Specific and Asks, 'Are You a Cardmember?'" *New York Times*, April 6, 2007, http://www.nytimes.com/2007/04/06/business/media/06adco.html?scp=7&sq=american+express+marketing&st=nyt (accessed on April 14).

One-to-Many:
Advertising, Public Relations, and Consumer Sales Promotion

Marc Brownstein

Profile | Info

▼ A **Decision Maker** at Brownstein Group Brand Communication

Marc Brownstein is president and CEO of Brownstein Group Brand Communication. He went to his first client meeting at the age of 3 when his father, founder of what was then Brownstein Advertising, had unexpected babysitting duties and brought his son along. After graduating from Penn State, Marc spent most of his early years at Ogilvy & Mather, becoming one of the youngest members of the agency's new business development team. He has created award-winning campaigns for AT&T, American Express, *Sports Illustrated*, Hershey Foods, Hallmark, and Campbell Soup Company. In 1989, Brownstein joined the firm his father founded and assumed the responsibilities of creative director and later, president and CEO of Brownstein Group (BG). The agency has grown fivefold since Marc took over the agency's leadership, and BG is considered an innovator in digital advertising and social media. The agency's clients include Microsoft, IKEA, Gore-Tex, and Comcast.

Marc serves on the board of directors of the National Multiple Sclerosis Society; the American Association of Advertising Agencies (AAAA); Philly Ad Club; and the Young Presidents' Organization (YPO Philadelphia and YPO International). He speaks regularly before industry groups and is a blogger for *Advertising Age* magazine. The Boy Scouts of America honored Marc in 2007 with its annual Good Scout Award for his community and business leadership. Penn State also named him an "Alumni Fellow" in 2009, the highest honor awarded by the Alumni Association.

💬 Marc's Info ✏️

What do I do when I'm not working?
A) Spend time with my family and get some form of exercise: working out at the gym, biking, golf, tennis.

First job out of school?
A) Copywriter.

Career high?
A) Winning the Microsoft business when all odds were against us.

A job-related mistake I wish I hadn't made?
A) Waiting too long to fire a high-level executive.

Business book I'm reading now?
A) *The Outliers*, by Malcolm Gladwell.

My hero?
A) Steve Jobs—he changed how we live.

My motto to live by?
A) 1. Never discount an underdog. 2. Don't listen when others say the odds are against you. 3. Always remember that dreams DO come true.

What drives me?
A) Winning.

My management style?
A) I give people the opportunity to be entrepreneurial, unless they prove otherwise.

Don't do this when interviewing with me?
A) Make the mistake of not visiting our company's Web site first.

My pet peeve?
A) People who don't make eye contact when speaking to me.

Here's my problem...

In the first quarter of 2010 one of Marc's clients (a large consumer communications company) was under siege. Its primary competitor was relentlessly attacking the company with clever advertising in major markets across the United States that took direct aim at a new product the client had launched.

Marc's agency took exception to these unfair attacks and his account team proactively approached the client with three possible responses. Each of these solutions was based on a strategic direction the agency formulated. The group proposed a multi-pronged counterattack on multiple platforms including TV spots, outdoor billboards, print ads, online banner ads, and a landing page for the client's Web site.

The decision to develop these options was a risky one since the client had not requested the work and there was no budget provided to lay out these solutions. If the client didn't approve the work, Marc's agency would have invested over $200,000 worth of services for which it would not be compensated.

Still, Marc felt the competitor's campaign demanded an aggressive response. He created three integrated teams within the agency; each included creatives, PR specialists, strategists, and account managers. He gave each team 24 hours to propose an idea. Each team then presented its idea.

Things to remember

Marc and his team need to define their client's image and clearly show how it differs from competing brands. They have a variety of possible communications tools they might use to accomplish this.

The team needs to counterattack in response to a competitor's messages. They need to decide how aggressive they should be and whether they should "go negative."

As consumers increasingly become involved in spreading messages about the brands they like and don't like, many marketers try to harness this power to their own advantage. However, this strategy can backfire if customers aren't motivated enough to participate or even worse if they spread negative opinions to others.

2 Option

Fire back. This concept took direct aim at the competition's brand name and product claims. The messages mocked the rival's brand name, and they aimed to create doubt in consumers' minds about whether their product really possessed the supposedly superior product benefits it claimed. This was a very hard-hitting campaign that was also highly memorable—but it also posed a bigger risk. A direct attack response was not typical of the client's company culture; they didn't believe in starting ad wars that duked it out between two brands (like Coke vs. Pepsi). This aggressive approach would draw a lot of attention to the client and probably launch a bitter battle with the rival. However, the team argued that the competitor was already firing at them so they had no choice but to respond forcefully.

3 Option

Launch a guerrilla marketing strategy that attacked the rival more subtly than a major ad campaign. The idea was to stage a mock product comparison on the streets of various U.S. cities. Consumers would compare both products, while hidden cameras videotaped their reactions. The team intended to use this footage to launch a viral campaign that encouraged people to share the clips with their friends via *YouTube* and also post them on the client's Web site. Ads would follow to promote the mock comparisons; these would provide a link to the videos, and a strong PR campaign would work in tandem to drum up awareness of the clips among the public. The team believed this approach would send the message that the client's product is superior—but that people should draw their own conclusions rather than let advertising draw it for them. This was clearly an unconventional campaign that might make the client a bit nervous; but then again the team knew that the client wanted to ramp up its brand's "cool factor." However, the idea's success depended on the quality of the videotaped reactions people would provide. If they weren't as provocative as the team hoped, they wouldn't generate much buzz and the campaign wouldn't go viral after all.

Now, put yourself in Marc's shoes: Which option would you choose, and why?

Marc considered his **Options** 1·2·3

1 Option

Clearly define the new product. This campaign focused solely on defining exactly what the client's new product is and why it's better than the competing product. The team believed that the current advertising—which another ad agency had created—didn't do a very good job of explaining the product. The messages consumers were seeing left them confused about just what the product does and why it's superior to the competition. To respond to the rival's attack, new messages needed to inject clarity into the information people were getting. However, the client might not agree with this assessment because they had already approved the current campaign. The team's judgment was subjective; there was no formal research that actually demonstrated whether people were confused by the campaign. There's always a risk when an agency has to tell a client that its current advertising doesn't work very well.

You Choose

Which **Option** would you choose, and **why**?
1. ☐YES ☐NO   2. ☐YES ☐NO   3. ☐YES ☐NO

See what **option** Marc chose on **page 412** ➡

1

OBJECTIVE

Tell what advertising is, describe the major types of advertising, and discuss some of the criticisms of advertising.
(pp. 380–386)

Advertising: The Image of Marketing

Advertising is so much a part of marketing that many people think of the two as the same thing. Remember, product, price, and distribution strategies are just as important as marketing communications. And, as we saw in Chapter 12, there are many ways to get a message out to a target audience in addition to advertising. Make no mistake—traditional advertising is still important, even during hard economic times. In 2009, U.S. marketers spent just over $125 billion on advertising, down 12.3 percent from $142.9 billion in 2008.[1] As a result, U.S. advertising and marketing firms cut 7.9% of their staff or over 58,000 jobs.[2]

In today's competitive environment even the big guys like Procter & Gamble and General Motors are rethinking how much they want to invest in pricey ad campaigns as they search for alternative ways to get their messages out there. Indeed, while total ad spending declined, spending on Internet advertising increased 7.3 percent among all advertisers and a whopping 34 percent among the top 100 U.S. advertisers.[3]

One thing is sure—as the media landscape continues to change, so will advertising. Sales of Internet-ready and 3-D TVs are booming, as is the number of households with digital video recorders (DVRs) that let viewers skip through the commercials. Nielsen reported that in the first quarter of 2010, 138 million consumers watched video on the Internet and 20.3 million viewed mobile video.[4]

With all of this bleak news, is traditional advertising dead? Don't write any obituaries yet. Mass media communications are still the best way to reach a large audience. For that reason, producers of FMCGs (fast-moving consumer goods) such as P&G and Unilever will continue to rely on these traditional channels of communication to reach their customers. They will just be more creative as they mix-and-match different platforms to reach various target markets.

Indeed, wherever we turn advertising bombards us. Television commercials, radio spots, banner ads, and huge billboards scream, "Buy me!" Advertising, as we said in Chapter 12, is nonpersonal communication an identified sponsor pays for that uses mass media to persuade or inform an audience.[5] Advertising can be fun, glamorous, annoying, informative—and hopefully an effective way to let consumers know what a company is selling and why people should run out and buy it *today*. Advertising is also a potent force that creates desire for products; it transports us to imaginary worlds where the people are happy, beautiful, or rich. In this way, advertising allows the organization to communicate its message in a favorable way and to repeat the message as often as it deems necessary to have an impact on receivers.

A long-running Virginia Slims cigarettes advertising campaign proclaimed, "You've come a long way, baby!" We can say the same about advertising itself. Advertising has been with us a long time. In ancient Greece and Rome, ad messages appeared on walls, were etched on stone tablets, or were shouted by criers, interspersed among announcements of successful military battles or government proclamations. Would the ancients have be-

Check out chapter 13 **Study Map** on page 412

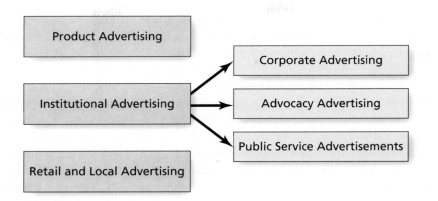

Figure 13.1 📷 *Snapshot* | Types of Advertising

Advertisements that an organization runs can take many different forms.

lieved that today we get messages about products almost wherever we are, whether we cruise down the road or around the Web? Some of us even get advertising messages on our mobile phones or in public restrooms. It's hard to find a place where ads don't try to reach us.

Types of Advertising

Although almost every business advertises, some industries are bigger spenders than others. Retail advertising tops the list with spending on measured advertising (magazines, newspapers, radio, television, and Internet) of over $15 billion in 2009, down 11.5 percent from 2008. The automotive industry with its recent problems cut measured ad spending 23 percent to a little over $12 billion in 2009. In contrast, the telecommunications industry's 2009 spending was up 1.5 percent from the previous year to $10.2 billion while medicine and remedies and financial services finished up the top five ad spenders with a little over $8 billion each, down 4.9 and 16.4 percent respectively.[6] Because they spend so much on advertising, marketers must decide which type of ad will work best to get their money's worth given their organizational and marketing goals. As 📷 Figure 13.1 shows, the advertisements an organization runs can take many forms, so let's review the most common kinds.

Product Advertising

When people give examples of advertising, they are likely to recall the provocative poses in Victoria's Secret ads or the cheeky reminders from the GEICO gecko. These are examples of **product advertising**, where the message focuses on a specific good or service. While not all advertising features a product or a brand, most of the advertising we see and hear is indeed product advertising.

Institutional Advertising

Rather than a focus on a specific brand, **institutional advertising** promotes the activities, personality, or point of view of an organization or company. **Corporate advertising** promotes the company as a whole instead of the firm's individual products. Some firms, in fact, do not advertise specific products at all but have built their businesses with only corporate advertising. Cisco, for example, uses corporate advertising to brand itself as "the human network." Other firms like Dow Chemical Co. use corporate advertising in addition to product advertising. Dow boosted its brand equity 25 percent through its "Human Element" corporate advertising campaign that said it is the "human element" that can solve some of the world's problems such as climate change and lack of clean water.[7]

product advertising
Advertising messages that focus on a specific good or service.

institutional advertising
Advertising messages that promote the activities, personality, or point of view of an organization or company.

corporate advertising
Advertising that promotes the company as a whole instead of a firm's individual products.

We make it like you'd make it.

The all-natural goodness of ripe tomatoes and fresh basil. Just what you'd put in your homemade sauce.

CLASSICO

Product advertising focuses on a specific good or service.

advocacy advertising
A type of public service advertising where an organization seeks to influence public opinion on an issue because it has some stake in the outcome.

public service advertisements (PSAs)
Advertising run by the media for not-for-profit organizations or to champion a particular cause without charge.

advertising campaign
A coordinated, comprehensive plan that carries out promotion objectives and results in a series of advertisements placed in media over a period of time.

Marc Brownstein

APPLYING ▽ Advertising Campaign

Marc's agency is responsible for creating a series of messages over a period of time for its telecommunications client. ➡

limited-service agency
An agency that provides one or more specialized services, such as media buying or creative development.

full-service agency
An agency that provides most or all of the services needed to mount a campaign, including research, creation of ad copy and art, media selection, and production of the final messages.

account executive (account manager)
A member of the account management department who supervises the day-to-day activities of the account and is the primary liaison between the agency and the client.

Some institutional messages state an organization's position on an issue to sway public opinion, a strategy we call **advocacy advertising**. For example, U.S. governors joined together in a campaign to get Congress to pass climate change legislation. The campaign included a 30-second TV commercial starring three governors, including California governor and *Terminator* movie star Arnold Schwarzenegger.[8]

Other messages take the form of **public service advertisements (PSAs)** that the media run free of charge. These messages promote not-for-profit organizations that serve society in some way, or they champion an issue such as increasing literacy or discouraging drunk driving. Advertising agencies often take on one or more public service campaigns on a *pro bono* (for free, not the U2 singer) basis. Little League baseball aired a 15-second PSA on ESPN that featured a 10-year old at the plate. In the stands the father yells, "Come on, son. Hit the ball." The boy rolls his eyes, turns around to face his dad, and yells back, "DAD, IS THAT THE BEST YOU CAN DO?! THAT'S PATHETIC. I DON'T EVEN KNOW WHY YOU BOTHER SHOWING UP! WHY CAN'T YOU BE MORE LIKE JIMMY'S DAD?! ALL THE OTHER PARENTS ARE GOING TO LAUGH AT YOU! YOU MAKE ME SICK!" The ad ends with a supertitle, "Now you know how it feels. Just let them play."[9]

Retail and Local Advertising

Both major retailers and small, local businesses advertise to encourage customers to shop at a specific store or use a local service. Local advertising informs us about store hours, location, and products that are available or on sale. These ads may take the form of popup ads online or perhaps newspaper circulars that fill out your Sunday newspaper.

Who Creates Advertising?

An **advertising campaign** is a coordinated, comprehensive plan that carries out promotion objectives and results in a series of advertisements placed in various media over a period of time. Although a campaign may be based around a single ad idea, most use multiple messages with all ads in the campaign having the same look-and-feel. Some campaigns run for only a short period of times while others remain with us for many years. Take, for example, GEICO's advertising campaigns. In recent years the insurance company has mounted a total of four different advertising campaigns; the messages often run simultaneously. These four are (1) the GEICO gecko campaign, (2) the caveman campaign that even spawned a short-lived TV sitcom ("so easy a caveman can do it"), (3) the "money you could be saving" campaigns with the googly-eyed dollar bills, and (4) the "Rhetorical Questions" campaign that includes ads featuring Charlie Daniels, Elmer Fudd, and the Waltons. While all of these campaigns promote the same company and its products and all use the same tag line, "Fifteen minutes could save you 15 percent or more on car insurance," they are each creatively distinct. Each includes multiple ads (there have been at least 22 caveman TV commercials), but each ad is obviously part of a coordinated campaign.

Although some firms create their own advertising in-house, in many cases several specialized companies work together to develop an advertising campaign. Typically the firm retains one or more outside *advertising agencies* to oversee this process. A **limited-service agency** provides one or more specialized services, such as media buying or creative development. In contrast, a **full-service agency** supplies most or all of the services a campaign requires, including research, creation of ad copy and art, media selection, and production of the final messages. The largest global agencies are Dentsu (based in Japan), McCann Worldwide Group, BBDO Worldwide, and DDB Worldwide, each with over 2 billion in billings.[10]

A campaign has many elements; it requires the services of many different people to pull it all together. Big or small, an advertising agency hires a range of specialists to craft a message and make the communication concept a reality:

- *Account management:* The **account executive**, or account manager, is the "soul" of the operation. This person supervises the day-to-day activities on the account and is the primary liaison between the agency and the client. The account executive has to ensure that the client is happy while verifying that people within the agency execute the desired strategy. The **account planner** combines research and account strategy to act as the voice of the consumer in creating effective advertising. It is the job of the account planner to use market data, qualitative research, and product knowledge to become intimately familiar with the consumer and to translate what customers are looking for to the creative teams who create the ads.

- **Creative services:** *Creatives* are the "heart" of the communication effort. These are the people who actually dream up and produce the ads. They include the agency's creative director, copywriters, and art director. Creatives are the artists who breathe life into marketing objectives and craft messages that (hopefully) will interest consumers.

- **Research and marketing services:** *Researchers* are the "brains" of the campaign. They collect and analyze information that will help account executives develop a sensible strategy. They assist creatives in getting consumer reactions to different versions of ads or by providing copywriters with details on the target group.

- *Media planning:* The **media planner** is the "legs" of the campaign. He helps to determine which communication vehicles are the most effective and recommends the most efficient means to deliver the ad by deciding where, when, and how often it will appear.

As we saw in Chapter 12, more and more agencies practice *integrated marketing communication (IMC)*, in which advertising is only one element of a total communication plan. Because IMC includes more than just advertising, client teams composed of people from account services, creative services, media planning, research, public relations, sales promotion, and direct marketing may work together to develop a plan that best meets the communication needs of each client.

User-Generated Advertising Content

The latest promotional craze is to let your customers actually create your advertising for you. **User-generated content (UGC),** also known as **consumer-generated media (CGM),** includes the millions of online consumer comments, opinions, advice, consumer-to-consumer discussions, reviews, photos, images, videos, podcasts and webcasts, and product-related stories available to other consumers through digital technology. Marketers that embrace this strategy understand that it's okay to let people have fun with their products. For example, join the millions of others who checked out the infamous YouTube videos where "mad scientists" mix Mentos candies with Diet Coke for explosive results (such as **http://www.youtube.com/watch?v5hKoB0MHVBvM**).

Marketers need to monitor (and sometimes encourage) UGC for two reasons. First, consumers are more likely to trust messages from fellow consumers than what companies tell them. In fact, they're more likely to say they "trust completely" product information they receive from other consumers than from any other source.[11] Second, we've already seen in the last chapter how social media is proliferating everywhere; a person who searches online for a company or product name is certain to access any number of blogs, forums, homegrown commercials, or online complaint sites that the product manufacturer had nothing to do with. Some companies resist this trend when they restrict access to their material or even sue consumers who talk about them because they fear they will lose control over their brand messages. They really need to get over it and recognize that in our digital world their messages (like your Facebook page) are almost impossible to control. In Web 2.0, you're either on the train or under it!

To take advantage of this phenomenon, some marketers encourage consumers to contribute their own **do-it-yourself (DIY) ads.** When Frito-Lay sponsored a contest for 2010 Super Bowl ads, two of the winners, "House Rules" and "Underdog," turned out to be the

account planner
A member of the account management department who combines research and account strategy to act as the voice of the consumer in creating effective advertising.

creative services
The agency people (creative director, copywriters, and art director) who dream up and produce the ads.

research and marketing services
Advertising agency department that collects and analyzes information that will help account executives develop a sensible strategy and assist creatives in getting consumer reactions to different versions of ads.

media planners
Agency personnel who determine which communication vehicles are the most effective and efficient to deliver the ad.

user-generated content (UGC) or consumer-generated media (CGM)
Online consumer comments, opinions, advice and discussions, reviews, photos, images, videos, podcasts, webcasts, and product, related stories available to other consumers.

do-it-yourself (DIY) ads
Product ads that are created by consumers.

Marc Brownstein

APPLYING ▼ Consumer-Generated Media

Marc's team needs to decide if it wants to rely on consumers to help it define and spread the word about the client. ➧

most watched ads of the game.[12] In its "Priceless" campaign, MasterCard invited consumers to write their own ad copy for two filmed commercials—all entries had to end with the word "Priceless." Converse allowed customers to send homemade commercials to its Web site, then ran several of them on television.[13] Other companies that have experimented with do-it-yourself (DIY) advertising are L'Oréal ("You Make the Commercial"), JetBlue ("Travel Stories"), and McDonald's ("Global Casting").[14]

For advertisers do-it-yourself advertising offers several benefits. First, consumer-generated spots cost only one-quarter to one-third as much as professional TV and Internet ads—about $60,000 compared to the $350,000 or more to produce a traditional 30-second spot. This can be especially important for smaller businesses and emerging brands. Equally important, even to large companies with deep pockets, is the feedback on how consumers see the brand and the chance to gather more creative ideas to tell the brand's story.[15]

crowdsourcing
A practice in which firms outsource marketing activities (such as selecting an ad) to a community of users.

Crowdsourcing is a practice in which firms outsource marketing activities (such as selecting an ad) to a community of users, that is, a crowd. When the D.C. Lottery created a new game with new ways to win, it decided to update its 28-year-old logo at the same time. To get the public involved and to select a logo that would be inviting to lottery "customers," the organization invited visitors to its Web site to vote on which of six logos they preferred.[16]

To get the ball rolling, an agency typically solicits ideas from online communities that people access because they are fans of a product or a specific brand. The idea behind crowdsourcing is that if you want to know what consumers think and what they like, the most logical thing to do is to ask them. First the agency shares a challenge with a large number of people who have varying degrees of expertise. Whether motivated by money, competition, or obsession, individuals then submit their solution to the problem.

Kraft, a global marketer of fast-moving-consumer goods including Lacta, a chocolate brand in Greece, recently enlisted a crowdsourcing technique to develop a branded film. Kraft first asked consumers to submit real love tales that might be the subject of a short film that would feature Lacta. A story about two strangers, a young soldier and a musician, meeting on a train was the winner out of the 1,307 real love tales submitted. Next Kraft used online polls for voters to select screen tests, names of characters, and costumes. The film created so much buzz that when Greece's #1 TV station ran the film for free, over 335,000 people watched it.[17]

Ethical Issues in Advertising

Advertising, more than any other part of marketing, has been sharply criticized for decades. Such criticism certainly may be based less on reality than on the high visibility of advertising and the negative attitudes of consumers who find ads an intrusion in their lives. The objections to advertising are similar to those some people have to marketing in general as we discussed in Chapter 1. Here are the main ones:

- *Advertising is manipulative:* Advertising causes people to behave like robots and do things against their will—to make purchases they would not otherwise make were it not for the ads. However, consumers are not robots. Since they are consciously aware of appeals made in advertising, they are free to choose whether to respond to an ad or not. Of course, consumers can and often do make bad decisions that advertising may influence, but that is not the same as manipulation.

- *Advertising is deceptive and untruthful:* Deceptive advertising means that an ad falsely represents the product and that consumers believe the false information and act on it. Indeed, there is some false or deceptive advertising, but as a whole advertisers try to present their brands in the best possible light while being truthful. In the United States, both government regulation and the industry itself strongly encourage honesty.

    To protect consumers from being misled, the Federal Trade Commission (FTC) has specific rules regarding unfair or deceptive advertising. Some deceptive ads make statements that can be proven false. For example, the FTC fined Volvo and its ad agency $150,000 each for an ad containing a "rigged" demonstration. The Volvo "Bear Food"

Ripped from the Headlines

Ethics/Sustainable Decisions in the Real World

Many consumers today are concerned about **greenwashing**; a practice in which companies promote their products as environmentally friendly when in truth the brand provides little ecological benefit. This practice may refer to a company that boasts in its corporate image advertising of the cutting-edge research it does to save the planet when in fact this work accounts for only a small fraction of its activities. Hotels claim they are "green" because they allow guests to choose not to have clean sheets and clean towels in their rooms every day. And grocery stores claim to be green because you can return your plastic bags there.

Critics of greenwashing single out Huggies Pure and Natural disposable diapers because the brand claims to be more environmentally friendly and safer for a baby. Its advertising claims that it offers parents the "pure bliss of a diaper that

includes gentle, natural materials." However, the only real difference in the Pure and Natural Huggies from the original is a piece of organically grown cotton fabric that is on the outside of the diaper, not where it touches the baby's skin.

But are such claims ethical? Are consumers being deceived into buying products that they think make a real difference to the environment when in reality the products are not substantially different? Those who are accused of greenwashing would argue that even small efforts toward "going green" are important and that such claims are justified. If you were a marketer, would you try to promote your product as more environmentally friendly even though differences between your product and those of the competition are very minor?

ETHICS CHECK: ✎
Find out what other students taking this course **would do** and **why** on **www .mypearsonmarketinglab .com**

If you worked for an advertising agency, would you approve an ad that implies a product is environmentally friendly when there is little to support such claims?

☐ **YES** ☐ **NO**

---

ad campaign showed a monster truck running over a row of cars and crushing all but the Volvo station wagon. The Volvos, however, had been structurally reinforced, while the structural supports in some of the other cars had been cut.[18]

In addition to fining firms for deceptive advertising, the FTC also has the power to require firms to run **corrective advertising**, messages that clarify or qualify previous claims.[19] Yaz, a best-selling birth control pill by Bayer, was accused of overstating its ability to improve women's moods and clear up acne and not adequately communicating the drug's health risks. As a result the Food and Drug Administration and the attorneys general of 27 states required Bayer to spend $20 million over six years in corrective advertising, telling consumers that they should not take the pill to cure pimples or premenstrual syndrome.

Other ads, although not illegal, may create a biased impression of products when they use **puffery**—claims of superiority that neither sponsors nor critics of the ads can prove are true or untrue. For example, Nivea bills itself as "the world's number 1 name in skin care," Neutrogena claims that its cream cleanser produces "the deepest feeling clean," and DuPont says that its Stainmaster Carpet is "a creation so remarkable, it's practically a miracle."

Does this mean that puffery is an unethical marketing practice? Not really. In fact, both advertisers and consumers generally accept puffery as a normal part of the advertising game. Although a little exaggeration may be reasonable, in most cases the goal is to create marketing communications that are both honest and that present the products in the most positive way possible. This approach works to the firm's advantage in the long run since it prevents consumers from becoming overly cynical about the claims it makes.

- *Advertising is offensive and in bad taste:* To respond to this criticism, we need to recognize that what is offensive or in bad taste to one person may not be to another. Yes, some TV commercials are offensive to some people, but then news and program content in the media can be and often is even more explicit or in poor taste. While advertisers seek to go the distance using humor, sex appeals, or fear appeals to get audiences' attention, most shy away from presenting messages that offend the very audience they want to buy their products.

- *Advertising creates and perpetuates stereotypes:* Some advertising critics assert that advertising portrays certain groups of consumers in negative ways. For example, advertising has portrayed women more often as homemakers than as industry leaders. While there is evidence that advertising (and media program content) is guilty of perpetuating stereotypes, it is important to recognize that these stereotypes already exist in the culture. Advertising doesn't create them so much as it reflects them.

greenwashing
A practice in which companies promote their products as environmentally friendly when in truth the brand provides little ecological benefit.

corrective advertising
Advertising that clarifies or qualifies previous deceptive advertising claims.

puffery
Claims made in advertising of product superiority that cannot be proven true or untrue.

- *Advertising causes people to buy things they don't really need:* The truth of this criticism depends on how you define a "need." If we believe that all consumers need is the basic functional benefits of products—the transportation a car provides, the nutrition we get from food, and the clean hair we get from shampoo—then advertising may be guilty as charged. If, on the other hand, you think you need a car that projects a cool image, food that tastes fantastic, and a shampoo that makes your hair shine and smell ever so nice, then advertising is just a vehicle that communicates those more intangible benefits.

2 Develop the Advertising Campaign

OBJECTIVE

Describe the process of developing an advertising campaign and how marketers evaluate advertising.
(pp. 386–402)

The advertising campaign is about much more than creating a cool ad and hoping people notice it. The campaign should be intimately related to the organization's overall communication goals. That means the firm (and its outside agency if it uses one) must have a good idea of whom it wants to reach, what it will take to appeal to this market, and where and when it should place its messages. Let's examine the steps required to do this, as  Figure 13.2 shows.

Step 1: Understand the Target Audience

The best way to communicate with an audience is to understand as much as possible about them and what turns them on and off. An ad that uses the latest "hip-hop" slang may relate to teenagers but not to their parents—and this strategy may backfire if the ad copy reads like an "ancient" 40-year-old trying to sound like a 20-year-old.

As we discussed in Chapter 7, marketers often identify the target audience for an advertising campaign from research. Researchers (like Jim Multari, the director of research for PBS Kids Sprout) try to get inside the customer's head to understand just how to create a message that he will understand and to which he will respond. For example, an account executive working on a campaign for Pioneer Stereo was assigned to hang out with guys who were likely prospects to buy car stereos. His observations resulted in an advertising campaign that incorporated the phrases they actually used to describe their cars: "My car is my holy temple, my love shack, my drag racer of doom."[20]

Figure 13.2 *Process* | Steps to Develop an Advertising Campaign

Developing an advertising campaign includes a series of steps that will ensure that the advertising meets communication objectives.

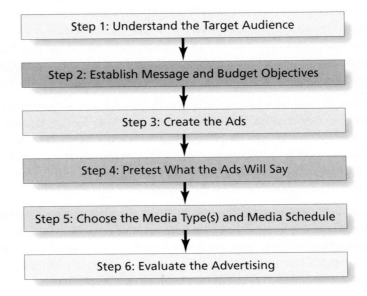

Step 2: Establish Message and Budget Objectives

Advertising objectives should be consistent with the overall communication plan. That means that both the underlying message and its costs need to relate to what the marketer is trying to say about the product and what the marketer is willing or able to spend. Thus, advertising objectives generally will include objectives for both the message and the budget.

Set Message Objectives

As we noted earlier, because advertising is the most visible part of marketing, many people assume that marketing *is* advertising. In truth, advertising alone is quite limited in what it can achieve. What advertising *can* do is inform, persuade, and remind. Accordingly, some advertisements are informational—they aim to make the customer knowledgeable about features of the product or how to use it. At other times, advertising seeks to persuade consumers to like a brand or to prefer one brand over the competition. But many, many ads simply aim to keep the name of the brand in front of the consumer—reminding consumers that this brand is the one to choose when they look for a soft drink or a laundry detergent.

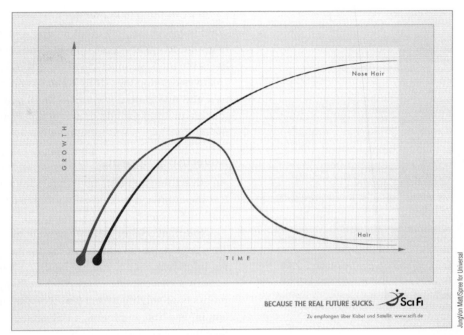

This German ad speaks to many of the viewers the SciFi channel hopes to reach.

Set Budget Objectives

Advertising is expensive. Procter & Gamble, which leads all U.S. companies in advertising expenditures, spends almost $5 billion per year while second- and third-place ad spenders AT&T and General Motors each spend well over $3 billion each.[21]

An objective of many firms is to allocate a percentage of the overall communication budget to advertising, depending on how much and what type of advertising the company can afford. The major approaches and techniques to setting overall promotional budgets, such as the percentage-of-sales and objective-task methods we discussed in Chapter 12, also set advertising budgets.

Major corporations like General Motors advertise heavily on expensive media such as television to promote multiple products throughout the year. Other companies may be more selective, and smaller firms may want to put their advertising dollars into cheaper media outlets such as direct mail or trade publications. Or a firm may decide to blow its entire advertising budget in one grand gesture—as the Web site host company **GoDaddy.com** does when it buys airtime during the Super Bowl.

Step 3: Create the Ads

The creation of the advertising begins when an agency formulates a **creative strategy**, which gives the advertising "creatives" (art directors, copywriters, photographers, and others) the direction and inspiration they need to begin the creative process. The strategy is summarized in a written document known as a **creative brief**, a rough blueprint that guides but does not restrict the creative process. It provides only the most relevant information and insights about the marketing situation, the advertising objective, the competition, the advertising target and, most importantly, the message that the advertising must deliver.

creative strategy
The process that turns a concept into an advertisement.

creative brief
A guideline or blueprint for the marketing communication program that guides the creative process.

It's one thing to know *what* a company wants to say about itself or its products and another to figure out *how* to say it. The role of the creative brief is to provide the spark that helps the ad agency come up with "the big idea," the visual and/or verbal concept that delivers the message in an attention-getting, memorable, and relevant manner. From this the creatives develop the ads by combining already-known facts, words, pictures, and ideas in new and unexpected ways. Specifically, to come up with finished ads, they must consider four elements of the ads shown in 📷 Figure 13.3: the appeal, the format, the tonality, and the creative tactics and techniques.[22]

Advertising Appeals

advertising appeal
The central idea or theme of an advertising message.

An **advertising appeal** is the central idea of the ad and the basis of the advertising messages. It is the approach used to influence the consumer. Generally, we think of appeals as informational or emotional.

Informational or rational appeals relate to consumers' practical need for the product. They emphasize the features of the product and/or the benefits we receive from using it. Often informational appeals are based on a **unique selling proposition (USP)** that gives consumers a clear, single-minded reason why the advertiser's product is better than other products at solving a problem. For example, "M&Ms melt in your mouth, not in your hands" is a USP. In general, a USP strategy is effective if there is some clear product advantage that consumers can readily identify and that is important to them.

unique selling proposition (USP)
An advertising appeal that focuses on one clear reason why a particular product is superior.

Because consumers often buy products based on social or psychological needs, advertisers frequently use emotional appeals instead where they try to pull our heartstrings rather than make us think differently about a brand. Emotional appeals focus on an emotional or social benefit the consumer may receive from the product such as safety, love, excitement, pleasure, respect, or approval.

reminder advertising
Advertising aimed at keeping the name of a brand in people's minds to be sure consumers purchase the product as necessary.

Of course, not all ads fit into these two appeal categories. Well-established brands often use **reminder advertising** just to keep their name in people's minds or to be sure that consumers repurchase the product as necessary. For example, Arm & Hammer baking soda re-

Figure 13.3 📷 *Snapshot* | Creative Elements of Advertising
Creating good ads includes making decisions about the four different ad elements.

Creative Element	Element Options
Appeals	Rational (Unique Selling Proposition) Emotional Reminder Advertising Teaser Ads
Execution Formats	Comparison Demonstration Testimonial Slice of Life Lifestyle
Tonality	Straightforward Humor Dramatic Romantic Apprehension/Fear
Creative Tactics and Techniques	Animation and Art Celebrities Music, Jingles, and Slogans

minds us to replace the open box many of us keep in our refrigerators to absorb odors on a regular basis.

Sometimes advertisers use **teaser** or **mystery ads** to generate curiosity and interest in a to-be-introduced product. Teaser ads draw attention to an upcoming ad campaign without mentioning the product. Before the creative team can craft and polish the words and visuals to bring the big idea to life, they still must choose the most appropriate format and tonality of the advertising. We'll turn to those ideas next.

Execution Formats

Execution format describes the basic structure of the message. Some of the more common formats, sometimes used in combination, include:

- *Comparison:* A comparative advertisement explicitly names one or more competitors. Pizza Hut's recent "America's Favorite Pizza" spots claimed that consumers preferred its hand-tossed pizzas 2 to 1 over both number two Domino's and number three Papa John's. Ads showed rival pizza delivery drivers eating Pizza Hut pizza at the Pizza Hut driver's home. Papa John's countered with claims that its crust was made fresh while Pizza Hut's was frozen.[23]

  Comparative ads can be very effective, but there is a risk of turning off consumers who don't like the negative tone. While in many countries comparative advertising is illegal, it's a widely used tactic in the United States. This format is best for brands that have a smaller share of the market and for firms that can focus on a specific feature that makes them superior to a major brand. When market leaders use comparative advertising, there is the risk consumers will feel they are "picking on the little guy." One exception is the "cola wars" advertising by Coca-Cola and Pepsi. In the recent Pepsi Max ad which features the song "Why Can't We Be Friends?" by War, delivery drivers for Coke and Pepsi meet in a diner; the Coke driver samples Pepsi Max and prefers it.

- *Demonstration:* The ad shows a product "in action" to prove that it performs as claimed: "It slices, it dices!" Demonstration advertising is most useful when consumers are unable to identify important benefits except when they see the product in use.

- *Testimonial:* A celebrity, an expert, or a "man in the street" states the product's effectiveness. The use of a *celebrity endorser* is a common but expensive strategy.

- *Slice of life:* A *slice-of-life* format presents a (dramatized) scene from everyday life. Slice-of-life advertising can be effective for everyday products such as peanut butter and headache remedies that consumers may feel good about if they see "real" people buy and use them.

- *Lifestyle:* A *lifestyle* format shows a person or persons attractive to the target market in an appealing setting. The advertised product is "part of the scene," implying that the person who buys it will attain the lifestyle. For example, a commercial on MTV might depict a group of "cool" California skateboarders who take a break for a gulp of milk and say, "It does a body good."

Tonality

Tonality refers to the mood or attitude the message conveys. Some common tonalities include:

- *Straightforward:* Straightforward ads simply present the information to the audience in a clear manner. Informative ads are frequently used in radio but less often in TV.

Margin definitions

teaser or **mystery advertising**
Ads that generate curiosity and interest in a to-be-introduced product by drawing attention to an upcoming ad campaign without mentioning the product.

execution format
The basic structure of the message such as comparison, demonstration, testimonial, slice-of-life and lifestyle.

tonality
The mood or attitude the message conveys (straightforward, humor, dramatic, romantic, sexy, and apprehension/fear).

Humorous, witty or outrageous ads can be an effective way to break through advertising clutter.

FRESH STEP® is a registered trademark of the Clorox Pets Company. Used with permission.

Marc Brownstein

Marc's team must make a crucial decision regarding the "tone" of the messages it launches to combat a competitor's critical advertising. This tonality might be positive or negative, so they have to decide what kind of emotional response (if any) they want to arouse in current and potential subscribers. ⇒

- *Humor:* Humorous, witty or outrageous ads can be an effective way to break through advertising clutter. But humor can be tricky, because what is funny to one person may be offensive or stupid to another. Different cultures also have different senses of humor. A recent Reebok commercial showed women at a basketball game checking out the all-male cheerleading squad. The spot was witty, but people from countries that don't feature cheerleaders at sports events (you don't find too many pom-poms at soccer matches) might not "get it."

  Perhaps the major benefit of humorous advertising is that it attracts consumers' attention and leaves them with a pleasant feeling. Of course, humor in advertising can backfire. In the United Kingdom, a Renault Megane 225 ad that featured people in everyday situations shaking uncontrollably as the car passed was banned by the government's Office of Communications: Viewers complained that the ad mocked people with illnesses such as Parkinson's disease.[24]

- *Dramatic:* A dramatization, like a play, presents a problem and a solution in a manner that is often exciting and suspenseful—a fairly difficult challenge in 30 or 60 seconds.

- *Romantic:* Ads that present a romantic situation can be especially effective at getting consumers' attention and at selling products people associate with dating and mating. That's why fragrance ads often use a romantic format.

- *Sexy:* Some ads appear to sell sex rather than products. In a Guess jeans ad, a shirtless man lies near an almost shirtless woman. Ads such as these rely on sexuality to get consumers' attention. *Sex appeal* ads are more likely to be effective when there is a connection between the product and sex (or at least romance). For example, sex appeals will work well with a perfume but are less likely to be effective when you're trying to sell a lawn mower.

- *Apprehension/Fear:* Some ads highlight the negative consequences of *not* using a product. Some *fear appeal* ads focus on physical harm, while others try to create concern for social harm or disapproval. Mouthwash, deodorant, and dandruff shampoo makers and life insurance companies successfully use fear appeals. So do ads aimed at changing behaviors, such as messages discouraging drug use or encouraging safe sex. In general, fear appeals can be successful if the audience perceives there to be an appropriate level of intensity in the fear appeal. For example, horrible photos of teens lying on the highway following an auto accident can be quite effective in PSAs designed to persuade teens not to drink and drive, but they are likely to backfire if an insurance company tries to "scare" people into buying life insurance.

Courtesy of Procter & Gamble Co.

Gillette uses a romantic theme in China.

Creative Tactics and Techniques

In addition to ad formats and tonality, the creative process may also include a number of different creative tactics and techniques. Some of these are

- *Animation and art:* Not all ads are executed with film or photography. Sometimes a creative decision is made to use art, illustration, or animation to achieve the desired look of a print ad or TV commercial or to attract attention. For example, Coke used the popular Simpsons cartoon characters in its Super Bowl ads in 2010.[25]

- *Celebrities.* Sometimes they just appear in testimonials, or for endorsements such as Marie Osmond's pitches for NutriSystem. Other times using a celebrity is simply a casting decision—a technique to make an ad more interesting or appealing, such as when the actor Luke Wilson shows up in commercials for AT&T mobile phones.

- *Music, jingles and slogans.* **Jingles** are original words and music written specifically for advertising executions. Many of us remember classic ad jingles such as "I wish I were an Oscar Mayer Wiener" (Oscar Mayer) and ad slogans such as "Finger lickin' good" (KFC), "Got milk?" (initially created for the California Milk Processor Board), and "Just do it" (Nike). Jingles aren't used as often as they were in the past, but many advertisers still like to set their slogan to original music at the end of a commercial. These are called "musical buttons" or "tags." A currently popular technique is to add a few appropriate measures of a popular song near the end of a commercial to emphasize the message.

    Slogans link the brand to a simple linguistic device that is memorable (jingles do the same but set the slogan to music). We usually have no trouble reciting successful slogans (sometimes years after the campaign has ended); think of such die-hards as "Please don't squeeze the Charmin," "Double your pleasure, double your fun," and "Even a caveman can do it." Firms such as Clorox, Allstate, and Procter & Gamble find that the songs they use in their commercials can become popular on their own; now they offer consumers the opportunity to purchase full-length versions of the music.[26]

jingles
Original words and music written specifically for advertising executions.

slogans
Simple, memorable linguistic devices linked to a brand.

Step 4: Pretest What the Ads Will Say

Now that the creatives have performed their magic, how does the agency know if the campaign ideas will work? Advertisers try to minimize mistakes by getting reactions to ad messages before they actually place them. Much of this **pretesting**, the research that goes on in the early stages of a campaign, centers on gathering basic information that will help planners be sure they've accurately defined the product's market, consumers, and competitors. As we saw in Chapter 4, this information comes from quantitative sources, such as surveys, and qualitative sources, such as focus groups.

pretesting
A research method that seeks to minimize mistakes by getting consumer reactions to ad messages before they appear in the media.

In these two executions from the U.K. the creatives borrow a nostalgic look from an earlier era.

In addition, some researchers use physiological measures to pretest ads. For example, the ad agency Bark Group employs eye movement tracking, skin responses, and brain responses to gauge consumers' emotional responses to ads in order to produce ad campaigns that result in a stronger emotional reaction.[27] The idea is to be able to identify the colors, sounds, images and words that elicit the strongest responses—even in some cases when viewers aren't consciously aware of how they're feeling.

Step 5: Choose the Media Type(s) and Media Schedule

media planning
The process of developing media objectives, strategies, and tactics for use in an advertising campaign.

Media planning is a problem-solving process that gets a message to a target audience in the most effective way. Planning decisions include audience selection and where, when, and how frequent the exposure should be. Thus, the first task for a media planner is to find out when and where people in the target market are most likely to be exposed to the communication. Many college students read the campus newspaper in the morning (believe it or not, sometimes even during class!), so advertisers may choose to place ad messages aimed at college students there.

There is no such thing as one perfect medium for advertising. The choice depends on the specific target audience, the objective of the message, and, of course, the budget. For the advertising campaign to be effective, the media planner must match the profile of the target market with specific media vehicles. For example, many Hispanic-American consumers, even those who speak English, are avid users of Spanish-language media. Marketers that wish to reach this segment might allocate a relatively large share of their advertising budget to buying Spanish-language newspapers, magazines, TV, and Spanish webcasts available to broadband Internet users.

The choice of the right media mix is no simple matter, especially as new options including videos and DVDs, video games, personal computers, the Internet, MP3 players, hundreds of new TV channels, and even satellite radio now vie for our attention. Consider that in 1965, advertisers could reach 80 percent of 18- to 49-year-olds in the United States with three 60-second TV spots! That kind of efficiency is just a pipe dream in today's highly fragmented media marketplace.

Where to Say It: Traditional Mass Media

What does a 50-inch plasma TV with Dolby Surround Sound have in common with a matchbook? Each is a media vehicle that permits an advertiser to communicate with a potential customer. Depending on the intended message, each medium has its advantages and disadvantages. In this section we'll take a look at the major categories of traditional mass media; then we'll look at Internet advertising and some less-traditional indirect forms of advertising. Table 13.1 summarizes some of the pros and cons of each type.

- *Television:* Because of television's ability to reach so many people at once, it's often the medium of choice for regional and national companies. However, advertising on a television network can be very expensive. The cost to air a 30-second ad on a popular prime-time network TV show one time normally ranges between $200,000 and $750,000 or more depending on the size of the show's audience. In 2008, ads for a near-finale episode of *American Idol*, the number one TV show for four years, went for $1 million or more.[28] Advertisers may prefer to buy cable, satellite, or local television time rather than network time because it's cheaper or because they want to reach a more targeted market, such as "foodies," who are into cooking. Nevertheless, 78 percent of advertisers say TV advertising has become less effective as DVRs and video-on-demand grow in popularity.[29]

  While viewing of traditional broadcast TV is down dramatically in recent years, people spend a lot more time watching cable and satellite channels. This explains why the companies that own broadcast networks also are buying up major cable channels—General Electric's NBC owns MSNBC, CNBC, Bravo, SciFi, and USA TV channels; Walt Disney Co., which owns ABC, also owns ESPN and ABC Family and also is a partial

Table 13.1 | Pros and Cons of Media Vehicles

Vehicle	Pros	Cons
Television	<ul><li>TV is extremely creative and flexible.</li><li>Network TV is the most cost-effective way to reach a mass audience.</li><li>Cable and satellite TV allow the advertiser to reach a selected group at relatively low cost.</li><li>A prestigious way to advertise.</li><li>Can demonstrate the product in use.</li><li>Can provide entertainment and generate excitement.</li><li>Messages have high impact because of the use of sight and sound.</li></ul>	<ul><li>The message is quickly forgotten unless it is repeated often.</li><li>The audience is increasingly fragmented.</li><li>Although the relative cost of reaching the audience is low, prices are still high on an absolute basis—often too high for smaller companies. A 30-second spot on a prime-time TV sitcom costs well over $250,000.</li><li>Fewer people view network television.</li><li>People switch from station to station and zap commercials.</li><li>Rising costs have led to more and shorter ads, causing more clutter.</li></ul>
Radio	<ul><li>Good for selectively targeting an audience.</li><li>Is heard outside the home.</li><li>Can reach customers on a personal and intimate level.</li><li>Can use local personalities.</li><li>Relatively low cost, both for producing a spot and for running it repeatedly.</li><li>Because of short lead time, radio ads can be modified quickly to reflect changes in the marketplace.</li><li>Use of sound effects and music allows listeners to use their imagination to create a vivid scene.</li></ul>	<ul><li>Listeners often don't pay full attention to what they hear.</li><li>Difficulty in buying radio time, especially for national advertisers.</li><li>Not appropriate for products that must be seen or demonstrated to be appreciated.</li><li>The small audiences of individual stations means ads must be placed with many different stations and must be repeated frequently.</li></ul>
Newspapers	<ul><li>Wide exposure provides extensive market coverage.</li><li>Flexible format permits the use of color, different sizes, and targeted editions.</li><li>Provides the ability to use detailed copy.</li><li>Allows local retailers to tie in with national advertisers.</li><li>Readers are in the right mental frame to process advertisements about new products, sales, etc.</li><li>Timeliness, i.e., short lead time between placing ad and running it.</li></ul>	<ul><li>Most people don't spend much time reading the newspaper.</li><li>Readership is especially low among teens and young adults.</li><li>Short life span—people rarely look at a newspaper more than once.</li><li>Offers a very cluttered ad environment.</li><li>The reproduction quality of images is relatively poor.</li><li>Not effective to reach specific audiences.</li></ul>
Magazines	<ul><li>Audiences can be narrowly targeted by specialized magazines.</li><li>High credibility and interest level provide a good environment for ads.</li><li>Advertising has a long life and is often passed along to other readers.</li><li>Visual quality is excellent.</li><li>Can provide detailed product information with a sense of authority.</li></ul>	<ul><li>With the exception of direct mail, it is the most expensive form of advertising. The cost of a full-page, four-color ad in a general-audience magazine typically exceeds $100,000.</li><li>Long deadlines reduce flexibility.</li><li>The advertiser must generally use several magazines to reach the majority of a target market.</li><li>Clutter.</li></ul>
Directories	<ul><li>Customers actively seek exposure to advertisements.</li><li>Advertisers determine the quality of the ad placement because larger ads get preferential placement.</li></ul>	<ul><li>Limited creative options.</li><li>May be a lack of color.</li><li>Ads are generally purchased for a full year and cannot be changed.</li></ul>

(continued)

Table 13.1 | Pros and Cons of Media Vehicles *(continued)*

Vehicle	Pros	Cons
Out-of-home media	• Most of the population can be reached at low cost. • Good for supplementing other media. • High frequency when signs are located in heavy traffic areas. • Effective for reaching virtually all segments of the population. • Geographic flexibility.	• Hard to communicate complex messages because of short exposure time. • Difficult to measure advertisement's audience. • Controversial and disliked in many communities. • Cannot pinpoint specific market segments.
Internet Web sites	• Can target specific audiences and individualize messages. • Web user registration and cookies allow marketers to track user preferences and Web site activity. • Is interactive—consumers can participate in the ad campaign; can create do-it-yourself ads. • An entertainment medium allowing consumers to play games, download music, etc. • Consumers are active participants in the communication process, controlling what information and the amount and rate of information they receive. • Web sites can facilitate both marketing communication and transactions. • Consumers visit Web sites with the mindset to obtain information. • Banners can achieve top of mind awareness (TOMA), even without click-throughs.	• Limited to Internet users only. • Banners, pop-ups, unsolicited e-mail, etc., can be unwanted and annoying. • Declining click-through rates for banners—currently less than 0.03 percent. • If Web pages take too long to load, consumers will abandon the site. • *Phishing* is e-mail sent by criminals to get consumers to go to phony Web sites that will seek to gain personal information such as credit card numbers. • Because advertisers' costs are normally based on the number of click-throughs, competitors may engage in click fraud by clicking on a sponsored link. • Difficult to measure effectiveness.
Place-based media	• Effective for certain markets such a pharmaceutical companies to reach their target audience. • In retail locations it can reach customers immediately before purchase; this provides a last opportunity to influence the purchase decision. • In locations such as airports, it receives a high level of attention because of lack of viewer options.	• Limited audience. • Difficult to measure effectiveness.
Branded entertainment	• Brand presented in a positive context. • Brand message presented in a covert fashion. • Less intrusive and thus less likely to be avoided. • Connection with a popular movie plot or TV program and with entertaining characters can help a brand's image. • Can build emotional connection with the audience. • Can create a memorable association that serves to enhance brand recall.	• Little control of how the brand is positioned—is in the hands of the director. • Difficult to measure effectiveness. • Costs of placement can be very high.
Advergaming	• Companies can customize their own games or incorporate brands into existing popular games. • Some game producers now actively pursue tie-ins with brands. • Millions of gamers play an average of 40 hours per game before they tire of it. • Millions of consumers have mobile phones "in their hands."	• Audience limited to gamers.
Mobile phones	• A large variety of different formats using different mobile phone apps.	• Consumers may be unwilling to receive messages through their phones.

Sources: Adapted from J. Thomas Russell and Ron Lane, *Kleppner's Advertising Procedure*, 15th ed. (Upper Saddle River, NJ: Prentice Hall, 2002); Terence A. Shimp, *Advertising, Promotion and Supplemental Aspects of Integrated Marketing Communications*, 8th ed. (Australia: Thomson Southwestern, 2010); and William Wells, John Burnett, and Sandra Moriarty, *Advertising: Principles and Practice*, 6th ed. (Upper Saddle River, NJ: Prentice Hall, 2003).

owner for Lifetime, A&E, and E! cable channels; and Viacom Inc. owns MTV, VH1, Comedy Central, Showtime, The Movie Channel, and Nickelodeon along with CBS.[30]

- *Radio:* Radio as an advertising medium dates back to 1922, when a New York City apartment manager went on the air to advertise properties for rent. One advantage of radio advertising is flexibility. Marketers can change commercials quickly, often on the spot by an announcer and a recording engineer.[31]

- *Newspapers:* The newspaper is one of the oldest communication platforms. Retailers in particular have relied on newspaper ads since before the turn of the 20th century to inform readers about sales and deliveries of new merchandise. While most newspapers are local, *USA Today*, the *Wall Street Journal*, and the *New York Times* have national circulations and provide readerships in the millions. Newspapers are an excellent medium for local advertising and for events (such as store sales) that require a quick response. Today, most newspapers also offer online versions of their papers to expand their exposure. Some, such as the *New York Times*, offer online subscribers downloads of the actual newspaper including all the ads at a much lower cost than the paper version. Rates for newspapers vary depending on the circulation of the paper. Most newspapers help advertisers in putting their ads together, a real advantage to the small business. However, the newspaper industry is in serious trouble as more people choose to get their news online and many major papers are closing their doors or struggling.

- *Magazines:* Today, in addition to general audience magazines such as *Readers Digest*, there are literally thousands of special-interest magazines. Approximately 92 percent of adults look through at least one magazine per month. New technology such as *selective binding* allows publishers to personalize their editions so that they can include advertisements for local businesses in issues they mail to specific locations. For advertisers, magazines also offer the opportunity for multipage spreads as well as the ability to include special inserts so they can deliver samples of products such as perfumes and other "scratch-and-sniff" treats. Kimberly Clark's Viva brand paper towels, for example, included samples of the product stitched into copies of *Readers Digest* as part of a six-page spread.[32]

Where to Say It: Digital Media

The term **digital media** refers to any media that are digital rather than analog. The more popular types of digital media advertisers use today include Web sites, mobile or cellular phones, and digital video such as YouTube.

Owned, Paid, and Earned Media

Internet media can be classified as owned, paid, and earned.[33] Companies can control their **owned media** that includes Web sites, blogs, Facebook, and Twitter accounts. The advantage of these owned media is that they are effective means for companies to build relationships with their customers. **Paid media**, the most similar model to traditional media, includes display ads, sponsorships, and paid key word searches. Consumers generally dislike the paid ads making their effectiveness less of a sure thing. **Earned media** refers to word of mouth (WOM) or buzz using social media. The positive of earned media is that it is the most credible to consumers. The challenge is that marketers have no control over earned media; they can only listen and respond.

Website Advertising

Online advertising no longer is a novelty; companies now spend over $21 billion a year to communicate via digital media. Major firms like General Mills and Kraft Foods are boosting their spending and the number of brands they promote online.[34] The reason? Fifteen percent of the time U.S. consumers spend with all media is now online—and of course for some segments such as college students, that figure is much higher.[35]

digital media
Media that are digital rather than analog including Web sites, mobile or cellular phones, and digital video such as YouTube.

owned media
Internet sites such as Web sites, blogs, Facebook, and Twitter accounts that are owned by an advertiser.

paid media
Internet media such as display ads, sponsorships, and paid key word searches that are paid for by an advertiser.

earned media
Word-of-mouth or buzz using social media where the advertiser has no control.

Alaska Airlines developed a system to create unique ads for individual Web surfers based on their geographic location, the number of times that person has seen an Alaska Airlines ad, the consumer's purchase history with the airline, and his experience with lost bags, delays, and flight cancellations. The program can offer different prices to different customers, even prices below the lowest published fares.[36]

Online advertising offers several advantages over other media platforms. First, the Internet provides new ways to finely target customers. Web user registrations and *cookies* allow sites to track user preferences and deliver ads based on previous Internet behavior. In addition, because the Web site can track how many times an ad is "clicked," advertisers can measure in real time how people respond to specific online messages.

Finally, online advertising can be interactive—it lets consumers participate in the advertising campaign, and in some cases they can even become part of the action. Viewers who logged on to a special Web site were able to "direct" TV commercials for the Ford Probe by picking the cast and plotlines that Ford's ad agency then used to create actual spots. Similarly, during its "**whatever.com**" campaign, Nike sent consumers to the Web to pick the endings of three cliffhanger TV spots.[37]

Specific forms of Internet advertising include banners, buttons, pop-up ads, search engines and directories, and e-mail:

banners
Internet advertising in the form of rectangular graphics at the top or bottom of Web pages.

buttons
Small banner-type advertisements that can be placed anywhere on a Web page.

pop-up ad
An advertisement that appears on the screen while a Web page loads or after it has loaded.

search engines
Internet programs that search for documents with specified keywords.

Web directory
Internet program that lists sites by categories and subcategories.

e-mail advertising
Advertising messages sent via e-mail to large numbers of people simultaneously.

spam
The use of electronic media to send unsolicited messages in bulk.

- **Banners**, rectangular graphics at the top or bottom of Web pages, were the first form of Web advertising.

- **Buttons** are small banner-type advertisements that a company can place anywhere on a page.

- A **pop-up ad** is an advertisement that appears on the screen while a Web page loads or after it has loaded. Because these messages take up part of the screen's "real estate" while surfers wait for the desired page to load, they are difficult to ignore. Many surfers find pop-ups a nuisance, so most Internet access software provides an option that blocks all pop-ups. Web advertisers are typically charged only if people actually click through to the ad.

- **Search engines and directory listings** are ways for people to find Web pages of interest to them. A Web **search engine** is a program that searches for documents with specified keywords. Because there are millions of Web pages that include a particular word or phrase, most search engines use some method to rank their search results and provide users with the most relevant results first. As we discussed in Chapter 5, firms are increasingly paying search engines for more visible or higher placement on results lists. Google, which has 65% of all U.S. web searches, has total global revenues of nearly $30 billion. In June, 2010, BP spent nearly $3.6 million for Google advertising following the Gulf oil spill while Google's top client, AT&T spent $8.08 million on Google's AdWords to support its launch of the iPhone 4.[38] Unlike search engines, a **Web directory** does not display lists of Web pages based on keywords but instead lists sites by categories and subcategories. Google, for example, offers its users the Google Directory in addition to its search engine. Who have you Googled today?

- **E-mail advertising** that transmits messages to very large numbers of inboxes simultaneously is one of the easiest ways to communicate with consumers—it's basically the same price whether you send ten messages or ten thousand. Recipients might be drawn from an organization's list or they may have "opted-in" to receive notifications of a company's discounts and promotions. One downside to this platform is the explosion of **spam**. The industry defines this practice as sending unsolicited e-mail to five or more people not personally known to the sender. Many Web sites that offer e-mail give surfers the opportunity to refuse unsolicited e-mail via junk e-mail blockers. This **permission marketing** strategy gives the consumer the power to *opt in* or out. Marketers in the United States send about 200 billion e-mails to consumers every year, so they hope that a good portion of these will be opened and read rather than being sent straight to the recycle bin.[39]

Mobile Advertising

The Mobile Marketing Association defines **mobile advertising** as "a form of advertising that is communicated to the consumer via a handset."[40] Mobile marketing offers advertisers a variety of ways to speak to customers including Mobile Web sites, mobile applications, mobile messaging, and mobile video and TV.

Mobile advertising has just begun to boom, much energized by Apple's iPhone and all the apps that go with it. Begun with Apple's iAd, today's mobile advertising has moved from static tiny static banner ads to rich media that brings motion, interactivity, sound, video, or Flash, to mobile advertising.[41] In the U.K., Kellogg's used mobile advertising for its "The Big Bake" campaign.[42] Messages on Kellogg's cereal boxes encouraged consumers to use their mobile phones to send in photos of themselves cooking recipes that include Kellogg's cereals. Winners of the contest were given the opportunity to star in a Kellogg's TV or print ad. And, before Oprah left TV, she made herself available to fans through a smartphone app that included a weekly calendar of what was on the show, information about availability of reservations for the show, and access to articles and photos from **Oprah.com** and *O* magazine and to her tweets.[43]

Newer phones with global positioning system (GPS) features that pinpoint your location allow additional mobile advertising opportunities. Outdoor apparel retailer North Face, for example, used location-based mobile ads to lure consumers to its stores.[44] When customers who opt in are close to one of the chain's stores, they receive a text message about new arrivals or an in-store promotion such as a free water bottle with a purchase.

Video Sharing: Check It Out on YouTube

Video sharing describes the strategy of uploading video recordings or **vlogs** (pronounced vee-logs) to Internet sites such as YouTube so that thousands or even millions of other Internet users can check them out. These videos are a powerful way to break through the clutter. To understand how, let's take a look at how Blendtec, a small electric blender manufacturer, used this strategy to grab a lot of attention quickly and cheaply. The company uploaded a vlog that showed its president dropping a brand-new iPhone into one of its appliances—presto! Within 24 hours, over a million people had watched as presto! purée of phone resulted.[45]

For marketers, YouTube provides vast opportunities to build relationships with consumers. For example, Home Depot provides do-it-yourselfers with free educational videos that promote Home Depot products while these vlogs position the company as a trusted expert. The University of Phoenix uses YouTube to post hundreds of video testimonials. The Boone Oakley advertising agency has established its Web site on YouTube. The interactive video allows potential clients to view its work in an easily accessible way and is especially appealing to companies that want a nontraditional marketing communications program.

Where to Say It: Branded Entertainment

As we noted earlier, more and more marketers rely on paid *product placements* in TV shows and movies to grab the attention of consumers who tune out traditional ad messages as fast as they see them. These placements are an important form of **branded entertainment**, a strategy where marketers integrate products into all sorts of venues including movies, television shows, videogames, novels, and even retail settings. For one promotion a group of 7-Eleven convenience stores literally became Kwik-E-Marts just like the store Homer loves

permission marketing
E-mail advertising in which on-line consumers have the opportunity to accept or refuse the unsolicited e-mail.

mobile advertising
A form of advertising that is communicated to the consumer via a handset.

video sharing
Uploading video recordings on to Internet sites such as YouTube so that thousands or even millions of other Internet users can see them.

vlogs
Video recordings shared on the Internet.

branded entertainment
A form of advertising in which marketers integrate products into entertainment venues.

The Cutting Edge

Augmented Reality

Ever wonder how they make those yellow first-down lines in televised football games that spectators in the stadium can't see? Or how about the trail of the puck in broadcasts of hockey games? The answer is **augmented reality** (AR), a form of technology where a view of a real-world environment joins a layer of virtual computer-generated imagery to create a mixed reality.

Adidas is one of several companies experimenting with AR in its marketing program.[46] **Adidas.com** uses augmented reality to create three online games for Adidas sneaker customers. One is a skateboard game where the gamer's

sneaker navigates through the city. Other Adidas games include a *Star Wars*–like game and a music game. To play all three games, the consumer holds the tongue of the sneaker up to a computer webcam and an implanted code activates a virtual 3-D world that the person sneaks into. The iPhone now offers users at least ten AR apps. Hold your phone up to the stars and the app will map the constellations with their names for you while the Firefighter 360 game app sets your location on fire and then allows you to put the fire out and save passers-by to make you a hero.[47]

---

augmented reality
A form of technology where a view of a real-world environment joins a layer of virtual computer-generated imagery to create a mixed reality.

to frequent in the TV show *The Simpsons*. Real-world customers could buy such exotic delicacies as "Squishees," "Buzz Cola," and "Krusty-Os cereal." The KFC fast-food chain paid two cities in Indiana to put founder Colonel Sanders's face on their hydrants and fire extinguishers to promote its new "fiery" chicken wings.[48] And the Twentieth Century Fox movie studio even managed to place a plug for the romantic comedy *I Love You, Beth Cooper* in a high school valedictorian's speech (she got paid $1,800 to mention one of the main characters).[49] Product placement has also moved to social media as many firms are paying YouTube celebrities to push their products. Because consumers trust what these YouTubers say, companies including giants AT&T, GE, Ford, Colgate, Lancôme Paris, McDonalds, and Coca-Cola are paying $75,000 or more to some YouTube stars.[50]

Is branded entertainment a solid strategy? The idea is that when consumers see a popular celebrity who uses a specific brand in their favorite movie or TV program, they might develop a more positive attitude toward that brand. Successful brand placements include the BMW Z3 James Bond drove, the Nike shoes Forrest Gump wore, and the Ray-Ban sunglasses Tom Cruise sported in *Risky Business*. Audi recently promoted its R8 sports car in the movie *Iron Man*: Superhero Tony Stark drives the car, while Gwyneth Paltrow as Virginia "Pepper" Potts drives the Audi S5 sports sedan.[51]

But placing a Pepsi can in a TV show is only one form of branded entertainment. Today advertisers also take a more active role in developing new television programs to showcase their products. For example, TNT and Dodge paired up to produce *Lucky Chance*, a branded miniseries about an undercover Drug Enforcement Agency agent who drives a 2009 Dodge Challenger to transport money to a mob boss.[52]

advergaming
Brand placements in video games.

Beyond movies and television shows, what better way to promote to the video generation than through brand placements in video games? The industry calls this technique **advergaming**. If you are a video game hound, watch for placements of real-life brands such as Ford, Radio Shack, General Motors, Toyota, and Sony embedded in the action of your game. Quiksilver, a clothing manufacturer for extreme-sport participants, now puts its shirts and shorts into video games such as Tony Hawk's *Pro Skater 3*.

Where to Say It: Support Media

support media
Media such as directories or out-of-home media that may be used to reach people who are not reached by mass media advertising.

While marketers (and consumers) normally think of advertising as mass media messages, in reality many of the ads we see today show up in our homes, our workplaces, and in public venues like restroom walls, on signs that trail behind airplanes, or in movies and television programs. **Support media** reach people who may not have been reached by mass media advertising, and these platforms also support the messages traditional media delivers. Here we'll look at some of the more important support media advertisers use.

- **Directories:** Directory advertising is the most "down-to-earth," information-focused advertising medium. In 1883, a printer in Wyoming ran out of white paper while printing part of a telephone book, so he substituted yellow paper instead. Today, the Yellow

Pages, including the online Yellow Pages, posts revenues of more than $16 billion in the United States and over $45 billion globally.[53] Often consumers look through directories just before they are ready to buy.

- **Out-of-home media** includes outdoor advertising (billboards and signs), transit advertising (signs placed inside and/or outside buses, taxis, trains, train stations, and airports) and other types of messages that reach people in public places. In recent years, outdoor advertising has pushed the technology envelope with **digital signage** that enables the source to change the message at will. In a first for out-of-home media, CBS Outdoor installed a high-definition 3-D projection display in New York's Grand Central Terminal where 70,000 commuters a day were able to view 3-D commercials (yes, with 3-D glasses) for Visa.[54] Of course, many consumers dislike out-of-home media, especially outdoor advertising, because they feel it is unattractive.

- **Place-based media** like "The Airport Channel" transmit messages to "captive audiences" in public places, such as doctors' offices and airport waiting areas. Place-based video screens are now in thousands of shops, offices, and health clubs across the country including stores like CompUSA, Best Buy, Borders, Foot Locker, and Target. The Walmart TV Network has more than 125,000 screens in 2,850 Walmart stores, and patients who wait in over 10,800 doctors' offices watch medical programming and ads. NBC Universal has its shows on screens installed in office building elevators and on United Airlines flights.[55]

- And now, some retailers can even follow you around the store to deliver more up-close and personal messages: *RFID* technology (radio frequency identification) uses tiny sensors embedded in packages or store aisles to track customers as they pass. An unsuspecting shopper might hear a beep to remind him that he just passed his family's favorite peanut butter.[56] You're not paranoid; they really *are* watching you!

out-of-home media
Communication media that reach people in public places.

digital signage
Out-of-home media that use digital technology to change the message at will.

place-based media
Advertising media that transmit messages in public places, such as doctors' offices and airports, where certain types of people congregate.

When to Say It: Media Scheduling

After she chooses the advertising media, the planner then creates a **media schedule** that specifies the exact media the campaign will use as well as when and how often the message should appear. Figure 13.4 shows a hypothetical media schedule for the promotion of a new video game. Note that much of the advertising reaches its target audience in the months just before Christmas, and that much of the expensive television budget focuses on advertising during specials just prior to the holiday season.

The media schedule outlines the planner's best estimate of which media will be most effective to attain the advertising objective(s) and which specific media vehicles will do the most effective job. The media planner considers qualitative factors such as the match between the demographic and psychographic profile of a target audience and the people a media vehicle

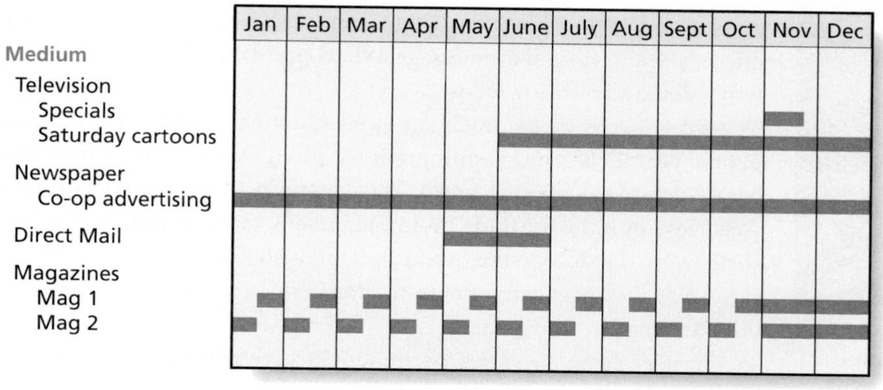

media schedule
The plan that specifies the exact media to use and when to use it.

Figure 13.4 *Snapshot* | Media Schedule for a Video Game

Media planning includes decisions on where, when, and how much advertising to do. A media schedule such as this one for a video game shows the plan visually.

reach
The percentage of the target market that will be exposed to the media vehicle.

frequency
The average number of times a person in the target group will be exposed to the message.

gross rating points (GRPs)
A measure used for comparing the effectiveness of different media vehicles: average reach × frequency.

cost per thousand (CPM)
A measure used to compare the relative cost-effectiveness of different media vehicles that have different exposure rates; the cost to deliver a message to 1,000 people or homes.

The long-running Got Milk? campaign avoids advertising wear-out because it uses a steady stream of different celebrities (all with milk mustaches, of course) over time.

reaches, the advertising patterns of competitors, and the capability of a medium to adequately convey the desired information. The planner must also consider factors such as the compatibility of the product with editorial content. For example, viewers might not respond well to a lighthearted ad for a new snack food during a somber documentary on world hunger.

There are also a number of quantitative factors, which the media planner uses to develop the media schedule. **Reach** is the percentage of the target market that will be exposed to the media vehicle at least once during a given period of time, usually four weeks. For example, if the target market includes 100 million adults age 18 and over and a specific TV program has an audience that includes 5 million adults in this age group, the program has a reach of 5. Developing a media plan with high reach is particularly important for widely used products when the message needs to get to as many consumers as possible.

Frequency is the average number of times that an individual or a household will be exposed to the message. Note that this is the *average*. For example, while some members of a target market may be exposed to an ad 2 or 4 or 20 times and others see an ad only once, the average and thus the frequency might be 4. High levels of frequency are important for products that are complex or those that are targeted to relatively small markets for which multiple exposures to the message are necessary to make an impact.

Gross rating points (GRPs) are a measure of the quantity of media included in the media plan. Just as we talk about buying 15 gallons of gas or a pound of coffee, media planners talk about a media schedule that includes the purchase of 250 gross rating points of radio and 700 GRPs of TV. We calculate gross rating points by multiplying a media vehicle's rating by the number of planned ad insertions. As we see in Table 13.2, if 30 percent of a target audience watches *American Idol* and you place eight ads on the show, you buy 240 GRPs of that show.

Although some media vehicles deliver more of your target audience, they may not be cost-efficient. More people will see a commercial aired during the Super Bowl than during a 3:00 A.M. rerun of a Tarzan movie. But the advertiser could run late-night commercials every night for a year for the cost of one 30-second Super Bowl spot. To compare the relative cost-effectiveness of different media and of spots run on different vehicles in the same medium, media planners use a measure they call **cost per thousand (CPM)**. This figure reflects the cost to deliver a message to 1,000 people.

Assume that the cost of each 30-second commercial on *American Idol* is $400,000 but the number of target audience members the show reaches is 20 million or 20,000 × 1,000. The CPM of *American Idol* is $400,000/20,000 = $20 CPM. Compare this to the cost of advertising in *Fortune* magazine: A full-page 4-color ad costs approximately $115,000 and the readership includes approximately 2 million members of our target audience. The cost per thousand for *Fortune* is $115,000/2000 = $57.50. Thus, *American Idol*, while having a much higher total cost, actually is a more efficient buy.

Media Scheduling: How Often to Say It

After she decides where and when to advertise, the planner must decide how often she wants to send the message. What time of day? And what overall pattern will the advertising follow?

A *continuous schedule* maintains a steady stream of advertising throughout the year. This is most appropriate for products that we buy on a regular basis, such as shampoo or bread. The American Association of Advertising Agencies, an industry trade group, maintains that continuous advertising sustains market leadership even if total industry sales fall.[57] On the downside, some messages can suffer from *advertising wear-out* because people tune out the same old ad messages.

A *pulsing schedule* varies the amount of advertising throughout the year based on when the product is likely to be in demand. A suntan lotion might

Table 13.2 | A (Hypothetical) Media Schedule

Media Vehicle	Rating (Percentage of Target Audience Reached)	Number of Ad Insertions During the Period	GRPs (Rating × Number of Insertions)
American Idol TV show	30	8 (2 ads on each week's show for 4 weeks)	240 GRPs
NBC Nightly News	10	40 (2 ads each weeknight for 4 weeks)	400
The Today Show	20	40 (2 ads each weekday morning for 4 weeks)	800
Newsweek magazine	20	4 (1 ad in each of 4 editions during the 4-week period)	80
Fortune magazine	12	2 (1 ad in each of the 2 editions each month)	24
USA Today newspaper	7	8 (1 ad each Monday and Thursday during the 4-week period)	56
Total GRPs			1600

advertise year-round but more heavily during the summer months. *Flighting* is an extreme form of pulsing, in which advertising appears in short, intense bursts alternating with periods of little to no activity. It can produce as much brand awareness as a steady dose of advertising at a much lower cost if consumers noticed the messages from the previous flight and these made an impact.

Step 6: Evaluate the Advertising

John Wanamaker, a famous Philadelphia retailer, once complained, "I am certain that half the money I spend on advertising is completely wasted. The trouble is, I don't know which half."[58] Now that we've seen how advertising is created and executed, let's step back and see how we decide if it's working.

There's no doubt that a lot of advertising is ineffective. Ironically, as marketers try harder and harder to reach their customers, these efforts can backfire. Many consumers have a love–hate relationship with advertising. Over half the respondents in a survey said they "avoid buying products that overwhelm them with advertising and marketing," and 60 percent said their opinion of advertising "is much more negative than just a few years ago."[59] With so many messages competing for the attention of frazzled customers, it's especially important for firms to evaluate their efforts to increase the impact of their messages. How can they do that?

Posttesting means conducting research on consumers' responses to advertising messages they have seen or heard (as opposed to *pretesting*, which as we've seen collects reactions to messages *before* they're actually placed in "the real world"). Ironically, many creative ads that are quirky or even bizarre make an advertising agency look good within the industry (and on the résumé of the art director), but are ultimately unsuccessful because they don't communicate what the company needs to say about the product itself. We may remember that weird ad, but have no idea what product it advertised.

Three ways to measure the impact of an advertisement are *unaided recall*, *aided recall*, and *attitudinal measures*:

1. **Unaided recall** tests by telephone survey or personal interview whether a person remembers seeing an ad during a specified period without giving the person the name of the brand.

posttesting
Research conducted on consumers' responses to actual advertising messages they have seen or heard.

unaided recall
A research technique conducted by telephone survey or personal interview that asks whether a person remembers seeing an ad during a specified period without giving the person the name of the brand.

aided recall

A research technique that uses clues to prompt answers from people about advertisements they might have seen.

attitudinal measures

A research technique that probes a consumer's beliefs or feelings about a product before and after being exposed to messages about it.

public relations (PR)

Communication function that seeks to build good relationships with an organization's publics, including consumers, stockholders, and legislators.

publicity

Unpaid communication about an organization that appears in the mass media.

crisis management

The process of managing a company's reputation when some negative event threatens the organization's image.

2. An **aided recall** test uses the name of the brand and sometimes other clues to prompt answers. For example, a researcher might show a group of consumers a list of brands and ask them to choose which items they have seen advertised within the past week.

3. **Attitudinal measures** probe a bit more deeply by testing consumers' beliefs or feelings about a product before and after they are exposed to messages about it. If, for example, Pepsi's messages about "freshness-dating" make enough consumers believe that the freshness of soft drinks is important, marketers can consider the advertising campaign successful.

3 Public Relations

OBJECTIVE

Explain the role of public relations and the steps in developing a public relations campaign.
(pp. 402–408)

Public relations (PR) is the communication function that seeks to build good relationships with an organization's *publics*; these include consumers, stockholders, legislators, and other stakeholders in the organization. Today marketers use PR activities to influence the attitudes and perceptions of various groups not only toward companies and brands but also toward politicians, celebrities, and not-for-profit organizations.

The basic rule of good PR is, *Do something good, and then talk about it*. A company's efforts to get in the limelight—and stay there—can range from humanitarian acts to sponsoring band tours. The big advantage of this kind of communication is that when PR messages are placed successfully, they are more credible than if the same information appeared in a paid advertisement. As one marketing executive observed, "There's a big difference between hearing about a product from a pitchman and from your trusted local anchorman."[60]

Public relations strategies are crucial to an organization's ability to establish and maintain a favorable image. *Proactive PR* activities stem from the company's marketing objectives. For example, marketers create and manage **publicity**, unpaid communication about an organization that gets media exposure. It's interesting to note that this aspect of PR is blending into other promotional strategies as social media continue to mushroom. Essentially, buzz marketing is also one form of public relations because it tries to motivate consumers to talk up a brand or service to one another (ideally for free).

As many of the other function of public relations blend into buzz marketing activities, perhaps the most important function it still "owns" is **crisis management**. This refers to the process of managing a company's reputation when some negative and often unplanned event threatens the organization's image. Think about the unfortunate BP executives, for example, who had to communicate to the public as the explosion of an oil rig in the Gulf of Mexico took the shape of an epic environmental disaster, or those who had to reassure a formerly loyal Toyota customer base that faulty accelerator pedals would not in fact cause their cars to speed out of control.

The goal in such situations is to manage the flow of information to address concerns so that consumers don't panic and distributors don't abandon the product. Although some organizations don't seem to learn this lesson, typically the best strategy is to be honest about the problem and to quickly take responsibility for correcting it. For example, a few years ago PepsiCo was rocked by claims that consumers had found hypodermic needles in Diet Pepsi cans. The company assembled a crisis team to map out a response and supplied video footage of its bottling process to show that it was impossible for foreign objects to find their way into cans before they were sealed at the factory. The claims proved false, and PepsiCo ran follow-up ads reinforcing the findings. Pepsi's calm, coordinated response averted a PR disaster.

Even a single negative event can cause permanent damage to a company, the success of its products, and its stockholder equity. While it didn't have the magnitude of a massive oil spill such as the one BP confronted, Wendy's was faced with a similar public image disaster when a customer said she found a finger in a bowl of its chili.[61] The woman and her husband were both sent to prison after investigators discovered that he had actually obtained the finger from a co-worker who had lost it in a workplace accident. While the claim proved false, it still cost the company $2.5 million in lost sales.[62] In another incident, a man stuffed a dead mouse in a Taco Bell burrito in an attempt to extort money from the fast-food chain.[63] Supersize that!

Public relations professionals know that when a firm handles a crisis well, it can minimize damage and help the company make things right. Thus, a vitally important role of PR is to prepare a *crisis-management plan*. This is a document that details what an organization will do *if* a crisis occurs—who will be the spokesperson for the organization, how the organization will deal with the press, and what sort of messages it will deliver to the press and the public.

Plan a Public Relations Campaign

A **public relations campaign** is a coordinated effort to communicate with one or more of the firm's publics. This is a three-step process that develops, executes, and evaluates PR objectives. Let's review each step and then we'll examine some of the more frequently used objectives and tactics shown in 📷 Figure 13.5.

Like an advertising campaign, the organization must first *develop* clear objectives for the PR program that define the message it wants people to hear. For example the International Apple Institute, a trade group devoted to increasing the consumption of apples, had to decide if a campaign should focus on getting consumers to cook more with apples, drink more apple juice, or simply to buy more fresh fruit. Because fresh apples brought a substantially higher price per pound to growers than apples used for applesauce or apple juice, the group decided to push the fresh fruit angle. It used the theme "An apple a day . . ." (sound familiar?) as it mounted a focused campaign to encourage people to eat more apples by placing articles in consumer media extolling the fruit's health benefits.

Execution of the campaign means deciding precisely how to communicate the message to the targeted public(s). An organization can get out its positive messages in many ways: news conferences, sponsorship of charity events, and other attention-getting promotions.

public relations campaign
A coordinated effort to communicate with one or more of the firm's publics.

Figure 13.5 📷 *Snapshot* | Objectives and Tactics of Public Relations
Successful PR campaigns include clearly defined objectives and the use of the right PR activities.

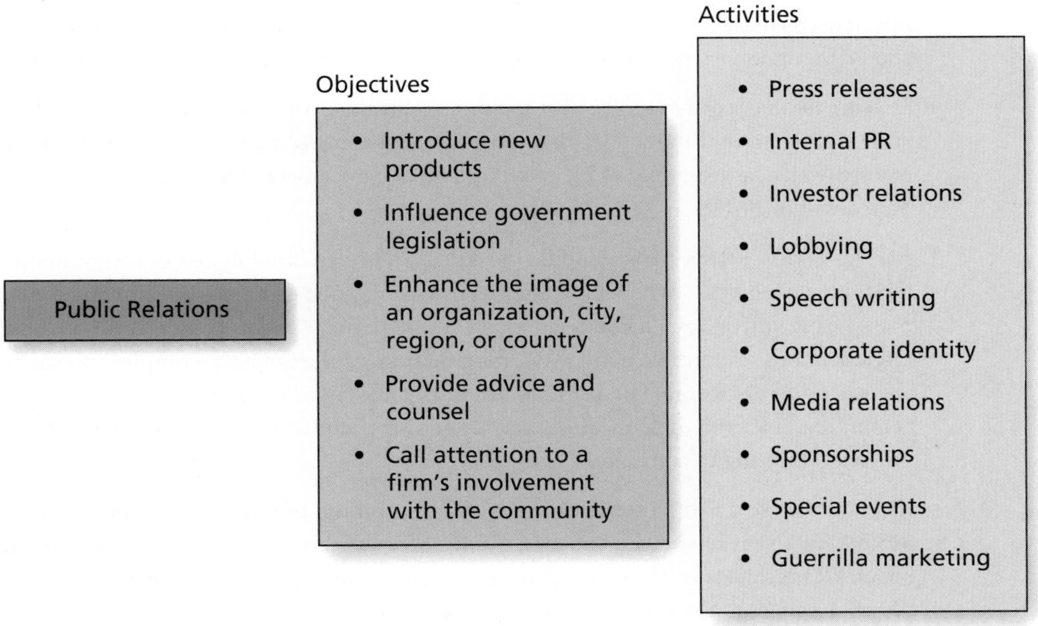

Public Relations

Objectives
- Introduce new products
- Influence government legislation
- Enhance the image of an organization, city, region, or country
- Provide advice and counsel
- Call attention to a firm's involvement with the community

Activities
- Press releases
- Internal PR
- Investor relations
- Lobbying
- Speech writing
- Corporate identity
- Media relations
- Sponsorships
- Special events
- Guerrilla marketing

One of the barriers to greater reliance on PR campaigns is *evaluation*; compared to many other forms of marketing communications, it's difficult to devise metrics to gauge their effectiveness. Who can say precisely what impact an appearance by Steve Carell on *The Tonight Show* to plug his new movie exerts on ticket sales, or whether Virgin's sponsorship of the London Marathon boosted purchases of airline tickets? It is possible to tell if a PR campaign gets media exposure, though compared to advertising it's much more difficult to assess bottom-line impact. Table 13.3 describes some of the most common PR measurement techniques.

Public Relations Objectives

Marketing communication experts know that PR strategies are best used in concert with advertising, sales promotion, and personal selling to send a consistent message to customers and other stakeholders. As part of the total marketing communication plan, they often rely on PR to accomplish the following objectives:

- *Introduce new products to retailers and consumers.* To make the most of the introduction of the iPad in January 2010, Apple staged a live press conference hosted by CEO Steve Jobs in his trademark blue jeans and black turtleneck.[64]

- *Influence government legislation.* Airplane maker Boeing spent over a decade in public relations activities to persuade regulators that jetliners with two engines are as safe as those with three or four engines even for nonstop international flights, some as long as 16 hours.[65]

- *Enhance the image of an organization.* The Ladies Professional Golf Association (LPGA) used a variety of public relations and other promotion activities—from product endorsements to player blogs to sexy calendars—in its "These Girls Rock" campaign. The program to change the image of ladies' golf to a hip sport seems to be working, as both tournament attendance and television audiences have increased.[66]

- *Provide advice and counsel.* Because of their expertise and understanding of the effects of communication on public opinion, PR professionals also provide *advice and counsel* for top management. When a firm needs to shut down a plant or to build a new one, to discontinue a product or add to the product line, to fire a vice president, or to give an award to an employee who spends hundreds of hours a year doing volunteer work in his community, it needs the advice of its PR staff. What is the best way to handle the situation? How should the announcement be made? Who should be told first? What is to be said and how?

- *Enhance the image of a city, region, or country.* To promote Vancouver, British Columbia, and Canada around the world, the not-for-profit business organization Tourism Vancouver used a large variety of PR activities to make the most of the Winter Olympics in Vancouver in 2010.[67]

- *Manage a crisis.* PR specialists handle the crucial but often difficult task of communicating with stakeholders when something goes wrong, such as when BP is involved in a massive oil spill or Toyota issues a massive recall of cars with faulty accelerator pedals. Organizations respond in many ways, ranging from (unfortunately) complete denial or silence to full disclosure. For example, when Toyota started to receive reports of unsafe cars in the U.K., the director of the carmaker's operations there posted a five-minute video apologizing to consumers.[68]

- *Call attention to a firm's involvement with the community.* U.S. marketers spend about $15 billion a year to sponsor sporting events, rock concerts, museum exhibits, and the ballet. PR specialists work behind the scenes to ensure that sponsored events receive ample press coverage and exposure. We'll talk more about sponsorships later in this section.

Table 13.3 | Measuring the Effectiveness of Public Relations (PR) Tactics

Method	Description	Example	Pros	Cons
Personal (subjective) evaluation of PR activities	Evaluation of PR activities by superiors may occur at all levels of the organization.	Items in employee annual reviews relate to the successful fulfillment of PR role.	Simple and inexpensive to complete; assures an annual assessment will be completed.	Subjective nature of the evaluation may result in biased appraisal. Employees may focus on the annual review to the exclusion of some important PR goals.
Matching of PR activity accomplishments with activity objectives	Simple counts of actual PR activities accomplished compares with activity goals set for the period.	Goal: to obtain publication of three feature articles in major newspapers in the first quarter of the year. Result: four articles published.	Focuses attention on the need for quantitative goals for PR activities and achievements. Easy and inexpensive to measure.	Focuses on activity goals rather than image or communication goals. Ignores image perception or attitudes of the firm's publics.
Evaluation of communication objectives through opinion surveys among the firm's publics	Surveys are used to determine if image/communication goals are met within key groups.	Goal: to achieve an improved image of the organization among at least 30 percent of financial community stakeholders.	Causes PR professionals to focus on actual communication results of activities.	May be difficult to measure changes in perceptions among the firm's publics. Factors not under the control of PR practitioners may influence public perceptions. It is relatively expensive. Results may take many months, thus preventing corrective actions in PR activities.
Measurement of coverage in print and broadcast media, especially those generated by PR activities	Systematic measurement of coverage achieved in print media (column inches/pages) and broadcast media (minutes of air time).	Total number of column inches of newspaper articles resulting from PR releases. Total number of articles including those not from PR releases. Total amount of positive print and broadcast coverage. Total amount of negative print and broadcast coverage. Ratio of negative to positive print and broadcast coverage.	Very objective measurements with little opportunity for bias. Relatively inexpensive.	Does not address perceptions, attitudes, or image issues of the organization.
Impression measurement	Measure the size of the audience for all print and broadcast coverage. Often assessment includes comparisons in terms of advertising costs for same number of impressions.	Network news coverage during the time period equaled over 15 million gross impressions. This number of impressions through advertising would have cost $4,500,000.	Objective, without any potential bias in measurement; provides a monetary measure to justify the expenditures of the PR office or consultant. Relatively inexpensive.	Does not differentiate between negative and positive news coverage. Does not consider responses of publics to the coverage. Assumes advertising and PR communication activities are equal.

Public Relations Tactics

In order to accomplish their objectives, PR professionals choose from a variety of tactics as shown in 📷 Figure 13.5. These activities include press releases, activities aimed at specific internal and external stakeholder groups, speech writing and corporate communications, sponsorships and special events, and guerilla marketing activities.

Press Release

press release
Information that an organization distributes to the media intended to win publicity.

The most common way for PR specialists to communicate is by a **press release**. This is a report of some event or activity that an organization writes and sends to the media in the hope that it will be published for free. A newer version of this idea is a *video news release* (*VNR*) that tells the story in a film format instead. Some of the most common types of press releases include the following:

- *Timely topics* deal with topics in the news, such as Levi Strauss's efforts to promote "Casual Fridays" to boost sales of its Dockers and Slates casual dress pants by highlighting how different corporations around the country are adopting a relaxed dress code.

- *Research project stories* are published by universities to highlight breakthroughs by faculty researchers.

- *Consumer information releases* provide information to help consumers make product decisions, such as helpful tips from Butterball about how to prepare dishes for Thanksgiving dinner.

Internal PR and External Stakeholders

internal PR
PR activities aimed at employees of an organization.

Internal PR activities target employees; they often include company newsletters and closed-circuit television to keep people informed about company objectives, successes, or even plans to "downsize" the workforce. Often company newsletters also are distributed outside the firm to suppliers or other important publics.

investor relations
PR activities such as annual and quarterly reports aimed at a firm's investors.

Investor relations activities focus on communications to those whose financial support is critical; this is especially vital for publicly held companies. It is the responsibility of the PR department to develop and distribute annual and quarterly reports and to provide other essential communications with individual and corporate stockholders, with investment firms, and with capital market organizations.

lobbying
Talking with and providing information to government officials in order to influence their activities relating to an organization.

Lobbying means talking with and providing information to government officials to persuade them to vote a certain way on pending legislation or even to initiate legislation or regulations that would benefit the organization.

Speech Writing and Corporate Communications

speech writing
Writing a speech on a topic for a company executive to deliver.

An important job of a firm's PR department is **speech writing**; specialists provide speeches for company executives to deliver. While some executives do actually write their own speeches, it is more common for a speechwriter on the PR staff to develop an initial draft of a speech to which the executive might add her own input. PR specialists also provide input on **corporate identity** materials, such as logos, brochures, building design, and even stationery that communicates a positive image for the firm.

corporate identity
Materials such as logos, brochures, building design, and stationery that communicate an image of the organization.

One of the tasks of the PR professional is to develop close **media relations** to ensure the organization will receive the best media exposure possible for positive news, such as publicizing the achievements of an employee who has done some notable charity work or for a product the company developed that saved someone's life. And, as we've seen, good media relations can be even more important when things go wrong. News editors are less inclined to present a story of a crisis in its most negative way if they have a good relationship with PR people in the organization.

media relations
A PR activity aimed at developing close relationships with the media.

Sponsorships and Special Events

Sponsorships are PR activities through which companies provide financial support to help fund an event in return for publicized recognition of the company's contribution. Many companies today find that their promotion dollars are well spent to sponsor a golf tournament, a NASCAR driver, a symphony concert, or global events such as the Olympics or World Cup soccer competition. These sponsorships are particularly effective because they allow marketers to reach customers during their leisure time; people often appreciate these efforts because the financial support makes the events possible in the first place.

A related task is to plan and implement **special events**. Companies find special events useful for a variety of purposes. For example, a firm might hold a press conference to increase interest and excitement in a new product or other company activity. A city or state may hold an annual event such as the strawberry festivals in Florida and California or the National Cherry Blossom Festival in Washington, D.C. to promote tourism. A company outing like the huge road rallies Harley-Davidson's Harley Owner's Group (H.O.G.) sponsors reinforces loyalty toward an existing product. Other special events aim simply to create buzz and generate publicity. For New York City

McDonald's, a sponsor of the FIFA World Cup since 1994, built on its sponsorship to create promotions in its restaurants around the world. McDonald's global Player Escort Program sent 1,408 children ages 6 to 10 to the World Cup where they escorted players onto the field for all 64 FIFA matches. In Brazil, McDonald's restaurants offered customers sandwiches with flavors from countries competing in the World Cup. World Cup beverage cups were available for customers in some countries, including China and the United States, and some locations in Europe offered consumers a World Cup burger, which was 40 percent larger than McDonald's Big Mac.[69]

shoppers, Unilever created its "All Small & Mighty Clothes Bus," a 40-foot bus it covered in all the shirts, shorts, and socks that one bottle of super-concentrated All laundry detergent can wash. Consumers who spotted the bus during its 12-day campaign could "clean up" if they entered a sweepstakes to win a $5,000 shopping spree or $200 gift cards.[70]

Guerrilla Marketing

Organizations with tiny advertising budgets need to develop innovative—and cheap—ways to capture consumers' attention. **Guerrilla marketing** activities are an increasingly popular way to accomplish this objective. No, this term doesn't refer to marketers making monkeys out of themselves (that's "gorilla marketing"). A guerrilla marketing strategy involves "ambushing" consumers with promotional content in places where they don't expect to encounter these messages. These activities include putting advertising stickers on apples, placing product-related messages on the backs of theater tickets and flags on golf courses, or even staging elaborate dance routines in train stations. T-Mobile pulled this off at the Liverpool station in the U.K. as 350 pedestrians suddenly congregated in the center and launched into an elaborate group routine as the song *Shout!* played on huge speakers (check out the video at **http://www.youtube.com/watch?v5VQ3d3KigPQM&feature5player_embedded#at530**).

Today, big companies buy into guerrilla marketing strategies big time. Burger King recently decided to increase sales in its Asia-Pacific stores by 25 percent. The company sent CDs with quirky marketing suggestions to local restaurant managers. These included putting "I♥BK" on T-shirts and placing the shirts on Ronald McDonald, placing large footprints from McDonald's stores to Burger King outlets, placing signs on empty benches saying "gone to BK—Ronald," and placing large signs at BK locations that are near KFC locations that read, "It's why the chicken crossed the road."[71]

Companies use guerrilla marketing to promote new drinks, cars, clothing styles, or even computer systems. Much to the annoyance of city officials in San Francisco and Chicago, IBM painted hundreds of "Peace Love Linux" logos on sidewalks to publicize the company's adoption of the Linux operating system. Even though the company got hit with

sponsorships
PR activities through which companies provide financial support to help fund an event in return for publicized recognition of the company's contribution.

special events
Activities—from a visit by foreign investors to a company picnic—that are planned and implemented by a PR department.

guerrilla marketing
Marketing activity in which a firm "ambushes" consumers with promotional content in places they are not expecting to encounter this kind of activity.

a hefty bill to pay for cleaning up the "corporate graffiti," one marketing journalist noted that they "got the publicity they were looking for."[72] Given the success of many of these campaigns that operate on a shoestring budget, expect to see even more of these tactics as other companies climb on the guerrilla bandwagon.

4 Sales Promotion

OBJECTIVE

Explain what sales promotion is, and describe the different types of consumer sales promotion activities.
(pp. 408–411)

sales promotion
Programs designed to build interest in or encourage purchase of a product during a specified period.

Sometimes when you walk through your student union on campus you might get assaulted by a parade of people eager for you to enter a contest, taste a new candy bar, or take home a free T-shirt with a local bank's name on it. These are examples of **sales promotion**, programs that marketers design to build interest in or encourage purchase of a good or service during a specified period.[73]

How does sales promotion differ from advertising? Both are paid messages from identifiable sponsors to change consumer behavior or attitudes. In some cases, a traditional advertising medium actually publicizes the sales promotion, as when Denny's restaurant used Super Bowl advertising to tell consumers about its free breakfast offer. But while marketers carefully craft advertising campaigns to create long-term positive feelings about a brand, company, or store, sales promotions are more useful if the firm has an *immediate* objective, such as bolstering sales for a brand quickly or encouraging consumers to try a new product.

Marketers today place an increasing amount of their total marketing communication budget into sales promotion. Several reasons account for this increase. First, due to the growth of very large grocery store chains and mass merchandisers such as Walmart, there has been a shift in power in the channels. These large chains can pressure manufacturers to provide deals and discounts. A second reason for the growth in sales promotion is declining consumer brand loyalty. This means that consumers are more likely to purchase products based on cost, value, or convenience. Thus a special sales promotion offer is more likely to cause price-conscious customers to switch brands.

Marketers target sales promotion activities either to ultimate consumers or to members of the channel such as retailers that sell their products. Thus we divide sales promotion into two major categories: consumer-oriented sales promotion and trade-oriented sales promotion. In this chapter we will talk about the consumer type. We'll talk about the trade type in Chapter 14. You'll see some examples of common consumer-oriented sales promotions in Table 13.4.

Sales Promotion Directed toward Consumers

As we said, one of the reasons for an increase in sales promotion is because it works. For consumer sales promotion, the major reason for this is that most promotions temporarily change the price/value relationships. A coupon for 50 cents off the price of a bottle of ketchup reduces the price while a special "25 percent more" jar of peanuts increases the value. And if you get a free hairbrush when you buy a bottle of shampoo, this also increases the value. Even the prize in the bottom of the box of cereal increases its value exponentially as every mother (unfortunately) knows. As shown in 📷 Figure 13.6, we generally classify consumer sales promotions as either price-based or attention-getting promotions.

Price-Based Consumer Sales Promotion

Many sales promotions target consumers where they live—their wallets. They emphasize *short-term price reductions* or *rebates* that encourage people to choose a brand—at least during the deal period. Price-based consumer promotions, however, have a downside similar

Table 13.4 | Consumer Sales Promotion Techniques: A Sampler

Technique	Description	Example
Coupons (newspaper, magazine, in-the-mail, on product packages, in-store, and on the Internet)	Certificates for money off on selected products, often with an expiration date, are used to encourage product trial.	Crest offers $5 off its WhiteStrips.
Price-off packs	Specially marked packages offer a product at a discounted price.	Tide laundry detergent is offered in a specially marked box for 50 cents off.
Rebates/refunds	Purchasers receive a cash reimbursement when they submit proofs of purchase.	Uniroyal offers a $40 mail-in rebate for purchasers of four new Tiger Paw tires.
Continuity/loyalty programs	Consumers are rewarded for repeat purchases through points that lead to reduced price or free merchandise.	Airlines offer frequent fliers free flights for accumulated points; a carwash offers consumers a half-price wash after purchasing 10 washes.
Special/bonus packs	Additional amount of the product is given away with purchase; it rewards users.	Maxell provides 10 free blank CDs with purchase of a pack of 50.
Contests/sweepstakes	Offers consumers the chance to win cash or merchandise. Sweepstakes winners are determined strictly by chance. Contests require some competitive activity such as a game of skill.	Publisher's Clearing House announces its zillionth sweepstakes.
Premiums: Free premiums include in-pack, on-pack, near pack, or in-the-mail premiums; consumers pay for self-liquidating premiums	A consumer gets a free gift or low-cost item when a product is bought; reinforces product image and rewards users.	A free makeup kit comes with the purchase of $20 worth of Clinique products.
Samples (delivered by direct mail, in newspapers and magazines door-to-door, on or in product packages, and in-store)	Delivering an actual or trial-sized product to consumers in order to generate trial usage of a new product.	A free small bottle of Clairol Herbal Essences shampoo arrives in the mail.

to trade promotions that involve a price break. If a company uses them too frequently, this "trains" its customers to purchase the product at only the lower promotional price. Price-based consumer sales promotion includes the following:

- *Coupons:* Try to pick up any Sunday newspaper without spilling some coupons. These certificates, redeemable for money off a purchase, are the most common price promotion. Indeed, they are the most popular form of sales promotion overall. Companies distribute billions of them annually in newspapers, magazines, in the mail, in stores, by e-mail, and through the Internet. One company, Val-Pak, has created an entire business

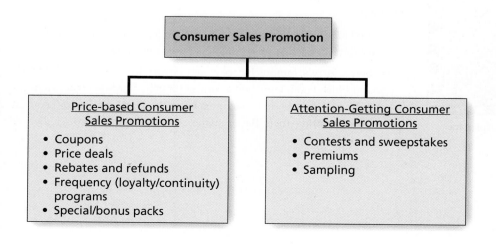

Figure 13.6 📷 *Snapshot* | Types of Consumer Sales Promotions

Consumer sales promotions are generally classified as price-based or attention-getting promotions.

around coupons. You've probably received a Val-Pak envelope in the mail—it's the one with dozens of coupons and other offers inside. Even industries such as pharmaceuticals that never tried this approach before now use it in a big way. This industry mails coupons that customers can redeem for free initial supplies of drugs. Coupons are also available through sites such as **Viagra.com** and **Purplepill.com**. Companies use the coupons to prompt patients to ask their physician for the specific brand instead of a competing brand or a more economical generic version.[74]

- *Price deals, refunds, and rebates:* In addition to coupons, manufacturers often offer a temporary price reduction to stimulate sales. This price deal may be printed on the package itself, or it may be a price-off flag or banner on the store shelf. Alternatively, companies may offer refunds or **rebates** that allow the consumer to recover part of the purchase price via mail-ins to the manufacturer. Today, many retailers such as Best Buy print the rebate form for you along with your sales receipt. After you mail it in, you can track whether the check has been sent to you by visiting the retailer's Web site.

rebates
Sales promotions that allow the customer to recover part of the product's cost from the manufacturer.

frequency programs
Consumer sales promotion programs that offer a discount or free product for multiple purchases over time; also referred to as loyalty or continuity programs.

- *Frequency (loyalty/continuity) programs:* **Frequency programs**, also called *loyalty* or *continuity programs*, offer a consumer a discount or a free product for multiple purchases over time. Mike Gunn, former vice president of marketing at American Airlines, is widely credited with developing this concept in the early 1980s when he coined the phrase "frequent flyer" miles. Of course, all the other airlines were quick to follow suit, as were a host of other firms, including retailers, auto rental companies, hotels, restaurants—you name it, and they have a customer loyalty program. Virgin Atlantic has gone one step farther with its frequent flyer program, which allows Virgin Atlantic Flying Club members the chance to redeem miles for a trip to outer space—only 2 million miles required![75] La Croissanterie, a French-style fast-food chain in Paris, offers an enhanced customer loyalty program that allows customers to identify themselves with a paper pass, a smart-phone application or their public transportation pass—no problem if you happen to leave the loyalty card at home.[76]

  - *Special/bonus packs:* Another form of price promotion involves giving the shopper more product instead of lowering the price.[77] How nice to go to Walgreen's and find an 8-ounce bottle of Nivea lotion packaged with another 4 ounces free! A special pack also can be in the form of a unique package such as a reusable decorator dispenser for hand soap.

Ben & Jerry's uses a game as part of its campaign to combat global warming.

Attention-Getting Consumer Sales Promotions

Attention-getting consumer promotions stimulate interest in a company's products. Some typical types of attention-getting promotions include the following:

- *Contests and sweepstakes:* According to their legal definitions, a contest is a test of skill, while a sweepstakes is based on chance.

  - Ben & Jerry's, famous for ice cream flavors such as Chunky Monkey and Phish Food, launched a contest for consumers to create an original flavor ice cream. Consumers enter the "Do Us a Flavor" contest by submitting their flavor name and description through Ben & Jerry's Web site.[78]

- As part of the kickoff of Disney's global marketing campaign themed "Where Dreams Come True," Disney offered consumers an online *Keys to the Magic Kingdom* sweepstakes. The winning family received a trip to Walt Disney World Resort and a day at the Magic Kingdom.[79]

- Oreo included consumers as not only the contestants, but also the judges in its Oreo & Milk Jingle Contest. The top five contestants' renditions of the Oreo song were posted on the **Oreo.com** Web site. Consumers entered part of an Oreo package UPC to vote for their favorite; the winner received $10,000 and a recording session for an Oreo radio spot and a trip to Los Angeles to visit with *American Idol* judge Randy Jackson.[80]

Cooking contest (such as the "Bourboncuing" contest sponsored by Jim Beam) are a popular way to let consumers "strut their stuff" and create a buzz about the company's products.

- *Premiums:* **Premiums** are items you get free when you buy a product. The prize in the bottom of the box of cereal—the reason many college students open the box from the bottom—is a premium. Prepaid phone cards have become highly popular premiums. Companies that jump on the phone card bandwagon offer cards emblazoned with pictures of sports heroes, products, and rock bands. Phone cards make ideal premiums because they are compact, they can display brand logos or attractive graphics, and they provide opportunities for repeat exposure. And an important benefit for the marketer is the ability to build databases by tracking card usage.[81] Your "good neighbor" State Farm agent used to send you a calendar on your birthday—now you're likely to get a phone card with 30 long-distance minutes on it, adorned with a reminder of your agent's phone number to be sure you won't forget who sent it to you.

premiums
Items offered free to people who have purchased a product.

- *Sampling:* How many starving college students at one time or another have managed to scrape together an entire meal by scooping up free food samples at their local grocery store? Some stores, like Publix and Sam's Club, actually promote Saturdays as sampling day in their advertising. **Product sampling** encourages people to try a product by distributing trial-size and sometimes regular-size versions in stores, in public places such as student unions, or through the mail. Many marketers now distribute free samples through sites on the Internet.[82] Companies like Procter & Gamble, Unilever, S.C. Johnson, and GlaxoSmithKline are readily taking advantage of Web sites such as **www .freesamples.com** and **www.startsampling.com** that distribute the firms' samples and then follow up with consumer-satisfaction surveys.

product sampling
Distributing free trial-size versions of a product to consumers.

Now, that you've learned about advertising, public relations, and consumer sales promotion, read "Real People, Real Choices: How It Worked Out" to see how it worked out for The Brownstein Group.

Oscar Mayer created an eye-catching promotion with its Weinermobile—guaranteed to draw attention from hot dog lovers.

Here's my choice...

Real **People**, Real **Choices**

1 Option **2** Option **3** Option

Why do you think Marc chose option #1?

How It Worked Out at Brownstein Group

The client agreed with Marc, as its account executives felt their first priority was to clearly define the brand in the wake of the attacks by the rival. Marc's agency rolled out an advertising campaign that used an educational approach to better explain what the new brand was and why it should be important to consumers. Ads appeared in print, outdoor, online, and on radio. As a result of this campaign, which "punched the bully in the nose," the attack ads from the competition soon subsided.

To learn the whole story, visit www.mypearsonmarketinglab.com.

Brand **YOU**!

Create an award-winning advertising campaign for your personal brand.

Think of your cover letter and résumé as your advertising . . . the award is landing the job you want. Learn simple tips that can make your cover letter and résumé more powerful and stand out in the crowd. Check out the cover letter and résumé examples in Chapter 13 of *Brand You*.

Objective Summary ➡ Key Terms ➡ Apply

CHAPTER 13
Study Map

1. Objective Summary (pp. 380–386)

Tell what advertising is, describe the major types of advertising, and discuss some of the criticisms of advertising.

Advertising is nonpersonal communication from an identified sponsor using mass media to persuade or influence an audience. Advertising informs and reminds consumers and creates consumer desire. Product advertising is used to persuade consumers to choose a specific product or brand. Institutional advertising is used to develop an image for an organization or company (corporate advertising), to express opinions (advocacy advertising), or to support a cause (public service advertising). Retail and local advertising informs customers about where to shop. Most firms rely on the services of advertising agencies to create successful advertising campaigns. Full-service agencies include account management, creative services, research and marketing services, and media planning, while limited-service agencies provide only one or a few services.

User-generated content (UGC), also known as consumer-generated media (CGM), includes online consumer comments, opinions, advice, consumer-to-consumer discussions, reviews, photos, images, videos, podcasts and webcasts, and product-related stories available to other consumers through digital technology. To take advantage of this phenomenon, some marketers encourage consumers to contribute their own do-it-yourself (DIY) ads. Crowdsourcing is a practice in which firms outsource marketing activities (such as selecting an ad) to a community of users, that is, a crowd.

Advertising has been criticized for being manipulative, for being deceitful and untruthful, for being offensive and in bad taste, for creating and perpetuating stereotypes, and for causing people to buy things they don't really need. While some advertising may justify some of these criticisms, most advertisers seek to provide honest ads that don't offend the markets they seek to attract.

Key Terms

product advertising, p. 381

institutional advertising, p. 381

corporate advertising, p. 381

advocacy advertising, p. 382

public service advertisements (PSAs), p. 382

advertising campaign, p. 382

limited-service agency, p. 382

full-service agency, p. 382

account executive, p. 382

account planner, p. 383

creative services, p. 383

research and marketing services, p. 383

media planner, p. 383

user-generated content (UGC) or consumer-generated media (CGM), p. 383

do-it-yourself (DIY) ads, p. 383

crowdsourcing, p. 384

greenwashing, p. 385

corrective advertising, p. 385

puffery, p. 385

2. Objective Summary (pp. 386–402)

Describe the process of developing an advertising campaign and how marketers evaluate advertising.

Development of an advertising campaign begins with understanding the target audiences and developing objectives for the message and the ad budget. To create the ads, the agency develops a creative strategy that is summarized in a creative brief. To come up with finished ads, they must decide on the appeal, the format, the tonality and the creative tactics and techniques. Pretesting advertising before placing it in the media prevents costly mistakes.

Media planning gets a message to a target audience in the most effective way. The media planner must decide whether to

place ads in traditional mass media or in digital media including Web site advertising, mobile advertising, and video sharing, variously referred to as owned media, paid or bought media, and earned media. Product placements, a type of branded entertainment, integrate products into movies, television shows, video games, novels, and even retail settings. Support media include directories, out-of-home media, and place-based media. A media schedule specifies the exact media the campaign will use and when and how often the message should appear.

The final step in any advertising campaign is to evaluate its effectiveness. Marketers evaluate advertising through posttesting. Posttesting research may include aided or unaided recall tests that examine whether the message had an influence on the target market.

Key Terms

creative strategy, p. 387

creative brief, p. 387

advertising appeal, p. 388

unique selling proposition (USP), p. 388

reminder advertising, p. 388

teaser or mystery advertising, p. 389

execution format, p. 389

tonality, p. 389

jingles, p. 391

slogans, p. 391

pretesting, p. 391

media planning, p. 392

digital media, p. 395

owned media, p. 395

paid media, p. 395

earned media, p. 395

banners, p. 396

buttons, p. 396

pop-up ad, p. 396

search engines, p. 396

Web directory, p. 396

e-mail advertising, p. 396

spam, p. 396

permission marketing, p. 397

mobile advertising, p. 397

video sharing, p. 397

vlogs, p. 397

branded entertainment, p. 397

augmented reality, p. 398

advergaming, p. 398

support media, p. 398

out-of-home media, p. 399

digital signage, p. 399

place-based media, p. 399

media schedule, p. 399

reach, p. 400

frequency, p. 400

gross rating points (GRPs), p. 400

cost per thousand (CPM), p. 400

posttesting, p. 401

unaided recall, p. 401

aided recall, p. 402

attitudinal measures, p. 402

3. Objective Summary (pp. 402–408)

Explain the role of public relations and the steps in developing a public relations campaign.

The purpose of PR is to build good relationships between an organization and its various publics and to establish and maintain a favorable image. Crisis management is the process of managing a company's reputation when some negative and often unplanned event threatens the organization's image.

The steps in a PR campaign begin with setting objectives, creating and executing a campaign strategy, and planning how the PR program will be evaluated. Public relations is useful to introduce new products; influence legislation; enhance the image of a city, region, or country; polish the image of an organization; provide advice and counsel; and call attention to a firm's community involvement.

PR specialists often use print or video news releases to communicate timely topics, research stories, and consumer information. Internal communications with employees include company newsletters and internal TV programs. Other PR activities include investor relations, lobbying, speech writing, developing corporate identity materials, media relations, arranging sponsorships and special events, and guerrilla marketing activities.

Key Terms

public relations (PR), p. 402

publicity, p. 402

crisis management, p. 402

public relations campaign, p. 403

press release, p. 406

internal PR, p. 406

investor relations, p. 406

lobbying, p. 406

speech writing, p. 406

corporate identity, p. 406

media relations, p. 406

sponsorships, p. 407

special events, p. 407

guerrilla marketing, p. 407

4. Objective Summary (pp. 408–411)

Explain what sales promotion is, and describe the different types of consumer sales promotion activities.

Sales promotions are programs that marketers design to build interest in or encourage purchase of a good or service during a specified period. Marketers target sales promotion activities either to ultimate consumers or to members of the channel such as retailers that sell their products. Price-based consumer sales promotion include coupons; price deals, refunds, and rebates; frequency (loyalty/continuity) programs; and special/bonus packs. Attention-getting consumer sales promotions include contests and sweepstakes, premiums, and sampling.

Key Terms

sales promotion, p. 408

rebates, p. 410

frequency programs, p. 410

premiums, p. 411

product sampling, p. 411

Chapter **Questions** and **Activities**

Questions: Test Your Knowledge

1. What is advertising and what types of advertising do marketers use most often? What is an advertising campaign?

2. Firms may seek the help of full-service or limited-service advertising agencies for their advertising. Describe each. What are the different departments of a full-service agency?

3. What is consumer-generated advertising and why is it growing in importance? What is crowdsourcing and how is it used in advertising?

4. What are some of the major criticisms of advertising? What is corrective advertising? What is puffery?

5. Describe the steps in developing an advertising campaign. What is a creative brief? What is meant by the appeal, execution format, tonality, and creative tactics used in an ad campaign?

6. What is media planning? What are the strengths and weaknesses of traditional media, that is, television, radio, newspapers, and magazines?

7. What is digital media? How do marketers use Web site advertising, mobile advertising, and video sharing in their digital media activities? What are owned, paid, and earned media?

8. How do marketers use branded entertainment and support media such as directories, out-of-home media, and place-based media to communicate with consumers?

9. How do marketers pretest their ads? How do they posttest ads?

10. What is media planning? How do media planners use reach, frequency, gross rating points, and cost per thousand in developing effective media schedules? What are continuous, flighting, and pulsing media schedules?

11. What is the purpose of public relations? What is a crisis-management plan? What are the some of the objectives of PR? Describe some of the activities that are part of PR.
12. What is sales promotion? Explain some of the different types of consumer sales promotions marketers frequently use.

Activities: Apply What You've Learned

1. Assume that you are a member of the marketing department for a firm that produces several brands of household cleaning products. Your assignment is to develop recommendations for several consumer sales promotion activities that will be used in introducing a new laundry detergent. Develop an outline of your recommendations for these sales promotions. In a role-playing situation, present and defend your recommendations to your boss.
2. As an account executive for an advertising agency, you have been assigned to a new client, a company that has developed a new energy soft drink. As you begin development of the creative strategy, you are considering different types of ad execution formats and tonality:
   a. Comparative advertising
   b. A fear appeal
   c. A celebrity endorsement
   d. A slice-of-life ad
   e. Sex appeal
   f. Humor
   Outline the strengths and weaknesses of using each of these appeals for advertising the new soft drink. Using your recommendations, develop an outline for a TV commercial for the new product. Develop a report of your recommendations.
3. Assume that you are the head of PR for a regional fast-food chain that specializes in fried chicken and fish. A customer has claimed that he became sick when he ate a fried roach that was in his chicken dinner at one of your restaurants. As the director of PR, what recommendations do you have for how the firm might handle this crisis?
4. As we discussed in this chapter, many consumers are highly critical of advertising. In order to better understand this, conduct a short survey of (1) your college classmates and (2) a different group of consumers such as your parents and their friends. In the survey ask the respondents about the criticisms of advertising discussed in this chapter, that is, that advertising (1) is manipulative, (2) is deceptive and untruthful, (3) is offensive and in bad taste, (4) creates and perpetuates stereotypes, and (5) causes people to buy things they don't really need. Be sure to ask respondents to give you examples of ads that they feel fall in these categories. Develop a report that summarizes your results and compares the attitudes of the two consumer groups.

5. Watch three of your favorite TV programs. While you watch the programs, take notes on each product placement in the programs. Be sure to record how many seconds (approximately) the product is in view and where the product is located (e.g., was an actor holding the product, was it in the background, on a table, etc.). Develop a report that summarizes your findings.
6. As an alternate activity for #5 above, view a new hit movie and develop a report on the product placements in the movie.
7. Look through some magazines to find an ad that fits each of the following categories:
   a. USP strategy
   b. Demonstration
   c. Testimonial
   d. Slice-of-life
   e. Sex -oriented
   f. Humor-oriented
   Critique each ad. Tell who the target market appears to be. Describe how the message is executed. Discuss what is good and bad about the ad. Do you think the ad will be effective? Why or why not?

Marketing Metrics Exercise

Media planners use a variety of metrics to help in making decisions on what TV show or which magazines to include in their media plans. Two of these are gross rating points (GRPs) and cost per thousand (CPM).

Assume you are developing a media plan for a new brand of gourmet frozen meals. Your target market includes females ages 25–64. Following is a list of six possible media buys you are considering for the media plan. The plan is based on a four-week period.

1. Calculate the GRPs for each media buy based on the information given.
2. Calculate the CPM for each media buy.
3. Based on the cost of each buy, the reach or rating of each buy, and any qualitative factors that you feel are important, select four of the media buys that you would recommend.
4. Tell why you would select the four.

Media Vehicle	Rating	Cost per Ad or Insertion	Number of Insertions	CPM	GRPs for This Number of Insertions
American Idol	30	$500,000	4 (1 per weekly episode)		
NCIS	20	$400,000	4 (1 per weekly episode)		
CBS Evening News	12	$150,000	20 (1 per weeknight news program)		
Time magazine	5	$40,000	4 (1 per weekly publication)		
Better Homes and Gardens magazine	12	$30,000	1 (1 per monthly publication)		
USA Today	4	$10,000	12 (3 ads per week)		

Choices: What Do You Think?

1. Firms are increasing their use of search engine marketing in which they pay search engines such as Google and Bing for priority position listings. And social media sites such as Twitter are generating revenue by offering to sell "search words" to firms so that their posting appears on top. Are such practices ethical? Are consumers being deceived when a firm pays for priority positioning?

2. Because of concerns about the effectiveness of mass media advertising, more and more firms are using product placements, also referred to as branded entertainment, to put their product in front of consumers. But is this practice really ethical? Are consumers deceived when they see a can of diet Coke on the *American Idol* judges' table? Or what about the can of Dr. Pepper on the table of Tony Stark's house in *Iron Man 2*? Does the average consumer believe the can is there because it is the favorite of a TV or movie celebrity or are most consumers savvy enough to recognize it as a paid product placement? Should the government regulate product placements, perhaps requiring TV programs and movies to inform consumers about the paid placements? Are consumers really harmed by such practices?

3. Some people are turned off by advertising because they say it is deceptive or offensive, that it creates stereotypes and causes people to buy things they don't need. Others argue that advertising is beneficial and actually provides value for consumers. What are some arguments on each side? How do you feel?

4. Today, advertisers are spending less on mass media advertising and more on alternative media, that is, online, mobile, entertainment, and digital out-of-home media. How has this affected the advertising industry so far, and do you think this will affect it in the future? What are some ways that advertising has so far responded to this? What ideas do you have for how they can respond in the future?

5. User-generated content (UGC), also known as consumer-generated media (CGM) includes online consumer comments, opinions, advice, consumer-to-consumer discussions, reviews, photos, images, videos, podcasts and webcasts, and product-related stories available to other consumers through digital technology. What are the problems and benefits for marketers of UCG? How should marketers respond to UCG? Do you think marketers should encourage UCG or attempt to discourage it? Why do you feel that way?

6. Companies sometimes teach consumers a "bad lesson" with the overuse of sales promotions. As a result, consumers expect the product always to be "on deal" or have a rebate available. What are some examples of products for which this has occurred? How do you think companies can prevent this?

7. Some critics denounce PR specialists, calling them "flacks" or "spin doctors" whose job is to hide the truth about a company's problems. What is the proper role of PR within an organization? Should PR specialists try to put a good face on bad news?

Miniproject: Learn by Doing

The purpose of this miniproject is to give you an opportunity to experience the advertising creative process.

1. First, you should create (imagine) a new brand of an existing product (such as a laundry detergent, toothpaste, perfume, or soft drink). If you are doing a marketing plan project in your course, you might use the same product for this miniproject.

2. Next, you should decide on your creative strategy. What appeal, execution format, tonality, and creative tactics do you think are best?

3. Create a series of at least three magazine ads for your product, using the appeal you selected. Your ads should have a headline, a visual, and copy to explain your product and to persuade customers to purchase your brand.

4. Present your ads to your class. Explain your ad execution and the reasons for the various decisions you made in developing the ads.

Marketing in **Action** Case Real Choices at JetBlue

When low-cost carrier JetBlue Airways began operations in 1999, it promised customers cheap fares combined with exceptional service. JetBlue planes offer more leg room and all seats on JetBlue planes offer passengers 36-channel DIRECTV® service on seat-back screens.

For seven years, JetBlue, with a few exceptions, kept its promise to passengers and shot to the top of customer satisfaction surveys J.D. Power and Associates conducted. On Valentine's Day, 2007, however, the airline suffered the worst crisis in its history. Due to an unexpected New York ice storm, nine JetBlue planes full of passengers were stranded on the tarmac for over 6 hours—one plane and its 130 passengers sat on the tarmac for 10 hours. The planes left the gate and then found they couldn't take off, but the airlines, feeling that the storm would let up by midmorning, did not allow the planes to return to the gate. In the end, the wheels of the planes were frozen in the slush, unable to move.

In the next few days things got even worse for JetBlue as a snowball effect (pardon the pun) from the storm caused hundreds of flights to be cancelled—JetBlue's flight attendants and pilots were not where they were needed, and the company's communication system staff people were not trained to tell them what to do. At some airports, police had to be called in to help calm down the irate customers.

While the airline was far less than satisfactory in its response to the Valentine's Day ice storm, its response to the crisis was a model of excellent PR. Seeking to swiftly respond to the crisis and appease angry customers, CEO David Neeleman quickly apologized to customers and explained what went wrong. He said he felt "mortified" and "humiliated." To get his message across, he appeared on CNN's *American Morning, Today, Fox and Friends*, and *Squawk Box* early the next day. But JetBlue did more than just apologize to consumers. The airline offered passengers who were stranded on JetBlue planes for three hours or more a full refund plus a free round-trip ticket to any JetBlue destination. In all, the airline spent $30 million on vouchers for passengers of the 1,102 cancelled flights.

In addition to its immediate response to the February cancellations, JetBlue cited its dedication to "bringing humanity back to air travel" and established a Customer Bill of Rights retroactive to February 14. The Bill of Rights outlines what Jet-Blue will provide to its customers in cases of flight cancellations, departure delays, overbookings (customers who are denied boarding will receive $1,000), and even when the DIRECTV® is inoperable.

But will these changes satisfy customers? Most customers reacted with caution, saying that they would be watching the airline to see if it lived up to its promises. Other stranded passengers were less positive, and some vowed never to fly JetBlue again.

Will the Bill of Rights allow JetBlue to gain the level of customer loyalty it enjoyed before the crisis? While most customers of delayed flights may be satisfied, others may not. What about customers whose delays fall 10 minutes short of receiving a full-price trip voucher? And what will happen when another crisis occurs? JetBlue must continue to develop customer service and PR programs if it is to stay in the air for the long haul.

You Make the Call

1. What is the decision facing JetBlue?
2. What factors are important in understanding this decision situation?
3. What are the alternatives?
4. What decision(s) do you recommend?
5. What are some ways to implement your recommendation?

Based on: Bloomberg News, "Airlines' Proposals on Long Runway Delays," *New York Times* (February 23, 2007), http://www.nytimes.com/2007/02/23/business/23air.html?scp5162&sq5jetblue&st5nyt (accessed April 21, 2008); Jeff Bailey, "JetBlue Cancels More Flights in Storm's Wake," *New York Times* (February 18, 2007), http://www.nytimes.com/2007/02/18/business/18jetblue.html?scp5173&sq5jetblue&st5nyt (accessed April 21, 2008); Jeff Bailey, "JetBlue's C.E.O. Is 'Mortified' After Fliers Are Stranded," *New York Times* (February 19, 2007), http://www.nytimes.com/2007/02/19/business/19jetblue.html?scp5170&sq5jetblue&st5nyt (accessed April 21, 2008); Jeff Bailey, "Long Delays Hurt Image of JetBlue," *New York Times* (February 17, 2007), http://www.nytimes.com/2007/02/17/business/17air.html?scp5174&sq5jetblue&st5nyt (accessed April 21, 2008); "JetBlue's Customer Bill of Rights," http://www.jetblue.com/about/ourcompany/promise/index.html (accessed April 21, 2008).

One-to-One:
Trade Promotion, Direct Marketing, and Personal Selling

Real People **Profiles**

Jeffrey Brechman

Profile

▼ A Decision Maker at Woodtronics

Jeffrey Brechman is a principal at Woodtronics Inc., a company that designs and builds trading room furniture and command centers and network operation control centers for financial institutions, the military, and police and fire departments. Jeffrey moved into his career in an unconventional way. After a short stint in college, he started a painting business and wasn't thrilled about what he was doing. He got into a conversation about his career aspirations with a woman whose house he was painting. She, in turn, set up a meeting with her husband, who happened to be president of a company that manufactured and sold trading room console furniture. Trading room furniture is a very specialized niche business. It needs to accommodate a lot of electronic equipment to let brokers monitor the market, but also to take up a minimum amount of space so that brokerage houses can fit as many brokers as is comfortably possible in expensive floor space.

Info

💬 Jeffrey's Info

What do I do when I'm not working?
 A) Spend time with my family and play golf.

First job out of school?
 A) Telemarketer for American Automobile Association.

Career high?
 A) Telling my family about the first deal I won, not the actual win itself.

Business book I'm reading now?
 A) *Secrets of the Millionaire Mind: Mastering the Inner Game of Wealth* by T. Harv Eker.

My hero?
 A) My grandfather.

My motto to live by?
 A) Treat everyone as an equal.

What drives me?
 A) To be able to provide not only for my family but the employees that work for me.

My management style?
 A) I let the situation drive my style . . . stern when needed.

Here's my problem...

Jeffrey landed his first job as a sales executive in New York after that meeting. He worked hard to prove himself to this firm and he became its top salesperson in his very first year. He worked at that first company for four years, but then a competing company approached him to revitalize its business in the New York metropolitan area. This new company was losing money and was not a major competitor in the industry because it was not managed properly and it wasn't making sales it should have been winning. Jeffrey believed he could turn the company around, so he swallowed hard and moved to the competitor—Woodtronics. Within two years the company's sales had tripled, and it's now one of the leading manufacturers in the trading desk furniture industry. The turnaround came by carefully examining each area of the business and building on employees' strengths as well as improving products and customer service. In 2006, Woodtronics also opened an office in London to allow the growing company to expand its business overseas.

An architect had a client in Chicago who was using one of Woodtronics' best-selling trading desk products. The architect liked the product so much that he recommended it to another important client in Jersey City who would also be installing trading desks. Of course, Jeffrey was thrilled with the referral; this new client represented a major sale for Woodtronics. However, in the meantime the company had developed a prototype of a new model it called Evolution that Jeffrey believed would provide an even better solution for this new client. The Evolution technology platform is specifically designed for high-density technology trading environments; it maximizes work-surface area, allows for easier integration of new flat screen technology into the furniture, features a high-volume integrated heat removal system to increase the comfort for users, and also offers innovative designs to hide cumbersome computer cables, yet still provides access to them when needed.

Woodtronics really preferred to sell this new product, but the architect was hesitant to recommend it because he had used the older product in a prior project and it had worked out well for him. And this project would be the first large-scale installation, so he was afraid that his client would be a "guinea pig" by taking a chance on a product without a proven track record. To complicate the issue, the Jersey City client had shown a lack of enthusiasm for the original product because it didn't exactly meet his project's needs.

As a principal of the company, Jeffrey is personally involved in every one of its major sales. He had described the new product to the Jersey City client who was interested in learning more—but the architect was still resisting. Jeffrey had to make a critical sales decision or risk losing out completely on this large sale. Which product should he try to sell?

Things to remember

Woodtronics operates solely in business-to-business contexts, so the company relies primarily on personal selling to get and retain clients.

Jeffrey has both an ethical and a financial responsibility to do what's best for the client. He needs to recommend the Woodtronics product solution that will be most likely to meet the client's needs rather than just generating more business down the road with other clients.

Jeffrey considered his **Options** 1·2·3

Option 1

Push the original product even though this was not the best solution for the client. This approach would maintain the important relationship Jeffrey already had with the architect. But the new client wasn't satisfied with the current product, so the company's reputation was at risk if it offered a product it knew was not completely in line with the client's needs.

Option 2

Sell the client using the prototype of the Evolution platform, arguing that this alternative would better meet his needs in terms of both price and functionality. This option would let Jeffrey lead with his best, state-of-the-art product. But he would risk alienating the architect who had been so helpful in bringing new business to Woodtronics.

Option 3

Concentrate on raising the architect's comfort level with the new Evolution product and hope that he would be persuaded to recommend it to the new client instead. This option would deliver the right solution to the client and of course deliver a major sale to Woodtronics. If it succeeded, Jeffrey might even further boost the architect's confidence in Woodtronics to deliver the best solutions for his other clients down the road. But the architect was set on using the tried-and-true product; there was a real risk he would walk away from Woodtronics and find a competitor that didn't want to "field-test" a new product on one of his clients.

Now, put yourself in Jeffrey's shoes: Which option would you choose, and why?

You Choose

Which **Option** would you choose, and **why**?

1. ☐YES ☐NO   2. ☐YES ☐NO   3. ☐YES ☐NO

See what **option** Jeffrey chose and its success on **page 439**

trade promotions
Promotions that focus on members of the "trade," which include distribution channel members, such as retail salespeople or wholesale distributors, that a firm must work with in order to sell its products.

1

OBJECTIVE

Identify the sales promotion elements for B2B. (pp. 420–423)

Trade Sales Promotion: Targeting the B2B Customer

In Chapter 13 you learned about a variety of sales promotion techniques aimed directly at consumers. Now, we turn our attention to a different type of approach to sales promotion in which the consumer is decidedly *not* the primary target. Here, the target is the B2B customer—located somewhere within the supply chain. Such entities are traditionally referred to as "the trade." Hence, **trade promotions** focus on members of the supply chain, which include distribution channel members, such as retail salespeople or wholesale distributors with whom a firm must work to sell its products. (We'll discuss these and other distribution channel members in more detail in Chapters 15 and 16.)

Trade promotions take one of two forms: (1) those designed as discounts and deals, and (2) those designed to increase industry visibility. Let's take a look at both types of trade promotions in more detail. To help you follow along, 📷 Figure 14.1 portrays several of the most important types of trade sales promotion approaches, and Table 14.1 provides more details about each approach. You will note that some of the techniques, although primarily targeted to the trade, also appeal to consumers.

Figure 14.1 📷 *Snapshot* | Trade Sales Promotions

Trade sales promotions come in a variety of forms. Some are designed as discounts and deals for channel members and some are designed to increase industry visibility.

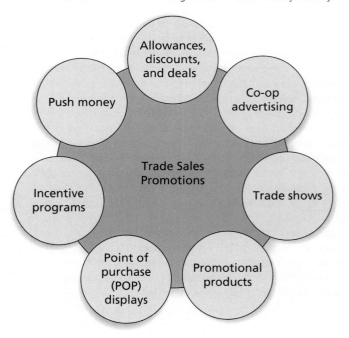

Check out chapter 14 Study Map on page 440

Table 14.1 | Characteristics of Trade Sales Promotion Approaches

Technique	Primary Target	Description	Example
Allowances, discounts, and deals	Trade	Retailers or other organizational customers receive discounts for quantity purchases or for providing special merchandising assistance.	Retailers get a discount for using a special Thanksgiving display unit for Pepperidge Farm Stuffing Mix.
Co-op Advertising	Trade and consumers	Manufacturers pay part of the cost of advertising by retailers who feature the manufacturer's product in their ads.	Toro pays half of the cost of Brad's Hardware Store newspaper advertising that features Toro lawn mowers.
Trade shows	Trade	Many manufacturers showcase their products to attendees.	The National Kitchen and Bath Association trade shows allow manufacturers to display their latest wares to owners of kitchen and bath remodeling stores.
Promotional products	Trade and consumers	A company builds awareness and reinforces its image by giving out "premiums" with its name on them.	Coors distributors provide bar owners with highly sought-after "Coors Light" neon signs. Caterpillar gives customers caps with the Caterpillar logo.
Point-of-purchase (POP) displays	Trade and consumers	In-store exhibits attract consumers' attention. Many POP displays also serve a merchandising function.	The Behr's paint display in Home Depot stores allow consumers to select from over 1,600 colors including 160 Disney colors.
Incentive programs	Trade	A prize is offered to employees who meet a prespecified sales goal or who are top performers during a given period.	Mary Kay cosmetics awards distinctive pink cars to its top-selling representatives.
Push money	Trade	A particular type of incentive program in which salespeople are given a bonus for selling a specific manufacturer's product.	A retail salesperson at a cosmetics counter gets $5 every time she sells a bottle of Glow perfume by JLo.

Discount Promotions

Discount promotions (deals) reduce the cost of the product to the distributor or retailer or help defray its advertising expenses. Firms design these promotions to encourage stores to stock the item and be sure it gets a lot of attention.

Allowances, Discounts, and Deals

One form of trade promotion is a short-term *price break*. A manufacturer can reduce a channel partner's costs with a sales promotion that discounts its products. For example, a manufacturer can offer a **merchandising allowance** to reimburse the retailer for in-store support of a product, such as when a store features an off-shelf display for a brand. Another way in which a manufacturer can reduce a channel partner's cost is with a **case allowance** that provides a discount to the retailer or wholesaler during a set period based on the sales volume of a product the retailer or wholesaler orders from the manufacturer.

However, allowances and deals have a downside. As with all sales promotion activities, the manufacturer expects these to be of limited duration, after which the distribution channel partner will again pay full price for the items. Unfortunately, some channel members engage in a practice the industry calls *forward buying*: They purchase large quantities of the product during a discount period, warehouse them, and don't buy them again until the manufacturer offers another discount. Some large retailers and wholesalers take this to an extreme when they engage in *diverting*. This describes an ethically questionable practice where the retailer buys the product at the discounted promotional price and warehouses it. Then, after the promotion has expired, the retailer sells the hoarded inventory to other retailers at a price that is lower than the manufacturer's nondiscounted price but high enough

merchandising allowance
Reimburses the retailer for in-store support of the product.

case allowance
A discount to the retailer or wholesaler based on the volume of product ordered.

to turn a profit. Obviously, both forward buying and diverting go against the manufacturer's intent in offering the sales promotion.

Co-op Advertising

co-op advertising
A sales promotion where the manufacturer and the retailer share the cost.

Another type of trade allowance is **co-op advertising**. These programs offer to pay the retailer a portion, usually 50 percent, of the cost of any advertising that features the manufacturer's product. Co-op advertising is a win–win situation for manufacturers because most local media vehicles offer lower rates to local businesses than to national advertisers. Both the retailer and the manufacturer pay for only part (normally half) of the advertising, plus the manufacturer gets the lower rate. Normally the amount available to a retailer for co-op advertising is limited to a percentage of the purchases the retailer makes during a year from the manufacturer.

Sales Promotion Designed to Increase Industry Visibility

Other types of trade sales promotions increase the visibility of a manufacturer's products to channel partners within the industry. Whether it is an elaborate exhibit at a trade show or a coffee mug with the firm's logo it gives away to channel partners, these aim to keep the company's name topmost when distributors and retailers decide which products to stock and push. These forms of sales promotion include the following:

trade shows
Events at which many companies set up elaborate exhibits to show their products, give away samples, distribute product literature, and troll for new business contacts.

- *Trade shows:* The thousands of industry **trade shows** in the United States and around the world each year are major vehicles for manufacturers to show off their product lines to wholesalers and retailers. Usually large trade shows are held in big convention centers where many companies set up elaborate exhibits to show their products, give away samples, distribute product literature, and troll for new business contacts. Today we also see more and more online trade shows that allow potential customers to preview a manufacturer's products remotely. This idea is growing in popularity, though many industry people find it a challenge to "schmooze" in cyberspace (it's also a little harder to collect all the great *swag* [promotional products] they give out at real-life shows!). An important benefit of traditional trade shows is the opportunity to develop customer leads that the company then forwards to its sales force for follow-up.

promotional products
Goodies such as coffee mugs, T-shirts, and magnets given away to build awareness for a sponsor. Some freebies are distributed directly to consumers and business customers; others are intended for channel partners such as retailers and vendors.

- *Promotional products:* We have all seen them: coffee mugs, visors, T-shirts, ball caps, key chains, refrigerator magnets, and countless other doodads emblazoned with a company's logo. They are examples of **promotional products**. Unlike licensed merchandise we buy in stores, sponsors give away these goodies to build awareness for their organization or specific brands. In many industries, companies vie for the most impressive promotional products and offer their business customers and channel partners upscale items such as watches, polar fleece jackets, and expensive leather desk accessories.

Point-of-purchase (POP) displays
In-store displays and signs.

- **Point-of-purchase (POP) displays**: Point-of-purchase materials include signs, mobiles, banners, shelf ads, floor ads, lights, plastic reproductions of products, permanent and temporary merchandising displays, in-store television, and shopping card advertisements. Manufacturers spend over $17 billion annually on POP displays because it keeps the name of the brand in front of the consumer, reinforces mass-media advertising, calls attention to other sales promotion offers, and stimulates impulse purchasing. Generally, manufacturers must give retailers a promotion allowance for use of POP materials. For retailers, the POP displays are useful if they encourage sales and increase revenues for the brand.

  It's a challenge for marketers to come up with new and innovative POP displays that will grab attention, such as the now classic promotion Bausch & Lomb ran in Spain some years ago. The company wanted to encourage consumers with good vision to buy contact lenses that changed their eye color. By letting shoppers upload their pictures to a computer in the store and digitally altering the photos, the promotion allowed people to see how they would look with five different eye colors without actually inserting the contacts.[1]

- *Incentive programs:* In addition to motivating distributors and customers, some promotions light a fire under the firm's own sales force. These incentives, or **push money**, may come in the form of cash bonuses, trips, or other prizes. Mary Kay Corporation—the in-home party plan cosmetics seller—is famous for giving its more productive distributors pink cars to reward their efforts. Another cosmetics marketer that uses a retail store selling model, Clinique, provides push money to department store cosmeticians to demonstrate and sell the full line of Clinique products. This type of incentive has the nickname *SPIF* for "sales promotion incentive funds." Even Starbucks has gotten into the incentive program business by offering gift cards that companies can purchase and provide for their salespeople to give clients as a small "thank you" for closing a sale.

push money
A bonus paid by a manufacturer to a salesperson, customer, or distributor for selling its product.

2

Direct Marketing

Are you one of those people who love to get lots of catalogs in the mail, pore over them for hours, and then order just exactly what you want without leaving home? Do you download music from iTunes or order books from **Amazon.com**? Have you ever responded to an infomercial on TV? All these are examples of direct marketing, the fastest-growing type of marketing communication.

Direct marketing refers to "any direct communication to a consumer or business recipient that is designed to generate a response in the form of an order, a request for further information, or a visit to a store or other place of business for purchase of a product."[2] The Direct Marketing Association (DMA) reports that direct-marketing-driven sales represent about 10 percent of the total U.S. gross domestic product (GDP)—an astounding figure! Spending on direct marketing is increasing, while at the same time spending on traditional advertising has declined—especially fueled by ad cutbacks during the recent economic downturn. And the projections for growth in outlays on direct marketing during the decade beginning in 2010 are very bullish.[3]

Clearly, direct marketing has the potential for high impact. Let's look at the four most popular types of direct marketing as portrayed in 📷 Figure 14.2: mail order (including catalogs and direct mail), telemarketing, direct-response advertising, and M-commerce. We'll start with the oldest—buying through the mail—which is still incredibly popular!

direct marketing
Any direct communication to a consumer or business recipient designed to generate a response in the form of an order, a request for further information, and/or a visit to a store or other place of business for purchase of a product.

Mail Order

In 1872, Aaron Montgomery Ward and two partners put up $1,600 to mail a one-page flyer that listed their merchandise with prices, hoping to spur a few more sales for their retail store.[4] The mail-order industry was born, and today consumers can buy just about anything through the mail. Mail order comes in two forms: catalogs and direct mail.

A **catalog** is a collection of products offered for sale in book form, usually consisting of product descriptions accompanied by photos of the items. Catalogs came on the scene within a few decades of the invention of movable type over 500 years ago, but they've come a long way since then.[5]

The early catalogs Montgomery Ward and other innovators such as Sears and JC Penney pioneered targeted people in remote areas who lacked access to stores. Today, the catalog customer is likely to be an affluent career woman with access to more than enough stores but without the time or desire to go to them. According to the DMA, over two-thirds of U.S. adults order from a catalog at least once a year.[6] Catalog mania extends well beyond clothing and cosmetics purchases. PC marketers HP and Dell both aggressively send out promotional catalogs that feature their own products along with accessories from a variety of manufacturers.

catalog
A collection of products offered for sale in book form, usually consisting of product descriptions accompanied by photos of the items.

Figure 14.2 📷 *Snapshot* | Key Forms of Direct Marketing

Key forms of direct marketing are mail order (including catalogs and direct mail), telemarketing, direct-response advertising, and M-commerce.

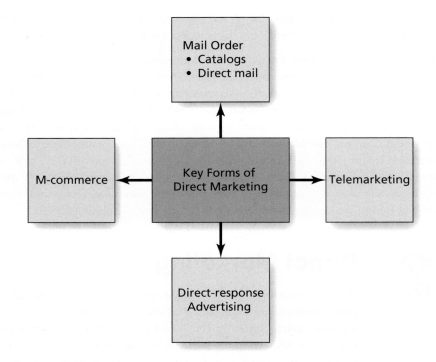

Many stores use catalogs to complement their in-store efforts—Neiman-Marcus is famous for featuring one-of-a-kind items like diamond-encrusted bras or miniature working versions of Hummers in its mailings as a way to maintain the store's image as a purveyor of unique and upscale merchandise. These upscale features change regularly, and avid Neiman's fans love to get the new catalog to find out what the next one is.

A catalog strategy allows the store to reach people in the United States who live in areas too small to support a store. But also, more and more U.S. firms use catalogs to reach overseas markets as well. Companies like Lands' End and Eddie Bauer do brisk sales in Europe and Asia, where consumers tend to buy more goods and services through the mail in the first place than do Americans. Lands' End opened a central warehouse in Berlin and attacked the German market with catalogs. The company trained phone operators in customer service and friendliness and launched an aggressive marketing campaign to let consumers know of the Lands' End lifetime warranty (German catalog companies require customers to return defective merchandise within two weeks to receive a refund). Although local competitors protested and even took the company to court, the case was settled in the American company's favor, and the Yankee invasion continues.

Catalog Choice started in 2007 as a Web site that enabled consumers to opt out of receiving catalogs by big companies (much like a "do not call" list for telemarketers). By 2010 the Web site (**www.catalogchoice.org**) claimed to be used by over 1.2 million people in communicating with nearly 3,000 catalogers! Part of the site's motivation is to reduce the waste unwanted paper catalogs create. Back when the 2007 holiday season came around, many catalog marketers initially didn't heed the requests of the consumers who signed up at Catalog Choice and mailed to them anyway. Since then, additional pressure has been put on the catalogers to comply and the Direct Marketing Association (DMA) itself has begun an initiative to help firms better police their own practices.[7]

Direct Mail

direct mail
A brochure or pamphlet that offers a specific good or service at one point in time.

Unlike a catalog retailer that offers a variety of merchandise through the mail, **direct mail** is a brochure or pamphlet that offers a specific good or service at one point in time. A direct mail offer has an advantage over a catalog because the sender can personalize it. Charities, political groups, and other not-for-profit organizations also use a lot of direct mail.

Just as with e-mail spamming, many Americans are overwhelmed with direct-mail offers—"junk mail"—that mostly end up in the trash. Traditional direct mail marketers are finding it increasingly difficult to get their promotional pieces to rise above the din of competitors' offers. A perfect example of overwhelming direct mail was the seemingly endless offers for new credit cards that bombarded consumers earlier in the 2000s, often resulting in the receipt of multiple promotional letters the same week (or even the same day!). However, this trend was cut short by the tightened credit markets and new regulations of the financial markets that followed the recession that began in 2008. The direct-mail industry constantly works on ways to monitor what companies send through the mail and provides some help when it allows consumers to "opt out" of at least some mailing lists.

Telemarketing

Telemarketing is direct marketing an organization conducts over the telephone (but why do they always have to call during dinner?). It might surprise you to learn that telemarketing actually is more profitable for business markets than for consumer markets. When business-to-business marketers use the telephone to keep in contact with smaller customers, it costs far less than a face-to-face sales call, yet still lets small customers know they are important to the company.

The Federal Trade Commission (FTC) established the *National Do Not Call Registry* to allow consumers to limit the number of telemarketing calls they receive. The idea is that telemarketing firms check the registry at least every 31 days and clean their phone lists accordingly. Consumers responded very positively to the regulation, and over 100 million have posted their numbers on the Registry to date. Some direct marketers initially challenged this action; they argued that it would put legitimate companies out of business while unethical companies would not abide by the regulation and continue to harass consumers. However, the National Do Not Call Registry, along with similar operations at the state level, now is an accepted part of doing business through direct marketing. The FTC maintains a list of violators on its Web site.[8]

The major issue on the horizon for telemarketers is whether they will be able to access cell phone numbers, as many consumers fear. In fact, rumors crop up from time to time that it's now necessary to place your cell number on the Do Not Call lists to avoid telemarketing calls (so far, that's not true). Especially for many young people, their cell phone often is their *only* phone, which makes the lack of penetration of this media a glaring hole in a telemarketing strategy.[9]

telemarketing
The use of the telephone to sell directly to consumers and business customers.

Direct-Response Advertising

Direct-response advertising allows the consumer to respond to a message by immediately contacting the provider to ask questions or order the product. This form of direct marketing can be very successful. Although for many companies the Internet has become the medium of choice for direct marketing, this technique is still alive and well in magazines, newspapers, and television.

As early as 1950, the Television Department Stores channel brought the retailing environment into the television viewer's living room when it offered a limited number of products the viewer could buy when he or she called the advertised company. Television sales picked up in the 1970s when two companies, Ronco Incorporated (you may have seen Ron Popeil on TV) and K-Tel International began to hawk products such as the Kitchen Magician, Pocket Fisherman, Mince-O-Matic, and Miracle Broom on television sets around the world.[10] And who can forget the late Billy Mays' enthusiastic hawking of Oxy Clean, Jupiter Jack, and nearly 20 other products on TV? Make a simple phone call and one of these wonders could be yours. **Direct-response TV (DRTV)** includes short commercials of less than two minutes, 30-minute or longer infomercials, and the shows home shopping networks such as

direct-response advertising
A direct marketing approach that allows the consumer to respond to a message by immediately contacting the provider to ask questions or order the product.

direct-response TV (DRTV)
Advertising on TV that seeks a direct response, including short commercials of less than two minutes, 30-minute or longer infomercials, and home shopping networks.

Ripped from the Headlines

Ethical/Sustainable Decisions in the Real World

Every once in a while in most Web surfers' lives, a suggestion pops up on the screen that leads them to wonder: How did they know that about me? The moment can seem magical, and a bit creepy. Consider this one. A female shopper at the retail site **FigLeaves.com** takes a close look at a silky pair of women's slippers. Next a recommendation appears for a man's bathrobe. This could seem terribly wrong—unless, of course, it turns out to be precisely what she wanted. This type of surprising connection will happen more often as e-marketers adopt a new generation of *predictive technology* fueled by growing rivers of behavioral data, from mouse clicks to search queries—all crunched by ever more powerful computers.

So, why the bathrobe? The e-commerce data cruncher for FigLeaves has found that certain types of female shoppers at certain times of the week are likely to be shopping for men. As mar-

keters scrutinize shoppers in greater detail, they're edging closer to their ultimate goal: teaching computers to blend data smarts with something close to the savvy of a flesh-and-blood sales clerk. Just as in the customer's first five minutes in a store when the salesperson is observing the customer's body language and tone of voice, now machines are being taught to pick up those same insights from movements online.

This dissection of online shopping comes amid growing fears about invasions of privacy online and especially concerns about social media sites like Facebook's access to our personal data and online behaviors. But unlike the most controversial advertising technology, which tracks Web surfers' wanderings from site to site, many of these "preference prediction" methods limit their scrutiny to behavior on a retailer's own Web page. Much of the analysis looks simply at the patterns of clicks, purchases, and other variables, without including personal information about the shopper. In most cases, personal details are incorporated only if a customer registers on the site and supplies them.

ETHICS CHECK: ↖
Find out what other students taking this course **would do** and **why** on **www .mypearsonmarketinglab .com**

Should firms be able to use your online activities to attempt to predict your buying behavior? Does "being watched" (virtually at least) make you feel uncomfortable?

☐**YES** ☐**NO**

infomercials
Half-hour or hour-long commercials that resemble a talk show but actually are sales pitches.

m-commerce
Promotional and other e-commerce activities transmitted over mobile phones and other mobile devices, such as smartphones and personal digital assistants (PDAs).

QVC and HSN broadcast. Top-selling DRTV product categories include exercise equipment, self-improvement products, diet and health products, kitchen appliances, and music.

The primitive sales pitches of the old days have largely given way to the slick **infomercials** we all know and love (?) today. These half-hour or hour-long commercials resemble a talk show, often with heavy product demonstration and spirited audience participation, but of course they really are sales pitches. Although some infomercials still carry a low-class, sleazy stereotype, in fact, over the years numerous heavyweights from Apple Computer to Volkswagen have used this format.

M-Commerce

One final type of direct marketing is m-commerce. The "m" stands for "mobile," but it could also stand for massive—because that's how big the market will be for this platform. **M-commerce** refers to the promotional and other e-commerce activities transmitted over mobile phones and other mobile devices, such as smartphones and personal digital assistants (PDAs). With over 4.5 billion mobile phones in use worldwide—more and more of them Internet-enabled—it makes sense that marketers would want to reach out and touch this large audience.[11] In fact, nearly 70 percent of the world's population has a mobile phone today! In Russia there are far more mobile phones in use than there are people! The top five countries in total mobile phones in use are (the second number is the percentage of population with a mobile phone):

1. China—786 million, 59.6 percent

2. India—636 million, 53.8 percent

3. United States—286 million, 91.0 percent

4. Russia—214 million, 147.3 percent

5. Brazil—185 million, 96.6 percent[12]

M-commerce through text messages (such as an ad for a concert or a new restaurant) is known as *short-messaging system* (SMS) marketing. In terms of unwanted "junk mail," m-commerce has the same potential dark side as other forms of direct marketing such as snail mail and e-mail. And the rise of the all-in-one smartphone on which the user engages in 24/7 social networking has created an up-and-coming industry of social networking activity tracking and analytics such as Google Analytics and similar programs. The feature on ethics and sustainability highlights the new-age science of *predicting* Web buying behavior.

3 Personal Selling: Adding the Personal Touch to the Promotion Mix

OBJECTIVE

Appreciate the important role of personal selling and how it fits into the promotion mix.
(pp. 427–431)

We saw in Chapter 13 that companies increasingly supplement traditional advertising with other communication methods, such as public relations campaigns and various forms of social media, as they work harder and harder to cut through the clutter of competitors' marketing communications. In this chapter, so far we've looked at two other forms of promotion—trade-directed sales promotion and direct marketing. Now we turn our attention to one of the most visible, and most expensive, forms of marketing communication—personal selling.

Personal selling occurs when a company representative interacts directly with a customer or prospective customer to communicate about a good or service. This form of promotion is a far more intimate way to talk to customers. Another advantage of personal selling is that salespeople are the firm's eyes and ears in the marketplace. They learn which competitors talk to customers, what they offer, and what new rival goods and services are on the way—all valuable competitive intelligence.

personal selling
Marketing communication by which a company representative interacts directly with a customer or prospective customer to communicate about a good or service.

Many organizations rely heavily on personal selling because at times the "personal touch" carries more weight than mass-media material. For a business-to-business market situation, the personal touch translates into developing crucial relationships with clients. Also, many industrial goods and services are too complex or expensive to market effectively in impersonal ways (such as through mass advertising). An axiom in marketing is *the more complex, technical, and intangible the product, the more heavily firms tend to rely on personal selling to promote it.*

Personal selling has special importance for students (that's *you*) because many graduates with a marketing background will enter professional sales jobs. The U.S. Bureau of Labor Statistics estimates job growth of 9 percent for sales representatives in manufacturing and wholesaling between 2006 and 2016. For technical and scientific products, the growth projection rises to 10 percent. Overall, sales job growth ranks high among all occupations surveyed.[13] Jobs in selling and sales management often provide high upward mobility if you are successful, because firms value employees who understand customers and who can communicate well with them. The old business adage "nothing happens until something is sold" translates into many firms placing quite a bit of emphasis on personal selling in their promotion mixes. And the sales role is even more crucial during tricky economic times, when companies look to their salespeople to drum up new business and to maintain the business they already have.

Sold on selling? All right, then let's take a close look at how personal selling works and how professional salespeople develop long-term relationships with customers.

The Role of Personal Selling in the Marketing Mix

When a woman calls the MGM Grand Hotel in Vegas' 800 number to book a room for a little vacation trip and comes away with not just a room but with show tickets, a massage booking at the hotel spa, and a reservation for dinner at Emeril's, she deals with a salesperson. When she sits in on a presentation at work by a Web site renewal consultant who proposes a new content management system for her firm's Web site, she deals with a salesperson. And when that same woman agrees over lunch at a swanky restaurant to invest some of her savings with a financial manager's recommended mutual fund, she also deals with a salesperson.

For many firms, some element of personal selling is essential to land a commitment to purchase or a contract, so this type of marketing communication is a key to the success of their overall marketing plan. To put the use of personal selling into perspective, 📷 Figure 14.3 illustrates some of the factors that make it a more or less important element in an organization's promotion mix.

In general, a personal selling emphasis is more important when a firm engages in a *push strategy*, in which the goal is to "push" the product through the channel of distribution so that it is available to consumers. As a vice president at Hallmark Cards once observed, "We're not selling *to* the retailer, we're selling *through* the retailer. We look at the retailer as a pipeline to the hands of consumers."[14]

Personal selling also is likely to be crucial in business-to-business contexts where the firm must interact directly with a client's management to clinch a big deal—and often when intense negotiations about price and other factors will occur before the customer signs on the dotted line. In consumer contexts, inexperienced customers may need the hands-on assistance that a professional salesperson provides. Firms that sell goods and services consumers buy infrequently—houses, cars, computers, lawn mowers, even college educations—often rely heavily on personal selling. (*Hint:* Your school didn't pick just any student at random to conduct campus tours for prospective attendees.) Likewise, firms whose goods or services are complex or very expensive often need a salesperson to explain, justify, and sell them—in both business and consumer markets.

If personal selling is so useful, why don't firms just scrap their advertising and sales promotion budgets and hire more salespeople? There are some drawbacks that limit the role personal selling plays in the marketing communication mix. First, when the dollar amount of individual purchases is low, it doesn't make sense to use personal selling—the cost per contact with each customer is very high compared to other forms of promotion. Analysts esti-

Figure 14.3 📷 *Snapshot* | Factors That Influence a Firm's Emphasis on Personal Selling

A variety of factors influence whether personal selling is a more or less important element in an organization's overall promotion mix.

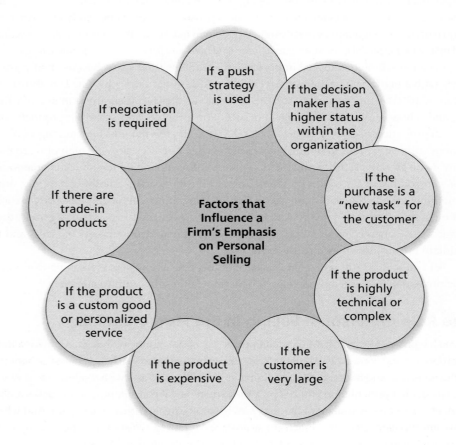

mate that in 2010 the average total cost for a sales call with a *consultative* (problem-solving) approach to selling was about $350, and this cost will continue to increase at a rate of 5 percent per year. And, of course this figure is an *average*—depending on the industry, some sales calls are much more expensive to make. The per-contact cost of a national television commercial is minuscule by comparison. A 30-second prime-time commercial may run $300,000 to $500,000 (or even around $3 million during the Super Bowl), but with millions of viewers, the cost per contact may be only $10 or $15 per 1,000 viewers.[15] For low-priced consumer goods, personal selling to end users simply doesn't make good financial sense.

Ironically, consumer resistance to telemarketing gives a powerful boost to a form of selling that has been around for a long time: direct selling. *Direct selling is not the same thing as direct marketing.* Direct sellers bypass channel intermediaries and sell directly from manufacturer to consumer through personal, one-to-one contact. Typically, independent sales representatives sell in person in a customer's home or place of business. Tupperware, Avon, Mary Kay, and the Pampered Chef are some well-known examples. Many direct selling firms use a *party plan* approach where salespeople demonstrate products in front of groups of neighbors or friends. Direct selling is on a big upswing, with domestic sales volume doubling in the past 10 years to over $30 billion annually. We'll discuss direct selling in more detail in Chapter 16.[16]

Salespeople—even the really energetic types—can make only so many calls a day. Thus, reliance on personal selling is effective only when the success ratio is high. Telemarketing, sometimes called teleselling, involves person-to-person communication that takes place on the phone. Because the cost of field salespeople is so high, telemarketing continues to grow in popularity (much to the dismay of many prospects when calls interrupt their dinner). Of course, as we've seen, no-call legislation and do-not-call lists at the state and federal levels have given consumers a powerful weapon to ward off unwanted telephone selling.

Technology and Personal Selling

Personal selling is supposed to be, well, "personal." By definition, a company uses personal selling for marketing communications in situations when one person (the salesperson) interacts directly with another person (the customer or prospective customer) to communicate about a good or service. All sorts of technologies can enhance the personal selling process, and clearly today the smartphone is the communication hub of the relationship between salesperson and client. However, as anyone making sales calls knows, technology itself cannot and should not *replace* personal selling. As we'll discuss later in this chapter, today a key role of personal selling is to manage customer *relationships*—and remember, relationships occur between people, not between computers (as much as you love your Facebook friends or checking in on Foursquare).

However, there's no doubt that a bevy of technological advancements makes it easier for salespeople to do their jobs more effectively. One such technological advance is *customer relationship management (CRM) software*. For years now, *account management software* such as ACT and GoldMine has helped salespeople manage their client and prospect base. These programs are inexpensive, easy to navigate, and they allow salespeople to track all aspects of customer interaction. Currently, many firms turn to *cloud computing* CRM applications, which are more customizable and integrative than ACT or GoldMine, yet are less expensive than major companywide CRM installations. A market leader in such products is **SalesForce .com**, which is particularly user-friendly for salespeople. A key benefit of cloud computing versions of CRM systems is that firms "rent" them for a flat fee per month (at SalesForce .com, monthly prices are as low as $20 per user) so they avoid major capital outlays.[17] Recently, some sales organizations have turned to a new-generation system called *partner relationship management (PRM)* that links information between selling and buying firms. PRM

Salesforce.com is a popular CRM application.

differs from CRM in that both supplier and buyer firms share at least some of their databases and systems to maximize the usefulness of the data for decision-making purposes. Firms that share information are more likely to work together toward win–win solutions.

Beyond CRM and PRM, numerous other technology applications enhance personal selling, including teleconferencing, videoconferencing, and improved corporate Web sites that offer FAQ (frequently asked questions) pages to answer customers' queries. Many firms also use intranets and blogs to facilitate access to internal and external communication.

Voice-over Internet protocol (VoIP)—systems that rely upon a data network to carry voice calls—get a lot of use in day-to-day correspondence between salespeople and customers. With VoIP, the salesperson on the road can just plug into a fast Internet connection and then start to make and receive calls just as if she is in the office. Unlike mobile phones, there are no bad reception areas, and unlike hotel phones there are no hidden charges. One popular VoIP product is Skype, whose tagline is "The whole world can talk for free." According to its Web site, Skype "is a little piece of software that allows you to make free calls to other Skype users and really cheap calls to ordinary phones." Skype even offers bargain rates to fixed lines and cell phones outside the United States.[18]

Thanks to Skype, webcams, instant messaging, and the like, customers of all types are becoming more comfortable with the concept of doing business with a salesperson who is not actually in the same room. As such, a good portion of the future of face-to-face sales calls may occur on your own computer screen. Consider the following hypothetical transaction related to buying a set of solar panels for your roof—a complex and expensive purchase:

The sales consultant calls at an appointed time. You open her e-mail message, click a link to start the presentation, and a picture of your roof appears, courtesy of satellite imaging. Colorful charts show past electricity bills and the savings from a solar-panel system. A series of spreadsheets examine the financing options available—and these are dynamic documents, not static images, so the salesperson can tinker with the figures right before your eyes. Would more panels be justified? A few keystrokes later, new charts displayed the costs and savings. Could they be shifted to another part of the roof? With a mouse, she moves some black panels from the east to the west side. How about more cash upfront? She scrolls to the spreadsheets, highlights three payment options, and computes the numbers over the next 15 years. In less than an hour, the exchange is over.

Perhaps for a few days or a week you mull over the choices and study the fine print in the contract, but the sale was essentially closed by the time you hung up the phone. You decided to make a major, complex purchase, worth thousands of dollars, without ever meeting anyone in the flesh and without holding any product in your hands. And unlike many purchases, you had no *buyer's remorse* despite the fact it was done online—or maybe *because* it was online.[19]

For years now, all of us have been shopping online, taking in the bargains and wide selection, usually for relatively straightforward products and services and without any human contact unless a problem arises with the ordering technology itself. The brave new world of virtual selling adds another dimension and is yet another example of how the Internet transforms business and remakes job descriptions. These more sophisticated virtual selling capabilities won't replace all face-to-face salesperson/client encounters any more than e-commerce replaced brick-and-mortar retailers. But smart sales organizations can find the right blend of technology and personal touch, tailored to their particular clientele and product offerings, that makes the most of building strong customer relationships.

The Cutting Edge

When Your Salesperson Is an Avatar

Spend some time on the Web site of Tekno Bubbles (**www.teknobubbles .com**), and you are sure to encounter Dr. Funk. An aging hippie with wild hair and a penchant for tie-dyed clothes, the doctor is a key member of the company's sales force. He greets visitors and describes the company's soap bubbles, which glow when exposed to black light. "We can get you hooked up with some bubbles so you can check them out for yourself," Dr. Funk says as he directs visitors to the site's online store. There, he will suggest complementary items that can be found on the site, such as bubble-blowing machines and remote-controlled timers.

Dr. Funk doesn't work in Tekno Bubbles' St. Louis office—or, for that matter, in any physical location. His sales pitch is exclusively online. That's because Dr. Funk is an *avatar*, an animated online character used to represent a person or brand. Broad public awareness of just what an avatar is took a quantum leap with the success of its namesake movie directed by James Cameron, and now even many fuddy-duddy Baby Boomers understand. Originally confined to virtual worlds such as Second Life, avatars are increasingly making their way onto commercial Web sites as businesses seek new ways to interact with customers. By performing tasks such as greeting visitors and fulfilling orders, avatars can enhance a Web site's sales and service, reduce the costs of live customer support and, as with Dr. Funk, provide a sense of personality and playfulness.

In the first six months after Dr. Funk's debut online sales have increased from 30 percent of Tekno Bubbles' gross revenue to 50 percent. The company has also begun integrated marketing communication by using images of Dr. Funk in offline promotions, including trade show displays. The key is that he's able to effectively touch the market the firm wants to touch. Still, avatars aren't for everyone. They tend to work best when the Web site is a company's main venue for purchases, lead gathering, or customer assistance. At least so far, they have been better suited for companies that sell to consumers rather than to other businesses.[20]

4
OBJECTIVE
Identify the different types of sales jobs.
(pp. 431–433)

The Landscape of Modern Personal Selling

Given what you've read about personal selling so far, you can begin to see why professional salespeople have very dynamic career opportunities. In this section you'll get a feel for what today's jobs are like and two distinct ways salespeople approach their role.

Types of Sales Jobs

There are several different types of sales jobs from which you can choose, each with its own unique characteristics. Maybe you aspire to work in sales someday, or perhaps you've already held a sales job at some point. Let's look more closely at some of the different types of sales positions. Figure 14.4 summarizes the most important types.

As you might imagine, sales jobs vary considerably. The person who processes a Dell computer purchase over the phone (if anybody orders them by phone anymore instead of online) is primarily an **order taker**—a salesperson who processes transactions the customer initiates. Many retail salespeople are order takers, but often wholesalers, dealers, and distributors also employ salespeople to assist their business customers. Because little creative selling is involved in order taking, this type of sales job typically is the lowest-paid sales position.

In contrast, a **technical specialist** contributes considerable expertise in the form of product demonstrations, recommendations for complex equipment, and setup of machinery. The technical specialist provides *sales support* rather than actually closing the sale. She promotes the firm and tries to stimulate demand for a product to make it easier for colleagues to actually seal the deal.

Then there is the **missionary salesperson** whose job is to stimulate clients to buy. Like technical specialists, missionary salespeople promote the firm and encourage demand for its goods and services but don't actually take orders.[21] Pfizer salespeople do missionary sales work when they call on physicians to influence them to prescribe the latest and greatest Pfizer medications instead of competing drugs. However, no sale actually gets made until doctors call prescriptions into pharmacies, which then place orders for the drug through their wholesalers.

order taker
A salesperson whose primary function is to facilitate transactions that the customer initiates.

technical specialist
A sales support person with a high level of technical expertise who assists in product demonstrations.

missionary salesperson
A salesperson who promotes the firm and tries to stimulate demand for a product but does not actually complete a sale.

Figure 14.4 📷 *Snapshot* | Types of Sales Jobs

A wide range of different types of sales jobs are available, each of which has different job requirements and responsibilities.

new-business salesperson
The person responsible for finding new customers and calling on them to present the company's products.

order getter
A salesperson who works to develop long-term relationships with particular customers or to generate new sales.

team selling
The sales function when handled by a team that may consist of a salesperson, a technical specialist, and others.

The **new-business salesperson** is responsible for finding new customers and calls on them to present the company's products. As you might imagine, gaining the business of a new customer usually means that the customer stops doing business with one of the firm's competitors (and they won't give up without a fight). New-business selling requires a high degree of creativity and professionalism, so this type of salesperson is usually very well paid. Once a new-business salesperson establishes a relationship with a client, he or she often continues to service that client as the primary contact as long as the client continues to buy from the company. In that long-term-relationship-building role, this type of salesperson is an **order getter**. Order getters are usually the people most directly responsible for a particular client's business; they may also hold the title of "account manager."[22]

More and more, firms find that the selling function works best via **team selling**. A selling team may consist of a salesperson, a technical specialist, someone from engineering and design, and other players who work together to develop products and programs that satisfy the customer's needs. When the company includes people from a range of areas it often calls this group a *cross-functional team*.

Two Approaches to Personal Selling

Personal selling is one of the oldest forms of marketing communication. Unfortunately, over the years smooth-talking pitchmen who will say anything to make a sale have tarnished its image. Pulitzer Prize–winning playwright Arthur Miller's famous character Willie Loman in *Death of a Salesman*—a must-read for generations of middle- and high-school students—didn't help. Willie Loman (as in "low man" on the totem pole—get it?) is a pathetic, burned-out peddler who leaves home for the road on Monday morning and returns late Friday evening selling "on a smile and a shoeshine." His personal life is in shambles with two dysfunctional sons and a disaffected wife who hardly knows him. Great public relations for selling as a career, right?

Fortunately, personal selling today is nothing like Miller's harsh portrayal. Selling has moved from a transactional, hard-sell approach to an approach based on relationships with customers. Let's see how.

Transactional Selling: Putting on the Hard Sell

Willy Loman practiced a high-pressure, hard-sell approach. We've all been exposed to the pushy electronics salesperson that puts down the competition when she tells shoppers that if they buy elsewhere they will be stuck with an inferior home theater system that will fall apart in six months. Or how about the crafty used car salesman who plays the good cop/bad cop game: She gives you an awesome price, but then sadly informs you her boss, the sales manager, won't go for such a sweet deal. These hard-sell tactics reflect **transactional selling**, an approach that focuses on making an immediate sale with little concern for developing a long-term relationship with the customer.

As customers, the hard sell makes us feel manipulated and resentful, and it diminishes our satisfaction and loyalty. It's a very short-sighted approach to selling. As we said earlier in the book, constantly finding new customers is much more expensive than getting repeat business from the customers you already have. And the behaviors transactional selling promotes (that is, doing anything to get the order) contribute to the negative image many of us have of salespeople as obnoxious and untrustworthy. Such salespeople engage in these behaviors because they don't care if they ever have the chance to sell to you again. This is really bad business!

Relationship Selling: Building Long-Term Customers

Relationship selling is the process by which a salesperson secures, develops, and maintains long-term relationships with profitable customers.[23] Today's professional salesperson is more likely to practice relationship selling than transactional selling. This means that the salesperson tries to develop a mutually satisfying, win–win relationship with the customer. Securing a customer relationship means converting an interested prospect into someone who is convinced that the good or service holds value for her. Developing a customer relationship means ensuring that you and the customer work together to find more ways to add value to the transaction. Maintaining a customer relationship means building customer satisfaction and loyalty—thus, you can count on the customer to provide future business and stick with you for the long haul. And if doing business with the customer isn't profitable to you, unless you're a charitable organization you would probably like to see that customer go somewhere else.

transactional selling
A form of personal selling that focuses on making an immediate sale with little or no attempt to develop a relationship with the customer.

relationship selling
A form of personal selling that involves securing, developing, and maintaining long-term relationships with profitable customers.

creative selling process
The process of seeking out potential customers, analyzing needs, determining how product attributes might provide benefits for the customer, and then communicating that information.

prospecting
A part of the selling process that includes identifying and developing a list of potential or prospective customers.

5
OBJECTIVE

List the steps in the creative selling process.
(pp. 433–436)

The Creative Selling Process

Many people find selling to be a great profession, partly because something different is always going on. Every customer, every sales call, and every salesperson is unique. Some salespeople are successful primarily because they know so much about what they sell. Others are successful because they've built strong relationships with customers so that they're able to add value to both the customer and their own firm—a win–win approach to selling. Successful salespeople understand and engage in a series of activities to make the sales encounter mutually beneficial.

A salesperson's chances of success increase when she undergoes a systematic series of steps we call the **creative selling process**. These steps require the salesperson to seek out potential customers, analyze their needs, determine how product attributes provide benefits, and then decide how best to communicate this to prospects. As 📷 Figure 14.5 shows, there are seven steps in the process. Let's take a look at each.

Step 1: Prospect and Qualify

Prospecting is the process by which a salesperson identifies and develops a list of *prospects* or *sales leads* (potential customers). Leads come from existing customer lists, telephone directories, commercially available databases, and of course through diligent use of Web search engines like Google. The local library usually owns directories of businesses (including

Figure 14.5 🔀 *Process* | Steps in the Creative Selling Process

In the creative selling process, salespeople follow a series of steps to build relationships with customers.

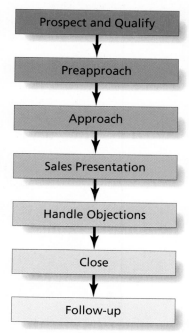

those state and federal agencies publish) and directories of association memberships. Sometimes companies generate sales leads through their advertising or sales promotion when they encourage customers to request more information.

As you learned earlier in this chapter, trade shows also are an important source of sales leads, as are visits to your company's Web site by potential customers. Accela Communications is one company that tracks these responses for its clients in order to generate leads. Sales organizations turn to Accela to monitor, analyze, and summarize visitors to a company's Web site—in essence, to develop prospect lists. Accela then turns these lists over to salespeople for follow-up by phone or in person.[24]

Another way to generate leads is through *cold calling*, in which the salesperson simply contacts prospects "cold," without prior introduction or arrangement. It always helps to know the prospect, so salespeople might rely instead on *referrals*. Current clients who are satisfied with their purchase often recommend a salesperson to others—yet another reason to maintain good customer relationships.

However, the mere fact that someone is willing to talk to a salesperson doesn't guarantee a sale. After they identify potential customers, salespeople need to *qualify* these prospects to determine how likely they are to become customers. To do this they ask questions such as the following:

- Are the prospects likely to be interested in what I'm selling?
- Are they likely to switch their allegiance from another supplier or product?
- Is the potential sales volume large enough to make a relationship profitable?
- Can they afford the purchase?
- If they must borrow money to buy the product, what is their credit history?

Step 2: Preapproach

preapproach
A part of the selling process that includes developing information about prospective customers and planning the sales interview.

In the **preapproach** stage, you compile background information about prospective customers and plan the sales interview. Firms don't make important purchases lightly, and it's often difficult even to get an appointment to see a prospect. It's foolish for a salesperson to blindly call on a qualified prospect and risk losing the sale because of a lack of preparation. Salespeople try to learn as much as possible about qualified prospects early on. They may probe a prospect's prior purchase history, current needs, or, in some cases, even try to learn about their personal interests.

Salespeople can draw information about a prospect from a variety of sources. In the case of larger companies, they can find financial data, names of top executives, and other information about a business from outlets such as *Standard & Poor's 500 Directory* or Dun & Bradstreet's *Million Dollar Directory*. They can also find a great deal of information for the preapproach on customers' Web sites. And the inside scoop on a prospect often comes from informal sources such as noncompeting salespeople who have dealt with the prospect before.

Of course, if the salesperson's firm has a CRM system, she can use it to see whether the database includes information about the prospect. Say, for example, a salesperson at Mike's Bikes plans to call on a buyer at Greg's Vacation Rentals to see about selling some new bikes for guests to use at Greg's various resort properties. If Mike's has had a CRM system in place for some time, any contacts with customers and potential customers (prospects) are recorded in the database. The salesperson can simply run an inquiry about Greg's Vacation Rentals and with luck, the CRM database will deliver information on the company, prior purchases from Mike's, when and why customers stopped buying from the company, and perhaps even the preferences of the particular buyer.

Step 3: Approach

After the salesperson lays the groundwork with the preapproach, it's time to **approach**, or contact, the prospect. During these important first minutes several key events occur. The salesperson tries to learn even more about the prospect's needs, create a good impression, and build rapport. If the salesperson found prospect Anne Fahlgren through a referral, she will probably say so to Anne up front: "Melissa Sabella with Prentice Industries suggested I call on you."

During the approach, the customer decides whether the salesperson has something to offer that is of potential value. The old saying "You never get a second chance to make a good first impression" rings true here. A professional appearance tells the prospect that the salesperson means business and is competent to handle the sale.

Step 4: Sales Presentation

Many sales calls involve a formal **sales presentation**, which lays out the benefits of the product and its advantages over the competition. When possible and appropriate, salespeople should incorporate a great PowerPoint presentation integrated with some sound and media into their sales presentations to jazz things up. The focus of the sales presentation should always be on ways the salesperson, her goods and services, and her company can add value to the customer (and in a business-to-business setting, to the customer's company). It is important for the salesperson to present this value proposition clearly and to invite the customer's involvement in the conversation. Let the customer ask questions, give feedback, and discuss her needs. Canned approaches to sales presentations are a poor choice for salespeople who want to build long-term relationships. In fact, sales managers rate *listening* skills, not talking skills, as the single most important attribute they look for when they hire relationship salespeople.[25] In a sales call, it's a good idea to put the *80/20 rule* to work—that is, spend 80 percent of your time listening to the client and assessing his needs and only 20 percent talking (note: this rule-of-thumb is a spinoff of the 80/20 rule for market segmentation we discussed in Chapter 7).

A good salesperson is well groomed and wears appropriate business dress. She doesn't chew gum, use poor grammar or inappropriate language, mispronounce the customer's name, or seem uninterested in the call. Visible tattoos, body piercings, and the like are controversial in professional selling.

approach
The first step of the actual sales presentation in which the salesperson tries to learn more about the customer's needs, create a good impression, and build rapport.

sales presentation
The part of the selling process in which the salesperson directly communicates the value proposition to the customer and invites two-way communication.

Step 5: Handle Objections

It's rare when a prospect accepts everything the salesperson offers without question. The effective salesperson anticipates *objections*—reasons why the prospect is reluctant to make a commitment—and she's prepared to respond with additional information or persuasive arguments. Actually, the salesperson should welcome objections because they show that the prospect is at least interested enough to consider the offer and seriously weigh its pros and cons. Handling the objection successfully can move a prospect to the decision stage. For example, the salesperson might say, "Ms. Bloom, you've said before that you don't have room to carry our new line of trail bikes, although you mentioned that you may be losing some sales by carrying only one brand with very few different models. If we could come up with an estimate of how much business you're losing, I'll bet you'd consider making room for our line, wouldn't you?"

Step 6: Close the Sale

The win–win nature of relationship selling should take some of the pressure off salespeople to make "the dreaded close." But there still comes a point in the sales call at which one or the other party has to move toward gaining commitment to the objectives of the call—presumably

close
The stage of the selling process in which the salesperson actually asks the customer to buy the product.

a purchase. This is the decision stage, or **close**. Directly asking the customer for her business doesn't need to be painful or awkward: If the salesperson has done a great job in the previous five steps of the creative selling process, closing the sale should be a natural progression of the dialogue between the buyer and seller.

There are a variety of approaches salespeople use to close the sale:

- A *last objection close* asks customers if they are ready to purchase, providing the salesperson can address any concerns they have about the product: "Are you ready to order if we can prove our delivery time frames meet your expectations?"

- An *assumptive* or *minor points close* mean the salesperson acts as if the purchase is inevitable with only a small detail or two to be settled: "What quantity would you like to order?"

- A *standing-room-only* or *buy-now close* injects some urgency when the salesperson suggests the customer might miss an opportunity if she hesitates: "This price is good through Saturday only, so to save 20 percent we should book the order now." When making such closes, salespeople must be sure the basis they state for buying now is truthful or they'll lose a valuable relationship for the price of a one-time sale!

Step 7: Follow-up

follow-up
Activities after the sale that provide important services to customers.

Understanding that the process doesn't end after the salesperson earns the client's business is basic to a relationship selling perspective that emphasizes the importance of long-term satisfaction. The **follow-up** after the sale includes arranging for delivery, payment, and purchase terms. It also means the salesperson makes sure the customer received delivery and is satisfied. Follow-up also allows the salesperson to *bridge* to the next purchase. Once a relationship develops, the selling process is only beginning. Even as one cycle of purchasing draws to a close, a good salesperson already lays the foundation for the next one.

6 Sales Management

OBJECTIVE
Explain the role of sales management.
(pp. 436–439)

sales management
The process of planning, implementing, and controlling the personal selling function of an organization.

Few, if any, firms succeed with just one star salesperson. Personal selling is a team effort that requires careful planning to be sure that the organization makes salespeople available when and where customers need them. **Sales management** is the process of planning, implementing, and controlling the personal selling function. Let's review some of the major decisions sales managers who oversee this function must make as Figure 14.6 outlines.

Set Sales Force Objectives

Sales force objectives state what management expects the sales force to accomplish and when. Sales managers develop sales force performance objectives such as "acquire 100 new customers," "generate $100 million in sales," or even "reduce travel expenses by 5 percent." Firms that engage in relationship selling also state objectives that relate to customer satisfaction, loyalty, and retention (or turnover). Other common objectives are new customer development, new product suggestions, training, reporting on competitive activity, and community involvement.

Sales managers also work with their salespeople to develop *individual* objectives. There are two types of individual objectives. *Performance objectives* are readily measurable outcomes, such as total sales and total profits per salesperson. *Behavioral objectives* specify the actions salespeople must accomplish, such as the number of prospects she should identify, the number of sales calls, and the number of follow-up contacts she should make.

Create a Sales Force Strategy

A sales force strategy establishes important specifics such as the structure and size of a firm's sales force. Each salesperson is responsible for a set group of customers—his or her **sales territory**. The territory structure allows salespeople to have an in-depth understanding of customers and their needs through frequent contact, both business and personal. The most common way to allot territories is geographic to minimize travel and other field expenses. The firm usually defines a *geographic sales force structure* according to how many customers reside in a given area. If the product line is diverse or technically complex, however, a better approach may be to structure sales territories in terms of different classes of goods and services; this approach enables the sales force to provide more focused product expertise to customers. Kraft Foods has separate sales forces for its major product areas, such as beverages, cheese and dairy, and grocery items.

Still another sales structure is *industry specialization* in which salespeople focus on a single industry or a small number of industries. Firms often refer to such large clients as *key accounts* or *major accounts*. P&G uses cross-functional key account teams to focus on each of its major customers. For Lakeland, Florida–based Publix Supermarkets (one of the top 10 ranked supermarket chains in the United States by revenue), P&G fields a team of over 100 people headed by a top-level executive—customer managers, accountants, logistics people, and more—all of whom reside right in Central Florida to be right where the Publix action is. The idea behind this concentration on key accounts is the old *80/20 rule* again —that is, if 20 percent of your customers account for 80 percent of your sales (and profits), those 20 percent deserve the bulk of your personal selling attention.

Putting salespeople out into the field is a very expensive proposition that greatly impacts a company's profitability. Remember, cost-per-customer-contact is higher by a wide margin for personal selling than for any other form of promotion. Thus, it's really important to determine the optimal number of salespeople you put into the field. A larger sales force may increase sales, but at what cost? A smaller sales force will keep costs down. But this lean and mean approach could backfire if competitors move in with larger teams; they will be in a better position to develop strong customer relationships because each of their salespeople doesn't have to call on as many customers.

Recruit, Train, and Reward the Sales Force

Because the quality of a sales force can make or break a firm, a top priority for sales managers is to recruit and hire the right set of people to do the job. The ideal candidates exhibit good listening skills, effective follow-up skills, the ability to adapt their sales style from situation to situation, tenacity (sticking with a task), and a high level of personal organization.[26] Companies screen potential salespeople to reveal these skills, along with useful information about interests and capabilities. Pencil-and-paper tests determine quantitative skills and competencies in areas that interviews can't easily assess.

Are successful salespeople born or made? Probably elements of both inherent ability and trainable skills contribute to career success. *Sales training* teaches salespeople about the organization and its goods and services and helps them to develop the skills, knowledge, and attitudes they require to succeed. And training doesn't end once a person "graduates" into the organization. *Professional development* activities continually prepare salespeople personally and professionally for new challenges such as promotions and management responsibilities. They try to develop the salesperson more broadly than knowledge or skills training. Many sales organizations turn to outside consultants to help them develop sales

Figure 14.6 *Process* | The Sales Management Process
Sales management includes four major areas of decision-making.

Set Sales Force Objectives

↓

Create a Sales Force Strategy

↓

Recruit, Train, and Reward the Sales Force

↓

Evaluate the Sales Force

sales territory
A set of customers, often defined by geographic boundaries, for whom a particular salesperson is responsible.

force training and development programs. Sometimes a boost in creative thinking from the outside can do wonders to develop more productive salespeople. Today, with budgets tighter than ever, sales organizations expect identifiable returns on investments in training, and outside firms often deliver these quantifiable results.

Of course, a good way to motivate salespeople is to pay them well. This can mean tying compensation to performance. A *straight commission plan* is based solely on a percentage of sales the person closes. Under a *commission-with-draw plan*, earnings come from commission plus a regular payment, or "draw," that may be charged against future commissions if current sales are inadequate to cover the draw. With a *straight salary plan*, the salesperson is paid a set amount regardless of sales performance. Sometimes a company augments a straight salary plan with a *quota-bonus plan*, in which it pays salespeople a salary *plus* a bonus for her sales that exceed an assigned quota or if she sells certain goods and services that are new or relatively more profitable.

Sales contests provide prizes (cash or otherwise) for selling specific goods and services during a specific period and can kick-start a short-term sales boost. Popular prizes for contest winners include cruises, resort vacations, and products winners select from prize catalogs. However, it's easy for a firm to overuse sales contests; these incentives might motivate salespeople to simply wait to sell some goods and services until the contest period kicks in, so in reality there is no net increase in sales.

Although many salespeople like to work independently, supervision is essential to an effective sales force. Sales managers often require salespeople to develop monthly, weekly, or daily *call reports*, where they document information about customers they called on and how the call went. Today most salespeople generate these call reports electronically, often on their laptop computer as a part of the firm's overall CRM initiative. They allow the sales manager to track what the salespeople do in the field, and they provide marketing managers with timely information about customers' responses, competitive activity, and any changes in the firm's customer base.

Evaluate the Sales Force

A sales manager's job isn't complete until she evaluates the total effort of the sales force. First, it is important to determine whether the sales force meets its objectives. If it is not, the sales manager must figure out the causes. Is the problem due to flaws in the design and/or implementation of the sales force strategy? Or did uncontrollable factors contribute? An overall downturn in the economy such as the one that began in 2008 with the subprime mortgage loan crisis, a big drop in housing prices, and a huge escalation in the price of gasoline can make it impossible for the best sales force to meet its original sales objectives.

Managers normally measure individual salesperson performance against sales quotas for individual sales territories, even when compensation plans do not include bonuses or commissions based on the quotas. They may also include quantitative measures such as number of sales calls and sales reports the group completed when they evaluate performance. In addition to quantitative measures, many firms also evaluate their salespeople on qualitative indicators of performance, such as salesperson attitude, product knowledge, and communication skills. Increasingly, as firms focus on relationship selling, several important customer metrics such as customer satisfaction, loyalty, and retention/turnover are key measures of superior salesperson performance.

Finally, the company can consider the salesperson's expense account for travel and entertainment since the best sales record can mean little to a company's bottom line if the salesperson gouges the company with outrageous expenses. You think *you're* creative when you spend money? Here are some classic expenses a few salespeople actually submitted, according to *Sales and Marketing Management* magazine:[27]

- Chartering a private plane to make an appointment after missing a regularly scheduled flight

- A $2,300 round of golf for four people

- A set of china for a salesperson's wife to use for a client dinner party

- Season baseball tickets for $6,000

- A three-day houseboat rental with a crew and chef for $30,000

Here's my choice. . .

Real **People**, Real **Choices**

Why do you think Jeffrey chose option #2?

1 Option   2 Option   3 Option

How It Worked Out at Woodtronics

Jeffrey went directly to the client with a mockup of the new Evolution platform. He didn't let the architect know he had done this until he was confident that the client was completely satisfied with the new alternative. Woodtronics got the sale; what's more, the client decided to purchase the new product within a week of seeing the demo.

To learn the whole story, visit www.mypearsonmarketinglab.com.

Brand **YOU**!

Personal selling works!

No one can sell your brand better than you can.

Sell yourself by connecting with people you know. Networking helps you access the hidden job market . . . 80 percent of jobs are filled through networking. You know more people than you realize. And those people can lead you to more people. And before you know it, you'll be interviewing! Master the skill of networking in person and on social networking sites in Chapter 14 of *Brand You*.

Objective Summary ➡ Key Terms ➡ Apply

Study Map

1. Objective Summary (pp. 420–423)

Identify the sales promotion elements for B2B.

A sales promotion is a short-term program designed to build interest in or encourage purchase of a product. Trade sales promotions come in a variety of forms. Some are designed as discounts and deals, including co-op advertising, for channel members and some are designed to increase industry visibility. Approaches aimed at increasing industry visibility include trade shows, promotional products, point of purchase (POP) displays, incentive programs, and push money.

Key Terms

trade promotions, p. 420

merchandising allowance, p. 421

case allowance, p. 421

co-op advertising, p. 422

trade shows, p. 422

promotional products, p. 422

point-of-purchase (POP) displays, p. 422

push money, p. 423

2. Objective Summary (pp. 423–427)

Understand the elements of direct marketing.

Direct marketing refers to any direct communication designed to generate a response from a consumer or business customer. Some of the types of direct marketing activities are mail order (catalogs and direct mail), telemarketing, and direct-response advertising, including infomercials and home shopping networks.

Key Terms

direct marketing, p. 423

catalog, p. 423

direct mail, p. 424

telemarketing, p. 425

direct-response advertising, p. 425

direct-response TV (DRTV), p. 425

infomercials, p. 426

M-commerce, p. 426

3. Objective Summary (pp. 427–431)

Appreciate the important role of personal selling and how it fits into the promotion mix.

Personal selling occurs when a company representative interacts directly with a prospect or customer to communicate about a good or service. Many organizations rely heavily on this approach because at times the "personal touch" can carry more weight than mass-media material. Generally, a personal selling effort is more important when a firm engages in a push strategy, in which the goal is to "push" the product through the channel of distribution so that it is available to consumers. Today's salespeople are less likely to use transactional selling (hard-sell tactics) in favor of relationship selling, in which they pursue win–win relationships with customers.

Key Term

personal selling, p. 427

4. Objective Summary (pp. 431–433)

Identify the different types of sales jobs.

Order takers process transactions that the customer initiates. *Technical specialists* are very involved in giving product demonstrations, giving advice and recommendations, and product setup. *Missionary salespeople* work to stimulate purchase, but don't take actual orders. *New-business salespeople*, or *order getters*, are responsible for finding new customers and calling on them to present the company's products. And finally, *team selling* has become very prevalent in many industries as a way to bring together the expertise needed to better satisfy customer needs. *Transactional selling* focuses on making an immediate sale with little concern for developing a long-term relationship with the customer. It is sometimes called the "hard sell" approach. In contrast, *relationship selling* involves securing, developing, and maintaining long-term relationships with profitable customers. Developing a customer relationship means ensuring that you and the customer find more ways to add value over time.

Key Terms

order taker, p. 431

technical specialist, p. 431

missionary salesperson, p. 431

new-business salesperson, p. 432

order getter, p. 432

team selling, p. 432

transactional selling, p. 433

relationship selling, p. 433

approach, p. 435

sales presentation, p. 435

close, p. 436

follow-up, p. 436

5. Objective Summary (pp. 433–436)

List the steps in the creative selling process.

The steps in the personal selling process include prospecting and qualifying, preapproach, approach, sales presentation, handling objections, close, and follow-up. These steps combine to form the basis for communicating the company's message to the customer. Learning the intricacies of each step can aid the salesperson in developing successful relationships with clients and in bringing in the business for their companies.

Key Terms

creative selling process, p. 433

prospecting, p. 433

preapproach, p. 434

6. Objective Summary (pp. 436–439)

Explain the role of sales management.

Sales management includes planning, implementing, and controlling the selling function. The responsibilities of a sales manager include the following: creating a sales force strategy, including the structure and size of the sales force; recruiting, training, and compensating the sales force; and evaluating the sales force.

Key Terms

sales management, p. 436

sales territory, p. 437

Chapter **Questions** and **Activities**

Concepts: Test Your Knowledge

1. Explain some of the different types of trade sales promotions marketers frequently use.
2. What is direct marketing? Describe the more popular types of direct marketing.
3. What is m-commerce?
4. What role does personal selling play within the marketing function?
5. What is relationship selling? How does it differ from transactional selling?
6. What is prospecting? What does it mean to qualify the prospect? What is the preapproach? Why are these steps in the creative selling process that occur before you ever even contact the buyer so important to the sale?
7. What are some ways you might approach a customer? Would some work better in one situation or another?
8. What is the objective of the sales presentation? How might you overcome buyer objections?
9. Why is follow-up after the sale so important in relationship selling?
10. Describe the role of sales managers. What key functions do they perform?

Activities: Apply What You've Learned

1. Assume that you are a member of the marketing department for a firm that produces several brands of household cleaning products. Your assignment is to develop recommendations for trade sales promotion activities for a new laundry detergent. Develop an outline of your recommendations for these sales promotions. In a role-playing situation, present and defend your recommendations to your boss.
2. Timing is an important part of a sales promotion plan. Trade sales promotions must be properly timed to ensure channel members fully maximize the opportunity to sell your product. Assume that the introduction of the new laundry detergent in question 1 is planned for April 1. Place the activities you recommended in question 1 onto a 12-month calendar of events. (Hint: The calendar needs to start *before* the product introduction.) In a role-playing situation, present your plan to your boss. Be sure to explain the reasons for your timing of each trade sales promotion element.
3. Consider carefully the potentially annoying downsides of various forms of direct marketing to consumers. As a marketer, what would you do to ensure that your firm's direct marketing efforts don't turn customers off your product?

4. For you personally, what are the pros and cons of personal selling as a potential career choice? Make a list under the two columns and be as specific as you can in explaining each pro and con.

5. Assume a firm that publishes university textbooks has just hired you as a field salesperson. Your job requires that you call on university faculty members to persuade them to adopt your textbooks for their classes. As part of your training, your sales manager has asked you to develop an outline of what you will say in a typical sales presentation. Write that outline.

6. This chapter introduced you to several key success factors sales managers look for when hiring relationship salespeople. Are there other key success factors you can identify for relationship salespeople? Explain why each is important.

Marketing Metrics Exercise

How does a firm know whether a salesperson is effective? Obviously, the short answer is that she produces high sales volume and meets or exceeds sales goals. But just increasing total dollar or unit sales volume is not always a good indicator of salesperson success. The problem is, everything else being equal, salespeople who are compensated strictly on sales volume will simply sell whatever products are easiest to sell to maximize total sales. But these may not be the products with the highest profit margins, and they may not be the goods and services the firm identifies as key to future success in the market.

Because of the problems with using raw sales volume as the sole indicator of salesperson success, some firms turn to a variety of other metrics, including input and output measures. Input measures are effort measures—things that go into selling, such as the number and type of sales calls, expense account management, and a variety of nonselling activities such as follow-up work and client service. Output measures, or the results of the salesperson's efforts, include sales volume but these also can be the number of orders, size of orders, number of new accounts, level of repeat business, customer profitability, and customer satisfaction.

Ultimately, the best approach to measure salesperson success is to use a variety of metrics that are consistent with the goals of the firm, to ensure the salesperson understands the goals and related metrics, and to link rewards to the achievement of those goals.

If you were a professional salesperson, what type of metrics would you prefer to be evaluated against? Why?

Choices: What Do You Think?

1. M-commerce allows marketers to engage in *location commerce* when they can identify where consumers are and send them messages about a local store. Do you think consumers will respond positively to this? What do you think are the benefits for consumers of location commerce? Do you see any drawbacks (such as invasion of privacy)?

2. In general, professional selling has evolved from hard-sell to relationship selling. Do organizations still use the hard-sell style? If so, what types? What do you think the future holds for these organizations? Will the hard sell continue to succeed—that is, are there instances in which transactional selling is still appropriate? If so, when?

3. One reason experts cite for the increase in consumer online shopping is the poor quality of service available at retail stores. What do you think about the quality of service you get from most retail salespeople with whom you come into contact? What are some ways retailers can improve the quality of their sales associates?

4. Based on the salesperson compensation figures the chapter supplies, do you think professional salespeople are appropriately paid? Why or why not? What is it that salespeople do that warrants their compensation?

5. Would training and development needs of salespeople vary depending on how long they have been in the business? Why or why not? Would it be possible (and feasible) to have different training programs for salespeople who are at different career stages?

6. What would be the best approach for a sales manager to determine the appropriate rewards program to implement for her salespeople? What issues are important when she decides what rewards to offer?

Miniproject: Learn by Doing

The purpose of this miniproject is to help you understand the advantages of following the creative selling process.

1. With several of your classmates, create a new product in a category that most college students buy regularly (for example, toothpaste, shampoo, pens, pencils, soft drinks . . . anything that interests you that might be sold through a drugstore like Walgreens). Make up a new brand name and some creative features and benefits of the new product you come up with.

2. Develop a plan for executing each of the steps in the creative selling process. Carefully ensure that you cover all the bases of how you would go about selling your product to an organizational buyer at Walgreens for distribution to all stores.

3. Report on your plan to your class, and ask the other students for feedback on whether your approach will convince the Walgreens buyer to make a purchase.

Marketing in **Action** Case   Real Choices at Frito-Lay

Chips, chips, and even more chips! This might be the mantra for Frito-Lay salespeople as they carry out their daily assignments. Although it may not seem like it on the surface, it is a challenge to be effective in the salty snack sales environment. As with most forms of selling, the secret to success lies in finding ways to be both efficient and effective. There is only so much shelf space for all those tempting crunchy bags in grocery and convenience stores, and lots of manufacturers that want their products to be on them. The salty snack industry includes potato chips; tortilla chips; snack nuts and seeds (including corn nuts); popcorn; pretzels; extruded cheese; snacks; corn snacks; and other. Total retail sales in the United States totaled over $17 billion in 2009.

Frito-Lay is one of the world's leading producers of salty snacks. Frito-Lay North America is a division of PepsiCo, Inc. Based in Plano, Texas, the company's most popular brands include Fritos, Lay's, Doritos, Cheetos, and Tostitos. In 1932, C. E. Doolin purchased the recipe for Fritos and began to sell corn chips in San Antonio from his Ford Model T. In the same year, Herman W. Lay began his potato chip business in Nashville by purchasing a snack food manufacturer.

The Frito Company and the H. W. Lay Company merged in 1961 to become Frito-Lay, Inc. Eventually, in 1965 Frito-Lay, Inc. and the Pepsi-Cola Company combined and created PepsiCo, Inc. Today, PepsiCo is organized into four divisions: Frito-Lay North America, PepsiCo Beverages North America, PepsiCo International, and Quaker Foods North America.

In the retail atmosphere, Frito-Lay faces competition from many sources. This includes large multinational companies such as ConAgra (DAVID Seeds, Crunch 'n Munch, Orville Redenbacher), Kraft Foods (Nabisco, Honey Maid), and Procter & Gamble (Pringles). In addition there are numerous regional manufacturers such as Cape Cod Potato Chip (chips, popcorn), Snyder's of Hanover (chips, pretzels), and Jay's Foods (chips, popcorn).

Relationships with retailers are critical as all these formidable competitors jockey for limited shelf space. The leadership of Frito-Lay's sales organization believes that knowledge manage-

ment is the key to success so that salespeople in the field can constantly update what they know about each store and tailor their offerings accordingly. The challenge is that important information must be captured in many different places and systems. This can inhibit the sharing of knowledge across members of the sales organization.

Frito-Lay's solution was to develop a knowledge management portal on the company's intranet. The portal provides a central point of access to the database that integrates customer and internal corporate information. The goals for the Frito-Lay portal are to provide knowledge that is more efficient, make use of customer-specific data, and promote team collaboration. Given the company's size, this is no easy task.

During the mid-2000s, the salty snack market grew slowly, and changes in consumers' eating habits might provide an even slower future. A trend toward healthier snacking and concerns about weight loss will increase the competitiveness among the different snack food sales organizations. Salespeople have to continue to develop customer loyalty as consumers experiment with new products to enhance the at-home experience. Frito-Lay needs to decide just what pieces of information its sales force needs to know while not burdening them with too much data to be effective.

You Make the Call

1. What is the decision facing Frito-Lay?
2. What factors are important in understanding this decision situation?
3. What are the alternatives?
4. What decision(s) do you recommend?
5. What are some ways to implement your recommendation?

Based on: Esther Shein, "Frito-Lay Sales Force Sells More Through Information Collaboration," *CIO.com*, May 01, 2001 (http://www.cio.com/article/30167/Case_Study_Frito_Lay_Sales_Force_Sells_More_Through_Information_Collaboration); Frito-Lay, *Wikipedia*, http://en.wikipedia.org/wiki/Frito-Lay (accessed July 14, 2010); Kat Fay, "Salty Snacks," *PreparedFoods.com*, April 1, 2009 (http://www.preparedfoods.com/Articles/Feature_Article/BNP_GUID_9-5-2006_A_100000000000000569180); Sonia Reyes, "Strategy: Frito-Lay Gets Wise to Rival's Revamp," *Brandweek*, June 21, 2004 (http://www.allbusiness.com/marketing-advertising/branding-brand-development/4686710-1.html).

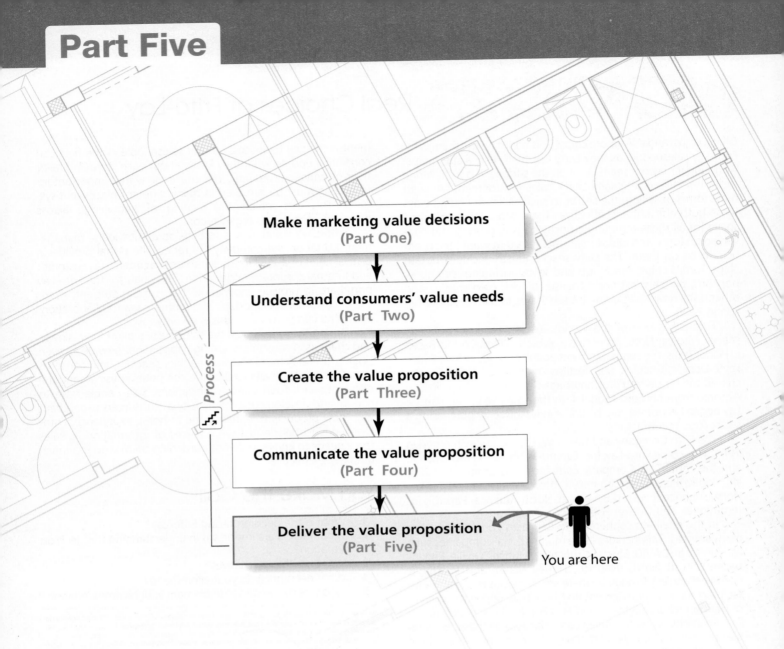

Make marketing value decisions
(Part One)

Understand consumers' value needs
(Part Two)

Create the value proposition
(Part Three)

Communicate the value proposition
(Part Four)

Deliver the value proposition
(Part Five)

Process

You are here

Deliver the Value Proposition

Part Five
Overview

You're almost there! Your remaining decisions involve choices about how to deliver the value proposition to your market. Chapter 15 explains the main options related to the supply chain for your value offering, different types of distribution channels that are available, and how to select and plan a channel strategy. You'll also learn some interesting things about logistics and transportation. Then, in Chapter 16 you have the opportunity to focus on all types of retailing from traditional stores to direct selling to e-commerce.

Marketing Plan Connection:
Tricks of the Trade

Supply Chain Strategies

Recall that the Appendix at the end of the book provides you with an abbreviated marketing plan example for the fictitious S&S Smoothie Company. That plan is flagged to indicate what elements from the plan correspond to each of the Parts within the book. In addition, in Chapter 2 you found a tear-out guide called "Build a Marketing Plan," which can be used as a template for marketing planning. It is also cross-referenced to chapters by section of the marketing plan.

In the chapters within Part Five, the key learning elements deal with the place "P" of the marketing mix 4Ps—physical distribution or, using the term more common today, the supply chain. Retailing as a particular supply chain element is also featured. Like most firms, S&S the success of S&S Smoothie's marketing plan weighs heavily on how effectively they can deliver value through their supply chain.

Recall that S&S Smoothie seeks to position its products as the first-choice smoothie beverage for the serious health-conscious consumer, including those who are seeking to lower their carbohydrate intake. The justification for this positioning is as follows: Many smoothie beverages are available. The S&S Smoothie formula provides superior flavor and nutrition in a shelf-stable form. S&S Smoothie has developed its product (including packaging) and pricing in support of this positioning strategy. As noted earlier, S&S Smoothie's physical distribution approach is primarily through health clubs and gyms, and small upscale specialty food stores. S&S Smoothie plans to expand its target reseller market to include the following:

1. Hotels and resorts in the United States and in targeted international markets
2. Golf and tennis clubs
3. College campuses

To increase leverage in larger health clubs, S&S Smoothie will offer free refrigerated display units. This will encourage the facility to maintain a high level of inventory of S&S Smoothie beverages.

Implementation

Now that all the marketing mix elements have been brought to bear to establish S&S Smoothie's new positioning, the next step of the marketing plan identifies the all-important Action Plan. As you saw in Chapter 2, Table 2.4, an Action Plan systematically details the activities necessary to implement all marketing strategies. In addition, the Action Plan includes the individual(s) responsible for each item, timing, budget, and measurement and control. Table A.4 from the S&S Smoothie Appendix in the back of the book shows an example of one objective (to increase distribution venues) and the action items S&S Smoothie will use to accomplish this objective.

Measurement and Control Strategies

For S&S Smoothie, a variety of activities will ensure effective measurement of the success of the marketing plan and allow the firm to make adjustments as necessary. These include targeted market research and trend analysis.

Research

Firms need continuous market research to understand brand awareness and brand attitudes among their target markets. S&S Smoothie will therefore continue its program of focus group research and descriptive studies of its target consumer and reseller markets.

Trend Analysis

S&S Smoothie will do a monthly trend analysis to examine sales by reseller type, geographic area, chain, agent, and distributor. These analyses will allow S&S Smoothie to take corrective action when necessary.

Deliver Value through Supply Chain Management, Channels of Distribution, and Logistics

Heather Mayo

Profile

▼ A **Decision Maker** at Sam's Club

With over 16 years of operations and merchandising experience in the warehouse club industry, Heather Mayo has responsibility for Sam's Club grocery business with sales of over $5 billion. As vice president of merchandising, she focuses on creating solutions to meet the needs of the 47 million members Sam's serves in over 600 locations across the country. Additionally, she represented the company as a supplier diversity lead on Walmart's Supplier Diversity Internal Steering Committee and was captain of Walmart's Packaging Sustainable Value Network. Most recently, she has added the role of executive sponsor of the Wood and Paper Sustainable Value Network. In February 2009, she was honored as Divisional Merchandise Manager of the Year for Sam's Club.

Prior to joining Sam's in 2004, Heather was an executive consultant/associate partner focusing on business strategy for IBM. In this capacity, she provided business advice and counsel to C-level executives of *Fortune* 500 companies regarding strategic direction and operational capability of their business, marketplace, and partners. Notable clients included REI, Godiva, Hallmark, the United States Mint, and Coca-Cola.

Additionally, Heather has 10 years' experience with a wholesale club competitor where she successfully managed 33 businesses representing the petroleum, financial, travel, communications, automotive, insurance and foodservice industries. In this capacity as assistant vice president of specialty business, she identified, developed, and implemented entrepreneurial business concepts and lucrative strategic partnerships for increased revenue, visibility, and customer satisfaction. Heather successfully negotiated multimillion-dollar contracts with both local and national companies, resulting in significant mutually rewarding financial gain.

She holds a bachelor of science degree in business management from Bentley College in Waltham, Massachusetts.

Info

💬 Heather's Info

First job out of school?
A) After my junior year in college, I had an internship with Honeywell scheduling production of mainframe computer systems. Two weeks into the job, I was asked to stay on full time and they paid for me to complete my senior year at night. I also entered their management development program at that time.

Career high?
A) Becoming an officer at Walmart.

My motto to live by?
A) If it is to be, it's up to me.

What drives me?
A) The opportunity to make a positive difference both personally and professionally.

My management style?
A) Open, inclusive, collaborative, supportive, and results-driven.

Don't do this when interviewing with me?
A) Don't come in unprepared. Do your homework on the company, competition, and the position you are applying for. Also, be prepared to interview me. You need to make sure the position and company culture are in alignment with your personal and professional values and goals in order to be truly successful.

Here's my problem...

Like other high-volume retailers that operate on razor-thin margins, Sam's Club always looks for ways to shave costs and improve efficiency in order to distribute large amounts of grocery and other items to its hundreds of stores quickly and inexpensively. Heather, at the time, oversaw the dairy category along with eight other merchandise categories for Sam's Club. Collectively, her team had the responsibility to source over 600 items, negotiate costs, and specify delivery methods and prices for the chain's more than 47 million club members across the United States.

Things to remember

Every link in the distribution chain adds cost to the final product.

Big companies like Sam's Club operate with very high volumes, so shaving a few cents off at different stages in a distribution process can result in significant savings.

Distribution processes are entrenched and it's costly to make changes. Also, consumers are reluctant to accept changes to products like milk cartons that they buy on a regular basis over a long period of time.

Ironically, milk is one of the most basic staple items the team stocks in its stores, but it is difficult to supply economically because it takes up a lot of space and is highly perishable. Heather and her team tried to address the problem of the high cost of shipping milk using traditional distribution methods. Shippers and end consumers tend to stick with what they know, and what they know is that the milk people use every day will come out of familiar gallon jugs just as it always has—the jug's design has not changed since 1953!

But Heather knew that something had to give. Competitors were cutting costs and using milk as a *loss leader* (where they deliberately sold the product below cost) in order to drive traffic into their stores. Sam's was at a competitive disadvantage, and it was losing market share on an important staple item. Sam's had to look closely at every step in the supply chain to look for ways to trim costs. Heather realized that the tried-and-true method of shipping milk to stores is inefficient and that this could be a link in the chain that she might tighten.

Typically a dairy truck will "weight out" before it "cubes out"; this means it hits the maximum weight it can carry well before it's full of jugs. In early 2007 the company was approached by one of its supplier partners that had developed a simple change to the design of the gallon milk jug that would allow it to *palletize* the product. This means that the supplier ships the item on a 40″ × 48″ platform (pallet), and a forklift or pallet jack moves the entire pallet from warehouse to truck and then from truck to cooler in the store.

The design modification also would eliminate the need to *back haul* empty racks and cases (milk crates) to the supplier to clean and reload; typically the empties need to be trucked back where they came from at great expense. This innovation promised to make milk cheaper to ship, so Sam's Club could reduce its *food miles* (an industry term that refers to how far the product has to travel from supplier to retailer). The company could deliver fresher milk to its stores so the product had a longer shelf life when it was put out in the dairy case. And this change would allow the company to pass the cost savings on to its members to the tune of 10 to 20 cents per gallon.

These new square or *case-less* milk jugs did not require crates or racks for shipping and storage. Instead, the newly designed milk gallon was self-stacking; the spout is flatter and each gallon can rest on another during transport, as well as while on display in the store. The company estimated that trucks used for shipping from the processor to a club could accommodate 9 percent more product—a total of 4,704 gallons per truck or approx-imately 384 more containers—without any metal racks. In addition, the flat top and wider spout do not come in contact with equipment during the fill process. This reduces the risk of possible contamination or the introduction of bacteria that shortens shelf life. To be sure, the new-and-improved technique had a lot of advantages over the tried-and-true, but Heather knew she would have to swim against the tide if she advocated the change. You always have to think twice before you mess with such an important and traditional product!

Heather considered her **Options** 1·2·3

1 Option

Continue doing business as usual and don't make any changes. Sam's Club's distribution network was very familiar with the current system so workers would not have to be retrained to handle a different process. Similarly, the club managers wouldn't have to learn a new way to receive and merchandise a staple product. Club members would continue to find what they expected to see on the dairy shelves.

However, storage space is at a premium in the packed Sam's Club stores. Under the current system the club has to store empty milk crates and racks until the milk supplier picks them up. Racks and crates tend to get stolen when they are placed outside for suppliers to pick up. The receiving process is slow because an employee needs to physically lift every crate and count it to verify the correct amount of product is there. In addition, floor space in the cooler is very tight as this is where product is stored *and* sold. Workers need to carefully maneuver milk rack "bossies" around in order to be able to stock other dairy items and get to needed stock for replenishment.

2 Option

Sam's Club's parent, Walmart, maintains large perishable distribution centers where full trucks of milk could be delivered and then reshipped to the appropriate locations. Walmart's fleet of trucks could help realize economies of scale as deliveries to stores would be made 24/7. Since the trucks deliver many other dairy products as well as milk, the trucks could be loaded more efficiently if the warehouse workers loaded different kinds of refrigerated products together—the heavier milk jugs could be intermingled with lighter, smaller containers of butter, and so forth, so the trucks could be more tightly packed without exceeding weight restrictions. On the other hand, this process would involve shipping the milk products twice: once to the distribution center and then to the Sam's Club stores. Each time the product is touched adds cost to the process. And multiple touches also multiply the opportunities for product damage.

3 Option

Change Sam's Club product and pallet configuration to embrace the new case-less design. This change would result in delivery of better quality milk products with a longer shelf life and reduce the retail price members paid for gallons of milk. The net result would be 9 percent more product on a truck, a 50 percent cut in the number of weekly deliveries each store would

You Choose

Which option would you choose, and why?

1. ☐YES ☐NO **2.** ☐YES ☐NO **3.** ☐YES ☐NO

See what **option** Heather chose on **page 473** ➡

supply chain
All the activities necessary to turn raw materials into a good or service and put it in the hands of the consumer or business customer.

Check out chapter 15 **Study Map** on page 474

require, and elimination of 32,000 deliveries in one year. On the green front, the supplier would save 100,000 gallons of water every day because it wouldn't have to clean and sanitize returnable milk crates. The new container is recyclable; pallets are used for other products, while shrink wrap and cardboard are recycled at each club location. And less labor is required at the club store to restock the milk jugs.

On the other hand, change can be difficult: The store managers would have to learn a new way to merchandise the product. Club shoppers would have to accept a radically different container in place of their beloved milk jug. And if Sam's Club converted to this process, it would be dependent on the supplier that invented it to stay in business and maintain its capacity to supply the needs of the business.

Now, put yourself in Heather's shoes. Which option would you choose, and why?

1

OBJECTIVE

Understand the concept of a supply chain.

(pp. 448–450)

Place: The Final Frontier

Sam's Club and its sister company, Walmart, are models of global supply chain effectiveness. Walmart is increasing the proportion of goods that it buys directly from manufacturers, rather than through third-party procurement companies or suppliers. As part of its effort to combine purchasing for the 15 countries in which it operates, Walmart has established four global merchandising centers for general goods and clothing. These include a center in Mexico City focused on emerging markets and a center in the UK to serve its George brand. It is also shifting to direct purchasing of its fresh fruit and vegetables on a global basis, and it plans to do the same for sheets and towels for its stores in the United States, Canada, and Mexico: its Faded Glory clothing line: licensed Disney character clothing: and eventually through other categories, including seafood, frozen food, and dry packaged groceries.[1]

Walmart clearly understands the potential for supply chain practices to enhance organizational performance and profits, and other firms benchmark against them for best practices. The truth is distribution may be the "final frontier" for marketing success. After years of hype, many consumers no longer believe that "new and improved" products really *are* new and improved. Nearly everyone, even upscale manufacturers and retailers, tries to gain market share through aggressive pricing strategies. Advertising and other forms of promotion are so commonplace they have lost some of their impact. Even hot new social media strategies can't sell overpriced or unavailable products, at least for long. Marketers have come to understand that *place* (the "distribution P") may be the only one of the *Four Ps* to offer an opportunity for really long-term competitive advantage—especially since many consumers now expect "instant gratification" by getting just what they want when the urge strikes.

That's why savvy marketers are always on the lookout for novel ways to distribute their products. This chapter is about the science and art of getting goods and services to customers. A large part of the marketer's ability to deliver a value proposition rests on the ability to understand and develop effective supply chain strategies, which is the major first topic in the chapter. The **supply chain** includes all the activities necessary to turn raw materials into a good or service and put it into the hands of the consumer or business customer. Often, of course, firms may decide to bring in outside companies to accomplish these activities—this is *outsourcing*, which as we learned about back in Chapter 6 occurs when firms obtain outside vendors to provide goods or services that might otherwise be supplied in-house. In the case of supply chain functions, outsource firms are most likely organizations with whom the company has developed some form of partnership or cooperative business arrangement.

Next, we talk about *distribution channels* and the *wholesaling intermediaries* therein. Distribution channels are a subset of the supply chain and are important because a large part of the marketer's ability to deliver the value proposition rests on the ability to understand and develop effective distribution strategies. Finally, we look at different *channels of distribution* and then *logistics management*, which is the process of actually moving goods through the supply chain. We will define each of these terms in greater detail in subsequent sections of this chapter, but for now let's look at the broader activities of the supply chain.

Supply Chain Management

The supply chain also encompasses all activities necessary to convert raw materials into a good or service and put it in the hands of the consumer or business customer. Thus, **supply chain management** is the coordination of flows among the firms in a supply chain to maximize total profitability. These "flows" include not only the physical movement of goods but also the sharing of information about the goods—that is, supply chain partners must synchronize their activities with one another. For example, they need to communicate information about which goods they want to purchase (the procurement function), about which marketing campaigns they plan to execute (so that the supply chain partners can ensure there will be enough product to supply the increased demand that results from the promotion), and about logistics (such as sending advance shipping notices to alert their partners that products are on their way). Through these information flows, a company can effectively manage all the links in its supply chain, from sourcing to retailing.

In his book *The World Is Flat: A Brief History of the Twenty-First Century*, which we discussed way back in Chapter 3, Thomas Friedman addresses a number of high-impact trends in global supply chain management.[2] One such development is the trend whereby companies we traditionally know for other things remake themselves as specialists who take over the coordination of clients' supply chains for them. UPS is a great example of this trend. UPS, which used to be "just" a package delivery service, today is much, much more because it specializes in **insourcing**. This process occurs when companies contract with a specialist who services their supply chains. Unlike the *outsourcing process* where a company delegates nonessential tasks to subcontractors, insourcing means that the client company brings in an external company to run its essential operations. Although we tend to associate UPS with those little brown trucks zipping around town delivering boxes, the company now also performs the following functions for some of its clients:

- If your Toshiba laptop needs repair, you drop it off at a UPS store. It's shipped to a UPS unit where UPS employees (not Toshiba technicians) actually get your machine booted back up.

- When you order a pizza from Papa John's, it's UPS that dispatches the drivers and schedules the delivery of pizza sauce, dough, and so on that the local store uses to make your "everything except anchovies."

- Order a pair of shoes at **Nike.com** and a UPS employee fills the order, bags it, labels it, and delivers it to your house.

The major difference between a supply chain and a channel of distribution is the number of members and their functions. A supply chain is broader; it consists of those firms that supply the raw materials, component parts, and supplies necessary for a firm to produce a good or service *plus* the firms that facilitate the movement of that product to the ultimate users of the product. This last part—the firms that get the product to the ultimate users—is the **channel of distribution**. (There will be more on channels of distribution in a bit.)

Heather Mayo
APPLYING ▽ Supply Chain Management

Heather's decision regarding how Sam's Club gets its milk into consumers' refrigerators has ramifications for the chain's price competitiveness, the impact on the environment, and customer loyalty. ➡

supply chain management
The management of flows among firms in the supply chain to maximize total profitability.

insourcing
A practice in which a company contracts with a specialist firm to handle all or part of its supply chain operations.

channel of distribution
The series of firms or individuals that facilitates the movement of a product from the producer to the final customer.

Figure 15.1 *Process* | HP's Supply Chain

The supply chain for computer maker HP's line of notebooks includes firms that supply component parts for the machines as well as retailers such as Best Buy. Each firm in the chain adds value through its inputs to provide the notebook the consumer wants at the lowest cost.

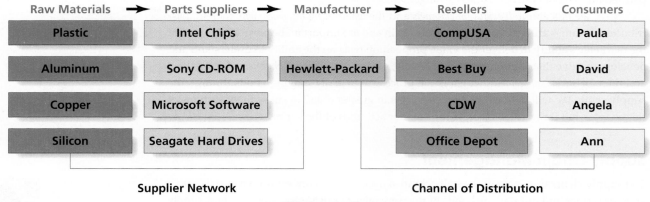

The Supply Chain

Now, let's take a closer look at one company's supply chain—Hewlett-Packard's (HP) line of laptop computers we show in *Figure 15.1*. HP use hundreds of suppliers to manufacture its laptops, and it sells them through online and brick-and-mortar retailers worldwide. And it's noteworthy that the role of individual firms within the supply chain depends on your perspective. If we look at HP's supply chain, Intel is a supplier, and Best Buy is a member of its channel of distribution. From Intel's perspective, however, HP is a customer. From the perspective of Best Buy, HP is a supplier.

In our example, Intel takes raw materials such as silicon and adds value when it turns them into chips, which it brands with names such as "Core," "Centurion," "Celeron," and "Pentium." Intel then ships chips to HP, which combines them with the other components of a computer (and places the famous "Intel Inside" stickers on the outside), again adding value. Best Buy takes the finished product and adds value when it provides display, sales support, repair service, and financing for the customer.

Now that you understand the basics of the value chain and the supply chain, let's dig into the nitty-gritty and understand how products actually get from point A to point B.

2 Distribution Channels: Get It There

OBJECTIVE

Explain what a distribution channel is and what functions distribution channels perform.
(pp. 450–453)

So you've created your product—priced it, too. And you've done the research to understand your target market—you've even set up a Facebook page to attract legions of brand fans. Sorry, you're still not done—now you need to get what you make out into the marketplace. As we noted earlier, a channel of distribution is a series of firms or individuals that facilitates the movement of a product from the producer to the final customer. In many cases, these channels include an organized network of producers (or manufacturers), wholesalers, and retailers that develop relationships and work together to make products conveniently available to eager buyers.

Distribution channels come in different shapes and sizes. The bakery around the corner where you buy your cinnamon rolls is a member of a channel, as is the baked goods section at the local supermarket, the Starbucks that sells biscotti to go with your double mocha cappuccino, and the bakery outlet store that sells day-old rolls at a discount.

A channel of distribution consists of, at a minimum, a producer—the individual or firm that manufactures or produces a good or service—and a customer. This is a *direct channel*. For example, when you buy a loaf of bread at a mom-and-pop bakery, you're buying through a direct channel. Firms that sell their own products through Web sites, catalogs, toll-free numbers, or factory outlet stores use direct channels.

But life (and marketing) usually isn't that simple: Channels often are *indirect* because they include one or more **channel intermediaries**—firms or individuals such as wholesalers, agents, brokers, and retailers who in some way help move the product to the consumer or business user. For example, a baker may choose to sell his cinnamon buns to a wholesaler that will in turn sell boxes of buns to supermarkets and restaurants that in turn sell them to consumers. Another older term for intermediaries is *middlemen*.

Functions of Distribution Channels

Channels that include one or more organizations or intermediaries often can accomplish certain distribution functions more effectively and efficiently than can a single organization. As we saw in Chapter 3, this is especially true in international distribution channels where differences among countries' customs, beliefs, and infrastructures can make global marketing a nightmare. Even small companies can succeed in complex global markets when they rely on distributors that know local customs and laws.

Overall, channels provide the time, place, and ownership utility we described in Chapter 1. They make desired products available when, where, and in the sizes and quantities that customers desire. Suppose, for example, you want to buy that perfect bouquet of flowers for a special someone. You *could* grow them yourself or even "liberate" them from a cemetery if you were *really* desperate (very classy!). Fortunately, you can probably accomplish this task with just a simple phone call or a few mouse clicks, and "like magic" a local florist delivers a bouquet to your honey's door.

Distribution channels provide a number of logistics or physical distribution functions that increase the efficiency of the flow of goods from producer to customer. How would we buy groceries without our modern system of supermarkets? We'd have to get our milk from a dairy, our bread from a bakery, our tomatoes and corn from a local farmer, and our flour from a flour mill. And forget about specialty items such as Twinkies or Coca-Cola. The companies that make these items would have to handle literally millions of transactions to sell to every individual who craves a junk-food fix.

Distribution channels create *efficiencies* because they reduce the number of transactions necessary for goods to flow from many different manufacturers to large numbers of customers. This occurs in two ways. The first is **breaking bulk**. Wholesalers and retailers purchase large quantities (usually cases) of goods from manufacturers but sell only one or a few at a time to many different customers. Second, channel intermediaries reduce the number of transactions when they **create assortments**—they provide a variety of products in one location—so that customers can conveniently buy many different items from one seller at one time.

 Figure 15.2 provides a simple example of how distribution channels work. This simplified illustration includes five producers and five customers. If each producer sold its product to each individual customer, 25 different transactions would have to occur—not exactly an efficient way to distribute products. But with a single intermediary who buys from all five manufacturers and sells to all five customers, we quickly cut the number of transactions to 10. If there were 10 manufacturers and 10 customers, an intermediary would reduce the number of transactions from 100 to just 20. Do the math: Channels are efficient.

The transportation and storage of goods is another type of physical distribution function. Retailers and other channel members move the goods from the production point to other locations where they can hold them until consumers want them. Channel intermediaries also perform a number of **facilitating functions** that make the purchase process easier for customers and manufacturers. For example, intermediaries often provide customer services such

Sometimes firms "delegate" part of the distribution function to the customer. And many customers are happy to cooperate when they can save on shipping charges and get that 60" LCD TV set up immediately.

channel intermediaries
Firms or individuals such as wholesalers, agents, brokers, or retailers who help move a product from the producer to the consumer or business user. An older term for intermediaries is middlemen.

breaking bulk
Dividing larger quantities of goods into smaller lots in order to meet the needs of buyers.

creating assortments
Providing a variety of products in one location to meet the needs of buyers.

facilitating functions
Functions of channel intermediaries that make the purchase process easier for customers and manufacturers.

Heather Mayo

APPLYING ▽ Utility

Sam's Club's dairy distribution channel provides utility to shoppers who no longer need to obtain milk directly from farms. ➡

Figure 15.2 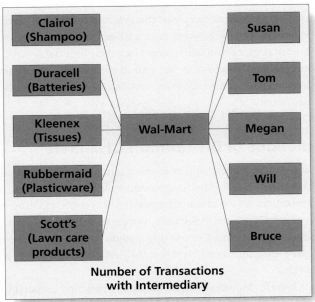 *Process* | Reducing Transactions via Intermediaries

One of the functions of distribution channels is to provide an assortment of products. Because the customers can buy a number of different products at the same location, this reduces the total costs of obtaining a product.

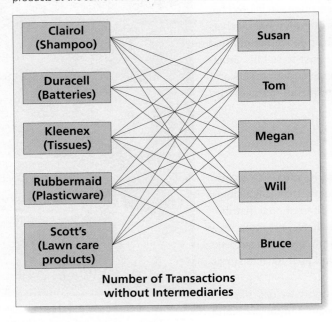

Some wholesalers and retailers assist the manufacturer when they provide setup, repair, and maintenance service for products they handle. Best Buy's Geek Squad is a perfect example.

as offering credit to buyers. Many of us like to shop at department stores because if we are not happy with the product we can take it back to the store where cheerful customer service personnel are happy to give us a refund (at least in theory). These same customer services are even more important in business-to-business markets where customers purchase larger quantities of higher-priced products. And channel members perform a risk-taking function. If a retailer buys a product from a manufacturer and it just sits on the shelf because no customers want it, he is stuck with the item and must take a loss. Perishable items present an even greater risk of spoilage.

Finally, intermediaries perform communication and transaction functions. Wholesalers buy products to make them available for retailers and they sell products to other channel members. Retailers handle transactions with final consumers. Channel members can provide two-way communication for manufacturers. They may supply the sales force, advertising, and other types of marketing communication necessary to inform consumers and persuade them that a product will meet their needs. And the channel members can be invaluable sources of information on consumer complaints, changing tastes, and new competitors in the market.

The Internet in the Distribution Channel

Obviously, many consumers choose the Internet to shop for everything from tulip bulbs to exotic vacations. By using the Internet, even small firms with limited resources enjoy the same market opportunities as their largest competitors to make their products available to customers around the globe.

E-commerce creates radical changes in distribution strategies. Manufacturing firms like Dell, HP, and Apple in the personal computer space rely heavily on Internet-driven direct-to-end-user distribution strategies, although all three are very active outside this channel (consider Apple Stores and Dell Kiosks). In most cases, though, end users still don't obtain products directly from manufacturers. Rather, goods flow from manufacturers to intermediaries and then on to the final customers.

With the Internet, this need for intermediaries and much of what we assume about the need and benefits of channels changes. As you know, an increasing number of consumers buy (or pirate?) their music as an Internet download, making retail music stores less necessary. Then too, as more and more consumers have access to faster broadband Internet service, downloadable movies soon will become the norm.[3]

In the future, channel intermediaries that physically handle the product may become obsolete. Already companies are eliminating many traditional intermediaries because they find that they don't add enough value in the distribution channel—a process we call **disintermediation (of the channel of distribution)**. For marketers, disintermediation reduces costs in many ways: fewer employees, no need to buy or lease expensive retail property in high-traffic locations, and no need to furnish a store with fancy fixtures and decor. You can also see this process at work when you pump your own gas, withdraw cash from an ATM, or use your electronic pass for expressway tolls instead of forking over your money to a flesh-and-blood attendant who sits in a toll booth. Are there any full-service gas stations left?

Some companies use the Internet to make coordination among members of a supply chain more effective in ways that end consumers never see. These firms develop better ways to implement **knowledge management**, which refers to a comprehensive approach that collects, organizes, stores, and retrieves a firm's information assets. These assets include both databases and company documents and the practical knowledge of employees whose past experience may be relevant to solving a new problem. If a firm shares this knowledge with other supply chain members, this more strategic management of information results in a win-win situation for all the partners.

But as with most things cyber, the Internet as a distribution channel brings pain with pleasure. One of the more vexing problems with Internet distribution is the potential for **online distribution piracy**, which is the theft and unauthorized repurposing of intellectual property via the Internet. The college textbook industry has high potential for online piracy. It's not uncommon for U.S.-produced textbooks to make their way to unscrupulous individuals outside the country who translate the core content into the native language and post it online for distribution. And obviously, unauthorized downloads of music is a predominant issue for the "recording" industry—to the point where the whole nature of the industry has turned topsy-turvy. Many in the music business are rethinking exactly what—and where—is the value-added for what they do. If the value is just to sell CDs in plastic cases, the industry is likely doomed. More and more musical artists opt to defect from traditional record labels and introduce their tunes online, where they can control some or all of the channel of distribution.[4]

So far, we've learned what a distribution channel is and about some of the functions it performs. Now let's find out about different types of channel intermediaries and channel structures.

Recording artist Aimee Mann licenses her music rather than work with a major record label in order to retain creative control over her product.

disintermediation (of the channel of distribution)
The elimination of some layers of the channel of distribution in order to cut costs and improve the efficiency of the channel.

knowledge management
A comprehensive approach to collecting, organizing, storing, and retrieving a firm's information assets.

online distribution piracy
The theft and unauthorized repurposing of intellectual property via the Internet.

3 Wholesaling Intermediaries

OBJECTIVE

Discuss the types of wholesaling intermediaries found in distribution channels.

(pp. 453–457)

How can you get your hands on a new Lady Gaga T-shirt? You could pick one up at your local music store, at a trendy clothing store like Hot Topic or maybe at its online store. You might join hoards of other "little monsters" and buy an "official Lady Gaga concert T-shirt" from vendors during a show. Alternatively, you might get a "deal" on a bootlegged, unauthorized version of the same shirt a shady guy who stands *outside* the concert venue sells from a battered suitcase. Perhaps you shop online at **www.ladygaga.com**. Each of these distribution alternatives traces a different path from producer to consumer. Let's look

Figure 15.3 📷 *Snapshot* | Key Types of Intermediaries

Intermediaries can be independent or manufacturer-owned.

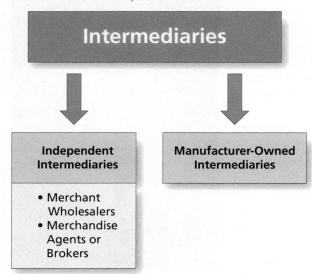

wholesaling intermediaries

Firms that handle the flow of products from the manufacturer to the retailer or business user.

independent intermediaries

Channel intermediaries that are not controlled by any manufacturer but instead do business with many different manufacturers and many different customers.

merchant wholesalers

Intermediaries that buy goods from manufacturers (take title to them) and sell to retailers and other business-to-business customers.

take title

To accept legal ownership of a product and assume the accompanying rights and responsibilities of ownership.

at the different types of wholesaling intermediaries and at different channel structures. We'll hold off focusing on retailers, which are usually the last link in the chain, until the next chapter.

Wholesaling intermediaries are firms that handle the flow of products from the manufacturer to the retailer or business user. There are many different types of consumer and business-to-business wholesaling intermediaries. Some of these are independent, but manufacturers and retailers can own them, too. 📷 Figure 15.3 portrays key intermediary types and Table 15.1 summarizes the important characteristics of each.

Independent Intermediaries

Independent intermediaries do business with many different manufacturers and many different customers. Because no manufacturer owns or controls them, they make it possible for many manufacturers to serve customers throughout the world while they keep prices low.

Merchant wholesalers are independent intermediaries that buy goods from manufacturers and sell to retailers and other business-to-business customers. Because merchant wholesalers **take title** to the goods (that is, they legally own them), they assume certain risks and can suffer losses if products are damaged, become outdated or obsolete, are stolen, or just don't sell. On the other hand, because they own the products, they are free to develop their own marketing strategies including setting the prices they charge their customers. Wait, it gets better: There are several different kinds of merchant wholesalers:

- *Full-service merchant wholesalers* provide a wide range of services for their customers, including delivery, credit, product-use assistance, repairs, advertising, and other promotional support—even market research. Full-service wholesalers often have their own sales force to call on businesses and organizational customers. Some general merchandise wholesalers carry a large variety of different items, whereas specialty wholesalers carry an extensive assortment of a single product line. For example, a candy wholesaler carries only candy and gum products, but he stocks enough different varieties to give your dentist nightmares for a year.

- In contrast, *limited-service merchant wholesalers* provide fewer services for their customers. Like full-service wholesalers, limited-service wholesalers *take title* to merchandise but are less likely to provide services such as delivery, credit, or marketing assistance to retailers. Specific types of limited-service wholesalers include the following:

- *Cash-and-carry wholesalers* provide low-cost merchandise for retailers and industrial customers that are too small for other wholesalers' sales representatives to call on. Customers pay cash for products and provide their own delivery. Some popular cash-and-carry product categories include groceries, office supplies, and building materials.

- *Truck jobbers* carry their products to small business customer locations for their inspection and selection. Truck jobbers often supply perishable items such as fruit and vegetables to small grocery stores. For example, a bakery truck jobber calls on supermarkets, checks the stock of bread on the shelves, removes outdated items, and suggests how much bread the store needs to reorder.

- *Drop shippers* are limited-function wholesalers that take title to the merchandise but never actually take possession of it. Drop shippers take orders from and bill retailers and industrial buyers, but the merchandise is shipped directly from the manufacturer. Because they take title to the merchandise, they assume the same risks as

Table 15.1 | Types of Intermediaries

Intermediary Type	Description	Advantages
Independent Intermediaries	Do business with many different manufacturers and many different customers	Used by most small- to medium-sized firms
• **Merchant Wholesalers**	Buy (take title to) goods from producers and sell to organizational customers; either full or limited function	Allow small manufacturers to serve customers throughout the world with competitive costs
• Cash-and-carry wholesalers	Provide products for small-business customers who purchase at wholesaler's location	Distribute low-cost merchandise for small retailers and other business customers
• Truck jobbers	Deliver perishable food and tobacco items to retailers	Ensure perishable items are delivered and sold efficiently
• Drop shippers	Take orders from and bill retailers for products drop-shipped from manufacturer	Facilitate transactions for bulky products
• Mail-order wholesalers	Sell through catalogs, telephone, or mail order	Provide reasonably priced sales options to small organizational customers
• Rack jobbers	Provide retailers with display units, check inventories, and replace merchandise for the retailers	Provide merchandising services to retailers
• **Merchandise Agents and Brokers**	Provide services in exchange for commissions	Maintain legal ownership of product by the seller
• Manufacturers' agents	Use independent salespeople; carry several lines of noncompeting products	Supply sales function for small and new firms
• Selling agents, including export/import agents	Handle entire output of one or more products	Handle all marketing functions for small manufacturers
• Commission merchants	Receive commission on sales price of product	Provide efficiency primarily in agricultural products market
• Merchandise brokers, including export/import brokers	Identify likely buyers and bring buyers and sellers together	Enhance efficiency in markets where there are many small buyers and sellers
Manufacturer-Owned Intermediaries	Limit operations to one manufacturer	Create efficiencies for large firms
• **Sales branches**	Maintain some inventory in different geographic areas (similar to wholesalers)	Provide service to customers in different geographic areas
• **Sales offices**	Carry no inventory; availability in different geographic areas	Reduce selling costs and provide better customer service
• **Manufacturers' showrooms**	Display products attractively for customers to visit	Facilitate examination of merchandise by customers at a central location

other merchant wholesalers. Drop shippers are important to both the producers and the customers of bulky products, such as coal, oil, or lumber.

• *Mail-order wholesalers* sell products to small retailers and other industrial customers, often located in remote areas, through catalogs rather than a sales force. They usually carry products in inventory and require payment in cash or by credit card before shipment. Mail-order wholesalers supply products such as cosmetics, hardware, and sporting goods.

• *Rack jobbers* supply retailers with specialty items such as health and beauty products and magazines. Rack jobbers get their name because they own and maintain the product display racks in grocery stores, drugstores, and variety stores. These wholesalers visit retail customers on a regular basis to maintain levels of stock and refill their racks with merchandise. Think about how quickly magazines turn over on the rack—without an expert who pulls old titles and inserts new ones, retailers would have great difficulty ensuring you can buy the current issue of *US* magazine on the first day it hits the streets.

Merchandise Agents or Brokers

merchandise agents or **brokers**
Channel intermediaries that provide services in exchange for commissions but never take title to the product.

Merchandise agents or **brokers** are a second major type of independent intermediary. Agents and brokers provide services in exchange for commissions. They may or may not take possession of the product, but they *never* take title; that is, they do not accept legal ownership of the product. Agents normally represent buyers or sellers on an ongoing basis, whereas clients employ brokers for a short period of time.

- *Manufacturers' agents*, or *manufacturers' reps*, are independent salespeople who carry several lines of noncompeting products. They have contractual arrangements with manufacturers that outline territories, selling prices, and other specific aspects of the relationship but provide little if any supervision. Manufacturers normally compensate agents with commissions based on a percentage of what they sell. Manufacturers' agents often develop strong customer relationships and provide an important sales function for small and new companies.

- *Selling agents*, including *export/import agents*, market a whole product line or one manufacturer's total output. They often work like an independent marketing department because they perform the same functions as full-service wholesalers but do not take title to products. Unlike manufacturers' agents, selling agents have unlimited territories and control the pricing, promotion, and distribution of their products. We find selling agents in industries such as furniture, clothing, and textiles.

- *Commission merchants* are sales agents who receive goods, primarily agricultural products such as grain or livestock, on *consignment*—that is, they take possession of products without taking title. Although sellers may state a minimum price they are willing to take for their products, commission merchants are free to sell the product for the highest price they can get. Commission merchants receive a commission on the sales price of the product.

- *Merchandise brokers*, including export/import brokers, are intermediaries that facilitate transactions in markets such as real estate, food, and used equipment, in which there are lots of small buyers and sellers. Brokers identify likely buyers and sellers and bring the two together in return for a fee they receive when the transaction is completed.

Manufacturer-Owned Intermediaries

Sometimes manufacturers set up their own channel intermediaries. In this way, they can operate separate business units that perform all the functions of independent intermediaries while at the same time they can still maintain complete control over the channel.

- *Sales branches* are manufacturer-owned facilities that, like independent wholesalers, carry inventory and provide sales and service to customers in a specific geographic area. We find sales branches in industries such as petroleum products, industrial machinery and equipment, and motor vehicles.

- *Sales offices* are manufacturer-owned facilities that, like agents, do not carry inventory but provide selling functions for the manufacturer in a specific geographic area. Because they allow members of the sales force to locate close to customers, they reduce selling costs and provide better customer service.

- *Manufacturers' showrooms* are manufacturer-owned or leased facilities in which products are permanently displayed for customers to visit. Merchandise marts are often multiple buildings in which one or more industries hold trade shows and many manufacturers have permanent showrooms. Retailers can visit either during a show or all year long to see the manufacturer's merchandise and make business-to-business purchases.

4

Types of Distribution Channels

Firms face many choices when they structure distribution channels. Should they sell directly to consumers and business users? Would they benefit if they included wholesalers, retailers, or both in the channel? Would it make sense to sell directly to some customers but use retailers to sell to others? Of course, there is no single best channel for all products. The marketing manager must select a channel structure that creates a competitive advantage for the firm and its products based on the size and needs of the target market. Let's consider some of the factors these managers need to think about.

When they develop distribution (place) strategies, marketers first consider different **channel levels**. This refers to the number of distinct categories of intermediaries that make up a channel of distribution. Many factors have an impact on this decision. What channel members are available? How large is the market? How frequently do consumers purchase the product? What services do consumers require? Figure 15.4 summarizes the different structures a distribution channel can take. The producer and the customer are always members, so the shortest channel possible has two levels. Using a retailer adds a third level, a wholesaler adds a fourth level, and so on. Different channel structures exist for both consumer and business-to-business markets.

And what about services? As we saw in Chapter 11, services are intangible, so there is no need to worry about storage, transportation, and the other functions of physical distribution. In most cases, the service travels directly from the producer to the customer. However, an intermediary we call an *agent* can enhance the distribution of some services when he helps the parties complete the transaction. Examples of these agents include insurance agents, stockbrokers, and travel agents (no, not everyone books their travel online).

channel levels
The number of distinct categories of intermediaries that populate a channel of distribution.

Consumer Channels

As we noted earlier, the simplest channel is a direct channel. Why do some producers sell directly to customers? One reason is that a direct channel may allow the producer to serve its customers better and at a lower price than is possible if it included a retailer. A baker who uses a direct channel makes sure his customers chew on fresher bread than if he sells the loaves through a local supermarket. Furthermore, if the baker sells the bread through a supermarket, the price will be higher because of the supermarket's costs of doing business and its need to make its own profit on the bread. In fact, sometimes this is the *only* way to sell the product, because using channel intermediaries may boost the price above what consumers are willing to pay.

Another reason to use a direct channel is *control*. When the producer handles distribution, it maintains control of pricing, service, and delivery—all elements of the transaction. Because distributors and dealers carry many products, it can be difficult to get their sales forces to focus on selling one product. In a direct channel, a producer works directly with customers so it gains insights into trends, customer needs and complaints, and the effectiveness of its marketing strategies.

Figure 15.4 📷 *Snapshot* | Different Types of Channels of Distribution

Channels differ in the number of channel members that participate.

Major Types of Channels of Distribution

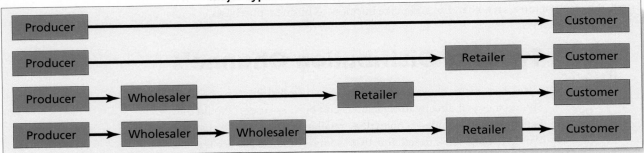

Typical Consumer Channels

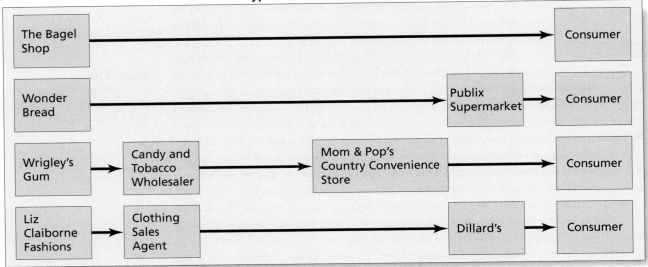

Business-to-Business Channels

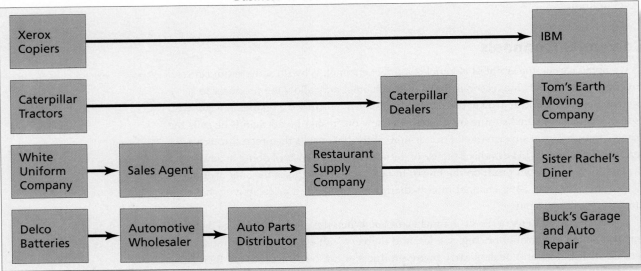

Why do producers choose to use indirect channels to reach consumers? A reason in many cases is that customers are familiar with certain retailers or other intermediaries—it's where they always go to look for what they need. Getting customers to change their normal buying behavior—for example, convincing consumers to buy their laundry detergent or frozen pizza from a catalog or over the Internet instead of from the corner supermarket—can be difficult.

In addition, intermediaries help producers in all the ways we described earlier. By creating utility and transaction efficiencies, channel members make producers' lives easier and enhance their ability to reach customers. The *producer–retailer–consumer channel* in ▣ Figure 15.4 is the shortest indirect channel. Panasonic uses this channel when it sells flat-screen TVs through large retailers such as Best Buy. Because the retailers buy in large volume, they can obtain inventory at a low price and then pass these savings on to shoppers (this is what gives them a competitive advantage over smaller, more specialized stores that don't order so many items). The size of these retail giants also means they can provide the physical distribution functions such as transportation and storage that wholesalers handle for smaller retail outlets.

The *producer–wholesaler–retailer–consumer channel* is a common distribution channel in consumer marketing. A single ice-cream factory supplies, say, four or five regional wholesalers. These wholesalers then sell to 400 or more retailers such as grocery stores. The retailers, in turn, each sell the ice cream to thousands of customers. In this channel, the regional wholesalers combine many manufacturers' products to supply grocery stores. Because the grocery stores do business with many wholesalers, this arrangement results in a broad selection of products.

Entrepreneurs Richie Lodico and Vinny Barbieri, owners of Eastern Meat Farms, Inc., discovered in the very early days of the Internet (they started their online business in 1995) that an online direct channel is a great way to continually expand their business globally. For years prior to going online, Lodico and Barbieri shipped sausages and cheeses across the country, but they didn't feel there was enough volume to justify the expense of direct marketing. However, with the advent of the Internet, **www.salami.com** was born (the URL alone must be worth a fortune today!). The company ships each order using Styrofoam and ice packs to ensure that customers from around the globe receive high-quality, fresh products, often for less than half the price they would have to pay for similar delicacies locally. Hot dog![5]

The Cutting Edge

Google Sells Adroid Phones Direct to Consumers

The wireless industry sells phones through several channels: company-owned stores, third-party retailers like Best Buy and RadioShack, and online, where customer telephone service is an option. Google thought it could sell phones in a new way—without retail stores or customer-service reps to hold shoppers' hands through the experience. Think again: Just eight days after Google opened its online store to sell the new Nexus One Smartphone (which runs their Android operating system) directly to customers, its support forums became overloaded with complaints. Customers vented about coverage and delivery problems, network compatibility, dropped calls, and operation woes.

Even though the Nexus One was initially offered at a discounted $179 with a two-year contract from T-Mobile, T-Mobile wasn't involved in the marketing, delivery, or customer service, beyond wireless service issues. Issues were posted on a support forum, where Google promised an e-mail response within

48 hours. Based on the volume on Google's message forums the first week, Google no doubt had a lot of e-mail to reply to. "This is an epic failure for Google," says Rob Enderle, an independent analyst. "t tried to create an Apple-like experience, but it's so far off from the Apple experience, it's not even on the same planet." In a statement, Google said it works "quickly to solve any customer-support issues as they come up." It said phone manufacturer HTC would provide telephone support for "device troubleshooting and warranty, repairs and returns."

Charles Golvin, an analyst at Forrester Research, says Google "clearly neglected" to realize what was involved in being a retailer. "It needs to make sure the experience gets better going forward." Google, says Enderle, has a massive Web presence, and if it doesn't want to offer phone support as the carriers do, it could have used Web tools and social networking to better communicate with customers. Clearly, intermediaries can add a great deal of value to customers within a channel.[6]

B2B Channels

B2B distribution channels, as the name suggests, facilitate the flow of goods from a producer to an organizational or business customer. Generally, business-to-business channels parallel consumer channels in that they may be direct or indirect. For example, the simplest indirect channel in industrial markets occurs when the single intermediary—a merchant wholesaler we refer to as an *industrial distributor* rather than a retailer—buys products from a manufacturer and sells them to business customers.

Direct channels are more common to business-to-business markets than to consumer markets. As we saw in Chapter 6, this is because B2B marketing often means a firm sells high-dollar, high-profit items (a single piece of industrial equipment may cost hundreds of thousands of dollars) to a market made up of only a few customers. In such markets, it makes sense financially for a company to develop its own sales force and sell directly to customers—in this case the investment in an in-house sales force pays off.

Dual and Hybrid Distribution Systems

Figure 15.4 illustrates how simple distribution channels work. But, once again we are reminded that life (or marketing) is rarely that simple: Producers, dealers, wholesalers, retailers, and customers alike may actually participate in more than one type of channel. We call these *dual* or *multiple distribution systems.*

The pharmaceutical industry provides a good example of multiple-channel usage. Pharmaceutical companies distribute their products in at least three types of channels. First, they sell to hospitals, clinics, and other organizational customers directly. These customers buy in quantity, and they purchase a wide variety of products. Because hospitals and clinics dispense pills one at a time rather than in bottles of 50, these outlets require different product packaging than when the manufacturer sells medications to other types of customers. Pharmaceuticals' second channel is an indirect consumer channel where the manufacturer sells to large drug store chains, like Walgreens, that distribute the medicines to their stores across the country. Alternatively, some of us would rather purchase our prescriptions in a more personal manner from the local independent drugstore where we can still get an ice-cream soda while we wait. In this version of the indirect consumer channel, the manufacturer sells to drug wholesalers that, in turn, supply these independents. Finally, third-party payers such as HMOs, PPOs, and insurance companies represent a third type of channel to which pharmaceutical companies also sell directly. After health care reform in the United States fully kicks in, who knows what the channel configuration might be!

Instead of serving a target market with a single channel, some companies combine channels—direct sales, distributors, retail sales, and direct mail—to create a **hybrid marketing system.**[7] For example, at one time you could buy a Xerox copier only directly through a Xerox salesperson. Today, unless you are a very large business customer, you likely will purchase a Xerox machine from a local Xerox authorized dealer, or possibly through the Xerox "Online Store." Xerox turned to an enhanced dealer network for distribution because such hybrid marketing systems offer companies certain competitive advantages, including increased coverage of the market, lower marketing costs, and a greater potential for customization of service for local markets.

Distribution Channels and the Marketing Mix

How do decisions regarding place relate to the other *three Ps*? For one, place decisions affect pricing. Marketers that distribute products through low-priced retailers such as Walmart, T.J. Maxx, and Marshalls will have different pricing objectives and strategies than will those that sell to specialty stores or traditional department stores. And of course the nature of the product itself influences the retailers and intermediaries that we use. Manufacturers select

hybrid marketing system
A marketing system that uses a number of different channels and communication methods to serve a target market.

mass merchandisers to sell mid-price-range products while they distribute top-of-the-line products such as expensive jewelry through high-end department and specialty stores.

Distribution decisions can sometimes give a product a distinct position in its market. For example, Enterprise Rent-a-Car avoids being overly dependent on the cutthroat airport rental car market as it opens retail outlets in primary locations in residential areas and local business centers. This strategy takes advantage of the preferences of customers who are not flying and who want short-term use of a rental vehicle, such as when their primary vehicle is in the repair shop. Enterprise built such a successful following around this business model that loyal customers began to clamor for more Enterprise counters at airports, which the company is all too happy to provide. Now Enterprise is a rising competitive threat to traditional airport car rental agencies such as Hertz and Avis.

Ethics in the Distribution Channel

Companies' decisions about how to make their products available to consumers through distribution channels can create ethical dilemmas. For example, because their size gives them great bargaining power when they negotiate with manufacturers, many large retail chains force manufacturers to pay a **slotting allowance**—a fee in exchange for agreeing to place a manufacturer's products on a retailer's valuable shelf space. Although the retailers claim that such fees pay the cost of adding products to their inventory, many manufacturers feel that slotting fees are more akin to highway robbery. Certainly, the practice prevents smaller manufacturers that cannot afford the slotting allowances from getting their products into the hands of consumers.

Another ethical issue involves the sheer size of a particular channel intermediary—be it manufacturer, wholesaler, retailer, or other intermediary. Giant retailer Walmart, increasingly criticized for forcing scores of independent competitors (i.e., "mom-and-pop stores") to go out of business, has begun a very visible program to help its smaller rivals. The program offers financial grants to hardware stores, dress shops, and bakeries near its new urban stores, training on how to survive with a Walmart in town, and even free advertising in Walmart stores. Of course, Walmart hopes to benefit from the program in cities like Los Angeles and New York, where its plan to build new stores in urban neighborhoods has met high resistance from local communities.[8]

Overall, it is important for all channel intermediaries to behave and treat each other in a professional, ethical manner—and to do no harm to consumers (financially or otherwise) through their channel activities. Every intermediary in the channel wants to make money, but behavior by one to maximize its financial success at the expense of others' success is a doomed approach, as ultimately cooperation in the channel will break down. Instead, it behooves intermediaries to work cooperatively in the channel to distribute products to consumers in an efficient manner—making the channel a success for everybody participating in it (including consumers)!

slotting allowance
A fee paid in exchange for agreeing to place a manufacturer's products on a retailer's valuable shelf space.

5
OBJECTIVE
List the steps to plan a distribution channel strategy.
(pp. 461–467)

Plan a Channel Strategy

Do customers want products in large or small quantities? Do they insist on buying them locally, or will they purchase from a distant supplier? How long are they willing to wait to get the product? Inquiring marketers want to know!

Distribution planning works best when marketers follow the steps in Figure 15.5. In this section, we will first look at how manufacturers decide on distribution objectives and then examine what influences distribution decisions. Finally, we'll talk about how firms select different distribution strategies and tactics.

Figure 15.5 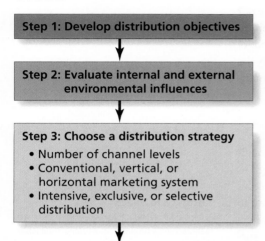 *Process* | Steps in Distribution Planning

Distribution planning begins with setting channel objectives and includes developing channel strategies and tactics.

Firms that operate within a channel of distribution—manufacturers, wholesalers, and retailers—do *distribution planning*. In this section, our perspective focuses on distribution planning by producers and manufacturers rather than intermediaries because they, more often than intermediaries, take a leadership role to create a successful distribution channel.

Step 1: Develop Distribution Objectives

The first step to decide on a distribution plan is to develop objectives that support the organization's overall marketing goals. How can distribution work with the other elements of the marketing mix to increase profits? To increase market share? To increase sales volume? In general, the overall objective of any distribution plan is to make a firm's product available when, where, and in the quantities customers want at the minimum cost. More specific distribution objectives, however, depend on the characteristics of the product and the market.

For example, if the product is bulky, a primary distribution objective may be to minimize shipping costs. If the product is fragile, a goal may be to develop a channel that minimizes handling. In introducing a new product to a mass market, a channel objective may be to provide maximum product exposure or to make the product available close to where customers live and work. Sometimes marketers make their product available where similar products are sold so that consumers can compare prices.

Step 2: Evaluate Internal and External Environmental Influences

After they set their distribution objectives, marketers must consider their internal and external environments to develop the best channel structure. Should the channel be long or short? Is intensive, selective, or exclusive distribution best? Short, often direct channels may be better suited for business-to-business marketers for whom customers are geographically concentrated and require high levels of technical know-how and service. Companies frequently sell expensive or complex products directly to final customers. Short channels with selective distribution also make more sense with perishable products, since getting the product to the final user quickly is a priority. However, longer channels with more intensive distribution are generally best for inexpensive, standardized consumer goods that need to be distributed broadly and that require little technical expertise.

The organization must also examine issues such as its own ability to handle distribution functions, what channel intermediaries are available, the ability of customers to access these intermediaries, and how the competition distributes its products. Should a firm use the same retailers as its competitors? It depends. Sometimes, to ensure customers' undivided attention, a firm sells its products in outlets that don't carry the competitors' products. In other cases, a firm uses the same intermediaries as its competitors because customers expect to find the product there. For example, you will find Harley-Davidson bikes only in selected Harley "boutiques" and Piaggio's Vespa scooters only at Vespa dealers (no sales through Walmart for those two!), but you can expect to find Coca-Cola, Colgate toothpaste, and a Snickers bar in every possible outlet that sells these types of items.

Finally, when they study competitors' distribution strategies, marketers learn from their successes and failures. If the biggest complaint of competitors' customers is delivery speed, developing a system that allows same-day delivery can make the competition pale in comparison.

Step 3: Choose a Distribution Strategy

Planning a distribution strategy means making at least three decisions. First, of course, distribution planning includes decisions about the number of levels in the distribution channel. We discussed these options in the earlier section on consumer and business-to-business channels, illustrated by 📷 Figure 15.4. Beyond the number of levels, distribution strategies also involve decisions about channel relationships—that is, whether a conventional system or a highly integrated system will work best—and the distribution intensity or the number of intermediaries at each level of the channel.

Conventional, Vertical, or Horizontal Marketing System?

Participants in any distribution channel form an interrelated system. In general, these marketing systems take one of three forms: conventional, vertical, or horizontal.

1. A **conventional marketing system** is a multilevel distribution channel in which members work independently of one another. Their relationships are limited to simply buying and selling from one another. Each firm seeks to benefit, with little concern for other channel members. Even though channel members work independently, most conventional channels are highly successful. For one thing, all members of the channel work toward the same goals—to build demand, reduce costs, and improve customer satisfaction. And each channel member knows that it's in everyone's best interest to treat other channel members fairly.

   > **conventional marketing system**
   > A multiple-level distribution channel in which channel members work independently of one another.

2. A **vertical marketing system (VMS)** is a channel in which there is formal cooperation among channel members at two or more different levels: manufacturing, wholesaling, and retailing. Firms develop vertical marketing systems as a way to meet customer needs better by reducing costs incurred in channel activities. Often, a vertical marketing system can provide a level of cooperation and efficiency not possible with a conventional channel, maximizing the effectiveness of the channel while also maximizing efficiency and keeping costs low. Members share information and provide services to other members; they recognize that such coordination makes everyone more successful when they want to reach a desired target market.

   > **vertical marketing system (VMS)**
   > A channel of distribution in which there is formal cooperation among members at the manufacturing, wholesaling, and retailing levels.

In turn there are three types of vertical marketing systems: administered, corporate, and contractual:

   a. In an *administered VMS*, channel members remain independent but voluntarily work together because of the power of a single channel member. Strong brands are able to manage an administered VMS because resellers are eager to work with the manufacturer so they will be allowed to carry the product.

   b. In a *corporate VMS*, a single firm owns manufacturing, wholesaling, and retailing operations. Thus, the firm has complete control over all channel operations. Retail giant Macy's, for example, owns a nationwide network of distribution centers and retail stores.

   c. In a *contractual VMS*, cooperation is enforced by contracts (legal agreements) that spell out each member's rights and responsibilities and how they will cooperate. This arrangement means that the channel members can have more impact as a group than they could alone. In a wholesaler-sponsored VMS, wholesalers get retailers to work together under their leadership in a voluntary chain. Retail members of the chain use a common name, cooperate in advertising and other promotion, and even develop their own private-label products. Examples of wholesaler-sponsored chains are IGA (Independent Grocers' Alliance) food stores and Ace Hardware stores.

In other cases, retailers themselves organize a cooperative marketing channel system. A *retailer cooperative* is a group of retailers that establish a wholesaling operation to help them compete more effectively with the large chains. Each retailer owns shares in the wholesaler operation and is obligated to purchase a certain percentage of its inventory from the cooperative operation. Associated Grocers and True Value Hardware stores are examples of retailer cooperatives.

Franchise organizations are a third type of contractual VMS. Franchise organizations include a *franchiser* (a manufacturer or a service provider) who allows an entrepreneur (the *franchisee*) to use the franchise name and marketing plan for a fee. In these organizations, contractual arrangements explicitly define and strictly enforce channel cooperation. In most franchise agreements, the franchiser provides a variety of services for the franchisee, such as helping to train employees, giving access to lower prices for needed materials, and selecting a good location. In return, the franchiser receives a percentage of revenue from the franchisee. Usually the franchisees are obligated to follow the franchiser's business format very closely in order to maintain the franchise.

From the manufacturer's perspective, franchising a business is a way to develop widespread product distribution with minimal financial risk while at the same time maintaining control over product quality. From the entrepreneur's perspective, franchises are a helpful way to get a start in business.

horizontal marketing system
An arrangement within a channel of distribution in which two or more firms at the same channel level work together for a common purpose.

3. In a **horizontal marketing system**, two or more firms at the same channel level agree to work together to get their product to the customer. Sometimes unrelated businesses forge these agreements. Most airlines today are members of a horizontal alliance that allows them to cooperate when they provide passenger air service. For example, American Airlines is a member of the oneworld® alliance, which also includes British Airways, Cathay Pacific, Finnair, Iberia, JAL, LAN, Malev, Mexicana, Qantas, and Royal Jordanian Airways. These alliances increase passenger volume for all airlines because travel agents who book passengers on one of the airline's flights will be more likely to book a connecting flight on the other airline. To increase customer benefits, they also share frequent-flyer programs and airport clubs.[9]

Intensive, Exclusive, or Selective Distribution?

How many wholesalers and retailers should carry the product within a given market? This may seem like an easy decision: Distribute the product through as many intermediaries as possible. But guess again. If the product goes to too many outlets, there may be inefficiency and duplication of efforts. For example, if there are too many Honda dealerships in town, there will be a lot of unsold Hondas sitting on dealer lots and no single dealer will be successful. But if there are not enough wholesalers or retailers to carry a product, this will fail to maximize total sales of the manufacturer's products (and its profits). If customers have to drive hundreds of miles to find a Honda dealer, they may instead opt for a Toyota, Mitsubishi, Mazda, or Nissan. Thus, a distribution objective may be to either increase or decrease the level of distribution in the market.

The three basic choices are intensive, exclusive, and selective distribution. Table 15.2 summarizes five decision factors—company, customers, channels, constraints, and competition—and how they help marketers determine the best fit between distribution system and marketing goals.

intensive distribution
Selling a product through all suitable wholesalers or retailers that are willing to stock and sell the product.

Intensive distribution aims to maximize market coverage by selling a product through all wholesalers or retailers that will stock and sell the product. Marketers use intensive distribution for products such as chewing gum, soft drinks, milk, and bread that consumers quickly consume and must replace frequently. Intensive distribution is necessary for these products because availability is more important than any other consideration in customers' purchase decisions.

exclusive distribution
Selling a product only through a single outlet in a particular region.

In contrast to intensive distribution, **exclusive distribution** means to limit distribution to a single outlet in a particular region. Marketers often sell pianos, cars, executive training programs, television programs, and many other products with high price tags through exclusive distribution arrangements. They typically use these strategies with products that are high-priced and have considerable service requirements, and when a limited number of buyers exist in any single geographic area. Exclusive distribution enables wholesalers and retailers to better recoup the costs associated with long-selling processes for each customer and, in some cases, extensive after-sale service.

Table 15.2	Characteristics That Favor Intensive versus Exclusive Distribution	
Decision Factor	**Intensive Distribution**	**Exclusive Distribution**
Company	Oriented toward mass markets	Oriented toward specialized markets
Customers	High customer density	Low customer density
	Price and convenience are priorities	Service and cooperation are priorities
Channels	Overlapping market coverage	Nonoverlapping market coverage
Constraints	Cost of serving individual customers is low	Cost of serving individual customers is high
Competition	Based on a strong market presence, often through advertising and promotion	Based on individualized attention to customers, often through relationship marketing

Of course, not every situation neatly fits a category in Table 15.2. (You didn't *really* think it would be that simple, did you?) For example, consider professional sports. Customers might not shop for games in the same way they shop for pianos. They might go to a game on impulse, and they don't require much individualized service. Nevertheless, professional sports use exclusive distribution. A team's cost of serving customers is high because of those million-dollar player salaries and multimillion-dollar stadiums.

The alert reader (and/or sports fan) may note that there are some exceptions to the exclusive distribution of sports teams. New York has two football teams and two baseball teams, Chicago fields two baseball teams, and so on. We call market coverage that is less than intensive distribution but more than exclusive distribution **selective distribution**. This model fits when demand is so large that exclusive distribution is inadequate, but selling costs, service requirements, or other factors make intensive distribution a poor fit. Although a White Sox baseball fan may not believe that the Cubs franchise is necessary (and *vice versa*), Major League Baseball and even some baseball fans think the Chicago market is large enough to support both teams.

Selective distribution strategies are suitable for so-called *shopping products,* such as household appliances and electronic equipment for which consumers are willing to spend time visiting different retail outlets to compare alternatives. For producers, selective distribution means freedom to choose only those wholesalers and retailers that have a good credit rating, provide good market coverage, serve customers well, and cooperate effectively. Wholesalers and retailers like selective distribution because it results in higher profits than are possible with intensive distribution, in which sellers often have to compete on price.

selective distribution
Distribution using fewer outlets than intensive distribution but more than exclusive distribution.

Step 4: Develop Distribution Tactics

As with planning for the other marketing Ps, the final step in distribution planning is to develop the distribution tactics necessary to implement the distribution strategy. These decisions are usually about the type of distribution system to use, such as a direct or indirect channel or a conventional or an integrated channel. Distribution tactics relate to the implementation of these strategies, such as how to select individual channel members and how to manage the channel.

These decisions are important because they often have a direct impact on customer satisfaction—nobody wants to have to wait for something they've bought! When Toyota first introduced the now wildly successful Scion, the company wisely came up with a new approach to distribute this youth-oriented vehicle that differs from its traditional Toyota distribution system. The company's overall goal was to cut delivery time to its impatient young customers to no more than a week by offering fewer model variations and doing

Ripped from the Headlines

Ethical/Sustainable Decisions in the Real World

Walmart announced in early 2010 that it would cut some 20 million metric tons of greenhouse gas emissions from its supply chain by the end of 2015—the equivalent of removing more than 3.8 million cars from the road for a year. The company plans to achieve that goal in part by pressing its suppliers to rethink how they source, manufacture, package, and transport their goods. Essentially, the chain is asking suppliers to examine the carbon lifecycle of their products, from the raw materials used in manufacturing all the way through to the recycling phase. Walmart's sustainability executives will work with suppliers to help them figure out what measures to take. But any costs related to making products more energy-efficient—redesigning packaging or using a different fertilizer—will be the responsibility of each supplier, not of Walmart.

ETHICS CHECK: ☜

Find out what other students taking this course **would do** and **why** on **www .mypearsonmarketinglab .com**

The initiative is good for the environment, but it's also good for Walmart as it follows the sustainability mantra of "doing well by doing good." Driving costs out of the supply chain could result in savings for Walmart that the stores can pass along to consumers—enabling the company to enhance its reputation as a destination for rock-bottom prices. Walmart said supplier participation in its effort to reduce greenhouse gas emissions would not be mandatory. But the giant retailer—with sales of more than $400 billion—made it clear that it was interested in doing business only with suppliers that share its goals. Critics argue, though, that rather than change its business model, Walmart pressures suppliers to change theirs—which can lead them to cut corners and produce shoddier products.

For its part, Walmart has started many environmental initiatives in recent years that include improving the efficiency of its truck fleet; creating a global index to measure the environmental impact of products; and changing the labels on clothing it sells to indicate the products can be washed in cold water (therefore lowering customers' electricity bills). The company said the 20 million metric tons of greenhouse gas emissions it intends to cut from its supply chain by the end of 2015 is 150 percent of the estimated growth in carbon emissions from its own operations over the next five years.

Should Walmart aggressively force its suppliers to comply with its green goals?

☐YES ☐NO

more customization *at the dealer* rather than at the factory. The continuing resounding success of the Scion brand shows the power of tailoring distribution tactics differently for different markets.[10]

Select Channel Partners

When firms agree to work together in a channel relationship, they become partners in what is normally a long-term commitment. Like a marriage, it is important to both manufacturers and intermediaries to select channel partners wisely, or they'll regret the match-up later (and a divorce can be really expensive!). In evaluating intermediaries, manufacturers try to answer questions such as the following: Will the channel member contribute substantially to our profitability? Does the channel member have the ability to provide the services customers want? What impact will a potential intermediary have on channel control?

For example, what small to midsize firm wouldn't jump at the chance to have retail giant Walmart distribute its products? With Walmart as a channel partner, a small firm could double, triple, or quadruple its business. Actually, some firms that recognize size means power in the channel actually decide against selling to Walmart because they are not willing to relinquish control of their marketing decision making. There is also a downside to choosing one retailer and selling only through that one retailer. If that retailer stops carrying the product, for example, the company will lose its one and only customer (perhaps after relinquishing other smaller customers), and it will be back to square one.

Another consideration in selecting channel members is competitors' channel partners. Because people spend time comparing different brands when purchasing a shopping product, firms need to make sure they display their products near similar competitors' products. If most competitors distribute their electric drills through mass merchandisers, a manufacturer has to make sure its brand is there also.

A firm's dedication to social responsibility may also be an important determining factor in the selection of channel partners. Many firms run extensive programs to recruit minority-owned channel members. Starbucks' famous organizational commitment to good corporate citizenship translates in one way into its "supplier diversity program" that works to help minority-owned business thrive.[11]

Manage the Channel

Once a manufacturer develops a channel strategy and aligns channel members, the day-to-day job of managing the channel begins. The **channel leader**, sometimes called a *channel captain*, is the dominant firm that controls the channel. A firm becomes the channel leader because it has power relative to other channel members. This power comes from different sources:

- A firm has *economic power* when it has the ability to control resources.

- A firm such as a franchiser has *legitimate power* if it has legal authority to call the shots.

- A producer firm has *reward* or *coercive power* if it engages in exclusive distribution and has the ability to give profitable products and to take them away from the channel intermediaries.

In the past, producers traditionally held the role of channel captain. Procter & Gamble, for example, developed customer-oriented marketing programs, tracked market trends, and advised retailers on the mix of products most likely to build sales. As large retail chains evolved, giant retailers such as Best Buy, Home Depot, Target, and Walmart began to assume a leadership role because of the sheer size of their operations. Today it is much more common for the big retailers to dictate their needs to producers instead of producers controlling what products they offer to retailers.

Because producers, wholesalers, and retailers depend on one another for success, channel cooperation helps everyone. Channel cooperation is also stimulated when the channel leader takes actions that make its partners more successful. High intermediary profit margins, training programs, cooperative advertising, and expert marketing advice are invisible to end customers but are motivating factors in the eyes of wholesalers and retailers.

Of course, relations among members in a channel are not always full of sweetness and light. Because each firm has its own objectives, channel conflict may threaten a manufacturer's distribution strategy. Such conflict most often occurs between firms at different levels of the same distribution channel. Incompatible goals, poor communication, and disagreement over roles, responsibilities, and functions cause conflict. For example, a producer is likely to feel the firm would enjoy greater success and profitability if intermediaries carry only its brands, but many intermediaries believe they will do better if they carry a variety of brands.

In this section, we've been concerned with the distribution channels firms use to get their products to customers. In the next section, we'll look at the area of logistics—physically moving products through the supply chain.

channel leader
A firm at one level of distribution that takes a leadership role, establishing operating norms and processes based on its power relative to other channel members.

Logistics: Implement the Supply Chain

OBJECTIVE

Explain logistics and how it fits into the supply chain concept.
(pp. 467–472)

Some marketing textbooks tend to depict the practice of marketing as 90 percent planning and 10 percent implementation. Not so! In the "real world" (our world) many managers argue that this ratio should be reversed. Marketing success is very much the art of getting the timing right and delivering on promises—*implementation*.

That's why marketers place so much emphasis on efficient **logistics**: the process of designing, managing, and improving the movement of products through the supply chain. Logistics includes purchasing, manufacturing, storage, and transport. From a company's viewpoint, logistics takes place both *inbound* to the firm (raw materials, parts, components, and supplies) and *outbound* from the firm (work-in-process and finished goods). Logistics is

logistics
The process of designing, managing, and improving the movement of products through the supply chain. Logistics includes purchasing, manufacturing, storage, and transport.

also a relevant consideration regarding product returns, recycling and material reuse, and waste disposal—*reverse logistics*.[12] As we saw in earlier chapters, that's becoming even more important as firms start to more seriously consider *sustainability* as a competitive advantage and put more effort into maximizing the efficiency of recycling to save money and the environment at the same time. So you can see logistics is an important issue across all elements of the supply chain. Let's examine this process more closely.

The Lowdown on Logistics

Have you ever heard the saying, "An army travels on its stomach"? *Logistics* was originally a term the military used to describe everything needed to deliver troops and equipment to the right place, at the right time, and in the right condition. In business, logistics is similar in that its objective is to deliver exactly what the customer wants—at the right time, in the right place, and at the right price. The application of logistics is essential to the efficient management of the supply chain.

physical distribution
The activities that move finished goods from manufacturers to final customers, including order processing, warehousing, materials handling, transportation, and inventory control.

The delivery of goods to customers involves **physical distribution**, which refers to the activities that move finished goods from manufacturers to final customers. Physical distribution activities include order processing, warehousing, materials handling, transportation, and inventory control. This process impacts how marketers physically get products where they need to be, when they need to be there, and at the lowest possible cost. Effective physical distribution is at the core of successful logistics.

When a firm does logistics planning, however, the focus also should be on the customer. When managers thought of logistics as physical distribution only, the objective was to deliver the product at the lowest cost. Today, forward-thinking firms consider the needs of the customer first. The customer's goals become the logistics provider's goals. And this means that when they make most logistics decisions, firms must decide on the best trade-off between low costs and high customer service. The appropriate goal is not just to deliver what the market needs at the lowest cost but rather to provide the product at the lowest cost possible *as long as the firm meets delivery requirements*. Although it would be nice to transport all goods quickly by air, that is certainly not practical. But sometimes air transport is necessary to meet the needs of the customer, no matter the cost.

Logistics Functions

When they develop logistics strategies, marketers must make decisions related to the five functions of logistics 📷 Figure 15.6 depicts: order processing, warehousing, materials handling, transportation, and inventory control. For each decision, managers need to consider how to minimize costs while maintaining the service customers want.

Order Processing

order processing
The series of activities that occurs between the time an order comes into the organization and the time a product goes out the door.

Order processing includes the series of activities that occurs between the time an order comes into the organization and the time a product goes out the door. After a firm receives an order it typically sends it electronically to an office for record keeping and then on to the warehouse to fill it. When the order reaches the warehouse, personnel there check to see if the item is in stock. If it is not, they put the order on back-order status. That information goes to the office and then to the customer. If the item is available, the company locates it in the warehouse, packages it for shipment, and schedules it for pickup by either in-house or external shippers.

enterprise resource planning (ERP) systems
A software system that integrates information from across the entire company, including finance, order fulfillment, manufacturing, and transportation and then facilitates sharing of the data throughout the firm.

Fortunately, many firms automate this process with **enterprise resource planning (ERP) systems**. An ERP system is a software solution that integrates information from across the entire company, including finance, order fulfillment, manufacturing, and transportation. Data need to be entered into the system only once, and then the organization automatically shares this information and links it to other related data. For example, an ERP system ties information on product inventories to sales information so that a sales representative can immediately tell a customer whether the product is in stock.

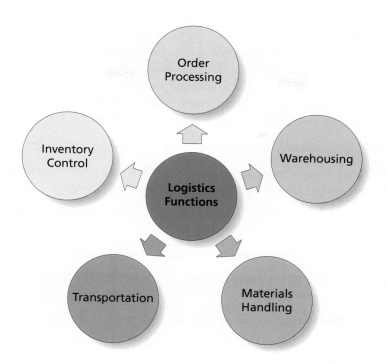

Figure 15.6 📷 *Process* | The Five Functions of Logistics

When they develop logistics strategies, marketers must make decisions related to order processing, warehousing, materials handling, transportation, and inventory control.

Warehousing

Whether we deal with fresh-cut flowers, canned goods, or computer chips, at some point goods (unlike services) must be stored. Storing goods allows marketers to match supply with demand. For example, toys and other gift items are big sellers at Christmas, but toy factories operate 12 months of the year. **Warehousing**—storing goods in anticipation of sale or transfer to another member of the channel of distribution—enables marketers to provide *time utility* to consumers by holding on to products until consumers need them.

Part of developing effective logistics means making decisions about how many warehouses we need and where and what type of warehouse each should be. A firm determines the location of its warehouse(s) by the location of customers and access to major highways, airports, or rail transportation. The number of warehouses often depends on the level of service customers require. If customers generally demand fast delivery (today or tomorrow at the latest), then it may be necessary to store products in a number of different locations from which the company can quickly ship the goods to the customer.

Firms use private and public warehouses to store goods. Those that use *private warehouses* have a high initial investment, but they also lose less of their inventory due to damage. *Public warehouses* are an alternative; they allow firms to pay for a portion of warehouse space rather than having to own an entire storage facility. Most countries offer public warehouses in all large cities and many smaller cities to support domestic and international trade. A *distribution center* is a warehouse that stores goods for short periods of time and that provides other functions, such as breaking bulk.

Materials Handling

Materials handling is the moving of products into, within, and out of warehouses. When goods come into the warehouse, they must be physically identified, checked for damage, sorted, and labeled. Next they are taken to a location for storage. Finally, they are recovered from the storage area for packaging and shipment. All in all, the goods may be handled over a dozen separate times. Procedures that limit the number of times a product must be handled decrease the likelihood of damage and reduce the cost of materials handling.

warehousing
Storing goods in anticipation of sale or transfer to another member of the channel of distribution.

materials handling
The moving of products into, within, and out of warehouses.

Heather Mayo

APPLYING ▽ Materials Handling

Heather needs to consider whether a new process that reduces the times a milk carton is handled is worth the hassles it may create if Sam's Club changes its distribution strategy for milk. ➡

transportation
The mode by which products move among channel members.

Transportation

Logistics decisions take into consideration options for **transportation**, the mode by which products move among channel members. Again, making transportation decisions entails a compromise between minimizing cost and providing the service customers want. As Table 15.3 shows, modes of transportation, including railroads, water transportation, trucks, airways, pipelines, and the Internet, differ in the following ways:

- *Dependability:* The ability of the carrier to deliver goods safely and on time

- *Cost:* The total transportation costs to move a product from one location to another, including any charges for loading, unloading, and in-transit storage

- *Speed of delivery:* The total time to move a product from one location to another, including loading and unloading

- *Accessibility:* The number of different locations the carrier serves

- *Capability:* The ability of the carrier to handle a variety of different products such as large or small, fragile, or bulky

- *Traceability:* The ability of the carrier to locate goods in shipment

Each mode of transportation has strengths and weaknesses that make it a good choice for different transportation needs. Table 15.3 summarizes the pros and cons of each mode.

- *Railroads:* Railroads are best to carry heavy or bulky items, such as coal and other mining products, over long distances. Railroads are about average in their cost and provide moderate speed of delivery. Although rail transportation provides dependable, low-cost service to many locations, trains cannot carry goods to every community.

Table 15.3 | A Comparison of Transportation Modes

Transportation Mode	Dependability	Cost	Speed of Delivery	Accessibility	Capability	Traceability	Most Suitable Products
Railroads	Average	Average	Moderate	High	High	Low	Heavy or bulky goods, such as automobiles, grain, and steel
Water	Low	Low	Slow	Low	Moderate	Low	Bulky, nonperishable goods, such as automobiles
Trucks	High	High for long distances; low for short distances	Fast	High	High	High	A wide variety of products, including those that need refrigeration
Air	High	High	Very fast	Low	Moderate	High	High-value items, such as electronic goods and fresh flowers
Pipeline	High	Low	Slow	Low	Low	Moderate	Petroleum products and other chemicals
Internet	High	Low	Very fast	Potentially very high	Low	High	Services such as banking, information, and entertainment

- *Water:* Ships and barges carry large, bulky goods and are very important in international trade. Water transportation is relatively low in cost but can be slow.

- *Trucks:* Trucks or motor carriers are the most important transportation mode for consumer goods, especially for shorter hauls. Motor carrier transport allows flexibility because trucks can travel to locations missed by boats, trains, and planes. Trucks also carry a wide variety of products, including perishable items. Although costs are fairly high for longer-distance shipping, trucks are economical for shorter deliveries. Because trucks provide door-to-door service, product handling is minimal, and this reduces the chance of product damage.

- *Air:* Air transportation is the fastest and also the most expensive transportation mode. It is ideal to move high-value items such as important mail, fresh-cut flowers, and live lobsters. Passenger airlines, air-freight carriers, and express delivery firms, such as FedEx, provide air transportation. Ships remain the major mover of international cargo, but air transportation networks are becoming more important as international markets continue to develop.

- *Pipeline:* Pipelines carry petroleum products such as oil and natural gas and a few other chemicals. Pipelines flow primarily from oil or gas fields to refineries. They are very low in cost, require little energy, and are not subject to disruption by weather.

- *The Internet:* As we discussed earlier in this chapter, marketers of services such as banking, news, and entertainment take advantage of distribution opportunities the Internet provides.

Inventory Control: JIT, RFID, and Fast Fashion

Another component of logistics is **inventory control**, which means developing and implementing a process to ensure that the firm always has sufficient quantities of goods available to meet customers' demands—no more and no less. That explains why firms work so hard to track merchandise so they know where their products are and where they are needed in case a low-inventory situation appears imminent.

Some companies are even phasing in a sophisticated technology (similar to the EZ Pass system many drivers use to speed through tollbooths) known as **radio frequency identification (RFID)**. RFID lets firms tag clothes, pharmaceuticals, or virtually any kind of product with tiny chips that contain information about the item's content, origin, and destination. This technology has the potential to revolutionize inventory control and help marketers ensure that their products are on the shelves when people want to buy them. Great for manufacturers and retailers, right? But some consumer groups are creating a backlash against RFID, which they refer to as "spy chips." Through blogs, boycotts, and other anti-company initiatives, these groups proclaim RFID a personification of the privacy violations George Orwell predicted in his classic book *1984*.[13]

Firms store goods (that is, they create an *inventory*) for many reasons. For manufacturers the pace of production may not match seasonal demand. It may be more economical to produce snow skis year-round than to produce them only during the winter season. For channel members that purchase goods from manufacturers or other channel intermediaries, it may be economical to order a product in quantities that don't exactly parallel demand. For example, delivery costs make it prohibitive for a retail gas station to place daily orders for just the amount of gas people will use that day. Instead, stations usually order truckloads of gasoline, holding their inventory in underground tanks. The consequences of stockouts may be very negative. Hospitals must keep adequate supplies of blood, IV fluids, drugs, and other supplies on hand to meet emergencies, even if some items go to waste.

Inventory control has a major impact on the overall costs of a firm's logistics initiatives. If supplies of products are too low to meet fluctuations in customer demand, a firm may

inventory control
Activities to ensure that goods are always available to meet customers' demands.

radio frequency identification (RFID)
Product tags with tiny chips containing information about the item's content, origin, and destination.

have to make expensive emergency deliveries or lose customers to competitors. If inventories are above demand, unnecessary storage expenses and the possibility of damage or deterioration occur. To balance these two opposing needs, manufacturers turn to **just in time (JIT)** inventory techniques with their suppliers. JIT sets up delivery of goods just as they are needed on the production floor. This minimizes the cost of holding inventory while it ensures the inventory will be there when customers need it.

A supplier's ability to make on-time deliveries is the critical factor in the selection process for firms that adopt this kind of system. JIT systems reduce stock to very low levels, or even zero, and time deliveries very carefully to maintain just the right amount of inventory. The advantage of JIT systems is the reduced cost of warehousing. For both manufacturers and resellers that use JIT systems, the choice of supplier may come down to one whose location is nearest. To win a large customer, a supplier may even have to be willing to set up production facilities close to the customer to guarantee JIT delivery.[14]

Supply Chain Metrics

Companies track a wide range of metrics within the supply chain area. Some of the most common ones are the following:

- On-time delivery

- Forecast accuracy

- Value-added productivity per employee

- Returns processing cost as a percentage of product revenue

- Customer order actual cycle time

- Perfect order measurement

Let's take a look at the last measure in more detail. The **perfect order measurement** calculates the error-free rate of each stage of a purchase order.[15] This measure helps managers track the multiple steps involved in getting a product from a manufacturer to a customer so that they can pinpoint processes they need to improve. For example, a company can calculate its error rate at each stage and then combine these rates to create an overall metric of order quality. Suppose the company identifies the following error rates:

- Order entry accuracy: 99.95 percent correct (five errors per 1,000 order lines)

- Warehouse pick accuracy: 99.2 percent

- Delivered on time: 96 percent

- Shipped without damage: 99 percent

- Invoiced correctly: 99.8 percent

The company can then combine these individual rates into an overall perfect order measurement by multiplying them together: $99.95 \times 99.2 \times 96 \times 99 \times 99.8 = 94.04$ percent.

just in time (JIT)
Inventory management and purchasing processes that manufacturers and resellers use to reduce inventory to very low levels and ensure that deliveries from suppliers arrive only when needed.

perfect order measurement
A supply chain metric that tracks multiple steps in getting a product from a manufacturer to a customer.

Here's my choice. . .

Real **People**, Real **Choices**

1 Option   2 Option   **3** Option

Why do you think
Heather chose option #3?

How It Worked Out at Sam's Club

Sam's Club launched the caseless program. But Sam's had to teach shoppers how to use the new jug—if they lifted and poured as they did with the old container, the milk would dribble down the side. Since the initial launch, the jug has gone through numerous versions to improve "pourability," so the spillage problem has been eliminated. The switch was so large-scale and innovative that more than 1,000 news stories about it ran around the world.

To learn the whole story, visit www.mypearsonmarketinglab.com.

Brand **YOU**!

Special delivery.

Deliver value to your prospective employer starting with your interview. Uncover some of the best secrets to a successful interview from employers and executives. Impress your interviewer with the exact balance of research, preparation, personality, and all the right questions. Get the inside track in Chapter 15 of *Brand You*.

| Kim Richmond Fourth Edition |

Brand YOU

MARKETING 7E **real** People, **real** Choices

Solomon | Marshall | Stuart

Objective Summary ➝ Key Terms ➝ Apply

1. Objective Summary (pp. 448–450)

Understand the concept of a supply chain.

The value chain consists of five primary activities (inbound logistics, operations, outbound logistics, marketing and sales, and service) and four support activities (procurement, technology development, human resource management, and firm infrastructure). The process is called a value chain because each of these activities adds value to the product the customer eventually buys. Whereas the value chain is an overarching concept of how firms create value, the supply chain also encompasses components external to the firm itself, including all activities that are necessary to convert raw materials into a good or service and put it in the hands of the consumer or business customer.

Key Terms

supply chain, p. 448

supply chain management, p. 449

insourcing, p. 449

channel of distribution, p. 449

2. Objective Summary (pp. 450–453)

Explain what a distribution channel is and what functions distribution channels perform.

A distribution channel is a series of firms or individuals that facilitates the movement of a product from the producer to the final customer. Channels provide time, place, and ownership utility for customers and reduce the number of transactions necessary for goods to flow from many manufacturers to large numbers of customers by breaking bulk and creating assortments. Channel members make the purchasing process easier by providing important customer services. Today the Internet is becoming an important player in distribution channels.

Key Terms

channel intermediaries, p. 451

breaking bulk, p. 451

create assortments, p. 451

facilitating functions, p. 451

disintermediation (of the channel of distribution), p. 453

knowledge management, p. 453

online distribution piracy, p. 453

3. Objective Summary (pp. 453–457)

Discuss the types of wholesaling intermediaries found in distribution channels.

Wholesaling intermediaries are firms that handle the flow of products from the manufacturer to the retailer or business user. Merchant wholesalers are independent intermediaries that take title to a product and include both full-function wholesalers and limited-function wholesalers. Merchandise agents and brokers are independent intermediaries that do not take title to products. Manufacturer-owned channel members include sales branches, sales offices, and manufacturers' showrooms.

Key Terms

wholesaling intermediaries, p. 454

independent intermediaries, p. 454

merchant wholesalers, p. 454

take title, p. 454

merchandise agents or brokers, p. 456

4. Objective Summary (pp. 457–461)

Describe the types of distribution channels and how *place* fits in with the other three Ps in the marketing mix.

Distribution channels vary in length from the simplest two-level channel to longer channels with three or more channel levels. Distribution channels include direct distribution in which the producer sells directly to consumers, and indirect channels, which may include a retailer, wholesaler, or other intermediary. Decisions on what channels to utilize affect the price you can charge as well as overall positioning strategy for a product. The marketing mix is called a "mix" because each ingredient impacts the others as well as the whole marketing strategy.

Key Terms

channel levels, p. 457

hybrid marketing system, p. 460

slotting allowance, p. 461

5. Objective Summary (pp. 461–467)

List the steps to plan a distribution channel strategy.

Marketers begin channel planning by developing channel objectives and considering important environmental factors. The next step is to decide on a distribution strategy, which involves determining the type of distribution channel that is best. Distribution tactics include the selection of individual channel members and management of the channel.

Key Terms

conventional marketing system, p. 463

vertical marketing system (VMS), p. 463

horizontal marketing system, p. 464

intensive distribution, p. 464

exclusive distribution, p. 464

selective distribution, p. 465

channel leader, p. 467

6. Objective Summary (pp. 467–472)

Explain logistics and how it fits into the supply chain concept.

Logistics is the process of designing, managing, and improving supply chains, including all the activities that are required to move products through the supply chain. Logistics contributes to the overall supply chain through activities including order processing, warehousing, materials handling, transportation, and inventory control.

Key Terms

logistics, p. 467

physical distribution, p. 468

order processing, p. 468

enterprise resource planning (ERP) systems, p. 468

warehousing, p. 469

materials handling, p. 469

transportation, p. 470

inventory control, p. 471

radio frequency identification (RFID), p. 471

just in time (JIT), p. 472

perfect order measurement, p. 472

Chapter Questions and Activities

Concepts: Test Your Knowledge

1. What is a value chain?
2. What is a supply chain, and how is it different from a channel of distribution?
3. What is a channel of distribution? What are channel intermediaries?
4. Explain the functions of distribution channels.
5. List and explain the types of independent and manufacturer-owned wholesaling intermediaries.
6. What factors are important in determining whether a manufacturer should choose a direct or indirect channel? Why do some firms use hybrid marketing systems?
7. What are conventional, vertical, and horizontal marketing systems?
8. Explain intensive, exclusive, and selective forms of distribution.
9. Explain the steps in distribution planning.
10. What is logistics? Explain the functions of logistics.
11. What are the advantages and disadvantages of shipping by rail? By air? By ship? By truck?

Activities: Apply What You've Learned

1. Assume that you have recently been hired by a firm that manufactures furniture. You feel that marketing should have an input into supplier selection for the firm's products, but the purchasing department says that should not be a concern for marketing. You need to explain to the department head the importance of the value chain perspective. In a role-playing exercise, explain to the purchasing agent the value chain concept, why it is of concern to marketing, and why the two of you should work together.

2. Assume that you are the director of marketing for a firm that manufactures cleaning chemicals used in industries. You have traditionally sold these products through manufacturer's reps. You are considering adding a direct Internet channel to your distribution strategy, but you aren't sure whether this will create channel conflict. Make a list of the pros and cons of this move. What do you think is the best decision?

3. As the one-person marketing department for a candy manufacturer (your firm makes high-quality, hand-dipped chocolates using only natural ingredients), you are considering making changes in your distribution strategy. Your products have previously been sold through a network of food brokers that call on specialty food and gift stores. But you think that perhaps it would be good for your firm to develop a corporate vertical marketing system (that is, vertical integration). In such a plan, a number of company-owned retail outlets would be opened across the country. The president of your company has asked that you present your ideas to the company executives. In a role-playing situation with one of your classmates, present your ideas to your boss, including the advantages and disadvantages of the new plan compared to the current distribution method.

4. Assume that your firm recently gave you a new marketing assignment. You are to head up development of a distribution plan for a new product line—a series of do-it-yourself instruction videos for home gardeners. These videos would show consumers how to plant trees, shrubbery, and bulbs; how to care for their plants; how to prune; and so on. You know that as you develop a distribution plan it is essential that you understand and consider a number of internal and external environmental factors. Make a list of the information you will need before you can begin to write the distribution plan. How will you adapt your plan based on each of these factors?

5. Visit the Web site for UPS (**www.ups.com**). UPS has positioned itself as a full-service provider of logistics solutions. After reviewing its Web site, answer the following questions:
   a. What logistics services does UPS offer its customers?
   b. What does UPS say to convince prospective customers that its services are better than those of the competition?

Marketing Metrics Exercise

Companies track a wide range of metrics within the supply chain area. Some of the most common ones are the following:

- On-time delivery
- Forecast accuracy
- Value-added productivity per employee
- Returns processing cost as a percentage of product revenue
- Customer order actual cycle time
- Perfect order measurement

Let's take a look at the last measure in more detail. The perfect order measurement calculates the error-free rate of each stage of a purchase order—basically you are looking for a perfect order process (or at least as close to one as you can get)! It helps managers track the multiple steps involved in getting a product from a manufacturer to a customer in order to pinpoint processes that need improvement—a bit like TQM we learned about earlier. For example, a company can calculate its error rate at each stage and then combine these rates to create an overall metric of order quality. As an example, let's suppose the company identifies the following error rates:

- Order entry accuracy: 99.95 percent correct (five errors per 1,000 order lines)

- Warehouse pick accuracy: 99.2 percent
- Delivered on time: 96 percent
- Shipped without damage: 99 percent
- Invoiced correctly: 99.8 percent

The company can then combine these individual rates into an overall perfect order measurement by multiplying them together: $99.95 \times 99.2 \times 96 \times 99 \times 99.8 = 94.04$ percent.

Given this particular example, what are some things the manufacturer might work on to bring the overall perfect order measurement higher? What would be the advantages to the firm of investing in making this already good number even better for customers?

Choices: What Do You Think?

1. The supply chain concept looks at both the inputs of a firm and the firms that facilitate the movement of the product from the manufacturer to the consumer. Do you think *marketers* should be concerned with the total supply chain concept? Why or why not?

2. Sometimes people will say, "The reason products cost so much is because of all the intermediaries." Do intermediaries increase the cost of products? Would consumers be better off or worse off without intermediaries?

3. Many entrepreneurs choose to start a franchise business rather than "go it alone." Do you think franchises offer the typical businessperson good opportunities? What are some positive and negative aspects of purchasing a franchise?

4. As colleges and universities are looking for better ways to satisfy their customers, an area of increasing interest is the distribution of their product—education. Describe the characteristics of your school's channel(s) of distribution. What types of innovative distribution might make sense for your school to try?

5. "Music, video, or textbook downloading (even when done clandestinely) is just a way to create a more efficient supply chain because it 'cuts out the middleman' (stores that sell music, video, and books, for example)." Do you agree? Why or why not?

Miniproject: Learn by Doing

In the United States, the distribution of most products is fairly easy. There are many independent intermediaries (wholesalers, dealers, distributors, and retailers) that are willing to cooperate to get the product to the final customer. Our elaborate interstate highway system combines with rail, air, and water transportation to provide excellent means for moving goods from one part of the country to another. In many other countries, the means for distribution of products are far less efficient and effective.

For this miniproject, you should first select a consumer product, probably one you normally purchase. Then use either library sources or other people or both (retailers, manufacturers, dealers, classmates, and so on) to gather information to do the following:

1. Describe the path the product takes to get from the producer to you. Draw a model to show each of the steps the product takes. Include as much as you can about transportation, warehousing, materials handling, order processing, inventory control, and so on.

2. Select another country in which the same or a similar product is sold. Describe the path the product takes to get from the producer to the customer in that country.

3. Determine if the differences between the two countries cause differences in price, availability, or quality of the product.

4. Prepare and present a summary of your findings.

Marketing in **Action** Case   Real Choices at Walmart

Walmart began as "Walton's Five and Dime" in Bentonville, Arkansas, operated by Sam Walton. Walton was able to be successful against the market by achieving higher sales volume through competitive pricing. In 1962, the first Wal-Mart Discount City store opened in Rogers, Arkansas. Through careful expansion and effective merchandising, Wal-Mart Stores, Inc. (branded as Walmart since 2008), has become the world's largest public corporation by revenue according to *Forbes* magazine. While beginning as a discount general merchandise store, it has also become the largest grocery retailer in the United States. In addition, Walmart is the largest majority private employer in the United States.

In the past, Walmart has requested and was granted different concessions from members of its supply chain, such as environmentally friendly packaging, cooperative advertising, and radio frequency identification tags on products. Due to its enormous size and purchasing power, Walmart is able to make burdensome demands on its suppliers. This allows the company to achieve its main customer objective of providing the lowest possible price for its general merchandise and groceries. One of the challenges of this type of strategy is that it may be impossible to obtain because it has no endpoint. Therefore, Walmart is constantly pressuring suppliers to continually lower their price to the firm.

In its latest efforts to reduce its costs, Walmart wants to provide transportation services for its domestic suppliers. Walmart searches for those situations where it believes that it can provide delivery services for less money than the supplier charges. The company intends to use its scale to take advantage of shipping efficiencies that will ultimately lead to lower prices offered to customers. This process will lead to lower margins for the suppliers by eliminating an opportunity to provide services. Since Walmart generally represents a notable part of the suppliers' sales, they may offer little resistance. For instance, Walmart accounts for over 30 percent of Vlasic's pickle business. It is unlikely that Vlasic will not go along with the new policies.

When it comes to handling, moving, and tracking merchandise, Walmart has a reputation that includes continuous improvement in its methods. Walmart has a fleet of 6,500 trucks and 55,000 trailers that would be supplemented with contractors to pick up products from the manufacturer and deliver the items to its regional centers and individual stores. Walmart would receive lower wholesale prices from the manufacturer as compensation for its transportation services. However, some retailers are complaining that the discount requested by Walmart is more than the cost of transporting goods by the manufacturer. This new arrangement represents another point of tension in its supplier relationships.

Walmart is not able to provide transportation services for all of its business partners' products. Therefore, Walmart still has to effectively manage these relationships. Having a relationship with Walmart affords each supplier an opportunity for increased sales and market share growth. Does this potential success come at too high a cost to the supplier? For many companies, they will have to pass on the additional costs from Walmart to partners in other supply chains in which they participate. Nevertheless, for many suppliers, they believe that they may have no choice in the matter. It has been stated before that "For many suppliers, though, the only thing worse than doing business with Wal-Mart may be not doing business with Wal-Mart."

You Make the Call

1. What is the decision facing Walmart?
2. What factors are important in understanding this decision situation?
3. What are the alternatives?
4. What decision(s) do you recommend?
5. What are some ways to implement your recommendation?

Based on: Chris Burritt, Carol Wolf, and Matthew Boyle, "Why Wal-Mart Wants to Take the Driver's Seat," *Bloomberg BusinessWeek*, May 27, 2010, pp. 17–18; Walmart, *Wikipedia*, http://en.wikipedia.org/wiki/Wal-Mart (accessed June 28, 2010); Charles Fishman, "The Wal-Mart You Don't Know," *Fast Company*, December 1, 2003 (http://www.fastcompany.com/magazine/77/walmart.html).

Retailing:
Bricks and Clicks

Stan Clark

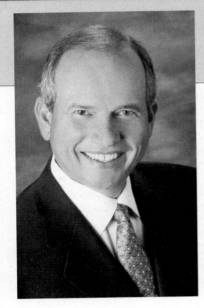

Profile

Info

▼ A **Decision Maker** at Eskimo Joe's

Stan Clark is a native of Tulsa, Oklahoma. He graduated from Oklahoma State University in May 1975 with a bachelor of science degree in business administration. For more than a decade, Stan's entrepreneurial success story has captivated audiences all over Oklahoma and across the country. Among other honors he was a Regional Finalist for *Inc.* magazine's Entrepreneur of the Year.

💬 Stan's Info

First job out of school?
A) Eskimo Joe's. I graduated from OSU in May 1975 and opened Joe's about two weeks later. To do that, I turned down an assistantship to go into the OSU MBA program!

Career high?
A) During his 1990 commencement address at Lewis Field at OSU, President George Bush mentioned Eskimo Joe's in his speech. In 2006, George W. Bush did the same thing.

A job-related mistake I wish I hadn't made?
A) Killing the annual Joe's Anniversary Party in 1993. It attracted tens of thousands of people but was getting unwieldy.

Business book I'm reading now?
A) *Hug Your Customers* by Jack Mitchell and *Discovering the Soul of Service* by Len Berry.

My hero?
A) My dad, who inspired me to be an entrepreneur, and my mom, who gave me a positive outlook on life.

My motto to live by?
A) Live passionately, and make a difference.

Here's my problem. . .

Stan Clark, the colorful entrepreneur behind the toothy grin of the Eskimo Joe caricature and his dog Buffy, faced a big problem. In 1975, Stan opened Eskimo Joe's bar in Stillwater, Oklahoma—the home of Oklahoma State University. By the mid-1980s the watering hole had become a huge favorite among OSU students. Situated right across from the OSU campus, Joe's carved out a niche as "the" place to go for beer, music, pool, and foosball in this college town. Trading on the popularity of the bar as well as its quirky logo, Stan had also begun to sell some logo apparel over the counter. Before long, students, friends, parents, alums, and other visitors simply couldn't get enough of the T-shirts sporting the wide smiles by the boy and his faithful dog. For Stan, life was good and also lots of fun.

So what could possibly go wrong? Try the fact that Oklahoma had just passed a statewide "liquor by the drink" law. Prior to this, Oklahoma had a patchwork quilt of post–Prohibition era liquor laws including "club card" requirements at bars and bring-your-own-bottle rules. Liquor by the drink opened up normal serving of beer, wine, and spirits at any establishment with a proper state liquor license—however, part of the new law was an increase in the legal drinking age from 18 to 21. Oops . . . a beer bar in a college town when you have to be 21 to drink? Not exactly an attractive business proposition. But, in the eight years since Eskimo Joe's opening, Stan had come to understand that the place represented a whole lot more to people than just pitchers of cold Bud on hot summer nights. There was a certain mystique and a strong sense of community around the brand that made it more than just a place to drink. Brisk sales of T-shirts and other clothing over the counter were evidence that people saw something else in the retailer—something that made them want to wear these items again and again. The affection and interest reached almost cult-like proportions and were not limited to Stillwater or even to Oklahoma. Stan had hit on something big, but what could he do? Big Brother in the person of the State of Oklahoma was about to regulate him right out of his core business.

Stan had to take a couple of steps back, take a new look at his business, and think about what he might do to ensure that his retail enterprise would survive the new law. The situation could be life or death for Eskimo Joe's.

Things to remember

Stan Clark successfully positioned Eskimo Joe's as the place go for beer, music and good times near the campus of Oklahoma State University. Then, in the mid-1980s the State of Oklahoma raised the legal drinking age from 18 to 21—and Stan had a big problem.

In the ten or so years it took to build the brand, Eskimo Joe's also developed a certain mystique—its toothy spokescharacters appeared on T-shirts all over the world. Clearly people had developed a loyalty and affection for the brand that went well beyond just a place that sold pizza and beer.

As Stan decided how address the new change in his environment he had to think hard about just what he was selling in addition to brews and slices—and repackage those qualities for a new generation.

what type of menu fare would be most appealing to that customer. This was a risky proposition, since restaurants open and close all the time. On the other hand, if Stan could morph the location into a restaurant that also happens to serve alcohol (which, under the new liquor law, would be legal—and potentially quite profitable), he would hopefully be able to continue to build the fledgling logo apparel business around the new restaurant theme, à la the Hard Rock Café.

2. Option **Continue operating as a beer bar at the core and work to offset declining beer sales with an increase in apparel sales.** From 1975 to 1984, Joe's was "Stillwater's Jumpin' Little Juke Joint." It was by far one of the highest-volume beer bars in the region, and it had built its entire reputation on this image.

As the number-one competitor in this market space, Stan had every reason to believe that the weaker competitors would be forced out of business by the law change, leaving their share of the market to him. Stan could continue to operate the bar in much the way it had always been operated, and if he liked he could use it as a cash cow to generate revenues and then invest the money elsewhere for growth. The upside of this plan would be that any attempt to rebrand Eskimo Joe's as something other than what it had always been would be risky. However, the downside was the unknown of what it would mean to a retailer over the long run to lose its primary customer base of 18- to 20-year-olds in a town brimming with college students.

3. Option **Close Eskimo Joe's bar and refocus resources on building the growing apparel business.** The cult-like status of the Eskimo Joe's brand and image may have begun at the physical location of the bar in Stillwater, but the way to replicate and perpetrate it on a national or international scale is by marketing the now-hip logo. Stan could build a small retail clothing boutique in Stillwater but turn primarily to direct marketing through catalogs focused on his target primary age and demographic groups. A key benefit of this approach is avoiding any unexpected problems with the bar that might occur in the liquor law transition, especially the very negative publicity that would result if Joe's got caught selling beer to underage drinkers. The Eskimo Joe spirit would be maintained through the direct marketing and also through accompanying word of mouth. On the downside, to Joe's loyal fans, closing Stillwater's "Jumpin' Little Juke Joint" would be like Harley-Davidson ceasing to make motorcycles: Who wants the logo apparel when there's no product or place that still sports it? However, this option was tempting in that it would redirect Stan's resources to the high-growth (and high-profit-margin) apparel retailing sector.

Now, put yourself in Stan's shoes: Which option would you choose, and why?

Stan considered his **Options** 1·2·3

1. Option **Convert the beer bar into a full-service restaurant that focuses on selling great food.** This option assumes that the equity of the Eskimo Joe's brand would transfer into a brand-new market and product space. To accomplish this transformation, Stan would have to extensively remodel the facility. He would have to figure out who the new target market is and

You Choose

Which **Option** would you choose, and **why**?

1. ☐YES ☐NO **2.** ☐YES ☐NO **3.** ☐YES ☐NO

See what **option** Stan chose and its success on **page 504**

retailing
The final stop in the distribution channel in which organizations sell goods and services to consumers for their personal use.

1

Retailing:
Special Delivery

Shop 'til you drop! For many people, obtaining the product is only half the fun. Others, of course, would rather walk over hot coals than spend time in a store. Marketers like Stan Clark need to find ways to deliver goods and services that please both types of consumers. **Retailing** is the final stop on the distribution path—the process by which organizations sell goods and services to consumers for their personal use.

As we said in Chapter 15, planning for distribution of product offerings includes decisions about where to make the product available. Thus when marketers of consumer goods and services plan their distribution strategy, they talk about the retailers they will include in their channel of distribution. This, of course, means they need to understand retailing and the retailer landscape.

Of course, retailers also develop their own marketing plans. While our sample marketing plan represents the plan of a producer, the same elements are also seen in marketing plans for retailers. They must decide which consumer groups they can best serve, what product assortment and services they will provide for their customers, what pricing policies they will adopt, how they will promote their retail operations, and where they will locate their retail outlets. This chapter will explore the many different types of retailers as we keep one question in mind: How does a retailer—whether store or nonstore (selling via television, phone, or the Internet)—lure the consumer? The answer to this question isn't getting any easier as the competition for customers continues to heat up, fueled by the explosion of Web sites that sell branded merchandise (or that auction it like eBay), the "overstoring" of many areas as developers continue to build elaborate malls and strip shopping centers, and improvements in communications and distribution that make it possible for retailers from around the world to enter local markets. So, this chapter has plenty "in store" for us. Let's start with an overview of where retailing has been and where it's going.

Retailing: A Mixed (Shopping) Bag

Retailing is big business. Despite nearly two years of economic downturn, in 2009 U.S. retail sales totaled more than $4.5 trillion.[1] Over 1 million retail businesses employ over 14.5 million workers—more than 1 of every 10 U.S. workers.[2] Although we tend to associate huge stores such as Walmart and Sears with retailing activity, in reality most retailers are small businesses. Certain retailers, such as Home Depot, also are wholesalers because they provide goods and services to businesses as well as to end consumers.

As we said in Chapter 15 retailers belong to a channel of distribution, and as such they provide time, place, and ownership utility to customers. Some retailers save people time or money when they provide an assortment of merchandise under one roof. Others search the world for the most exotic delicacies; they allow shoppers access to goods they would otherwise never see. Still others, such as Barnes & Noble café/bookstores, provide us with interesting environments in which to spend our leisure time and, they hope, our money.

Check out chapter 16 Study Map on page 505

Globally, retailing may have a very different face. In some European countries, don't even think about squeezing a tomato to see if it's too soft or picking up a cantaloupe to see if it smells ripe. Such mistakes will quickly gain you a reprimand from the store clerk who will choose which oranges and bananas you should have. In developing countries like those in Asia, Africa, and South America, retailing often includes many small butcher shops where sides of beef and lamb proudly hang in store windows so everyone will be assured that the meat comes from healthy animals; vendors sell lettuce, tomatoes, and cucumbers on the sidewalk or neatly stack watermelons on a donkey cart; and women sell small breakfast items they cook out of the front of their homes for workers and schoolchildren who pass by in the mornings. Neat store shelves stacked with bottles of shampoo may be replaced by hanging displays that hold one-use size sachets of shampoo—the only size that a woman can afford to buy and then only for special occasions. Street vendors may sell cigarettes one at a time. The local pharmacist also gives customers injections and recommends antibiotics and other medicines for patients who come in with a complaint and who can't afford to see a doctor. Don't feel like cooking tonight? There's no drive-through window for pick up but even better—delivery from McDonald's, Hardees, KFC, Pizza Hut, Fuddruckers, Chili's, and a host of local restaurants via motor scooters that dangerously dash in and out of traffic is just a few minutes away. You can even order your Big Mac or a spicy vegetable dragon roll for delivery online through sites such as Egypt's **www.otlob.com** or Mumbai's **www.foodkamood.com**

The Evolution of Retailing

Retailing has taken many forms over time, including the peddler who hawked his wares from a horse-drawn cart, a majestic urban department store, an intimate boutique, and a huge "hyperstore" that sells everything from potato chips to snow tires. But now the cart you see at your local mall that sells new-age jewelry or monogrammed golf balls to passersby has replaced the horse-drawn cart. As the economic, social, and cultural pictures change, different types of retailers emerge—and they often squeeze out older, outmoded types. How can marketers know what the dominant types of retailing will be tomorrow or 10 years from now?

The Wheel of Retailing

One of the oldest and simplest explanations for these changes is the **wheel-of-retailing hypothesis**. Figure 16.1 shows that new types of retailers begin at the entry phase where they find it easiest to enter the market with low-end strategies as they offer goods at lower prices than their competitors.[3] After they gain a foothold, they gradually trade up. They improve their facilities and increase the quality and assortment of merchandise. Finally, retailers move on to a high-end strategy with even higher prices, better facilities, and amenities such as parking and gift wrapping. Upscaling results in greater investment and operating costs, so the store must raise its prices to remain profitable, which then makes it vulnerable to still newer entrants that can afford to charge lower prices. And so the wheel turns.

That's the story behind Pier 1 Imports. Pier 1 started as a single store in San Mateo, California, that sold low-priced beanbags, love beads, and incense to post–World War II baby boomers. These days it sells quality home furnishings and decorative accessories to the same customers, who are now the most affluent segment of the American population.[4] Today, even low-cost retailer Walmart is moving up, as it tries to broaden its appeal to upscale shoppers. The retail giant opened a new upscale supercenter in Plano, Texas, that boasts a Wi-Fi-enabled coffee shop, a sushi bar, quieter cash registers, and grocery selections that include more than 1,200 choices of wine and gourmet cheeses.[5]

New ways to sell products constantly appear. American Airlines is testing the concept of selling goods and services (other than pillows and blankets) on its flights. The carrier has

wheel-of-retailing hypothesis
A theory that explains how retail firms change, becoming more upscale as they go through their life cycle.

Figure 16.1 📷 *Snapshot* | The Wheel of Retailing

The Wheel of Retailing explains how retailers change over time.

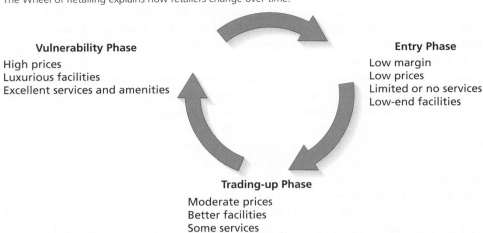

Vulnerability Phase
High prices
Luxurious facilities
Excellent services and amenities

Entry Phase
Low margin
Low prices
Limited or no services
Low-end facilities

Trading-up Phase
Moderate prices
Better facilities
Some services
Increased quality merchandise

started by selling Heathrow Express train tickets on London-bound flights, and it offers items from the SkyMall catalog on 165 of its planes. Other options on the table include Broadway show tickets.[6]

Retailers, however, must be careful not to move too quickly and too far from their roots. Earlier attempts by Walmart to upgrade its clothing lines from basic T-shirts, tank tops, and tube socks to brand-name apparel alienated many of its loyal core customers who found the new items out of reach. Today Walmart reinvents its clothing offerings with higher fashion apparel while it maintains its focus on everyday apparel.[7]

The wheel of retailing helps us explain the development of some but not all forms of retailing. For example, some retailers never trade up; they simply continue to occupy a niche as discounters. Others, such as upscale specialty stores, start out at the high end. Of course, some retailers move down after they experience success at the high end. Sometimes they open sister divisions that sell lower-priced products (as when Gap Stores opened Old Navy), or they develop outlets that sell lower-priced versions of their own products (as when Nordstrom creates the Nordstrom Rack or Anne Taylor opens Anne Taylor Loft).

The Retail Life Cycle

Of course, retailers sell products. But in a way retailers also *are* products because they provide benefits such as convenience or status to consumers, and they must offer a competitive advantage over other retailers to survive. And sometimes *where* a product is bought either adds to or takes away from its allure (which explains why some people secretly replace shopping bags from bargain stores with those from upscale stores to create the "right" impression).

retail life cycle
A theory that focuses on the various stages that retailers pass through from introduction to decline.

So, another way to understand how retailers evolve is the **retail life cycle** shown in 📷 Figure 16.2. Like the *product life cycle* we discussed in Chapter 9, this perspective recognizes that (like people, soft-drink brands, and vacation destinations) retailers are born, they grow and mature, and eventually most die or become obsolete. The life cycle approach allows us to categorize retail stores by the conditions they face at different points in the cycle.[8]

In the *introduction* stage, the new retailer often is an aggressive entrepreneur who takes a unique approach to doing business. This may mean it competes on the basis of low price, as the wheel of retailing suggests. However, the new guy on the block may also enter the market by offering a distinctive assortment or a different way to distribute items, such as through the Internet. Internet grocery stores, for example, are in the introduction stage. In the introduction stage, profits usually are low because of high development costs. As the business enters the *growth* stage, the retailer (hopefully) catches on with shoppers, and sales and profits rise. But a new idea doesn't stay new for long. Others start to copy it and competition

Figure 16.2 📷 *Snapshot* | The Retail Life Cycle

The Retail Life Cycle explains how retailers are born, grow, mature, and (most) die.

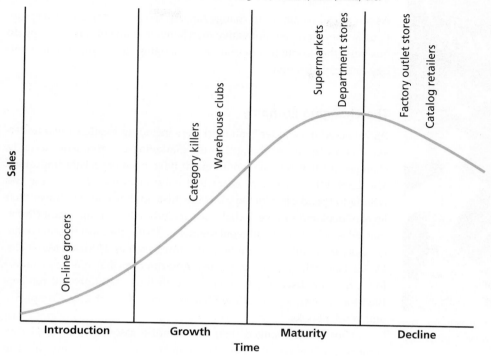

increases, so the store needs to expand what it offers. Often the retailer responds by opening more outlets and develops systems to distribute goods to these new stores—which may in turn cut profits, as the firm invests in new buildings and fixtures.

By the time the business reaches the *maturity* stage, many other individual retailers have copied the unique idea of the original entrepreneur to form an entire industry. The industry probably has overexpanded and intense competition makes it difficult to maintain customer loyalty. Profits decline as competitors resort to price cutting to keep their customers. We observe this pattern in department stores like Macy's and fast-food chains like McDonald's.

During the maturity stage, firms seek to increase their share of the market or to attract new customers. That has been the case with fast-food retailers for a number of years. In order to meet changing customer tastes, KFC offers grilled chicken for customers who want a finger-lickin' lower fat meal. For low-carb consumers who want less bread, McDonald's sells a Big Mac Wrap and KFC's menu includes the "Double Down" sandwich without any bread (just pure fried chicken on a fried chicken roll!). Supermarkets have responded to consumers' demand for healthy, locally grown food with more organic alternatives.

Other retailers use mergers to survive when their retail category matures. **Mergers** are when two or more separately owned retail firms combine. For example, Sears, a department store chain, recently merged with Kmart, a discount chain. Another strategy a firm in a mature industry may choose is **downsizing** where it closes unprofitable stores or sells off entire divisions. Federated Department Stores, for example, became Macy's, Inc. and combined its different department stores under two names, Bloomingdales and Macy's, as it did away with less successful chains such as Stern's, Marshall Field's, and Filene's. In the *decline* stage, retail businesses, like the general store or the peddler, become obsolete as newer ways of doing business emerge. Of course, the outmoded retailer does not have to fold its tent at this stage. Marketers who anticipate these shifts can avert decline if they change to meet the times. Some retailers, such as Starbucks, find growth opportunities in foreign markets. Starbucks now operates over 16,000 stores in 50 countries.[9]

mergers
When two or more separately owned retail firms combine.

downsizing
When a firm in a mature industry closes or sells off unprofitable stores or entire divisions.

Like other marketers, retailers need to stay on top of cultural trends that affect demand for the merchandise they sell, such as fur-free vegan, or sustainable products.

The Evolution Continues: What's "In Store" for the Future?

As our world continues to change rapidly, retailers scramble to keep up. Four factors motivate innovative merchants to reinvent the way they do business: the economic environment, changing demographics, technology, and globalization.

The Changing Economy

As we noted in Chapter 5, all marketers including retailers must understand and respond to changes in the marketing environment. Recently, changes in the economic environment have been especially important. The 2008–2010 downturn meant that consumers worldwide were less willing to spend discretionary income. Instead they chose to lower their level of debt and to save. Retail sales, including the all-important Christmas sales, fell in nearly all retail segments.[10] Sales for most upscale retailers were especially vulnerable while stores such as TJ Maxx, Marshalls, Dollar General, and online retailer **Amazon.com** that offer consumers low prices or discounted merchandise thrived. A number of retailers filed for bankruptcy including Sharper Image, Circuit City, CompUSA, and Waldenbooks.[11]

Other stores changed their merchandise assortment to meet consumers' preferences. Private-label brands reached an all-time high in sales in 2009—on average 17.5 percent of a basket of U.S. groceries consisted of store brands.[12] Walmart and other mass merchandisers responded to this trend by allocating more shelf space to their own private-label brands and less to national brands. (As we noted in Chapter 11, Walmart later found this strategy aggravated many consumers and hurt overall sales and the chain has now returned many items to its shelves.[13]) Even the convenience store chain 7-Eleven plans to release two private label wines that will sell for $3.99 a bottle. A zesty chardonnay with your corn dog?[14]

Demographics

As we noted in Chapter 7, keeping up with changes in population characteristics is at the heart of many marketing efforts. Retailers can no longer afford to stand by and assume that their customer base is the same as it has always been. They must come up with new ways to sell their products to diverse groups.

Here are some of the ways changing demographics are altering the face of retailing:

- *Convenience for working consumers:* Some retailers expand their operating hours and services to meet the needs of working consumers who have less time to shop. Other retailers, including dry cleaners and pharmacies, add drive-up windows. In some areas, mobile furniture stores replace design studios; designers pick out 8 or 10 sofas from their large inventories and bring them to your home so you can see how each will actually look in your living room. And walk-in medical clinics located at retailer, pharmacy, or grocery stores not only provide convenience but also save both patients and insurers money on routine care.[15]

- *Recognize ethnic diversity:* Although members of every ethnic group can usually find local retailers that cater to their specific needs, larger companies must tailor their strategies to the cultural makeup of specific areas. For example, in Texas, California, and Florida, where there are large numbers of customers who speak only Spanish, many retailers make sure that there are sales associates who *habla Español*.

Technology

In addition to demographics, technology is revolutionizing retailing. As we all know, the Internet has brought us the age of e-tailing. Whether it's a store that sells only on the Web or a traditional retailer such as Banana Republic, J. Crew, or Eskimo Joe's that also sells on the Web, retailing is steadily evolving from bricks to clicks. Our personal computers have turned our homes into virtual malls. While many traditional retailers saw sales decline in 2008 and 2009, online retailer **Amazon.com's** business grew. Fourth-quarter 2009 sales, which included the Christmas season, were 42 percent above the previous year.[16]

Some of the most profound changes are not even visible to shoppers, such as advanced electronic **point-of-sale (POS) systems**. These devices contain computer brains that collect sales data and connect directly into the store's inventory-control system. Stores may use POS systems to create **perpetual inventory unit control systems** that keep a running total on sales, returns, transfers to other stores, and so on. This technology allows stores to develop computerized **automatic reordering systems** that are automatically activated when inventories reach a certain level.[17] The store of the future will use RFID tags (and other technology) to assist the shopper in ways we haven't even thought of. For example, an RFID tag on a bottle of wine can tip off a nearby plasma screen that will project an ad for Barilla pasta and provide a neat recipe for fettuccine with bell peppers and shrimp. Don't remember what number printer ink cartridge you need? No problem. In-store kiosks will allow consumers to ask questions of a product "expert" in another city via a video-enabled screen, alleviating customer complaints about lack of knowledgeable store personnel while they create a cost-efficient way to provide expertise to dozens of customers at one time.[18]

Some restaurants already use technology to let diners order their food tableside directly from a screen complete with photos of the dishes it offers. The *e-menus* help customers because they can see what every item on the menu will look like and, hopefully, avoid a surprise when the waiter arrives.[19] This innovation also increases sales for the restaurant—who can avoid that mouth-watering picture of the four-layer chocolate cake with peppermint-stick ice cream on top?

Of course, technology is important to service industries also. Banking, for example, has become much simpler for both consumers and business customers because of electronic banking. For many years electronic banking has offered ATMs and Web sites where consumers can check their bank balance or transfer funds. Today, most banks offer automatic bill-pay services. With bill pay services, consumers can schedule their rent or credit card or other payment online and the bank will write the check and mail it.

point-of-sale (POS) systems
Retail computer systems that collect sales data and are hooked directly into the store's inventory-control system.

perpetual inventory unit control system
Retail computer system that keeps a running total on sales, returns, transfers to other stores and so on.

automatic reordering system
Retail reordering system that is automatically activated when inventories reach a certain level.

Globalization

As we saw in Chapter 3, the world is becoming a much smaller (and flatter) place. Retailers are busy expanding to other countries and they bring with them innovations and new management philosophies. McDonald's, T.G.I. Friday's, and Starbucks join the Hard Rock Café as they become global success stories for U.S. retailers. Similarly, Spanish fashion retailers Zara and Mango are now global brands, while Swedish home goods company IKEA furnishes homes around the world. Even French hyperstore chain Carrefours has stores in Europe, South America, Asia, North Africa and the United States.

Still, retailers need to adjust to different conditions around the world. In countries in the Middle East with large Muslim populations, you won't find the riblet basket

One form of retailing can be at different points in its life cycle in different business environments. In China, the department store is still in its growth stage. Chains like PCD are benefiting from a boom in China's retail market and from shoppers' growing love affair with luxury items. They flock to department stores to buy them because e-commerce isn't well established in the mainland—and department stores have a reputation for avoiding the sale of counterfeit goods that pop up elsewhere around the country.[20]

on Applebee's menu, and McDonald's offers customers McArabia Kofta sandwiches. And some countries require that certain percentages, often over half, of goods sold in retail stores are locally produced.

Ethical Problems in Retailing

shrinkage
Losses experienced by retailers due to shoplifting, employee theft, and damage to merchandise.

Retailers must deal with ethical problems that involve both their customers and their employees. Losses due to **shrinkage** are a growing problem. Shrinkage is the term retailers use to describe stock losses due to shoplifting, employee theft, and damage to merchandise. A 2009 worldwide survey of large retailers in 41 countries found that shrinkage cost retailers $114.8 billion or 1.43 percent of all retail sales.[21] That's $208.39 per family.

Shoplifting

Shoplifting has grown in recent years to giant proportions. In 2009, shoplifting in the United States was estimated at $15.1 billion or more than 35 percent of all shrinkage.[22]

These thefts in turn drive consumer prices up and hurt the economy, and sometimes even cause smaller retailers to go out of business. For department stores, discount stores, and specialty stores, the items lifted include high-price-tag electronics, clothing, and jewelry. For food stores, razor blades, condoms, pregnancy tests, cigarettes, and pain relievers are shoplifters' common targets. The problem is so bad that many small stores now keep high-theft items such as analgesics under lock and key.

At its worst, shoplifting can be an organized criminal activity. Groups of thieves that use store floor plans and foil-lined bags to evade security sensors get away with thousands of dollars in goods in a single day. One survey reported that 92 percent of retailers said they had been the victim of organized retail crime.[23] When Mervyn's stores in Los Angeles found that its inventories of Levi's jeans were mysteriously shrinking, surveillance cameras filmed organized gangs of thieves who whisked the jeans off shelves to waiting cars. Mervyn's estimated the stores lost more than $1 million before the company stopped the thieves.[24] Ironically, the growth of online retailing boosts shoplifting from bricks and mortar stores because it facilitates a wide distribution of stolen goods—no longer do thieves have to fence their loot in the local market. One Houston, Texas, theft ring unloaded $258,000 worth of goods it stole from Target before it was caught.[25] Of course, some shoplifting is more amateurish and nakedly obvious—as when a nude man walked into a Missouri convenience store on a hot August day and did a hula dance to divert attention while his partner stole a case of beer from the store.[26] (Do not try this at home!)

Employee Theft

A second major source of shrinkage in retail stores is employee theft of both merchandise and cash. On a case by case basis, dishonest employees steal 6.6 times the amount shoplifters do.[27] A current trend in employee theft involves the use of store gift cards. Saks, for example, caught a sales clerk ringing up $130,000 in false merchandise returns and putting the money on a gift card.[28] Employees not only have access to products, but they also are familiar with the store's security measures. "Sweethearting" is an employee practice in which a cashier consciously undercharges, gives a cash refund, or allows a friend to walk away without paying for items.[29] Sometimes a dishonest employee simply carries merchandise out the back door to a friend's waiting car.

Retail Borrowing

retail borrowing
Consumer practice of purchasing a product with the intent to return the nondefective merchandise for a refund after it has fulfilled the purpose for which it was purchased.

A third source of shrinkage is an unethical consumer practice the industry calls **retail borrowing**. Merchants over recent decades have developed liberal policies of accepting returns from customers because the product performs unsatisfactorily or even if the customer simply changes her mind. Retail borrowing refers to the return of nondefective merchandise for

Ripped from the Headlines

Ethical/Sustainable Decisions in the Real World

Retailers know that if they create a better shopping experience for their customers, they create higher sales for themselves. But retailers need to know what's wrong in order to "fix" it. What if customers find the aisles in stores too narrow, the merchandise on the top shelves too hard to reach, or no place to sit to tie a shoelace? Today hundreds of retailers around the world use *observational research technology* to improve the way they serve customers. This means they install video cameras, motion sensors, and other monitoring devices in their stores not to catch thieves, but to observe how their customers shop and then to make improvements.[31] But some critics are concerned about customer privacy. People don't know they are being taped. We all behave differently when we think we are alone (which is the argument for using the technology in the first place). And what will happen when facial recognition technology allows a store to identify the individual customers they watch? Should retailers use cameras to monitor their shoppers without letting them know? Why or why not?

> **ETHICS CHECK:** ↖
> Find out what other students taking this course **would do** and **why** on **www .mypearsonmarketinglab .com**

> If you were a retailer looking to improve your store for your customers, would you install video cameras, motion sensors, and other monitoring devices to monitor customers' behavior without their knowledge or consent?
>
> ☐YES ☐NO

a refund after it has fulfilled the purpose for which it was purchased.[30] Popular objects for retail borrowing include a dress for a high school prom, a new suit for a job interview, and a boom box for a weekend picnic on the beach. One study suggests that 12 percent of merchandise returns involve an intent to deceive the retailer. For the consumer the practice provides short-term use of a product for a specific occasion at no cost. For the retailer, the practice results in lower total sales and often in damaged merchandise, unsuitable for resale.

Ethical Treatment of Customers

On the other side of the retail ethics issue is how retailers and their employees treat customers. While it may be illegal if a store doesn't provide equal access to consumers of different ethnic groups, behavior that discourages customers who appear economically disadvantaged or socially unacceptable is not. As a classic scene in the movie *Pretty Woman* starring Julia Roberts depicted, stores that seek to maintain an image of elite sophistication may not offer assistance to customers who enter the premises not meeting the requirements for that image—or they may actually ask the customer to leave.

Similarly, many would suggest that retailers have an obligation not to sell products to customers if the products can be harmful. For example, for many years some teens and young adults abused potentially harmful over-the-counter medicines. While government regulations removed many of these drug products from store shelves in recent years, retailers still have to carefully police their distribution. The same is true for products such as alcohol and cigarettes, which by law are limited to sale to adult customers.

2

OBJECTIVE

Understand how we classify retailers.

(pp. 487–493)

From Mom-and-Pop to Super Walmart: How Marketers Classify Retail Stores

The field of retailing covers a lot of ground—from mammoth department stores to sidewalk vendors to Web sites to bars like Eskimo Joe's. Retail marketers need to understand all the possible ways they might offer their products in the market, and they also need a way to benchmark their performance relative to other similar retailers.

Classify Retailers by What They Sell

Stan Clark's dilemma boils down to what Eskimo Joe's should sell—beer, food, clothing, some mixture of these? One of the most important strategic decisions a retailer makes is *what* to sell—its **merchandise mix**. This choice is similar to settling on a market segment (as we

merchandise mix
The total set of all products offered for sale by a retailer, including all product lines sold to all consumer groups.

discussed in Chapter 7: If a store's merchandise mix is too limited, it may not have enough potential customers, whereas if it is too broad, the retailer runs the risk of being a "jack of all trades, master of none." Because what the retailer sells is central to its identity, one way we describe retailers is in terms of their merchandise mix.

While we learned in Chapter 9 that a manufacturer's product line consists of product offerings that satisfy a single need, in retailing a *product line* is a set of related products a retailer offers, such as kitchen appliances or leather goods. The *Census of Retail Trade* that the U.S. Bureau of the Census conducts classifies all retailers by North American Industry Classification System (NAICS) codes (the same system we described in Chapter 6 that classifies industrial firms). A retailer that wants to identify direct competition simply looks for other firms with the same NAICS classification codes.

However, a word of caution: As retailers experiment with different merchandise mixes, it's getting harder to make these direct comparisons. For example, even though marketers like to distinguish between food and nonfood retailers, in reality these lines are blurring. **Combination stores** offer consumers food and general merchandise in the same store. **Supercenters** such as Super Walmart Supercenters are large combination stores that combine an economy supermarket with other lower-priced merchandise. Other retailers like Target, CVS, and Walgreens drugstores carry limited amounts of food. In Japan, the major department stores have one floor that, like freestanding supermarkets, sells meats, vegetables, and other fresh food items, while another entire floor offers store customers a wide range of prepared foods ready for the modern Japanese working woman (or man) to carry home for dinner.

Classify Retailers by Level of Service

Retailers differ in the amount of service they provide for consumers. Firms recognize that there is a trade-off between service and low prices, so they tailor their strategies to the level of service they offer. Customers who demand higher levels of service must be willing to pay for that service, and those who want lower prices must be willing to give up services. Unfortunately, some consumers don't understand this trade-off and still insist on top-level service while they pay bottom-dollar prices!

Retailers like Sam's Club that promise cut-rate prices often are self-service operations. When customers shop at *self-service retailers*, they make their product selection without any assistance, they often must bring their own bags or containers to carry their purchases, and they may even handle the checkout process with self-service scanners. Contrast that experience to visiting a *full-service retailer*. Many of us prefer to shop at major department stores like Bloomingdale's and specialty stores like Victoria's Secret because they provide supporting services such as gift wrapping, and they offer trained sales associates who can help us select that perfect gift. Other specialized services are available based on the merchandise the store offers. For example, many full-service clothing retailers will provide alteration services. Retailers like Macy's, Bed Bath and Beyond, and Best Buy that carry china, silver, housewares, appliances, electronics and other items brides (and grooms) might want also offer special bridal consultants and bridal gift registries.

Limited-service retailers fall in between self-service and full-service retailers. Stores like Walmart, Target, Old Navy, and Kohl's offer credit and merchandise return but little else. Customers select merchandise without much assistance, preferring to pay a bit less rather than be waited on a bit more.

Classify Retailers by Merchandise Selection

Another way to classify retailers is in terms of the selection they offer. A retailer's **merchandise assortment**, or selection of products it sells, has two dimensions: breadth and depth. These concepts strongly resemble the produce lines we discussed in Chapter 9. **Merchandise breadth**, or variety, is the number of different product lines available. A *narrow*

---

combination stores
Retailers that offer consumers food and general merchandise in the same store.

supercenters
Large combination stores that combine economy supermarkets with other lower-priced merchandise.

merchandise assortment
The range of products a store sells.

merchandise breadth
The number of different product lines available.

Figure 16.3 📷 *Snapshot* | Classification of Book Retailers by Merchandise Selection

Marketers often classify retail stores on the breadth and depth of their merchandise assortment. In this figure, we use the two dimensions to classify types of bookstores that carry science fiction books.

	Breadth	
	Narrow	Broad
Shallow	**Airport Bookstore:** A few *Lord of the Rings* books	**Sam's Club:** A few *Lord of the Rings* books and a limited assortment of *Lord of the Rings* T-shirts and toys
Deep	**www.legendaryheroes.com:** Internet retailer selling only merchandise for *Lord of the Rings, The Highlander, Zena: Warrior Princess, Legendary Swords, Conan,* and *Hercules*	**www.Amazon.com:** Literally millions of current and out-of-print books plus a long list of other product lines including electronics, toys, apparel, musical instruments, jewelry, motorcycles and ATVs

(Depth is the vertical axis label shown on the left.)

assortment, such as we encounter in convenience stores, means that shoppers will find only a limited selection of product lines such as candy, cigarettes, and soft drinks. A *broad assortment,* such as a warehouse store like COSTCO or Sam's Club offers, means there is a wide range of items from eyeglasses to barbecue grills.

Merchandise depth is the variety of choices available within each specific product line. A *shallow assortment* means that the selection within a product category is limited, so a factory outlet store may sell only white and blue men's dress shirts (all made by the same manufacturer, of course) and only in standard sizes. In contrast, a men's specialty store may feature a *deep assortment* of dress shirts (but not much else) in varying shades and in hard-to-find sizes.

📷 Figure 16.3 illustrates these assortment differences for one product, science fiction books.

merchandise depth
The variety of choices available for each specific product line.

convenience stores
Neighborhood retailers that carry a limited number of frequently purchased items and cater to consumers willing to pay a premium for the ease of buying close to home.

supermarkets
Food stores that carry a wide selection of edibles and related products.

Major Types of Retailers

Now that we've seen how retailers differ in the breadth and depth of their assortments, let's review some of the major forms these retailers take. Table 16.1 provides a list of these types and their characteristics.

Convenience Stores

Convenience stores carry a limited number of frequently purchased items, including basic food products, newspapers, and sundries. They cater to consumers willing to pay a premium for the ease of buying staple items close to home. In other words, convenience stores meet the needs of those who are pressed for time, who buy items in smaller quantities, or who shop at irregular hours. But these stores are starting to change, especially in urban areas, where many time-pressed shoppers prefer to visit these outlets even for specialty items. Store chains such as 7-Eleven and Wawa now offer customers a coffee bar, fresh sandwiches, and pastries.

Supermarkets

Supermarkets are food stores that carry a wide selection of edible and nonedible products. Although the large supermarket is a fixture in the United States, it has not caught

Think convenience stores are just for convenience and a late night gallon of milk? Maverik Country Stores, Inc. doesn't think so. The 187-store chain transformed itself from an Old West country store to match its slogan, "Adventure's First Stop." Customers from soccer moms to mountain bikers think it's a fun place. The Adventure First Stop stores feature cascading waterfalls of fountain drinks, a winding river of coffee, and snowy mountains made of frozen yogurt. Unique names are also a part of the fun. Destination areas of the stores include Bodacious Bean coffee stations, Fountain Falls beverage dispensers, Big Moon restrooms (no comment), Big Bear Bakery, and Room with a Brew walk-in beer coolers. The stores even wrap their fuel pumps and tanker delivery trucks in murals of sports images such as jet skis and snowmobiles.[32]

Steven K. Doi/ZUMA Press/Newscom

Table 16.1 | Major Types of Retailers Different retailers offer varying product assortments, levels of service, store sizes, and prices

Type	Merchandise	Level of service	Size	Prices	Examples
Convenience stores	Limited number of choices in narrow number of product lines; frequently purchased and emergency items	Self-service	Small	Low-priced items sold at higher than average prices	7-Eleven
Supermarkets	Large selection of food items and limited selection of general merchandise	Limited service	Medium	Moderate	Publix, Kroger
Box stores	Limited selection of food items; many store brands	Self-service Bag your own purchases	Medium	Low	ALDI
Specialty stores	Large selection of items in one or a few product lines	Full service	Small and medium	Moderate to high	Claire's (accessories), Yankee Candle Co., Things Remembered
Category killers	Large selection of items in one or a few product lines	Full service	Large	Moderate	Toys "R" Us, Home Depot and Best Buy
Leased departments	Limited selection of items in a single product line	Usually full service	Small	Moderate to high	Picture Me portrait studios in Walmart Stores
Variety stores	Small selection of items in limited product lines; low-priced items; may have a single price point	Self-service	Small	Low	Dollar General, Dollar Tree
General merchandise discount stores	Large selection of items in a broad assortment of product lines	Limited service	Large	Moderate to low	Walmart, Kmart
Off-price retailers	Moderate selection of limited product lines; buy surplus merchandise	Limited service	Moderate	Moderate to low	T.J. Maxx, Marshall's
Warehouse clubs	Moderate selection of limited product lines; many items in larger than normal sizes	Self-service	Large	Moderate to low	Costco, Sam's Club, BJ's
Factory outlet stores	Limited selection from a single manufacturer	Limited service	Small	Moderate to low	Gap Outlet, Liz Claiborne Outlet, Coach Outlet
Department stores	Large selection or many product lines	Full service	Large	Moderate to high	Macy's, Bloomingdales, Nordstrom
Hypermarkets	Large selection of items in food and a broad assortment of general merchandise product lines	Self-service	Very large	Moderate to low	Carrefour

on to the same extent in other parts of the world. In many European countries, for example, consumers walk or bike to small stores near their homes. They tend to have smaller food orders per trip and to shop more frequently, partly because many lack the freezer space to store a huge inventory of products at home. Although wide variety is less important than quality and local ambiance to Europeans, their shopping habits are starting to change as huge hypermarkets become popular around the globe.

Box Stores

Box stores are food stores that have a limited selection of items, few brands per item, and few refrigerated items. Generally they are open fewer hours than supermarkets and are smaller and carry fewer items than warehouse clubs. Items are displayed in open boxes (hence the name) and customers bag their own purchases. ALDI stores, for example, carry only about 1,400 regularly stocked items, while a typical supermarket may carry up to 50,000 items.[33] (About 95 percent of ALDI items are store brands with a few national brands that are special-buy purchases and are available for limited periods.)

The **category killer** is one type of specialty store that has become especially important in retailing today. A category killer is a very large specialty store that carries a vast selection of products in its category. Some examples of category killers are Home Depot, Toys "R" Us, Best Buy and Staples.

Specialty Stores

Specialty stores have narrow and deep inventories. They do not sell a lot of product lines, but they offer a good selection of brands within the lines they do sell. For many women with less-than-perfect figures, shopping at a store that sells only swimsuits means there will be an adequate selection so they can find a suit that really fits. The same is true for larger, taller men who can't find suits that fit in regular department stores but have lots of choices in stores that cater to big-and-tall guys. Specialty stores can tailor their assortment to the specific needs of a targeted consumer, and they often offer a high level of knowledgeable service.

box stores
Food stores that have a limited selection of items, few brands per item, and few refrigerated items.

category killer
A very large specialty store that carries a vast selection of products in its category.

specialty stores
Retailers that carry only a few product lines but offer good selection within the lines that they sell.

Leased Departments

Leased departments are departments within a larger retail store that an outside firm rents. This arrangement allows larger stores to offer a broader variety of products than they would otherwise carry. Some examples of leased departments are in-store banks, photographic studios, pet departments, jewelry departments, and watch and shoe repair departments.

leased departments
Departments within a larger retail store that an outside firm rents.

Variety Stores

Variety stores originated as the five-and-dime or dime stores that began in the late 1800s. In these early variety stores such the iconic Woolworth's, all items sold for a nickel or a dime. Today's variety stores carry a variety of inexpensive items from kitchen gadgets to toys to candy and candles. It's tough to buy something for a dime today, but many variety stores still stick to a single price point and some offer products that don't cost more than a dollar. Some examples of today's variety stores include Dollar General Stores, Family Dollar stores, and Dollar Tree.

variety stores
Stores that carry a variety of inexpensive items.

Discount Stores

General merchandise discount stores, such as Target, Kmart, and Walmart, offer a broad assortment of items at low prices and with minimal service and are the dominant outlet for many products. Discounters are tearing up the retail landscape because they appeal to price-conscious shoppers who want easy access to a lot of merchandise. Kohl's, for example, is

general merchandise discount stores
Retailers that offer a broad assortment of items at low prices with minimal service.

Step into middle England's
best loved department store,
stroll through haberdashery to
the audio visual department
where an awfully well brought
up young man will bend over
backwards to find the right TV
for you **then go to dixons.co.uk
and buy it.**

Dixons.co.uk
The last place you want to go

Simon Dicketts-Creative Director; Orlando Warner-Creative Director

A British discount store.

off-price retailers
Retailers that buy excess merchandise from well-known manufacturers and pass the savings on to customers.

warehouse clubs
Discount retailers that charge a modest membership fee to consumers who buy a broad assortment of food and nonfood items in bulk and in a warehouse environment.

factory outlet store
A discount retailer, owned by a manufacturer, that sells off defective merchandise and excess inventory.

department stores
Retailers that sell a broad range of items and offer a good selection within each product line.

hypermarkets
Retailers with the characteristics of both warehouse stores and supermarkets; hypermarkets are several times larger than other stores and offer virtually everything from grocery items to electronics.

one of the nation's fastest-growing retailers. These stores increasingly carry designer-name clothing at bargain prices as companies like Liz Claiborne create new lines just for discount stores.[34]

Some discount stores, such as T.J. Maxx, Marshalls, HomeGoods, and A.J. Wright, are **off-price retailers**. These stores obtain surplus merchandise from manufacturers and offer brand-name, fashion-oriented goods at low prices. **Warehouse clubs** such as COSTCO and BJ's are a newer version of the discount store. These establishments do not offer any of the amenities of a full-service store. Customers buy many of the products in larger-than-normal packages and quantities—nothing like laying in a three-year supply of paper towels or five-pound boxes of pretzels, even if you have to build an extra room in your house to store all this stuff! These clubs often charge a membership fee to consumers and small businesses. A recent survey showed that the typical warehouse shopper shops about once a month, is intrigued by bulk buying, hates long lines, and is drawn to the club retailer because of specific product areas such as fresh groceries.[35]And, consistent with the wheel of retailing, even these stores "trade up" in terms of what they sell today; shoppers can purchase fine jewelry and other luxury items at many warehouse clubs. The **factory outlet store** is still another type of discount retailer. A manufacturer owns these stores. Some factory outlets enable the manufacturer to sell off defective merchandise or excess inventory, while others carry items not available at full-price retail outlets and are designed to provide an additional distribution channel for the manufacturer. Although the assortment is not wide because a store carries products only one manufacturer makes, we find most factory outlet stores in *outlet malls* where a large number of factory outlet stores cluster together in the same location.

Department Stores

Department stores sell a broad range of items and offer a deep selection organized into different sections of the store. Grand department stores dominated urban centers in the early part of the twentieth century. In their heyday, these stores sold airplanes and auctioned fine art. Lord & Taylor even offered its customers a mechanical horse to ensure the perfect fit of riding habits.

In many countries, department stores continue to thrive and they remain consumers' primary place to shop. In Japan, department stores are always crowded with shoppers who buy everything from a takeaway sushi dinner to a string of fine pearls. In Spain, a single department store chain, El Corte Inglés, dominates retailing. Its branch stores include store-size departments for electronics, books, music, and gourmet foods, and each has a vast supermarket covering one or two floors of the store.

In the United States, however, department stores have struggled in recent years. On the one hand, specialty stores lure department-store shoppers away with deeper, more cutting-edge fashion selections and better service. On the other hand, department stores have also been squeezed by discount stores and catalogs that offer the same items at lower prices because they don't have the expense of rent, elaborate store displays and fixtures, or high salaries for salespeople.

Hypermarkets

Hypermarkets combine the characteristics of warehouse stores and supermarkets. A European invention, these are huge establishments several times larger than other stores. A supermarket might be 40,000 to 50,000 square feet, whereas a hypermarket takes up 200,000 to 300,000 square feet, or four football fields. They offer one-stop shopping, often for over 50,000 items, and feature restaurants, beauty salons, and children's play areas. Hypermarkets such as those the French firm Carrefour runs are popular in Europe and Latin America where big stores are somewhat of a novelty. More recently, Carrefour is expanding to developing countries such as China where a burgeoning population and a lack of large retailers provide hyper-opportunities. Hypermarkets have been less successful in the United States where many other shopping options including discount stores, malls, and supermarkets are available. Consumers in the United States find the hypermarkets to be too large and shopping in them too time-consuming.

3 Nonstore Retailing

Stores like the Limited succeed because they put cool merchandise in the hands of young shoppers who can't get it elsewhere. But competition for shoppers' dollars comes from sources other than traditional stores that range from bulky catalogs to dynamic Web sites. Debbie in Dubuque can easily log on to **alloy.com** at 3:00 A.M. and order the latest belly-baring fashions without leaving home.

As the founder of the Neiman-Marcus department store once noted, "If customers don't want to get off their butts and go to your stores, you've got to go to them."[36] Indeed, many products are readily available in places other than stores. Think of the familiar Avon lady who sells beauty products to millions of women around the world. Avon allows customers to place orders by phone, fax, or catalog or through a sales representative.

Avon's success at giving customers alternatives to traditional store outlets illustrates the increasing importance of **nonstore retailing**, which is any method a firm uses to complete an exchange that does not require a customer to visit a store. Indeed, many conventional retailers—from upscale specialty stores such as Tiffany's to discounter Walmart—offer nonstore alternatives such as catalogs and Web sites for customers who want to buy their merchandise. For other companies, such as Internet retailer **Amazon.com**, nonstore retailing is their entire business. Catalog companies have, perhaps, had the easiest time making the transition to the Web. Many have been able to use their experience delivering goods directly to consumers and make a successful jump to online sales. In Chapter 14 we talked about direct marketing done through the mail, telephone, and television. In this section, we'll look at other types of nonstore retailing shown 📷 in Figure 16.4: direct selling, automatic vending, and B2C e-commerce.

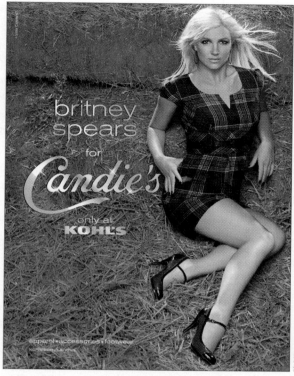

Discount department stores like Kohl's are a go-to source for fashion today.

nonstore retailing
Any method used to complete an exchange with a product end user that does not require a customer visit to a store.

direct selling
An interactive sales process in which a salesperson presents a product to one individual or a small group, takes orders, and delivers the merchandise.

Direct Selling

Direct selling occurs when a salesperson presents a product to one individual or a small group, takes orders, and delivers the merchandise. The Direct Selling Association reported that in 2009, 15 million people engaged in direct selling in the United States and these activities generated $29.6 billion in sales.[37] Of this, 66.3 percent of revenues came from face-to-face sales and 25.7 percent from party plan or group sales. Female salespeople accounted for 86.4 percent of all direct salespeople. The major product categories for direct sales include home/family care products (such as cleaning products), wellness products (such as weight loss products), and personal care products (such as cosmetics, jewelry, and skin care products).

Figure 16.4 📷 *Snapshot* | Types of Nonstore Retailing

Traditional retailers must compete with a variety of nonstore retailers from automatic vending to dynamic Web sites.

Direct Selling
- Door to door
- Parties and networks
- Multilevel networks and activities

Automatic Vending

B2C E-Commerce

Door-to-Door Sales

Door-to-door selling is still popular in some countries, such as China. But it's declining in the United States, where two-income households are the norm, because fewer people are home during the day, and those who *are* home are reluctant to open their doors to strangers. Door-to-door selling is illegal in communities that have **Green River Ordinances**; they prohibit door-to-door selling unless prior permission is given by the household.

Parties and Networks

At *home shopping parties* a company representative makes a sales presentation to a group of people who have gathered in the home of a friend.[38] One reason that these parties are so effective is that people who attend may get caught up in the "group spirit," and buy things they would not normally purchase if they were alone—even Botox injections to get rid of those nasty wrinkles. We call this sales technique a **party plan system**. Perhaps the most famous home shopping parties were the Tupperware parties popular in the 1950s.

Multilevel Marketing

Another form of direct selling, which the Amway Company epitomizes, is **multilevel marketing** or **network marketing**. In this system, a *master distributor* recruits other people to become distributors. The master distributor sells the company's products to the people she entices to join, and then she receives commissions on all the merchandise sold by the people she recruits. Today, Amway has over 3 million independent business owners who distribute personal care, home care, and nutrition and commercial products in more than 80 countries and territories.[39] Amway and other similar network marketers use revival-like techniques to motivate distributors to sell products and find new recruits.[40]

One of the advantages of *multilevel marketing* is that it allows firms to reach consumers who belong to tightly knit groups that are not so easy to reach. Salt Lake City–based Nu Skin Enterprises relies on Mormons to sell its products in Mormon communities. Shaklee (which sells food supplements, cleaning products, and personal care items) recruits salespeople in isolated religious communities, including Amish and Mennonite people (who receive "bonus buggies" instead of cars as prizes for superior salesmanship).[41]

Despite the growing popularity of this technique, some network systems are illegal. They are really **pyramid schemes**: illegal scams that promise consumers or investors large profits from recruiting others to join the program rather than from any real investment or sale of goods to the public. Often large numbers of people at the bottom of the pyramid pay money to advance to the top and to profit from others who might join. At recruiting meetings, pyramid promoters create a frenzied, enthusiastic atmosphere complete with promises of easy money. Some pyramid schemes are disguised as multilevel marketing—that is, people entering the pyramid do not pay fees to advance, but they are forced to buy large, costly quantities of merchandise. Of course, in these organizations, little or no effort ever goes into actually marketing the products.[42] That's one of the crucial differences between pyramid schemes and legitimate network marketers.

Automatic Vending

Coin-operated vending machines are a tried-and-true way to sell convenience goods, especially cigarettes and drinks. These machines are appealing because they require minimal space and personnel to maintain and operate. Some of the most interesting innovations are state-of-the-art vending machines that dispense everything from Ore-Ida French fries to software. French consumers purchase Levi's jeans from a machine called Libre Service that offers the pants in 10 different sizes. In the United States, vending machines that utilize touch screens and credit cards dispense pricey items like digital cameras and Elizabeth Arden cosmetics.[43]

Green River Ordinances
Community regulations that prohibit door-to-door selling unless prior permission is given by the household.

party plan system
A sales technique that relies heavily on people getting caught up in the "group spirit," buying things they would not normally buy if they were alone.

multilevel or **network marketing**
A system in which a master distributor recruits other people to become distributors, sells the company's product to the recruits, and receives a commission on all the merchandise sold by the people recruited.

pyramid schemes
An illegal sales technique that promises consumers or investors large profits from recruiting others to join the program rather than from any real investment or sale of goods to the public.

In general, however, vending machines are best suited to the sales of inexpensive merchandise and food and beverages. Most consumers are reluctant to buy pricey items from a machine. New vending machines may spur more interest, however, as technological developments loom on the horizon, including video kiosk machines that let people see the product in use, have the ability to accept credit cards as payment, and have inventory systems that signal the operator when malfunctions or stockouts occur.

B2C E-Commerce

Business-to-consumer (B2C) e-commerce is online exchange between companies and individual consumers. Forrester Research reports that in 2009 shoppers bought $155 billion worth of consumer goods online.[44] Furthermore, Forrester estimates $917 billion in offline consumer sales were Web-influenced. These two categories accounted for 42 percent of all retail sales. Forrester also estimates that offline Web-influenced sales will increase to $1.4 trillion by 2014 while online sales will top $250 billion.[45]

A number of factors prevent online sales from growing even more. Most consumers prefer stores where they can touch and feel items and avoid issues with returns and shipping costs. Also, many consumers don't like to buy online because they want the product immediately. To address some of these issues, retailers such as Best Buy have merged their online and in-store sales functions. Consumers can select an item and pay for it online, then pick it up at their local store within hours—no wandering over the store to find the item or waiting in line to pay and no concerns about stockouts. We'll talk more about these limitations and the benefits of B2C e-commerce next.

business-to-consumer (B2C) e-commerce
On-line exchanges between companies and individual consumers.

Benefits of B2C E-Commerce

For both consumers and marketers, B2C e-commerce provides a host of benefits and some limitations. Table 16.2 lists some of these.

Table 16.2 | Benefits and Limitations of E-Commerce

Benefits	Limitations
For the consumer:	**For the consumer:**
Shop 24 hours a day	Lack of security
Less traveling	Fraud
Can receive relevant information in seconds from any location	Can't touch items
More product choices	Exact colors may not reproduce on computer monitors
More products available to less developed countries	Expensive to order and then return
Greater price information	Potential breakdown of human relationships
Lower prices, so less affluent can purchase	**For the marketer:**
Participate in virtual auctions	Lack of security
Fast delivery	Must maintain site to reap benefits
Electronic communities	Fierce price competition
For the marketer:	Conflicts with conventional retailers
The world is your marketplace	Legal issues not resolved
Decreases costs of doing business	
Very specialized businesses can be successful	
Real-time pricing	

The Cutting Edge

Be Your Own Virtual Stylist

Think shopping's a bore? Hate hours of trying on outfits to see what looks best? **Coutourious.com** is changing that.[46] Sign on to **Coutourious.com** and you can become your own clothing stylist by virtually styling 3-D models. Visitors to the site first choose a photo of a model with a body style like their own. Next they select tops, bottoms, dresses, shoes, bags, accessories, and other items from 100 brands and place them on a fairly realistic model—just the way they want it. To enhance the experience, Couturious even made styles from six designers that were shown at New York City's Fall 2010 Fashion Week but not yet in stores available to site visitors. The best part—for both Couturious and you—is that you can buy the clothes online and then share your outfit with friends on Facebook or Twitter.

experiential shoppers
Consumers who engage in on-line shopping because of the experiential benefits they receive.

From the consumer's perspective, electronic marketing increases convenience as it breaks down many of the barriers time and location cause. You can shop 24/7 without leaving home. Consumers in even the smallest of communities can purchase funky shoes or a hot swimsuit from **Bloomingdales.com** just like big-city dwellers. In less-developed countries, the Internet lets consumers purchase products that may not be available at all in local markets. The Web site Ideeli offers its customers the chance to buy heavily discounted luxury items in a kind of online "blue-light special" on your cell phone. Thus, the Internet can improve the quality of life without the necessity of developing costly infrastructure, such as opening retail stores in remote locations.

For some consumers, online shopping provides an additional benefit because it fulfills their experiential needs, that is, their desire to shop for fun. Consumers who are collectors or who enjoy hobbies are most likely to be **experiential shoppers**. While most online consumers engage in goal-directed behavior—they wish to satisfy their shopping goal as quickly as possible—between 20 and 30 percent of online consumers shop online because they enjoy the "thrill of the hunt" as much as or more than the actual acquisition of the item. Experiential shoppers linger at sites longer and a desire to be entertained is what motivates them. Consequently, marketers who wish to attract these customers must design Web sites that offer surprise, uniqueness, and excitement.

Marketers realize equally important benefits from e-commerce. Because an organization can reach such a large number of consumers via electronic commerce, it is possible to develop very specialized businesses that could not be profitable if limited by geographic constraints. The Internet provides an excellent opportunity to bring merchants with excess merchandise and bargain-hunting consumers together.[47] When retailers become concerned that, due to economic downturns or other factors, consumers may not buy enough, they may utilize online liquidators such as **Overstock.com** and Bluefly that offer consumers great bargains on apparel and accessories, items retailers refer to as "distressed inventory."

Even high fashion designers whose retail outlets we associate with Rodeo Drive in Los Angeles, Fifth Avenue in New York, and the Magnificent Mile in Chicago are setting up shop on the Internet to sell $3,000 skirts and $5,000 suits.[48] Forrester Research predicts that soon luxury apparel online sales will approach $1 billion per year. Armani, for example, offers its entire Emporio collection at **EmporioArmani.com**. The high-end Neiman Marcus department store finds it can easily sell items like $7,900 Valentino gowns and $5,500 Carolina Herrera jackets online.

As we discussed in Chapter 11, one of the biggest advantages of e-commerce is that it's easy to get price information. Want to buy a new Hellboy action figure, a mountain bike, an MP3 player, or just about anything else you can think of? Instead of plodding from store to store to compare prices, many Web surfers use search engines or "shop bots" like **Ask.com** that compile and compare prices from multiple vendors. With readily available pricing information, shoppers can browse brands, features, reviews, and information on where to buy that particular product. This means that consumers can find all of this information in one central location, which makes shopping more efficient.

E-commerce also allows businesses to reduce costs. Compared to traditional bricks-and-mortar retailers, e-tailers' costs are minimal—no expensive mall sites to maintain and no sales associates to pay. And, for some products, such as computer software and digitized music, e-commerce provides fast, almost instantaneous delivery. Music fans responded by buying over 30 million downloads from sites including iTunes, Dell, and Walmart. Newer entertainment downloads have gone a step further with sites such as iTunes that offer online shoppers the opportunity to purchase or rent movies. Just download a flick to your iPod, plug it into your new flat-screen TV, and pop some corn. You're set for the evening.

Limitations of B2C E-Commerce

But, all is not perfect in the virtual world. E-commerce does have its limitations. One drawback compared to shopping in a store is that customers must wait a few days to receive most products, which are often sent via private delivery services, so shoppers can't achieve instant gratification by walking out of a store clutching their latest "finds."

Of course, some e-commerce sites still suffer from poor design that people find irritating. Customers are less likely to return to sites that are difficult to navigate or that don't provide easy access to customer-service personnel such as the online chats that better sites provide. Customers are often frustrated with sites where their shopping baskets "disappear" as soon as they leave the site. Retailers need to take these navigational problems seriously. When consumers have problems shopping on a site, they are less likely to return to shop another day.

Security is a concern to both consumers and marketers. We hear horror stories of consumers whose credit cards and other identity information have been stolen. Although in the United States an individual's financial liability in most theft cases is limited because credit card companies usually absorb most or all of the loss, the damage to one's credit rating can last for years.

Consumers also are concerned about Internet fraud. Although most of us feel competent to judge a local bricks-and-mortar business by its physical presence, by how long it's been around, and from the reports of friends and neighbors who shop there, we have little or no information on the millions of Internet sites offering their products for sale—even though sites like eBay and the Better Business Bureau try to address these concerns by posting extensive information about the reliability of individual vendors.

Another problem is that people need "touch-and-feel" information before they buy many products. Although it may be satisfactory to buy a computer or a book on the Internet, buying clothing and other items for which touching the item or trying it on is essential may be less attractive. As with catalogs, even though most online companies have liberal return policies, consumers can still get stuck with large delivery and return shipping charges for items that don't fit or simply aren't the right color.

Developing countries with primarily cash economies pose yet another obstacle to the global success of B2C e-commerce. In these countries, few people use credit cards, so they can't easily pay for items they purchase over the Internet. Furthermore, banks are far less likely to offer consumers protection against fraudulent use of their cards, so a hacked card number can literally wipe you out. For consumers in these countries, there are a growing number of alternatives for safely paying for online purchases. PayPal is a global leader in online payments. Founded in 1998 and acquired by eBay in 2002, PayPal has 81 million active accounts and services customers in 190 markets and 24 currencies around the world.[49] Twitpay is a service that permits consumers to send payments using the social network site Twitter. Twitpay's RT2Give™ service offers consumers the opportunity to easily make payments to nonprofits. After the disastrous earthquake in Haiti in 2010, consumers were able to donate money to the Red Cross for Haiti via Twitter.

As major marketers beef up their presence on the Web, they worry that inventory they sell online will *cannibalize* their store sales (we discussed the strategic problem of cannibalization in Chapter 9). This is a big problem for companies like bookseller Barnes & Noble, which has to be careful as it steers customers toward its Web site and away from its chain of stores bursting with inventory. Barnes & Noble has to deal with competitors such as Amazon (with 40 million worldwide customers and annual sales of not only books but myriad products from apparel to cell phones of over $14.84 billion in 2007), which sells its books and music exclusively over its six global Web sites and so doesn't have to worry about this problem.[50] Of course, today books, including textbooks like this one, have gone digital and can be purchased and downloaded online. Tablet eBook readers such as Amazons Kindle, Sony's Reader™, and Apple's iPad have made eBooks even more attractive.

B2C's Effect on the Future of Retailing

Does the growth of B2C e-commerce mean the death of bricks-and-mortar stores as we know them? Don't plan any funerals for your local stores prematurely. Although some argue that virtual distribution channels will completely replace traditional ones because of their cost advantages, this is unlikely. For example, although a bank saves 80 percent of its costs when customers do business online from their home computers, Wells Fargo found that it could not force its customers to use PC-based banking services. For now, clicks will have to coexist with bricks.

However, this doesn't mean that physical retailers can rest easy. Stores as we know them will continue to evolve to lure shoppers away from their computer screens. In the future, the trend will be *destination retail*; that is, consumers will visit retailers not so much to buy a product but for the entertainment they receive from the total experience. Many retailers are already developing ways to make the shopping in bricks-and-mortar stores an experience rather than just a place to pick up stuff. At the General Mills Cereal Adventure in the Mall of America, children of all ages cavort in the Cheerios Play Park and the Lucky Charms Magical Forest.

4

Develop a Store Positioning Strategy: Retailing as Theater

OBJECTIVE

Understand the importance of store image to a retail positioning strategy and explain how a retailer can create a desirable image in the marketplace.
(pp. 498–504)

A "destination retail" strategy reminds us that shopping often is part buying, part entertainment, and part social outlet. So far we've seen that we distinguish stores in several ways, including the types of products they carry and the breadth and depth of their assortments. But recall that a store is itself a product that adds to or subtracts from the goods the shopper came to buy there.

When we decide which store to patronize, many of us are less likely to say, "I'll go there because their assortment is broad," and more likely to say, "That place is so cool. I really like hanging out there." Stores can entertain us, bore us, make us angry, or even make us sad (unless it's a funeral parlor, that last kind probably won't be in business for long). In today's competitive marketplace, retailers have to do more than offer good inventory at reasonable prices. They need to position their stores so that they offer a competitive advantage over other stores that also vie for the shopper's attention—not to mention the catalogs, Web sites, and shopping channels that may offer the same or similar merchandise. Let's see next how bricks-and-mortar retailers compete against these alternatives.

Walk into REI, a Seattle-based retailer with over 70 stores in 24 states, and you'll find gear for camping, climbing, cycling, skiing, outdoor cross-training, paddling, snow sports, and travel. REI is more than that, though. The Seattle store, for example, features a 65-foot-high, artificial climbing rock, while other REI stores include a vented area for testing camp stoves and an outdoor trail to check out mountain bikes. Buying a water pump? Test it in an indoor river. Want to try out those boots before you walk in them? Take a walk on hiking boot test trails.[51]

Many retailers recognize that much of what they do is theater. Shoppers are an audience to entertain. The "play" can cleverly use stage sets (store design) and actors (salespeople) that together create a "scene." For example, think about buying a pair of sneakers. Athletic shoe stores are a far cry from the old days, when a tired shoe salesman (much like Al Bundy in the TV show *Married with Children*) waded through box after box of shoes as kids ran amuck across dingy floors.

Now salespeople (actors) dress in costumes such as black-striped referee outfits at stores like Foot Locker. Foot Locker stores are ablaze with neon, and they display their shoes in clear acrylic walls so they appear to be floating.[52] All these special effects make the buying occasion less about buying and more about having an experience. As one marketing strategist commented, "The line between retail and entertainment is blurring." In this section, we'll review some of the tools available to the retailing playwright.

Store Image

When people think of a store, they often have no trouble describing it in the same terms they might use to describe a person. They might come up with labels like *exciting, boring, old-fashioned, tacky,* or *elegant.* **Store image** is how the target market perceives the store—its market position relative to the competition. Restaurants provide a good example. While Outback's décor attempts to look like an Australian steakhouse complete with "Kookaburra Wings" and "Jackaroo Chops" on the menu, Olive Garden restaurants use foliage, stucco walls, and Italian background music to remind the diner of an Italian farmhouse. Just as brand managers do for products, store managers work hard to create a distinctive and appealing personality.

To appreciate this idea, consider the dramatic makeover now in place at Selfridges, long a well-known but dowdy British department store chain. At the newly renovated flagship store in London, shoppers can wander over to a body-piercing salon where store associates are teenagers in dreadlocks. Periodic events that scream cutting-edge accent the store's makeover, including the "Body Craze" promotion when thousands of shoppers flocked to see 650 naked people ride the escalators.[53] Not every store can have (or wants to have) naked people running around the store, but even more modest strategies to enliven the atmosphere make a big difference. When a retailer decides to create a desirable store image, it has many tools including those shown in 📷 Figure 16.5 at its disposal. Ideally, all these elements work together to create a clear, coherent picture that meets consumers' expectations of what that particular shopping experience should be.

Store Design: Set the Stage

The elements of store design should correspond to management's desired image. A bank lobby needs to convey respectability and security because people need to be reassured about the safety of their money. In contrast, a used bookstore might create a disorderly look so that shoppers think treasures lie buried beneath piles of tattered novels.

Atmospherics is the use of color, lighting, scents, furnishings, sounds, and other design elements to create a desired setting. Marketers manipulate these elements to create a certain "feeling" for the retail environment.[54] Today many retailers seek to create a "playground" for adults in their stores, often through the sophisticated use of lighting, more intimate retail spaces, and even strategic smells they pump into the space.[55]

store image
The way the marketplace perceives a retailer relative to the competition.

atmospherics
The use of color, lighting, scents, furnishings, and other design elements to create a desired store image.

The marquee of the Planet Hollywood restaurant in Myrtle Beach, S.C. is, quite naturally, a very large replica of a planet that can be seen from blocks away.

Andre Jenny/Newscom

Figure 16.5  *Snapshot* | Elements of a Store Image

A store's image is how the target market perceives the store relative to the competition. Marketers have many tools to use in creating a desirable store image.

> **Set the Stage: Store Design**
> - Atmospherics
> - Traffic flow design
> - Visual merchandising
> - Music
> - Color and lighting

> Store Personnel

> Pricing Policy

traffic flow

The direction in which shoppers will move through the store and which areas they will pass or avoid.

At Levi's Stores and other retailers, consumers experience a Jetsons-like virtual fitting room. A shopper steps into the cylindrical unit where holographic imaging technology performs a 360-degree body scan in less than 10 seconds. The customer then gets a printout with the store's styles and sizes that will best fit his particular body type.[56]

Here are some other design factors that retailers consider:

- *Store layout:* This is the arrangement of merchandise in the store. The placement of fixtures such as shelves, racks, and cash registers is important because store layout determines **traffic flow**—how shoppers will move through the store and which areas they will pass or avoid. A typical strategy is to place staple goods shoppers purchase more frequently in more remote areas. Retailers stock impulse goods in spots shoppers will pass on their way to look for something else to encourage them to stop and check them out.

A *grid layout* we usually find in supermarkets and discount stores consists of rows of neatly spaced shelves that are at right angles or parallel to one another. This configuration is useful when management wants to move shoppers systematically down each aisle, being sure that they pass through such high-margin sections as deli and meat. Figure 16.6 illustrates how a grid layout in a supermarket helps regulate traffic flow.

In contrast, department and specialty stores typically use a *free-flow layout* because it is more conducive to browsing. A retailer might arrange merchandise in circles or arches or perhaps in separate areas, each with its own distinct image and merchandise mix.

- *Visual merchandising:* Just as we form impressions of people from their home decor, our feelings about stores are affected by furnishings, fixtures (shelves and racks that display

Figure 16.6 *Snapshot* | Grid Layout

A grid layout encourages customers to move up and down the ailes, passing many different products, and supermarkets and many discount stores often use it.

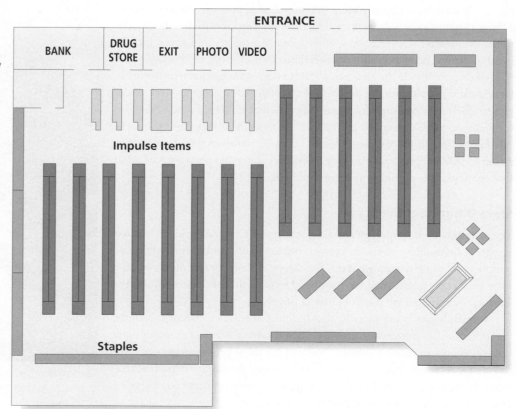

merchandise), and even how much "stuff" is packed into the sales area. **Visual merchandising** includes all the things customers see both inside and outside the store. Generally, clutter conveys a store with lower-priced merchandise. Upscale stores allocate space for sitting areas, dressing rooms, and elaborate displays of merchandise. Before customers even enter the store, the **storefront** or physical exterior and the sign that shows the store's name, called a **marquee,** contribute to the store's image. Retailers try to create a unique design that customers will associate with the personality of the store. The Toys "R" Us marquee, for example, uses a backward "R," reminiscent of a mistake a child learning to write the alphabet might make.

- *The sound of music:* An elegant restaurant softly playing Mozart in the background is worlds apart from a raucous place such as the Hard Rock Café, where loud rock-and-roll is essential to the atmosphere. The music a store plays has become so central to its personality that many retailers, including Ralph Lauren, Victoria's Secret, Au Bon Pain, Starbucks, and Pottery Barn, even sell the soundtracks specially designed for them.[57] Muzak, the premier provider of commercial music for over 70 years, uses its library of over three million songs to create "audio architecture" for businesses including retail stores. For a clothing store, the music may be fun and upbeat, while a bar may want romantic music to encourage late-night couples to stay and have another drink.[58]

- *Color and lighting:* Marketers use color and lighting to set a mood. Red, yellow, and orange are warm colors (fast-food chains use a lot of orange to stimulate hunger), whereas blue, green, and violet signify elegance and cleanliness. Light colors make one feel more serene, whereas bright colors convey excitement.

Store Personnel

Store personnel (the actors) should complement a store's image. Each employee has a part to play, complete with props and costumes. Movie theaters often dress ushers in tuxedos, and many stores provide employees with scripts to use when they present products to customers.

Although the presence of knowledgeable sales personnel is important to shoppers, they generally rate the quality of service they receive from retail personnel as low. Retailers work hard to maintain service quality, though they often find that the rapid turnover of salespeople makes this a difficult goal to achieve. Perhaps they can learn from Japanese retailers. A visitor to a Japanese restaurant or store is greeted by an enthusiastic, cheerful, polite, and immaculately dressed employee who, no matter how busy she is, says *"Irasshaimase"* and bows to welcome the customer.

Some U.S. firms have turned superior customer service into a competitive advantage. Nordstrom's chain of department stores is legendary for its service levels. In fact, some "Nordies" have even been known to warm up customers' cars while they pay for their merchandise! The store motivates its employees by paying them substantially more than the average rate and deducting sales commissions if customers return the merchandise. This policy encourages the salesperson to be sure the customer is satisfied the first time.

Pricing Policy: How Much for a Ticket to the Show?

When consumers form an image of a store in their minds, the *price points*, or price ranges, of its merchandise often play a role. A chain of off-price stores in the Northeast called Daffy's advertises with such slogans as, "Friends Don't Let Friends Pay Retail," implying that anyone who buys at the full, nondiscounted price needs help. Discount stores and general merchandisers are likely to compete on a price basis by offering brand names for less.

In recent years, consumers' desires for bargains have hurt department stores. Many retailers responded by running frequent sales, a strategy that often backfired because they trained consumers to buy *only* when the store held a sale. Some stores have instead reduced the number of sales they run in favor of lowering prices across the board. As we saw in Chapter 11, some stores, including Home Depot and Walmart, offer an *everyday-low-pricing*

visual merchandising
The design of all the things customers see both inside and outside the store.

storefront
The physical exterior of a store.

marquee
The sign that shows a store's name.

(EDLP) strategy; they set prices that are between the list price the manufacturer suggests and the deeply discounted price stores that compete on price only offer.

Build the Theater: Store Location

Any real estate agent will tell you the three most important factors when they sell a home are "location, location, and location." The same is true in retailing. Walmart's success is due not only to what it is but also to *where* it is. It was the first large discount retailer to locate in small and rural markets. When they choose a site, Walmart's planners consider factors such as proximity to highways and major traffic routes. By carefully selecting "undiscovered" areas, the company has been able to negotiate cheap leases in towns with expanding populations. This is an important strategic advantage for Walmart because it means access to markets hungry for a store that offers such a wide assortment of household goods. In this section we'll review some important aspects of retail locations.

Types of Store Locations

As 📷 Figure 16.7 shows, there are four basic types of retail locations. Stores locate in a business district, in a shopping center, as a freestanding entity, or in a nontraditional location.

central business district (CBD)
The traditional downtown business area found in a town or city.

- *Business districts:* A **central business district (CBD)** is the traditional downtown business area you'll find in a town or city. Many people are drawn to the area to shop or work, and public transportation is usually available. CBDs have suffered in recent years because of concerns about security, lack of parking, and the lack of customer traffic on evenings and weekends. To combat these problems, cities typically provide incentives such as tax breaks to encourage the opening of stores and entertainment areas such as Boston's Quincy Marketplace. These vibrant developments or *festival marketplaces* have done a lot to reverse the fortunes of aging downtown areas from Boston to Baltimore.

shopping center
A group of commercial establishments owned and managed as a single property.

popup store
A temporary retail space a company erects to build buzz for its products.

- *Shopping centers:* A **shopping center** is a group of commercial establishments owned and managed as a single property. They range in size and scope from *strip centers* to massive *superregional centers* such as Minneapolis's Mall of America, which offers 4.2 million square feet of shopping plus such attractions as a seven-acre Knott's Camp Snoopy Theme Park. Strip centers offer quick and easy access to basic conveniences such as dry cleaners and video rentals, though shoppers seeking more exotic goods need to look elsewhere. Shopping malls offer variety and the ability to combine shopping with entertainment. Rents tend to be high in shopping malls, making it difficult for many stores to be profitable. In addition, small specialty stores may find it hard to compete with a mall's *anchor stores*, the major department stores that typically draw many shoppers.

  A *lifestyle center* combines the feel of a neighborhood park with the convenience of a strip mall. These more intimate centers typically are located in affluent neighborhoods and feature expensive landscaping; they are an appealing way for retailers to blend in to upscale residential areas. Retailers including Williams-Sonoma and Talbot's invest heavily in this concept.[59]

A **popup store** is a temporary retail space a company erects to build buzz for its products. As the sour economy creates a glut of commercial real estate, this concept is an increasingly popular way to test new product ideas or perhaps even to test if a neighborhood will be a good fit for a new store. A range of marketers, from eBay and Seven for All Mankind to upscale Hermés, have bought into the concept.

- *Freestanding retailers:* Some stores, usually larger ones such as IKEA, occupy their own facility. These retailers benefit from lower rents and fewer parking problems. However, the store must be attractive enough on its own to be a destination point for shoppers, because it can't rely on spillover from consumers visiting other stores at the same place.

Figure 16.7 📷 *Snapshot* | Types of Store Locations

Different types of store locations are best for different types of retailers. Retailers choose from among central business districts, shopping centers, freestanding stores, and nontraditional locations.

A central business district is often found in downtown areas. Although U.S. retailers have been deserting impoverished center cities in droves for the past 20 years, these downtown areas are now staging a comeback. Sophisticated developments such as festival marketplaces including New York City Street Seaport, Union Station in St. Louis, Harborplace in Baltimore, and Boston s Fanueil Hall (shown here) are contributing to the renaissance of American cities.

A shopping center is a group of commercial establishments owned and managed as a single property. They range in size from strip centers to superregional centers such as the Mall of America, which covers 4.2 million square feet of shopping space. Shopping malls offer the ability to combine shopping with entertainment.

A freestanding store is not located near other stores. This locational strategy, used by some big chains like Kids "R" Us, has the advantage of offering a lack of direct competition, lower rents, and adaptability. The store has the freedom to alter its selling space to accommodate its own needs. On the other hand, the store had better be popular because it cannot rely on the drawing power of neighbor stores to provide it with customer traffic.

A nontraditional location offers products to shoppers in convenient places. For example, Taco Bell now has locations inside Target stores as it tempts shoppers to take a taquito break.

- *Nontraditional store locations:* Innovative retailers find new ways to reach consumers. For example, many entrepreneurs use *carts* or *kiosks* to sell their products. Carts are small, movable stores that can be set up in many locations including inside malls, in airports, or in other public facilities. Kiosks are slightly larger than carts and offer store-like facilities, including telephone hookups and electricity. Carts and kiosks are relatively inexpensive and a good way for new businesses to get started.

Site Selection: Choose Where to Build

A story from the past is that Sam Walton, the founder of Walmart, used to fly over an area in a small plane until he found a spot that appealed to him. Now factors such as long-term population patterns, the location of competitors, and the demographic makeup of an area enter into retailers' decisions. The choice of where to open a new store should reflect the company's overall growth strategy. It should be consistent with long-term goals and be in a place that allows the company to best support the outlet. For example, a chain with stores and an extensive warehouse system in the Northeast may not be wise to open a new store in California because the store would be an "orphan," cut off from the company's supply lines.

Location planners look at many factors when they select a site. They want to find a place that is convenient to customers in the store's **trade area**, the geographic zone that accounts

trade area
A geographic zone that accounts for the majority of a store's sales and customers.

for the majority of its sales and customers.[60] A *site evaluation* considers specific factors such as traffic flow; number of parking spaces available; ease of delivery access; visibility from the street; local zoning laws that determine the types of buildings, parking, and signage allowed; and cost factors such as the length of the lease and the amount of local taxes. Planners also consider population characteristics such as *age profile* (is the area witnessing an influx of new families?), *community life cycle* (is the community relatively new, stable, or in decline?), and *mobility* (how often do people move into and out of the area?). This information is available from a variety of sources, including the U.S. Bureau of the Census; the buying power index (BPI) the trade magazine *Sales & Marketing Management* publishes each year; and research firms such as Urban Decision Systems and Nielsen Claritas that analyze many forms of demographic data to create profiles of selected areas.

Planners also have to consider the degree of competition they will encounter if they locate in one place versus another. One strategy that fast-food outlets follow is to locate in a *saturated trade area*. This is a site where a sufficient number of stores already exist so that high customer traffic is present but where the retailer believes it can compete successfully if it goes head-to-head with the competition. As one fast-food industry executive put it, "Customers are lazybones. They absolutely will not walk one more step. You literally have to put a store where people are going to smack their face against it." However, that task is getting harder and harder because at this point many of the good sites are already taken: The United States has 277,208 fast-food outlets from coast to coast—one for every 1,000 people in the country. Subway Restaurants opens a new store in the United States every three hours on average. Starbucks unveils a new store every 11 hours, and Quiznos Sub opens a new door every 16 hours.[61]

Another strategy is to find an *understored trade area*, where too few stores exist to satisfy the needs of the population (this was Walmart's strategy), and the retailer can establish itself as a dominant presence in the community. Over time, these areas may become *overstored* so that too many stores exist to sell the same goods. Those that can't compete are forced to move or close, as has happened to many small mom-and-pop stores that can't beat the Walmarts of the world at their sophisticated retailing games.

Now that you've learned about retailing, read "Real People, Real Choices: How It Worked Out" to see which strategy Stan Clark of Eskimo Joe's selected.

Here's my choice. . .

Real **People**, Real **Choices**

1 Option   **2** Option   **3** Option

Why do you think Stan chose option 1?

How It Worked Out at Eskimo Joe's

Stan reopened Eskimo Joe's as a trendy restaurant. Today the company consists of three restaurants that locals call "The Three Amigos." The original Eskimo Joe's, located right across from campus, still serves up burgers, cheese fries, and other fun fare, while Mexico Joe's offers south-of-the-border food, and Joseppi's is a family-style Italian place. And the rise of online shopping and the continued cult-like status of the logo have driven Stan's Eskimo Joe's clothing business to unanticipated heights.

To learn the whole story, visit www.mypearsonmarketinglab.com.

Brand **YOU**!

You're hired!

You successfully created and communicated your personal brand. Now you have job offers to consider. How do you orchestrate the timing so you get all your offers at the same time? How do you determine which offer is really best for you? How do you negotiate and finalize the offer you want? Enjoy reading Chapter 16 in *Brand You* where your job search comes together.

Kim Richmond Fourth Edition

YOU

MARKETING 7E **real** People, **real** Choices

Solomon | Marshall | Stuart

Objective Summary ➡ Key Terms ➡ Apply

CHAPTER 16
Study Map

---

1. Objective Summary (pp. 480–487)

Define retailing; understand how retailing evolves and appreciate some ethical issues in retailing.

Retailing is the process by which goods and services are sold to consumers for their personal use. The wheel-of-retailing hypothesis suggests that new retailers compete on price and over time become more upscale, leaving room for other new, low-price entrants. The retail life cycle theory suggests that retailing institutions are introduced, grow, reach maturity, and then decline. Three factors that motivate retailers to evolve are changing economic conditions, demographics, technology, and globalization. Some of the ethical issues retailers face include shrinkage due to shoplifting, employee theft, and retail borrowing. Retailers and their employees must also be cognizant of the ethical treatment of customers.

Key Terms

retailing p. 480

wheel-of-retailing hypothesis, p. 481

retail life cycle, p. 482

mergers p. 483

downsizing p. 483

point-of-sale (POS) systems, p. 485

perpetual inventory unit control system p. 485

automatic reordering system p. 485

shrinkage, p. 486

retail borrowing p. 486

2. Objective Summary (pp. 487–493)

Understand how we classify retailers.

Retailers are classified by NAICS codes based on product lines sold; however, new retail models such as combination stores offer consumers more than one product line. Retailers may also be classified by the level of service offered (self-service, full-service, and limited-service retailers) and by the merchandise assortment offered. Merchandise assortment is described in terms of breadth and depth, which refer to the number of product lines sold and the amount of variety available for each. Thus, stores are classified as convenience stores, supermarkets, box stores, specialty stores, category killers, leased departments, variety stores, general merchandise discount stores, off-price retailers, warehouse clubs, department stores, and hypermarkets.

Key Terms

merchandise mix, p. 487

combination stores p. 488

supercenters p. 488

merchandise assortment, p. 488

merchandise breadth, p. 488

merchandise depth, p. 489

convenience stores, p. 489

supermarkets, p. 489

box stores p. 491

category killer, p. 491

specialty stores, p. 491

leased departments p. 491

variety stores p. 491

general merchandise discount stores, p. 491

off-price retailers, p. 492

warehouse clubs, p. 492

factory outlet store, p. 492

department stores, p. 492

hypermarkets, p. 492

3. Objective Summary (pp. 493–498)

Describe the more common forms of nonstore retailing including B2C e-commerce.

The two more common types of nonstore retailing are direct selling and automatic vending machines. In direct selling, a salesperson presents a product to one individual or a small group, takes orders, and delivers the merchandise. Direct selling includes door-to-door sales and party or network sales. State-of-the-art self-service vending machines can dispense products from French fries to iPods.

B2C e-commerce, online exchanges between companies and consumers, is growing rapidly. For consumers, B2C benefits include greater convenience, greater product variety, and increased price information. For marketers, B2C offers a world market, decreased costs of doing business, opportunities for specialized businesses, and real-time pricing. The downside of B2C e-commerce for consumers includes having to wait to receive products, security issues, and the inability to touch and feel products. For Internet-only marketers, success on the Internet may be difficult to achieve, whereas cannibalization may be a problem with traditional retailers' online operations.

Key Terms

nonstore retailing, p. 493

direct selling, p. 493

Green River Ordinances p. 494

party plan system, p. 494

multilevel or network marketing, p. 494

pyramid schemes, p. 494

business-to-consumer (B2C) e-commerce, p. 495

experiential shoppers p. 496

4. Objective Summary (pp. 498–504)

Understand the importance of store image to a retail positioning strategy and explain how a retailer can create a desirable image in the marketplace.

Store image is how the target market perceives the store relative to the competition and results from many different elements working together to create the most desirable shopping experience and to ensure that shoppers view a store favorably relative to the competition. Color, lighting, scents, furnishings, and other design elements, called atmospherics, are used to create a "feel" for a store environment. Use of atmospherics includes decisions on (1) store layout, which determines traffic flow and influences the desired customer behavior in the store; (2) the use of store fixtures and open space; (3) the use of sound to attract (or repel) certain types of customers; and (4) the use of color and lighting that can influence customers' moods. The number and type of store personnel, pricing of products sold in the store, and store location contribute to a store's image. The major types of retail locations include central business districts, shopping centers, freestanding retailers, and nontraditional locations such as kiosks.

Key Terms

store image, p. 499

atmospherics, p. 499

traffic flow p. 500

visual merchandising p. 501

storefront p. 501

marquee p. 501

central business district (CBD), p. 502

shopping center, p. 502

popup store, p. 502

trade area, p. 503

Chapter **Questions** and **Activities**

Questions: Test Your Knowledge

1. Define retailing. What is the role of retailing in today's world?
2. How do the wheel-of-retailing and retail life cycle theories explain the evolution of retailing? How do the economic environment, demographics, technology, and globalization affect the future of retailing?
3. Explain retail store shrinkage and the ways shrinkage normally occurs. What are some of the ethical issues in retailers' treatment of consumers? What is "sweethearting"?
4. How do marketers classify retail stores? Explain merchandise breadth and depth.
5. Describe the differences in merchandise assortments for convenience stores, supermarkets, box stores, specialty stores, category killers, leased departments, variety stores,

general merchandise discount stores, off-price retailers, warehouse clubs, department stores, and hypermarkets.

6. Explain the different types of direct selling. What is the difference between a multilevel network and a pyramid scheme?

7. What is the role of automatic vending in retailing?

8. What is B2C e-commerce? What are some benefits of B2C e-commerce for consumers and for marketers? What are the limitations of B2C e-commerce?

9. What are some possible effects of B2C e-commerce on traditional retailing?

10. How is store-positioning strategy like theater?

11. What is store image? Why is it important?

12. What is meant by store atmospherics? How can the elements of atmospherics be used to increase the store's success? How are store personnel part of a store's image?

13. What is visual merchandising? How do a retailer's store front and marquee participate in development of a store's image?

14. What are some of the different types of store locations? What are their advantages and disadvantages?

Activities: Apply What You've Learned

1. Assume you are a business consultant for a chain of 37 traditional department stores located in 12 midwestern U.S. cities. In recent years, the stores have seen declining revenues as specialty stores and hypermarkets have begun to squeeze the department stores out. The chain has asked you for suggestions on how to increase its business. Develop an outline of your recommendations and present your plan to your class.

2. Assume that you are the director of marketing for a national chain of convenience stores. Your firm has about 200 stores located in 43 states. The stores are fairly traditional both in design and in the merchandise they carry. Because you want to be proactive in your marketing planning, you are concerned that your firm may need to consider making significant changes because of the current demographic, technological, and global trends in the marketplace. You think it is important to discuss these things with the other executives at your firm. Develop a presentation that includes the following:
   a. A discussion of the demographic changes that will impact your stores
   b. A discussion of the technological changes that will impact your stores
   c. A discussion of how global changes may provide problems and opportunities for your organization
   d. Your recommendations for how your firm might meet the challenges faced in each of these areas

3. As a college graduate, you and a friend think the career you really would enjoy means being your own boss—you want to start your own business. You feel that e-commerce is the place for you to make your fortune. You and your friend are considering two options: (1) an online business that sells custom-made blue jeans based on customers' measurements, and (2) an online business that sells gourmet foods from around the world. In a role-playing exercise, debate with your friend the pros and cons of each of these two online retail businesses and make a decision about which is better.

4. All your life you've wanted to be an entrepreneur and to own your own business. Now you're ready to graduate

from college, and you've decided to open a combination coffee shop and bookstore in a location near your college. You know that to attract both the college-student market and other customers from the local community, it will be necessary to carefully design the store image. Develop a detailed plan that specifies how you will use atmospherics to create the image you desire.

5. In your job with a marketing consulting firm, you often are asked to make recommendations for store location. Your current client is a local caterer that is planning to open a new retail outlet for selling take-out gourmet dinners. You are examining the possible types of locations: the central business district, a shopping center, a freestanding entity, or some nontraditional location. Outline the advantages and disadvantages of each type of location for a catering business. In a role-playing exercise, present your recommendations to your client.

6. Retailers are faced with the problem of shrinkage and what to do about it. Shrinkage comes, of course, from shoplifting and employee theft. More subtle, however, is shrinkage that involves customers such as "sweethearting" and "retail borrowing." Many consumers feel such practices are okay. Conduct a survey of students in your school to study these two sources of shrinkage. You might want to include questions about the following:
   a. If and how frequently students engage in such practices
   b. The attitudes of students as to whether such practices are unethical and why or why not
   c. What harm comes from such practices
   d. What respondents think retailers should do to prevent such shrinkage

Develop a report on your findings and present it to your class.

7. One problem that traditional retailers face when they open online stores is cannibalization. Select a traditional retailer where you and your fellow students might normally shop that also sells products online. You might, for example, select Best Buy, Banana Republic, the Gap, or Walmart. Visit the retailer's online store and make notes on the site's product offering, pricing, customer service policies, and so on. (If the store you have chosen offers many different product lines, you might wish to limit your research to one or two different product lines.) Then visit the store and compare what is offered there with the online offerings. Develop a report that summarizes your findings and discusses the potential for cannibalization and its implications for the retailer.

Marketing Metrics Exercise

Inventory management is an important aspect of retail strategy. For example, it is important to know when it is time to reorder and how much to order at a time.

This is the **reorder point**. As consumers buy a product day after day, the inventory level declines. The question for retailers is how low they should allow the inventory level to decline before they place an order, that is, when is it time to reorder? If you order too late, you take a chance of losing sales because you are out of stock. If you order too soon, consumer tastes may change and you will be stuck with excess and unsellable merchandise. The decision of when to order and how much to order is critical to a retailer's bottom line.

The simplest formula to determine the reorder point is

Reorder point = Usage Rate × Lead Time

But, of course, a retailer can't exactly estimate the usage rate, so it needs to keep some "safety stock" on hand. Then the formula becomes

Reorder point = (Usage Rate × Lead Time) + Safety Stock

The Healthy Day Organic Food Store sells 20 containers of yogurt a day. It takes 6 days to place an order and receive a new shipment of yogurt. But to be prepared for the possibility of extra sales or a late shipment, they need to have a safety stock equal to three days' sales.

What is the reorder point for yogurt for Healthy Day Organic Food Store?

Choices: What Do You Think?

1. Pyramid-scheme promoters specialize in recruiting new members of the pyramid with exciting, even frenzied meetings where potential members are made fearful that they may pass up a great opportunity if they don't join. Why do people continue to be lured into these schemes? What do you think should be done to stop these unethical promoters?

2. Most retail store shrinkage can be attributed to shoplifting, employee theft, and retail borrowing. What are some ways that retail store managers can limit or stop shrinkage? What are some problems inherent in security practices? Should retailers create stricter merchandise return policies?

3. Experts predict the future of B2C e-commerce to be very rosy indeed, with exponential increases in Internet sales of some product categories within the next few years. What effect do you think the growth of e-retailing will have on traditional retailing? In what ways will this be good for consumers, and in what ways will it not be so good?

4. The wheel-of-retailing theory suggests that the normal path for a retailer is to enter the marketplace with lower-priced goods and then to increase quality, services, and prices. Why do you think this happens? Is it the right path for all retailers? Why or why not?

5. Walmart has become a dominant retailer in the American marketplace, accounting for over 30 percent of the total sales of some products. Is this a good thing for consumers? For the retail industry as a whole? Some communities try to prevent Walmart from building a store in their area. Why do you think people feel this way?

6. Macy's and other stores have used vending machines to sell electronics such as iPods. What are some other opportunities for vending-machine sales? What are the negative and positive elements of vending-machine sales?

Miniproject: Learn by Doing

This project is designed to help you understand how store atmospherics play an important role in consumers' perceptions of a retail store.

1. First, select two retail outlets where students in your college are likely to shop. It will be good if you can select two outlets that you feel are quite different in terms of store image but that sell the same types of products. You might consider two specialty women's clothing stores, two jewelry stores, two department stores, or two coffee shops.

2. Visit each of the stores, and write a detailed description of the store atmosphere—the storefront and marquee, colors, materials used, types of displays, lighting fixtures, product displays, store personnel, and so on.

3. Survey some of the students in your college. Develop a brief questionnaire asking about the perceptions of the two stores you are studying. You may want to ask about things such as the quality of merchandise, prices, competence and friendliness of the store personnel, the attitude of management toward customer service, and so on. What is the "personality" of each store?

4. Develop a report of your findings. Compare the description of the stores with the results of the survey. Attempt to explain how the different elements of the store atmosphere create each store's unique image.

Marketing in **Action** Case Real Choices at IKEA

How would you go about becoming one of the wealthiest people in the world? Ingvar Kamprad did it by flying coach, taking public transportation, driving 10-year-old automobiles, moving from Sweden to Switzerland (for lower taxes) . . . oh, and incidentally, founding IKEA—now the world's largest furniture store.

Kamprad founded IKEA in Sweden in 1943 when he was just 17 years old and while the world was caught up in World War II. He began by dealing pens, picture frames, wallets, and other bargain items out of a catalog. In 1951 he started to sell furniture made by local carpenters, and in 1957 he opened his first IKEA furniture store in Sweden. Today, IKEA, with 23 billion in sales and 280 retail outlets in 26 countries, is the world's largest home furnishing company that is known for its contemporary designs, affordable prices, and loyal customers.

IKEA retail locations are gigantic—roughly three times the size of a typical Home Depot—and they focus exclusively on the furniture and home decorating market. IKEA's size and focus limit the *breadth* of items it offers, but they do provide a great deal of merchandise *depth* including furniture, decorative accessories, and lighting fixtures for all rooms of the house. While the company has historically made only low-priced, flat-packed furniture, it recently introduced a new 82-piece collection it calls Stockholm to offer its shoppers more expensive furniture made from higher quality materials.

In designing its store layout, IKEA is responding to consumer interest in one-stop shopping—finding what the consumer wants in one store rather than having to visit numerous stores. Also, IKEA makes it easier for customers to shop once they enter the store. It sets up furniture displays in "lifestyle" themes that show the type of furniture that singles, couples, or young families might need. The company also uses vignette displays to suggest how a customer can put together various items to create a certain look. These types of displays are perfect for the generation that is no longer interested in buying furniture to last a lifetime but rather that fits their lifestyle now.

IKEA has enjoyed great success throughout its history, and that success has not come by accident—IKEA got to where it is today through great marketing planning. Presently, one of the most important decisions facing IKEA is how and where it should look to expand its business and its revenues. The company has announced its desire to add new store locations in Russia, Germany, France, China, Italy, Japan, U.K., Finland, Spain, and Switzerland.

But IKEA is more than just a bricks-and-mortar retailer. In recent years the firm has also become a popular online store. Its Web site is very popular; it got 450 million hits during the year 2007 alone. Despite its renown among online furniture shoppers, IKEA recently announced plans to focus on the in-store experience as "the only sales channel." It doesn't plan to invest more money in home shopping or online sales channels. The company bases this decision on its belief that the chain can give customers the best offers and the lowest prices when it makes its products available only through its bricks-and-mortar stores. Despite IKEA's successful history, there are no guarantees for the future in the hyper-competitive world of retailing. Is focusing solely on the in-store experience the right decision? Can IKEA reach its growth and revenue goals without online sales? In the U.S. alone, Internet sales of home furnishings are over $150 billion a year, and industry experts forecast continued annual growth at double-digit rates. Would IKEA be better advised to continue to push online sales at least in some areas of the world?

You Make the Call

1. What is the decision facing IKEA?
2. What factors are important to understand this decision situation?
3. What are the alternatives?
4. What decision(s) do you recommend?
5. What are some ways to implement your recommendation?

Based on: Cora Daniels and Adam Edström, "Create IKEA, Make Billions, Take Bus," *Fortune* (May 3, 2004): 44; Emma Hall and Normandy Madden, "IKEA Courts Buyers with Offbeat Ideas," *Advertising Age* (April 12, 2004): 10; "IKEA Report," *Datamonitor* (February 10, 2008), www .datamonitor.com; Jon Ortiz, "Customers Drawn to IKEA 'Experience,'" *The Sacramento Bee* (February 26, 2006): D1; Luisa Kroll and Allison Fass, "The World's Billionaires," Forbes.com, http://www.forbes.com/billionaires (accessed June 19, 2006); Marianne Rohrlich, "Currents: Furniture; IKEA for the Post-Collegiate Crowd: Fancier Finishes and Less Work," *New York Times* (April 26, 2007), http://query.nytimes.com/ gst/fullpage.html?res59D00E4DF153EF935A15757C0A9619C8B63&scp53&sq5ikea&st5nyt (accessed May 1, 2008); Mei Fong, "IKEA Hits Home in China," *Wall Street Journal Online* (March 3, 2006): B1; Mike Duff, "IKEA Eyes Aggressive Growth," *DSN Retailing Today* (January 27, 2003): 3, 22; "News," *Chain Store Age* (February 2008): 50; "Welcome Inside, Yearly summary FY09," http://www.ikea.com/ms/en_US/ about_ikea/pdf/Welcome_inside_2010.pdf.

Marketing Plan: The S&S Smoothie Company

Executive Summary

Situation Analysis

S&S Smoothie Company is an entrepreneurial organization that produces fruit-and-yogurt–based beverages with superior flavor and nutritional content and unique packaging. Within the United States, S&S has targeted a consumer market of younger, health-conscious, upscale consumers who frequent gyms and health clubs, and two broad reseller markets: (1) gyms and health clubs, and (2) smaller upscale food markets. S&S distributes its product through manufacturers' agents in the United States, Canada, and the United Kingdom and through Internet sales. An analysis of the internal and external environments indicates the firm enjoys important strengths in its product, its employees, and its reputation, while weaknesses are apparent in its limited size, financial resources, and product capabilities. S&S faces a supportive external environment, highlighted by a growing interest in healthy living, and limited threats, primarily from potential competitive growth.

Marketing Objectives

The S&S marketing objectives are to increase awareness, gross sales (50 percent), and distribution, and to introduce two new product lines over the next three years:

- A line of gourmet flavored smoothies
- A line of low-carb smoothies

Marketing Strategies

To accomplish its growth goals, S&S will direct its marketing activities toward the following strategies:

1. *Target Market Strategy:* S&S will continue to target its existing consumer markets while expanding its organizational markets to include hotels and resorts, golf and tennis clubs, and university campuses.

2. *Positioning Strategy:* S&S will continue to position its products as the first-choice smoothie beverage for the serious health-conscious consumer, including those who are seeking to lower their carbohydrate intake.

3. *Product Strategy:* S&S will introduce two new product lines, each identifiable through unique packaging/labeling:
   a. **S&S Smoothie Gold:** a product similar to the original S&S Smoothie beverages but in six unique flavors
   b. **Low-Carb S&S Smoothie:** a product with 50 percent fewer grams of carbohydrates

4. *Pricing Strategy:* S&S will maintain the current pricing strategy for existing and new products.

5. *Promotion Strategy:* S&S will augment current personal selling efforts with television and magazine advertising, with sponsorships of marathons in major cities, and with a sampling program.

6. *Supply Chain Strategy:* S&S will expand its distribution network to include the organizational markets targeted. In addition, to encourage a high level of inventory in larger health clubs, S&S Smoothie will offer free refrigerated display units.

Implementation and Control

The Action Plan details how the marketing strategies will be implemented, including the individual(s) responsible, the timing of each activity, and the budget necessary. The measurement and control strategies provide a means of measurement of the success of the plan.

The following sections provide typical content for a marketing plan. Note that in the right margin the relevant book part for each section is referenced. Please refer to each part opener for "Tricks of the Trade" for developing content for the related marketing plan section.

Situation Analysis

The S&S Smoothie Company[1] was founded in September 2004 in New York with the goal of creating and marketing healthy "smoothie" beverages for sale to health-conscious consumers. S&S Smoothie expects to take advantage of an increasing desire for healthy foods both in the United States and internationally—and to ride the wave of consumer interest in low-carb alternatives. While there are other companies both large and small competing in this market, S&S Smoothie feels it has the expertise to create and market superior products that will appeal to its target market.

Internal Environment

PART ONE

Mission Statement

The strategic direction and actions of the S&S Smoothie Company are driven by its mission:

> S&S Smoothie seeks to meet the needs of discriminating, health-conscious consumers for high-quality, superior-tasting smoothie beverages and other similar products.

Organizational Structure

As an entrepreneurial company, S&S Smoothie does not have a very sophisticated organizational structure. Key personnel include the following:

- Patrick Small, founder and co-president. Small is responsible for the creation, design, packaging, and production management of all S&S Smoothie products.

- William "Bill" Sartens, founder and co-president. Sartens is responsible for international and domestic distribution and marketing.

[1]S&S Smoothie Company is a fictitious company created to illustrate a sample marketing plan.

- Gayle Humphries, chief financial officer. Humphries develops financial strategy and keeps the company's books.

- Alex Johnson, national sales manager. Johnson is responsible for maintaining the sales force of independent sales reps. He also advises on product development.

- Bob LeMay, Pam Sartens, and Paul Sartens, shareholders. Next to Patrick Small and William Sartens, Bob, Pam, and Paul own the largest number of shares. They consult and sit on the company's board of directors. Bob is a lawyer and also provides legal services.

Corporate Culture

S&S Smoothie is an entrepreneurial organization. Thus, a key element of the internal environment is a culture that encourages innovation, risk taking, and individual creativity. The company's beginning was based on a desire to provide a unique, superior product, and company decisions have consistently emphasized this mission.

Current Products

The original S&S Smoothie product, introduced in mid-2004, is a fruit-and-yogurt–based beverage that contains only natural ingredients (no additives) and is high in essential nutrients. Because of the company's patented manufacturing process, S&S Smoothie beverages do not have to be refrigerated and have a shelf life of over a year. Therefore, the product can be shipped and delivered via nonrefrigerated carriers. S&S Smoothie currently sells its beverages exclusively through gyms, health clubs, and smaller upscale food markets. As a producer of dairy-based beverages, S&S Smoothie's NAICS (North American Industry Classification System) classification is 311511, Fluid Milk Manufacturers.

At present, the single product line is the S&S Smoothie fruit and yogurt beverage. This healthy beverage product has a flavor and nutritional content that makes it superior to competing products. The present product comes in five flavors: strawberry, blueberry, banana, peach, and cherry. S&S offers each in a 12-ounce and a 20-ounce size. S&S packages the product in a unique hourglass-shaped, frosted glass bottle with a screw-off cap. The bottle design makes the product easy to hold, even with sweaty hands after workouts. The frosted glass allows the color of the beverage to be seen, but at the same time it communicates an upscale image. The labeling and lid visually denote the flavor with an appropriate color. Labeling includes complete nutritional information. In the future, S&S Smoothie plans to expand its line of products to grow its market share of the health drink market.

The suggested retail prices for S&S Smoothie beverages are $4.00 for the 12-oz. size and $6.00 for the 20-oz. container. S&S's prices to distributors are $1.20 and $1.80, respectively.

At present, S&S Smoothie outsources actual production of the product. Still, the company takes care to oversee the entire production process to ensure consistent quality of its unique product. With this method of production, variable costs for the 12-ounce S&S Smoothie beverages are $0.63, and variable costs for the 20-ounce size are $0.71.

Markets

The consumer market for S&S Smoothie products is made up of anyone who is interested in healthy food and a healthy lifestyle. Although according to published research nearly 70 percent of American consumers say they are interested in living a healthy lifestyle, the number of those who actually work to achieve that goal is much smaller. It is estimated that approximately 80 million Americans actually engage in exercise and/or follow nutritional plans that would be described as healthy. As experts expect the trend toward healthier living to grow globally, the domestic market and the international market for S&S Smoothie products are expected to expand for some time.

Table A.1 | Company Sales Performance

Year	Gross Sales
2004	$ 287,850
2005	$ 638,770
2006	$1,211,445
2007	$1,586,228
2008	$1,918,376
2009	$1,895,120

Customers/Sales

Sales of S&S Smoothie products showed steady growth through 2008 but suffered some decline due to a downturn in the economy in 2009. Actual sales figures for 2004 through 2009 are shown in Table A.1.

These sales figures plus S&S customer research show a strong and growing loyal customer base. This customer asset is important to the future of S&S. Nevertheless, research indicates that only about half of all consumers in the target market are aware of the S&S brand.

Within the U.S. consumer market, S&S Smoothie targets upscale consumers who frequent gyms and health clubs. Based on research conducted by S&S Smoothie, these consumers are primarily younger; however, there is also an older segment that seeks to be physically fit and that also patronizes health clubs.

Distribution

In order to reach its target market, S&S Smoothie places primary distribution emphasis on health clubs and other physical fitness facilities and small, upscale specialty food markets. The company began developing channel relationships with these outlets through individual contacts by company personnel. As sales developed, the company solicited the services of manufacturers' agents and specialty food distributors. Manufacturers' agents are individuals who sell products for a number of different noncompeting manufacturers. By contracting with these agents in various geographic regions, the company can expand its product distribution to a significant portion of the United States and Canada. Similar arrangements with agents in the United Kingdom have allowed it to begin distribution in that country.

The company handles large accounts such as Gold's Gym and World Gyms directly. While total sales to these chains are fairly substantial, when considering the large number of facilities within each chain the sales are very small with much room for growth.

The Internet is a secondary channel for S&S Smoothie. Online retail outlets currently account for only 5 percent of S&S Smoothie sales. Although this channel is useful for individuals who wish to purchase S&S Smoothie products in larger quantities, S&S does not expect that online sales will become a significant part of the business in the near future.

External Environment

PART ONE

Competitive Environment

S&S Smoothie faces several different levels of competition. Direct competitors are companies that also market smoothie-type beverages and include the following:

1. Franchise smoothie retail operations

2. Online-only smoothie outlets

3. Other smaller manufacturers

4. Larger companies such as Nestlé that produce similar products

Indirect competition comes from the following:

1. Homemade smoothie drinks made from powders sold in retail outlets and over the Internet

2. Homemade smoothie drinks made using a multitude of available recipes

3. Other healthy beverages, such as juices

4. A growing number of energy drinks that are especially popular with younger consumers

Economic Environment

S&S Smoothie first introduced its products during a period of economic downturn following the dot.com bust and 9/11. Despite this, the product quickly gained momentum and sales steadily increased. As the economy of the United States has suffered a severe recession during recent years, sales have correspondingly shown some decreases. Analysts estimate that the recovery will be slow and take a number of years, during which time GDP and consumer sales will increase at a similarly low pace.

Technological Environment

Because S&S Smoothie produces a simple food product, technological advances have minimum impact on the firm's operations. Nevertheless, the use of current technology enables and enhances many of the company's activities. For example, S&S Smoothie uses the Internet to enhance its operations in two ways. As noted previously, the Internet provides an additional venue for sales. In addition, manufacturers' agents and channel members can keep in contact with the company, allowing for fewer problems with deliveries, orders, and so on. Finally, in recent years, the company has established a presence on social media sites Facebook and Twitter through which it can communicate with consumers in a more personal way while monitoring consumers' feedback communication.

Political and Legal Environment

Because they are advertised as nutritional products, all S&S Smoothie products must be approved by the FDA. Labeling must include ingredients and nutritional information, also regulated by the FDA. In addition, S&S Smoothie products are regulated by the U.S. Department of Agriculture.

While there are no specific regulations about labeling or advertising products as low-carb, there is potential for such regulations to come into play in the future. In addition, there are numerous regulations that are country-specific in current and prospective global markets of which the company must constantly remain aware. Any future advertising campaigns developed by S&S Smoothie will have to conform to regulatory guidelines both in the United States and internationally.

Sociocultural Environment

S&S Smoothies uses marketing research to monitor the consumer environment. This research shows that changing cultural values and norms continue to provide an important opportunity for S&S Smoothie. The trend toward healthy foods and a healthier lifestyle has grown dramatically for the past decade or longer. In response to this, the number of health clubs across the country and the number of independent resorts and spas that offer patrons a healthy holiday have also grown. In addition, many travelers demand that hotels offer health club facilities.

During the past decade, consumers around the globe have become aware of the advantages of a low-carbohydrate diet. Low-carb menu items abound in restaurants, including fast-food chains such as McDonald's. A vast number of low-carb foods, including low-carb candy, fill supermarket shelves.

There are approximately 125 million American adults aged 15 to 44. Demographers project that this age group will remain stable for the foreseeable future, with an increase of less than 8 percent projected to 2025. Similarly, incomes should neither decrease nor increase significantly in the near future in this segment of the population.

SWOT Analysis

The SWOT analysis provides a summary of the strengths, weaknesses, opportunities, and threats identified by S&S Smoothie through the analysis of its internal and external environments.

Strengths

The following are the strengths identified by S&S Smoothie:

- A creative and skilled employee team

- A high-quality product recipe that provides exceptional flavor with high levels of nutrition

- Because of its entrepreneurial spirit, the ability to remain flexible and to adapt quickly to environmental changes

- A strong network of manufacturers' agents and distributors

- The growth of a reputation of a high-quality product among health clubs, other retail outlets, and targeted consumer groups

Weaknesses

The following are the weaknesses identified by S&S Smoothie:

- Limited financial resources for growth and for advertising and other marketing communications

- Little flexibility in terms of personnel due to size of the firm

- Reliance on external production to maintain quality standards and to meet any unanticipated surges in demand for the product

Opportunities

The following are the opportunities identified by S&S Smoothie:

- A strong and growing interest in healthy living among both young, upscale consumers and older consumers

- Continuing consumer interest in low-carb alternatives that offers opportunities for additional product lines

Threats

The following are the threats identified by S&S Smoothie:

- The potential for competitors, especially those with large financial resources who can invest more in promotion, to develop products that consumers may find superior

- The continuation of a slowed economy that might affect sales

- Fizzling of the low-carb craze if other forms of dieting gain in popularity

- Increase in popularity of energy drinks like Rockstar, etc.

Marketing Objectives

The following are the marketing objectives set by S&S Smoothie:

- To increase the awareness of S&S Smoothie products by at least 10 percent among the target market

- To increase gross sales by 50 percent over the next two years

- To introduce two new product lines: a line of low-carb smoothies and a line of gourmet flavored smoothies

- To increase distribution of S&S Smoothie products to include new retail outlets both in the United States and globally

Marketing Strategies

Target Markets

Consumer Markets

S&S Smoothies will continue to target its existing consumer markets. Company research shows that the primary consumer target market for S&S Smoothie beverages can be described as follows:

Demographics

- Male and female teens and young adults

- Ages: 15–39

- Household income: $50,000 and above

- Education of head of household: College degree or above

- Primarily located in midsize to large urban areas or college towns

Psychographics

- Health-conscious, interested in living a healthy lifestyle

- Spend much time and money taking care of their bodies

- Enjoy holidays that include physical activities

- Live very busy lives and need to use time wisely to enjoy all they want to do

- Enjoy spending time with friends

- According to the VALS2™ typology, many are in the Achievers and Experiencers categories

Media Habits

- Individuals in the target market are more likely to get their news from television or the Internet than from newspapers. They are likely to view not only the news channels but also the financial news networks.

- The consumers prefer watching edgier shows such as *Weeds* and *Californication*.

- They are likely to have satellite radio installed in their automobiles.

- They are heavy users of social media, spending between 2 and 3 hours a day on sites including Facebook, Twitter, LinkedIn, and Foursquare.

- Frequently read magazines such as *Men's Health*, *BusinessWeek*, *Sports Illustrated*, and *The New Yorker*.

Organizational Markets

In the past, S&S Smoothie has targeted two categories of reseller markets: (1) health clubs and gyms, and (2) small, upscale specialty food markets. To increase distribution and sales of its products, S&S Smoothie will target the following in the future:

1. Hotels and resorts in the United States and in selected international markets

2. Golf and tennis clubs

3. College and university campuses

Upscale young professionals frequently visit hotels and resorts, and they demand that even business travel should include quality accommodations and first-rate health club facilities. The membership of golf and tennis clubs, while including many older consumers, also is an excellent means of providing products conveniently for the targeted groups. College and university students, probably more than any other consumer group, are interested in health and in their bodies. In fact, many universities have built large, fairly elaborate health and recreational facilities as a means of attracting students. Thus, providing S&S Smoothie beverages on college campuses is an excellent means of meeting the health beverage needs of this group.

Positioning the Product

PART TWO

S&S Smoothie seeks to position its products as the first-choice smoothie beverage for the serious health-conscious consumer, including those who are seeking to lower their carbohydrate intake. The justification for this positioning is as follows: Many smoothie beverages are available. The S&S Smoothie formula provides superior flavor and nutrition in a shelf-stable form. S&S Smoothie has developed its product, packaging, pricing, and promotion to communicate a superior, prestige image. This positioning is thus supported by all its marketing strategies.

Product Strategies

PART THREE

To increase its leverage in the market and to meet its sales objectives, S&S Smoothie needs additional products. Two new product lines are planned:

1. *S&S Smoothie Gold:* This product will be similar to the original S&S Smoothie beverage but will come in six unique flavors:

   a. Piña colada

   b. Chocolate banana

   c. Apricot nectarine madness

   d. Pineapple berry crush

   e. Tropical tofu cherry

   f. Peaches and dreams

   The nutritional content, critical to the success of the new products, will be similar to that of the original S&S Smoothie beverages. Nutritional information is shown in Table A.2.

Table A.2 | Nutritional Information: S&S Smoothie Beverage

	S&S Smoothie Gold		Low-Carb S&S Smoothie	
	Amount per Serving	% Daily Value	Amount per Serving	% Daily Value
Calories	140		130	
Calories from fat	6		7	
Total fat	< 0.5 g	1%	< 0.5 g	1%
Saturated fat	< 0.5 g	2%	< 0.5 g	2%
Cholesterol	6 mg	2%	6 mg	2%
Sodium	70 mg	3%	70 mg	3%
Potassium	100 mg	3%	100 mg	3%
Total carbs	20 g	8%	10 g	4%
Dietary fiber	5 g	20%	5 g	20%
Protein	25 g	50%	25 g	50%
Vitamin A		50%		50%
Vitamin C		50%		50%
Calcium		20%		20%
Iron		30%		30%
Vitamin D		40%		40%
Vitamin E		50%		50%
Thiamin		50%		50%
Riboflavin		50%		50%
Niacin		50%		50%
Vitamin B^6		50%		50%
Vitamin B^{12}		50%		50%
Biotin		50%		50%
Pantothenic acid		50%		50%
Phosphorus		10%		10%
Iodine		50%		50%
Chromium		50%		50%
Zinc		50%		50%
Folic acid		50%		50%

Serving Size: 12 ounces
For 20-ounce sizes, multiply the amounts by 1.67.

The packaging for the new S&S Smoothie product will also be similar to that used for the original product, utilizing the unique, easy-to-hold, hourglass-shaped, frosted glass bottle and providing the new beverage with the same upscale image. To set the product apart from the original-flavor Smoothie beverages in store refrigerator cases, labels will include the name of the beverage and the logo in gold lettering. The bottle cap will be black.

2. *Low-Carb S&S Smoothie:* As shown in Table A.2, the Low-Carb S&S Smoothie beverage will have approximately 50 percent fewer grams of carbohydrates than the original

Smoothie beverage or the S&S Smoothie Gold. Low-Carb S&S Smoothie will come in the following four flavors:

a. Strawberry

b. Blueberry

c. Banana

d. Peach

Packaging for the Low-Carb S&S Smoothie will be similar to other S&S Smoothie beverages but will include the term "Low-Carb" in large type. The label will state that the beverage has 50 percent fewer carbs than regular smoothies.

Pricing Strategies

PART THREE

The current pricing strategy will be maintained for existing and new products. This pricing is appropriate for communicating a high-quality product image for all S&S Smoothie products. The company feels that creating different pricing for the new beverages would be confusing and create negative attitudes among consumers. Thus, there is no justification for increasing the price of the new products.

Pricing through the channel including margins is shown in Table A.3.

Table A.3 | Pricing of S&S Smoothie Beverages

	12 oz	20 oz
Suggested retail price	$4.00	$6.00
Retailer margin	50%/$2.00	50%/$3.00
Price to retail outlets (health clubs, etc.)	$2.00	$3.00
Distributor/sales agent margin	40%/$0.80	40%/$1.20
Price to distributor/discount to sales agent	$1.20	$1.80
Variable costs	$0.63	$0.71
S&S contribution margin	$0.57	$1.09

S&S Smoothie will continue to outsource actual production of the new offerings as it does with its existing product. As noted earlier, with this method of production, variable costs for the 12-ounce S&S Smoothie beverages are $0.63 and variable costs for the 20-ounce size are $0.71. Anticipated annual fixed costs for S&S Smoothie office space, management salaries, and expenses related to sales, advertising and other marketing communications are as follows:

Salaries and employee benefits	$525,000
Office rental, equipment, and supplies	$124,600
Expenses related to sales (travel, etc.)	$132,000
Advertising and other marketing communications	$450,000
Total fixed costs	**$1,231,600**

Sales of the two sizes of all S&S products are expected to be approximately equal; that is, half of sales will be for the 12-ounce size and half will be for the 20-ounce size. Thus, there will be an average contribution margin of $0.83 per bottle. Based on this, to achieve break-even, S&S Smoothie must sell

$$\frac{\$1,231,600}{.83} = 1,483,856$$

Again, assuming equal sales of the two sizes of products, the break-even point in dollars is $2,225,784.

PART FOUR

Promotion Strategies

In the past, S&S Smoothie has used mainly personal selling to promote its products to the trade channel. To support this effort, signage has been provided for the resellers to promote the product at the point of purchase. Posters and stand-alone table cards show appealing photographs of the product in the different flavors and communicate the brand name and the healthy benefits of the product. Similar signage will be developed for use by resellers who choose to stock the S&S Smoothie Gold and the Low-Carb Smoothies.

Selling has previously been handled by a team of over 75 manufacturers' agents who sell to resellers. In addition, in some geographic areas, an independent distributor does the selling. To support this personal selling approach, S&S Smoothie plans for additional promotional activities to introduce its new products and meet its other marketing objectives. These include the following:

1. *Television advertising:* S&S Smoothie will purchase a limited amount of relatively inexpensive and targeted cable channel advertising. A small number of commercials will be shown during prime-time programs with high viewer ratings by the target market. Television advertising can be an important means of not only creating awareness of the product, but also enhancing the image of the product. Indeed, consumers are prone to feel that if a product is advertised on prime-time TV, it must be a good product.

2. *Magazine advertising:* Because consumers in the target market are not avid magazine readers, magazine advertising will be limited and will supplement other promotion activities. During the next year, S&S Smoothie will experiment with limited magazine advertising in such titles as *Men's Health*. The company will also investigate the potential of advertising in university newspapers.

3. *Sponsorships:* S&S Smoothie will attempt to sponsor several marathons in major cities. The advantage of sponsorships is that they provide visibility for the product while at the same time showing that the company supports activities of interest to the target market.

4. *Digital Marketing:* S&S Smoothie will continue its use of social media to communicate with consumers and to monitor customers' postings about S&S products. In addition, S&S TV commercials will be available on the company Web site and on YouTube. In the latter part of the year, the company will sponsor a do-it-yourself ad competition through its Web site. The winning ads will be aired on cable TV.

5. *Sampling:* Sampling of S&S Smoothie beverages at select venues will provide an opportunity for prospective customers to become aware of the product and to taste the great flavors. Sampling will include only the two new products being introduced. Venues for sampling will include the following:
   a. Marathons
   b. Weight-lifting competitions
   c. Gymnastics meets
   d. Student unions located on select college campuses

Supply Chain Strategies

As noted earlier, S&S Smoothie distributes its beverages primarily through health clubs and gyms, and small, upscale specialty food stores. S&S Smoothie plans to expand its target reseller market to include the following:

1. Hotels and resorts in the United States and in targeted international markets

2. Golf and tennis clubs

3. College campuses

To increase leverage in larger health clubs, S&S Smoothie will offer free refrigerated display units. This will encourage the facility to maintain a high level of inventory of S&S Smoothie beverages.

Implementation

The action plan details the activities necessary to implement all marketing strategies. In addition, the action plan includes the timing for each item, the individual(s) responsible, and the budgetary requirements. Table A.4 shows an example of one objective (to increase distribution venues) and the action items S&S Smoothie will use to accomplish it.[2]

Table A.4 | Action Items to Accomplish Marketing Objective Regarding Supply Chain

Objective: Increase Distribution Venues

Action Items	Beginning Date	Ending Date	Responsible Party	Cost	Remarks
1. Identify key hotels and resorts, golf clubs, and tennis clubs where S&S Smoothies might be sold	July 1	September 1	Bill Sartens (consulting firm will be engaged to assist in this effort)	$25,000	Key to this strategy is to selectively choose resellers so that maximum results are obtained from sales activities. Because health club use is greater during the months of January to May, efforts will be timed to have product in stock no later than January 15.
2. Identify 25 key universities where S&S Smoothies might be sold	July 1	August 1	Bill Sartens	0	Information about colleges and universities and their health club facilities should be available on the university Web pages.
3. Make initial contact with larger hotel and resort chains	September 1	November 1	Bill Sartens	Travel: $10,000	
4. Make initial contact with larger individual (nonchain) facilities	September 1	November 1	Bill Sartens	Travel: $5,000	
5. Make initial contact with universities	August 15	September 15	Manufacturers' agents	0	Agents will be assigned to the 25 universities and required to make an initial contact and report back to Bill Sartens on promising prospects.
6. Follow up initial contacts with all potential resellers and obtain contracts for coming six months	September 15	Ongoing	Bill Sartens, manufacturers' agents	$10,000	$10,000 is budgeted for this item, although actual expenditures will be on an as-needed basis, as follow-up travel cannot be preplanned.

---

[2]Note that the final marketing plan should include objectives, action items, timing information, and budget information necessary to accomplish all marketing strategies. We have only one objective in this sample marketing plan.

Measurement and Control Strategies

A variety of activities will ensure effective measurement of the success of the marketing plan and allow the firm to make adjustments as necessary. These include targeted market research and trend analysis.

Research

Firms need continuous market research to understand brand awareness and brand attitudes among their target markets. S&S Smoothie will therefore continue its program of focus group research and descriptive studies of its target consumer and reseller markets.

Trend Analysis

S&S Smoothie will do a monthly trend analysis to examine sales by reseller type, geographic area, chain, agent, and distributor. These analyses will allow S&S Smoothie to take corrective action when necessary.

▶ Notes

CHAPTER 1

1. John W. Schouten, "Selves in Transition: Symbolic Consumption in Personal Rites of Passage and Identity Reconstruction," *Journal of Consumer Research*, March 17, 1991, 412–25; Michael R. Solomon, "The Wardrobe Consultant: Exploring the Role of a New Retailing Partner," *Journal of Retailing* 63 (1987): 110–28; Michael R. Solomon and Susan P. Douglas, "Diversity in Product Symbolism: The Case of Female Executive Clothing," *Psychology & Marketing* 4 (1987): 189–212; Joseph Z. Wisenblit, "Person Positioning: Empirical Evidence and a New Paradigm," *Journal of Professional Services Marketing* 4, no. 2 (1989): 51–82.

2. "Marketing Definitions," MarketingPower.com, http://www.marketingpower.com/AboutAMA/Pages/DefinitionofMarketing.aspx (accessed September 19, 2008).

3. Michael R. Solomon, "Deep-Seated Materialism: The Case of Levi's 501 Jeans," in *Advances in Consumer Research*, ed. Richard Lutz (Las Vegas, NV.: Association for Consumer Research, 1986), 13: 619–22.

4. Sheila Shayon, "Break Me Off a Piece of That WASABI Kit-Kat Bar!" *Brandchannel* (March 8, 2010), http://www.brandchannel.com/home/post/2010/03/08/Break-Me-Off-A-Piece-Of-That-WASABI-Kit-Kat-Bar!.aspx, (accessed June 8, 2010).

5. Peter F. Drucker, *Management: Tasks, Responsibilities, Practices* (New York: Harper & Row, 1972), 64–65.

6. Jenna Wortham, "A Netflix Model for Haute Couture," *The New York Times* (November 8, 2009), http://www.nytimes.com/2009/11/09/technology/09runway.html, (accessed August 17, 2010).

7. "Henry Ford and the Model T," in *Forbes Greatest Business Stories* (New York: Wiley, 1996), www.wiley.com/legacy/products/subject/business/forbes/ford.html.

8. Theodore Levitt, "Marketing Myopia," *Harvard Business Review*, July–August 1960, 45–56.

9. Rahul Jacob, "How to Retread Customers," *Fortune*, Autumn/Winter 1993, 23–24; http://www.directtire.com, (accessed June 7, 2010).

10. Ian Mount, "Rise of the Instapreneur," *Wired*, December 2007, 129; http://www.spreadshirt.com/create-your-own-t-shirt-C59, (accessed June 7, 2010).

11. Paula D. Englis, Basil G. Englis, Michael R. Solomon, and Aard Groen, "Strategic Sustainability and Triple Bottom Line Performance in Textiles: Implications of the Eco-Label for the EU and Beyond," Business as an Agent of World Benefit Conference, United Nations and the Academy of Management, Cleveland, OH, 2006.

12. Stephanie Rosenbloom, "Walmart Unveils Plan to Make Supply Chain Greener," *New York Times* (February 25, 2010), http://www.nytimes.com/2010/02/26/business/energy-environment/26walmart.html, (accessed June 8, 2010).

13. Sarah Mahone, "Yahoo Is Latest Brand to Join Random Acts," *Marketing Daily* (December 23, 2009), http://www.mediapost.com/publications/?fa=Articles.printEdition&art_send_date=2009-12-23&art_type=16, (accessed June 8, 2010).

14. Cf. M. K. Khoo, S.G. Lee, and S.W. Lye, "A Design Methodology for the Strategic Assessment of a Product's Eco-Efficiency," *International Journal of Production Research* 39 (2001): 245–74; C. Chen, "Design for the Environment: A Quality-Based Model for Green Product Development," *Management Science* 47, no. 2 (2001): 250–64; McDonough Braungart Design, *Chemistry's Design Paradigm*, (retrieved April 15, 2006), from http://www.mbdc.com/c2c_home.htm; Elizabeth Corcoran, "Thinking Green," *Scientific American* 267, no. 6 (1992): 44–46; Amitai Etzioni, "The Good Society: Goals Beyond Money," *The Futurist* (2001): 68–69; M. H. Olson, "Charting a Course for Sustainability," *Environment* 38, no. 4 (1996): 10–23.

15. Sindya N. Bhanoo, "Those Earth-Friendly Products? Turns Out They're Profit-Friendly as Well," *New York Times* (June 12, 2010), B3.

16. Gail Nickel-Kailing, "Green Marketing: What Works, What Doesn't," WhatTheyThink.com, January 22, 2010, http://blogs.whattheythink.com/going-green/2010/01/green-marketing-what-works-what-doesn%E2%80%99t (accessed May 4, 2010).

17. Jeff Lowe, *The Marketing Dashboard: Measuring Marketing Effectiveness* (Venture Communications, February 2003), www.brandchannel.com/images/papers/dashboard.pdf; G. A. Wyner, "Scorecards and More: The Value Is in How You Use Them," *Marketing Research*, Summer, 6–7; C. F. Lundby and C. Rasinowich, "The Missing Link: Cause and Effect Linkages Make Marketing Scorecards More Valuable," *Marketing Research*, Winter 2003, 14–19.

18. Sal Randazzo, "Advertising as Myth-Maker; Brands as Gods and Heroes," *Advertising Age*, November 8, 1993, 32.

19. Lee D. Dahringer, "Marketing Services Internationally: Barriers and Management Strategies," *Journal of Service Marketing* 5 (1991): 5–17.

20. Jesse McKinley, "Don't Call It 'Pot' in This Circle; It's a Profession," *New York Times* (April 23, 2010), http://www.nytimes.com/2010/04/24/us/24pot.html, (accessed June 8, 2010).

21. Quoted in Sarah Varney, "Calif. Pot Movement Adopts Glossier Approach," *NPR* (June 10, 2010), http://www.npr.org/templates/story/story.php?storyId=127727563&ft=1&f=1006, (accessed June 10, 2010).

22. Stuart Elliott, "Introducing Kentucky, the Brand," *New York Times Online* (June 9, 2004), www.nyt.com.

23. Jennifer Wright, "Russia's News Agency Allegedly Looking to Rebrand Stalin," *Brandchannel* (November 9, 2009), http://www.brandchannel.com/home/post/2009/11/09/Russias-News-Agency-Allegedly-Looking-To-Rebrand-Stalin.aspx, (accessed June 8, 2010).

24. http://nakedjen.blogs.com/, (accessed June 7, 2010).

25. Clive Thompson, "Almost Famous," *Wired*, December 2007, 84.

26. http://www.harley-davidson.com/en_US/Content/Pages/Events/Sturgis.html, (accessed June 8, 2010).

27. Caroline McCarthy, "Delete 10 Facebook Friends, Get a Free Whopper," *CNet* (January 8, 2009), http://news.cnet.com/delete-10-facebook-friends-get-a-free-whopper/, (accessed June 8, 2010).

28. Michael E. Porter, *Competitive Advantage: Creating and Sustaining Superior Performance* (New York: Free Press, 1985).

29. Karlene Lukovitz, "Ghirardelli Streams User Content in Times Square," *Marketing Daily* (March 9, 2010), http://www.mediapost.com/publications/index.cfm?fa=Articles.showArticle&art_aid=123852, (accessed June 8, 2010).

30. Mark Penn, "Microtrends: On the Web, Amateurs Rivaling Professionals," *Wall Street Journal* (October 28, 2009), http://online.wsj.com/article/SB125668986047512001.html, (accessed June 8, 2010).

31. James Yang, "Here's an Idea: Let Everyone Have Ideas," *New York Times* (March 30, 2006).

32. Some material adapted from a presentation by Matt Leavey, Prentice Hall Business Publishing, July 18, 2007.

33. This section adapted from Michael R. Solomon, *Consumer Behavior: Buying, Having and Being*, 8th ed. (Upper Saddle River, NJ: Pearson Education, 2008).

34. Jeff Surowiecki, *The Wisdom of Crowds* (New York: Anchor, 2005); Jeff Howe, "The Rise of Crowdsourcing," *Wired* (June 2006), http://www.wired.com/wired/archive/14.06/crowds.html, (accessed October 3, 2007).

35. Kunur Patel, "That Coke Can You're Holding Could Be Your New Media Channel: StickyBits App Lets Users 'Check In' to Objects Via

Barcodes," *Advertising Age* (April 28, 2010), http://adage.com/digital/article?article_id=143566, (accessed June 8, 2010).

36. Tom Espiner, "IE Slips Further as Firefox, Safari, Chrome Gain," *CNET* (February 2, 2009), http://news.cnet.com/8301-1023_3-10154447-93.html, (accessed June 8, 2010).

37. Joseph Rhee, Asa Eslocker and Mark Schone, "Former Toyota Lawyer Tells ABC News Automaker Hides Safety Problems," (February 10, 2010), *ABC News*, http://abcnews.go.com/Blotter/exclusive-toyota-lawyer-tells-abc-news-automaker-hides/story?id=9751262, (accessed June 8, 2010); Rich Blake, Boycotting BP: Who Gets Hurt?," (June 2, 2010), *ABC News*, http://abcnews.go.com/Business/bp-boycotts-spreading-frustration-oil-spill-boils/story?id=10800309, (accessed June 8, 2010).

38. Larry Edwards, "The Decision Was Easy," *Advertising Age*, August 26, 1987, 106. For research and discussion related to public policy issues, see Paul N. Bloom and Stephen A. Greyser, "The Maturing of Consumerism," *Harvard Business Review*, November/December 1981, 130–39; George S. Day, "Assessing the Effect of Information Disclosure Requirements," *Journal of Marketing*, April 1976, 42–52; Dennis E. Garrett, "The Effectiveness of Marketing Policy Boycotts: Environmental Opposition to Marketing," *Journal of Marketing* 51 (January 1987): 44–53; Michael Houston and Michael Rothschild, "Policy-Related Experiments on Information Provision: A Normative Model and Explication," *Journal of Marketing Research* 17 (November 1980): 432–49; Jacob Jacoby, Wayne D. Hoyer, and David A. Sheluga, *Misperception of Televised Communications* (New York: American Association of Advertising Agencies, 1980); Gene R. Laczniak and Patrick E. Murphy, *Marketing Ethics: Guidelines for Managers* (Lexington, MA: Lexington Books, 1985): 117–23; Lynn Phillips and Bobby Calder, "Evaluating Consumer Protection Laws: Promising Methods," *Journal of Consumer Affairs* 14 (Summer 1980): 9–36; Donald P. Robin and Eric Reidenbach, "Social Responsibility, Ethics, and Marketing Strategy: Closing the Gap between Concept and Application," *Journal of Marketing* 51 (January 1987): 44–58; Howard Schutz and Marianne Casey, "Consumer Perceptions of Advertising as Misleading," *Journal of Consumer Affairs* 15 (Winter 1981): 340–57; and Darlene Brannigan Smith and Paul N. Bloom, "Is Consumerism Dead or Alive? Some New Evidence," in *Advances in Consumer Research*, ed. Thomas C. Kinnear (Provo, UT: Association for Consumer Research, 1984): 569–73.

39. This section adapted from Michael R. Solomon, *Consumer Behavior: Buying, Having and Being*, 8th ed. (Upper Saddle River, NJ: Pearson Education, 2008).

40. William Leiss, Stephen Kline, and Sut Jhally, *Social Communication in Advertising: Persons, Products, and Images of Well-Being* (Toronto: Methuen, 1986); Jerry Mander, *Four Arguments for the Elimination of Television* (New York: William Morrow, 1977).

41. William Leiss, Stephen Kline, and Sut Jhally, *Social Communication in Advertising: Persons, Products, and Images of Well-Being* (Toronto: Methuen, 1986).

42. Quoted in Leiss et al., *Social Communication*, 11 (Toronto: Methuen, 1986).

43. Parts of this section are adapted from Michael R. Solomon, *Consumer Behavior: Buying, Having, and Being*, 7th ed. (Upper Saddle River, NJ: Prentice Hall, 2007).

44. Thomas C. O'Guinn and Ronald J. Faber, "Compulsive Buying: A Phenomenological Explanation," *Journal of Consumer Research* 16 (September 1989): 154.

45. Associated Press, "Center Tries to Treat Web Addicts," *New York Times* (September 5, 2009), http://www.nytimes.com/2009/09/06/us/06internet.html, (accessed June 8, 2010); Samantha Manas, "Addicted to Chapstick: The World of Chapstick Addicts Revealed," *Associated Content* (July 5, 2006), http://www.associatedcontent.com/article/41148/addicted_to_chapstick.html (accessed May 13, 2008).

46. "Advertisers Face Up to the New Morality: Making the Pitch," *Bloomberg* (July 8, 1997).

47. Gerry Khermouch, "Virgin's 'Va Va' Bottle Has 'Voom'; First Ads via Long Haymes Carr," *Brandweek*, July 10, 2000, 13.

48. Michael McCarthy, "Adidas Puts Computer on New Footing," *USA Today.com* (March 3, 2005): http://www.usatoday.com/money/industries/2005-03-02-smart-usat_x.htm (accessed May 13, 2008).

49. http://green.yahoo.com/pledge/, (accessed August 30, 2010).

50. http://www.carbonfootprint.com/carbonfootprint.html, (accessed August 30, 2010).

CHAPTER 2

1. Claudia Parsons, "From Madoff to Merrill Lynch: Where Was the Ethics Officer," *New York Times Online*, December 9, 2009 (accessed January 25, 2010).

2. "Dow Chemical Company Code of Business Conduct," Dow, http://www.dow.com/about/aboutdow/code_conduct/ethics_conduct.htm (accessed January 12, 2010).

3. MADD Mission Statement, http://www.madd.org/About-Us/About-Us/Mission-Statement.aspx (accessed January 14, 2010).

4. "About Xerox," Xerox, http://www.xerox.com/about-xerox/enus.html (accessed January 20, 2010).

5. A.G. Lafley and Ram Charan, *The Game Changer* (New York: Crown Business, 2008).

6. "Cheerios and Cholesterol," Cheerios, http://www.cheerios.com/ourcereals/cheerios/cheeriosandcholesterol.aspx (accessed January 19, 2010); "About Quaker," Quaker, http://www.quakeroats.com/about-quaker-oats/content/quaker-history.aspx#yr15 (accessed January 19, 2010).

7. Anath Hartman, "Senior Citizens Wowed by Nintendo's Wii," *Gazette.Net*, December 20, 2007, http://www.gazette.net/stories/122007/laurnew142319_32358.shtml (accessed December 29, 2007).

8. Michael Arndt, "McDonald's 24/7," *BusinessWeek*, February 5, 2007, 64–72.

9. American Airlines Wine Selection, http://www.aa.com/intl/cn/aboutUs_en/pr20090803.jsp (accessed January 20, 2010).

10. Gordon A. Wyner, "Beyond ROI: Make Sure the Analytics Address Strategic Issues," *Marketing Management* 15 (May/June 2006): 8–9.

11. Tim Ambler, "Don't Cave In to Cave Dwellers," *Marketing Management*, September/October 2006, 25–29.

12. "What Else Can Social Media Do for Your Campaign?" www.marketingvox.com/what-else-can-social-marketing-do-for-your-campaign?, January 7, 2010 (accessed February 2, 2010).

CHAPTER 3

1. Carol Matlack, "Auchan: Walmart's Tough New Global Rival," *BusinessWeek*, October 23, 2009, at http://www.businessweek.com/globalbiz/content/oct2009/gb20091023_414708.htm (accessed January 18, 2010).

2. World Trade Organization, "International Trade Statistics 2010," http://www.wto.org/english/res_e/booksp_e/anrep_e/world_trade_report10_e.pdf (accessed August 26, 2010).

3. The Associated Press, "Walmart Pulling Jewelry Cited in AP Cadmium Report," *New York Times*, January 11, 2010, http://www.nytimes.com/aponline/2010/01/11/health/AP-US-Cadmium-Jewelry.html?pagewanted=2&sq=unsafe%20products&st=cse&scp=1 (accessed January 22, 2009).

4. Mark Bursa, "China Automotive Market Review: Management Briefing: Major Developments at Other Chinese automakers," *Just-Auto*, October 2007, 20–23.

5. "Chinese Automaker Coming to the U.S.," MSN.com, http://autos.msn.com/as/article.aspx?xml=Geely&shw=autoshow2006 (accessed May 15, 2008).

6. World Trade Organization, "The WTO in Brief," 2009, http://www.wto.org/english/res_e/doload_e/inbr_e.pdf (accessed January 24, 2010).

7. David Nowak, Associated Press, "Microsoft: Pirated Software Still Sold in Russia," MSNBC.com, February 8, 2010, http://www.msnbc.msn.com/id/35298730/ns/technology_and_science-security/ (accessed February 12, 2010).

8. Roberta Rampton, "Russia Cuts U.S. Poultry, Pork 2010 Import Quotas," *Reuters*, Dec. 18, 2009, http://www.reuters.com/article/idUSTRE5BH4LR20091219 (accessed 1/24/2010).

9. **The Associated Press, "WTO Panel to Look into US Tariffs on Chinese Tires," *The New York Times*, January 11, 2010,** http://www.nytimes.com/aponline/2010/01/11/business/AP-EU-WTO-US-China.html?_r=1&scp=1&sq=tariffs&st=cse (accessed January 24, 2010).

10. "The Big Mac Index, Taste and See, Burgernomics Shows the Chinese Yuan Is Still Undervalued," Economist.Com, http://www.economist.com/daily/chartgallery/displaystory.cfm?story_id=15210330 (accessed January 24, 2010).

11. International Trade Center UNCTAD/WTO, "Successful Exporters from LDCs Beat the Odds," ITC News Release, May 2001, http://www.intracen.org/DocMan/PRSR1534.htm (accessed February 12, 2010).

12. Julia Bonstein, "European Firms Eye Developing World," *BusinessWeek*, January 16, 2008, http://www.businessweek.com/globalbiz/content/jan2008/gb20080116_886509.htm (accessed January 24, 2010).

13. G8 Information Center, "What Is the G8?" http://www.g7.utoronto.ca/what_is_g8.html (accessed February 12, 2010).

14. "Corporate Facts: Walmart by the Numbers," Walmart, http://walmartstores.com/FactsNews/FactSheets/#CorporateFacts (accessed January 24, 2010).

15. EB Eggs, "About Eggland's Best," http://www.egglandsbest.com/egglands-eggs/why-egglands/about-us.aspx (accessed January 24, 2010).

16. Jason Leow and Jane Zhang, "Product-Safety Pacts Put Greater Burden on Beijing," *Wall Street Journal*, December 12, 2007, A13.

17. The Associated Press, "China Executes Two for Role in Tainted Milk Scandal," USA Today, November 24, 2009, http://www.usatoday.com/news/world/2009-11-24-china-taintedmilk-deaths_N.htm (accessed February 12, 2010).

18. "United States: Tightening a Loose Noose; Iran," *The Economist*, November 3, 2007, 57.

19. Helene Cooper and Mark Landler, "U.S. Eyes New Sanctions over Iran Nuclear Program," *New York Times*, February 9, 2010, http://www.nytimes.com/2010/02/10/world/middleeast/10sanctions.html?scp=4&sq=iran%20nuclear%20program&st=cse (accessed February 12, 2010).

20. Peter Ford, "China Yanks 'Avatar' for Homegrown Film," *Christian Science Monitor*, January 19, 2010, http://www.csmonitor.com/World/Asia-Pacific/2010/0119/China-yanks-Avatar-for-homegrown-film (accessed February 1, 2010).

21. Thomas L. Friedman, "U.S. Prods Indonesia on Rights," *New York Times*, January 18, 1994, D1(2).

22. Amy Merrick, "Gap Offers Unusual Look at Factory Conditions," *Wall Street Journal–Eastern Edition*, May 12, 2004, A1–A12.

23. "Gap: Report of Kids' Sweatshop 'Deeply Disturbing,'" *CNN.com*, http://www.cnn.com/2007/WORLD/asiapcf/10/29/gap.labor/index.html (accessed January 10, 2008); Amelia Gentleman, "Gap Campaigns Against Child Labor," *New York Times*, November 16, 2007, http://www.nytimes.com/2007/11/16/business/worldbusiness/16gap.html (accessed Jan 10, 2008).

24. Tim McKeough, "A Stylish Way to Help the Homeless," *New York Times*, September 9, 2009, http://www.nytimes.com/2009/09/10/garden/10open.html?_r=1 (accessed February 1, 2010).

25. David Carr, "Romance, in *Cosmo's* World, Is Translated in Many Ways," May 26, 2002, *New York Times*, sec. 1, 1, adapted from Michael R. Solomon, *Consumer Behavior: Buying, Having, and Being*, 6th ed. (Upper Saddle River, NJ: Prentice Hall, 2003).

26. Richard W. Pollay, "Measuring the Cultural Values Manifest in Advertising," *Current Issues and Research in Advertising* 6 (1983): 71–92.

27. Deborah Ball, "Women in Italy Like to Clean but Shun the Quick and Easy," *Wall Street Journal*, April 25, 2006, A1.

28. Daniel Goleman, "The Group and the Self: New Focus on a Cultural Rift," December 25, 1990, *New York Times Online*, http://query.nytimes.com/gst/fullpage.html?res=9C0CE3DD1330F936A15751C1A966958260&scp=1&sq=The+Group+and+the+Self%3A+New+Focus+on+a+Cultural+Rift&st=nyt, 37; Harry C. Triandis, "The Self and Social Behavior in Differing Cultural Contexts," *Psychological Review* 96 (July 1989): 506; Harry C. Triandis et al., "Individualism and Collectivism: Cross-Cultural Perspectives on Self-Ingroup Relationships," *Journal of Personality and Social Psychology* 54 (February 1988): 323.

29. Adapted from Michael R. Solomon, *Consumer Behavior: Buying, Having, and Being*, 7th ed. (Upper Saddle River, NJ: Prentice Hall, 2007).

30. "Foreign Corrupt Practices Act of 1977 (As Amended)," U.S. Department of Justice, http://www.usdoj.gov/usao/eousa/foia_reading_room/usam/title9/47mcrm.htm (accessed May 15, 2008).

31. Tom Gilbert, "An 'Idol' by Any Other Name," *Television Week*, May 29, 2006, 2.

32. Aric Chen, "Li Ning and Ziba Design Want to Build China's First Truly Global Brand," Fastcompany.com, October, 2009, http://www.fastcompany.com/magazine/139/retail-therapy-li-ning-and-ziba-design.html (accessed January 31 2010).

33. McDonald's Corporation, "About McDonald's," www.mcdonalds.com/corp/about.html (accessed May 15, 2008).

34. Saritha Rai, "Tastes of India in U.S. Wrappers," *New York Times*, April 29, 2003, http://query.nytimes.com/gst/fullpage.html?res=9C03E6D6133DF93AA15757C0A9659C8B63.

35. John Tozzi, "Is It Time to Buy a Franchise?" *BusinessWeek*, March 10, 2008, http://www.businessweek.com/smallbiz/content/mar2008/sb2008036_478890_page_2.htm (accessed February 12, 2010).

36. Douglas McIntyre, "GM Forecasts 2 Million Car Sales in China This Year," *DailyFinance*, http://www.dailyfinance.com/story/company-news/gm-forecasts-2-million-car-sales-in-china-this-year/19329149/ (accessed February 1, 2010).

37. Catherine McColl, "Saris and Levi's—the Indo-Western Youth Trend," Canvas8.com, August 4, 2009, http://docs.google.com/viewer?a=v&pid=sites&srcid=cGVhcnNvbi5jb218cmVhbC1wZW9wbGUtcmVhbC1jb2xsYWJvcmF0aW9ufGd4OjM0MWQxZDExNTUwOTAyZTk (accessed January 31, 2010).

38. Jim Thompson, "Twenty Years Later: What McDonald's in Russia Says About the Brand's Future," *Brandchannel.com*, February 1, 2010, http://www.brandchannel.com/home/post/2010/02/01/Twenty-Years-Later-What-McDonalds-In-Russia-Says-About-The-Brands-Future.aspx (accessed February 1, 2010.)

39. Brian Stelter, "Betting the Situation Will Not Get Lost in Translation," *New York Times* (March 22, 2010).

40. Richard C. Morais, "The Color of Beauty," *Forbes*, November 27, 2000, 170–76.

41. Catherine McColl, "Saris and Levi's."

42. Valentina Vescovi and Aixa Rocca, "In Argentina, Pepsi Becomes 'Pecsi'," *Advertising Age*, July 15, 2009.

43. Julie Jargon, "Kraft Reformulates Oreo, Scores in China," *Wall Street Journal* (May 1, 2008), http://online.wsj.com/article/SB120958152962857053.html, (accessed September 1, 2010).

44. Catherine McColl, "Saris and Levi's."

45. International Energy Agency, "Access to Electricity," World Energy Outlook, 2009, http://www.iea.org/weo/electricity.asp (accessed February 16, 2010).

46. Aaron O. Patrick, "World Cup's Advertisers Hope One Size Fits All: Month-Long Tournament Sets Off Scramble to Reach Huge Global TV Audience," *Wall Street Journal*, March 28, 2006: B7.

47. Natalie Zmuda, "Coke Set to Reveal 'Open Happiness' Campaign," *Advertising Age*, January 14, 2009, http://adage.com/article?article_id=133781 (accessed February 16, 2010); Natalie Zmuda, "Sprite Launches 'The Spark,' Its First Global Ad Campaign," *Advertising Age*, February 11, 2010, http://adage.com/article?article_id=142073 (accessed February 16, 2010).

48. Reuters, "U.S. Steelmakers File China Dumping Complaint," April 9, 2009, http://www.reuters.com/article/idUSPEK34053520090409 (accessed February 1, 2010).

49. Bloomberg News, "China to Tax Some Imports from U.S. and Russia," *New York Times*, December 10, 2009, http://www.nytimes.com/2009/12/11/business/global/11steel.html?scp=1&sq=chinese%20dumping%20steel&st=cse (accessed February 12, 2010).

50. Choe Sang-Hun, "Walmart Selling Stores and Leaving South Korea,"*New York Times Online*, May 23, 2006.

51. Jennifer Corbett Dooren, "Alcohol Ads Impact Consumption among the Young, Study Shows," *Wall Street Journal*, January 2, 2006.

52. Quoted in Rob Walker, "McDonald's: When a Brand Becomes a Stand-In for a Nation," *New York Times Online*, March 30, 2003, http://query.nytimes.com/gst/fullpage.html?res=9E01E5D81639F933A05750C0A9659C8B63&scp=1&sq=When%20a%20brand%20becomes%20a%20stand%20%20in%20for%20a%20nation&st=cse.

CHAPTER 4

1. Alan J. Greco and Jack T. Hogue, "Developing Marketing Decision Support Systems in Consumer Goods Firms," *Journal of Consumer Marketing* 7 (1990): 55–64.

2. "The Simply Everything Plan," Sprint.com, http://www.sprintspecialoffers.com/everything/?id12=UHP_Masthead_040708_SimplyEverything (accessed February 8, 2010).

3. Marketing Evaluations Inc., "The Q Scores Company," www.qscores.com (accessed February 8, 2010).

4. Pan-Ning Tan, Michael Steinbach, and Vipin Kumar, *Introduction to Data Mining* (New York: Addison Wesley, 2005).

5. Catherine Holahan, "Battling Data Monsters at Yahoo!" *BusinessWeek*, 14 December 2007, www.businessweek.com/technology/content/dec2007/tc20071213_341756.htm?chan=search (accessed February 8, 2010); Catherine Holahan, "Facebook: Marketers Are Your 'Friends,'" *BusinessWeek*, 7 November 2007, www.businessweek.com/technology/content/nov2007/tc20071116_289111.htm?chan=search (accessed February 8, 2010).

6. Arik Hesseldahl, "A Rich Vein for 'Reality Mining'," *BusinessWeek* Online, April 24, 2008 (accessed February 25, 2010).

7. Tan et al., *Introduction to Data Mining*.

8. Nate Nead, "Customer Acquisition vs. Retention," 9 November 2009, http://www.digitalsignage.com/blog/2009/11/09/signage-customer-acquisition-vs-retention/ (accessed February 7, 2010).

9. Robert Nelson, "Sprint May Cancel Your Service If You Call Customer Service Too Often," 6 July 2007, http://www.gadgetell.com/tech/comment/sprint-may-cancel-your-service-if-you-call-customer-service-to-often/ (accessed February 7, 2010); Samar Srivasta, "Sprint Drops Clients Over Excessive Inquiries" 7 July 2007, *Wall Street Journal*, http://online.wsj.com/public/article_print/SB118376389957059668-IpRTFYVQbLGbXKvlbPELi83M_8A_20080710 .html (accessed February 7, 2010).

10. Hamilton Nolan, "Mercedes Launches PR Push," *PR Week*, February 6, 2006, 3.

11. http://www.smrb.com/web/guest/core-solutions/national-consumer-study (accessed March 1, 2010).

12. Michael R. Solomon, *Conquering Consumerspace: Marketing Strategies for a Branded World* (New York: AMACOM Books, 2003).

13. Emily Steel, "The New Focus Groups: Online Networks," *The Wall Street Journal*, January 28, 2009, B6.

14. Matt Richtel, "The Parable of the Beer and Diapers," *TheRegister.com*, August 15, 2006, http://www.theregister.co.uk/2006/08/15/beer_diapers/ (accessed February 10, 2010).

15. World Business Academy, "'Spellcasters': The Hunt for the 'Buy-Button' in Your Brain," *Truthout.org*, January 22, 2010, http://www.truthout.org/spellcasters-the-hunt-buy-button-your-brain56278 (accessed February 8, 2010).

16. Direct Marketing Association, "Where Marketers Can Obtain State Do-Not-Call Lists," www.the-dma.org/government/donotcalllists.shtml (accessed February 7, 2010).

17. The Praxi Group, Inc., "Research Overview: Telephone versus Online Research—Advantages and Pitfalls," *praxigroup.net* (Fall 2007), http://www.praxigroup.net/TPG%20Phone%20Versus%20Online%20WP.pdf (accessed February 7, 2010).

18. Basil G. Englis and Michael R. Solomon, "Life/Style OnLine ©: A Web-Based Methodology for Visually-Oriented Consumer Research," *Journal of Interactive Marketing* 14:1 (2000): 2–14; Basil G. Englis, Michael R. Solomon, and Paula D. Harveston, "Web-Based, Visually Oriented Consumer Research Tools," *Online Consumer Psychology: Understanding and Influencing Consumer Behavior in the Virtual World*, ed. Curt Haugtvedt, Karen Machleit, and Richard Yalch (Hillsdale, NJ: Lawrence Erlbaum Associates, 2005).

19. "Nielsen Begins Largest Ever Expansion of Its National U.S. Television Ratings Panel," http://en-us.nielsen.com/main/news/news_releases/2007/september/Nielsen_Begins_Largest_Ever_Expansion_of_Its_National_U_S__Television_Ratings_Panel, September 26, 2007 (accessed March 2, 2010).

20. Tim Callahan, "Building on Success to Deliver Better Insights," http://us.acnielsen.com/pubs/2004_q4_ci_building.shtml (accessed June 10, 2008).

21. Brian Steinberg, "Olympics Give NBC Universal First Crack at Cross-Media Metric: Network to Provide Data on Audiences across All Screens," *Advertising Age Online*, August 14, 2008, http://adage.com/mediaworks/article?article_id=130314 (accessed February 26, 2010).

22. Steven Baker, "The Web Knows What You Want," BusinessWeek Online, August 5, 2009, businessweek.com/.../b414004848688... (accessed February 27, 2010).

23. Jack Neff, "Chasing the Cheaters That Undermine Online Research," *Advertising Age*, March 31, 2008, 12.

24. Bruce L. Stern and Ray Ashmun, "Methodological Disclosure: The Foundation for Effective Use of Survey Research," *Journal of Applied Business Research* 7 (1991): 77–82.

25. Michael E. Ross, "It Seemed Like a Good Idea at the Time," *MSNBC.com*, April 22, 2005, http://www.msnbc.msn.com/id/7209828/ (accessed February 8, 2010).

26. Gary Levin, "New Adventures in Children's Research," *Advertising Age*, August 9, 1993, 17.

27. 2009 Honomichl Top 50 Report, *Marketing News*, June 30, 2009, http://www.marketingpower.com/ResourceLibrary/Publications/MarketingNews/2009/43/6_30_09/Hono%20full.pdf (accessed February 10, 2010).

CHAPTER 5

1. James R. Bettman, "The Decision Maker Who Came In from the Cold," Presidential Address, in *Advances in Consumer Research*, vol. 20, ed. Leigh McAllister and Michael Rothschild (Provo, UT: Association for Consumer Research, 1990); John W. Payne, James R. Bettman, and Eric J. Johnson, "Behavioral Decision Research: A Constructive Processing Perspective," *Annual Review of Psychology*

4 (1992): 87–131; for an overview of recent developments in individual choice models, see Robert J. Meyer and Barbara E. Kahn, "Probabilistic Models of Consumer Choice Behavior," in *Handbook of Consumer Behavior*, ed. Thomas S. Robertson and Harold H. Kassarjian (Englewood Cliffs, NJ: Prentice Hall, 1991), 85–123.

2. Richard Pérez-Peña, "Newspaper Guild Files Labor Complaint against Reuters over Compensation Cuts," *New York Times*, February 17, 2010, http://mediadecoder.blogs.nytimes.com/ (accessed February 4, 2010); Stephanie Clifford, "Cable Companies Target Commercials to Audience," *New York Times*, March 3, 2009, http://www.nytimes.com/2009/03/04/business/04cable.html?_r=1 (accessed February 4, 2010).

3. Amanda Mark, "Under Armour's Star Presence," *Multichannel Merchant News*, November 1, 2000 http://multichannelmerchant.com/news/marketing_armours_star_presence/ (accessed May 1, 2008).

4. Michael Lev, "No Hidden Meaning Here: Survey Sees Subliminal Ads," *New York Times*, May 3, 1991, D7.

5. "ABC Rejects KFC Commercial, Citing Subliminal Advertising," *The Wall Street Journal Interactive Edition*, March 2, 2006.

6. Stuart Elliott, "TV Commercials Adjust to a Shorter Attention Span," *New York Times Online*, April 8, 2005.

7. Robert M. McMath, "Image Counts," *American Demographics*, May 1998, 64.

8. Abraham H. Maslow, *Motivation and Personality*, 2nd ed. (New York: Harper & Row, 1970).

9. Robert A. Baron and Donn Byrne, *Social Psychology: Understanding Human Interaction*, 5th ed. (Boston: Allyn & Bacon, 1987).

10. Ryan Nakashima, "Disney to create lab to test ads for ABC, ESPN," *USA Today* May 12, 2008, http://www.usatoday.com/tech/products/2008-05-12-1465558386_x.htm (accessed February 24, 2010).

11. http://www.jfmvipclub.com/ jfm_styleguide.pdf (accessed February 24, 2010).

12. Benjamin D. Zablocki and Rosabeth Moss Kanter, "The Differentiation of Life-Styles," *Annual Review of Sociology* (1976): 269–97; Ben Detrick, "Skateboarding Rolls Out of the Suburbs," *New York Times*, November 11, 2007, http://www.nytimes.com/2007/11/11/fashion/11skaters.html?scp=1&sq=skateboarding&st=nyt (accessed February 10, 2008).

13. Andrea Chang, "Mattel Taps into Social Media Craze with Puppy Tweets," *Los Angeles Times*, February 11, 2010, http://articles.latimes.com/2010/feb/11/business/la-fi-puppy-tweets11-2010feb11 (accessed February 20, 2010).

14. Alfred S. Boote, "Psychographics: Mind over Matter," *American Demographics*, April 1980, 26–29; William D. Wells, "Psychographics: A Critical Review," *Journal of Marketing Research*, 12 (May 1975): 196–213.

15. Alan R. Hirsch, "Effects of Ambient Odors on Slot-Machine Usage in a Las Vegas Casino," *Psychology & Marketing* 12, no. 7 (October 1995): 585–94.

16. James Vlahos, "Scent and Sensibility," *New York Times*, September 9, 2007, http://query.nytimes.com/gst/fullpage.html?res=9D07EFDC1E3AF93AA3575AC0A9619C8B63&scp=1&sq=scent%20and%20sensibility&st=cse (accessed February 1, 2008).

17. Marianne Meyer, "Attention Shoppers!" *Marketing and Media Decisions* 23 (May 1988): 67.

18. GFK Group, "Many German Consumers Decide at the Supermarket Shelves," *Market Research world*, March 2009, http://www.marketresearchworld.net/index.php?option=com_content&task=view&id=2564&Itemid=77 (accessed February 21, 2010).

19. Eben Shapiro, "Need a Little Fantasy? A Bevy of New Companies Can Help," *New York Times*, March 10, 1991, F4.

20. Quoted in John P. Cortez, "Ads Head for Bathroom," *Advertising Age*, May 18, 1992, 24.

21. Kerry Capel, "The Arab World Wants Its MTV," *Business Week*, October 11, 2007, http://www.businessweek.com/globalbiz/content/oct2007/gb20071011_342851.htm.

22. Adapted from Michael R. Solomon, *Consumer Behavior: Buying, Having, and Being*, 9th ed.,(Upper Saddle River, NJ: Prentice Hall, 2010

23. Richard W. Pollay, "Measuring the Cultural Values Manifest in Advertising," *Current Issues and Research in Advertising* (1983): 71–92.

24. Emily Bryson York, "General Mills Targets Three Groups to Fuel Growth," *Advertising Age*, February 16, 2010, http://adage.com/article?article_id=142138 (accessed February 20, 2010).

25. Ben Berkon, "Coca-Cola Comes Clean about Going Green at Olympic Games," *BrandChannel*, February 1, 2010, http://www.brandchannel.com/home/post/2010/02/01/Coca-Cola-Comes-Clean-About-Going-Green-At-Olympic-Games.aspx (accessed February 3, 2010).

26. Stuart U. Rich and Subhash C. Jain, "Social Class and Life Cycle as Predictors of Behavior," *Journal of Marketing Research* 5 (February 1968): 41–49.

27. Nathan Kogan and Michael A. Wallach, "Risky Shift Phenomenon in Small Decision-Making Groups: A Test of the Information Exchange Hypothesis," *Journal of Experimental Social Psychology* 3 (January 1967): 75–84; Arch G. Woodside and M. Wayne DeLozier, "Effects of Word-of-Mouth Advertising on Consumer Risk Taking," *Journal of Advertising* (Fall 1976): 12–19.

28. Carlo Dellaverson, "Tailgating: It's Bigger Business Than You Think," CNBC.com, December 21, 2006, http://www.cnbc.com/id/16315025/for/cnbc (accessed May 6, 2008).

29. Everett M. Rogers, *Diffusion of Innovations*, 3rd ed. (New York: Free Press, 1983).

30. Kathleen Debevec and Easwar Iyer, "Sex Roles and Consumer Perceptions of Promotions, Products, and Self: What Do We Know and Where Should We Be Headed," in *Advances in Consumer Research*, vol. 13, ed. Richard J. Lutz (Provo, UT: Association for Consumer Research, 1986), 210–14; Lynn J. Jaffe and Paul D. Berger, "Impact on Purchase Intent of Sex-Role Identity and Product Positioning," *Psychology & Marketing* (Fall 1988): 259–271.

31. Jennie Yabroff, "Girls Going Mild(er): A New 'Modesty Movement' Aims to Teach Young Women They Don't Have to Be Bad, or Semiclad," *Newsweek* (July 23, 2007), http://boards.youthnoise.com/eve/forums/a/tpc/f/573295355/m/38310644 (accessed July 18, 2007).

32. Vivian Manning-Schaffel, "Metrosexuals: A Well-Groomed Market?" brandchannel.com, http://brandchannel.com/features_effect.asp?pf_id=315 (accessed May 22, 2006).

33. Diego Rinallo, "Metro/Fashion/Tribes of Men: Negotiating the Boundaries of Men's Legitimate Consumption" in B. Cova, R. Kozinets, and A. Shankar, eds., *Consumer Tribes: Theory, Practice and Prospects* (Burlington, MA: Elsevier/Butterworth-Heinemann, 2007); Susan Kaiser, Michael R. Solomon, Janet Hethorn, Basil Englis, Van Dyk Lewis, and Wi-Suk Kwon, "Menswear, Fashion, and Subjectivity," paper presented in Special Session: Susan Kaiser, Michael Solomon, Janet Hethorn, and Basil Englis (Chairs), "What Do Men Want? Media Representations, Subjectivity, and Consumption," at the ACR Gender Conference, Edinburgh, Scotland, June 2006.

34. Catharine Skipp and Arian Campo-Flores, "Looks: A Manly Comeback," *Newsweek* (August 20, 2007), http://services.newsweek.com/search.aspx?offset=0&pageSize=10&sortField=pubdatetime&sortDirection=descending&mode=summary&q=Looks%2C+a+manly+comeback (accessed August 17, 2007).

35. "National Poll Reveals the Emergence of a 'New Man,'" Miller Brewing Co., PR Newswire, http://goliath.ecnext.com/coms2/summary_0199-5364500_ITM (accessed May 14, 2008).

CHAPTER 6

1. http://www.boeing.com/commercial/prices/ (accessed March 10, 2010).
2. F. Robert Dwyer and John F. Tanner, *Business Marketing: Connecting Strategy, Relationships, and Learning* (Boston: McGraw-Hill, 2008); Edward F. Fern and James R. Brown, "The Industrial/Consumer Marketing Dichotomy: A Case of Insufficient Justification," *Journal of Marketing*, Spring 1984, 68–77.
3. Porche, "All Boxter Models," www.porsche.com/usa/models/boxster/ (accessed February 22, 2010).
4. U.S. Census Bureau, *The 2008 Statistical Abstract of the United States*; U.S. Census Bureau, "The 2008 Statistical Abstract," www.census.gov/compendia/statab/ (accessed February 22, 2010).
5. U.S. Census Bureau, "North America Industry Classification System (NAICS)," www.census.gov/eos/www/naics/ (accessed February 23, 2010).
6. Carol Krol, "Companies Use Fun and Games to Find Serious Business," *B to B*, December 10, 2007, www.btobonline.com/apps/pbcs.dll/article?AID=/20071210/FREE/71210001/1109/FREE&template=printart (accessed February 22, 2010); Andy Sernovits and Guy Kawasaki, *Word of Mouth Marketing: How Smart Companies Get People Talking* (New York: Kaplan Publishing, 2006).
7. Ben Hanna, "Audience Characteristics and Social Media Use," *B2B: The Magazine for Marketing Strategists Online*, btobonline.com/apps/pbcs.dll/article?, January 18, 2010 (accessed March 12, 2010).
8. Steve Fretzin, "Forget Facebook and Twitter . . . For B2B It's All About LinkedIn," *Enterprise Management Quarterly Online*, www.emqus.com/index.php?/emq/article/forget_facebook_and_twit, January 25, 2010 (accessed March 18, 2010); "B2B Goes 007," *Marketing Profs Articles*, www.marketingprofs.com/short-articles/1589/b2b-goes-007, January 21, 2010 (accessed March 18, 2010); Gavin O'Malley, "LinkedIn Debuts B2B Network," *Media Post's Online Media Daily*, www.mediapost.com/publications/?fa=Articles.san&s=93229&Nid=48626&p=407056, October 27, 2008 (accessed March 18, 2010).
9. April Joyner, "Nice Meeting Your Avatar: Industry Trade Shows Go Virtual," *INC* Online, http://www.inc.com/magazine/20090501/sales-and-marketing-nice-meeting-your-avatar.html, May 1, 2009 (accessed March 22, 2010).
10. Aflac, "Aflac for Business," www.aflac.com/business/default.aspx (accessed February 23, 2010).
11. Chris Lake, "10 Kickass Crowdsourcing Sites for Your Business," *Econsultancy Digital Marketers United*, http://econsultancy.com/blog/4355-10-kickass-crowdsourcing-sites-for-your-business, posted August 4, 2009 (accessed March 16, 2010).
12. Patrick LaPointe, *Marketing by the Dashboard Light: How to Get More Insight, Foresight, and Accountability from Your Marketing Investments*, (New York: ANA, 2005).

CHAPTER 7

1. Ellen Neuborne and Kathleen Kerwin, "Generation Y," *BusinessWeek Online* February 15, 1999, http://www.businessweek.com/1999/99_07/b3616001.htm (accessed May 23, 2008); David Browne, "Harry Potter Is Their Peter Pan," *The New York Times*, July 22, 2009, http://www.nytimes.com/2009/07/23/fashion/23nostalgia.html (accessed March 9, 2010).
2. "Converse's All-Star Image," *BusinessWeek Online*, April 25, 2008, www.businessweek.com/innovate/content/apr2008/id20080425_383266.htm?chan=search (accessed February 25, 2010).
3. Conway Lackman and John M. Lanasa, "Family Decision-Making Theory: An Overview and Assessment," *Psychology & Marketing* 10 (March/April 1993): 81–93.

4. Christopher Palmeri, "Holiday Hits: Music, Toys, and Games," *BusinessWeek Online*, December 19, 2007, www.businessweek.com/bwdaily/dnflash/content/dec2007/db20071218_252797.htm?chan=search (accessed February 18, 2010).
5. Mary Beth Grover, "Teenage Wasteland," *Forbes*, July 28, 1997, 44–45; Bloomberg News, "Adult Concerns Are Pinching Teen Spending," *Boston.com*, July 3, 2008, http://www.boston.com/business/articles/2008/07/03/adult_concerns_are_pinching_teen_spending/ (accessed March 9, 2010).
6. Amy Barrett, "To Reach the Unreachable Teen," *BusinessWeek*, September 18, 2000, 78–80.
7. Bruce Horovitz, "Gen Y: A Tough Crowd to Sell," *USA Today*, May 21, 2002, www.usatoday.com/money/covers/2002-04-22-geny.htm (accessed March 22, 2006); Tricia Ellis-Christensen, "What Is Generation Y?" *Wise Geek*, March 1, 2010, http://www.wisegeek.com/what-is-generation-y.htm (accessed March 9, 2010).
8. Alan Cohen, "Swimming against the Tide," *Fast Company*, January 2005, 80–84.
9. Sharon Jayson, "A Detailed Look at Millennials," *USA Today*, February 24, 2010, 10B.
10. Aaron Baar, "Ford Builds Buzz around Upcoming Fiesta," *MediaPost News*, February 20, 2009, http://www.mediapost.com/publications/?fa=Articles.showArticle&art_aid=100693 (accessed April 16, 2010).
11. Douglas Coupland, *Generation X: Tales for an Accelerated Culture* (New York: St. Martin's Press, 1991).
12. Quoted in Karen Lowry Miller, "You Just Can't Talk to These Kids," *BusinessWeek*, April 19, 1993, 104.
13. Robert Scally, "The Customer Connection: Gen X Grows Up, They're in Their 30s Now," *Discount Store News*, archived in *Bnet.com*, October 25, 1999, 38, http://findarticles.com/p/articles/mi_m3092/is_20_38/ai_57443548?tag=content;col1 (accessed June 25, 2008).
14. Scally, "The Customer Connection: Gen X Grows Up, They're in Their 30s Now"; Marshall Lager, "The Slackers' X-cellent Adventure," *DestinationCRM.com*, November 2008, http://www.destinationcrm.com/Articles/Editorial/Magazine-Features/The-Slackerse28099-X-cellent-Adventure-51406.aspx (accessed February 12, 2010).
15. U.S. Census Bureau, "Resident Population by Age and Sex 1980–2006," www.census.gov/compendia/statab/tables/08s0007.pdf (accessed March 31, 2008).
16. Jeffrey Zaslow, "Get Back to Where You Once Belonged," *Wall Street Journal Online*, January 20, 2010, http://online.wsj.com/article/SB10001424052748704561004575012964067490650.html (accessed April 26, 2010).
17. Jennifer Lawrence, "Gender-Specific Works for Diapers—Almost Too Well," *Advertising Age*, February 8, 1993, S–10; Rachel Perls, "Why Is Blue for Boys and Pink for Girls?" *Hue.com* March 16, 2007, http://hueconsulting.blogspot.com/2007/03/why-is-blue-for-boys-and-pink-for-girls.html (accessed March 1, 2010).
18. Michael Flocker, *The Metrosexual Guide to Style: A Handbook for the Modern Man* (Cambridge, MA: Da Capo Press, 2003); Lizzie Elzingre, "The Metrosexual Man," *Suite101.com*, May 22, 2009, http://mens-cosmetic-health.suite101.com/article.cfm/the_metrosexual_man (accessed March 1, 2010).
19. "Metrosexual," Urban Dictionary, www.urbandictionary.com/define.php?term=metrosexual (accessed March 11, 2010).
20. Sam Roberts, "More Men Marrying Wealthier Wives," *New York Times Online*, January 8, 2010, http://www.nytimes.com/2010/01/19/us/19marriage.html (accessed April 29, 2010).
21. "Glass Baby Bottles in Demand," *BrandPackaging.com*, June 1, 2008, www.brandpackaging.com/CDA/Articles/Trends_Next_Now/

BNP_GUID_9-5-2006_A_10000000000000352222 (accessed March 1, 2010).

22. Alex Williams, "What Women Want: More Horses," *New York Times Online*, wJune, www.nytimes.com/2005/06/12/fashion/sundaystyles/12cars.html?ex=1276228800&en=7ea4473d0aa65bb0&ei=5090&partner=rssuserland&emc=rss (accessed February 12, 2010).

23. "Water," Voss of Norway, www.vosswater.com (accessed March 12, 2010).

24. David Leonhardt and Geraldine Fabrikant, "Rise of the Super-Rich Hits a Sobering Wall," *New York Times Online*, August 20, 2009, http://www.nytimes.com/2009/08/21/business/economy/21inequality.html (accessed April 23, 2010).

25. Jack Neff, "Survey Finds the Rich Returning to Familiar Spending Habits," *Advertising Age Online*, September 15, 2009, http://adage.com/article?article_id=139009 (accessed April 14, 2010).

26. Michael E. Ross, "At Newsstands, Black Is Plentiful," *New York Times*, December 26, 1993, F6; "Listings of Weekly, Monthly and Quarterly African American Magazines," *BlackNews.com*, http://www.blacknews.com/directory/black_african_american_magazines.shtml (accessed February 25, 2010).

27. Brad Edmondson, "Asian Americans in 2001," *American Demographics*, February 1997, 16–17.

28. Greg Johnson and Edgar Sandoval, "Advertisers Court Growing Asian Population: Marketing, Wide Range of Promotions Tied to New Year Typify Corporate Interest in Ethnic Community," *Los Angeles Times* (February 4, 2000): C1.

29. Alice Z. Cuneo and Jean Halliday Ford, "Penney's Targeting California's Asian Populations," *Advertising Age* (January 4, 1999): 28.

30. Dorinda Elliott, "Objects of Desire," *Newsweek* (February 12, 1996): 41.

31. "United States Census 2000," U.S. Census Bureau, www.census.gov/main/www/cen2000.html (accessed March 22, 2006); Elinor Kinnier, "Five Trends Emerging Among U.S. Hispanics: The New General Market," *Associate Management Group* April, 2008, http://www.amg-inc.com/AMG/news/4-08-5trends-hispanicmkt.html (accessed February 25, 2010).

32. Lucette B. Comer and J. A. F. Nicholls, "Communication between Hispanic Salespeople and Their Customers: A First Look," *Journal of Personal Selling & Sales Management* 20 (Summer 2000): 121–27; Elena del Valle, "Relationship Building and Brand Loyalty," *HispanicMPR* (January 21, 2009), http://www.hispanicmpr.com/2009/01/21/relationship-building-and-brand-loyalty/ (accessed March 12, 2010).

33. See Lewis Alpert and Ronald Gatty, "Product Positioning by Behavioral Life Styles," *Journal of Marketing* 33 (April 1969): 65–69; Emanuel H. Demby, "Psychographics Revisited: The Birth of a Technique," *Marketing News*, January 2, 1989, 21; and William D. Wells, "Backward Segmentation," in *Insights into Consumer Behavior*, ed. Johan Arndt (Boston: Allyn & Bacon, 1968), 85–100.

34. Chrissie Thompson, "Buick Counting on Greg and Laurie Robbins," *Automotive News* (May 10,2010), http://www.autonews.com/article/20100510/BLOG06/100519991/1259#ixzz0ne PMDEVF, (accessed May 11, 2010).

35. For other examples of applications see "Representative VALS™ Projects," SRI Consulting Business Intelligence, http://www.sric-bi.com/VALS/projects.shtml#positioning (accessed February 29, 2008).

36. Neal E. Boudette, "Navigating Curves: BMW's Push to Broaden Line Hits Some Bumps in the Road," *Wall Street Journal*, January 10, 2005, A1.

37. "Four Distinct Types of Consumers Emerging from the Recession, Study by Decitica Reveals," *PR Newswire* January 10, 2009, http://www.prnewswire.com/news-releases/four-distinct-types-of-consumers-emerging-from-the-recession-study-by-decitica-reveals-69080587.html (accessed April 20, 2010).

38. Judann Pollack, "Kraft's Miracle Whip Targets Core Consumers with '97 Ads," *Advertising Age*, February 3, 1997, 12.

39. Chris Anderson, *The Long Tail: Why the Future of Business Is Selling Less of More* (New York: Hyperion, 2006).

40. "Lesson 3c: Language & Location Targeting," Google Learning Center, http://adwords.google.com/support/aw/bin/static.py?page=guide.cs&guide=22793&topic=22804 (accessed March 12, 2010).

41. Anthony Ramirez, "New Cigarettes Raising Issue of Target Market," *New York Times*, February 18, 1990, 28.

42. "Our Business," Toyota, http://www.toyota.com/about/our_business/index.html (accessed February 22, 2010).

43. www.blacksocks.com (accessed March 12, 2010); Jack Ewing, "A Web Outfit with Socks Appeal," *BusinessWeek Online* July 24, 2002, http://www.businessweek.com/technology/content/jul2002/tc20020724_9718.htm?chan=search (accessed March 22, 2008).

44. Chip Bayers, "The Promise of One to One (a Love Story)," *Wired*, May 1998, 130.

45. Andrea K. Walker, "Under Armour in Public Eye," *The Baltimore Sun* (July 24, 2008), www.commercialalert.org/issues/culture/product-placement/under-armour-in-public-eye (accessed March 1, 2010).

46. Arundhati Parmar, "Where Are They Now? Revived, Repositioned Products Gain New Life," *Marketing News* (April 14, 2003): 1(3).

47. For an example of how consumers associate food brands with a range of female body shapes, see Martin R. Lautman, "End-Benefit Segmentation and Prototypical Bonding," *Journal of Advertising Research*, June/July 1991, 9–18.

48. "A Crash Course in Customer Relationship Management," *Harvard Management Update*, March 2000 (Harvard Business School reprint U003B); Nahshon Wingard, "CRM Definition—Customer-Centered Philosophy," *CRM Definition*, October 26, 2009, http://www.crmdefinition.com/2009/10/crm-definition-customer-centered-philosophy/ (accessed March 12, 2010).

49. Don Peppers and Martha Rogers, *The One-to-One Future* (New York: Doubleday, 1996).

50. Don Peppers, Martha Rogers, and Bob Dorf, "Is Your Company Ready for One-to-One Marketing?" *Harvard Business Review*, January–February 1999, 151–60.

51. Quoted in Cara B. DiPasquale, "Navigate the Maze," Special Report on 1:1 Marketing, *Advertising Age*, October 29, 2001, S1(2).

52. Leonard L. Berry, *On Great Service: A Framework for Action* (New York: The Free Press, 1995); Paul T. Ringenbach, *USAA: A Tradition of Service* (San Antonio, TX: Donning, 1997).

53. Barney Beal, "CRM, Customer Service Still Driving Technology Spending," SearchCRM.com, January 18, 2007, http://searchcrm.techtarget.com/news/article/0,289142,sid11_gci1239727,00.html (accessed March 12, 2010).

54. Jeff Kang, "Amazon.com and Customer Relationship Management," Iconocast, www.iconocast.com/ZZZZResearch/eMarketing_amazon.pdf (accessed April 8, 2008).

55. Michael Bush and Rupal Parekh, "More Marketers Want to Get to Know You," *Advertising Age Online*, August 25, 2008, http://adage.com/article?article_id=130497 (accessed May 3, 2010).

56. Robert C. Blattberg, Gary Getz, and Mark Pelofsky, "Want to Build Your Business? Grow Your Customer Equity," *Harvard Management Update*, August 2001 (Harvard Business School reprint U0108B), 3; "What Are Your Customers Really Worth?" *Forbes.com*, March 6, 2007, http://www.forbes.com/2007/03/06/gm-schwab-bmw-ent-manage-cx_kw_0306whartoncustomers.html (accessed January 8, 2010).

CHAPTER 8

1. Woodstream Corp., *Victor*, www.victorpest.com (accessed March 27, 2010).
2. Microsoft Corp., "Communities," www.microsoft.com/communities/default.mspx (accessed March 27, 2010).
3. iRobot Corp., *iRobot*, http://store.irobot.com/home/index.jsp (accessed May 5, 2010).
4. "The Story of Cotton," Cotton's Journey, www.cottonsjourney.com/Storyofcotton/page7.asp (accessed March 12, 2010).
5. "Lexus Self-Parking Car Video and Review," GIZMODO http://gizmodo.com/gadgets/clips/lexus-self-parking-car-video-and-review-196551.php (accessed March 13, 2010).
6. "Radar Car Collision Systems Put to Test," *Gizmag*, February 25, 2008, www.gizmag.com/radar-car-collision-prevention-systems-put-to-the-test/8813/ (accessed March 23, 2010).
7. Apple Inc., *iPod Classic Features*, www.apple.com/ipodclassic/features.html (accessed March 28, 2010).
8. Tim Ambler, *Marketing and the Bottom Line*, 2nd ed. (Edinburgh Gate, UK: FT Press, 2004), 172.
9. Mary Bellis, "History of Sony Playstation," About.com: Inventors, http://inventors.about.com/library/inventors/bl_playstation.htm (accessed March 28, 2010); "Sony Playstation," CyberiaPC.com, www.cyberiapc.com/vgg/sony_ps.htm (accessed March 28, 2010); Steven L. Ken, *The Ultimate History of Video Games: From Pong to Pokemon—The Story Behind the Craze That Touched Our Lives and Changed the World* (Pittsburgh, PA: Three Rivers Press, 2001).
10. Natalie Zmuda, "Facebook Turns Focus Group with Splenda Product-Sampling App," *Advertising Age Online*, July 13, 2009, http://adage.com/digital/article?article_id=137851, (accessed May 12, 2010).
11. Allison Enright, "There's Nothing Mellow about Sharp's New Marketing Mix," *Marketing News Exclusives*, April 1, 2010.
12. Simon Pitman, "Pfizer Sues P&G over Mouthwash Ad Claims," CosmeticsDesign.com, March 6, 2006, www.cosmeticsdesign.com/news/ng.asp?n=66236-pfizer-proctor-gamble-lawsuit-mouthwash (accessed March 19, 2010).
13. Brad Stone, "Analysts Ask If the iPad Can Live Up to Its Hype," *The New York Times Online*, March 28, 2010, http://www.nytimes.com/2010/03/29/technology/29apple.html (accessed May 12, 2010).
14. Malcolm Gladwell, *The Tipping Point* (Newport Beach, CA: Back Bay Books, 2002).
15. Amazon.com, http://www.amazon.com/Sharp-UXP115-Phone-Fax-Copier/dp/B0006HERX8/ref=sr_1_3?ie=UTF8&s=electronics&qid=1269880958&sr=8-3 (accessed March 15, 2010).
16. Enright, "There's Nothing Mellow about Sharp's new Marketing Mix."
17. "Jetta," VW, http://www.vw.com/jetta/en/us/ (accessed March 18, 2010); Neal E. Boudette and Lee Hawkins, "Volkswagen Eyes Young Parents with Newest Version of Jetta," *Wall Street Journal*, January 11, 2005, D.9.
18. "Products," Tamagotchi Connections, www.tamagotchi.com (accessed March 18, 2010).
19. Amy Gilroy, "More Players Enter Portable Nav Market," *TWICE*, April 5, 2004, 28(2); Pioneer Electronics Co., "XM NavTraffic," Pioneer: Car Electronics, www.pioneerelectronics.com/pna/article/0,,2076_3149_269505659,00.html (accessed April 4, 2006).
20. Bill Gerba, "Gamestop Trials Dell Kiosks," *Interactive Kiosk News*, September 30, 2005, http://kiosknews.blogspot.com/2005/09/gamestop-trials-dell-kiosks.html (accessed March 18, 2010); "Dell Completes Acquisition of Alienware," Allbusiness.com, May 9, 2006, http://www.allbusiness.com/company-activities-management/company-structures-ownership/5475507-1.html (accessed March 18, 2010).
21. Everett Rogers, *Diffusion of Innovations* (New York: Free Press, 1983), 247–251.
22. Sources used in this section: "Wi-Fi's Big Brother," *Economist*, March 13, 2004, 65; William J. Gurley, "Why Wi-Fi Is the Next Big Thing," *Fortune*, March 5, 2001, 184; Joshua Quittner, "Cordless Capers," *Time*, May 1, 2000, 85; Scott Van Camp, "Intel Switches Centrino's Gears," *Brandweek*, April 26, 2004, 16; Benny Evangelista, "SBC Park a Hot Spot for Fans Lugging Laptops," *San Francisco Chronicle*, April 26, 2004, A1; Todd Wallack, "Santa Clara Ready for Wireless," *San Francisco Chronicle*, April 19, 2004, D1; Glenn Fleishman, "Three Essays on Muni-Fi You Should Read," WNN Wi-Fi Net News, http://wifinetnews.com.
23. Christine Chen and Tim Carvell, "Hall of Shame," *Fortune*, November 22, 1999, 140.
24. Rogers, *Diffusion of Innovations*, Chapter 6.

CHAPTER 9

1. David Kiley, "The MINI Bulks Up," *BusinessWeek* Online, January 17, 2006, www.businessweek.com/autos/content/jan2006/bw20060117_818487.htm?chan=search (accessed April 8, 2010).
2. Pepperidge Farm, www.pfgoldfish.com/default.aspx (accessed April 8, 2010).
3. Dawn, www.dawn-dish.com/en_US/home.do (accessed April 8, 2010).
4. Rolls-Royce Motor Cars, www.rolls-roycemotorcars.com (accessed April 8, 2010).
5. Matt Stone, "First Drive: 2009 Hyundai Sonata," *MotorTrend Online*, http://www.motortrend.com/roadtests/sedans/112_0804_2009_hyundai_sonata/index.html (accessed April 9, 2010); Joann Muller and Robyn Meredity, "Last Laugh," *Forbes*, April 18, 2005, 98.
6. Daniel Thomas, "Relaunches: New Life or Last Gasps?" *Marketing Week*, January 29, 2004, 20(2).
7. Lea Goldman, "Big Gulp," *Forbes*, January 10, 2005, 68.
8. Geoffrey Colvin, "The Ultimate Manager," *Fortune*, November 22, 1999, 185–87.
9. "General Information on ISO," ISO, www.iso.org/iso/support/faqs/faqs_general_information_on_iso.htm (accessed April 7, 2010).
10. Al Ries and Laura Ries, *The Origin of Brands* (New York: Collins, 2005).
11. Stuart Elliot, "KFC Has Consumers Remembering KGC," *New York Times*, November 25, 2009, http://mediadecoder.blogs.nytimes.com/2009/11/25/kfc-has-consumers-remembering-kgc/#more-20217 (accessed April 8, 2010).
12. Laurie Burkitt and Ken Bruno, "New, improved . . . and failed," *MSNBC.com*, March, 24, 2010, http://www.msnbc.msn.com/id/36005036/ns/business-forbescom/ (accessed April 4, 2010).
13. Brad Stone, "For Apple, iPad Said More Than Intended," New York Times Online, January 29, 2010, http://www.nytimes.com/2010/01/29/technology/29name.html, (accessed May 24, 2010).
14. "'Apple' wins logo lawsuit against Beatles," MacNN.com, May 8, 2006, www.macnn.com/articles/06/05/08/apple.wins.logo.lawsuit (accessed April 8, 2010).
15. "The Most Famous Name in Music," *Music Trades*, September 2003, 118(12).
16. Suzanne Vranica, "McDonald's Vintage T-Shirts Sizzle," *Wall Street Journal Online* (April 27, 2006), http://www.post-gazette.com/pg/06117/685629-28.stm (accessed April 8, 2010).
17. Susan Fournier, "Consumers and Their Brands: Developing Relationship Theory in Consumer Research," *Journal of Consumer Research* 24 (March 1998): 343–373.
18. Stuart Elliott, "For One Production Company, It's All About the Power of Storytelling," *New York Times Online*, November 16, 2008, http://www.nytimes.com/2008/11/17/business/media/17adcol.html, (accessed May 31, 2010).

19. Kevin Lane Keller, "The Brand Report Card," *Harvard Business Review*, January–February 2000 (Harvard Business School reprint R00104).

20. Karl Greenberg, "Dodge Cars to Target Lifestyles, Ram Becomes Sub-Brand," *Marketing Daily/MediaPost*, November 4, 2009, http://www.mediapost.com/publications/?art_aid=116815&fa=Articles.showArticle (accessed May 15, 2010).

21. Nicholas Casey, "Can New Quiksilver Line Reach Beyond the Beach," *Wall Street Journal Online*, March 6, 2008, http://online.wsj.com/article_email/SB120476311128015043-lMyQjAxMDI4MDA0NjcwNjYzWj.html (accessed April 2, 2010).

22. John D. Stoll, "Eight-Brand Pileup Dents GM's Turnaround Efforts," *Wall Street Journal Online*, March 4, 2008, http://online.wsj.com/article_email/SB120456874600508063-lMyQjAxMDI4MDA0NTUwNjU4Wj.html (accessed April 1, 2010).

23. "Psst! Wanna See Loblaws' New Products?" *Private Label Buyer*, January 2003, 10(1); Len Lewis, "Turf War!" *Grocery Headquarters*, November 2002, 13(6).

24. "Why Not Try a Nurse in a Box," Clarkhoward, January 11, 2007, http://clarkhoward.com/shownotes/category/11/65/315/ (accessed April 19, 2010); "Pharmacy," Walmart.com, www.walmart.com/cp/Pharmacy/5431 (accessed April 9, 2010).

25. "TGI Friday's Worldwide: Menus," TGI Fridays, http://www.tgifridays.com/menus/Menus.aspx (accessed April 8, 2010); "Ultimate Recipe Showdown Winners on Friday's Menu," http://weblogs.sun-sentinel.com/features/food/restaurants/blog/2009/02/ultimate_recipe_showdown_winne_1.html (accessed June 22, 2010).

26. "Harry Potter," Lego, http://parents.lego.com/awards/awards.aspx?id=legoharrypotter (accessed April 2, 2010).

27. D. C. Denison, "The Boston Globe Business Intelligence Column," *Boston Globe*, May 26, 2002.

28. "Putting Zoom into Your Life," *Time International*, March 8, 2004, 54.

29. Stephanie Thompson, "Brand Buddies," *Brandweek*, February 23, 1998, 26–30; Jean Halliday, "L.L. Bean, Subaru Pair for Co-Branding," *Advertising Age*, February 21, 2000, 21.

30. "EquiTrend," Harris Interactive, www.harrisinteractive.com/Products/MultiClient/EquiTrend.aspx (accessed April 6, 2010).

31. "Best Global Brands for 2009," Interbrand, http://www.interbrand.com/best_global_brands.aspx (accessed June 11, 2010).

32. Kusum L. Ailawadi, Donald R. Lehmann, and Scott A. Neslin, "Revenue Premium as an Outcome Measure of Brand Equity," *Journal of Marketing* 67 (October 2003): 1–17.

33. Pringles, http://www.pringles.com/pages/index.shtml (accessed May 28, 2010).

34. "A Package that Lights Up the Shelf," *New York Times* online, March 4, 2008, http://www.nytimes.com/2008/03/04/business/media/04adco.html?ex=1205298000&en=844d46791650b628&ei=5070&emc=etal (accessed April 10, 2010).

35. Aaron Baar, "Accidental Purchases: Blame Package Design," *Marketing Daily/MediaPost News*, October 29, 2010, (accessed May 23, 2010).

36. "Labels to Include Trans Fat," *San Fernando Valley Business Journal*, January 19, 2004, 15.

37. Professor Jakki Mohr, University of Montana, personal communication (April 2004).

CHAPTER 10

1. Bureau of Labor Statistics, "Employment Situation Summary: The Employment Situation: April 2008," www.bls.gov/news.release/empsit.nr0.htm (accessed May 10, 2008).

2. John A. Czepiel, Michael R. Solomon, and Carol F. Surprenant, eds., *The Service Encounter: Managing Employee/Customer Interaction in Service Businesses* (Lexington, MA: D.C. Heath, 1985).

3. Cengiz Haksever, Barry Render, Roberta S. Russell, and Robert G. Murdick, *Service Management and Operations* (Englewood Cliffs, NJ: Prentice Hall, 2000), 25–26.

4. David H. Maister, "The Psychology of Waiting Lines," in Czepiel et al., *The Service Encounter*, 113–24.

5. Lou W. Turley and Douglas L. Fugate, "The Multidimensional Nature of Service Facilities: Viewpoints and Recommendations," *Journal of Services Marketing* 6 (Summer 1992): 37–45.

6. http://businesscenter.jdpower.com/news/pressrelease.aspx?ID=2010092 (accessed June 20, 2010).

7. Roger Yu, "Airlines Put Mobile Agents into Service," *USA Today*, July 7, 2010, http://www.usatoday.com/money/industries/travel/2010-07-07-airlineagents07_ST_N.htm (accessed July 8, 2010).

8. Cynthia Webster, "Influences upon Consumer Expectations of Services," *Journal of Services Marketing* 5 (Winter 1991): 5–17.

9. Valarie A. Zeithaml, Mary Jo Bitner, and Dwayne Gremler, *Services Marketing*, 4th ed. (Englewood Cliffs, NJ: Prentice Hall, 2005).

10. A. Parasuraman, Leonard L. Barry, and Valarie A. Zeithaml, "SERVQUAL: A Multiple-Item Scale for Measuring Consumer Perceptions of Service Quality," *Journal of Retailing* 64 (1, 1988): 12–40; A. Parasuraman, Leonard L. Barry, and Valarie A. Zeithaml, "Refinement and Reassessment of the SERVQUAL Scale," *Journal of Retailing* 67 (4, 1991): 420–50.

11. Valarie A. Zeithaml, Leonard L. Berry, and A. Parasuraman, "Communication and Control Processes in the Delivery of Service Quality," *Journal of Marketing* 52 (April 1988): 35–48.

12. Jody D. Nyquist, Mary F. Bitner, and Bernard H. Booms, "Identifying Communication Difficulties in the Service Encounter: A Critical Incident Approach," in Czepiel et al., *The Service Encounter*, 195–212.

13. Nyquist et al., "Identifying Communication Difficulties in the Service Encounter," 195–212.

14. Kristin Anderson and Ron Zemke, *Delivering Knock Your Socks Off Service* (New York: American Management Association, 1998).

15. Michael R. Solomon, "The Wardrobe Consultant: Exploring the Role of a New Retailing Partner," *Journal of Retailing* 63 (Summer 1987): 110–128.

16. Irving J. Rein, Philip Kotler, and Martin R. Stoller, *High Visibility* (New York: Dodd, Mead, 1987).

17. "Million Back Comic for President," *BBC News Online*, October 29, 2007, http://news.bbc.co.uk/1/hi/world/americas/7068040.stm, (accessed April 8, 2010).

18. Michael R. Solomon, "Celebritization and Commodification in the Interpersonal Marketplace," unpublished manuscript, Rutgers University, 1991.

19. "New York Rolls Out Tourism Ad Campaign," CNN.com, November 8, 2001, http://cnn.com/travel.

20. "Annual Report 2004–2005," *NYC & Company Online*, www.nycvisit.com/_uploads/docs/AnnualReport2004-2005.pdf (accessed March 30, 2008).

21. Gustav Niebuhr, "Where Religion Gets a Big Dose of Shopping-Mall Culture," *New York Times*, April 16, 1995, 1(2).

22. Stephen L. Vargo and Robert F. Lusch, "Evolving to a New Dominant Logic for Marketing," *Journal of Marketing* 68 (January 2004): 1–17.

23. "Search Hyatt Hotels & Resorts," www.hyatt.com/hyatt/features/hotel-search-results.jsp?No=10&type=clear&N=409 (accessed March 22, 2010).

CHAPTER 11

1. John Dawes, "Sibling Rivalry: When Companies Offer Discounts, They Too Often Ignore the Impact on Other Products They Sell," *The Wall Street Journal*, August 17, 2009, http://online.wsj.com/article/SB10001424052970203353904574149120051802950.html?

KEYWORDS=Sibling+Rivalry%3A+When+Companies+Offer+Discounts (accessed March 5, 2010).

2. http://en.wikipedia.org/wiki/Teen_Buzz (accessed June 30, 2006).

3. Wendy Zellner, "Is JetBlue's Flight Plan Flawed?" *BusinessWeek*, February 16, 2004, 56–58.

4. MCBS News.com, "Aloha Airlines Files for Bankruptcy, Again," March 21, 2008, http://www.cbsnews.com/stories/2008/03/21/business/main3956412.shtml (accessed March 5, 2010).

5. Nick Bunkley and Bill Vlasic, "G.M. to Close Saturn after Deal Fails," *New York Times*, September 30, 2009, http://www.nytimes.com/2009/10/01/business/01auto.html?scp=6&sq=saturn&st=cse (accessed March 3, 2010).

6. Claire Cain Miller, "At Checkout, More Ways to Avoid Cash or Plastic," *The New York Times*, November 15, 2009, http://www.nytimes.com/2009/11/16/technology/start-ups/16wallet.html?_r=1&scp=1&sq=at%20chekcout%20more%20ways%20to%20avoid&st=cse (accessed March 3, 2010).

7. Chris Woodyard, "High-Tech Gear Disables Car If Borrower Misses Payment," *USA Today*, March 31, 2008, http://www.usatoday.com/money/autos/2008-03-30-repo-device-car-loans_n.htm (accessed March 31, 2008).

8. Jack Neff, "Walmart Reversal Marks Victory for Brands," *Advertising Age*, March 22, 2010, http://adage.com/article?article_id=142904 (accessed September 5, 2010).

9. Ellen Byron, "P&G Meets Frugal Shoppers Halfway," *Wall Street Journal*, January 29, 2010, http://online.wsj.com/article/SB10001424052748704878904575030850236465716.html?KEYWORDS=PG+Meets+Frugal+Shoppers+Halfway (accessed March 4, 2010); James Surowiecki, "Inconspicuous Consumption," *The New Yorker*, October 12, 2009, http://www.newyorker.com/talk/financial/2009/10/12/091012ta_talk_surowiecki (accessed March 4, 2010).

10. Claire Cain Miller, "Will the Hard-Core Starbucks Customer Pay More? The Chain Plans to Find Out," *New York Times*, August 20, 2009, http://www.nytimes.com/2009/08/21/business/21sbux.html?scp=1&sq=Will%20the%20Hard-Core%20Starbucks%20Customer%20Pay%20More?%20The%20Chain%20Plans%20to%20Find%20Out&st=cse (accessed March 3, 2010).

11. Jennifer Waters, "It's a New Day for Credit Cards," *The Wall Street Journal*, February 21, 2010, http://online.wsj.com/article/SB126670472534749217.html?KEYWORDS=credit+card+rate+regulations (accessed March 3, 2010).

12. Avery Johnson, "Medical Insurers Slam Proposed Supervision," *The Wall Street Journal*, February 23, 2010, http://online.wsj.com/article/SB10001424052748703494404575081892597070352.html?KEYWORDS=regulation+of+health+insurance+rates (accessed March 3, 2010); Sheryl Gay Stolberg and Robert Pear, "Obama Signs Health Care Overhaul Bill, With a Flourish," *New York Times*, March 24, 2010, A19.

13. Quoted in Mercedes M. Cardonna, "Affluent Shoppers Like Their Luxe Goods Cheap," *Advertising Age*, December 1, 2003, 6.

14. Steward Washburn, "Pricing Basics: Establishing Strategy and Determining Costs in the Pricing Decision," *Business Marketing*, July 1985, reprinted in Valerie Kijewski, Bob Donath, and David T. Wilson, eds., *The Best Readings from Business Marketing Magazine* (Boston: PWS-Kent, 1993), 257–69.

15. Robin Cooper and W. Bruce Chew, "Control Tomorrow's Costs through Today's Design," *Harvard Business Review*, January–February 1996, 88–97.

16. Nikki Swartz, "Rate-Plan Wisdom," *Telephony Online*, June 15, 2000, http://telephonyonline.com/wireless/mag/wireless_rateplan_wisdom/ (accessed May 28, 2008).

17. Carol Angrisani, "How Low Can You Go?" *Supermarket News*, August 6, 2007, 37–38; Al Heller, "The New Science of Pricing," *Supermarket News*, March 19, 2007, 14–18.

18. Mel Martin, "Could iPad Prices Drop the Way the iPhone Did after Launch?" February 8, 2010, http://www.tuaw.com/2010/02/08/could-ipad-prices-drop-the-way-the-iphone-did-after-launch/ (accessed March 3, 2010); Ipad, http://www.apple.com/ipad/pricing/ (accessed March 3, 2010).

19. "HP 17bII+ Financial Business Calculator—overview and features," HP United States, http://h10010.www1.hp.com/wwpc/us/en/sm/WF05a/215348-215348-64232-20036-215349-384708.html (accessed March 20 2008).

20. "International Commercial Terms," Export 911, http://www.export911.com/e911/export/comTerm.htm (accessed May 27, 2008).

21. "iTunes Music Store Downloads Top a Quarter Billion Songs," press release, January 24, 2005, Apple http://www.apple.com/pr/library/2005/jan/24itms.html (accessed May 25, 2008).

22. Emma Ritch, "Mobile Music Is Shooting Up the Charts," *San Jose Business Journal*, March 31, 2008, http://www.mlive.com/business/ambizdaily/bizjournals/index.ssf?/base/abd-3/1206949203163950.xml (accessed March 30, 2008).

23. This section is adapted from Chris Anderson, "Free! Why $0.00 is the Future of Business," *Wired*, March 2008, 140, 10.

24. David Ackerman and Gerald Tellis, "Can Culture Affect Prices? A Cross-Cultural Study of Shopping and Retail Prices," *Journal of Retailing* 77 (2001): 57–82.

25. Shankar Vedantam, "Eliot Spitzer and the Price-Placebo Effect," *WashingtonPost.com*, March 17, 2008, http://www.washingtonpost.com/wp-dyn/content/article/2008/03/16/AR2008031602168.html (accessed May 27, 2008).

26. William J. Boyes, Allen K. Lynch, and William Stewart, "Why Odd Pricing?" *Journal of Applied Social Psychology*, 37 (5) (May 2007): 1130–1140; Robert M. Schindler and Thomas M. Kibarian, "Increased Consumer Sales Response through Use of 99-Ending Prices," *Journal of Retailing* 72 (1996): 187–99.

27. Sarah Kershaw, "Using Menu Psychology to Entice Diners," *The New York Times*, December 22, 2009, http://www.nytimes.com/2009/12/23/dining/23menus.html?scp=1&sq=Using%20Menu%20Psychology%20to%20Entice%20Diners&st=cse (accessed March 3, 2010).

28. Stephanie Rosenbloom, "Back-to-School Discounts Are Deeper, More Creative," *The New York Times*, August 14, 2008, http://www.nytimes.com/2008/08/15/business/15retail.html?scp=1&sq=Back-to-School%20Discounts%20Are%20Deeper,%20More%20Creative&st=cse (accessed March 4, 2010).

29. Steve Lohr, "LCD Makers Fined $585 Million for Price Fixing," *The New York Times*, November 13, 2008, http://www.nytimes.com/2008/11/13/technology/13iht-13panel.17777580.html (accessed March 2, 2010).

30. BBC News, "Dutch Brewers Fined over Cartel," April 27, 2007, http://news.bbc.co.uk/2/hi/business/6566827.stm (accessed March 3, 2010).

31. Adam Bryant, "Aisle Seat Bully?" *Newsweek*, May 24, 1999, 56.

CHAPTER 12

1. http://adage.com/digital/article?article_id=121406.

2. Schultz, Don E. and Heidi Schultz (2003), *IMC. The next generation. Five steps for delivering value and measuring returns using marketing communication*, New York: McGraw Hill, 20-21.

3. Barbara Lippert, "Windows Debut: Almost 7th Heaven," *Adweek*, October 26, 2009, http://www.adweek.com/aw/content_display/creative/critique/e3i7a4f853fe57e4c0b5bf8e3a501635ead (accessed May 12, 2009).

4. Gert Assmus, "An Empirical Investigation into the Perception of Vehicle Source Effects," *Journal of Advertising* 7 (Winter 1978): 4–10; for a more thorough discussion of the pros and cons of different media, see Stephen Baker, *Systematic Approach to Advertising Creativity* (New York: McGraw-Hill, 1979).

5. Charlene Li and Josh Bernoff, *Groundswell: Winning in a World Transformed by Social Technologies* (Boston, MA: Harvard Business School Publishing, 2008), 9.

6. Meghan Keane, "Pepsi Refresh: Will the Social Media Halo Extend to Soda Sales?" EConsultancy, February 5, 2010, http://econsultancy.com/blog/5391-pepsi-refresh-will-the-halo-extend-to-soda (accessed March 5, 2010).

7. Natalie Zmuda, "Pepsi Expands Refresh Project," *Advertising Age,* September 07, 2010, http://adage.com/article?article_id=145773 (accessed September 20, 2010).

8. Lois Geller, "Wow—What a Buzz," *Target Marketing*, June 2005, 21.

9. Dale Buss, "Volvo Wants You to See Its 'Naughty' Side," *Brandchannel*, March 4, 2010, http://www.brandchannel.com/ home/post/2010/03/04/Volvo-Wants-You-to-See-its-e28098Naughtye 28099-Side.aspx, (accessed March 10, 2010).

10. Matthew Creamer, "In Era of Consumer Control, Marketers Crave the Potency of Word-of-mouth," *Advertising Age*, November 28, 2005, 32.

11. Todd Wasserman, "Word Games," *Brandweek*, April 24, 2006, 24.

12. Todd Wasserman, "Blogs Cause Word-of-Mouth Business to Spread Quickly," *Brandweek*, October 3, 2005, 9.

13. Richard Read, "2010 Honda Accord Crosstour Sideswiped by Facebook, Twitter," The Car Connection, September 3, 2009, http://www.thecarconnection.com/marty-blog/1034885_2010-honda-accord-crosstour-sideswiped-by-facebook-twitter, (accessed March 20, 2010).

14. Wasserman, "Blogs Cause Word-of-Mouth Business to Spread Quickly."

15. Abe Sauer, "Smith Vs. Southwest: Twitter Again Central to National Debate," *Brandchannel*, February 16, 2010, http://www.brandchannel.com/home/post/2010/02/16/Smith-Vs-Southwest-Twitter-Again-Central-To-National-Debate.aspx (accessed March 5, 2010).

16. Suzanne Vranica, "Getting Buzz Marketers to Fess Up," *Wall Street Journal*, February 9, 2005, B9.

17. Todd Wasserman, "Word Games," *Brandweek*, April 24, 2006, 24.

18. Tamar Weinbert, *The New Community Rules: Marketing on the Social Web* (Sebastopol, CA: O'Reilly Media, 2009).

19. Andrew McMains, "Consumers Party On for Major Brands," *Adweek*, February 1, 2010, http://www.adweek.com/aw/content_display/news/client/e3i9765415345582f6e24e7539db4803cb2 (accessed March 5, 2010).

20. Aaron Baar, "Ford Builds Buzz Around Upcoming Fiesta," *Media Post News*, February 20, 2009, http://www.mediapost.com/publications/?fa=Articles.showArticle&art_aid=100693 (accessed March 5, 2010).

21. Erik Sass, "20% of Social Network Users Have Shared Negative Brand Experiences," *Social Media and Marketing Daily* (April 29, 2010), http://www.mediapost.com/publications/?fa=Articles.showArticle&art_aid=127224, (accessed April 30, 2010).

22. Sheila Shayon, "Reluctant Romance: Franchise Brands and Social Media," *Brandchannel*, January 27, 2010, http://www.brandchannel.com/home/post/2010/01/27/Reluctant-Romance-Franchise-Brands-And-Social-Media.aspx (accessed March 5, 2010).

23. Myra Frazier, "The Networked Boomer Woman: Hear Us Roar," *Brandchannel*, December 18, 2009, http://www.brandchannel.com/features_effect.asp?pf_id=496 (accessed April 4, 2010).

24. "Facebook Is College Students' GoTo," *Research Brief from the Center for Media Research* (December 18, 2009), http://www.mediapost.com/publications/?fa=Articles.showArticle&art_aid=119049, (accessed April 30, 2010).

25. Karlene Lukovitz, "Facebook Helps Burgerville Woo Young Adults" (March 18, 2010), *Marketing Daily*, http://www.mediapost.com/publications/?fa=Articles.showArticle&art_aid=124407, (accessed April 30, 2010).

26. Claire Cain Miller, "Twitter Unveils Plans to Draw Money from Ads," *The New York Times*, April 13, 2010, B1.

27. Sheila Shavon, "One in Five Tweets Is Brand-Related," *Brandchannel*, February 12, 2010, http://www.brandchannel.com/home/post/2010/02/12/One-In-Five-Tweets-Is-Brand-Related.aspx (accessed March 20, 2010).

28. Tamar Weinbert, *The New Community Rules: Marketing on the Social Web* (Sebastopol, CA: O'Reilly Media, 2009).

29. Claire Cain Miller, "Twitter Unveils Plans to Draw Money from Ads," *The New York Times*, April 13, 2010, B1.

30. Sheila Shayon, "Kwedit Promise: You Can Keep That Virtual Puppy, for a Price," *Brandchannel*, February 8, 2010, http://www.brandchannel.com/home/post/2010/02/08/Kwedit-Promise-You-Can-Keep-That-Virtual-Puppy-For-A-Price.aspx (accessed March 5, 2010).

31. Dawn C. Chmielewski, "Disney Hopes Kids Will Take Online World of Cars Out for a Spin," *Los Angeles Times*, February 24, 2010, http://articles.latimes.com/2010/feb/24/business/la-fi-ct-disney24-2010feb24 (accessed March 20, 2010).

32. Elizabeth Olson, "Marketing Fanciful Items in the Lands of Make Believe," *New York Times,* September 7, 2010, B3.

33. Natalie Zmuda, "An App for That, Too: How Mobile Is Changing Shopping," *Advertising Age* (March 1, 2010), http://adage.com/print?article_id=142318, (accessed March 14, 2010); Jenna Wortham, "Telling Friends Where You Are (or Not)," *New York Times* (March 14, 2010), http://www.nytimes.com/2010/03/15/technology/15locate.html, (accessed April 30, 2010).

34. Brad Stone and Barrett Sheridan, "The Retailer's Clever Little Helper," *Bloomberg Businessweek*, August 30–September 5, 2010, 31–32.

35. "Five Ways Businesses Can Leverage Foursquare in Marketing Efforts, from Affect Strategies," *BusinessWire* (April 16, 2010), http://www.businesswire.com/portal/site/home/permalink/?ndmViewId=news_view&newsId=20100416005542&newsLang=en (accessed April 30, 2010).

36. John Borland, "All Eyes on New DVDs' Format War," *CNET News.com* http://news.cnet.com/All-eyes-on-new-DVDs-format-war/2100-1026_3-5783387.html, July 11, 2005 (accessed July 1, 2006).

37. Stuart Elliott, "Yes, It Was a Bad Year for Ad Spending, But It Got Less Worse in the Fourth Quarter," *New York Times, March 17, 2010,* http://mediadecoder.blogs.nytimes.com/2010/03/17/yes-it-was-a-bad-year-for-ad-spending-but-it-got-less-worse-in-the-fourth-quarter/?scp=8&sq=TV%20advertising%20down&st=cse (accessed May 12, 2010).

38. Center for Media Research, "Traditional Marketing Budgets Lose to Interactive," *Research Brief* (July 14, 2009), http://www.mediapost.com/publications/?fa=Articles.showArticle&art_aid=109611, (accessed May 12, 2010).

39. Elaine Wong, "Kraft Spreads the Word about Athenos with Sampling Effort," *Brandweek*, February 20, 2010, http://www.brandweek.com/bw/content_display/news-and-features/direct/e3i5207f9d259b81f621f2445ead779f22e (accessed February 25, 2010).

40. Sheila Shavon, "Del Taco Goes Online To Bring Customers In Stores," Brandchannel, March 1, 2010, http://www.brandchannel.com/home/post/2010/03/01/Del-Taco-Goes-Online-To-Bring-Customers-In-Stores.aspx (accessed March 10, 2010).

41. Patricia Odell, "Ghirardelli Gives Out One Million Chocolates," *Promo,* March 11, 2010, http://promomagazine.com/eventmarketing/news/0311-ghirardelli-gives-chocolates/ (accessed March 15, 2010); Barry, Silverstein, "Ghirardelli "Million Moments" Combines Live Streaming With Sweepstakes," *Brandchannel*, March 9, 2010, http://www.brandchannel.com/home/post/2010/03/09/Ghirardelli-Million-Moments-Combines-Live-Streaming-With-Sweepstakes.aspx, (accessed March 15, 2010).

CHAPTER 13

1. Bradley Johnson, "Top 100 Outlays Plunge 10% But Defying Spend Trend Can Pay Off,"*Advertising Age*, June 21, 2010, 1, 10–11.
2. Bradley Johnson, "Agency Report 2010," *Advertising Age*, April 26, 2010, 22–33.
3. Bradley Johnson, "Top 100 Outlays Plunge 10% But Defying Spend Trend Can Pay Off:" *Advertising Age*, June 21, 2010, 1, 10–11.
4. "What Consumers Watch: Nielsen's Q1 2010 Three Screen Report," Nielsen Wire, June 11, 2010, http://blog.nielsen.com/nielsenwire/online_mobile/what-consumers-watch-nielsens-q1-2010-three-screen-report/ (accessed October 10, 2010).
5. William Wells, John Burnett, and Sandra Moriarty, *Advertising: Principles and Practice*, 5th ed. (Englewood Cliffs, NJ: Prentice Hall, 2000).
6. Bradley Johnson, "Top 100 Outlays Plunge 10% But Defying Spend Trend Can Pay Off"" *Advertising Age*, June 21, 2010, 1, 10–11.
7. Rance Crain, "Dow's Corporate Ads Have Great Chemistry, But Will Respect Follow?" *Advertising Age*, August 6, 2007, http://adage.com/columns/article?article_id=119676 (accessed May 22, 2010).
8. John M. Broder, "Governors Join in Creating Regional Pacts on Climate Change," *New York Times*, November 15, 2007, http://www.nytimes.com/2007/11/15/washington/15climate.html?scp=1&sq=governors+join+in+creating+regional&st=nyt (accessed June 9, 2008).
9. Bob Garfield, "PSA Won't Change Perennial Parental Bleacher Creatures," *Advertising Age*, April 14, 2008, http://adage.com/garfield/post?article_id=126354&search_phrase=PSA (accessed April 19, 2008).
10. Bradley Johnson, "Agency Report 2010," *Advertising Age*, April 26, 2010, 22–33.
11. "CGM Overview," Nielsen BuzzMetrics, http://www.nielsenbuzzmetrics.com/cgm.
12. Stuart Elliott, "Do It Yourself Super Ads," *The New York Times*, February 9, 2010, B3.
13. Julie Bosman, "Chevy Tries a Write-Your-Own-Ad Approach, and the Potshots Fly," *New York Times*, April 4, 2006, Section C, 1.
14. "Customer-Made," Trend-watching.com, www.trendwatching.com/briefing/; "Generation C," http://www.trendwatching.com/trends/GENERATION_C.htm.
15. Karen E. Klein, "Should Your Customers Make Your Ads?" *Business Week Online*, January 3, 2008, 9.
16. Abe Sauer, "D.C. Lottery Gambles on New Logo," *Brandchannel*, February 23, 2010, http://www.brandchannel.com/home/post/2010/02/23/DC-Lottery-Gambles-On-New-Logo.aspx (accessed March 15, 2010).
17. Emma Hall, "In Greece, Kraft Scores a Hit for Lacta Chocolate with Crowdsourced Film," *Advertising Age*, March 24, 2010, http://adage.com/globalnews/article?article_id=142953 (accessed March 25, 2010).
18. Federal Trade Commission, *FTC Policy Statement on Deception*, October 14, 1983, www.ftc.gov/bcp/policystmt/ad-decept.htm (accessed July 2, 2006); Dorothy Cohen, *Legal Issues in Marketing Decision Making* (Cincinnati: South-Western College Publishing, 1995).
19. Natasha Singer, "A Birth Control Pill That Promised Too Much," *The New York Times*, February 11, 2009, B1.
20. Leslie Kaufman, "Enough Talk," *Newsweek*, August 18, 1997, 48–49.
21. "Index to the 100 Leading National Advertisers," *Advertising Age*, June 20, 2007, http://adage.com/datacenter/article?article_id=118652&search_phrase=top+ad+spenders+2007 (accessed April 21, 2008).
22. Peter Cornish, personal communication, March 2010.
23. Kate Macarthur, "Why Big Brands Are Getting into the Ring," *Advertising Age*, May 22, 2007, http://adage.com/print?article_id=116722 (accessed April 21, 2008).
24. Jeremy Lee, "Ofcom Bans Follow-Up Renault Megane Spot," *Campaign*, August 6, 2004, 10.
25. Russ Josephs, "I'd Like to Buy the World a (Virtual) Coke, and Keep It Company," *Brandchannel*, January 28, 2010, http://www.brandchannel.com/home/post/2010/01/29/Ie28099d-Like-To-Buy-The-World-A-%28Virtual%29-Coke-And-Keep-It-Company.aspx (accessed April 15, 2010).
26. Stephanie Kant, "Magic of Clorox Sells for a Song," *Wall Street Journal*, March 28, 2008, http://online.wsj.com/article/SB120666813235770629.html (accessed April 17, 2008).
27. James Berrinder, "Tech Box Neuromarketing: Ad Agency Bark Gets Emotional with Neuromarketing technology," Research-live.com, 28 April 2010, http://www.research-live.com/news/new-business/ad-agency-bark-gets-emotional-with-neuromarketing-technology/4001806.article (accessed April 15, 2010).
28. Christopher Rocchio, "Report: Writers Strike Spikes 'American Idol' Ad Rates to $1 Million Plus," *Radio-TV World*, January 14, 2008, http://www.realitytvworld.com/news/report-writers-strike-spikes-american-idol-ad-rates-1-million-plus-6390.php (accessed April 21, 2008).
29. "TV Advertising Is Less Effective: Survey," *PROMO Magazine*, www.promomagazine.com/news/tvadvertising_survey_032406/index/html (accessed July 29, 2006).
30. "Who Owns What," *Columbia Journalism Review*, http://www.cjr.org/resources/ (accessed April 18, 2008).
31. Phil Hall, "Make Listeners Your Customers," *Nation's Business*, June 1994, 53R.
32. Jack Neff, "Viva Viva! K-C Boosts Brand's Marketing," *Advertising Age*, June 11, 2007, 4.
33. Sean Corcoran, "Defining Earned, Owned and Paid Media," Forrester Blogs, December 16, 2009, http://blogs.forrrester.com/interactive_marketing/2009/12/defining-earned-owned-and-paid-media.html (accessed April 27, 2010).
34. "Internet Advertising Revenues Again Reach New Highs, Estimated to Pass $21 Billion in 2007 and Hit Nearly $6 Billion in Q4 2007, February 25, 2008," press release, Interactive Advertising Bureau, http://www.iab.net/about_the_iab/recent_press_releases/press_release_archive/press_release/195115 (accessed April 21, 2008).
35. Kevin J. Delaney, "Once Wary Industry Giants Embrace Internet Advertising," *Wall Street Journal*, April 17, 2006, A1.
36. Louise Story, "Online Pitches Made Just for You," *New York Times*, March 6, 2008, 7.
37. Michael McCarthy, "Companies Are Sold on Interactive Ad Strategy," *USA Today*, March 3, 2000, 1B.
38. Michael Learmonth, "Inside the Black Box: What Big Brands Are Spending on Google," *Advertising Age*, September 6, 2010, 1, 20.
39. Ann M. Mack, "Got E-Mail," *Brandweek*, March 20, 2000, 84–88.
40. Mobile Marketing Association, "Mobile Marketing Industry Glossary," http://mmaglobal.com/uploads/glossary.pdf (accessed April 27, 2010).
41. Kunur Patel, "How the iAd Gave mobile marketing needed Shot in Arm," *Advertising Age*, September 13, 2010, M-2–M-3; Rich Karpinski, "Why Mobile Advertising Networks Are on the Cust of Real Change," *Advertising Age*, September 13, 2010, M-2–M-3.
42. Dan Butcher, "Kellogg Runs MMS Campaign for Cereal Recipes," MobileMarketer.com, April 9, 2009, http://www.mobilemarketer.com/cms/news/messaging/3002.html (accessed April 27, 2010).
43. Giselle Tsirulnik, "Oprah Grows Mobile Media Empire," MobileMarketer.com, April 26, 2010, http://www.mobilemarketer.com/cms/news/media/6075.html (accessed April 27, 2010).

44. Claire Cain Miller, "Take a Step Closer for an Invitation to Shop," *The New York Times*, February 24, 2010, B4.

45. Lon Safko and David K. Brake, *The Social Media Bible* (Hoboken, NJ: John Wiley & Sons).

46. Sheila Shavon, "Adidas Steps into the World of Augmented Reality," Brandchannel.com, January 27, 2010, http://www.brandchannel.com/home/post/2010/01/27/Adidas-Steps-Into-The-World-Of-Augmented-Reality.aspx (accessed April 15, 2010).

47. Amy-Mae Elliott, "10 Amazing Augmented Reality iPhone Apps," *Mashable*, http://mashable.com/2009/12/05/augmented-reality-iphone/ (accessed April 15, 2010).

48. Bruce Schreiner and Emily Fredrix, "KFC Pays Indiana Cities for 'Fiery' Ad Space" (January 6, 2010), Indystar.com, (accessed January 25, 2010).

49. Ethan Smith and Sabrina Shankman, "Fellow Graduates, Before We Greet the Future, a Word from My Sponsor," *Wall Street Journal* (July 28, 2009), . . . wsj.com/.../SB124873785621885167 . . ., (accessed July 28, 2009).

50. Irina Slutsky, "Meet YouTube's Most In-Demand Brand Stars," *Advertising Age*, September 13, 2010, 8.

51. Karl Greenberg, "Audi Ties R8 to Promotion of 'Iron Man,' Due Out May 2," *Marketing Daily*, April 23, 2008, http://publications.mediapost.com/index.cfm?fuseaction=Articles.san&s=81185&Nid=41887&p=941737 (accessed April 23, 2008).

52. Andrew Hampp, "In This Year's Upfront, It's All About Branded Entertainment," *Advertising Age*, May 26, 2008, http://adage.com/print?article_id=127312 (accessed June 6, 2008).

53. "Interactive Advertising Revenues to Reach $147B Globally, $62.4B in US," The Kelsey Group, http://www.marketingcharts.com/direct/interactive-advertising-revenues-to-reach-147b-globally-624b-in-us-3567/ (accessed April 21, 2008).

54. www.adweek.com/aw/content_display/news/agency/e3i9ee4b481143e87d75b75c7e38e0a3f84, (accessed March 15, 2010).

55. Louise Story, "Away from Home, TV Ads Are Inescapable," *New York Times*, March 2, 2007, 6.

56. Jeremy Wagstaff, "Loose Wire—Bootleg Backlash: Software Industry Groups Are Snooping for People Using Pirated Software; But Their Assumptions about Who's a Pirate Seem Awfully Mixed Up," July 31, 2003, *Far Eastern Economic Review*, 31.

57. Bristol Voss, "Measuring the Effectiveness of Advertising and PR," *Sales & Marketing Management*, October 1992, 123–24.

58. This remark has also been credited to a British businessman named Lord Leverhulme; see Charles Goodrum and Helen Dalrymple, *Advertising in America: The First 200 Years* (New York: Harry N. Abrams, 1990).

59. Stuart Elliott, "New Survey on Ad Effectiveness," April 14, 2004, http://query.nytimes.com/search/query?frow=0&n=10&srcht=s&query=new+survey+on+ad+effectiveness&srchst=nyt&submit.x=0&submit.y=0&submit=sub&hdlquery=&bylquery=&daterange=full&mon1=01&day1=01&year1=1981&mon2=06&day2=09&year2=2008.

60. Kate Fitzgerald, "Homemade Bikini Contest Hits Bars, Beach for 10th Year," *Advertising Age*, April 13, 1998, 18.

61. Alan J. Liddle, "Guilty Pleas End Wendy's Finger-Pointing, But Will They Inspire Leniency in Sentencing," *Nation's Restaurant News*, September 19, 2005, 202; Jonathan Birchall, "Jail for Wendy's Finger Claim Couple," *Financial Times*, January 19, 2006, 25.

62. "Jail for Wendy's Finger Scam Couple," CBS News, January 18, 2006, http://www.cbsnews.com/stories/2006/01/18/national/main1218315.shtml (accessed June 9, 2008).

63. "Man Who Put Dead Mouse in Burrito at Taco Bell Given Prison Time," FoxNews.com, http://www.foxnews.com/story/0,2933,197993,00.html (accessed June 9, 2008).

64. The Star-Ledger Continuous News Deal, "Apple iPad tablet is unveiled at live press conference," January 27, 2010, http://www.nj.com/business/index.ssf/2010/01/apple_ipad_tablet_is_unveiled.html (accessed March 15, 2010).

65. Andy Pasztor, "FAA Ruling on Long-Haul Routes Would Boost Boeing's Designs," *Wall Street Journal*, June 5, 2006, A.3.

66. Amy Chozick, "Star Power: The LPGA Is Counting on a New Marketing Push to Take Women's Golf to the Next Level," *Wall Street Journal*, June 12, 2006, R.6.

67. Michael R. Solomon, Greg W. Marshall and Elnora W. Stuart, *Marketing: Real People, Real Choices*, 6th ed. (2009).

68. Carol Driver, "Five-Minute YouTube apology from Toyota boss as first lawsuit filed over faulty pedal recall," *Daily Mail*, February 5, 2010, http://www.dailymail.co.uk/news/article-1248588/Five-minute-YouTube-apology-Toyota-boss-lawsuit-filed-faulty-pedal-recall.html (accessed March 15, 2010).

69. Jaimie Seaton, "Burger King Guns for Rivals in Guerilla Push," *Media*, September 9, 2005, 6.

70. Quoted in Michelle Kessler, "IBM Graffiti Ads Gain Notoriety," *USA Today*, April 26, 2001, 3B.

71. Howard Stumpf and John M. Kawula, "Point of Purchase Advertising," in *Handbook of Sales Promotion*, ed. S. Ulanoff (New York: McGraw-Hill, 1985); Karen A. Berger, *The Rising Importance of Point-of-Purchase Advertising in the Marketing Mix* (Englewood Cliffs, NJ: Point-of-Purchase Advertising Institute).

72. Gardiner Harris, "Drug Makers Offer Consumers Coupons for Free Prescriptions—But Patients Still Have to Get Their Physician's Approval, and Most Don't Pay for Pills," *The Wall Street Journal*, March 13, 2002, B1.

73. "Virgin Atlantic Rolls Out Space Miles," *PROMO Magazine*, http://promomagazine.com/incentives/virgin_atlantic_miles_011106/index.html (accessed June 12, 2006).

74. Michael Fielding, "C'est Délicieux," *Marketing News*, September 15, 2010, 10.

75. This section based on material presented in Don E. Schultz, William A. Robinson, and Lisa A. Petrison, *Sales Promotion Essentials*, 2nd ed. (Lincolnwood, IL: NTC Business Books, 1993).

76. "Ben & Jerry's Launches Ice Cream Flavor Contest," *PROMO Magazine*, http://promomagazine.com/news/benjerry_contest_031606/index.html (accessed March 16, 2006).

77. "Lengthy Research Leads Disney to Global 'Dreams' Theme," *PROMO Magazine*, http://promomagazine.com/research/disney_research_061206/index.html (accessed June 12, 2006).

78. "Consumers Vote for Oreo Idol," *PROMO Magazine*, http://promomagazine.com/contests/news/oreo_idol_contest_061206/index.html (accessed June 9, 2008).

79. Kerry J. Smith, "It's for You," *PROMO Magazine*, August 1994, 41(4); Sharon Moshavi, "Please Deposit No Cents," *Forbes*, August 16, 1993, 102.

80. Amanda Beeler, "Package-Goods Marketers Tune In Free-Sampling Sites," *Advertising Age*, June 12, 2000, 58.

CHAPTER 14

1. "Bausch & Lomb Makes Eyes with Consumers in Spain," *PROMO Magazine*, October 1994, 93.

2. Direct Marketing Association, www.the-dma.org/index.php (accessed May 2, 2010).

3. David Liberman, "Ad Spending Forecast to Shift to More Direct Marketing," *USA Today Online*, http://www.usatoday.com/money/media/2008-08-04-media-forecast_N.htm, August 5, 2008 (accessed June 12, 2010).

4. Frances Huffman, "Special Delivery," *Entrepreneur*, February 1993, 81(3).

5. Paul Hughes, "Profits Due," *Entrepreneur*, February 1994, 74(4).

6. *DMA Statistical Fact Book*, 31st ed. (New York: Direct Marketing Association, 2010).

7. Burt Helm, "Cutting the Stack of Catalogs," *BusinessWeek* Online, December 20, 2007, http://www.businessweek.com/magazine/content/07_53/b4065035213195.htm?chan=search (accessed May 5, 2010).

8. Federal Trade Commission, National Do Not Call Registry, www.ftc.gov/donotcall (accessed May 8, 2010).

9. Robert Longley, "Truth about Cell Phones and the Do Not Call Registry," *About.com: U.S. Government Information*, April 2005, http://www.ftc.gov/donotcall (accessed May 10, 2010).

10. Alison J. Clarke, "'As Seen on TV': Socialization of the Tele-Visual Consumer," paper presented at the Fifth Interdisciplinary Conference on Research in Consumption, University of Lund, Sweden, August 1995.

11. *Measuring the Information Society 2010*, Geneva, Switzerland: International Telecommunications Union, 2010; "Mobile Phone Use Reaches 50% Worldwide," *Romow Shopping Blog*, February 28, 2008, http://www.romow.com/shopping-blog/mobile-phone-use-reaches-50-worldwide/ (accessed April 30, 2010).

12. http://en.wikipedia.org/wiki/List_of_countries_by_number_of_mobile_phones_in_use (accessed July 15, 2010).

13. Bureau of Labor Statistics, *Occupational Outlook Handbook 2008–09*, www.bls.gov/oco/ocos119.htm#outlook (accessed May 3, 2010).

14. Quoted in Jaclyn Fierman, "The Death and Rebirth of the Salesman," *Fortune*, July 25, 1994, 38(7), 88.

15. "Super Bowl Commercials Cost Plenty, Deliver Little," *TransWorldNews*, February 4, 2008, www.transworldnews.com/NewsStory.aspx?id=35308&cat=2 (accessed May 1, 2010).

16. Direct Selling Association, www.dsa.org (accessed May 6, 2010); Scott Reeves, "'Do Not Call' Revives Door-to-Door Sales," *Marketing News*, December 8, 2003, 13; Maria Puente, "Direct Selling Brings It All Home," *USA Today*, October 28, 2003, 5D.

17. Salesforce.com, www.salesforce.com (accessed May 1, 2010).

18. Skype, www.skype.com (accessed May 1, 2010).

19. Adapted from Mitchell Schnurman, "The Game-Changing Reality of Virtual Sales Pitches," *Fort Worth Star-Telegram Online*, April 9, 2010, www.star-telegram.com/2010/04/09/2103717_p2/the-game-changing-reality-of-virtual.html (accessed May 1, 2010).

20. April Joyner, "An Animated Salesperson," *Inc. Online*, June 1, 2010, http://www.inc.com/magazine/20100601/an-animated-salesperson.html (accessed June 3, 2010).

21. Dan C. Weilbaker, "The Identification of Selling Abilities Needed for Missionary Type Sales," *Journal of Personal Selling & Sales Management*, 10 (Summer 1990), 45–58.

22. Derek A. Newton, *Sales Force Performance and Turnover* (Cambridge, MA: Marketing Science Institute, 1973), 3.

23. Mark W. Johnston and Greg W. Marshall, *Relationship Selling*, 3rd ed. (Boston: McGraw-Hill, 2010).

24. Accela Communications, www.accelacommunications.com (accessed May 6, 2010).

25. Greg W. Marshall, Daniel J. Goebel, and William C. Moncrief, "Hiring for Success at the Buyer-Seller Interface," *Journal of Business Research* 56 (April 2003): 247–55.

26. Marshall et al., "Hiring for Success at the Buyer-Seller Interface."

27. Adapted from Erin Strout, "The Top 10 Most Outrageous T&E Expenses," *Sales & Marketing Management*, February 2001, 60.

CHAPTER 15

1. Jonathan Birchall, "Walmart Aims to Cut Supply Chain Cost," FT.com, January 3, 2010, http://www.ft.com/cms/s/0/891c7878-f895-11de-beb8-00144feab49a.html (accessed June 28, 2010).

2. Thomas L. Friedman, *The World Is Flat 3.0: A Brief History of the Twenty-First Century* (New York: Picador, 2007).

3. "How It Works," Netflix, www.netflix.com/HowItWorks (accessed May 7, 2010).

4. David Byrne, "David Byrne's Survival Strategies for Emerging Artists—and Megastars," *Wired* 16.01, December 18, 2007, www.wired.com/entertainment/music/magazine/16-01/ff_byrne/ (accessed May 1, 2010).

5. "About us," Eastern Meat Farms, Inc., www.salami.com/ordereze/AboutUs.aspx (accessed May 1, 2010).

6. Jefferson Graham, "Google May Be Missing the Middleman After All," *USA Today*, January 13, 2010, 3B.

7. Rowland T. Moriarty and Ursula Moran, "Managing Hybrid Marketing Systems," *Harvard Business Review* (November–December 1990), 2–11.

8. Michael Barbaro, "Walmart Offers Aid to Rivals," *New York Times*, April 5, 2006, Section C, page 1.

9. Oneworld, www.oneworld.com/home.cfm (accessed May 1, 2010).

10. John Neff, "Scion May Break Promise to Itself, Add Fourth Model," *AutoBlog*, May 25, 2007, http://www.autoblog.com/2007/05/25/scion-may-break-promise-to-itself-add-fourth-model/ (accessed May 1, 2010).

11. "About us," Starbucks, www.starbucks.com/about-us (accessed May 1, 2010).

12. Toby B. Gooley, "The Who, What, and Where of Reverse Logistics," *Logistics Management* 42 (February 2003), 38–44; James R. Stock, *Development and Implementation of Reverse Logistics Programs* (Oak Brook, IL: Council of Logistics Management, 1998), 20.

13. "Spychipped Levi's Brand Jeans Hit the U.S.," RFID Nineteen Eighty-Four, April 27, 2006, www.spychips.com/press-releases/levis-secret-testing.html (accessed May 1, 2010): Katherine Albrecht and Liz McIntyre, *Spychips: How Major Corporations and Government Plan to Track Your Every Purchase and Watch Your Every Move* (New York: Plume, 2006).

14. Faye W. Gilbert, Joyce A. Young, and Charles R. O'Neal, "Buyer-Seller Relationships in Just-in-Time Purchasing Environments," *Journal of Organizational Research* 29 (February 1994), 111–120.

15. "Perfect Order Measure," Supply Chain Metric.com, www.supplychainmetric.com/perfect.htm (accessed May 5, 2010).

CHAPTER 16

1. U.S. Census Bureau, "Advance Monthly Sales for Retail and Food Services, December 2007," http://www.census.gov/marts/www/download/pdf/adv0712.pdf (accessed April 26, 2008).

2. U.S. Department of Labor, "Employment, Hours, and Earnings from the Current Employment Statistics survey (National)" (accessed March 10, 2010), http://data.bls.gov/PDQ/servlet/SurveyOutputServlet?&series_id=CEU4200000001.

3. Stanley C. Hollander, "The Wheel of Retailing," *Journal of Retailing*, July 1960, 41.

4. "About Us," Pier 1 imports, www.pier1.com/company/history.aspx (accessed June 25, 2006).

5. "Walmart Opens Supercenter for Upscale Shoppers," *PROMO Magazine*, http://promomagazine.com/news/Walmart_supercenter_033006/index.html (accessed June 12, 2006); Stuart Elliott and Michael Barbaro, "Walmart on the Hunt for an Extreme Makeover," *New York Times*, May 4, 2006, Section C1.

6. Christine Negroni, "Airline Tests Retail Sales at 35,000 Feet," *New York Times* (November 16, 2009), http://www.nytimes.com/2009/11/17/business/17sales.html (accessed March 22, 2010).

7. Ann Zimmerman and Cheryl Lu-Lien Tan, "After Misstep, Walmart Revisits Fashion," *Wall Street Journal*, April 24, 2008, http://online.wsj.com/article/SB120899828876040063.html (accessed April 29, 2008).

8. William R. Davidson, Albert D. Bates, and Stephen J. Bass, "The Retail Life Cycle," *Harvard Business Review*, November–December 1976, 89.

9. "Company Profile," http://assets.starbucks.com/assets/company-profile-feb10.pdf (accessed March 10, 2010).

10. Stephanie Rosenbloom and Jack Healy, "Retailers Post Weak Earnings and July Sales," *The New York Times*, August 13, 2009, http://www.nytimes.com/2009/08/14/business/14shop.html?scp=2&sq=christmas%20sales%20percentage%20of%20annual&st=cse (accessed March 15, 2010).

11. Bruce Lambert, "Once Robust, Retail Scene on the Island Is Smarting," *The New York Times*, May 7, 2009, http://www.nytimes.com/2009/05/10/nyregion/long-island/10rooseveltli.html?scp=5&sq=retail%20bankruptcies&st=cse (accessed March 15, 2010).

12. John Jannarone, "Walmart Spices Up Private Label," *The Wall Street Journal*, February 6, 2010, http://online.wsj.com/article/SB10001424052748704533204575047110888997700.html?KEYWORDS=Walmart+shelf+space (accessed March 15, 2010).

13. Jack Neff, "Walmart Reversal Marks Victory for Brands," *Advertising Age*, March 22, 2010, http://adage.com/article?article_id=142904 (accessed September 30, 2010).

14. Stephanie Startz, "7-Eleven Recommends a Zesty Chardonnay with Your Corn Dog, Sir," *Brandchannel* (November 6, 2009), http://www.brandchannel.com/home/post/2009/11/06/7-Eleven-Recommends-A-Zesty-Chardonnay-With-Your-Corn-Dog-Sir.aspx, (accessed March 22, 2010).

15. Thomas M. Anderson, "Checkups on the Run," *Kiplinger Personal Finance*, May 2006, 96.

16. Bloomberg News, "Amazon's Holiday Sales Buoyed Profit," *The New York Times*, January 28, 2010, http://www.nytimes.com/2010/01/29/business/29amazon.html?scp=1&sq=amazon.com%20sales&st=cse (accessed March 15, 2010).

17. Barry Berman and Joel R. Evans, *Retail Management: A Strategic Approach*, 11th ed. (Upper Saddle River, NJ: Pearson Education 2010).

18. Mya Frazier, "The Store of the Future," *Advertising Age*, January 16, 2006, 1, 23.

19. Rebecca Harrison, "Restaurants Try E-Menus," *Reuters*, February 25, 2008, http://uk.reuters.com/article/internetNews/idUKL204599320080226

20. Bruce Einhorn and Wing-Gar Cheng, "China: Where Retail Dinosaurs Are Thriving," *BusinessWeek*, January 21, 2010.

21. Center for Retail Research, "Key Findings from the Global Retail Theft Barometer 2009," http://www.retailresearch.org/global_theft_baromter/2009keyfindings.php (accessed March 12, 2010).

22. Center for Retail Research, "Key Findings from the Global Retail Theft Barometer 2009," http://www.retailresearch.org/global_theft_baromter/2009keyfindings.php (accessed March 12, 2010).

23. Kathy Grannis, "Troubled Economy Increases Shoplifting Rates, According to National Retail Security Survey," National Retail Federation, June 16, 2009, http://www.nrf.com/modules.php?name=News&op=viewlive&sp_id=746 (accessed March 12, 2010).

24. Jessica Silver-Greenberg, "Shoplifters Get Smarter," *BusinessWeek*, November 19, 2007, http://www.businessweek.com/magazine/content/07_47/b4059051.htm?chan=search (accessed May 1, 2008).

25. Jessica Silver-Greenberg, "Shoplifters Get Smarter," *BusinessWeek*, November 19, 2007 (accessed May 1, 2008), http://www.businessweek.com/magazine/content/07_47/b4059051.htm?chan=search.

26. "Weird But True, the Naked Truth," *Convenience Store News*, October 22, 2007, 13.

27. "Shoplifter and Dishonest Employee Theft on Rise," Jack L. Hayes International, Inc., http://www.hayesinternational.com/thft_srvys.html (accessed May 1, 2008).

28. Steven Greenhouse, "Shoplifters? Studies Say Keep an Eye on Workers," *The New York Times*, December 29, 2009, http://www.nytimes.com/2009/12/30/business/30theft.html?scp=6&sq=shoplifting&st=cse (accessed March 12, 2010).

29. Kelly Gates and Dan Alaimo, "Solving Shrink," *Supermarket News*, October 22, 2007, 43.

30. Francis Piron and Murray Young, "Retail Borrowing: Insights and Implications on Returning Used Merchandise," *International Journal of Retail & Distribution Management*, Vol. 28, No. 1, 2000, 27–36.

31. Stephanie Rosenbloom, "In Bid to Sway Sales, Cameras Track Shoppers," *The New York Times*, March 19, 2010, http://www.nytimes.com/2010/03/20/business/20surveillance.html?th&emc=th (accessed March 20, 2010).

32. Linda Lisanti, "Adventure's Next Stop," *Convenience Store News*, March 3, 2008, 28–34; Michael Browne, "Maverik's Big Adventure," *Convenience Store News*, November 15, 2005, 50–54.

33. "About ALDI," http://www.aldifoods.com/us/html/company/about_aldi_ENU_HTML.htm?WT.z_src=main (accessed March 28, 2010).

34. Mark Albright, "Kohl's Debut with Fresh New Look," *The St. Petersburg Times*, September 28, 2006, 1D.

35. "Proof of Club Popularity in the 64-Ounce Pudding," *DSN Retailing Today*, December 19, 2005, 64.

36. Quoted in Stratford Sherman, "Will the Information Superhighway Be the Death of Retailing?" *Fortune*, April 18, 1994, 99(5), 110.

37. Direct Selling Association, Research Services Center, "Direct Selling by the Numbers, Calendar Year 2008," http://www.dsa.org/research/industry-statistics/#SALES (accessed March 18, 2010).

38. Direct Selling Association, "Direct Selling by the Numbers—Calendar Year 2006."

39. "About Amway," Amway, www.amway.com/en/General/About-Amway-10725.aspx (accessed June 25, 2006).

40. "Amway Corporation Company Profile," *Yahoo Finance*, http://biz.yahoo.com/ic/103/103441.html (accessed June 27, 2008).

41. H. J. Shrager, "Close Social Networks of Hasidic Women, Other Tight Groups, Boost Shaklee Sales," *Wall Street Journal*, November 19, 2001, www.wsj.com

42. "Pyramid Schemes," Direct Selling Association, www.dsa.org/aboutselling/consumer/dis_pyramid.cfm (accessed June 25, 2006).

43. Aili McConnon, "Vending Machines Go Luxe," *BusinessWeek*, January 29, 2008, 17.

44. Erick Schonfeld, "Forrester Forecast: Online Retail Sales Will Grow to $250 Billion by 2014," TechCrunch, March 8, 2010, http://techcrunch.com/2010/03/08/forrester-forecast-online-retail-sales-will-grow-to-250-billion-by-2014/ (accessed March 18, 2010).

45. Helen Leggatt, "Double-Digit Growth Ahead for U.S. and European Online Retail," *BizReport*, March 9, 2010, http://www.bizreport.com/2010/03/double-digit_growth_ahead_for_us_and_european_online_retail.html (accessed March 18, 2010).

46. Leena Rao, "Like.com Expands Digital Fashion Empire with Virtual Styling Tool Couturious," *TechCrunch*, February 23, 1010, http://techcrunch.com/2010/02/23/like-com-expands-digital-fashion-empire-with-virtual-styling-tool-couturious/ (accessed February 25, 2010).

47. Bob Tedeschi, "A Quicker Resort This Year to Deep Discounting," *New York Times*, December 17, 2007, http://www.nytimes.com/2007/12/17/technology/17ecom.html?scp=41&sq=forrester+research&st=nyt (accessed May 1, 2008).

48. Bob Tedeschi, "$7,900 Valentino Gowns, a Click Away," *New York Times*, November 5, 2007, http://www.nytimes.com/2007/12/17/technology/17ecom.html?_r=1&scp=41&sq=forrester+research&st=nyt&oref=slogin (accessed May 1, 2008).

49. "Fact Sheet," PayPal, https://www.paypal-media.com/documentdisplay.cfm?DocumentID=2258 (accessed March 28, 2010).

50. "Amazon.com Announces Fourth Quarter Sales up 42% to $5.7 Billion; 2007 Free Cash Flow More Than Doubles, Surpassing $1 Billion for the First Time," Press Releases, Amazon.com, http://phx.corporate-ir.net/phoenix.zhtml?c=176060&p=irol-newsArticle&ID=1102343&highlight= (accessed June 27, 2008).

51. Randy Hurlow, "REI to Open Store in Pittsburg," Industry News, Outdoor Industry Association, June 22, 2004, http://outdoorindustry.com/media.outdoor.php?news_id=640&sort_year=2006 (accessed June 27, 2008).

52. "A Wide World of Sports Shoes: Fixtures Enhance Appeal of World Foot Locker," *Chain Store Age Executive*, January 1993, 176–81.

53. Tracie Rozhon, "High Fashion, from Front Door to the Top Floor," *New York Times*, July 31, 2003, http://www.nytimes.com/2003/07/31/business/high-fashion-from-front-door-to-the-top-floor.html?scp=1&sq=High+Fashion%2C+from+Front+Door+to+the+Top+Floor&st=nyt (accessed December 29, 2010).

54. L. W. Turley and Ronald E. Milliman, "Atmospheric Effects on Shopping Behavior: A Review of the Experimental Evidence," *Journal of Business Research* 49 (2000): 193–211.

55. Eric Newman, "Retail Design for 2008: Thinking Outside the Big Box," *Brandweek*, December 17, 2007, 26.

56. Samantha Murphy, "A Contemporary Future," *Chain Store Age*, April 2007, 62.

57. Julie Flaherty, "Music to a Retailer's Ears; Sorry, Springsteen Won't Be Playing at Pottery Barn Today," *New York Times*, July 4, 2001, http://www.nytimes.com/2001/07/04/business/music-retailer-s-ears-sorry-springsteen-won-t-be-playing-pottery-barn-today.html?src=pm (accessed December 29, 2010).

58. http://www.muzak.com/muzak.html (accessed March 21, 2010); CBS TV, *Sunday Morning*, "Sound of Muzak," March 21, 2010.

59. Lorrie Grant, "Shopping in the Great Outdoors," *USAToday*, August 3, 2004, http://www.usatoday.com/money/industries/retail/2004-08-03-lifestyle-center_x.htm (accessed December 29, 2010).

60. Michael Levy and Barton A. Weitz, *Retailing Management*, 3rd ed. (Boston: Irwin/McGraw-Hill, 1998).

61. Quoted in Shirley Leung, "A Glutted Market Is Leaving Food Chains Hungry for Sites," *Wall Street Journal*, September 1, 2003.

Glossary

80/20 rule A marketing rule of thumb that 20 percent of purchasers account for 80 percent of a product's sales.

A

account executive (account manager) A member of the account management department who supervises the day-to-day activities of the account and is the primary liaison between the agency and the client.

account planner A member of the account management department who combines research and account strategy to act as the voice of the consumer in creating effective advertising.

action plans Individual support plans included in a marketing plan that provide the guidance for implementation and control of the various marketing strategies within the plan. Action plans are sometimes referred to as "marketing programs."

actual product The physical good or the delivered service that supplies the desired benefit.

advergaming Brand placements in video games.

advertising appeal The central idea or theme of an advertising message.

advertising campaign A coordinated, comprehensive plan that carries out promotion objectives and results in a series of advertisements placed in media over a period of time.

advertising Nonpersonal communication from an identified sponsor using the mass media.

advocacy advertising A type of public service advertising where an organization seeks to influence public opinion on an issue because it has some stake in the outcome.

affect The feeling component of attitudes; refers to the overall emotional response a person has to a product.

AIDA model The communication goals of attention, interest, desire, and action.

aided recall A research technique that uses clues to prompt answers from people about advertisements they might have seen.

AIOs Measures of consumer activities, interests and opinions used to place consumers into dimensions.

amafessionals Consumers who contribute ideas to online forums for the fun and challenge rather than to receive a paycheck, so their motivation is to gain *psychic income* rather than financial income.

anticonsumption The deliberate defacement of products.

AOR (Agency of Record) relationship A relationship where the client pays a monthly retainer fee to an agency for creative services.

approach The first step of the actual sales presentation in which the salesperson tries to learn more about the customer's needs, create a good impression, and build rapport.

atmospherics The use of color, lighting, scents, furnishings, and other design elements to create a desired store image.

attention economy A company's success is measured by its share of mind rather than share of market, where companies make money when they attract eyeballs rather than just dollars.

attention The extent to which a person devotes mental processing to a particular stimulus.

attitude A learned predisposition to respond favorably or unfavorably to stimuli on the basis of relatively enduring evaluations of people, objects, and issues.

attitudinal measures A research technique that probes a consumer's beliefs or feelings about a product before and after being exposed to messages about it.

attributes Include features, functions, benefits, and uses of a product. Marketers view products as a bundle of attributes that includes the packaging, brand name, benefits, and supporting features in addition to a physical good.

augmented product The actual product plus other supporting features such as a warranty, credit, delivery, installation, and repair service after the sale.

augmented reality A form of technology where a view of a real-world environment joins a layer of virtual computer-generated imagery to create a mixed reality.

augmented services The core service plus additional services provided to enhance value.

automatic reordering system Retail reordering system that is automatically activated when inventories reach a certain level.

avatars Graphic representations of users of virtual worlds.

average fixed cost The fixed cost per unit produced.

B

baby boomers The segment of people born between 1946 and 1964.

back-translation The process of translating material to a foreign language and then back to the original language.

backward invention strategy Product strategy in which a firm develops a less advanced product to serve the needs of people living in countries without electricity or other elements of a developed infrastructure.

bait-and-switch An illegal marketing practice in which an advertised price special is used as bait to get customers into the store with the intention of switching them to a higher-priced item.

banners Internet advertising in the form of rectangular graphics at the top or bottom of Web pages.

basing-point pricing A pricing tactic in which customers pay shipping charges from set basing-point locations, whether the goods are actually shipped from these points or not.

BCG growth–market share matrix A portfolio analysis model developed by the Boston Consulting Group that assesses the potential of successful products to generate cash that a firm can then use to invest in new products.

behavior The doing component of attitudes; involves a consumer's intention to do something, such as the intention to purchase or use a certain product.

behavioral learning theories Theories of learning that focus on how consumer behavior is changed by external events or stimuli.

behavioral segmentation A technique that divides consumers into segments on the basis of how they act toward, feel about, or use a good or service.

behavioral targeting The marketing practice by which marketers deliver advertisements for products a consumer is looking for by watching what the consumer does online.

benefit The outcome sought by a customer that motivates buying behavior—that satisfies a need or want.

bottom-up budgeting techniques Allocation of the promotion budget based on identifying promotion goals and allocating enough money to accomplish them.

box stores Food stores that have a limited selection of items, few brands per item, and few refrigerated items.

brand ambassadors or **brand evangelists** Loyal customers of a brand recruited to communicate and be salespeople with other consumers for a brand they care a great deal about.

brand competition When firms offering similar goods or services compete on the basis of their brand's reputation or perceived benefits.

brand equity The value of a brand to an organization.

brand extensions A new product sold with the same brand name as a strong existing brand.

brand loyalty A pattern of repeat product purchases, accompanied by an underlying positive attitude toward the brand, based on the belief that the brand makes products superior to those of its competition.

brand manager An individual who is responsible for developing and implementing the marketing plan for a single brand.

brand meaning The beliefs and associations that a consumer has about the brand.

brand personality A distinctive image that captures a good's or service's character and benefits.

brand storytelling Marketers seek to engage consumers with compelling stories about brands.

brand A name, a term, a symbol, or any other unique element of a product that identifies one firm's product(s) and sets it apart from the competition.

branded entertainment A form of advertising in which marketers integrate products into entertainment venues.

brandfests Events companies host to thank customers for their loyalty.

break-even analysis A method for determining the number of units that a firm must produce and sell at a given price to cover all its costs.

break-even point The point at which the total revenue and total costs are equal and beyond which the company makes a profit; below that point, the firm will suffer a loss.

breaking bulk Dividing larger quantities of goods into smaller lots in order to meet the needs of buyers.

bribery When someone voluntarily offers payment to get an illegal advantage.

BRIC countries Refers to Brazil, Russia, India, and China, the largest and fastest growing of the developing countries with over 40 percent of the world's population

business analysis The step in the product development process in which marketers assess a product's commercial viability.

business cycle The overall patterns of change in the economy—including periods of prosperity, recession, depression, and recovery—that affect consumer and business purchasing power.

business ethics Rules of conduct for an organization.

business plan A plan that includes the decisions that guide the entire organization.

business planning An ongoing process of making decisions that guides the firm both in the short term and for the long term.

business portfolio The group of different products or brands owned by an organization and characterized by different income-generating and growth capabilities.

business-to-business (B2B) e-commerce Internet exchanges between two or more businesses or organizations.

business-to-business (B2B) markets The group of customers that include manufacturers, wholesalers, retailers, and other organizations.

business-to-business marketing The marketing of goods and services from one organization to another.

business-to-consumer (B2C) e-commerce On-line exchanges between companies and individual consumers.

buttons Small banner-type advertisements that can be placed anywhere on a Web page.

buyclass One of three classifications of business buying situations that characterizes the degree of time and effort required to make a decision.

buying center The group of people in an organization who participate in a purchasing decision.

buzz Word-of-mouth communication that customers view as authentic.

C

cannibalization The loss of sales of an existing brand when a new item in a product line or product family is introduced.

capacity management The process by which organizations adjust their offerings in an attempt to match demand.

captive pricing A pricing tactic for two items that must be used together; one item is priced very low, and the firm makes its profit on another, high-margin item essential to the operation of the first item.

case allowance A discount to the retailer or wholesaler based on the volume of product ordered.

case study A comprehensive examination of a particular firm or organization.

cash cows SBUs with a dominant market share in a low-growth-potential market.

cash discounts A discount offered to a customer to entice them to pay their bill quickly.

catalog A collection of products offered for sale in book form, usually consisting of product descriptions accompanied by photos of the items.

category killer A very large specialty store that carries a vast selection of products in its category.

causal research A technique that attempts to understand cause-and-effect relationships.

central business district (CBD) The traditional downtown business area found in a town or city.

channel intermediaries Firms or individuals such as wholesalers, agents, brokers, or retailers who help move a product from the producer to the consumer or business user. An older term for intermediaries is middlemen.

channel leader A firm at one level of distribution that takes a leadership role, establishing operating norms and processes based on its power relative to other channel members.

channel levels The number of distinct categories of intermediaries that populate a channel of distribution.

channel of distribution The series of firms or individuals that facilitates the movement of a product from the producer to the final customer.

classical conditioning   The learning that occurs when a stimulus eliciting a response is paired with another stimulus that initially does not elicit a response on its own but will cause a similar response over time because of its association with the first stimulus.

close   The stage of the selling process in which the salesperson actually asks the customer to buy the product.

co-op advertising   A sales promotion where the manufacturer and the retailer share the cost.

cobranding   An agreement between two brands to work together to market a new product.

code of ethics   Written standards of behavior to which everyone in the organization must subscribe.

cognition   The knowing component of attitudes; refers to the beliefs or knowledge a person has about a product and its important characteristics.

cognitive dissonance   The anxiety or regret a consumer may feel after choosing from among several similar attractive choices.

cognitive learning theory   Theory of learning that stresses the importance of internal mental processes and that views people as problem solvers who actively use information from the world around them to master their environment.

collectivist cultures   Cultures in which people subordinate their personal goals to those of a stable community.

combination stores   Retailers that offer consumers food and general merchandise in the same store.

commercialization   The final step in the product development process in which a new product is launched into the market.

communication model   The process whereby meaning is transferred from a source to a receiver.

comparison shopping agents or shopbots   Web applications that help online shoppers find what they are looking for at the lowest price and provide customer reviews and ratings of products and sellers

compatibility   The extent to which a new product is consistent with existing cultural values, customs, and practices.

competitive intelligence (CI)   The process of gathering and analyzing publicly available information about rivals.

competitive-parity budgeting method   A promotion budgeting method in which an organization matches whatever competitors are spending.

complexity   The degree to which consumers find a new product or its use difficult to understand.

component parts   Manufactured goods or subassemblies of finished items that organizations need to complete their own products.

concentrated targeting strategy   Focusing a firm's efforts on offering one or more products to a single segment.

consumer behavior   The process involved when individuals or groups select, purchase, use, and dispose of goods, services, ideas, or experiences to satisfy their needs and desires.

consumer goods   The goods individual consumers purchase for personal or family use.

consumer orientation   A business approach that prioritizes the satisfaction of customers' needs and wants.

consumer satisfaction/dissatisfaction   The overall feelings or attitude a person has about a product after purchasing it.

consumer-generated content   Everyday people functioning in marketing roles, such as participating in creating advertisements, providing input to new product development, or serving as wholesalers or retailers.

consumer   The ultimate user of a good or service.

consumerism   A social movement that attempts to protect consumers from harmful business practices.

continuous innovation   A modification of an existing product that sets one brand apart from its competitors.

contribution per unit   The difference between the price the firm charges for a product and the variable costs.

control   A process that entails measuring actual performance, comparing this performance to the established marketing objectives, and then making adjustments to the strategies or objectives on the basis of this analysis.

convenience product   A consumer good or service that is usually low-priced, widely available, and purchased frequently with a minimum of comparison and effort.

convenience sample   A nonprobability sample composed of individuals who just happen to be available when and where the data are being collected.

convenience stores   Neighborhood retailers that carry a limited number of frequently purchased items and cater to consumers willing to pay a premium for the ease of buying close to home.

conventional marketing system   A multiple-level distribution channel in which channel members work independently of one another.

convergence   The coming together of two or more technologies to create a new system with greater benefits than its separate parts.

cookies   Text files inserted by a Web site sponsor into a Web surfer's hard drive that allows the site to track the surfer's moves.

core product   All the benefits the product will provide for consumers or business customers.

core service   The basic benefit of having a service performed.

corporate advertising   Advertising that promotes the company as a whole instead of a firm's individual products.

corporate identity   Materials such as logos, brochures, building design, and stationery that communicate an image of the organization.

corrective advertising   Advertising that clarifies or qualifies previous deceptive advertising claims.

cost per thousand (CPM)   A measure used to compare the relative cost-effectiveness of different media vehicles that have different exposure rates; the cost to deliver a message to 1,000 people or homes.

cost-plus pricing   A method of setting prices in which the seller totals all the costs for the product and then adds an amount to arrive at the selling price.

countertrade   A type of trade in which goods are paid for with other items instead of with cash.

creating assortments   Providing a variety of products in one location to meet the needs of buyers.

creative brief   A guideline or blueprint for the marketing communication program that guides the creative process.

creative selling process The process of seeking out potential customers, analyzing needs, determining how product attributes might provide benefits for the customer, and then communicating that information.

creative services The agency people (creative director, copywriters, and art director) who dream up and produce the ads.

creative strategy The process that turns a concept into an advertisement.

credence qualities Product characteristics that are difficult to evaluate even after they have been experienced.

crisis management The process of managing a company's reputation when some negative event threatens the organization's image.

critical incident technique A method for measuring service quality in which marketers use customer complaints to identify critical incidents—specific face-to-face contacts between consumer and service providers that cause problems and lead to dissatisfaction.

cross-elasticity of demand When changes in the price of one product affect the demand for another item.

cross-sectional design A type of descriptive technique that involves the systematic collection of quantitative information.

crowdsourcing A practice in which firms outsource marketing activities (such as selecting an ad) to a community of users.

cultural diversity A management practice that actively seeks to include people of different sexes, races, ethnic groups, and religions in an organization's employees, customers, suppliers, and distribution channel partners.

cultural values A society's deeply held beliefs about right and wrong ways to live.

culture The values, beliefs, customs, and tastes a group of people values.

custom marketing strategy An approach that tailors specific products and the messages about them to individual customers.

custom research Research conducted for a single firm to provide specific information its managers need.

customer equity The financial value of a customer relationship throughout the lifetime of the relationship.

customer reference program A formalized process by which customers formally share success stories and actively recommend products to other potential clients, usually facilitated through an on-line community.

customer relationship management (CRM) A systematic tracking of consumers' preferences and behaviors over time in order to tailor the value proposition as closely as possible to each individual's unique wants and needs. CRM allows firms to talk to individual customers and to adjust elements of their marketing programs in light of how each customer reacts.

D

data mining Sophisticated analysis techniques to take advantage of the massive amount of transaction information now available.

decline stage The final stage in the product life cycle, during which sales decrease as customer needs change.

decoding The process by which a receiver assigns meaning to the message.

demand-based pricing A price-setting method based on estimates of demand at different prices.

demand Customers' desires for products coupled with the resources needed to obtain them.

demographics Statistics that measure observable aspects of a population, including size, age, gender, ethnic group, income, education, occupation, and family structure.

department stores Retailers that sell a broad range of items and offer a good selection within each product line.

derived demand Demand for business or organizational products caused by demand for consumer goods or services.

descriptive research A tool that probes more systematically into the problem and bases its conclusions on large numbers of observations.

developed country A country that boasts sophisticated marketing systems, strong private enterprise, and bountiful market potential for many goods and services.

developing countries Countries in which the economy is shifting its emphasis from agriculture to industry.

differential benefit Properties of products that set them apart from competitors' products by providing unique customer benefits.

differentiated targeting strategy Developing one or more products for each of several distinct customer groups and making sure these offerings are kept separate in the marketplace.

diffusion The process by which the use of a product spreads throughout a population.

digital media Media that are digital rather than analog including Web sites, mobile or cellular phones, and digital video such as YouTube.

digital signage Out-of-home media that use digital technology to change the message at will.

direct mail A brochure or pamphlet that offers a specific good or service at one point in time.

direct marketing Any direct communication to a consumer or business recipient designed to generate a response in the form of an order, a request for further information, and/or a visit to a store or other place of business for purchase of a product.

direct selling An interactive sales process in which a salesperson presents a product to one individual or a small group, takes orders, and delivers the merchandise.

direct-response advertising A direct marketing approach that allows the consumer to respond to a message by immediately contacting the provider to ask questions or order the product.

direct-response TV (DRTV) Advertising on TV that seeks a direct response, including short commercials of less than two minutes, 30-minute or longer infomercials, and home shopping networks.

discontinuous innovation A totally new product that creates major changes in the way we live.

discretionary income The portion of income people have left over after paying for necessities such as housing, utilities, food, and clothing.

disintermediation (of the channel of distribution) The elimination of some layers of the channel of distribution in order to cut costs and improve the efficiency of the channel.

disintermediation A service that requires the customer to obtain an outcome without the intervention of a human provider.

distinctive competency   A superior capability of a firm in comparison to its direct competitors.

diversification strategies   Growth strategies that emphasize both new products and new markets.

do-it-yourself (DIY) ads   Product ads that are created by consumers.

dogs   SBUs with a small share of a slow-growth market. They are businesses that offer specialized products in limited markets that are not likely to grow quickly.

downsizing   When a firm in a mature industry closes or sells off unprofitable stores or entire divisions.

dumping   A company tries to get a toehold in a foreign market by pricing its products lower than it offers them at home.

durable goods   Consumer products that provide benefits over a long period of time, such as cars, furniture, and appliances.

dynamic pricing   A pricing strategy in which the price can easily be adjusted to meet changes in the marketplace.

dynamically continuous innovation   A change in an existing product that requires a moderate amount of learning or behavior change.

E

e-commerce   The buying or selling of goods and services electronically, usually over the Internet.

e-mail advertising   Advertising messages sent via e-mail to large numbers of people simultaneously.

early adopters   Those who adopt an innovation early in the diffusion process, but after the innovators.

early majority   Those whose adoption of a new product signals a general acceptance of the innovation.

earned media   Word-of-mouth or buzz using social media where the advertiser has no control.

economic communities   Groups of countries that band together to promote trade among themselves and to make it easier for member nations to compete elsewhere.

economic infrastructure   The quality of a country's distribution, financial, and communications systems.

elastic demand   Demand in which changes in price have large effects on the amount demanded.

embargo   A quota completely prohibiting specified goods from entering or leaving a country.

emergency products   Products we purchase when we're in dire need.

encoding   The process of translating an idea into a form of communication that will convey meaning.

enterprise resource planning (ERP) systems   A software system that integrates information from across the entire company, including finance, order fulfillment, manufacturing, and transportation and then facilitates sharing of the data throughout the firm.

environmental stewardship   A position taken by an organization to protect or enhance the natural environment as it conducts its business activities.

environmentalism   A broad philosophy and social movement that seeks conservation and improvement of the natural environment.

equipment   Expensive goods that an organization uses in its daily operations that last for a long time.

ethnocentrism   The tendency to prefer products or people of one's own culture.

ethnography   An approach to research based on observations of people in their own homes or communities.

evaluative criteria   The dimensions consumers use to compare competing product alternatives.

exchange   The process by which some transfer of value occurs between a buyer and a seller.

exclusive distribution   Selling a product only through a single outlet in a particular region.

execution format   The basic structure of the message such as comparison, demonstration, testimonial, slice-of-life and lifestyle.

experience qualities   Product characteristics that customers can determine during or after consumption.

experiential shoppers   Consumers who engage in on-line shopping because of the experiential benefits they receive.

experiments   A technique that tests predicted relationships among variables in a controlled environment.

exploratory research   A technique that marketers use to generate insights for future, more rigorous studies.

export merchants   Intermediaries a firm uses to represent it in other countries.

exposure   The extent to which a stimulus is capable of being registered by a person's sensory receptors.

expropriation   When a domestic government seizes a foreign company's assets without any reimbursement.

external environment   The uncontrollable elements outside an organization that may affect its performance either positively or negatively.

extortion   When someone in authority extracts payment under duress.

extranet   A private, corporate computer network that links company departments, employees, and databases to suppliers, customers, and others outside the organization.

F

F.O.B. delivered pricing   A pricing tactic in which the cost of loading and transporting the product to the customer is included in the selling price and is paid by the manufacturer.

F.O.B. origin pricing   A pricing tactic in which the cost of transporting the product from the factory to the customer's location is the responsibility of the customer.

facilitating functions   Functions of channel intermediaries that make the purchase process easier for customers and manufacturers.

factory outlet store   A discount retailer, owned by a manufacturer, that sells off defective merchandise and excess inventory.

family brand   A brand that a group of individual products or individual brands share.

family life cycle   A means of characterizing consumers within a family structure on the basis of different stages through which people pass as they grow older.

feedback   Receivers' reactions to the message.

fixed costs   Costs of production that do not change with the number of units produced.

focus group   A product-oriented discussion among a small group of consumers led by a trained moderator.

folksonomy   A classification system that relies on users rather than preestablished systems to sort contents.

follow-up   Activities after the sale that provide important services to customers.

Four Ps   Product, price, promotion, and place.

franchising A form of licensing involving the right to adapt an entire system of doing business.

free trade zones Designated areas where foreign companies can warehouse goods without paying taxes or customs duties until they move the goods into the marketplace.

freenomics A business model that encourages giving products away for free because of the increase in profits that can be achieved by getting more people to participate in a market.

freight absorption pricing A pricing tactic in which the seller absorbs the total cost of transportation.

frequency programs Consumer sales promotion programs that offer a discount or free product for multiple purchases over time; also referred to as loyalty or continuity programs.

frequency The average number of times a person in the target group will be exposed to the message.

full-service agency An agency that provides most or all of the services needed to mount a campaign, including research, creation of ad copy and art, media selection, and production of the final messages.

functional planning A decision process that concentrates on developing detailed plans for strategies and tactics for the short term, supporting an organization's long-term strategic plan.

G

gap analysis A marketing research method that measures the difference between a customer's expectation of a service quality and what actually occurred.

gender roles Society's expectations regarding the appropriate attitudes, behaviors, and appearance for men and women.

General Agreement on Tariffs and Trade (GATT) International treaty to reduce import tax levels and trade restrictions.

general merchandise discount stores Retailers that offer a broad assortment of items at low prices with minimal service.

Generation X The group of consumers born between 1965 and 1978.

Generation Y The group of consumers born between 1979 and 1994.

generational marketing Marketing to members of a generation, who tend to share the same outlook and priorities.

generic branding A strategy in which products are not branded and are sold at the lowest price possible.

geocoding Customizing Web advertising so that people who log on in different places will see ad banners for local businesses.

geodemography A segmentation technique that combines geography with demographics.

geospatial platforms Digital applications that integrate sophisticated GPS technology to enable users to alert friends of their exact whereabouts via their mobile phones.

good A tangible product that we can see, touch, smell, hear, or taste.

government markets The federal, state, county, and local governments that buy goods and services to carry out public objectives and to support their operations.

gray market goods Items manufactured outside a country and then imported without the consent of the trademark holder.

green marketing A marketing strategy that supports environmental stewardship, thus creating a differential benefit in the minds of consumers.

Green River Ordinances Community regulations that prohibit door-to-door selling unless prior permission is given by the household.

greenwashing A practice in which companies promote their products as environmentally friendly when in truth the brand provides little ecological benefit.

gross domestic product (GDP) The total dollar value of goods and services produced by a nation within its borders in a year.

gross margin The markup amount added to the cost of a product to cover the fixed costs of the retailer or wholesaler and leave an amount for a profit.

gross national product (GNP) The value of all goods and services produced by a country's citizens or organizations, whether located within the country's borders or not.

gross rating points (GRPs) A measure used for comparing the effectiveness of different media vehicles: average reach × frequency.

groundswell A social trend in which people use technology to get the things they need from each other, rather than from traditional institutions like corporations.

Group of 8 (G8) An informal forum of the eight most economically developed countries that meets annually to discuss major economic and political issues facing the international community.

growth stage The second stage in the product life cycle, during which consumers accept the product and sales rapidly increase.

guerrilla marketing Marketing activity in which a firm "ambushes" consumers with promotional content in places they are not expecting to encounter this kind of activity.

H

heuristics A mental rule of thumb that leads to a speedy decision by simplifying the process.

hierarchy of effects A series of steps prospective customers move through, from initial awareness of a product to brand loyalty.

hierarchy of needs An approach that categorizes motives according to five levels of importance, the more basic needs being on the bottom of the hierarchy and the higher needs at the top.

horizontal marketing system An arrangement within a channel of distribution in which two or more firms at the same channel level work together for a common purpose.

hybrid marketing system A marketing system that uses a number of different channels and communication methods to serve a target market.

hypermarkets Retailers with the characteristics of both warehouse stores and supermarkets; hypermarkets are several times larger than other stores and offer virtually everything from grocery items to electronics.

I

idea generation The first step of product development in which marketers brainstorm for products that provide customer benefits and are compatible with the company mission.

idea marketing Marketing activities that seek to gain market share for a concept, philosophy, belief, or issue by using elements of the marketing mix to create or change a target market's attitude or behavior.

import quotas Limitations set by a government on the amount of a product allowed to enter or leave a country.

impulse products A product people often buy on the spur of the moment.

impulse purchase A purchase made without any planning or search effort.

independent intermediaries Channel intermediaries that are not controlled by any manufacturer but instead do business with many different manufacturers and many different customers.

individualist cultures   Cultures in which people tend to attach more importance to personal goals than to those of the larger community.

industrial goods   Goods individuals or organizations buy for further processing or for their own use when they do business.

inelastic demand   Demand in which changes in price have little or no effect on the amount demanded.

infomercials   Half-hour or hour-long commercials that resemble a talk show but actually are sales pitches.

information search   The process whereby a consumer searches for appropriate information to make a reasonable decision.

innovation   A product that consumers perceive to be new and different from existing products.

innovators   The first segment (roughly 2.5 percent) of a population to adopt a new product.

inseparability   The characteristic of a service that means that it is impossible to separate the production of a service from the consumption of that service.

insourcing   A practice in which a company contracts with a specialist firm to handle all or part of its supply chain operations.

instapreneur   A businessperson who only produces a product when it is ordered.

institutional advertising   Advertising messages that promote the activities, personality, or point of view of an organization or company.

intangibility   The characteristic of a service that means customers can't see, touch, or smell good service.

intangibles   Experience-based products.

integrated marketing communication (IMC)   A strategic business process that marketers use to plan, develop, execute, and evaluate coordinated, measurable, persuasive brand communication programs over time to targeted audiences.

intelligent agents   Computer programs that find sites selling a particular product.

intensive distribution   Selling a product through all suitable wholesalers or retailers that are willing to stock and sell the product.

internal environment   The controllable elements inside an organization, including its people, its facilities, and how it does things that influence the operations of the organization.

internal PR   PR activities aimed at employees of an organization.

internal reference price   A set price or a price range in consumers' minds that they refer to in evaluating a product's price.

interpretation   The process of assigning meaning to a stimulus based on prior associations a person has with it and assumptions he or she makes about it.

intranet   An internal corporate communication network that uses Internet technology to link company departments, employees, and databases.

introduction stage   The first stage of the product life cycle in which slow growth follows the introduction of a new product in the marketplace.

inventory control   Activities to ensure that goods are always available to meet customers' demands.

investor relations   PR activities such as annual and quarterly reports aimed at a firm's investors.

involvement   The relative importance of perceived consequences of the purchase to a consumer.

ISO 14000   Standards of the International Organization for Standardization concerned with "environmental management" aimed at minimizing harmful effects on the environment.

ISO 9000   Criteria developed by the International Organization for Standardization to regulate product quality in Europe.

J

jingles   Original words and music written specifically for advertising executions.

joint demand   Demand for two or more goods that are used together to create a product.

joint venture   A strategic alliance in which a new entity owned by two or more firms allows the partners to pool their resources for common goals.

just in time (JIT)   Inventory management and purchasing processes that manufacturers and resellers use to reduce inventory to very low levels and ensure that deliveries from suppliers arrive only when needed.

K

knockoff   A new product that copies, with slight modification, the design of an original product.

knowledge management   A comprehensive approach to collecting, organizing, storing, and retrieving a firm's information assets.

Kyoto Protocol   A global agreement among countries that aims at reducing greenhouse gases that create climate change.

L

laggards   The last consumers to adopt an innovation.

late majority   The adopters who are willing to try new products when there is little or no risk associated with the purchase, when the purchase becomes an economic necessity, or when there is social pressure to purchase.

learning   A relatively permanent change in behavior caused by acquired information or experience.

leased departments   Departments within a larger retail store that an outside firm rents.

least developed country (LDC)   A country at the lowest stage of economic development.

level of economic development   The broader economic picture of a country.

licensing agreement   An agreement in which one firm gives another firm the right to produce and market its product in a specific country or region in return for royalties.

licensing   An agreement in which one firm sells another firm the right to use a brand name for a specific purpose and for a specific period of time.

lifestyle   The pattern of living that determines how people choose to spend their time, money, and energy and that reflects their values, tastes, and preferences.

lifetime value of a customer   The potential profit a single customer's purchase of a firm's products generates over the customer's lifetime.

limited-service agency   An agency that provides one or more specialized services, such as media buying or creative development.

list price or manufacturer's suggested retail price (MSRP)   The price the end customer is expected to pay as determined by the manufacturer; also referred to as the suggested retail price. The appropriate price for the end customer to pay as determined by the manufacturer.

lobbying   Talking with and providing information to government officials in order to influence their activities relating to an organization.

local content rules   A form of protectionism stipulating that a certain proportion of a product must consist of components supplied by industries in the host country or economic community.

logistics   The process of designing, managing, and improving the movement of products through the supply chain. Logistics includes purchasing, manufacturing, storage, and transport.

long tail A new approach to segmentation based on the idea that companies can make money by selling small amounts of items that only a few people want, provided they sell enough different items.

longitudinal design A technique that tracks the responses of the same sample of respondents over time.

loss-leader pricing The pricing policy of setting prices very low or even below cost to attract customers into a store.

M

m-commerce Promotional and other e-commerce activities transmitted over mobile phones and other mobile devices, such as smartphones and personal digital assistants (PDAs).

maintenance, repair, and operating (MRO) products Goods that a business customer consumes in a relatively short time.

mall-intercept A study in which researchers recruit shoppers in malls or other public areas.

marginal analysis A method that uses cost and demand to identify the price that will maximize profits.

marginal cost The increase in total cost that results from producing one additional unit of a product.

marginal revenue The increase in total income or revenue that results from selling one additional unit of a product.

market development strategies Growth strategies that introduce existing products to new markets.

market fragmentation The creation of many consumer groups due to a diversity of distinct needs and wants in modern society.

market manager An individual who is responsible for developing and implementing the marketing plans for products sold to a particular customer group.

market penetration strategies Growth strategies designed to increase sales of existing products to current customers, nonusers, and users of competitive brands in served markets.

market position The way in which the target market perceives the product in comparison to competitors' brands.

market segment A distinct group of customers within a larger market who are similar to one another in some way and whose needs differ from other customers in the larger market.

market All the customers and potential customers who share a common need that can be satisfied by a specific product, who have the resources to exchange for it, who are willing to make the exchange, and who have the authority to make the exchange.

marketing concept A management orientation that focuses on identifying and satisfying consumer needs to ensure the organization's long-term profitability.

marketing decision support system (MDSS) The data, analysis software, and interactive software that allow managers to conduct analyses and find the information they need.

marketing information system (MIS) A process that first determines what information marketing managers need and then gathers, sorts, analyzes, stores, and distributes relevant and timely marketing information to system users.

marketing intelligence system A method by which marketers get information about everyday happenings in the marketing environment.

marketing mix A combination of the product itself, the price of the product, the place where it is made available, and the activities that introduce it to consumers that creates a desired response among a set of predefined consumers.

marketing plan A document that describes the marketing environment, outlines the marketing objectives and strategy, and identifies who will be responsible for carrying out each part of the marketing strategy.

marketing research ethics Taking an ethical and above-board approach to conducting marketing research that does no harm to the participant in the process of conducting the research.

marketing research The process of collecting, analyzing, and interpreting data about customers, competitors, and the business environment in order to improve marketing effectiveness.

marketing scorecards Feedback vehicles that report (often in quantified terms) how the company or brand is actually doing in achieving various goals.

marketing An organizational function and a set of processes for creating, communicating, and delivering value to customers and for managing customer relationships in ways that benefit the organization and its stakeholders.

marketplace Any location or medium used to conduct an exchange.

markup An amount added to the cost of a product to create the price at which a channel member will sell the product.

marquee The sign that shows a store's name.

mass communication Relates to television, radio, magazines, and newspapers.

mass customization An approach that modifies a basic good or service to meet the needs of an individual.

mass market All possible customers in a market, regardless of the differences in their specific needs and wants.

mass-class The hundreds of millions of global consumers who now enjoy a level of purchasing power that's sufficient to let them afford high-quality products—except for big-ticket items like college educations, housing, or luxury cars.

materials handling The moving of products into, within, and out of warehouses.

maturity stage The third and longest stage in the product life cycle, during which sales peak and profit margins narrow.

media blitz A massive advertising campaign that occurs over a relatively short time frame.

media planners Agency personnel who determine which communication vehicles are the most effective and efficient to deliver the ad.

media planning The process of developing media objectives, strategies, and tactics for use in an advertising campaign.

media relations A PR activity aimed at developing close relationships with the media.

media schedule The plan that specifies the exact media to use and when to use it.

medium A communication vehicle through which a message is transmitted to a target audience.

merchandise agents or brokers Channel intermediaries that provide services in exchange for commissions but never take title to the product.

merchandise assortment The range of products a store sells.

merchandise breadth The number of different product lines available.

merchandise depth The variety of choices available for each specific product line.

merchandise mix The total set of all products offered for sale by a retailer, including all product lines sold to all consumer groups.

merchandising allowance Reimburses the retailer for in-store support of the product.

merchant wholesalers Intermediaries that buy goods from manufacturers (take title to them) and sell to retailers and other business-to-business customers.

mergers When two or more separately owned retail firms combine.

message The communication in physical form that goes from a sender to a receiver.

metrics Measurements or "scorecards" marketers use to identify the effectiveness of different strategies or tactics.

metrosexual A straight, urban male who is keenly interested in fashion, home design, gourmet cooking, and personal care.

microcultures Groups of consumers who identify with a specific activity or art form.

mission statement A formal statement in an organization's strategic plan that describes the overall purpose of the organization and what it intends to achieve in terms of its customers, products, and resources.

missionary salesperson A salesperson who promotes the firm and tries to stimulate demand for a product but does not actually complete a sale.

mobile advertising A form of advertising that is communicated to the consumer via a handset.

modified rebuy A buying situation classification used by business buyers to categorize a previously made purchase that involves some change and that requires limited decision making.

monopolistic competition A market structure in which many firms, each having slightly different products, offer unique consumer benefits.

monopoly A market situation in which one firm, the only supplier of a particular product, is able to control the price, quality, and supply of that product.

motivation An internal state that drives us to satisfy needs by activating goal-oriented behavior.

multichannel promotional strategy A marketing communication strategy where they combine traditional advertising, sales promotion, and public relations activities with online buzz-building activities.

multilevel or network marketing A system in which a master distributor recruits other people to become distributors, sells the company's product to the recruits, and receives a commission on all the merchandise sold by the people recruited.

multiple sourcing The business practice of buying a particular product from several different suppliers.

myths Stories containing symbolic elements that express the shared emotions and ideals of a culture.

N

national or manufacturer brands Brands that the product manufacturer owns.

nationalization When a domestic government reimburses a foreign company (often not for the full value) for its assets after taking it over.

need The recognition of any difference between a consumer's actual state and some ideal or desired state.

new dominant logic for marketing A reconceptualization of traditional marketing to redefine service as the central (core) deliverable and the actual physical products purveyed as comparatively incidental to the value proposition.

new product development (NPD) The phases by which firms develop new products including idea generation, product concept development and screening, marketing strategy development, business analysis, technical development, test marketing, and commercialization.

new-business salesperson The person responsible for finding new customers and calling on them to present the company's products.

new-task buy A new business-to-business purchase that is complex or risky and that requires extensive decision making.

noise Anything that interferes with effective communication.

nondurable goods Consumer products that provide benefits for a short time because they are consumed (such as food) or are no longer useful (such as newspapers).

nonprobability sample A sample in which personal judgment is used to select respondents.

nonstore retailing Any method used to complete an exchange with a product end user that does not require a customer visit to a store.

North American Industry Classification System (NAICS) The numerical coding system that the United States, Canada, and Mexico use to classify firms into detailed categories according to their business activities.

not-for-profit institutions The organizations with charitable, educational, community, and other public service goals that buy goods and services to support their functions and to attract and serve their members.

O

objective-task method A promotion budgeting method in which an organization first defines the specific communication goals it hopes to achieve and then tries to calculate what kind of promotion efforts it will take to meet these goals.

observability How visible a new product and its benefits are to others who might adopt it.

observational learning Learning that occurs when people watch the actions of others and note what happens to them as a result.

off-price retailers Retailers that buy excess merchandise from well-known manufacturers and pass the savings on to customers.

oligopoly A market structure in which a relatively small number of sellers, each holding a substantial share of the market, compete in a market with many buyers.

on-line auctions E-commerce that allows shoppers to purchase products through online bidding.

online distribution piracy The theft and unauthorized repurposing of intellectual property via the Internet.

open source model A practice used in the software industry in which companies share their software codes with one another to assist in the development of a better product.

operant conditioning Learning that occurs as the result of rewards or punishments.

operational planning A decision process that focuses on developing detailed plans for day-to-day activities that carry out an organization's functional plans.

operational plans Plans that focus on the day-to-day execution of the marketing plan. Operational plans include detailed directions for the specific activities to be carried out, who will be responsible for them, and time lines for accomplishing the tasks.

opinion leader A person who is frequently able to influence others' attitudes or behaviors by virtue of his or her active interest and expertise in one or more product categories.

order getter A salesperson who works to develop long-term relationships with particular customers or to generate new sales.

order processing The series of activities that occurs between the time an order comes into the organization and the time a product goes out the door.

order taker A salesperson whose primary function is to facilitate transactions that the customer initiates.

organizational markets Another name for business-to-business markets.

out-of-home media Communication media that reach people in public places.

outsourcing The business buying process of obtaining outside vendors to provide goods or services that otherwise might be supplied in-house.

owned media Internet sites such as Web sites, blogs, Facebook, and Twitter accounts that are owned by an advertiser.

P

package The covering or container for a product that provides product protection, facilitates product use and storage, and supplies important marketing communication.

paid media Internet media such as display ads, sponsorships, and paid key word searches that are paid for by an advertiser.

party plan system A sales technique that relies heavily on people getting caught up in the "group spirit," buying things they would not normally buy if they were alone.

patent A legal mechanism to prevent competitors from producing or selling an invention, aimed at reducing or eliminating competition in a market for a period of time.

penetration pricing A pricing strategy in which a firm introduces a new product at a very low price to encourage more customers to purchase it.

perceived risk The belief that choice of a product has potentially negative consequences, whether financial, physical, and/or social.

percentage-of-sales budgeting method A method for promotion budgeting that is based on a certain percentage of either last year's sales or on estimates of the present year's sales.

perception The process by which people select, organize, and interpret information from the outside world.

perceptual map A technique to visually describe where brands are "located" in consumers' minds relative to competing brands.

perfect competition A market structure in which many small sellers, all of whom offer similar products, are unable to have an impact on the quality, price, or supply of a product.

perfect order measurement A supply chain metric that tracks multiple steps in getting a product from a manufacturer to a customer.

perishability The characteristic of a service that makes it impossible to store for later sale or consumption.

permission marketing E-mail advertising in which on-line consumers have the opportunity to accept or refuse the unsolicited e-mail.

perpetual inventory unit control system Retail computer system that keeps a running total on sales, returns, transfers to other stores and so on.

personal selling Marketing communication by which a company representative interacts directly with a customer or prospective customer to communicate about a good or service.

personality The set of unique psychological characteristics that consistently influences the way a person responds to situations in the environment.

physical distribution The activities that move finished goods from manufacturers to final customers, including order processing, warehousing, materials handling, transportation, and inventory control.

physical URLs New apps that enable user-generated clouds of content to form around products; barcode scans allow the user to upload content or see what others have already uploaded.

place marketing Marketing activities that seek to attract new businesses, residents, or visitors to a town, state, country, or some other site.

place-based media Advertising media that transmit messages in public places, such as doctors' offices and airports, where certain types of people congregate.

place The availability of the product to the customer at the desired time and location.

Point-of-purchase (POP) displays In-store displays and signs.

point-of-sale (POS) systems Retail computer systems that collect sales data and are hooked directly into the store's inventory-control system.

pop-up ad An advertisement that appears on the screen while a Web page loads or after it has loaded.

popular culture The music, movies, sports, books, celebrities, and other forms of entertainment consumed by the mass market.

popup store A temporary retail space a company erects to build buzz for its products.

portfolio analysis A management tool for evaluating a firm's business mix and assessing the potential of an organization's strategic business units.

positioning Develop a marketing strategy to influence how a particular market segment perceives a good or service in comparison to the competition.

posttesting Research conducted on consumers' responses to actual advertising messages they have seen or heard.

preapproach A part of the selling process that includes developing information about prospective customers and planning the sales interview.

predatory pricing Illegal pricing strategy in which a company sets a very low price for the purpose of driving competitors out of business.

predictive technology Analysis techniques that use shopping patterns of large numbers of people to determine which products are likely to be purchased if others are.

premiums Items offered free to people who have purchased a product.

press release Information that an organization distributes to the media intended to win publicity.

prestige products Products that have a high price and that appeal to status-conscious consumers.

pretesting A research method that seeks to minimize mistakes by getting consumer reactions to ad messages before they appear in the media.

price bundling Selling two or more goods or services as a single package for one price.

price elasticity of demand The percentage change in unit sales that results from a percentage change in price.

price leadership A pricing strategy in which one firm first sets its price and other firms in the industry follow with the same or very similar prices.

price lining The practice of setting a limited number of different specific prices, called price points, for items in a product line.

price-fixing The collaboration of two or more firms in setting prices, usually to keep prices high.

price The assignment of value, or the amount the consumer must exchange to receive the offering.

primary data Data from research conducted to help make a specific decision.

private exchanges Systems that link an invited group of suppliers and partners over the Web.

private-label brands Brands that a certain retailer or distributor owns and sells.

probability sample A sample in which each member of the population has some known chance of being included.

problem recognition The process that occurs whenever the consumer sees a significant difference between his current state of affairs and some desired or ideal state; this recognition initiates the decision-making process.

processed materials Products created when firms transform raw materials from their original state.

producers The individuals or organizations that purchase products for use in the production of other goods and services.

product adaptation strategy Product strategy in which a firm offers a similar but modified product in foreign markets.

product adoption The process by which a consumer or business customer begins to buy and use a new good, service, or idea.

product advertising Advertising messages that focus on a specific good or service.

product category managers Individuals who are responsible for developing and implementing the marketing plan for all the brands and products within a product category.

product competition When firms offering different products compete to satisfy the same consumer needs and wants.

product concept development and screening The second step of product development in which marketers test product ideas for technical and commercial success.

product development strategies Growth strategies that focus on selling new products in existing markets.

product invention strategy Product strategy in which a firm develops a new product for foreign markets.

product life cycle (PLC) A concept that explains how products go through four distinct stages from birth to death: introduction, growth, maturity, and decline.

product line length Determined by the number of separate items within the same category.

product line A firm's total product offering designed to satisfy a single need or desire of target customers.

product management The systematic and usually team-based approach to coordinating all aspects of a product's marketing initiative including all elements of the marketing mix.

product mix width The number of different product lines the firm produces.

product mix The total set of all products a firm offers for sale.

product quality The overall ability of the product to satisfy customers' expectations.

product review sites Social media sites that enable people to post stories about their experiences with products and services.

product sampling Distributing free trial-size versions of a product to consumers.

product specifications A written description of the quality, size, weight, and other details required of a product purchase.

product A tangible good, service, idea, or some combination of these that satisfies consumer or business customer needs through the exchange process; a bundle of attributes including features, functions, benefits, and uses.

production orientation A management philosophy that emphasizes the most efficient ways to produce and distribute products.

promotion mix The major elements of marketer-controlled communication, including advertising, sales promotion, public relations, personal selling, and direct marketing.

promotion The coordination of a marketer's communication efforts to influence attitudes or behavior.

promotional products Goodies such as coffee mugs, T-shirts, and magnets given away to build awareness for a sponsor. Some freebies are distributed directly to consumers and business customers; others are intended for channel partners such as retailers and vendors.

prospecting A part of the selling process that includes identifying and developing a list of potential or prospective customers.

protectionism A policy adopted by a government to give domestic companies an advantage.

prototypes Test versions of a proposed product.

psychographics The use of psychological, sociological, and anthropological factors to construct market segments.

public relations (PR) Communication function that seeks to build good relationships with an organization's publics, including consumers, stockholders, and legislators.

public relations campaign A coordinated effort to communicate with one or more of the firm's publics.

public service advertisements (PSAs) Advertising run by the media for not-for-profit organizations or to champion a particular cause without charge.

publicity Unpaid communication about an organization that appears in the mass media.

puffery Claims made in advertising of product superiority that cannot be proven true or untrue.

pull strategy The company tries to move its products through the channel by building desire for the products among consumers, thus convincing retailers to respond to this demand by stocking these items.

push money A bonus paid by a manufacturer to a salesperson, customer, or distributor for selling its product.

push strategy The company tries to move its products through the channel by convincing channel members to offer them.

pyramid schemes An illegal sales technique that promises consumers or investors large profits from recruiting others to join the program rather than from any real investment or sale of goods to the public.

Q

quantity discounts A pricing tactic of charging reduced prices for purchases of larger quantities of a product.

question marks SBUs with low market shares in fast-growth markets.

R

radio frequency identification (RFID) Product tags with tiny chips containing information about the item's content, origin, and destination.

raw materials Products of the fishing, lumber, agricultural, and mining industries that organizational customers purchase to use in their finished products.

reach The percentage of the target market that will be exposed to the media vehicle.

rebates Sales promotions that allow the customer to recover part of the product's cost from the manufacturer.

receiver The organization or individual that intercepts and interprets the message.

reciprocity A trading partnership in which two firms agree to buy from one another.

reference group An actual or imaginary individual or group that has a significant effect on an individual's evaluations, aspirations, or behavior.

relationship selling A form of personal selling that involves securing, developing, and maintaining long-term relationships with profitable customers.

relative advantage The degree to which a consumer perceives that a new product provides superior benefits.

reliability The extent to which research measurement techniques are free of errors.

reminder advertising Advertising aimed at keeping the name of a brand in people's minds to be sure consumers purchase the product as necessary.

repositioning Redoing a product's position to respond to marketplace changes.

representativeness The extent to which consumers in a study are similar to a larger group in which the organization has an interest.

research and marketing services Advertising agency department that collects and analyzes information that will help account executives develop a sensible strategy and assist creatives in getting consumer reactions to different versions of ads.

research design A plan that specifies what information marketers will collect and what type of study they will do.

resellers The individuals or organizations that buy finished goods for the purpose of reselling, renting, or leasing to others to make a profit and to maintain their business operations.

retail borrowing Consumer practice of purchasing a product with the intent to return the nondefective merchandise for a refund after it has fulfilled the purpose for which it was purchased.

retail life cycle A theory that focuses on the various stages that retailers pass through from introduction to decline.

retailer margin The margin added to the cost of a product by a retailer.

retailing The final stop in the distribution channel in which organizations sell goods and services to consumers for their personal use.

retro brand A once-popular brand that has been revived to experience a popularity comeback, often by riding a wave of nostalgia.

return on investment (ROI) The direct financial impact of a firm's expenditure of a resource such as time or money.

return on marketing investment (ROMI) Quantifying just how an investment in marketing has an impact on the firm's success, financially and otherwise.

reverse marketing A business practice in which a buyer firm attempts to identify suppliers who will produce products according to the buyer firm's specifications.

S

sachets Single use packages of products such as shampoo often sold in developing countries.

sales management The process of planning, implementing, and controlling the personal selling function of an organization.

sales presentation The part of the selling process in which the salesperson directly communicates the value proposition to the customer and invites two-way communication.

sales promotion Programs designed to build interest in or encourage purchase of a product during a specified period.

sales territory A set of customers, often defined by geographic boundaries, for whom a particular salesperson is responsible.

sampling The process of selecting respondents for a study.

search engine marketing (SEM) Search marketing strategy in which marketers pay for ads or better positioning.

search engine optimization (SEO) A systematic process of ensuring that your firm comes up at or near the top of lists of typical search phrases related to your business.

search engines Internet programs that search for documents with specified keywords.

search marketing Marketing strategies that involve the use of Internet search engines.

search qualities Product characteristics that the consumer can examine prior to purchase.

seasonal discounts Price reductions offered only during certain times of the year.

secondary data Data that have been collected for some purpose other than the problem at hand.

segment profile A description of the "typical" customer in a segment.

segmentation variables Dimensions that divide the total market into fairly homogeneous groups, each with different needs and preferences.

segmentation The process of dividing a larger market into smaller pieces based on one or more meaningfully shared characteristics.

selective distribution Distribution using fewer outlets than intensive distribution but more than exclusive distribution.

self-concept An individual's self-image that is composed of a mixture of beliefs, observations, and feelings about personal attributes.

selling orientation A managerial view of marketing as a sales function, or a way to move products out of warehouses to reduce inventory.

sensory marketing Marketing techniques that link distinct sensory experiences such as a unique fragrance with a product or service.

service encounter The actual interaction between the customer and the service provider.

services Intangible products that are exchanged directly between the producer and the customer.

servicescape The actual physical facility where the service is performed, delivered, and consumed.

SERVQUAL A multiple-item scale used to measure service quality across dimensions of tangibles, reliability, responsiveness, assurance, and empathy.

share of customer The percentage of an individual customer's purchase of a product that is a single brand.

shopping center A group of commercial establishments owned and managed as a single property.

shopping products Goods or services for which consumers spend considerable time and effort gathering information and comparing alternatives before making a purchase.

shrinkage Losses experienced by retailers due to shoplifting, employee theft, and damage to merchandise.

single sourcing The business practice of buying a particular product from only one supplier.

situation analysis An assessment of a firm's internal and external environments.

Six Sigma A process whereby firms work to limit product defects to 3.4 per million or fewer.

skimming price A very high, premium price that a firm charges for its new, highly desirable product.

slogans   Simple, memorable linguistic devices linked to a brand.

slotting allowance   A fee paid in exchange for agreeing to place a manufacturer's products on a retailer's valuable shelf space.

social class   The overall rank or social standing of groups of people within a society according to the value assigned to factors such as family background, education, occupation, and income.

social marketing concept   A management philosophy that marketers must satisfy customers' needs in ways that also benefit society and also deliver profit to the firm.

social media   Internet-based platforms that allow users to create their own content and share it with others who access these sites.

social networking   Online platforms that allow a user to represent him- or herself via a profile on a Web site and provide and receive links to other members of the network to share input about common interests.

social networks   Sites used to connect people with other similar people.

social norms   Specific rules dictating what is right or wrong, acceptable or unacceptable.

source   An organization or individual that sends a message.

spam   The use of electronic media to send unsolicited messages in bulk.

special events   Activities—from a visit by foreign investors to a company picnic—that are planned and implemented by a PR department.

specialty products   Goods or services that has unique characteristics and is important to the buyer and for which she will devote significant effort to acquire.

specialty stores   Retailers that carry only a few product lines but offer good selection within the lines that they sell.

speech writing   Writing a speech on a topic for a company executive to deliver.

sponsored search ads   Paid ads that appear at the top or beside the Internet search engine results.

sponsorships   PR activities through which companies provide financial support to help fund an event in return for publicized recognition of the company's contribution.

stakeholders   Buyers, sellers, or investors in a company, community residents, and even citizens of the nations where goods and services are made or sold—in other words, any person or organization that has a "stake" in the outcome.

standard of living   An indicator of the average quality and quantity of goods and services consumed in a country.

staple products   Basic or necessary items that are available almost everywhere.

stars   SBUs with products that have a dominant market share in high-growth markets.

status symbols   Visible markers that provide a way for people to flaunt their membership in higher social classes (or at least to make others believe they are members).

store image   The way the marketplace perceives a retailer relative to the competition.

storefront   The physical exterior of a store.

straight extension strategy   Product strategy in which a firm offers the same product in both domestic and foreign markets.

straight rebuy   A buying situation in which business buyers make routine purchases that require minimal decision making.

strategic alliance   Relationship developed between a firm seeking a deeper commitment to a foreign market and a domestic firm in the target country.

strategic business units (SBUs)   Individual units within the firm that operate like separate businesses, with each having its own mission, business objectives, resources, managers, and competitors.

strategic planning   A managerial decision process that matches an organization's resources and capabilities to its market opportunities for long-term growth and survival.

sub-branding   Creating a secondary brand within a main brand that can help differentiate a product line to a desired target group.

subculture   A group within a society whose members share a distinctive set of beliefs, characteristics, or common experiences.

subliminal advertising   Supposedly hidden messages in marketers' communications.

supercenters   Large combination stores that combine economy supermarkets with other lower-priced merchandise.

supermarkets   Food stores that carry a wide selection of edibles and related products.

supply chain management   The management of flows among firms in the supply chain to maximize total profitability.

supply chain   All the activities necessary to turn raw materials into a good or service and put it in the hands of the consumer or business customer.

support media   Media such as directories or out-of-home media that may be used to reach people who are not reached by mass media advertising.

sustainability   A product design focus that seeks to create products that meet present consumer needs without compromising the ability of future generations to meet their needs.

SWOT analysis   An analysis of an organization's strengths and weaknesses and the opportunities and threats in its external environment.

syndicated research   Research by firms that collect data on a regular basis and sell the reports to multiple firms.

T

take title   To accept legal ownership of a product and assume the accompanying rights and responsibilities of ownership.

target costing   A process in which firms identify the quality and functionality needed to satisfy customers and what price they are willing to pay before the product is designed; the product is manufactured only if the firm can control costs to meet the required price.

target market   The market segments on which an organization focuses its marketing plan and toward which it directs its marketing efforts.

target marketing strategy   Dividing the total market into different segments on the basis of customer characteristics, selecting one or more segments, and developing products to meet the needs of those specific segments.

targeting   A strategy in which marketers evaluate the attractiveness of each potential segment and decide in which of these groups they will invest resources to try to turn them into customers.

tariffs   Taxes on imported goods.

team selling   The sales function when handled by a team that may consist of a salesperson, a technical specialist, and others.

teaser or **mystery advertising**   Ads that generate curiosity and interest in a to-be-introduced product by drawing attention to an upcoming ad campaign without mentioning the product.

technical development   The step in the product development process in which company engineers refine and perfect a new product.

technical specialist   A sales support person with a high level of technical expertise who assists in product demonstrations.

telemarketing   The use of the telephone to sell directly to consumers and business customers.

test marketing   Testing the complete marketing plan in a small geographic area that is similar to the larger market the firm hopes to enter.

time poverty Consumers' belief that they are more pressed for time than ever before.

tipping point In the context of product diffusion, the point when a product's sales spike from a slow climb to an unprecedented new level, often accompanied by a steep price decline.

tonality The mood or attitude the message conveys (straightforward, humor, dramatic, romantic, sexy, and apprehension/fear).

top-down budgeting Allocation of the promotion budget based on management's determiniation of the total amount to be devoted to marketing communication.

total costs The total of the fixed costs and the variable costs for a set number of units produced.

total quality management (TQM) A management philosophy that focuses on satisfying customers through empowering employees to be an active part of continuous quality improvement.

touchpoint Any point of direct interface between customers and a company (online, by phone, or in person).

trade area A geographic zone that accounts for the majority of a store's sales and customers.

trade discounts Discounts off list price of products to members of the channel of distribution who perform various marketing functions.

trade promotions Promotions that focus on members of the "trade," which include distribution channel members, such as retail salespeople or wholesale distributors, that a firm must work with in order to sell its products.

trade shows Events at which many companies set up elaborate exhibits to show their products, give away samples, distribute product literature, and troll for new business contacts.

trademark The legal term for a brand name, brand mark, or trade character; trademarks legally registered by a government obtain protection for exclusive use in that country.

traffic flow The direction in which shoppers will move through the store and which areas they will pass or avoid.

transactional selling A form of personal selling that focuses on making an immediate sale with little or no attempt to develop a relationship with the customer.

transportation The mode by which products move among channel members.

trial pricing Pricing a new product low for a limited period of time in order to lower the risk for a customer.

trialability The ease of sampling a new product and its benefits.

triple bottom line orientation A business orientation that looks at financial profits, the community in which the organization operates, and creating sustainable business practices.

twitter A free microblogging service that lets users post short text messages with a maximum of 140 characters.

U

U.S. Generalized System of Preferences (GSP) A program to promote economic growth in developing countries by allowing duty-free entry of goods into the U.S.

unaided recall A research technique conducted by telephone survey or personal interview that asks whether a person remembers seeing an ad during a specified period without giving the person the name of the brand.

undifferentiated targeting strategy Appealing to a broad spectrum of people.

unfair sales acts State laws that prohibit suppliers from selling products below cost to protect small businesses from larger competitors.

uniform delivered pricing A pricing tactic in which a firm adds a standard shipping charge to the price for all customers regardless of location.

unique selling proposition (USP) An advertising appeal that focuses on one clear reason why a particular product is superior.

Universal Product Code (UPC) The set of black bars or lines printed on the side or bottom of most items sold in grocery stores and other mass-merchandising outlets. The UPC, readable by scanners, creates a national system of product identification.

unobtrusive measures Measuring traces of physical evidence that remain after some action has been taken.

unsought products Goods or services for which a consumer has little awareness or interest until the product or a need for the product is brought to her attention.

usage occasions An indicator used in behavioral market segmentation based on when consumers use a product most.

user-generated content (UGC) or **consumer-generated media (CGM)** Online consumer comments, opinions, advice and discussions, reviews, photos, images, videos, podcasts, webcasts, and product, related stories available to other consumers.

utility The usefulness or benefit consumers receive from a product.

V

validity The extent to which research actually measures what it was intended to measure.

VALS™ (Values and Lifestyles) A psychographic system that divides the entire U.S. population into eight segments.

value chain A series of activities involved in designing, producing, marketing, delivering, and supporting any product. Each link in the chain has the potential to either add or remove value from the product the customer eventually buys.

value pricing or **everyday low pricing (EDLP)** A pricing strategy in which a firm sets prices that provide ultimate value to customers.

value proposition A marketplace offering that fairly and accurately sums up the value that will be realized if the good or service is purchased.

value The benefits a customer receives from buying a good or service.

variability The characteristic of a service that means that even the same service performed by the same individual for the same customer can vary.

variable costs The costs of production (raw and processed materials, parts, and labor) that are tied to and vary depending on the number of units produced.

variety stores Stores that carry a variety of inexpensive items.

venture teams Groups of people within an organization who work together to focus exclusively on the development of a new product.

vertical marketing system (VMS) A channel of distribution in which there is formal cooperation among members at the manufacturing, wholesaling, and retailing levels.

video sharing Uploading video recordings on to Internet sites such as YouTube so that thousands or even millions of other Internet users can see them.

viral marketing Marketing activities that aim to increase brand awareness or sales by consumers passing a message along to other consumers.

virtual goods Digital products bought and sold in virtual worlds that don't exist in the real world.

virtual goods Digital products consumers buy for use in online contexts.

virtual worlds Online, highly engaging digital environments where avatars live and interact with other avatars in real time.

visual merchandising The design of all the things customers see both inside and outside the store.

vlogs Video recordings shared on the Internet.

W

want   The desire to satisfy needs in specific ways that are culturally and socially influenced.

warehouse clubs   Discount retailers that charge a modest membership fee to consumers who buy a broad assortment of food and nonfood items in bulk and in a warehouse environment.

warehousing   Storing goods in anticipation of sale or transfer to another member of the channel of distribution.

Web 2.0   The new generation of the World Wide Web that incorporates social networking and user interactivity.

Web directory   Internet program that lists sites by categories and subcategories.

wheel-of-retailing hypothesis   A theory that explains how retail firms change, becoming more upscale as they go through their life cycle.

wholesaler margin   The amount added to the cost of a product by a wholesaler.

wholesaling intermediaries   Firms that handle the flow of products from the manufacturer to the retailer or business user.

wisdom of crowds   Under the right circumstances, groups are smarter than the smartest people in them, meaning that large numbers of consumers can predict successful products.

word-of-mouth communication   When consumers provide information about products to other consumers.

World Trade Organization (WTO)   An organization that replaced GATT; the WTO sets trade rules for its member nations and mediates disputes between nations.

world trade   The flow of goods and services among different countries—the value of all the exports and imports of the world's nations.

Y

yield management pricing   A practice of charging different prices to different customers in order to manage capacity while maximizing revenues.

▶Index

SUBJECT INDEX